Contest Theory
Incentive Mechanisms and Ranking Methods

Contests are prevalent in many areas, including sports, rent-seeking, patent races, innovation inducement, labor markets, scientific projects, crowdsourcing and other online services, and allocation of computer system resources. This book provides unified, comprehensive coverage of contest theory as developed in economics, computer science, and statistics, with a focus on online services applications, allowing professionals, researchers, and students to learn about the underlying theoretical principles and to test them in practice.

The book sets contest design in a game-theoretic framework that can be used to model a wide range of problems and efficiency measures such as total and individual output and social welfare, and it offers insight into how the structure of prizes relates to desired contest design objectives. Methods for rating the skills and ranking of players are presented, as are proportional allocation and similar allocation mechanisms, simultaneous contests, sharing utility of productive activities, sequential contests, and tournaments.

Milan Vojnović is a researcher at Microsoft Research, Cambridge, United Kingdom. He is also an affiliated lecturer at the University of Cambridge, with a courtesy appointment with the Statistical Laboratory. He obtained a Ph.D. in Technical Sciences from École Polytechnique Fédérale de Lausanne with a thesis on resource allocation problems in communication networks, and a M.Sc. in Electrical Engineering from the University of Split, Croatia. His research covers a broad range of subjects that includes resource allocation, machine learning and data science, and game theory. He won several awards, including several best paper awards at various scientific conferences, the 2005 ERCIM Cor Baayen Award, and the 2010 ACM SIGMETRICS Rising Star Researcher Award.

To Sandra, Srđan, and Mirta

Contest Theory

Incentive Mechanisms and Ranking Methods

Milan Vojnović

Microsoft Research

CAMBRIDGE
UNIVERSITY PRESS

CAMBRIDGE
UNIVERSITY PRESS

32 Avenue of the Americas, New York, NY 10013-2473, USA

Cambridge University Press is part of the University of Cambridge.

It furthers the University's mission by disseminating knowledge in the pursuit of
education, learning, and research at the highest international levels of excellence.

www.cambridge.org
Information on this title: www.cambridge.org/9781107033139

First published 2015

Printed in the United States of America

A catalog record for this publication is available from the British Library.

Library of Congress Cataloging in Publication Data

Vojnović, Milan
Contest theory : incentive mechanisms and ranking methods / Milan Vojnović,
Microsoft Research, Cambridge, UK.
pages   cm
Includes bibliographical references and index.
ISBN 978-1-107-03313-9 (hardback : alk. paper)
1. Game theory.   I. Title.
QA269.V634   2016
519.3 – dc23   2015027578

ISBN 978-1-107-03313-9 Hardback

Contents

v

Preface

Contests are systems in which participants, whom I refer to as players, invest efforts in order to win one or more prizes. A distinctive feature of a contest is that each player invests effort but may not be awarded a prize. This makes the area of contest design a subset of *auction theory* where the aim is to design an auction that achieves a desired goal without necessarily restricting the design to one in which everybody pays. The area is also different from that of *mechanism design* where the goal is to design a mechanism that optimizes a given objective subject to the constraint that the mechanism is *truthful*, i.e., players truthfully report their private information. In general, no such constraint is imposed for a contest design problem, and in fact, many contest designs are non-truthful. Another important feature of a contest is that contestants are rewarded with respect to their *relative performance*, e.g., allocating an award to the best performing player or based on the rank of individual production outputs. This is different from traditional compensation schemes based on some estimate of absolute performance output. The theory of contest design has been developed over the last hundred years or so; in the early days it was predominantly studied in the areas of statistics, political economy and public choice, and the research was motivated by the need to understand and study various competitions, such as sport competitions, rent-seeking, lobbying, conflicts, arm races, R&D competitions, and, more recently, online marketplaces and resource allocation mechanisms. The development of the theory and experimental evaluation have been especially advanced over recent years in the areas of theoretical computer science and management sciences, fueled by the needs of various applications in the context of Internet online services. Here we find a wide variety of contests offering either monetary rewards or reputation. For example, soliciting solutions to tasks through open calls to large communities, so-called *crowdsourcing*, has emerged as a method of choice for solving a wide range of tasks, including web design, software development, algorithmic and data mining challenges, and various other tasks that require human intelligence.

This book was written to provide an exposition of some of the central concepts in contest design. It should be accessible to any senior-level undergraduate and graduate student equipped with a basic knowledge of mathematics and probability theory. It is also written for a scientist or an engineer from any area where the aspects of contest design are of interest, including, but not limited to, computer science, economics, social sciences, operations research, and any engineering discipline. The book would be useful not only to those who are interested in contest theory and its development in its own right but also to those who care more about applications and want to learn some of their theoretical underpinnings. These theoretical foundations provide insights and guidelines for system design, and motivate the design of various hypotheses to be evaluated by experimental research. The goal was to put in one place the results developed by different communities over many years and, to make some of the domain-specific concepts in the areas of computer science and economics more widely accessible. The focus of this book is on principles that underpin various contest architectures that are of interest in applications, especially those that arise in the context of Internet online services. The book could be used as the main material to support a stand-alone course on the topic of contest theory, or parts of the book could be used to complement a course on a related subject. The book would also serve well as a research monograph because it provides a thorough overview of basic concepts and coverage of many references, and as such it would be a good starting point to pursue new research in the area.

Structure of the Book

Chapter 1 provides an introduction and preview. Throughout the book, we examine various contest architectures and study their equilibrium properties under two standard informational assumptions: (i) a game with complete information where the abilities of the players are common knowledge and (ii) a game with incomplete information where the abilities of the players are private information. Both these assumptions are of interest for modeling contests that arise in practice. Several quantities are of interest in equilibrium, including the total effort, maximum individual effort, and social efficiency. Chapter 2 begins by considering one of the most basic contest designs – the standard all-pay contest – where the entire prize is awarded to the player who invests the largest effort. This simple contest design already provides us with an abundance of interesting results and serves well to introduce and study basic concepts of equilibria. Chapter 3 takes one step forward in considering a natural extension of awarding one or more placement prizes depending on the rank of invested efforts. Here an interesting question is how to allocate a prize purse so as to optimize a given objective. We find conditions under which it is optimal to allocate only the first place prize. Chapter 4 considers a class of smooth allocation of prizes, where a prize is allocated according to a smooth function of the invested efforts. This class of contests includes as a special case the well-known Tullock contest and, in particular, the allocation proportional to invested efforts. In Chapter 5, we consider systems of simultaneous contests where each player has a choice to invest his or her effort in one of several simultaneous contests. This serves as a natural model of crowdsourcing systems, which are now in prevalent use in the context of Internet online services. Chapter 6 covers sequential contests where, for example, players make sequential effort investments competing for one prize, or multiple prizes are awarded in a sequential manner. Chapter 7 gives an account of utility sharing and social welfare, where the efforts invested by the players amount to a utility of production, which is shared among the contributors according to a given allocation mechanism. Our goal in this chapter is to gain some understanding of the social efficiency of equilibria under simple utility sharing mechanisms. Chapter 8 studies the design of single-elimination tournaments with respect to various objectives. It discusses designing a tournament plan that specifies the seeding and schedule of matches and presents reasoning about which tournament plan is better. In Chapter 9, we discuss the main principles of rating systems for estimation of the skills of players; these systems have been in active use for the rating of chess players and in other sport competitions, rating of players in online computer games, and rating of coders in competition-based software development platforms. Chapter 10 covers the area of ranking and aggregation of judgments. The Appendix provides a review of various mathematical concepts that are used in the book.

Presentation Style

The presentation style is standard exposition structured around theorems, which helps highlight the main results. Most of the theorems are presented with proofs. A discussion of insights and implications of a theorem is usually presented following the proof of the theorem. An effort was made to keep the complexity of notation at a minimum level, while still allowing for some level of mathematical precision. Throughout the book, simple drawings are used to quickly explain or support some of the key ideas. The main results of each chapter are highlighted in a summary section near the end of each chapter. This is followed by selected exercises that vary in difficulty. Some of the exercises are simple and serve the purpose of checking basic understanding. Others are more involved, and usually their aim is to cover some known interesting results that did not fit in the main text. Each chapter ends with bibliographical notes that not only refer to the sources used in the content of the chapter but also put the results in a historical context and provide pointers to related references.

Use of the Book in Courses

This book could be used as the main material to teach a stand-alone course on the theory of contests as part of various programs in computer science, economics, electrical engineering, mathematics, and statistics. It could also be used to support parts of a course on a related subject, such as courses on economics and computation, online marketplaces, and special topics in economics, game theory, and statistics. The book contains a substantial amount of material and can well support a one-semester course. The delivery of the course can be tailored to specific audiences by the choice of presentation style and putting more emphasis on one type of applications than another. The students are expected to have some prior knowledge of basic real analysis and some elements of probability theory. The course could be delivered as part of a senior-level undergraduate program or a graduate program.

This book was used as the main reference for the course "Contest Theory," a 16-lecture course of a master's program in mathematics at the University of Cambridge. The content covered in the course varied from one year to the next. The core material that was covered included standard all-pay contests, rank-order allocation of prizes, smooth allocation of prizes, and simultaneous contests, as well as basic principles of rating systems. Each of these topics was taught using a subset of the material of the corresponding book chapter. The selection of these topics allowed there to be a flow of thought throughout the course. The students were given a good exposition of various notions of strategic equilibria and their efficiency for games of concern. The lectures on rating systems gave students some exposure to standard probabilistic models and statistical inference methods that underlie the design of popular rating systems.

Dependence Graph

Most of the chapters can be read individually because they are self-contained. However, there are some dependencies of which the reader should be aware, especially, a novice reader. Figure 0.1 depicts dependencies between individual chapters. Chapter 2 contains results about standard all-pay contests, which are invoked in several subsequent chapters. Chapter 3 is concerned with a generalization of the standard all-pay contest to one or more prizes. Hence, it would help the reader to go through Chapter 2 first. Chapter 4 can be read independently of any other chapter because it covers a class of prize allocation mechanisms introduced in the given chapter. Chapter 5 covers a generalization to a system of simultaneous contests and, in particular, a system of simultaneous all-pay contests, so there is some dependency with Chapter 2. Chapters 9 and 10 are somewhat distinct from the other chapters – the focus in these

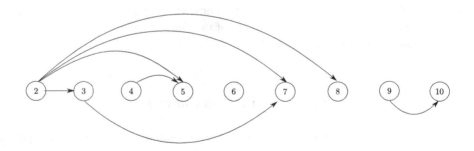

2.   standard all-pay contest
3.   rank-order allocation of prizes
4.   smooth allocation of prizes
5.   simultaneous contests
6.   utility sharing and social welfare
7.   sequential contests
8.   tournaments
9.   rating systems
10. ranking and aggregation of judgments

Figure 0.1. Dependence graph.

two chapters is on statistical estimation of skills and ranking of the players and not so much on consideration of their strategic behavior.

Acknowledgments

I would like to express my gratitude to several people who provided useful feedback for specific chapters of this book, including Dan Alistarh, Sofia Ceppi, Subhasish M. Chowdhury, Thore Graepel, Tobias Harks, Ian Kash, Thành Nguyen, David Parkes, Ella Segev, Vasilis Syrgkanis, and several anonymous reviewers.

I am very grateful to my collaborators who worked with me on projects that involved studying various models of contests. In particular, I would like to mention Dominic DiPalantino, Nan Li, Thành Nguyen, and Vasilis Syrgkanis who as part of their internship worked with me at Microsoft Research. They provided me with a great deal of inspiration and a source of knowledge.

I owe a special debt to James Norris for providing me with the opportunity to teach a course at the University of Cambridge and the faculty board for appointing me as an Affiliated Lecturer at the university. I am indebted to Frank Kelly who recommended the course for Part III of Mathematical Tripos, a one-year master's program in mathematics whose tradition and prestige are world renowned. Felix Fischer, Frank Kelly, James Norris, and Richard Weber kindly shared with me their teaching experience, which helped me to adjust to a new and challenging environment. This was especially useful to someone like me whose previous teaching experience was limited to computer science and engineering programs, where ordinarily one more often uses a presentation slide deck than a piece of chalk and blackboard. Felix Fischer was my de facto mentor, guiding me throughout with useful advice and feedback, showing me how to maneuver through the university system, and acting as a checker for my course exam sheets. Last but not least, the book benefited greatly from the feedback of students, both in class during lectures and individually. The course was attended by truly inspiring and bright young mathematicians with a wide range of backgrounds and interests.

I am indebted to Lauren Cowles, my book editor at Cambridge University Press, who helped me throughout the book production process with moral support, soliciting anonymous feedback for individual chapters, and taking a personal interest by reading some of the chapters and providing me with her own reviews. The initial book proposal, review, and contract agreement were handled by Ada Brunstein who at that time was with Cambridge University Press – I thank her and Cambridge University Press for sharing a view of a need for this book, taking the proposal through a successful review process, and, finally, signing a contract. I would also like to thank the book copy-editor, Gail Naron Chalew, for her meticulous reviews, and the production project manager, Minaketan Dash, for handling everything so kindly and professionally.

The idea of writing this book was born in late 2011. It was an ambitious and demanding, but rewarding journey. It allowed me to focus on and learn a great deal of new things, exploring far beyond my initial knowledge. I am grateful to Microsoft Research for providing me with a stimulating work environment that helped toward putting this book together. This book was written in my office, at home, in cafe bars, at airports, on planes, and in hotels in many different countries while on trips of business and pleasure. Specific parts of the book evoke personal memories of the various moments and places when they were written.

The production of this book would not have been possible without continued support, interest, and encouragement from my family – my wife and two children. They shared a great deal of the book writing project with me through all the time I was tied up to a desk, often during weekends and while on holidays, which deprived us of many other things we could be doing together.

Since this book is as much about reasoning about investments of efforts, I end with the hope that the reader will find the end product worthy of all the effort put into its production.

Milan Vojnović
May, 2015

CHAPTER 1
Introduction and Preview

This book synthesizes what one may refer to as *contest theory*, understood in a broad sense to encompass scientific methods and theories for the better understanding and informed design of contests. Its goal is to provide a contest designer with a set of theoretical results and methods that can be used for the design of contests. An ambitious aspiration is to provide a toolkit for a contest designer of a similar kind to what control theory offers to engineers for the design of control systems. This is, undoubtedly, a challenging task, primarily because of the complexity of user behavior and incentives that play a key role in most of the systems of concern. This book covers a wide range of models developed in different areas of science including computer science, economics, and statistics.

Generally speaking, we refer to *contests* as situations in which individuals invest efforts toward winning one or more prizes, those investments of efforts are costly and irreversible, and prizes are allocated based on the relative values of efforts. A prize is understood in a broad sense to refer to a notion of value that is general enough to include not only monetary prizes but also social reputation and gratitude. How to allocate a prize purse to competitors in a contest was studied as early as 1902 by Galton, who reasoned about the question, "what is the most suitable proportion between the values of first and second prizes?" assuming a statistical model according to which individual production outputs are independent and identically distributed random variables with a given distribution. An economist's approach is to assume that contestants are rational players who strategically invest efforts with a selfish goal of maximizing their individual payoffs, which combine in some way the value of winning a prize and the cost of production. The study of a contest as a game using the framework of *game theory* allows us to reason about properties that arise in a strategic equilibrium. The design of a contest needs to ensure that proper incentives are put in place to achieve a desired objective. Commonly studied objectives include the total effort invested by contestants, the maximum individual effort over all contestants, and the social welfare defined as the value of the prizes to those who win them.

A canonical auction theory model of a contest is that of an *all-pay auction*. In an all-pay auction, each player incurs a cost equal to his or her invested bid, and a prize is

1

allocated according to an allocation mechanism that specifies the winning probabilities for every given vector of bids. This simple model of a contest offers plenty of interesting equilibrium properties and allows one to study how the choice of a prize allocation mechanism affects a quantity of interest in a strategic equilibrium. A natural contest design is to offer several placement prizes. Contest architectures can also have more sophisticated structures. For example, a contest owner may award prizes only if the individual performance outputs meet a certain level of quality. Other examples include contests that are structured as a composition of simple contests; for example, a system of *simultaneous contests* where each player strategically decides in which contests to invest efforts; a system of *sequential contests* where the competition proceeds through multiple rounds, each consisting of one or more simple contests; or a *single-elimination tournament* that is yet another instance of a composition of simple contests.

In this book, we cover a general theory of contests that provides models for a wide range of situations. We use the term *online contests* to refer to a broad range of systems that arise in the context of Internet online services whose design is based on some elements of contests. Many Internet services can be modeled in this way.

A general question that serves as a motivation for much of this book is as follows:

How should a contest be designed so as to achieve a given objective?

In designing a contest, one may need to address a broad range of design choices. In this book, we focus on theoretical foundations to provide a better understanding of the implications of various contest design choices. Specific questions of interest concern properties of production outputs and are naturally studied in the framework of game theory, drawing from the areas of auction theory, rent-seeking, algorithmic mechanism design, and social choice. Other questions may have little to do with the strategic behavior of players and require methodologies from other scientific disciplines. For example, the estimation of skills of players based on observed outcomes in contests requires methods from statistics. Another example of a contest design problem that is not necessarily studied as a strategic game is that of seeding of a single-elimination tournament, which under certain conditions boils down to a sorting problem with noisy observations. Figure 1.1 indicates some of the well-established areas from which one may draw methodologies to reason about contests.

This book puts together in one place a wide range of theoretical results that have been developed over many years by different scientific communities, including various branches of economic theory such as political economy; theory of games, and in particular auction theory; computer science; and statistics. The original studies were motivated by applications as diverse as animal conflicts, auctions for selling various kinds of goods, political lobbying, research and development races, production in firms, and Internet online services, to name a few.

Three particular fields are of special interest in the theory of contests: economics, computer science, and statistics. Here we highlight some of the main contributions in these areas.

Economic theory established much of the theory of contests, particularly, in the context of game theory, auction theory, and studies of rent-seeking activities in public choice theory. It introduced the area of *mechanism design*, which is a field in game theory that studies solution concepts for games with private information where the goal

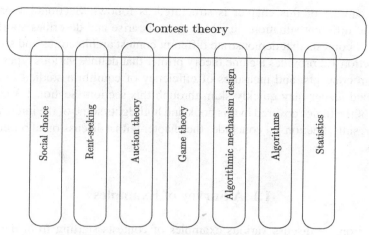

Figure 1.1. Some pillars of contest theory.

is to design a mechanism to achieve a desired objective. The foundations of mechanism design theory were laid down in a series of works starting in the 1960s with major contributions by Leonid Hurwicz, Eric Maskin, and Rodger Myerson, who together won the 2007 Nobel Memorial Prize in Economic Sciences for this line of work. The optimum auction design with respect to social welfare was established by Vickrey (1961) and with respect to revenue by Myerson (1981). A complete characterization of the equilibrium of the all-pay auction with complete information was established by Baye et al. (1996). A model of rent-seeking, commonly referred to as *the Tullock contest*, was formulated by Tullock (1980). This model formally corresponds to an all-pay auction with a specific form of a prize allocation mechanism.

Computer science introduced the use of analytical tools from theoretical computer science such as *worst-case complexity* and *approximation ratio* to study mechanism design questions. The concept of a worst-case equilibria was introduced by Koutsoupias and Papadimitriou (1999). This has been followed by many studies of the social efficiency of various games using the concept of *the price of anarchy*, defined as the ratio of the optimum social welfare and the social welfare in a worst-case equilibrium. The term *algorithmic mechanism design* was coined by Nisan and Ronen (1999, 2001) to refer to a theoretical computer science approach to mechanism design questions using concepts such as communication complexity, approximation algorithms, and worst-case analysis.

Statistics has been used to reason about contests as early as in the aforementioned study by Galton (1902). Statistical methods have played a major role in the study of tournament plans and, in particular, seeding procedures, with theoretical foundations laid down in the works of Chung and Hwang (1978), Hwang (1982), Israel (1982), and Horen and Riezman (1985) and continued developments being made since then. Statistical methods for ranking of alternatives based on pair comparisons were developed by Thurstone (1927) and Zermelo (1929) and subsequently studied by Bradley and Terry (1952, 1954) and many others. This work laid foundations for the design of rating systems that are in popular use today in sport competitions, crowdsourcing services, and online computer games.

The remainder of this chapter is structured as follows. Section 1.1 provides an overview of different situations in which contests arise and describes some concrete examples of contests that demonstrate different contest architectures and structures of prizes. Section 1.2 provides a game theory primer that defines various types of games, equilibrium concepts, and measures of efficiency of equilibria studied in this book. An informed reader may quickly skim through this section. Section 1.3 provides an overview of the topics covered in this book and highlights some of the interesting questions and results. Section 1.4 concludes the chapter with a discussion of bibliographical references.

1.1 A Survey of Examples

In this section we discuss various examples of contests starting from the more traditional ones including sport contests, rent-seeking, patent races, labor markets, and scientific research projects, and then go on to discuss online contests in the context of crowdsourcing services and other types of competitions.

1.1.1 Sport Contests

Sport competitions have a long and rich history and a wide range of contest architectures, structures of prizes, and methods for rating and ranking of players and teams of players. The ancient Olympic Games were held at Olympia as early as 776 BC and were abolished in 393 AD. The games organized at Olympia led to the development of the Panhellenic Games, which were held at Olympia and three other sites. At the Panhellenic Games there was only one winner, awarded a wreath or crown of leaves. The modern Olympic Games were inaugurated in 1896, with the first, second, and third placed athletes awarded with, respectively, gold, silver, and bronze medals. Finley and Pleket (2005) and Swaddling (2011) are good sources for these historical facts. Evidence of the use of prizes in ancient Greece can also be found in Homer's *Iliad* II. 23, 249–897, in the funeral games instituted by Achilles in honor of Patroclus: these games consisted of the chariot race, boxing, wrestling, foot race, single combat, discus, shooting with arrows, darting, and javelin. According to Papakonstantinou (2002), the winners were awarded various kinds of valuable objects: "the circulation of these valuable objects was an integral part of aristocratic gift-exchange and that therefore such prizes reaffirmed social hierarchies and consolidated networks of power relationships of the Homeric elites."

The use of prizes in various sports has prevailed to date, with a wide range in the number and values of prizes being awarded. For example, in the game of football in Europe (soccer), only one club wins the title of a national season champion, but this is not the only prize. The final outcome is a league table ranking where the position of a team in the ranking is associated with various kinds of prizes. A number of top-ranked teams often qualify to participate in international competitions such as the UEFA Championship League and UEFA Europa League. On the other hand, a number of teams at the bottom of the league table are relegated to a lower league. The league table ranking typically positively correlates with the monetary prizes awarded to the

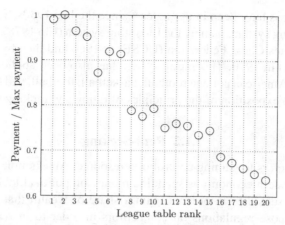

Figure 1.2. Broadcast payments made to the clubs in the premiership league season 2013/2014 versus the league table rank: the maximum payment is of value $97,544,336 (Barclays Premier League (2014)).

teams. For example, in the Barclays Premier League, according to a contract, the UK broadcast revenue is distributed to the 20 clubs of the league such that 50% of the revenue is split equally among the clubs, 25% of the revenue is split based on merit payments, i.e., depending on where a club finishes in the final league table, and the final 25% is paid in facility fees each time a club's match is broadcast in the United Kingdom. All international broadcast revenue and central commercial revenues are split equally among the 20 clubs. See Figure 1.2 for the values of payments to clubs in the premiership league season 2013/2014 depending on their placement in the final league table. The prizes generally play an important role as an incentive mechanism in sport contests. An interesting historical example of the design of prizes in the context of the game of soccer is the introduction of the system known as the *three points for a win*, where in a match, the winner is awarded three points and the loser zero points, and in the case of a draw outcome each team is awarded one point. This system replaced the original two points for a win system in England in 1981 and was adopted by most European national leagues by the mid-1990s. The new system was introduced under a premise that it would encourage more attacking play because teams would not settle for a draw if they have the prospect of gaining two extra points.

Sport contests have served as a motivation for the development of various contest design methodologies. A prominent example is the design of tournament plans and scheduling of contests. A formal study of the question of how to design a tournament plan using statistics was attempted already in 1883 by Charles Dodgson (better known by his pen name Lewis Carroll) in his article "Lawn Tennis Tournaments: The True Method of Assigning Prizes with a Proof of the Fallacy of the Present Method." A testimony to the richness of the research in this area is an extensive annotated biography of scheduling in sports by Kendall et al. (2010). The design of tournament plans is discussed in Chapter 8. Economic models have also been applied to various sport contests, some of which are covered in Chapters 2, 3, 4, and 7; see the survey by Szymanski (2003). The design of systems ranking and rating skills of players has also been greatly influenced by sport competitions. For example, the methods for rating skills of players in the game of chess have been in use at least since the late 1930s. The currently most popular chess rating system, namely the Elo rating system (Elo 1978), was first adopted by the United States Chess Federation (UCSF) in 1960 and then by the World Chess Federation (FIDE) in 1970. This rating system has also been applied in several other sports, including American college football, basketball, football, and tennis. Chapters 9 and 10 provide an exposition of the principles of rating and ranking methods.

1.1.2 Rent-Seeking

The term "rent" refers to gaining control of a resource. An example of a rent-seeking activity in our modern economy is spending money on political lobbying for government benefits or subsidies in order to gain a share of wealth that has already been created, or to impose regulations on competitors in order to increase market share. Rent-seeking activities may result in social efficiency loss, reduced wealth creation, government revenue losses, and income inequality. In economics, rent-seeking activities were first studied by Tullock (1967), while the term *rent-seeking* was coined later in the work of Krueger (1974). The model of rent-seeking introduced by Tullock (1980) has elicited general interest as a model of a contest. The key property captured by this model is that a contestant increases his or her chance of winning the prize by increasing his or her effort investment, but it is not guaranteed that the one who invests the most wins the prize. Chapter 4 provides a comprehensive coverage of this and more general families of such models.

1.1.3 Patent Races

Firms invest in research and development (R&D) under both technological and market uncertainties. There is uncertainty about the relationship between a firm's investment in R&D and the time at which the innovation may be introduced by the firm. The market uncertainty occurs because no firm can be sure when any of its rivals' R&D efforts will be successful. Patent races are common in pharmaceutical, software, and other industries and are often referred to as *R&D races* or *research contests*. A classic model of a patent race, which we discuss in Chapter 4, was pioneered by Loury (1979) and subsequently studied by Lee and Wilde (1980) and Dasgupta and Stiglitz (1980). The practice of using patents as a mechanism to promote innovation is under much debate among economists, e.g., Stiglitz (2008). One of the main concerns is that giving exclusive rights to corporations enforces monopoly and social inequality, especially between the developed and the developing world. Some economists, e.g., Stiglitz (2006), have advocated the use of alternative mechanisms such as innovation inducement prizes.

1.1.4 Innovation Inducement Prizes

As a way to promote innovation, governments and private parties award prizes for solutions to predefined scientific or technological problems or for demonstrations of the feasibility of specified unprecedented accomplishments. We refer to these as *innovation inducement prizes*. For concreteness, we next discuss a selection of such prizes from a large number of representative examples.

The Netflix prize challenge is a contest that was run from October 2, 2006, to September 21, 2009; it sought to substantially improve the accuracy of predictions about how much someone is going to enjoy a movie based on his or her movie preferences. This is an example of a contest awarding the main prize subject to a minimum required level of quality. To qualify for the grand prize in the amount of $1,000,000, the accuracy of a submitted prediction was required to be at least 10% better than the accuracy of a benchmark prediction method.

The DARPA Network Challenge was launched in 2009 with the broad goal of exploring the role of the Internet and social networking in real-time communications, wide-area collaborations, and practical actions required to solve broad-scope, time-critical problems. A cash prize in the amount of $40,000 was offered to the team that could first identify the locations of 10 red balloons moored at different locations across the United States.

Kaggle is a platform for hosting challenges on data science problems, which offer a wide range of monetary prizes. The users are also awarded reputation points based on the outcomes in contests; these points are discounted over time. The number of points earned by a team member for participation in a contest is based on several factors including the placement of the team, the number of competing teams, and the number of team members.

X Prize is a non-profit organization founded in 1995 that designs and manages public competitions intended to bring about major breakthroughs for the benefit of humanity. The X Prize competitions are typically big projects with prizes in the order of millions of dollars.

Challenge.gov is a platform established in 2010 for hosting challenge and prize competitions, all of which are run by various agencies across the U.S. federal government. These include technical, scientific, ideation, and creative competitions where the government seeks innovative solutions from the public, with the goal of bringing the best ideas and talent together to solve mission-centric problems.

1.1.5 Labor Markets

Contest theory provides models for labor compensations in firms that reward employees using prizes such as bonuses, stock shares, and job title promotions, often based on an individual's performance relative to that of his or her co-workers. Typically, there is a limited prize budget, such as a percentage of a firm's annual revenue or a fixed number of stock shares, as well as a limited number of available positions at each level of an organization hierarchy. The question is how to design a promotion system to induce employees to work the hardest, or perhaps to maximize the chance of promoting the best worker. A first formal study of these questions using economic theory was given by Lazear and Rosen (1981) in which they compared compensation schemes that pay according to an individual's ordinal rank of performance to those that pay based on an individual's absolute production output. In Chapters 2 through 8, we cover a wide range of models of contests that award prizes based on the relative performance of contestants, which are of interest in the context of labor markets.

1.1.6 Scientific Projects

Academic research is mostly realized through scientific projects funded by various non-profit and profit organizations. Scientists form teams to work on projects that result in publications and other deliverables. An illustration of the scale of scientific collaborations is presented in Figure 1.3 showing co-authorship of publications in computer science. Contributors to a project receive shares of scientific credit, whose values depend on the resulting impact and perhaps on the values of individual contributions and other factors. The impact is measured through performance indicators such as the number of citations and other indicators of societal impact. How should scientific credit be allocated to incentivize production that has high social value? Such questions were considered in studies of the allocation of scientific credit and division of cognitive labor, such as Merton (1968, 1973) and Kitcher (1990, 1993). Chapter 6 discusses the social efficiency of a model of a general production system in which individuals invest efforts in one or more available projects under different assumptions on how the efforts invested relate to the value of the utility produced and different utility sharing mechanisms.

1.1.7 Crowdsourcing Services

Crowdsourcing is the process of obtaining needed services, ideas, or content by soliciting contributions from a large group of people, especially from an online community, rather than from traditional employees or supplies. The first definition of the term "crowdsourcing" was posted in a blog by Howe (2006a) on June 2, 2006, which

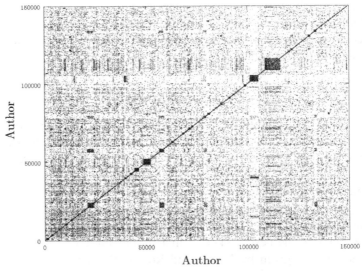

Figure 1.3. Co-authorship of journal articles published in 2010 according to DBLP: each point (x, y) represents co-authorship of a journal article by authors x and y.

was soon followed by a popular book by Howe (2006b) on this subject. The term *competition-based* crowdsourcing refers to soliciting solutions to various tasks through organizing contests. The sponsor (a private person or a company) identifies a specific problem, offers a cash prize, and broadcasts an invitation to submit solutions. Contests work well in situations when it is not clear what combination of skills or technical approach will lead to the best solution for a problem at hand, or the sponsor lacks information about which specific workers are most skillful for the given problem. The term *paid-labor* crowdsourcing refers to online labor marketplaces for matching workers and jobs where the compensation for labor is typically based an a priori agreed contract between an employer and a worker or a team of workers. An important feature of a crowdsourcing platform is that it typically hosts a number of open contests at any given time, providing workers with alternative options for effort investments.

Competition-Based Crowdsourcing Services

We discuss here two examples of competition-based crowdsourcing platforms, which help illustrate the type of tasks, the structure and value of prizes, and participation in contests.

TopCoder is a competition-based software development crowdsourcing platform using monetary and reputation prizes. Contests are held for the design, development, specification, and architecture of software development tasks. Table 1.1 provides some summary statistics. Such contests typically offer two prizes, splitting a prize purse between the first and the second place prize in the ratio 2:1. See Figure 1.4 for a

Table 1.1. Statistics of participation in some crowdsourcing contests[a]

Category	Tasks	Users	Mean User/Task	Median User/Task
TopCoder				
Design	2,041	535	2.35	2
Development	2,147	1,450	3.47	2
Specification	199	71	2.33	2
Architecture	378	94	1.83	2
Taskcn				
Website	13,673	1,946	11.70	7
Design	11,306	3,388	17.51	13
Coding	896	4,758	7.15	4
Writing	3,398	6,328	50.75	15
Multimedia	155	2,305	15.98	9
Other	1,824	3,768	17.14	11

[a] (TopCoder) data covering approximately a 10-year period from early 2003 until early 2013, (Taskcn) data covering approximately a 7-year period from mid-2006 until early 2013.

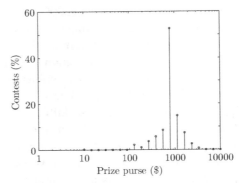

Figure 1.4. TopCoder histogram of prize values.

histogram of the values of prizes. The algorithmic contests award rating scores using TopCoder's own rating system, which is described in Chapter 9. An annual tournament, the TopCoder Open Tournament, is held for algorithmic competitions, which is an illustrative example of a tournament design with multiple elimination stages. See Figure 1.6 for a graphical representation of this tournament design.

Taskcn is a platform for soliciting solutions to various tasks such as website design, design, coding, writing, multimedia, and other types of tasks. Tasks typically attract in the order of ten submissions and some, such as writing a slogan, attract a considerably larger number of submissions. Table 1.1 shows statistics of participation in contests, and Figure 1.5 shows participation of users in contests over month-long periods in a year.

The key feature of competition-based crowdsourcing is the all-pay nature of contests: online workers invest irreversible efforts in producing solutions to tasks, and only those whose solutions are selected as the winning solutions for a given task are awarded a prize. Chapters 2, 3, and 4 discuss models of all-pay contests under different prize allocation mechanisms that specify the relation between the values of effort investments and the winning probabilities. Another key feature of competition-based crowdsourcing is that, typically, at any given time there are a multitude of open contests in which a user may participate. Chapter 5 covers models of simultaneous contests that are of interest in such scenarios.

Paid-Labor Crowdsourcing Services

We now discuss three representative examples of paid-labor crowdsourcing platforms that are described next.

Amazon Mechanical Turk is a crowdsourcing Internet marketplace where requesters post tasks known as HITs (Human Intelligence Tasks). HITs are typically simple tasks such as choosing a preferred photo for a storefront, writing a product description, and categorizing restaurants. Workers (sometimes referred to as Turkers) select and complete tasks for a given monetary payment.

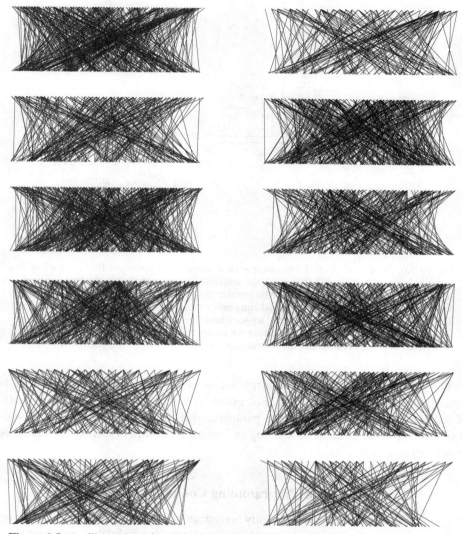

Figure 1.5. An illustration of participation of online workers in contests as observed in the competition-based crowdsourcing service Taskcn for web development tasks in each month of the year 2010. Each bipartite graph shows participation of workers in contests in a month where the bottom vertices represent workers and the top vertices represent contests.

Crowdflower is a platform for soliciting solutions to various kinds of tasks such as categorization, search relevance, content generation, listing verification and enrichment, attribute collection, image moderation, sentiment analysis, and transcription.

Upwork is an online staffing platform where contingent workers, contractors, and freelancers offer their skills and services and where organizations and individuals can post their requirements. Specific areas of expertise include web development, a wide variety of software development skills, graphic design, writing and administrative support.

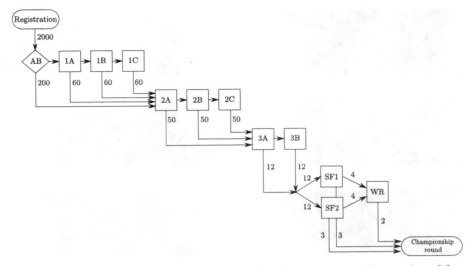

Figure 1.6. TopCoder Open Tournament – an elimination tournament that consists of five competition rounds: rounds 1 through 3, the semi-final round, and the championship round. A set of up to 2,000 top-ranked coders who register for participation qualify to participate. The top 200 ranked coders receive a bye and automatically advance to round 2 of the tournament. The first three rounds proceed in several stages where in each a given number of coders advance to the next round. The championship round is a competition among eight coders who were not eliminated in an earlier round of the tournament.

The models of paid-labor online platforms are not the focus of this book, but some issues are of relevance here. For example, Chapter 10 covers an "aggregation of judgments" problem that can be paraphrased as a classification problem, which is of interest in the context of labeling of images and other objects using paid-labor crowdsourcing platforms.

1.1.8 Programming Competitions

Programming competitions are typically hosted and administered by commercial companies as a means to identify top engineering talent for potential recruitment, or by professional organizations for increasing activity in their areas of interest. Some well-known examples are listed in Table 1.2 along with a description of the structure and values of prizes.

Table 1.2. Structures of prizes in some programming contests

	Place					
Contest	1st	2nd	3rd	4th	5th	6th–25th
Facebook Hacker Cup	$5,000	$2,000	$1,000	$100	$100	
Google Code Jam	$10,000	$2,000	$1,000	$100	$100	$100
Microsoft Imagine Cup	$50,000	$10,000	$5,000			

A well-known programming competition run by a professional organization is ACM-ICPC International Collegiate Programing Contest, an annual multi-tiered competitive programming competition among the universities of the world. In 2014, the teams finishing in the top four positions were awarded gold medals, teams finishing in fifth through eighth place were awarded silver medals, and teams finishing in ninth through twelfth place received bronze medals. The highest scoring team was crowned the world champion.

1.1.9 Collaborative Online Communities

Online collaborative communities are formed around specific or general areas of interest. The participants in these online communities share knowledge and consume information. The rewards are typically non-monetary such as satisfying an information need or gaining status or reputation. We discuss a selection of representative examples of such online communities.

Quora is a question-and-answer (Q&A) website where questions are created, answered, edited, and organized by its community of users. Questions and answers are then aggregated into topics. Users can collaborate by editing questions and suggesting edits of other users' answers.

Stackoverflow is a Q&A website on a wide range of topics in computer programming. Users can gain or lose reputation points based on the quality of the answers and questions they provide.

Yahoo! Answers is a Q&A website using a reputation system that rewards active participation and valuable contributions.

Wikipedia is a collaboratively edited, multi-lingual, free Internet encyclopedia.

A common feature of these online collaboration services is that users invest efforts in production activities such as asking or answering questions, which creates utility to the entire community, using incentive mechanisms such as awarding attention and reputation points. Chapter 6 is concerned with a general model of production that is of interest here. A design goal for some of these systems is to elicit user contributions for a specific production activity so as to reach a desired outcome in a short period of time. For example, one important goal of online Q&A forums is to find a good-quality answer to a question soon after its submission. Section 7.4 studies the efficiency of various prize allocation mechanisms in a model of sequential aggregation of production, which is motivated by online Q&A sites and other similar services.

1.1.10 Online Computer Games

Online computer games feature a variety of contests including those among two or more individual players or teams of players. An important component of an online computer game is the system for rating skills of players, which is used for various purposes such as the creation of leaderboards and matching players with similar skills. The design of

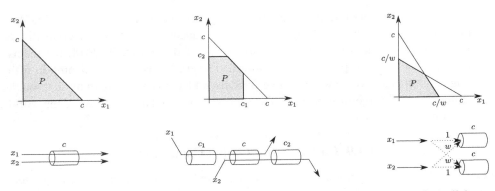

Figure 1.7. Three examples of resource allocation problems: (left) two flows through one link, (middle) two flows and three links, and (right) a workflow assignment with costs per unit flow w and 1.

rating systems has advanced significantly because of specific requirements of online computer games; in these scenarios, the design of a rating system needs to enable the rating of skills of players who engage in contests among two or more players and among teams of players. This is unlike traditional scenarios for which the first rating systems were designed, such as the game of chess, where players confront each other in contests between two players. Chapter 9 covers the fundamental principles that underlie the design of modern rating systems and, in particular, describes a rating system specifically designed for some popular online computer games.

1.1.11 Resource Allocation

In the context of Internet data transport control protocols, the resource allocation problem was first formulated as a utility optimization problem by Kelly (1997), which has been subsequently studied by many. A transport control protocol (TCP) is a widely deployed Internet protocol designed for reliable end-to-end data transfer between sender and receiver end hosts. Any communication over the Internet that requires reliable transport of data, meaning that the data must be transferred without corruption or loss, is typically carried via a TCP connection. An important part of a TCP is the congestion control protocol that regulates the transfer of data packets to avoid congestion in network devices such as Internet routers. Thus, we can think of each TCP connection as of an agent that competes for network resources. Recently, similar resource allocation problems have been studied in the context of data centers with a distinctive feature of allocating multiple types of resources such as CPU, storage, and network bandwidth, e.g., Ghodsi et al. (2011), Parkes et al. (2012), and Joe-Wong et al. (2012). Figure 1.7 shows some simple illustrative examples of resource allocation problems. Chapter 4 covers resource allocation mechanisms such as proportional allocation.

1.2 Games, Equilibrium, and Efficiency

The study of the strategic aspects of contests in this book usually goes through the following steps:

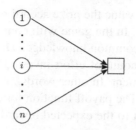

Figure 1.8. A single contest.

(i) We formulate a game-theoretic model for the contest under consideration.
(ii) We study the question of the existence and uniqueness of a strategic equilibrium.
(iii) If a strategic equilibrium exists, we provide a characterization of it and analyze its efficiency.

In this section, we provide an introduction to games and equilibrium concepts and to the notions of efficiency studied in this book. The informed reader may either skim this section or proceed directly to Section 1.3.

1.2.1 Normal Form Games

In this section, we consider a *strategic game* that is a model of decision making in which each decision maker chooses his or her action once, and all actions are made simultaneously; in the terminology of von Neumann and Morgenstern (1944), referred to as a *normal form game*.

Games with Complete Information

Definition 1.1 (normal form game with complete information). A *normal form game with complete information*, sometimes also referred to as a *normal form game with perfect information*, consists of the following elements:

(i) A finite *set of players*: $N = \{1, 2, \ldots, n\}$.
(ii) For every player $i \in N$, a set $\mathcal{B}_i$ of *strategies*. The set of strategies of all players is denoted with $\mathcal{B} = \times_{i \in N} \mathcal{B}_i$, and we refer to $\mathbf{b} \in \mathcal{B}$ as a *strategy vector*. If for every player $i \in N$, the set $\mathcal{B}_i$ of strategies is finite, the strategic game is said to be finite.
(iii) For every player $i \in N$, the *payoff* of player i is given by a *payoff function* $s_i : \mathcal{B} \to \mathbf{R}$.

A normal form game is defined by

$$G = (N, \{\mathcal{B}_i, \ i \in N\}, \{s_i, \ i \in N\}).$$

Example 1.2 (standard all-pay contest). The standard all-pay contest consists of a set of two or more players who simultaneously invest efforts $\mathbf{b} = (b_1, b_2, \ldots, b_n)$ where each b_i takes values in $\mathbf{R}_+$. A prize is awarded to the player who invests the largest effort with a uniform random tie break, so the winning probabilities of players are given by

$$x_i(\mathbf{b}) = \begin{cases} \frac{1}{|W(\mathbf{b})|}, & \text{if } i \in W(\mathbf{b}) \\ 0, & \text{otherwise} \end{cases} \qquad (1.1)$$

where $W(\mathbf{b}) = \{j \in N \mid b_j \geq b_l \text{ for every } l \in N\}$.

The players are assumed to value the prize according to positive real-valued *valuation parameters* $v_1, v_2, \ldots, v_n$. In the game with complete information, the values of valuations are assumed to be common knowledge. The production cost of a player is assumed to be linear in the amount of effort invested by this player, with a unit cost incurred per unit effort investment. In other words, players are assumed to incur unit marginal costs of production. The payoff function for each player is assumed to be of *quasi-linear* form with respect to the expected reward and the production cost and is defined by

$$s_i(\mathbf{b}) = v_i x_i(\mathbf{b}) - b_i, \quad \text{for } i \in N. \tag{1.2}$$

Pure-strategy Nash equilibrium The concept of a pure-strategy Nash equilibrium is defined as follows.

Definition 1.3 (pure-strategy Nash equilibrium). A *pure-strategy Nash equilibrium* of a normal form game with complete information $G = (N, (\mathcal{B}_i, i \in N), (s_i, i \in N))$ is a strategy vector $\mathbf{b} \in \mathcal{B}$ such that for every player $i \in N$, we have

$$s_i(b_i, \mathbf{b}_{-i}) \geq s_i(a_i, \mathbf{b}_{-i}), \quad \text{for all } a_i \in \mathcal{B}_i.$$

In other words, a strategy vector $\mathbf{b} \in \mathcal{B}$ is a pure-strategy Nash equilibrium if under this strategy vector no player has a beneficial unilateral deviation.

Definition 1.3 can be restated in the following way. For every $\mathbf{b}_{-i} \in \mathcal{B}_{-i}$ define $\beta_i(\mathbf{b}_{-i})$ to be the set of best response strategies for player i given that other players deploy strategies $\mathbf{b}_{-i}$, i.e.,

$$\beta_i(\mathbf{b}_{-i}) = \{b_i \in \mathcal{B}_i \mid s_i(b_i, \mathbf{b}_{-i}) \geq s_i(a_i, \mathbf{b}_{-i}), \quad \text{for all } a_i \in \mathcal{B}_i\}.$$

We refer to the-set valued function β_i as the *best-response function* of player i. A pure-strategy Nash equilibrium is a strategy vector $\mathbf{b} \in \mathcal{B}$ such that

$$b_i \in \beta_i(\mathbf{b}_{-i}), \quad \text{for all } i \in N.$$

Mixed-strategy Nash equilibrium The concept of a mixed-strategy Nash equilibrium formulates a stable state in a strategic game in which players deploy randomized strategies. Let $G = (N, \{\mathcal{B}_i, i \in N\}, \{s_i, i \in N\})$ be a normal form game. Let $\Delta(\mathcal{B}_i)$ denote the set of probability distributions over $\mathcal{B}_i$, and let $\Delta(\mathcal{B}) = \times_{i \in N} \Delta(\mathcal{B}_i)$. We refer to each $a_i \in \Delta(\mathcal{B}_i)$ as a *mixed strategy* of player i. A mixed strategy a_i that puts all of its mass into any specific element in $\mathcal{B}_i$ is referred to as a pure strategy. It is assumed that players choose their strategies independently and that every player i chooses his or her strategy according to a probability distribution in $\Delta(\mathcal{B}_i)$. A set of mixed strategies induces a distribution on the set of strategy vectors $\mathcal{B}$ that is of product form. Given mixed strategies $\mu = (\mu_1, \mu_2, \ldots, \mu_n) \in \Delta(\mathcal{B})$, we define the expected payoffs under these mixed strategies as follows:

$$\bar{s}_i(\mu) = \mathbf{E}_{\mathbf{b} \sim \mu}[s_i(\mathbf{b})].$$

Definition 1.4 (mixed-strategy Nash equilibrium). A *mixed-strategy Nash equilibrium* of a normal form game with complete information $G = (N, \{\mathcal{B}_i, i \in N\},$

$\{s_i, \ i \in N\})$ is a pure-strategy Nash equilibrium of the normal form game with complete information $\bar{G} = (N, \{\Delta(\mathcal{B}_i), \ i \in N\}, \{\bar{s}_i, \ i \in N\})$.

If the sets of strategies are finite, then for a mixed strategy $\mu \in \Delta(\mathcal{B})$, the payoff functions can be represented as follows:

$$\bar{s}_i(\mu) = \sum_{\mathbf{b} \in \mathcal{B}} \prod_{j \in N} \mu_j(b_j) s_i(\mathbf{b}), \quad \text{for } i \in N.$$

The following lemma provides an alternative definition of a mixed-strategy Nash equilibrium that often proves useful in characterizing mixed-strategy equilibria of specific strategic games.

Lemma 1.5. *Let $G = (N, (\mathcal{B}_i, \ i \in N), (s_i, \ i \in N))$ be a strategic game. Then $\mu \in \Delta(\mathcal{B})$ is a mixed-strategy Nash equilibrium of the strategic game G if, and only if, the following two conditions hold.*

  (i) *For every player $i \in N$ no strategy in $\mathcal{B}_i$ yields a larger payoff than the equilibrium payoff, given that other players play according to mixed strategies μ_{-i}.*

  (ii) *The set of strategies that yield a payoff smaller than the equilibrium payoff has a measure zero with respect to μ_i, given that other players play according to mixed strategies μ_{-i}.*

The necessary and sufficient conditions for mixed strategies to be a mixed-strategy Nash equilibrium given in Lemma 1.5 imply that every strategy in the support of any player's equilibrium mixed strategy yields that player the same expected payoff.

Example 1.6 (standard all-pay contest cont'd). Consider the normal form game that models the standard all-pay contest, introduced in Example 1.2. Suppose that players deploy mixed strategies such that player i plays according to a mixed strategy B_i that is a distribution on $\mathbf{R}_+$. Then, $(B_1, B_2, \ldots, B_n)$ is a mixed-strategy equilibrium if, and only if, for every player $i \in N$, we have

$$\mathbf{E}[s_i(\mathbf{b})] \geq \mathbf{E}[s_i(\mathbf{b}) \mid b_i = a_i], \quad \text{for every } a_i \in \mathbf{R}_+.$$

If the inequality is strict for some $a_i \in \mathbf{R}_+$, then a_i is not in the support of distribution B_i.

For every normal form game, the set of mixed-strategy Nash equilibria contains the set of pure-strategy Nash equilibria. There exist normal form games for which the set of pure-strategy Nash equilibria is empty, and the set of mixed-strategy Nash equilibria is not. In Chapter 2, we shall show that the game that models the standard all-pay contest is such a normal form game.

Correlated equilibrium The concept of a mixed-strategy Nash equilibrium assumes that players deploy independent randomized strategies, which induce a joint distribution over the set of all possible strategy vectors of players. This is generalized by the concept of a correlated equilibrium that allows for randomized strategies that are not necessarily independent.

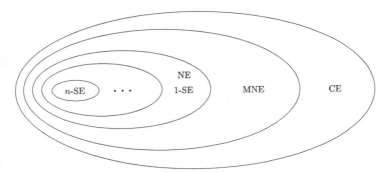

Figure 1.9. Relations between different equilibria.

Definition 1.7 (correlated equilibrium). For a normal form game $G = (N, \{\mathcal{B}_i, \ i \in N\}, \{s_i, \ i \in N\})$, a *correlated equilibrium* is every probability distribution μ over the set of pure strategies $\mathcal{B}$ such that for every player $i \in N$,

$$\mathbf{E}_{\mathbf{b} \sim \mu}[s_i(\mathbf{b})] \geq \mathbf{E}_{\mathbf{b}_{-i} \sim \mu_{-i}}[s_i(a_i, \mathbf{b}_{-i})], \quad \text{for all } a_i \in \mathcal{B}_i.$$

Strong equilibrium The concept of a strong equilibrium is used to model stability with respect to coalitional deviations.

Definition 1.8 (strong equilibrium). A strategy vector is a *strong equilibrium* if there is no coalitional deviation such that every player in the coalition receives a larger payoff after this deviation: a strategy vector $\mathbf{b} \in \mathcal{B}$ is a strong equilibrium if for every non-empty coalition of players $C \subseteq N$,

$$s_i((\mathbf{b}_C, \mathbf{b}_{N \setminus C})) \geq s_i((\mathbf{b}'_C, \mathbf{b}_{N \setminus C})), \quad \text{for some } i \in C, \text{ for every } \mathbf{b}'_C \in \times_{j \in C} \mathcal{B}_j. \quad (1.3)$$

A strong equilibrium requires from a strategy vector to be resilient to coalitional deviations for every non-empty subset of players. A natural generalization is to restrict the size of the coalition so that is at most some parameter k. A strategy vector $\mathbf{b} \in \mathcal{B}$ is said to be a *k-strong equilibrium* if condition (1.3) holds for every non-empty coalition of size at most k, i.e., for every $C \subseteq N$ such that $|C| \leq k$. This concept accommodates a pure-strategy Nash equilibrium as a special case for $k = 1$, and a strong equilibrium as a special case for $k = n$. Figure 1.9 summarizes relations between different types of equilibria.

Games with Incomplete Information

A *normal form game with incomplete information* (sometimes also referred to as a normal form game with imperfect information) consists of the following elements:

   (i) A set of players $N = \{1, 2, \ldots, n\}$.
  (ii) Every player $i \in N$ is of type t_i that takes values from a set of types $\mathcal{T}_i$ assumed to be a complete, separable metric space. We let $\mathcal{T} = \times_{i \in N} \mathcal{T}_i$.
 (iii) For every player $i \in N$, the set of feasible strategies is a set $\mathcal{B}_i(t_i)$ given that player i is of type t_i. We let $\mathcal{B}(\mathbf{t}) = \times_{i \in N} \mathcal{B}_i(t_i)$, for $\mathbf{t} \in \mathcal{T}$, and $\mathcal{B} = \times_{i \in N} \{b_i \in \mathcal{B}_i(t_i) \mid t_i \in \mathcal{T}_i\}$.
 (iv) For every player $i \in N$, the payoff of this player for a type vector $\mathbf{t} \in \mathcal{T}$ and a strategy vector $\mathbf{b} \in \mathcal{B}(\mathbf{t})$ is given by the *payoff function* $s_i : \mathcal{T} \times \mathcal{B} \to \mathbf{R}$.

(v) *A prior distribution* μ on $\mathcal{T}$. Associated with μ is a marginal distribution on each $\mathcal{T}_i$ that is denoted by μ_i: $\mu_i(S) = \mu(\mathcal{T}_1, \ldots, \mathcal{T}_{i-1}, S, \mathcal{T}_{i+1}, \ldots, \mathcal{T}_n)$, for every $S \subseteq \mathcal{T}_i$. The prior distribution μ is assumed to be public information.

(vi) For every player $i \in N$, the type t_i is private information.

A normal form game with incomplete information is defined by

$$G = (N, \{\mathcal{T}_i, \ i \in N\}, \{\mathcal{B}_i, \ i \in N\}, \{s_i, \ i \in N\}).$$

A *pure strategy* of a player in a normal form game with incomplete information G is specified by a function $\beta_i : \mathcal{T}_i \to \mathcal{B}_i$. We refer to $\beta = (\beta_i, \ i \in N)$ as a pure-strategy vector. Here $\beta_i(t_i)$ is the strategy deployed by player $i \in N$ given that his or her type is t_i.

Bayes-Nash equilibrium The concept of a Bayes-Nash equilibrium is defined as follows.

Definition 1.9 (Bayes-Nash equilibrium). A pure strategy β is a *Bayes-Nash equilibrium* if there exists no player $i \in N$ who can increase his or her expected payoff by deploying a strategy different than β_i, while all other players play according to β_{-i}. More formally, a pure-strategy profile β is a Bayes-Nash equilibrium if for every player $i \in N$, we have

$$\mathbf{E}[s_i(t_i, \beta(t_i)) \mid t_i = t] \geq \mathbf{E}[s_i(t_i, (b_i, \beta_{-i}(\mathbf{t}_{-i}))) \mid t_i = t, b_i = b],$$

$$\text{for every } b \in \mathcal{B}_i(t) \text{ and } t \in \mathcal{T}_i.$$

Example 1.10 (standard all-pay contest cont'd). The standard all-pay contest, defined in Example 1.2, can be studied as a normal form game with incomplete information by interpreting the valuation parameters of players as the types of players. Such a game is often referred as a game with *private valuations*.

A commonly studied case is that of *independent and identically distributed valuations* according to a distribution function F whose support is a compact interval in $\mathbf{R}_+$, say $[0, 1]$. This corresponds to a normal form game with incomplete information with identical marginal prior distributions $\mu_i([0, v_i]) \equiv F(v_i)$, and the product-form prior distribution $\mu([0, v_1], [0, v_2], \ldots, [0, v_n]) \equiv F(v_1)F(v_2) \cdots F(v_n)$. This is the case studied throughout the book unless otherwise stated.

1.2.2 Extensive Form Games

An *extensive form game* is a description of the sequential structure of the decision-making process faced by players in a strategic situation. The model allows us to study solutions in which players make decisions in a sequential manner and possibly have a chance to revise their decision. This stands in contrast to the model of normal form games where players make decisions simultaneously and once for all at the beginning of the game.

Complete Information

We consider an extensive form game in which each player has complete information about the payoff functions of all players and all previous actions undertaken by players at each point of the game.

Definition 1.11 (extensive game with complete information). An *extensive game with complete information* consists of the following elements:

(i) A set of players $N = \{1, 2, \ldots, n\}$.

(ii) A set H that contains sequences of the form $\mathbf{h}^k = (\mathbf{b}^1, \mathbf{b}^2, \ldots, \mathbf{b}^k)$, for $k = 1, 2, \ldots, K$, where $\mathbf{b}^j = (b_1^j, b_2^j, \ldots, b_n^j)$ is a strategy vector of the players at stage $1 \leq j \leq k$, such that

$$\mathbf{h}^0 = \emptyset \text{ and } \mathbf{h}^k = (\mathbf{h}^{k-1}, \mathbf{b}^k), \quad \text{for } k = 1, 2, \ldots, K,$$

which we refer to as *histories* and we refer to K as the *horizon* of the game. If K is finite, then the game is said to be a *finite horizon game*.

The set of strategies available to player $i \in N$ in stage k of the game, is denoted by $\mathcal{B}_i(\mathbf{h}^k)$, given that the history is $\mathbf{h}^k$ and denote $\mathcal{B}(\mathbf{h}^k) = \times_{i \in N} \mathcal{B}_i(\mathbf{h}^k)$. Each set of strategies $\mathcal{B}_i(\mathbf{h}^k)$ is assumed to contain the strategy "no play in this stage," denoted by $\perp$, which can be the only strategy available to the player for some history $\mathbf{h}^k$.

We define H_k to be the set of all possible histories in stage k of the game, which can be defined recursively as follows:

$$H^0 = \emptyset, \, H^k = \{(\mathbf{h}^{k-1}, \mathbf{b}^k) \mid \mathbf{h}^{k-1} \in H^{k-1} \text{ and } \mathbf{b}^k \in \mathcal{B}(\mathbf{h}^k)\}.$$

The set H^K is the set of all possible *terminal histories*. The set of all possible histories is defined by $H = \cup_{k=0}^K H^k$.

(iii) For every player $i \in N$ a *pure strategy at stage k of the game* is defined by a mapping

$$\beta_i^k : H^k \to \mathcal{B}_i(H^k)$$

where $\mathcal{B}_i(H^k) = \cup_{\mathbf{h}^k \in H^k} \mathcal{B}_i(\mathbf{h}^k)$. A *pure strategy of player i* is given by a sequence $(\beta_i^1, \beta_i^2, \ldots, \beta_i^K)$, i.e., a collection of maps from all possible histories into available strategies.

(iv) The *payoff* of every player $i \in N$ is a function $s_i : H^K \to \mathbf{R}$ that maps each terminal history $\mathbf{h}^K \in H^K$ to a real value. With a slight abuse of notation, we denote by $s_i(\beta)$ the payoff to player i under strategy vector $\beta = (\beta_i^k, \, k = 1, 2, \ldots, K, \, i = 1, 2, \ldots, n)$.

Given an extensive form game, the game starting from any given stage until the termination of this extensive form game is referred to as a subgame, which is formally defined as follows.

Definition 1.12 (subgame). The *subgame* of the extensive form game with complete information $G = (N, H, \{s_i, \, i \in N\})$ that follows the history $\mathbf{h}^k$ is the extensive form game

$$G(\mathbf{h}^k) = (N, H(\mathbf{h}^k), \{s_i(\cdot \mid \mathbf{h}^k), \, i \in N\})$$

where $H(\mathbf{h}^k) = \{(\mathbf{h}, \mathbf{g}) \in H \mid \mathbf{h} = \mathbf{h}^k\}$ and $s_i(\mathbf{b} \mid \mathbf{h}^k) = s_i((\mathbf{h}^k, \mathbf{b}))$ for $(\mathbf{h}^k, \mathbf{b}) \in H^K$.

Subgame perfect Nash equilibrium The concept of a subgame perfect Nash equilibrium is defined as follows:

Definition 1.13 (subgame perfect Nash equilibrium). *A subgame perfect Nash equilibrium of an extensive form game with complete information* $G = (N, H, \{s_i, \ i \in N\})$ *is a pure-strategy* β *that is a Nash equilibrium for every subgame* $G(\mathbf{h}^k)$ *of* G.

A subgame perfect equilibrium of a finite horizon extensive form game can be computed by backward induction. First compute the best-response strategy vectors in the last subgame of the game for every possible history in that subgame. Then, proceed backward toward the first stage of the game by computing the best-response strategy vectors in each subgame of the game for every given history in that subgame and using the already computed best-response strategy vectors in subsequent subgames of the game.

Example 1.14 (Stackelberg equilibrium). Consider a two-player extensive form game with complete information in which one of the players has the role of a "leader" who chooses first his or her action from a given set $\mathcal{B}_1$ and then the other player has the role of a "follower" who, once informed about the leader's choice, chooses his or her action from a given set $\mathcal{B}_2$.

A strategy vector (b_1, b_2) is a *Stackelberg equilibrium* if for the leader we have

$$s_1(b_1, \beta_2(b_1)) \geq s_1(b_1', \beta_2(b_1')), \quad \text{for every } b_1' \in \mathcal{B}_1$$

where $\beta_2(b_1)$ is a best response of the follower given that the leader opted for action b_1:

$$s_2(b_1, \beta_2(b_1)) \geq s_2(b_1, b_2'), \text{ for every } b_2' \in \mathcal{B}_2.$$

An important fact for a finite extensive form game with complete information is that β is a subgame perfect Nash equilibrium if, and only if, it satisfies the *one-stage-deviation condition*, which means that no player can gain by unilaterally deviating from β in a single stage and conforming to β thereafter.

Theorem 1.15 (one-stage-deviation principle). *A strategy* β *is a subgame perfect Nash equilibrium if, and only if, there exists no player* $i \in N$ *and no strategy* $\tilde{\beta}_i$ *that agrees with* β_i *except at a single* k *and* $\mathbf{h}^k$ *and that is such that* $\tilde{\beta}_i$ *is a better response to* β_{-i} *than* β_i *conditional on reaching the history* $\mathbf{h}^k$.

The statement of Theorem 1.15 extends to infinite-horizon extensive form games under the assumption that the payoff functions are *continuous at infinity*, i.e.,

$$\lim_{k \to \infty} \sup_{\mathbf{h}, \mathbf{g} \in H : \mathbf{h}^k = \mathbf{g}^k} |s_i(\mathbf{h}) - s_i(\mathbf{g})| = 0, \quad \text{for every } i \in N.$$

A commonly studied family of payoff functions is the *discounted sum of stage payoffs*:

$$s_i((\mathbf{b}^1, \mathbf{b}^2, \ldots)) = \sum_{k=1}^{\infty} \delta_i^k s_i^k(\mathbf{b}^k), \text{ for } i \in N \tag{1.4}$$

where δ_i is a discount factor in $(0, 1)$ and $s_i^k(\mathbf{b}^k)$ are the stage payoffs assumed to be uniformly bounded, i.e., there exists $c > 0$ such that $|s_i^k(\mathbf{b}^k)| \leq c$, for every $\mathbf{b}^k \in \mathcal{B}(H^k)$, k, and $i \in N$. The payoff functions from this family are continuous at infinity.

Games with Incomplete Information

Definition 1.16. An *extensive form game with incomplete information* consists of the following elements:

  (i) A set of players $N = \{1, 2, \ldots, n\}$.

  (ii) Every player $i \in N$ is of *type* t_i that takes values from a set $\mathcal{T}_i$. We let $\mathcal{T} = \times_{j \in N} \mathcal{T}_j$.

  (iii) The histories are defined in the same way as for the extensive form game with complete information (Definition 1.11).

  (iv) The *strategy* played by player $i \in N$ at stage k is denoted by b_i^k and takes values in the set of strategies $\mathcal{B}_i(t_i, \mathbf{h}^k)$.

  (v) The *prior distribution* μ of the types is defined as for the normal form game with incomplete information, but under the additional assumption that it is of the product form:

$$\mu(t_1, t_2, \ldots, t_n) = \mu_1(t_1)\mu_2(t_2) \cdots \mu_n(t_n).$$

  (vi) For every player $i \in N$ and stage k, $\mu_i(\mathbf{t}_{-i} \mid t_i, \mathbf{h}^k)$ denotes player i's *posterior distribution* of the types of other players, conditional on the history $\mathbf{h}^k$ and his or her own type t_i.

A distributional strategy β_i maps the set of possible histories and types into the strategy sets such that $\beta_i(b_i^k \mid \mathbf{h}^k, t_i)$ is the probability that player i plays strategy b_i^k at stage k, given the history $\mathbf{h}^k$ and type of this player t_i. Player i's payoff is denoted by $s_i(\mathbf{t}, \mathbf{h}^{K+1})$, for $i \in N$.

In addition, we make the following assumptions:

(C1) Posterior types are independent and identically distributed:

$$\mu_i(\mathbf{t}_{-i} \mid t_i, \mathbf{h}^k) = \prod_{j \neq i} \mu_i(t_j \mid \mathbf{h}^k), \quad \text{for all } \mathbf{t}, k, \text{ and } \mathbf{h}^k.$$

(C2) Posterior distributions of types are updated according to Bayes's rule whenever possible: for every pair of players $i, j \in N$, history $\mathbf{h}^k$ at stage k, and strategy $b_j^k \in \mathcal{B}_j(t_j, \mathbf{h}^k)$, if there exists $\hat{t}_j$ such that $\mu_i(\hat{t}_j \mid \mathbf{h}^k) > 0$ and $\beta_j(b_j^k \mid \hat{t}_j, \mathbf{h}^k) > 0$, then

$$\mu_i(t_j \mid (\mathbf{h}^k, \mathbf{b}^k)) = \frac{\mu_i(t_j \mid \mathbf{h}^k)\beta_j(b_j^k \mid \mathbf{h}^k, t_j)}{\sum_{\hat{t}_j} \mu_i(\hat{t}_j \mid \mathbf{h}^k)\beta_j(b_j^k \mid \mathbf{h}^k, \hat{t}_j)}, \quad \text{for all } t_j.$$

If player $j \in N$ does not deviate at stage k, the posterior updating is not influenced by the strategies deployed by other players:

$$\mu_i(t_j \mid (\mathbf{h}^k, \mathbf{b}^k)) = \mu_i(t_j \mid (\mathbf{h}^k, \hat{\mathbf{b}}^k)), \text{ if } b_j^k = \hat{b}_j^k.$$

(C4) For every pair of players $i, j \in N$ has the posterior distributions of the type of every other player are equal:

$$\mu_i(t_l \mid \mathbf{h}^k) = \mu_j(t_l \mid \mathbf{h}^k), \quad \text{for every history } \mathbf{h}^k \text{ and type } t_l \in \mathcal{T}_l.$$

A *perfect Bayesian equilibrium* is a (μ, β) that satisfies (C1)–(C4) and

$$s_i(\beta \mid \mathbf{h}^k, t_i, \mu(\cdot \mid \mathbf{h}^k)) \geq s_i((\beta_i', \beta_{-i}) \mid \mathbf{h}^k, t_i, \mu(\cdot \mid \mathbf{h}^k)),$$

for every $i \in N$, $t_i \in \mathcal{T}_i$, and $\mathbf{h}^k$

where $s_i(\beta \mid \mathbf{h}^k, \mu(\cdot \mid \mathbf{h}^k))$ is the expected payoff of a player with type t_i under strategy β conditional on the history $\mathbf{h}^k$.

1.2.3 Efficiency Measures

Throughout this book we consider three standard notions of efficiency of a strategic equilibrium, each defined as a function of the vector of efforts invested in a strategic equilibrium. These functions quantify the value of utility of a given vector of efforts to either the contest owner or the contestants or both. For concreteness, in this section, we define these notions of efficiency for a normal form game that has the payoff functions of this form: for every vector of efforts $\mathbf{b} \in \mathcal{B}$,

$$s_i(v_i, \mathbf{b}) = u_i(v_i, \mathbf{b}) - b_i, \qquad \text{for } i \in N$$

where v_i is a parameter in $\mathbf{R}_+$ and $u_i : \mathbf{R}_+ \times \mathcal{B}_i \to \mathbf{R}_+$ is a given function. This accommodates the normal form game that models the standard all-pay contest that we introduced in Example 1.2.

Total Effort

A natural quantity of interest is the *total effort* invested by the contestants in an equilibrium. If the game has a pure-strategy Nash equilibrium $\mathbf{b} \in \mathcal{B}$, then we consider the total effort $R = \sum_{i \in N} b_i$. If the game has a mixed-strategy Nash equilibrium, then we primarily consider the *expected total effort* in this equilibrium:

$$R = \mathbf{E}\left[\sum_{i \in N} b_i\right].$$

Similarly, for the game with incomplete information, if the game has a Bayes-Nash equilibrium, we primarily consider the expected total effort in this equilibrium.

The total effort corresponds to a standard measure of efficiency in auction theory: in the class of all-pay auctions, it corresponds to the *revenue* of the auctioneer. The total effort is also a central quantity studied in the context of rent-seeking activities, e.g., in the case of a political lobbying process, it corresponds to the total revenue of a politician who collects outlays from all lobbyists.

Maximum Individual Effort

Another natural measure of efficiency is the *maximum individual effort* over all contestants. If the game has a pure-strategy Nash equilibrium $\mathbf{b} \in \mathcal{B}$, then we consider the maximum individual effort $R_1 = \max_{i \in N} b_i$. If the game has a mixed-strategy Nash equilibrium, then we primarily consider the *expected maximum individual effort* in this equilibrium:

$$R_1 = \mathbf{E}\left[\max_{i \in N} b_i\right].$$

Similarly, for the game with incomplete information, if the game has a Bayes-Nash equilibrium, we primarily consider the expected maximum individual effort in this equilibrium.

This measure of efficiency is of particular interest in the context of competition-based crowdsourcing services where, ordinarily, submissions of solutions for a task are solicited from the online community with the goal of ultimately making use only of the winning solution.

Social Welfare, Social Efficiency, and the Price of Anarchy

The social welfare of a strategy vector $\mathbf{b} \in \mathcal{B}$ is defined as the total utility realized by players:

$$u(\mathbf{v}, \mathbf{b}) = \sum_{i \in N} u_i(v_i, \mathbf{b}).$$

For a given valuation vector $\mathbf{v}$, the optimum social welfare is the maximum value of the social welfare at a strategy vector, i.e., the social welfare of a strategy $\beta^*(\mathbf{v}) \in \mathcal{B}$ such that

$$u(\mathbf{v}, \beta^*(\mathbf{v})) \geq u(\mathbf{v}, \mathbf{b}), \quad \text{for all } \mathbf{b} \in \mathcal{B}.$$

For example, for the case of the standard all-pay contest introduced in Example 1.2, the optimum social welfare is equal to the value of the largest valuation: $u(\mathbf{v}, \beta^*(\mathbf{v})) = \max_{i \in N} v_i$.

The *social efficiency* of a pure-strategy Nash equilibrium $\mathbf{b} \in \mathcal{B}$ is defined as the ratio of the social welfare of the strategy vector $\mathbf{b}$ and the optimum social welfare: $u(\mathbf{v}, \mathbf{b})/u(\mathbf{v}, \beta^*(\mathbf{v}))$. The *worst-case social efficiency* of a game is defined as the social efficiency of a worst-case pure-strategy Nash equilibrium for a worst-case valuation vector. The *price of anarchy* is defined as the reciprocal of the worst-case social efficiency. The concept of the *price of stability* follows the same definition, but considers the best-case pure-strategy Nash equilibrium. The *strong price of anarchy* and *k-strong price of anarchy* are defined analogously but the Nash equilibrium is replaced by the strong equilibrium and k-strong equilibrium, respectively.

All these quantities are defined analogously for a mixed-strategy Nash equilibrium by considering the expected social welfare $\mathbf{E}_{\mathbf{b} \sim \mu}[u(\mathbf{v}, \mathbf{b})]$ of a mixed-strategy Nash equilibrium μ.

For the game with incomplete information with valuations according to a prior distribution F, we consider the expected social welfare $\mathbf{E}[u(\mathbf{v}, \beta(\mathbf{v}))]$ of a Bayes-Nash equilibrium β and redefine the optimum social welfare to be the expected value $\mathbf{E}[u(\mathbf{v}, \beta^*(\mathbf{v}))]$.

1.3 Overview of the Book

In this section, we highlight some of the interesting questions and results for each topic studied in this book.

1.3.1 Standard All-Pay Contests

Consider a single-prize contest among two or more players who simultaneously invest efforts toward winning the prize. The prize is awarded according to an allocation mechanism that specifies the winning probabilities for each vector of invested efforts. Each player has his or her own valuation of the prize and incurs a cost of production according to a given production cost function. Specifically, we study a normal form game with the set $N = \{1, 2, \ldots, n\}$ of two or more players, the strategy sets $\mathcal{B}_i = \mathbf{R}_+$ for $i \in N$, and the *quasi-linear* payoff functions

$$s_i(\mathbf{b}) = v_i x_i(\mathbf{b}) - c_i(b_i), \quad \text{for } i \in N \tag{1.5}$$

where v_i is a valuation parameter in $\mathbf{R}_+$, $x_i : \mathbf{R}_+^n \to [0, 1]$ is the winning probability function, $c_i : \mathbf{R}_+ \to \mathbf{R}_+$ is the production cost function, and $\mathbf{b} = (b_1, b_2, \ldots, b_n)$ is the vector of effort investments. We can interpret the valuation v_i of a player i as a measure of the ability (or skill) of this player.

The given normal form game allows us to model contests with different types of prize allocation mechanisms and production cost functions. A natural prize allocation mechanism to study is the one that awards the prize to the player who invests the largest effort with a uniform random tie break in case of ties. Such a prize allocation mechanism is sometimes referred as being with *perfect discrimination* as it assumes that a player who invests the largest effort can be identified based on the observed production outputs. Another type of prize allocation mechanism assumes the winning probabilities of players to be smooth functions of the effort investments. Such allocation mechanisms are sometimes referred to as allocation mechanisms with *imperfect discrimination* because the prize is not necessarily allocated to the player who invests the largest effort. The production costs can also be of different types, including production costs that increase linearly in the invested effort or according to a function with increasing or decreasing increments, or a player may incur zero production cost as long as his or her effort investment is within a given effort budget and is, otherwise, infinite.

We study specific instances of normal form games with complete information and with incomplete information. The assumption of complete information accommodates situations in which players possess perfect information about their own abilities and the abilities of other players. This is a plausible assumption to model situations in which prior to a contest, players are informed about which contestants are going to participate and about their abilities based on publicly available records of historical individual performance. In some online contests, the information about who is going to participate in a given contest is made available to the public following a contest registration phase, and the information about the abilities of the contestants can be readily accessible through historical individual performance records available from user profile pages. The assumption of incomplete information accommodates situations in which players are uncertain about the abilities of other players. For example, in an online service, each user may have a good idea about the statistics pertaining to the ability of the user population as a whole, but may be uncertain about which particular other users are going to participate in any given contest.

The *standard all-pay contest*, as described in Example 1.2, awards a single prize to a player who invests the largest effort, and players incur unit marginal costs of production. Chapter 2 is devoted to the normal form game that models the standard all-pay contest covering both the game with complete information and the game with incomplete information.

The game that models the standard all-pay contest with complete information has no pure-strategy Nash equilibrium. Instead the game has a mixed-strategy Nash equilibrium that for some valuation vectors is unique and for others has a continuum of mixed-strategy Nash equilibria. In Section 5.2.2, we provide a complete characterization of mixed-strategy Nash equilibria and the efficiency of these equilibria. These mixed-strategy Nash equilibria have several interesting properties. The set of players who invest a strictly positive effort with a strictly positive probability includes only the players whose valuations are greater than or equal to the second largest valuation. The expected total effort can decrease with the value of the highest valuation of a player. The expected total effort can increase by excluding some players from the competition; in particular, by excluding the highest valuation player. If the objective of the contest owner is to maximize the best individual production output, the all-pay contest may be considered to be an inefficient means toward this goal. One may a priori think that there exist instances under which the expected maximum individual effort can be an arbitrarily small fraction of the expected total effort. This, however, is not true for the standard the all-pay contest. The expected maximum individual effort is guaranteed to be at least half of the expected total effort in every mixed-strategy Nash equilibrium.

The game that models the standard all-pay contest with incomplete information where the valuation parameters are private information and are independent and identically distributed according to a prior distribution has a unique symmetric Bayes-Nash equilibrium, which is shown in Section 2.2. The symmetric equilibrium strategy is for each player to invest effort equal to the expected value of a random variable that is equal to the largest valuation among all other players if this is smaller than or equal to the valuation parameter of this player, and otherwise invest a zero effort. Similarly to the mixed-strategy Nash equilibria of the game with complete information, the second highest valuation plays an important role in the game with incomplete information: the expected total effort in the symmetric Bayes-Nash equilibrium is equal to the expected value of the second highest valuation. For every prior distribution, the expected maximum individual effort is guaranteed to be at least half of the expected total effort in the symmetric Bayes-Nash equilibrium.

1.3.2 Rank-Order Allocation of Prizes

A natural generalization of a single-prize all-pay contest is to allow for several placement prizes based on the rank of individual effort investments. This is the topic studied in Chapter 3. Suppose that the values of the placement prizes are $w_1 \geq w_2 \geq \cdots \geq w_n \geq 0$ where w_j is the value of the prize awarded to the player who makes the j-th largest effort investment. We refer to such a prize allocation mechanism as a *rank-order allocation of prizes*.

Given a desired objective and a prize budget, is it optimal to split the prize budget over several placement prizes or, on the contrary, is it better to devote the entire prize budget to the first place prize? Under certain conditions, there is a clear-cut answer to this question. Suppose that the game is with incomplete information with independent and identically distributed valuation parameters according to a prior distribution, that players incur unit marginal costs of production, and that the objective is to maximize the expected total effort in the symmetric Bayes-Nash equilibrium. Then, we will see that it is optimal to allocate the entire prize budget to the first place prize. In other words, under the given conditions, the optimal allocation of prizes is of the *winner-take-all* type. This remains true even for other objectives, such as maximizing the expected maximum individual effort and for the more general class of increasing concave production cost functions, i.e., players incur (weakly) diminishing marginal costs of production. On the other hand, if the production cost functions are convex, then there exist instances under which splitting a prize budget over more than one place prize is strictly preferable to allocating the entire prize budget to the first place prize.

In our preceding discussion we identified asserted conditions under which it is optimal to offer only the first place prize with respect to maximizing either the expected total effort or the expected maximum individual effort. This was for the game with incomplete information, in which players are uncertain about the abilities of other players, which are assumed to be private parameters with identical prior distributions. This is an important assumption here. In the case of non-identical prior distributions, devoting the entire prize budget to the first place prize is not always optimal. In Section 3.2.1, we describe an instance with players of asymmetric abilities in which it is strictly preferred to split a prize budget between the first and the second place prize rather than to direct the entire prize budget to the first place prize.

Optimal All-Pay Contest Design

Is it possible to make a better allocation of the prize budget by allowing for a more general class of prize allocation mechanisms, in particular, by allowing for not rewarding players at all under certain conditions? The answer to this question is affirmative for both objectives of maximizing the expected total effort and the expected maximum individual effort. The analysis follows from the celebrated work by Myerson (1981) on optimum auction design, which we review in Section 3.1.5. The key concept here is that of a *virtual valuation* that is defined in Definition 3.25. The optimal all-pay contest design is the standard all-pay contest with a minimum required effort.

1.3.3 Smooth Allocation of Prizes

A lot of research has been devoted to the study of allocation mechanisms according to a smooth function of invested efforts, which is the topic of Chapter 4. A well-known example is that of proportional allocation, which assigns a given prize to players in proportion to individual effort investments. Proportional allocation has been extensively studied in the context of the allocation of infinitely divisible resources such as network bandwidth, which we briefly discussed in Section 1.1.11. The smooth allocation of prizes may reflect a deliberate choice of using a randomized allocation with the goal of improving on an objective such as the total effort or the maximum individual effort. The smooth allocation of prizes may also be a consequence of a stochastic production where the prize is awarded to the player who makes the largest production output, which is a noisy observation of his or her effort investment. A prize allocation mechanism that does not necessarily allocate the prize to the player who invests the largest effort is similar in spirit to the use of reserve prices in auctions, where the highest bidder is allocated the prize only if his or her bid is larger than a reserve price. Specific smooth prize allocation mechanisms can be derived from a set of axioms (Section 4.2.1) and various models of stochastic production (Section 4.2.2).

A contest with a smooth prize allocation can exhibit very different equilibrium properties than the standard all-pay contest. Unlike the standard all-pay contest, there exists a smooth allocation of prizes that guarantees the existence of a pure-strategy Nash equilibrium. In Section 4.3 we establish conditions for the existence and uniqueness of a pure-strategy Nash equilibrium for a broad family of general-logit contest success functions, which accommodates as special cases proportional allocation and other types of smooth allocation of prizes. In general, smooth allocation of prizes is prone to social efficiency loss because it may not award the prize to the player who values it the most. However, we shall see that for several specific types of smooth allocation mechanisms, the social efficiency is guaranteed to be at least a constant that is independent of the number of players and the values of the valuation parameters.

We devote particular attention to proportional allocation, which is covered in depth in Section 4.4. The total effort in a pure-strategy Nash equilibrium under proportional allocation is within constant factors of the second highest valuation. For any contest where a single prize is allocated according to proportional allocation, the social efficiency of a pure-strategy Nash equilibrium is guaranteed to be at least $3/4$. The following two properties stand in contrast to those in the game that models the standard all-pay contest: under proportional allocation, the exclusion of some players cannot increase the total effort in a pure-strategy Nash equilibrium, and there are instances in which the maximum individual effort can be an arbitrarily small fraction of the total effort in a pure-strategy Nash equilibrium. Several generalizations of proportional allocation are also studied to some depth, including the ratio-form contest success function, weighted proportional allocation, and weighted valuation allocation, which are defined and studied in Sections 4.5, 4.6, and 4.7, respectively.

Is it possible that a smooth allocation of prizes yields a larger total effort than the standard all-pay contest? The answer is yes. There exist smooth allocations of prizes under which the total effort in a pure-strategy Nash equilibrium is a factor of the second largest valuation that is increasing in the ratio of the largest and the second largest valuation. This naturally leads one to ask: does there exist a smooth allocation of prizes under which the total effort in a pure-strategy Nash equilibrium is guaranteed to be at least a constant factor of the highest valuation? The answer is no. In Section 4.8, we show that the ratio of the total effort and the largest valuation of a player is upper bounded by a function that decreases in the ratio of the largest and the second largest valuation parameter.

1.3.4 Simultaneous Contests

In a system of simultaneous contests, players strategically decide in which contests to participate and how much effort to invest in each selected contest by leveraging available information such as the values of the prizes offered by individual contests

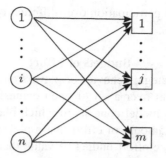

Figure 1.10. A system of simultaneous contests: circles represent players, squares represent contests, and edges represent options for effort investments.

and prior beliefs about the abilities of the players. Figure 1.10 shows an illustration. For any given contest, the presence of other contests provides players with outside options, which in general have a significant effect on the equilibrium outcome. Systems of simultaneous contests are rather common in practice. A prominent example is that of crowdsourcing online platforms that typically host hundreds of open contests at any given time, as demonstrated by the examples in Section 4.7. Online workers incur production costs and can work only on a limited number of projects over a period of time. How do strategic players invest efforts in scenarios with a multitude of open contests? This question is considered in Chapter 5 for different types of prize allocation mechanisms and production costs.

Simultaneous Standard All-Pay Contests

In the game of simultaneous standard all-pay contests each contest awards a prize of an arbitrary value to a player who invests the largest effort in this contest with a uniform random tie break. If the players incur linear production costs, then the game separates into a collection of independent games, one for each contest. In this case, the analysis of equilibrium boils down to that covered in Chapter 3. Another case of interest is when each player incurs a linear production cost but can participate only in a limited number of contests; in particular, we consider the case in which each player can participate in at most one contest. In Section 5.2, we consider both pure- and mixed-strategy Nash equilibria for the game with complete information and a symmetric Bayes-Nash equilibrium for the game with incomplete information. The analysis reveals several interesting properties that arise in equilibria. In particular, in the symmetric Bayes-Nash equilibrium of the game with incomplete information, players choose contests to participate in according to mixed strategies. The relation between the values of the prizes and the participation of players over contests admits an explicit characterization, which is independent of the underlying prior distribution of the valuation parameters. There is a partition of players into classes with respect to their abilities such that a player of a higher ability class selects a contest from a smaller set of contests that offer the top values of prizes than a lower ability class player. A contest is selected by players with a positive probability only if the value of the prize offered by this contest is large enough relative to the values of larger prizes offered by other contests and the overall level of competition. If a contest receives a strictly positive expected participation, then the expected participation in this contest is larger than in any other contest that offers a smaller prize. The expected participation over different contests is more balanced the larger the number of players.

Budgets of Effort

What is the equilibrium strategic behavior of players endowed with budgets of effort that they can arbitrarily split over a set of open contests? The assumption of effort budgets is a natural way to model contests in which players need to produce over a fixed time interval and the amount of effort that a player can produce over this time interval is represented by the effort budget of value that is allowed to be specific to him or her. The assumption of effort budgets also accommodates scenarios in which each player can devote a limited number of working hours, which amount to a budget of effort specific to this player. We shall study three prize allocation mechanisms: the prize allocation as in the standard all-pay contest (Section 5.3), proportional allocation (Section 5.4), and equal sharing allocation (Section 5.5).

The game that models simultaneous standard all-pay contests with effort budgets was studied as early as Borel (1921). Following the work by Gross and Wagner (1950), this game is often referred to as the (continuous) *Colonel Blotto game*. The classic Colonel Blotto game is a game between two colonels, each endowed with a number of troops that they simultaneously distribute across a given number of battlefields. A battlefield is won by the colonel who puts a larger number of troops on that battlefield, and the war is won by the colonel who wins a larger number of battlefields. The class of games of simultaneous contests with players endowed with budgets has a rich set of equilibrium properties. A pure-strategy Nash equilibrium is not guaranteed to exist. There are instances as simple as two contests and two players, which have a continuum of mixed-strategy Nash equilibria. For the case of players with symmetric budgets, there exists a Nash equilibrium in which each player invests his or her entire effort in one contest whenever the number of players is sufficiently large. The expected participation in a contest is proportional to the value of the prize offered by this contest, asymptotically as the number of players grows large. This stands in contrast with the case of standard all-pay contests in which players incur linear production costs.

For the game that models simultaneous contests that award prizes according to proportional allocation, which we study in Section 5.4, we find conditions for the existence of a pure-strategy Nash equilibrium. This pure-strategy Nash equilibrium, in general, need not be unique. The worst-case social efficiency can be arbitrarily low, which is in sharp contrast to the case of players with linear production costs, which we show has the worst-case social efficiency of at least 3/4.

For the game that models a system of simultaneous contests that award prizes according to equal sharing allocation, which we study in Section 5.5, we show that it is a potential game and, thus, has a pure-strategy Nash equilibrium.

1.3.5 Utility Sharing and Welfare

Consider a general production system in which individuals invest efforts over a set of production activities. Suppose that the effort investments put into any given production activity generate a utility of production for this activity. The contributors to a given activity share the utility of production according to a utility sharing mechanism. For example, the utility of production could be shared equally among contributors to this activity. Alternatively, a utility sharing mechanism may award a higher share to an individual who contributed more in a given activity. An example is a utility sharing mechanism according to proportional allocation where each individual contributor receives a share of the production utility that is proportional to his or her contribution. An investment of efforts over a set of production activities results in a social utility of production. In Chapter 6, we consider individuals who make strategic effort investments over a set of production activities with the selfish goal of maximizing their individual payoffs, which combine in some way the value of the received utility and the incurred cost of production. We consider such a production system in a strategic equilibrium in which no individual can benefit by unilaterally deviating from his or her effort investment. Since individuals may form coalitions, we also consider strategic equilibria that are robust to coalitional deviations. A general question that we study is: how efficient is a system of production with respect to the social utility of production in a strategic equilibrium?

The system of production just introduced is defined so broadly that it can serve as a model of many production systems encountered in practice. In the context of online services, users invest efforts in various production activities such as contributing and sharing knowledge, answering questions, contributing to discussions in online forums, and recommending items such as news articles and products. Contributors to such online activities receive credits in the form of attention and visibility in the online community. Users can choose from a large set of different activities that differ in the level of attention received from the online community, depending not only on the general interest of the activity but also on the quality of the production efforts invested in the given activity. The general system of production can also serve as a model of many production systems in practice beyond the context of online services. For example, employees in a firm may have some level of freedom in the choice of projects to work on. The amount of credits received for contribution to a project may depend on the ultimate success of the project, which depends on individual contributions put into the project. Another prominent example is that of the advancement of science through collaborations on research projects. Scientists have a great amount of control over which projects to work on and over the choice of collaborators to work with on these projects. The order of the author names on a research publication provides a means to communicate the relative levels of individual contributions, and is done according to different norms specific to particular research communities. For example, the mathematical and theoretical computer science communities, as a norm, use alphabetical order of author names, which may be seen as an implementation of equal sharing of credits. There are also research communities such as in some applied research areas of computer science and other engineering disciplines in which a norm is to use author order in decreasing contribution order.

There are several principal factors that can contribute to a socially inefficient production, including the type of project utility functions, the type of production cost functions, the choice of the utility sharing mechanism, and the vector of the abilities of individuals across different production activities. In Section 6.2, we discuss several examples that demonstrate how a combination of the form of project utility functions, production cost functions, and utility sharing mechanisms can yield either a socially efficient or a socially inefficient production. In Chapter 6, we discuss general conditions under which a production is guaranteed to be socially efficient.

1.3.6 Sequential Contests

All models of contests that we discussed thus far have one thing in common: they all assume that players invest efforts simultaneously all at once. This is different from the contest designs that involve some elements of sequential play, which are discussed in Chapter 7. The general goal of our analysis is to establish the existence of a subgame perfect Nash equilibrium for the underlying extensive form games, characterize the equilibrium whenever one exists, and compare it with the corresponding normal form game whenever such a comparison is appropriate.

Sequential Moves

What is the equilibrium strategic behavior that arises in a single-prize contest in which players sequentially invest efforts? This is a question studied in Section 7.1. We consider two types of sequential effort investments: sequential play-once and sequential play-twice. In a sequential play-once contest, players invest efforts sequentially one after the other according to a given order of play. In a sequential play-twice contest, the contest consists of multiple rounds, in each round all players make simultaneous effort investments, and the prize is allocated according to a prize allocation mechanism based on the individual total effort investments made over all rounds. We primarily consider the case of two-player contests, which allows for analysis of the subgame perfect Nash equilibrium.

The sequential play version of the standard all-pay contest is studied in Section 7.1.1. We find that the order in which players invest efforts has an important role on the equilibrium outcome. In general, a smaller effort investment is elicited when the weaker player plays first. In the game with incomplete information, the equilibrium outcome critically depends on the prior distribution of the valuation parameter of the player who plays second. If this prior distribution is strictly concave, then there exists a non-trivial subgame perfect Bayes-Nash equilibrium. On the other hand, if this prior distribution is convex, then both players invest zero efforts.

Both the sequential play-once and the sequential play-twice contests with smooth prize allocation according to a general-logit contest success function are studied in Section 7.1.2. Again, we find that the case with the weaker player playing first, in general, results in smaller effort investments. There is a continuum of subgame perfect Nash equilibria for the sequential play-twice contest. The largest value of the maximum individual effort is achieved in a sequential play-once contest. If two players have a choice to decide whether to make effort investments either simultaneously or sequentially with playing once or twice, then it is a pure-strategy Nash equilibrium that both players decide to compete in a sequential play-twice contest.

The War of Attrition

A classic version of the game of the war of attrition consists of two players who compete for a prize in a contest in which the one who waits longer collects the prize and both players incur a cost equal to the length of time taken to resolve the contest. This game was introduced as a model of animal conflicts by Maynard Smith (1974) and was subsequently studied by Bishop and Cannings (1978), Bishop et al. (1978), and others. The player who invests the larger effort wins the prize, and both players incur a cost equal to the smaller of the two efforts. The game resembles that of the second-price auction in which the highest bidder wins and pays the second highest bid, with the notable exception that the game of the war of attrition is an all-pay auction. What strategic behavior arises in equilibrium in such a game with complete information about the valuations of the players? What if the game is with incomplete information? These questions are studied in Section 7.2. A natural generalization is also considered that allows for one or more prizes of identical values, with the contest ending as soon as the number of players who still remain in the competition becomes equal to the number of available prizes.

The Tug of War

The winner in a match between two players is often determined based on the outcomes in one or more rounds of play between the two players. Such contests are common in sport contests in which the winner must win a larger number of rounds than the opponent. For example, in a match between two chess players, a round is a game of chess, and in a match between two tennis players, a round is a set. In the context of crowdsourcing services, a task may consist of several subtasks, and the best solution for the task may be the one that has the largest number of subtasks selected to be of the best quality. How is the strategic behavior of players affected by extending a single-round contest to a multi-round contest? What is the equilibrium strategic behavior in a multi-round contest? Section 7 addresses these questions for a basic multi-round contest design where each round corresponds to a standard all-pay contest. Overall, the analysis reveals that the multi-round contest design favors the stronger player.

Sequential Aggregation of Production

Consider a contest in which players make effort investments in a project over a sequence of rounds that accumulate into a total effort investment. The simplest case of interest is where each player is endowed with a unit effort that he or she can strategically invest in one of the available rounds. The total effort invested in the project amounts to a utility of production that is given by an increasing utility function of the total effort investment. The contest ends in the earliest round in which the value of the utility of production reaches a threshold value. This threshold value is assumed to be private information to the contest owner, and players hold beliefs about this value according to a prior distribution. At the end of the contest, a prize of given value is allocated to players who invested their efforts according to a prize allocation mechanism. For example, a simple prize allocation mechanism is the *first to pass the post* that splits the prize equally among the players who invest in the last round of the contest. The goal is to incentivize players to make early effort investments. Such contests appear in the context of user-generated content in Internet online services, for example, where the project corresponds to answering a question posted to an online Q&A forum. What prize allocation mechanisms incentivize players to make their effort investments in the first round of the contest? Do such mechanisms exist at all for a given family of utility of production functions? Section 7.4 addresses this kind of questions.

Sequential Allocation of Prizes

Consider a sequential allocation of prizes of identical values through one or more rounds using a mechanism described as follows. The number of rounds and, for each round, the number of prizes to award are given. In each round, the prizes of the given round are awarded to players who exhibit the best performance in the given round with each such player being awarded one prize. In each round, the participants in the given round make simultaneous effort investments. We consider unit-demand players, meaning that a player has the same valuation for any subset of one or more prizes. A unit-demand player has no incentive to compete further, having already won a prize. The contest rules do not allow a player to further compete after he or she wins a prize, if this ever happens. While such a contest design may at first appear not very familiar, it is, in fact, commonly used in practice. For example, it exactly specifies a qualifying stage in a tournament, which is used to select players to advance to the next stage of the tournament. We have already encountered one such example in the design of the TopCoder Open Tournament, which is described in Figure 1.6. What is the equilibrium strategic behavior of players under such a sequential allocation of prizes? How do the effort investments compare to that in a single-round contest design? Section 7.5 provides some answers to these questions.

1.3.7 Tournaments

A tournament is a contest architecture that is composed of one or more rounds, each holding some number of contests. In a single-elimination tournament, the winners in a round advance to the next round, and all other players are eliminated from further competition. A single-elimination tournament for pairwise contests is defined by a tournament plan. A tournament plan is given by a directed tree that originates from a root node and has as many leaf nodes as there are players, and a seeding of players that specifies an assignment of players to the leaf nodes of the tree. For example, if the number of players is a power of two, a tournament plan can be specified by a balanced binary tree and an assignment of players to the leaves of this tree.

A good seeding procedure should possess some intuitively compelling properties. For example, a seeding procedure should be fair in the sense of maximizing the probability that the strongest player wins the tournament, assuming the existence of a player who has a higher chance of winning in a contest against any other player. A standard practice is to choose a seeding with the goal of minimizing the chance of early upsets, where a weaker player knocks out a stronger player in an early round of the tournament. Such a practice is followed by the standard seeding procedure, which assigns players to seeding positions such that strong players confront each other only in later rounds of the tournament. For example, in a four-player tournament, the standard seeding procedure matches the strongest player with the weakest player. How can so far vaguely defined notions of goodness of a seeding procedure be formulated into some more exact and verifiable criteria? In Chapter 8 we study approaches to address this question.

A framework to study tournament plans is based on a statistical model whose foundations were developed as early as in works by Chung and Hwang (1978), Israel (1982), Hwang (1982), Horen and Riezman (1985), and many subsequent studies, which we discuss in Section 8.2. In this statistical model, the win-or-lose outcomes of matches between pairs of players are assumed to be independent Bernoulli random variables with parameters according to a given matrix of winning probabilities. The matrix of winning probabilities is assumed to satisfy certain conditions that ensure the existence of a ranking of players such that every player of a given rank has a larger or equal winning probability against any player of a lower rank. In such a framework, one may analyze a given seeding procedure with respect to the following criteria: (i) *delayed confrontation* – does the seeding procedure guarantee that any two players from the set of top 2^q players can only confront each other in a round in which the number of players who still remain in the competition is smaller than or equal to 2^q?; (ii) *monotonicity* – is the probability that a player wins the tournament at least as large as that of every weaker player?; and (iii) *envy-freeness* – is it true that no player prefers the seeding position of a weaker player? Some of these properties can fail to hold for some common seeding procedures. For example, the monotonicity property is not guaranteed to hold for the standard seeding procedure.

Another framework to study tournament plans is to formulate an underlying strategic game under different assumptions about the allocation of prizes, production costs, and the information available to players, which is the topic of Section 8.3. The study of tournament plans as strategic games was pursued as early as by Rosen (1986). We discuss some of the results that provide insights into the optimal allocation of prizes and allow for a comparison with alternative contest architectures such as awarding a single prize in a one-round contest.

1.3.8 Rating Systems

An important problem in practice is rating skills of players based on observed outcomes in contests. This is of interest for various purposes such as ranking players in decreasing order of skills for creating leaderboards and seeding of tournaments and matching players of similar skills with the underlying goal of scheduling interesting matches with uncertain outcomes. There are several desiderata in the design of a rating system, which should be based on some well-defined principles. Simple and intuitive principles are ordinarily preferred over more complicated ones. A rating system often needs to allow for sparsity of observed contest outcomes. In many competitions involving contests between pairs of players, only a small fraction of all possible pairwise contests are held between pairs of players. This is often for the simple reason that the total number of all possible pairwise contests can be so large that it is practically infeasible to realize all pairwise contests. The missing comparisons are also a typical case in situations in which there is less control over the scheduling of matches. For example, in many crowdsourcing services, participation in contests is often to a large extent based on choices made by contestants.

There are a few popular rating systems that are in common use today such as the Elo rating system (Elo 1978), which has been in common use for rating chess players; the TopCoder rating system, which has been used for rating coders; and TrueSkill, which has been used for rating online computer game players. These rating systems differ in various aspects such as in allowing for two-player or multi-player contests, allowing for competitions among individual players or teams of players, and providing only point estimates of the skills of players or providing also confidence intervals for these estimates. However, all these rating systems have one thing in common: they are all based on an underlying probabilistic model with a number of unknown parameters, including the parameters that represent skills of individual players and the uncertainty of individual performance. The statistical model that underlies the design of popular rating systems stems from the early work in statistics in the late 1920s, starting with the work by Thurstone (1927) and Zermelo (1929); has been further developed in subsequent studies by Bradley and Terry (1952, 1954) and many others until the present time.

In Chapter 9, we provide a thorough overview of different families of models and statistical estimation methods, and describe the main principles of some popular rating systems.

1.3.9 Ranking and Aggregation of Judgments

A basic ranking problem is to find an aggregate ranking of players for a given set of input rankings. A related problem is to find a ranking of players for a given tournament matrix that contains information about the outcomes in contests between pairs of players. Another problem of interest is to identify an underlying ground-truth ranking from a given set of noisy observations of this ground-truth ranking. These are the topics discussed in Chapter 10.

Rank Aggregation

The *rank aggregation* problem asks us to find an aggregate ranking of a set of alternatives that is in some sense most congruent with a given set of input rankings over the set of alternatives. For example, the input rankings may correspond to the observed placements of players in a series of contest outcomes among these players, and the goal is to find an aggregate ranking of players that is in some sense most congruent with the given set of contest outcomes. If the input rankings are for a set of two alternatives, then finding an aggregate ranking is a simple matter: just output the input ranking that appears most often in the set of input rankings with a uniform random tie break. If the input rankings are for a set of three or more alternatives, then finding an aggregate ranking becomes a tricky matter, even for the case of only three alternatives. A related question is to select a single alternative as the winner, for a given a set of input rankings over a set of alternatives. This problem is non-trivial as well. An approach to formulate the rank aggregation problem is to admit a loss function and then define the aggregate ranking to be an optimal ranking with respect to minimizing this loss function. For example, a commonly studied loss function is defined as the sum of distances between a given aggregate ranking and each input ranking. A well-known case is the Kemeny rank aggregation where the distance function is the Kendall's τ distance, which for a pair of rankings is defined as the number of pairwise disagreements between the two rankings. These topics are discussed in Section 10.2.

A related ranking problem is the *minimum feedback arc set in tournaments*, which is addressed in Section 10.2.2 and is described as follows. Suppose there is a tournament graph, defined as a directed graph where the vertices of this graph correspond to alternatives and the graph has a directed edge (u, v) if alternative v is preferred over alternative u. For example, a tournament graph can be used as a representation of win-or-lose outcomes in two-player contests. The goal is to find a ranking of alternatives that minimizes the number of edges from a lower ranked alternative to a higher ranked alternative. In other words, the goal is to find a ranking of alternatives that minimizes the number of pairwise disagreements with the rankings of pairs of alternatives given by the input tournament graph. Such a ranking of alternatives is known to be a maximum likelihood estimate under a statistical model that defines a noisy observation of a given tournament graph. The *standard ranking procedure* is to assign each alternative with a *point score*, defined as the number of alternatives that are less preferable than the given alternative, and then to rank alternatives in decreasing order of the point scores. For example, for a tournament graph that represents win-or-lose contest outcomes, the point score of a player corresponds to the number of wins achieved by this player. The standard ranking procedure is a constant factor approximation algorithm for the minimum feedback arc set in tournaments.

The standard ranking procedure is so prevalent that it is worth understanding under what conditions it enjoys certain optimality properties. Suppose that outcomes in contests are according to a statistical model where those outcomes are independent and according to distributions with unknown parameters representing skills of players. Then, it can be shown that for the standard ranking procedure to be optimal with respect to minimizing a loss function from a broad family of loss functions, it is sufficient that the distributions of the contest outcomes come from a specific family of distributions. This, in fact, can also be shown to be a necessary condition. These topics are studied in Section 10.2.2.

Aggregation of Judgments

Consider a binary classification problem where the goal is to classify an object into one of two possible classes. Suppose there exists a ground truth that specifies which one of the two classes is the true class. The ground truth, however, is unknown. The goal is to correctly classify the object based on a set of noisy judgments. This type of classification problems arises in various situations. For example, consider the problem of determining the winner in a contest between two players using a panel of experts who make their judgments based on observed performances of the two players, e.g., as in a boxing match or ice skating. Another prominent example is that of classification (or labeling) of various objects such as images and text performed by (less-than-expert) online workers for a given task wage in paid-labor crowdsourcing services. The individual accuracies of experts may vary greatly from one expert to another. A simple statistical model of judgments by a set of experts is to assume that individual judgments are independent and each given expert states the ground truth with a probability that is a parameter representative of the accuracy of this expert. How should the input judgments be aggregated to classify the object with the best possible probability of correct classification? If there is a budget for the number of classification tasks that can be performed (or money that can be invested), how should the tasks be assigned to experts and the input judgments aggregated? These are the topics discussed in Section 10.4.

1.3.10 Appendix

The last chapter provides a review of mathematical background and some more technical material. This chapter consists of three parts. In the first part, we provide a review of some elements of real analysis, convex functions, convex optimization, some special functional equations, and fixed point theorems. In the second part, we cover some elements of probability and statistics including the basic concept of a distribution, expected values and order statistics that are used throughout the book, a catalog of distributions on a simplex that are used in the context of Colonel Blotto games, and some properties of Gaussian distributions that are used in rating systems. The last part covers some special types of normal form games including concave games, potential games, and smooth games. The first two types of games, concave and potential games, have known results on the existence of a strategic equilibria that are used in some parts of the book. The framework of smooth games allows for deriving bounds on the efficiency for various notions of strategic equilibria without explicitly characterizing the underlying equilibria.

1.4 Bibliographical Notes

The study of strategic games and equilibrium has a long and rich history. The concept of Nash equilibrium was first formalized in the context of strategic games by Nash (1950b). The basic idea goes back as early as Cournot (1838). Bayesian games were first formally introduced and studied by Harsanyi (1967, 1968a,b). The concepts of correlated and strong equilibria were introduced by Aumann (1974). von Stackelberg (1934) studied a two-stage extensive form game with complete information, and following this work we refer to Stackelberg equilibria. The concepts of perfect Bayesian and sequential equilibria were introduced and studied by Kreps and Wilson (1982a,b). Maynard Smith (1982) introduced the concepts of evolutionary and evolutionarily stable strategies. Koutsoupias and Papadimitriou (1999) introduced the notion of the price of anarchy, which has been subsequently studied by many. The concept of the strong price of anarchy is by Andelman et al. (2009). There are several good textbooks on game theory, including Moulin (1986), Fudenberg and Tirole (1991), Myerson (1991), Osborne and Rubinstein (1994), Osborne (2003), and Maschler et al. (2013). Hartline (2012) provides a nice exposition to Bayesian mechanism design and covers many of the recent developments. Vohra (2011) is an advanced-level book on mechanism design based on linear programming techniques.

The formal study of auctions was initiated by the work of Vickrey (1961). The optimal auction design in games with incomplete information was established by Myerson (1981), and also Riley and Samuelson (1981). A complete characterization of the mixed-strategy equilibria for the all-pay auction game with complete information was given by Baye et al. (1996). The all-pay contest with the ratio-form contest success function was introduced by Tullock (1980) as a model of rent-seeking activities and has been subsequently studied by many, especially in the context of public choice literature. An early work on allocation of several prizes in an all-pay contest with unit marginal production costs is due to Glazer and Hassin (1988). There are several good books on auction theory. Krishna (2002) provides a nice introduction and good coverage of standard auctions, in particular, all-pay auctions with incomplete information. Milgrom (2004) provides nice coverage of a broad range of auctions. Klemperer (2004) is a good source on the theory and practice of auctions.

There are numerous research publications on contest theory, developed in the context of economic theory, in particular, political economy and public choice. A search of JSTOR digital library, conducted in early April 2014, for journal articles using search keywords "rent seeking", returned as many as 40,208 entries! Among these entries, 318 had either of the two keywords in the title. On the other hand, there are very few books devoted to contest theory. Some aspects of contest theory are covered in various surveys, including Riley (1987), Nitzan (1994), Szymanski (2003), Corchón (2007), and Sisak (2009). The two edited volumes by Congleton et al. (2008a,b) contain an introduction and reprints of 96 articles published up to 2005 meant to represent major contributions in "40 years of research on rent seeking." An earlier edited volume is by Rowley et al. (1988). Konrad (2009) is one of the very few books on strategic aspects of contests; it focuses more on a higher level discussion of the results and intuition and somewhat less on detailed mathematical analysis.

Some of the topics of interest for strategic aspects of contests can be found covered across various references. There are several books of interest written by computer scientists. Nisan et al. (2007) provides nice coverage of various topics in the area of algorithmic game theory. Parkes and Seuken (2016) provides an introduction to various topics in the area of economics and computation. Law and Ahn (2011) gives a nice exposition of various issues around the design of "human computation" systems. There are several books written by economists that contain elements of relevance to contest theory. Laffont and Martimort (2001) is a book on the theory of incentives. Cournot (1838), Friedman (1977), and Dasgupta and Heal (1979) are standard references on the topic of public goods and Cournot oligopolies. Moulin (1986) is a book on game theory and social sciences. Tirole (1988) is a book on the theory of industrial organizations, in which chapter 10 on research and development technologies is of particular interest. Hirshleifer and Riley (1992) provides interesting perspectives on the role of uncertainty in various economic models, in which chapter 7 provides relevant discussion of some models of research and innovation, and chapter 10 considers the economics of contests with plenty of insightful discussions based on simple contests such as two-player contests or contests with arbitrary number of players but symmetric valuations. Some models of contests are formulated and studied in the context of the studies of division of cognitive labor, e.g., in Kitcher (1993). Frank (1985) provides interesting perspectives on the role of status and how it may shape human behavior. Berry and Johari (2013) and Kelly and Yudovina (2014) provide nice expositions to the topic of network resource allocation.

Let me point out some relevant books for the topics of rating systems and ranking and aggregation of judgments that we cover in Chapter 9 and Chapter 10, respectively. David (1963) is an early book on the method of pair of comparisons and the design of tournaments, which we cover in Chapter 8. McCullagh and Nelder (1989) is a monograph devoted to the topic of generalized linear models. Several books on categorical or rank data, e.g., by Marden (1995), Tutz (2012), and Agresti (2013), are also of interest here. Langville and Meyer (2012) provides an introduction to rating and ranking systems. The problem of ranking of alternatives is closely related to social choice theory and voting theory, which are topics with long and rich histories; see Arrow (1951), Moulin (1988), Laslier (1997), Taylor (2005), and the references therein.

Lastly, let me mention some references in popular literature on the topic of contests and prizes, which may serve as a source of anecdotal evidence, inspiration, or just some fun reading. Dixit and Nalebuff (2008) is a popular book written for a broad audience on various game theory models. Frank and Cook (2010) is a popular book arguing about the winner-take-all nature of modern society. English (2005) provides plenty of stories about prizes in literature and the arts. The research study by McKinsey & Company (2009) focuses on the use of prizes for innovation, provides evidence of their continued growth, and discuses many case studies.

CHAPTER 2
Standard All-Pay Contest

In this chapter we consider a contest design that is often encountered in practice. The contest is among two or more players who compete for a single prize, and the prize is awarded to the best performing player, i.e., it is of the *winner-take-all* type. We shall refer to this basic contest design as the *standard all-pay contest*. We consider a normal form game that models the standard all-pay contest and study the properties of interest in a strategic equilibrium of this game.

The game that models the standard all-pay contest consists of a set $N = \{1, 2, \ldots, n\}$ of two or more players. The players simultaneously make their effort investments $\mathbf{b} = (b_1, b_2, \ldots, b_n) \in \mathbf{R}_+^n$. A unit prize is awarded to the player who invests the largest effort with a uniform random tie break. Specifically, given a vector of efforts $\mathbf{b}$, player i wins the prize with probability

$$x_i(\mathbf{b}) = \begin{cases} \frac{1}{|W(\mathbf{b})|}, & \text{if } i \in W(\mathbf{b}) \\ 0, & \text{otherwise} \end{cases} \tag{2.1}$$

where $W(\mathbf{b}) = \{j \in N \mid b_j \geq b_l \text{ for every } l \in N\}$.

The players value the prize according to strictly positive valuations $\mathbf{v} = (v_1, v_2, \ldots, v_n)$, which we shall refer to as the *valuation vector* of the game. Each player is assumed to incur a production cost that is a linear function of his or her own effort investment. Specifically, the marginal costs of production are assumed to be symmetric over players, and without loss of generality, we assume that each player has a unit marginal cost of production. The payoff functions are of the following quasi-linear form:

$$s_i(\mathbf{b}) = v_i x_i(\mathbf{b}) - b_i, \quad \text{for } i \in N. \tag{2.2}$$

The valuation parameter of a player can be interpreted as a quantity that reflects the *ability* of this player. It can also be interpreted as the reciprocal of his or her marginal cost of production. This holds because of the structure of the payoff functions, which are linear in both the valuation and the production cost, and thus, the game is strategically equivalent to another game that has the payoff functions of the form $\tilde{s}_i(\mathbf{b}) = x_i(\mathbf{b}) - c_i b_i$, where $c_i = 1/v_i$, for $i \in N$.

This chapter consists of two parts. In Section 2.1, we consider the game with complete information where the abilities of the players are common knowledge among the players. In Section 2.2, we consider the game with incomplete information where the ability of each player is private information, and each player holds a belief about the abilities of other players according to a prior distribution.

2.1 Game with Complete Information

In the game with complete information, the valuation vector $\mathbf{v} = (v_1, v_2, \ldots, v_n)$ is common knowledge. The contest owner is not required to be informed about the valuations of players because by definition he or she is committed to using the prize allocation mechanism specified in (2.1), which is conditional only on the invested efforts and is prior-free with respect to the valuations of the players. We shall first show that a pure-strategy Nash equilibrium does not exist and then go on to study the mixed-strategy Nash equilibria.

2.1.1 Non-Existence of a Pure-Strategy Nash Equilibrium

A strategy vector $\mathbf{b} = (b_1, b_2, \ldots, b_n) \in \mathbf{R}_+^n$ is a pure-strategy Nash equilibrium, defined in Definition 1.3, if under this strategy vector no player can increase his or her payoff by unilaterally deviating to playing a different pure strategy.

Theorem 2.1. *For the game with complete information that models the standard all-pay contest, for every valuation vector of two or more players, there exists no pure-strategy Nash equilibrium.*

Proof. Suppose that a strategy vector $\mathbf{b} = (b_1, b_2, \ldots, b_n)$ is a pure-strategy Nash equilibrium.

There cannot exist a player $i \in N$ such that $0 < b_i < \max_{j \in N} b_j$. This is because any such player i would incur a strictly negative payoff $s_i(\mathbf{b}) = -b_i < 0$, and thus, would be better off by investing no effort $b_i = 0$, in which case $s_i(\mathbf{b}) = 0$. Therefore, it must be that whenever $b_i > 0$, then $b_i = \max_{j \in N} b_j$. In other words, it must be that each player invests either 0 or $\max_{j \in N} b_j$.

If there is a unique player who invests the largest effort, then this player has a beneficial unilateral deviation to invest less. By lowering his or her effort by an infinitesimally small amount, the player still wins the prize but at a smaller production cost, which yields a higher payoff. If there are two or more players who invest the largest effort, then each of these players has a beneficial unilateral deviation to increase his or her effort by an infinitesimally small amount. This guarantees that each such player receives his or her full valuation of the prize with an infinitesimally small increase in the production cost, which yields a higher payoff to this player. We have thus shown that it must be that $\mathbf{b} = (0, 0, \ldots, 0)$.

The proof is completed by showing that $\mathbf{b} = (0, 0, \ldots, 0)$ cannot be a pure-strategy Nash equilibrium. Under this strategy vector, every player has a benefical unilateral deviation to increase his or her effort from value zero by an infinitesimally small amount, which increases his or her payoff from value zero to a strictly positive value. $\qquad \square$

2.1.2 Mixed-Strategy Nash Equilibrium

In the game that models the standard all-pay contest, a mixed-strategy of a player $i \in N$ is a distribution function $B_i : \mathbf{R} \to [0, 1]$. The concept of a mixed-strategy Nash equilibrium for a normal form game is introduced in Definition 1.4. For the game that models the standard all-pay contest, mixed strategies $B_1, B_2, \ldots, B_n$ constitute a mixed-strategy Nash equilibrium, if given that all players invest efforts according to these mixed strategies, then no player has a beneficial unilateral deviation to playing according to a different mixed strategy. The characterization of a mixed-strategy Nash equilibrium in Lemma 1.5 can be restated as follows.

Lemma 2.2. *Any given mixed strategies $B_1, B_2, \ldots, B_n$ are a mixed-strategy Nash equilibrium if, and only if, for every player $i \in N$,*

$$\mathbf{E}[s_i(\mathbf{b})] \geq \mathbf{E}[s_i(\mathbf{b}) \mid b_i = x], \quad \text{for every } x \in \mathbf{R}_+$$

and the equality holds for every $x \in \mathbf{R}_+$ that is in the support of distribution B_i, i.e., it has either an atom or strictly positive density at point x.

A player is said to be *active* if his or her mixed strategy invests a strictly positive effort with a strictly positive probability. Otherwise, the player is said to be *inactive*. A player is said to *randomize continuously* on a set $A \subseteq \mathbf{R}$, if this player deploys a mixed-strategy distribution that is continuous and strictly increasing almost everywhere on A. We denote with $\underline{b}_i$ and $\bar{b}_i$ the lower end and the upper end of the support of the mixed-strategy distribution of player i, respectively.

2.1.3 Two Players

Throughout this book, we first consider the special case of a contest between two players and then go on to consider the more general case of a contest among two or more players. This helps us to quickly get an idea about the underlying equilibrium. Understanding the properties of equilibria for a game that models a two-player contest is also of interest in its own right because two-player contests are very common in practice. In the case of the standard all-pay contest, we shall see that a two-player contest also has a very special role: for every given valuation vector of the game, with two or more players, there always exists a mixed-strategy Nash equilibrium in which two players are active and other players are inactive. In the next theorem, we show that in the game that models a standard all-pay contest between two players, there is a unique mixed-strategy Nash equilibrium that is as illustrated in Figure 2.1, and characterize several quantities of interest in this equilibrium.

Theorem 2.3. *Consider the game that models a two-player standard all-pay contest with valuation parameters $v_1 \geq v_2 > 0$. There is a unique mixed-strategy Nash equilibrium, which has the following properties.*

(i) *The mixed strategies:*

$$B_1(x) = \frac{x}{v_2} \text{ and } B_2(x) = \frac{v_1 - v_2 + x}{v_1}, \quad \text{for } x \in [0, v_2].$$

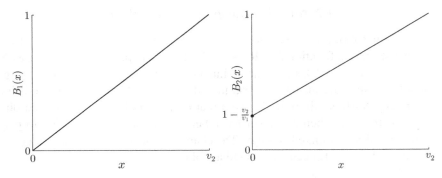

Figure 2.1. The mixed-strategy equilibrium distributions of efforts in a two-player contest.

(ii) *The winning probabilities:*

$$\mathbf{E}[x_1(\mathbf{b})] = 1 - \frac{v_2}{2v_1} \ and \ \mathbf{E}[x_2(\mathbf{b})] = \frac{v_2}{2v_1}.$$

(iii) *The expected payoffs:*

$$\mathbf{E}[s_1(\mathbf{b})] = v_1 - v_2 \ and \ \mathbf{E}[s_2(\mathbf{b})] = 0.$$

(iv) *The expected efforts:*

$$\mathbf{E}[b_1] = \frac{v_2}{2} \ and \ \mathbf{E}[b_2] = \frac{v_2}{v_1}\frac{v_2}{2}.$$

(v) *The expected total effort:*

$$R = \frac{v_2}{2}\left(1 + \frac{v_2}{v_1}\right).$$

(vi) *The expected maximum individual effort:*

$$R_1 = \frac{v_2}{2}\left(1 + \frac{1}{3}\frac{v_2}{v_1}\right).$$

(vii) *The social efficiency:*

$$1 - \frac{1}{2}\frac{v_2}{v_1}\left(1 - \frac{v_2}{v_1}\right).$$

Proof. Here we prove that the asserted pair of mixed strategies is a mixed-strategy Nash equilibrium and sketch a proof for the uniqueness of this mixed-strategy Nash equilibrium. The other claims of the theorem follow by straightforward integral calculus.

The expected payoff for a player conditional on his or her effort investment is given by

$$\mathbf{E}[s_1(b_1, b_2) \mid b_1 = x] = v_1 B_2(x) - x \ and \ \mathbf{E}[s_2(b_1, b_2) \mid b_2 = x] = v_2 B_1(x) - x$$

(2.3)

for player 1 and player 2, respectively. Since neither player has an incentive to invest more than v_2, we have $B_1(v_2) = 1$ and $B_2(v_2) = 1$. Combining with (2.3), we have

$$\mathbf{E}[s_1(b_1, b_2) \mid b_1 = v_2] = v_1 - v_2 \ and \ \mathbf{E}[s_2(b_1, b_2) \mid b_2 = v_2] = 0. \quad (2.4)$$

It suffices to check that the asserted mixed strategies validate the condition in Lemma 2.2 where the equalities hold for the values of the expected pay-offs $\mathbf{E}[s_1(b_1, b_2)] = v_1 - v_2$ and $\mathbf{E}[s_2(b_1, b_2)] = 0$. From $\mathbf{E}[s_1(b_1, b_2) \mid b_1 = x] = v_1 B_2(x) - x = v_1 - v_2$, we obtain

$$B_2(x) = \frac{v_1 - v_2 + x}{v_1}, \quad \text{for } x \in [0, v_2].$$

Similarly, from $\mathbf{E}[s_2(b_1, b_2) \mid b_2 = x] = v_2 B_1(x) - x = 0$, we obtain

$$B_1(x) = \frac{x}{v_2}, \quad \text{for } x \in [0, v_2].$$

The uniqueness of the mixed-strategy Nash equilibrium can be established by using contradiction to show that for a pair of mixed strategies to be a mixed-strategy Nash equilibrium, if one of the players randomizes continuously on an interval, then the other player must also randomize continuously on this interval. One can then argue, again using contradiction, that both players randomize continuously on the interval $[0, v_2]$. From this and the condition in Lemma 2.2, for a pair of mixed strategies to be a mixed-strategy Nash equilibrium, it follows that it must be that for every $x \in [0, v_2]$,

$$\mathbf{E}[s_1(b_1, b_2)] = \mathbf{E}[s_1(b_1, b_2) \mid b_1 = x] \text{ and } \mathbf{E}[s_2(b_1, b_2)] = \mathbf{E}[s_2(b_1, b_2) \mid b_2 = x].$$

Combining this with (2.3) and (2.4), it follows that there is a unique pair of mixed strategies (B_1, B_2) that is a mixed-strategy Nash equilibrium. □

We discuss some interesting observations derived from Theorem 2.3 for the mixed-strategy Nash equilibrium of the game that models a two-player standard all-pay contest. We refer to player 1 as the high-ability player and player 2 as the low-ability player. The strategy deployed by the low-ability player may be interpreted as trying to lower the effort of the high-ability player by not competing with some probability. The winning probabilities depend only on the ratio of the valuations and not on their absolute values. The expected payoff for the high-ability player is equal to the difference between the largest and the second largest valuation and the expected payoff of the low-ability player is zero. We shall see that this property carries over to every mixed-strategy Nash equilibrium in the general case of two or more players. The expected individual efforts are such that each player invests a fraction of his or her own valuation, where the value of this fraction is the same for both players, equal to $v_2/(2v_1)$. Hence, the larger the competition imbalance, the smaller the expected fraction of the valuations of players exerted from the players. For every fixed ability of the low-ability player, both the expected total effort and the expected maximum individual effort decrease with the ability of the high-ability player. This may appear as counter-intuitive because one would expect that replacing the high-ability player with a higher ability player should result in a larger expected total effort and a larger expected maximum individual effort, which in Chapter 4 is shown to hold for some other prize allocation mechanisms.

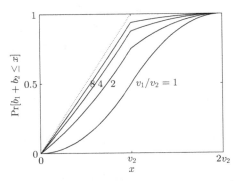

Figure 2.2. The mixed-strategy equilibrium distribution of the total effort in a two-player contest.

The total effort in the mixed-strategy Nash equilibrium has the following distribution:

$$\mathbf{Pr}[b_1 + b_2 \leq x] = \begin{cases} \left(1 - \frac{v_2}{v_1}\right)\frac{x}{v_2} + \frac{v_2}{v_1}\frac{1}{2}\left(\frac{x}{v_2}\right)^2, & \text{for } 0 \leq x \leq v_2 \\ 1 - \frac{v_2}{v_1}\frac{1}{2}\left(2 - \frac{x}{v_2}\right)^2, & \text{for } v_2 < x \leq 2v_2, \end{cases} \tag{2.5}$$

which is left as Exercise 2.1 for the reader to show. From this, we observe that for any fixed value of the ability of the low-ability player, the total effort is stochastically decreasing in the ability of the high-ability player, i.e. for every fixed value v_2, for every given point x, the probability that the total effort is less than or equal to x is non-decreasing in v_1. In one of the extreme cases, for two players of equal abilities, the total effort is a sum of two uniform random variables on $[0, v_2]$. In the other extreme case, as the ability of the high-ability player grows asymptotically large for the fixed ability of the low-ability player, the total effort is a uniform random variable on $[0, v_2]$, which corresponds to the distribution of the effort investment of the high-ability player. See Figure 2.2 for an illustration.

Finally, we note that some amount of social efficiency loss occurs because the players use mixed strategies, and thus, the prize is not necessarily allocated to the player with the largest valuation. This efficiency loss is, however, bounded: the worst-case valuation vector is such that $v_2 = v_1/2$ in which case the social efficiency is $7/8 = 87.5\%$.

2.1.4 General Case of Two or More Players

In this section, we consider the general case of an arbitrary valuation vector for two or more players and provide necessary and sufficient conditions for the existence and uniqueness as well as a full characterization of mixed-strategy Nash equilibria. We shall show that for every valuation vector, a mixed-strategy Nash equilibrium exists. Whether a mixed-strategy Nash equilibrium is unique, however, depends on the valuation vector.

Types of Valuation Vectors

We distinguish the following three mutually exclusive types of valuation vectors:

Type A There is unique pair of players whose individual valuations are larger than the valuation of any other player:

$$v_1 \geq v_2 > v_3 \geq \cdots \geq v_n > 0, \quad \text{for } n \geq 2.$$

Type B There is a unique player with the largest valuation and two or more players whose valuations are equal to the second largest distinct value of the valuations:

$$v_1 > v_2 = \cdots = v_k > v_{k+1} \geq \cdots \geq v_n > 0, \quad \text{for } 2 < k \leq n.$$

Type C There are three or more players with the largest value of the valuations:

$$v_1 = \cdots = v_k > v_{k+1} \geq \cdots \geq v_n > 0 \text{ and } 2 < k \leq n.$$

We shall show that the properties of equilibrium depend on the type of the valuation vector. If the valuation vector is of Type A, then there is a unique equilibrium. If the valuation vector is of Type B, then there is a continuum of equilibria. If the valuation vector is of Type C, then there is a unique symmetric equilibrium as well as a continuum of asymmetric equilibria. There is a unique mixed-strategy Nash equilibrium only in the case when there is a unique pair of players whose individual valuations are larger than the valuation of any other player. In this case, the equilibrium is exactly the same as in a two-player contest between the two players with the largest valuations. In any other case, there are a multiplicity of equilibria.

Specific Examples

In this section we demonstrate the existence of multiple and a continuum of mixed-strategy Nash equilibria for some special valuation vectors. The first case that we consider is a Type C valuation vector where there are three or more players with symmetric values of valuations. The second case is a Type B valuation vector where there is a unique player with the largest valuation and two or more players with symmetric values of valuations. In this section, we claim properties about equilibria without providing proofs, which is left to the reader as Exercise 2.2. The reader who is less experienced with dealing with the concept of equilibria may find it useful to work out the exercise before moving forward to the next section, where we pursue a more involved analysis for the general case of arbitrary valuation vectors.

Symmetric valuations Consider the case of two or more players with symmetric valuation parameters: $v_1 = v_2 = \cdots = v_n > 0$. In this case, there is a unique symmetric mixed-strategy Nash equilibrium in which each player deploys the same mixed strategy:

$$B_i(x) = \left(\frac{x}{v_1}\right)^{\frac{1}{n-1}}, \quad \text{for } i \in N \text{ and } x \in [0, v_1]. \tag{2.6}$$

See Figure 2.3 for an illustration. This, however, is not the only mixed-strategy Nash equilibrium. Another mixed-strategy Nash equilibrium is for the set of active players A being an arbitrary subset of two or more players, and the active players deploying symmetric mixed strategies:

$$B_i(x) = \begin{cases} \left(\frac{x}{v_1}\right)^{\frac{1}{|A|-1}}, & \text{if } i \in A \\ 1, & \text{if } i \in N \setminus A \end{cases} \quad \text{for } x \in [0, v_1].$$

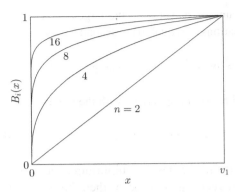

Figure 2.3. The symmetric mixed-strategy Nash equilibrium for a given number of active players.

There are as many such mixed-strategy Nash equilibria as there are different subsets of two or more players; thus, as many as $2^n - n - 1$ in total. The symmetric mixed-strategy Nash equilibrium in (2.6) is a special instance of such equilibria in which all players are active.

All these mixed-strategy Nash equilibria are payoff equivalent, a property that we shall show to hold in general when we consider arbitrary valuation vectors. For the specific case under consideration, the expected payoff of each player is equal to zero. The mixed-strategy Nash equilibria under consideration are also equivalent with respect to the expected total effort

$$R = v_1, \tag{2.7}$$

which is a property that does not hold in general for asymmetric valuation vectors. The mixed-strategy Nash equilibria under consideration are, however, not equivalent with respect to the expected maximum individual effort, which decreases with the number of active players in the following way:

$$R_1 = \frac{v_1}{2}\left(1 + \frac{1}{2|A| - 1}\right).$$

There also exist asymmetric mixed-strategy Nash equilibria in which some players deploy different mixed strategies than other players. In fact, there is a continuum of asymmetric mixed-strategy Nash equilibria, which we demonstrate by exhibiting such kind of equilibrium. Suppose there are a real number $a \in (0, 1]$ and two integers k and m such that $k \geq 2$ and $2 \leq k + m \leq n$. The set of active players is an arbitrary subset of $k + m$ players. The set of active players is split in an arbitrary way such that k players deploy the same mixed strategy and the remaining m players deploy the same mixed strategy. Without loss of generality, consider the case where players 1 through k deploy the same strategy, and players $k + 1$ through $k + m$ deploy the same strategy. We claim that the following mixed strategies are a mixed-strategy Nash equilibrium:

$$B_i(x) = \begin{cases} \left(\frac{x}{v_1 a^m}\right)^{\frac{1}{k-1}}, & \text{if } i = 1, 2, \ldots, k \\ a, & \text{if } i = k + 1, \ldots, k + m \\ 1, & \text{if } i = k + m + 1, \ldots, n \end{cases} \quad \text{for } 0 \leq x \leq a^{k+m-1} v_1$$

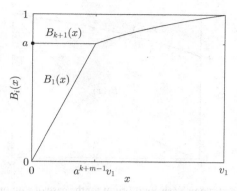

Figure 2.4. The continuum of mixed-strategy Nash equilibria parameterized with $a \in [0, 1]$.

and

$$
B_i(x) = \begin{cases} \left(\frac{x}{v_1}\right)^{\frac{1}{k+m-1}}, & \text{if } i = 1, 2, \ldots, k \\ \left(\frac{x}{v_1}\right)^{\frac{1}{k+m-1}}, & \text{if } i = k+1, \ldots, k+m \quad \text{for } a^{k+m-1} v_1 < x \le v_1, \\ 1, & \text{if } i = k+m+1, \ldots, n \end{cases}
$$

which specifies a continuum of mixed-strategy Nash equilibria parametrized with $a \in (0, 1]$. Figure 2.4 shows an illustration.

An asymmetric type of valuation vectors Consider now a Type B valuation vector where $v_1 > v_2 = \cdots = v_n > 0$. We demonstrate the existence of multiple mixed-strategy Nash equilibria for the mixed strategies of the following form: given an integer $1 \le k < n$, the set of active players consists of player 1 and an arbitrary subset of k players from the set $\{2, 3, \ldots, n\}$ who are assumed to deploy symmetric mixed strategies. Without loss of generality, assume that players 2 through $k + 1$ are active. We claim that the following mixed strategies are a mixed-strategy Nash equilibria:

$$
B_i(x) = \begin{cases} \frac{x}{v_2}\left(1 - \frac{v_2}{v_1} + \frac{x}{v_1}\right)^{\frac{1}{k}-1}, & \text{for } i = 1 \\ \left(1 - \frac{v_2}{v_1} + \frac{x}{v_1}\right)^{\frac{1}{k}}, & \text{for } i = 2, \ldots, k+1 \quad \text{for } x \in [0, v_2]. \quad (2.8) \\ 1, & \text{for } i = k+2, \ldots, n \end{cases}
$$

These mixed-strategy Nash equilibria are not equivalent with respect to the expected total effort, which decreases with the number of active players. See Figure 2.3 for an illustration. The interested reader may either check this on his or her own or consult the derivations and Equation (2.44) in Section 2.44 where we use the specific valuation vector under consideration to obtain bounds on the total effort for general valuation vectors.

Characterization of Mixed-Strategy Nash Equilibria

In this section we provide a full characterization of mixed-strategy Nash equilibria for each type of valuation vector. We first discuss some obervations about the mixed-strategy Nash equilibria and introduce some conventions.

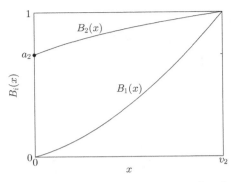

Figure 2.5. The mixed-strategy Nash equilibrium for the case of a unique player of the highest ability and other players of identical lower abilities where players 2 through k are active and play the same strategy, which has an atom at the effort of value zero of mass $a_2 = (1 - v_2/v_1)^{1/k}$.

Given a mixed-strategy Nash equilibrium, every mixed strategy derived from it by interchanging the strategies between any two players whose valuations are equal is a mixed-strategy Nash equilibrium. For example, in Type C, any permutation of the mixed strategies among the players with the largest valuation is a mixed-strategy Nash equilibrium. For easy of exposition, we shall refer to specific players while discussing the mixed-strategy Nash equilibrium. For example, for a mixed-strategy Nash equilibrium in Type C in which only a pair of players is active, we shall refer to players 1 and 2 as the active players, and the reader should bear in mind that any property asserted to hold for these two players also holds for an arbitrary pair of active players among the players with the largest valuation. For the valuation vectors such that there are two or more players with the largest valuation, we shall see that at least one of these players places no atom at effort of value zero. By convention, and again without loss of generality, we assume that player 1 is such a player.

The mixed-strategy Nash equilibria of the game with complete information that models the standard all-pay contest is fully characterized as follows.

Type A:

- The only active players are players 1 and 2: both randomize continuously over $(0, v_2]$, and player 2 invests zero effort with probability $1 - v_2/v_1$.

Type B:

- Player 1 randomizes continuously on $[0, v_2]$.
- Each player 2 through k employs a mixed strategy whose support is contained in $[0, v_2]$ and may have an atom at 0. The mass of this atom may differ across players but $\prod_{i=2}^{n} B_i(0) = 1 - v_2/v_1$.
- For every player $i \in N$, $B_i(x) = B_i(0)$ for every $x \in [0, d_i]$, for some $d_i \geq 0$, where $d_i = 0$ for at least one player $i \neq 1$ and every player $i \in N$ randomizes continuously on $(d_i, v_2]$.
- When two or more players among players 2 through k randomize continuously on a common interval, then they do so in an identical manner.
- Each player $k + 1$ through n invests zero effort with probability 1.

Type C:

- At least two players among players 1 through k randomize continuously on $[0, v_1]$.
- Each player 1 through k randomizes continuously on $[d_i, v_i]$, for some $d_i \geq 0$ and invests a zero effort with a strictly positive probability if $d_i > 0$.
- Players $k + 1$ through n invest zero effort with probability 1.

We observe that under a valuation vector of Type A where there is a unique pair of players whose individual valuations are larger than that of any other player, only these two players are active. This is the only case where the mixed-strategy Nash equilibrium is unique. This mixed-strategy Nash equilibrium corresponds to that of a two-player contest between the two players with the largest valuations. Under a valuation vector of either Type B or Type C, there exists a continuum of mixed-strategy Nash equilibria. The case when only a pair of players with the largest values of valuations is active is a mixed-strategy Nash equilibrium for every valuation vector. We shall see that this equilibrium is extremal with respect to the expected total effort and the expected maximal individual effort. We shall also see that there is a *payoff equivalence*: for a given valuation vector, the expected payoffs of players assume the same values in every mixed-strategy Nash equilibrium of the game under the given valuation vector. If there is a unique player with the largest valuation, then his or her expected payoff is equal to the difference between the largest and the second largest valuation, and is equal to zero for every other player. Otherwise, if there are at least two players with the largest valuation, then the expected payoff of every player is zero.

The properties summarized above follow from the characterization of the mixed-strategy Nash equilibria that is given in the next theorem.

Theorem 2.4. *Consider the game with complete information that models the standard all-pay contest among two or more players with a valuation vector such that $v_1 \geq v_2 > 0$ and if $n > 2$, $v_1 \geq v_2 = \cdots = v_k > v_{k+1} \geq \cdots \geq v_n \geq 0$, for some $2 \leq k \leq n$. Then, every mixed-strategy Nash equilibrium specified by distributions $B_1, B_2, \ldots, B_n$ have the following properties:*

- (i) $0 \leq \underline{b}_i \leq \bar{b}_i \leq v_i$, *for every* $i \in N$.
- (ii) $\underline{b}_i = 0$, *for every* $i \in N$.
- (iii) $\bar{b}_i \leq v_2$, *for every* $i \in N$, *where the equality holds for at least two players.*
- (iv) $\bar{b}_i = 0$, *for every* $i > k$.
- (v) B_i *has no atom in* $(0, v_2]$, *for every* $i \in N$.
- (vi) *Player 1 has no atom at point 0, i.e.* $B_1(0) = 0$.
- (vii) *If B_i is strictly increasing on $(a, b) \in (0, v_2)$, then it is strictly increasing on (a, v_2), for every player $\{2, 3, \ldots, k\}$.*
- (viii) *Player 1 and at least one player 2 through k randomize continuously on $(0, v_2]$.*
- (ix) $\mathbf{E}[s_1(\mathbf{b})] = v_1 - v_2$.
- (x) $\mathbf{E}[s_i(\mathbf{b})] = 0$, *for every* $i \neq 1$.
- (xi) $\prod_{i=2}^{n} B_i(0) = 1 - v_2/v_1$.

Proof. Suppose that the players deploy mixed strategies $B_1, B_2, \ldots, B_n$ and that this is a mixed-strategy Nash equilibrium. We next prove that these mixed strategies satisfy the properties asserted in the theorem by proving each of the properties in the order

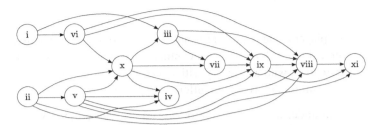

Figure 2.6. The graph of dependencies: each fact is represented by a vertex, and a directed edge from a vertex a to a vertex b means that fact a is used in the proof of fact b.

they are stated. For some of these properties, the proof makes use of some of the other properties asserted in the theorem, which is as summarized in Figure 2.6.

Proof of Fact (i). For every player of the game, investing a value larger than the valuation parameter of this player yields a negative payoff to this player. However, every player is guaranteed a non-negative payoff by investing zero value. Therefore, it must be that every player's mixed strategy has the upper end of its support smaller than or equal to the valuation parameter of this player. The effort investments of negative values are ruled out by definition. Hence, every player's mixed strategy has the lower end of its support larger than or equal to zero.

Proof of Fact (ii). We first establish a lemma that we use to prove the fact under consideration.

Lemma 2.5. *If a pair of distributions B_i and B_j have lower ends of their supports such that $\underline{b}_j \leq \underline{b}_i$ and B_i has no atom at point $\underline{b}_j$, then $\underline{b}_j = 0$ and B_j has no mass in $(0, \underline{b}_i)$. If, in addition, B_i has no atom at point $\underline{b}_i$, then B_j has no mass in $(0, \underline{b}_i]$. See Figure 2.7 for an illustration.*

Proof. By assumption $\bar{b}_j \leq \bar{b}_i$ and $B_i(\underline{b}_j) = 0$. Hence, by the mixed-strategy Nash equilibrium condition in Lemma 2.2, we have

$$\mathbf{E}[s_j(\mathbf{b})] = \mathbf{E}[s_j(\mathbf{b}) \mid b_j = \underline{b}_j] = -\underline{b}_j.$$

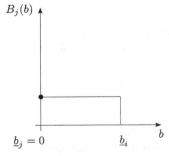

Figure 2.7. The property asserted in Lemma 2.5.

On the other hand, by the assumption $B_i(\underline{b}_j) = 0$ and the mixed-strategy Nash equilibrium condition in Lemma 2.2, we have

$$\mathbf{E}[s_j(\mathbf{b}) \mid b_j = \underline{b}_j] = \mathbf{E}[s_j(\mathbf{b})] \geq \mathbf{E}[s_j(\mathbf{b}) \mid b_j = 0] = 0.$$

Since every player's effort investment is non-negative, it follows that $\underline{b}_j = 0$. By the same arguments, we have $\mathbf{E}[s_j(\mathbf{b}) \mid b_j = x] = -x < 0$, whenever $\underline{b}_j = 0 < x < \underline{b}_i$, and $0 \leq \mathbf{E}[s_j(\mathbf{b})]$ because each player is guaranteed a non-negative payoff by investing zero value. From this it follows that B_j is constant on $(0, \underline{b}_i)$.

The second claim of the lemma follows by the same arguments except for making use of the given extra assumption to deduce that B_j is constant on $(0, \underline{b}_i]$. □

We use a contradiction to show that if there exists at least one player whose mixed strategy has a strictly positive lower end of its support, then this cannot be a mixed-strategy Nash equilibrium. We separately consider the following two possible cases: (i) there is a unique player whose mixed strategy has a strictly positive lower end of its support, and (ii) there are at least two such players.

Suppose that there exists a unique player $i \in N$ such that $\underline{b}_i > 0$; thus $\underline{b}_i > \underline{b}_j = 0$, for every $j \neq i$. If B_i has no atom at point $\underline{b}_i$, then by Lemma 2.5, it follows that for every player $j \neq i$, B_j has zero mass on the interval $(0, \underline{b}_i]$. This, in turn, implies

$$\mathbf{E}[s_i(\mathbf{b})] = \mathbf{E}[s_i(\mathbf{b}) \mid b_i = \underline{b}_i] < \mathbf{E}[s_i(\mathbf{b}) \mid b_i = x], \quad \text{for every } 0 < x < \underline{b}_i \quad (2.9)$$

which is a contradiction to the mixed-strategy Nash equilibrium condition in Lemma 2.2. If, on the other hand, B_i has an atom at point $\underline{b}_i$, then every player $j \neq i$ who would put some mass on $\underline{b}_i$ will increase his or her expected payoff by relocating some of this mass to a larger value. Hence,

$$B_j \text{ has no atom at point } \underline{b}_i, \quad \text{for every } j \neq i. \quad (2.10)$$

Since $\underline{b}_i > \underline{b}_j$ for all $j \neq i$, we have that B_i has no atom at point $\underline{b}_j = 0$, and thus, by Lemma 2.5, we have

$$B_j(0) = \lim_{x \uparrow \underline{b}_i} B_j(x), \quad \text{for every } j \neq i. \quad (2.11)$$

By putting together relations (2.10) and (2.11), we deduce that for every player $j \neq i$, B_j has no mass on the interval $(0, \underline{b}_i]$. This, again, implies (2.9), which is a contradiction to the mixed-strategy Nash equilibrium condition in Lemma 2.2.

Suppose now that the set S defined by $S = \{i \in N \mid \underline{b}_i > 0\}$ contains two or more players. By similar arguments as in the previous case, it is easy to observe that it suffices to consider the case in which $\underline{b}_i = \underline{b}_j$, for every $i, j \in S$. For at least one player $i \in S$, it must hold that $B_i(\underline{b}_i) = 0$, because otherwise, each $j \in S$ could gain by increasing $\underline{b}_j$ for a small amount. This means that there exist $i, j \in S$ such that $\underline{b}_i = \underline{b}_j > 0$ and $B_i(\underline{b}_j) = 0$, which is a contradiction to the fact asserted in Lemma 2.5.

Proof of Fact (iii). By Fact (i), every player $i \in N$ has the support of its mixed strategy contained in $[0, v_i]$. Since, by assumption, the valuation parameter of each player $i \neq 1$ is smaller than or equal to v_2, it suffices to consider only player 1. Player 1 has no incentive to invest a value in $(v_2, v_1]$ because any such choice is strictly dominated by investing an infinitesimally smaller value.

There must exist a player $i \in N$ such that $\bar{b}_i = v_2$. Otherwise, player 2 would be guaranteed a strictly positive expected payoff by investing any value in $(\max_{j \in N} \bar{b}_j, v_2)$. This is a contradiction to Fact (x) that in every mixed-strategy Nash equilibrium, the expected payoff of player 2 is equal to zero.

There must exist at least two players whose mixed strategies have v_2 in their supports. Otherwise, if $\bar{b}_i = v_2$ for some player $i \in N$ and $\bar{b}_j < v_2$ for every other player $j \neq i$, then player i would have an incentive to reduce the upper end of the support of his or her mixed strategy.

Proof of Fact (iv). We first establish two lemmas.

Lemma 2.6. *There exists at least one player whose mixed strategy has no atom at point* 0.

Proof. Suppose on the contrary that $B_i(0) > 0$ for every $i \in N$. For every player $i \in N$, we have

$$\mathbf{E}[s_i(\mathbf{b}) \mid b_i = 0] = v_i \frac{1}{n} \prod_{j \neq i} B_j(0) \tag{2.12}$$

and, for every small enough $\epsilon > 0$,

$$\mathbf{E}[s_i(\mathbf{b}) \mid b_i = \epsilon] \geq v_i \prod_{j \neq i} B_j(0) - \epsilon > v_i \frac{1}{n} \prod_{j \neq i} B_j(0) = \mathbf{E}[s_i(\mathbf{b}) \mid b_i = 0]. \tag{2.13}$$

Since by the mixed-strategy Nash equilibrium condition in Lemma 2.2, $\mathbf{E}[s_i(\mathbf{b}) \mid b_i = 0] = \mathbf{E}[s_i(\mathbf{b})] \geq \mathbf{E}[s_i(\mathbf{b}) \mid b_i = \epsilon]$, and by relations (2.12) and (2.13), $\mathbf{E}[s_i(\mathbf{b}) \mid b_i = 0] < \mathbf{E}[s_i(\mathbf{b}) \mid b_i = \epsilon]$, we have a contradiction. $\square$

Lemma 2.7. *For every two players* $i, j \in N$ *their expected payoffs satisfy:*

(i) *If* $v_i \geq v_j$, *then* $\mathbf{E}[s_i(\mathbf{b})] \geq \mathbf{E}[s_j(\mathbf{b})]$.
(ii) *If* $v_i > v_j$, *then either* $\mathbf{E}[s_i(\mathbf{b})] > \mathbf{E}[s_j(\mathbf{b})]$, *or* $\mathbf{E}[s_i(\mathbf{b})] = \mathbf{E}[s_j(\mathbf{b})] = 0$ *and* $\bar{b}_j = 0$.

Proof. First note that for every two players $i, j \in N$, their respective expected payoffs conditional on their individual effort investments can be written as

$$\mathbf{E}[s_i(\mathbf{b}) \mid b_i = x] = \begin{cases} v_i \frac{1}{n} B_j(0) A(0), & \text{if } x = 0 \\ v_i B_j(x) A(x) - x, & \text{if } x > 0 \end{cases} \tag{2.14}$$

and

$$\mathbf{E}[s_j(\mathbf{b}) \mid b_j = x] = \begin{cases} v_j \frac{1}{n} B_i(0) A(0), & \text{if } x = 0 \\ v_j B_i(x) A(x) - x, & \text{if } x > 0 \end{cases} \tag{2.15}$$

where

$$A(x) = \begin{cases} 1, & \text{if } n = 2 \\ \prod_{l \in N \setminus \{i, j\}} B_l(x), & \text{if } n > 2 \end{cases} \tag{2.16}$$

For the first claim, suppose that on the contrary $v_i \geq v_j$ and $\mathbf{E}[s_i(\mathbf{b})] < \mathbf{E}[s_j(\mathbf{b})]$. Then, combining the latter inequality with the mixed-strategy Nash equilibrium condition in Lemma 2.2, we have

$$\mathbf{E}[s_i(\mathbf{b})] < \mathbf{E}[s_j(\mathbf{b})] = \mathbf{E}[s_j(\mathbf{b}) \mid b_j = \bar{b}_j].$$

On the other hand, by the assumption $v_i \geq v_j$ and the relations (2.14) and (2.15), we have

$$\mathbf{E}[s_j(\mathbf{b}) \mid b_j = \bar{b}_j] \leq \lim_{x \downarrow \bar{b}_j} \mathbf{E}[s_i(\mathbf{b}) \mid b_i = x].$$

Hence, it follows that

$$\mathbf{E}[s_i(\mathbf{b})] < \mathbf{E}[s_i(\mathbf{b}) \mid b_i = x], \text{ for some } x > \bar{b}_j \qquad (2.17)$$

which is a contradiction to the mixed-strategy Nash equilibrium condition in Lemma 2.2.

We now prove the second claim. By the first claim, it suffices to show that if under $v_i > v_j$, it holds that $\mathbf{E}[s_i(\mathbf{b})] = \mathbf{E}[s_j(\mathbf{b})]$, then it must be that $\bar{b}_j = 0$. Suppose on the contrary that $v_i > v_j$, $\mathbf{E}[s_i(\mathbf{b})] = \mathbf{E}[s_j(\mathbf{b})]$, and $\bar{b}_j > 0$. Then, combining with the mixed-strategy Nash equilibrium condition in Lemma 2.2, we have

$$\mathbf{E}[s_i(\mathbf{b})] = \mathbf{E}[s_j(\mathbf{b})] = \mathbf{E}[s_j(\mathbf{b}) \mid b_j = \bar{b}_j].$$

On the other hand, by Fact (ii) $\prod_{l \neq m} B_l(x) > 0$, for every $x > 0$, and every player $m \in N$. Combining this with the assumptions $v_i > v_j$ and $\bar{b}_j > 0$, and the relations (2.14) and (2.15), we obtain

$$\mathbf{E}[s_j(\mathbf{b}) \mid b_j = \bar{b}_j] < \lim_{x \downarrow \bar{b}_j} \mathbf{E}[s_i(\mathbf{b}) \mid b_i = x].$$

Hence, it follows that the relation in (2.17) holds, which is a contradiction. □

By Fact (x), $\mathbf{E}[s_i(\mathbf{b})] = 0$ for every $i \neq 1$, which combined with the assumption $v_2 > v_{k+1}$ and Lemma 2.7, implies $\bar{b}_j = 0$ for every $j \in \{k+1, \ldots, n\}$.

Proof of Fact (v). Suppose that there exists a player $i \in N$ such that B_i has an atom at a point $x^* \in (0, v_2]$. By Fact (ii), $\prod_{l \neq j} B_l(x) > 0$, for every $x > 0$ and every player $j \in N$. It follows that for every player $j \neq i$, $\prod_{l \neq j} B_l(x)$ has an upward jump at $x = x^*$. This implies that every player $j \neq i$ such that $x^* < v_j$ can gain by transferring the mass of its mixed-strategy distribution from a neighborhood below x^* to point x^*, if there is any. For the case $x^* = v_j$, it pays for player j to transfer the mass of its mixed-strategy distribution from a neighborhood below x^* to zero. It follows that there is a neighborhood below x^* in which no player $j \neq i$ puts a positive mass. This implies that player i has an incentive to move the mass of its mixed-strategy distribution from point x^* to a lower value, which is a contradiction to the hypothesis that B_i has an atom at point x^*.

Proof of Fact (vi). We show that $B_1(0) = 0$ by considering two different cases for the valuation vector.

Consider first the case $v_1 > v_2$. Suppose on the contrary that $B_1(0) > 0$. Then, by Lemma 2.2 and Lemma 2.6, we have

$$\mathbf{E}[s_1(\mathbf{b})] = \mathbf{E}[s_1(\mathbf{b}) \mid b_1 = 0] = v_1 \frac{1}{n} \prod_{j \neq 1} B_j(0) = 0. \tag{2.18}$$

On the other hand, by Lemma 2.2 and Fact (i), for every small enough $\epsilon > 0$,

$$\mathbf{E}[s_1(\mathbf{b})] \geq \mathbf{E}[s_1(\mathbf{b}) \mid b_1 = v_2 + \epsilon] = v_1 - v_2 - \epsilon > 0. \tag{2.19}$$

When relations (2.18) and (2.19) are put together we have a contradiction.

Consider now the case $v_1 = v_2$, where we distinguish the following two subcases:

If $v_1 = v_2 = \cdots = v_n$, it immediately follows that $B_1(0) = 0$ because by Lemma 2.6, $B_i(0) = 0$ for some player $i \in N$, and obviously such a player has a valuation parameter of value v_1; by convention, player 1 is assumed to be such a player.

If $v_1 = v_2 = \cdots = v_k > v_{k+1}$, for $2 \leq k < n$, we proceed as follows. It suffices to show that $B_i(0) = 0$ for some $i \in \{1, 2, \ldots, k\}$. Suppose on the contrary that $B_i(0) > 0$ for every $i \in \{1, 2, \ldots, k\}$. Then, by Lemma 2.2 and Lemma 2.6, we have

$$\mathbf{E}[s_i(\mathbf{b})] = \mathbf{E}[s_i(\mathbf{b}) \mid b_i = 0] = v_1 \frac{1}{n} \prod_{j \neq i} B_j(0) = 0, \text{ for every } i \in \{1, 2, \ldots, k\}.$$

Combining with Lemma 2.7, it follows that $\mathbf{E}[s_i(\mathbf{b})] = 0$ for every $i \in N$ and that $\bar{b}_i = 0$ for every $i \in \{k+1, k+2, \ldots, n\}$. Thus, it follows that the mixed strategy of every player has an atom at 0, which is a contradiction to the fact asserted in Lemma 2.6.

Proof of Fact (vii). We first establish two lemmas.

Lemma 2.8. *For every non-empty interval* $(a, b] \in (0, v_2]$, *there exists a pair of players* $i, j \in N$, $i \neq j$, *such that both* B_i *and* B_j *have a strictly positive mass on* $(a, b]$.

Proof. The proof is by contradiction by considering the following two cases.

Suppose first that there exists a non-empty interval $(a, b] \in (0, v_2]$ such that $B_j(b) - B_j(a) = 0$ for every player $j \in N$. By Fact (iii), there exists a player $i \in N$ such that $\bar{b}_i = v_2$. Hence, it must be that $b < v_2$ and that there exists a value $x \in (b, v_2)$ such that $B_i(x)$ increases at x for some player $i \in N$. Let x^* be the smallest such value and let $i \in N$ be a player such that B_i increases at point x^*. Then, we have $\mathbf{E}[s_i(\mathbf{b}) \mid b_i = x^*] = v_i \prod_{j \neq i} B_j(a) - x^* < v_i \prod_{j \neq i} B_j(a) - a = \mathbf{E}[s_i(\mathbf{b}) \mid b_i = a]$, where the equalities hold because by Fact (v) every player's mixed strategy has no atoms in $(0, v_2]$. Since B_i increases at x^*, by the mixed-strategy Nash equilibrium condition in Lemma 2.2, $\mathbf{E}[s_i(\mathbf{b})] = \mathbf{E}[s_i(\mathbf{b}) \mid b_i = x^*]$. It follows that $\mathbf{E}[s_i(\mathbf{b})] < \mathbf{E}[s_i(\mathbf{b}) \mid b_i = a]$, which is a contradiction to the mixed-strategy Nash equilibrium condition in Lemma 2.2.

Suppose now that there exists a non-empty interval $(a, b] \in (0, v_2]$ such that $B_i(b) - B_i(a) > 0$ for some player $i \in N$, and $B_j(b) - B_j(a) = 0$, for every other player $j \neq i$. Then, $\mathbf{E}[s_i(\mathbf{b}) \mid b_i = x] = v_i \prod_{j \neq i} B_j(a) - x < v_i \prod_{j \neq i} B_j(a) - a = \mathbf{E}[s_i(\mathbf{b}) \mid b_i = a]$, for every $x \in (a, b]$, where the equalities hold because by Fact (v) every player's mixed strategy has no atoms in $(0, v_2]$. By the assumption $B_i(b) - B_i(a) > 0$,

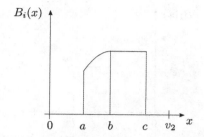

Figure 2.8. The assumed condition for contradiction.

there exists $x \in (a, b]$ such that B_i increases at x. Let x^* be one such value. By the mixed-strategy Nash equilibrium condition in Lemma 2.2, we have $\mathbf{E}[s_i(\mathbf{b})] = \mathbf{E}[s_i(\mathbf{b}) \mid b_i = x^*]$. It follows that $\mathbf{E}[s_i(\mathbf{b})] < \mathbf{E}[s_i(\mathbf{b}) \mid b_i = a]$, which, again, is a contradiction. $\qquad\square$

Lemma 2.9. *Suppose that both B_i and B_j increase at a point $x \in (0, v_2]$, for $i, j \in \{2, 3, \ldots, k\}$. Then, $B_i(x) = B_j(x)$.*

Proof. By the assumption of the lemma, x is in the support of both B_i and B_j, and by Fact (x) $\mathbf{E}[s_i(\mathbf{b})] = \mathbf{E}[s_j(\mathbf{b})] = 0$. Therefore, by the mixed-strategy Nash equilibrium condition in Lemma 2.2, we have

$$\mathbf{E}[s_i(\mathbf{b}) \mid b_i = x] = \mathbf{E}[s_j(\mathbf{b}) \mid b_j = x] = 0.$$

This implies

$$A(x)B_i(x) = A(x)B_j(x) = \frac{x}{v_2}$$

where $A(x)$ is defined in (2.16). It follows that $B_i(x) = B_j(x)$. $\qquad\square$

The proof of the fact under consideration follows by a contradiction. Suppose on the contrary that there exists a player $i \in \{2, 3, \ldots, k\}$ such that B_i is strictly increasing on an interval $(a, b] \in (0, v_2)$ and is constant on $(b, c]$, for some $b < c \le v_2$. See Figure 2.8 for an illustration.

By Lemma 2.8, there exists $\epsilon > 0$ such that there are two players, say j and l, such that both B_j and B_l are strictly increasing on $[b, b + \epsilon]$. At least one of these two players is in the set $\{2, 3, \ldots, k\}$, and, without loss of generality, assume that j is such a player. By Lemma 2.9 and Fact (ii), we have

$$B_j(b) = B_i(b) > 0.$$

Since B_i is increasing at point b and is constant on $(b, b + \epsilon]$, by Lemma 2.2, we have

$$\mathbf{E}[s_i(\mathbf{b}) \mid b_i = b] \ge \mathbf{E}[s_i(\mathbf{b}) \mid b_i = x], \text{ for every } x \in (b, b + \epsilon]. \qquad (2.20)$$

On the other hand, since B_j is strictly increasing on $[b, b + \epsilon]$, by Lemma 2.2, we have

$$\mathbf{E}[s_j(\mathbf{b})] = \mathbf{E}[s_j(\mathbf{b}) \mid b_j = x], \text{ for every } x \in [b, b + \epsilon]. \qquad (2.21)$$

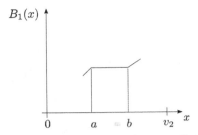

Figure 2.9. The assumed gap for contradiction.

By Fact (x),

$$\mathbf{E}[s_i(\mathbf{b})] = \mathbf{E}[s_j(\mathbf{b})] = 0. \tag{2.22}$$

From (2.20), (2.21), and (2.22), we have

$$\mathbf{E}[s_i(\mathbf{b}) \mid b_i = x] \le \mathbf{E}[s_j(\mathbf{b}) \mid b_j = x], \text{ for every } x \in (b, b + \epsilon].$$

This implies that $\prod_{m \ne i} B_m(x) \le \prod_{m \ne j} B_m(x)$ and, hence, $B_j(x) \le B_i(x)$, for every $x \in (b, b + \epsilon]$. This is a contradiction to that $B_i(b) = B_j(b)$, B_j is strictly increasing on $[b, b + \epsilon]$ and B_i is constant on $(b, b + \epsilon]$.

Proof of Fact (viii). By Facts (ii) and (iii), $\underline{b}_1 = 0$ and $\bar{b}_1 \le v_2$. Suppose there exists a non-empty interval $(a, b) \in [0, v_2]$ such that $B_1(x)$ increases at points a and b and is constant on (a, b).

By Lemma 2.8, for every small enough $\epsilon > 0$, there are two players $i, j \in \{2, 3, \ldots, k\}$ such that both B_i and B_j are strictly increasing on $(a, a + \epsilon)$. Combined with Fact (vii), both B_i and B_j are strictly increasing on (a, b). Combining this further with Lemma 2.9, we have $B_i(x) = B_j(x)$, for $x \in [a, b]$. From Fact (v), Fact (x) and Lemma 2.2, we have

$$\prod_{m \ne i} B_m(x) = \prod_{m \ne j} B_m(x) = \frac{x}{v_2}, \text{ for } x \in [a, b]. \tag{2.23}$$

By Lemma 2.2, $\mathbf{E}[s_1(\mathbf{b})] = \mathbf{E}[s_1(\mathbf{b}) \mid b_1 = x]$, for $x = a, b$, because both a and b are in the support of B_1. By Fact (ix), $\mathbf{E}[s_1(\mathbf{b})] = v_1 - v_2$. Therefore,

$$\prod_{m \ne 1} B_m(x) = \frac{v_1 - v_2 + x}{v_1}, \text{ for } x = a, b. \tag{2.24}$$

From (2.23) and (2.24) and the observation that $B_i(x) = B_j(x)$ for $x \in [a, b]$, we obtain

$$B_1(x) B_j(x) \prod_{m \notin \{1, i, j\}} B_m(x) = \frac{x}{v_2}, \text{ for } x = a, b \tag{2.25}$$

and

$$B_j(x)^2 \prod_{m \notin \{1, i, j\}} B_m(x) = \frac{v_1 - v_2 + x}{v_1}, \text{ for } x = a, b. \tag{2.26}$$

From (2.25) and (2.26), it follows that

$$\frac{B_j(a) \prod_{m \notin \{1,i,j\}} B_m(a)}{B_j(b) \prod_{m \notin \{1,i,j\}} B_m(b)} = \frac{a}{b} \quad \text{and} \quad \frac{B_j(a)^2 \prod_{m \notin \{1,i,j\}} B_m(a)}{B_j(b)^2 \prod_{m \notin \{1,i,j\}} B_m(b)} = \frac{v_1 - v_2 + a}{v_1 - v_2 + b}.$$

Hence,

$$B_j(a) = B_j(b)\frac{b(v_1 - v_2 + a)}{a(v_1 - v_2 + b)} \geq B_j(b),$$

which is a contradiction to that $a < b$ and that B_j is strictly increasing on $(a, b]$.

We next show that at least one player among players 2 through k randomizes continuously on $[0, v_2]$. Without loss generality, assume that this is player 2. Applying Lemma 2.8 along with the part of Fact (viii) that player 1 randomizes continuously on $(0, v_2]$, it follows that for every $\epsilon > 0$, $B_2(\epsilon) - B_2(0) > 0$. Using Fact (vii), it follows that player 2 randomizes continuously on $(0, v_2]$.

Proof of Fact (ix). By Fact (v) every player's mixed strategy has no atoms in $(0, v_2]$, and by Fact (iii) every player's mixed strategy has its support contained in $[0, v_2]$. Therefore, by the mixed-strategy Nash equilibrium condition in Lemma 2.2, we have

$$\mathbf{E}[s_1(\mathbf{b})] \geq \mathbf{E}[s_1(\mathbf{b}) \mid b_1 = v_2] = v_1 \prod_{j \neq 1} B_j(v_2) - v_2 = v_1 - v_2.$$

It thus suffices to show that the point v_2 is in the support of player 1's mixed strategy. Since by Fact (v) player 1's mixed strategy has no atom at point v_2, we need to show that B_1 is strictly increasing on $(v_2 - \epsilon, v_2]$ for every small enough $\epsilon > 0$.

Note that by Fact (iii), Fact (vii), and Lemma 2.8, there exists a player $m \in \{2, 3, \ldots, k\}$ who randomizes continuously on $(0, v_2]$.

Since by Fact (vi) $B_1(0) = 0$ and by Fact (v) every player's mixed strategy has no atoms in $(0, v_2]$, it follows that B_1 is increasing at some point $x \in (0, v_2)$. At every such point x, we have

$$\mathbf{E}[s_1(\mathbf{b}) \mid b_1 = x] = v_1 \prod_{j \neq 1} B_j(x) - x \geq \mathbf{E}[s_1(\mathbf{b}) \mid b_1 = v_2] = v_1 - v_2.$$

Therefore, we have

$$v_1 \prod_{j \neq 1} B_j(x) - x \geq v_1 - v_2. \tag{2.27}$$

On the other hand, since player m randomizes continuously on $(0, v_2]$ and by Fact (x) $\mathbf{E}[s_m(\mathbf{b})] = 0$, by the mixed-strategy Nash condition in Lemma 2.2, we have

$$\mathbf{E}[s_m(\mathbf{b})] = \mathbf{E}[s_m(\mathbf{b}) \mid b_m = x] = v_2 \prod_{j \neq m} B_j(x) - x = 0. \tag{2.28}$$

From (2.27) and (2.28), we obtain

$$\prod_{j \neq m} B_j(x) - \prod_{j \neq 1} B_j(x) \leq \frac{v_2 - x}{v_1} \left(1 - \frac{v_1}{v_2} \right) \leq 0.$$

Therefore, $\prod_{j \neq 1} B_j(x) \geq \prod_{j \neq m} B_j(x)$, from which it follows that $B_1(x) \leq B_m(x)$. Since B_2 has support $[0, v_2]$ and neither distribution B_1 nor B_m has atoms in $(0, v_2]$, it follows that B_1 is strictly increasing on $(v_2 - \epsilon, v_2]$, for every small enough $\epsilon > 0$.

Proof of Fact (x). Consider an arbitrary player $i \neq 1$. If player i has an atom at point 0, then by Lemma 2.2 and Lemma 2.6, we have

$$\mathbf{E}[s_i(\mathbf{b})] = \mathbf{E}[s_i(\mathbf{b}) \mid b_i = 0] = v_i \frac{1}{n} \prod_{j \neq i} B_j(0) = 0.$$

If, otherwise, player i has no atom at point 0, we proceed as follows. Using Fact (ii) that tells us that point 0 is in the support of player i's mixed strategy, and Fact (v) that tells us that every player's mixed strategy has no atoms in $(0, v_2]$, and the mixed-strategy Nash equilibrium condition in Lemma 2.2, it follows that there exists $\epsilon > 0$ such that

$$\mathbf{E}[s_i(\mathbf{b})] = \mathbf{E}[s_i(\mathbf{b}) \mid b_i = x] = v_i \prod_{j \neq i} B_j(x) - x, \text{ for every } x \in (0, \epsilon].$$

Now, by Fact (vi) $B_1(0) = 0$, hence $v_i \prod_{j \neq i} B_j(x) - x$ goes to 0 in the limit as x goes to zero. It follows that $\mathbf{E}[s_i(\mathbf{b})] = 0$.

Proof of Fact (xi). From Facts (v), (viii), and (ix), and the condition for the mixed-strategy Nash equilibrium in Lemma 2.2, we have

$$v_1 - v_2 = \mathbf{E}[s_1(\mathbf{b})] = \mathbf{E}[s_1(\mathbf{b}) \mid b_1 = x] = v_1 \prod_{i \neq 1} B_i(x) - x, \text{ for every } x \in (0, v_2],$$

which yields the claim of Fact (xi) by taking the limit as x goes to 0 from above. □

2.1.5 Equilibrium Mixed-Strategy Distributions

In this section we provide explicit characterization of the mixed-strategy Nash equilibrium distributions, which follows from the properties of mixed-strategy Nash equilibria in Theorem 2.4.

We introduce some new notation. Let a_i be the probability that player i invests zero effort, i.e., $B_i(0) = a_i$. In every mixed-strategy Nash equilibrium, player 1 randomizes continuously on $(0, v_2]$ and hence $a_1 = 0$; players $k + 1$ through n invest zero efforts with probability 1 and, hence, $a_{k+1} = \cdots = a_n = 1$. Let d_i denote the smallest positive value of effort such that player i randomizes continuously on $(d_i, v_2]$. Without loss of generality, we assume that

$$0 = a_1 \leq a_2 \leq \cdots \leq a_k \leq a_{k+1} = \cdots = a_n = 1$$
$$0 = d_1 = d_2 \leq \cdots \leq d_k \leq d_{k+1} = \cdots = d_n = v_2$$

where $0 = d_1 = d_2$ because at least two players randomize continuously on $(0, v_2]$ and $d_{k+1} = \cdots = d_n = v_2$ because each player $k + 1$ through n invests a zero effort with probability 1.

The distributions of the effort investments in a mixed-strategy Nash equilibrium are characterized for every possible type of a valuation vector as follows.

Type A: In this case, the only active players are players 1 and 2. The equilibrium effort distributions are unique and correspond to those of a two-player contest in Theorem 2.3.

Type B: In this case,

$$d_j = \begin{cases} 0, & \text{if } j = 1, 2 \\ (v_1 - v_2)\left(\dfrac{a_j^{j-1}}{\prod_{l=2}^{j} a_l} - 1\right), & \text{if } j = 3, \ldots, k \\ v_2, & \text{if } j = k+1, \ldots, n \end{cases} \tag{2.29}$$

and, for $d_j < x \leq d_{j+1}, 1 < j \leq k$,

$$B_i(x) = \begin{cases} \left(\dfrac{\prod_{l=2}^{j} a_l}{1 - \frac{v_2}{v_1}}\right)^{\frac{1}{j-1}} \dfrac{x}{v_2} \left(\dfrac{v_1 - v_2 + x}{v_1}\right)^{\frac{1}{j-1} - 1}, & \text{if } i = 1 \\ \left(\dfrac{\prod_{l=2}^{j} a_l}{1 - \frac{v_2}{v_1}}\right)^{\frac{1}{j-1}} \left(\dfrac{v_1 - v_2 + x}{v_1}\right)^{\frac{1}{j-1}}, & \text{if } i = 2, \ldots, j \\ a_i, & \text{if } i = j+1, \ldots, n \end{cases} \tag{2.30}$$

where $a_1, a_2, \ldots, a_n$ satisfy

$$\prod_{j=2}^{n} a_j = 1 - \frac{v_2}{v_1}. \tag{2.31}$$

Type C: In this case,

$$d_j = \begin{cases} 0, & \text{if } j = 1, 2 \\ v_1 \prod_{l=2}^{k} a_l \dfrac{a_j^{j-1}}{\prod_{l=2}^{j} a_l}, & \text{if } j = 3, \ldots, k \\ v_1, & \text{if } j = k+1, \ldots, n \end{cases} \tag{2.32}$$

and, for $d_j < x \leq d_{j+1}, 1 < j \leq k$,

$$B_i(x) = \begin{cases} \left(\dfrac{\prod_{l=1}^{j} a_l}{\prod_{l=1}^{k} a_l}\right)^{\frac{1}{j-1}} \left(\dfrac{x}{v_1}\right)^{\frac{1}{j-1}}, & \text{if } i = 1, \ldots, j \\ a_i, & \text{if } i = j+1, \ldots, n. \end{cases} \tag{2.33}$$

Figure 2.10 shows a graph of the distribution of effort investment of a player in a mixed-strategy Nash equilibrium.

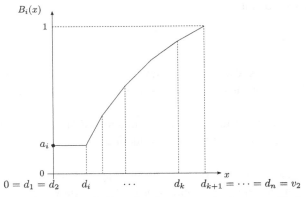

Figure 2.10. The distribution of effort of a player in a mixed-strategy Nash equilibrium.

We shall show that the asserted mixed-strategy distributions are indeed a mixed-strategy Nash equilibrium for Type B valuation vectors. The same arguments apply for a Type C valuation vector and are thus omitted. Let us consider x such that $d_j \leq x < d_{j+1}$. Note that (i) players 1 through j randomize continuously on $(d_j, v_2]$; (ii) players $j + 1$ through k select no effort in $(d_j, d_{j+1}]$ with probability 1, and hence $B_i(x) = a_i$, for $x \in (d_j, d_{j+1}]$ and $i = j + 1, \ldots, k$; and (iii) players $k + 1$ through n invest zero effort with probability 1. The expected payoff of player 1 is $v_1 - v_2$, and the expected payoff of any other player is zero, which yields that for every $x \in (d_j, d_{j+1}]$,

$$v_1 \prod_{l \neq 1} B_l(x) - x = v_1 - v_2 \text{ and } v_2 \prod_{l \neq i} B_l(x) - x = 0, \quad \text{for } i = 2, \ldots, j.$$

From this, we observe that

$$B_1(x) = \frac{v_1}{v_1 - v_2 + x} \prod_{l \in N} B_l(x) \tag{2.34}$$

and

$$B_i(x) = \frac{v_2}{x} \prod_{l \in N} B_l(x), \quad \text{for } i = 2, \ldots, j. \tag{2.35}$$

Now,

$$\prod_{i \in N} B_i(x) = B_1(x) \cdot \prod_{i=2}^{j} B_i(x) \cdot \prod_{i=j+1}^{n} a_i$$

$$= \frac{v_1}{v_1 - v_2 + x} \prod_{i \in N} B_i(x) \cdot \left(\frac{v_2}{x} \prod_{i \in N} B_i(x) \right)^{j-1} \cdot \frac{\frac{v_1 - v_2}{v_2}}{\prod_{i=2}^{j} a_i}.$$

Hence,

$$\prod_{i \in N} B_i(x) = \left(\frac{\prod_{i=2}^{j} a_i}{1 - \frac{v_2}{v_1}} \right)^{\frac{1}{j-1}} \frac{x}{v_2} \left(\frac{v_1 - v_2 + x}{v_1} \right)^{\frac{1}{j-1}}.$$

Combining the last identity with (2.34) and (2.35), we obtain the characterization of the equilibrium distribution of effort in equation (2.30). It remains only to show that (2.32) holds as asserted. By Theorem 2.4, the mixed-strategy distribution $B_i(x)$ is continuous on $(0, v_2]$ for all $i \in N$. From this, the expression in (2.29) follows by requiring that $B_i(x)$ in (2.30) is continuous at $x = d_j$, for $i \leq j$.

2.1.6 The Effort of the Highest Ability Player

In this section we consider the effort investment of the highest ability player in a mixed-strategy Nash equilibrium. Besides being of interest in its own right, this is of special interest for characterizing some other quantities of interest. We shall see in Section 2.1.7 and Section 2.1.8 that the distribution of the effort investment of the highest ability player plays a key role in determing the properties of the total effort and the maximum individual effort in a mixed-strategy Nash equilibrium, respectively. Under a valuation vector of either Type B or Type C, there is a continuum of mixed-strategy Nash equilibria. Hence, it is of interest to understand how the distribution of effort of the highest ability player compares for different mixed-strategy Nash equilibria. It suffices to consider only the case of three or more players with a valuation vector of either Type B or Type C because only in this case do there exist multiple mixed-strategy Nash equilibria.

Corollary 2.10. *For every mixed-strategy Nash equilibrium for the game that models the standard all-pay contest with three or more players with valuation parameters $v_1 \geq v_2 \geq \cdots \geq v_n > 0$ of either Type B or Type C, we have the following two properties:*

(i) *The effort of a player with the largest valuation is stochastically smaller than or equal to that in a mixed-strategy Nash equilibrium where only players 1 and 2 are active.*

(ii) *The effort of a player with the largest valuation is stochastically larger than or equal to that in a mixed-strategy Nash equilibrium of the game with the valuation vector $(v_1, v_2, \ldots, v_2)$ where players 2 through n play symmetric strategies.*

Proof. We only prove the case for a valuation vector of Type B because the other case for a valuation vector of Type C follows similarly.

Consider the first claim of the corollary. By Theorem 2.3, for the mixed-strategy Nash equilibrium in which only players 1 and 2 are active, we have $B_1(x) = x/v_2$ for $x \in [0, v_2]$. Combining this with the fact that for every mixed-strategy Nash equilibrium, the distribution of effort of player 1 is of the form as in equation (2.30), it suffices to show that for $d_j < x \leq d_{j+1}$ and $1 < j \leq k$,

$$\left(\frac{\prod_{l=2}^{j} a_l}{1 - \frac{v_2}{v_1}} \right)^{\frac{1}{j-1}} \frac{x}{v_2} \left(\frac{v_1 - v_2 + x}{v_1} \right)^{\frac{1}{j-1}-1} \geq \frac{x}{v_2}.$$

This is indeed true because by (2.31),

$$1 - \frac{v_2}{v_1} = \prod_{l=2}^{n} a_l \leq \prod_{l=2}^{j} a_l$$

and

$$\left(\frac{v_1 - v_2 + x}{v_1}\right)^{\frac{1}{j-1}-1} \geq 1, \quad \text{for all } 0 \leq x \leq v_2,$$

where in both relations equality holds for $j = 2$.

Consider now the second claim of the corollary. Using (2.30), it suffices to show that for $d_j < x \leq d_{j+1}$ and $1 < j \leq k$,

$$\left(\frac{\prod_{l=2}^{j} a_l}{1 - \frac{v_2}{v_1}}\right)^{\frac{1}{j-1}} \frac{x}{v_2} \left(\frac{v_1 - v_2 + x}{v_1}\right)^{\frac{1}{j-1}-1} \leq \left(\frac{\prod_{l=2}^{j+1} a_l}{1 - \frac{v_2}{v_1}}\right)^{\frac{1}{j}} \frac{x}{v_2} \left(\frac{v_1 - v_2 + x}{v_1}\right)^{\frac{1}{j}-1}.$$

This is equivalent to

$$\left(\prod_{l=2}^{j} a_l\right) \frac{v_1 - v_2 + x}{v_1 - v_2} \leq a_{j+1}^{j-1}$$

which by the definition of d_{j+1} and a_{j+1} corresponds to $B_{j+1}(d_{j+1}) \leq a_{j+1}$, and thus holds true. This shows that $B_1(x)$ is maximized by taking $j = k$ and $d_1 = \cdots = d_k$, and in this case we have

$$B_1(x) = \frac{x}{v_2} \left(\frac{v_1 - v_2 + x}{v_1}\right)^{\frac{1}{k-1}-1}, \quad \text{for } x \in [0, v_2]. \tag{2.36}$$

Since the right-hand side in (2.3) is non-decreasing in k, it is maximized by taking $k = n$, i.e. $v_2 = \cdots = v_n$. $\qquad\square$

Expected Effort of the Highest Ability Player

Corollary 2.11 (upper bound). *For every value of the valuation parameters $v_1 \geq v_2 \geq \cdots \geq v_n > 0$ of two or more players and every mixed-strategy Nash equilibrium under these values of the valuation parameters, the expected effort of player 1 satisfies*

$$\mathbf{E}[b_1] \leq \frac{1}{2} v_2.$$

Proof. By Corollary 2.10, in every mixed-strategy Nash equilibrium, the effort of player 1 is stochastically smaller than or equal to that in the mixed-strategy Nash equilibrium in which only players 1 and 2 are active. By Theorem 2.3, in a mixed-strategy Nash equilibrium in which only players 1 and 2 are active, the expected effort of player 1 is equal to $v_2/2$. Hence, for every valuation vector and every mixed-strategy Nash equilibrium under this valuation vector, the expected effort of player 1 satisfies $\mathbf{E}[b_1] \leq v_2/2$. $\qquad\square$

Corollary 2.12 (lower bound). *For every value of the valuation parameters $v_1 \geq v_2 \geq \cdots \geq v_n > 0$ of two or more players and every mixed-strategy Nash equilibrium under these values of the valuation parameters, the expected effort of player 1* *satisfies*

$$\mathbf{E}[b_1] \geq v_2 \left(\frac{v_1}{v_2} - 1\right)\left(\frac{v_1}{v_2}\log\left(\frac{\frac{v_1}{v_2}}{\frac{v_1}{v_2}-1}\right) - 1\right).$$

Furthermore, this bound is tight for the valuation parameters $v_1 \geq v_2 = \cdots = v_n$ asymptotically as the number of players n grows large.

Proof. By Corollary 2.10, the effort invested by player 1 in a mixed-strategy Nash equilibrium is stochastically larger than or equal to that in the mixed-strategy Nash equilibrium under the valuation vector $(v_1, v_2, v_2, \ldots, v_2)$ in which players 2 through n play according to symmetric strategies. For the valuation vector $(v_1, v_2, v_2, \ldots, v_2)$, there is a unique mixed-strategy Nash equilibrium such that players 2 through n play according to symmetric strategies, which is given by

$$B_i(x) = \begin{cases} \frac{x}{v_2}\left(\frac{v_1}{v_1-v_2+x}\right)^{\frac{n-2}{n-1}}, & \text{for } i = 1 \\ \left(\frac{v_1-v_2+x}{v_1}\right)^{\frac{1}{n-1}}, & \text{for } i = 2, \ldots, n \end{cases}, \quad x \in [0, v_2]. \qquad (2.37)$$

These distributions follow from (2.8) for the case when all players are active.

By the telescope formula applied to distribution B_1 given in (2.37) and a straightforward but tedious integration, we obtain

$$\mathbf{E}[b_1] = v_2\left[1 - \int_0^1 \left(\frac{v_1/v_2}{v_1/v_2 - 1 + x}\right)^{\frac{n-2}{n-1}} x\,dx\right] = v_2 f(v_1/v_2, n)$$

where

$$f(x, n) = 1 - x\left(1 - \frac{1}{n}\right)\left[x - (x-1)\left(n - (n-1)\left(1 - \frac{1}{x}\right)^{\frac{1}{n-1}}\right)\right].$$

From (2.37), observe that the effort of player 1 is stochastically decreasing in n, i.e. for every $x \in [0, v_2]$, $B_1(x)$ is non-decreasing in the number of players n. Hence,

$$\mathbf{E}[b_1] \geq v_2 \lim_{n\to\infty} f(v_1/v_2, n) = v_2(v_1/v_2 - 1)\left(v_1/v_2 \log\left(\frac{v_1/v_2}{v_1/v_2 - 1}\right) - 1\right). \quad (2.38)$$

$\square$

Figure 2.11 shows a graph for the lower bound on the expected effort of the highest ability player asserted in Corollary 2.12. Notice that this lower bound goes to zero in the limit of players of equal abilities. This should not be surprising. We know that in the case of two or more players with symmetric valuations in the mixed-strategy Nash equilibrium where players play symmetric strategies, each player has the expected effort of value v_1/n, which for any fixed value of $v_1 > 0$ goes to zero asymptotically as the number of players n grows large.

2.1.7 Total Effort

Theorem 2.13. *For every value of the valuation parameters $v_1 \geq v_2 \geq \cdots \geq v_n > 0$ of two or more players, and every mixed-strategy Nash equilibrium under these values*

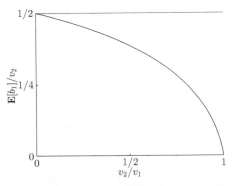

Figure 2.11. The expected effort of the highest ability player normalized by the second largest valuation is in the region between the two curves.

of the valuation parameters, the expected total effort satisfies the following identity:

$$R = \frac{v_2}{v_1}v_2 + \left(1 - \frac{v_2}{v_1}\right)\mathbf{E}[b_1]. \tag{2.39}$$

Proof. Suppose that $B_1, B_2, \ldots, B_n$ is a mixed-strategy Nash equilibrium. By Theorem 2.4, $\mathbf{E}[s_1(\mathbf{b})] = v_1 - v_2$ and $\mathbf{E}[s_i(\mathbf{b})] = 0$ for $i \neq 1$. Hence

$$v_1\mathbf{E}[x_1(\mathbf{b})] - \mathbf{E}[b_1] = v_1 - v_2 \tag{2.40}$$

and

$$v_i\mathbf{E}[x_i(\mathbf{b})] - \mathbf{E}[b_i] = 0, \quad \text{for } i = 2, \ldots, n. \tag{2.41}$$

Summing up the expected payoffs of all players and using the identities (2.40) and (2.41), we obtain that the expected total effort is

$$\sum_{i \in N}\mathbf{E}[b_i] = v_1(\mathbf{E}[x_1(\mathbf{b})] - 1) + \sum_{i=2}^{n}v_i\mathbf{E}[x_i(\mathbf{b})] + v_2. \tag{2.42}$$

By Theorem 2.4, each player $i \in N$ whose valuation parameter is smaller than v_2 has the winning probability $\mathbf{E}[x_i(\mathbf{b})] = 0$ because each such player invests zero effort, and at least one player invests a strictly positive effort. Therefore,

$$\sum_{i=2}^{n}v_i\mathbf{E}[x_i(\mathbf{b})] = v_2(1 - \mathbf{E}[x_1(\mathbf{b})]).$$

Combining this with (2.42), we obtain

$$\sum_{i \in N}\mathbf{E}[b_i] = v_1(\mathbf{E}[x_1(\mathbf{b})] - 1) + v_2(2 - \mathbf{E}[x_1(\mathbf{b})]). \tag{2.43}$$

From the identity in (2.40), we have

$$\mathbf{E}[x_1(\mathbf{b})] = \frac{v_1 - v_2 + \mathbf{E}[b_1]}{v_1}$$

which combined with (2.43) establishes the identity asserted in the theorem. □

Theorem 2.13 tells us that given a valuation vector in every mixed-strategy Nash equilibrium, under this valuation vector, the expected total effort is determined by the expected effort of the highest ability player. From identity (2.39), we observe that for every valuation vector such that the highest ability player is non-unique, the expected total effort is equal to the largest valuation $R = v_1$. In general, the expected total effort can differ from one mixed-strategy Nash equilibrium to another: in the parlance of auction theory, there is no *revenue equivalence*. We next establish some simple and upper and lower bounds for the expected total effort. This will reveal that for every given valuation vector for two or more players, the expected total effort is within a constant factor of the second largest valuation.

Upper Bound

Corollary 2.14. *For every value of the valuation parameters $v_1 \geq v_2 \geq \cdots \geq v_n > 0$ of two or more players and every mixed-strategy Nash equilibrium under these values of the valuation parameters, the expected total effort is the largest in the equilibrium in which only players 1 and 2 are active. Therefore,*

$$R \leq \frac{v_2}{2}\left(1 + \frac{v_2}{v_1}\right) \leq v_2.$$

Proof. The asserted upper bound follows from the identity in Theorem 2.13 that relates the expected total effort and the expected effort of player 1 and the upper bound in Corollary 2.11 for the expected effort of player 1 as given here:

$$R = \frac{v_2}{v_1}v_2 + \left(1 - \frac{v_2}{v_1}\right)\mathbf{E}[b_1]$$

$$\leq \frac{v_2}{v_1}v_2 + \left(1 - \frac{v_2}{v_1}\right)\frac{v_2}{2}$$

$$= \frac{v_2}{2}\left(1 + \frac{v_2}{v_1}\right).$$

$\square$

Lower Bound

Corollary 2.15. *For every value of the valuation parameters $v_1 \geq v_2 \geq \cdots \geq v_n > 0$ of two or more players and every mixed-strategy Nash equilibrium under these values of the valuation parameters, the expected total effort is at least as large as half of the second largest valuation, i.e.,*

$$R \geq \frac{1}{2}v_2.$$

Furthermore, this lower bound is tight: for every $\epsilon \in (0, 1)$, there exists a valuation vector such that under this valuation vector, the expected total effort satisfies $R \leq (1 + \epsilon)v_2/2$.

Proof. The asserted lower bound follows from the identity in Theorem 2.13 that relates the expected total effort and the expected effort of player 1 and the lower bound in

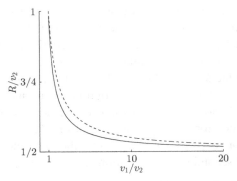

Figure 2.12. The lower bound on the expected total effort normalized by the second largest valuation for any number of two or more players and given value of v_1/v_2 is depicted by the solid curve. The same but for the case of two players is depicted by the dashed curve.

Corollary 2.12 for the expected effort of player 1 as given here:

$$R = \frac{v_2}{v_1}v_2 + \left(1 - \frac{v_2}{v_1}\right)\frac{\mathbf{E}[b_1]}{v_2}$$

$$\geq v_2 \frac{1 + \left(\frac{v_1}{v_2} - 1\right)^2 \left[\frac{v_1}{v_2}\log\left(\frac{\frac{v_1}{v_2}}{\frac{v_1}{v_2}-1}\right) - 1\right]}{\frac{v_1}{v_2}} \qquad (2.44)$$

$$\geq \frac{1}{2}v_2$$

where the first equality is from Theorem 2.13, the first inequality is by (2.38), and the last inequality is equivalent to $\log(1 + 1/(x-1)) \geq 1/(x-1) - 1/(2(x-1)^2)$, which is indeed true as can be verified by limited Taylor development of the function $\log(1+x)$ at $x = 0$. See Figure 2.12 for a graph of the lower bound in (2.44).   □

2.1.8 Maximum Individual Effort

We consider here the expected maximum individual effort in a mixed-strategy Nash equilibrium. In general, the expected maximum individual effort can differ from one mixed-strategy Nash equilibrium to another. We have already observed this to be the case for symmetric valuations in Section 2.1.4, where the expected maximum individual effort is decreasing in the number of active players. Our goal in this section is to derive lower and upper bounds for the expected maximum individual effort that for a given valuation vector hold in every mixed-strategy Nash equilibrium under this valuation vector.

A key property that we exploit is the following relation between the distribution of the maximum individual effort and the distribution of the effort of the highest ability player:

$$\mathbf{Pr}\left[\max_{i \in N} b_i \leq x\right] = \frac{v_1 - v_2 + x}{v_1}B_1(x), \qquad (2.45)$$

which follows by noting that $\mathbf{Pr}[\max_{i \in N} b_i \leq x] = \prod_{i \in N} B_i(x)$ and that $\prod_{i \in N} B_i(x)$ and $B_1(x)$ satisfy the relation given in (2.34). The relation (2.45) implies that some of the properties that we know to hold for the mixed strategy of the highest ability player in a mixed-strategy Nash equilibrium are inherited by the distribution of the maximum individual effort. For example, it is readily observed that both claims in Corollary 2.10 for the effort of the highest ability player directly imply the corresponding claims for the maximum individual effort.

Upper Bound

Corollary 2.16. *For every value of the valuation parameters $v_1 \geq v_2 \geq \cdots \geq v_n > 0$ of two or more players and every mixed-strategy Nash equilibrium under these values of the valuation parameters, the expected maximum individual effort is largest in the equilibrium in which only players 1 and 2 are active. Therefore,*

$$R_1 \leq \frac{v_2}{2}\left(1 + \frac{1}{3}\frac{v_2}{v_1}\right) \leq \frac{2}{3}v_2.$$

Proof. The first part of the claim is immediate from the relation in (2.45) and the result in Corollary 2.10 that says that for every mixed-strategy Nash equilibrium, the effort of player 1 is stochastically larger than or equal to that in the mixed-strategy Nash equilibrium when only players 1 and 2 are active. The asserted upper bound follows from the characterization of the expected maximum individual effort in Theorem 2.3 for a contest between two players. □

Lower Bound

Corollary 2.17. *For every value of the valuation parameters $v_1 \geq v_2 \geq \cdots \geq v_n > 0$ of two or more players and every mixed-strategy Nash equilibrium under these values of the valuation parameters, the expected maximum individual effort is at least as large as half of the second largest valuation, i.e.,*

$$R_1 \geq \frac{1}{2}v_2.$$

This bound is tight for the case $v_2 = \cdots = v_n$ asymptotically as the number of players n grows large.

Proof. Both claims in Corollary 2.10 for the effort of the highest ability player hold as well for the maximum individual effort. Hence, for every given valuation parameter $v_1 \geq v_2 \geq \cdots \geq v_n > 0$ and every mixed-strategy Nash equilibrium under these valuation parameters, the maximum individual effort is stochastically larger than or equal to that in the mixed-strategy Nash equilibrium under the valuation vector $(v_1, v_2, v_2, \ldots, v_2)$ with players 2 through n playing symmetric strategies, given by (2.37). Therefore, we have

$$\mathbf{Pr}\left[\max_{i \in N} b_i \leq x\right] \leq \frac{x}{v_2}\left(\frac{v_1 - v_2 + x}{v_1}\right)^{\frac{1}{n-1}}, \quad \text{for } x \in [0, v_2]. \qquad (2.46)$$

For every fixed value $x \in [0, v_2]$, the right-hand side in equation (2.46) is increasing in the number of players n, and thus the expected maximum individual effort is decreasing in the number of players n. Furthermore, from (2.46), note that

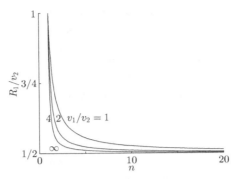

Figure 2.13. Lower bound for the expected maximum individual effort versus the number of players.

$\mathbf{Pr}[\max_{i \in N} b_i \leq x] \leq x/v_2$, which is tight asymptotically as the number of players n grows large. Hence,

$$R_1 = \int_0^{v_2} \left(1 - \mathbf{Pr}\left[\max_{i \in N} b_i \leq x \right] \right) dx \geq \int_0^{v_2} \left(1 - \frac{x}{v_2} \right) dx = \frac{v_2}{2}$$

where the inequality is tight asymptotically as the number of players n grows large.

By a straightforward but tedious integral calculus, we obtain that for the game with the valuation vector $(v_1, v_2, v_2, \ldots, v_2)$, in the mixed-strategy Nash equilibrium where players 2 through n play symmetric strategies, we have

$$\frac{R_1}{v_2} = 1 - \frac{v_1}{v_2} \frac{n-1}{n} \left\{ 1 - \frac{v_1}{v_2} \frac{n-1}{2n-1} \left(1 - \left(1 - \frac{v_2}{v_1} \right)^{\frac{2n-1}{n-1}} \right) \right\} \qquad (2.47)$$

where the right-hand side of the equality is decreasing in the number of players n and goes to $1/2$ as n grows large. Figure 2.13 shows an illustration. $\square$

Total vs. Maximum Individual Effort

Contests that elicit contributions from all the players but make use only of the best submitted solution may be considered wasteful, since the maximum individual effort may be a small portion of the total invested effort. This waste of effort, however, is bounded in any mixed-strategy Nash equilibrium of the game that models the standard all-pay contest as shown in the following corollary.

Corollary 2.18. *For any valuation vector with two or more players and any mixed-strategy Nash equilibrium of the game that models the standard all-pay contest, the expected maximum individual effort is at least half of the expected total effort.*

Proof. The claim is an immediate consequence of Corollary 2.14 and Corollary 2.17. $\square$

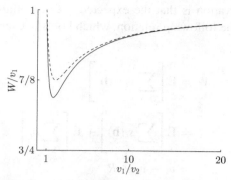

Figure 2.14. The lower bound on the social efficiency for any number of two or more players for given v_2/v_1 is depicted by the solid curve. The same but for the case of two players is depicted by the dashed line.

2.1.9 Social Efficiency

In a standard all-pay contest, the prize is not guaranteed to be allocated to the highest ability player. The prize may be awarded to a player of lower ability due to the use of randomized strategies. We have already considered the extent of the social efficiency loss in Section 2.1.3 for the case of a two-player contest. In the next theorem, we provide a tight characterization of the worst-case social efficiency for arbitrary valuation vectors.

Theorem 2.19. *For the game that models a standard all-pay contest among two or more players with valuation parameters $v_1 \geq v_2 \geq \cdots \geq v_n > 0$, the expected social welfare W in every mixed-strategy Nash equilibrium of the game and the optimum social welfare v_1 satisfy*

$$W \geq f\left(\frac{v_2}{v_1}\right) v_1$$

where

$$f(x) = x + \frac{(1-x)^2}{x} \log\left(\frac{1}{1-x}\right).$$

This lower bound is tight for the valuation parameters such that $v_1 \geq v_2 = \cdots = v_n$ for asymptotically large number of players n.

Furthermore, the worst-case social efficiency is $\eta = f(a)$, which is for the valuation parameters such that $v_2 = \cdots = v_n = av_1$, where a is the unique strictly positive solution to the equation

$$1 - a = \exp\left(-\frac{a}{1-a^2}\right).$$

By numerical computations, we have

$$a = 0.56939710218357 \text{ and } f(a) = 0.843771826857562.$$

See Figure 2.14 for a graphical illustration.

Proof. The key observation is that the expected social welfare W and the expected total effort R satisfy the following relation, which holds in every mixed-strategy Nash equilibrium:

$$W = \mathbf{E}\left[\sum_{i \in N} v_i x_i(\mathbf{b})\right]$$

$$= \mathbf{E}\left[\sum_{i \in N} s_i(\mathbf{b})\right] + \mathbf{E}\left[\sum_{i \in N} b_i\right]$$

$$= v_1 - v_2 + R$$

where the last equation follows from the expected payoff equivalence of the standard all-pay contest. Combined with Corollary 2.15, this immediately yields a lower bound of $1/2$.

A tighter lower bound is obtained as follows:

$$\frac{W}{v_1} = 1 - \frac{v_2}{v_1} + \frac{v_2}{v_1}\frac{R}{v_2}$$

$$\geq 1 - \frac{v_2}{v_1} + \frac{v_2}{v_1}\frac{1 + \left(\frac{v_1}{v_2} - 1\right)^2\left(\frac{v_1}{v_2}\log\left(\frac{\frac{v_1}{v_2}}{\frac{v_1}{v_2}-1}\right) - 1\right)}{\frac{v_1}{v_2}}$$

$$= \frac{1 + \left(\frac{v_1}{v_2} - 1\right)^2\log\left(\frac{\frac{v_1}{v_2}}{\frac{v_1}{v_2}-1}\right)}{\frac{v_1}{v_2}} \tag{2.48}$$

$$= f\left(\frac{v_2}{v_1}\right) \tag{2.49}$$

where the inequality is by (2.44).

The worst-case efficiency bound follows by minimizing $f(v_2/v_1)$ over $v_2/v_1 \in (0, 1]$. Note that

$$f'(x) = \frac{1}{x} - \frac{1 - x^2}{x^2}\log\left(\frac{1}{1-x}\right).$$

Hence, it follows that $f'(a) = 0$ is equivalent to

$$(1 - a^2)\log\left(\frac{1}{1-a}\right) = a.$$

It is readily checked that this is equivalent to the equation asserted in the theorem. $\qquad\square$

2.2 Game with Incomplete Information

In this section we consider the game that models the standard all-pay contest with incomplete information where the valuation parameters of the players are private information. The players are assumed to hold prior beliefs about the values of the valuation parameters of other players according to a prior distribution. For most of this section, we shall consider the case where the valuation parameters are independent and identically distributed random variables according to a prior distribution F, which has no atoms above zero and has strictly positive density function on the support $[0, 1]$.

We consider the Bayes-Nash equilibrium of this game, which is defined in Definition 1.9. A pure-strategy Bayes-Nash equilibrium is given by strategies $(\beta_1, \beta_2, \ldots, \beta_n)$ where for every $i \in N$, $\beta_i : [0, 1] \to \mathbf{R}_+$ specifies the effort investment of player i for every possible value of the valuation parameter of this player. For every player $i \in N$, let $\beta_{-i}(\mathbf{v}_{-i}) = (\beta_j(v_j), j \neq i)$ be the strategies deployed by other players. Strategies $(\beta_1, \beta_2, \ldots, \beta_n)$ are a pure-strategy Bayes-Nash equilibrium if under these strategies, no player can unilaterally increase his or her expected payoff by deviating to a different strategy, i.e., for every player $i \in N$,

$$\mathbf{E}[s_i(v_i, (\beta_i(v_i), \beta_{-i}(\mathbf{v}_{-i})))] \geq \mathbf{E}[s_i(v_i, (b_i, \beta_{-i}(\mathbf{v}_{-i}))) \mid b_i = x], \quad \text{for every } x \in \mathbf{R}_+$$

where the equality holds at every point $x \in \mathbf{R}_+$ at which β_i increases. Strategies $(\beta_1, \beta_2, \ldots, \beta_n)$ are said to be a symmetric Bayes-Nash equilibrium if every player $i \in N$ plays according to the same strategy $\beta : [0, 1] \to \mathbf{R}_+$.

2.2.1 Revenue Equivalence

One of the most important results from auction theory is the revenue equivalence theorem that we present in this section and leverage in some of our subsequent analysis.

Consider a generalization of the game that models the standard all-pay contest that allows for a more general allocation specified by given functions $x_i : \mathbf{R}_+^n \to [0, 1]$ and that allows the players to incur more general costs according to given payment functions $c_i : \mathbf{R}_+^n \to \mathbf{R}_+$. The payoff functions of the players are assumed to be of the quasi-linear form:

$$s_i(v_i, \mathbf{b}) = v_i x_i(\mathbf{b}) - c_i(\mathbf{b}), \quad \text{for } i \in N. \tag{2.50}$$

The game that models the standard all-pay contest is a special case in which the allocation is of the specific winner-take-all form as given in (2.1) and the payments incurred by the players correspond to their respective individual effort investments. Following the standard terminology in auction theory, an auction is said to be a *standard auction* if it allocates the item to the highest bidder. The standard all-pay contest is, thus, a standard auction.

With a slight abuse of notation, given strategies $(\beta_1, \beta_2, \ldots, \beta_n)$, we denote with $x_i(x)$ the expected allocation to player i conditional on his or her valuation parameter being of value x, i.e.,

$$x_i(x) = \mathbf{E}[x_i(\beta_1(v_1), \beta_2(v_2), \ldots, \beta_n(v_n)) \mid v_i = x].$$

Similary, we define $c_i(x)$ to be the expected payment and $s_i(x)$ to be the expected payoff of player i, conditional on his or her valuation parameter being of value x.

Theorem 2.20 (revenue equivalence). *Assume that the valuation parameters are independent and identically distributed according to distribution F that has no atoms above zero and has strictly positive density on the support $[0, 1]$. Then, every symmetric* *and strictly increasing equilibrium of any standard auction, such that the expected payment of a player with valuation zero is zero, yields the same expected payment.*

Furthermore, the expected payment by player i conditional on his or her valuation parameter being of value v_i is given by

$$c_i(v_i) = \int_0^{v_i} x \, dF(x)^{n-1}.$$

Proof. Suppose that $\beta : [0, 1] \to \mathbf{R}_+$ is a strictly increasing function that is assumed to be a symmetric Bayes-Nash equilibrium strategy. Fix an arbitrary player $i \in N$. Consider a unilateral deviation of player i from playing $\beta(v_i)$ to playing a different strategy $\beta(v)$ for some $v \neq v_i$. Player i wins in the event that his or her bid $\beta(v)$ exceeds the highest competing bid $\max_{j \neq i} b_j$. Let us denote with $G(v)$ the probability of this event. Since all players $j \neq i$ play according to the symmetric strategy function β, which is assumed to be strictly increasing, player i wins if the valuations of all other players are smaller than v. Thus, we have

$$G(v) = F(v)^{n-1}.$$

The expected payoff for player i conditional on his or her valuation being of value v_i and that he or she bids $\beta(v)$ is

$$s_i(v_i, v) = v_i G(v) - c_i(v).$$

Since β is assumed to be an equilibrium strategy, it is optimal for player i to bid $v = v_i$, and thus it must hold $\partial s_i(v_i, v)/\partial v = 0$ at $v = v_i$. Since

$$\frac{\partial}{\partial v} s_i(v_i, v) = v_i G'(v) - \frac{d}{dv} c_i(v),$$

it follows that

$$\frac{d}{dv} c_i(v) = v G'(v).$$

By integrating and making use of the assumption that the expected payment of a player with valuation zero is zero, we have

$$c_i(v_i) = \int_0^{v_i} x G'(x) \, dx. \tag{2.51}$$

The right-hand side is independent of the allocation mechanism; hence, the expected payment by player i is as given in (2.51) for every mechanism that satisfies the assumptions of the theorem. □

One way to think of the expected payment in Theorem 2.20 from the perspective of a player as the expected value of a random variable that is equal to the maximum valuation parameter of a competitor to this player, if this maximum value is smaller than or equal to the valuation of this player, and is otherwise equal to zero, i.e.,

$$c_i(v) = \mathbf{E}\left[\left(\max_{j \in N\setminus\{i\}} v_j \right) \mathbf{1} \left(\max_{j \in N\setminus\{i\}} v_j \leq v \right) \mid v_i = v \right]. \tag{2.52}$$

There is a fundamental relation between the expected payoff and the winning probability conditional on the valuation of this player that is given in the following corollary.

Corollary 2.21. *For every standard auction with $n \geq 2$ players whose valuations are independent and identically distributed according to distribution function F, the expected payoff for each player $i \in N$ conditional on his or her valuation is equal to*

$$s_i(v_i) = \int_0^{v_i} x_i(v) \, dv.$$

Proof. By the definition of the payoff functions,

$$s_i(v_i) = v_i x_i(v_i) - c_i(v_i), \quad \text{for } i \in N.$$

By the revenue equivalence Theorem 2.20,

$$c_i(v_i) = \int_0^{v_i} v \, dx_i(v), \quad \text{for } i \in N.$$

Hence, by partial integration,

$$s_i(v_i) = v_i x_i(v_i) - \int_0^{v_i} v \, dx_i(v) = \int_0^{v_i} x_i(v) \, dv, \quad \text{for } i \in N.$$

$\square$

2.2.2 Symmetric Bayes-Nash Equilibrium

Theorem 2.22. *For the game with incomplete information that models the standard all-pay contest with $n \geq 2$ players whose valuations are independent and identically distributed according to prior distribution F that has no atoms above zero and has strictly positive density function on the support $[0, 1]$, there exists a unique symmetric Bayes-Nash equilibrium strategy given by*

$$\beta(v) = \int_0^v x \, dF(x)^{n-1}, \quad \text{for } v \in [0, 1]. \tag{2.53}$$

Proof. Suppose first that players deploy a common strategy β that maps each point in the set of valuations $[0, 1]$ to an effort investment in $\mathbf{R}_+$, which is strictly increasing and such that $\beta(0) = 0$. Since the standard all-pay contest is a standard auction in which every player's payment is equal to his or her bid, by the revenue equivalence of standard auctions in Theorem 2.20, it follows that there is a unique symmetric Bayes-Nash strategy β and that it is equal to that in (2.53).

We can check that the strategy β in (2.53) is a symmetric Bayes-Nash equilibrium as follows. Suppose that all players play according to the strategy β, except for player i who plays according to a strictly increasing strategy β_i. Player i wins if $\beta_i(v_i) > \beta(v_j)$, for every $j \neq i$, i.e., if $v_j < v_i^*$, for every $j \neq i$, where v_i^* is uniquely defined by $\beta_i(v_i) = \beta(v_i^*)$; if β_i is equal to β, then $v_i^* = v_i$.

By the definition of the payoff functions and the revenue equivalence theorem, we have

$$s_i(v_i, v_i^*) = v_i G(v_i^*) - \int_0^{v_i^*} x G'(x) \, dx.$$

From this, by integration by parts, we have

$$s_i(v_i, v_i^*) = (v_i - v_i^*)G(v_i^*) + \int_0^{v_i^*} G(x)\,dx.$$

Now, note

$$s_i(v_i, v_i) - s_i(v_i, v_i^*) = (v_i^* - v_i)G(v_i^*) - \int_{v_i}^{v_i^*} G(x)\,dx = \int_{v_i}^{v_i^*}(G(v_i^*) - G(x))\,dx \geq 0,$$

which shows that player i cannot benefit by unilaterally deviating to a different strictly increasing strategy than β, which thus shows that β is a symmetric Bayes-Nash equilibrium.

The uniqueness of a symmetric Bayes-Nash equilibrium follows by showing that in every symmetric Bayes-Nash equilibrium the strategy deployed by the players must be such that (i) it is equal to zero at point 0 and (ii) it is strictly increasing on $[0, 1]$. Condition (i) follows straightforwardly from the definition of the payoff functions, and condition (ii) is shown to hold as follows.

We first show that in every Bayes-Nash equilibrium, each player deploys a non-decreasing strategy. Suppose on the contrary that there exists a player $i \in N$ whose strategy β_i is a correspondence that maps each point in the set of valuations $[0, 1]$ to a set of effort investments that is not non-decreasing, i.e., there exist values of valuations $0 \leq v < v^* \leq 1$ and values of effort investments $b > b^*$ such that $b \in \beta_i(v)$ and $b^* \in \beta_i(v^*)$. Suppose that the strategies β_j for players $j \neq i$ are arbitrarily fixed.

With a slight abuse of notation, for every player $j \in N$, we denote with $s_j(v_j, x)$ the expected payoff for this player conditional on his or her valuation being of value v_j and his or her strategy b_j being of value x, i.e.,

$$s_j(v_j, x) = v_j \mathbf{E}[x_j(\mathbf{b}) \mid b_j = x] - x, \text{ for } j \in N.$$

From this, we have

$$s_i(v^*, b) - s_i(v, b) = (v^* - v)\mathbf{E}[x_i(\mathbf{b}) \mid b_i = b] \tag{2.54}$$

and

$$s_i(v^*, b^*) - s_i(v, b^*) = (v^* - v)\mathbf{E}[x_i(\mathbf{b}) \mid b_i = b^*]. \tag{2.55}$$

Now, note that (i) $b^* \in \beta_i(v^*)$ implies $s_i(v^*, b) \leq s_i(v^*, b^*)$, (ii) $b \in \beta_i(v)$ implies $s_i(v, b) \leq s_i(v, b^*)$, and (iii) $b > b^*$ implies $\mathbf{E}[x_i(\mathbf{b}) \mid b_i = b] \geq \mathbf{E}[x_i(\mathbf{b}) \mid b_i = b^*]$. Combining with relations (2.54) and (2.55), it follows that

$$\mathbf{E}[x_i(\mathbf{b}) \mid b_i = b] = \mathbf{E}[x_i(\mathbf{b}) \mid b_i = b^*],$$

$$s_i(v^*, b) = s_i(v^*, b^*),$$

and

$$s_i(v, b) = s_i(v, b^*).$$

From these equations, we deduce that $b = b^*$ because

$$0 = s_i(v^*, b) - s_i(v^*, b^*)$$

$$= (v^*\mathbf{E}[x_i(\mathbf{b}) \mid b_i = b] - b) - (v^*\mathbf{E}[x_i(\mathbf{b}) \mid b_i = b^*] - b^*) = b^* - b,$$

which is a contradiction.

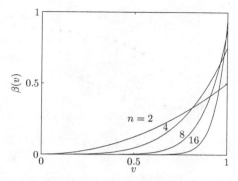

Figure 2.15. The symmetric Bayes-Nash equilibrium strategy for a uniform prior distribution and the number of players n as indicated in the figure.

We now establish that for every symmetric Bayes-Nash equilibrium, players deploy a strictly increasing strategy. Suppose on the contrary that in a symmetric Bayes-Nash equilibrium, each player plays according to a strategy β that is increasing but not strictly so, i.e., there exist values of valuations $0 \le v < v^* < 1$ such that $\beta(x)$ is constant on the interval $[v, v^*]$. Let b^* be such that $\beta(x) = b^*$ for $x \in [v, v^*]$.

Since the valuation parameters are assumed to be independent and identically distributed random variables, and each player deploys a common strategy β that maps each value in the set of valuations $[0, 1]$ to a value of effort investment, the effort investments $b_1, b_2, \ldots, b_n$ are independent and identically distributed random variables with distribution $B(x) = \Pr[\beta(v_i) \le x]$. By the assumption that distribution F has strictly positive density function on $[0, 1]$, it follows that B has an atom at point b^*.

Consider an arbitrary player $i \in N$. By the definition of the prize allocation mechanism, if there are two or more players who invest the highest effort, the prize is allocated uniformly at random to one of these players. Since every player's effort investment is according to distribution B that has an atom at b^*, if player i invests effort of value b^*, the event that this is the highest effort investment and in a tie with another player's effort investment occurs with a strictly positive probability. On the other hand, if player i invests an infinitesimally larger amount than b^*, then a tie occurs with zero probability. It follows that player i's winning probability $\mathbf{E}[x_i(\mathbf{b}) \mid b_i = x]$ has an upward jump at point $x = b^*$. This implies that player i's expected payoffs satisfy $s_i(v_i, x) > s_i(v_i, b^*)$ for some $x > b^*$, which is a contradiction to that b^* is a best response. $\qquad\square$

Example 2.23 (uniform prior). Suppose that the prior distribution is uniform on $[0, 1]$. Then,

$$\beta(v) = \left(1 - \frac{1}{n}\right) v^n, \quad \text{for } v \in [0, 1].$$

See Figure 2.15 for graphs of the function β for a few different values of the number of players.

2.2.3 Total Effort

Theorem 2.24. *For the game that models the standard all-pay contest among $n \ge 2$ players with independent and identically distributed valuations according to a prior*

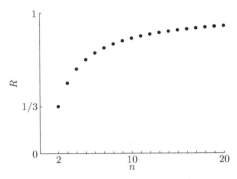

Figure 2.16. The expected total effort versus the number of players for a uniform prior distribution.

distribution F that has no atoms above zero and has strictly positive density function on the support $[0, 1]$, *the total expected effort in the symmetric Bayes-Nash equilibrium is equal to the expected value of the second largest valuation, i.e.,*

$$R = \mathbf{E}[v_{(n,2)}].$$

Proof. By the revenue equivalence in Theorem 2.20, the expected payment by player $i \in N$ is

$$c_i(v_i) = \mathbf{E}\left[\left(\max_{j \neq i} v_j\right) \mathbf{1}\left(\max_{j \neq i} v_j < v_i\right) \mid v_i\right].$$

Therefore, the expected total effort is

$$R = \sum_{i \in N} \mathbf{E}[c_i(v_i)]$$

$$= \sum_{i \in N} \mathbf{E}\left[\left(\max_{j \neq i} v_j\right) \mathbf{1}\left(\max_{j \neq i} v_j < v_i\right)\right]$$

$$= \mathbf{E}\left[\sum_{i \in N}\left(\max_{j \neq i} v_j\right) \mathbf{1}\left(\max_{j \neq i} v_j < v_i\right)\right]$$

$$= \mathbf{E}[v_{(n,2)}].$$

$\square$

By Theorem 2.24 and elementary analysis of order statistics, we have

$$R = n \int_0^1 x(1 - F(x)) \, dF(x)^{n-1}. \tag{2.56}$$

An alternative characterization can be obtained by elementary algebraic manipulations (Exercise 2.8) and is given as follows:

$$R = 1 - \int_0^1 [nF(x)^{n-1} - (n-1)F(x)^n] \, dx. \tag{2.57}$$

Example 2.25 (uniform prior revisited). For a uniform prior distribution on $[0, 1]$, the expected total effort is

$$R = 1 - \frac{2}{n+1}.$$

See Figure 2.16 for a graph.

2.2.4 Maximum Individual Effort

Theorem 2.26. *For the game that models the standard all-pay contest among $n \geq 2$ players with independent and identically distributed valuations according to a prior distribution F that has no atoms above zero and has strictly positive density on the support $[0, 1]$, the expected maximum individual effort in the symmetric Bayes Nash equilibrium is equal to*

$$R_1 = \int_0^1 x(1 - F(x)^n) \, dF(x)^{n-1}.$$

Proof. Using Theorem 2.22 and $v_{(n,1)} \sim F^n$, we have

$$R_1 = \mathbf{E}[\beta(v_{(n,1)})]$$

$$= \int_0^1 \int_0^x y \, dF(y)^{n-1} \, dF(x)^n$$

$$= \int_0^1 \int_0^1 \mathbf{1}(y \leq x) y \, dF(y)^{n-1} \, dF(x)^n$$

$$= \int_0^1 \left(\int_y^1 dF(x)^n \right) y \, dF(y)^{n-1}$$

$$= \int_0^1 y(1 - F(y)^n) \, dF(y)^{n-1}.$$

$\square$

An alternative characterization of the expected maximum individual effort follows from Theorem 2.26 and simple calculus:

$$R_1 = \frac{n}{2n - 1} - \int_0^1 \left(F(x)^{n-1} - \frac{n-1}{2n-1} F(x)^{2n-1} \right) dx. \tag{2.58}$$

From the last expression and some simple calculus of order statistics, we obtain

$$R_1 = \mathbf{E}[v_{(n-1,1)}] - \frac{n-1}{2n-1} \mathbf{E}[v_{(2n-1,1)}]. \tag{2.59}$$

The reader may work out Exercise 2.8 to derive identities (2.58) and (2.59). Since the integrand in the right-hand side of equation (2.58) is non-negative, we have the following upper bound that holds for the expected maximum individual effort, in general, for every prior distribution.

Corollary 2.27. *For the game that models the standard all-pay contest with $n \geq 2$ players whose valuation parameters are independent and identically distributed according to a prior distribution that has no atoms above zero and has strictly positive density function on the support $[0, 1]$, the expected maximum individual effort in the symmetric Bayes-Nash equilibrium satisfies*

$$R_1 \leq \frac{1}{2} \left(1 + \frac{1}{2n - 1} \right).$$

In particular, the expected maximum individual effort is at most $2/3$, which is the upper bound for the case of two players, and the upper bound decreases with the number of players, going to $1/2$ asymptotically for a large number of players. For a sequence of prior distributions that concentrates around a given value $\bar{v} \in (0, 1]$, the

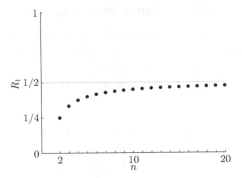

Figure 2.17. The expected maximum individual effort versus the number of players for a uniform prior distribution.

expected maximum individual effort converges to $(\bar{v}/2)(1 + 1/(2n - 1))$. This shows that the upper bound in Corollary 2.27 is asymptotically tight for a sequence of prior distributions that concentrates around the largest possible value of a valuation of a player.

Example 2.28 (uniform prior revisited). For a uniform prior distribution on $[0, 1]$, we have

$$R_1 = \frac{1}{2}\left(1 - \frac{1}{n}\right).$$

See Figure 2.17 for a graph.

Total vs. Maximum Individual Effort

An interesting question is how the expected maximum individual effort compares to the expected total effort in a symmetric Bayes-Nash equilibrium. For the special case of a uniform prior distribution, from Example 2.25 and Example 2.28, we observe that the expected maximum individual effort is a fraction of the expected total effort that decreases with the number of players (see Figure 2.18 for a graph). An interesting fact is that for the case of a uniform prior distribution, the expected maximum individual

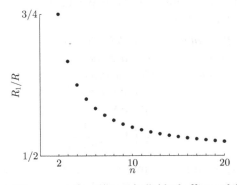

Figure 2.18. The ratio of the expected maximum individual effort and the expected total effort versus the number of players for a uniform prior distribution.

effort is at least half of the expected total effort for every given number of players. This fact is shown to hold in much more generality for every prior distribution in the following theorem.

Theorem 2.29. *For the game with incomplete information that models the standard all-pay contest among two or more players whose valuation parameters are independent and identically distributed according to a prior distribution that has no atoms above zero and has strictly positive density function on the support* $[0, 1]$, *in the symmetric Bayes-Nash equilibrium, the expected maximum individual effort is at least half of the expected total effort.*

Furthermore, the factor of $1/2$ *is tight asymptotically as the number of players grows large.*

Proof. The first claim follows from the following sequence of relations:

$$2R_1 - R = 2 \int_0^1 \beta(x) \, dF(x)^n - n \int_0^1 \beta(x) \, dF(x)$$

$$= 2n \int_0^1 \beta(x) F(x)^{n-1} \, dF(x) - n \int_0^1 \beta(x) \, dF(x)$$

$$= n \int_0^1 \beta(x)(2F(x)^{n-1} - 1) \, dF(x)$$

$$= n \int_0^1 \gamma(y) y^{n-1} (2y^{n-1} - 1) \, dy$$

$$= n \left[\int_0^{y^*} \gamma(y) y^{n-1} (2y^{n-1} - 1) \, dy + \int_{y^*}^1 \gamma(y) y^{n-1} (2y^{n-1} - 1) \, dy \right]$$

$$\geq n \left[\gamma(y^*) \int_0^{y^*} y^{n-1} (2y^{n-1} - 1) \, dy + \gamma(y^*) \int_{y^*}^1 y^{n-1} (2y^{n-1} - 1) \, dy \right]$$

$$= n\gamma(y^*) \int_0^1 y^{n-1} (2y^{n-1} - 1) \, dy$$

$$= \gamma(y^*) \frac{1}{2n - 1}$$

$$\geq 0 \tag{2.60}$$

where $\gamma(y) = \beta(F^{-1}(y))/y^{n-1}$, y^* is the solution of $2y^{*n-1} - 1 = 0$, and the inequality (2.60) follows from the facts that $\gamma(y)$ is non-negative and increasing, and $y^{n-1}(2y^{n-1} - 1) \leq 0$ for $y \in [0, y^*]$ and $y^{n-1}(2y^{n-1} - 1) \geq 0$ for $y \in [y^*, 1]$.

We next establish the asserted tightness. Using the change of variables $y = F(x)^{n-1}$ and $H_n(y) = F^{-1}(y^{\frac{1}{n-1}})$, from Theorem 2.24 and Theorem 2.26, it follows that

$$R(n) = n \int_0^1 H_n(y) \left(1 - y^{\frac{1}{n-1}} \right) dy \quad \text{and} \quad R_1(n) = \int_0^1 H_n(y) \left(1 - y^{\frac{n}{n-1}} \right) dy.$$

Note that $\lim_{n\to\infty} H_n(y) = 1$, for every $y \in (0, 1]$. Using this, we observe

$$\lim_{n\to\infty} R(n) = \int_0^1 \left[\lim_{n\to\infty} n\left(1 - y^{\frac{1}{n-1}}\right)\right] dy$$

$$= \int_0^1 [-\log(y)]\, dy$$

$$= \int_0^\infty y e^{-y}\, dy$$

$$= 1.$$

Similarly, we have

$$\lim_{n\to\infty} R_1(n) = \int_0^1 (1-y)\, dy = \frac{1}{2}.$$

$\square$

2.2.5 Minimum Required Effort

In this section we consider the standard all-pay contest with the additional assumption that the prize is allocated to the player who invests the largest effort but only if his or her effort is larger than an a priori specified value of minimum required effort. Otherwise, if each individual effort is smaller than the minimum required effort, then the prize is witheld by the contest owner. The minimum required effort is a parameter of the allocation mechanism whose value is common knowledge. The standard all-pay contest studied thus far in this chapter is a special case with the value of the minimum required effort parameter equal to zero. The game that models the standard all-pay contest with a minimum required effort formally corresponds to a standard all-pay auction with a reserve price, which is known to be optimal with respect to revenue under some conditions. We shall make use of the characterization of the symmetric Bayes-Nash equilibrium of this extended prize allocation mechanism later in Chapter 3, where we also discuss in more detail its optimality properties with respect to the expected total effort and the expected maximum individual effort.

Theorem 2.30. *Consider the game with incomplete information that models the standard all-pay contest with a minimum required effort of value $\underline{b} \in [0, 1]$ where the valuation parameters are independent and identically distributed according to a prior distribution F that has no atoms above zero and has strictly positive density function on the support $[0, 1]$. Then, such a game has a symmetric Bayes-Nash equilibrium, which is given by*

$$\beta(v) = \begin{cases} 0, & if\ 0 \le v < \underline{v} \\ \int_0^v \max\{x, \underline{v}\}\, dF(x)^{n-1}, & if\ \underline{v} \le v \le 1 \end{cases} \tag{2.61}$$

where $\underline{v}$ is given by

$$\underline{v} F(\underline{v})^{n-1} = \underline{b}. \tag{2.62}$$

Proof. By the revenue equivalence given in Theorem 2.20, the expected payment by a player with valuation v_i in an all-pay and a second-price auction are equivalent. Since

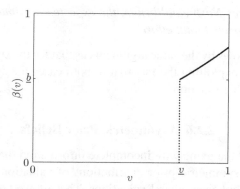

Figure 2.19. The symmetric Bayes-Nash equilibrium strategy for the game that models the standard all-pay contest with a minimum effort requirement under a uniform prior distribution.

in an all-pay auction, the player pays his or her own bid, it must be that $\beta(v_i)$ is equal to his or her expected payment under the second-price auction. In a second-price auction with a reserve price, the winner is the highest bidder, and his or her payment is the larger of the second highest bid and the reserve price. None of the other players make a payment. In the symmetric Bayes-Nash equilibrium of the second-price auction with a reserve value $\underline{v}$, each player bids his or her own valuation. Hence, in a second-price auction with a reserve value $\underline{v}$, the expected payment by a player conditional on the valuation parameter of this player being of value v is equal to

$$c_i(v) = \begin{cases} 0, & \text{if } 0 \le v < \underline{v} \\ \mathbf{E}[\max\{\max_{j \ne i} v_j, \underline{v}\}\mathbf{1}(\max_{j \ne i} v_j \le v_i) \mid v_i = v], & \text{if } \underline{v} \le v \le 1. \end{cases}$$

The expression asserted in (2.61) follows by noting that

$$\mathbf{E}\left[\max\left\{\max_{j \ne i} v_j, \underline{v}\right\}\mathbf{1}\left(\max_{j \ne i} v_j \le v_i\right) \mid v_i = v\right] = \int_0^v \max\{x, \underline{v}\}\, dF(x)^{n-1}, \quad \text{for } v \ge \underline{v}.$$

Since the reserve value $\underline{v}$ and the minimum required effort $\underline{b}$ satisfy the relation $\underline{b} = \beta(\underline{v})$, and by (2.61), $\beta(\underline{v}) = \underline{v}F(\underline{v})^{n-1}$, it follows that $\underline{v}F(\underline{v})^{n-1} = \underline{b}$. $\qquad\square$

Example 2.31 (uniform prior revisited). For a uniform prior distribution on $[0, 1]$, we have

$$\beta(v) = \begin{cases} 0, & \text{if } 0 \le v < \underline{v} \\ \frac{1}{n}\underline{v}^n + \left(1 - \frac{1}{n}\right)v^n, & \text{if } \underline{v} \le v \le 1 \end{cases}$$

where

$$\underline{v} = \underline{b}^{1/n}.$$

See Figure 2.19 for a graph.

Total vs. Maximum Individual Effort

Theorem 2.32. *Consider the game with incomplete information that models the standard all-pay contest with a minimum required effort, where the valuation parameters are independent and identically distributed according to a prior distribution that has no atoms above zero and has strictly positive density function on the support $[0, 1]$. Then,* *in the symmetric Bayes-Nash equilibrium, the expected maximum individual effort is at least half of the expected total effort.*

Proof. The proof follows by the same arguments as that for the standard-all pay contest in Theorem 2.29, by exploiting the fact that in both cases the symmetric equilibrium strategy is an increasing function. ☐

2.2.6 Asymmetric Prior Beliefs

So far we considered the game with incomplete information that models the standard all-pay contest with symmetric prior distributions of valuations, where players hold symmetric beliefs about each others' valuations. This allowed us to obtain an explicit characterization of a Bayes-Nash equilibrium and establish several properties in this equilibrium. The case that allows for asymmetric prior distributions is substantially more difficult to characterize. In this section we manage to establish an explicit characterization of a Bayes-Nash equilibrium for the case of two players whose prior distributions of valuations are allowed to be asymmetric.

Theorem 2.33. *Consider the game with incomplete information that models the standard all-pay contest between two players with private valuations that are assumed to be independent random variables according to prior distributions F_1 and F_2 for player 1 and player 2, respectively. Assume that both prior distributions have no atoms above zero and have strictly positive density functions on the support $[0, 1]$. Then, there exists a unique Bayes-Nash equilibrium, which is given by*

$$\beta_1(v) = \int_0^v \varphi(x) F_1'(x)\,dx \text{ and } \beta_2(v) = \beta_1(\varphi^{-1}(v)), \quad \text{for } v \in [0, 1] \quad (2.63)$$

where φ is the solution of the ordinary differential equation

$$\varphi'(v) = \frac{\varphi(v) F_1'(v)}{v F_2'(\varphi(v))} \quad (2.64)$$

with the boundary condition $\varphi(1) = 1$.

Proof. We shall only provide a sketch of the proof. Suppose that a pair of strategies (β_1, β_2) is a Bayes-Nash equilibrium. The expected payoff for a player conditional on the value of his or her effort investment and that the opponent plays according his or her assumed Bayes-Nash equilibrium strategy is given by

$$\mathbf{E}[s_1(v_1, (b_1, \beta_2(v_2)) \mid b_1 = x] = v_1 F_2(\beta_2^{-1}(x)) - x, \quad \text{for player 1}$$

and

$$\mathbf{E}[s_2(v_2, (\beta_1(v_1), b_2)) \mid b_2 = x] = v_2 F_1(\beta_1^{-1}(x)) - x, \quad \text{for player 2.}$$

Since in a Bayes-Nash equilibrium the expected payoff of each player $i \in \{1, 2\}$ is a constant at every point $b_i \in [0, \max_{v \in [0,1]} \beta_i(v)]$, it is necessary that at every such point $\partial \mathbf{E}[s_i(v_i, (b_i, \beta_j(v_j)) \mid b_i]/\partial b_i = 0$ for $j \in \{1, 2\}, j \neq i$. Hence, we have the following two necessary conditions:

$$v_1 F_2'(\beta_2^{-1}(b_1))\beta_2^{-1'}(b_1) = 1 \quad (2.65)$$

and

$$v_2 F_1'(\beta_1^{-1}(b_2))\beta_1^{-1'}(b_2) = 1. \tag{2.66}$$

Given that player $i \in \{1, 2\}$ plays according to a strictly increasing strategy function $\beta_i : [0, 1] \rightarrow \mathbf{R}_+$, his or her effort investment is a random variable with distribution

$$B_i(b_i) = F_i(\beta_i^{-1}(b_i)). \tag{2.67}$$

We now state five intuitive properties that can be shown to hold in a Bayes-Nash equilibrium, which for brevity we omit to prove here.

$$B_1 \text{ and } B_2 \text{ have identical supports.} \tag{2.68}$$

$$B_1 \text{ and } B_2 \text{ are continuous on } [0, \beta_1(1)] \text{ and } [0, \beta_2(1)], \text{ respectively.} \tag{2.69}$$

$$\text{If } v_i > v_i', \text{ then } F_j(\beta_i(v_i)) \geq F_j(\beta_i(v_i')) \text{ for } i, j \in \{1, 2\} \text{ and } i \neq j. \tag{2.70}$$

$$B_i \text{ has support } [0, \max_{v \in [0,1]} \beta_i(v)], \quad \text{for } i = 1 \text{ and } 2. \tag{2.71}$$

$$\text{If } F_1(0) = 0 \text{ and } F_2(0) = 0, \text{ then either } B_1(0) = 0 \text{ or } B_2(0) = 0. \tag{2.72}$$

Let us define a mapping $\varphi : [0, 1] \rightarrow [0, 1]$ by

$$\beta_1(v) = \beta_2(\varphi(v)), \quad \text{for } v \in [0, 1]. \tag{2.73}$$

By the properties (2.68)–(2.72), φ is a well-defined mapping from $[0, 1]$ onto $[0, 1]$. By (2.70), φ must be strictly increasing except possibly at $\varphi^{-1}(0)$. Hence,

$$\varphi'(v) = \beta_2^{-1'}(\varphi(v))\beta_1'(v), \quad \text{for } v \in [0, 1] \setminus \{\varphi^{-1}(0)\}. \tag{2.74}$$

Conditions (2.65) and (2.66) can be, respectively, written as

$$\beta_2^{-1'}(\beta_1(v_1)) = \frac{1}{v F_2'(\varphi(v_1))} \tag{2.75}$$

and

$$\beta_1'(v_1) = \varphi(v_1) F_1'(v_1) \tag{2.76}$$

where to obtain the last identity we use the elementary fact $\beta_1'(v) = 1/\beta_1^{-1'}(\beta_1(v))$.

Using (2.74), condition (2.75) can be equivalently expressed as

$$\varphi'(v_1) = \frac{\varphi(v_1) F_1'(v_1)}{v_1 F_2'(\varphi(v_1))}.$$

The boundary condition $\varphi(1) = 1$ follows from the facts (2.68), (2.70), and (2.71). $\square$

Example 2.34 (symmetric prior distributions). For the case of symmetric prior distributions, $\varphi(v) = v$ for $v \in [0, 1]$, and thus the strategies asserted in Theorem 2.33 boil down to those asserted for the symmetric Bayes-Nash equilibrium in Theorem 2.22 for the case of two players.

By the property asserted in (2.72), whenever both prior distributions have no atom at zero, at most one player has an atom at an effort investment of value zero. From (2.63) and (2.67), observe that

$$B_2(0) = F_2(\varphi(0)).$$

Example 2.35 (asymmetric prior distributions). Suppose that $F_1(v) = v^{\alpha_1}$ and $F_2(v) = v^{\alpha_2}$ for $v \in [0, 1]$, for the values of parameters $\alpha_1 > \alpha_2 \geq 1$.

If $\alpha_2 = 1$, then we have

$$\varphi(v) = e^{-\frac{\alpha_1}{\alpha_1 - 1}(1 - v^{\alpha_1 - 1})}.$$

In this case, player 2 invests zero effort with probability

$$B_2(0) = e^{-\frac{\alpha_1}{\alpha_1 - 1}}.$$

Otherwise, if $\alpha_2 \neq 1$, then we have

$$\varphi(v) = \left(1 - \frac{\alpha_1(\alpha_2 - 1)}{\alpha_1 - 1} + \frac{\alpha_1(\alpha_2 - 1)}{\alpha_1 - 1} v^{\alpha_1 - 1} \right)^{\frac{1}{\alpha_2 - 1}}.$$

In this case, player 2 invests zero effort with probability

$$B_2(0) = \left(\frac{\alpha_1 - \alpha_2}{\alpha_2(\alpha_1 - 1)} \right)^{\frac{\alpha_2}{\alpha_2 - 1}}.$$

Summary

Standard all-pay contest with complete information: $n \geq 2$ players with valuation parameters $v_1 \geq v_2 \geq \cdots \geq v_n > 0$.

There exists no pure-strategy Nash equilibrium.

In general there exists a continuum of mixed-strategy Nash equilibria.

The mixed-strategy Nash equilibrium is unique only for a valuation vector such that there is a pair of players whose values of valuation parameters are larger than that of any other player. In this case, the only active players in equilibrium are the two players with the two largest valuations. For other valuation vectors, there exists a continuum of mixed-strategy Nash equilibria.

In every equilibrium, the set of active players can contain only those whose valuation is at least v_2.

Payoff equivalence: in every equilibrium, the expected payoff of player 1 is equal to $v_1 - v_2$ and that of every other player is equal to zero.

For every valuation vector, it is always an equilibrium that only two players with the largest valuation parameters are the active players, and other players are inactive. This equilibrium outcome is special in that it yields the largest expected total effort among all equilibria for the given valuation vector.

The expected total effort in a contest between two players:

$$R = \frac{v_2}{2} \left(1 + \frac{v_2}{v_1} \right)$$

The expected total effort in a two-player contest is decreasing in the valuation parameter v_1.

The smallest expected total effort is for the equilibrium under valuation parameters $v_1 \geq v_2 = \cdots = v_n$ where players 2 through n play symmetric strategies that continuously randomize over $[0, v_2]$.

The expected total effort bounds:

$$\frac{1}{2}v_2 \leq R \leq v_2$$

where the lower bound is achieved for the valuation parameters $v_1 \geq v_2 = \cdots = v_n$, asymptotically as the number of players n grows large and an asymptotically small ratio of the valuation parameters v_2/v_1.

The expected maximum individual effort bounds:

$$\frac{1}{2}v_2 \leq R_1 \leq \frac{2}{3}v_2$$

The worst-case social welfare is at least $\eta \approx 84.38\%$ of the optimum social welfare. The worst-case is for valuation parameters $v_1 > v_2 = \cdots = v_n = 1$, for a unique value of the ratio $v_1/v_2 > 1$.

Standard all-pay contest with incomplete information: $n \geq 2$ players with private valuations that are assumed to be independent and identically distributed according to a prior distribution F on the support $[0, 1]$.

The exists a symmetric pure-strategy Bayes-Nash equilibrium, and this is the only Bayes-Nash equilibrium.

The symmetric pure-strategy Bayes-Nash equilibrium strategy:

$$\beta(v) = \int_0^v x \, dF(x)^{n-1}, \quad \text{for } v \in [0, 1].$$

The expected total effort is equal to the expected value of the second largest valuation:

$$R = \mathbf{E}[v_{(n,2)}].$$

The expected maximum individual effort is at most 2/3 of the maximum possible valuation.

The expected maximum individual effort is at least half of the expected total effort, which is tight asymptotically as the number of players grows large.

Exercises

2.1 Two players: total effort Show that the distribution asserted in Equation (2.5) is the distribution of the total effort in the mixed-strategy Nash equilibrium of the game that models the standard all-pay contest between two players.

2.2   **Multiplicity of mixed-strategy Nash equilibria** Show that the mixed-strategy Nash equilibria asserted in Section 2.1.4 are indeed mixed-strategy Nash equilibria.

2.3   **Total payoff** Consider the game with complete information that models the standard all-pay contest among two or more players with symmetric valuation parameters $v_1 = v_2 = \cdots = v_n > 0$ in the symmetric mixed-strategy Nash equilibrium. Let $p(n)$ be the probability of the event that the total payoff of all the players is non-negative, i.e.,

$$p(n) = \mathbf{Pr}\left[\sum_{i=1}^{n} s_i(\mathbf{b}) \geq 0\right].$$

Let $\Gamma(x)$ be the Gamma function $\Gamma(x) = \int_0^\infty y^{x-1} e^{-y} dy$ and let γ be the Euler's constant $\gamma = \lim_{x\to\infty}[1 + 1/2 + \cdots + 1/x - \log(x)]$.

Prove the following claims:

(a) $p(n) = \frac{n-1}{n}\Gamma\left(\frac{n}{n-1}\right)^{n-1}$.
(b) $p(n)$ is increasing in n.
(c) $p(2) = 1/2$ and $\lim_{n\to\infty} p(n) = e^{-\gamma} \approx 0.5615$.
(d) The total effort is smaller than or equal to the prize value, i.e., $\sum_{i=1}^{n} b_i \leq v_1$, with probability at least $1/2$.

2.4   **Exclusion** Consider the game that models the standard all-pay contest among two or more players with valuation parameters $v_1 \geq v_2 \geq \cdots \geq v_n > 0$. Assume that the content owner is informed about the values of the valuation parameters and his or her goal is to restrict the participation to a subset of players that maximizes the minimum expected total effort over mixed-strategy Nash equilibria of the game. Prove the following claims.

(a) The expected total effort is maximized by restricting the participation to a subset of players $\{k, k+1, \ldots, l\}$ where k is an integer such that $1 \leq k < n$,

$$\frac{v_{k+1}}{2}\left(1 + \frac{v_{k+1}}{v_k}\right) \geq \frac{v_{i+1}}{2}\left(1 + \frac{v_{i+1}}{v_i}\right), \quad \text{for } 1 \leq i < n, \qquad (2.77)$$

and l is some integer such that $k < l \leq n$.

Under such restricted participation, the expected total effort is

$$\frac{v_{k+1}}{2}\left(1 + \frac{v_{k+1}}{v_k}\right). \qquad (2.78)$$

(b) If the highest ability player is non-unique, i.e., $v_1 = v_2 \geq v_3 \geq \cdots \geq v_n > 0$, then the expected total effort cannot be increased by excluding some players.
(c) Suppose that there is a unique player of the highest ability and at least two players of the second highest ability, i.e., $v_1 > v_2 = v_3 \geq \cdots \geq v_n > 0$. Then, a larger expected total effort is achieved by excluding the highest ability player.
(d) The expected total effort in every mixed-strategy Nash equilibrium of the game in which all players are allowed to participate is at least $1/2$ of the the maximum expected total effort by allowing some of the players to be excluded. There exist valuation parameters such that the expected total effort in the former case can be made arbitrarily close to $1/2$ of the expected total effort in the latter case.

2.5   **Exclusion (cont'd)** Consider the same problem as in Exercise 2.4, but with the objective of maximizing the expected maximum individual effort. Prove the following claims.

(a) All the claims in Exercise 2.4 hold for the expected maximum individual effort with the following three changes: equation (2.77) is replaced by

$$\frac{v_{k+1}}{2}\left(1+\frac{v_{k+1}}{3v_k}\right) \geq \frac{v_{i+1}}{2}\left(1+\frac{v_{i+1}}{3v_i}\right), \quad \text{for every } 1 \leq i < n,$$

equation (2.78) is replaced by

$$\frac{v_{k+1}}{2}\left(1+\frac{v_{k+1}}{3v_k}\right)$$

and in Claim (d) 1/2 is replaced by 3/4.

(b) If exclusion of a highest ability player is not beneficial with respect to the expected total effort, then this is so with respect to the expected maximum individual effort.

(c) If exclusion of a highest ability player is beneficial with respect to the maximum individual effort, then this is so with respect to the expected total effort.

2.6 Budget caps Consider the game with complete information that models the standard all-pay contest between two players with valuations $v_1 \geq v_2 > 0$ where the effort investment of each player is capped by value $c > 0$. Show that the following claims hold in a mixed-strategy Nash equilibrium.

(a) The mixed-strategy Nash equilibria are given as follows:

(1) Case $c < v_2/2$: both players invest effort of value c with probability 1.

(2) Case $c = v_2/2$: there exists a continuum of mixed-strategy Nash equilibria in which player 1 invests effort of value c with probability 1, and player 2 invests effort of value zero with probability α and otherwise invests effort of value c, for any given value $0 \leq \alpha \leq 1 - v_2/v_1$.

(3) Case $v_2/2 < c < v_2$: the two players invest efforts according to the mixed strategies

$$B_1(x) = \begin{cases} \frac{x}{v_2}, & \text{if } 0 \leq x < 2c - v_2 \\ \frac{2c-v_2}{v_2}, & \text{if } 2c - v_2 \leq x < c \\ 1, & \text{if } x \geq c \end{cases}$$

and

$$B_2(x) = \begin{cases} 1 - \frac{v_2}{v_1} + \frac{v_2}{v_1}\frac{x}{v_2}, & \text{if } 0 \leq x < 2c - v_2 \\ 1 - \frac{v_2}{v_1} + \frac{v_2}{v_1}\frac{2c-v_2}{v_2}, & \text{if } 2c - v_2 \leq x < c \\ 1, & \text{if } x \geq c. \end{cases}$$

(4) Case $c \geq v_2$: the mixed strategies are as in the mixed-strategy Nash equilibrium of the game that models the standard all-pay contest without the budget caps, which are given in Theorem 2.3.

See Figure 2.20 for graphs.

(b) The expected individual efforts are

$$\mathbf{E}[b_1] = \begin{cases} c, & \text{if } 0 \leq c \leq v_2/2 \\ \frac{v_2}{2}, & \text{if } v_2/2 < c \leq v_2 \end{cases}$$

and

$$\mathbf{E}[b_2] = \begin{cases} c, & \text{if } 0 \leq c < v_2/2 \\ (1-\alpha)c, & \text{if } c = v_2/2 \\ \frac{v_2^2}{2v_1}, & \text{if } v_2/2 < c \leq v_2. \end{cases}$$

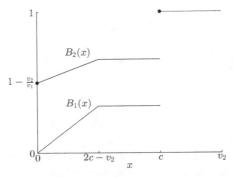

Figure 2.20. The mixed-strategy Nash equilibrium strategies for the case $v_2/2 < c < v_2$: both B_1 and B_2 have an atom at c with masses $2\left(1 - \frac{c}{v_2}\right)$ and $\frac{2v_2}{v_1}\left(1 - \frac{c}{v_2}\right)$, respectively.

(c) The expected total effort is

$$R = \begin{cases} 2c, & \text{if } 0 \le c < v_2/2 \\ (2 - \alpha)c, & \text{if } c = v_2/2 \\ \frac{v_2}{2}\left(1 + \frac{v_2}{v_1}\right), & \text{if } v_2/2 < c. \end{cases}$$

See Figure 2.21 for a graph.

(d) The expected payoffs are

$$\mathbf{E}[s_1(\mathbf{b})] = \begin{cases} \frac{v_1}{2} - c, & \text{if } 0 \le c < v_2/2 \\ \frac{(1+\alpha)v_1 - v_2}{2}, & \text{if } c = v_2/2 \\ v_1 - v_2, & \text{if } c > v_2/2 \end{cases}$$

and

$$\mathbf{E}[s_2(\mathbf{b})] = \begin{cases} \frac{v_2}{2} - c, & \text{if } 0 \le c < v_2/2 \\ 0, & \text{if } c \ge v_2/2. \end{cases}$$

2.7   Budget cap only for the low-ability player Consider the same game as in Exercise 2.6 but under the assumption that only the effort of player 2 is capped with value $c \ge 0$. Prove the following claims.

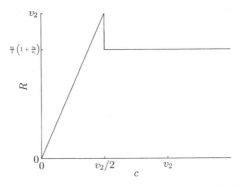

Figure 2.21. The expected total effort in a mixed-strategy Nash equilibrium.

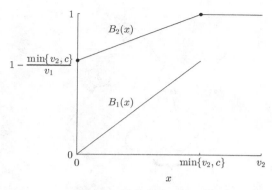

Figure 2.22. The mixed-strategy Nash equilibrium strategies where the effort investment of the low-ability player is capped with value c.

(a) There is a unique mixed-strategy Nash equilibrium, which is given by

$$B_1(x) = \begin{cases} \frac{x}{v_2}, & \text{if } 0 \le x < \min\{v_2, c\} \\ 1, & \text{if } x \ge \min\{v_2, c\} \end{cases}$$

and

$$B_2(x) = \begin{cases} 1 - \frac{\min\{v_2, c\}}{v_1} + \frac{x}{v_1}, & \text{if } 0 \le x \le \min\{v_2, c\} \\ 1, & \text{if } x \ge \min\{v_2, c\} \end{cases}.$$

See Figure 2.22 for a graphical representation.

(b) The expected individual efforts are

$$\mathbf{E}[b_1] = \frac{\min\{v_2, c\}}{2} \left(2 - \frac{\min\{v_2, c\}}{v_2} \right) \text{ and } \mathbf{E}[b_2] = \frac{\min\{v_2, c\}^2}{2v_1}.$$

(c) The expected total effort is

$$R = \frac{\min\{v_2, c\}}{2} \left(2 - \left(\frac{1}{v_2} - \frac{1}{v_1} \right) \min\{v_2, c\} \right).$$

2.8 Game with incomplete information Show that in the game with incomplete information that models the standard-all pay contest, in the symmetric Bayes-Nash equilibrium the expected total effort is as given in Equation (2.57), and the expected maximum individual effort is as given in Equation (2.58) and Equation (2.59).

2.9 Revelation of information Suppose that a contest owner commits to run a standard all-pay contest among two or more players whose valuation parameters are a priori private information and are independent and identically distributed random variables according to a prior distribution. The contest owner is informed about the values of the valuation parameters just before the contest takes place. Before this happens, the contest owner needs to decide whether to run the contest with the valuation parameters made public information to the players, or to run the contest such that the players are not informed about the values of the valuation parameters of other players. Prove the following claims.

(a) The contest owner has no incentive to make the values of the valuation parameters public with respect to the objective of maximizing the expected total effort in equilibrium of the two respective games.

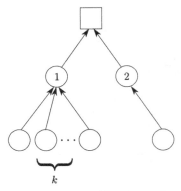

Figure 2.23. A two-player contest with asymmetric prior distributions.

(b) If the values of the valuation parameters are made public information, then the expected total effort in a mixed-strategy Nash equilibrium is at least half of the expected total effort in the symmetric Bayes-Nash equilibrium of the game in which the valuation parameters are private information.

2.10 Uncertain number of competitors Consider the game with incomplete information that models the standard all-pay contest with private valuations that are independent and identically distributed according to a prior distribution F with support $[0, 1]$. The number of players $|N|$ who participate in the contest is an independent random variable according to a prior distribution. The distribution of the number of participants in the contest, conditional on that any given player participates in the contest, is assumed to be independent of the identity of this player. Prove the following claims.

(a) The game has a symmetric Bayes-Nash equilibrium, which is given by

$$\beta(v) = \mathbf{E}\left[\int_0^v x \, dF(x)^{|N|-1} \mid |N| \geq 1\right].$$

(b) The expected total effort is

$$R = \mathbf{E}[|N|]\mathbf{E}\left[\frac{v_{(|N|,2)}}{|N|} \mid |N| \geq 1\right].$$

(c) The ex-ante expected total effort in the game where the number of participants is not revealed to the players is larger than in the game where the number of participants is revealed to the players if, and only if,

$$\mathbf{E}[|N| \mid |N| \geq 1]\mathbf{E}\left[\frac{v_{(|N|,2)}}{|N|} \mid |N| \geq 1\right] > \mathbf{E}[v_{(|N|,2)} \mid |N| \geq 1].$$

This condition holds whenever the prior distribution of valuations is sufficiently concentrated around a value, for any distribution of the number of players that has a strictly positive mass on at least two values larger than zero. The condition fails to hold if the prior distribution of valuation is sufficiently spread: check this to be the case for a uniform prior distribution of valuations on $[0, 1]$ and the number of players being equal to 1 with probability $1 - p$ or 2 with probability p, for every value $0 \leq p \leq 1$.

2.11 Asymmetric prior beliefs Consider the game with incomplete information that models the standard all-pay contest between two players. Suppose that player 1 is selected from a pool of k players as the player with the largest valuation where the valuations of the players in the pool are independent and identically distributed random variables according to a uniform prior distribution on $[0, 1]$. The value of the parameter k is common knowledge, but the valuation of player 1 remains unknown to player 2. The valuation of player 2 is according to an independent sample from a uniform prior distribution on $[0, 1]$. See Figure 2.23 for an illustration.

Show that the expected individual efforts in the Bayes-Nash equilibrium satisfy

$$\lim_{k \to \infty} \mathbf{E}[b_1] = 1 - \frac{2}{e} \approx 0.26 \text{ and } \lim_{k \to \infty} \mathbf{E}[b_2] = \frac{1}{2} \left(1 - \frac{1}{e} \right)^2 \approx 0.2.$$

2.3 Bibliographical Notes

The game with complete information that models the standard all-pay contest was studied, for example, by Moulin (1986), Dasgupta (1986), Hillman and Samet (1987), Hillman (1988), Hillman and Riley (1989), Ellingsen (1991), Baye et al. (1993), and Baye et al. (1996). The non-existence of pure-strategy Nash equilibrium, shown in Theorem 2.1, is from Hillman and Samet (1987). Moulin (1986) was the first to analyze the standard all-pay contest with more than two players with symmetric valuations and to characterize the symmetric mixed-strategy Nash equilibrium. Hillman and Samet (1987) showed that there are valuation vectors with two or more players with the largest valuation, under which there exists a symmetric mixed-strategy Nash equilibrium as well as multiple asymmetric mixed-strategy Nash equilibria, where some players of the largest valuation invest zero effort with probability one. Hillman and Riley (1989) were the first to show that there is a unique mixed-strategy Nash equilibrium under valuation vectors with a unique pair of players with the largest valuations. A complete characterization of all mixed-strategy equilibria was established by Baye et al. (1996), who showed that with more than two players there generally exists a continuum of mixed-strategy Nash equilibria. Theorem 2.4 and the characterization of the equilibrium mixed strategy distributions are from Baye et al. (1996). The relationship between the expected total effort and the expected effort of a player with the largest valuation in a mixed-strategy Nash equilibrium, which we showed in Theorem 2.13, was first established by Baye et al. (1993). Exercise 2.3, which is concerned with the distribution of the total payoff in a mixed-strategy Nash equilibrium, is from Baye et al. (1999). The exclusion principle in Exercise 2.4 was obtained by Baye et al. (1993), and is specific to the winner-take all prize allocation as discussed in Gale and Stegeman (1994). The effect of budget caps was first studied by Che and Gale (1998) in the context of political lobbying and later by Kvasov (2007). Exercise 2.6 is based on the study in Che and Gale (1998). Bertoletti (2006) studied the game with complete information that models the standard all-pay contest with reserve prices.

The study of the game with incomplete information that models the standard all-pay contest has also a long and rich history. Some early work includes Nalebuff and Stiglitz (1983), who studied contests as a scheme for competitive compensation in economics with imperfect information, and Singh and Wittman (1988), who studied a two-player contest with valuations and efforts from sets of two elements and where valuations are allowed to be statistically dependent. Krishna (2002) provides a nice textbook account on auction theory, with a good coverage of all-pay auctions. The revenue equivalence theorem, Theorem 2.20, is originally from Myerson (1981). Comparison of the expected total effort and the expected maximum individual effort was first studied by Chawla et al. (2012). The first part of the claim in Theorem 2.29 is from Chawla et al. (2012). The existence and uniqueness of Bayes-Nash equilibrium were studied by Maskin and Riley (1984), Weber (1985), Amann and Leininger (1996), Maskin and Riley (2003), McAdams (2007), Bhattacharya et al. (2010), and Chawla and Hartline (2013). Maskin and Riley (1984) proved the existence of Bayes-Nash equilibrium for the n-player case and the uniqueness of equilibrium for the two-player case with continuous prior distributions. The existence and uniqueness of the Bayes-Nash equilibrium in a n-player contest with independent and identically distributed valuations were established by Chawla and Hartline (2013). Several authors considered the case of asymmetric prior distributions of valuations, including Marshall et al. (1994), Amann and Leininger (1996), and Fibich and Gavish (2012). Theorem 2.33 is from Amann and Leininger (1996). The effects of the uncertainty about the number of competitors on the equilibrium properties in the first-price and the second-price auctions were studied by various, authors including Matthews (1987), McAfee and McMillan (1987), Harstad et al. (1990), and Levin and Ozdenoren (2004).

Last but not least, we point to Muller and Schotter (2010) and the survey by Dechenaux et al. (2012) for experimental evaluations of all-pay contests.

CHAPTER 3
Rank-Order Allocation of Prizes

In this chapter we consider contests that award one or more placement prizes based on the rank of individual performance. Such contests are rather common. The number of placement prizes and how the prize purse is split over a given number of placement prizes vary widely from one contest to another. Perhaps the most common contest design is to award only the first place prize, thus rewarding only the best performing contestant. Another common practice is to award two prizes: the first place prize and the runner-up prize to the best performing and the second best performing contestant, respectively. Also common are designs with three placement prizes: the first place prize to the best performing player, the second place prize to the second best performing player, and the third place prize to the third best performing player. A case that also often arises in practice is a contest that offers one or more prizes of identical values. For example, such prizes can be positions in the next stage of a tournament, admissions to a school program, or research papers accepted for inclusion in a conference program. The rank-based allocation of prizes that is considered in this chapter can be seen as a generalization of that studied in Chapter 2, where the focus was on contests that award only the first place prize. One might expect that devoting some amount of a prize purse to the runner-up and perhaps also to other placement prizes would incentivize lower ability contestants to try harder and as a result yield overall higher performance.

Our goal in this chapter is to characterize strategic behavior in contests that award one or more placement prizes. We shall pay particular attention to identifying conditions under which it is optimal for a contest owner to offer only the first place prize and when it is better to split a prize purse across several placement prizes. There are two important factors here: the informational assumptions about abilities of players and the nature of production costs. We shall see that if players are ex-ante identical with respect to their abilities and the production of each player exhibits a weakly diminishing marginal cost of production, it is optimal for the contest owner to allocate the entire prize purse to the first place prize with respect to both the expected total effort and the expected maximum individual effort in an equilibrium. On the other hand, if the production costs of the players have increasing marginal costs of production, then there are cases when it is optimal to split a prize purse across more than one placement prize. We shall focus on two natural optimality criteria in an equilibrium: the expected total effort and the expected maximum individual effort. Both these criteria are natural and of interest in practice.

We study a normal form game with the set $N = \{1, 2, \ldots, n\}$ of two or more players who simultaneously invest efforts of values $\mathbf{b} = (b_1, b_2, \ldots, b_n) \in \mathbf{R}_+^n$ and receive one of n placement prizes based on the rank of their individual efforts. The value of the effort of a player is said to be of rank j if the individual efforts can be sorted in decreasing order such that the effort of this player is the j-th largest. Let $\mathbf{v}_i = (v_{i,j}, j = 1, 2, \ldots, n) \in \mathbf{R}_+^n$ be the valuation vector of player $i \in N$, where $v_{i,j}$ is the valuation of winning the jth place prize for player $i \in N$. Given a vector of efforts $\mathbf{b}$, the allocation of prizes is given by $x(\mathbf{b}) = (x_{i,j}(\mathbf{b}), i, j = 1, 2, \ldots, n)$, where $x_{i,j}(\mathbf{b}) = 1$, if player i is allocated the j-th place prize, and $x_{i,j}(\mathbf{b}) = 0$, otherwise. Player i is assumed to incur a cost of production according to a given production cost function $c_i : \mathbf{R}_+ \to \mathbf{R}_+$ of his or her own value of invested effort. The payoff functions of players are given by

$$s_i(\mathbf{v}_i, \mathbf{b}) = \sum_{j=1}^{n} v_{i,j} x_{i,j}(\mathbf{b}) - c_i(b_i), \quad \text{for } i \in N. \tag{3.1}$$

The type of valuation vectors that is studied in this chapter is of the following form. Suppose a vector of values of the placement prizes $\mathbf{w} = (w_1, w_2, \ldots, w_n) \in \mathbf{R}_+^n$ is given, where w_j is the value of the j-th place prize. The values of the placement prizes are assumed to be decreasing in the placement, i.e., it holds that $w_1 \geq w_2 \geq \cdots \geq w_n$. We shall consider allocation of a given prize purse over the placement prizes, and in this case, without loss of generality, assume that the prize purse is of unit value, i.e. $\sum_{j=1}^{n} w_j = 1$. Each player $i \in N$ is associated with a valuation parameter v_i, which can be interepreted as the valuation per unit of a prize value. The valuation vector is then defined by $v_{i,j} = v_i w_j$ for player $i \in N$ and the prize of placement $j = 1, 2, \ldots, n$. The payoff functions of players admit the following form:

$$s_i(v_i, \mathbf{b}) = v_i \sum_{j=1}^{n} w_j x_{i,j}(\mathbf{b}) - c_i(b_i), \quad \text{for } i \in N. \tag{3.2}$$

Such defined payoff functions accommodate the game that models the standard all-pay contest, which we studied in Chapter 2, as a special case where $w_1 > w_2 = \cdots = w_n = 0$ and the production cost functions are assumed to be identical and linear. We shall pay special attention to the case of linear production cost functions, and in particular to linear production functions where each player incurs a unit marginal cost of production.

This chapter is split in two parts. In the first part, we consider the game with incomplete information, and in the second part, we consider the game with complete information.

3.1 Game with Incomplete Information

We consider the game with incomplete information with the payoff functions of players given by (3.2) where the valuation parameters of players are private information and are assumed to be independent and identically distributed random variables according to a given prior distribution F. The prior distribution F is assumed to be atomless with the support $[0, 1]$. We study properties of the game in a symmetric Bayes-Nash equilibrium where each player plays according to a strictly increasing strategy $\beta : [0, 1] \to \mathbf{R}_+$, which specifies the value of effort investment by a player for every given value of the valuation parameter of this player. The probability that a player whose valuation parameter is of value v wins the j-th place prize is equal to the probability of the event that there are $j - 1$ players whose valuation parameters are larger than v and $n - j$ players whose valuation parameters are smaller than v. Specifically, the probability that a player with a valuation parameter of value $v \in [0, 1]$ wins the placement prize $j = 1, 2, \ldots, n$ is equal to

$$x_j(v) = \mathbf{E}[x_{i,j}(\mathbf{b}) \mid v_i = v] = \binom{n-1}{j-1} F(v)^{n-j}(1 - F(v))^{j-1}. \quad (3.3)$$

Note that the probability of winning the first place prize by a player with the valuation parameter of value $v \in [0, 1]$ is $x_1(v) = F(v)^{n-1}$. This is exactly the expression that we already encountered in Section 2.2 where the focus was on contests that only award the first place prize.

A key role in the characterization of a symmetric Bayes-Nash equilibrium is played by the order statistics of the valuation parameters. For every given vector of valuations $\mathbf{v} = (v_1, v_2, \ldots, v_n)$, we denote the rearrangement of the elements of this vector in decreasing order as $(v_{(n,1)}, v_{(n,2)}, \ldots, v_{(n,n)})$. We denote with $F_{n,j}$ the distribution function of the j-th largest valuation and denote with $f_{n,j}$ the density function of this distribution, which is given by

$$f_{n,j}(x) = \frac{n!}{(j-1)!(n-j)!} F(x)^{n-j}(1 - F(x))^{j-1} f(x), \quad \text{for } x \in \mathbf{R}. \quad (3.4)$$

3.1.1 Symmetric Bayes-Nash Equilibrium

Theorem 3.1. *Consider the game that models the rank-order all-pay contest with the values of placement prizes $w_1 \geq w_2 \geq \cdots \geq w_n \geq 0$. There exists a symmetric Bayes-Nash equilibrium, which is given by*

$$\beta(v) = \sum_{j=1}^n w_j \int_0^v x \, dx_j(x), \quad for \ v \in [0, 1] \quad (3.5)$$

where $x_j(x)$ is the probability of winning the j-th place prize by a player with the valuation parameter of value x given by (3.3).

Proof. Suppose that $\beta : [0, 1] \to \mathbf{R}_+$ is a strictly increasing symmetric Bayes-Nash equilibrium strategy. We show that it is of the form asserted in the theorem. The expected payoff of player $i \in N$ conditional on his or her effort investment being of value x is equal to

$$\mathbf{E}[s_i(v_i, \mathbf{b}) \mid b_i = x] = v_i \sum_{j=1}^n w_j x_j(\beta^{-1}(x)) - x.$$

Let $v = \beta^{-1}(x)$. Since β is assumed to be a symmetric Bayes-Nash equilibrium, it must hold that

$$\frac{\partial}{\partial b_i} \mathbf{E}[s_i(v_i, \mathbf{b}) \mid b_i = x] = \frac{dv}{db_i} \cdot v_i \sum_{j=1}^{n} w_j x'_j(v) - 1 = 0, \quad \text{for } v = v_i.$$

From this, we obtain

$$\frac{d}{dv}\beta(v) = \sum_{j=1}^{n} w_j v x'_j(v).$$

The assertion of the theorem follows by integrating the last expression and the boundary condition that a player with the valuation parameter of value zero invests the effort of value zero.   □

An alternative characterization of the symmetric Bayes-Nash equilibrium is given by

$$\beta(v) = \sum_{j=1}^{n-1}(w_j - w_{j+1}) \int_0^v x \, dF_{n-1,j}(x), \quad \text{for } v \in [0, 1]. \tag{3.6}$$

This follows from the expression in (3.5) and by making use of the identities

$$x'_j(x) = \begin{cases} f_{n-1,1}(x), & \text{if } j = 1 \\ f_{n-1,j}(x) - f_{n-1,j-1}(x), & \text{if } 1 < j < n \\ -f_{n-1,n-1}(x), & \text{if } j = n, \end{cases}$$

which are easy to establish from (3.3) and making use of equation (3.4).

Note that the symmetric Bayes-Nash equilibrium strategy in (3.6) is a convex combination of the symmetric Bayes-Nash equilibrium strategies in contests that offer prizes of unit values to the players who make the j largest effort investments, for $1 \le j < n$.

From Theorem 3.1, we observe that it is never beneficial to allocate some amount of a prize budget to the lowest-placement prize with respect to the invested efforts in equilibrium.

Corollary 3.2. *For every game with incomplete information that models the rank-order contest with two or more players, allocating a strictly positive portion of a prize budget to the lowest placement prize decreases the equilibrium effort for every realized value of the valuation parameter of a player.*

Proof. This is immediate from the characterization of the symmetric Bayes-Nash equilibrium strategy in (3.5) and the fact that

$$x'_n(x) = -f_{n-1,n-1}(x) < 0 \text{ for every } x \in [0, 1).$$

□

Examples

In this section, we consider the symmetric Bayes-Nash equilibrium strategy in Theorem 3.1 in terms of three specific ways of splitting a prize purse over a given

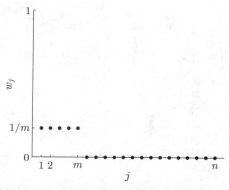

Figure 3.1. The uniform split of a unit prize budget over a given number of prizes m.

number of placement prizes. We revisit some of these examples later when we examine the expected total effort and the expected maximum individual effort.

Example 3.3 (uniform split of a prize budget over a given number of prizes).
Consider the splitting of a unit prize budget over a given number of prizes $m \geq 1$ so that $w_1 = \cdots = w_m = 1/m > w_{m+1} = \cdots = w_n = 0$ (see Figure 3.1). The symmetric Bayes-Nash equilibrium is equal to

$$\beta(v) = \frac{1}{m} \int_0^v x \, dF_{n-1,m}(x). \tag{3.7}$$

This accommodates awarding only the first place prize as a special case; then the expression in (3.7) boils down to that already encountered in Theorem 3.1.

Example 3.4 (linearly decreasing prizes). Consider splitting a unit prize budget over the placement prizes such that the values of prizes decrease linearly with the rank: for a given value of the lowest placement prize $w_n \in [0, 1/n]$, the values of the placement prizes are given by $w_j = w_n + a(n - j)$ for $j = 1, 2, \ldots, n$, where $a = 2(1 - nw_n)/[n(n - 1)]$ (see Figure 3.2). The symmetric Bayes-Nash equilibrium strategy in (3.6) boils down to

$$\beta(v) = \frac{2(1 - nw_n)}{n} \int_0^v x \, dF(x), \quad \text{for } v \in [0, 1].$$

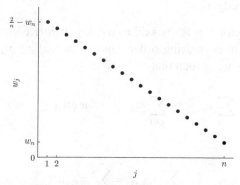

Figure 3.2. Linearly decreasing values of the placement prizes.

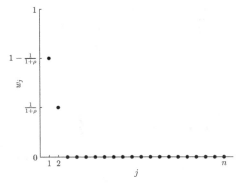

Figure 3.3. Two prizes with the values of the first place prize and the second place prize $\rho : 1$.

Example 3.5 (two prizes). Consider splitting a unit prize budget over two first place-ment prizes so that $w_1 \geq w_2 \geq w_3 = \cdots = w_n = 0$ and $w_1/w_2 = \rho$, for given parameter $\rho \geq 1$ (see Figure 3.3). In other words, a unit prize budget is split between the first and the second place prize such that they are of respective values $1 - 1/(1 + \rho)$ and $1/(1 + \rho)$. Such allocation of a prize budget has as the extreme points the uniform split of the prize budget over the first two placements for $\rho = 1$ and awarding only the first place prize asymptotically in the limit as ρ grows large. The symmetric Bayes-Nash equilibrium strategy is given by

$$\beta(v) = \int_0^v x \, dF(x)^{n-1} - \frac{1}{1+\rho} \left(n \int_0^v x \, dF(x)^{n-1} - (n-1) \int_0^v x \, dF(x)^{n-2} \right).$$

Single-Crossing Property of Equilibrium Strategies

In this section, we compare two symmetric Bayes-Nash equilibrium strategies in the games with different splits of a prize purse over given number of placement prizes. In particular, we consider splits of a prize budget that stand in a majorization order and show that such a majorization order implies a single-crossing property for the respective symmetric Bayes-Nash equilibrium strategies. The concept of single-crossing functions is also used later in Section 3.1.4 as a step in establishing comparison results for the expected total effort and the expected maximum individual effort under different ways of allocating a prize budget.

Definition 3.6. A vector $\mathbf{x} \in \mathbf{R}^n$ is said to *weakly majorize* vector $\mathbf{y} \in \mathbf{R}^n$ if $\mathbf{x}$ and $\mathbf{y}$ have rearrangements in decreasing order denoted as $x_{(n,1)} \geq x_{(n,2)} \geq \cdots \geq x_{(n,n)}$ and $y_{(n,1)} \geq y_{(n,2)} \geq \cdots \geq y_{(n,n)}$ such that

$$\sum_{j=1}^{i} x_{(n,j)} \geq \sum_{j=1}^{i} y_{(n,j)}, \quad \text{for all } 1 \leq i < n$$

and

$$\sum_{j=1}^{n} x_{(n,j)} = \sum_{j=1}^{n} y_{(n,j)}.$$

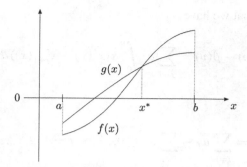

Figure 3.4. f is single-crossing with respect to g.

In the context of vectors of values of placement prizes, a vector of placement prizes weakly majorizes another vector of placement prizes if its total value of the top j placement prizes is larger than or equal to that in the other vector, for every $j = 1, 2, \ldots, n$. The allocation of the entire prize budget to the first place prize weakly majorizes every possible way of splitting a given prize budget over a given number of placement prizes. The uniform split of prizes over a given number of placement prizes, as discussed in Example 3.3, weakly majorizes every uniform split of prizes over a larger number of placement prizes. The splitting of a prize budget over two first placement prizes as discussed in Example 3.5 weakly majorizes any such splitting of the prize budget that allocates a smaller portion of the prize budget to the first place prize.

Definition 3.7. A function $f : [a, b] \to \mathbf{R}$ is said to be *single-crossing* with respect to a function $g : [a, b] \to \mathbf{R}$, if there exists $x^* \in [a, b]$ such that

$$f(x) \leq g(x) \text{ for } x \in [a, x^*] \text{ and } f(x) \geq g(x) \text{ for } x \in (x^*, b].$$

See Figure 3.4 for an illustration.

In the following theorem, we establish that if two vectors of values of prizes satisfy the majorization order then this implies that the respective symmetric Bayes-Nash equilibrium strategies satisfy the single-crossing property.

Theorem 3.8. *For two vectors of prizes* $\mathbf{w}$ *and* $\tilde{\mathbf{w}}$ *such that* $\mathbf{w}$ *weakly majorizes* $\tilde{\mathbf{w}}$, *the symmetric Bayes-Nash equilibrium strategy in the game with the values of prizes according to vector* $\mathbf{w}$ *is single-crossing with respect to that in the game with the values of prizes according to vector* $\tilde{\mathbf{w}}$.

Proof. From the characterization of the symmetric Bayes-Nash equilibrium strategy in (3.5) and the telescope formula, we have

$$\beta(v) = \sum_{j=1}^{n} \left(\sum_{i=1}^{j} w_i \right) \left(\int_0^v x \, dx_j(x) - \int_0^v x \, dx_{j+1}(x) \right),$$

where by convention $x_{n+1}(x) = 0$ for $x \in [0, 1]$. Let $\tilde{\beta}$ be the symmetric Bayes-Nash equilibrium strategy in the game with the placement prizes according to the vector of prizes $\tilde{w}$. It follows that we have

$$\beta(v) - \tilde{\beta}(v) = \sum_{j=1}^{n} a_j \int_0^v x(x'_j(x) - x'_{j+1}(x)) \, dx,$$

where

$$a_j = \sum_{i=1}^{j} w_i - \sum_{i=1}^{j} \tilde{w}_i \geq 0, \quad \text{for } j = 1, 2, \ldots, n.$$

From this, we observe that it suffices to show that for every $1 \leq i < j \leq n$, x'_i is single-crossing with respect to x'_j, i.e., there exists $x_{i,j} \in [0, 1]$ such that

$$x'_i(x) - x'_j(x) \leq 0, \quad \text{for } x \in [0, x_{i,j}] \text{ and } x'_i(x) - x'_j(x) \geq 0, \quad \text{for } (x_{i,j}, 1].$$

By a straightforward calculus, we have

$$x'_i(x) - x'_j(x) = \phi_{i,j}(x) x^{n-j-1}(1-x)^{i-2}$$

where

$$\phi_{i,j}(x) = \binom{n-1}{i-1} x^{j-i}(n-i-(n-1)x) - \binom{n-1}{j-1}(1-x)^{j-i}(n-j-(n-1)x).$$

Note that $x'_i(x) - x'_j(x) \leq 0$ if, and only if, $\phi_{i,j}(x) \leq 0$, which is equivalent to

$$\binom{n-1}{i-1} x^{j-i} \leq \binom{n-1}{j-1}(1-x)^{j-i} \frac{n-j-(n-1)x}{n-i-(n-1)x}.$$

The left-hand side in the last inequality is increasing in x and the right-hand side is decreasing in x, at $x = 0$ the inequality holds true, and at $x = 1$ the inequality does not hold. Hence, it follows that there exists a unique point $x_{i,j} \in [0, 1]$ such that the inequality holds for every $x \in [0, x_{i,j}]$ and it does not hold for every $x \in (x_{i,j}, 1]$, which establishes the claim. $\square$

The comparison result in Theorem 3.8 implies that reallocating some amount of a prize budget from a lower to a higher position prize has the effect of increasing the effort of a higher valuation player and decreasing the effort of a lower valuation player. Figure 3.5 illustrates the single-crossing property for the equilibrium strategies under the splitting of a unit prize budget over two first placement prizes that we discussed in Example 3.5.

Corollary 3.9 (symmetric values of a given number of prizes). *Suppose that $\beta_{n,m}$ is the symmetric Bayes-Nash equilibrium strategy in the game with incomplete information that models the rank-order all-pay contest with $n > m$ players and the values of prizes $w_1 = \cdots = w_m = 1/m > w_{m+1} = \cdots = w_n = 0$. Then, $\beta_{n,m}$ is single-crossing with respect to $\beta_{n,m'}$ for every m' such that $m < m' < n$.*

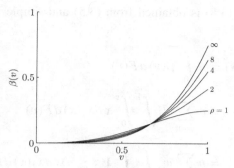

Figure 3.5. The symmetric Bayes-Nash equilibrium strategies for the split of a unit prize budget over two first placement prizes in the ratio $\rho : 1$ and a uniform prior distribution: the equilibrium strategy in the game with the split of prizes $\rho : 1$ is single-crossing with respect to the equilibrium strategy in the game with the split of prizes $\rho' : 1$ for every $\rho' \in [1, \rho)$.

We next make note of a comparison property that holds for the equilibrium strategies with respect to the number of players.

Theorem 3.10. *Consider the game with incomplete information that models the rank-order all-pay contest with the values of position prizes given by $w_1 \geq w_2 \geq \cdots \geq w_m > 0$ for an integer $m \geq 1$. The symmetric Bayes-Nash equilibrium strategy in the game with $n > m$ players is single-crossing with respect to that in the game with n' players such that $m \leq n' < n$.*

Proof. Using the characterization of the symmetric Bayes-Nash equilibrium in (3.6), we note that it suffices to show that $f_{n,j}$ is single-crossing with respect to $f_{n',j}$, for $1 \leq j \leq m$. From (3.4), notice that $f_{n,j}(x) - f_{n',j}(x) \leq 0$ is equivalent to

$$F(x)^{n-n'} \leq \frac{n'!(n-j)!}{n!(n'-j)!}.$$

From this it follows that there exists $x^* \in [0, 1]$ such that $f_{n,j}(x) - f_{n',j}(x) \leq 0$ if $x \in [0, x^*]$ and $f_{n,j}(x) - f_{n',j}(x) > 0$ if $x \in (x^*, 1]$. $\square$

An illustration of the comparison claim asserted in Theorem 3.10 can be found in Figure 2.15 for the case of awarding only the first place prize and a uniform prior distribution.

3.1.2 Total Effort

The expected total effort in the symmetric Bayes-Nash equilibrium specified in Section 3.1.1 can be represented as follows:

$$R(\mathbf{w}) = n \sum_{j=1}^{n} w_j \int_0^1 x(1 - F(x))dx_j(x) \tag{3.8}$$

where recall that $x_j(x)$ is the probability of winning the j-th place by a player with the valuation parameter of value x given in (3.3).

The expression in (3.8) is obtained from (3.5) and simple integration, which we perform as follows:

$$R(\mathbf{w}) = n \int_0^1 \beta(v) \, dF(v)$$

$$= n \sum_{j=1}^n w_j \int_0^1 \int_0^v x \, dx_j(x) \, dF(v)$$

$$= n \sum_{j=1}^n w_j \int_0^1 \int_0^1 \mathbf{1}(x \le v) x \, dx_j(x) \, dF(v)$$

$$= n \sum_{j=1}^n w_j \int_0^1 \left(\int_x^1 F'(v) \, dv \right) x \, dx_j(x)$$

$$= n \sum_{j=1}^n w_j \int_0^1 x(1 - F(x)) \, dx_j(x).$$

An alternative way to represent the expected total effort in the symmetric Bayes-Nash equilibrium is in terms of the order statistics of the valuations of the players:

$$R(\mathbf{w}) = \sum_{j=1}^{n-1} (w_j - w_{j+1}) j \, \mathbf{E}[v_{(n,j+1)}]. \tag{3.9}$$

This is obtained by noting that $R(\mathbf{w}) = n \int_0^1 \beta(v) dF(v)$, using the expression in Equation (3.6), and making use of the following easy-to-establish fact:

$$\int_0^1 \int_0^v x \, dF_{n-1,j}(x) \, dF(v) = \frac{j}{n} \int_0^1 x \, dF_{n,j+1}(x) = \frac{j}{n} \mathbf{E}[v_{(n,j+1)}].$$

Examples
Example 3.11 (uniform split of a prize budget revisited). For the case introduced in Example 3.3, the expected total effort is given by

$$R(n, m) = \mathbf{E}[v_{(n,m+1)}]. \tag{3.10}$$

For the standard all-pay contest $w_1 = 1$ and $w_i = 0$, for $i \ne 1$, and thus, in this case the expression in (3.9) boils down to $R = \mathbf{E}[v_{(n,2)}]$, which we know to be true by the revenue equivalence Theorem 2.20.

Example 3.12 (linearly decreasing prizes revisited). For the case introduced in Example 3.4, the expected total effort is given by

$$R(n, w_n) = (1 - n w_n) \mathbf{E}[v_{(2,2)}].$$

If no part of a unit prize budget is allocated to the lowest placement prize, i.e., $w_n = 0$, then we have

$$R = \mathbf{E}[v_{(2,2)}].$$

In this case, the expected total effort in invariant to the number of players. It corresponds to the expected total effort in the symmetric Bayes-Nash equilibrium of the game that models the standard all-pay contest with two players.

Example 3.13 (two prizes revisited). For the case introduced in Example 3.5, the expected total effort is given by

$$R(n, \rho) = \left(1 - \frac{2}{1 + \rho}\right) \mathbf{E}[v_{(n,2)}] + \frac{2}{1 + \rho}\mathbf{E}[v_{(n,3)}].$$

In this case, the expected total effort is a convex combination of the expected second largest valuation and the expected third largest valuation. It is a smooth interpolation between these two expected values, which are achieved in the two extreme cases asymptotically as the value of ρ grows large and for the value $\rho = 1$, respectively.

3.1.3 Maximum Individual Effort

The expected maximum individual effort in the symmetric Bayes-Nash equilibrium specified in Section 3.1.1 can be represented as follows:

$$R_1(\mathbf{w}) = \sum_{j=1}^{n} w_j \int_0^1 x(1 - F(x)^n)\, dx_j(x), \tag{3.11}$$

where, again, recall that $x_j(x)$ is the probability of winning the j-th place by a player with the valuation parameter of value x given in (3.3).

The expression in (3.11) follows by this series of equations:

$$R_1(\mathbf{w}) = n \int_0^1 \beta(v)F(v)^{n-1}\, dF(v)$$

$$= \sum_{j=1}^{n} w_j \int_0^1 \int_0^v x\, dx_j(x)\, dF(v)^n$$

$$= \sum_{j=1}^{n} w_j \int_0^1 \int_0^1 \mathbf{1}(x \le v)x\, dx_j(x)\, dF(v)^n$$

$$= \sum_{j=1}^{n} w_j \int_0^1 \left(\int_x^1 dF(v)^n\right) x\, dx_j(x)$$

$$= \sum_{j=1}^{n} w_j \int_0^1 x(1 - F(x)^n)\, dx_j(x).$$

An alternative representation of the expected maximum individual effort is given as follows:

$$R_1(\mathbf{w}) = \sum_{j=1}^{n-1} (w_j - w_{j+1})(\mathbf{E}[v_{(n-1,j)}] - c_{n,j}\mathbf{E}[v_{(2n-1,j)}]) \tag{3.12}$$

where $c_{n,j} = \binom{n-1}{j}/\binom{2n-1}{j}$. This can be easily derived from $R_1(\mathbf{w}) = \int_0^1 \beta(v)\, dF^n(x)$ and the expression for the Bayes-Nash equilibrium strategy in (3.6).

Examples

Example 3.14 (uniform split of a prize budget revisited). For the case introduced in Example 3.3, the expected maximum individual effort is given by

$$R_1(n, m) = \frac{1}{m}(E[v_{(n-1,m)}] - c_{n,m}E[v_{(2n-1,m)}]).$$ (3.13)

For the case of awarding only the first place prize, the expression in (3.13) boils down to the one that we already noted in Equation (2.59).

Example 3.15 (linearly decreasing prizes revisited). For the case introduced in Example 3.4, the expected maximum individual effort is given by

$$R_1(n, w_n) = \frac{2(1 - nw_n)}{n}\left(E[v_1] - \frac{1}{n+1}E[v_{(n+1,1)}]\right).$$

3.1.4 Optimality of Awarding Only the First Place Prize

How should a contest owner split a prize budget over different placement prizes to achieve the goal of maximizing the expected total effort or the expected maximum effort in equilibrium? Should the contest owner allocate the entire prize budget to the first place prize, or should a part of the prize budget be allocated to other placement prizes? For the specific ways of splitting a prize budget in Examples 3.11, 3.12, and 3.13, we observe that allocating the entire prize budget to the first place prize is optimal for the goal of maximizing the expected total effort. The same observation holds for the specific ways of splitting a prize budget in Examples 3.14 and 3.15 for the goal of maximizing the expected maximum individual effort. In this section, we show that for the game that models the rank-order all-pay contest with linear production costs, it is always optimal to allocate the entire prize budget to the first place prize with respect to both objectives. In Section 3.1.6 we consider the same question for a more general class of prize allocation rules than the rank-order allocation of prizes, which for example, allow the contest designer to withhold the prize.

Total Effort

Theorem 3.16. *For every game with incomplete information that models the rank-order all-pay contest with two or more players whose valuation parameters are independent and identically distributed according to a prior distribution and such that players incur identical linear production costs, it is optimal to allocate entire prize purse to the first place prize with respect to the expected total effort in the symmetric Bayes-Nash equilibrium.*

Proof. Let us define $G_j(x)$ to be the probability of the event that for $n - 1$ independent samples from a uniform distribution $[0, 1]$, $j - 1$ of the samples are of value larger than x and $n - j$ of the samples are of value smaller than or equal to x, i.e.,

$$G_j(x) = \binom{n-1}{j-1}x^{n-j}(1 - x)^{j-1}, \quad \text{for } x \in [0, 1] \text{ and } 1 \le j \le n.$$ (3.14)

From the characterization of the expected total effort in the symmetric Bayes-Nash equilibrium in (3.8) and the change of variables $y = F(x)$, we have

$$R = \sum_{j=1}^{n} a_j w_j$$ (3.15)

where

$$a_j = \int_0^1 F^{-1}(x) h_j(x)\,dx \text{ and } h_j(x) = (1-x)G'_j(x).$$

We shall show that $a_1 > a_j$, for all $1 < j \le n$, which in view of (3.15) implies that it is optimal to allocate the entire prize budget to the first place prize.

First, we note that h_1 is single-crossing with respect to h_j. Indeed, $h_1(x) - h_j(x) \le 0$ is equivalent to $G'_1(x) \le G'_j(x)$, which is further equivalent to

$$(n-1)x^{j-1} \le \binom{n-1}{j-1}[(n-j)-(n-1)x](1-x)^{j-2}.$$

Since the left-hand side in the last equation is increasing in x and the right-hand side in the last equation is decreasing in x, it follows that $G'_1(x) \le G'_j(x)$ if, and only if, $x \in [0, x^*]$, for some $x^* \in [0, 1]$.

Second, observe that

$$\begin{aligned}
a_1 - a_j &= \int_0^1 F^{-1}(x)(h_1(x) - h_j(x))\,dx \\
&= \int_0^{x^*} F^{-1}(x)(h_1(x) - h_j(x))\,dx + \int_{x^*}^1 F^{-1}(x)(h_1(x) - h_j(x))\,dx \\
&\ge \int_0^{x^*} F^{-1}(x^*)(h_1(x) - h_j(x))\,dx + \int_{x^*}^1 F^{-1}(x^*)(h_1(x) - h_j(x))\,dx \\
&= F^{-1}(x^*) \int_0^1 (h_1(x) - h_j(x))\,dx.
\end{aligned}$$

Let $f(a, b) = \int_0^1 x^{a-1}(1-x)^{b-1}dx = \frac{(a-1)!(b-1)!}{(a+b-1)!}$, for two integers a and b greater than or equal to 1. Note that

$$\begin{aligned}
\int_0^1 h_j(x)\,dx &= \binom{n-1}{j-1} \int_0^1 [(n-j)-(n-1)x]x^{n-j-1}(1-x)^{j-1}dx \\
&= \binom{n-1}{j-1}[(n-1)f(n-j,j) - (n-1)f(n-j+1,j)] \\
&= \frac{1}{(j-1)!} - \frac{n-1}{n}.
\end{aligned}$$

From this we observe that $\int_0^1 h_j(x)dx$ is strictly decreasing in j, and thus

$$\int_0^1 (h_1(x) - h_j(x))\,dx > 0, \quad \text{for every } n \ge 2 \text{ and } 1 < j \le n. \qquad (3.16)$$

$\square$

Theorem 3.16 shows that it is optimal to allocate the entire prize budget to the first place prize. One might have a priori expected that awarding several prizes might encourage lower ability players to compete more intensively and that this, as a result, would yield a larger expected total effort. This, however, is false under the assumption that prior distributions are identical, and thus, ex-ante, the players are statistically indistinguishable with respect to their abilities, and production costs are linear. If production costs are non-linear, then it may be optimal to reward several placement prizes; for example, if the marginal costs of production are strictly increasing. An example with asymmetric values of the valuation parameters of the players in which it is suboptimal to allocate the entire prize budget to the first place prize is provided in Section 3.2.2. In Section 3.1.8, we consider the effects of non-linear production costs.

Maximum Individual Effort

Theorem 3.17. *For every game with incomplete informatiom that models the rank-order all-pay contest with two or more players whose valuation parameters are independent and identically distributed according to a prior distribution, and players incur identical linear production costs, it is optimal to allocate the entire prize purse to the first place prize with respect to the expected maximum individual effort in the symmetric Bayes-Nash equilibrium.*

Proof. The proof follow the same steps as that of Theorem 3.16. From (3.11), observe that

$$R_1 = \sum_{j=1}^{n} a_j w_j$$

where

$$a_j = \int_0^1 h_j(x)\, dx \text{ and } h_j(x) = (1 - x^n) G'_j(x).$$

By exactly the same arguments as in the proof of Theorem 3.16, we observe that h_1 is single-crossing with respect to h_j and

$$a_1 - a_j \geq F^{-1}(x^*) \int_0^1 (h_1(x) - h_j(x))\, dx.$$

It remains to show (3.16) for functions h_1 and h_j as defined locally in this proof. Note that

$$\int_0^1 h_j(x)\, dx = \binom{n-1}{j-1} \int_0^1 (1 - x^n)[(n - j) - (n - 1)x]x^{n-j-1}(1 - x)^{j-2} dx$$

$$= \binom{n-1}{j-1}[(n - j)f(n - j, j - 1) - (n - 1)f(n - j + 1, j - 1)$$

$$-(n - j)f(2n - j, j - 1) - (n - j)f(2n - j + 1, j - 1)]$$

$$= \binom{n-1}{j-1}[(n - 1)f(2n - j + 1, j - 1) - (n - j)f(2n - j, j - 1)]$$

$$= \frac{n!}{(2n - 1)!}\frac{(2n - j - 1)!}{(n - j)!}$$

$$= \frac{n!}{(2n - 1)!}(2n - j - 1)(2n - j)\cdots(n - j + 1).$$

Again, we observe that $\int_0^1 h_j(x) dx$ decreases in j, which completes the proof. □

3.1.5 Optimal Auction Design

In this section we discuss the celebrated result of auction theory: the optimal auction design with respect to the expected profit to the auctioneer in a Bayes-Nash equilibrium. We then use this in our study of the optimal all-pay contest design in Section 3.1.6.

Assume that the valuation parameters $v_1, v_2, \ldots, v_n$ of the players are independent and identically distributed random variables with given prior distribution functions $F_1, F_2, \ldots, F_n$. Each prior distribution function F_i is assumed to have support $V_i = [\underline{v}_i, \bar{v}_i]$, for $-\infty < \underline{v}_i < \bar{v}_i < \infty$ and density function f_i that is assumed to be a strictly positive and continuous function on V_i. Let $V = V_1 \times V_2 \times \cdots \times V_n$ and $V_{-i} = V_1 \times V_2 \times \cdots \times V_{i-1} \times V_{i+1} \times \cdots \times V_n$.

Consider the class of *direct revelation mechanisms* where players simultaneously and confidentially submit their valuations to the auctioneer. The auctioneer then determines an *outcome* $(\mathbf{x}, \mathbf{p})$ that consists of *allocation* $\mathbf{x} = (x_1, x_2, \ldots, x_n)$ and *payment* $\mathbf{p} = (p_1, p_2, \ldots, p_n)$, where $\mathbf{x} : V \to \mathbf{R}^n$ and $\mathbf{p} : V \to \mathbf{R}^n$. We refer to $(\mathbf{x}, \mathbf{p})$ as an *auction mechanism*. Given an auction mechanism $(\mathbf{x}, \mathbf{p})$, let $\bar{x}_i(v)$ be the expected allocation and $\bar{p}_i(v)$ be the expected payment by player i conditional on his or her valuation parameter being of value v, i.e.,

$$\bar{x}_i(v) = \mathbf{E}[x_i(\mathbf{v}) \mid v_i = v] \text{ and } \bar{p}_i(v) = \mathbf{E}[p_i(\mathbf{v}) \mid v_i = v].$$

Let $s_i(v_i, v)$ be the expected payoff for player $i \in N$ conditional on his or her valuation parameter being of value v_i and he or she playing as if his or her valuation parameter is of value $v \in V_i$, i.e.,

$$s_i(v_i, v) = v_i \bar{x}_i(v) - \bar{p}_i(v).$$

The expected payoff $s_i(v_i)$ of player $i \in N$ conditional on his or her valuation parameter being of value v_i is given by $s_i(v_i) = s_i(v_i, v_i)$, i.e.,

$$s_i(v_i) = v_i \bar{x}_i(v_i) - \bar{p}_i(v_i). \tag{3.17}$$

The expected payoff of the auctioneer is

$$s_0(r) = \mathbf{E}\left[\sum_{i \in N} p_i(\mathbf{v})\right] + r\left(1 - \mathbf{E}\left[\sum_{i \in N} x_i(\mathbf{v})\right]\right) \tag{3.18}$$

where r represents the value of the item to the auctioneer.

Necessary and Sufficient Conditions for a Bayes-Nash Equilibrium

An auction mechanism $(\mathbf{x}, \mathbf{p})$ is said to be a *feasible auction mechanism* if it satisfies the following conditions:

(RC) Resource constraint The allocation is at most of unit value:

$$x_i(\mathbf{v}) \geq 0, \quad \text{for all } i \in N, \sum_{j \in N} x_j(\mathbf{v}) \leq 1, \quad \text{for } \mathbf{v} \in V. \tag{3.19}$$

(IR) Individual rationality Every player has a non-negative expected payoff:

$$s_i(v_i) \geq 0, \quad \text{for all } v_i \in V_i \text{ and } i \in N. \tag{3.20}$$

(IC) Incentive compatibility Every player has no beneficial unilateral deviation from truthfully reporting his or her valuation:

$$s_i(v_i, v_i) \geq s_i(v_i, v) \text{ for very } v \in V_i \text{ and } i \in N. \tag{3.21}$$

The following theorem shows that for every feasible auction mechanism, the payment **p** is fully determined by the allocation **x**. This has an important implication for the design of an optimal feasible auction mechanism: it suffices to optimize only over the set of feasible allocations.

Theorem 3.18 (feasible auctions). *An auction mechanism* $(\mathbf{x}, \mathbf{p})$ *is feasible if, and only if, for every player* $i \in N$, *the following conditions hold:*

(M) *The expected allocation* $\bar{x}_i(v_i)$ *is increasing in* v_i *on the set* V_i;
(P) *The expected payment is*

$$\bar{p}_i(v_i) = v_i \bar{x}_i(v_i) - \int_{\underline{v}_i}^{v_i} \bar{x}_i(v) \, dv - [\underline{v}_i \bar{x}_i(\underline{v}_i) - \bar{p}_i(\underline{v}_i)], \quad \text{for every } v_i \in V_i;$$

(IR') $s_i(\underline{v}_i) \geq 0$;
(RC) $x_i(\mathbf{v}) \geq 0$, *and* $\sum_{j \in N} x_j(\mathbf{v}) \leq 1$, *for every* $\mathbf{v} \in V$.

Proof. The direct implication is proven as follows. We first show that condition (IC) implies condition (M). The expected payoff $s_i(v_i, v)$ can be expressed as follows:

$$s_i(v_i, v) = v_i \bar{x}_i(v) - \bar{p}_i(v)$$
$$= v \bar{x}_i(v) - \bar{p}_i(v) + (v_i - v) \bar{x}_i(v)$$
$$= s_i(v) + (v_i - v) \bar{x}_i(v).$$

From this, observe that (IC) is equivalent to

$$s_i(v_i) \geq s_i(v) + (v_i - v) \bar{x}_i(v), \quad \text{for every } v_i, v \in V_i, \text{ and } i \in N. \tag{3.22}$$

From (3.22), it follows that for every $i \in N$ and $v_i, v \in V_i$,

$$(v_i - v) \bar{x}_i(v) \leq s_i(v_i) - s_i(v) \leq (v_i - v) \bar{x}_i(v_i). \tag{3.23}$$

This implies that for every v and $v_i \in V_i$ such that $v < v_i$, we have $\bar{x}_i(v) \leq \bar{x}_i(v_i)$. Hence, the monotonicity condition (M) holds true.

We next show that condition (IC) implies condition (P). Let $v_i - v = \delta > 0$. From (3.23), we have

$$\bar{x}_i(v) \delta \leq s_i(v + \delta) - s_i(v) \leq \bar{x}_i(v + \delta) \delta.$$

By letting δ go to zero, we obtain

$$s_i(v_i) - s_i(\underline{v}_i) = \int_{\underline{v}_i}^{v_i} \bar{x}_i(v) \, dv.$$

Combining this with the definition of the expected payoff in Equation (3.17), we obtain condition (P).

It remains to observe that condition (IR) implies condition (IR'), and that (RC) obviously holds true, which completes the proof of the direct part.

The converse is proved as follows. Condition (RC) implies

$$\bar{x}_i(v) \geq 0, \quad \text{for every } v \in V_i \text{ and } i \in N. \tag{3.24}$$

Conditions (P), (IR'), and (RC) imply (IR) by the following relations:

$$s_i(v_i) = v_i \bar{x}_i(v_i) - \bar{p}_i(v_i) = s_i(\underline{v}_i) + \int_{\underline{v}_i}^{v_i} \bar{x}_i(x)\,dx \geq 0,$$

where the first equality is by the definition of the expected payoff in (3.17), the second equality is by (P), and the inequality holds true because by (IR') $s_i(\underline{v}_i) \geq 0$ and by (3.24) $\int_{\underline{v}_i}^{v_i} \bar{x}_i(x)dx \geq 0$.

Conditions (M) and (P) imply (IC) as follows. For every v', $v \in V_i$ such that $v' \leq v$, we have

$$\begin{aligned}
s_i(v) &= v\bar{x}_i(v) - \bar{p}_i(v) \\
&= s_i(v') + \int_{v'}^{v} \bar{x}_i(x)\,dx \\
&\geq s_i(v') + (v - v')\bar{x}_i(v'), \tag{3.25}
\end{aligned}$$

where the second equality is by condition (P) and the inequality is by the monotonicity condition (M). The inequality in (3.25) shows that condition (3.22) holds true, which is equivalent to (IC). □

From Theorem 3.18, we observe that the expected total payment for every feasible auction mechanism $(\mathbf{x}, \mathbf{p})$ is completely determined by the allocation function $\mathbf{x}$ and the expected payoffs received by players at the lowest possible values of their valuations, i.e., $s_i(\underline{v}_i)$, for $i \in N$. The auctioneer must obtain the same expected payment for any two feasible auction mechanisms that are such that the allocation is fully to a player with the largest valuation and each player has zero expected payoff if his or her valuation parameter is at its lowest possible value.

Optimal Auction

In this section, we formulate the optimal auction as a solution of an optimization problem. A key role in this formulation has the concept of a virtual valuation, which we define first.

Definition 3.19 (virtual valuation). For every player $i \in N$, we refer to $\psi_i(v_i)$ as the *virtual valuation* of player i where ψ_i is *the virtual valuation function* given by

$$\psi_i(v) = v - \frac{1 - F_i(v)}{f_i(v)}, \quad \text{for } v \in V_i.$$

Theorem 3.20 (optimal auction). *Suppose that* $\mathbf{x}$ *maximizes*

$$\mathbf{E}\left[\sum_{i \in N}(\psi_i(v_i) - r)x_i(\mathbf{v})\right] \tag{3.26}$$

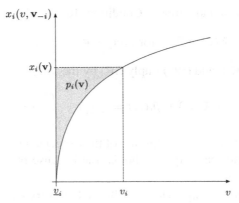

Figure 3.6. The payment is determined by the allocation.

subject to constraints (M) and (RC) and that payment is given by

$$p_i(\mathbf{v}) = v_i x_i(\mathbf{v}) - \int_{\underline{v}_i}^{v_i} x_i(v, \mathbf{v}_{-i}) \, dv, \quad \textit{for all } i \in N \textit{ and } \mathbf{v} \in V. \qquad (3.27)$$

Then, $(\mathbf{x}, \mathbf{p})$ *is an optimal auction mechanism. See Figure 3.6.*

Proof. From (3.18), we have

$$s_0(r) = \mathbf{E}\left[\sum_{i \in N}(v_i - r)x_i(\mathbf{v})\right] - \mathbf{E}\left[\sum_{i \in N}(v_i x_i(\mathbf{v}) - p_i(\mathbf{v}))\right] + r. \qquad (3.28)$$

We have the following series of equations:

$$\mathbf{E}[v_i x_i(\mathbf{v}) - p_i(\mathbf{v})] = \mathbf{E}\left[v_i \bar{x}_i(v_i) - \bar{p}_i(v_i)\right]$$

$$= a_i \bar{x}_i(\underline{v}_i) + \mathbf{E}\left[\int_{\underline{v}_i}^{v_i} \bar{x}_i(v) \, dv\right] - \bar{p}_i(\underline{v}_i)$$

$$= s_i(\underline{v}_i) + \mathbf{E}\left[\int_{\underline{v}_i}^{v_i} \bar{x}_i(v) \, dv\right]$$

$$= s_i(\underline{v}_i) + \mathbf{E}\left[\int_{\underline{v}_i}^{\bar{v}_i} \bar{x}_i(v)\mathbf{1}(v \leq v_i) \, dv\right]$$

$$= s_i(\underline{v}_i) + \int_{\underline{v}_i}^{\bar{v}_i} \bar{x}_i(v)(1 - F_i(v)) \, dv$$

$$= s_i(\underline{v}_i) + \mathbf{E}\left[\bar{x}_i(v_i)\frac{1 - F_i(v_i)}{f_i(v_i)}\right]$$

$$= s_i(\underline{v}_i) + \mathbf{E}\left[x_i(\mathbf{v})\frac{1 - F_i(v_i)}{f_i(v_i)}\right] \qquad (3.29)$$

where the second equality is by (P) in Lemma 3.18, the third equality is by the expression in (3.17), and other equalities follow by simple algebraic manipulations.

Combining (3.28) and (3.29), we obtain

$$s_0(r) = \mathbf{E}\left[\sum_{i \in N}(\psi_i(v_i) - r)x_i(\mathbf{v})\right] + r - \sum_{i \in N} s_i(\underline{v}_i). \tag{3.30}$$

The only term in the last expression that depends on the payment function $\mathbf{p}$ is $\sum_{i \in N} s_i(\underline{v}_i)$. Under the payment function in (3.27), condition (P) in Lemma 3.18 holds with $s_i(\underline{v}_i) = \underline{v}_i\bar{x}_i(\underline{v}_i) - \bar{p}_i(\underline{v}_i) = 0$, and thus $\sum_{i \in N} s_i(\underline{v}_i) = 0$, which in view of condition (IR') in Theorem 3.18 is the value of $\sum_{i \in N} s_i(\underline{v}_i)$ that maximizes the expected payoff to the auctioneer in (3.30). Therefore, we showed that maximizing the auctioneer's expected payoff is equivalent to maximizing the objective function (3.26) subject to constraints (M), (RC), and (3.27). □

Optimal Auction: Regular Case

In this section, we characterize the format of an optimal auction mechanism in the case when the virtual valuation functions satisfy a regularity condition that is given in the following definition.

Definition 3.21. A distribution function F_i is said to be *regular* if the virtual valuation function $\psi_i(v)$ is increasing in v on the set V_i. An auction is said to be regular if F_i is regular for every player $i \in N$.

From Theorem 3.20, we observe that for a regular auction, the optimal auction mechanism $(\mathbf{x}, \mathbf{p})$ is such that the auctioneer keeps the item if $\psi_i(v_i) < r$, for every $i \in N$, and allocates the item to a player $i \in N$ with the largest virtual valuation $\psi_i(v_i)$ otherwise. The payment function $\mathbf{p}$ is specified by (3.27). If each virtual valuation function is a strictly increasing function, the optimal auction mechanism $(\mathbf{x}, \mathbf{p})$ can be represented as follows: for $i \in N$,

$$x_i(\mathbf{v}) = \begin{cases} 1, & \text{if } v_i > \theta_i(\mathbf{v}_{-i}) \\ 0, & \text{otherwise} \end{cases} \text{ and } p_i(\mathbf{v}) = \begin{cases} \theta_i(\mathbf{v}_{-i}), & \text{if } x_i(\mathbf{v}) = 1 \\ 0, & \text{otherwise} \end{cases} \tag{3.31}$$

where

$$\theta_i(\mathbf{v}_{-i}) = \inf\left\{v \in V_i \mid \psi_i(v) \geq r \text{ and } \psi_i(v) \geq \max_{j \in N} \psi_j(v_j)\right\}. \tag{3.32}$$

If, in addition, the valuation parameters are a sequence of independent and identically distributed random variables according to a prior distribution F with a strictly increasing virtual valuation function denoted by ψ, the optimal auction mechanism is the one specified by (3.31) with

$$\theta_i(\mathbf{v}_{-i}) = \max\left\{\max_{j \neq i} v_j, \psi^{-1}(r)\right\}, \quad \text{for } i \in N.$$

In other words, the optimal auction mechanism is such that the item is allocated to the player with the largest valuation subject to a reserve price of value $\psi^{-1}(r)$ and only this player makes a payment, which is for the amount equal to the maximum between the second largest valuation and the reserve price $\psi^{-1}(r)$. From Theorem 3.20, we note that for the case when the valuation parameters of the players are independent and identically distributed random variables with a regular prior distribution, the expected payoff for the auctioneer under the optimum auction mechanism is equal to

$$s_0(r) = \mathbf{E}[\max\{\psi(v_{(n,1)}) - r, 0\}]. \qquad (3.33)$$

Example 3.22 (uniform prior distribution). Suppose that the valuations are independent and identically distributed random variables according to a uniform prior distribution on [0, 1]. The virtual valuation function is given by

$$\psi(v) = 2v - 1, \quad \text{for } v \in [0, 1].$$

The virtual valuation function is increasing; hence, the auction is regular. In this case the optimal auction allocates the item to a player $i \in N$ with the largest valuation, and the only payment is made by this player, which is for the amount $\max\{\max_{j \neq i} v_j, (1 + r)/2\}$.

If the auctioneer's valuation is equal to zero, then his or her expected payoff under the optimum auction mechanism is of value

$$1 - \frac{2}{n + 1} + \frac{1}{n + 1} \frac{1}{2^n}.$$

The alert reader would have noticed that this is indeed larger than the expected total payment in a standard all-pay auction with no reserve price that is of value $1 - 2/(n + 1)$ (see Example 2.25).

Optimal Auction: General Case

In the general case that allows for a virtual valuation function to be non-regular, the optimal auction is obtained by using the concept of ironing a virtual valuation function that we describe as follows. For every player $i \in N$, let

$$h_i(x) = \psi_i(F_i^{-1}(x)) \text{ and } H_i(x) = \int_0^x h_i(y)\,dy, \quad \text{for } x \in [0, 1].$$

We denote with $\bar{H}_i(x)$ the convex closure of the function $H_i(x)$, i.e., the point-wise largest convex function on [0, 1] such that $\bar{H}_i(x) \leq H_i(x)$, for every $x \in [0, 1]$, and denote with $\bar{h}_i(x)$ its derivative, i.e., $\bar{h}_i(x) = \bar{H}_i'(x)$ for $x \in [0, 1]$.

Definition 3.23. For every player $i \in N$, we refer to $\bar{\psi}_i(v_i)$ as the *ironed virtual valuation* that is defined by

$$\bar{\psi}_i(v) = \bar{h}_i(F_i(v)), \quad \text{for } v \in V_i.$$

For every virtual valuation function ψ_i, the ironed virtual valuation function $\bar{\psi}_i$ is regular. If a virtual valuation function ψ_i is regular, then function H_i is convex, and hence, its convex closure is the function H_i. In this case, the ironed virtual valuation is equal to the virtual valuation itself. Figure 3.7 illustrates the construction of the ironed virtual valuation function for a specific non-regular virtual valuation function.

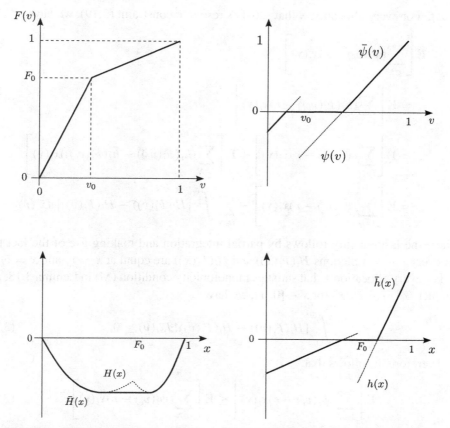

Figure 3.7. An illustration of the definition of the ironed virtual valuation function $\bar{\psi}$ for a non-regular virtual valuation function ψ.

Let $W(\mathbf{v})$ be the set of players whose ironed virtual valuations are larger than or equal to that of any other player and are larger than or equal to the reserve value, i.e.,

$$W(\mathbf{v}) = \left\{ i \in N \mid \bar{\psi}_i(v_i) = \max_{j \in N} \bar{\psi}_j(v_j) \geq r \right\}.$$

The following theorem specifies an optimal auction mechanism for the general case.

Theorem 3.24. *Suppose that $(\mathbf{x}^*, \mathbf{p}^*)$ satisfies, for every $i \in N$ and $\mathbf{v} \in V$,*

$$x_i^*(\mathbf{v}) = \begin{cases} \frac{1}{|W(\mathbf{v})|}, & \textit{if } i \in W(\mathbf{v}) \\ 0, & \textit{otherwise} \end{cases} \tag{3.34}$$

and

$$p_i^*(\mathbf{v}) = v_i x_i(\mathbf{v}) - \int_{\underline{v}_i}^{v_i} x_i(v, \mathbf{v}_{-i}) dv. \tag{3.35}$$

Then $(\mathbf{x}^*, \mathbf{p}^*)$ is an optimal auction mechanism.

Proof. For every allocation **x** that satisfies resource constraint (3.19), we have

$$\mathbf{E}\left[\sum_{i\in N}(\psi_i(v_i) - r)x_i(\mathbf{v})\right]$$

$$= \mathbf{E}\left[\sum_{i\in N}(h_i(F_i(v_i)) - r)x_i(\mathbf{v})\right]$$

$$= \mathbf{E}\left[\sum_{i\in N}(\bar{\psi}_i(v_i) - r)x_i(\mathbf{v})\right] + \mathbf{E}\left[\sum_{i\in N}(h_i(F_i(v_i)) - \bar{h}_i(F_i(v_i)))x_i(\mathbf{v})\right]$$

$$= \mathbf{E}\left[\sum_{i\in N}(\bar{\psi}_i(v_i) - r)x_i(\mathbf{v})\right] - \sum_{i\in N}\int_{\underline{v}_i}^{\bar{v}_i}[H_i(F_i(v)) - \bar{H}_i(F_i(v))]\,d\bar{x}_i(v)$$

where the last equality follows by partial integration and making use of the fact that for every $i \in N$, functions $H_i(F_i(x))$ and $\bar{H}_i(F_i(x))$ are equal at $x = \underline{v}_i$ and $x = \bar{v}_i$.

For every allocation **x** that satisfies monotonicity condition (M) in Lemma 3.18, and the fact $H_i(x) \geq \bar{H}_i(x)$ for $x \in [0, 1]$, we have

$$\int_{\underline{v}_i}^{\bar{v}_i}[H_i(F_i(v)) - \bar{H}_i(F_i(v))]d\bar{x}_i(v) \geq 0. \tag{3.36}$$

Therefore, it follows that

$$\mathbf{E}\left[\sum_{i\in N}(\psi_i(v_i) - r)x_i(\mathbf{v})\right] \leq \mathbf{E}\left[\sum_{i\in N}(\bar{\psi}_i(v_i) - r)x_i(\mathbf{v})\right]. \tag{3.37}$$

Since function $\bar{H}_i$ is a convex closure of function H_i, $\bar{H}_i''(x) = 0$ for every $x \in [0, 1]$ such that $H_i(x) > \bar{H}_i(x)$. This implies that if $H_i(F_i(v)) > \bar{H}_i(F_i(v)) > 0$ for some $v \in [0, 1]$, then functions $\bar{\psi}_i$ and $\bar{x}_i^*$ are constant in some neighborhood of the point v, and thus equality holds in (3.36) under the allocation $\mathbf{x}^*$. Therefore, we have

$$\mathbf{E}\left[\sum_{i\in N}(\psi_i(v_i) - r)x_i^*(\mathbf{v})\right] = \mathbf{E}\left[\sum_{i\in N}(\bar{\psi}_i(v_i) - r)x_i^*(\mathbf{v})\right]. \tag{3.38}$$

Using the fact that $\mathbf{x}^*$ allocates the item to a player with maximal value of $\bar{\psi}_i(v_i) - r$ if this value is positive, and does not allocate the item otherwise, it follows that for every allocation **x** that satisfies resource constraint (3.19), we have

$$\mathbf{E}\left[\sum_{i\in N}(\bar{\psi}_i(v_i) - r)x_i^*(\mathbf{v})\right] \geq \mathbf{E}\left[\sum_{i\in N}(\bar{\psi}_i(v_i) - r)x_i(\mathbf{v})\right]. \tag{3.39}$$

From (3.37), (3.38), and (3.39), it follows that for every allocation **x** that satisfies conditions in Lemma 3.18, we have

$$\mathbf{E}\left[\sum_{i\in N}(\psi_i(v_i) - r)x_i(\mathbf{v})\right] \leq \mathbf{E}\left[\sum_{i\in N}(\psi_i(v_i) - r)x_i^*(\mathbf{v})\right]$$

which shows that $(\mathbf{x}^*, \mathbf{p}^*)$ is an optimal auction. $\qquad\qquad\square$

3.1.6 Optimal All-Pay Contest

In this section we use the framework of the optimal auction design that we introduced in Section 3.1.5 to consider the optimal all-pay contest design with respect to both the expected total effort and the expected maximum individual effort in a Bayes-Nash equilibrium. We consider the game with incomplete information where the valuation parameters are independent and identically distributed according to a regular prior distribution function F on the support $[0, 1]$, and consider the symmetric Bayes-Nash equilibrium. The game that models the rank-order all-pay contest formally corresponds to an all-pay auction where the payment of a bidder corresponds to his or her bid. By Theorem 3.18, the symmetric Bayes-Nash equilibrium strategy is given by

$$\beta(v_i) = v_i \bar{x}_i(v_i) - \int_0^{v_i} \bar{x}_i(x)\,dx, \quad \text{for } v_i \in [0, 1], \tag{3.40}$$

where recall that $\bar{x}_i(v)$ is the expected allocation to player i conditional on his or her valuation parameter being of value v.

A central role in the characterization of an optimal all-pay contest is played by the concept of an n-virtual valuation function that is defined as follows.

Definition 3.25 (n-virtual valuation function). For a given distribution F that has density function f and an integer $n \geq 1$, the n-*virtual valuation function* is defined by

$$\psi(v; n) = v F(v)^{n-1} - \frac{1 - F(v)^n}{n f(v)}.$$

The definition of an n-virtual valuation function can be seen as a generalization of that of a virtual valuation function in Definition 3.19, which is recovered as a special case for $n = 1$. We use $\psi(v)$ as the shorthand notation for the 1-virtual valuation function $\psi(v; 1)$. The generalized definition of a virtual valuation function allows us to characterize the optimal contest design with respect to the objective of maximizing the expected maximum individual effort.

Example 3.26 (uniform prior distribution). For a uniform prior distribution on $[0, 1]$, the n-virtual valuation function is

$$\psi(v; n) = \left(1 + \frac{1}{n}\right) v^n - \frac{1}{n}.$$

See Figure 3.8 for graphs of the n-virtual valuation function for particular values of parameter n.

In the following lemma we characterize the expected total effort in symmetric Bayes-Nash equilibrium of an all-pay contest.

Lemma 3.27 (total effort). *For the all-pay contest with an allocation* $\mathbf{x}$ *in the symmetric Bayes-Nash equilibrium where the players play strategy (3.40), the expected total effort is given by*

$$R = \mathbf{E}\left[\sum_{i \in N} x_i(\mathbf{v})\psi(v_i)\right].$$

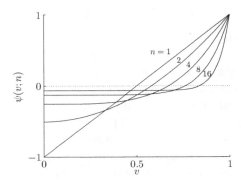

Figure 3.8. The n-virtual valuation function for a uniform prior distribution for a few particular values of parameter n.

Proof. This follows from $R = \mathbf{E}[\sum_{i \in N} \beta(v_i)]$ where β is the strategy given in (3.40) and using simple algebra. $\qquad\square$

A similar characterization holds for the expected maximum individual effort that is given in the following lemma.

Lemma 3.28 (maximum individual effort). *For the all-pay contest with an allocation* **x** *in the symmetric Bayes-Nash equilibrium where the players play strategy (3.40), the expected maximum individual effort is given by*

$$R_1 = \mathbf{E}\left[\sum_{i \in N} x_i(\mathbf{v})\psi(v_i; n)\right].$$

Proof. The assertion follows by the following sequence of equalities:

$$R_1 = \sum_{i \in N} \mathbf{E}\left[\beta(v_i)\mathbf{1}(v_i \geq \max_{j \neq i} v_j)\right]$$

$$= \sum_{i \in N} \int_0^1 \beta(v)F(v)^{n-1}dF(v)$$

$$= \sum_{i \in N} \int_0^1 \left[v\bar{x}_i(v) - \int_0^v \bar{x}_i(x)\,dx\right]F(v)^{n-1}dF(v)$$

$$= \sum_{i \in N} \int_0^1 v\bar{x}_i(v)F(v)^{n-1}\,dF(v) - \int_0^1 \left[\int_0^1 \mathbf{1}(x \leq v)F(v)^{n-1}dF(v)\right]\bar{x}_i(x)\,dx$$

$$= \sum_{i \in N} \int_0^1 v\bar{x}_i(v)F(v)^{n-1}dF(v) - \int_0^1 \frac{1 - F(x)^n}{n}\bar{x}_i(x)\,dx$$

$$= \sum_{i \in N} \int_0^1 \bar{x}_i(v)\left[vF(v)^{n-1} - \frac{1 - F(v)^n}{nF'(v)}\right]dF(v)$$

$$= \sum_{i \in N} \int_0^1 \bar{x}_i(v)\psi(v; n)\,dF(v)$$

$$= \mathbf{E}\left[\sum_{i \in N} \bar{x}_i(v_i)\psi(v_i; n)\right]$$

$$= \mathbf{E}\left[\sum_{i \in N} x_i(\mathbf{v})\psi(v_i; n)\right].$$

$\square$

Optimal All-Pay Contest: Regular Case

We now consider the optimal all-pay contest with respect to maximum individual effort for the case of a prior distribution that satisfies a regularity condition introduced in the next definition.

Definition 3.29. A distribution function F is said to be *n-regular* with respect to maximum individual effort if its n-virtual valuation function $\psi(v; n)$ is an increasing function. The distribution F is said to be regular with respect to maximum individual effort if it is n-regular for every integer $n \geq 1$.

The optimal all-pay contest with respect to the objective of maximizing the expected maximum individual effort in a symmetric Bayes-Nash equilibrium is given in the following theorem.

Theorem 3.30 (optimal all-pay contest). *Consider an all-pay contest among $n \geq 2$ players whose valuations are independent and identically distributed according to a prior distribution F that is n-regular with respect to maximum individual effort. Then, the optimal all-pay contest with respect to maximizing the expected maximum individual effort in a symmetric Bayes-Nash equilibrium is the standard all-pay contest with the minimum required effort of value $\psi^{-1}(0; n)F^{n-1}(\psi^{-1}(0; n))$.*

Proof. From the characterization of the expected maximum individual effort in Lemma 3.28, we observe that it is optimal to fully allocate the prize to the player with the largest n-virtual valuation provided that this value is positive, i.e., the valuation parameter of the player is larger than or equal to $\psi^{-1}(0; n)$. This can be implemented by the standard all-pay contest with a minimum required effort that we studied in Section 2.2.5. By Theorem 2.30, for the standard all-pay contest with a minimum required effort, the minimum required valuation r and the minimum required effort b stand in the following relation: $b = rF(r)^{n-1}$. $\square$

Example 3.31 (uniform prior distribution revisited). For a uniform prior distribution on $[0, 1]$, the n-virtual valuation function is given in Example 3.26. The minimum required valuation is of value $\psi^{-1}(0; n) = 1/(n + 1)^{1/n}$ and the minimum required effort is of value $1/(n + 1)$. The optimum expected maximum individual effort is

$$R_1 = \frac{1}{2}\left(1 - \frac{1}{n + 1}\right).$$

Compare this optimum value with the expected maximum individual effort in the symmetric Bayes-Nash equilibrium of the game that models the standard all-pay contest, which in Example 2.28, we showed to be of value $(1 - 1/n)/2$. Thus, we observe that the optimal expected maximum individual effort is $1/(1 - 1/n^2)$ factor of that in the game that models the standard all-pay contest, which achieves the largest value of $4/3$ for the case of two players and diminishes to value 1 asymptotically as the number of players grows large.

Sufficient Conditions for Regularity A sufficient condition for a distribution F to be regular with respect to maximum individual effort is that it has an increasing hazard rate.

Lemma 3.32. *Suppose that F is a distribution such that its hazard rate function $h(v) = f(v)/(1 - F(v))$ is increasing. Then, F is regular with respect to the maximum individual effort.*

Proof. From the definition of n-virtual valuation in Definition 3.25, we have

$$\psi(v; n) = vF(v)^{n-1} - \frac{1 - F(v)^n}{nf(v)}$$

$$= vF(v)^{n-1} - \frac{1 - F(v)}{nf(v)} \frac{1 - F(v)^n}{1 - F(v)}$$

$$= vF(v)^{n-1} - \frac{1 - F(v)}{nf(v)} \sum_{i=0}^{n-1} F(v)^i$$

$$= F(v)^{n-1} \left(v - \frac{1}{h(v)} \frac{1}{n} \sum_{i=0}^{n-1} \frac{1}{F(v)^i} \right).$$

Since the hazard rate function $h(v)$ is assumed to be an increasing function, we readily observe that the right-hand side in the last equality is increasing in v. $\square$

Optimal All-Pay Contest: General Case

In the general case in which the prior distribution F is allowed not to be n-regular, the optimal all-pay contest is derived by applying the ironing procedure described in Section 3.1.5 to the n-virtual valuation function $\psi(v; n)$ to obtain the ironed n-virtual valuation function $\bar{\psi}(v; n)$. The optimal mechanism allocates the prize to the player with the larest value of the ironed n-virtual valuation subject to the minimum required valuation of value $\bar{\psi}^{-1}(0; n)$. In every given interval on which the ironed n-virtual valuation function is constant, the symmetric Bayes-Nash equilibrium strategy (3.40) is constant (with a random tie break in the case of ties). See Figure 3.9 for an illustration.

The optimal all-pay contest can be implemented as follows. Let $\beta^{-1}(b) = \max\{v \in [0, 1] \mid \beta(v) \le b\}$ be the pseudo-inverse function of function $\beta(v)$. Then, the optimal all-pay contest is a standard all-pay contest that allocates the prize based on the transformed efforts $\beta(\beta^{-1}(b_i))$ subject to the minimum required effort of value $\bar{\psi}^{-1}(0; n)F^{n-1}(\bar{\psi}^{-1}(0; n))$.

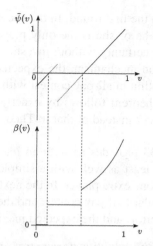

Figure 3.9. The ironing procedure.

3.1.7 Approximation Guarantees of the Standard All-Pay Contest

The standard all-pay contest is in general suboptimal with respect to both the expected total effort and the expected maximum individual effort in a Bayes-Nash equilibrium, and one can do better by using the optimal all-pay contest design. For example, if the prior distribution is regular with respect to maximum individual effort, by Theorem 3.30, the optimal all-pay contest is the standard all-pay contest with a minimum required effort. However, the standard all-pay contest may be preferred for its simplicity and the fact is that it is prior free - it requires only identifying the best performing player based on the observed invested efforts. It is thus of interest to understand how the standard all-pay contest compares with the optimal all-pay contest with respect to the expected total effort and the expected maximum individual effort.

Theorem 3.33. *Suppose that the valuation parameters of the players are independent and identically distributed according to a regular prior distribution. Then, the expected total effort in the symmetric Bayes-Nash equilibrium of the game that models the standard all-pay contest with $n + 1$ players is at least as large as the expected total effort in the symmetric Bayes-Nash equilibrium of the optimal all-pay contest with n players.*

Furthermore, under the stronger assumption that the prior distribution is regular with respect to maximum individual effort, the same comparison claim holds with respect to the expected maximum individual effort.

Proof. We first prove the claim for the expected total effort. In a standard all-pay contest with $n + 1$ players, by Theorem 3.16, it is optimal to allocate the entire prize to a player who invests the largest effort with respect to the expected total effort. Now, consider an alternative prize allocation mechanism that also allocates the entire prize purse to a single player, but uses the following two-round allocation mechanism. The expected total effort under this alternative allocation mechanism is smaller than or equal to that under the allocation mechanism as in the standard all-pay contest. In the first round, an optimal all-pay contest is run among a subset of n players. If the prize remains unallocated, then, in the second round, it is allocated to the player who was kept out of the competition in the first round. In the second round, the expected effort of the player is zero because he or she is the only player in that round, and thus he or she receives the prize with certainty without investing any effort. Therefore, under this alternative prize allocation mechanism, the expected total effort is precisely the expected total effort of the optimum all-pay contest with n players.

The second claim of the theorem follows by exactly the same arguments and by using the result in Theorem 3.17 instead of that in Theorem 3.16.   □

The result in Theorem 3.33 provides us with an interesting insight that a contest owner is guaranteed to do at least as well with a simpler, prior-free standard all-pay contest design by employing one extra player. In the next theorem we further compare the game that models the standard all-pay contest and the optimal all-pay contest with respect to the expected total effort and the expected maximum individual effort.

Theorem 3.34. *Suppose that the valuation parameters are independent and identically distributed according to a prior distribution function F.*

  (i) *If F is regular, then the expected total effort in the symmetric Bayes-Nash equilibrium of the game that models the standard all-pay contest is at least factor $1 - 1/n$ of the expected total effort in the symmetric Bayes-Nash equilibrium of the optimal all-pay contest.*

 (ii) *If F is regular with respect to the maximum individual effort, then the expected maximum individual effort in the symmetric-Bayes Nash equilibrium of the game that models the standard all-pay contest is at least factor $(1 - 1/n)/2$ of the expected total effort in the symmetric Bayes-Nash equilibrium of the optimal all-pay contest.*

Proof. We first prove the claim of the theorem that is concerned with the expected total effort. Let $R(n)$ be the expected total effort in the symmetric Bayes-Nash equilibrium in the game with incomplete information that models the standard all-pay contest with n players. Let $R^*(n)$ be the expected total effort in the symmetric Bayes-Nash equilibrium of the optimal all-pay contest for n players. By Theorem 3.33, we have

$$R(n) \geq R^*(n - 1). \tag{3.41}$$

Using (3.33), for every $n \geq 1$,

$$\frac{R^*(n)}{n} = \frac{1}{n}\mathbf{E}[\psi(v_{(n,1)})\mathbf{1}(\psi(v_{(n,1)}) \geq 0)] = \int_{\psi^{-1}(0)}^{1} \psi(v)F(v)^{n-1}\, dF(v),$$

which is decreasing in n, and thus

$$\frac{R^*(n-1)}{n-1} \geq \frac{R^*(n)}{n}, \quad \text{for every } n \geq 2. \tag{3.42}$$

Combining the relations (3.41) and (3.42), we obtain the first claim of the theorem.

We next prove the claim of the theorem that is concerned with the expected maximum individual effort. Let $R_1(n)$ be the expected maximum individual effort in the symmetric Bayes-Nash equilibrium of the game with incomplete information that models the standard all-pay contest with n players. The claim follows by the inequalities

$$R_1(n) \geq \frac{1}{2} R(n)$$

$$\geq \frac{1}{2} \left(1 - \frac{1}{n} \right) R^*(n)$$

where the first inequality is by Theorem 2.29 and the second inequality is by the first claim of the present theorem. □

3.1.8 Non-Linear Production Costs

In this section we consider the rank-order all-pay contest in which players incur production costs according to a given production cost function $c : \mathbf{R}_+ \to \mathbf{R}_+$, which is assumed to be continuously differentiable, strictly increasing, and such that $c(0) = 0$. This is a generalization of our considerations thus far, in which the production cost functions were assumed to be identical and linear. Our focus is on showing that, for the family of concave production costs, it is optimal for the contest owner to allocate the entire prize budget to the first place prize with respect to both the expected total effort and the expected maximum individual effort in a Bayes-Nash equilibrium. This is a generalization of the respective statements in Theorem 3.16 and Theorem 3.17 that were derived under the assumption that the production cost functions of the players are symmetric and linear. We shall then show that under convex production cost functions, there are cases in which it is optimal to split a prize budget over more than one placement prize.

In a similar way as for the case of linear production cost functions in Theorem 3.1, we can show that the following is a symmetric Bayes-Nash equilibrium strategy:

$$\beta(v) = c^{-1} \left(\sum_{j=1}^{n} w_j \int_0^v x \, dx_j(x) \right), \quad \text{for } v \in [0, 1]. \tag{3.43}$$

Concave Production Costs

Theorem 3.35 (Total effort). *For every rank-order all-pay contest with two or more players whose valuations are independent and identically distributed according to a given prior distribution such that the players incur production costs according to a production cost function c that is continuously differentiable, increasing, and concave, it is optimal to fully allocate a prize purse to the first place prize with respect to the expected total effort in the symmetric Bayes-Nash equilibrium.*

Proof. The main idea of the proof is the same as that of Theorem 3.16, and the differences lie in the details, which we outline as follows. Using (3.43), the expected total effort is given by

$$R(\mathbf{w}) = n \int_0^1 c^{-1} \left(\sum_{j=1}^{n} w_j \int_0^v x \, dx_j(x) \right) dF(v). \tag{3.44}$$

The key point is to consider a reallocation of an infinitesimal amount of the prize value at place $i \neq 1$ to the prize value at place 1 and show that this increases the expected total effort. Notice that

$$dR(\mathbf{w}) = \frac{\partial}{\partial w_1} R(\mathbf{w}) dw_1 + \frac{\partial}{\partial w_i} R(\mathbf{w}) dw_i,$$

and since $dw_1 + dw_i = 0$, we have

$$\frac{d}{dw_1} R(\mathbf{w}) = \frac{\partial}{\partial w_1} R(\mathbf{w}) - \frac{\partial}{\partial w_i} R(\mathbf{w}).$$

From (3.44), we obtain that for every $i \in N$,

$$\frac{\partial}{\partial w_i} R(\mathbf{w}) = n \int_0^1 \gamma(v) \int_0^v x \, dx_i(x), \tag{3.45}$$

where recall that $x_i(x)$ is the probability of winning the i-th place prize by a player with the valuation parameter of value x given by (3.3), and by definition

$$\gamma(v) = c^{-1'} \left(\sum_{j=1}^n w_j \int_0^v x \, dx_j(x) \right).$$

Using (3.45), it follows that

$$\frac{d}{dw_1} R(\mathbf{w}) = n \int_0^1 \gamma(v) \left(\int_0^v x \, dx_1(x) - \int_0^v x \, dx_i(x) \right) dF(v)$$

$$= n \int_0^1 \int_0^1 \gamma(v) \mathbf{1}(x \leq v)(x \, dx_1(x) - x \, dx_i(x)) \, dF(v)$$

$$= n \int_0^1 \left(\int_x^1 \gamma(v) dF(v) \right) x \, (dx_1(x) - dx_i(x))$$

$$= n \int_0^1 \phi(x)(1 - x)(G_1'(x) - G_i'(x)) \, dx \tag{3.46}$$

where the last equality is by the change of variables and recalling the definition of function G_j in (3.14), and defining the function $\phi(x)$ as follows:

$$\phi(x) = F^{-1}(x) \frac{\int_x^1 \gamma(F^{-1}(y)) \, dy}{1 - x}. \tag{3.47}$$

From (3.46), $dR(\mathbf{w})/dw_1 > 0$ provided that function $\phi(x)$ is strictly increasing on $[0, 1]$ and that function $G_1'(x)$ is single-crossing with respect to function $G_i'(x)$. The latter condition is easy to establish. To see that the former condition holds, note that under the assumption that the production cost function c is concave, $\gamma(x)$ is increasing in x. This implies that

$$\frac{\int_x^1 \gamma(F^{-1}(y)) \, dy}{1 - x}$$

is increasing in x, and hence in view of (3.47) and the fact that $F^{-1}(x)$ is strictly increasing in x, it follows that $\phi(x)$ is strictly increasing on $[0, 1]$.   □

We next show that the statement in Theorem 3.35 holds also with respect to the maximum individual effort.

Theorem 3.36 (maximum individual effort). *For every rank-order all-pay contest with two or more players whose valuations are independent and identically distributed according to a given prior distribution such that the players incur production costs according to a production cost function c that is continuously differentiable, increasing, and concave, it is optimal to fully allocate a prize purse to the first place prize with respect to the expected maximum individual effort in the symmetric Bayes-Nash equilibrium.*

Proof. Most of the proof is a carbon copy of that of Theorem 3.35, so we only point out the differences. First, we consider the expected maximum individual effort that is given by

$$R_1(\mathbf{w}) = \int_0^1 c^{-1}\left(\sum_{j=1}^n w_j \int_0^v x\, dx_j(x)\right) dF(v)^n. \tag{3.48}$$

Second, using the same steps as those used to derive (3.46), we obtain

$$\frac{d}{dw_1}R_1(\mathbf{w}) = \int_0^1 \phi(x)(1 - x^n)[G_1'(x) - G_i'(x)]\, dx$$

where we redefine

$$\phi(x) = F^{-1}(x)\frac{\int_x^1 \gamma(F^{-1}(y))\, dy^n}{1 - x^n}.$$

The rest follows by exactly the same arguments. $\qquad\square$

Convex Production Costs

If the production costs of the players are according to a convex production cost function, then the expected total effort in the symmetric Bayes-Nash equilibrium is a concave function of the values of the placement prizes. Let us define $\delta w_j = w_j - w_{j+1}$, for $j = 1, 2, \ldots, n$, with $w_{n+1} := 0$. From (3.44), it follows that

$$R(\delta\mathbf{w}) = n\int_0^1 c^{-1}\left(\sum_{j=1}^n \bar{a}_j(v)\delta w_j\right) dF(v) \tag{3.49}$$

where

$$\bar{a}_j(v) = \int_0^v x f_{n-1,j}(x)\, dx.$$

The function $R(\delta\mathbf{w})$ is concave. Indeed, since $c(x)$ is assumed to be a convex function, $c^{-1}(x)$ is a concave function. Function $c^{-1}\left(\sum_{j=1}^n \bar{a}_j(v)\delta w_j\right)$ is a composition of a concave function and an affine function, and thus, it is itself a concave function. Function $R(\delta\mathbf{w})$ is a convex combination of concave functions, and thus it is itself a concave function.

Suppose now that our objective is to maximize the expected total effort subject to a unit prize budget. This problem corresponds to the following convex optimization problem:

$$\text{maximize} \quad R(\delta\mathbf{w})$$
$$\text{subject to} \quad \sum_{j=1}^{n} j\delta w_j \leq 1 \tag{3.50}$$
$$\delta\mathbf{w} \in \mathbf{R}_+^n.$$

Note that for maximizing the expected maximum individual effort, the same formulation holds by using the expression in (3.44), with replacing $F(v)$ with $F(v)^n$ in (3.49) and elsewhere.

We next demonstrate that in the case of strictly convex production cost functions, it can be beneficial to split a prize purse over two or more placement prizes with respect to maximizing the expected total effort.

Example 3.37. Suppose that the prior distribution is uniform on $[0, 1]$, and consider splitting a unit prize purse over two first placement prizes; hence, $\delta w_1 = 2w_1 - 1$ and $\delta w_2 = 1 - w_1$, for $1/2 \leq w_1 \leq 1$. Under these assumptions, by (3.49), the expected total effort in the symmetric Bayes-Nash equilibrium is given by

$$R(w_1) = n \int_0^1 c^{-1}\left(\bar{a}_1(v)(2w_1 - 1) + \bar{a}_2(v)(1 - w_1)\right) dv$$

where

$$\bar{a}_1(v) = \left(1 - \frac{1}{n}\right) v^n \text{ and } \bar{a}_2(v) = (n - 2)v^{n-1}\left(1 - \left(1 - \frac{1}{n}\right)v\right).$$

Suppose now that the production cost function is of the form $c(x) = x^\alpha$, for $x \in \mathbf{R}_+$, for parameter $\alpha \geq 1$. We show that for every fixed $\alpha > 1$ and every sufficiently large number of players n, a larger total expected effort is achieved in the symmetric Bayes-Nash equilibrium by evenly splitting the prize purse over the two first placement prizes than by assigning the entire prize purse to the first place prize. It suffices to show that for every fixed $\alpha > 1$, $R(1/2) > R(1)$ in the limit of asymptotically large number of players n.

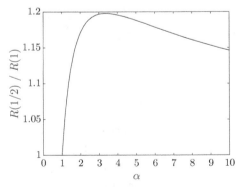

Figure 3.10. The ratio of the expected total effort under an even split of a unit prize purse over two first placement prizes and the expected total effort under assigning the entire prize purse to the first place prize, for the production cost function $c(x) = x^\alpha$, in the limit of asymptotically large number of players n.

For the case in which the entire prize purse is assigned to the first place prize, we have

$$R(1) \sim \alpha, \quad \text{for large } n.$$

On the other hand, for the case of splitting the prize purse evenly over the first two placement prizes, we have

$$R(1/2) \sim \alpha \left(\frac{e\alpha}{2}\right)^{1/\alpha} \Gamma\left(\frac{1}{\alpha} + 1, \frac{1}{\alpha}\right), \quad \text{for large } n$$

where $\Gamma(s, x)$ is the incomplete Gamma function $\Gamma(s, x) = \int_x^\infty y^{s-1} e^{-y} dy$. Figure 3.10 shows that $R(1/2) > R(1)$ in the limit of asymptotically large number of players n.

3.2 Game with Complete Information

In this section we consider the game with complete information that models the rank-order all-pay contest where the valuation parameters are common knowledge. In Section 2.1, we considered the game with complete information for the special case where only the first place prize is awarded and observed that a pure-strategy Nash equilibrium does not exist; we therefore focused on the study of mixed-strategy Nash equilibria. We also observed that the general case of arbitrary values of the valuation parameters that are allowed to be tied in every possible way necessitates a rather involved analysis in order to fully characterize mixed-strategy Nash equilibria, and we found that there are valuation vectors under which there is a continuum of mixed-strategy Nash equilibria. For these reasons, in this section we study the game with complete information that models the rank-order all-pay contest under specific assumptions on the valuation parameters and the values of the placement prizes. In particular, we shall study two cases: the case of symmetric values of a given number of top placement prizes with arbitrary but distinct values of the valuation parameters, and the case of arbitrary values of the placement prizes and symmetric values of the valuation parameters of the players. The first case is of special interest because it commonly arises in practice. The assumption that the valuation parameters of the players are distinct greatly simplifies the analysis because it prevents the occurrence of a multiplicity of equilibria when the valuation parameters of some players are identical. In the case where the valuation parameters of the players are assumed to be distinct, note that their values are allowed to be arbitrarily close to each other.

3.2.1 Symmetric Valuation Parameters

In the special case of symmetric values of the valuation parameters and symmetric production costs of players, the payoff functions given in (3.2) boil down to the following form:

$$s_i(\mathbf{b}) = \sum_{j=1}^{n} w_j x_{i,j}(\mathbf{b}) - c(b_i), \quad \text{for } i \in N.$$

The production cost function $c : \mathbf{R}_+ \to \mathbf{R}_+$ is assumed to be increasing and such that $c(0) \geq 0$. The case of a strictly positive production cost at zero effort investment allows us to accomodate the scenarios in which participation involves a fixed cost, for example, because of missed opportunities in some outside options. We assume that the participation cost $c(0)$ is smaller than the value of the largest placement prize w_1. Otherwise, it is a dominant strategy for each player not to participate in the contest.

Suppose that the players invest efforts according to a symmetric mixed strategy given by a distribution B. The expected payoff for each player $i \in N$ conditional on the value of his or her effort investment is given by

$$\mathbf{E}[s_i(\mathbf{b}) \mid b_i = x] = \sum_{j=1}^{n} w_j G_j(B(x)) - c(x), \quad \text{for } x \in \mathbf{R}_+ \text{ and } i \in N \quad (3.51)$$

where function G_j is defined in (3.14).

Theorem 3.38. *Consider the rank-order all-pay contest with the values of the placement prizes $w_1 \geq w_2 \geq \cdots \geq w_n \geq 0$. Suppose that the valuation parameters are of unit values and that each player incurs a cost of production according to a production cost function $c : \mathbf{R}_+ \to \mathbf{R}_+$, which is assumed to be increasing and positive valued. Then, there is a unique symmetric mixed-strategy Nash equilibrium strategy B that is given by*

$$\sum_{j=1}^{n} w_j G_j(B(x)) = c(x) - f(c(0), w_n), \quad \text{for } x \in [0, \bar{b}] \quad (3.52)$$

where

$$f(c(0), w_n) = \min\{c(0) - w_n, 0\}$$

and $\bar{b}$ is the solution to $c(\bar{b}) = w_1 + f(c(0), w_n)$.

Proof. We only provide a sketch of the proof. For every symmetric mixed-strategy Nash equilibrium, the payoff of a player, given by (3.51), must be invariant to the value of his or her effort investment for every value that is in the support of the equilibrium symmetric mixed strategy, assuming that all other players invest efforts according to the given symmetric mixed strategy.

If $c(0) \leq w_n$, then no player loses by participating, and thus $B(0) = 0$. For every point x in the support of the distribution B, we have

$$\mathbf{E}[s_i(\mathbf{b}) \mid b_i = x] = \mathbf{E}[s_i(\mathbf{b}) \mid b_i = 0] = \sum_{j=1}^{n} w_j G_j(0) - c(0) = w_n - c(0). \quad (3.53)$$

Combining with (3.51) we obtain the asserted expression in (3.52). The upper end of the support, $\bar{b}$, follows from the identity in (3.53) at the point $x = \bar{b}$ and the fact that

$$\mathbf{E}[s_i(\mathbf{b}) \mid b_i = \bar{b}] = \sum_{j=1}^{n} w_j G_j(B(\bar{b})) - c(\bar{b}) = \sum_{j=1}^{n} w_j G_j(1) - c(\bar{b}) = w_1 - c(\bar{b}).$$

If $w_n < c(0) < w_1$, then in a mixed-strategy Nash equilibrium, the expected payoff of each player must be non-negative because each player is guaranteed the expected payoff of value zero by not participating in the contest. The expected payoff of value zero is achieved by each player under the given mixed strategy. $\square$

Corollary 3.39. *For the case of allocating a unit prize purse fully to the first place prize, we have*

$$B(x) = c(x)^{\frac{1}{n-1}}, \quad for \ x \in [0, c^{-1}(1)].$$

Total Effort

The expected total effort in the symmetric mixed-strategy Nash equilibrium specified in Theorem 3.38 is given by

$$R(\mathbf{w}) = n \int_{B(0)}^{1} c^{-1} \left(f(c(0), w_n) + \sum_{j=1}^{n} w_j G_j(x) \right) dx, \tag{3.54}$$

which follows from

$$R(\mathbf{w}) = n \int_{0}^{\bar{b}} x \, dB(x) = n \int_{B(0)}^{1} B^{-1}(x) \, dx$$

and noting from (3.52) that

$$B^{-1}(x) = n \int_{B(0)}^{1} c^{-1} \left(f(c(0), w_n) + \sum_{j=1}^{n} w_j G_j(x) \right) dx, \quad for \ x \in [B(0), 1]. \tag{3.55}$$

We next identify a set of conditions under which it is optimal for the contest owner to offer only the first place prize by a comparison in which we fix the expected total value of assigned prizes. The total value of assigned prizes can be smaller than the total value of the placement prizes because the number of players who decide to participate in the contest may end up being smaller than the number of available placement prizes. The number of participants in the contest in a mixed-strategy Nash equilibrium is a random variable. In a symmetric mixed-strategy Nash equilibrium where each player plays according to a mixed strategy specified by distribution B is a binomial random variable with parameters n and $1 - B(0)$. Therefore, the expected value of the assigned prizes satisfies

$$\bar{w} = \sum_{j=1}^{n} w_j \sum_{i=j}^{n} \binom{n}{i} B(0)^{n-i} (1 - B(0))^i. \tag{3.56}$$

In the case in which players play according to mixed strategies such that each player participates in the contest with probability 1, the expected total value of assigned prizes is equal to the total value of the placement prizes.

Theorem 3.40. *Suppose that the production cost function is continuously differentiable and concave. Then, for every fixed value of the total value of assigned prizes, the expected total effort in the symmetric mixed-strategy Nash equilibrium is largest when the entire prize purse is allocated to the first place prize.*

Proof. By the telescope formula, we have

$$R(\mathbf{w}) = n \int_{0}^{\bar{b}} (1 - B(x)) \, dx. \tag{3.57}$$

We show that by reallocating an infinitesimal value from the first place prize to the j-th place prize, for every $1 < j \le n$, while keeping the expected total value of assigned prizes fixed, decreases the value of the expected total effort.

We first make the following three claims:

Claim 1 Let x_l be the probability that a player wins the l-th place prize, i.e.,

$$x_l = \int_0^{\bar{b}} G_l(B(x)) \, dB(x) = \int_{B(0)}^1 G_l(x) \, dx, \tag{3.58}$$

and let $\mu_l(x)$ be a density function defined by

$$\mu_l(x) = \frac{G_l(B(x))B'(x)}{x_l}, \quad \text{for } x \in [0, \bar{b}]. \tag{3.59}$$

Then, we have

$$dR(\mathbf{w}) = n \int_0^{\bar{b}} \frac{1}{c'(x)} (\mu_1(x)x_1 dw_1 + \mu_j(x)x_j dw_j) \, dx. \tag{3.60}$$

Claim 2 $x_1 dw_1 + x_j dw_j \le 0$.

Claim 3 Function μ_1 is single-crossing with respect to function μ_j.

The proof of the theorem follows from the asserted claims as follows:

$$dR(\mathbf{w}) = n \int_0^{\bar{b}} \frac{1}{c'(x)} (\mu_1(x)x_1 dw_1 + \mu_j(x)x_j dw_j) \, dx$$

$$\le -n x_j dw_j \int_0^{\bar{b}} \frac{1}{c'(x)} (\mu_1(x) - \mu_j(x)) \, dx$$

$$< -n x_j dw_j \left(\int_0^{x^*} \frac{1}{c'(x^*)} (\mu_1(x) - \mu_j(x)) \, dx + \int_{x^*}^{\bar{b}} \frac{1}{c'(x^*)} (\mu_1(x) - \mu_j(x)) \, dx \right)$$

$$= -n x_j dw_j \frac{1}{c'(x^*)} \int_0^{\bar{b}} (\mu_1(x) - \mu_j(x)) \, dx$$

where the first equality is by Claim 1, the first inequality is by Claim 2, and the third inequality holds for some $x^* \in [0, \bar{b}]$ by the assumption that c is a concave function (hence $1/c'(x)$ is an increasing function) and by Claim 3. Since μ_1 and μ_j are density functions with all the mass on $[0, \bar{b}]$, we have $\int_0^{\bar{b}} (\mu_1(x) - \mu_j(x)) \, dx = 0$. Hence, it follows that $dR(\mathbf{w})/dw_j < 0$.

We next prove Claim 1 and Claim 2. The proof of Claim 3 is easy and thus omitted.

Proof of Claim 1 From (3.57), we have

$$dR(\mathbf{w}) = n \int_0^{\bar{b}} \left(\frac{\partial(1 - B(x))}{\partial w_1} dw_1 + \frac{\partial(1 - B(x))}{\partial w_j} dw_j \right) dx. \tag{3.61}$$

By taking a partial derivative in (3.52) with respect to w_l, and a derivative in (3.52) with respect to x, we respectively obtain

$$\frac{\partial(1 - B(x))}{\partial w_l} = \frac{G_l(B(x))}{\sum_{i=1}^{n} w_i G_i'(B(x))} \quad \text{and} \quad \sum_{i=1}^{n} w_i G_i'(B(x)) = \frac{c'(x)}{B'(x)}.$$

Therefore, we have

$$\frac{\partial(1 - B(x))}{\partial w_l} = \frac{G_l(B(x))B'(x)}{c'(x)}. \tag{3.62}$$

Combining with (3.61), we obtain

$$dR(\mathbf{w}) = n \int_0^{\bar{b}} \frac{1}{c'(x)} [G_1(B(x))dw_1 + G_j(B(x))dw_j]B'(x) \, dx.$$

Using a change of variables along with the definitions (3.58) and (3.59), we obtain the asserted expression in (3.60).

Proof of Claim 2 A sufficient condition for the claim under consideration is

$$\frac{1}{x_j}\frac{\partial \bar{w}}{\partial w_j} \geq \frac{1}{x_1}\frac{\partial \bar{w}}{\partial w_1}. \tag{3.63}$$

This follows from the assumption that the expected total assigned value of prizes is fixed, and thus

$$d\bar{w} = \frac{\partial \bar{w}}{\partial w_1}dw_1 + \frac{\partial \bar{w}}{\partial w_j}dw_j = 0,$$

which combined with (3.63) and assumption $dw_j \geq 0$ implies

$$\frac{1}{x_1}\frac{\partial \bar{w}}{\partial w_1}(x_1 \, dw_1 + x_j \, dw_j) \leq 0$$

from which the assertion of the claim follows because the term $(1/x_1)\partial \bar{w}/\partial w_1$ is positive.

In the remainder of the proof we establish relation (3.63). From (3.56), we obtain

$$\frac{\partial \bar{w}}{\partial w_l} = \frac{\partial}{\partial w_l}\left(\sum_{k=1}^{n} w_k \sum_{i=k}^{n}\binom{n}{i}B(0)^{n-i}(1 - B(0))^i\right)$$

$$= \sum_{i=l}^{n}\binom{n}{i}B(0)^{n-i}(1 - B(0))^i - \sum_{k=1}^{n}w_k\frac{d}{dB(0)}\left(\sum_{i=k}^{n}\binom{n}{i}B(0)^{n-i}(1 - B(0))^i\right)$$

$$\times \frac{\partial(1 - B(0))}{\partial w_l}$$

$$= n\int_{B(0)}^{1}G_l(x)dx + n\sum_{i=1}^{n}w_i G_l(B(0))\frac{\partial(1 - B(0))}{\partial w_l}$$

$$= nx_l + nc(0)\frac{\partial(1 - B(0))}{\partial w_l}$$

$$= nx_l + nc(0)\frac{G_l(B(0))B'(0)}{c'(x)}$$

where the third equality follows by elementary properties of order statistics and the last equality is by identity (3.62).

It follows that condition (3.63) is equivalent to

$$\frac{x_j}{x_1} \leq \frac{G_j(B(0))}{G_1(B(0))}.$$

This indeed holds true because by definition (3.58), we have

$$\frac{x_j}{x_1} = \frac{\int_{B(0)}^1 G_j(x)\,dx}{\int_{B(0)}^1 G_1(x)\,dx} \leq \max_{x \in [B(0),1]} \frac{G_j(x)}{G_1(x)} = \max_{x \in [B(0),1]} \binom{n-1}{j-1}\left(\frac{1-x}{x}\right)^{j-1} = \frac{G_j(B(0))}{G_1(B(0))}.$$

$\square$

The alert reader would have noted that the claim in Theorem 3.40 bears quite some similarity to claim in Theorem 3.35, which is for the game with incomplete information. A notable difference is that in the present case, we allow for participation costs. In both cases, the players are ex-ante symmetric with respect to their abilities: in the case of Theorem 3.35 this is because of identical prior distributions and in Theorem 3.40 this is because the valuation parameters are assumed to have identical values.

Example 3.41 (linear production costs). Consider the case of a linear production cost function $c(x) = x/a$, for $a > 0$, and without loss of generality assume that the expected total value of assigned prizes is of unit value. In this case, the participation cost is zero, and thus $f(c(0), w_n) = -w_n$. From (3.54), we obtain

$$R(\mathbf{w}) = a\left(\sum_{j=1}^{n-1} w_j - (n-1)w_n\right). \tag{3.64}$$

In this example, the problem of maximizing the expected total effort in the symmetric mixed-strategy Nash equilibrium under a unit total prize budget corresponds to maximizing the linear objective function in (3.64) subject to the constraints $w_1 \geq w_2 \geq \cdots \geq w_n \geq 0$ and $\sum_{i=1}^n w_i \leq 1$. Obviously, the optimal solution is to split the prize budget over all but the last place prize in an arbitrary way subject to that every placement prize is at least as large as every lower placement prize, and to allocate no prize to the lowest place prize. In particular, an optimal allocation is to allocate the entire prize budget to the first place prize.

Maximum Individual Effort

The expected maximum individual effort in the symmetric mixed-strategy Nash equilibrium specified in Theorem 3.38 is given by

$$R_1(\mathbf{w}) = \int_{B(0)}^1 c^{-1}\left(f(c(0), w_n) + \sum_{j=1}^n w_j G_j(x)\right) x^{n-1}\,dx, \tag{3.65}$$

which follows from (3.55) and

$$R_1(\mathbf{w}) = \int_0^{\bar{b}} x\,dB(x)^n = n\int_{B(0)}^1 B^{-1}(x)x^{n-1}\,dx.$$

Example 3.42 (linear production costs). The expected maximum individual effort given in (3.65) boils down to

$$R_1(\mathbf{w}) = a \left(\sum_{j=1}^{n-1} a_j w_j - a_n w_n \right)$$

where

$$a_j = \begin{cases} \frac{1}{n} \frac{(2n-j-1)(2n-j-2)\cdots(n-j+1)}{(2n-1)(2n-2)\cdots(n+1)}, & \text{if } 1 \le j < n \\ \frac{1}{n} \left(1 - \frac{(n-1)(n-2)\cdots 1}{(2n-1)(2n-2)\cdots(n+1)} \right), & \text{if } j = n. \end{cases}$$

Again, similarly to the expected total effort, the expected maximum individual effort is a linear function of the values of the placement prizes. A notable difference is that allocating the entire prize purse to the first place prize is a unique optimal allocation of the prize purse, because $a_1, a_2, \ldots, a_{n-1}$ is a strictly decreasing sequence.

We now identify a set of conditions under which it is optimal to assign the entire prize purse to the first place prize with respect to the objective of maximizing the expected maximum individual effort in the symmetric mixed-strategy Nash equilibrium.

Theorem 3.43. *Consider the rank-order all-pay contest with the production cost function c that is increasing, positive valued, continuously differentiable, and log-concave. For every fixed value of the expected total value of assigned prizes, the expected maximum individual effort in the symmetric mixed-strategy Nash equilibrium is largest when the entire prize budget is allocated to the first place prize.*

Proof. The proof follows exactly the same steps as that of Theorem 3.40 with a few differences that we describe here. We instead consider the expected maximum individual effort given by

$$R_1(\mathbf{w}) = \int_0^{\bar{b}} (1 - B(x)^n) \, dx. \tag{3.66}$$

By the same arguments, we obtain

$$dR_1(\mathbf{w}) = n \int_0^{\bar{b}} \frac{B(x)^{n-1}}{c'(x)} (\mu_1(x) x_1 dw_1 + \mu_j(x) x_j dw_j) \, dx.$$

The only difference from (3.60) is the extra factor $B(x)^{n-1}$ in the integrand. For the proof to carry over, we need $B(x)^{n-1}/c'(x)$ to increase in x. It suffices to show that this is implied by the assumption that $c'(x)/c(x)$ is decreasing in x. From (3.52), we can write

$$\frac{c'(x)}{B(x)^{n-1}} = \frac{c'(x)}{c(x)} \left(\sum_{j=1}^n w_j \binom{n-1}{j-1} \left(\frac{1-B(x)}{B(x)} \right)^{j-1} + \frac{f(c(0), w_n)}{B(x)^{n-1}} \right).$$

Since the term in the brackets is decreasing in x, it follows that $c'(x)/c(x)$ decreasing in x is a sufficient condition for $B(x)^{n-1}/c'(x)$ to be increasing in x, which holds by the assumption that function c is log-concave. $\square$

Table 3.1. Examples of log-concave production cost functions

	$c(x)$	$\frac{c'(x)}{c(x)}$	
Linear	$ax + d$	$\frac{a}{ax+d}$	for $a > 0, d \geq 0$
Power	$(ax + d)^\alpha$	$\frac{a}{ax+d}$	for $a, \alpha > 0, d \geq 0$
Exponential	e^{ax+d}	a	for $a > 0$
Logarithmic	$a \log(x + d)$	$a\frac{\log(x+d)}{x+d}$	for $a, d > 0$

The assumptions on the production cost function c in Theorem 3.43 are weaker than those in Theorem 3.40. Indeed, assuming that the production cost function c is concave implies that $c'(x)/c(x)$ is decreasing, which is equivalent to saying that function c is log-concave. The converse, however, is not true; there are functions that are convex and log-concave. For example, for the production cost functions in Table 3.1, both the power function for $\alpha \geq 0$ and the exponential function are convex and log-concave. There also exist instances of convex functions that are not log-concave. One such example is the production cost function $c(x) = 1/(d - x)^\alpha$ for $0 \leq x < d$ and $c(x) = +\infty$, otherwise, for parameters $d > 0$ and $\alpha > 0$.

3.2.2 Asymmetric Valuations and Awarding More than One Prize

Awarding only the first place prize is optimal with respect to maximizing the expected total effort in a symmetric mixed-strategy Nash equilibrium, as we showed in Theorem 3.40. The same optimality property was also shown to hold in Theorem 3.16, for the game with incomplete information in the symmetric Bayes-Nash equilibrium. Both these results were established under a symmetry assumption about the valuation parameters, which are assumed to have identical values in Theorem 3.40 and to have identical prior distributions in Theorem 3.16. We shall now show that, if the valuation parameters are asymmetric, then the contest owner may benefit by splitting a prize purse over two or more placement prizes. We shall show this for a simple but representative example where a unit prize purse is split between the first two placement prizes, the first place prize and a runner-up prize, according to the proportions w and $1 - w$, where $1/2 \leq w \leq 1$. This accommodates an even splitting of the prize purse between the first place and the runner-up prize as one extreme point, for $w = 1/2$, and allocating the entire prize purse to the first place prize as the other extreme point, for $w = 1$.

Suppose that there are three players: one high-ability player and two equally able players of lower ability. Specifically, assume that $v = v_1 > v_2 = v_3 = 1$ (see Figure 3.11). Assume that the players incur identical linear production costs with unit marginal production costs. We next show that there exists a mixed-strategy Nash equilibrium in which the lower ability players deploy symmetric strategies, which admits the following limit for asymptotically large values of parameter v:

(i) If $w = 1/2$, for $x \in [0, 1/2]$,

$$B_1(x) = \mathbf{1}(x \geq 1/2) \text{ and } B_2(x) = 2x; \tag{3.67}$$

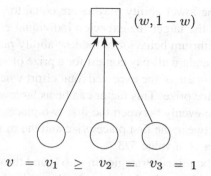

$$v = v_1 \geq v_2 = v_3 = 1$$

Figure 3.11. A contest with two prizes of values $(w, 1 - w)$ and three players, one high-ability player and two players of identical lower ability.

(ii) If $1/2 < w < 1$, for $x \in [0, w]$,

$$B_1(x) = \max \left\{ \frac{1}{2w - 1} x - \frac{1 - w}{2w - 1}, 0 \right\} \text{ and } B_2(x) = \min \left\{ \frac{1}{1 - w} x, 1 \right\};$$

(3.68)

(iii) If $w = 1$, for $x \in [0, 1]$,

$$B_1(x) = x \text{ and } B_2(x) = 1.$$

(3.69)

See Figure 3.12 for graphs of these limit mixed strategies. For these limit mixed strategies, the expected individual efforts are given by

$$\mathbf{E}[b_1] = \frac{1}{2} \text{ and } \mathbf{E}[b_2] = \frac{1 - w}{2}$$

and the expected total effort is given by

$$R = \frac{3}{2} - w.$$

Note that the following properties hold in the given limit. The expected effort investment of the high-ability player is invariant to the way the prize purse is split between the two first placement prizes, assuming the value of $1/2$ for any possible split of the prize purse. The runner-up prize incentivizes the two lower ability players to invest effort. In the case when the entire prize budget is allocated to the first place prize, the expected

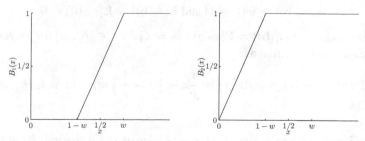

Figure 3.12. The limit mixed-strategy Nash equilibrium strategies for the contest with two prizes and three players in the limit of large ability of the high-ability player.

effort investments of the lower ability players are equal to zero. The larger the value of the runner-up prize, the larger the expected individual efforts of the lower ability players. The limit equilibrium behavior of the low-ability players is as if only the two of them compete in a standard all-pay contest for a prize of value $1 - w$. The expected total effort is a factor $3 - 2w$ of the expected total effort when the entire prize purse is allocated to the first place prize. This factor can be as large as 2, which is achieved by splitting the prize purse evenly between the first two placement prizes. For a popular split of a prize purse between the first place prize and the runner-up prize according to the ratio $2 : 1$, the factor is of value $5/3$.

We next show that the mixed strategies in (3.67) and through (3.69) are indeed the limit of mixed strategies in a mixed-strategy Nash equilibrium, asymptotically as the value of the valuation parameter v grows large. Given a pair of mixed strategies B_1 and B_2, suppose that player 1 plays the mixed strategy B_1 and players 2 and 3 both play the mixed strategy B_2. The expected payoffs of the players, conditional on their individual effort investments, are given by

$$\mathbf{E}[s_i(\mathbf{b}) \mid b_i = x] = \begin{cases} vwx_{1,1}(x) + v(1-w)x_{1,2}(x) - x, & \text{for } i = 1 \\ wx_{i,1}(x) + (1-w)x_{i,2}(x) - x, & \text{for } i = 2, 3 \end{cases} \quad (3.70)$$

where the first place prize winning probabilities are given by

$$x_{i,1}(x) = \begin{cases} B_2(x)^2, & \text{for } i = 1 \\ B_1(x)B_2(x), & \text{for } i = 2, 3 \end{cases} \quad (3.71)$$

and the runner-up prize winning probabilities are given by

$$x_{i,2}(x) = \begin{cases} 2B_2(x)(1 - B_2(x)), & \text{for } i = 1 \\ B_1(x)(1 - B_2(x)) + B_2(x)(1 - B_1(x)), & \text{for } i = 2, 3. \end{cases} \quad (3.72)$$

The supports of distributions B_1 and B_2 must be contained in $[0, w]$ because neither player has an incentive to invest more than w. Player 1 has the expected payoff of value at least $w(v - 1)$ because he or she is guaranteed this value by investing the effort of value w.

We next show that a specific pair of distributions B_1 and B_2 is a mixed-strategy Nash equilibrium. Suppose that (i) B_1 and B_2 have respective supports $[\underline{b}_1, w]$ and $[\bar{b}_2, w]$, (i) both B_1 and B_2 have strictly positive density functions on their supports, (iii) B_1 has no atoms in its support, and (iv) B_2 may have an atom at 0 and it has the lower-end of its support $\bar{b}_2 = 0$. For such mixed strategies, by the mixed-strategy Nash equilibrium condition in Lemma 2.2, we have that

$$\mathbf{E}[s_1(\mathbf{b})] = w(v - 1) \text{ and } \mathbf{E}[s_2(\mathbf{b})] = \mathbf{E}[s_3(\mathbf{b})] = 0$$

and that the condition $\mathbf{E}[s_i(\mathbf{b})] = \mathbf{E}[s_i(\mathbf{b}) \mid b_i = x]$ for $x \in [\underline{b}_i, w]$ for player $i = 1$ and 2 can be respectively written as

$$(3w - 2)B_2(x)^2 + 2(1 - w)B_2(x) = \frac{1}{v}x + \left(1 - \frac{1}{v}\right)w, \quad \text{for } x \in [\underline{b}_1, w], \quad (3.73)$$

and

$$B_1(x)((3w - 2)B_2(x) + 1 - w) = x - (1 - w)B_2(x), \quad \text{for } x \in [0, w]. \quad (3.74)$$

We separately consider the three cases in (3.67), (3.68), and (3.69) as follows.

Case $w = 1/2$ In this case, it is readily checked that $B_1(x) = 0$ for $x \in [0, 1/2)$, $B_1(x) = 1$ for $x \geq 1/2$, and $B_2(x) = 2x$ for $x \in [0, 1/2]$ satisfy (3.73) and (3.74), which conform to the asserted limits in (3.67).

Case $1/2 < w < 1$ Since B_1 has no atom in its support, we have $B_1(x) = 0$ for $0 \leq x \leq \underline{b}_1$. Combining with (3.74), we obtain $B_2(x) = x/(1 - w)$, for $x \in [0, \underline{b}_1]$. The right-hand side in equation (3.73) is equal to w, asymptotically in the limit of large value of parameter v. It follows that in this limit, $B_2(x) = 1$, for $x \in [\underline{b}_1, w]$ is a solution to equation (3.73).

From (3.74) and $B_2(x) = 1$ for $x \in [\underline{b}_1, 1]$, we obtain

$$B_1(x) = \frac{1}{2w - 1}x - \frac{1 - w}{2w - 1}, \quad \text{for } x \in [\underline{b}_1, w]. \tag{3.75}$$

Since $B_1(x) = 0$ for $0 \leq x \leq \underline{b}_1$, we have $\underline{b}_1 = 1 - w$. This completes showing that for the given case, the limit mixed strategies are as asserted in (3.68).

Case $w = 1$ From (3.73) and (3.74), it readily follows that $\underline{b}_1 = 0$ and

$$B_1(x) = x\sqrt{\frac{v}{x + v - 1}} \quad \text{and } B_2(x) = \sqrt{\frac{x + v - 1}{v}}, \quad \text{for } x \in [0, 1]. \tag{3.76}$$

In the limit of large values of parameter v, we have $B_1(x) = x$ and $B_2(x) = 1$ for $x \in [0, 1]$, which corresponds to the limit asserted in (3.69).

Two Prizes of Values $2 : 1$

As an example, we compare allocating the entire prize purse to the first place prize with the popular choice of splitting a prize purse between the first place prize and the runner-up prize according to the ratio $2 : 1$ for an arbitrary ability of the high-ability player.

For the allocation of entire prize purse to the first place prize, we have the mixed-strategy Nash equilibrium strategies given by (3.76). By a straightforward integration, we obtain the expected individual efforts:

$$\mathbf{E}[b_i] = \begin{cases} 1 - 2v + \frac{4}{3}v^2\left(1 - \left(1 - \frac{1}{v}\right)^{3/2}\right), & \text{for } i = 1 \\ 1 - \frac{2}{3}v\left(1 - \left(1 - \frac{1}{v}\right)^{3/2}\right), & \text{for } i = 2, 3. \end{cases}$$

For the case of splitting the prize purse between the two first placement prizes according to the ratio $2 : 1$, from (3.73) and (3.74), we obtain

$$B_i(x) = \begin{cases} \max\left\{\frac{3}{2}\frac{2v-1}{v}x - \frac{v-1}{v}, 0\right\}, & \text{for } i = 1 \\ \min\left\{3x, \frac{3}{2v}x + \frac{v-1}{v}\right\}, & \text{for } i = 2, 3, \end{cases}$$

Again, by a straightforward integration, we have the expected individual efforts:

$$\mathbf{E}[b_i] = \begin{cases} \frac{1}{3}\left(1 + \frac{v-1}{2v-1}\right), & \text{for } i = 1 \\ \frac{v}{3(2v-1)}, & \text{for } i = 2, 3. \end{cases}$$

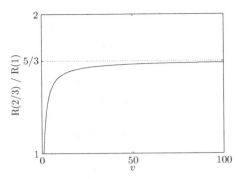

Figure 3.13. The ratio of the expected total effort in the equilibrium of the game with two prizes of values $2:1$ and the expected total effort in the equilibrium of the game with single prize versus the valuation v of the high-ability player.

The ratio of the expected total effort under the two prizes and the expected total effort under one prize monotonically increases to the limit value $5/3$ with the ability of the high-ability player as shown in Figure 3.13.

3.2.3 Symmetric Values of Prizes

In this section we consider the game that models the rank-order allocation of prizes that are of identical values, so that $w_1 = w_2 = \cdots = w_m > w_{m+1} = \cdots = w_n = 0$, for a given number of prizes $1 \le m < n$. Without loss of generality, we assume that each prize is of unit value. The case when the number of prizes is larger than or equal to the number of players is trivial, as in this case it is a dominant strategy for every player to invest an effort of value zero. The valuation parameters are assumed to have distinct values and, without loss of generality, we assume $v_1 > v_2 > \cdots > v_n > 0$. The payoff functions of the players are given as follows

$$s_i(\mathbf{b}) = v_i \sum_{j=1}^{m} x_{i,j}(\mathbf{b}) - b_i, \quad \text{for } i \in N.$$

Theorem 3.44. *For the game with complete information that models the rank-order all-pay contest among two or more players with the valuation parameters $v_1 > v_2 > \cdots > v_n > 0$ and given number of $1 \le m < n$ prizes of unit values, there exists a unique mixed-strategy Nash equilibrium, which is characterized as follows:*

(i) *The mixed-strategy of player i is given by*

$$B_i(x) = \begin{cases} 1 - \dfrac{v_i}{\left(\prod_{l=j}^{m} v_l\right)^{\frac{1}{m-j+1}}} \left(1 - \dfrac{x}{v_{m+1}}\right)^{\frac{1}{m-j+1}}, & \text{if } i \ge j \\ 0, & \text{otherwise} \end{cases} \quad \text{for } \underline{b}_j \le x < \underline{b}_{j-1}$$

(3.77)

where

$$\underline{b}_i = \begin{cases} \left(1 - \prod_{j=i}^{m} \frac{v_j}{v_i}\right) v_{m+1}, & \text{if } 1 \le i < m \\ 0, & \text{if } m \le i \le n \end{cases}$$

(3.78)

and

$$\bar{b}_i = \begin{cases} v_{m+1}, & \text{if } 1 \le i \le m+1 \\ 0, & \text{if } m+1 < i \le n. \end{cases} \tag{3.79}$$

(ii) *The expected payoffs for the players are*

$$\mathbf{E}[s_i(\mathbf{b})] = \max\{v_i - v_{m+1}, 0\}, \quad \text{for } i \in N. \tag{3.80}$$

Proof. Recall that a player is said to be active if his or her mixed strategy is such that a strictly positive effort investment is made with a strictly positive probability. We denote the set of active players by $\hat{N}$ and denote with $\hat{n}$ the number of active players. We denote with $x_i(x)$ the probability that player i wins a prize conditional on his or her effort investment being of value x. The proof follows by the following claims.

Claim 1: *Every player's mixed strategy has no atoms above zero.* Suppose on the contrary that there exists a player $i \in N$ such that B_i has an atom at a point $x^* > 0$. Note that it must be that $x_i(x^*) > 0$; otherwise, playing x^* would yield a strictly negative payoff to player i while he or she is guaranteed a non-negative payoff by investing zero effort. Consider an arbitrary player $j \ne i$. Note that $x_j(x^*) > \lim_{\epsilon \downarrow 0} x_j(x^* - \epsilon)$. Therefore, there exists a small enough $\delta > 0$ such that

$$v_j x_j(x^*) - x^* > v_j x_j(x) - x, \text{ for every } x \in [x^* - \delta, x^*).$$

From this, we conclude that every player $j \ne i$ plays a mixed strategy that has no mass on $[x^* - \delta, x^*)$. Hence, player i can increase his or her expected payoff by moving the mass placed at point x^* to a lower value, which is a contradiction to that his or her mixed strategy has an atom at point x^*.

Claim 2: *The number of active players is equal to $m + 1$.* Let us define $\bar{b} = \max_{i \in N} \bar{b}_i$. Note that $\bar{b}$ is larger than zero. Otherwise, every player would have an incentive to unilaterally increase the upper end of the support of his or her mixed strategy.

We first show that $\hat{n} \ge m + 1$. We claim that there are at least $m + 1$ players whose mixed strategies have upper ends of supports equal to $\bar{b}$. Suppose on the contrary that there are fewer than $m + 1$ such players. By Claim 1 every player's mixed strategy has no atoms above zero. It follows that there exists a player j such that $\bar{b}_j < \bar{b}$ and whose winning probability satisfies $x_j(\bar{b}_j) = 1$. Hence, every player $i \in N$ such that $\bar{b}_i = \bar{b}$ can increase his or her expected payoff by lowering the upper end of the support of his or her mixed strategy, which is a contradiction.

We next show that $\hat{n} \le m + 1$, by a contradiction. Suppose that $\hat{n} > m + 1$. For every active player $i \in \hat{N}$, we have

$$\begin{aligned} v_i x_i(\underline{b}_i) - \underline{b}_i &\ge v_i x_i(\bar{b}) - \bar{b} \\ &= v_i - \bar{b} \\ &\ge \min_{j \in \hat{N}} v_j - \bar{b} \\ &\ge 0 \end{aligned} \tag{3.81}$$

where the first equality holds because by Claim 1 every player's mixed strategy Nash equilibrium has no atoms above zero and $\bar{b} > 0$ so $x_i(\bar{b}) = 1$, the second inequality is strict for all but one active player because the valuation parameters assume distinct values, and the last inequality is because the valuation parameter of every active player must be larger than or equal to $\bar{b}$. Under assumption $\hat{n} > m + 1$, from (3.81), it follows that $x_i(\underline{b}_i) > 0$ for at least $m + 1$ players. Since by Claim 1 every player's mixed strategy has no atoms above zero, it follows that (i) there are at least two active players with an atom at value zero, and (ii) there are at most m players who invest a strictly positive value with probability 1. From this it follows that $x_i(0) > 0$ for every active player $i \in \hat{N}$. This is a contradiction because every player with the mixed strategy that has value zero in its support would benefit by unilaterally deviating from investing zero value to investing an infinitesimally small value.

Claim 3: *The set of active players consists of players 1 through $m + 1$.* By Claim 2, the number of active players is $m + 1$. Since $x_i(\underline{b}_i) \geq 1 - \bar{b}/v_i \geq 0$, for every active player $i \in \hat{N}$, and $x_i(\underline{b}_i) = 0$ for at least one active player $i \in \hat{N}$, it follows that $\bar{b} = \min_{i \in \hat{N}} v_i$. We claim that $v_i < \bar{b}$ for every inactive player $i \in N$. Suppose on the contrary that $v_j > \bar{b}$ for an inactive player $j \in N$. Then, this player would realize a strictly positive payoff by investing value $\bar{b}$ with probability 1, which is a contradiction. This shows that the set of active players is $\hat{N} = \{1, 2, \ldots, m + 1\}$.

Claim 4: *For every active player $i \in \hat{N}$, B_i has the upper end of its support equal to v_{m+1}.* This claim follows from the proof of Claim 3.

Claim 5: *For every active player $i \in \hat{N}$, B_i is strictly increasing on $[\underline{b}_i, \bar{b}_i]$.* Suppose on the contrary that for an active player $i \in \hat{N}$, there exists a non-empty interval $(a, b) \in [\underline{b}_i, \bar{b}_i]$ such that B_i has zero mass on (a, b) and it has point b in its support. Since by Claim 2 there are $m + 1$ active players, it follows that $x_j(a) = x_j(b)$ for every active player $j \in \hat{N}$, and, hence, $v_j x_j(a) - a > v_j x_j(b) - b$ for every active player $j \in \hat{N}$. This implies that point b is not in the support of player i's mixed strategy, which is a contradiction.

Claim 6: *The expected payoffs are as given in (3.80).* It suffices to consider only an active player as the payoffs of inactive players are obviously zero. Consider an arbitrary active player $i \in \hat{N}$. By Claim 1 and Claim 4, $x_i(v_{m+1}) = 1$. By Claim 4 and Claim 5,

$$\mathbf{E}[s_i(\mathbf{b}) \,|\, b_i = x] = v_i x_i(x) - x = v_i x_i(\bar{b}) - \bar{b} = v_i - v_{m+1}, \text{ for every } x \in [\underline{b}_i, v_{m+1}].$$

Since for every x in the support of player i's mixed strategy it must hold $\mathbf{E}[s_i(\mathbf{b})] = \mathbf{E}[s_i(\mathbf{b}) \mid b_i = x]$, it follows that $\mathbf{E}[s_i(\mathbf{b})] = v_i - v_{m+1}$.

Claim 7: *The mixed strategies satisfy (3.77) on their supports.* Consider an arbitrary active player $i \in \hat{N}$. By Claims 4, 5, and 6,

$$x_i(x) = 1 - \frac{v_{m+1} - x}{v_i}, \text{ for every } x \in [\underline{b}_i, v_{m+1}]. \tag{3.82}$$

Since there are m prizes and by Claim 2 there are $m + 1$ active players, every given active player wins a prize if, and only if, his or her effort is not the smallest among the effort investments made by the active players, i.e.

$$x_i(x) = 1 - \prod_{j \in N \setminus \{i\}: B_j(x) < 1} (1 - B_j(x)).$$ (3.83)

Combining (3.82) and (3.83), we obtain

$$\frac{v_{m+1} - x}{v_i} = \prod_{j \in N \setminus \{i\}: B_j(x) < 1} (1 - B_j(x)).$$

By multiplying both sides of the last equation with $1 - B_i(x)$, we obtain

$$(1 - B_i(x))(v_{m+1} - x) = \phi(x)v_i$$ (3.84)

where $\phi(x)$ is defined by

$$\phi(x) = \prod_{j \in N: B_j(x) < 1} (1 - B_j(x)).$$

From (3.84), note that for every pair of active players $k, l \in \hat{N}$ such that $v_k > v_l$, and a point x such that both B_k and B_l increase at x, $B_k(x) < B_l(x)$. Combining this with Claim 5, it follows that

$$0 \le \underline{b}_{m+1} \le \underline{b}_m < \cdots < \underline{b}_1 < v_{m+1}.$$ (3.85)

Using this observation, we can write

$$\phi(x) = \prod_{l=j}^{m+1} (1 - B_l(x)), \text{ for } \underline{b}_j \le x < \underline{b}_{j-1}.$$

From (3.84), it follows that, for $\underline{b}_j \le x < \underline{b}_{j-1}$,

$$\phi(x) = \prod_{i=j}^{m+1} (1 - B_i(x)) = \phi(x)^{m-j+2} \frac{\prod_{i=j}^{m+1} \frac{v_i}{v_{m+1}}}{\left(1 - \frac{x}{v_{m+1}}\right)^{m-j+2}}$$

and, thus,

$$\phi(x) = v_{m+1} \frac{\left(1 - \frac{x}{v_{m+1}}\right)^{1 + \frac{1}{m-j+1}}}{\left(\prod_{i=j}^{m} v_i\right)^{\frac{1}{m-j+1}}}.$$

Combining with (3.84), we obtain that the mixed strategies satisfy (3.77) on their supports.

Claim 8: *The mixed strategies have the lower ends of their supports as given in (3.78).* From (3.85), we have that $\underline{b}_i > 0$ for every active player $i < m$. Hence, in this case, by Claim 1, $B_i(\underline{b}_i) = 0$, which along with (3.77) uniquely defines the value of $\underline{b}_i$. For player m, from (3.77), $B_m(\underline{b}_m) = \underline{b}_m / v_{m+1}$. Hence, it follows that $\underline{b}_m = 0$. Combining this with (3.85), it follows that $\underline{b}_{m+1} = 0$. $\square$

We now highlight some of the properties of the mixed-strategy Nash equilibrium given in Theorem 3.44. The mixed strategy of every player has the support contained

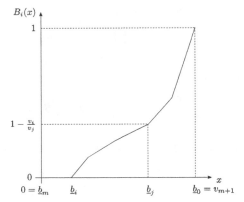

Figure 3.14. The mixed-strategy Nash equilibrium strategy of an active player $1 \leq i \leq m + 1$.

in $[0, v_{m+1}]$. There are exactly $m + 1$ active players and these are the players with $m + 1$ highest valuations. There are exactly two players who randomize continuously on $[0, v_{m+1}]$ and these are the two active players with the lowest valuations, namely players m and $m + 1$. There is exactly one active player who invests zero effort with a positive probability and this is the active player with the lowest valuation, namely player $m + 1$. See Figure 3.14 for a graph of the equilibrium mixed strategy of an active player. The alert reader would have already noted the relation with the game that models the standard all-pay contest with only the first place prize, which we studied in Chapter 2. Under the assumption that the valuation parameters assume distinct values, for the case of awarding only the first place prize, the characterization of the mixed-strategy Nash equilibrium in Theorem 3.44 boils down to that for the standard all-pay contest that awards only the first place prize. Figure 3.15 shows the equilibrium mixed strategies for a specific example of awarding three placement prizes.

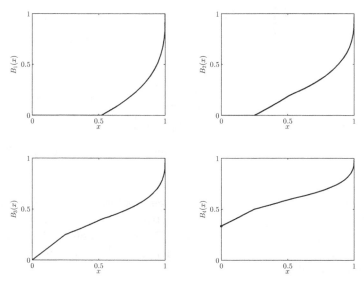

Figure 3.15. The mixed-strategy Nash equilibrium strategies for the case of a contest with three prizes of symmetric values and five players with linearly decreasing values of the valuation parameters.

Expected Individual Efforts

The expected individual efforts in the mixed-strategy Nash equilibrium of active players are given as follows: for player 1,

$$\mathbf{E}[b_1] = v_{m+1}\left(1 - \frac{1}{m+1}\prod_{l=1}^{m}\frac{v_l}{v_1}\right), \tag{3.86}$$

for players $i \in \{2, 3, \ldots, m\}$,

$$\mathbf{E}[b_i] = v_{m+1}\left(1 - \prod_{l=i}^{m}\frac{v_l}{v_i}\right)$$

$$+ v_i\left(\frac{m}{m+1}\prod_{l=1}^{m+1}\frac{v_l}{v_1} + \sum_{j=2}^{i}\frac{m-j+1}{m-j+2}\left(\prod_{l=j}^{m+1}\frac{v_l}{v_j} - \prod_{l=j}^{m+1}\frac{v_l}{v_{j-1}}\right)\right), \tag{3.87}$$

and, for player $m+1$,

$$\mathbf{E}[b_{m+1}] = \frac{v_{m+1}}{v_m}\mathbf{E}[b_m]. \tag{3.88}$$

The expressions for the expected individual efforts in (3.86) and (3.87) can be derived by a straightforward but tedious calculus using the telescope formula for the expected value of a random variable and the characterization of the mixed-strategy Nash equilibrium strategies in Theorem 3.44. The expression for the expected effort of player $m+1$ in (3.88) follows by noting that from (3.84), we have

$$(1 - B_{m+1}(x)) = \frac{v_{m+1}}{v_m}(1 - B_m(x)), \quad \text{for } x \in [0, v_{m+1}]$$

and, thus,

$$\mathbf{E}[b_{m+1}] = \int_0^{v_{m+1}}(1 - B_{m+1}(x))\,dx$$

$$= \frac{v_{m+1}}{v_m}\int_0^{v_{m+1}}(1 - B_m(x))\,dx$$

$$= \frac{v_{m+1}}{v_m}\mathbf{E}[b_m].$$

The expected effort of the highest-valuation player has the following properties. For the special case of awarding only the first place prize, the expression in (3.86) boils down to $\mathbf{E}[b_1] = v_2/2$, which indeed corresponds to the one that we already encountered in Theorem 2.3. From (3.86), it is readily observed that for the set of valuation vectors that have fixed values of the valuations v_1 and v_{m+1}, player 1 invests the largest expected effort when the valuation parameters of players 2 through m have nearly identical values near to value v_{m+1}. On the other hand, his or her expected effort is lowest when players 2 through m have nearly identical values of the valuation parameters near to value v_2.

An alternative representation of the expected individual efforts of players 1 through m is readily obtained from (3.86) and (3.87), and is given as follows:

$$\mathbf{E}[b_i] = v_{m+1}\left(1 - \lambda_{i,i}(\mathbf{v}) + \sum_{j=1}^{i} a_{i,j}\lambda_{i,j}(\mathbf{v})\right), \quad \text{for } i \in \{1, 2, \ldots, m\} \qquad (3.89)$$

where

$$\lambda_{i,j}(\mathbf{v}) = \frac{v_i}{v_j}\prod_{l=j}^{m}\frac{v_l}{v_j} \qquad (3.90)$$

and

$$a_{i,j} = \begin{cases} \frac{1}{(m-j+2)(m-j+1)}, & \text{if } 1 \leq j < i \\ \frac{m-j+1}{m-j+2}, & \text{if } j = i. \end{cases} \qquad (3.91)$$

Using the characterization of the expected individual efforts in (3.89), we can obtain the following lower bounds.

Corollary 3.45. *The expected individual efforts of active players admit the following lower bounds:*

$$\mathbf{E}[b_i] \geq v_{m+1}\left(1 - \frac{1}{m-i+2}\right), \quad \text{for } i \in \{1, 2, \ldots, m+1\}.$$

Proof. For every player $i \in \{1, 2, \ldots, m\}$, using (3.89) and (3.90), we have

$$\frac{\mathbf{E}[b_i]}{v_{m+1}} = 1 - \lambda_{i,i}(\mathbf{v}) + \sum_{j=1}^{i} a_{i,j}\lambda_{i,j}(\mathbf{v})$$

$$\geq 1 \cdot (1 - \lambda_{i,i}(\mathbf{v})) + a_{i,i}\lambda_{i,i}(\mathbf{v})$$

$$\geq a_{i,i}$$

$$= 1 - \frac{1}{m-i+2}.$$

For player $m + 1$, we have the trivial lower bound of value zero. $\square$

The lower bounds in Corollary 3.45 imply that for each player 1 through m, the expected effort is at least a half of the maximum possible individual effort in the equilibrium. This, however, is not guaranteed for player $m + 1$, whose expected effort can be an arbitrarily small fraction of the maximum possible individual effort in equilibrium.

Total Effort

In this section we provide simple and tight lower and upper bounds for the expected total effort in terms of the number of prizes m and the $(m + 1)$-st largest value of the valuation parameter of a player.

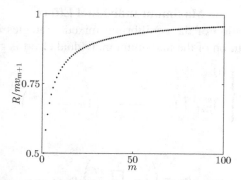

Figure 3.16. Lower bound on the expected total effort.

Corollary 3.46. *The expected total effort in the mixed-strategy Nash equilibrium satisfies*

$$(m + 1 - H_{m+1})v_{m+1} \leq R \leq mv_{m+1}$$

where H_{m+1} is the $(m + 1)$-st harmonic number.

Proof. The lower bound follows from the fact $R \geq \sum_{i=1}^{m} \mathbf{E}[b_i]$ and Corollary 3.45. The upper bound follows from the expected payoffs of players in the mixed-strategy Nash equilibrium as follows. From Theorem 3.44, we have

$$\mathbf{E}[s_i(\mathbf{b})] = v_i\mathbf{E}[x_i(\mathbf{b})] - \mathbf{E}[b_i] = \max\{v_i - v_{m+1}, 0\}, \quad \text{for } i \in N.$$

Hence,

$$R = \sum_{i=1}^{n} \mathbf{E}[b_i] = v_{m+1}\sum_{i=1}^{m+1}\left(\left(1 - \frac{v_i}{v_{m+1}}\right) + \frac{v_i}{v_{m+1}}\mathbf{E}[x_i(\mathbf{b})]\right)$$

$$\leq v_{m+1}\sum_{i=1}^{m+1}\mathbf{E}[x_i(\mathbf{b})] = mv_{m+1}.$$

□

The bounds in Corollary 3.46 tell us that mv_{m+1} is a good approximation of the expected total effort. See Figure 3.16 for a graph of the lower bound. The lower bound implies $R \geq mv_{m+1}/2$, which generalizes the lower bound established for the game that models the standard all-pay contest in Corollary 2.15 to the case of one or more prizes of identical values. The lower bound in Corollary 3.46 implies $R \geq m(1 - \log(m + 1)/m)v_{m+1}$. Therefore, we have

$$R = mv_{m+1}\left(1 - O\left(\frac{\log m}{m}\right)\right).$$

The quantity mv_{m+1} relates to the expected total effort in the symmetric Bayes-Nash equilibrium of the game with incomplete information that is of value $m\mathbf{E}[v_{(n,m+1)}]$, which follows from Example 3.11; the extra factor of value m in comparison to the expression in Example 3.11 is because each prize is assumed to be of value 1, while in Example 3.11, each prize is of value $1/m$.

Maximum Individual Effort

From the characterization of the equilibrium mixed strategies in Theorem 3.44, we obtain that the distribution of the maximum individual effort is given by

$$\mathbf{Pr}\left[\max_{i \in N} b_i \leq x\right] = \begin{cases} 0, & \text{for } 0 \leq x \leq \underline{b}_1 \\ \prod_{i=1}^{m+1}\left(1 - \frac{v_i}{\left(\prod_{l=1}^{m} v_l\right)^{\frac{1}{m}}}\left(1 - \frac{x}{v_{m+1}}\right)^{\frac{1}{m}}\right), & \text{for } \underline{b}_1 < x \leq v_{m+1} \end{cases}$$

(3.92)

where

$$\underline{b}_1 = \left(1 - \prod_{i=1}^{m} \frac{v_i}{v_1}\right) v_{m+1}.$$

The expected maximum individual effort satisfies, for the case of a single prize,

$$R_1 = \frac{v_2}{2}\left(1 + \frac{v_2}{3v_1}\right)$$

(3.93)

and, for the case of two or more prizes,

$$R_1 = v_{m+1}\left(1 - m\int_0^1 (1-t)\left(\prod_{i=2}^{m} \frac{v_i t}{v_1}\left(1 - \frac{v_i t}{v_1}\right)\right)\left(1 - \frac{v_{m+1}t}{v_1}\right) dt\right).$$

(3.94)

Example 3.47. For the limit valuation vector such that $v_1 = \cdots = v_m \geq v_{m+1}$, the expected maximum individual effort is given by

$$R_1 = v_{m+1}\left(1 - \frac{1}{\binom{2m+1}{m}}\frac{\left(2 - \frac{v_{m+1}}{v_1}\right)m + 1}{m + 1}\right).$$

In particular, if $v_1 = \cdots = v_m = v_{m+1}$, we have

$$R_1 = v_{m+1}\left(1 - \frac{1}{\binom{2m+1}{m}}\right).$$

(3.95)

Example 3.48. For the limit valuation vector such that $v_1 \geq v_2 = \cdots = v_m = v_{m+1}$, the expected maximum individual effort can be expressed as

$$R_1 = v_{m+1}\left(1 - \frac{1}{\binom{2m+1}{m}}\frac{a\left(\frac{v_{m+1}}{v_1}, m\right)m + b\left(\frac{v_{m+1}}{v_1}, m\right)}{m + 1}\right)$$

(3.96)

where

$$a(t, m) = \frac{2t\,B(t; m, m+1) - B(t; m+1, m+1)}{t^2},$$

$$b(t, m) = \frac{B(t; m, m+1)}{t}$$

and $B(t; x, y)$ is the incomplete beta function.

The expected maximum individual effort satisfies the following bounds.

Corollary 3.49. *For the expected maximum individual effort in the mixed-strategy Nash equilibrium, we have that*

$$\left(1 - \frac{1}{m+1}\right) v_{m+1} \le R_1 \le v_{m+1}.$$

Proof. The asserted upper bound is a straightforward implication of Theorem 3.44 because the mixed strategies have supports contained in $[0, v_{m+1}]$. The lower bound is established as follows

$$\mathbf{E}\left[\max_{i \in N} b_i\right] \ge \mathbf{E}[b_1] \ge \left(1 - \frac{1}{m+1}\right) v_{m+1}$$

where the second inequality is by Corollary 3.45. □

Social Welfare

We consider the social welfare W defined as the expected valuation of prizes by those who win them in the mixed-strategy Nash equilibrium, i.e. $W = \sum_{i \in N} v_i \mathbf{E}[x_i(\mathbf{b})]$. The optimum social welfare W^* is obtained by assigning the prizes to m players with the highest valuations, i.e. $W^* = \sum_{i=1}^{m} v_i$.

Corollary 3.50. *The social welfare in the mixed-strategy Nash equilibrium is at least $1 - (H_{m+1} - 1)/m$ of the optimum social welfare.*

Proof. Using the characterization of the expected payoffs in Theorem 3.44, in the mixed-strategy Nash equilibrium, the expected social welfare W and the expected total effort R satisfy

$$W - R = \sum_{i \in N} \mathbf{E}[s_i(\mathbf{b})] = \sum_{i=1}^{m} v_i - m v_{m+1}.$$

Therefore, we have

$$\frac{W}{W^*} = \frac{\sum_{i=1}^{m} v_i - m v_{m+1} + R}{\sum_{i=1}^{m} v_i} \ge \frac{R}{m v_{m+1}} \ge 1 - \frac{H_{m+1} - 1}{m}$$

where the first inequality is because by Corollary 3.46 the expected total effort R satisfies $R \le m v_{m+1}$ and the fact $\sum_{i=1}^{m} v_i \ge m v_{m+1}$, and the second inequality is by the lower-bound for the expected total effort in Corollary 3.46. □

The social efficiency lower bound in Corollary 3.50 increases with the number of prizes from value $1/2$ for the case of a single prize to value 1 as the number of prizes grows large. This lower bound is exactly equal to the lower bound derived from Corollary 3.46 for the ratio of the expected total effort R and the value $m v_{m+1}$. Figure 3.16 shows a graph of this lower bound versus the number of prizes.

Summary

Game with incomplete information: the rank-order all-pay contest among $n \ge 2$ players with private valuation parameters that are independent and identically distributed random variables according to prior distribution F with the support

[0, 1]. The values of the placement prizes are $w_1 \geq w_2 \geq \cdots \geq w_n \geq 0$. The production cost functions are assumed to be linear with unit marginal cost of production.

There exists a unique symmetric Bayes-Nash equilibrium, which is given by

$$\beta(v) = \sum_{j=1}^{n-1}(w_j - w_{j+1}) \int_0^v x \, dF_{n-1,j}(x).$$

The expected total effort is given by

$$R(\mathbf{w}) = \sum_{j=1}^{n-1}(w_j - w_{j+1}) j \mathbf{E}[v_{(n,j+1)}].$$

The expected maximum individual effort is given by

$$R_1(\mathbf{w}) = \sum_{j=1}^{n-1}(w_j - w_{j+1}) \left(\mathbf{E}[v_{(n-1,j)}] - \frac{(n-1)!(2n-1-j)!}{(n-1-j)!(2n-1)!} \mathbf{E}[v_{(2n-1,j)}] \right).$$

For the rank-order prize allocation where the contest owner commits to assign the entire prize purse to the players, it is optimal to assign the entire prize purse to the first place prize with respect to both maximizing the expected total effort and the expected maximum individual effort in the symmetric Bayes-Nash equilibrium. These optimality properties hold more generally for increasing concave production cost functions.

The n-virtual valuation function is defined by

$$\psi(v; n) = v F(v)^{n-1} - \frac{1 - F(v)^n}{n f(v)}.$$

A distribution F is said to be n-regular with respect to maximum individual effort if $\psi(v; n)$ is a monotone increasing function. If this holds for every positive integer n, then F is said to be regular with respect to maximum individual effort.

Optimal contest design for a 1-regular prior distribution is to award the entire prize purse to the player who invests the largest effort subject to a minimum required effort of value $\psi^{-1}(0; 1) F^{-1}(\psi^{-1}(0; 1))$.

Optimal contest design for a regular prior distribution with respect to maximum individual effort is to award the entire prize purse to the player who invests the largest effort subject to a minimum required effort of value $\psi^{-1}(0; n) F^{-1}(\psi^{-1}(0; n))$.

Approximation guarantees of the standard all-pay contest: the expected total effort in the game that models the standard all-pay contest with $n + 1$ players is at least as large as the expected total effort in the optimal all-pay contest with n players. The expected total effort in the game that models the standard all-pay contest with n players is at least a factor $1 - 1/n$ of the expected total effort in the optimal all-pay contest with n players.

Assigning the entire prize purse to the first place prize is not optimal in general with respect to either the expected total effort or the expected maximum individual effort. It can be suboptimal in the case of convex production cost functions.

Game with complete information: the rank-order all-pay contest with $n \geq 2$ whose valuation parameters $v_1 \geq v_2 \geq \cdots \geq v_n > 0$ are common knowledge.

Under the assumption that the values of the valuation parameters are identical and that production costs are according to a concave function, it is optimal to assign the entire prize purse to the first place prize with respect to the objective of maximizing the expected total effort in the symmetric mixed-strategy Nash equilibrium.

Under the assumption that the values of the valuation parameters are identical and the weaker assumption that costs of production are according to a log-concave production cost function, it is optimal to assign the entire prize purse to the first place prize with respect to the objective of maximizing the expected maximum individual effort in the symmetric mixed-strategy Nash equilibrium.

Assigning the entire prize purse to the first place prize is not optimal in general. It can be beneficial to split a prize purse over two or more prizes in the case of asymmetric values of the valuation parameters of the players. Splitting a prize purse over two or more placement prizes can incentivize lower ability players to invest more effort.

For the case of identical values of $m \geq 1$ placement prizes, under the assumption that the values of valuation parameters are arbitrary but distinct, there exists a unique mixed-strategy Nash equilibrium.

The expected total effort satisfies

$$(m + 1 - H_{m+1})v_{m+1} \leq R \leq mv_{m+1}.$$

The expected maximum individual effort satisfies

$$(1 - 1/(m + 1))v_{m+1} \leq R_1 \leq v_{m+1}.$$

The expected social welfare is at least $1 - (H_{m+1} - 1)/m$ factor of the optimum social welfare.

Exercises

3.1 **The limit of many players** Consider the game that models a contest among $n \geq 2$ players with rank-order allocation of prizes of values $w_1 \geq w_2 \geq \cdots \geq w_k > w_{k+1} = \cdots = w_n = 0$, for a fixed integer k such that $1 \leq k < n$. The valuation parameters of the players are private information and are independent and identically distributed according to a prior distribution with support $[0, 1]$. The players incur unit marginal costs of production. Prove that the following claims hold in the symmetric Bayes-Nash equilibrium asymptotically as n grows large.

(a) The expected value of the i-th largest effort satisfies

$$\lim_{n \to \infty} \mathbf{E}[b_{(n,i)}] = \sum_{j=1}^{k} \frac{1}{2^{j+i-1}} \binom{j+i-2}{j-1} w_j.$$

(b) For the case of awarding only the first place prize, we have

$$\lim_{n \to \infty} \mathbf{E}[b_{(n,i)}] = \frac{1}{2^i} w_1.$$

(c) The expected maximum individual effort satisfies

$$\lim_{n \to \infty} R_1 = \sum_{j=1}^{k} \frac{1}{2^j} w_j.$$

(d) The expected total effort satisfies

$$\lim_{n \to \infty} R = \sum_{j=1}^{k} w_j.$$

3.2 **Two prizes** Consider the game that models a contest among $n \geq 2$ players with rank-order allocation of two prizes of values $w_1 \geq w_2 > 0$. The valuation parameters are assumed to be private information and are independent and identically distributed random variables according to prior distribution F, which has strictly positive density and no atoms in $[0, 1]$. The players incur unit marginal costs of production.

Show that for any values of the two prizes such that the value of the first prize is at least twice the value of the second prize, the expected total effort in the symmetric Bayes-Nash equilibrium is at least $1/3$ of that in the same contest that allocates the entire prize purse to the first prize.

3.3 **Maximum individual effort vs. total effort** Show that there exists a rank-order all-pay contest among $n \geq 2$ players such that in the symmetric Bayes-Nash equilibrium, the expected maximum individual effort R_1 and the expected total effort R satisfy $R_1/R = O(1/n)$. Note that this is in contrast to the contest that offers only the first place prize, in which case $R_1/R \geq 1/2$.

3.4 **Parallel contest architecture** Consider the game with incomplete information that models the standard all-pay contest with $n \geq 2$ players and a unit-valued prize, where the number of players is a multiple of a positive integer m. Consider also another game that partitions the set of players over m simultaneous standard all-pay contests, each awarding a prize of value $1/m$, such that there are n/m participants in each of these contests. See Figure 3.17 for an illustration. Prove that the following claims hold in the symmetric Bayes-Nash equilibria of the two games.

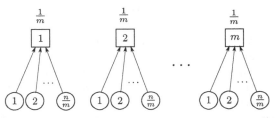

Figure 3.17. A parallel contest architecture that evenly partitions the players over m simultaneous standard all-pay contests, each offering a prize of value $1/m$.

(a) The expected total effort in the single contest architecture is larger than or equal to that in the parallel contest architecture.

(b) The expected maximum individual effort in the single contest architecture is larger than or equal to that in the parallel contest architecture.

3.5 Convex production functions Derive the equations and the asymptotic limits asserted in Example 3.37.

3.6 Symmetric valuations Suppose that a contest owner offers only the first place prize of the amount w_1 in a rank-order all-pay contest with $n \geq 2$ players with symmetric valuations and symmetric production costs according to a production cost function c that is continuous, increasing, and such that $0 \leq c(0) \leq w_1$. Prove that the following properties hold in the symmetric mixed-strategy Nash equilibrium.

(a) Any given player does not enter the competition with probability

$$B(0) = \left(\frac{c(0)}{w_1} \right)^{\frac{1}{n-1}}.$$

(b) The expected value of the prize assigned to the players is

$$\bar{w} = w_1 \left(1 - \left(\frac{c(0)}{w_1} \right)^{\frac{n}{n-1}} \right).$$

(c) The expected maximum individual effort is

$$R_1(w_1) = \int_0^{c^{-1}(w_1)} \left(1 - \left(\frac{c(x)}{w_1} \right)^{\frac{n}{n-1}} \right) dx.$$

3.7 Optimal prize allocation and convex production costs Consider a rank-order all-pay contest among two or more players with symmetric valuations and symmetric production costs according to a function c that is continuously differentiable, increasing, and such that $c(0) = 0$. Suppose that the contest owner has a unit prize purse and his or her objective is to maximize the expected total effort in the symmetric mixed-strategy Nash equilibrium. Prove the following claims.

(a) For the case of two players, it is optimal to allocate the entire prize purse to the first place prize, and in this case the expected total effort is

$$2 \int_0^1 c^{-1}(x) \, dx.$$

(b) For the case of three players and the additional assumption that the production cost function is strictly convex, it is optimal to evenly split the prize purse between the first place and the runner-up prize.

3.8 Conference program design problem Suppose that a conference program committee has to decide how many papers to accept for inclusion in the conference program and it makes this decision public information prior to the paper submission deadline. Suppose that the goal of the program committee is to maximize the overall technical quality of the conference program. Could you formulate a game-theoretic model and based on this model provide a solution to the problem? Consider the same question but for the goal of maximizing the best paper quality.

3.9 Contests for status Consider the game with incomplete information that models a rank-order all-pay contest with status prizes defined as follows. The placement positions are partitioned into a given number k of status levels defined by separators $0 = n_0 < n_1 < \cdots < n_{k-1} < n_k = n$. A function $u(x, y)$ is given that is assumed to be decreasing in x and y. The values of prizes are given by

$$w_j = u(n_{l-1}, n_l), \quad \text{for } n_{l-1} < j \leq n_l \text{ and } 1 \leq l \leq k.$$

The total value of status prizes is equal to

$$u^* = \sum_{l=1}^{k} (n_l - n_{l-1}) u(n_{l-1}, n_l).$$

If $u^* = 0$, we say that the status prizes are of zero-sum. An example of zero-sum status prizes are the status prizes defined as the difference between the number of players of a lower status and the number of players of a higher status, in which case $u(x, y) = (n - x) - y$.

Prove that in symmetric Bayes-Nash equilibrium we have the following properties.

(a) The expected total effort is given by

$$R = \sum_{l=1}^{k-1} (u(n_{l-1}, n_l) - u(n_l, n_{l+1})) n_l \mathbf{E}[v_{(n,n_l+1)}].$$

Hence, in particular, for the case of two status levels,

$$R = \frac{n_1(nu(0, n_1) - u^*)}{n - n_1} \mathbf{E}[v_{(n,n_1+1)}],$$

and for the partition into status levels of the finest grain, we have

$$R = \sum_{l=1}^{n-1} (u(l - 1, l) - u(l, l + 1)) l \mathbf{E}[v_{(n,l+1)}].$$

(b) If, in addition, $u(x, y)$ is a convex function such that $u(x, y) \leq u(x + a, y - a)$ for every $a \leq y$, then the optimal partition into status levels with respect to maximizing the expected total effort awards only one top status prize.

(c) Suppose now that in addition to zero-sum status prizes there are also monetary prizes of total value $w > u(0, 1)$. Then, the maximum expected total effort is achieved by partition into two status levels and awarding monetary prizes such that $w - u(0, 1)$ is allocated to the top status player and the remaining amount is evenly split among other players. In this case, the expected total effort is of value

$$R = w\mathbf{E}[v_{(n,2)}].$$

3.10 Francis Galton's difference problem Suppose that the performance outputs of two or more individuals are according to a sequence $b_1, b_2, \ldots, b_n$ of independent and identically distributed random variables with distribution F. The larger value of individual performance output indicates better performance. A prize purse of unit value is split between the first place and the second place prize with the value of the first place prize given by

$$w_1 = \frac{b_{(n,1)} - b_{(n,3)}}{b_{(n,1)} - b_{(n,3)} + b_{(n,2)} - b_{(n,3)}}$$

where $b_{(n,j)}$ denotes the j-th largest individual performance output. Prove the following claims.

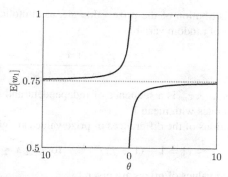

Figure 3.18. The expected value of the first prize under Francis Galton's prize allocation, for asymptotically large n vs. parameter θ.

(a) The asymptotic distribution of the first prize value, as n grows large, is

$$\lim_{n \to \infty} \mathbf{Pr}[w_1 \le x] = H(x; \theta)$$

where $H(x; \theta)$ is given for different domains of maximal attraction of distribution F as follows:

• Type 1 $(-\infty < \theta < 0)$:

$$H(x; \theta) = 1 + 2\theta \frac{1-x}{x} \int_1^\infty u^\theta \left(\frac{1-x}{x} u + 1 - \frac{1-x}{x} \right)^{\theta - 1} du, \quad \text{for } \frac{1}{2} \le x \le 1$$

• Type 2 $(0 < \theta < \infty)$:

$$H(x; \theta) = 1 - 2\theta \frac{1-x}{x} \int_0^1 u^\theta \left(\frac{1-x}{x} u + 1 - \frac{1-x}{x} \right)^{\theta - 1} du, \quad \text{for } \frac{1}{2} \le x \le 1$$

• Type 3:

$$H(x; +\infty) = 2x - 1, \quad \text{for } \frac{1}{2} \le x \le 1.$$

(b) For a type-2 domain of maximal attraction of distribution F with parameter $\theta = 1$, we have

$$H(x; 1) = 2 - 1/x, \quad \text{for } 1/2 \le x \le 1.$$

For $n > 2$ and F being a uniform distribution on $[0, 1]$, we have $\mathbf{Pr}[w_1 \le x] = H(x; 1)$.

(c) In the limit of large n, the expected value of the first prize is such that for $-\infty < \theta < 0$, the expected first prize increases from $3/4$ to 1, and for $0 < \theta < \infty$, it increases from $1/2$ to $3/4$. See Figure 3.18 for a graph.

3.11 Generalized Francis Galton's prize allocation Consider a generalization of Francis Galton's prize allocation to $2 \le m < n$ prizes with the share of the j-th place prize given by

$$w_j = \frac{b_{(n,j)} - b_{(n,m+1)}}{b_{(n,1)} - b_{(n,m+1)} + \cdots + b_{(n,m)} - b_{(n,m+1)}}, \quad \text{for } j = 1, 2, \ldots, m.$$

Assume that the distribution F has the domain of maximal attraction of type 3. Prove the following claims.

(a) The limit distribution of the prize value w_j, asymptotically as n grows large, is equal to that of random variable

$$\frac{\frac{1}{j}z_j + \frac{1}{j+1}z_{j+1} + \cdots + \frac{1}{m}z_m}{z_1 + z_2 + \cdots + z_m}$$

where $z_1, z_2, \ldots, z_m$ is a sequence of independent and exponentially distributed random variables with mean 1.

(b) The distributions of the differences of prize values are given by

$$\mathbf{Pr}[w_j - w_{j+1} \leq x] = 1 - (1 - jx)^{m-1}, \quad \text{for } 0 \leq x \leq 1/j \text{ and } j = 1, 2, \ldots, m.$$

(c) The expected values of prizes are given by

$$\mathbf{E}[w_j] = \frac{H_m - H_{j-1}}{m}, \quad \text{for } j = 1, 2, \ldots, m$$

where H_l is the l-th harmonic number.

3.3 Bibliographical Notes

The efficiency of prize allocation with respect to the total expected effort has been studied by many because this objective is of special interest in various contexts such as lobbying and rent-seeking contests where one cares about the total amount of received payments. Recently, more attention has been devoted to efficiency with respect to the maximum individual effort because this metric is of special interest in the context of crowdsourcing services. The problem of designing a contest with the goal of maximizing the expected total effort was studied by several authors. Glazer and Hassin (1988) studied both the game with complete information and the game with incomplete information. For the game with complete information, they showed that uniformly splitting a prize budget over all but the lowest placement prize is optimal with respect to the expected total effort in a mixed-strategy Nash equilibrium under several assumptions, including that the players have identical valuation parameters, strictly concave utility functions, and linear production costs. This is indeed an optimal allocation of a prize purse as discussed in Example 3.41. For the game with incomplete information and linear production cost functions, Glazer and Hassin (1988) showed that it is optimal to allocate the entire prize purse to the first place prize with respect to the expected total effort in the symmetric Bayes-Nash equilibrium. This result is presented in Theorem 3.16. The game with incomplete information was further studied by Moldovanu and Sela (2001) who characterized the symmetric Bayes-Nash equilibrium, showed that assigning the entire prize purse to the first place prize is optimal more generally for increasing concave production cost functions, and provided a necessary and sufficient condition for optimality of offering two or more placement prizes in the case of convex production cost functions. These results are discussed in Section 3.1.8. The concept of majorization in Definition 3.6 is originally from Hardy et al. (1952). Krishna and Morgan (1998) also studied the problem of how to allocate a prize purse over a given number of placement prizes for contests with two, three, and four players with identical values of the valuation parameters, identical convex production cost functions, and a stochastic production where the output of each player is a sum of his or her invested effort and an independent random variable with zero mean and even density function. Under the assumptions therein, it was shown that it is optimal to offer only the first place prize for the cases of two and three players and to split the price purse between two prizes for the case of four players. Moldovanu and Sela (2006) studied different contest architectures that define how a prize purse is allocated to contestants, e.g., uniformly splitting the prize purse over a given number of placement prizes or using a parallel contest architecture that splits the set of players and the prize purse evenly over a given number of standard all-pay contests. Exercise 3.4 is from Moldovanu and Sela (2006). The characterization of the expected individual efforts in the symmetric Bayes-Nash equilibrium in the limit of many players, in Exercise 3.1, is from Archak and Sundararajan (2009).

Optimal contest design with respect to the expected total effort rests on the framework established in the seminal work by Myerson (1981) on revenue optimal auction design, which we discussed in Section 3.1.5. The comparison result that the expected revenue in a standard auction with $n + 1$ bidders is at least as large as that in the optimal auction with n bidders is due to Bulow and Klemperer (1996) and holds under more general conditions than stated in Theorem 3.33, allowing for affiliated valuations. Laffont and Robert (1996) showed that the optimal auction when bidders have (common knowledge) caps can be implemented by an all-pay auction with specific choice of a reserve price. The optimal contest design with respect to the expected maximum individual effort was first considered by Chawla et al. (2012). The result on the optimality of allocating the entire prize purse to the first place prize, stated in Theorem 3.17, is from Chawla et al. (2012). The part of Theorem 3.33 that is concerned with the expected maximum individual effort and Theorem 3.34 are from Chawla et al. (2012), as is the sufficient condition requiring monotonicity of the hazard rate.

The game with complete information with players of identical abilities and identical production costs that we covered in Section 3.2.1 was studied by Ghosh and McAfee (2012). A full characterization of equilibrium in the game with complete information with players of identical abilities and linear production costs was given in Barut and Kovenock (1998). The results in Section 3.2.1 are based on the work by Ghosh and McAfee (2012). The game with complete information with prizes of identical values and linear production cost functions that is discussed in Section 3.2.3 is based on the work by Clark and Riis (1998a). In particular, Theorem 3.44 is from Clark and Riis (1998a). Most of the characterization results provided in this chapter are new.

Contests for status, which correspond to rank-order all-pay contests with zero-sum prizes, were studied, for example, by Moldovanu et al. (2007) and Auriol and Renault (2008). Exercise 3.9 is based on the work by Moldovanu et al. (2007). A rank-order allocation of prizes where prizes are allowed to admit negative values (a.k.a. punishments) was studied by Moldovanu et al. (2012) in the game with incomplete information. There it was shown that the optimal prize structure is related to the curvature properties of the prior distribution and that, under certain conditions, punishing the low-performing players is more effective than rewarding the top-performing players with respect to the objective of maximizing the expected total effort.

The question of how to split a prize purse was studied mathematically as early as by Galton (1902), who considered an allocation rule that splits a prize purse between two individuals who exhibit the best performance output where the split is in proportion to the excess of their individual outputs with respect to that of the third best-performing individual. Galton (1902) showed that under the assumption that individual outputs are independent and identically distributed random variables from a specific family of distributions, the expected portion of the prize purse allocated to the first prize is 3/4; he also provided some empirical evidence suggesting that the first place prize is uniformly distributed on the interval [1/2, 1]. More recently, Wright (1983) showed that the latter is in fact the exact limit distribution for every distribution of the output that has a type-3 domain of maximal attraction. Exercise 3.10 covers these findings for every type of maximal attraction. Exercise 3.11 is concerned with a natural generalization to two or more prizes.

The optimal allocation of prizes with respect to the objective of maximizing the expected maximum individual effort was studied in the context of economics and theory of firms, e.g., see Levitt (1995), Singh and Wittman (1988), Nalebuff and Stiglitz (1983), and O'Keeffe et al. (1984). Lazear and Rosen (1981) studied a competition-based worker compensation scheme where each worker is rewarded based on the ordinal rank of his or her individual output, and compared this with the traditional payment-based compensation scheme where each worker is rewarded a fixed reward per unit output.

CHAPTER 4

Smooth Allocation of Prizes

In this chapter we consider a class of contests where a prize is allocated to players according to an allocation mechanism that is a smooth function of invested efforts, with one exception: the corner case in which none of the players invest efforts. The smooth allocation mechanism differs from the rank-order allocation of prizes considered in previous two chapters where the allocation is according to a discontinuous function of effort investments. Smooth allocation of prizes may occur not only because of factors such as *stochastic production*, where individual production outputs depend on the invested efforts, but also because of exogenous random effects, or *imperfect discrimination*, where the ranking of players is according to some noisy observations of individual production outputs. As a result of such random effects, the probability of winning a prize may well end up being a smooth function of invested efforts. A smooth allocation of prizes may have desirable properties and for this reason may be imposed by the contest design. For example, one of the key features of the smooth allocation of prizes is that the best performing player may not be allocated the prize with some probability, which may intensify the competition and, as a result, elicit larger effort investments. Our overarching goal in this chapter is to characterize strategic behavior in contests under the smooth allocation of prizes and evaluate properties of interest for particular forms of contest success functions with respect to induced efforts and social efficiency. We present a set of axioms and some probabilistic justifications that serve as a motivation for particular forms of smooth prize allocation. This puts in the spotlight a contest success function that admits a *general-logit* form, which allocates the prize in proportion to increasing functions of individual effort investments. The general-logit function accommodates several interesting and well-studied special cases such as *proportional allocation*, where the prize is allocated in proportion to individual efforts, or more generally, the *ratio form* where the prize is allocated in proportion to a power function of the invested effort. At the end of the chapter, we discuss contest success functions of *difference form* where the contest success function is a function of the difference of individual efforts.

4.1 Contests with Smooth Allocation of Prizes

Consider a contest with a set of two or more players $N = \{1, 2, \ldots, n\}$ and a valuation vector such that $v_1 \geq v_2 \geq \cdots \geq v_n > 0$. Players simultaneously make effort investments $\mathbf{b} = (b_1, b_2, \ldots, b_n)$. A prize of unit value is awarded according to allocation $x(\mathbf{b}) = (x_1(\mathbf{b}), x_2(\mathbf{b}), \ldots, x_n(\mathbf{b}))$. Notice that $x_i(\mathbf{b})$ can be interpreted as either the probability of player i winning a unit indivisible prize or as the portion of an infinitely divisible unit prize. Following standard terminology used in the theory of contests, we shall refer to $x(\mathbf{b})$ as a *contest success function*. Players are assumed to incur identical linear costs of production with a unit marginal cost of production. The payoffs of players are given by

$$s_i(\mathbf{b}) = v_i x_i(\mathbf{b}) - b_i, \quad \text{for } i \in N. \tag{4.1}$$

The payoff functions are quasi-linear in the utility and the cost in the same way as for the standard all-pay contest in Chapter 2. The difference is in the definition of the allocation $x(\mathbf{b})$, which in this chapter is assumed to satisfy certain conditions that accommodate a large class of contest success functions and that are not satisfied by the standard all-pay contest. Specifically, $x(\mathbf{b})$ is assumed to satisfy the following three conditions, for all $\mathbf{b} \in \mathbf{R}_+^n$:

(R) Regularity:
    (i) $x_i(\mathbf{b}) \geq 0$ for all $i \in N$.
    (ii) $\sum_{i \in N} x_i(\mathbf{b}) \leq 1$.
    (iii) If $b_i > 0$, then $x_i(\mathbf{b}) > 0$, for $i \in N$.

(M) Monotonicity:
    (i) $x_i(\mathbf{b})$ is strictly increasing in b_i, for all $i \in N$.
    (ii) $x_i(\mathbf{b})$ is decreasing in b_j for every $i, j \in N$ such that $j \neq i$.

(S) Smoothness:
    (i) $x_i(\mathbf{b})$ is differentiable in b_j, for $i, j \in N$, for every $\mathbf{b} \in \mathbf{R}_+^n$ such that $\sum_{l \in N} b_l > 0$.

An allocation is said to be *anonymous* if it is independent of players' identities, which is formally introduced by the following condition:

(A) Anonymity: $x_i(b_1, b_2, \ldots, b_n) = x_{\pi(i)}(b_{\pi(1)}, b_{\pi(2)}, \ldots, b_{\pi(n)})$ for every permutation π of the elements $1, 2, \ldots, n$.

We say that the prize is always allocated fully to the players if $\sum_{i \in N} x_i(\mathbf{b}) = 1$, for all $\mathbf{b} \in \mathbf{R}_+^n$. This condition is validated by most of the contest success functions considered in this chapter. The case when the prize is not always allocated fully to players accommodates cases where the contest owner reserves the right to withhold the prize for some vectors of effort investments. This is a natural mechanism to elicit higher investments, similar to the use of reserve prices in auctions. The contest success function in the standard all-pay contest is neither monotonically strictly increasing nor smooth.

Under the conditions of monotonicity and smoothness, we have

$$\frac{\partial}{\partial b_i} x_i(\mathbf{b}) \geq 0 \text{ and } \frac{\partial}{\partial b_j} x_i(\mathbf{b}) \leq 0, \quad \text{for } j \neq i.$$

Anonymous prize allocation rules are entirely meritocratic in that the prize is awarded based exclusively on the invested efforts and not on the identities of players. A contest success function may be non-anonymous for various reasons, including the asymmetry of production abilities and the use of discrimination mechanisms such as handicapping and head starts. Our main focus in this chapter is on properties of a pure-strategy Nash equilibrium, whenever one exists. Under the conditions of monotonicity and smoothness, for every pure-strategy Nash equilibrium vector of efforts **b**, one of the following two conditions hold for every player $i \in N$:

$$\frac{\partial}{\partial b_i} s_i(\mathbf{b}) = 0 \text{ and } b_i > 0, \tag{4.2}$$

$$\frac{\partial}{\partial b_i} s_i(\mathbf{b}) \leq 0 \text{ and } b_i = 0, \tag{4.3}$$

and the payoff for every player $i \in N$ is non-negative:

$$s_i(\mathbf{b}) \geq 0. \tag{4.4}$$

4.1.1 A Catalog of Contest Success Functions

In this section we introduce several special families of contest success functions that have been studied extensively in the literature and are analyzed later in the chapter.

General-Logit Form

A contest success function $x : \mathbf{R}_+^n \to [0, 1]^n$ is said to be of *general-logit form* if, given a collection of functions $f_j : \mathbf{R}_+ \to \mathbf{R}_+$, for $j \in N$, it has the following form:

$$x_i(\mathbf{b}) = \frac{f_i(b_i)}{\sum_{j \in N} f_j(b_j)}, \quad \text{for } i \in N \tag{4.5}$$

whenever $\sum_{j \in N} b_j > 0$, and $x_i(\mathbf{b}) = 1/n$, for $i \in N$, otherwise.

The value of function $f_i(b_i)$ can be interpreted as the production output of player i given that this player invests effort of value b_i. We shall refer to f_i as the *production function* of player $i \in N$. The general-logit form corresponds to an allocation in proportion to individual production outputs. A general-logit contest success function always allocates the prize fully to the players, i.e., $\sum_{i \in N} x_i(\mathbf{b}) = 1$, and a strictly positive effort guarantees a strictly positive probability of winning provided that $f_i(b_i) > 0$, for $b_i > 0$. The monotonicity condition holds if the production function of each player is strictly increasing, while the smoothness condition holds if the production function of each player is continuously differentiable.

A general-logit contest success function is anonymous if all production functions are identical, say f for each player, and in this case,

$$x_i(\mathbf{b}) = \frac{f(b_i)}{\sum_{j \in N} f(b_j)}, \quad \text{for } i \in N \tag{4.6}$$

whenever $\sum_{j \in N} b_j > 0$, and $x_i(\mathbf{b}) = 1/n$, for $i \in N$, otherwise.

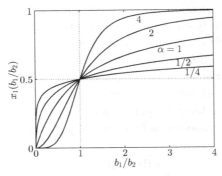

Figure 4.1. Examples of the ratio-form contest success function for a two-player contest for different values of the return to scale parameter.

Ratio Form

A contest success function is said to be of *ratio form* if it is of general-logit form (4.5) with the production functions of the form $f_i(b) = a_i b^\alpha$, for given parameters $\alpha > 0$ and $a_i > 0$, for $i \in N$. Therefore, in this case,

$$x_i(\mathbf{b}) = \frac{a_i b_i^\alpha}{\sum_{j \in N} a_j b_j^\alpha}, \quad \text{for } i \in N \tag{4.7}$$

whenever $\sum_{j \in N} b_j > 0$, and $x_i(\mathbf{b}) = 1/n$, for $i \in N$, otherwise.

We shall refer to a_i as *the relative ability* of player i and to α as *the return to scale* parameter. A ratio-form contest success function that satisfies the condition of anonymity is given by

$$x_i(\mathbf{b}) = \frac{b_i^\alpha}{\sum_{j \in N} b_j^\alpha}, \quad \text{for } i \in N \tag{4.8}$$

whenever $\sum_{j \in N} b_j > 0$, and $x_i(\mathbf{b}) = 1/n$, for $i \in N$, otherwise.

The production output of each player increases with the invested effort according to *decreasing returns* if $0 < \alpha < 1$, to *constant returns* if $\alpha = 1$, and to *increasing returns* if $\alpha > 1$. The ratio-form function is of the soft-max type: the larger the return to scale parameter, the larger the probability of winning for a player who invests the largest effort. On the other hand, the smaller the return to scale parameter, the more balanced the winning probabilities of players are. See Figure 4.1 for an illustration of the contest success functions of a two-player contest.

Proportional

A contest success function is said to be a *weighted proportional allocation* if it is of the ratio form (4.7) with the return to scale parameter equal to 1, i.e., given by

$$x_i(\mathbf{b}) = \frac{a_i b_i}{\sum_{j \in N} a_j b_j}, \quad \text{for } i \in N \tag{4.9}$$

whenever $\sum_{j \in N} b_j > 0$, and $x_i(\mathbf{b}) = 1/n$, for $i \in N$, otherwise.

We shall refer to the anonymous version as *proportional allocation*, which is given by

$$x_i(\mathbf{b}) = \frac{b_i}{\sum_{j \in N} b_j}, \quad \text{for } i \in N \qquad (4.10)$$

whenever $\sum_{j \in N} b_j > 0$, and $x_i(\mathbf{b}) = 1/n$, for $i \in N$, otherwise.

Weighted Valuation

A contest success function is said to be a *weighted valuation allocation* if for every given positive real numbers $a_1, a_2, \ldots, a_n$, it is of the form

$$x_i(\mathbf{b}) = \frac{b_i}{\sum_{j \in N} b_j} a_i, \quad \text{for } i \in N \qquad (4.11)$$

whenever $\sum_{j \in N} b_j > 0$, and $x_i(\mathbf{b}) = 1/n$, for $i \in N$, otherwise.

This contest success function does not guarantee the regularity condition $\sum_{i \in N} x_i(\mathbf{b}) \le 1$ for every $\mathbf{b} \in \mathbf{R}_+^n$. It allows us to study contests in which the contest owner deploys a mechanism to regulate individual marginal costs of production with an underlying objective, for example, to maximize the total effort or maximum individual effort in an equilibrium. The contest owner may use a choice of weights to maximize his or her desired objective subject to the regularity condition $\sum_{i \in N} x_i(\mathbf{b}) \le 1$ in an equilibrium.

4.2 Why a Particular Choice of a Contest Success Function?

In this section we provide justification for some forms of contest success functions using two approaches: (i) an axiomatic approach where a particular form of a contest success function follows from a set of axioms and (ii) an uncertainty approach where a particular form of a contest success function is derived from a model of stochastic production.

4.2.1 Axiomatic Approach

Given a vector of efforts $\mathbf{b} \in \mathbf{R}_+^n$ and a subset of players $N' \subseteq N$, let $\mathbf{b}_{N'}$ be a vector in $\mathbf{R}_+^n$ whose elements $i \in N'$ are equal to the corresponding elements in $\mathbf{b}$, and all other elements are equal to zero (we write $\mathbf{b}$ in lieu of $\mathbf{b}_N$). Let $x_i(\mathbf{b}_{N'})$ be the winning probability for player $i \in N'$ when the set of players allowed to participate in the contest is restricted to N'. We introduce the following three axioms:

(IR) **Independence of Irrelevant Alternatives:** For every non-empty subset $N' \subseteq N$ and $\mathbf{b} \in \mathbf{R}_+^n$ such that $\sum_{j \in N'} b_j > 0$,

$$x_i(\mathbf{b}_{N'}) = \frac{x_i(\mathbf{b})}{\sum_{j \in N'} x_j(\mathbf{b})}, \quad \text{for } i \in N',$$

which is assumed to be independent of the efforts of players not in the set N'.

(SC) **Scale Invariance:** For every $\lambda > 0$, $x_i(\lambda \mathbf{b}) = x_i(\mathbf{b})$ for all $i \in N$.

(SH) **Shift Invariance:** $x_i(\mathbf{b}) = x_i(\mathbf{b} + c\mathbf{1})$ for $c \in \mathbf{R}$ such that $b_i + c \ge 0$, for all $i \in N$.

The independence of irrelevant alternatives means that allocation $x(\mathbf{b})$ must be such that under the restriction to allocate the prize within an arbitrary non-empty subset of players N', the winning probabilities must be proportional to $x_i(\mathbf{b})$, for $i \in N'$, and these winning probabilities cannot depend on the efforts invested by players outside N'. The scale invariance means that the winning probabilities are insensitive to the measurement units of individual production outputs. The shift invariance means that the winning probabilities are insensitive to translations of the vector of efforts.

Theorem 4.1 (general-logit form). *A contest success function satisfies regularity, monotonicity, and independence of irrelevant alternatives if, and only if, it is of the general-logit form.*

Proof. It is readily observed that a general-logit contest success function satisfies regularity, monotonicity, and independence of irrelevant alternatives, so we only show that such a contest success function must be of a general-logit form. Without loss of generality, suppose that $\mathbf{b}$ is such that $b_1 > 0$. By the regularity condition (R-iii), $x_1(\mathbf{b}) > 0$, and (R-ii), $\sum_{j \in N} x_j(\mathbf{b}) = 1$; thus $1 - \sum_{j \in N \setminus \{1,i\}} x_j(\mathbf{b}) > 0$. By the independence of irrelevant alternatives (IR), we have

$$x_i(\mathbf{b}_{\{1,i\}}) = \frac{x_i(\mathbf{b})}{1 - \sum_{j \in N \setminus \{1,i\}} x_l(\mathbf{b})} \text{ and } x_1(\mathbf{b}_{\{1,i\}}) = \frac{x_1(\mathbf{b})}{1 - \sum_{j \in N \setminus \{1,i\}} x_l(\mathbf{b})}.$$

Combined with the regularity condition (R-ii) and that in a two-player contest $x_1(\mathbf{b}_{\{1,i\}}) + x_i(\mathbf{b}_{\{1,i\}}) = 1$, we have

$$\frac{x_i(\mathbf{b})}{x_1(\mathbf{b})} = \frac{x_i(\mathbf{b}_{\{1,i\}})}{x_1(\mathbf{b}_{\{1,i\}})} = \frac{x_i(\mathbf{b}_{\{1,i\}})}{1 - x_i(\mathbf{b}_{\{1,i\}})}. \qquad (4.12)$$

Let us fix b_1 to an arbitrary strictly positive value and define $f_i(b_i) = x_i(\mathbf{b}_{\{1,i\}})/(1 - x_i(\mathbf{b}_{\{1,i\}}))$. From the last relation, it follows that

$$\frac{x_i(\mathbf{b})}{x_1(\mathbf{b})} = f_i(b_i).$$

From this, $1 = \sum_{i \in N} x_i(\mathbf{b}) = x_1(\mathbf{b}) \sum_{i \in N} f_i(b_i)$, and thus

$$x_i(\mathbf{b}) = \frac{f_i(b_i)}{\sum_{j \in N} f_j(b_j)}, \qquad \text{for } i \in N.$$

$\square$

We shall next show that the ratio-form family of contest success functions is a special family of contest success functions.

Theorem 4.2 (ratio form). *A contest success function satisfies regularity, monotonicity, independence of irrelevant alternatives, and scale invariance if, and only if, it is of the ratio form.*

Proof. It is readily observed that a ratio-form contest success function satisfies regularity, monotonicity, independence of irrelevant alternatives, and scale invariance, so we only prove the converse. As in the proof of Theorem 4.1, assume that the vector of efforts $\mathbf{b}$ is such that $b_1 > 0$. Let us define $h_i(x) = x_i(1, 0, \ldots, 0, x, 0, \ldots, 0)/x_1(1, 0, \ldots, 0, x, 0, \ldots, 0)$, for $i \in N$.

From (4.12) and the scale-invariance axiom, we have

$$\frac{x_i(\mathbf{b})}{x_1(\mathbf{b})} = h_i(b_i) = h_i\left(\frac{b_i}{b_1}\right), \quad \text{for } i \in N. \tag{4.13}$$

Hence,

$$x_i(\mathbf{b}) = x_1(\mathbf{b}) \cdot h_i\left(\frac{b_i}{b_1}\right), \quad \text{for } i \in N.$$

Combining this with the regularity condition $\sum_{i=1}^{n} x_i(\mathbf{b}) = 1$, we obtain

$$x_1(\mathbf{b}) = \frac{1}{1 + \sum_{j=2}^{n} h_j\left(\frac{b_j}{b_1}\right)} \quad \text{and } x_i(\mathbf{b}) = \frac{h_i\left(\frac{b_i}{b_1}\right)}{1 + \sum_{j=2}^{n} h_j\left(\frac{b_j}{b_1}\right)}, \quad \text{for } i \neq 1.$$

Therefore, by the axiom of independence of irrelevant alternatives,

$$\frac{x_i(\mathbf{b})}{1 - x_1(\mathbf{b})} = \frac{h_i\left(\frac{b_i}{b_1}\right)}{\sum_{j=2}^{n} h_j\left(\frac{b_j}{b_1}\right)} = \frac{h_i(b_i)}{\sum_{j=2}^{n} h_j(b_j)}, \quad \text{for } i \in N.$$

The last equation implies

$$\frac{h_i\left(\frac{b_i}{b_1}\right)}{h_i(b_i)} = \frac{h_k\left(\frac{b_k}{b_1}\right)}{h_k(b_k)}, \quad \text{for all } i, k \in N. \tag{4.14}$$

From (4.14), we observe that the value of the left-hand side in (4.14) must be invariant to the value of b_i; hence, for every $b_i \in \mathbf{R}_+$,

$$\frac{h_i\left(\frac{b_i}{b_1}\right)}{h_i(b_i)} = \frac{h_i\left(\frac{1}{b_1}\right)}{h_i(1)}, \quad \text{for all } i \in N. \tag{4.15}$$

Let us define $u = b_i$, $v = 1/b_1$ and $g_i(x) = h_i(x)/h_i(1)$, for $i \in N$. Then equation (4.15) can be written as

$$g_i(uv) = g_i(u)g_i(v).$$

This is the Cauchy's multiplicative functional equation, as defined in Section 11.1.8, which has a unique solution $g_i(x) = x^{\alpha_i}$, for constant $\alpha_i > 0$, because $g_i(x)$ is a strictly increasing function. Indeed, $x_i(\mathbf{b})$ is increasing in b_i and decreasing in b_j for every $j \neq i$. Hence, it follows that $h_i(x)$ is strictly increasing in x, which implies that $g_i(x)$ is strictly increasing in x. It follows that $h_i(x) = c_i x^{\alpha_i}$, for $\alpha_i, c_i > 0$. From (4.14), we have $\alpha_i = \alpha$, for $\alpha > 0$ and all $i \in N$. □

Theorem 4.3. *A contest success function satisfies regularity, monotonicity, independence of irrelevant alternatives, and shift invariance if, and only if, it is a general-logit contest success function with $f_i(b) = a_i e^{\alpha b}$, for some $\alpha > 0$, and $a_i > 0$, $i \in N$.*

Proof. Let us define $\hat{b}_i = e^{b_i}$ and $\hat{x}_i(\hat{b}_1, \ldots, \hat{b}_n) = x_i(b_1, \ldots, b_n)$, for $i \in N$. It is readily observed that $\hat{x}$ inherits regularity, monotonicity, and independence of irrelevant alternatives from x. Furthermore, by the shift invariance of x, for every $c \in \mathbf{R}$ such that $\mathbf{b} + \mathbf{1}c \geq 0$,

$$\hat{x}_i(\hat{b}_1, \ldots, \hat{b}_n) = x_i(b_1, \ldots, b_n)$$
$$= x_i(b_1 + c, \ldots, b_n + c)$$
$$= \hat{x}_i(e^c \hat{b}_1, \ldots, e^c \hat{b}_n).$$

Hence, $\hat{x}$ is scale invariant. By Theorem 4.2, it must be that $\hat{x}_i(\hat{\mathbf{b}}) = a_i \hat{b}_i^\alpha / \sum_{j \in N} a_j \hat{b}_j$ where $\alpha > 0$ and $a_j > 0$, $j \in N$. Therefore, $x_i(\mathbf{b}) = a_i e^{\alpha b_i} / \sum_{j \in N} a_j e^{\alpha b_j}$, for $i \in N$. $\square$

Note that under the conditions of Theorem 4.3, the allocation to each player depends only on the difference between the effort invested by this players and the individual efforts of other players.

4.2.2 Uncertainty Approach

In this section we show how some instances of the ratio-form contest success functions arise under some models of stochastic production, where the production output of an individual is determined by his or her invested effort and a stochastic component. This stochastic component of production is assumed to be due to some source of uncertainty. It could be an internal source of uncertainty where the quality of production by an individual exhibits some level of inconsistency from one production output to another. It could also be due to an external source, such as a procedure for ranking players based on observed individual production outputs that is flawed by estimation errors.

Model 1 Consider a multiplicative-noise model of production where the production output of an individual is a product of his or her invested effort and a positive-valued random variable drawn independently from a distribution. Specifically, we assume that the production output of player i is $z_i b_i$, where z_i is an independent sample from a distribution G_i and b_i is the effort investment. A question arises whether there exist distributions $G_1, G_2, \ldots, G_n$ for which the contest success functions are of the ratio form. The answer to this question is affirmative.

Assume that $z_1, z_2, \ldots, z_n$ is a sequence of independent random variables where the distribution of z_i is an inverse exponential distribution $\mathbf{Pr}[z_i \leq z] = e^{-\frac{a_i}{z^\alpha}}$, for $z > 0$, for given parameters α and $a_i \geq 0$. Then, the contest success function of each player is of the ratio form:

$$x_i(\mathbf{b}) = \mathbf{Pr}[\cap_{j \neq i} \{z_i b_i > z_j b_j\}] = \frac{a_i b_i^\alpha}{\sum_{j=1}^n a_j b_j^\alpha}, \quad \text{for } i \in N$$

whenever $\sum_{j \in N} b_j > 0$.

This follows by the following series of equalities:

$$x_i(\mathbf{b}) = \mathbf{E}\left[\prod_{j \neq i} \mathbf{Pr}\left[z_i b_i > z_j b_j \mid z_i\right]\right]$$

$$= \int_0^\infty \prod_{j \neq i} \mathbf{Pr}[z b_i > z_j b_j] \, d\mathbf{Pr}[z_i \leq z]$$

$$= \int_0^\infty \prod_{j \neq i} e^{-\frac{a_j b_j^\alpha}{b_i^\alpha z^\alpha}} \cdot \frac{\alpha a_i}{z^{\alpha+1}} e^{-\frac{a_i}{z^\alpha}} \, dz$$

$$= \int_0^\infty e^{-\frac{\sum_{j=1}^n a_j b_j^\alpha}{b_i^\alpha z^\alpha}} \frac{\alpha a_i}{z^{\alpha+1}} \, dz$$

$$= \frac{a_i b_i^\alpha}{\sum_{j=1}^n a_j b_j^\alpha} \int_0^\infty \frac{\alpha \sum_{j=1}^n a_j b_j^\alpha}{b_i^\alpha z^{\alpha+1}} e^{-\frac{\sum_{j=1}^n a_j b_j^\alpha}{b_i^\alpha z^\alpha}} \, dz$$

$$= \frac{a_i b_i^\alpha}{\sum_{j=1}^n a_j b_j^\alpha}.$$

The claim also holds for the production function defined by $f(b, z) = \log(b) + z$ where $z_1, z_2, \ldots, z_n$ is a sequence of independent and identically distributed random variables according to a Gumbel distribution $\mathbf{Pr}[z_i \leq z] = e^{-a_i e^{-\alpha z}}$, for $z \geq 0$.

Model 2 Consider a multiplicative-noise model of production where the production output of player i is given by $z_i a_i b_i^\alpha$, where $z_1, z_2, \ldots, z_n$ are independent random variables with exponential distributions with mean 1, $b_1, b_2, \ldots, b_n$ are the effort investments, and $a_1, a_2, \ldots, a_n, \alpha > 0$ are the parameters of the model. For the case of two players, the winning probabilities are of the ratio form

$$x_1(b_1, b_2) = \frac{a_1 b_1^\alpha}{a_1 b_1^\alpha + a_2 b_2^\alpha} \quad \text{and} \quad x_2(b_1, b_2) = \frac{a_2 b_2^\alpha}{a_1 b_1^\alpha + a_2 b_2^\alpha}$$

whenever $b_1 + b_2 > 0$.

If the number of players is larger than two, then the contest success functions are not of the ratio form.

Model 3 Consider a scenario where each worker is assigned a task to complete and a prize is awarded to the worker who is first to complete his or her assigned task. Suppose that $a_i b_i^\alpha$ is the amount of work processed by worker i per unit time, for parameters $\alpha \geq 0$ and $a_i > 0$, where b_i is the amount of effort put in by worker i. Suppose also that each worker i is assigned a task that requires a total amount of work z_i where $z_1, z_2, \ldots, z_n$ is a sequence of independent and identically distributed random variables with exponential distribution with mean 1. For the purpose of our model, we can also assume that workers are of identical abilities so that b_i^α is the production rate of worker i and his or her assigned task requires an amount of work z_i, assumed to be an independent sample from an exponential distribution of mean $1/a_i$. Under these assumptions, the contest success functions are of the ratio form:

$$x_i(\mathbf{b}) = \mathbf{Pr}\left[\bigcap_{j \neq i}\left\{\frac{z_i}{a_i b_i^\alpha} \leq \frac{z_j}{a_j b_j^\alpha}\right\}\right] = \frac{a_i b_i^\alpha}{\sum_{j=1}^n a_j b_j^\alpha}, \quad \text{for } i \in N$$

whenever $\sum_{j \in N} b_j > 0$.

Model 4 In this model the production output of each worker is an independent sample from a distribution that we define as follows. Suppose we have a distribution F that has a density on an interval in $\mathbf{R}_+$. Each worker i is assumed to be of ability $a_i b_i^\alpha$, where b_i is his or her effort investment and $a_i > 0$ and $\alpha \geq 0$ are the parameters of the model. The production output p_i of worker i is assumed to be an independent sample from distribution $F(x)^{a_i b_i^\alpha}$. If $a_i b_i^\alpha$ are integers, then this models a scenario where each worker i submits $a_i b_i^\alpha$ solutions whose qualities are according to independent samples from distribution F, and the worker who submits the best quality solution wins the competition and is awarded the prize. In this case, the contest success functions are of the ratio form:

$$x_i(\mathbf{b}) = \mathbf{Pr}[\cap_{j \neq i}\{p_i \geq p_j\}] = \int_0^\infty \left(\prod_{j \neq i} F(x)^{a_j b_j^\alpha}\right) dF(x)^{a_i b_i^\alpha}$$

$$= \frac{a_i b_i^\alpha}{\sum_{j=1}^n a_j b_j^\alpha}, \quad \text{for } i \in N \tag{4.16}$$

whenever $\sum_{j \in N} b_j > 0$.

4.3 General-Logit Contest Success Functions

In this section we provide a set of sufficient conditions for the existence of a pure-strategy Nash equilibrium and present some interesting properties of a pure-strategy Nash equilibrium whenever one exists in a contest where the prize is allocated according to a general-logit contest success function in equation (4.5), which we recall here:

$$x_i(\mathbf{b}) = \frac{f_i(b_i)}{\sum_{j \in N} f_j(b_j)}, \quad \text{for } i \in N$$

whenever $\sum_{j \in N} b_j > 0$, and $x_i(\mathbf{b}) = 1/n$, for $i \in N$, otherwise.

Conditions (4.2), (4.3), and (4.4) for a vector of efforts $\mathbf{b}$ to be a pure-strategy Nash equilibrium correspond to the following condition: for every player $i \in N$ either (4.17) or (4.18) holds:

$$v_i f_i'(b_i)(1 - x_i(\mathbf{b})) = \sum_{j \in N} f_j(b_j) \text{ and } b_i > 0 \tag{4.17}$$

$$v_i f_i'(0) \leq \sum_{j \in N} f_j(b_j) \text{ and } b_i = 0 \tag{4.18}$$

and

$$v_i f_i(b_i) \geq b_i \sum_{j \in N} f_j(b_j). \tag{4.19}$$

4.3.1 Existence and Uniqueness of a Pure-Strategy Nash Equilibrium

We first discuss a special case of anonymous contest success functions and identical values of valuation parameters. This special case yields an elegant analysis, allows us to demonstrate cases for which a pure-strategy Nash equilibrium does not exist, and suggests a set of sufficient conditions for its existence. We shall then provide a set of sufficient conditions for the existence and uniqueness of a pure-strategy Nash equilibrium in the general case.

A Warm-Up: Symmetric Valuations and Production Functions

Suppose that the valuation parameters are symmetric $v_1 = v_2 = \cdots = v_n > 0$ and that the contest success functions are of anonymous general-logit form with production function f. If a vector of efforts $\mathbf{b} = (b_1, b_2, \ldots, b_n)$ is a pure-strategy Nash equilibrium, then for each player $i \in N$ either condition (4.2) or condition (4.3) holds, and the payoffs are non-negative (4.4). By the symmetry of the payoff functions, the vector $\mathbf{b}$ satisfies $b_1 = b_2 = \cdots = b_n$, and thus $x_i(\mathbf{b}) = 1/n$, for all $i \in N$. Conditions (4.2)-(4.4) boil down to the following two conditions:

$$v_1 f'(b_1)(n - 1) = n^2 f(b_1) \tag{4.20}$$

$$v_1 \frac{1}{n} - b_1 \geq 0. \tag{4.21}$$

We define $\phi(x) = f(x)/f'(x)$. The conditions (4.20) and (4.21) are equivalent to

$$\phi(b_1) = \left(1 - \frac{1}{n}\right) \frac{v_1}{n} \text{ and } b_1 \leq \frac{v_1}{n}. \tag{4.22}$$

Condition (4.22) admits a simple geometric interpretation, which is sketched in Figure 4.2. If a vector of efforts $\mathbf{b} = (b_1, b_1, \ldots, b_1)$ is a pure-strategy Nash equilibrium, then $(b_1, \phi(b_1))$ must be a point at the intersection of the graph of function ϕ and the line segment with the end points A and B. The curvature properties of ϕ play an important role here. A sufficient condition for the existence of a unique pure-strategy Nash equilibrium is that the production function f is concave, which we explain as follows. Observe that f is concave if, and only if, $\phi'(x) \geq 1$, for all $x \geq 0$. Thus ϕ is increasing because f is assumed to be increasing and by the assumed concavity f' is decreasing. Figure 4.2 shows that for any concave production function f there always exists a unique intersection of the graph of function ϕ and the line segment with the end points A and B because the function ϕ never lies below the line through the points $(0, 0)$ and (v_1, v_1), and the line segment with the end points A and B always intersects that line.

On the other hand, if f is not concave, then a pure-strategy Nash equilibrium is not guaranteed to exist. In particular, if f is convex, then the graph of $\phi(x)$ lies at or below the line through the points $(0, 0)$ and (v_1, v_1) on the interval $[0, v_1/n]$, and it

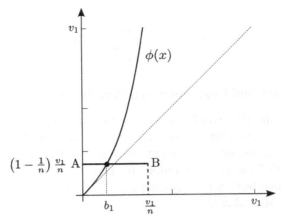

Figure 4.2. An example for which a pure-strategy Nash equilibrium exists under symmetric valuations.

may never cross the line segment from point A to point B. As an example, consider the production function $f(x) = x^\alpha$ as in the ratio-form contest success function, which is strictly convex for the return to scale parameter $\alpha > 1$. In this case, condition (4.22) is equivalent to $\alpha \leq 1/(1 - 1/n)$. Thus, for any fixed value of the return to scale parameter $\alpha > 1$, (4.22) fails to hold for any sufficiently large number of players n, in which case a pure-strategy Nash equilibrium does not exist.

General Asymmetric Valuations and Production Functions

In the preceding section we showed that for the special case of symmetric valuation parameters and symmetric production cost functions, a sufficient condition for the existence of a pure-strategy Nash equilibrium is that the production function is concave. We shall now show that this holds in much more generality for arbitrary valuation parameters and production functions that are allowed to be asymmetric.

Theorem 4.4. *Consider a contest among two or more players with valuation parameters $v_1 \geq v_2 \geq \cdots \geq v_n > 0$ where a unit prize is allocated according to a general-logit form contest success function with production functions f_i that are increasing, twice differentiable, and concave with $f_i(0) = 0$, and the players incur linear production costs with unit marginal costs. Then, there exists a unique pure-strategy Nash equilibrium.*

Proof. The existence of a pure-strategy Nash equilibrium can be established by making use of a result on the existence of pure-strategy Nash equilibrium for concave games, which is presented in Section 11.3.1. For the given game to be a concave game, we would need to show that (i) each payoff function $s_i(\mathbf{b})$ is continuous, (ii) each payoff function $s_i(\mathbf{b})$ is a concave function in b_i for every fixed $\mathbf{b}_{-i}$, and (iii) $\mathbf{b}$ is in a set that is convex, closed, and bounded. Conditions (ii) and (iii) can be shown to hold, but condition (i) fails to hold because of the discontinuity of each payoff function at $\mathbf{b} = (0, 0, \ldots, 0)$. A standard trick is to consider an ϵ-perturbed game, for parameter

$\epsilon \geq 0$, with the payoff functions

$$s_i^\epsilon(\mathbf{b}) = v_i \frac{f_i(b_i)}{\sum_{j \in N} f_j(b_j) + \epsilon} - b_i, \quad \text{for } i \in N.$$

For this perturbed game, condition (i) obviously holds for every $\epsilon > 0$ by the assumption that each production function f_i is continuous. Condition (ii) is shown to hold for every $\epsilon \geq 0$ as follows. Note that

$$\frac{\partial}{\partial b_i} s_i^\epsilon(\mathbf{b}) = v_i \frac{f_i'(b_i)}{\sum_{l \in N} f_l(b_l) + \epsilon} \left(1 - \frac{f_i(b_i)}{\sum_{l \in N} f_l(b_l) + \epsilon}\right) - 1.$$

Since the production functions are assumed to be concave, $f_i'(b_i)$ is decreasing in b_i, which combined with the fact that $f(b_i)$ is increasing, implies that $f_i'(b_i)/(\sum_{l \in N} f_l(b_l) + \epsilon)$ is decreasing in b_i and that $1 - f_i(b_i)/(\sum_{l \in N} f_l(b_l) + \epsilon)$ is decreasing in b_i. Therefore, it follows that $\partial s_i^\epsilon(\mathbf{b})/\partial b_i$ is decreasing in b_i, i.e., $s_i(\mathbf{b})$ is concave in b_i. Condition (iii) holds by the condition of non-negativity of payoffs in (4.4), from which we conclude that $0 \leq b_i \leq v_i$, for every $i \in N$. Hence $\mathbf{b}$ is in the set $[0, v_1] \times [0, v_2] \times \cdots \times [0, v_n]$, that is convex, closed, and bounded.

We next show an alternative way of proving the existence of a pure-strategy Nash equilibrium that also establishes its uniqueness. The proof formulates a constructive method for computation of the pure-strategy Nash equilibrium, which amounts to finding a unique solution of a fixed-point equation for the total effort investment of the players. For every given value of the total effort, each individual effort is a unique solution of a fixed-point equation.

First, note that the game is strategically equivalent to a game with the payoff functions

$$\hat{s}_i(\hat{\mathbf{b}}) = \frac{\hat{b}_i}{\sum_{j \in N} \hat{b}_j} - c_i(\hat{b}_i), \quad \text{for } i \in N,$$

which are derived from the original payoff functions by the change of variables $\hat{b}_i = f_i(b_i)$ and defining $c_i(x) = f_i^{-1}(x)/v_i$, for $i \in N$. Since $f_i(x)$ is a concave function, $c_i(x)$ is a convex function.

A vector of efforts $\mathbf{b}$ is a pure-strategy Nash equilibrium if, and only if, the corresponding vector $\hat{\mathbf{b}}$ satisfies the following conditions: $\hat{b}_i = 0$ and $(\partial/\partial \hat{b}_i)\hat{s}_i(\hat{\mathbf{b}}) \leq 0$, or $\hat{b}_i > 0$ and $(\partial/\partial \hat{b}_i)\hat{s}_i(\hat{\mathbf{b}}) = 0$, and $\hat{s}_i(\hat{\mathbf{b}}) \geq 0$, for every player $i \in N$. The first two conditions are equivalent to

$$\hat{b}_i = 0 \text{ and } \hat{b}c_i'(0) \geq 1, \text{ or } \hat{b}_i > 0 \text{ and } \hat{b}^2 c_i'(\hat{b}_i) = \hat{b} - \hat{b}_i$$

where $\hat{b} = \sum_{j \in N} \hat{b}_j$. It follows that $\hat{b}_i = \beta_i(\hat{b})$, for $i \in N$, where $\beta_i(\hat{b}) = 0$ if $\hat{b}c_i'(0) \geq 1$, and $\beta_i(\hat{b})$ is the unique value $x > 0$ such that $\hat{b}^2 c_i'(x) = \hat{b} - x$, otherwise. Let us define $\varphi(x) = \sum_{i \in N} \beta_i(x) - x$. Since $\hat{\mathbf{b}}$ must be such that $\sum_{i \in N} \beta_i(\hat{b}) = \hat{b}$, where recall $\hat{b} = \sum_{i \in N} \hat{b}_i$, $\mathbf{b}$ is a pure-strategy Nash equilibrium if, and only if,

$$\varphi(\hat{b}) = 0 \tag{4.23}$$

and

$$\hat{\mathbf{b}} = (\beta_1(\hat{b}), \beta_1(\hat{b}), \ldots, \beta_n(\hat{b})).$$

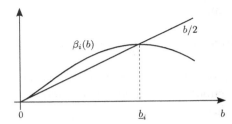

Figure 4.3. The equilibrium effort of a player versus the total effort.

We shall next show that there exists $0 < \hat{b}_* < \hat{b}^*$ such that (i) $\varphi(x) > 0$ for $0 < x < \hat{b}_*$, (ii) $\varphi(x)$ is decreasing for $\hat{b}_* < x \le \hat{b}^*$, and (iii) $\varphi(x) < 0$, for $x > \hat{b}^*$. This implies the existence of a unique value $\hat{b}$ such that $\varphi(\hat{b}) = 0$ and thus the existence of a unique pure-strategy Nash equilibrium given by $\beta_i(\hat{b})$, for $i \in N$. We first state and prove the following two claims.

Claim 4.5. For every player $i \in N$, $\beta_i(b)$ is strictly increasing at every value b such that $\beta_i(b) > b/2$, and is decreasing, otherwise. See Figure 4.3.

Claim 4.6. For every player $i \in N$, $\beta_i(b) > b/2$ is equivalent to $2bc_i'(b/2) < 1$.

The assertion in Claim 4.5 is immediate by inspection of the first derivative of $\beta_i(b)$, which is equal to

$$\beta_i'(b) = \frac{2\beta_i(b) - b}{b(1 + b^2 c_i''(\beta_i(b)))}. \tag{4.24}$$

On the other hand, the assertion in Claim 4.6 is immediate by noting from the definition of $\beta_i(b)$ that $b^2 c_i'(\beta_i(b)) + \beta_i(b) = b$, and that the left-hand side in the last equation is increasing in $\beta_i(b)$, which follows by the fact that c_i is a convex function.

An implication of Claim 4.5 is that for every player $i \in N$, there exists a unique value $\underline{b}_i$ such that $\beta_i(\underline{b}_i) = \underline{b}_i/2$. An implication of Claim 4.6 is that for every player $i \in N$, $\beta_i(\hat{b}) > \hat{b}/2$ for $0 \le \hat{b} < \underline{b}_i$, and $\beta_i(\hat{b}) < \hat{b}/2$ for $\hat{b} > \underline{b}_i$. Without loss of generality, we assume that the players are enumerated such that $\underline{b}_1 \ge \underline{b}_2 \ge \cdots \ge \underline{b}_n$.

Any value $\hat{b}$ that satisfies condition (4.23) must also satisfy $\hat{b} \ge \underline{b}_2$. This is shown by contradiction as follows. Suppose that $\hat{b} < \underline{b}_2$ and $\varphi(\hat{b}) = 0$. By Claim 4.5, we have $\beta_1(\hat{b}) > \hat{b}/2$ and $\beta_2(\hat{b}) > \hat{b}/2$. This implies $\varphi(\hat{b}) > 0$, a contradiction.

We next show that $\varphi(\hat{b})$ is strictly decreasing at every value $\hat{b} \ge \underline{b}_2$. Assume that $\hat{b} \ge \underline{b}_2$. Notice the fact that by Claim 4.5, for every player $i \ne 1$, $\beta_i(\hat{b})$ is decreasing at $\hat{b}$. Where $\beta_1(\hat{b})$ is decreasing at $\hat{b}$, we obviously have that $\varphi(\hat{b})$ is decreasing at $\hat{b}$. Otherwise, where $\beta_1(\hat{b})$ is not decreasing at $\hat{b}$, we have

$$\varphi'(\hat{b}) = \sum_{i \in N} \beta_i'(\hat{b}) - 1 \le \beta_1'(\hat{b}) - 1 \le \frac{2\beta_1(\hat{b}) - \hat{b}}{\hat{b}} - 1 = 2\frac{\beta_1(\hat{b}) - \hat{b}}{\hat{b}} < 0,$$

where the first inequality follows by the fact that $\beta_i'(\hat{b}) < 0$ for every $i \ne 1$, the second inequality follows from equation (4.24) and the fact that c_i is a convex function, and the last inequality follows by noting from the definition of β_i that $\hat{b} - \beta_i(\hat{b}) = \hat{b}^2 c_i'(\beta_i(\hat{b})) > 0$.

It remains only to show that $\varphi(\hat{b}^*) < 0$ for some value $\hat{b}^* > \underline{b}_2$. By Claim 4.5, for every player $i \in N$, $\beta_i(\hat{b}) \le \hat{b}$ and $\beta_i(\hat{b})$ is decreasing for every value $\hat{b} \ge \underline{b}_1$. It follows that $\beta_i(\hat{b}) \le \underline{b}_1$ for every $\hat{b} \ge \underline{b}_1$ and $i \in N$. Therefore, $\varphi(\hat{b}) \le n\underline{b}_1 - \hat{b} < 0$ for every value $\hat{b} > n\underline{b}_1$.

$\square$

4.3.2 Properties of a Pure-Strategy Nash Equilibrium

In this section we discuss some interesting properties that hold in a pure-strategy Nash equilibrium, under the sufficient conditions in Theorem 4.4 that ensure the existence of such an equilibrium.

Theorem 4.7. *For any n-player contest with valuation parameters $v_1 \ge v_2 \ge \cdots \ge v_n > 0$ where the contest success functions are of general-logit form with production functions such that f_i is increasing, twice differentiable, and concave with $f_i(0) = 0$, for all $i \in N$, the following properties hold in a pure-strategy Nash equilibrium.*

(i) *At least two players invest strictly positive efforts. Hence, for a two-player contest, both players invest strictly positive efforts.*

(ii) *If the valuation vector is such that $v_1 \ge v_2 = \cdots = v_n > 0$ and $n \ge 2$, then every player invests a strictly positive effort.*

(iii) *If $f_i'(0) = +\infty$, then player i invests a strictly positive effort.*

The proof of Theorem 4.7 is left as Exercise 4.2. The last claim in Theorem 4.7 has the following implication for the family of contest success functions of the ratio form. Recall that for a ratio-form contest success function, the production functions are $f_i(b) = a_i b_i^\alpha$, for $a_i > 0$ and $\alpha > 0$. These production functions are concave if, and only if, $0 < \alpha \le 1$. For the case $0 < \alpha < 1$, the production cost functions are strictly concave, and thus by Theorem 4.4, there is a unique pure-strategy Nash equilibrium. Since in this case each f_i satisfies the condition $f_i'(0) = +\infty$, by Theorem 4.7, in the pure-strategy Nash equilibrium every player invests a strictly positive effort. On the other hand, for the case $\alpha = 1$, there exist pure-strategy Nash equilibria in which some players invest a zero effort. A full characterization of pure-strategy Nash equilibria in this case is provided in Section 4.4. An obvious implication is that for any anonymous general-logit contest success function such that the production function f satisfies $f'(0) = \infty$, every player invests a strictly positive effort in any pure-strategy Nash equilibrium.

For the broad class of contests with general-logit contest success functions, there is a non-trivial upper bound on the invested effort for each player that holds in any pure-strategy Nash equilibrium. To show this, let us define $\phi_i(x) = f_i(x)/f_i'(x)$, for $i \in N$. Note that $\phi_i(x)$ is an increasing function for any production function $f_i(x)$ that is increasing and concave.

Theorem 4.8. *Consider an n-player contest with valuation parameters $v_1 \ge v_2 \ge \cdots \ge v_n > 0$ and contest success functions that are of general-logit form with production functions such that f_i assumed to be increasing, continuously differentiable, and concave with $f_i(0) = 0$, for $i \in N$. Then, in any pure-strategy Nash equilibrium, the* *individual efforts satisfy*

$$0 \leq b_i \leq \phi_i^{-1}\left(\frac{v_i}{4}\right), \quad \text{for } i \in N$$

where ϕ_i^{-1} is the inverse function of ϕ_i. This implies $b_i \leq v_i/4$, for every $i \in N$.

Proof. From (4.17), if $b_i > 0$, then

$$v_i x_i(\mathbf{b})(1 - x_i(\mathbf{b})) = \phi_i(b_i). \tag{4.25}$$

From this observe that $v_i/4 \geq \phi_i(b_i)$ because $0 \leq x_i(\mathbf{b}) \leq 1$ and $x(1-x) \leq 1/4$ for every $x \in \mathbf{R}$. Since $\phi_i(x)$ is an increasing function, it follows that $b_i \leq \phi_i^{-1}(v_i/4)$, which proves the first claim.

The second claim is immediate from the assumption that $f_i(x)$ is an increasing concave, continuously differentiable function and $f_i(0) = 0$:

$$\phi_i(b_i) = \frac{f_i(b_i)}{f_i'(b_i)} \geq \frac{f_i'(b_i)b_i}{f_i'(b_i)} = b_i,$$

which combined with the first claim of the theorem $v_i/4 \geq \phi_i(b_i)$ establishes the second claim of the theorem. □

Theorem 4.8 implies that in every pure-strategy Nash equilibrium, the maximum individual effort is at most one-quarter of the largest valuation. If the player with the largest valuation is non-unique, i.e., $v_1 = v_2$, then the maximum individual effort is at most $v_2/4$. Compare this with the standard all-pay contest for which in Corollary 2.17 we observed the expected maximum individual effort to be at least $v_2/2$ in any mixed-strategy Nash equilibrium.

4.4 Proportional Allocation

In this section we shall consider contests with the contest success functions according to proportional allocation. This prize allocation mechanism has attracted considerable attention in the literature. In part of our analysis, we shall allow for utility functions $u_i : \mathbf{R}_+ \to \mathbf{R}_+$ to be strictly increasing, concave, and such that $u_i(0) = 0$. Doing so accommodates, as a special case, linear utility functions $u_i(x) = v_i x$, for $v_i > 0$. We devote particular attention to linear utility functions, for which we provide an explicit characterization of a pure-strategy Nash equilibrium. The payoff functions of the players are given by

$$s_i(\mathbf{b}) = \begin{cases} u_i\left(\frac{b_i}{\sum_{j \in N} b_j}\right) - b_i, & \text{if } b_i > 0 \\ u_i(0), & \text{if } b_i = 0 \end{cases}, \quad \text{for } i \in N. \tag{4.26}$$

4.4.1 Two Players

Theorem 4.9. *Consider a two-player contest with valuation parameters $v_1 \geq v_2 > 0$ where a unit prize is allocated according to proportional allocation. Then, there is a unique pure-strategy Nash equilibrium $\mathbf{b} = (b_1, b_2)$ that satisfies the following properties.*

(i) *The individual efforts:*

$$b_1 = v_2 \left(\frac{v_1}{v_1 + v_2} \right)^2 \text{ and } b_2 = \frac{v_2}{v_1} b_1.$$

(ii) *The winning probabilities:*

$$x_1(\mathbf{b}) = \frac{v_1}{v_1 + v_2} \text{ and } x_2(\mathbf{b}) = \frac{v_2}{v_1 + v_2}.$$

(iii) *The payoffs:*

$$s_1(\mathbf{b}) = v_1 \left(\frac{v_1}{v_1 + v_2} \right)^2 \text{ and } s_2(\mathbf{b}) = v_2 \left(\frac{v_2}{v_1 + v_2} \right)^2.$$

(iv) *The total effort:*

$$R = v_2 \frac{v_1}{v_1 + v_2}.$$

(v) *The maximum individual effort:*

$$R_1 = v_2 \left(\frac{v_1}{v_1 + v_2} \right)^2.$$

(vi) *The social efficiency:*

$$1 - \frac{v_2}{v_1} \left(1 - \frac{v_2}{v_1} \right) \frac{v_1}{v_1 + v_2}.$$

(vii) *The competitive balance:*

$$\frac{x_2(\mathbf{b})}{x_1(\mathbf{b})} = \frac{v_2}{v_1}.$$

The proof of Theorem 4.9 is left to the reader as Exercise 4.3.

The winning probabilities and the payoffs are proportional to the valuation parameters of the players. The worst-case social efficiency is for the ratio of the valuations $v_2/v_1 = \sqrt{2} - 1$ and is equal to $\sqrt{2}(2 - \sqrt{2}) \approx 83\%$. It is interesting to compare this with the corresponding quantities in the mixed-strategy Nash equilibrium of the game where the prize is allocated as in the standard all-pay contest, which we considered in Theorem 2.3. For the purpose of our discussion, we shall refer to player 1 as the high-ability player and to player 2 as the low-ability player. The effort of the high-ability player is strictly increasing in his or her ability while the expected effort of the high-ability player under the standard all-pay contest is insensitive to his or her ability. The effort of the low-ability player decreases with the ability of the high-ability player, which goes in the same direction as for the expected effort of the low-ability player under the standard all-pay contest. The total effort is strictly increasing with the ability of the high-ability player, which stands in sharp contrast to the standard all-pay contest, where the expected total effort is decreasing in the ability of the high-ability player. If the asymmetry between the valuation parameters is sufficiently large, the total effort is larger than the expected total effort in the standard all-pay contest.

4.4.2 Existence, Uniqueness, and Characterization of a Nash Equilibrium

Theorem 4.10. *Assume that the number of players n is two or more and the utility functions in (4.26) are such that u_i is strictly increasing, concave, and continuously differentiable, for every player $i \in N$. Then, there exists a unique pure-strategy Nash equilibrium $\mathbf{b} \in \mathbf{R}_+^n$ that satisfies $\sum_{i \in N} b_i > 0$ and $x_i = b_i / \sum_{j \in N} b_j$ where x_i are the winning probabilities that are a unique solution of the following convex optimization problem:*

$$
\begin{aligned}
\text{maximize} \quad & \sum_{i \in N} \hat{u}_i(x_i) \\
\text{subject to} \quad & \sum_{i \in N} x_i \leq 1 \\
& x_i \geq 0, \ i \in N
\end{aligned}
\tag{4.27}
$$

where

$$
\hat{u}_i(x_i) = (1 - x_i) u_i(x_i) + x_i \left(\frac{1}{x_i} \int_0^{x_i} u_i(z)\, dz \right) \text{ for } i \in N.
$$

For the special case of linear utility functions $u_i(x_i) = v_i x_i$, we have

$$
\hat{u}_i(x_i) = v_i x_i \left(1 - \frac{1}{2} x_i \right).
\tag{4.28}
$$

Proof. The proof follows by the following claims. □

Claim 4.11. If $\mathbf{b} \in \mathbf{R}_+^n$ is a pure-strategy Nash equilibrium, then at least two elements of $\mathbf{b}$ are strictly positive.

Consider a vector of efforts $\mathbf{b}$ such that $b_j = 0$ for all $j \neq i$, for an arbitrarily fixed player $i \in N$. If $b_i > 0$, then player i receives the same allocation by reducing b_i slightly and thus increases his or her payoff, so such a vector cannot be a pure-strategy Nash equilibrium. If $b_i = 0$, then player i can increase his or her payoff by investing an infinitesimally small amount because the utility function u_i is strictly increasing. Thus, for every pure-strategy Nash equilibrium $\mathbf{b}$, it must be that $b_j > 0$ for some $j \neq i$. Since this holds for every player $i \in N$, at least two elements of the vector $\mathbf{b}$ must be strictly positive.

Claim 4.12. If $\mathbf{b} \in \mathbf{R}_+^n$ has at least two strictly positive elements, then the payoff function $s_i(b_i, \mathbf{b}_{-i})$ is strictly concave and continuously differentiable in b_i, for all fixed $\mathbf{b}_{-i}$.

From (4.26), $s_i(\mathbf{b}) = u_i(b_i / (b_i + \sum_{j \neq i} b_j)) - b_i$. By Claim 4.11, $\sum_{j \neq i} b_j > 0$ and thus $b_i / (b_i + \sum_{j \neq i} b_j)$ is an increasing function of b_i. Claim 4.12 then follows from the assumption that u_i is an increasing concave and differentiable function.

Claim 4.13. A vector $\mathbf{b}$ is a pure-strategy Nash equilibrium if, and only if, at least two elements of $\mathbf{b}$ are strictly positive, and for each $i \in N$,

$$
\begin{aligned}
u_i'\left(\frac{b_i}{\sum_{j \in N} b_j} \right)\left(1 - \frac{b_i}{\sum_{j \in N} b_j} \right) &= \sum_{j \in N} b_j, \quad \text{if } b_i > 0 \\
u_i'(0) &\leq \sum_{j \in N} b_j, \quad \text{if } b_i = 0.
\end{aligned}
\tag{4.29}
$$

Let **b** be a pure-strategy Nash equilibrium. By Claim 4.12, $s_i(b'_i, \mathbf{b}_{-i})$ is strictly concave and continuously differentiable in b'_i. Thus, b_i must be a unique maximizer of $s_i(b'_i, \mathbf{b}_{-i})$ over $b'_i \geq 0$, and must satisfy

$$\frac{\partial}{\partial b_i} s_i(\mathbf{b}) = 0, \quad \text{if } b_i > 0 \quad \text{and} \quad \frac{\partial}{\partial b_i} s_i(\mathbf{b}) \leq 0, \quad \text{if } b_i = 0.$$

By plugging in (4.26) and multiplying by $\sum_{j \in N} b_j$, we obtain the asserted conditions.

Claim 4.14. Function $\hat{u}_i$ is strictly concave and increasing on $[0, 1]$.

This is easily observed from $\hat{u}'_i(x_i) = (1 - x_i)u'_i(x_i)$. Since u_i is strictly increasing, we have $u'_i(x_i) > 0$, and thus $\hat{u}_i$ is strictly increasing on $[0, 1]$. Since u_i is concave, u'_i is decreasing, and thus $\hat{u}'_i$ is strictly decreasing on $[0, 1]$, i.e., strictly concave on $[0, 1]$.

Claim 4.15. There exists a unique vector **x** and $\lambda > 0$ such that

$$\begin{aligned} (1 - x_i)u'_i(x_i) &= \lambda, \quad \text{if } b_i > 0, \\ u'_i(0) &\leq \lambda, \quad \text{if } b_i = 0, \\ \sum_{j \in N} x_j &= 1, \end{aligned} \tag{4.30}$$

and **x** is a unique solution to (4.27).

By Claim 4.14, $\hat{u}_i$ is continuous and strictly concave over the convex, compact feasible set for every $i \in N$; thus (4.27) has a unique solution. This solution satisfies the optimality conditions that consist of the first two relations in (4.30) and $\sum_{j \in N} x_j \leq 1$. Because $\hat{u}_i$ is strictly increasing for every player i, the last relation in (4.30) must hold. The uniqueness of λ follows because at least one x_i must be strictly positive at the unique solution of (4.27).

Claim 4.16. If $(\mathbf{x}, \lambda)$ satisfies (4.30), then $\mathbf{b} = \lambda \mathbf{x}$ is a pure-strategy Nash equilibrium.

From $\mathbf{b} = \lambda \mathbf{x}$ and the last relation in (4.30), we obtain

$$\lambda = \sum_{i \in N} b_i \quad \text{and} \quad x_i = \frac{b_i}{\sum_{j \in N} b_j}. \tag{4.31}$$

Substituting these into (4.30), we obtain the pure-strategy Nash equilibrium conditions in (4.29).

Claim 4.17. If **b** is a pure-strategy Nash equilibrium, then **x** and λ defined by (4.31) are the unique solution of (4.30).

This is a converse to the statement under Claim 4.16, which can be established by reversing the arguments used to show Claim 4.16.

Claim 4.18. There exists a unique pure-strategy Nash equilibrium **b**, and the vector **x** defined by (4.31) is the unique solution of the optimization problem (4.27).

The existence follows from Claims 4.15 and 4.16, while its uniqueness follows from Claim 4.17. The assertion that **x** is a solution to (4.27) follows from Claims 4.15 and 4.17.

4.4.3 Linear Utility Functions

An explicit characterization of the pure-strategy Nash equilibrium can be obtained for the case of linear utility functions by solving the optimization problem (4.27).

Theorem 4.19. *Consider an n-player contest with two or more players and valuation parameters $v_1 \geq v_2 \geq \cdots \geq v_n > 0$ where a unit prize is awarded according to proportional allocation. Then, there is a unique pure-strategy Nash equilibrium that is specified as follows:*

$$b_i = \begin{cases} \left(1 - \frac{1}{\hat{n}}\right) \bar{v}(\mathbf{v}) \left(1 - \left(1 - \frac{1}{\hat{n}}\right) \bar{v}(\mathbf{v})\frac{1}{v_i}\right), & \text{for } i = 1, 2, \ldots, \hat{n} \\ 0, & \text{otherwise} \end{cases}$$

where

$$\hat{n} = \max \left\{ i \in N \mid v_i > \frac{i-2}{\sum_{j=1}^{i-1} \frac{1}{v_j}} \right\} \tag{4.32}$$

and

$$\bar{v}(\mathbf{v}) = \frac{\hat{n}}{\sum_{i=1}^{\hat{n}} \frac{1}{v_i}}.$$

Proof. From (4.27) and (4.28), a necessary and sufficient optimality condition is that there exists $\lambda > 0$ such that

$$v_i(1 - x_i) = \lambda, \quad \text{if } x_i > 0, \tag{4.33}$$

$$v_i \leq \lambda, \quad \text{if } x_i = 0. \tag{4.34}$$

Thus, $x_i > 0$ for $i = 1, 2, \ldots, \hat{n}$ and $x_i = 0$, otherwise, for some integer $1 \leq \hat{n} \leq n$. Combining this observation with (4.33) and $\sum_{i \in N} x_i = 1$, we obtain

$$\lambda = \left(1 - \frac{1}{\hat{n}}\right) \bar{v}(\mathbf{v}). \tag{4.35}$$

Therefore,

$$x_i = \begin{cases} 1 - \left(1 - \frac{1}{\hat{n}}\right) \frac{\bar{v}(\mathbf{v})}{v_i}, & \text{if } i = 1, 2, \ldots, \hat{n} \\ 0, & \text{otherwise.} \end{cases}$$

Now, using (4.34) and (4.35), $\hat{n}$ is given as asserted in the theorem.

For the last step, by Claim 4.16, $\mathbf{b} = \lambda \mathbf{x}$ is the pure-strategy Nash equilibrium. $\square$

As a corollary of the last theorem, we have the following two properties that hold for every pure-strategy Nash equilibrium.

Corollary 4.20. *In every pure-strategy Nash equilibrium, (i) there are at least two active players, i.e., $\hat{n} \geq 2$, and (ii) for each active player, the valuation parameter is at least half of the second largest valuation parameter, i.e., $v_i \geq v_2/2$, for all $i = 1, 2, \ldots, \hat{n}$.*

Total Effort

The total effort in the pure-strategy Nash equilibrium admits the following closed-form expression that is obtained by summing up the individual equilibrium efforts in Theorem 4.19:

$$R(\mathbf{v}) = \left(1 - \frac{1}{\hat{n}}\right) \bar{v}(\mathbf{v}). \qquad (4.36)$$

In other words, the expected total effort is equal to the product of $1 - 1/\hat{n}$ and the harmonic mean of the valuation parameters of active players.

We next show simple lower and upper bounds for the total effort.

Corollary 4.21. *The total effort in the pure-strategy Nash equilibrium satisfies $v_{\hat{n}+1} \le R < v_{\hat{n}}$. Since the number of active players $\hat{n}$ is two or more, $R < v_2$.*

Proof. By the definition of $\hat{n}$ in (4.32), we have

$$v_{\hat{n}+1} \le \frac{\hat{n} - 1}{\sum_{j=1}^{\hat{n}} \frac{1}{v_j}} = R,$$

which establishes the lower bound.

The upper bound is established as follows. Again, by the definition of $\hat{n}$ in (4.32), we have

$$v_{\hat{n}} > \frac{\hat{n} - 2}{\sum_{j=1}^{\hat{n}-1} \frac{1}{v_j}}.$$

By multiplying both sides of the last equation with $\sum_{j=1}^{\hat{n}-1} 1/v_j$ and adding $v_{\hat{n}}/v_{\hat{n}} = 1$ to both sides, it follows that

$$v_{\hat{n}} > \frac{\hat{n} - 1}{\sum_{j=1}^{\hat{n}} \frac{1}{v_j}} = R,$$

which establishes the upper bound. □

Corollary 4.22. *For every given valuation vector for two or more players, the total effort in the pure-strategy Nash equilibrium is at least half of the second highest valuation, i.e.,*

$$R \ge \frac{1}{2}v_2.$$

Proof. Consider the conditions (4.33) and (4.34) for a vector of efforts $\mathbf{b}$ to be a pure-strategy Nash equilibrium, where $\mathbf{b} = \lambda\mathbf{x}$ and $\lambda = R$. Suppose first that (4.33) holds for player 2. By condition (4.33) and the assumption $v_1 \ge v_2$, it follows that $x_2 \le x_1$, which in turn, combined with $\sum_{i \in N} x_i = 1$, implies $x_2 \le 1/2$. Using this along with (4.33), we obtain

$$R = v_2(1 - x_2) \ge \frac{1}{2}v_2.$$

Suppose now that (4.34) holds for player 2. Since in this case $b_2 = 0$, we have $x_2 = 0$, and thus from (4.34) we immediately obtain $R \geq v_2$, which implies the asserted lower bound. $\hspace{1cm} \square$

An important implication of the last two corollaries is that under proportional allocation, the total effort in a pure-strategy Nash equilibrium is within constant factors of the second highest valuation. A similar type of guarantee is shown to hold in expectation for the standard all-pay contest in Chapter 2, where in any mixed-strategy Nash equilibrium, the expected total effort is within constant factors of the second highest valuation.

Total Effort Cannot Be Increased by Exclusion

For the standard all-pay contest, there exist valuation vectors under which the contest owner can earn a larger expected total effort by excluding some of the players from participation, and this exclusion may even involve a player of the highest ability (see Exercise 2.4). We shall show that exclusion is never beneficial when a prize is awarded according to proportional allocation. Suppose that the contest owner shortlists a set of players to compete in the contest, and let $\mathbf{z} \in \{0, 1\}^n$ indicate the subset of selected players: $z_i = 1$ if player i is selected and $z_i = 0$ otherwise. By (4.36), the total effort in the pure-strategy Nash equilibrium of the contest with the set of contestants given by $\mathbf{z}$ is

$$R(\mathbf{z}) = \frac{\sum_{i=1}^{n} z_i - 1}{\sum_{i=1}^{n} \frac{1}{v_i} z_i}.$$

The problem of maximizing the total effort in a pure-strategy Nash equilibrium corresponds to the following integer programming problem:

$$\begin{aligned} \text{maximize} \quad & R(\mathbf{z}) \\ \text{over} \quad & \mathbf{z} \in \{0, 1\}^n \end{aligned} \tag{4.37}$$

Corollary 4.23. *For any valuation vector for two or more players under proportional allocation, the largest total effort in the pure-strategy Nash equilibrium is achieved when all players are allowed to compete.*

Proof. We find an optimal solution of the integer programming problem (4.37) in two steps. In the first step, we fix an integer $m \in \{1, \dots, n\}$ and solve the given optimization problem subject to the constraint $\sum_{i=1}^{n} z_i = m$. In the second step, we optimize over the value of m. For the first step, it is obvious that an optimal solution is $z_i = 1$ for $i = 1, 2, \dots, m$ and $z_i = 0$ otherwise. In the second step, we must maximize the function $g(m) = (m - 1)/\sum_{i=1}^{m} 1/v_i$ over $m \in \{1, 2, \dots, n\}$. Note that

$$g(m) - g(m - 1) > 0 \Leftrightarrow v_m > \frac{m - 2}{\sum_{i=1}^{m-1} \frac{1}{v_i}}.$$

Combining with the definition of $\hat{n}$ in (4.32), it follows that function $g(m)$ is maximized at $m = \hat{n}$. This shows that it is optimal to restrict the set of participants to the set of active players in the pure-strategy Nash equilibrium in a contest where all players are allowed to compete, i.e., $z_i = 1$, for $i = 1, 2, \dots, \hat{n}$, and $z_i = 0$ otherwise. In this case, the total effort is exactly equal to that in the case where all players are allowed to compete, so an optimal solution is to let all players compete.   □

Under restrictions of participation to a subset of two or more players with largest values of valuation parameters, the lowest total effort in a pure-strategy Nash equilibrium is achieved by restricting the participation to a pair of players with the largest values of the valuation parameters. This is in contrast to the standard-all pay contest, where in Corollary 2.10, we found that the largest expected total effort is achieved in the mixed-strategy Nash equilibrium where the set of active players consists of a pair of players with the largest values of the valuation parameters.

Maximum Individual Effort

From the characterization of the pure-strategy Nash equilibrium in Theorem 4.19, we observe that the maximum individual effort corresponds to the individual effort of a player of the highest valuation, and by definition player 1 is always one such player. Combining this with (4.36), the maximum individual effort can be represented as follows:

$$R_1(\mathbf{v}) = R(\mathbf{v}) \left(1 - \frac{R(\mathbf{v})}{v_1} \right). \tag{4.38}$$

The maximum individual effort is not guaranteed to be within constant factors of the total effort. This can be seen already for the simple case of an n-player contest with symmetric valuation parameters $\mathbf{v} = (1, 1, \ldots, 1)$. Under this valuation vector, the total effort is $R(\mathbf{v}) = 1 - 1/n$, while the maximum individual effort is $R_1(\mathbf{v}) = (1 - 1/n)/n$. Hence, $R_1(\mathbf{v})/R(\mathbf{v}) = 1/n$, which can be made arbitrarily small by taking a large enough number of players n. This is unlike the guarantee provided by the standard all-pay contest that, in every mixed-strategy Nash equilibrium, the expected maximum individual effort is at least half of the expected total effort, which we established in Corollary 2.18.

The exclusion of some players from the competition can be beneficial with respect to the maximum individual effort. As a simple example, note that by excluding from participation all but a pair of players with the largest valuation parameters, the maximum individual effort is guaranteed to be larger than or equal to $v_2/4$. We already observed that there exist valuation vectors with the value of v_2 fixed, for which the maximum individual effort can be made arbitrarily small when all players are allowed to participate.

4.4.4 Social Welfare

When a prize is allocated according to proportional allocation, it is not necessarily assigned fully to the player who values it the most, so there is in general some social efficiency loss. However, this efficiency loss is bounded for a broad class of utility functions.

Theorem 4.24. *Assume that utility functions u_i are increasing, concave, and continuously differentiable, and $u_i(0) = 0$, for all $i \in N$. Then, the social welfare in the pure-strategy Nash equilibrium is at least $3/4$ of the maximum social welfare.*

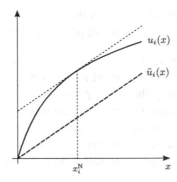

Figure 4.4. Linear utility function $\tilde{u}_i$ derived from the utility function u_i.

This bound is tight: for every $\epsilon > 0$, there exists an instance with a sufficiently large number of players and (linear) utility functions such that the social welfare in the pure-strategy Nash equilibrium is at most $3/4 + \epsilon$ of the maximum social welfare.

A worst case is for linear utility functions $u_i(x) = v_i x$ with the valuation vector such that $v_1 = 1$ and $v_2 = \cdots = v_n = 1/2$, and a sufficiently large number of players n. Such a valuation vector with a unique high-ability player and all other players of some common lower ability often arises as a worst case with respect to the social efficiency; we have already encountered such a valuation vector as the worst case in Section 2.1.9 for the standard all-pay contest. For the given valuation vector, under proportional allocation, the winning probability of the high-ability player is $x_1 = n/(2n-1)$, while the winning probabilities of other players are $x_i = 1/(2n-1)$, for $i = 2, 3, \ldots, n$. For the given valuation vector, the social efficiency goes to $3/4$ asymptotically as the number of players n grows, which is left to the reader as Exercise 4.8.

Proof. The proof rests on two key observations. The first observation is that the necessary and sufficient condition (4.30) for an allocation $\mathbf{x}^N$ to be a pure-strategy Nash equilibrium involves only first derivatives of utility functions u_i, for $i \in N$. From this, we have the following lemma.

Lemma 4.25. *The pure-strategy Nash equilibrium allocation $\mathbf{x}^N$ corresponds to that of a new game with linear utility functions $\tilde{u}_i(x_i) = v_i x_i$, where $v_i = u_i'(x_i^N)$, for $i \in N$. See Figure 4.4.*

The second observation is noted in the following lemma.

Lemma 4.26. *Suppose that $u_i(0) \geq 0$, for all $i \in N$, and let $\mathbf{x}^S$ be any socially optimal allocation. Then, for any feasible allocation $\mathbf{x}$, i.e., such that $\mathbf{x} \in \mathbf{R}_+^n$ and $\sum_{j \in N} x_j \leq 1$, we have*

$$\frac{\sum_{i \in N} u_i(x_i)}{\sum_{i \in N} u_i(x_i^S)} \geq \frac{\sum_{i \in N} u_i'(x_i)x_i}{\max_{i \in N} u_i'(x_i)}.$$

Proof. By the assumption that each utility function is continuously differentiable and concave, we have $u_i(x_i^S) \leq u_i(x_i) + u_i'(x_i)(x_i^S - x_i)$, for all $x_i \geq 0$ and $i \in N$. From this, it follows that

$$\frac{\sum_{i \in N} u_i(x_i)}{\sum_{i \in N} u_i(x_i^S)} \geq \frac{\sum_{i \in N}(u_i(x_i) - u_i'(x_i)x_i) + \sum_{i \in N} u_i'(x_i)x_i}{\sum_{i \in N}(u_i(x_i) - u_i'(x_i)x_i) + \sum_{i \in N} u_i'(x_i)x_i^S}.$$

Since $\sum_{i \in N} x_i^S = 1$,

$$\sum_{i \in N} u_i'(x_i) x_i^S \leq \max_{i \in N} u_i'(x_i).$$

Therefore,

$$\frac{\sum_{i \in N} u_i(x_i)}{\sum_{i \in N} u_i(x_i^S)} \geq \frac{\sum_{i \in N}(u_i(x_i) - u_i'(x_i)x_i) + \sum_{i \in N} u_i'(x_i)x_i}{\sum_{i \in N}(u_i(x_i) - u_i'(x_i)x_i) + \max_{i \in N} u_i'(x_i)}.$$

Again, invoking the concavity of the utility functions and together with the assumption that $u_i(0) \geq 0$, we have $u_i'(x_i)x_i \leq u_i(x_i)$, for all $x_i \geq 0$, and thus $\sum_{i \in N}(u_i(x_i) - u_i'(x_i)x_i) \geq 0$. Therefore we conclude that

$$\frac{\sum_{i \in N} u_i(x_i)}{\sum_{i \in N} u_i(x_i^S)} \geq \frac{\sum_{i \in N} u_i'(x_i)x_i}{\max_{i \in N} u_i'(x_i)}$$

which completes the proof. □

We see from Lemma 4.25 and Lemma 4.26 that to study the worst-case social efficiency, it suffices to consider only linear utility functions. The rest of the proof amounts to identifying a set of linear utility functions that yield the smallest social efficiency. Given a valuation vector $\mathbf{v}$, let $\mathbf{x}^N(\mathbf{v})$ be the allocation in a pure-strategy Nash equilibrium and $\mathbf{x}^S(\mathbf{v})$ be a socially optimal allocation. From Lemma 4.26, we observe that

$$\frac{\sum_{i \in N} u_i(x_i^N(\mathbf{v}))}{\sum_{i \in N} u_i(x_i^S(\mathbf{v}))} \geq \min_{\mathbf{a} \in \mathbf{R}_+^n} \sum_{i \in N} \frac{a_i}{\max_{j \in N} a_j} x_i^N(\mathbf{a}). \tag{4.39}$$

Without loss of generality, let us assume $1 = a_1 \geq a_2 \geq \cdots \geq a_n > 0$. Using the characterization of the pure-strategy Nash equilibrium in Theorem 4.19, note that the objective function in the optimization problem in (4.39) corresponds to

$$1 + \sum_{i=2}^{\hat{n}} a_i - \frac{\hat{n}(\hat{n} - 1)}{1 + \sum_{i=2}^{\hat{n}} \frac{1}{a_i}}$$

which we need to minimize over $\mathbf{a} \in \mathbf{R}_+^n$ subject to constraint $1 = a_1 \geq a_2 \geq \cdots \geq a_n > 0$. We are going to do this in two steps. In the first step, we optimize subject to the constraint that $\hat{n}$ is fixed to an integer m such that $1 \leq m \leq n$. In the second step, we optimize over the value of m. Given that the value of $\hat{n}$ is fixed to m, the objective function is a convex function and the function is symmetric, so the optimal solution is such that $a_2 = \cdots = a_m$. Hence, the optimization corresponds to minimizing $\eta_m(a_2)$ over $a_2 \in [0, 1]$, where $\eta_m(a_2) = 1 + (m - 1)a_2 - m/(1/(m - 1) + 1/a_2)$. For every fixed value of $0 < a_2 \leq 1$, the objective function $\eta_m(a_2)$ decreases with m; thus the optimum value of m is n. It follows that the worst-case social efficiency is the solution of the following optimization problem:

$$\begin{aligned} \text{minimize} \quad & \eta_n(a_2) \\ \text{over} \quad & 0 \leq a_2 \leq 1. \end{aligned}$$

There is a unique solution to this problem, which is given as follows:

$$a_2(n) = \sqrt{n - 1}\left(\sqrt{n} - \sqrt{n - 1}\right).$$

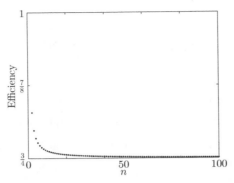

Figure 4.5. Lower bound for the social efficiency under proportional allocation.

The efficiency lower bound follows by showing that $\eta_n(a_2(n)) \geq 3/4$, for all $n \geq 2$, which is implied by the following facts: (i) $a_2(n) \geq 1/2$, for all $n \geq 2$, (ii) $\eta_n(a_2)$ is increasing in a_2, for all $0 < a_2 \leq 1$, and (iii) $\eta_n(1/2) = 1 - (n-1)/[2(2n+1)] \geq 3/4$, for all $n \geq 2$. $\qquad\square$

Under the assumptions of Theorem 4.24, the social efficiency is guaranteed to be at least $3/4$ for any valuation vector of two or more players. Moreover, this is asymptotically achieved for the valuation vector $(1, 1/2, \ldots, 1/2)$ as the number of players n grows large. In the proof of the theorem, we find that for any given number of two or more players n, the social efficiency is at least $\eta_n(v_2(n))$, and this is exactly achieved for the valuation vector $(1, v_2(n), \ldots, v_2(n))$. Figure 4.5 shows this lower bound on the social efficiency.

Polyhedral Resources

In the previous section, we showed that for allocation of a single prize according to proportional allocation, the worst-case social efficiency is at least a strictly positive constant. The single prize contest can be seen as a resource allocation problem where the allocation $x = (x_1, x_2, \ldots, x_n) \in \mathbf{R}_+^n$ must satisfy the simple polyhedral constraint $\sum_{i \in N} x_i \leq 1$. Consider now the case of more general polyhedral resource constraints $\sum_{i \in N} a_{i,j} x_i \leq 1$, for $j = 1, 2, \ldots, m$, for given $(a_{i,j}) \in \mathbf{R}_+^{n \times m}$ and integer $m \geq 1$. Such a generalization is of interest in practice, for example, for allocation of computer and network resources. For the case of general polyhedral resources, the social efficiency of a pure-strategy Nash equilibrium can be arbitrarily small.

Theorem 4.27. *For the case of general polyhedral resources and proportional allocation, there exist instances for which in a pure-strategy Nash equilibrium, the social welfare is $O(1/\sqrt{n})$ of the optimum social welfare.*

Proof. We establish the lower bound for an instance with n players and $n-1$ contests, where each contest offers a unit prize. There are two different types of players: players 1 through $n-1$ all compete in different contests, and player n competes in all $n-1$ contests. See Figure 4.6 for an illustration.

A vector of efforts $\mathbf{b}$ such that all individual efforts are equal to 0 is not a pure-strategy Nash equilibrium because any player could increase the payoff by raising

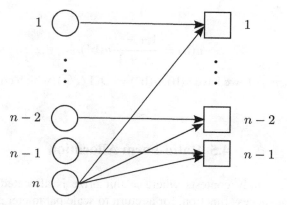

Figure 4.6. An instance with n players and $n-1$ contests.

his or her effort. It must be that $b_n > 0$ because, otherwise, each player $i \neq n$ such that $b_i > 0$ would have a beneficial unilateral deviation to decrease his or her effort investment. Similarly, it must be that $\sum_{j=1}^{n-1} b_j > 0$ because, otherwise, player n could decrease his or her effort for a small enough amount and still receive the prize of 1 at each contest. By the fact $\sum_{j=1}^{n-1} b_j > 0$, it follows that $b_i > 0$, for every $i \neq n$, because otherwise if there exists a player in this set with zero effort, then this player could increase his or her payoff by increasing his or her effort for a small enough amount. Since $x_i(\mathbf{b}) = b_i / \sum_{j=1}^{n} b_j$ and in a pure-strategy Nash equilibrium $x_i(\mathbf{b}) + x_n(\mathbf{b}) = 1$, for all $i \neq n$, we have

$$s_i(\mathbf{b}) = v_i \left(1 - \frac{b_n}{\sum_{j=1}^{n} b_j} \right) - b_i, \quad \text{for } i \neq n, \quad \text{and} \quad s_n(\mathbf{b}) = v_n \frac{b_n}{\sum_{j=1}^{n} b_j} - b_n.$$

Suppose now that the valuation parameters are given by $v_i = 1$ for $i \neq n$ and $v_n = a_n$ for a positive-valued parameter a_n such that $a_n < n - 1$. From condition (4.2), we have $\partial s_i(\mathbf{b})/\partial b_i = 0$, for every $i = 1, 2, \ldots, n$. Since $\partial s_i(\mathbf{b})/\partial b_i = b_n / \sum_{j=1}^{n} b_j - 1$, for $i \neq n$ and $\partial s_n(\mathbf{b})/\partial b_n = a_n \sum_{j=1}^{n-1} b_j / \sum_{j=1}^{n} b_j - 1$, we have

$$a_n \sum_{j=1}^{n-1} b_j = \left(\sum_{j=1}^{n} b_j \right)^2 \quad \text{and} \quad b_n = \left(\sum_{j=1}^{n} b_j \right)^2.$$

From this, we have $b_n = a_n^2/(a_n + 1)^2$ and $\sum_{j=1}^{n-1} b_j = a_n/(a_n + 1)^2$. Therefore,

$$x_i(\mathbf{b}) = \frac{1}{a_n + 1}, \quad \text{for } i \neq n \quad \text{and} \quad x_n(\mathbf{b}) = \frac{a_n}{a_n + 1}.$$

The social welfare in the pure-strategy Nash equilibrium $\mathbf{b}$ is

$$u(\mathbf{b}) = \sum_{i=1}^{n} v_i x_i(\mathbf{b}) = \frac{a_n^2 + n - 1}{a_n + 1}.$$

The optimal social welfare is to allocate fully to players 1 through $n - 1$, and thus

$$u(\mathbf{b}^*) = n - 1.$$

Therefore,

$$u(\mathbf{b}) = \frac{1 + \frac{a_n^2}{n-1}}{a_n + 1} u(\mathbf{b}^*).$$

By taking $a_n = \sqrt{n-1}$, we have $u(\mathbf{b})/u(\mathbf{b}^*) = O(1/\sqrt{n})$, which completes the proof.
□

4.5 Ratio-Form Allocation

In this section we study contests where a unit prize is allocated according to the ratio-form contest success function, for a return to scale parameter $\alpha > 0$,

$$x_i(\mathbf{b}) = \frac{b_i^\alpha}{\sum_{j=1}^n b_j^\alpha}, \quad \text{for } i \in N,$$

whenever $\sum_{j \in N} b_j > 0$, and $x_i(\mathbf{b}) = 1/n$, for $i \in N$, otherwise.

This form of a contest success function has been studied by many in the context of rent-seeking and public choice, where it is often referred to as Tullock contest success function.

4.5.1 Two Players

Theorem 4.28. *Consider the game that models a two-player all-pay contest with valuation parameters $v_1 \geq v_2 > 0$ under a ratio-form contest success function with the return to scale parameter $\alpha > 0$. Then, there exists a pure-strategy Nash equilibrium if, and only if,*

$$\alpha \leq 1 + \left(\frac{v_2}{v_1}\right)^\alpha. \tag{4.40}$$

Moreover, if a pure-strategy Nash equilibrium exists, it is unique and is characterized as follows.

(i) *The individual efforts:*

$$b_1 = v_1 \frac{\alpha \left(\frac{v_1}{v_2}\right)^\alpha}{\left(\left(\frac{v_1}{v_2}\right)^\alpha + 1\right)^2} \text{ and } b_2 = v_2 \frac{\alpha \left(\frac{v_1}{v_2}\right)^\alpha}{\left(\left(\frac{v_1}{v_2}\right)^\alpha + 1\right)^2}.$$

(ii) *The winning probabilities:*

$$x_1(\mathbf{b}) = \frac{v_1^\alpha}{v_1^\alpha + v_2^\alpha} \text{ and } x_2(\mathbf{b}) = \frac{v_2^\alpha}{v_1^\alpha + v_2^\alpha}.$$

(iii) *The total effort:*

$$R = v_1 \left(1 + \frac{v_2}{v_1}\right) \frac{\alpha \left(\frac{v_1}{v_2}\right)^\alpha}{\left(\left(\frac{v_1}{v_2}\right)^\alpha + 1\right)^2}.$$

(iv) *The maximum individual effort:*

$$R_1 = \frac{1}{1 + \frac{v_2}{v_1}} R.$$

(v) *The social efficiency:*

$$1 - \frac{1 - \frac{v_2}{v_1}}{\left(\frac{v_1}{v_2}\right)^{\alpha} + 1}.$$

(vi) *The competitive balance:*

$$\frac{x_2(\mathbf{b})}{x_1(\mathbf{b})} = \left(\frac{v_2}{v_1}\right)^{\alpha}.$$

Proof. First we note that in every pure-strategy Nash equilibrium each player invests a strictly positive effort. If both players invest zero effort, then either of them would increase his or her payoff by unilaterally increasing his or her effort investment to some small strictly positive value. If one of the players invests zero effort, then the other player would have an incentive to reduce any strictly positive effort investment to a smaller value. Hence, it must be that in every pure-strategy Nash equilibrium $\mathbf{b} = (b_1, b_2)$, we have that $b_1 > 0$ and $b_2 > 0$. A necessary condition for $\mathbf{b}$ to be a pure-strategy Nash equilibrium is that for every player i, it either holds $\partial s_i(\mathbf{b})/\partial b_i = 0$ and $b_i > 0$, or $\partial s_i(\mathbf{b})/\partial b_i \leq 0$ and $b_i = 0$. Hence, it follows that a necessary condition is that $\partial s_1(\mathbf{b})/\partial b_1 = 0$ and $\partial s_2(\mathbf{b})/\partial b_2 = 0$. By a simple calculus, this is equivalent to the following two conditions

$$v_1 \alpha \frac{b_1^{\alpha-1} b_2^{\alpha}}{(b_1^{\alpha} + b_2^{\alpha})^2} = 1 \text{ and } v_2 \alpha \frac{b_1^{\alpha} b_2^{\alpha-1}}{(b_1^{\alpha} + b_2^{\alpha})^2} = 1. \tag{4.41}$$

From the last two equations, it follows that

$$\frac{b_1}{v_1} = \frac{b_2}{v_2}. \tag{4.42}$$

Combining with (4.41), we have

$$b_1 = \frac{v_1}{v_2} b_2 \text{ and } b_2 = v_2 \frac{\alpha \left(\frac{v_1}{v_2}\right)^{\alpha}}{\left(1 + \left(\frac{v_1}{v_2}\right)^{\alpha}\right)^2}. \tag{4.43}$$

Since each player is guaranteed a payoff of zero by investing effort of zero value, in every pure-strategy Nash equilibrium $\mathbf{b}$, it is a necessary condition that $s_1(\mathbf{b}) \geq 0$ and $s_2(\mathbf{b}) \geq 0$. Using (4.43), this is equivalent to the condition in (4.40).

The sufficiency of the condition (4.40) is established as follows. By a simple calculus, we have

$$\frac{\partial^2}{\partial b_2^2} s_2(\mathbf{b}) = v_2 \alpha \frac{b_1^{\alpha} b_2^{2(\alpha-1)}}{(b_1^{\alpha} + b_2^{\alpha})^3} \left((\alpha - 1)\left(\frac{b_1}{b_2}\right)^{\alpha} - 1 - \alpha\right).$$

From this, note that for every fixed value $b_1 > 0$, the following condition

$$(\alpha - 1)\left(\frac{b_1}{b_2}\right)^{\alpha} \leq 1 \tag{4.44}$$

is a sufficient condition for $\partial^2 s_2(\mathbf{b})/\partial b_2^2 < 0$, i.e. for $s_2(\mathbf{b})$ to be a strictly concave function in b_2. Since in every pure-strategy Nash equilibrium $\mathbf{b} = (b_1, b_2)$, it must hold that $b_1 \geq b_2$, note that condition (4.44) is also a sufficient condition for $s_1(\mathbf{b})$ to be

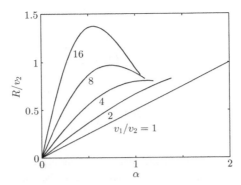

Figure 4.7. Total effort in pure-strategy Nash equilibrium vs. the return to scale parameter α, for five different ratios of the highest and the smallest valuation.

a strictly concave function in b_1, for every fixed value $b_2 > 0$. It follows that under condition (4.44), there exists a pure-strategy Nash equilibrium, and moreover, that it is unique. Combining (4.42) and (4.44), it follows that (4.40) is also a sufficient condition.

The asserted expressions for the winning probabilities, total effort, social efficiency, and competitive balance follow easily from (4.43).

$\square$

A sufficient condition for (4.40) to hold is that $0 < \alpha \leq 1$. This sufficient condition is equivalent to saying that the ratio-form production functions are concave, and we know already from the more general result in Theorem 4.4 that in this case a pure-strategy Nash equilibrium exists. If $\alpha > 1$, condition (4.40) is equivalent to $v_1/v_2 \leq 1/(\alpha - 1)^{1/\alpha}$. Observe that for any fixed value of $\alpha > 1$, the condition fails to hold whenever the asymmetry of the values of the valuation parameters is large enough. This means that condition $0 < \alpha \leq 1$ is necessary to guarantee existence of a pure-strategy Nash equilibrium for all valuation vectors. If $\alpha > 2$, then a pure-strategy Nash equilibrium does not exist for any valuation vector.

It is noteworthy that for each player, the effort invested is proportional to his or her valuation parameter. The effect of the return to scale parameter on the winning probabilities is very much as one would expect: the smaller the parameter α, the more balanced the winning probabilities are. In the limit of small α, the winning probability of each player tends to $1/2$, and thus this limit corresponds to an unbiased lottery. The total effort depends on the parameter α in a more intricate way. If the asymmetry of the valuation parameters is small enough, then the total effort increases with α for all values of α for which a pure-strategy Nash equilibrium exists. On the other hand, if the asymmetry of the valuation parameters is large enough, then the total effort achieves its maximum value at a unique value of α strictly within the interval of values of α for which a pure-strategy Nash equilibrium exists. Moreover, the larger the asymmetry of the valuation parameters, the smaller the value of the parameter α at which the total effort achieves its largest value. Figure 4.7 shows an illustration. There is an intuitive explanation for the last observation: the larger the asymmetry between the abilities of players, the smaller the value of the return to scale parameter needs to be to balance the competition to a level at which the total effort is maximized. Note that, in any case, in the limit of small α, the total effort tends to zero, which is indeed intuitive because in this limit, the prize allocation is virtually an unbiased lottery under which the best response for each player is to invest no effort. The maximum individual effort is equal to the total effort up to a factor that depends on the ratio of the valuation parameters, but not on the return to scale parameter α. Notice that the maximum individual effort is guaranteed to be at least half of the total effort, for all $\alpha > 0$ for which a pure-strategy Nash equilibrium exists. Finally, social efficiency increases with the return to scale parameter α. This is also intuitive: the larger the value of α, the more biased the allocation is to award the prize to the player who invests larger effort, and in the pure-strategy Nash equilibrium, this player is indeed the player with the larger valuation. For the limit of small α, the social efficiency is $(1 + v_2/v_1)/2$, which corresponds to the social efficiency of an unbiased lottery, under which each player is equally likely to win the prize.

4.5.2 Existence and Uniqueness of a Pure-Strategy Nash Equilibrium

Corollary 4.29. *For every contest among two or more players with valuation parameters $v_1 \geq v_2 \geq \cdots \geq v_n > 0$ that awards a unit prize according to a ratio-form contest success function with the return to scale parameter $0 < \alpha \leq 1$, there exists a unique pure-strategy Nash equilibrium.*

This corollary is derived from the results in the preceding sections as follows. Under the assumption that $0 < \alpha \leq 1$, the conditions of Theorem 4.4 are validated, and thus, there exists a pure-strategy Nash equilibrium. From the same theorem, if $0 < \alpha < 1$, there is a unique pure-strategy Nash equilibrium. The remaining case, $\alpha = 1$, corresponds to proportional allocation, and thus by Theorem 4.19, there exists a unique pure-strategy Nash equilibrium in this case as well.

4.5.3 Total Effort

Corollary 4.30. *Consider a two-player all-pay contest with valuation parameters $v_1 \geq v_2 > 0$ and a ratio-form contest success function with the return to scale parameter $0 < \alpha \leq 1$. Then, in the unique pure-strategy Nash equilibrium, the total effort satisfies*

$$R \geq \frac{\alpha}{2} v_2.$$

Furthermore, this bound is tight: it is achieved for two players with identical valuations.

Proof. The assertion follows from the following series of inequalities:

$$\frac{R}{v_2} = (1 + v_1/v_2) \frac{\alpha(v_1/v_2)^\alpha}{(1 + (v_1/v_2)^\alpha)^2} \geq \alpha \frac{(v_1/v_2)^\alpha}{1 + (v_1/v_2)^\alpha} \geq \frac{\alpha}{2}.$$

$\square$

In the remainder of this section, we shall consider the following question: what is the largest total effort that a contest owner can extract in a pure-strategy Nash equilibrium under a ratio-form contest success function? In Section 4.5.1, we noted that there exists a unique value of the return to scale parameter that maximizes the total effort in a pure-strategy Nash equilibrium. The return to scale parameter provides a means to make the competition more balanced in the case of asymmetric valuation parameters and to achieve a higher total effort. We shall show that the total effort in a pure-strategy Nash equilibrum under a ratio-form contest success function is not guaranteed to be within constant factors of the highest valuation. Specifically, there exists a constant $C > 0$ such that

$$\frac{R}{v_1} \leq C \frac{1}{\log(v_1/v_2)}, \quad \text{for every large enough } v_1/v_2.$$

Theorem 4.31. *Consider a two-player contest with valuation parameters $v_1 \geq v_2 > 0$ that awards a unit prize according to a ratio-form contest success function with the return to scale parameter α such that the necessary and sufficient condition (4.40) for the existence of a pure-strategy Nash equilibrium holds. Then, the total effort in the pure-strategy Nash equilibrium satisfies*

$$\frac{R}{v_1 + v_2} \leq \psi(v_1/v_2) \tag{4.45}$$

where

$$\psi(x) = \begin{cases} 1 - \frac{1}{\vartheta(x)}, & \text{if } x \leq \theta \\ \frac{C}{\log(x)}, & \text{otherwise} \end{cases}$$

and where $\vartheta(x)$ is given by $\vartheta = 1 + (1/x)^\vartheta$, $\theta = (1+a)^{\frac{1+a}{2+a}}$, $C = (1+a)/(a(a+2))$, and a is the unique solution of $\log(a + 1) = 1 + 2/a$.

Furthermore, the upper bound is tight: for the case $v_1/v_2 \leq \theta$, it is achieved asymptotically as α tends to $\vartheta(v_1/v_2)$ from below, and otherwise, it is achieved for $\alpha = \log(1 + a)/\log(v_1/v_2)$.

The upper bound in Theorem 4.31 implies an upper bound for the maximum individual effort, because by Theorem 4.28 we have that $R_1/v_1 = R/(v_1 + v_2)$.

Proof. Let us define $\rho = v_1/v_2$. From Theorem 4.28, it follows that $R/(v_1 + v_2) = R_1/v_1 = f_\rho(\alpha)$, where

$$f_\rho(\alpha) = \frac{\alpha \rho^\alpha}{(\rho^\alpha + 1)^2}.$$

We need to consider the following optimization problem:

$$\begin{aligned} \text{maximize} \quad & f_\rho(\alpha) \\ \text{over} \quad & 0 \leq \alpha \leq 1 + (1/\rho)^\alpha. \end{aligned} \tag{4.46}$$

For the unconstrained version of the problem, the optimum value α is the solution of

$$\frac{d}{d\alpha} \log f_\rho(\alpha) = \frac{1}{\alpha} + \log(\rho) - 2\frac{\log(\rho)\rho^\alpha}{1 + \rho^\alpha} = 0,$$

which is equivalent to

$$\log(\rho^\alpha) = 1 + \frac{2}{\rho^\alpha - 1}.$$

Using the notation $a = \rho^\alpha - 1$ we note that $a > 0$ is the unique solution of

$$\log(1 + a) = 1 + 2/a. \tag{4.47}$$

Hence, for the unconstrained version of the problem, the optimum value of the return to scale parameter is

$$\alpha^* = \frac{\log(1+a)}{\log(\rho)}. \tag{4.48}$$

We now consider the effect of the constraint in the optimization problem (4.46). Note that the constraint in (4.46) is equivalent to $\alpha \le \vartheta(\rho)$. Therefore, if $\alpha^* \le \vartheta(\rho)$, then α^* is the solution, and otherwise, $\vartheta(\rho)$ is the solution to the problem (4.46). Notice that $\log(\rho) = -\log(\vartheta(\rho) - 1)/\vartheta(\rho)$, and using this along with (4.48) note that $\alpha^* \le \vartheta(\rho)$ is equivalent to $\vartheta(\rho) \le 1 + 1/(1+a)$. Since $\vartheta(\rho)$ is decreasing in ρ, we have that $\alpha^* \le \vartheta(\rho)$ is equivalent to $\rho \ge (1+a)^{(1+a)/(2+a)}$, where the right-hand side in the last inequality corresponds to the definition of θ in the theorem.

For the case $\rho \ge \theta$, the maximizer is α^* and by using (4.48) and (4.47), we obtain $f_\rho(\alpha^*)/(v_1 + v_2) = C/\log(\rho)$. Otherwise, for the case $\rho < \theta$, the maximizer is $\vartheta(\rho)$ and we obtain $f_\rho(\vartheta(\rho))/(v_1 + v_2) = 1 - 1/\vartheta(\rho)$. This completes the proof of the theorem. $\qquad\square$

In the discussion following Theorem 4.28, we noted that to guarantee existence of a pure-strategy Nash equilibrium for all valuation vectors, it is necessary that $0 \le \alpha \le 1$. It is thus of interest to consider what is the largest total effort that can be achieved in a pure-strategy Nash equilibrium subject to the additional constraint $0 \le \alpha \le 1$. The answer to this question is provided in the following corollary.

Corollary 4.32. *Consider a two-player contest with valuation parameters $v_1 \ge v_2 > 0$ that awards a unit prize according to a ratio-form contest success function with the return to scale parameter α such that $0 \le \alpha \le 1$. Then, the total effort in the pure-strategy Nash equilibrium satisfies*

$$\frac{R}{v_1} \le \begin{cases} \frac{1}{1 + v_1/v_2}, & \text{if } 1 \le v_1/v_2 \le 1 + a \\ \frac{C}{\log(v_1/v_2)}, & \text{if } 1 + a < v_1/v_2 \end{cases}$$

where a and C are absolute positive constants defined in Theorem 4.31. If $1 \le v_1/v_2 \le 1 + a$, the optimal value of the return to scale parameter is $\alpha = 1$, and otherwise, $\alpha = \log(1+a)/\log(v_1/v_2)$.

Proof. The key point is to observe that $dR(\alpha)/d\alpha \ge 0$ is equivalent to $(v_1/v_2)^\alpha + 1 \ge ((v_1/v_2)^\alpha - 1)\log((v_1/v_2)^\alpha)$. From this, we deduce that R is increasing in α on $[0, 1]$ if, and only if, $v_1/v_2 + 1 \ge (v_1/v_2 - 1)\log(v_1/v_2)$. Then, note that the last condition holds if, and only if, $1 \le v_1/v_2 \le 1 + a$. If the condition does not hold, then the optimum value is achieved at the value $\alpha \in [0, 1)$ as in Theorem 4.31 where the second case holds since $v_1/v_2 > 1 + a > \theta$. $\qquad\square$

The bounds for the total effort in Corollary 4.32 are discussed as follows. For the valuation vectors such that $1 \le v_1/v_2 \le 1 + a$, the total effort is increasing in the return to scale parameter α, for all $0 < \alpha < 1$, and hence it achieves the largest value at $\alpha = 1$. Otherwise, the total effort achieves the largest value at a value of α smaller than 1, specifically, at $\alpha = \log(1 + a)/\log(v_1/v_2)$. For the ratio-form contest success functions with the return to scale parameter $0 < \alpha \le 1$, the total effort in a pure-strategy Nash equilibrium is the largest under proportional allocation for any valuation vector

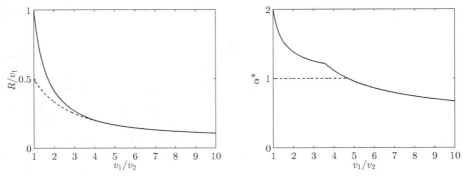

Figure 4.8. The total effort upper bound (left) and the optimal return to scale parameter (right) vs. the valuation ratio v_1/v_2. The dashed lines are for the case under the additional constraint $0 \le \alpha \le 1$.

$1 \le v_1/v_2 \le 1 + a \approx 4.68$. Figure 4.8 shows how, for the cases in Theorem 4.31 and Corollary 4.32, the optimal total effort and the optimal value of the return to scale parameter depend on v_1/v_2.

4.6 Weighted Proportional Allocation

A weighted proportional allocation is a general-logit contest success function with linear production functions, i.e., $f_i(x) = a_i x$, for some constant $a_i > 0$ that is allowed to be player specific. The contest success functions are given by

$$x_i(\mathbf{b}) = \frac{a_i b_i}{\sum_{j \in N} a_j b_j}, \quad \text{for } i \in N \tag{4.49}$$

whenever $\sum_{j \in N} b_j > 0$, and $x_i(\mathbf{b}) = 1/n$, for $i \in N$, otherwise.

Relation to Proportional Allocation It is readily observed that the game with the payoff functions $s_i(\mathbf{b}) = u_i(x_i(\mathbf{b})) - b_i$, $i \in N$, is strategically equivalent to the game with payoff functions

$$\hat{s}_i(\hat{\mathbf{b}}) = a_i u_i(x_i(\hat{\mathbf{b}})) - \hat{b}_i,$$

where $\hat{\mathbf{b}}$ is a vector of normalized efforts defined by $\hat{b}_i = a_i b_i$, for $i \in N$, and with an abuse of notation $x_i(\mathbf{b})$ is as defined in (4.49) but with $a_1 = a_2 = \cdots = a_n = 1$. For linear utility functions $u_i(x) = v_i x$, this auxiliary game is equivalent to that of a contest where a unit prize is allocated according to proportional allocation and players incur linear production costs where the valuation parameters are $\hat{v}_i = a_i v_i$, for $i \in N$.

Lemma 4.33. *A contest among two or more players with valuation parameters $v_1 \ge v_2 \ge \cdots \ge v_n > 0$ where a unit prize is allocated according to a weighted proportional allocation with weights $a_i \ge 0$, for $i \in N$, has a unique pure-strategy Nash equilibrium. Moreover, in the pure-strategy Nash equilibrium, the invested efforts are $b_i = \hat{b}_i/a_i$, where $\hat{b}_i$, $i \in N$, are individual efforts in the unique pure-strategy Nash equilibrium in a contest where a unit prize is allocated according to proportional allocation to the players with valuation parameters $\hat{v}_i = a_i v_i$, for $i \in N$.*

We now focus on the pure-strategy Nash equilibrium of a game where the weights are chosen by the contest owner so as to maximize the total effort in the pure-strategy Nash equilibrium. This problem could be seen as a two-stage game where in the first stage, the contest owner selects and announces the weights to all players, and then, in the second stage, the players simultaneously make effort investments. In the first stage, the contest owner anticipates how the players are going to respond in the second stage, and thus can choose the weights that maximize the total effort exerted in the second stage of the game. This can be formally formulated as follows. Since in any pure-strategy Nash equilibrium, we have that either $\partial s_i(\mathbf{b})/\partial b_i \leq 0$ and $b_i = 0$ or $\partial s_i(\mathbf{b})/\partial b_i = 0$ and $b_i > 0$,

$$b_i = u_i'(x_i(\mathbf{b}))x_i(\mathbf{b})(1 - x_i(\mathbf{b})), \quad \text{for } i \in N. \tag{4.50}$$

Therefore, the total effort in a pure-strategy Nash equilibrium is

$$R(\mathbf{x}) = \sum_{i \in N} u_i'(x_i)x_i(1 - x_i).$$

The optimization problem of the contest owner is formulated as follows:

$$
\begin{aligned}
\text{maximize} \quad & R(\mathbf{x}) \\
\text{over} \quad & x_i \geq 0, i \in N \\
& \sum_{i \in N} x_i = 1.
\end{aligned}
\tag{4.51}
$$

Extremal Property of Linear Production Functions We shall now show that the class of linear production functions is a special class in the sense as described in the following theorem.

Theorem 4.34. *Consider a contest among two or more players with valuation parameters $v_1 \geq v_2 \geq \cdots \geq v_n > 0$ where a unit prize is allocated according to general-logit contest success functions with the production functions $f_i(x)$, $i \in N$, that are assumed to be increasing, concave, and such that $f_i(0) = 0$, for all $i \in N$. If $\mathbf{b}$ is a pure-strategy Nash equilibrium in this contest, then there exists a collection of linear production functions $\tilde{f}_i(x) = a_i x$, $a_i \geq 0$, such that $\mathbf{b}$ is a pure-strategy Nash equilibrium in the same contest but with the production functions $\tilde{f}_i(x)$, $i \in N$.*

Proof. We need to show that there exists a vector $\mathbf{a} \in \mathbf{R}_+^n$ such that conditions (4.17), (4.18), and (4.19) hold at point $\mathbf{b}$. Note that by setting $a_i = 0$, if $b_i = 0$, condition (4.18) is satisfied. Thus, it suffices to consider conditions (4.17) and (4.19) for $b_i > 0$. Using the shorthand notation $A(\mathbf{a}, \mathbf{b}) = \sum_{j \in N} a_j b_j$, it follows from (4.17) that a_i is a solution of the following quadratic equation: $a_i^2 - (A(\mathbf{a}, \mathbf{b})/b_i)a_i + A(\mathbf{a}, \mathbf{b})^2/(v_i b_i) = 0$. Since by Theorem 4.8, $b_i \leq v_i/4$, it follows that a_i is one of the following two solutions:

$$a_i = \frac{A(\mathbf{a}, \mathbf{b})}{2b_i}\left(1 \pm \sqrt{1 - \frac{4b_i}{v_i}}\right).$$

It readily follows that such a_i satisfies (4.19), i.e., $v_i a_i \geq A(\mathbf{a}, \mathbf{b})$. □

An important implication of the last theorem is given in the following corollary.

Corollary 4.35. *Suppose that our goal is to maximize a function $g(\mathbf{b})$ over the class of production functions $f_i(x)$, $i \in N$, which are increasing, concave, and $f_i(0) = 0$, for all $i \in N$, subject to that $\mathbf{b}$ is a pure-strategy Nash equilibrium in the contest with production functions $f_i(x)$, $i \in N$. Let OPT denote the optimal value, and let OPT' denote the optimum value by maximizing over the class of linear production functions. Then, OPT' $\geq$ OPT.*

The last corollary tells us that for the problem of maximizing the total effort in a pure-strategy Nash equilibrium over the class of production functions that are increasing, concave, and equal to zero at zero, it is non-restrictive to focus only on the linear production functions. Hence, the results that we shall establish for the maximum achievable total effort under weighted proportional allocation apply more generally as upper bounds to the broad class of general-logit contest success functions that validate the aforementioned conditions.

4.6.1 Two Players

Theorem 4.36. *Consider a two-player all-pay contest with valuation parameters $v_1 \geq v_2 > 0$ that awards a unit prize according to a weighted proportional allocation with weights that maximize the total effort in a pure-strategy Nash equilibrium. Then, there exists a unique pure-strategy Nash equilibrium $\mathbf{b} = (b_1, b_2)$ that has the following properties.*

(i) *The individual efforts:*

$$b_1 = \frac{v_1}{4} \text{ and } b_2 = \frac{v_2}{4}.$$

(ii) *The winning probabilities:*

$$x_1(\mathbf{b}) = \frac{1}{2} \text{ and } x_2(\mathbf{b}) = \frac{1}{2}.$$

(iii) *The total effort:*

$$R = \frac{v_1 + v_2}{4}.$$

(iv) *The maximum individual effort:*

$$R_1 = \frac{v_1}{4}.$$

(v) *The social efficiency:*

$$\frac{1}{2}\left(1 + \frac{v_2}{v_1}\right).$$

(vi) *The competitive balance:*

$$\frac{x_2(\mathbf{b})}{x_1(\mathbf{b})} = 1.$$

(vii) *The optimum discrimination weights:*

$$a_1 = \frac{1}{v_1} \text{ and } a_2 = \frac{1}{v_2}.$$

Notice that each player invests the largest possible value in a pure-strategy Nash equilibrium, achieving the upper bound in Theorem 4.8 that holds for arbitrary general-logit contest success functions with concave production functions. Notice also that the optimal weights achieve a perfect balance of the winning probabilities.

4.6.2 Characterization of Equilibrium for an Arbitrary Number of Players

In this section we provide a full characterization of the pure-strategy Nash equilibrium for a contest where a unit prize is allocated according to weighted proportional allocation with weights that maximize the total effort in a pure-strategy Nash equilibrium.

Theorem 4.37. *Consider a contest among two or more players with valuation parameters $v_1 \geq v_2 \geq \cdots \geq v_n > 0$ where a unit prize is allocated according to weighted proportional allocation with weights **a** chosen so that they maximize the total effort in the pure-strategy Nash equilibrium. Then, there exists a unique pure-strategy Nash equilibrium that is characterized as follows.*

(i) *The set of active players corresponds to that in the unique pure-strategy Nash equilibrium under proportional allocation.*

(ii) *The optimal weights are unique up to an arbitrary positive multiplicative constant and, up to a multiplicative constant, are given by*

$$a_i = \frac{1}{v_i + \frac{\hat{n}-2}{\sum_{j=1}^{\hat{n}} \frac{1}{v_j}}}, \quad \text{for } i \in N$$

where $\hat{n}$ is the number of active players in the contest where the prize is allocated according to proportional allocation.

(iii) *The individual efforts are given by*

$$b_i = \begin{cases} \frac{v_i}{4}\left(1 - \left(\frac{\hat{n}-2}{\sum_{j=1}^{\hat{n}} \frac{1}{v_j}} \frac{1}{v_i}\right)^2\right), & \text{if } i = 1, 2, \ldots, \hat{n} \\ 0, & \text{otherwise.} \end{cases}$$

Proof. By Lemma 4.33, for weighted proportional allocation with weights **a** and valuation vector **v**, there is a unique pure-strategy Nash equilibrium **b** that satisfies $b_i = \hat{b}_i/a_i$ where $\hat{\mathbf{b}}$ is the unique pure-strategy Nash equilibrium in an auxiliary contest where a unit prize is allocated according to proportional allocation with valuation parameters $\hat{v}_i = v_i a_i$, for $i \in N$. Using Theorem 4.19, we can deduce that in the unique pure-strategy Nash equilibrium in the auxiliary contest, the individual efforts $\hat{\mathbf{b}}$ are characterized as follows. Let us assume that players are enumerated such that $a_1 v_1 \geq a_2 v_2 \geq \cdots \geq a_n v_n$, and let $\hat{n}_c$ denote the number of active players in the auxiliary contest. Now, note that

$$\hat{n}_c = \max\left\{i \in N \mid a_i v_i > \frac{i-2}{\sum_{j=1}^{i-1} \frac{1}{a_j v_j}}\right\}$$

and that

$$b_i = \begin{cases} \frac{B(\mathbf{a})}{a_i}\left(1 - \frac{B(\mathbf{a})}{a_i v_i}\right), & \text{if } i = 1, 2, \ldots, \hat{n}_c \\ 0, & \text{otherwise} \end{cases} \qquad (4.52)$$

where

$$B(\mathbf{a}) = \sum_{i \in N} a_i b_i = \frac{\hat{n}_c - 1}{\sum_{i=1}^{\hat{n}_c} \frac{1}{a_i v_i}}.$$

It follows that the total effort can be expressed as

$$R(\mathbf{a}) = B(\mathbf{a}) \left(\sum_{i=1}^{\hat{n}_c} \frac{1}{a_i} - B(\mathbf{a}) \sum_{i=1}^{\hat{n}_c} \frac{1}{a_i^2 v_i} \right). \qquad (4.53)$$

We shall maximize the total effort over the weights $\mathbf{a}$. To this end, it is convenient to use the following change of variables, $z_i = 1/a_i$, and optimize over these new variables. By simple differential calculus, we have

$$\frac{\partial}{\partial z_i} R(\mathbf{z}) = -\frac{B(\mathbf{z})^2}{\hat{n}_c - 1} \frac{1}{v_i} \sum_{j=1}^{\hat{n}_c} z_j + B(\mathbf{z}) + 2B(\mathbf{z}) \frac{B(\mathbf{z})^2}{\hat{n}_c - 1} \frac{1}{v_i} \sum_{j=1}^{\hat{n}_c} \frac{z_j^2}{v_j} - 2B(\mathbf{z})^2 \frac{z_i}{v_i}.$$

A necessary optimality condition is $\partial R(\mathbf{z})/\partial z_i = 0$, from which we obtain

$$z_i = \frac{v_i}{2B(\mathbf{z})} + \frac{B(\mathbf{z})}{\hat{n}_c - 1} \sum_{j=1}^{\hat{n}_c} \frac{z_j^2}{v_j} - \frac{1}{2(\hat{n}_c - 1)} \sum_{j=1}^{\hat{n}_c} z_j = \frac{v_i}{2B(\mathbf{z})} + \frac{1}{2B(\mathbf{z})} \frac{\hat{n}_c - 2}{\sum_{j=1}^{\hat{n}_c} \frac{1}{v_j}}$$

where the last equality follows by making use of the fact $\sum_{i=1}^{\hat{n}_c} \frac{\partial}{\partial z_i} R(\mathbf{z}) = 0$.

Reverting back to our original variables, we obtain that optimal weights satisfy

$$\frac{1}{a_i} = \frac{1}{2B(\mathbf{a})} \left(v_i + \frac{\hat{n}_c - 2}{\sum_{j=1}^{\hat{n}_c} \frac{1}{v_j}} \right). \qquad (4.54)$$

We are now in a position to show that the assertions of the theorem hold. First, we recall that $b_i > 0$ is equivalent to

$$a_i v_i > \frac{i - 2}{\sum_{j=1}^{i-1} \frac{1}{a_j v_j}},$$

which by plugging the optimal weights (4.54) is easily shown to be equivalent to

$$v_i > \frac{i - 2}{\sum_{j=1}^{i-1} \frac{1}{v_j}}.$$

This is exactly the same condition that identifies the set of active players where the prize is allocated according to proportional allocation to players with the valuation vector $\mathbf{v}$.

Second, since the optimal weights are unique up to an arbitrary positive multiplicative constant, let $B(\mathbf{a}) = 1/2$, and then by (4.54), the optimal weights are as asserted in the theorem.

Finally, from (4.52) and the fact that for optimal weights $\hat{n}_c = \hat{n}$, we note that for $1 \le i \le \hat{n}$,

$$\frac{b_i}{v_i} = \frac{1}{2a_i v_i} \left(1 - \frac{1}{2a_i v_i} \right).$$

Plugging in the optimal weights given by (4.54), with $B(\mathbf{a}) = 1/2$, yields the asserted individual efforts. $\qquad\qquad\square$

We note that the optimal weight for each player is inversely proportional to $v_i + (1 - 2/\hat{n})\bar{v}(\mathbf{v})$, where $\bar{v}(\mathbf{v})$ is the harmonic mean of the valuation parameters of active players. In particular, for the case when only two players are active, this boils down to the weights that for each player are inversely proportional to his or her valuation parameter.

4.6.3 Total Effort

For the optimal weighted proportional allocation, the total effort is given as follows.

Corollary 4.38. *Under the assumptions of Theorem 4.37, we have*

$$R = \frac{1}{4} \left(\sum_{i=1}^{\hat{n}} v_i - \frac{(\hat{n}-2)^2}{\sum_{i=1}^{\hat{n}} \frac{1}{v_i}} \right).$$

Another interesting corollary is that the optimal weighted proportional allocation guarantees that the total effort is at least a constant factor of the highest valuation.

Corollary 4.39. *The optimal weighted proportional allocation has the total effort in the unique pure-strategy Nash equilibrium that satisfies*

$$R \ge \frac{1}{4}v_1.$$

The last inequality follows from

$$R = \frac{1}{4} \left(v_1 + \sum_{i=2}^{\hat{n}} v_i - \frac{(\hat{n}-2)^2}{\sum_{i=1}^{\hat{n}} \frac{1}{v_i}} \right)$$

$$\ge \frac{1}{4} \left(v_1 + \sum_{i=2}^{\hat{n}} v_i - (\hat{n}-1)\frac{\hat{n}-1}{\sum_{i=2}^{\hat{n}} \frac{1}{v_i}} \right)$$

$$\ge \frac{1}{4}v_1$$

where the last inequality is by the fact that the arithmetic mean is greater than or equal to the harmonic mean.

Note that this can be established alternatively by the following facts: (i) $R \ge b_1$, and (ii) $b_1 = v_1/4$ can be achieved by setting the weights to zero for all the players except for a pair of players with the largest valuation parameters, for whom the weights are set as in Theorem 4.36. The lower bound is achieved for the case of two players with an asymptotically small ratio of the second largest and the largest valuation parameters.

4.6.4 Maximum Individual Effort

First, we consider the maximum individual effort in a pure-strategy Nash equilibrium with the weights that maximize the total effort in the equilibrium. We shall show that there exist valuation vectors for which the maximal individual effort can be made arbitrarily small. Consider a valuation vector such that $v_1 \geq v_2 = \cdots = v_n > 0$. Using Theorem 4.37, it follows that the maximum individual effort is

$$b_1 = \frac{v_1}{4}\left(1 - \left(\frac{n-2}{1+(n-1)\frac{v_1}{v_2}}\right)^2\right).$$

Notice that this decreases to the limit value $(1 - (v_2/v_1)^2)v_1/4$ as the number of players n goes to infinity. Hence, while the total effort is guaranteed to be at least $v_1/4$, the maximum individual effort can be arbitrarily small for a sufficiently small gap between the highest and the second highest valuation.

Second, we consider the maximum individual effort with the weights that are chosen to maximize the maximum individual effort in the equilibrium. It is readily observed that it is optimal to exclude all players from the competition except a pair of players with the largest valuation parameters by setting the corresponding weights to zero and then optimizing the weights for the two selected players as in Theorem 4.36. This yields the maximum individual effort of $v_1/4$, which by Theorem 4.8 is the best possible effort for the class of contest success functions with concave production functions.

4.6.5 Social Welfare

Theorem 4.40. *For a weighted proportional allocation with weights that maximize the total effort in the pure-strategy Nash equilibrium, the social welfare is at least $1/2$ of the maximum social welfare. Moreover, the worst-case efficiency loss is achieved for a valuation vector such that $v_1 > v_2 = \cdots = v_n > 0$, for asymptotically large n and v_1/v_2.*

Proof. By the same argument as for proportional allocation in Section 4.4.4, the worst-case social welfare is for the class of linear utility functions. Thus, it suffices to consider the case $u_i(x) = v_i x$, for $x \geq 0$ and $v_i > 0$. In this case, the total effort maximization problem in (4.51) has a strictly concave objective function that has a unique maximum over the convex set specified by the constraints of the problem. The optimal solution $\mathbf{x}$ is such that for the Lagrange multiplier $\lambda > 0$, if $x_i > 0$ then $\partial R(\mathbf{x})/\partial x_i = v_i(1 - 2x_i) = \lambda$, and if $v_i < \lambda$ then $x_i = 0$. Therefore,

$$x_i = \frac{1}{2}\max\left\{1 - \frac{(1-2x_1)v_1}{v_i}, 0\right\}, \quad \text{for } i \in N. \tag{4.55}$$

Now, note the following series of relations:

$$u(\mathbf{x}) = v_1 x_1 + \sum_{i=2}^{n} v_i x_i$$

$$= v_1 x_1 + \sum_{i=2}^{n} v_i x_i \mathbf{1}(x_i > 0)$$

$$\geq v_1 x_1 + v_1 (1 - 2x_1) \sum_{i=2}^{n} x_i \mathbf{1}(x_i > 0)$$

$$= v_1 x_1 + v_1 (1 - 2x_1) \sum_{i=2}^{n} x_i$$

$$= v_1 x_1 + v_1 (1 - 2x_1)(1 - x_1)$$

$$= v_1 [1 - 2x_1 (1 - x_1)]$$

$$\geq \frac{1}{2} v_1$$

where the first inequality follows by noting from (4.55) that $v_i \geq v_1 (1 - 2x_1)$ whenever $x_i > 0$.

On the other hand, the maximum social welfare is achieved by allocating the entire prize to a player with the highest valuation, which yields the maximum social welfare in the amount of v_1. We have thus shown that the social welfare in the pure-strategy Nash equilibrium is at least $1/2$ of the maximum social welfare.

The tightness is established as follows. Suppose $v_1 \geq v_2 = \cdots = v_n > 0$. From (4.55) and $\sum_{i \in N} x_i = 1$, we have

$$x_i = \frac{1}{2} \left(1 - \frac{n - 2}{\frac{1}{v_1} + \frac{n-1}{v_2}} \frac{1}{v_i} \right) \quad \text{for } i \in N.$$

It follows that

$$u(\mathbf{x}) = \sum_{i=1}^{n} v_i x_i = v_1 \frac{1 + (n - 1)\frac{1}{2}\left(\frac{v_1}{v_2} + \frac{v_2}{v_1}\right)}{1 + (n - 1)\frac{v_1}{v_2}}.$$

Thus, the ratio of the social welfare in the pure-strategy Nash equilibrium and the maximum social welfare is equal to

$$\frac{1}{2} \frac{2 + (n - 1)\left(\frac{v_1}{v_2} + \frac{v_2}{v_1}\right)}{1 + (n - 1)\frac{v_1}{v_2}}.$$

It is readily observed that the last expression is decreasing in n and v_1/v_2 and hence can be arbitrarily near to $1/2$ by taking n and v_1/v_2 large enough. $\qquad\square$

4.7 Weighted Valuation Allocation

We consider a weighted valuation allocation that is defined by

$$x_i(\mathbf{b}) = \frac{b_i}{\sum_{j \in N} b_j} a_i, \quad \text{for } i \in N$$

whenever $\sum_{j \in N} b_j > 0$, and $x_i(\mathbf{b}) = 1/n$, for $i \in N$, otherwise. Here $\mathbf{a} = (a_1, a_2, \ldots, a_n)$ are positive real-valued weights such that the allocation is feasible. For allocation of a unit prize, this means that $\mathbf{a}$ is such that $\sum_{i \in N} x_i(\mathbf{b}) \leq 1$. In this section, we shall consider a more general case where the allocation is a point in a given convex polyhedral set P. The unit prize is a special case by defining $P = \{\mathbf{x} \in \mathbf{R}_+^n \mid \sum_{i=1}^n x_i \leq 1\}$.

Each player is assumed to value the prize according to a utility function $u_i : \mathbf{R}_+ \to \mathbf{R}_+$ of the allocation that is assumed to be increasing, concave, and continuously differentiable, for every player $i \in N$. For the case of linear utility functions, $u_i(x) = v_i x$ for a valuation parameter $v_i > 0$. Players are assumed to incur linear production costs with unit marginal costs. The payoff functions of the players are given by

$$s_i(\mathbf{b}) = u_i \left(\frac{b_i}{\sum_{j \in N} b_j} a_i \right) - b_i, \quad \text{for } i \in N.$$

Notice that for any fixed vector of weights $\mathbf{a}$ with at least two strictly positive elements, the game corresponds to that under proportional allocation. Specifically, for a contest with two or more players with valuation parameters $v_1 \geq v_2 \geq \cdots \geq v_n > 0$ where a unit prize is allocated according to a weighted valuation allocation with weights $\mathbf{a}$, the game corresponds to that of proportional allocation with valuation parameters $\hat{v}_i = v_i a_i$, for $i \in N$. Hence, by Theorem 4.19, we know that there exists a unique pure-strategy Nash equilibrium for this game.

We now analyze the game for the choice of weights $\mathbf{a}$ that maximizes the total effort in a pure-strategy Nash equilibrium. As for the previously studied case of weighted proportional allocation, this may be seen as a two-stage game. In the first stage, the contest owner selects the values of the weights and makes them public to all players anticipating how the players are going to respond in the second stage. In the second stage the players simultaneously invest efforts.

4.7.1 Two Players

Theorem 4.41. *Consider a two-player contest with valuation parameters $v_1 \geq v_2 > 0$ where a unit prize is allocated according to a weighted valuation allocation with weights (a_1, a_2) that maximize the total effort in a pure-strategy Nash equilibrium. Then, there is a unique pure-strategy Nash equilibrium with the following properties.*

(i) *The individual efforts:*

$$b_1 = v_1 \frac{1}{2 \left(1 + \sqrt{\frac{v_1}{v_2}} \right)} \text{ and } b_2 = v_2 \frac{1}{2 \left(1 + \sqrt{\frac{v_1}{v_2}} \right)}.$$

(ii) *The weights:*

$$a_1 = \frac{1}{2}\left(1 + \sqrt{\frac{v_2}{v_1}}\right) \text{ and } a_2 = \frac{1}{2}\left(1 + \sqrt{\frac{v_1}{v_2}}\right).$$

(iii) *The winning probabilities:*

$$x_1 = \frac{1}{2} \text{ and } x_2 = \frac{1}{2}.$$

(iv) *The total effort:*

$$R = \frac{1}{2}\sqrt{v_1 v_2}.$$

(v) *The social efficiency:*

$$\frac{1}{2}\left(1 + \frac{v_2}{v_1}\right).$$

(vi) *The competitive balance:*

$$\frac{x_2(\mathbf{b})}{x_1(\mathbf{b})} = 1.$$

We note that unlike a weighted proportional allocation, the total effort is not guaranteed to be at least a constant factor of the highest valuation. In this case the form of the allocation rule imposes a constraint on the choice of weights, while for weighted proportional allocation no such constraint is required except for non-negativity of weights. However, this prize allocation can yield a higher total effort than the second highest valuation, provided that the ratio of the highest and the second highest valuation is sufficiently large. Specifically, observe that the total effort is equal to half of the geometric mean of the valuation parameters of a pair of players with the largest valuation parameters. We shall find that in general the total effort is guaranteed to be within constant factors of the geometric mean of the valuation parameters of a pair of players with the largest valuation parameters, for every given valuation vector of two or more players. The efficiency and competitive balance turn out to be the same as for the optimum weighted proportional allocation.

4.7.2 Characterization of Equilibrium for an Arbitrary Number of Players

Theorem 4.42. *Suppose that utility function u_i is strictly increasing, continuously differentiable, and concave, for all $i \in N$. Then, for every vector of weights $\mathbf{a}$ with at least two strictly positive elements, there exists a unique pure-strategy Nash equilibrium. The total effort is maximized for the vector of weights*

$$a_i = x_i + \frac{R(\mathbf{x})}{u'_i(x_i)}, \quad \text{for } i \in N$$

where $\mathbf{x}$ is a unique allocation that maximizes the total effort $R(\mathbf{x})$ over the set of feasible allocations in P, with $R(\mathbf{x})$ given by

$$\sum_{i \in N} \frac{u'_i(x_i)x_i}{u'_i(x_i)x_i + R(\mathbf{x})} = 1. \tag{4.56}$$

The individual efforts satisfy

$$b_i = \frac{u_i'(x_i)x_i}{u_i'(x_i)x_i + R(\mathbf{x})} R(\mathbf{x}), \quad for\ i \in N. \tag{4.57}$$

Proof. The existence and uniquess of a pure-strategy Nash equilibrium for every vector of the weights **a** with at least two strictly positive elements follow by the equivalence to the game with proportional allocation and Theorem 4.19. Suppose that **b** is a pure-strategy Nash equilibrium. If $x_i(\mathbf{b}) > 0$, then $\partial s_i(\mathbf{b})/\partial b_i = 0$, which is equivalent to

$$u_i'(x_i)(a_i - x_i) = R(\mathbf{x}). \tag{4.58}$$

From the last identity, we obtain the asserted relation between weights **a** and allocation **x**. Using the fact $\sum_{i \in N} x_i(\mathbf{b})/a_i = 1$ and (4.58), we obtain that $R(\mathbf{x})$ is given as asserted in (4.56). Finally, the asserted individual efforts follow from the definition of the allocation rule $x_i(\mathbf{b}) = (b_i / \sum_{j \in N} b_j)a_i$, the fact $R(\mathbf{x}) = \sum_{j \in N} b_j$, and the relation between weights **a** and allocation **x**. □

Linear Utility Functions

Corollary 4.43. *Consider a contest among two or more players whose valuation parameters are $v_1 \geq v_2 \geq \cdots \geq v_n > 0$ where a unit prize is allocated according to a weighted valuation allocation with weights chosen to maximize the total effort in a pure-strategy Nash equilibrium. Then, there exists a unique pure-strategy Nash equilibrium whose properties are as follows.*

(i) *The weights:*

$$a_i = \begin{cases} R\frac{1}{\hat{n}-1}\sum_{j=1}^{\hat{n}} \frac{1}{\sqrt{v_j}} \frac{1}{\sqrt{v_i}}, & for\ i = 1, 2, \ldots, \hat{n} \\ \frac{R}{v_i}, & otherwise \end{cases} \tag{4.59}$$

where

$$\hat{n} = \max \left\{ i \in N \mid \sqrt{v_i} > \frac{i-2}{\sum_{j=1}^{i-1} \frac{1}{\sqrt{v_j}}} \right\}.$$

(ii) *The individual efforts:*

$$b_i = \begin{cases} R\left(1 - \frac{\hat{n}-1}{\sum_{j=1}^{\hat{n}} \frac{1}{\sqrt{v_j}}} \frac{1}{\sqrt{v_i}}\right), & for\ i = 1, 2, \ldots, \hat{n} \\ 0, & otherwise. \end{cases} \tag{4.60}$$

(iii) *The winning probabilities:*

$$x_i = \begin{cases} R\frac{1}{\sqrt{v_i}}\left(\frac{1}{\hat{n}-1}\sum_{j=1}^{\hat{n}} \frac{1}{\sqrt{v_j}} - \frac{1}{\sqrt{v_i}}\right), & for\ i = 1, 2, \ldots, \hat{n} \\ 0, & otherwise. \end{cases} \tag{4.61}$$

(iv) *The total effort:*

$$R = \frac{\hat{n} - 1}{\left(\sum_{i=1}^{\hat{n}} \frac{1}{\sqrt{v_i}}\right)^2 - (\hat{n} - 1)\sum_{i=1}^{\hat{n}} \frac{1}{v_i}}. \tag{4.62}$$

We say that a player is active if in the pure-strategy Nash equilibrium he or she invests a strictly positive effort. Note that the set of active players is as in a contest with proportional allocation with valuation parameters $\sqrt{v_1} \geq \sqrt{v_2} \geq \cdots \geq \sqrt{v_n} > 0$.

Proof. By Theorem 4.42, in the pure-strategy Nash equilibrium of the game, $\mathbf{x}$ is the optimal solution of the following optimization problem:

$$\text{maximize} \quad R(\mathbf{x})$$
$$\text{over} \quad \mathbf{x} \in [0, 1]^n$$
$$\sum_{i=1}^n x_i \leq 1,$$

where $R(\mathbf{x})$ is given by (4.56), which for the case of linear utility functions reads as follows:

$$\sum_{i \in N} \frac{v_i x_i}{v_i x_i + R(\mathbf{x})} = 1. \tag{4.63}$$

The Lagrangian function is $L(\mathbf{x}) = R(\mathbf{x}) + \lambda(1 - \sum_{i=1}^n x_i)$, for $\lambda > 0$. For an optimal solution $\mathbf{x}$, it either holds that

$$\frac{\partial}{\partial x_i} L(\mathbf{x}) = 0 \text{ and } x_i > 0 \text{ or } \frac{\partial}{\partial x_i} L(\mathbf{x}) \leq 0 \text{ and } x_i = 0. \tag{4.64}$$

Note that $\partial L(\mathbf{x})/\partial x_i = \partial R(\mathbf{x})/\partial x_i - \lambda$. By taking a partial derivative with respect to x_i on both sides in (4.56), we obtain

$$\frac{R(\mathbf{x})v_i}{(v_i x_i + R(\mathbf{x}))^2} = \frac{\partial R(\mathbf{x})}{\partial x_i} \cdot \sum_{j \in N} \frac{v_j x_j}{(v_j x_j + R(\mathbf{x}))^2}. \tag{4.65}$$

Using this, note that (4.64) corresponds to

$$\frac{v_i}{(v_i x_i + R(\mathbf{x}))^2} = \lambda \text{ and } x_i > 0, \quad \text{or} \quad \frac{v_i}{R(\mathbf{x})^2} \leq \lambda \text{ and } x_i = 0. \tag{4.66}$$

From this, it is not difficult to observe that $\mathbf{x}$ is such that $x_i > 0$, for $i = 1, 2, \ldots, \hat{n}$ and $x_i = 0$, otherwise, for some $\hat{n}$ such that $1 < \hat{n} \leq n$. If $x_i > 0$, then

$$x_i = \frac{1}{\sqrt{\lambda}} \frac{1}{\sqrt{v_i}} - \frac{R(\mathbf{x})}{v_i}.$$

Combining with $\sum_{i \in N} x_i = 1$, we obtain

$$x_i = \begin{cases} \dfrac{1 + R(\mathbf{x}) \sum_{j=1}^{\hat{n}} \frac{1}{v_j}}{\sum_{j=1}^{\hat{n}} \frac{1}{\sqrt{v_j}}} \dfrac{1}{\sqrt{v_i}} - \dfrac{R(\mathbf{x})}{v_i}, & i = 1, 2, \ldots, \hat{n} \\ 0, & \text{otherwise.} \end{cases}$$

The asserted expression for the total effort R in (4.62) follows by plugging in the last identity in (4.63). Using (4.62) with the last above identity yields (4.61). The asserted discrimination weights (4.59) and individual efforts (4.60) follow from (4.61) and the corresponding relations in Theorem 4.42. $\qquad \square$

4.7.3 Total Effort

The total effort in the unique pure-strategy Nash equilibrium is fully characterized by (4.62). Here we note that for an optimal choice of weights, the following bounds hold.

Corollary 4.44. *For every valuation vector such that* $v_1 \geq v_2 \geq \cdots \geq v_n > 0$, *for two or more players, the total effort satisfies*

$$\frac{1}{2}\sqrt{v_1 v_2} \leq R \leq \sqrt{v_1 v_2}.$$

Proof. For the lower bound, consider a restricted game under the constraint that the weights of all players other than players 1 and 2 are set to zero. The total effort in the pure-strategy Nash equilibrium of such a restricted game is clearly smaller than or equal to the total effort in the pure-strategy Nash equilibrium of the original game. The total effort in the restricted game corresponds to that in the original game but in which only players 1 and 2 are allowed to participate. By Theorem 4.41, the expected total effort in this game is $\sqrt{v_1 v_2}/2$.

For the upper bound, we shall show that for every valuation vector with fixed values of the valuation parameters v_1 and v_2, the total effort is smaller than or equal to that in the game under the valuation vector such that $v_1 \geq v_2 = \cdots = v_n$. The total effort under such a valuation vector is then shown to be smaller than or equal to $\sqrt{v_1 v_2}$. Consider the total effort in (4.62), which we rewrite as follows:

$$R = \frac{\hat{n} - 1}{\left(\frac{1}{\sqrt{v_1}} + \sum_{i=2}^{\hat{n}} \frac{1}{\sqrt{v_i}}\right)^2 - (\hat{n} - 1)\left(\frac{1}{v_1} + \sum_{i=2}^{\hat{n}} \frac{1}{v_i}\right)}. \tag{4.67}$$

We now maximize the right-hand side in equation (4.67) over the values of the valuation parameters of players 2 through $\hat{n}$ as follows. We fix $\hat{n}$ to an arbitrary integer that is larger than or equal to two and is smaller than or equal to the number of players n, and let c be such that $\sum_{i=2}^{\hat{n}} \frac{1}{v_i} = c(\hat{n} - 1)$. Note that $c \geq 1/v_2$. Under the given constraints, the right-hand side in equation (4.67) is a concave function in the values of the valuation parameters of players 2 through $\hat{n}$. Hence, it achieves its maximum value for the values of the valuation parameters of players 2 through $\hat{n}$ equal to $1/c$. Therefore, we have

$$R \leq \frac{\hat{n} - 1}{\left(\frac{1}{\sqrt{v_1}} + (\hat{n} - 1)\sqrt{c}\right)^2 - (\hat{n} - 1)\left(\frac{1}{v_1} + (\hat{n} - 1)c\right)}$$

$$= \frac{1}{2\sqrt{cv_2} - \frac{\hat{n}-2}{\hat{n}-1}\sqrt{\frac{v_2}{v_1}}}\sqrt{v_1 v_2}$$

$$\leq \frac{1}{2 - \frac{n-2}{n-1}\sqrt{\frac{v_2}{v_1}}}\sqrt{v_1 v_2} \tag{4.68}$$

where the last inequality follows by the facts $cv_2 \geq 1$ and $\hat{n} \leq n$. The expression in the right-hand side of the inequality (4.68) is exactly the total effort in the pure-strategy Nash equilibrium of the game with the valuation vector such that $v_1 \geq v_2 = \cdots = v_n$.

The proof is completed by noting that

$$\frac{1}{2 - \frac{n-2}{n-1}\sqrt{\frac{v_2}{v_1}}} \le \frac{1}{2 - \frac{n-2}{n-1}} = \frac{1}{1 + \frac{1}{n-1}} \le 1.$$

$\square$

The bounds in Corollary 4.44 are tight. The lower bound is achieved for the case of two players while the upper bound is achieved for the case of symmetric valuation parameters $v_1 = v_2 = \cdots = v_n > 0$ and asymptotically large number of players n. An important implication of the corollary is that the total effort is competitive to the geometric mean of the valuation parameters of a pair of players with the largest valuation parameters.

From the given bounds, it indeed holds

$$\frac{R}{v_1} = \Theta\left(\frac{1}{\sqrt{v_1/v_2}}\right).$$

4.7.4 Maximum Individual Effort

From (4.60), observe that the maximum individual effort in the unique-pure strategy Nash equilibrium with an optimal selection of weights with respect to the total effort is given as follows:

$$R_1 = R\left(1 - \frac{\hat{n} - 1}{\sum_{j=1}^{\hat{n}} \frac{1}{\sqrt{v_j}}} \frac{1}{\sqrt{v_1}}\right).$$

From this, we observe that

$$R_1 = R\left(1 - \frac{\hat{n} - 1}{1 + \sum_{j=2}^{\hat{n}} \sqrt{\frac{v_1}{v_j}}}\right)$$

$$\ge R\left(1 - \frac{1}{\frac{1}{n-1} + \sqrt{\frac{v_1}{v_2}}}\right)$$

$$\ge R\left(1 - \sqrt{\frac{v_2}{v_1}}\right)$$

where the first inequality holds with equality for the valuation vector such that $v_1 \ge v_2 = \cdots = v_n$, and the second inequality is asymptotically tight for large n. In view of Corollary 4.44, the maximum individual effort is at least a constant factor of the quantity $\sqrt{v_2}(\sqrt{v_1} - \sqrt{v_2})$.

4.7.5 Social Welfare

Theorem 4.45. *Consider a contest among two or more players with valuation parameters $v_1 \ge v_2 \ge \cdots \ge v_n > 0$ where a unit prize is allocated according to a weighted valuation allocation that maximizes the total effort in the pure-strategy Nash equilibrium. Then, the social welfare is at least $1/(1 + 2/\sqrt{3})$ of the maximum social welfare, i.e., approximately 46%.*

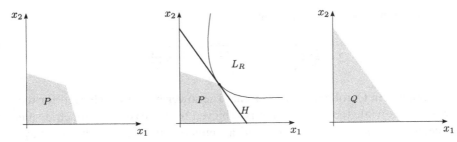

Figure 4.9. Reduction to a simpler constraint.

Moreover, the worst-case social efficiency is achieved for the valuation vector such that $v_1 > v_2 = \cdots = v_n = (2 - \sqrt{3})^2 v_1$ for every fixed $v_1 > 0$ and asymptotically large n.

Proof. Let R^* be the optimal total effort, i.e., $R^* = \max\{R(\mathbf{x}) : \mathbf{x} \in P\}$ where $R(\mathbf{x})$ is given by (4.63) and P is a given convex polyhedral set. Note that for every $\mu \in [0, R^*]$, $L_\mu := \{\mathbf{x} \in \mathbf{R}^n_+ : R(\mathbf{x}) \geq \mu\}$ is a convex set. Consider two convex sets L_{R^*} and P, and note that they intersect at $\mathbf{x}$ such that $R(\mathbf{x}) = R^*$ and they do not have any interior points in common. Let $\sum_{i \in N} q_i x_i = 1$ be the separating hyperplane for these two sets. Now, consider the same game, but with the set of feasible allocations defined as $Q = \{\mathbf{x} \in \mathbf{R}^n_+ : \sum_{i \in N} q_i x_i \leq 1\}$. Then, note that the allocation that maximizes $R(\mathbf{x})$ over Q is the same as in the original game. Since $P \subseteq Q$, the optimal social welfare in the new game is at least as large as in the original game. Therefore, it suffices to prove a lower bound on the efficiency for the class of games with the feasible set Q. See Figure 4.9 for an illustration.

Let us introduce the following change of variables: $\hat{v}_i = v_i/q_i$ and $\hat{x}_i = q_i x_i$, for $i \in N$. Note that $\hat{\mathbf{v}} = (\hat{v}_1, \hat{v}_2, \dots, \hat{v}_n)$ can be interpreted as a valuation vector and $\hat{\mathbf{x}} = (\hat{x}_1, \hat{x}_2, \dots, \hat{x}_n)$ corresponds to allocation of a unit prize, i.e., it holds that $\sum_{i \in N} \hat{x}_i \leq 1$. Let us also define $\hat{b}_i = b_i/R^*$, for $i \in N$, and note that

$$\sum_{i \in N} \hat{b}_i = 1. \qquad (4.69)$$

From (4.57), we have

$$\hat{b}_i = \frac{\hat{v}_i \hat{x}_i}{\hat{v}_i \hat{x}_i + R^*}, \qquad \text{for } i \in N. \qquad (4.70)$$

For the social welfare in the pure-strategy Nash equilibrium, we have

$$u(\mathbf{x}) = \sum_{i \in N} \hat{v}_i \hat{x}_i$$

$$= R^* \sum_{i \in N} \frac{\hat{b}_i}{1 - \hat{b}_i}$$

$$\geq R^* \left(\frac{\hat{b}_1}{1 - \hat{b}_1} + \sum_{i=2}^{n} \hat{b}_i \right)$$

$$= R^* \left(\frac{\hat{b}_1}{1 - \hat{b}_1} + 1 - \hat{b}_1 \right)$$

$$= R^* \frac{\hat{b}_1^2 - \hat{b}_1 + 1}{1 - \hat{b}_1} \qquad (4.71)$$

where the second equality is by (4.70) and the third equality is by (4.69).

Now, let us consider a socially optimal allocation $\mathbf{x}^*$, for which we have

$$u(\mathbf{x}^*) = \max_{\mathbf{x} \in \mathbf{R}_+^n : \sum_{i \in N} q_i x_i = 1} \sum_{i \in N} v_i x_i = \max_{\hat{\mathbf{x}} \in \mathbf{R}_+^n : \sum_{i \in N} \hat{x}_i = 1} \sum_{i \in N} \hat{v}_i \hat{x}_i = \hat{v}_1.$$

Using this along with (4.70), we have

$$u(\mathbf{x}^*) = \hat{v}_1 = \hat{v}_1 \sum_{i \in N} \hat{x}_i = \hat{v}_1 R^* \sum_{i \in N} \frac{\hat{b}_i}{\hat{v}_i (1 - \hat{b}_i)}. \tag{4.72}$$

We observed at the beginning of the proof that the pure-strategy Nash equilibrium allocation $\mathbf{x}$ maximizes $R(\mathbf{x})$ over $\mathbf{x} \in Q$ where $R(\mathbf{x})$ is given by (4.63). With our change of variables, the optimality conditions are as in (4.66), with v_i replaced by $\hat{v}_i$ and x_i replaced by $\hat{x}_i$. Combined with the identities (4.70), these conditions correspond to the following: there exists $\lambda > 0$ such that

$$\frac{\hat{v}_i (1 - \hat{b}_i)^2}{R^{*2}} = \lambda \text{ and } \hat{x}_i > 0, \quad \text{or} \quad \hat{x}_i = 0.$$

From this, we note that $\hat{v}_i (1 - \hat{b}_i)^2 = \hat{v}_1 (1 - \hat{b}_1)^2$ whenever $\hat{b}_1, \hat{b}_i > 0$; hence $\hat{v}_i (1 - \hat{b}_i) = \hat{v}_1 (1 - \hat{b}_1)^2 / (1 - \hat{b}_i)$. Replacing this in the optimal social welfare (4.72), we obtain

$$u(\mathbf{x}^*) = \hat{v}_1 R^* \sum_{i \in N} \frac{\hat{b}_i}{\hat{v}_i (1 - \hat{b}_i)}$$

$$= \frac{R^*}{(1 - \hat{b}_1)^2} \sum_{i \in N} \hat{b}_i (1 - \hat{b}_i)$$

$$\leq \frac{R^*}{(1 - \hat{b}_1)^2} \left(\hat{b}_1 (1 - \hat{b}_1) + \sum_{i=2}^{n} \hat{b}_i \right)$$

$$= \frac{R^*}{(1 - \hat{b}_1)^2} (\hat{b}_1 (1 - \hat{b}_1) + (1 - \hat{b}_1))$$

$$= R^* \frac{1 + \hat{b}_1}{1 - \hat{b}_1}.$$

Combining this with (4.71), we obtain

$$\frac{u(\mathbf{x})}{u(\mathbf{x}^*)} \geq \frac{\hat{b}_1^2 - \hat{b}_1 + 1}{\hat{b}_1 + 1}.$$

By a simple calculus, it is easy to show that the right-hand side is minimized at $\hat{b}_1 = \sqrt{3} - 1$ where it achieves the value $1/(1 + 2/\sqrt{3})$. □

4.8 Optimal Prior-Free Contest Design

In the preceding sections we studied the equilibrium properties of contests under different forms of contest success functions and provided characterizations of the largest total effort that can be extracted from the players under given contest success

Table 4.1. Total effort bounds for different
types of contest success functions

Contest type	R/v_1
Proportional	$O\left(\frac{1}{v_1/v_2}\right)$
Ratio form	$O\left(\frac{\alpha}{(v_1/v_2)^{2\alpha}}\right)$
Ratio-form optimal weights	$O\left(\frac{1}{\log(v_1/v_2)}\right)$
Weighted proportional	$O(1)$
Weighted valuation	$O\left(\frac{1}{\sqrt{v_1/v_2}}\right)$

functions. We found that the total effort in a pure-strategy Nash equilibrium is a fraction of the highest valuation that is decreasing with the ratio of the largest and the second largest valuation parameter. We summarize these results in Table 4.1.

For all the given contest success functions, the total effort is a fraction of the highest valuation, which decreases with the ratio of the highest and the second highest valuation v_1/v_2, except for weighted proportional allocation whose discrimination weights can be chosen to guarantee the total effort that is at least a constant factor of the highest valuation. We observe that proportional allocation has the fastest decrease, which is inversely proportional to the ratio v_1/v_2. The weighted valuation allocation improves this to an inverse square-root decrease with the ratio v_1/v_2. The ratio-form allocation can provide improvement for some values of the return to scale parameter α and yields the decrease that is inversely proportional to the logarithm of the ratio v_1/v_2, for the optimal choice of the parameter α. It is important to bear in mind that the ratio-form allocation, weighted proportional allocation, and weighted valuation allocation use an optimal setting of parameters that requires prior knowledge about the valuation vector.

An interesting question is what is the best possible total effort that can be achieved in a pure-strategy Nash equilibrium for the class of smooth contest success functions without any prior information about the valuation vector. In other words, we are interested in the best possible total effort for the class of prior-free contest success functions.

4.8.1 Always Allocating the Whole Prize to Contestants

In this section, we shall show that for a broad class of smooth contest success functions that satisfy some mild conditions, are prior free, and always fully allocate the prize to the contestants (withholding the prize by the contest owner is not permitted), the total effort in any pure-strategy Nash equilibrium satisfies

$$\frac{R}{v_1} = O\left(\frac{1}{\log(v_1/v_2)}\right)$$

where v_1 is the largest valuation and v_2 is the second largest valuation, for any large enough v_1/v_2. This is a fundamental bound on the total effort that cannot be surpassed by any contest success function from the given class of prior-free contest success functions. Note that, in particular, this implies that the total effort is not guaranteed to be with constant factors of the highest valuation. We shall then characterize a class of contest success functions under which the total effort in a pure-strategy Nash equilibrium can be arbitrarily close to the best possible total effort bound within a constant factor.

Theorem 4.46. *Consider a contest among two or more players where a unit prize is allocated according to contest success functions that are regular, anonymous, continuously differentiable, and such that for every valuation vector there exists a pure-strategy Nash equilibrium. Then, for every fixed constant $C > 0$, there exists a valuation vector $v_1 \geq v_2 \geq \cdots \geq v_n > 0$ such that in any pure-strategy Nash equilibrium the total effort satisfies*

$$R \leq C \frac{v_1}{\log\left(\frac{v_1}{v_2} + 1\right)}.$$

Proof. We shall show that this assertion holds for a two-player contest with valuation parameters $v_1 \geq v_2 > 0$, for any large enough v_1/v_2. The payoffs of the players are

$$s_1(b_1, b_2) = v_1 x_1(b_1, b_2) - b_1 \text{ and } s_2(b_1, b_2) = v_2(1 - x_1(b_1, b_2)) - b_2.$$

First, we show that in any pure-strategy Nash equilibrium, each player invests a strictly positive effort. Suppose that (b_1, b_2) is a pure-strategy Nash equilibrium; then $b_1 > 0$ and $b_2 > 0$. Indeed, $(b_1, b_2) = (0, 0)$ cannot be a pure-strategy Nash equilibrium because, by the assumptions of anonymity and that the prize is always fully allocated to players, the payoffs of players are $v_1/2$ and $v_2/2$; thus either player can unilaterally increase his or her payoff by investing an infinitesimally small effort. For $b_1 > 0$ and $b_2 = 0$, the payoffs of players 1 and 2 are $v_1 - b_1$ and 0, respectively, and player 1 has an incentive to decrease his or her effort to zero, which leads to $(0, 0)$ that we have shown is not a pure-strategy Nash equilibrium. A similar argument applies to the case in which $b_1 = 0$ and $b_2 > 0$.

Since $b_1 > 0$ and $b_2 > 0$, by the assumption that the contest success functions are continuously differentiable, it holds that $\partial s_1(\mathbf{b})/\partial b_1 = 0$ and $\partial s_2(\mathbf{b})/\partial b_2 = 0$, which is equivalent to

$$v_1 \frac{\partial}{\partial b_1} x_1(b_1, b_2) - 1 = 0 \tag{4.73}$$

$$-v_2 \frac{\partial}{\partial b_2} x_1(b_1, b_2) - 1 = 0. \tag{4.74}$$

In order to prove the claim asserted in the theorem by contradiction, suppose that there exists a constant $C > 0$ such that for every valuation vector such that $v_1 \geq v_2 > 0$, the total effort in any pure-strategy Nash equilibrium satisfies

$$R = b_1 + b_2 \geq C \frac{v_1}{\log(v_1/v_2 + 1)}.$$

This implies that

$$\frac{b_1}{v_1} \geq C_1 \frac{1}{\log(v_1/v_2 + 1)} \tag{4.75}$$

where $C_1 = C/2$. We claim that (4.75) implies

$$\left(\frac{b_1}{C_1 v_2} + 1\right) \log\left(\frac{b_1}{C_1 v_2} + 1\right) \geq \frac{v_1}{2v_2} \tag{4.76}$$

which is established at the end of the proof.

From (4.73) and (4.76), we obtain

$$\frac{\partial}{\partial b_1} x_1(b_1, b_2) \geq \frac{1}{2v_2} \frac{1}{\left(\frac{b_1}{C_1 v_2} + 1\right) \log\left(\frac{b_1}{C_1 v_2} + 1\right)}.$$

Using the last inequality, it follows that

$$1 \geq x_1(v_1, b_2) - x_1(v_2, b_2) = \int_{v_2}^{v_1} \frac{\partial}{\partial b_1} x_1(b_1, b_2) db_1$$

$$\geq \int_{v_2}^{v_1} \frac{1}{2v_2} \frac{1}{\left(\frac{b_1}{C_1 v_2} + 1\right) \log\left(\frac{b_1}{C_1 v_2} + 1\right)} db_1$$

$$= \frac{C_1}{2} \log\left(\log\left(\frac{\frac{v_1}{C_1 v_2} + 1}{\frac{1}{C_1} + 1}\right)\right)$$

which is false for every large enough v_1/v_2.

It remains to show that (4.75) implies (4.76). Indeed, we have

$$\left(\frac{b_1}{C_1 v_2} + 1\right) \log\left(\frac{b_1}{C_1 v_2} + 1\right) \geq \frac{b_1}{C_1 v_2} \log\left(\frac{b_1}{C_1 v_2} + 1\right)$$

$$\geq \frac{v_1}{v_2} \frac{1}{\log(v_1/v_2 + 1)} \log\left(\frac{v_1/v_2}{\log(v_1/v_2 + 1)} + 1\right)$$

$$\geq \frac{v_1}{2v_2}$$

where the second inequality is because the function that is lower bounded is increasing in b_1 and equation (4.75) holds, and the third inequality is by the fact that $(1/\log(x + 1)) \log(x/\log(x + 1) + 1) \geq 1/2$, for all $x \geq 0$. $\square$

Asymptotically Optimal Prior-Free Contest Design

We shall show that the upper bound for the total effort in a pure-strategy Nash equilibrium in Theorem 4.46 is achievable for the case of two players under a class of contest success functions that we introduce as follows. A key property of such a class of contest success functions is to ensure that the player with the lower valuation parameter wins with a sufficiently large probability. Suppose that a function $q : \mathbf{R}_+ \rightarrow [0, 1]$ is given that satisfies the following conditions:

(i) $q(0) = 0$.

(ii) $\lim_{x \to \infty} q(x) = 1$.

(iii) q is continuous, increasing, and differentiable.

(iv) $q(x) = 1 - q(1/x)$, for every $x \geq 0$.

Suppose that the contest success functions are defined by $x_1(b_1, b_2)$ and $x_2(b_1, b_2) = 1 - x_1(b_1, b_2)$, for player 1 and player 2, respectively, where

$$x_1(b_1, b_2) = \begin{cases} q\left(\frac{b_1}{b_2}\right), & \text{if } b_1 + b_2 > 0 \\ \frac{1}{2}, & \text{otherwise.} \end{cases} \tag{4.77}$$

Let us introduce the following additional condition on the function q: there exist constants $C > 0$, $\alpha > 0$ and $\rho \geq 1$ such that

$$q'(x) \geq \frac{C}{(x+1)\log^{1+\alpha}(x+1)}, \quad \text{for } x \geq \rho. \tag{4.78}$$

We give two examples of contest success functions that satisfy the given conditions.

Example 4.47. Suppose $q(x) = \phi(\log(x))$ where ϕ is a distribution function that has an even density function on the set of real numbers and satisfies

$$\phi'(x) \geq \frac{C}{x^{1+\alpha}}, \quad \text{for } x \geq \log(\rho).$$

Example 4.48. Suppose that $q(x) = \frac{1+g(x)-g(1/x)}{2}$ where

$$g(x) = 1 - \frac{1}{\log(\log(x+1)+1)+1}.$$

We are now in a position to state a theorem that shows that the upper bound on the total effort in Theorem 4.46 is nearly achievable.

Theorem 4.49. *Consider a two-player contest with valuation parameters $v_1 \geq v_2 > 0$ where a unit prize is allocated according to the contest success functions defined by (4.77) and $x_1(b_1, b_2) + x_2(b_1, b_2) = 1$. Then, there exists a unique pure-strategy Nash equilibrium. Suppose that q satisfies condition (4.78); then the total effort in the pure-strategy Nash equilibrium satisfies*

$$R \geq C\frac{v_1}{\log^{1+\alpha}(v_1/v_2 + 1)}, \quad \text{for } v_1/v_2 \geq \rho.$$

Proof. The payoffs of player 1 and player 2 are $s_1(\mathbf{b}) = v_1 q(b_1/b_2) - b_1$ and $s_2(\mathbf{b}) = v_2(1 - q(b_1/b_2)) - b_2$, respectively. In a pure-strategy Nash equilibrium, each player invests a strictly positive effort, and thus $\partial s_1(\mathbf{b})/\partial b_1 = 0$ and $\partial s_2(\mathbf{b})/\partial b_2 = 0$. The last two conditions are equivalent to

$$v_1 q'\left(\frac{b_1}{b_2}\right) = b_2 \quad \text{and} \quad v_2 q'\left(\frac{b_1}{b_2}\right) = \frac{b_2^2}{b_1}.$$

From this, we observe that

$$\frac{b_1}{b_2} = \frac{v_1}{v_2}.$$

Thus, it follows that there is a unique pure-strategy Nash equilibrium given by

$$b_1 = \frac{v_1}{v_2} v_1 q' \left(\frac{v_1}{v_2}\right) \text{ and } b_2 = v_1 q' \left(\frac{v_1}{v_2}\right)$$

and, the total effort is

$$R = b_1 + b_2 = v_1 q' \left(\frac{v_1}{v_2}\right) \left(\frac{v_1}{v_2} + 1\right)$$

which combined with the assumptions of the theorem yields the asserted result.   □

4.8.2 Allowing a Contest Owner to Withhold the Prize

In this section we consider a contest in which the contest owner is allowed to withhold the prize so that the allocation $\mathbf{x}$ satisfies $\sum_{i \in N} x_i(\mathbf{b}) \leq 1$, for all $\mathbf{b} \in \mathbf{R}_+^n$. Note that in the previous section this option was precluded by assuming that $\mathbf{x}$ is such that $\sum_{i \in N} x_i(\mathbf{b}) = 1$, for all $\mathbf{b} \in \mathbf{R}_+^n$. A question of interest is to characterize the largest total effort that can be achieved in a pure-strategy Nash equilibrium. In this section we shall show that there exist valuation vectors such that

$$\frac{R}{v_1} = O\left(\frac{1}{\log(v_1)}\right)$$

where v_1 is the largest valuation. In fact, we shall show that this is a fundamental bound that cannot be surpassed for a broad class of weakly monotonic auctions that is defined as follows. Consider an auction with a set of two or more players with valuation parameters $v_1 \geq v_2 \geq \cdots \geq v_n > 0$ that is defined by an allocation $(x_1(\mathbf{b}), x_2(\mathbf{b}), \ldots, x_n(\mathbf{b}))$ and payment $(c_1(\mathbf{b}), c_2(\mathbf{b}), \ldots, c_n(\mathbf{b}))$. The payoff functions of the players are given by

$$s_i(v_i, \mathbf{b}) = v_i x_i(\mathbf{b}) - c_i(\mathbf{b}), \quad \text{for } i \in N. \tag{4.79}$$

We denote with $\beta_i(v_i, \mathbf{b}_{-i})$ the set of best responses for player $i \in N$ given that his or her valuation parameter is of value v_i and that other players play $\mathbf{b}_{-i}$, i.e.,

$$\beta_i(v_i, \mathbf{b}_{-i}) = \operatorname{argmax}\{s_i(v_i, (a_i, \mathbf{b}_i)) \mid a_i \in \mathbf{R}_+\}.$$

An auction is said to be *weakly monotonic* if it satisfies the following conditions, for every player $i \in N$:

(i) The allocation function $x_i(\mathbf{b})$ is continuously differentiable in b_j for all $j \in N$.
(ii) For every strategy vector $\mathbf{b} \in \mathbf{R}_+^n$ such that $b_i < b_j$ for some $j \in N$,

$$x_i(b_i', \mathbf{b}_{-i}) \geq x_i(b_i, \mathbf{b}_{-i}) + \epsilon, \quad \text{for some } \epsilon > 0 \text{ and } b_i' \geq b_j.$$

(iii) The payment function $c_i(\mathbf{b})$ is continuously differentiable in b_j, for all $j \in N$.
(iv) For every player $j \in N$ and every $\mathbf{b} \in \mathbf{R}^n$,

$$c_i(b_i', \mathbf{b}_{-i}) \geq c_j(\mathbf{b}), \quad \text{for some } b_i' \in \mathbf{R}_+.$$

(v) The allocation and payment functions satisfy

$$x_i(0, \mathbf{b}_{-i}) = 0 \text{ and } c_i(0, \mathbf{b}_{-i}) = 0 \text{ whenever } \sum_{j \neq i} b_j > 0.$$

(vi) For every $\mathbf{b}_{-i} \in \mathbf{R}_+^{n-1}$, the best response $\beta_i(v_i, \mathbf{b}_{-i})$ is continuously differentiable in v_i.

Condition (ii) is a weak monotonicity condition for the allocation, while condition (iv) is a weak monotonicity condition for the payment. Condition (v) ensures that any best response of a player guarantees a non-negative payoff to this player. Condition (vi) requires that the best response of a player is continuously differentiable in the valuation of this player. This condition indeed holds for the class of smooth contests considered in this chapter with strictly concave payoffs.

Lemma 4.50. *Consider a two-player weakly monotonic auction. Then, there exists $t_0 > 0$ such that for every $t \geq t_0$, for the valuation vector $(v_1, v_2) = (t, v_2(t))$, there exists a pure-strategy Nash equilibrium $(b_1, b_2) = (b_1(t), 1)$.*

Proof. We first show that there exists $t_0 > 0$ such that for every $v_1 = t \geq t_0$ and $b_2 = 1$, any best response of player 1 is greater than 1, i.e. $b_1(t) := \beta_1(t, 1) > 1$. To contradict this claim, assume that for every $t_0 > 0$, there exists $t > t_0$ such that $b_1(t) < 1$. By condition (ii), there exists $\epsilon > 0$ and $b_1' \geq 1$ such that $x_1(b_1', 1) \geq x_1(b_1(t), 1) + \epsilon$. Since $t_0 > 0$ can be chosen arbitrarily, let $t_0 = c_1(b_1', 1)/\epsilon$. The payoff function of player 1 satisfies the following two inequalities:

$$s_1(t, (b_1(t), 1)) = tx_1(b_1(t), 1) - c_1(b_1(t), 1) \leq tx_1(b_1(t), 1)$$

and

$$s_1(t, (b_1', 1)) = tx_1(b_1', 1) - c_1(b_1', 1) \geq t(x_1(b_1(t), 1) + \epsilon) - c_1(b_1', 1).$$

From the last two relations, we obtain

$$s_1(t, (b_1(t), 1)) < s_1(t, (b_1', 1)),$$

which contradicts the assumption that $b_1(t)$ is a best response for player 1.

It remains to show that there exists $v_2(t) > 0$ such that $\beta_2(v_2(t), b_1(t)) = 1$. If $\beta_2(v_2, b_1(t)) < b_1(t)$, then there exists $v_2' > v_2$ such that $\beta_2(v_2', b_1(t)) \geq b_1(t) > 1$. Since $\beta_2(0, b_1(t)) = 0$, $\beta_2(v_2', b_1(t)) > 1$, and $\beta_2(v_2, b_1(t))$ is continuous in v_2, there exists $v_2(t) > 0$ such that $\beta_2(v_2(t), b_1(t)) = 1$. □

Theorem 4.51. *Consider a weakly monotonic auction among two or more players and let C be a positive valued constant. Then, there exists a valuation vector $v_1 \geq v_2 \geq \cdots \geq v_n > 0$ such that for every sufficiently large value of the valuation parameter v_1, the total payment R in a pure-strategy Nash equilibrium satisfies*

$$R \leq C \frac{v_1}{\log(v_1 + 1)}.$$

Proof. The proof is established for valuation vectors of a two-player auction. To arrive at a contradiction, assume that there exist $C > 0$ and $t_0 > 0$ such that for every $t \geq t_0$ for the valuation vector $(t, v_2(t))$ under which $(b_1, b_2) = (b_1(t), 1)$ is a pure-strategy Nash equilibrium, the total payment satisfies

$$c_1(b_1(t), 1) + c_2(b_2(t), 1) \geq C \frac{t}{\log(t + 1)}. \tag{4.80}$$

This implies that

$$c_1(b_1(t), 1) \geq \frac{C}{2} \frac{t}{\log(t+1)}.$$

Let $s_1(t)$ denote the payoff of player 1, i.e. $s_1(t) = s_1(t, (b_1(t), 1))$. By the envelope theorem, which is given in Section 11.1.7, we have

$$s_1(t) = s_1(t_0) + \int_{t_0}^t \frac{\partial}{\partial v_1} s_1(v, (b_1(v), 1)) dv.$$

From (4.79), we have

$$\frac{\partial}{\partial v_1} s_1(v_1, (b_1, 1)) = x_1(b_1, 1).$$

Therefore,

$$s_1(t) = s_1(t_0) + \int_{t_0}^t x_1(b_1(v), 1) dv.$$

Again, from (4.79), we have

$$s_1(t) = t x_1(b_1(t), 1) - c_1(b_1(t), 1).$$

Combining the last two identities, we obtain

$$c_1(b_1(t), 1) = t x_1(b_1(t), 1) - \int_{t_0}^t x_1(b_1(v), 1) dv - s_1(t_0).$$

From this, we observe that

$$\frac{d}{dt} x_1(b_1(t), 1) = \frac{1}{t} \frac{d}{dt} c_1(b_1(t), 1). \tag{4.81}$$

We note the following series of relations:

$$1 \geq x_1(b_1(t), 1) - x_1(b_1(t_0), 1)$$

$$= \int_{t_0}^t dx_1(b_1(v), 1)$$

$$= \int_{t_0}^t \frac{1}{v} dc_1(b_1(v), 1)$$

$$= \frac{c_1(b_1(v), 1)}{v} \Big|_{t_0}^t + \int_{t_0}^t \frac{c_1(b_1(v), 1)}{v^2} dv$$

$$\geq \int_{t_0}^t \frac{c_1(b_1(v), 1)}{v^2} dv$$

$$\geq \frac{C}{2} \int_{t_0}^t \frac{dv}{v \log(v+1)}$$

$$= \frac{C}{2} \log\left(\log\left(\frac{t+1}{t_0+1}\right)\right)$$

where the second equality is by (4.81), the third equality is by partial integration, and the third inequality is by the hypothesis (4.80). Hence, we showed that $(C/2) \log(\log((t +$

$1)/(t_0 + 1))) < 1$. This condition fails to hold true for every sufficiently large $t \geq t_0$, which establishes a contradiction to the assumption that the total payment satisfies (4.80) for every $t \geq t_0$. $\square$

4.9 Difference-Form Prize Allocation

In this section, we consider the class of contest success functions for which the winning probability of a player is a function of the differences between the effort invested by this player and those of other players. For example, any anonymous general-logit contest success function with production functions $f_j(x) = e^{\alpha_j x}$, $a_j > 0$, $j \in N$, is of difference form. We shall see that strategic behavior under difference-form contest success functions exhibits qualitative behavior that is very different from that under the contest success functions that we studied thus far in this chapter. We shall focus on the case of a two-player contest.

We consider a contest between two players whose valuation parameters are $v_1 \geq v_2 > 0$ and the contest success is of a difference form specified as follows. Let G be a distribution function that has a density g and is such that $G(x) + G(-x) = 1$, i.e., the density function g is an even function. The winning probabilities of the players are $(x_1(b_1, b_2), x_2(b_1, b_2)) = (G(b_1 - b_2), 1 - G(b_1 - b_2))$. This accommodates the case when G is a Gaussian distribution with mean 0 and variance σ^2, i.e., $G(x) = \Phi\left(x/\left(\sqrt{2}\sigma\right)\right)$ where Φ is the standard normal distribution, and the logistic distribution $G(x) = 1/(1 + e^{-\alpha x})$, for $\alpha > 0$. The payoffs of the players are given by

$$s_1(b_1, b_2) = v_1 G(b_1 - b_2) - b_1$$

$$s_2(b_1, b_2) = v_2(1 - G(b_1 - b_2)) - b_2.$$

We shall restrict our attention to the case $v_1 > v_2 > 0$, because it can be shown that in the case of two players with identical abilities in general there is a continuum of equilibria. We refer to player 1 as the strong player, and to player 2 as the weak player. To simplify matters even further, we shall assume that the density function $g(x)$ is strictly positive on $\mathbf{R}$, continuous, and strictly decreasing in $|x|$, and that $g(0)$ is bounded. In particular, this accommodates the two examples of probit and logit contest success functions. Let $g^{-1}(x)$ be the inverse of the function g restricted on $\mathbf{R}_+$. Then, there is a unique pure-strategy Nash equilibrium, which is given as follows:

$$(b_1, b_2) = \begin{cases} (0, 0), & \text{if } v_1 \leq 1/g(0) \\ (g^{-1}(1/v_1), 0), & \text{if } v_1 > 1/g(0) \end{cases}. \tag{4.82}$$

See Figure 4.10 for an illustration.

For the two examples of a probit and a logit difference-form contest success function, respectively, we have

$$1/g(0) = 2\sqrt{\pi}\sigma \quad g^{-1}(1/v_1) = 2\sigma\sqrt{\log\left(\frac{v_1}{2\sqrt{\pi}\sigma}\right)}$$

$$1/g(0) = 4/\alpha \quad g^{-1}(1/v_1) = \frac{1}{\alpha}\log\left(1/\left(1 - \frac{1}{2}\sqrt{\alpha v_1 - 4}\left(\sqrt{\alpha v_1} - \sqrt{\alpha v_1 - 4}\right)\right)\right).$$

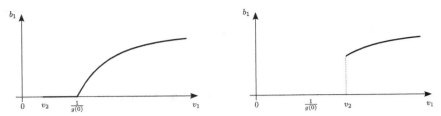

Figure 4.10. The equilibrium effort of the strong player under a difference-form contest success function.

There are two key observations to note here: (i) in any pure-strategy Nash equilibrium, there is at most one active player, and (ii) if the valuation parameter of the strong player is large enough, then this player *preempts* the weak player. This kind of strategic behavior was not observed under the contest success functions that we previously considered, where in every pure-strategy Nash equilibrium, at least two players were active. The strong player exerts a strictly positive effort only if his or her valuation parameter is larger than the threshold $\max\{v_2, 1/g(0)\}$. It is noteworthy that for large values of the largest valuation parameter, the effort exerted from the strong player is determined by the properties of the function $G(x)$ around $x = 0$. For the two examples of the probit and logit contest success functions, we, respectively, have $b_1 \sim 2\sigma \sqrt{\log(v_1)}$ and $b_1 \sim \frac{1}{\alpha} \log(v_1)$, asymptotically for large v_1.

Summary

Contest Success Functions

A contest success function that is regular, monotonic, and satisfies independence of irrelevant alternatives is a general-logit function.

If, in addition, scale invariance holds, then the contest success function is of the ratio form.

Proportional Allocation

Active players are those with $\hat{n}$ largest valuations where

$$\hat{n} = \max\left\{i \in N \mid v_i > \frac{i-2}{\sum_{j=1}^{i-1} \frac{1}{v_j}}\right\}.$$

Total effort:

$$R = \frac{\hat{n} - 1}{\sum_{i=1}^{\hat{n}} \frac{1}{v_i}}.$$

Total effort bounds: $\frac{1}{2}v_2 \leq R < v_2$.

Social efficiency is at least $3/4$, which is asymptotically achieved for the valuation vector such that $v_1 \geq v_2 = \cdots = v_n = v_1/2$ for every fixed $v_1 > 0$ as the number of players n grows large.

Ratio-Form Allocation

For $0 < \alpha < 1$, all players are active.

Total effort lower bound: $R \geq \frac{\alpha}{2} v_2$.

Total effort upper bound: $R = O\left(\frac{1}{\log(v_1/v_2)}\right)$, for every sufficiently large v_1/v_2.

Weighted Proportional Allocation

Active players are as under proportional allocation.

Total effort:

$$R = \frac{1}{4}\left(\sum_{i=1}^{\hat{n}} v_i - \frac{(\hat{n}-2)^2}{\sum_{i=1}^{\hat{n}} \frac{1}{v_i}}\right).$$

Total effort lower bound: $R \geq \frac{1}{4} v_1$.

Maximum individual effort: $R_1 = \frac{v_1}{4}$ by excluding all but a pair of players with largest valuations and optimal weights that maximize the total effort.

Social efficiency is at least $1/2$, which is asymptotically achieved for the valuation vector such that $v_1 \geq v_2 = \cdots = v_n > 0$ for asymptotically large n and v_1/v_2.

Weighted Valuation Allocation

Active players are those with $\hat{n}$ largest valuations where

$$\hat{n} = \left\{ i \in N \mid \sqrt{v_i} > \frac{i-2}{\sum_{j=1}^{i-1} \frac{1}{\sqrt{v_j}}} \right\}.$$

Total effort:

$$R = \frac{\hat{n}-1}{\left(\sum_{i=1}^{\hat{n}} \frac{1}{\sqrt{v_i}}\right)^2 - (\hat{n}-1)\sum_{i=1}^{\hat{n}} \frac{1}{v_i}}.$$

Total effort bounds: $\frac{1}{2}\sqrt{v_1 v_2} \leq R \leq \sqrt{v_1 v_2}$.

Social efficiency is at least $1/(1 + 2/\sqrt{3}) \approx 0.46$, which is asymptotically tight for the valuation vector such that $v_1 > v_2 = \cdots = v_n = (2 - \sqrt{3})^2 v_1$, for every fixed $v_1 > 0$ as the number of players n grows large.

Optimal Prior-Free Contest Design

For every contest with a contest success function that is regular, anonymous, and smooth and a constant $C > 0$, there exists a valuation vector such that in a pure-strategy Nash equilibrium, the total effort is

$$R \leq C\frac{v_1}{\log(v_1/v_2 + 1)}.$$

For a two-player contest, there exists a contest success function that for every $C > 0$ and $\alpha > 0$ guarantees the total effort

$$R \geq C\frac{v_1}{\log^{1+\alpha}(v_1/v_2 + 1)}$$

for sufficiently large v_1/v_2.

If the prize is allowed to be withheld by the contest owner, then the total effort satisfies

$$R \le C \frac{v_1}{\log(v_1 + 1)}$$

for every sufficiently large v_1.

Difference-Form Contest Success Function

In a contest with two players where the valuation of the stronger player is strictly larger than the valuation of the weaker player, the stronger player preempts the weaker player who invests zero effort.

If the valuations of the two players are equal then a continuum of equilibria may exist.

Exercises

4.1 **A model of stochastic production and general logit contest success function** Consider a model of stochastic production by a set $N = \{1, 2, \ldots, n\}$ of two or more individuals, which is defined as follows. A unit prize is awarded to the individual who first solves a task. The production times are assumed to be independent and exponentially distributed random variables with parameters $f_1(b_1), f_2(b_2), \ldots, f_n(b_n)$. We can interpret $f_i(b_i)$ as the speed of production of individual $i \in N$ given that he or she invests an effort of value b_i. If $\sum_{j \in N} f_j(b_j) = 0$, then the prize is awarded with equal probability to any of the individuals. Each individual $i \in N$ discounts the value of the prize exponentially with production time at a rate of value $\delta_i \ge 0$.

Show that the expected values received by the players are given by

$$x_i(\mathbf{b}) = \frac{f_i(b_i)}{\sum_{j \in N} f_j(b_j) + \delta_i}, \quad \text{for } i \in N$$

whenever $\sum_{j \in N} f_j(b_j) > 0$, and $x_i(\mathbf{b}) = 1/n$ for $i \in N$, otherwise.

4.2 **Some properties of pure-strategy Nash equilibrium** Prove each of the three claims asserted in Theorem 4.7.

4.3 **Proportional allocation: two players** Prove each of the claims asserted in Theorem 4.9.

4.4 **An extremal property of proportional allocation** Consider the game that models the contest among two or more players with identical values of valuation parameters $v_1 = v_2 = \cdots = v_n > 0$ and unit marginal costs of production that allocates a unit prize according to an anonymous general-logit contest success function with production function f that is increasing, concave, continuously differentiable, and such that $f(0) = 0$.

Show that for the given class of production functions, the largest total effort in the pure-strategy Nash equilibrium is achieved for linear production function $f(x) = x$, i.e., proportional allocation, and is in this case equal to

$$R = \left(1 - \frac{1}{n}\right) v_1.$$

4.5 **Some properties of equilibrium under general logit contest success function** Consider the game that models the contest among two or more players with valuation parameters

$v_1 \geq v_2 \geq \cdots \geq v_n > 0$ that awards a unit prize according to an anonymous general-logit contest success function with production function f that is increasing, continuously differentiable, concave, and $f(0) = 0$. Prove that the following two claims hold in the pure-strategy Nash equilibrium.

(a) The individual efforts of the players satisfy $b_1 \geq b_2 \geq \cdots \geq b_n$.
(b) If $xf'(x)/f(x)$ is increasing in x, then $b_1/v_1 \geq b_2/v_2 \geq \cdots \geq b_n/v_n$.

Note that $xf'(x)/f(x)$ is increasing for some common production functions, e.g., check that this is so for the ratio-form contest success function with production function $f(x) = x^\alpha$, for $0 < \alpha \leq 1$.

4.6 **General-logit contest success function: comparative analysis** Consider the game that models the two-player contest with valuation parameters $v_1, v_2 > 0$ and unit marginal costs of production that awards a unit prize according to a general-logit contest success function with production functions f_1 and f_2 that are assumed to be increasing, continuously differentiable, concave, and such that $f_1(0) = 0$ and $f_2(0) = 0$. For a pure-strategy Nash equilibrium $\mathbf{b} = (b_1, b_2)$ of this game, we refer to the player who is more likely to win as the favorite and to the other player as the underdog. Prove the following two claims.

(a) The effort of each player increases in the valuation parameter of the underdog player.
(b) The effort of the favorite player increases in his or her own valuation parameter, while that of the underdog player decreases.

4.7 **Proportional allocation: comparative analysis** Consider the game that models the contest among two or more players with valuation parameters $v_1 \geq v_2 \geq \cdots \geq v_n > 0$ where a unit prize is allocated according to proportional allocation. Prove that the following claims hold in the pure-strategy Nash equilibrium.

(a) The total effort is increasing in the valuation parameter of each active player.
(b) The effort of each active player is increasing in his or her own valuation.
(c) The larger the valuation of player 1, the smaller the effort of any other active player.
(d) The larger the valuation of an active player $i \neq 1$, the larger the effort of player 1, if, and only if, $v_1 > 2(1 - 1/\hat{n})\bar{v}(\mathbf{v})$, and the smaller the effort of any other active player j such that $j \neq 1$ and $j \neq i$.

4.8 **Proportional allocation: tightness of the** $3/4$ **worst-case social efficiency** Show that for an n-player contest with the valuation vector $(v_1, v_2, \ldots, v_n) = (1, 1/2, \ldots, 1/2)$ where a unit prize is allocated according to proportional allocation and players incur unit marginal costs of production, the social efficiency of the pure-strategy Nash equilibrium is $3/4$, asymptotically as the number of players n grows large.

4.9 **Proportional allocation: adding a player** Consider the game that models a contest among two or more players with valuation parameters $v_1 \geq v_2 \geq \cdots \geq v_n > 0$ and unit marginal costs of production that allocates a unit prize according to proportional allocation. Consider also another game that results by adding a new player a with valuation parameter v_a. Prove that the following comparison claims hold for the pure-strategy Nash equilibria of the two respective games.

(a) The total effort increases with the addition of player a if v_a is larger than the total effort in the game without player a, and, otherwise, it remains unchanged.

(b) The individual efforts of active players are affected by adding player a as follows. If v_a is smaller than or equal to the total effort in the game without player a, then the effort of each active player remains unchanged. Otherwise, we have the following two cases. The effort of each active player $i \neq 1$ decreases by adding player a. The effort of player 1 increases (decreases) if v_1 is larger (smaller) than the sum of the total efforts in the two games.

(c) The winning probability of each active player in the game without player a decreases by adding player a if v_a is larger than the total effort in the game without player a, and, otherwise, it remains unchanged.

(d) The same claim holds for the payoffs of the players as for the winning probabilities.

4.10 Multiple prizes: symmetric valuations Consider the game that models a contest among two or more players with unit-valued valuation parameters and unit marginal production costs that awards prizes $w_1 \geq w_2 \geq \cdots \geq w_n \geq 0$ using an anonymous general-logit contest success function with production function f as follows: the first prize is allocated to a player according to the general-logit contest success function applied to the set of all players, the second prize is allocated to a player according to the general-logit contest success function applied to the set of all players but excluding the player who won the first prize, and so on and so forth. The production function f is assumed to be increasing, continuously differentiable, concave, and such that $f(0) = 0$. Prove the following claims.

(a) There is a unique pure-strategy Nash equilibrium $\mathbf{b} = (b_1, b_2, \ldots, b_n)$ such that $b_1 = b_2 = \cdots = b_n$, where $b_1 = 0$, if $\sum_{j=1}^{n}(1 - (H_n - H_{n-j}))w_j \leq 0$, with H_l being the l-th harmonic number, and, otherwise, b_1 is the unique solution to the equation

$$\frac{f(b_1)}{f'(b_1)} = \frac{1}{n}\sum_{j=1}^{n}(1 - (H_n - H_{n-j}))w_j.$$

(b) Under the given assumptions on the production function, the largest total effort is achieved for a linear production function, i.e., proportional allocation. The same property holds also for the maximum individual effort.

(c) Given a prize budget, it is optimal to allocate the entire prize budget to the first prize with respect to both maximizing total effort and maximum individual effort.

(d) Each of the j^* largest prizes has a strictly effect and every other prize has a decreasing effect on both total effort and maximum individual effort, where j^* is the largest value of j such that $1 - (H_n - H_{n-j}) > 0$. The following asymptotic holds:

$$j^* \sim \left(1 - \frac{1}{e}\right)n \approx 0.63n, \quad \text{for large } n.$$

(e) In particular, for the case of proportional allocation and m identical prizes each of value w_1, the total effort is equal to

$$R(w_1, m) = (n - m)(H_n - H_{n-m})w_1.$$

4.11 Multiple prizes: asymmetric valuations Consider the game that models a contest among three players with valuation parameters $v = v_1 \geq v_2 = v_3 = 1$, who simultaneously invest efforts and incur unit marginal costs of production. A unit prize budget is split between the first place prize and the second place prize such that they are of values w and $1 - w$, for $1/2 \leq w \leq 1$, respectively. The winner of the first place prize is determined according to an anonymous general-logit contest success function applied to the efforts invested by all the players, and the winner of the second place prize is determined according to the given contest success function applied to the efforts invested by the two players who did not win the first place prize. The general-logit contest success function is assumed to be with production function f that is increasing, continuously differentiable, concave, and such that $f(0) = 0$. Prove the following three claims.

(a) The efforts of the players in the pure-strategy Nash equilibrium converge to $\mathbf{b} = (b_1, b_2, b_3)$ in the limit of asymptotically large value of the valuation parameter v, where $b_2 = b_3$, and b_1 and b_2 are the unique solution to the equations:

$$\frac{f(b_1)^2}{f'(b_1)} = 2(2w - 1)f(b_2)v \text{ and } \frac{f(b_2)}{f'(b_2)} = \frac{1 - w}{4}.$$

(b) The optimal split of the prize purse with respect to both total effort and maximum individual effort in the pure-strategy Nash equilibrium, asymptotically for large value of valuation parameter v, is such that a strictly positive, but smaller than half, portion of the prize purse is allocated to the second place prize.

(c) In particular, for the ratio-form contest success function, i.e., for production function $f(x) = x^\alpha$ with the return to scale parameter $0 < \alpha \leq 1$, it is optimal to allocate portion w^* to the first place prize given by

$$w^* = \frac{1}{2}\left(1 + \frac{1}{1 + \alpha}\right).$$

Thus, for proportional allocation, it is optimal to allocate $3/4$ of the prize purse to the first place prize ($3 : 1$ rule).

4.10 Bibliographical Notes

The axiomatic approach to justify particular forms of contest success functions was originally studied by Skaperdas (1996), and this was subsequently extended by Clark and Riis (1998b) who showed that the same set of axioms imply a more general family of ratio-form contest success functions, and not only anonymous ratio-form contest success functions. The results in Theorems 4.1, 4.2, and 4.3 closely follow those in Skaperdas (1996) and Clark and Riis (1998b). Kooreman and Schoonbeek (1997) pursued a similar axiomatic approach, but restricted to the case of two players. The axiom of independence of irrelevant alternatives originates from the theory of user choice models, e.g., Luce (1959). The uncertainty approach to justify the choice of a contest success function was studied by various authors, including a book exposition by Hirshleifer and Riley (1992). Models of stochastic production with additive noise were considered, e.g., by Levitt (1995), and with multiplicative noise, e.g., by O'Keeffe et al. (1984), Hillman and Riley (1989), Hirshleifer and Riley (1992), and Gerchak and He (2003). More recently, new developments were reported by Jia (2008), including that the ratio-form contest success function arises under a model of stochastic production as in Model 1 in Section 4.2.2. The observation that a ratio-form contest success function arises under a model of stochastic production with exponentially distributed multiplicative noise for the case of two players and not for a larger number of players (Model 2 in Section 4.2.2) was perhaps first reported by Hillman and Riley (1989). The model of stochastic production, Model 3, in Section 4.2.2 is a special case of the classic patent race game by Loury (1979). The model of stochastic production, Model 4, in Section 4.2.2 is from Fullerton and McAfee (1999). Survey expositions on the contest success functions include Skaperdas (1996), Garfinkel and Skaperdas (2007), and Corchón and Dahm (2010).

Contests with general-logit contest success functions were studied under various assumptions, e.g., by Rosen (1986), Dixit (1987), Baik and Jason (1992), and Münster (2006). The existence of a pure-strategy Nash equilibrium under the conditions in Theorem 4.4 follows from the work of Rosen (1965) on the more general class of concave games. The part of the same theorem on the uniqueness and the construction is from Szidarovszky and Okuguchi (1997). Some characterization results for general contest success functions with decreasing, constant, and increasing returns were provided in Cornes and Hartley (2005). The upper bounds on individual efforts in Theorem 4.8 are new. Special cases such as that of a two-player contest with the special form of production functions $f_i(x) = a_i f(x)$ were studied by Baik (1994). Dasgupta and Nti (1998) studied contests with linear production functions (also studied in Amegashie (2006) and Kolmar and Wagener (2012)) and showed that any equilibrium outcome under an anonymous contest success function with concave increasing production functions is also an equilibrium outcome in a contest under the suitable choice of linear production functions. This is generalized in Theorem 4.34 and Corollary 4.35 to general contest success functions. The special case of symmetric linear production functions was considered in various works to deal with the issue of discontinuity of proportional allocation at the point where all players invest zero effort, e.g., Maheswaran and Basar (2003), Johari and Tsitsiklis (2004), Zhang (2005), and Pálvölgi et al. (2012). Recently, this case was also studied by Wasser (2013) for games with complete and incomplete information. Münster (2006) studied the effect of uncertainty about the number of competitors in a contest with anonymous general-logit contest success functions.

Contests with proportional allocation were studied by many in the context of political economy, rent-seeking, lotteries, and resource allocation. Tullock (1975) introduced a game of a two-party conflict where the two parties participate in a lottery: "each party is permitted to buy as many lottery tickets as he wishes at one dollar each, the lottery tickets are put in a drum, one is pulled out, and whoever owns that ticket wins the prize." In the context of strategic rent-seeking, this allocation rule was studied by Tullock (1980), which prompted many subsequent studies, including Hillman and Katz (1984), Hillman and Riley (1989), Michaels (1988), Ellingsen (1991), Nitzan (1991a,b), Paul and Wilhite (1991), and Stein (2002). The contest with proportional allocation was used as a model to study various situations such as charitable fund-raising (Dudley 2002), allocation of resources in computer systems (Stoica et al. 1996), and allocation of network bandwidth in communication networks, e.g., Kelly (1997), Hajek and Gopalakrishnan (2002), and Johari and Tsitsiklis (2004). The characterizations of the set of active players and the total effort in Theorem 4.19 and equation (4.36) were already reported in Hillman and Riley (1989) and Ellingsen (1991). Corollary 4.21 and Exercise 4.7 are from Stein (2002). Fang (2002) studied how the strategic behavior under proportional allocation compares to that in a standard all-pay contest and showed that in contrast to standard all-pay contests, exclusion of some players cannot increase the total effort in equilibrium and that this even holds under budget limits. Corollary 4.23 is from Fang (2002). Characterization of the pure-strategy Nash equilibrium under proportional allocation and positive-valued, increasing, concave utility functions, in Theorem 4.10, is from Johari and Tsitsiklis (2004). The family of α-fair utility functions was first introduced in the context of network resource allocation by Mo and Walrand (2000) and La and Anantharam (2002). The correspondence of the allocation in a pure-strategy Nash equilibrium and the solution to the optimization problem in (4.27) is originally from Hajek and Gopalakrishnan (2002). The concept of an ϵ-perturbed game to establish the existence of a pure-strategy Nash equilibrium for the extended game was already used in Maheswaran and Basar (2003). The social efficiency lower bound in Theorem 4.24 is from Johari and Tsitsiklis (2004). An alternative proof was established by Correa et al. (2013) using a geometric argument that applies also to deriving the same quantitative bound for the game of non-atomic selfish routing, originally derived by Roughgarden and Tardos (2002). This worst-case social efficiency bound was extended to polyhedral constraints by Nguyen and Tardos (2007). The effects of the addition and removal of players were studied by Münster (2006), including the results in Exercise 4.9.

The study of the ratio-form contest success functions has a long and rich history in the context of economic theory, public choice, political economy, rent-seeking, lobbying, and resource allocation. The theory of rent-seeking originates from the work of Tullock (1967), Krueger (1974), and Posner (1975) and the introduction of strategic rent-seeking by Tullock (1980), which since then has been developed over the years including the works of Hillman and Katz (1984), Corcoran and Karels (1985), Higgins et al. (1885), Appelbaum and Katz (1986), Long and Vousden (1987), Hillman and Samet (1987), Allard (1988), Gradstein and Nitzan (1989), Katz et al. (1990), Ursprung (1990), Nitzan (1991a), Nitzan (1991b), and Leininger (1993). A contest with the ratio-form contest success function is commonly referred to as a Tullock contest, following the early work by Tullock (1967, 1980). This form of a contest success function was also considered in various other contexts including political campaigns by Snyder (1989), job promotions by Rosen (1986), commitments by Dixit (1987), and digital advertising by Mirrokni et al. (2010). Nitzan (1994) surveyed alternative ways to model rent-seeking contests, focusing on the relationship between the extent of the rent dissipation and the underlying contest characteristics such as the number of players, their attitudes toward risk and the asymmetry among the players. Appelbaum and Katz (1986) studied the strategic behavior in contests among players with symmetric valuation parameters. The fact that in a two-player contest the total effort in a pure-strategy Nash equilibrium is maximized for the return to scale parameter equal to 2 was observed by Moulin (1988). The characterization of equilibrium properties for players with symmetric valuations was done by Pérez-Castrillo and Verdier (1992) and for two players with asymmetric valuations by Baik (1994) and Nti (1999). The necessary and sufficient condition for the existence of a pure-strategy Nash equilibrium in a two-player contest with a ratio-form contest success function, given in Theorem 4.28, is from Nti (1999). The characterization of the maximum total effort in a pure-strategy Nash equilibrium in Theorem 4.31 was perhaps first obtained by Nti (2004). Comparison with the total effort in a standard all-pay contest was pursued by various authors, including Bos (2011). Baye et al. (1994) studied the mixed-strategy Nash equilibrium of a ratio-form contest with parameter $\alpha > 2$ and discrete strategy spaces. Malueg and Yates (2004) considered an incomplete information game in a two-player contest whose valuations are assumed to admit one of two values and are private information. A necessary and sufficient condition for the existence of a symmetric Bayes-Nash equilibrium is established in this work, as well as some interesting observations such as that the submitted effort of each player is a constant factor of his or her own valuation. Risk aversion was studied, e.g., by Hillman and Katz (1984), Hillman and Samet (1987), Long and Vousden (1987), Millner and Pratt (1991), Cornes and Hartley (2003), and Johari and Tsitsiklis (2004). Allocation of multiple prizes by successively applying a ratio-form contest success function over the set of players who have not yet been assigned a prize was studied, e.g., by Clark and Riis (1998c) and Szymanski and Valletti (2005). Exercise 4.10 is from Clark and Riis (1998c), and Exercise 4.11 is from Szymanski and Valletti (2005).

Contests that award a prize according to a weighted proportional allocation were studied by Gradstein (1998), Stein (2002), and Franke et al. (2011). Stein (2002) characterized the number of active players and the total effort in a pure-strategy Nash equilibrium. Franke et al. (2011) established several properties under relative abilities that maximize the total effort in a pure-strategy Nash equilibrium. The characterization of the total effort in Theorem 4.37 closely follows that of Franke et al. (2011).

Contests that award a prize according to a weighted valuation allocation were first studied in the context of public choice, e.g., Gradstein (1995, 1998). A characterization of the equilibrium properties for profit-maximizing choice of weights was derived by Nguyen and Vojnović (2010b), including the results in Theorem 4.42 and Theorem 4.45. Corollary 4.43 presents an explicit characterization under linear utility functions that is new. Another related work here is that of Ritz (2008), who observed that increasing the marginal production cost of each player by a common additive constant may increase the total effort in equilibrium, which can be seen as a manipulation of valuation parameters.

Optimal prior-free contest design was considered by Nguyen and Vojnović (2010a), including the upper bound on the total effort in a pure-strategy Nash equilibrium in Theorem 4.46 and the class of contest success functions that in two-player contests achieves this upper bound; it constitutes the basis of Theorem 4.49. The upper bound on the total effort for the class of weakly monotonic auctions, in Theorem 4.51, is from Nguyen and Vojnović (2011).

Strategic behavior in contests with difference-form contest success functions was studied by Nalebuff and Stiglitz (1983), Hirshleifer (1989), Baik (1998), and Che and Gale (2000). Nalebuff and Stiglitz (1983) considered difference-form contests with a winning gap where the winner is declared only if the largest invested effort is larger than the second largest invested effort for at least the value of a winning gap parameter; it was shown that there exist cases in which a strictly positive winning gap parameter improves the total effort. The discussion of the difference-form contest success functions in Section 4.9 is based on Baik (1998).

CHAPTER 5
Simultaneous Contests

In this chapter we consider normal form games that consist of a set of one or more contests each offering a prize of a certain value and a set of two or more players who simultaneously invest efforts across the set of available contests. We consider strategic players who aim at selfishly maximizing their individual payoffs. The payoff of each player is assumed to be quasi-linear in the total value of prizes won across different contests and the incurred cost of production. The values of prizes are allowed to assume arbitrary positive values, except when we consider the case of contests with identical values of prizes. The existence of multiple available contests provides players with alternative options for effort investment. From the perspective of any given contest, this provides players with outside options that may significantly affect the effort investments directed into the given contest.

The type of normal form games that we study in this chapter serves as a natural model of the competition-based crowdsourcing services that solicit contributions to projects from online communities through contests. In such crowdsourcing services there are typically several open contests at any given time, sometimes as many as in the order of hundreds. Each contest awards one or more prizes to the winning solutions selected from the set of solutions submitted to this contest. This selection is made according to a set of contest rules, which are public information, or at a discretion of a contest owner who identifies one or more best-quality submissions according to a criteria. Some of the competition-based crowdsourcing services allow workers to choose to participate in any of the open contests. Such a design rests on a premise that each individual worker may be in a best position to appreciate his or her ability to perform well in any given contest based on specification of the underlying project requirements and some prior sense about the competition. However, such an assignment of projects to workers may result in inefficiencies due to non-cooperative strategic behavior. Some projects may attract many while others may only attract a few workers.

There are several factors that can significantly affect strategic behavior in a game of simultaneous contests, including the choice of a prize allocation mechanism according to which prizes are allocated by individual contests, the nature of production costs incurred by players, the values of the prizes offered by individual contests, abilities or valuations of the players over different contests, and the amount of information available to players about the abilities of other players. We shall consider three types of a prize allocation mechanism: the mechanism that allocates the prize to a player who invests the highest effort in the given contest, the proportional allocation mechanism, and the equal sharing mechanism. We already studied the first two mechanisms in the case of a single contest in Chapter 2 and Chapter 4, respectively. We shall devote our attention here to two types of production cost functions. The first type assumes that each player can only afford to invest effort in one of the contests, in which he or she incurs a linear cost of production. This is motivated by situations in which a worker is able to produce a good-quality work by focusing on a limited number of open projects. The second type of production costs assumes that each player is endowed with a budget of effort that he or she strategically splits across a subset of available contests. This assumption is motivated by situations in which each given worker can invest only so much of a total effort depending on his or her ability or available time. For example, in the crowdsourcing scenarios, an online worker may be able to devote only a limited number of working hours in a week that he or she has to split across different projects. We shall primarily consider the case in which each player has a valuation that is in general allowed to be specific to him or her. The valuation parameter of a player can either be interpreted as a measure of the ability of this player or of how much this player values a unit of the prize offered by any given contest.

For all three types of prize allocation mechanisms, we shall consider the game with complete information where valuation parameters are common knowledge. For the prize allocation mechanism that awards the whole prize to the player who invests the largest effort, we shall also consider the game with incomplete information where valuations are private information. Both types of informational assumptions are of interest in practice. The game of simultaneous contests with complete information may serve as a model of situations in which competitors are informed about which opponents are going to participate in specific contests and about their individual abilities. For example, a contest may be organized such that in a registration phase workers indicate whether they are going to participate in the contest, and the ability of workers may be readily appreciated from publicly available worker profile pages that typically contain historical performance track records and rating scores computed based on their past performance. On the other hand, the game of incomplete information may well serve as a model of situations in which there is an uncertainty about which players would turn up to compete in any given contest.

Our goal in this chapter is to study strategic behavior of players in the games of simultaneous contests in an equilibrium. The first question to address for any type of game is whether an equilibrium exists. Given that an equilibrium exists, we are interested in characterizing the equilibrium points and evaluating efficiency with respect to the social welfare and the amount of total effort investment made across different contests. We also consider questions that are of interest specifically for the game of simultaneous contests, in particular, those that are concerned with the level of participation and effort investments across different contests for any given values of prizes offered by these contests in an equilibrium.

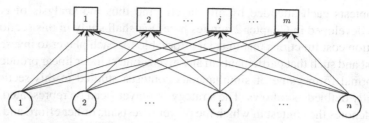

Figure 5.1. A system of simultaneous contests: circles represent players, squares represent contests, and edges represent options for effort investments.

5.1 Basic Concepts

A game of simultaneous contests consists of a set of $n \geq 2$ players and a set of $m \geq 1$ contests, where we denote the sets of players by $N = \{1, 2, \ldots, n\}$ and the set of contests by $M = \{1, 2, \ldots, m\}$ (see Figure 5.1). The effort investment of player i is denoted by $\mathbf{b}_i = (b_{i,j}, j \in M)$ and is assumed to take values in a strategy set $\mathcal{B}_i \subseteq \mathbf{R}_+^m$. The effort investments by all players across all contests are denoted by $\mathbf{b} = (b_{i,j}, \ i \in N, j \in M)$ in $\mathcal{B} = \mathcal{B}_1 \times \mathcal{B}_2 \times \cdots \times \mathcal{B}_n$. Each contest offers a prize that is allocated to participants in the given contest according to a prize allocation mechanism. The allocation mechanism of contest j is specified by $(x_{i,j}(\mathbf{b}), i \in N)$, where $x_{i,j}(\mathbf{b})$ denotes the allocation to player i and we assume $\sum_{i \in N} x_{i,j}(\mathbf{b}) = 1$. The payoff functions of players are defined as follows:

$$s_i(\mathbf{b}) = \sum_{j \in M} v_{i,j} x_{i,j}(\mathbf{b}) - c_i(\mathbf{b}_i), \quad \text{for } i \in N \tag{5.1}$$

where $v_{i,j} \geq 0$ denotes the valuation parameter of player i for winning the prize of contest j and $c_i : \mathbf{R}_+^m \to \mathbf{R}_+$ is the production cost incurred by player i for making the effort investment $\mathbf{b}_i$.

We shall pay particular attention to the following type of valuations of prizes. Contests are assumed to offer prizes of values $w_1 \geq w_2 \geq \cdots \geq w_m > 0$, and players are assumed to have valuations $v_1 \geq v_2 \geq \cdots \geq v_n > 0$ of a unit prize offered by any given contest. This is a special case of valuations of prizes by players of the form $v_{i,j} = v_i w_j$, for $i \in N$ and $j \in M$. The valuation parameter v_i of player i can be interpreted to quantify the ability of this player.

The definition of production costs is general enough to allow for the strategies of players to be restricted within a feasible set. For example, each player may incur an infinite production cost if investing a strictly positive effort in more than one contest or if the total effort investment of the player exceeds his or her budget of effort.

5.2 Standard All-Pay Contests

In this section we consider the game of simultaneous contests where each contest deploys the prize allocation mechanism as in the standard all-pay contest that we studied in Chapter 2. If the production cost functions of players are linear then the game of m simultaneous contests is strategically equivalent to that of m independent standard all-pay contests each attended by all players, and thus the analysis of equilibrium properties developed in Chapter 2 applies here. We shall study in this section the type of production cost functions that make it affordable for each player to invest in at most one contest and such that participants in any given contest incur linear production costs.

The normal form game of simultaneous contests, studied in this section, can be conveniently defined as follows. The strategy of player i can be represented by (a_i, b_i) where a_i denotes the contest in which the player invests his or her effort, and b_i denotes the amount of effort invested in contest a_i. We shall refer to $\mathbf{a} = (a_1, a_2, \ldots, a_n)$ as an *assignment* of players to contests. With a slight abuse of notation, we write $\mathbf{b} = (b_i, i \in N)$. The payoff functions can be written as follows:

$$s_i(\mathbf{a}, \mathbf{b}) = w_{a_i} v_i x_{i,a_i}(\mathbf{b}^{a_i}) - b_i, \quad \text{for } i \in N,$$

where $\mathbf{b}^j$ denotes the amounts of the effort investments by players who direct their efforts into contest j, i.e. $\mathbf{b}^j = (b_i, i \in N : a_i = j)$.

We observed in Chapter 2 that the game with complete information that models the standard all-pay contest, which is a special case of the normal form game considered in this section, does not have a pure-strategy Nash equilibrium. Therefore, here we shall consider the effort investments in a mixed-strategy Nash equilibrium. We shall next consider outcomes $(\mathbf{a}, \mathbf{b})$ in which the assignment of players to contests $\mathbf{a}$ is a pure-strategy Nash equilibrium.

5.2.1 Pure-Strategy Nash Equilibrium

Given any assignment of players to contests $\mathbf{a}$ there exists a mixed-strategy Nash equilibrium for the amounts of effort investments $\mathbf{b}$. Each contest, with the subset of players assigned to it, corresponds to an independent standard all-pay contest for which in Chapter 2 we showed that there exists a mixed-strategy Nash equilibrium and provided a complete characterization. In order to study mixed-strategy Nash equilibrium points $(\mathbf{a}, \mathbf{b})$, we need to consider the expected payoffs for players given an assignment of players to contests $\mathbf{a}$. The key observation here is that all mixed-strategy Nash equilibria of a standard all-pay contest are payoff equivalent: the expected payoff of a player with the largest valuation is equal to the difference between his or her valuation and the maximum valuation among all other players, and the expected payoff of each other player is equal to zero (see Lemma 2.4). Note that in each contest there is always at most one player with a strictly positive expected payoff. A player has a strictly positive expected payoff only if he or she is a unique player with the largest valuation among participants in a given contest, in which case his or her expected payoff is equal to the difference between the largest and the second largest valuation. The expected payoffs of players in any mixed-strategy Nash equilibrium, conditional on the assignment of players to contests being $\mathbf{a}$, are equal to

$$\mathbf{E}[s_i(\mathbf{a}, \mathbf{b}) \mid \mathbf{a}] = \begin{cases} w_{a_i}(v_1^{a_i}(\mathbf{a}) - v_2^{a_i}(\mathbf{a})), & \text{if } v_i = v_1^{a_i}(\mathbf{a}) \\ 0, & \text{otherwise} \end{cases}, \quad \text{for } i \in N$$

where $v_1^j(\mathbf{a})$ is the largest valuation of a player assigned to contest j if at least one player is assigned to contest j, and $v_1^j(\mathbf{a}) = 0$, otherwise; similarly, $v_2^j(\mathbf{a})$ is the largest valuation of a player assigned to contest j excluding a player with the largest valuation if at least two players are assigned to contest j, and $v_2^j(\mathbf{a}) = 0$, otherwise.

An assignment of players to contests **a** is a pure-strategy Nash equilibrium if, and only if, under the assignment of players **a** there exists no player with a beneficial unilateral deviation of switching to investing in a different contest, which is equivalent to the following condition:

$$
w_j(v_1^j(\mathbf{a}) - v_2^j(\mathbf{a})) \geq w_l(v_1^j(\mathbf{a}) - v_1^l(\mathbf{a})) \\
\text{and } v_2^j(\mathbf{a}) \leq v_1^l(\mathbf{a})
\quad , \quad \text{for all } j \neq l. \tag{5.2}
$$

To see that (5.2) is indeed a necesary and sufficient condition, consider an arbitrary contest j and the set of players assigned to this contest according to an assignment of players to contests **a**. A player in this contest of valuation $v_1^j(\mathbf{a})$ has no beneficial unilateral deviation if, and only if, he or she cannot gain a larger expected payoff by investing in a different contest, which corresponds to the inequality in the first line of condition (5.2). A player who is assigned to contest j and whose valuation is less than or equal to $v_2^j(\mathbf{a})$ has a zero expected payoff. Such a player cannot gain a strictly positive expected payoff by investing in a different contest if every other contest is assigned a player with a valuation larger than or equal to the valuation of this player, which is implied by the inequality in the second line of condition (5.2). Obviously the second line of condition (5.2) is necessary to prevent benefical unilateral deviations of players whose valuations are equal to $v_2^j(\mathbf{a})$ if there are any such players.

There always exists a pure-strategy Nash equilibrium assignment of players to contests, which follows by showing that the following type of an assignment is a pure-strategy Nash equilibrium. If the number of players is less than or equal to the number of contests, then assigning players in decreasing order of their valuations to contests in decreasing order of values of prizes such that players are assigned to different contests is a pure-strategy Nash equilibrium. Otherwise, if the number of players is larger than the number of contests, then assigning m players in decreasing order of their valuations to m contests in decreasing order of values of prizes, and assigning all other players in an arbitrary way, is a pure-strategy Nash equilibrium. See Figure 5.2 for an illustration. A notable feature of this type of assignment is that it tends to avoid competition between players of high valuations.

We consider the efficiency of equilibria with respect to the social welfare defined as the expected total utility of all players, and with respect to the total effort defined as the expected total effort invested by the players. The optimum social welfare, W^*, is given by

$$
W^* = \sum_{j=1}^{k} w_j v_j
$$

where $k = \min\{m, n\}$. For the expected total effort, we shall use the following benchmark value

$$
R^* = \begin{cases}
0, & \text{if } n \leq m \\
\sum_{j=1}^{n} w_j v_{m+j}, & \text{if } m < n < 2m \\
\sum_{j=1}^{m} w_j v_{m+j}, & \text{if } n \geq 2m
\end{cases} . \tag{5.3}
$$

This is a natural definition of a benchmark. For the special case of a single contest that offers a unit prize and two or more players it boils down to the value of the second

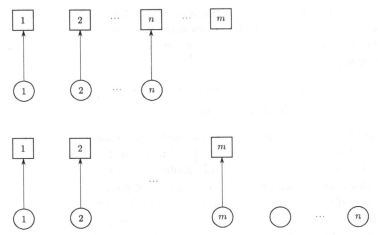

Figure 5.2. A pure-strategy Nash equilibrium assignment of players to contests: (top) $n \leq m$ and (bottom) $n > m$ where players $m + 1, m + 2, \ldots, n$ can be assigned to contests arbitrarily.

largest valuation v_2. In the general case, it is an upper bound for the expected total effort that can be achieved in any equilibrium of the game of simultaneous contests in which each individual contest obeys the assumptions of the standard-all pay contest.

When the number of players is smaller than the number of contests, then any pure-strategy Nash equilibrium assignment of players achieves the optimum social welfare and has the expected total effort equal to zero (due to a lack of competition), which is equal to the benchmark value. Otherwise, when the number of players is larger than the number of contests, then there may be some efficiency loss with respect to both social welfare and the expected total effort. The reader may try solving exercises 5.1 and 5.2.

There may also exist equilibrium assignments of players to contests under which there exists a pair of players, from the set of players with the m largest valuations, such that one of the two players has a larger valuation than the other player and is assigned to a contest of a lower prize than that of the other player. The existence of such an equilibrium is demonstrated in the following simple instance of two contests and four players.

Example 5.1 (two contests and four players). For the case of two contests and four players, there are eight possible equilibrium assignments of players to contests under conditions given in Figure 5.3.

It is left as Exercise 5.3 to show that for the case of two contests and four players, the social welfare in any equilibrium is at least $7/10$ of the optimal social welfare, and that the total effort invested in all contests in any equilibrium outcome is less than or equal to that under the assignment of players to contests $\mathbf{a} = (2, 1, 1, 2)$.

We end our discussion of pure-strategy Nash equilibrium assignments of players to contests by an example illustrating the special case of players with symmetric valuations.

Example 5.2 (symmetric valuations). For the case of players with symmetric valuations, assignments of players to contests in a pure-strategy Nash equilibrium can be described as follows. If the number of players is smaller than the number of contests,

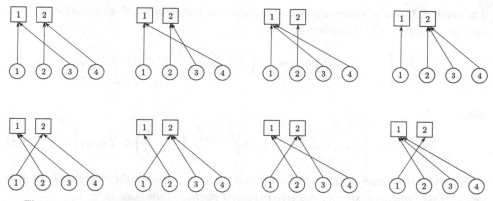

Figure 5.3. The equilibrium assignments of players to contests for the case of two contests and four players: (top) the four assignments are always equilibrium assignments; (bottom) the first and second assignments if $w_2(v_1 - v_4) \geq w_1(v_1 - v_2)$; and the third assigment if $w_2(v_1 - v_3) \geq w_1(v_1 - v_2)$, and the fourth assignment if $w_2 v_1 \geq w_1(v_1 - v_2)$.

then any assignment of players to a set of n contests that offer the largest values of prizes is a pure-strategy Nash equilibrium. Otherwise, any assignment of players to contests such that each contest is assigned at least one player is a pure-strategy Nash equilibrium. All these equilibrium outcomes achieve full social efficiency and have the expected total effort equal to the benchmark value.

5.2.2 Mixed-Strategy Nash Equilibrium

We consider the special case of players with symmetric valuations, for which we show that there exists a unique symmetric mixed-strategy Nash equilibrium and provide an explicit characterization of it. While all pure-strategy Nash equilibrium assignments of players to contests achieve full social efficiency (Example 5.2), we do expect some social efficiency loss in a mixed-strategy Nash equilibrium due to the use of mixed strategies. The use of mixed strategies implies that any given contest may not be assigned a player, with some probability, which amounts to some social efficiency loss. In this section, we shall study the efficiency of the symmetric mixed-strategy Nash equilibrium outcomes with respect to the total expected effort investment and the social welfare.

The following quantity will play an important role in the characterization of the symmetric mixed-strategy Nash equilibrium:

$$\Phi_j(\mathbf{w}, n) = \frac{1}{\frac{1}{j} \sum_{l=1}^{j} \left(\frac{1}{w_l}\right)^{1/(n-1)}} \quad \text{for } j = 1, 2, \ldots, m.$$

Note that $\Phi_j(\mathbf{w}, n)$ is the harmonic mean of the top j largest values of prizes raised to the power $1/(n - 1)$ where n is the number of players.

Existence and Characterization of a Mixed-Strategy Nash Equilibrium

The existence and uniqueness of a symmetric mixed-strategy Nash equilibrium and an explicit characterization of it are provided in the following theorem.

Theorem 5.3. *There exists a unique symmetric mixed-strategy Nash equilibrium* $\mathbf{p} = (p_1, p_2, \ldots, p_m)$, *which is given by*

$$p_j = \begin{cases} 1 - \left(1 - \frac{1}{\hat{m}}\right) \Phi_{\hat{m}}(\mathbf{w}, n) \left(\frac{1}{w_j}\right)^{1/(n-1)}, & \text{if } j = 1, 2, \ldots, \hat{m} \\ 0, & \text{otherwise} \end{cases} \qquad (5.4)$$

where

$$\hat{m} = \max \left\{ j \in \{1, 2, \ldots, m\} \mid w_j^{1/(n-1)} > \left(1 - \frac{1}{j}\right) \Phi_j(\mathbf{w}, n) \right\}. \qquad (5.5)$$

For every instance of the game with two or more contests there are at least two contests that attract a strictly positive expected participation, i.e., $\hat{m} \geq 2$.

Proof. Without loss of generality, assume that the valuation parameters are of unit values. Given that a contest is selected by one or more players, the competition in this contest is according to the standard all-pay contest with complete information, studied in Chapter 2.1 in its full generality. In the prevailing case, we have a special case of a standard all-pay contest with complete information and symmetric valuations: all players who participate in contest j have symmetric valuations of value w_j. By the characterization of the mixed-strategy Nash equilibrium in Lemma 2.4 (Section 2.1), the expected payoff for a player is equal to zero whenever the player is not the only participant in his or her selected contest and is obviously equal to the value of the prize of the selected contest, otherwise. In other words, the only way for a player to receive a strictly positive expected payoff for participating in a contest is for this player to be the only participant in the given contest, in which case the payoff accrued by this player is equal to the value of the prize offered by this contest.

A mixed strategy $\mathbf{p} = (p_1, p_2, \ldots, p_n)$ is a symmetric mixed-strategy Nash equilibrium if any given player cannot improve his or her expected payoff by unilaterally deviating to a different mixed strategy, given that all other players deploy the mixed strategy $\mathbf{p}$. The expected payoff for any given player for investing his or her effort in contest j is equal to

$$s_j = w_j(1 - p_j)^{n-1}.$$

For a mixed strategy $\mathbf{p}$ to be a mixed-strategy Nash equilibrium, there must exist $s^* > 0$ such that for every $j \in M$, either one of the following two conditions holds true:

$$p_j > 0 \text{ and } w_j(1 - p_j)^{n-1} = s^*, \quad \text{or} \quad p_j = 0 \text{ and } w_j \leq s^*. \qquad (5.6)$$

Since we assumed that $w_1 \geq w_2 \geq \cdots \geq w_m > 0$, (5.6) implies that $p_1 \geq p_2 \geq \cdots \geq p_m$. This is a rather intuitive property saying that in a mixed-strategy Nash equilibrium a contest that offers a prize with a value at least as large as that of another contest is selected by a player with a probability at least as large as that of the other contest.

Using (5.6), we can write

$$p_j = \max \left\{ 1 - \left(\frac{s^*}{w_j}\right)^{1/(n-1)}, 0 \right\}, \quad \text{for } j = 1, 2, \ldots, m.$$

Since $\sum_{j=1}^{m} p_j = 1$, we have that s^* is a solution of the equation

$$\sum_{j=1}^{m} \max \left\{ 1 - \left(\frac{s^*}{w_j} \right)^{1/(n-1)}, 0 \right\} = 1. \qquad (5.7)$$

Equation (5.7) has a unique solution, and hence, there is a unique symmetric mixed-strategy Nash equilibrium. To see this, note that the left-hand side of equation in (5.7) is a continuous, strictly decreasing function in s^* from value $m \geq 1$ at $s^* = 0$ to value 0 at $s^* = w_1$ and is equal to zero for $s^* \geq w_1$. It follows that there exists a unique positive value s^* that satisfies equation (5.7).

The symmetric mixed-strategy Nash equilibrium admits the form in (5.4) by defining $\hat{m}$ to be a positive integer such that $w_{\hat{m}+1} \leq s^* < w_{\hat{m}}$.

Since the left-hand side in (5.7) is decreasing in s^* from value $m \geq 1$ at $s^* = 0$ to value $1 - w_2/w_1 \leq 1$ at $s^* = w_2$, it follows that $s^* \leq w_2$, where the inequality is strict whenever $m \geq 2$. Hence, for every instance of the game with two or more contests, the number of contests that attract strictly positive expected participation is at least two in the symmetric mixed-strategy Nash equilibrium. $\qquad \square$

The strategic behavior of the players according to the symmetric mixed-strategy Nash equilibrium given in Theorem 5.3 admits an intuitive interpretation: each player aims at participating in a contest in which he or she would be the only participant. Such behavior should tend to balance the participation across different contests. From (5.4), we observe that a contest that offers a larger prize than another contest attracts larger expected participation whenever it attracts a non-zero expected participation. The larger the number of players, the more balanced is the expected participation across different contests. Specifically, it is easy to observe that in the limit of many players, the symmetric mixed-strategy Nash equilibrium is a uniform distribution on the set of available contests.

Example 5.4 (two contests). Consider the case of two contests $m = 2$ and $n \geq 2$ players. By Theorem 5.3, the symmetric mixed-strategy Nash equilibrium is given by

$$p_1 = \frac{w_1^{\alpha_n}}{w_1^{\alpha_n} + w_2^{\alpha_n}} \quad \text{and} \quad p_2 = 1 - p_1$$

where $\alpha_n = 1/(n-1)$. In the case of a competition between two players, each player selects a contest with probability proportional to the value of the prize offered by this contest. In the general case of two or more players, the larger the number of players, the less skewed is the mixed-strategy Nash equilibrium distribution. In the limit of many players, each contest is selected equally likely by any given player (see Figure 5.4).

Expected Payoffs

We establish two properties of the expected payoffs in the symmetric mixed-strategy Nash equilibrium.

The first property is a monotonicity with respect to the number of players: for any given values of prizes of two or more contests, the value of the expected payoff s^* in the symmetric mixed-strategy Nash equilibrium is decreasing in the number of players n. This property follows immediately by noting that for any given positive value s^*, the

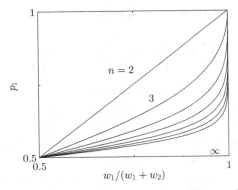

Figure 5.4. p_1 versus $w_1/(w_1 + w_2)$ for some values of the number of players n.

left-hand side in (5.7) is decreasing in the number of players n. This implies that the size of the support of the mixed-strategy Nash equilibrium distribution is increasing in the number of players.

The second property is an upper bound for the value of the expected payoff s^*: for any values of prizes $w_1 \geq w_2 \geq \cdots \geq w_m > 0$ such that $\sum_{j=1}^m w_j = 1$, the solution to equation (5.7) satisfies

$$s^* \leq \frac{1}{k}\left(1 - \frac{1}{k}\right)^{n-1} \tag{5.8}$$

where $k = \min\{m, n\}$.

The bound in (5.8) can be established as follows. Fix an integer t such that $1 \leq t \leq m$ and consider any values of prizes that satisfy

$$w_1 \geq w_2 \geq \cdots \geq w_t > s^* \geq w_{t+1} \geq \cdots \geq w_m. \tag{5.9}$$

Equation (5.7) can be written as

$$\sum_{j=1}^t \left(1 - \left(\frac{s^*}{w_j}\right)^{1/(n-1)}\right) = 1.$$

From this it follows that

$$s^* = \left(1 - \frac{1}{t}\right)^{n-1} \frac{1}{\left(\frac{1}{t}\sum_{j=1}^t \left(\frac{1}{w_j}\right)^{1/(n-1)}\right)^{n-1}}. \tag{5.10}$$

The right-hand side in equation (5.10) is a concave function of $\mathbf{w}$ that under the constraints $\sum_{j=1}^m w_j = 1$ and (5.9) achieves the maximum value for $w_j = 1/t$ for $j = 1, 2, \ldots, t$ and $w_j = 0$ otherwise. Hence, we have

$$s^* \leq \frac{1}{t}\left(1 - \frac{1}{t}\right)^{n-1}.$$

The right-hand side of the last inequality has the maximum value at $t = n$. Under the constraint $1 \leq t \leq m$, it has the maximum value at $t = \min\{m, n\}$.

Total Effort

Given that a contest j is selected by one or more players, the effort investments in this contest are according to the mixed-strategy Nash equilibrium strategies in the standard all-pay contest with complete information and symmetric valuations of value w_j. The expected total effort invested in contest j is equal to w_j conditional on the event that there are at least two participants in this contest, and is otherwise equal to zero. Therefore, the expected total efforts invested in individual contests are given by

$$R^j = w_j \left(1 - (1 - p_j)^n - np_j(1 - p_j)^{n-1}\right), \quad \text{for } j = 1, 2, \ldots, m. \quad (5.11)$$

We consider efficiency with respect to the expected total effort by comparing the expected total effort in the symmetric mixed-strategy Nash equilibrium

$$R = \sum_{j=1}^{m} R^j$$

with the benchmark value given by

$$R^* = \sum_{j=1}^{k} w_j$$

where $k = \min\{m, n\}$.

In the case when the number of players is smaller than the number of contests, there exist instances in which the efficiency with respect to the expected total effort can be arbitrarily small as demonstrated in the following example.

Example 5.5 (two players). Consider the case of $n = 2$ players and $m \geq 2$ contests that offer identical values of prizes. Without loss of generality, assume that each contest offers a prize of unit value. In the symmetric mixed-strategy equilibrium each player selects a contest to participate independently by choosing a contest uniformly at random from the set of available contests. In each given contest, a positive expected total effort is realized only if both players choose to make effort investments in this contest. This happens with probability $1/m^2$ for each given contest. Hence, we have $R = 1/m$. On the other hand, $R^* = 2$. This shows that the worst-case efficiency with respect to the expected total effort is less than or equal to $1/(2m)$, which can be made arbitrarily small by taking an instance with sufficiently large number of contests m.

The state of the affairs is qualitatively very different if the number of players is at least as large as the number of contests. By Example 5.5, the worst-case efficiency is at least as low as $1/4$, which is achieved in the instance of two players and two contests with symmetric values of prizes. The following theorem shows that this is in fact the worst-case efficiency for any values of prizes, provided that there are two or more players and the number of players is at least as large as the number of contests (see Figure 5.5).

Theorem 5.6. *Suppose that there are two or more players and that the number of players is larger than or equal to the number of contests. For any given values of prizes, the expected total effort in the symmetric mixed-strategy Nash equilibrium is at*

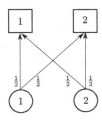

Figure 5.5. The worst-case instance for efficiency with respect to the expected total effort in the case of two or more players, and the number of players being at least as large as the number of contests: two players and two contests with symmetric values of prizes.

least 1/4 of the benchmark total effort. This efficiency lower bound is achieved in the instance of two players and two contests that offer symmetric values of prizes.

Proof. Without loss of generality, assume that $\sum_{j=1}^{m} w_j = 1$. Since the number of players is assumed to be larger than or equal to the number of contests, the value of the benchmark, R^*, is equal to 1. From (5.6) and (5.11), we have

$$R^j = \max\{w_j - (1 + (n-1)p_j)s^*, 0\}, \quad \text{for } j = 1, 2, \ldots, m.$$

Hence, it follows that

$$R = \sum_{j=1}^{m} \max\{w_j - (1 + (n-1)p_j)s^*, 0\} \geq 1 - (m+n-1)s^*.$$

Since the number of players is assumed to be at least as large as the number of contests, by (5.8), it follows that

$$R \geq 1 - \left(1 + \frac{n-1}{m}\right)\left(1 - \frac{1}{m}\right)^{n-1}. \tag{5.12}$$

The right-hand side in equation (5.12) is increasing in n, and hence

$$R \geq 1 - \left(2 - \frac{1}{m}\right)\left(1 - \frac{1}{m}\right)^{m-1}. \tag{5.13}$$

The right-hand side in equation (5.13) is increasing in m from value 1/4 for $m = 2$ to value $1 - 2/e \approx 0.264$ as m goes to infinity. See Figure 5.6 for an illustration. $\square$

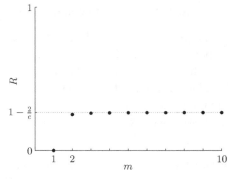

Figure 5.6. A lower bound on the expected total effort versus the number of contests m for the total prize of unit value.

Social Welfare

We now consider the social welfare defined as the expected value received by all players in the symmetric mixed-strategy Nash equilibrium. The prize of a contest is fully transfered to players whenever this contest is selected by at least one player, and otherwise, it is not transferred to the players at all. Hence, the expected social welfare in the symmetric mixed-strategy Nash equilibrium, W, is given by

$$W = \sum_{j=1}^{m} w_j \left(1 - (1 - p_j)^n\right). \tag{5.14}$$

The symmetric mixed-strategy Nash equilibrium in Theorem 5.3 is a unique symmetric mixed strategy that maximizes the expected social welfare given by (5.14) (Exercise 5.4). We shall consider the social efficiency by comparing the expected social welfare, W, in the symmetric mixed-strategy Nash equilibrium with the optimum social welfare, W^*, whose value is given by

$$W^* = \sum_{j=1}^{k} w_j \tag{5.15}$$

where $k = \min\{m, n\}$.

We first give an example that shows that the social welfare in the symmetric mixed-strategy Nash equilibrium can be as low as the factor $1 - 1/e$ (approx 0.63) of the optimum social welfare.

Example 5.7 (symmetric prizes). Consider any instance with symmetric values of prizes $w_1 = w_2 = \cdots = w_m > 0$, and without loss of generality assume that $\sum_{j=1}^{m} w_j = 1$. From (5.14) and (5.15), we obtain

$$\frac{W}{W^*} = \frac{1 - \left(1 - \frac{1}{m}\right)^n}{\min\left\{\frac{n}{m}, 1\right\}}$$

$$\geq \frac{1 - e^{-\frac{n}{m}}}{\min\left\{\frac{n}{m}, 1\right\}} \tag{5.16}$$

$$\geq 1 - \frac{1}{e}. \tag{5.17}$$

The lower bound (5.17) is achieved in the case when the number of contests is equal to the number of players, asymptotically for large number of players (see Figure 5.7).

In the following theorem we show that $1 - 1/e$ is the worst-case lower bound for the social efficiency of the symmetric mixed-strategy Nash equilibrium for any instance. See Figure 5.8 for an illustration.

Theorem 5.8. *For every given number of one or more contests with arbitrary positive values of prizes and any given number of one or more players, the expected social welfare in the symmetric mixed-strategy Nash equilibrium is at least $1 - 1/e$ (approx. 0.63) of the optimum social welfare. This efficiency lower bound is achieved in an instance with contests that offer symmetric values of prizes and with as many players as contests, asymptotically for large number of contests.*

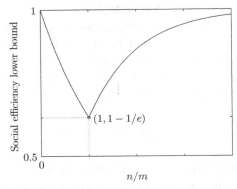

Figure 5.7. Social efficiency lower bound (5.16) versus the ratio of the number of players and the number of contests.

Proof. Without loss of generality, assume $\sum_{j=1}^{m} w_j = 1$. From (5.6) and (5.14), we have

$$W = s^* + \sum_{j=1}^{m} \max\{w_j - s^*, 0\}. \tag{5.18}$$

We first consider the case $n \geq m$. From (5.18), we have

$$W \geq 1 - (m - 1)s^*$$

and, from (5.15), $W^* = 1$. Combining this with (5.8), we have

$$\frac{W}{W^*} \geq 1 - \left(1 - \frac{1}{m}\right)^n \geq 1 - e^{-n/m} \geq 1 - \frac{1}{e}.$$

We next consider the other case $n < m$, which is a bit more involved. Fix a positive integer $1 \leq t \leq m$, and assume $w_1 \geq w_2 \geq \cdots \geq w_t > s^* \geq w_{t+1} \geq \cdots \geq w_m$. If $t \leq n$, then the analysis proceeds using the same steps as in the previously studied case. From now on assume that $t > n$. Fix a real number $x \in (0, 1]$ and assume that $\sum_{j=1}^{n} w_j = x$. From (5.15) and (5.18), it follows that

$$\frac{W}{W^*} \geq \frac{1 - (t - 1)s^*}{x}. \tag{5.19}$$

Using (5.10), observe that under the constraints $\sum_{j=1}^{t} w_j = 1$ and $\sum_{j=1}^{n} w_j = x$, the value of s^* is maximized by splitting the respective masses evenly so that $w_j = x/n$

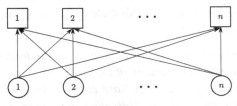

Figure 5.8. The worst-case instance for the social efficiency: an instance with contests that offer identical values of prizes with as many players as contests, for asymptotically large number of players n.

for $j = 1, 2, \ldots, n$ and $w_j = (1 - x)/(t - n)$ for $j = n + 1, n + 2, \ldots, t$. This yields

$$s^* \leq \left(\frac{t - 1}{n \left(\frac{n}{x}\right)^{1/(n-1)} + (t - n) \left(\frac{t-n}{1-x}\right)^{1/(n-1)}} \right)^{n-1}. \tag{5.20}$$

Let us use the simplifying notation $y = n/t$. From (5.19) and (5.20), it follows that

$$\frac{W}{W^*} \geq \frac{f(x, y)}{x} \tag{5.21}$$

where

$$f(x, y) = 1 - e^{-y} \frac{1}{\left(y \left(\frac{y}{x}\right)^{1/(n-1)} + (1 - y) \left(\frac{1-y}{1-x}\right)^{1/(n-1)} \right)^{n-1}}.$$

For every fixed value $y \in (0, 1)$, function $f(x, y)$ is decreasing in x if, and only if, $x \leq y$. In this case, $f(x, y)/x$ is decreasing in x. Hence, for every $y \in (0, 1)$ and $x \leq y$,

$$\frac{f(x, y)}{x} \geq \frac{f(y, y)}{y} = \frac{1 - e^{-y}}{y} \geq 1 - \frac{1}{e}. \tag{5.22}$$

Suppose now that $x > y$. In this case, function $f(x, y)$ is increasing in x. Note, however, that $f(x, y)$ is a convex function in x. It follows that $f(x, y)/x$ is increasing in x, and thus again the sequence of inequalities (5.22) holds. $\square$

5.2.3 Bayes-Nash Equilibrium

In this section we consider the game of simultaneous standard all-pay contests with incomplete information where the valuation parameters are private information and are independent and identically distributed random variables according to a prior distribution F that has no atoms above zero and has strictly positive density function on the support $[0, 1]$. With a slight abuse of notation, we let $w_1 > w_2 > \cdots > w_k > 0$ denote the distinct values of prizes offered by contests, and let m_j denote the number of contests that offer a prize of value w_j. We refer to each contest that offers a prize of value w_j as the contest of *class* j. We denote with M_j the number of contests that offer prizes of value larger than or equal to w_j, i.e., $M_j = \sum_{l=1}^{j} m_l$. Note that M_k is equal to the total number of contests m.

The strategy of each player consists of choosing one contest from the set of all contests, and making an effort investment into this contest. We consider symmetric mixed strategies $(\alpha, \beta) = (\alpha(v), \beta(v),$ for $v \in [0, 1])$, where $\alpha(v) = (\alpha_1(v), \alpha_2(v), \ldots, \alpha_k(v))$ with $\alpha_j(v)$ denoting the probability of choosing any given contest of class j and $\beta(v) = (\beta_1(v), \beta_2(v), \ldots, \beta_k(v))$ with $\beta_j(v)$ denoting the amount of effort investment of any given player who chose to participate in a contest of class j, for a player whose valuation parameter is equal to v. Each given player $i \in N$ chooses a contest of class a_i with probability $\alpha_j(v_i)m_j$, and in his or her chosen contest makes an effort investment of value $\beta_{a_i}(v_i)$.

A strategy (α, β) is a symmetric Bayes-Nash equilibrium if no player has a beneficial unilateral deviation from this strategy with respect to the expected payoff, assuming that all other players play according to the given strategy. The given normal form game has a symmetric Bayes-Nash equilibrium that can be characterized in an explicit form as follows. We shall make use of the quantities defined as follows:

$$\Phi_j = \frac{1}{\frac{1}{M_j} \sum_{l=1}^{j} m_l \left(\frac{1}{w_l}\right)^{1/(n-1)}}, \quad \text{for } j = 1, 2, \dots, k. \tag{5.23}$$

Note that Φ_j is the harmonic mean of the values of prizes offered by contests of class 1 through j raised to the power $1/(n-1)$.

The following theorem establishes that a symmetric Bayes-Nash equilibrium exists and provides an explicit characterization of it.

Theorem 5.9. *There exists a symmetric Bayes-Nash equilibrium (α, β) that is characterized as follows.*

(i) *Any given contest of class j is selected by any given player with probability*

$$p_j = \begin{cases} 1 - \left(1 - \frac{1}{M_k}\right) \Phi_{\hat{k}} \left(\frac{1}{w_j}\right)^{1/(n-1)}, & \text{if } 1 \le j \le \hat{k} \\ 0, & \text{otherwise} \end{cases} \tag{5.24}$$

where

$$\hat{k} = \max\left\{ j \in \{1, 2, \dots, k\} \mid w_j^{1/(n-1)} > \left(1 - \frac{1}{M_j}\right) \Phi_j \right\}.$$

(ii) *The set of values of the valuation parameters is partitioned into $\hat{k}$ disjoint intervals defined by the separators:*

$$\bar{v}_j = F^{-1}\left(1 - M_j\left(1 - \frac{w_j^{1/(n-1)}}{\Phi_j}\right)\right), \quad \text{for } j = 1, 2, \dots, \hat{k} \tag{5.25}$$

and

$$\bar{v}_j = 0, \quad \text{if } j > \hat{k}.$$

(iii) *Any given player, conditional on his or her valuation being equal to v, chooses any given contest of class j with probability*

$$\alpha_j(v) = \begin{cases} \frac{\Phi_l}{M_l} \left(\frac{1}{w_j}\right)^{1/(n-1)}, & \text{if } 1 \le j \le l \\ 0, & \text{otherwise} \end{cases}, \quad \text{if } \bar{v}_{l+1} \le v < \bar{v}_l. \tag{5.26}$$

(iv) *Any given player, conditional on his or her valuation being equal to v and the class of the contest selected by this player being equal to j, makes an effort investment in the amount of*

$$\beta_j(v) = w_j \int_0^v x \, dF_j(x)^{n-1}, \quad \text{for } v \in [0, 1] \tag{5.27}$$

where F_j is the distribution of the valuation of any given player from the perspective of a contest of class j that for $v \in [\bar{v}_{l+1}, \bar{v}_l]$ is given by

$$F_j(v) = \begin{cases} \Phi_l \left(\frac{1}{w_j}\right)^{1/(n-1)} \left(1 - \frac{1}{M_l} + \frac{1}{M_l} F(v)\right), & \text{if } 1 \le j \le l \\ 1, & \text{otherwise} \end{cases}. \tag{5.28}$$

Proof. The proof is organized in such a way that we first introduce some notation and basic facts, then state and prove several lemmas, which are then used to complete the proof of the theorem.

For any given player, we denote with p_j the probability that he or she chooses a given contest that belongs to class j. For any given player, conditional on his or her valuation parameter being of value v, we denote with $\alpha_j(v)$ the probability that he or she chooses a given contest that belongs to class j. Let G_j be the distribution of the valuation parameter of any given player, conditional on the event that he or she chosen to make effort investment in a contest of class j. For every given contest, conditioning on the event that a given player chosen to invest in some other contest is equivalent to this player having a valuation parameter of zero value. On the other hand, by definition, conditional on that the player chosen to invest in the given contest, the distribution of his or her valuation parameter is G_j. Hence, we can define F_j as the distribution of the valuation parameter of a player from the perspective of any given contest of class j, which is given by

$$F_j(v) = 1 - p_j + p_j G_j(v), \text{ for } v \in [0, 1].$$

We have the following relation:

$$p_j G_j(v) = \int_0^v \alpha_j(x) \, dF(x), \quad \text{for } v \in [0, 1], \tag{5.29}$$

which holds by the following two basic facts based on conditional probabilities:

$$\mathbf{Pr}[a_i = j, v_i \le v] = \mathbf{Pr}[v_i \le v \mid a_i = j]\mathbf{Pr}[a_i = j] = G_j(v)p_j$$

and

$$\mathbf{Pr}[a_i = j, v_i \le v] = \int_0^v \mathbf{Pr}[a_i = j \mid v_i = v] \, d\mathbf{Pr}[v_i \le v] = \int_0^v \alpha_j(x) \, dF(x).$$

Obviously, (5.29) implies

$$p_j = \int_0^1 \alpha_j(v) \, dF(v).$$

Using Corollary 2.21, the expected payoff for any given player for investing in any given contest of class j, conditional on the valuation parameter of this player being of value v, is equal to

$$s_j(v) = w_j \int_0^v (1 - p_j + p_j G_j(x))^{n-1} dx. \tag{5.30}$$

A strategy (α, β) is a symmetric Bayes-Nash equilibrium if the following condition holds true: for every $v \in (0, 1]$ there exists $s^*(v) > 0$ such that for every $j \in \{1, 2, \ldots, k\}$ one of the following two conditions holds true:

$$\alpha_j(v) > 0 \text{ and } s_j(v) = s^*(v), \text{ or } \alpha_j(v) = 0 \text{ and } s_j(v) < s^*(v). \tag{5.31}$$

From (5.30), we immediately observe that each expected payoff function $s_j(v)$ is a continuously differentiable, increasing, and convex function, because it is an integral of a non-negative and increasing function. Let $\bar{v}_j$ be the smallest value $v \in [0, 1]$ such that $s'_j(v) = w_j$, for $j \in \{1, 2, \ldots, k\}$. For every contest of class j, we have

$$w_j(1 - p_j)^{n-1} = s'_j(0) \le s'_j(v) \le s'_j(\bar{v}_j) = w_j \quad \text{for all } v \in [0, \bar{v}_j]$$

and

$$s'_j(v) = w_j \quad \text{for all } v \in [\bar{v}_j, 1].$$

We next state and prove several lemmas.

Lemma 5.10. *There exists a value $s^* > 0$ and $\hat{k} \in \{1, 2, \ldots, k\}$ such that*

$$w_1(1 - p_1)^{n-1} = w_2(1 - p_2)^{n-1} = \cdots = w_{\hat{k}}(1 - p_{\hat{k}})^{n-1} = s^* \qquad (5.32)$$

and

$$w_{\hat{k}+1} < s^*. \qquad (5.33)$$

Proof. We first establish that if for two contest classes j and l, $p_j > 0$ and $p_l > 0$, then $w_j(1 - p_j)^{n-1} = w_l(1 - p_l)^{n-1}$. If $p_j > 0$ and $p_l > 0$, then there exists $\epsilon \in (0, 1]$ such that

$$s_l(v) = s_j(v) \quad \text{for every } v \in [0, \epsilon]. \qquad (5.34)$$

Otherwise, we would have $s_j(v) \ne s_l(v)$ for every $v \in (0, 1]$, and in view of (5.31) this would imply that either $p_j = 0$ or $p_l = 0$, which is a contradiction. From (5.34), we have

$$\lim_{v \downarrow 0} \frac{1}{v} \int_0^v (s'_j(x) - s'_l(x)) \, dx = 0$$

which combined with (5.30) yields

$$w_j(1 - p_j)^{n-1} = w_l(1 - p_l)^{n-1}.$$

We now show that if for two contest classes j and l, $p_j = 0$ and $p_l > 0$, then $w_j < w_l(1 - p_l)^{n-1}$. From (5.31), we have $s_j(v) < s_l(v)$, for every $v \in (0, 1]$. Using (5.30), this is equivalent to

$$w_j < w_l \frac{1}{v} \int_0^v s'_l(x) \, dx \quad \text{for every } v \in (0, 1].$$

By letting v go to zero, we obtain

$$w_j < s'_l(0) = w_l(1 - p_l)^{n-1}.$$

$\square$

Lemma 5.11. *Suppose that for a pair of contest classes l and j, and $v \in [0, 1)$, the expected payoff functions s_l and s_j satisfy $s_l(v) = s^*(v)$ and $s'_j(v) < s'_l(v)$. Then, $s_j(x) < s^*(x)$, for every $x \in (v, 1]$.*

Proof. The proof is by contradiction as follows. Note that under condition $s_l(v) = s^*(v)$ and $s'_j(v) < s'_l(v)$, there exists $\epsilon > 0$ such that $s_j(x) < s_l(x)$ for $x \in (v, v + \epsilon]$. Suppose that there exists $z \in (v, 1]$ such that $s_j(z) = s^*(z)$ and let z be the smallest such value.

Since $s_j(x) < s^*(x)$ for $x \in (v, z)$, from (5.31), we have $\alpha_j(x) = 0$ for $x \in (v, z)$. Combining with (5.29) and (5.30), we obtain

$$s_j'(x) = s_j'(v) \quad \text{for } x \in [v, z]. \tag{5.35}$$

We have the following series of relations:

$$s^*(z) - s_j(z) \geq s_l(z) - s_j(z) \tag{5.36}$$

$$= s_l(v) - s_j(v) + \int_v^z (s_l'(x) - s_j'(x))\, dx$$

$$\geq \int_v^z (s_l'(x) - s_j'(x))\, dx \tag{5.37}$$

$$= \int_v^z (s_l'(x) - s_j'(v))\, dx \tag{5.38}$$

$$\geq (z - v)(s_l'(v) - s_j'(v)) \tag{5.39}$$

$$> 0 \tag{5.40}$$

where (5.36) is because by (5.31), $s^*(z) \geq s_l(z)$, (5.37) is because by (5.31) $s^*(z) \geq s_j(z)$ and the assumption $s^*(v) = s_l(v)$, (5.38) is by (5.35), (5.39) is by the differentiability and convexity of the payoff function $s_l(x)$, and the last equation (5.40) is by the assumption $s_j'(v) < s_l'(v)$.

By (5.40), $s_j(z) < s^*(z)$, which is a contradiction to the assumption that z is the smallest value greater than v such that $s_j(z) = s_j^*(z)$. □

Notice that from (5.31) and Lemma 5.11, we have

$$s_l(v) = s^*(v) \text{ and } s_j'(v) < s_l'(v) \;\Rightarrow\; \alpha_j(x) = 0 \quad \text{for } x \in (v, 1]. \tag{5.41}$$

Lemma 5.12. *The expected payoff functions satisfy*

$$s_j'(v) = \begin{cases} s_1'(v), & \text{if } 0 \leq v \leq \bar{v}_j \\ w_j, & \text{otherwise} \end{cases} \tag{5.42}$$

where

$$\bar{v}_j = 0, \text{ if } j > \hat{k}, \text{ and } 0 < \bar{v}_{\hat{k}} < \cdots < \bar{v}_2 < \bar{v}_1 = 1. \tag{5.43}$$

Proof. It suffices to consider a contest of class $j \in \{1, 2, \ldots, \hat{k}\}$ because, otherwise $p_j = 0$, which implies $s_j'(v) = w_j$ and, thus, (5.42) holds with $\bar{v}_j = 0$. The proof is by backward induction with respect to j.

Base case: $j = \hat{k}$. By (5.30) and Lemma 5.10, we have $s_1'(0) = s_2'(0) = \cdots = s_{\hat{k}}'(0)$. Let v be the smallest value in $[0, 1]$ such that $s_r'(v) < s_1'(v)$ for some $r \in \{2, \ldots, \hat{k}\}$. By (5.41), $\alpha_r(x) = 0$ for $x \in [v, 1]$. Combining with (5.29), it follows that $s_r'(x) = w_r$,

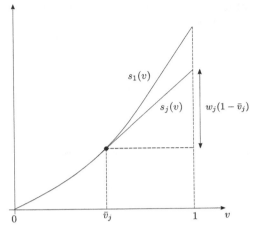

Figure 5.9. The expected payoff functions $s_1(v)$ and $s_j(v)$ for $1 < j \le k$.

for $x \in [v, 1]$. Since by assumption $w_1 > w_2 > \cdots > w_k$, it follows that r is equal to $\hat{k}$. This shows that (5.42) holds true for $j = \hat{k}$.

Induction step: Suppose that (5.42) is true for $j \in \{l + 1, \ldots, \hat{k}\}$, and we then show that this implies that it holds for $j = l$. By the induction hypothesis, $s_1'(x) = s_2'(x) = \cdots = s_{l+1}'(x)$, for $x \in [0, \bar{v}_{l+1}]$. Let v be the smallest value larger than $\bar{v}_{l+1}$ such that $s_r'(v) < s_1'(v)$ for some $r \in \{2, 3, \ldots, l\}$. By the same arguments as in the base case, it follows that $v = \bar{v}_r$, $s_r'(x) = w_r$, for $x \in [v, 1]$, and that $r = l$. This shows that (5.42) holds true for $j = l$. ☐

The result in Lemma 5.12 tells us that each expected payoff function $s_j(x)$ is equal to $s_1(x)$ for every x up to a point, and it then grows linearly with rate w_j. See Figure 5.9 for an illustration.

Lemma 5.13. *If* $1 \le j \le l \le \hat{k}$ *and* $v \in (\bar{v}_{l+1}, \bar{v}_l]$, *we have*

$$p_j(1 - G_j(v)) = 1 - \left(\frac{1}{w_j}\right)^{1/(n-1)} \Phi_l \left(1 - \frac{1}{M_l}(1 - F(v))\right). \quad (5.44)$$

Proof. Fix an arbitrary j, l, and v such that $1 \le j \le l \le \hat{k}$ and $v \in (\bar{v}_{l+1}, \bar{v}_l]$. From (5.30) and (5.42), we have

$$p_j(1 - G_j(v)) = 1 - \left(\frac{s_1'(v)}{w_j}\right)^{1/(n-1)}. \quad (5.45)$$

By definition of $\bar{v}_j$'s and Lemma 5.12, we have

$$G_r(v) = 1, \quad \text{for } l < r \le k.$$

Hence, we have

$$1 - F(v) = \sum_{r=1}^{k} m_r p_r (1 - G_r(v)) = \sum_{r=1}^{l} m_r p_r (1 - G_r(v)).$$

Combining with (5.45), we have

$$s_1'(v) = \left(\left(1 - \frac{1}{M_l}(1 - F(v)) \right) \Phi_l \right)^{n-1} \tag{5.46}$$

where Φ_l is defined in (5.26).

The equations (5.45) and (5.46) imply the equation in (5.44).   □

The proof of the theorem is completed as follows. The expression in (5.24) is obtained by Lemma 5.13 for value $v = 0$. The expression in (5.25) is obtained by Lemma 5.13 for value $v = \bar{v}_l$, and combining with (5.24). The expression in (5.26) is obtained by differentiating both sides in equation (5.29) to obtain

$$p_j G_j'(v) = \alpha_j(v) F'(v),$$

and by differentiating both sides in equation (5.44) to obtain

$$p_j G_j'(v) = \left(\frac{1}{w_j} \right)^{1/(n-1)} \frac{\Phi_l}{M_l} F'(v).$$

The expression in (5.28) follows from Lemma 5.13. The expression in (5.50) follows by Corollary 2.22 using the fact that the strategic behavior in each individual contest of class j seen in isolation is as in the game that models the standard all-pay contest with incomplete information where the valuation parameters are a sequence of independent and identically distributed random variables with prior distribution F_j.   □

Theorem 5.9 reveals several interesting properties of the strategic behavior in a symmetric Bayes-Nash equilibrium that we discuss as follows.

A contest attracts a strictly positive expected participation only if it offers a prize of a value that is sufficiently large relative to the values of other, higher valued prizes. There is an exception to this only if a unique contest offers a prize of the largest value, in which case all contests that offer the second largest prize attract a strictly positive participation. In particular, in the case of two simultaneous contests, both contests receive a strictly positive expected participation for any positive value of the second largest prize. In any symmetric Bayes-Nash equilibrium, at least two contests receive a strictly positive expected participation. The reader would have noticed that in the symmetric Bayes-Nash equilibrium, the probability that a player chooses to participate in a given contest corresponds to that in the mixed-strategy Nash equilibrium of the game with complete information and symmetric valuations (given in Theorem 5.3).

There is an endogenous partition of the set of valuations into intervals of valuations, which we refer to as classes. There are as many different classes of valuations as there are classes of contests that attract a strictly positive expected participation. A player is of class j if the value of his or her valuation falls in the j-th interval of largest valuations. A player is said to be of a higher class than another player if his or her valuation falls into an interval of larger valuations than that of the other player. All players of a given class have symmetric Bayes-Nash equilibrium strategies and invest in a contest of the same or higher class: each player of class 1 invests only in a contest of class 1, each player of class 2 invests only in a contest of either class 1 or class 2, and so on and so forth. The probability distribution according to which a player of

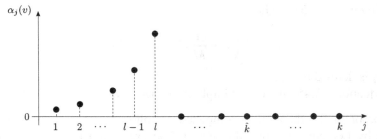

Figure 5.10. The probability that a player with the valuation parameter of value v, which is of class l, chooses a given contest of class j.

a given class chooses a contest to which to direct his or her effort has the following monotonicity property: a player of class l invests in a contest from the set of contests of class 1 through l in such a way that a larger mass is put on a contest of a lower class. See Figure 5.10 for an illustration.

From the perspective of any given contest, the existence of other contests presents players with outside options (opportunity to invest in other contests). The symmetric Bayes-Nash equilibrium of the game of simultaneous contests results in an endogenous distribution of valuations for any given contest of a given class (see Figure 5.11 for a graph). This distribution may have a mass at zero, representing the fact that a player may invest in a different contest. For any given contest, if a player invests in some other contest, then he or she can be seen as a player with a valuation of value zero from the perspective of this contest. These distributions of valuations admit a natural stochastic order: the distribution of valuations for a contest of a higher class is stochastically larger than the distribution of valuations for a contest of a lower class. For any given contest of class j, all players who invest in this contest have valuations smaller than or equal to $\bar{v}_j$, which is smaller the lower is the contest class.

The selection of contests in the symmetric Bayes-Nash equilibrium is according to a distribution that is parameterized with the values of prizes in such a way that only relative values matter and each individual prize value acts only through a transformed value, defined to be the actual prize value raised to the power $1/(n-1)$ where n is the number of players. This has the effect of balancing the transformed values of prizes

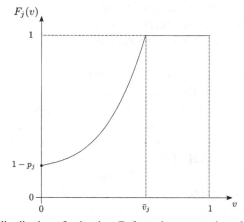

Figure 5.11. The distribution of valuation F_j from the perspective of a contest of class j.

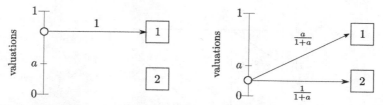

Figure 5.12. Strategic behavior in the symmetric Bayes-Nash equilibrium for the case of two contests: (left) class 1 behavior, and (right) class 2 behavior.

the larger the number of players. This results in an expected participation that is more balanced and over the same or a larger set of top prizes, the larger the number of players.

We revisit the case of two contests that we considered in Example 5.4 for the game with complete information and symmetric valuations.

Example 5.14 (two contests). Consider the case of two contests: $k = 2$, and $m_1 = m_2 = 1$. The symmetric Bayes-Nash equilibrium is completely determined by a single parameter, a, defined as follows:

$$a = \left(\frac{w_2}{w_1}\right)^{1/(n-1)}.$$

The value of parameter a is increasing in the ratio w_2/w_1 of the smaller to the larger prize value, and is increasing in the number of players n. The more balanced the values of the prizes, the larger the value of parameter a. The larger the number of players, the larger the value of parameter a, which is consistent with the aforementioned balancing effect with respect to the number of players.

There are two types of strategic behavior in the symmetric Bayes-Nash equilibrium: class 1 that consists of players whose valuations v_i satisfy $a < F(v_i) \le 1$, and class 2 that consists of players whose valuations v_i satisfy $0 < F(v_i) \le a$. See Figure 5.12 for an illustration. The expected portions of players of class 1 and class 2 are equal to $1 - a$ and a, respectively. Each player of class 1 invests his or her effort in contest 1 with probability 1, i.e.,

$$(\alpha_1(v_i), \alpha_2(v_i)) = (1, 0), \quad \text{if } a < F(v_i) \le 1,$$

while each player of class 2 invests his or her effort in a randomly selected contest according to the distribution

$$(\alpha_1(v_i), \alpha_2(v_i)) = \left(\frac{a}{1+a}, \frac{1}{1+a}\right), \quad \text{if } 0 < F(v_i) \le a.$$

A player invests in one of the two contests according to the distribution

$$(p_1, p_2) = \left(\frac{1}{1+a}, \frac{a}{1+a}\right).$$

This coincides with the mixed-strategy Nash equilibrium in the game with complete information with symmetric valuations; see Example 5.4. The probability distribution (p_1, p_2) is indeed consistent with the conditional probability distributions

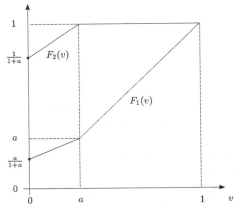

Figure 5.13. The distribution of valuation of a player from the perspective of each given contest for the example of two simultaneous contests and uniform prior distribution. The values of the two distributions at $v = 0$ and a are invariant to the choice of the prior distribution.

$(\alpha_1(v), \alpha_2(v))$, for $v \in [0, 1]$ as shown here:

$$p_1 = \int_0^1 \alpha_1(v) \, dF(v)$$

$$= \int_0^1 \frac{a}{1+a} \mathbf{1}(0 < F(v) \le a) \, dF(v) + \int_0^1 \mathbf{1}(a < F(v) \le 1) \, dF(v)$$

$$= \frac{a}{1+a} a + (1 - a)$$

$$= \frac{1}{1+a}.$$

For each given player, the distributions of the valuation parameter of this player from the perspective of contest 1 and contest 2, respectively, are given by

$$F_1(v) = \begin{cases} \frac{a}{1+a} F(v) + \frac{a}{1+a}, & \text{if } 0 \le F(v) \le a \\ F(v), & \text{if } a < F(v) \le 1 \end{cases}$$

and

$$F_2(v) = \begin{cases} \frac{1}{1+a} F(v) + \frac{1}{1+a}, & \text{if } 0 \le F(v) \le a \\ 1, & \text{if } a < F(v) \le 1 \end{cases}.$$

See Figure 5.13 for an illustration.

The Large System Limit

We consider a large system limit defined by assuming that prizes take values from a finite set, the number of contests that offer each distinct prize value scales proportionally with the the number of players, and the number of players n grows large. Such a limit is of interest in situations where there are many players and many contests that offer a few distinct values of prizes. For example, such a situation may arise in the context of crowdsourcing services where at any given time there are many active workers and many open projects that offer monetary prizes of a few distinct values.

The large system limit is defined, more formally, as follows: assume that there are fixed constants $\lambda > 0$ and $\mu_1, \mu_2, \ldots, \mu_k > 0$ such that

$$\lim_{n \to \infty} \frac{n}{m} = \lambda \text{ and } \lim_{n \to \infty} \frac{m_j}{m} = \mu_j, \quad \text{for } j = 1, 2, \ldots, k.$$

In other words, the number of contests is a constant factor, $1/\lambda$, of the number of players n, and the number of contests of class j is a constant fraction, μ_j, of the total number of contests asymptotically for large value of n. We shall denote with $\bar{\mu}_j$ the fraction of contests that are of class 1 through j, i.e., $\bar{\mu}_j = \sum_{i=1}^{j} \mu_i$. The following geometric means of prizes will play an important role:

$$\Gamma_j = \prod_{l=1}^{j} w_l^{\mu_l / \bar{\mu}_j}, \quad \text{for } 1 \le j \le k.$$

The characterization of the symmetric Bayes-Nash equilibrium in the large system limit follows as a corollary of Theorem 5.9 by computing the asymptotic limits of the quantities asserted therein.

Corollary 5.15. *In the large system limit, the symmetric Bayes-Nash equilibrium has the following properties.*

(i) *The expected number of players who invest in any given contest of class j is*

$$\lambda_j = \begin{cases} \frac{\lambda}{\bar{\mu}_k} + \log\left(\frac{w_j}{\Gamma_k}\right), & \text{if } 1 \le j \le \hat{k} \\ 0 & \text{otherwise} \end{cases} \tag{5.47}$$

where

$$\hat{k} = \max\left\{ j \in \{1, 2, \ldots, k\} \mid w_j > \Gamma_j e^{-\frac{\lambda}{\bar{\mu}_j}} \right\}.$$

(ii) *The set of valuations is partitioned into $\hat{k}$ intervals of valuations defined by the separators $0 = \bar{v}_k = \cdots = \bar{v}_{\hat{k}+1} < \bar{v}_{\hat{k}} < \cdots < \bar{v}_2 < \bar{v}_1 = 1$ where*

$$\bar{v}_j = \begin{cases} F^{-1}\left(1 - \frac{\bar{\mu}_j}{\lambda} \log\left(\frac{\Gamma_j}{w_j}\right)\right), & \text{if } 1 \le j \le \hat{k} \\ 0 & \text{otherwise.} \end{cases} \tag{5.48}$$

(iii) *Any given player, conditional on the valuation of this player being equal to v, choses a given contest of class j with probability $\alpha_j(v) = \alpha_j^*(v)/m + o(1/m)$ where*

$$\alpha_j^*(v) = \begin{cases} \frac{1}{\bar{\mu}_l}, & \text{if } 1 \le j \le l \\ 0 & \text{otherwise.} \end{cases}, \quad \text{if } \bar{v}_{l+1} \le v < \bar{v}_l \tag{5.49}$$

(iv) *Any given player, conditional on the valuation of this player being equal to v and the class of the contest selected by this player being equal to j, makes an effort investment in the amount of*

$$\beta_j(v) = w_j \int_0^v x \, dG(x), \quad \text{for } 0 \le v \le 1 \tag{5.50}$$

where

$$G(v) = \begin{cases} \frac{\Gamma_l}{w_j} e^{-\lambda \bar{\mu}_j (1 - F(v))} & \text{if } 1 \le j \le l \\ 1 & \text{otherwise} \end{cases}, \quad \text{if } \bar{v}_{l+1} \le v < \bar{v}_l. \tag{5.51}$$

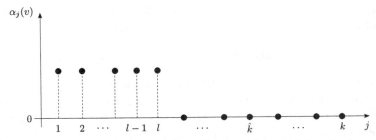

Figure 5.14. The large system limit of the probability that a player with the valuation parameter of value v, which is of class l, chooses a given contest of class j.

Proof. The proof is a straightforward exercise of deriving asymptotics of the equilibrium expressions asserted in Theorem 5.9. We shall only show how to derive the asymptotic expected number of participants in a contest because the other properties follow by similar arguments. We shall repeatedly use the following basic fact: for every fixed $a > 0$: $a^x = 1 + \log(a)x + o(x)$, for small x. Using this asymptote in (5.23), we obtain

$$\Phi_j = 1 + \frac{\log(\Gamma_j)}{n} + o(1/n).$$

Similarly, we have

$$\Phi_{\hat{k}}\left(\frac{1}{w_j}\right)^{1/(n-1)} = \left(1 + \frac{\log(\Gamma_j)}{n} + o(1/n)\right)\left(1 - \frac{\log(w_j)}{n} + o(1/n)\right)$$

$$= 1 + \log\left(\frac{\Gamma_{\hat{k}}}{w_j}\right)\frac{1}{n} + o(1/n).$$

Using this in (5.24), we obtain

$$np_j = \frac{1}{\bar{\mu}_{\hat{k}}} + \log\left(\frac{w_j}{\Gamma_{\hat{k}}}\right) + o(1), \quad \text{for } j = 1, 2, \ldots, \hat{k}.$$

$\square$

From (5.49) observe that in the large system limit, players of class l randomize their selection uniformly over the contests of class 1 through l (see Figure 5.14 for an illustration). From (5.47), the expected number of participants in a contest is logarithmic in the value of the prize offered by this contest.

Total Effort

In the symmetric Bayes-Nash equilibrium, the expected total effort invested in any given contest of class j is given by

$$R^j = \begin{cases} w_j\left(\bar{v}_j - \sum_{l=j}^{\hat{k}} \int_{\bar{v}_{l+1}}^{\bar{v}_l} \phi_{j,l}(x)\,dx\right), & \text{if } 1 \leq j \leq \hat{k} \\ 0, & \text{otherwise} \end{cases}$$

where

$$\phi_{j,l}(x) = n\left(\Phi_l\left(\frac{1}{w_j}\right)^{1/(n-1)}\right)^{n-1}\left(1 - \frac{1}{M_l}(1 - F(x))\right)^{n-1}$$
$$- (n-1)\left(\Phi_l\left(\frac{1}{w_j}\right)^{1/(n-1)}\right)^{n}\left(1 - \frac{1}{M_l}(1 - F(x))\right)^{n}.$$

A key observation is that each contest of class j is equivalent to a standard all-pay contest among n players with independent and identically distributed valuations according to distribution F_j, and the assertion follows from (5.28) and (2.57).

Maximum Individual Effort

In the symmetric Bayes-Nash equilibrium, the expected maximum individual effort invested in any given contest of class j is given by

$$R_1^j = \begin{cases} w_j\left(\frac{n}{2n-1}\bar{v}_j - \sum_{l=j}^{k}\int_{\bar{v}_{l+1}}^{\bar{v}_l}\phi_{j,l}(x)\,dx\right), & \text{if } 1 \le j \le \hat{k} \\ 0, & \text{otherwise} \end{cases}$$

where

$$\phi_{j,l}(x) = \left(\Phi_l\left(\frac{1}{w_j}\right)^{1/(n-1)}\right)^{n-1}\left(1 - \frac{1}{M_l}(1 - F(x))\right)^{n-1}$$
$$- \frac{n-1}{2n-1}\left(\Phi_l\left(\frac{1}{w_j}\right)^{1/(n-1)}\right)^{2n-1}\left(1 - \frac{1}{M_l}(1 - F(x))\right)^{2n-1},$$

which follows by the same arguments as for the expected total effort, but using (2.58).

5.3 Standard All-Pay Contests with Budgets

In this section we consider a normal form game of two or more simultaneous contests each offering a prize of positive value that is awarded to a player who makes the largest effort investment in this contest. Each player is endowed with a budget of effort that he or she can distribute in an arbitrary way over the set of contests. Specifically, each player i is endowed with a budget of effort of value $c_i > 0$, and his or her strategy set is given by $\mathcal{B}_i = \{\mathbf{b}_i \in \mathbf{R}_+^m \mid \sum_{j \in M} b_{i,j} \le c_i\}$. The payoff functions of the players are given by

$$s_i(\mathbf{b}) = \sum_{j=1}^{m} w_j x_{i,j}(\mathbf{b}), \quad \text{for } \mathbf{b} \in \mathcal{B}, \ i \in N. \tag{5.52}$$

The given normal form game defined by the given strategy sets and payoff functions has a rich set of equilibrium properties. A pure-strategy Nash equilibrium is not guaranteed to exist for simple instances of two-player games. A mixed-strategy

Nash equilibrium is in general non-unique, and there can exist a continuum of mixed-strategy Nash equilibria. In this section, we characterize mixed-strategy Nash equilibria for several special cases of interest. We shall first consider the case of two contests and two players allowing for arbitrary values of prizes and arbitrary values of budgets (Section 5.3.1). We shall see that already in this case there exists a continuum of mixed-strategy Nash equilibria and provide an explicit characterization of them. We shall then consider the case of one or more contests allowing for arbitrary values of prizes and two or more players with identical values of effort budgets (Section 5.3.2). We shall see that in this case there exist both a pure- and a mixed-strategy Nash equilibria in which each player directs his or her entire effort budget to one of the contests whenever the number of players is large enough. We shall then consider the case of one or more contests with identical values of prizes and two players with arbitrary values of budgets (Section 5.3.3). We shall see that in this case any mixed-strategy Nash equilibrium has a unique univariate marginal distribution for the effort investment of a player directed to any given contest, provided that the asymmetry of the effort budgets is not too large.

Before moving to the next section, we point out a strategic equivalence of the normal form game studied in this section and a classic game known as the continuous Colonel Blotto game.

Relation with Colonel Blotto games The normal form game defined by the given strategy sets and payoff functions accommodates the classic continuous Colonel Blotto game as a strategically equivalent game. The continuous Colonel Blotto game is a two-player zero-sum game described as follows. It consists of two players who simultaneously distribute their limited resources over a given set of contests. The winner in each contest is the player who invests the larger number of resources, and otherwise a draw takes place. For each contest, the winner wins a given number of points that may be specific to this contest, and the other player loses the same number of points. The winner of the game is the player who accumulates more points. In the narrative of the Colonel Blotto games, two colonels simultaneously distribute their troops across different battlefields, and in each battlefield the colonel who places a larger number of troops wins. The winner of the war is the colonel who wins in more battlefields. The game is clearly a zero-sum game because the total payoff earned by both players adds up to zero. The asserted strategic equivalence is shown as follows. For the case of two players, the payoff functions in (5.52) can be written in the following form:

$$s_1(\mathbf{b}) = \sum_{j=1}^{m} w_j u(b_{1,j} - b_{2,j}) \text{ and } s_2(\mathbf{b}) = \sum_{j=1}^{m} w_j u(b_{2,j} - b_{1,j}) \qquad (5.53)$$

where

$$u(x) = \begin{cases} 0, & \text{if } x < 0 \\ \frac{1}{2}, & \text{if } x = 0 \\ 1, & \text{if } x > 0 \end{cases} \qquad (5.54)$$

On the other hand, the payoff functions for the continuous Colonel Blotto game can be written as follows:

$$s_1(\mathbf{b}) = \sum_{j=1}^{m} w_j \operatorname{sgn}(b_{1,j} - b_{2,j}) \text{ and } s_2(\mathbf{b}) = \sum_{j=1}^{m} w_j \operatorname{sgn}(b_{2,j} - b_{1,j}) \quad (5.55)$$

where

$$\operatorname{sgn}(x) = \begin{cases} -1, & \text{if } x < 0 \\ 0, & \text{if } x = 0 \\ 1, & \text{if } x > 0 \end{cases}.$$

Since $\operatorname{sgn}(x) = 2u(x) - 1$ for all $x \in \mathbf{R}$, each payoff function in (5.55) is equal to the respective payoff function in (5.53) up to a multiplicative factor and an additive constant, which implies strategic equivalence of the two games.

5.3.1 Two Contests and Two Players

In this section we consider the game of simultaneous standard all-pay contests with budgets for the case of two players and two contests with arbitrary values of the effort budgets and the prizes.

Pure-Strategy Nash Equilibrium

The pure-strategy Nash equilibrium can be characterized as follows. Consider first the case of players with identical values of effort budgets, which without loss of generality are assumed to be of unit value. If the values of the prizes are identical then this is a degenerate case in which any split of efforts yields the same payoff to each player. Hence, any feasible effort investment is a pure-strategy Nash equilibrium. On the other hand, if the two contests offer different values of prizes, then there are three different cases to consider depending on those values. If $w_1/(w_1 + w_2) < 2/3$, a pure-strategy Nash equilibrium is for players to invest their entire effort budgets in different contests. In such a case neither player can benefit by reallocating some part of his or her budget from the contest that he or she invests in to the other contest. If $w_1/(w_1 + w_2) > 2/3$, a pure-strategy Nash equilibrium is for both players to invest their entire effort budgets in contest 1. In this case, again, neither player can benefit by unilaterally reallocating some part of his or her budget to the contest that offers the smaller prize. In the boundary case, when $w_1/(w_1 + w_2) = 2/3$, any outcome from the former two cases is a pure-strategy Nash equilibrium (see Figure 5.15). Note that if the values of the prizes are not very different, then the equilibrium outcomes are such that the players invest in different contests; otherwise, both players make all investment in the contest that offers the larger prize.

Consider now the case of asymmetric budgets $c_1 > c_2 > 0$. Obviously, the case $c_1 > 2c_2$ is trivial: it is a dominant strategy for player 1 to invest more than c_2 in each contest and thus win both prizes for any effort investment of player 2. If $c_1 \le 2c_2$, a pure-strategy Nash equilibrium is not guaranteed to exist. Consider the case of contests with identical values of prizes. In this case, for any given way player 2 splits his or her effort budget over the two contests, player 1 can redistribute his or her budget so as to

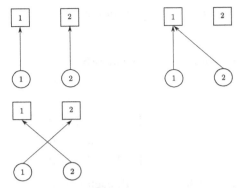

Figure 5.15. The pure-strategy Nash equilibrium outcomes for the game of two contests and two players with symmetric effort budgets: (left) $w_1/(w_1 + w_2) < 2/3$ and (right) $w_1/(w_1 + w_2) > 2/3$. If $w_1/(w_1 + w_2) = 2/3$, then any of the three outcomes is a pure-strategy Nash equilibrium.

guarantee the winning of both prizes. This, in turn, leaves player 2 with the smallest possible payoff, and his or her best response is to redistribute the effort investment in such a way as to win one of the contests. Continuing this sequence of best responses creates a never-ending cycle and thus shows the non-existence of a pure-strategy Nash equilibrium.

Mixed-Strategy Nash Equilibrium

We consider the case of two players with arbitrary distinct budgets $c_1 > c_2 > 0$ and two contests that offer arbitrary values of prizes $w_1 \geq w_2 > 0$. We shall show that there exists a mixed-strategy Nash equilibrium and, in fact, a continuum of mixed-strategy Nash equilibria.

We shall use the following notation. Let

$$k = \left\lfloor \frac{c_1}{c_1 - c_2} \right\rfloor$$

where $\lfloor x \rfloor$ is the largest integer smaller than or equal to x. Let $d_1 = c_1 - c_2$ be the difference of the effort budgets and $d_2 = c_2/(k-1)$ if $k > 1$ and $d_2 = 0$ otherwise. Let w be the ratio of values of prizes $w = w_1/w_2$.

Theorem 5.16. *For every real number $\delta \in (c_1 - kd_1, d_1)$, the following mixed strategies are a mixed-strategy Nash equilibrium:*

$$\mathbf{Pr}[(b_{1,1}, b_{1,2}) = (d_1 l + \delta, c_1 - (d_1 l + \delta))] = \frac{1}{Z} w^l, \quad \text{for } 0 \leq l < k \quad (5.56)$$

and

$$\mathbf{Pr}[(b_{2,1}, b_{2,2}) = (d_2 l, c_2 - d_2 l)] = \frac{1}{Z} w^{k-1-l}, \quad \text{for } 0 \leq l < k \quad (5.57)$$

where Z is a normalization constant equal to $\sum_{l=0}^{k-1} w^l$.

All mixed-strategy Nash equilibria given by (5.56) and (5.57) are payoff equivalent: the respective expected payoffs of player 1 and player 2 are given by

$$
\mathbf{E}[s_1(\mathbf{b})] = \begin{cases} w_1\left(1 + \frac{1}{k}\right), & \text{if } w = 1 \\ w_1 + w_2\frac{w-1}{w^k-1}, & \text{if } w > 1 \end{cases} \tag{5.58}
$$

and

$$
\mathbf{E}[s_2(\mathbf{b})] = \begin{cases} w_2\left(1 - \frac{1}{k}\right), & \text{if } w = 1 \\ w_2\frac{w^k-w}{w^k-1}, & \text{if } w > 1 \end{cases}. \tag{5.59}
$$

Proof. The following relations can be checked to hold under the assumption that $c_1 - kd_1 < \delta < d_1$:

$$
d_1(k-1) + \delta - b_{2,1} > 0, \quad \text{for all } 0 \le b_{2,1} \le c_2, \tag{5.60}
$$

$$
\delta - d_1 - b_{2,1} < 0, \quad \text{for all } 0 \le b_{2,1} \le c_2, \tag{5.61}
$$

$$
d_1 - d_2 \le 0, \tag{5.62}
$$

and

$$
d_1 - d_2 - b_{1,1} + d_2 k > 0, \quad \text{for all } 0 \le b_{1,1} < c_1. \tag{5.63}
$$

The expected payoff functions (5.53) can be written as follows:

$$
s_1(\mathbf{b}) = w_1 u(b_{1,1} - b_{2,1}) + w_2 u(b_{1,2} - b_{2,2}) \tag{5.64}
$$

$$
s_2(\mathbf{b}) = w_1 u(b_{2,1} - b_{1,1}) + w_2 u(b_{2,2} - b_{1,2}). \tag{5.65}
$$

We now show that if player 1 plays according to the mixed strategy in (5.56), then the expected payoff of player 2 is invariant to the strategy played by player 2. From (5.65), (5.60), and (5.61) it follows that the expected payoff for player 2 conditional on his or her effort investment in contest 1 is given by

$$
\mathbf{E}[s_2(\mathbf{b}) \mid b_{2,1} = x] = \frac{1}{Z}\sum_{l=0}^{k-1} w^l \left[w_1 u(x - d_1 l - \delta) + w_2 u(d_1(l-1) + \delta - x) \right]
$$

$$
= \frac{w_2}{Z}\sum_{l=0}^{k-1} w^{l+1} u(x - d_1 l - \delta)) + \frac{w_2}{Z}\sum_{l=0}^{k-1} w^l u(d_1(l-1) + \delta - x))
$$

$$
= \frac{w_2}{Z}\sum_{l=0}^{k-1} w^{l+1} u(x - d_1 l - \delta) + \frac{w_2}{Z}\sum_{l=-1}^{k-2} w^{l+1} u(d_1 l + \delta - x)
$$

$$
= \frac{w_2}{Z}\left(w^k u(x - d_1(k-1) - \delta) + \sum_{l=0}^{k-2} w^{l+1} + u(-d_1 + \delta - x) \right)
$$

$$
= \frac{w_2}{Z}\sum_{l=1}^{k-1} w^l.
$$

Therefore, the expected payoff of player 2 conditional on the value of the investment of this player is independent of this value and is equal to that given in (5.59).

Since the sum of the payoffs of the two players is equal to the sum of the prizes of the two contests, we have $\mathbf{E}[s_1(\mathbf{b})] + \mathbf{E}[s_2(\mathbf{b})] = w_1 + w_2$. Combining this with (5.59) we obtain

$$\mathbf{E}[s_1(\mathbf{b})] = w_2 \frac{\sum_{l=0}^{k} w^l}{\sum_{l=0}^{k-1} w^l} \qquad (5.66)$$

which is equivalent to (5.58).

We next show that player 1 cannot obtain a larger expected payoff by unilaterally deviating from the mixed strategy (5.56). From (5.64), (5.62), and (5.63), it follows that

$$\mathbf{E}[s_1(\mathbf{b}) \mid b_{1,1} = x] = \frac{1}{Z} \sum_{l=0}^{k-1} w^{k-1-l}[w_1 u(x - d_2 l) + w_2 u(d_1 + d_2 l - x)]$$

$$= \frac{w_2}{Z} \sum_{l=0}^{k-1} [w^{k-l} u(x - d_2 l) + w^{k-1-l} u(d_1 + d_2 l - x)]$$

$$= \frac{w_2}{Z} \sum_{l=0}^{k-1} w^{k-l} u(x - d_2 l) + \frac{w_2}{Z} \sum_{l=1}^{k} w^{k-l} u(d_1 - d_2 - (x - d_2 l))$$

$$= \frac{w_2}{Z} \left(w^k + \sum_{l=1}^{k-1} w^{k-l}[u(x - d_2 l) + u(d_1 - d_2 - (x - d_2 l))] + 1 \right)$$

$$\leq \frac{w_2}{Z} \left(w^k + \sum_{l=1}^{k-1} w^{k-l} + 1 \right)$$

$$= w_2 \frac{\sum_{l=0}^{k} w^l}{\sum_{l=0}^{k-1} w^l}$$

which in view of (5.66) shows that for any strategy deployed by player 1 the expected payoff is always less than or equal to that under the given mixed strategy. ☐

The mixed strategies (5.56) and (5.57) are such that each player randomizes on a support that consists of a lattice of k points (Figure 5.16). Player 1 randomizes over a lattice of points with distance $c_1 - c_2$ between consecutive points, with the smallest point placed at δ. Player 2 randomizes over a lattice of points with distance $c_2/(k-1)$ between consecutive points, with the smallest point placed at zero. Both supports are of size k, which is increasing in the ratio of the effort budgets c_2/c_1, from value 1 for $c_2/c_1 < 1/2$ to infinity as c_2/c_1 approaches 1 from below. In the case $c_2/c_1 < 1/2$, the equilibrium consists of trivial pure-strategy Nash equilibrium points that correspond to any split of the effort budgets such that player 1 beats player 2 in both contests by investing more than c_2 in each. We refer to the limit as c_2/c_1 approaches 1 from below as the limit of symmetric budgets.

If the two contests offer identical values of prizes, both players randomize uniformly over their respective supports. In particular, in the limit of symmetric budgets, the effort investment by each player in any given contest is according to a uniform distribution on $[0, c_1]$. On the other hand, if the two contests offer different values of prizes, the

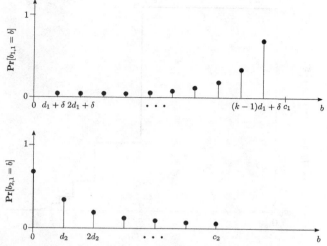

Figure 5.16. A mixed-strategy Nash equilibrium for the game with two contests and two players.

equilibrium distribution of the effort investment in the contest that offers the larger prize is geometrically increasing for the player with the larger effort budget (player 1) and is geometrically decreasing for the player with the smaller effort budget (player 2). In the limit of symmetric budgets, player 1 invests his or her entire effort budget to contest 1, and player 2 directs his or her entire effort budget to contest 2. In other words, in the limit of symmetric effort budgets, the player with the larger budget invests all effort to the contest that offers the larger prize, and the player with the smaller budget invests all effort to the contest that offers the smaller prize.

The mixed strategy of player 1 given in (5.56) is an infinite family of distributions parameterized with the real-valued parameter δ. Hence, there is a continuum of mixed-strategy Nash equilibria. However, all mixed-strategy Nash equilibria have equivalent expected payoffs, given by (5.56) and (5.57), for player 1 and player 2, respectively. The expected payoff of player 1 is guaranteed to be at least as large as the value of the larger prize, w_1. Since the total payoff of both players is equal to the sum of the values of the two prizes, the expected payoff of player 2 is smaller than or equal to the value of the smaller prize, w_2. The expected payoff of player 1 is increasing in the ratio of the smaller to the larger effort budget c_2/c_1. Obviously, in the case $c_2/c_1 < 1/2$, player 1 can invest more than the effort budget of player 2 in each contest, which guarantees that he or she wins in each contest, and hence achieves the highest possible payoff of value $w_1 + w_2$. In the limit of symmetric effort budgets, the expected payoff of player 1 tends to the value of the larger prize. As we already noted, in this limit case, player 1 invests all his or her effort in contest 1, and player 2 invests all his or her effort in contest 2. See Figure 5.17 for an illustration.

5.3.2 Symmetric Budgets

In this section we consider the case of players with symmetric budgets, which without loss of generality are assumed to be of unit value. The number of contests and values of

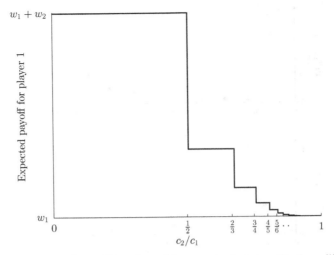

Figure 5.17. The expected payoff for player 1 in any mixed-strategy Nash equilibrim versus the ratio of the effort budgets c_2/c_1.

prizes are allowed to be arbitrary. We shall focus on special type of equilibria in which each player invests all effort into a single contest, which occurs under the condition that no player can benefit from unilaterally splitting his or her effort over two or more contests. This condition holds true provided that the number of players is sufficiently large. Intuitively, a player may benefit from splitting his or her effort over two or more contests if the overall competition is low, which gives a good chance for a player to be a sole participant in a contest, in which case an arbitrarily small effort investment into such a contest guarantees a win. We shall see that in both pure-strategy and mixed-strategy Nash equilibrium, the number of participants attracted by each contest tends to be proportional to the value of the prize of this contest as the number of players grows large. The other type of equilibria, in which some players split their efforts over two or more contests, is more complicated to study, and operates under additional assumptions considered in Section 5.3.1 and Section 5.3.3.

Pure-Strategy Nash Equilibria

For each given assignment of players to contests $\mathbf{a}$, we denote with $n_j(\mathbf{a})$ the number of players assigned to contest j, i.e., $n_j(\mathbf{a}) = \sum_{i=1}^{n} \mathbf{1}(a_i = j)$.

A set of necessary and sufficient conditions for an assignment of players to contests $\mathbf{a}$ to be a pure-strategy Nash equilibrium is given as follows. First, there must not exist a player who can benefit by unilaterally switching from investing his or her effort budget from one contest to another, which is equivalent to

$$\frac{w_j}{n_j(\mathbf{a})} \geq \frac{w_l}{n_l(\mathbf{a}) + 1}, \quad \text{for all } j \neq l. \tag{5.67}$$

Second, there must not exist a player who can benefit by splitting his or her effort budget over two or more contests, which corresponds to the following two conditions:

$$\begin{aligned}
&n_j(\mathbf{a}) = 0 \quad \text{for some } j \in \{1, 2, \ldots, m\} \\
\Rightarrow \quad &n_j(\mathbf{a}) = 0 \text{ or } n_j(\mathbf{a}) \geq 2 \quad \text{for all } j \in \{1, 2, \ldots, m\}
\end{aligned} \tag{5.68}$$

and

$$\frac{w_j}{n_j(\mathbf{a})} \geq \sum_{l=1}^{m} w_l \mathbf{1}(n_l(\mathbf{a}) = 0), \quad \text{for all } j = 1, 2, \ldots, m. \quad (5.69)$$

Condition (5.68) means that if there exists a contest into which none of the players have made an investment, then each contest that receives some effort investment must have received it from at least two players. Otherwise, if a player was the sole investor in a contest, then this player would benefit by reallocating some amount of his or her effort to a contest that received no investment prior to the deviation. Therefore, it remains only to consider the case when there exists a contest in which none of the players have invested, and each contest that received some investment did so from at least two players. In this case, condition (5.69) simply means that no player can benefit by splitting his or her effort budget over two or more contests. If splitting of the effort budget is beneficial, then a payoff-maximizing strategy is to invest a strictly positive effort in each contest. Such a strategy guarantees winning the prize of each contest that is unattended by a player prior to the deviation.

There are instances of games for which there exists no pure-strategy Nash equilibrium in which each player invests in one contest, i.e., there exists no assignment of players to contests $\mathbf{a}$ such that conditions (5.67), (5.68), and (5.69) are true. One such instance is given in the following example.

Example 5.17 (symmetric prizes). Consider any instance of the game with $m \geq 2$ simultaneous contests that offer symmetric values of prizes and such that the number of players n is smaller than the number of contests. Assuming that each player invests his or her entire effort budget in a single contest, it must be that each contest is attended by at most one player. Otherwise, each player who invests in a contest with two or more players would benefit by switching his or her effort budget to a contest that was unattended by a player prior to the deviation. Since the number of players is smaller than the number of contests, there exists at least one contest unattended by a player. Since each player is a sole participant in a contest, each can benefit by reallocating some amount of the effort budget to a contest unattended by a player.

The last example shows that for the case of contests with symmetric values of prizes in which each player invests in a single contest, for existence of a pure-strategy Nash equilibrium it is a necessary condition that the number of players is at least as large as the number of contests. For the case of contests that offer symmetric values of prizes, this condition is also sufficient, which follows easily by the following observation. For the case of contests with symmetric values of prizes, condition (5.67) boils down to

$$-1 \leq n_j(\mathbf{a}) - n_l(\mathbf{a}) \leq 1, \quad \text{for all } j \neq l.$$

This condition holds for any assignment vector $\mathbf{a}$ that is realized by assigning players in an arbitrary order to a contest with the least number of already assigned players. One such online assignment is a round-robin assignment, which assigns players to contests according to the following schedule:

$$1, 2, \ldots, m, 1, 2, \ldots, m, \ldots.$$

Under the condition that the number of players is at least as large as the number of contests, the assignment vector $\mathbf{a}$ is such that each contest is attended by at least one player, and thus trivially verifies conditions (5.68) and (5.69).

We now show that for arbitrary values of prizes and any given number of players there always exists an assignment of players to contests $\mathbf{a}$ that satisfies condition (5.67). Consider an assignment of players to contests defined as follows. Let $n_j(t)$ denote the number of players assigned to contest j just after the t-th assignment is made. Observe that $\sum_{j=1}^m n_j(t) = t$ holds. The t-th assignment is made by assigning an arbitrary unassigned player to a contest j such that

$$\frac{w_j}{n_j(t-1)+1} \geq \frac{w_l}{n_l(t-1)+1} \quad \text{for all } l \neq j. \tag{5.70}$$

This assignment rule prioritizes the assignment of a player to a contest that gives the largest payoff to the player just after the assignment is made. In the case of contests with symmetric values of prizes, such an assignment corresponds to assigning each player to a contest with the least number of already assigned players. It is left as an exercise to the reader to show that the assignment of players to contests that results from the prescribed assignment rule validates condition (5.67).

A sufficient condition for (5.67), (5.68), and (5.69) to hold true is to require that the number of players is sufficiently large so that each contest is attended by at least one player. In this case, no splitting of budget can be beneficial to a player and conditions (5.68), and (5.69) hold true. Such a sufficient condition is

$$n \geq \frac{\sum_{j=1}^m w_j}{w_m}$$

which boils down to the condition $n \geq m$ for the case of contests with identical values of prizes.

Note that from (5.67), we have

$$\frac{w_j}{\sum_{l=1}^m w_l} - \frac{1}{n} \leq \frac{n_j(\mathbf{a})}{n} \leq \frac{w_j}{\sum_{l=1}^m w_l}, \quad \text{for } j = 1, 2, \ldots, m.$$

Hence,

$$\lim_{n \to \infty} \frac{n_j(\mathbf{a})}{n} = \frac{w_j}{\sum_{l=1}^m w_l}, \quad \text{for } j = 1, 2, \ldots, m.$$

In other words, the participation in each contest is proportional to the value of the prize of this contest asymptotically as the number of players grows large.

Mixed-Strategy Nash Equilibria

We give a condition for the existence of a symmetric mixed-strategy Nash equilibrium in which each player invests his or her effort budget in a single contest, and provide an explicit characterization of it.

The following function is used in the characterization of the symmetric mixed-strategy Nash equilibrium, defined for every positive integer n as a parameter:

$$\phi_n(x) = \frac{1 - (1-x)^n}{nx}, \quad \text{for } 0 \leq x \leq 1. \tag{5.71}$$

See Figure 5.18 for a graph.

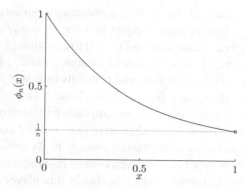

Figure 5.18. $\phi_n(x)$ versus x.

Theorem 5.18. *Suppose that* **p** *is given by*

$$p_j = \phi_n^{-1}\left(\min\left\{\frac{s^*}{w_j}, 1\right\}\right), \quad \text{for } j = 1, 2, \ldots, m \tag{5.72}$$

where s^* is uniquely defined by $\sum_{j=1}^{m} p_j = 1$, and the following condition holds true:

$$\frac{\sum_{j=1}^{m} w_j[(1 - p_j)^n + n(1 - p_j)^{n-1}]}{\sum_{j=1}^{m} w_j} \leq 1. \tag{5.73}$$

Then, **p** *is a symmetric mixed-strategy Nash equilibrium.*

Proof. Fix an arbitrary player, say player 1, and assume that all other players play according to a mixed strategy **p**. Let us first assume that player 1 invests all his or her effort in one contest, and consider later the case where he or she splits the effort budget over two or more contests. The expected payoff for player 1 for investing in contest j is given by

$$s_j = w_j \sum_{l=0}^{n-1} \frac{1}{l+1}\binom{n-1}{l} p_j^l (1 - p_j)^{n-1-l}.$$

From the last expression, by a straightforward calculus, we obtain

$$s_j = w_j \frac{1 - (1 - p_j)^n}{n p_j}. \tag{5.74}$$

Combining this with (5.71), we can write

$$s_j = w_j \phi_n(p_j) \quad \text{for } j = 1, 2, \ldots, m.$$

For the distribution **p** to be a mixed-strategy Nash equilibrium, there must exist $s^* > 0$ such that for every $j = 1, 2, \ldots, m$, one of the following two conditions holds true:

$$p_j > 0 \quad \text{and} \quad w_j \phi_n(p_j) = s^*, \quad \text{or} \quad p_j = 0 \quad \text{and} \quad w_j \leq s^*. \tag{5.75}$$

From this we obtain that **p** can be written in the form (5.72), and since **p** is a probability distribution, s^* is a solution to the equation

$$\sum_{j=1}^{m} \phi_n^{-1}\left(\min\left\{\frac{s^*}{w_j}, 1\right\}\right) = 1. \tag{5.76}$$

We claim that the left-hand side in (5.76) is a continuous, strictly decreasing function in s^* that takes a value greater than or equal to 1 for $s^* = w_1/n$ and has value 0 for $s^* = w_1$. Hence, there is a unique solution $s^* > 0$ to equation (5.76), and this solution satisfies $w_1/n \leq s^* \leq w_1$. The claim follows by the fact that $\phi_n : [0, 1] \to [1/n, 1]$ is a continuous, strictly decreasing function, and hence its inverse $\phi_n^{-1} : [1/n, 1] \to [0, 1]$ is a continuous, strictly decreasing function (see Figure 5.18).

Consider now the case where player 1 contemplates unilaterally deviating to a mixed strategy that splits his or her effort budget over two or more contests, assuming that all other players play according to the mixed strategy $\mathbf{p}$. By splitting the effort budget, the effort investment of player 1 in any given contest is smaller than 1, while any other player invests the effort in the amount of 1, should this player choose to participate in the given contest. The only way for player 1 to win in a contest is to be the sole participant in it. The expected payoff of player 1 achieves the largest possible value by investing a strictly positive effort in each contest, which yields the expected payoff of value

$$\sum_{j=1}^{m} w_j (1 - (1 - p_j)^{n-1}).$$

This quantity must be smaller than or equal to the expected payoff s^* that player 1 obtains by investing into one contest, such that each player invests his or her entire effort budget in one contest chosen independently according to the mixed strategy $\mathbf{p}$, i.e.,

$$\sum_{j=1}^{m} w_j (1 - (1 - p_j)^{n-1}) \leq s^*. \tag{5.77}$$

From (5.74), we have

$$n p_j s^* = w_j (1 - (1 - p_j)^n), \quad \text{for } j = 1, 2, \ldots, m.$$

Summing up, we obtain

$$s^* = \frac{1}{n} \sum_{j=1}^{m} w_j (1 - (1 - p_j)^n). \tag{5.78}$$

Using this, we obtain that (5.77) is equivalent to condition (5.73). $\qquad\square$

There exist instances for which condition (5.73) fails to be true, which is demonstrated by the following example.

Example 5.19 (symmetric values of prizes). Consider any instance of the game that models simultaneous contests with symmetric values of prizes. The symmetric mixed-strategy Nash equilibrium $\mathbf{p}$ is a uniform distribution on the set of available contests. Hence, condition (5.73) corresponds to

$$\left(1 - \frac{1}{m}\right)^n + n \left(1 - \frac{1}{m}\right)^{n-1} \leq 1. \tag{5.79}$$

Condition (5.79) holds true only if the number of players is large enough relative to the number of contests. For any fixed number of players, condition (5.79) becomes stronger the larger the number of contests, and it fails to hold for any sufficiently large number of contests. This admits a rather intuitive explanation: having fixed the

Table 5.1. Sufficient number of players for every player investing in one contest to be an equilibrium

m	1	2	3	4	5	6	7	8	9	10
n	1	3	6	9	13	17	22	26	31	35

number of players and then increasing the number of contests, the chance of any given contest ending up being unattended increases, and hence, at a certain point it becomes beneficial for a player to unilaterally deviate to investing a strictly positive amount in each contest. The least sufficient number of players, obtained from (5.79), is shown in Table 5.1 for some specific values of the number of contests.

Condition (5.79) is of more general interest than only for the case of contests with identical values of the prizes: it is a necessary condition for (5.73) to hold true for any values of prizes. This is because the left-hand side in (5.73) is a convex function in **p**, and hence, it is always greater than or equal to the value obtained for the uniform distribution over the set of available contests. It is readily seen that for condition (5.79) to hold true it is necessary that the number of players satisfies

$$n = \Omega(m \log(m)).$$

This means that the ratio of the number of players and the number of contest must grow with the number of contests at least as fast as $\Omega(\log(m))$, for the mixed strategy in Theorem 5.18 to be a mixed-strategy Nash equilibrium.

A sufficient condition for (5.79) to hold true is to require that the vector of prizes **w** satisfies

$$\frac{w_1}{\sum_{j=1}^m w_j} \geq 1 - \frac{1}{n+1}.$$

Under this condition, the symmetric mixed-strategy Nash equilibrium is such that $p_1 = 1$ and $p_2 = \cdots = p_m = 0$. This follows by noting that the left-hand side in equation (5.73) is a convex function in **p** and is thus smaller than or equal to the value obtained by putting all the unit mass on one of the contests, which in the mixed-strategy Nash equilibrium must be a contest with the largest prize.

Condition (5.73) holds true whenever the number of the players is large enough, for any fixed number of contests and values of the prizes. This follows since for any fixed value s^*, the left-hand side in (5.76) is decreasing in n, and hence the solution s^* to the equation (5.76) decreases in n. This implies that $p_j > 0$ for all $j = 1, 2, \ldots, m$, for every large enough n.

From (5.72) and (5.76), it follows that

$$\lim_{n \to \infty} p_j = \frac{w_j}{\sum_{l=1}^m w_l}, \quad \text{for } j = 1, 2, \ldots, m.$$

This limit stands in stark contrast to the case in which players incur linear costs of production, in which case the limit is such that players randomize uniformly over the set of available contests, which we established in Section 5.2.2.

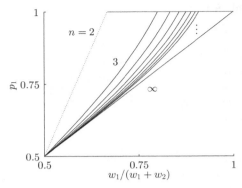

Figure 5.19. Two contests: p_1 versus $w_1/(w_1 + w_2)$ for specific values for the number of players (solid parts of curves indicate values for which condition (5.73) holds true).

Example 5.20 (two contests). Consider the case of two contests that offer prizes of values $w_1 \geq w_2 > 0$ and two or more players. Let $a = w_1/(w_1 + w_2)$. The symmetric mixed-strategy Nash equilibrium $\mathbf{p} = (p_1, 1 - p_1)$ is as follows: if $a < 1 - 1/(n + 1)$, then $1/2 \leq p_1 < 1$ is the unique solution of the equation

$$a(1 - p_1)(1 - (1 - p_1)^n) = (1 - a)p_1(1 - p_1^n),$$

and, otherwise, $p_1 = 1$.

For the special case of two players, the reader may check that

$$p_1 = \min\{3a - 1, 1\}$$

in which case condition (5.73) holds only if $2/3 \leq a \leq 1$; that is, $p_1 = 1$. For the case of three or more players, numerical evaluations show that condition (5.73) holds true for every $1/2 \leq a \leq 1$. See Figure 5.19 for a graph.

Social welfare We consider a social welfare function defined as the total expected value received by all players. Since the expected payoff of each player is equal to s^* in the symmetric mixed-strategy Nash equilibrium and players incur no production costs, we have

$$W = ns^*. \tag{5.80}$$

Combining with (5.78) or by arguing directly using the fact that the prize of each contest is fully transferred to players if, and only if, the contest is attended by at least one player, we have

$$W = \sum_{j=1}^{m} w_j(1 - (1 - p_j)^n).$$

The optimum value of the social welfare over all feasible effort investments subject to each player investing his or her entire effort in a single contest is equal to

$$W^* = \sum_{j=1}^{k} w_j$$

where $k = \min\{m, n\}$.

It is easy to show that the worst-case social efficiency is at least as small as $1 - 1/e$. To see this, consider the case of contests with identical values of prizes $w_1 = w_2 = \cdots = w_m$. Then, we have

$$\frac{W}{W^*} = \frac{1 - \left(1 - \frac{1}{m}\right)^n}{\min\left\{\frac{n}{m}, 1\right\}} \geq \frac{1 - e^{-\frac{n}{m}}}{\min\left\{\frac{n}{m}, 1\right\}} \geq 1 - \frac{1}{e}$$

which is tight for the instance where there are as many contests as there are players, asymptotically as the number of players grows large.

We next show that $1 - 1/e$ is the worst-case social efficiency for any values of the prizes.

Theorem 5.21. *The social welfare in every symmetric mixed-strategy Nash equilibrium is at least $1 - 1/e$ of the optimum social welfare.*

Proof. From (5.76) and (5.80), W is the unique solution of the following equation:

$$\sum_{j=1}^{m} \phi_n^{-1}\left(W/(nw_j)\right) \mathbf{1}(W/w_j < n) = 1. \tag{5.81}$$

Let us first consider the case $n \geq m$. Without loss of generality, assume that $\sum_{j=1}^{m} w_j = 1$. The left-hand side in equation (5.81) is decreasing in W. Hence, the inequality $W \geq 1 - 1/e$ is equivalent to saying

$$\sum_{j=1}^{m} \phi_n^{-1}\left((1 - 1/e)/w_j\right) \mathbf{1}((1 - 1/e)/w_j < n) \geq 1. \tag{5.82}$$

The left-hand side in the inequality in (5.82) is convex in $1/w_1, 1/w_2, \ldots, 1/w_m$, so it has the smallest value for $w_1 = w_2 = \ldots = w_m = 1/m$ subject to the constraint $\sum_{j=1}^{m} w_j = 1$. Hence, (5.82) is implied by

$$m\phi_n^{-1}\left((1 - 1/e)m\right) \geq 1,$$

which is equivalent to $(1 - 1/m)^n \leq 1/e$ that indeed holds true for every $n \geq m$.

For the case $n < m$, we proceed as follows. Without loss of generality, assume that $\sum_{j=1}^{n} w_j = 1$. It suffices to show that condition (5.82) holds true. Since each summation element in the left-hand side of the inequality in (5.82) is non-negative, the inequality is implied by

$$\sum_{j=1}^{n} \phi_n^{-1}\left((1 - 1/e)/w_j\right) \mathbf{1}((1 - 1/e)/w_j \leq n) \geq 1.$$

The rest of the proof follows exactly the same steps as in the previous case. $\square$

5.3.3 Symmetric Prizes: Two-Player Case

Consider the case of three or more contests with symmetric values of prizes, which are without loss of generality assumed to be of unit value, and two players with values of the effort budgets $c_1 > c_2 > 0$. We shall show that in general there exist multiple mixed-strategy Nash equilibria. However, all of them are equivalent with respect to the univariate marginal distributions of the effort investments in any given contest, provided that the number of contests is large enough.

Theorem 5.22. *For the case of three or more contests with symmetric values of prizes and two players with effort budgets $c_1 > c_2 > 0$, the following properties hold for any mixed-strategy Nash equilibrium.*

(i) **Case $1/m \leq c_2/c_1 < 1/(m-1)$:** *there can exist multiple mixed-strategy Nash equilibria, and the univariate marginal distributions of effort put by a player into a contest are not unique.*

(ii) **Case $1/(m-1) \leq c_2/c_1 < 2/m$:** *the univariate marginal distributions of effort by a player into a contest are unique and are given as follows: player 1 randomizes uniformly on $[0, c_2]$ with probability $2(1 - c_1/(mc_2))$ and invests c_2, otherwise; player 2 invests zero effort with probability $1 - 2/m$ and randomizes uniformly on $[0, c_2]$, otherwise.*

(iii) **Case $2/m \leq c_2/c_1$:** *the univariate marginal distributions of effort put by a player into a contest are unique and are given as follows: player 1 randomizes uniformly on the interval $[0, 2c_1/m]$; player 2 invests zero effort with probability $1 - c_2/c_1$, and randomizes uniformly on $[0, 2c_1/m]$, otherwise.*

Proof. Suppose that there exists a mixed-strategy Nash equilibrium with univariate marginal distributions denoted by $B_{i,j}(x)$, for $i = 1$ and 2, and $j = 1, 2, \ldots, m$. Let s_1^* and s_2^* be the expected payoffs in this equilibrium for player 1 and player 2, respectively. Then, it must hold that

$$s_1(\mathbf{b}_1) = \sum_{j=1}^{m} B_{2,j}(b_{1,j}) \leq s_1^*, \qquad \text{for all } \mathbf{b}_1 \in \mathcal{B}_1$$

$$s_2(\mathbf{b}_2) = \sum_{j=1}^{m} B_{1,j}(b_{2,j}) \leq s_2^*, \qquad \text{for all } \mathbf{b}_2 \in \mathcal{B}_2$$

where in the first equation the equality holds for every point $\mathbf{b}_1 \in \mathcal{B}_1$ in the support of the mixed-strategy distribution of player 1, and in the second equation the equality holds for every $\mathbf{b}_2 \in \mathcal{B}_2$ in the support of the mixed-strategy distribution of player 2. In any mixed-strategy Nash equilibrium, it must be that each player invests his or her entire effort. Otherwise, the expected payoff of this player would be strictly smaller than under the mixed-strategy Nash equilibrium specified in the theorem. Since each player maximizes his or her own expected payoff subject to a budget constraint, it follows that there exists a pair of Lagrange multipliers $\lambda_1 > 0$ and $\lambda_2 > 0$ such that

$$s_1^* = \lambda_1 \sum_{j=1}^{m} \int_0^{\infty} \left(\frac{1}{\lambda_1} B_{2,j}(b_{1,j}) - b_{1,j} \right) dB_{1,j}(b_{1,j}) + \lambda_1 c_1$$

$$s_2^* = \lambda_2 \sum_{j=1}^{m} \int_0^{\infty} \left(\frac{1}{\lambda_2} B_{1,j}(b_{2,j}) - b_{2,j} \right) dB_{2,j}(b_{2,j}) + \lambda_2 c_2.$$

From the last two identities, we observe that the expected payoffs are in one-to-one correspondence with those of the game with complete information that models the standard all-pay contest between two players with valuations $1/\lambda_1$ and $1/\lambda_2$ and caps on individual effort investments because of the effort budget constraints.

We next prove each of the claims of the theorem in reverse order:

Case $c_2/c_1 \geq 2/m$ In this case, we shall show that there exists a pair of Lagrange multipliers λ_1 and λ_2 such that $1/\lambda_1 \leq c_1$ and $1/\lambda_2 \leq c_2$, and thus the equilibrium mixed strategies correspond to those in the game that models the standard all-pay contest with valuations $1/\lambda_1$ and $1/\lambda_2$. Since each player invests his or her entire effort budget, the expected total effort invested by each player must be equal to his or her effort budget. By using the characterization of the mixed-strategy Nash equilibrium of the game that models the standard all-pay contest in Theorem 2.3, we obtain

$$c_1 = \sum_{j=1}^{m} \int_0^{1/\lambda_2} x \, dB_{1,j}(x) = m \int_0^{1/\lambda_2} x \frac{1}{1/\lambda_2} \, dx = \frac{m}{2\lambda_2}$$

$$c_2 = \sum_{j=1}^{m} \int_0^{1/\lambda_2} x \, dB_{2,j}(x) = m \int_0^{1/\lambda_2} x \frac{1}{1/\lambda_1} \, dx = \frac{m\lambda_1}{2\lambda_2^2}.$$

Therefore, $1/\lambda_1 = (c_1/c_2)(2c_1/m)$ and $1/\lambda_2 = 2c_1/m$. Combining this with the assumption $2/m \leq c_2/c_1$, we obtain $1/\lambda_1 \leq c_1$ and $1/\lambda_2 \leq c_2$.

Case $1/(m-1) < c_2/c_1 \leq 2/m$ In this case, the distributions in the previous case cannot be univariate marginal distributions of a mixed-strategy Nash equilibrium because in the corresponding standard all-pay contest the budget cap of player 2 would be smaller than the valuation of player 2. Hence, in the present case, we need to consider the standard all-pay contest with valuations $1/\lambda_1$ and $1/\lambda_2$ and a cap of value c_2 for the effort investment of player 2. Using the characterization of equilibrium in Exercise 2.7, it follows that player 1 puts a mass of weight $1 - c_2/(1/\lambda_2)$ on value c_2 and, otherwise, randomizes uniformly on $[0, c_2]$, and player 2 puts a mass of weight $1 - c_2/(1/\lambda_1)$ on value 0, and randomizes uniformly on $[0, c_2]$, otherwise. Again, the expected total effort invested by a player is equal to the budget of this player; hence

$$c_1 = \sum_{j=1}^{m} \int_0^{c_2} x \, dB_{1,j}(x) + c_2(1 - B_{1,j}(c_2)) = mc_2 \left(1 - \frac{c_2\lambda_2}{2}\right)$$

$$c_2 = \sum_{j=1}^{m} \int_0^{c_2} x \, dB_{2,j}(x) = \frac{m\lambda_1 c_2^2}{2}.$$

From this it follows that $1/\lambda_1 = mc_2/2$ and $1/\lambda_2 = mc_2^2/[2(mc_2 - c_1)]$.

Case $1/m < c_2/c_1 \leq 1/(m-1)$ The distributions in the previous case cannot be equilibrium strategies because therein player 1 invests an effort of value c_2 with probability $2c_1/(mc_2) - 1$, which in the prevailing case would be larger than 1. Since this case

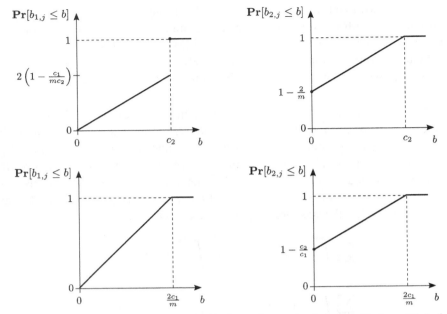

Figure 5.20. The univariate marginal distributions of any mixed-strategy Nash equilibria for the case (top) $1/(m-1) \leq c_2/c_1 < 2/m$ and the case (bottom) $2/m \leq c_2/c_1$.

accommodates the case of two contests and two players with the values of the budgets such that $c_2 < c_1 < 2c_2$, it follows from Theorem 5.16 that there exist multiple mixed-strategy Nash equilibria and that the univariate marginal distributions are not unique.   □

From Theorem 5.22 we observe that mixed-strategy Nash equilibria have equivalent univariate marginal distributions of the efforts invested in any given contest whenever $1/(m-1) \leq c_2/c_1$, i.e., the number of contests is large enough relative to the ratio of the effort budgets. In this case, there is a correspondence between the univariate marginal distributions and the distributions of a mixed-strategy Nash equilibrium in the game that models a standard all-pay contest. If $1/(m-1) \leq c_2/c_1 < 2/m$, the correspondence is to a standard all-pay contest between two players with valuations $mc_2/2$ and $mc_2^2/(2(mc_2 - c_1))$ for player 1 and player 2, respectively, and a cap of value c_2 for the effort investment by player 2. If $2/m \leq c_2/c_1$, the correspondence is to a standard all-pay contest with valuations $2c_1^2/(c_2m)$ and $2c_1/m$ for player 1 and player 2, respectively. See Figure 5.20 for a summarization.

Existence of Mixed-Strategy Nash Equilibria

In this section we establish the existence of mixed-strategy Nash equilibria for the game under consideration. For the first case in Theorem 5.22, we shall identify a pair of discrete mixed-strategy distributions and show that they are a mixed-strategy Nash equilibrium. For the last two cases in Theorem 5.22, we shall identify specific mixed-strategy distributions and show that if the players split their effort budgets over the contests according to these distributions, then their respective univariate marginal distributions of efforts correspond to those in Theorem 5.22. We shall make use of the catalog of distributions on a simplex in Appendix 11.2.3. For a gentle introduction, we first demonstrate how mixed strategies can be constructed for the special case of three contests for the last two cases in Theorem 5.22, and then subsequently cover the general case of three or more contests.

Special case: three contests Consider the case of three contests and two players with effort budgets of values as in the following two cases:

Case 1: $c_1/2 \leq c_2 < 2c_1/3$. The univariate marginal distributions of effort in this case are given in item (ii) of Theorem 5.22. For player 1 we need to establish the existence of a distribution on a 2-dimensional simplex such that if this player splits his or her effort budget over contests according to this distribution, then the univariate marginal distribution of his or her effort invested in any given contest is uniform on $[0, c_2)$ and has a mass of value $1 - 2(1 - c_1/(3c_2))$ at c_2. Such a distribution is the trivariate distribution that has a marginal distribution with a mass at a positive value, given in Appendix 11.2.3 for the value of the parameter $\theta = c_2/c_1$. For player 2 we need to show the existence of a distribution on a 2-dimensional simplex such that if this player splits his or her effort budget over contests according to this distribution, then the univariate marginal distribution of his or her effort invested in any given contest has a mass of value $1 - 2/m$ at zero value and is uniform on $(0, c_2]$. Such a distribution is the trivariate distribution that has a marginal distribution with a mass at zero value, given in Appendix 11.2.3 for the value of the parameter $\theta = 1$.

Case 2: $2c_1/3 \leq c_2$. The univariate marginal distributions of effort in this case are given in item (iii) of Theorem 5.22. For player 1 we need to show the existence of a distribution on a 2-dimensional simplex such that if this player splits his or her effort budget over contests according to this distribution, then the univariate marginal distribution of his or her effort invested in any given contest is uniform on $[0, 2c_1/3]$. Several such distributions are given in Appendix 11.2.3. For player 2 we need to show the existence of a distribution on a 2-dimensional simplex such that if this player splits his or her effort over contests according to this distribution, then the univariate marginal distribution of his or her effort invested in any given contest has a mass of value $1 - c_2/c_1$ at zero value and is uniform on $[0, 2c_1/3]$. Such a distribution is the trivariate distribution that has a marginal distribution with a mass at zero value, given in Appendix 11.2.3 for the value of the parameter $\theta = 2c_1/(3c_2)$.

General case: three or more contests The following theorem establishes the existence of mixed-strategy Nash equilibria for the general case of three or more contests.

Theorem 5.23. *For every game of three or more simultaneous contests that offer identical values of prizes and two players with effort budgets $c_1 > c_2 > 0$ such that $c_1 \leq mc_2$ there exists a mixed-strategy Nash equilibrium.*

Proof. We separately consider three different cases:

Case 1: $1/m \leq c_2/c_1 < 1/(m-1)$. We shall show that the mixed strategies as defined next are a mixed-strategy equilibrium. Suppose that player 1 chooses two contests by sampling uniformly at random without replacement from the set of all contests. He or she then splits a part of his or her effort budget of value $c_1 - (m - 2)c_2$ between the two chosen contests according to a uniform distribution over the points

$$\left(c_2 - \frac{i}{k-1}(mc_2 - c_1), c_2 - \left(1 - \frac{i}{k-1}\right)(mc_2 - c_1)\right), \quad \text{for } i = 0, 1, \ldots, k-1$$

where

$$k = \left\lceil \frac{c_2}{c_1 - (m-1)c_2} \right\rceil \tag{5.83}$$

and in each other contest invests an effort of value c_2. Suppose that player 2 chooses two contests by sampling uniformly at random without replacement from the set of all contests. He or she then splits his or her entire effort budget over the two chosen contests according to a uniform distribution over the points

$$\left(\left(1 - \frac{i}{k-1}\right)c_2, \frac{i}{k-1}c_2\right), \quad \text{for } i = 0, 1, \ldots, k-1.$$

We will show that under the given distributions, player 2 has no beneficial unilateral deviation; similar arguments can be used to show this also for player 1.

Note that each player has identical univariate marginal distributions of efforts invested in different contests that are defined as follows. For player 1, each univariate marginal distribution of effort has a mass of value $1 - 2(k-1)/(km)$ on the effort investment of value c_2 and a mass of value $2/(km)$ on each other point in its support. For player 2, each univariate marginal distribution of effort has a mass of value $1 - 2(k-1)/(km)$ on the effort investment of zero value and a mass of value $2/(km)$ on each other point in its support.

We now show that for the given mixed strategies, the expected payoff for player 2 is equal to

$$\frac{k-1}{k}\frac{2}{m}. \tag{5.84}$$

Consider an arbitrary contest $j \in \{1, 2, \ldots, m\}$. Let $W_{2,j}$ denote the event that player 2 wins in contest j. Note that player 2 wins in contest j if, and only if, player 1 chooses contest j and makes a smaller effort investment in this contest than player 2. The following relations can be checked to hold:

$$c_2 - \frac{k-i}{k-1}(mc_2 - c_1) < \frac{i}{k-1}c_2 \leq c_2 - \frac{k-1-i}{k-1}(mc_2 - c_1),$$
$$\text{for } i = 1, 2, \ldots, k-1.$$

Using this together with the assumption that player 1's mixed strategy is uniform over its support, it follows that for every $i \in \{0, 1, \ldots, k-1\}$, we have

$$\mathbf{Pr}\left[W_{2,j} \mid b_{2,j} = \frac{i}{k-1}c_2\right] = \mathbf{Pr}\left[b_{1,j} \leq c_2 - \frac{k-i}{k-1}(mc_2 - c_1)\right] = \frac{i}{k}\frac{2}{m},$$

and, by the same argument, we have

$$\mathbf{Pr}\left[W_{2,j} \mid b_{2,j} = \frac{k-1-i}{k-1}c_2\right] = \frac{k-1-i}{k}\frac{2}{m}.$$

Combining with the fact that player 2's mixed strategy is uniform over its support, it follows that

$$\mathbf{Pr}[W_{2,j}] = \frac{k-1}{k}\frac{2}{m^2}.$$

Since the expected payoff for a player is equal to the sum of his or her winning probabilities over all contests, it follows that the expected payoff for player 2 is as given in (5.84).

We next show that under the given mixed strategies, player 2 has no beneficial unilateral deviation. Suppose first that player 2 invests his or her effort budget over two contests. Consider the effort investment of player 2 in one of these contests. Player 2 has no incentive for this effort investment to be smaller than $c_1 - (m-1)c_2$ because player 1 invests at least as much in each contest with probability 1. By the definition of the support of player 1's mixed strategy, we observe that it suffices to consider the effort investment that is larger than $c_2 - ((k-1-i)/(k-1))(mc_2 - c_1)$ for an infinitesimally small amount, for a choice of an integer i such that $1 \le i < k-1$. For such an effort investment, the winning probability of player 2 is equal to

$$\frac{i+1}{k}\frac{2}{m}.$$

Note that the remaining effort budget of player 2 is of value smaller than

$$\frac{k-1-i}{k-1}(mc_2 - c_1) \le c_2 - \frac{i+1}{k-1}(mc_2 - c_1)$$

where the inequality holds because by the definition of k in (5.83), it holds that $k(mc_2 - c_1)/(k-1) \le c_2$. Using this observation and the assumption that player 1's mixed strategy is uniform over its support, it follows that player 2's winning probability in the other contest is at most

$$\frac{k-i-2}{k}\frac{2}{m}.$$

Hence, it follows that the expected payoff for player 2 is at most of value $((k-1)/k)(2/m)$, which is exactly the value of the expected payoff that he or she receives by playing the asserted equilibrium strategy.

Consider now the case where player 2 invests his or her effort over two or more contests. We can again consider one of these contests and assume that player 2 invests in this contest as in the previous case. The remaining effort budget can then be invested over one or more contests. The same argument can be repeated to establish that player 2 cannot obtain a larger expected payoff by splitting the remaining effort budget over two or more contests.

Case 2: $1/(m-1) \le c_2/c_1 < 2/m$. We now identify a mixed strategy for player 1 that has univariate marginal distributions as given in Theorem 5.22. Similar arguments can be used for player 2 as well. Recall that player 1 has univariate marginal distributions that are uniform on $[0, c_2)$ and have a mass of value $1 - 2(1 - c_1/(mc_2))$ at the effort investment of value c_2. We separately consider three different cases:

Subcase 2.1: $2 \le 2m - 2c_1/c_2 < 3$. Suppose that player 1 chooses a set of $2m - \lfloor 2c_1/c_2 \rfloor$ contests by sampling uniformly at random without replacement from the set of all contests. Note that the number of chosen contests is either 2 or 3. Suppose that in each non-chosen contest, player 1 invests the effort of value c_2. If the number of chosen contests is equal to 2, suppose that player 1 splits the remaining part of his or her effort budget of value c_2 uniformly at random over the two chosen contests. It should be easy to observe that each of his or her univariate marginal distributions has a mass of value $1 - 2/m$ at the effort investment of value c_2, and the remaining mass uniformly spread over $[0, c_2]$. If the number of chosen contests is equal to 3, suppose that player 1 splits the remaining part of his or her effort budget of value $c_1 - (m - 3)c_2$ over the set of chosen contests according to the trivariate distribution with a mass at a positive value as given in Appendix 11.2.3 with the value of the parameter $\theta = c_2/(c_1 - (m - 3)c_2)$. Since the set of the chosen contests is selected uniformly at random, the univariate marginal distributions are identical and are such that each has a mass of value

$$\frac{m - 3}{m} + \frac{3}{m} \left(1 - 2 \left(1 - \frac{1}{3\theta} \right) \right) = 1 - 2 \left(1 - \frac{c_1}{mc_2} \right)$$

at the effort investment of value c_2 and is uniform on $[0, c_2)$. This is exactly equal to the desired univariate marginal distribution.

Subcase 2.2: $3 \leq 2m - 2c_1/c_2 < 4$. Suppose that player 1 chooses a set of $2m - \lfloor 2c_1/c_2 \rfloor$ contests by sampling uniformly at random without replacement from the set of all contests. Note that the number of chosen contests is either 3 or 4. Suppose that in each non-chosen contest, player 1 invests the effort of value c_2. If the number of chosen contests is equal to 3, then a similar construction can be made as in Subcase 2.1. If the number of chosen contests is equal to 4, suppose that player 1 splits the remaining part of his or her effort budget of value $c_1 - (m - 4)c_2$ over the set of chosen contests according to the distribution quadruple with a mass at a positive value, given in Appendix 11.2.3 with the value of the parameter $\theta = c_2/(c_1 - (m - 4)c_2)$. By similar arguments as in Subcase 2.1, we obtain that the univariate marginal distributions are as desired.

Subcase 2.3: $4 \leq 2m - 2c_1/c_2 < m$. Suppose that $j - 1 \leq 2m - 2c_1/c_2 < j$, where j is an integer such that $4 < j \leq m$. Suppose that player 1 chooses a set of $2m - \lfloor 2c_1/c_2 \rfloor$ contests by sampling uniformly at random without replacement from the set of all contests. Note that the number of chosen contests is either $j - 1$ or j. Suppose that in each non-chosen contest, player 1 invests effort of value c_2. The remaining part of player 1's effort budget can be partitioned into pieces such that each can be allocated independently over different subsets of two or three contests from the set of chosen contests according to the mixed strategies that we identified in Subcase 2.1 and Subcase 2.2. Specifically, if the number of chosen contests is equal to j, the remaining part of the effort budget of value $c_1 - (m - j)c_2$ has to be invested over the set of chosen contests. Note that the condition $j - 1 \leq 2m - 2c_1/c_2 < j$ is equivalent to

$$\frac{j}{2} < \frac{c_1 - (m - j)c_2}{c_2} \leq \frac{j + 1}{2}.$$

From this observe that the remaining effort budget can be partitioned into pieces such that the value of each piece, say x, is such that either $1 < x/c_2 \leq 3/2$ or $3/2 < x/c_2 \leq 2$. For each of these two different cases, we can apply the mixed strategies identified in Subcase 2.1 and Subcase 2.2, respectively.

Case 3: $2/m \leq c_2/c_1$. We now identify a mixed strategy for player 2 that has univariate marginal distributions as given in Theorem 5.22. Similar arguments can be used for player 1 as well. Recall that player 2 has univariate marginal distributions that have a mass of value $1 - c_2/c_1$ at zero value and are uniform on $(0, 2c_1/m]$. We separately consider three different cases:

Subcase 3.1: $2/m \leq c_2/c_1 < 3/m$. Suppose that player 2 chooses a set of $\lceil mc_2/c_1 \rceil$ contests by sampling uniformly at random without replacement from the set of all contests. Note that the number of chosen contests is either 2 or 3. If the number of chosen contests is equal to 2, suppose that player 2 splits his or her effort budget uniformly at random over the two chosen contests. It should be easy to observe that this results in each univariate marginal distribution having a mass of value $1 - 2/m$ at zero value, and the remaining mass uniformly spread over $(0, c_2]$, which is the desired univariate marginal distribution. If the number of chosen contests is equal to 3, suppose that player 2 splits his or her effort budget over the chosen contests according to the trivariate distribution with marginal distribution that has a mass at zero, given in Appendix 11.2.3 for the value of the parameter $\theta = 2c_1/(mc_2)$. Such a mixed strategy has the univariate marginal distributions as desired.

Subcase 3.2: $3/m \leq c_2/c_1 < 4/m$. Suppose that player 2 chooses a set of $\lceil mc_2/c_1 \rceil$ contests by sampling uniformly at random without replacement from the set of all contests. Note that the number of chosen contests is either 3 or 4. If the number of chosen contests is equal to 3, then the mixed strategy identified in Subcase 3.1 has the desired univariate marginal distributions. If the number of chosen contests is equal to 4, suppose that player 2 splits his or her effort budget over the chosen contests according to the quadruple distribution with marginal distribution that has a mass at zero as given in Appendix 11.2.3 for the value of the parameter $\theta = 2c_1/(mc_2)$. Such a mixed strategy has the univariate marginal distributions as desired.

Subcase 3.3: $4/m \leq c_2/c_1 < 1$. Similarly as in Subcase 2.3, we show that player 2 can split his or her effort budget into pieces of values such that for each he or she can randomize independently according to the strategies identified in Subcase 3.1 and Subcase 3.2. If $4/m \leq c_2/c_1 < 5/m$, then player 2 can split his or her effort budget into two pieces of values $x = 2c_1/m$ and $y = c_2 - 2c_1/m$. Since $2/m \leq x/c_1 < 3/m$ and $2/m \leq y/c_1 < 3/m$, each piece can be allocated according to the mixed strategies in Subcase 3.1. If $5/m \leq c_2/c_1 < 6/m$, then player 2 can split his or her effort budget into two pieces of values $x = 3c_1/m$ and $y = c_2 - 3c_1/m$. Since $3/m \leq x/c_1 < 4/m$ and $2/m \leq y/c_1 < 3/m$ each piece can be allocated independently according to the mixed strategies in Subcase 3.2 and Subcase 3.1, respectively. Similar splitting of the effort budget can be done in general for $j/m \leq c_2/c_1 < (j+1)/m$, where j is an integer such that $4 \leq j < m$. $\qquad \square$

5.4 Proportional Allocation

In this section we consider a game of simultaneous contests where each individual contest allocates its prize according to proportional allocation. Specifically, this mechanism is defined by the allocation $\mathbf{x}_i(\mathbf{b}) = (x_{i,j}(\mathbf{b}), \ j \in M)$ where for $i \in N$ and $j \in M$,

$$x_{i,j}(\mathbf{b}) = \begin{cases} \dfrac{b_{i,j}}{\sum_{l \in N} b_{l,j}}, & \text{if } \sum_{l \in N} b_{l,j} > 0 \\ 0, & \text{otherwise.} \end{cases} \tag{5.85}$$

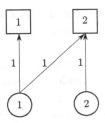

Figure 5.21. An instance with two contests and two players that has no pure-strategy Nash equilibrium. The values of the prizes and the effort budgets are arbitrary. The valuations are as indicated by the labels of the edges.

We assume that each player i receives a utility in the amount of $u_i(\mathbf{x}_i(\mathbf{b}))$, where $\mathbf{x}_i(\mathbf{b}) = (x_{i,j}(\mathbf{b}), \; j \in M)$, and u_i is an increasing, continuously differentiable, and concave function such that $u_i(\mathbf{0}) = 0$. In particular, this accommodates the special case of linear utility functions $u_i(\mathbf{x}_i) = \sum_{j \in M} v_{i,j} x_{i,j}$ where $v_{i,j} \geq 0$ is the valuation of player i of a unit prize offered by contest j. We shall consider the case of players endowed with effort budgets such that player i has the effort budget of value $c_i > 0$, and he or she incurs no production cost as long as his or her total effort investment remains within the given effort budget, and is infinite, otherwise. The payoff functions of the players are given by

$$s_i(\mathbf{b}) = u_i(\mathbf{x}_i(\mathbf{b})), \quad \text{for } i \in N. \tag{5.86}$$

In the case of utility functions that are separable across different contests and the production costs are linear, the game boils down to a collection of m independent contests each with the prize allocation according to proportional allocation. By Theorem 4.10, we know that in this case there exists a pure-strategy Nash equilibrium that is unique, and by Theorem 4.24, the social efficiency is at least 3/4. On the other hand, in the case in which players are endowed with effort budgets, it is a priori unclear whether a pure-strategy Nash equilibrium exists and, if it exists, how efficient it is. We shall show that under a set of mild conditions a pure-strategy Nash equilibrium exists and that the efficiency can be arbitrarily low, even under additional restrictions on how the values of the effort budgets relate to the values of the valuation parameters.

5.4.1 A Pure-Strategy Nash Equilibrium May Not Exist

In absence of any additional assumptions there exist instances of the normal form games under consideration that have no pure-strategy Nash equilibrium. One such instance is given in the following simple example.

Example 5.24 (two contests and two players). Consider an instance with two simultaneous contests, contest 1 and contest 2, with respective values of prizes w_1 and $w_2 > 0$, and two players, player 1 and player 2, with arbitrary values of budgets and constant marginal utilities of values $v_{1,1} = 1$, $v_{1,2} = 1$, $v_{2,1} = 0$, and $v_{2,2} = 1$. See Figure 5.21 for a graphical illustration. Obviously, it is a dominant strategy for player 2 to invest all of his or her effort budget to contest 2. If player 1 invests a strictly positive effort to contest 1, i.e., $b_{1,1} > 0$, then he or she receives the payoff in the amount of

$$s_1((b_{1,1}, c_1 - b_{1,1}), (0, c_2)) = w_1 + w_2 \frac{c_1 - b_{1,1}}{c_1 - b_{1,1} + c_2}. \quad (5.87)$$

The payoff function (5.87) is strictly decreasing in $b_{1,1}$ on $(0, \infty)$. This implies that it cannot be a pure-strategy Nash equilibrium for player 1 to invest a strictly positive effort in contest 1. On the other hand, if player 1 invests zero effort in contest 1, his or her payoff is equal to

$$s_1((0, c_1), (0, c_2)) = w_2 \frac{c_1}{c_1 + c_2}. \quad (5.88)$$

From (5.87) and (5.88), it is readily observed that there exists a value $b_{1,1} \in (0, c_1]$ such that player 1 strictly prefers investing $b_{1,1}$ to investing no effort in contest 1. Hence, it cannot be a pure-strategy Nash equilibrium for player 1 to invest zero effort in contest 1. It follows that there exist no pure-strategy Nash equilibria.

The non-existence of a pure-strategy Nash equilibrium in Example 5.24 is for an instance with linear utility functions such that there is a contest with only one player having a strictly positive valuation for a unit prize of this contest, namely contest 1 in the given example. If player 2 also had a unit valuation for a unit prize of contest 1, then there would have existed a pure-strategy Nash equilibrium, which moreover is unique. The existence and uniqueness of a pure-strategy Nash equilibrium in the case of linear utility functions with symmetric valuations can be established for an arbitrary number and values of prizes and an arbitrary number of players and values of their effort budgets, which we show in the following section.

5.4.2 Linear Utility Functions with Symmetric Valuations

Consider the case of linear utility functions with symmetric valuations, which without loss of generality are assumed to be of unit value:

$$u_i(\mathbf{x}_i) = \sum_{j=1}^{m} w_j x_{i,j}, \quad \text{for } i \in N.$$

This is a special case of interest in situations where players can split their effort budgets in an arbitrary way over the set of available contests and their marginal utilities are constant and uniform over different contests.

Theorem 5.25. *Any game of simultaneous contests that allocate prizes according to proportional allocation under the assumption that utility functions are linear with symmetric valuations has a unique pure-strategy Nash equilibrium in which each player splits his or her effort budget over contests in proportion to the values of the prizes, i.e.,*

$$b_{i,j} = \frac{w_j}{\sum_{l \in M} w_l} c_i, \quad \text{for all } i \in N \text{ and } j \in M. \quad (5.89)$$

Proof. Let us consider an ϵ-perturbed game by adding to each contest a fictitious player who makes an effort investment of $\epsilon > 0$ into this contest. This alleviates the discontinuity of the payoff functions at strategy vectors $\mathbf{b}$ such that $\sum_{i \in N} b_{i,j} = 0$ for some $j \in M$. We shall then consider the equilibria in the limit as the parameter ϵ goes to zero from above. For the ϵ-perturbed game, the payoff functions can be written as

$$s_i^\epsilon(\mathbf{b}) = \sum_{j \in M} w_j \frac{b_{i,j}}{\sum_{l \in N} b_{l,j} + \epsilon}, \quad \text{for } i \in N. \tag{5.90}$$

For every $\epsilon > 0$, the normal form game defined by the payoff functions (5.90) and the strategy sets $\mathcal{B}_i = \{\mathbf{b}_i \in \mathbf{R}_+^m \mid \sum_{j \in M} b_{i,j} \leq c_i\}$, for $i \in N$, is a concave game (Appendix 11.3.1). Thus, by Rosen's theorem (Theorem 11.51), it has a pure-strategy Nash equilibrium. It is a concave game because the payoff functions are increasing, continuously differentiable, and concave, and all the strategy sets are compact and convex.

We note the following fact:

$$\frac{\partial}{\partial b_{i,j}} s_i^\epsilon(\mathbf{b}) = \frac{w_j}{\sum_{l \in N} b_{l,j} + \epsilon} \left(1 - \frac{b_{i,j}}{\sum_{l \in N} b_{l,j} + \epsilon} \right), \quad \text{for } i \in N \text{ and } j \in M.$$

If a strategy vector $\mathbf{b}^\epsilon$ is a pure-strategy Nash equilibrium then for every player $i \in N$ there must exist $\lambda_i^\epsilon > 0$ such that one of the following two conditions holds true:

$$b_{i,j}^\epsilon > 0 \text{ and } \frac{w_j}{R_j^\epsilon + \epsilon} \left(1 - \frac{b_{i,j}^\epsilon}{R_j^\epsilon + \epsilon} \right) = \lambda_i^\epsilon, \text{ or } b_{i,j}^\epsilon = 0 \text{ and } \frac{w_j}{R_j^\epsilon + \epsilon} \leq \lambda_i^\epsilon \tag{5.91}$$

where R_j^ϵ is the total effort invested in contest j, i.e. $R_j^\epsilon = \sum_{i \in N} b_{i,j}^\epsilon$.

Conditions (5.91) correspond to the optimality conditions of the following optimization problem:

$$\begin{aligned} \text{maximize} \quad & \sum_{i \in N} s_i^\epsilon(\mathbf{b}) \\ \text{subject to} \quad & \mathbf{b} \in \times_{i \in N} \mathcal{B}_i. \end{aligned} \tag{5.92}$$

It is readily observed that (5.92) can be be written as the following convex optimization problem:

$$\begin{aligned} \text{maximize} \quad & \sum_{j \in M} w_j \frac{R_j^\epsilon}{R_j^\epsilon + \epsilon} \\ \text{subject to} \quad & R_j^\epsilon \in \mathbf{R}_+, \text{ for } j \in M \\ & \sum_{j \in M} R_j^\epsilon \leq c \end{aligned} \tag{5.93}$$

where $c = \sum_{i \in N} c_i$. There is a unique solution to the optimization problem (5.93) that is readily shown to be as follows:

$$R_j^\epsilon = \frac{w_j}{\sum_{l \in M} w_l} \sum_{i \in N} (c_i + \epsilon) - \epsilon, \quad \text{for } j \in M. \tag{5.94}$$

Notice that

$$\lim_{\epsilon \downarrow 0} R_j^\epsilon = \frac{w_j}{\sum_{l \in M} w_l} \sum_{i \in N} c_i, \quad \text{for } j \in M.$$

Since $w_j/(R_j^\epsilon + \epsilon) = w_k/(R_k^\epsilon + \epsilon)$, for all $j, k \in M$, (5.91) and (5.94) imply that it must hold that $b_{i,j}^\epsilon > 0$ for all $i \in N$ and $j \in M$. Otherwise, if there exist $i \in N$ and $j \in M$ such that $b_{i,j}^\epsilon = 0$, then (5.91) implies that $w_j/(R_j^\epsilon + \epsilon) < w_k/(R_k^\epsilon + \epsilon)$ for some $k \in M$, which is a contradiction. From the first condition in (5.91), and (5.94), we have that for every player $i \in N$,

$$\frac{b_{i,j}^\epsilon}{b_{i,k}^\epsilon} = \frac{w_j}{w_k}, \quad \text{for all } j, k \in M.$$

Combining with the budget constraints $\sum_{l \in M} b_{i,l}^\epsilon = c_i$ for all $i \in N$, we obtain that the pure-strategy Nash equilibrium is as asserted in (5.89). $\qquad\qquad\qquad\square$

The pure-strategy Nash equilibrium in the case of linear utility functions with symmetric valuations admits a simple interpretation: each player splits his or her effort budget over all available contests proportionally to the values of the prizes of individual contests. Combining this with that the sharing of prizes is according to proportional allocation, the share of the prize received by a player of any given contest is proportional to the value of his or her effort budget. The existence of a pure-strategy Nash equilibrium in the case of linear utility functions with symmetric valuations is ensured by the strong assumption that for each contest all players have strictly positive valuations, which prevents the non-existence observed in Example 5.24. It turns out that for existence of a pure-strategy Nash equilibrium in the case of linear utility functions (not necessarily symmetric), it suffices that each contest has at least two players with strictly positive valuations. This follows from a more general set of sufficient conditions for the existence of a pure-strategy Nash equilibrium that allow for a broader class of utility functions, which we present in the next section.

5.4.3 Sufficient Conditions for Existence of a Pure-Strategy Nash Equilibrium

A contest j is said to be *non-satiated* for player i if

$$\frac{\partial}{\partial x_{i,j}} u_i(\mathbf{x}_i) > 0, \quad \text{for every } \mathbf{x} \in \mathcal{X}$$

where

$$\mathcal{X} = \left\{ \mathbf{x} \in [0, 1]^{n \times m} \mid \sum_{i \in N} x_{i,j} = 1, \text{ for all } j \in M \right\}.$$

A game is said to be *strongly competitive* if each contest has at least two non-satiated players. For the special case of linear utility functions, the game is strongly competitive if, and only if, each contest has at least two players with strictly positive valuations of the prize of this contest.

In the next theorem we establish the existence of a pure-strategy Nash equilibrium for any normal form game under consideration when the utility functions satisfy a set of assumptions, including that the game is strongly competitive.

Theorem 5.26. *If each utility function u_i is increasing, continuously differentiable, and concave and the game is strongly competitive, then there exists a pure-strategy Nash equilibrium.*

Proof. We note that under proportional allocation mechanism, every player's payoff function is continuous on $\mathcal{B}$ except at every point $\mathbf{b} \in \mathcal{B}$ such that for some contest $j \in M$, $b_{i,j} = 0$ for every player $i \in N$. We consider an ϵ-*perturbed game* that is identical to the original game except that each contest is added a fictitious player who puts in an effort of value $\epsilon > 0$ in this contest. This ensures that every player's payoff function is continuous on $\mathcal{B}$. More formally, the ϵ-perturbed game is defined to be a normal form game $G^\epsilon = (N, \{s_i^\epsilon, i \in N\}, \{\mathcal{B}_i, i \in N\})$ such that every player $i \in N$ has the payoff function $s_i^\epsilon(\mathbf{b}) = u_i(\mathbf{x}_i^\epsilon(\mathbf{b}))$ and the allocation $\mathbf{x}_i^\epsilon(\mathbf{b}) = (x_{i,j}^\epsilon(\mathbf{b}), \ j \in M)$ that is defined by

$$x_{i,j}^\epsilon(\mathbf{b}) = \frac{b_{i,j}}{\sum_{l \in N} b_{l,j} + \epsilon}, \text{ for } j \in M. \tag{5.95}$$

The strategy sets are identical to those in the original game; thus, $\mathcal{B}_i = \{\mathbf{b}_i \in \mathbf{R}_+^m \mid \sum_{j \in M} b_{i,j} \leq c_i\}$, for $i \in N$.

For every $\epsilon > 0$, G^ϵ is a concave game; see Appendix 11.3.1 for a definition of a concave game. Thus, by Rosen's theorem (Theorem 11.51), G^ϵ has a pure-strategy Nash equilibrium. The ϵ-perturbed game G^ϵ is a concave game because each payoff function is increasing, continuously differentiable and concave, and each strategy set is compact and convex.

We denote with $\mathbf{b}^\epsilon$ a pure-strategy Nash equilibrium of the ϵ-perturbed game. Since the strategy sets are compact, there exists a strictly decreasing sequence ϵ_k of positive real numbers and a point $\mathbf{b}^* \in \mathcal{B}$ such that $\mathbf{b}^{\epsilon_k}$ converges to $\mathbf{b}^*$ as k goes to infinity. We shall show that $\mathbf{b}^*$ is a pure-strategy Nash equilibrium of the original game.

For every given $\epsilon > 0$, $\mathbf{b}^\epsilon$ is a pure-strategy Nash equilibrium, if there exist $\lambda_i^\epsilon > 0$ for $i \in N$, such that either

$$\frac{\partial}{\partial b_{i,j}} s_i^\epsilon(\mathbf{b}^\epsilon) = \lambda_i^\epsilon \text{ and } b_{i,j}^\epsilon > 0, \text{ or } \frac{\partial}{\partial b_{i,j}} s_i^\epsilon(\mathbf{b}^\epsilon) \leq \lambda_i^\epsilon \text{ and } b_{i,j}^\epsilon = 0. \tag{5.96}$$

We next establish several lemmas that are to be used later to prove the theorem.

Lemma 5.27. *For every $\epsilon > 0$, there exists $\bar{u} > 0$ such that $\frac{\partial}{\partial x_{i,j}} u_i(\mathbf{x}_i) \leq \bar{u}$, for every $\mathbf{x} \in \mathcal{X}$ such that $x_{i,j} \geq \epsilon$. Furthermore, there exists $\underline{u} > 0$ such that for every contest $j \in M$ that is non-satiated to player $i \in N$, $\frac{\partial}{\partial x_{i,j}} u_i(\mathbf{x}_i) \geq \underline{u}$, for every $\mathbf{x} \in \mathcal{X}$.*

Proof. The proof readily follows under the assumption that the utility functions are continuously differentiable and concave, and the condition for a contest to be non-satiated for a player. □

Lemma 5.28. *There exists $\bar{\lambda} > 0$ such that for every small enough $\epsilon > 0$, $\lambda_i^\epsilon \leq \bar{\lambda}$, for every $i \in N$.*

Proof. Note that for every pure-strategy Nash equilibrium point $\mathbf{b}^\epsilon$, each player $i \in N$ must invest an effort of value at least c_i/m in some contest. Consider an arbitrary player $i \in N$ and let $j \in M$ be such that $b_{i,j} \geq c_i/m$. From (5.96), if follows that

$$\lambda_i^\epsilon = \frac{\partial}{\partial x_{i,j}} u_i(\mathbf{x}_i^\epsilon(\mathbf{b}^\epsilon)) \cdot \frac{\sum_{l \neq i} b_{l,j}^\epsilon + \epsilon}{\left(\sum_{l \neq i} b_{l,j}^\epsilon + b_{i,j}^\epsilon + \epsilon\right)^2}. \tag{5.97}$$

We next show that the two factors in the right-hand side of equation (5.97) are uniformly bounded. We first show that this is so for the first factor. Since $b_{i,j}^\epsilon \geq c_i/m$, by the definition of proportional allocation mechanism, $x_{i,j}^\epsilon(\mathbf{b}^\epsilon) \geq (c_i/m)/(\sum_l c_l + \epsilon) \geq c_i/(2m \sum_l c_l)$, for every $\epsilon \in [0, \sum_l c_l]$. Combining with the assumption that the utility functions are concave, it follows that for every small enough $\epsilon > 0$,

$$\frac{\partial}{\partial x_{i,j}} u_i(\mathbf{x}_i^\epsilon(\mathbf{b}^\epsilon)) \leq \frac{\partial}{\partial x_{i,j}} u_i(\underline{\mathbf{x}}) \qquad (5.98)$$

where $\underline{\mathbf{x}}$ is defined by $\underline{x}_{i,j} = (\min_l c_l)/(2m \sum_l c_l)$, and $\underline{x}_{i,l} = 0$, for every contest $l \neq j$. From (5.98), it follows that $\partial u_i(\mathbf{x}_i^\epsilon(\mathbf{b}^\epsilon))/\partial x_{i,j}$ is uniformly bounded by a constant.

We now show that the second factor in the right-hand side of equation (5.97) is uniformly bounded. This follows from the following relations

$$\frac{\sum_{l \neq i} b_{l,j}^\epsilon + \epsilon}{\left(\sum_{l \neq i} b_{l,j}^\epsilon + b_{i,j}^\epsilon + \epsilon\right)^2} \leq \frac{1}{4\left(\sum_{l \neq i} b_{l,j}^\epsilon + b_{i,j}^\epsilon + \epsilon\right)}$$

$$\leq \frac{m}{4c_i}$$

$$\leq \frac{m}{4 \min_l c_l}$$

where the first inequality is obtained by maximizing the left-hand side of the inequality over the value of $\epsilon + \sum_{l \neq i} b_{l,j}^\epsilon$ and the second inequality is by the facts $\epsilon + \sum_{l \neq i} b_{l,j}^\epsilon + b_{i,j}^\epsilon \geq b_{i,j}^\epsilon \geq c_i/m$. $\qquad \square$

Lemma 5.29. *Suppose that the game is strongly competitive. Then, there exists $\underline{b} > 0$ such that for every small enough $\epsilon > 0$, $\sum_{i \in N} b_{i,j}^\epsilon \geq \underline{b}$, for every contest $j \in M$.*

Proof. Consider an arbitrary contest $j \in M$. Let N_j denote the set of players for which j is non-satiated. Since the game is strongly competitive, it holds that $|N_j| \geq 2$.

Consider first the case when there exists a player $i \in N_j$ such that $b_{i,j}^\epsilon = 0$. For every such player i, by (5.96), we have

$$\lambda_i^\epsilon \geq \frac{\partial}{\partial x_{i,j}} u_i(\mathbf{x}_i^\epsilon(\mathbf{b}^\epsilon)) \frac{1}{\sum_{l \neq i} b_{l,j}^\epsilon + \epsilon}.$$

Combining with Lemma 5.27 and Lemma 5.28, it follows that there exist constants $\underline{u}, \bar{\lambda} > 0$ such that

$$\sum_{l \in N} b_{l,j}^\epsilon \geq \frac{\underline{u}}{\bar{\lambda}} - \epsilon.$$

Hence, by choosing $\bar{b} = \underline{u}/(2\bar{\lambda})$, we have $\sum_{l \in N} b_{l,j}^\epsilon \geq \underline{b}$, for every small enough $\epsilon > 0$.

Consider now the case when $b_{i,j}^\epsilon > 0$, for every player $i \in N_j$. In this case, by (5.96), we have

$$\lambda_i^\epsilon = \frac{\partial}{\partial x_{i,j}} u_i^\epsilon(\mathbf{x}_i^\epsilon(\mathbf{b}^\epsilon)) \frac{\sum_{l \neq i} b_{l,j}^\epsilon + \epsilon}{\left(\sum_l b_{l,j}^\epsilon + \epsilon\right)^2}, \text{ for every } i \in N_j.$$

Combining with Lemma 5.27, it follows that

$$\sum_{i \in N_j} \lambda_i^\epsilon \geq \underline{u} \sum_{i \in N_j} \frac{\sum_{l \neq i} b_{l,j}^\epsilon + \epsilon}{\left(\sum_l b_{l,j}^\epsilon + \epsilon\right)^2}$$

$$= \underline{u} \frac{|N_j|(\sum_l b_{l,j}^\epsilon + \epsilon) - \sum_{i \in N_j} b_{i,j}^\epsilon}{\left(\sum_l b_{l,j}^\epsilon + \epsilon\right)^2}$$

$$\geq \underline{u} \frac{|N_j|(\sum_l b_{l,j}^\epsilon + \epsilon) - \sum_l b_{l,j}^\epsilon}{\left(\sum_l b_{l,j}^\epsilon + \epsilon\right)^2}$$

$$= \underline{u} \frac{(|N_j| - 1)(\sum_l b_{l,j}^\epsilon + \epsilon) + \epsilon}{\left(\sum_l b_{l,j}^\epsilon + \epsilon\right)^2}$$

$$\geq \underline{u} \frac{|N_j| - 1}{\sum_l b_{l,j}^\epsilon + \epsilon}.$$

Using Lemma 5.28 and the fact $|N_j| \geq 2$, it follows that $\sum_{l \in N} b_{l,j}^\epsilon \geq (1 - 1/|N_j|)\underline{u}/\bar{\lambda} - \epsilon \geq \underline{u}/(2\bar{u}) - \epsilon$. Thus, by choosing $\underline{b} = \underline{u}/(4\bar{\lambda})$, we have that $\sum_{l \in N} b_{l,j}^\epsilon \geq \underline{b}$, for every small enough $\epsilon > 0$. $\qquad \square$

Lemma 5.30. *Suppose that the game is strongly competitive. Then there exists* $\mathbf{b}^* \in \mathcal{B}$ *such that for every* $\delta > 0$,

$$\left| \frac{\partial}{\partial b_{i,j}} s_i^\epsilon(\mathbf{b}^\epsilon) - \frac{\partial}{\partial b_{i,j}} s_i(\mathbf{b}^*) \right| \leq \delta, \text{ for every small enough } \epsilon > 0.$$

Proof. Since the strategy sets are compact, we can choose a decreasing sequence ϵ_k such that $\mathbf{b}^{\epsilon_k}$ converges to a limit point $\mathbf{b}^* \in \mathcal{B}$ as k goes to infinity, where each $\mathbf{b}^{\epsilon_k}$ is a pure-strategy Nash equilibrium of the ϵ_k-perturbed game. Combining with Lemma 5.29, we have that there exists $\underline{b} > 0$ such that

$$\sum_{l \in N} b_{l,m}^{\epsilon_k} > \underline{b}, \text{ for } k \geq 1, \text{ and } \sum_{l \in N} b_{l,m}^* > \underline{b}, \text{ for every } m \in M. \qquad (5.99)$$

Consider an arbitrary player $i \in N$ and an arbitrary contest $j \in M$. Under (5.99), we have

$$\frac{\partial}{\partial b_{i,j}} s_i^{\epsilon_k}(\mathbf{b}^{\epsilon_k}) = \frac{\partial}{\partial x_{i,j}} u_i(\mathbf{x}_i^{\epsilon_k}(\mathbf{b}^{\epsilon_k})) \frac{\sum_{l \neq i} b_{l,j}^{\epsilon_k}}{(\sum_l b_{l,j}^{\epsilon_k})^2}, \text{ for every } k \geq 1$$

and

$$\frac{\partial}{\partial b_{i,j}} s_i(\mathbf{b}^*) = \frac{\partial}{\partial x_{i,j}} u_i(\mathbf{x}_i(\mathbf{b}^*)) \frac{\sum_{l \neq i} b_{l,j}^*}{(\sum_l b_{l,j}^*)^2}.$$

From (5.95) and (5.99), we note that $\mathbf{x}_i^{\epsilon_k}(\mathbf{b}^{\epsilon_k})$ converges to $\mathbf{x}_i(\mathbf{b}^*)$ as k goes to infinity. Hence, it follows that $\partial s_i^{\epsilon_k}(\mathbf{b}^{\epsilon_k})/\partial b_{i,j}$ converges to $\partial s_i(\mathbf{b}^*)/\partial b_{i,j}$ as k goes to infinity. $\qquad \square$

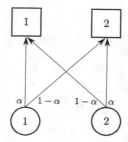

Figure 5.22. A system of two simultaneous contests and two players with valuations as indicated along with the edges.

We now complete the proof of the theorem. We need to show that a limit point $\mathbf{b}^*$ defined in the proof of Lemma 5.30 is a pure-strategy Nash equilibrium, i.e. that is satisfies the conditions in (5.96) with parameter ϵ set to zero therein. We fix an arbitrary player $i \in N$ and show that conditions (5.96) hold for this player as follows.

We first show that $\partial s_i(\mathbf{b}^*)/\partial b_{i,j} = \lambda_i$ for every $j \in M$ such that $b_{i,j}^* > 0$. Suppose on the contrary that there exist two contests j and $j' \in M$ such that $b_{i,j}^* > 0, b_{i,j'}^* > 0$, and $\partial s_i(\mathbf{b}^*)/\partial b_{i,j} \neq \partial s_i(\mathbf{b}^*)/\partial b_{i,j'}$. Then, by Lemma 5.30, it follows that for every small enough ϵ_k it holds that $b_{i,j}^{\epsilon_k} > 0, b_{i,j'}^{\epsilon_k} > 0$, and $\partial s_i^{\epsilon_k}(\mathbf{b}^{\epsilon_k})/\partial b_{i,j} \neq \partial s_i^{\epsilon_k}(\mathbf{b}^{\epsilon_k})/\partial b_{i,j'}$, which is a contradiction to that $\mathbf{b}^{\epsilon_k}$ is a pure-strategy Nash equilibrium of the ϵ_k-perturbed game.

We now show that $\partial s_i(\mathbf{b}^*)/\partial b_{i,j} \leq \lambda_i$ for every $j \in M$ such that $b_{i,j}^* = 0$. Suppose on the contrary that $\partial s_i(\mathbf{b}^*)/\partial b_{i,j} > \lambda_i$ and $b_{i,j}^* = 0$ for some $j \in M$. Then, by Lemma 5.30, it follows that there exists contest $j' \in M$ such that for every small enough ϵ_k, $\partial s_i^{\epsilon_k}(\mathbf{b}^{\epsilon_k})/\partial b_{i,j} > \lambda_i^{\epsilon_k} = \partial s_i^{\epsilon_k}(\mathbf{b}^{\epsilon_k})/\partial b_{i,j'}$ and $b_{i,j'}^{\epsilon_k} > 0$, which is a contradiction to that $\mathbf{b}^{\epsilon_k}$ is a pure-strategy Nash equilibrium of the ϵ_k-perturbed game. $\qquad\square$

5.4.4 Multiplicity of Pure-Strategy Nash Equilibria

Under conditions in Theorem 5.26, a pure-strategy Nash equilibrium is guaranteed to exist. However, it is not necessarily unique, which is demonstrated in this section.

Consider an instance with two contests and two players, with each contest offering a unit prize and each player having a unit budget of effort. The utility functions of the players are assumed to be linear such that for given parameter $0 < \alpha < 1$, we have $u_1(\mathbf{x}) = \alpha x_{1,1} + (1 - \alpha)x_{1,2}$ and $u_2(\mathbf{x}) = (1 - \alpha)x_{2,1} + \alpha x_{2,2}$. See Figure 5.22 for an illustration. This allows us to study situations in which players prefer different contests and these preferences are symmetric.

Conditions (5.96) for $\mathbf{b}$ to be a pure-strategy Nash equilibrium can be written as follows:

$$\alpha \frac{b_{2,1}}{(b_{1,1} + b_{2,1})^2} = (1 - \alpha)\frac{1 - b_{2,1}}{(2 - b_{1,1} - b_{2,1})^2}, \qquad (5.100)$$

$$(1 - \alpha)\frac{b_{1,1}}{(b_{1,1} + b_{2,1})^2} = \alpha \frac{1 - b_{1,1}}{(2 - b_{1,1} - b_{2,1})^2}. \qquad (5.101)$$

Let ρ denote the ratio of the total effort investments in contest 2 and contest 1, respectively, i.e. $\rho = (2 - b_{1,1} - b_{2,1})/(b_{1,1} + b_{2,1})$. From (5.100) and (5.101), we obtain

$$(\rho - 1)(\rho^2 + (1 - c(\alpha))\rho + 1) = 0 \tag{5.102}$$

where $c(\alpha) = 1/(2\alpha(1 - \alpha)) - 1$, and

$$b_{1,1}(\alpha) = \frac{\alpha}{\alpha + (1 - \alpha)\rho(\alpha)^2} \text{ and } b_{2,1}(\alpha) = \frac{1 - \alpha}{1 - \alpha + \alpha\rho(\alpha)^2}. \tag{5.103}$$

From (5.102), observe that $\rho = 1$ is a solution that corresponds to the symmetric equilibrium

$$(b_{1,1}(\alpha), b_{1,2}(\alpha)) = (\alpha, 1 - \alpha) \text{ and } (b_{2,1}(\alpha), b_{2,2}(\alpha)) = (1 - \alpha, \alpha).$$

This is an intuitively compelling equilibrium in which each player splits his or her effort budget over contests in proportion to his or her valuations of these contests.

There also exist two other equilibria if, and only if, $\rho^2 + (1 - c(\alpha))\rho + 1 = 0$ has a solution, which is equivalent to

$$\alpha \in \left[0, \frac{\sqrt{2} - 1}{2\sqrt{2}} \right] \cup \left[\frac{\sqrt{2} + 1}{2\sqrt{2}}, 1 \right].$$

The two equilibrium points are given by (5.103) for the values of the parameter

$$\rho(\alpha) = \frac{1 - 4\alpha(1 - \alpha) \pm \sqrt{1 - 8\alpha(1 - \alpha)}}{4\alpha(1 - \alpha)}.$$

These two equilibria are asymmetric. Under these equilibrium points, one of the contests receives a larger total effort than the other contest; see Figure 5.23. In one of the two asymmetric equilibria, contest 1 receives a much larger total effort than contest 2 as α goes to 0. In this limit case, player 1 receives half of the prize of contest 1 and the whole of the prize of contest 2.

5.4.5 Social Welfare

The social efficiency of the game of simultaneous contests with proportional allocation of prizes can be arbitrarily low already for simple instances, as demonstrated in the following example.

Example 5.31 (single contest). Consider a single contest and two players with linear utility functions with valuations $v_1 \geq v_2 > 0$ and effort budgets c_1 and $c_2 > 0$. The optimum social welfare is v_1 achieved by allocating the entire prize to player 1. There is a unique pure-strategy Nash equilibrium in which both players invest their entire effort budgets whose social welfare is

$$v_1 \frac{c_1}{c_1 + c_2} + v_2 \frac{c_2}{c_1 + c_2}.$$

The social efficiency of the pure-strategy Nash equilibrium can be made arbitrarily low by taking the valuation of player 2 being small enough relative to the valuation of player 1 and the budget of player 2 being large enough relative to the budget of player 1.

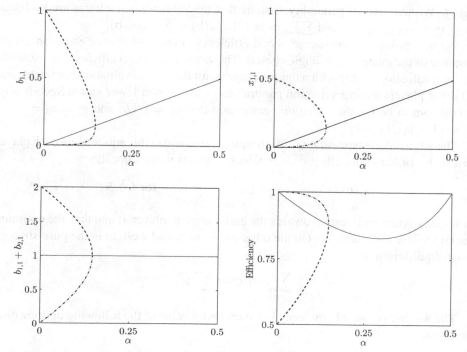

Figure 5.23. Some quantities in a pure-strategy Nash equilibrium vs. parameter α: (solid) symmetric pure-strategy Nash equilibrium, (dashed) one of two asymmetric pure-strategy Nash equilibria, and (dotted-dashed) the other asymmetric pure-strategy Nash equilibrium.

The social inefficiency exhibited in Example 5.31 is for a somewhat pathological case where the players with large valuations have small budget endowments. In this section we shall consider social efficiency under a condition on the relation between the values of the valuations and the budgets of the players that circumvents such pathological cases. In particular, we shall consider the instances in which the effort budget of each player is proportional to his or her valuation parameter. For the special instance in Example 5.31, this restriction ensures a social efficiency of at least $2/(\sqrt{2}+1) \approx 0.83$. This may lead one to conjecture that, in general, if the budgets of the players are proportional to their valuations, then the social efficiency is lower bounded by a constant. This, however, is not true. The efficiency can be arbitrarily low by allowing for an arbitrary number of players n, which we show in the next theorem.

Theorem 5.32. *Consider any instance of the game of one or more simultaneous contests that allocate prizes according to proportional allocation and with two or more players with linear utility functions of the form*

$$u_i(\mathbf{x}_i) = v_i \sum_{j \in M} x_{i,j}, \quad for\ i \in N$$

and the effort budgets proportional to valuations.

The social welfare in any pure-strategy Nash equilibrium is at least $1/\sqrt{2n}$ of the optimum social welfare. The worst-case social efficiency is smaller than or equal to $2/(\sqrt{n}+1)$.

Proof. Without loss of generality, assume that the valuation parameters are such that $v_1 \geq v_2 \geq \cdots \geq v_n > 0$ and $\sum_{i=1}^{n} v_i = 1$. Let $s(\mathbf{b}) = \sum_{i \in N} s_i(\mathbf{b})$.

We first prove the worst-case social efficiency bound, which we establish for an instance of the game with a single contest. The worst-case social efficiency is shown to be for a valuation vector with a unique player with the largest valuation parameter and all other players having valuation parameters of a common lower value. Specifically, it is shown to be for the valuation vector such that $v_1 = 1/\sqrt{n}$ and $v_2 = v_3 = \cdots = v_n = (1 - v_1)/(n - 1)$.

There is a unique pure-strategy Nash equilibrium, and in this equilibrium each player invests his or her entire effort budget, which amounts to the allocations

$$x_i(\mathbf{c}) = \frac{c_i}{\sum_{l \in N} c_l} = \frac{v_i}{\sum_{l \in N} v_l} = v_i, \quad \text{for } i \in N.$$

A socially optimal allocation awards the entire prize to player 1, and thus the optimum social welfare is of value v_1. On the other hand, the social welfare in the pure-strategy Nash equilibrium is

$$\sum_{i \in N} v_i x_i(\mathbf{c}) = \sum_{i \in N} v_i^2.$$

The worst-case social efficiency is the optimum value of the following optimization problem:

$$\begin{aligned} \text{minimize} \quad & \frac{\sum_{i=1}^{n} v_i^2}{v_1} \\ \text{subject to} \quad & 0 \leq v_i \leq v_1, \quad \text{for } i = 1, 2, \ldots, n \\ & \sum_{i=1}^{n} v_i = 1. \end{aligned}$$

Since v_1 is the maximum value of a set of n positive values whose sum is 1, we have $v_1 \geq 1/n$. Consider the given optimization problem for a fixed value of v_1 in $[1/n, 1]$. This is a convex optimization problem whose optimum solution is $v_2 = \cdots = v_n = (1 - v_1)/(n - 1)$. Hence, the worst-case social efficiency is obtained by minimizing

$$\frac{\sum_{i=1}^{n} v_i^2}{v_1} = \frac{v_1^2 + (1 - v_1)^2/(n - 1)}{v_1} = \frac{nv_1^2 - 2v_1 + 1}{(n - 1)v_1} \tag{5.104}$$

over the values $v_1 \in [1/n, 1]$. By some elementary calculus, it can be shown that (5.104) attains a minimum value at $v_1 = 1/\sqrt{n}$, which yields that the worst-case social efficiency is at least of value

$$\frac{2}{\sqrt{n} + 1} = \Theta(1/\sqrt{n}).$$

We now show that the lower bound in the theorem holds for any given valuation vector. Let $\mathbf{b}$ be the vector of efforts in a pure-strategy Nash equilibrium and $\mathbf{b}^*$ be a vector of efforts that maximizes the social welfare. We claim the following two relations:

$$s(\mathbf{b}) \geq \frac{m}{n} \tag{5.105}$$

and

$$\frac{s(\mathbf{b})}{s(\mathbf{b}^*)} \geq \frac{s(\mathbf{b}^*)}{2m}. \tag{5.106}$$

From (5.105) and (5.106),

$$\frac{s(\mathbf{b})}{s(\mathbf{b}^*)} \geq \min_{x \geq 0} \max \left\{ \frac{1}{nx}, \frac{x}{2} \right\} = \frac{1}{\sqrt{2n}}$$

which proves the assertion of the theorem.

It remains to establish claims (5.105) and (5.106). For brevity of notation, let us denote with c the total effort budget, i.e., $c = \sum_{i \in N} c_i$.

For claim (5.105), note that it is a feasible strategy for player i to invest efforts according to

$$b'_{i,j} = \frac{\sum_{l \neq i} b_{l,j}}{c - c_i} c_i$$

and, in this case,

$$x_{i,j}(\mathbf{b}'_i, \mathbf{b}_{-i}) = \frac{c_i}{c}, \quad \text{for all } j \in M.$$

Therefore,

$$s_i(\mathbf{b}) \geq s_i(\mathbf{b}'_i, \mathbf{b}_{-i}) = v_i \sum_{j \in M} x_{i,j}(\mathbf{b}'_i, \mathbf{b}_{-i}) = v_i \sum_{j \in M} \frac{c_i}{c} = m v_i^2.$$

From this, we have

$$s(\mathbf{b}) \geq \sum_{i \in N} m v_i^2 \geq \frac{m}{n}$$

which establishes claim (5.105).

For claim (5.106), suppose that player i unilaterally deviates to the following strategy:

$$b'_{i,j} = \frac{x_{i,j}(\mathbf{b}^*) \sum_{k \in N} b_{k,j}}{\sum_{l \in M} x_{i,l}(\mathbf{b}^*) \sum_{k \in N} b_{k,l}} c_i, \text{ for } j \in M.$$

Let $z_i = \sum_{j \in M} x_{i,j}(\mathbf{b}^*) \sum_{k \in N} b_{k,j}$ for $i \in N$, and note that $\sum_{i \in N} z_i = c$. Note that

$$x_{i,j}(\mathbf{b}'_i, \mathbf{b}_{-i}) = \frac{b'_{i,j}}{\sum_{l \in N} b_{l,j} - b_{i,j} + b'_{i,j}} \geq \frac{b'_{i,j}}{\sum_{l \in N} b_{l,j} + b'_{i,j}}$$

$$= \frac{x_{i,j}(\mathbf{b}^*) c_i}{x_{i,j}(\mathbf{b}^*) c_i + z_i} \geq \frac{c_i}{c_i + z_i} x_{i,j}(\mathbf{b}^*).$$

Hence,

$$s(\mathbf{b}) \geq \sum_{i \in N} s_i(\mathbf{b}'_i, \mathbf{b}_{-i}) \geq \sum_{i \in N} \frac{c_i}{c_i + z_i} s_i(\mathbf{b}^*).$$

Since

$$\min_{\mathbf{z} \in \mathbf{R}^n_+ : \sum_{i \in N} z_i = 1} \sum_{i \in N} \frac{c_i}{c_i + z_i} s_i(\mathbf{b}^*) = \frac{\left(\sum_{i \in N} \sqrt{c_i} \right)^2}{2c} s_i(\mathbf{b}^*)$$

and combining this with the assumption that the effort budget of a player is proportional to his or her valuation parameter and the fact that $s_i(\mathbf{b}^*) \leq mv_i$ for $i \in N$, we have

$$s(\mathbf{b}) \geq \frac{1}{2m} s(\mathbf{b}^*)^2$$

which establishes claim (5.106). $\qquad\square$

5.5 Equal Sharing Allocation

In this section we consider a game that models simultaneous contests where the prize of each contest is shared equally among the players who are regarded to be successful based on their effort investments. We consider a somewhat different model than so far in this chapter by assuming that players invest efforts over a given set of activities, where each effort of a player invested in an activity can be of use in one or more contests. Each contest is associated with a set of *successful vectors of efforts*. A player is said to be *successful* in a contest if his or her vector of efforts is in the set of successful vectors of efforts for this contest. The model accommodates the special case when each effort investment made by a player to a contest is of exclusive use for this contest by defining the activities to be in a one-to-one relation with the contests.

The game that we consider is a normal form game that we define as follows. The sets of players, activities, and contests are denoted by $N = \{1, 2, \ldots, n\}$, $K = \{1, 2, \ldots, k\}$, and $M = \{1, 2, \ldots, m\}$, respectively. Every player $i \in N$ has the strategy set $\mathcal{B}_i$ that is a convex subset of $\mathbf{R}_+^k$. For every contest $j \in M$, the set of successful vectors of efforts contains every vector $\mathbf{x} \in \mathbf{R}_+^k$ such that

$$\sum_{l \in K} f_{j,l}(x_l) \geq 1 \tag{5.107}$$

where $f_{j,l} : \mathbf{R}_+ \to \mathbf{R}_+$ is a given increasing function such that $f_{j,l}(0) = 0$, for every $l \in K$. Each contest $j \in M$ awards a prize of value $w_j > 0$ by equal sharing among the successful players in this contest. The efforts invested by players over different activities are denoted by $\mathbf{b} = (b_{i,l}, i \in N, l \in K)$. For every contest $j \in M$ and effort investments $\mathbf{b}$, we denote with $N_j(\mathbf{b})$ the set of successful players in contest j, i.e.,

$$N_j(\mathbf{b}) = \left\{ i \in N \mid \sum_{l \in K} f_{j,l}(b_{i,l}) \geq 1 \right\}$$

and denote with $n_j(\mathbf{b})$ the number of successful players in contest j.

The payoff functions of the players are given by

$$s_i(\mathbf{b}) = \sum_{j \in M: i \in N_j(\mathbf{b})} w_j \frac{1}{n_j(\mathbf{b})}, \quad \text{for } i \in N. \tag{5.108}$$

The normal form game as defined in this section allows contests to account only for effort investments made in some specific activities; see Figure 5.24 for an illustration. The special case in which any effort invested by a player in a contest is of exclusive

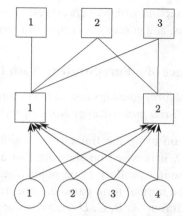

Figure 5.24. An example of a game with two activities: solid edges indicate that contest 1 accounts only for investments in activity 1 and both contest 2 and contest 3 account for investments in both activities.

use in this contest is accommodated by assuming that the activities are in a one-to-one correspondence with the contests and defining $f_{j,l}(x) = 0$ for every contest j and activity l that are not in correspondence.

We next discuss two examples. The first example is a game that we already encountered in Section 5.3.2.

Example 5.33 (standard all-pay contests and symmetric budgets). Consider the game that models simultaneous contests where each contest allocates a prize of certain value to a player who invests the largest effort in this contest with uniform random tie break, and each player is endowed with an effort budget of a common value that he or she can direct to one of the contests. Without loss of generality, assume that the effort budgets are of unit value. This game is a special case of the game defined in this section in which activities are in a one-to-one correspondence with contests, say such that every activity $j \in M$ is in correspondence with contest j, and for every $j \in M$ and $x \in \mathbf{R}_+$, $f_{j,j}(x) = x$ and $f_{j,l}(x) = 0$ for every $l \neq j$.

The second example illustrates the diversity of scenarios to which the model can be applied.

Example 5.34 (online news publishing game). Consider an online news publishing system that consists of publishers, news items, and readers. Suppose that each publisher can publish a given number of news items. Each reader has a personal preference for each of the news items, which is assumed to be known by the publishers. Suppose that each reader has a unit amount of attention that he or she splits uniformly over a subset of publishers who are regarded to post news items of interest to this reader. For example, a publisher may be regarded to post news items of interest to a reader, if he or she publishes at least a given number of news items that are relevant to the given reader. Suppose that publishers are strategic in deciding which news items to publish with a selfish goal of maximizing the amount of attention received from the readers. It should be clear that the given system can be modeled as a special instance of the game defined in this section with players corresponding to publishers, activities corresponding to news items, and contests corresponding to readers.

5.5.1 Existence of a Pure-Strategy Nash Equilibrium

Theorem 5.35. *The normal form game of simultaneous contests with equal sharing is a potential game; hence, it has a pure-strategy Nash equilibrium.*

Proof. The proof is based on using the framework of potential games presented in Section 11.3.2. Specifically, it is based on showing that a sufficient condition for a game to be a potential game in Corollary 11.63 holds true. This amounts to showing that for every instance of the normal form game of concern there exists a closed path of strategy vectors of length four A, B, C, D such that for every $i, l \in N$, $\mathbf{z} \in \mathcal{B}_{-\{i,l\}}$, $x_i, y_i \in \mathcal{B}_i$, and $x_l, y_l \in \mathcal{B}_l$, we have

$$[u_i(B) - u_i(A)] + [u_l(C) - u_l(B)] + [u_i(D) - u_i(C)] + [u_l(A) - u_l(D)] = 0$$

(5.109)

where $A = (x_i, x_l, \mathbf{z})$, $B = (y_i, x_l, \mathbf{z})$, $C = (y_i, y_l, \mathbf{z})$, and $D = (x_i, y_l, \mathbf{z})$. By Corollary 11.63, this is equivalent to saying that the normal form game is a potential game.

The payoff functions of the players can be written as

$$s_i(\mathbf{b}) = \sum_{j \in M} w_j \frac{n_j(\mathbf{b}_i, \mathbf{0})}{n_j(\mathbf{b}_{-\{i,l\}}, \mathbf{0}) + n_j(\mathbf{b}_l, \mathbf{0}) + 1}, \quad \text{for } i, l \in N, \ i \neq l.$$

We shall use the following shorthand notation:

$$\begin{aligned} x_i^j &= n_j(\mathbf{x}_i, \mathbf{0}) \\ y_i^j &= n_j(\mathbf{y}_i, \mathbf{0}) \end{aligned}, \quad \begin{aligned} x_l^j &= n_j(\mathbf{x}_l, \mathbf{0}) \\ y_l^j &= n_j(\mathbf{y}_l, \mathbf{0}) \end{aligned}, \quad \text{and} \quad z^j = n_j(\mathbf{b}_{-\{i,l\}}, \mathbf{0}).$$

Condition (5.109) corresponds to

$$\left[\sum_{j \in M} w_j \left(\frac{y_i^j}{z^j + x_l^j + 1} - \frac{x_i^j}{z^j + x_l^j + 1} \right) \right]$$

$$+ \left[\sum_{j \in M} w_j \left(\frac{y_l^j}{z^j + y_i^j + 1} - \frac{x_l^j}{z^j + y_i^j + 1} \right) \right]$$

$$+ \left[\sum_{j \in M} w_j \left(\frac{x_i^j}{z^j + y_l^j + 1} - \frac{y_i^j}{z^j + y_l^j + 1} \right) \right]$$

$$+ \left[\sum_{j \in M} w_j \left(\frac{x_l^j}{z^j + x_i^j + 1} - \frac{y_l^j}{z^j + x_i^j + 1} \right) \right] = 0,$$

which by simple algebraic manipulations is equivalent to

$$\sum_{j \in M} w_j a_j = 0$$

where

$$a_j = (y_i^j - x_i^j)(y_l^j - x_l^j)$$

$$\times \left(\frac{1}{(z^j + x_i^j + 1)(z^j + y_l^j + 1)} - \frac{1}{(z^j + x_i^j + 1)(z^j + y_i^j + 1)} \right). \quad (5.110)$$

We now show that $a_j = 0$ for every $j \in M$. Let us consider an arbitrary $j \in M$. If either $y_i^j = x_i^j$ or $y_l^j = x_l^j$ then obviously $a_j = 0$. Otherwise, we have that $y_i^j \neq x_i^j$ and $y_l^j \neq x_l^j$. There are four possible cases: $(x_i^j, y_i^j) = (0, 1)$ or $(1, 0)$, and $(x_l^j, y_l^j) = (0, 1)$ or $(1, 0)$. Since the last factor in (5.110) is a symmetric function in x_i^j and y_i^j, and in x_l^j and y_l^j, it suffices to consider the case $(x_i^j, y_i^j) = (0, 1)$ and $(x_l^j, y_l^j) = (0, 1)$. It is readily checked that in this case the last factor in (5.110) is equal to zero, and hence, $a_j = 0$. $\qquad \square$

5.5.2 Social Welfare

We consider the social efficiency with respect to the social welfare function $s(\mathbf{b}) = \sum_{i \in N} s_i(\mathbf{b})$, which using (5.108) is equal to

$$s(\mathbf{b}) = \sum_{j \in M} w_j \mathbf{1}(n_j(\mathbf{b}) > 0).$$

Theorem 5.36. *For the normal form game of simultaneous contests with equal sharing of prizes, the social welfare in any pure-strategy Nash equilibrium is at least $1/2$ of the optimum social welfare.*

Proof. We first show that for every $j \in M$ and $\mathbf{b}, \tilde{\mathbf{b}} \in \mathcal{B}$,

$$\sum_{i \in N_j(\tilde{\mathbf{b}}) \setminus N_j(\mathbf{b})} x_{i,j}(\tilde{\mathbf{b}}_i, \mathbf{b}_{-i}) \geq \mathbf{1}(n_j(\tilde{\mathbf{b}}) > 0) - \mathbf{1}(n_j(\mathbf{b}) > 0). \quad (5.111)$$

If $n_j(\mathbf{b}) > 0$, then (5.111) obviously holds because the left-hand side in equation (5.111) is non-negative and the right-hand side in equation (5.111) is at most zero. Otherwise, if $n_j(\mathbf{b}) = 0$, we have

$$\sum_{i \in N_j(\tilde{\mathbf{b}}) \setminus N_j(\mathbf{b})} x_{i,j}(\tilde{\mathbf{b}}_i, \mathbf{b}_{-i}) = \sum_{i \in N_j(\tilde{\mathbf{b}})} x_{i,j}(\tilde{\mathbf{b}}_i, \mathbf{0}) = n_j(\tilde{\mathbf{b}}) \geq \mathbf{1}(n_j(\tilde{\mathbf{b}}) > 0),$$

which shows that (5.111) holds true.

Using (5.111), we have

$$\sum_{i \in N} u_i(\tilde{\mathbf{b}}_i, \mathbf{b}_{-i}) = \sum_{i \in N} \sum_{j \in M} w_j x_{i,j}(\tilde{\mathbf{b}}_i, \mathbf{b}_{-i})$$

$$\geq \sum_{j \in M} w_j \sum_{i \in N_j(\tilde{\mathbf{b}}) \setminus N_j(\mathbf{b})} x_{i,j}(\tilde{\mathbf{b}}_i, \mathbf{b}_{-i})$$

$$\geq \sum_{j \in M} w_j \left(\mathbf{1}(n_j(\tilde{\mathbf{b}}) > 0) - \mathbf{1}(n_j(\mathbf{b}) > 0) \right)$$

$$\geq u(\tilde{\mathbf{b}}) - u(\mathbf{b}). \quad (5.112)$$

If $\mathbf{b}$ is a pure-strategy Nash equilibrium, then $u_i(\mathbf{b}) \geq u_i(\tilde{\mathbf{b}}_i, \mathbf{b}_{-i})$, for all $i \in N$, which combined with (5.112) implies that $u(\mathbf{b}) \geq u(\tilde{\mathbf{b}})/2$, for all $\tilde{\mathbf{b}} \in \mathcal{B}$. $\qquad\square$

The interested reader may note that showing that relation (5.112) holds for the given normal form game is equivalent to saying that the game is $(1, 1)$-smooth, a concept introduced in Appendix 11.3.2, which implies a worst-case social efficiency of at least $1/2$. The worst-case social efficiency bound in Theorem 5.36 is tight as demonstrated by the following example.

Example 5.37 (online news posting game revisited). Consider the online news posting game in Example 5.34 with n publishers, n news items, and $2n - 1$ readers such that n readers are interested in one common news item, say item 1, and other readers are interested in other different news items. The socially optimum outcome for publisers is to post different news items, which amounts to the social welfare of value $2n - 1$. A pure-strategy Nash equilibrium is a posting of news items such that each publisher posts news item 1, which realizes the social welfare of value n. Hence, the social efficiency of the given pure-strategy Nash equilibrium is

$$\frac{n}{2n - 1} = \frac{1}{2} + O(1/n).$$

Summary

Standard all-pay contests with complete information: $m \geq 1$ contests with values of prizes $w_1 \geq w_2 \geq \cdots \geq w_m > 0$ and $n \geq 2$ players with valuations $v_1 \geq v_2 \geq \cdots \geq v_n > 0$.

The case of players with linear production costs: strategically equivalent to m independent single contests each attended by all players.

The case of players with production costs that allow investing in at most one contest in which a linear production cost is incurred:

There exists a pure-strategy Nash equilibrium, which in general is not unique.

If $n < m$, it is always an equilibrium for players to be assigned in decreasing order of their valuations to n contests that offer the largest prizes in decreasing order of the values of prizes. Otherwise, if $n \geq m$, it is always an equilibrium for m players of largest valuations to be assigned in decreasing order of their valuations to m contests in decreasing order of values of the prizes, and for other players to be assigned arbitrarily.

Separation of high-ability players: high-ability players direct their efforts into different contests.

Mixed-strategy Nash equilibrium for the case of players with symmetric valuations:

$$p_j = \begin{cases} 1 - \left(1 - \frac{1}{\hat{m}}\right)\Phi_{\hat{m}}(\mathbf{w}, n)\left(\frac{1}{w_j}\right)^{1/(n-1)} & \text{if } j = 1, 2, \ldots, \hat{m} \\ 0 & \text{otherwise} \end{cases}$$

where

$$\hat{m} = \max \left\{ j \in \{1, 2, \ldots, m\} \mid w_j^{1/(n-1)} > \left(1 - \frac{1}{j}\right) \Phi_j(\mathbf{w}, n) \right\}$$

and

$$\Phi_j(\mathbf{w}, n) = \frac{1}{\frac{1}{j} \sum_{l=1}^{j} \left(\frac{1}{w_l}\right)^{1/(n-1)}} \quad \text{for } j = 1, 2, \ldots, m.$$

A contest is selected by a player with a strictly positive probability only if its offered prize is sufficiently large. At least two contests that offer the largest values of prizes are selected with a strictly positive probability.

The social welfare is guaranteed to be at least $1 - 1/e$ of the optimum social welfare.

The expected total effort invested in all contests is at least $1/4$ of a benchmark value.

Standard all-pay contests with incomplete information: $m \geq 1$ contests with $1 \leq k \leq m$ distinct values of prizes $w_1 > w_2 > \cdots > w_k > 0$ and $m_j \geq 1$ contests that offer a prize of value w_j, and $n \geq 2$ players.

The case of players with linear production costs: this is strategically equivalent to m independent single contests.

The case of players with production costs that allow investing in at most one contest in which a linear production cost is incurred:

There exists a symmetric Bayes-Nash equilibrium and it is unique.

The probability that a given contest is selected by a player is equal to that in the mixed-strategy Nash equilibrium of the game with complete information and symmetric valuations.

Segmentation of players into classes: there is a partition of players with respect to their valuations into classes such that each player of the same class deploys the same equilibrium strategy. The partition is defined by separators $0 = \bar{v}_k = \cdots = \bar{v}_{k+1} < \bar{v}_{\hat{k}} < \cdots < \bar{v}_1 = 1$, and class j consists of players whose valuation falls in the interval $(\bar{v}_{j+1}, \bar{v}_j]$.

Each player of class j focuses his or her selection of a contest on the top j class with respect to the value of the prizes, such that for any given contest the higher the class of this contest, the smaller the probability of selection.

The larger the number of players, the more balanced is the probability of selection across different contests. In the limit of many players where the number of contests of each given class scales proportionally with the number of players, each player of class j selects a contest uniformly from the set of contests that belong to the top j classes.

Standard all-pay contests with budgets: each player is endowed with a budget of effort that he or she can split arbitrarily across the set of available contests, and no production cost is incurred as long as the total investment by this player does not exceed his or her budget.

The given normal form game accommodates the well-known Colonel Blotto game as a strategically equivalent game.

A pure-strategy Nash equilibrium is not guaranteed to exist.

In general, there can exist multiple mixed-strategy Nash equilibria.

For the case of symmetric budgets there exist both pure-strategy and mixed-strategy Nash equilibria in which each player invests his or her entire effort in one contest provided that the number of players is large enough. In the limit of a large number of players, for any pure-strategy Nash equilibrium, the number of players who select any given contest is proportional to the value of the prize of this contest. Similarly, for the symmetric mixed-strategy Nash equilibrium each player selects any given contest with probability proportional to the value of the prize offered by this contest. The social welfare of the symmetric mixed-strategy Nash equilibrium is at least $1 - 1/e$ of the optimum social welfare.

For the case of symmetric values of prizes and two players there are in general multiple mixed-strategy Nash equilibria. However, if the values of the budgets are not very different, for any given number of prizes, the univariate distributions of the effort investments in a contest are unique.

Proportional allocation: $m \geq 1$ contests and $n \geq 2$ players. The utility functions of players are assumed to be increasing, continuously differentiable, concave, and of value zero at zero. This accommodates linear utility functions as a special case.

The case of players with linear production costs: the game is strategically equivalent to m independent contests.

The case of players endowed with budgets of efforts:

A pure-strategy Nash equilibrium is not guaranteed to exist.

For the case of linear utility functions, a sufficient condition for the existence of a pure-strategy Nash equilibrium is that each contest has at least two players with strictly positive valuations for this contest.

For the case of linear utility functions with symmetric valuations, there exists a pure-strategy Nash equilibrium, and in this equilibrium each player splits his or her effort budget over all available contests in proportion to the value of the prizes of individual contests.

In general, a sufficient condition for the existence of a pure-strategy Nash equilibrium is that the game is strongly-competitive, meaning that each contest has at least two players with strictly positive marginal valuations for this contest.

In general there can exist multiple pure-strategy Nash equilibria.

The social efficiency can be arbitrarily low. There exist instances with social efficiency $O(1/\sqrt{n})$.

Equal sharing allocation: $n \geq 1$ players, $m \geq 1$ contests with values of prizes $w_1 \geq w_2 \geq \cdots \geq w_m > 0$, and a set of $k \geq 1$ activities. The prize of each contest is shared equally among players who make sufficient investment in a subset of activities that is allowed to be specific to this contest.

The game is a potential game, and hence, it has a pure-strategy Nash equilibrium.

The social welfare is guaranteed to be at least $1/2$ of the optimum social welfare.

Exercises

5.1 **Total effort** Consider the game that models simultaneous standard all-pay contests with valuation parameters $v_1 \geq v_2 \geq \cdots \geq v_n \geq 0$ and values of prizes $w_1 \geq w_2 \geq \cdots \geq w_m \geq 0$. Prove the following claims.

   (a) There exists a pure-strategy Nash equilibrium assignment of players to contests under which the expected total effort is at least $1/2$ of the benchmark value given by (5.3). In particular, this is guaranteed by a round-robin assignment of players to contests, in decreasing order of valuation parameters and of values of prizes.

   (b) If $n \leq m$, then for every pure-strategy Nash equilibrium assignment of players to contests, the expected total effort is equal to zero. On the other hand, if $n > m$, for every pure-strategy Nash equilibrium assignment of players to contests, the expected total effort is at least $w_m v_{m+1}/2$. For every $\epsilon > 0$, there exists a valuation vector such that the expected total effort is at most $w_m v_{m+1}/2 + \epsilon$.

5.2 **Social welfare** Consider the game that models simultaneous standard all-pay contests with valuations $v_1 \geq v_2 \geq \cdots \geq v_n \geq 0$ and values of prizes $w_1 \geq w_2 \geq \cdots \geq w_m \geq 0$. Prove the following claims.

   (a) If $n \leq m$, then every pure-strategy Nash equilibrium assignment $\mathbf{a}$ of players to contests such that players $1, 2, \ldots, n$ are assigned to contests $1, 2, \ldots, n$, respectively, yields the maximum expected social welfare. On the other hand, if $n > m$, then every pure-strategy Nash equilibrium assignment $\mathbf{a}$ of players to contests such that players $1, 2, \ldots, m$ are assigned to contests $1, 2, \ldots, m$, respectively, has the expected social welfare that is at least factor $\eta \geq 5/6$ of the optimum expected social welfare, where η is defined in Theorem 2.19.

   (b) Suppose that $\mathbf{a}$ is a pure-strategy Nash equilibrium assignment of players to contests, and $v_1^j(\mathbf{a})$ is the largest valuation parameter of a player assigned to contest j. Then, $\mathbf{a}$ satisfies

$$\sum_{j=1}^{k} w_j v_1^j(\mathbf{a}) \geq \frac{1}{2} \sum_{j=1}^{k} w_j v_j$$

   where $k = \min\{n, m\}$.

   (c) The expected social welfare under any pure-strategy Nash equilibrium assignment $\mathbf{a}$ of players to contests is at least $\eta/2$ of the optimum expected social welfare.

5.3   Two contests and four players Consider the game of two simultaneous contests and four players as in Example 5.1 with pure-strategy Nash equilibrium assignments of players to contests as given in Figure 5.3. Prove the following claims.

(a) The assignments of players to contests $(1, 2, 1, 2)$, $(1, 2, 2, 1)$, $(1, 2, 1, 1)$, and $(1, 1, 2, 2)$ are always pure-strategy Nash equilibrium assignments. The assignments $(2, 1, 1, 2)$ and $(2, 1, 2, 2)$ are pure-strategy Nash equilibrium assignments if, and only if, $w_2(v_1 - v_4) \geq w_1(v_1 - v_2)$. The assignment $(2, 1, 2, 1)$ is a pure-strategy Nash equilibrium if, and only if, $w_2(v_1 - v_3) \geq w_1(v_1 - v_2)$. The assignment $(2, 1, 1, 1)$ is a pure-strategy Nash equilibrium if, and only if, $w_2 v_1 \geq w_1(v_1 - v_2)$.

(b) Whenever the assignment of players to contests $(2, 1, 1, 2)$ is a pure-strategy Nash equilibrium, it has the largest expected total effort over all equilibrium assignments of players to contests.

5.4   Social welfare and symmetric mixed strategies Consider the game that models simultaneous standard all-pay contests with a symmetric mixed-strategy Nash equilibrium as in Theorem 5.3. Prove that this mixed-strategy Nash equilibrium maximizes the expected social welfare over the set of all symmetric mixed strategies.

5.5   Simultaneous standard all-pay contests: identical values of prizes Consider the game that models simultaneous standard all-pay contests with symmetric values of prizes, assumed to be of unit value, with private valuations that are independent and identically distributed random variables with prior distribution F on $[0, 1]$. Prove that the following claims hold in the symmetric Bayes-Nash equilibrium.

(a) The expected total effort in every given contest is given by

$$R = 1 - \left(n \int_0^1 G(x)^{n-1} dx - (n - 1) \int_0^1 G(x)^n dx \right)$$

where

$$G(x) = 1 - \frac{1}{m} + \frac{1}{m} F(x).$$

(b) The expected maximum individual effort in every given contest is given by

$$R_1 = \frac{n}{2n - 1} - \left(\int_0^1 G(x)^{n-1} dx - \frac{n-1}{2n-1} \int_0^1 G(x)^{2n-1} dx \right).$$

(c) The expected payoff for every given player is given by

$$S = m \int_0^1 (1 - G(x)) G(x)^{n-1} dx.$$

5.6   Simultaneous standard all-pay contests: large system limit Consider the game as defined in Exercise 5.5 in the large system limit such that for a fixed constant $\lambda > 0$, $n \sim \lambda m$ as the number of players n grows large. Prove that the following asymptotic expressions hold.

(a) The expected total effort in every given contest satisfies

$$R \sim 1 - \int_0^1 e^{-\lambda(1 - F(x))} dx, \quad \text{for large } n.$$

(b) The expected maximum individual effort in every given contest satisfies

$$R_1 \sim \frac{1}{2} - \left(\int_0^1 e^{-\lambda(1-F(x))}dx - \frac{1}{2}\int_0^1 e^{-2\lambda(1-F(x))}dx \right), \quad \text{for large } n.$$

(c) The expected payoff for every given player satisfies

$$S \sim \int_0^1 (1 - F(x))e^{-\lambda(1-F(x))}dx, \quad \text{for large } n.$$

5.7 **Comparison of assignments of players to contests** Consider the game G that models simultaneous standard all-pay contests with symmetric values of prizes and players with private valuation parameters. Assume that the number of players n is a multiple of the number of contests m. Consider another game G^* that is identical to G except that the players are assigned to contests uniformly at random such that there are n/m players assigned to each contest. Prove that the following claims hold for the symmetric Bayes-Nash equilibrium of the two games.

(a) Suppose that the social welfare is defined as the valuation of the total value of prizes won by the players. The expected social welfare in game G is smaller than or equal to the expected social welfare in game G^*.

(b) The expected total effort in game G is larger than or equal to the expected total effort in game G^* if, and only if, the number of players is small enough.

(c) The same property holds for the expected maximal individual effort in a contest.

5.8 **Condition for the highest prize contests to attract all participation** Consider the game that models simultaneous standard all-pay contests with distinct values of prizes $w_1 > w_2 > \cdots > w_k$ such that there are m_j contests that offer a prize of value w_j, and n players with private valuation parameters. Prove the following claim: the contests that offer the largest prize value attract all participation if, and only if,

$$\frac{w_2}{w_1} \leq \left(1 - \frac{1}{m_1} \right)^{n-1}.$$

5.9 **Participation of players over contests** Consider the game that models simultaneous standard all-pay contests with distinct values of prizes $w_1 > w_2 > \cdots > w_k$ such that there are m_j contests that offer a prize of value w_j, and n players with private valuation parameters. Let $\mathbf{p} = (p_1, p_2, \ldots, p_k)$ be the probability distribution such that any given player decides to participate in any specific contest that offers a prize of value w_j with probability p_j in the symmetric Bayes-Nash equilibrium. Suppose that $\mathbf{p}$ satisfies

$$p_1 - p_2 \leq p_2 - p_3 \leq \cdots \leq p_{\hat{k}-1} - p_{\hat{k}} \qquad (5.113)$$

where $\hat{k}$ is the number of contest classes with a strictly positive probability of being selected by a player.

Prove the following claims.

(a) Condition (5.113) is equivalent to

$$\left(\frac{w_{j+2}}{w_{j+1}} \right)^{\frac{1}{n-1}} \left(2 - \left(\frac{w_{j+1}}{w_j} \right)^{\frac{1}{n-1}} \right) \leq 1, \quad \text{for } 1 \leq j < \hat{k} - 1.$$

(b) A sufficient condition for condition (5.113) to hold is that the values of prizes are such that

$$\frac{w_2}{w_1} \geq \frac{w_3}{w_2} \geq \cdots \geq \frac{w_k}{w_{k-1}}. \qquad (5.114)$$

(c) In particular, condition (5.114) holds for the following two cases:

- constant spread of prizes: $w_j = w_{j+1} + c$, for $c > 0$, and
- exponentially decreasing prizes: $w_j = \rho^{j-1} w_1$, for $0 < \rho < 1$ and $w_1 > 0$.

5.10 **Segregation of players to classes** Consider the game that models simultaneous standard all-pay contests with distinct values of prizes $w_1 > w_2 > \cdots > w_k$ such that there are m_j contests that offer a prize of value w_j, and n players with private valuation parameters. Recall that in the symmetric Bayes-Nash equilibrium there is a segregation of players in $\hat{k}$ classes such that players of class j direct all their efforts to contests that offer top j largest prizes. Prove that the following claims hold for the symmetric Bayes-Nash equilibrium.

(a) The number of players per class $n_1, n_2, \ldots, n_{\hat{k}}$ is a multinomial random variable with parameters $a_1, a_2, \ldots, a_{\hat{k}}$ that are given by

$$a_j = \left(w_j^{\frac{1}{n-1}} - w_{j+1}^{\frac{1}{n-1}} \right) \sum_{l=1}^{j} m_l \left(\frac{1}{w_l} \right)^{\frac{1}{n-1}}, \quad \text{for } j = 1, 2, \ldots, \hat{k}.$$

(b) If the values of prizes are such that $w_1 - w_2 \leq w_2 - w_3 \leq \cdots \leq w_{k-1} - w_k$, then the expected number of players in any given class is smaller than or equal to the expected number of players in any given lower class.

5.11 **Designing prizes for desired expected participation** Consider the game that models simultaneous standard all-pay contests with values of prizes $w_1 > w_2 > \cdots > w_k > 0$ such that there are m_j contests that offer a prize of value w_j, and n players with private valuations. Recall that M_j denotes the number of contests that offer a prize of value larger than or equal to w_j. Prove the following claims.

(a) Given a distribution $\mathbf{p} = (p_1, p_2, \ldots, p_k)$ such that $0 < p_k < \cdots < p_2 < p_1 < 1$, there exists a game that models simultaneous standard all-pay contests such that in the symmetric Bayes-Nash equilibrium of this game, any given player invests in any given contest that offers a prize of value w_j with probability p_j, if, and only if, the following condition holds:

$$\sum_{l=1}^{j-1} m_l p_l - (M_{j-1} - 1) p_j < 1, \quad \text{for } 1 < j \leq k.$$

(b) If this condition holds, setting the values of prizes such that, for an arbitrary constant $c > 0$,

$$w_j = c \left(\frac{1}{1 - p_j} \right)^{n-1}, \quad \text{for } j = 1, 2, \ldots, k$$

results in any given player deciding to participate in any given contest of class j with probability p_j in the symmetric Bayes-Nash equilibrium.

5.12 **Simultaneous contests with effort budgets** Consider the game that models simultaneous contests with players endowed with unit effort budgets as in Theorem 5.18. Prove the following claims.

(a) The symmetric mixed-strategy Nash equilibrium of the game coincides with the solution to the following convex optimization problem:

$$\text{maximize} \quad \sum_{j=1}^{m} w_j \Phi_n(p_j)$$
$$\text{subject to} \quad p_j \geq 0, \; j = 1, 2, \ldots, m$$
$$\sum_{j=1}^{m} p_j = 1$$

where $\Phi_n(x)$ is the primitive of function $\phi_n(x)$ given by (5.71).

(b) The following equation holds for every $j = 1, 2, \ldots, m$,

$$\Phi_n(p_j) = \frac{1}{n} \mathbf{E}[H_{N_j}],$$

where H_l is the l-th harmonic number and N_j is the number of participants in contest j, which in the symmetric mixed-strategy Nash equilibrium is a binomial random variable with parameters n and p_j.

5.13 Simultaneous contests with effort budgets: a monotonicity property Consider the game that models simultaneous contests with players endowed with unit effort budgets as in Theorem 5.18. Prove that the symmetric mixed-strategy Nash equilibrium $\mathbf{p} = (p_1, p_2, \ldots, p_m)$ is such that p_1 is decreasing in the number of players n.

5.14 The Kolkata paise restaurant problem There is a population of $n \geq 2$ people and $m \geq 2$ restaurants. All these people want to go to a restaurant. However, each restaurant j can serve at most k_j people. Moreover, the restaurants are allowed to differ in quality: each individual receives a utility of value w_j by being served at restaurant j. The individuals independently and simultaneously decide which restaurant to go to. If $n_j \leq k_j$ individuals come to restaurant j, then all of them are served, and otherwise, only k_j of them selected uniformly at random are served. Prove the following claims.

(a) There exists a unique symmetric mixed-strategy Nash equilibrium. In this mixed-strategy Nash equilibrium, each player decides to go to the restaurant drawn independently from distribution $\mathbf{p} = (p_1, p_2, \ldots, p_m)$ that is given by

$$p_j = \phi_{n,k_j}^{-1} \left(\min \left\{ \frac{s^*}{w_j}, 1 \right\} \right), \quad \text{for } j = 1, 2, \ldots, m,$$

where s^* is uniquely defined by $\sum_{j=1}^{m} p_j = 1$ and

$$\phi_{n,k}(x) = \frac{\mathbf{E}[\min\{X, k\}]}{nx}$$

with X a binomial random variable with parameters n and x.

(b) If $w_1 = w_2 = \cdots = w_m$ and $k_1 = k_2 = \cdots = k_m$, the expected social welfare in the symmetric mixed-strategy Nash equilibrium is at least $1 - 1/e$ of the optimum social welfare.

(c) In the limit of large number of players n, and having all other parameters fixed, we have

$$\lim_{n \to \infty} p_j = \frac{w_j k_j}{\sum_{l=1}^{m} w_l k_l}, \quad \text{for } j = 1, 2, \ldots, m.$$

5.15 Two simultaneous two contests and two players with effort budgets Consider the game that models two simultaneous contests that offer prizes of values $w_1 \geq w_2 > 0$ and two players with symmetric effort budgets. Prove that the symmetric mixed-strategy Nash equilibrium is for each player to decide in which contest to invest effort by sampling from distribution $\mathbf{p} = (p_1, p_2)$ given by

$$p_1 = \begin{cases} 3\frac{w_1}{w_1+w_2} - 1, & \text{if } \frac{w_1}{w_1+w_2} < \frac{2}{3} \\ 1, & \text{otherwise} \end{cases} \quad \text{and } p_2 = 1 - p_1.$$

5.16 **Simultaneous contests with effort budgets: comparison with an alternative formulation** Consider game G_n that models simultaneous contests with $n \geq 2$ players endowed with symmetric effort budgets as defined in Section 5.3.2. Consider also an alternative definition of game G_n^* that is identical to game G_n, with the only exception being that each contest in which no player participates awards its prize to a player selected uniformly at random from the set of all players. Prove that the symmetric mixed-strategy Nash equilibrium in game G_n^* is equivalent to that in game G_{n-1}, i.e., to the original game with one less player.

5.17 **Simultaneous contests: symmetric prizes and two players with budgets** Consider the game that models m simultaneous contests that award prizes of identical values and with two players endowed with effort budgets as defined in Section 5.3.3. Prove that in the mixed-strategy Nash equilibrium, in each given contest, the winning probabilities of the players are independent of the number of contests m whenever m is large enough.

5.18 **Proportional allocation** Consider the game as defined in Example 5.24, but with one extra player who invests a fixed strictly positive effort in contest 1. Prove that for such a redefined game, there exists a pure-strategy Nash equilibrium and, moreover, that it is unique.

5.6 Bibliographical Notes

To put this chapter in a broader perspective we briefly review simultaneous auctions that were studied under various assumptions in different contexts and then discuss work that is closely related to specific results presented in this chapter. An early game-theory model of simultaneous auctions was used by Engelbrecht-Wiggans and Weber (1979) to analyze a market with multiple single-unit auctions selling identical goods and multiple unit-demand buyers who strategically decide in which auctions to participate. Krishna and Rosenthal (1996) studied simultaneous auctions for selling complementary goods. An extension to common value items was shown in Rosenthal and Wang (1996). A related work is that on combinatorial auctions where each buyer values a set of items according to a valuation function defined over all possible subsets of items. Specifically, here we refer to auction mechanisms for selling items using simultaneous auctions where an auction is run for each item, and buyers simultaneously submit bids across the available auctions. A system of simultaneous Vickery auctions offering identical goods was studied by Gerding et al. (2008) under the assumption that there is a single strategic bidder who is competing with a set of other bidders each participating in one of the auctions chosen uniformly at random. Bikhchandani (1999) studied simultaneous auctions for selling heterogeneous items to multi-unit demand buyers in the complete information game where buyers' valuations are common knowledge and are allowed to depend on the subsets of items. Szentes (2007) studied the case of two simultaneous auctions and two buyers with complete information where the items on sale are either complements or substitutes. Hassidim et al. (2011) studied simultaneous single-item first-price auctions and obtained several results on the existence and efficiency of pure- and mixed-strategy Nash equilibria; they showed that if the valuations exhibit complementaries the social efficiency in a mixed-strategy Nash equilibrium can be $O(1/\sqrt{m})$ where m is the number of items on sale. Feldman et al. (2013) studied the cases of first-price and second-price auctions and showed that if the valuation functions are subadditive (a.k.a. complement-free), then the social efficiency in the Bayes-Nash equilibrium is 1/2 and 1/4 for the case of first-price and second-price auctions, respectively. A special type of valuations accommodates *majority games* where the utility for each player is to win some fixed number of auctions; for example in a pure majority game each player has a positive valuation for winning any subset of at least two auctions and zero otherwise. Majority games with first-price and second-price auctions were studied, e.g., by Szentes and Rosenthal (2003a,b). A special application scenario arises in the context of the *classical bankruptcy problem*, e.g., O'Neill (1982) and Atlamaz et al. (2011), where the problem is to divide an estate, such as an inheritance or the assets of a bankrupt firm, among a group of claimants who have legal entitlements to the estate.

A related work in economics is that on markets with switching costs where buyers or buyers and sellers incur switching costs by moving from one marketplace to another. For example, an early work in this area is by Klemperer (1987). McAfee (1993) studied a dynamic model with many sellers and many buyers in which buyers who fail to buy in the current period may attempt to do so in a future period, and sellers who fail to sell may sell in a future period. The buyers are assumed to know their private valuations before they choose among available auctions. An equilibrium was found where buyers randomize over the sellers they visit and sellers deploy second-price auctions with reserve prices. Peters and Severinov (1997) studied a large market where each seller sells one unit of a homogeneous good by offering an auction to buyers under two different assumptions: (i) buyers learn their valuations after meeting sellers and (ii) buyers know their valuations before they choose among available auctions as in McAfee (1993). In the latter game, buyers first simultaneously choose whether to participate in the market or pursue an outside alternative that guarantees a fixed payoff, then sellers simultaneously announce reserve prices, and then buyers simultaneously select one and only one seller as a potential trading partner and submit a bid to that seller. It was shown by Albrecht et al. (2012) that in the limit of many buyers and many sellers, a competitive matching equilibrium is characterized by a reserve price of zero. Pai (2009) studied a model where multiple sellers with limited supply strategically choose an auction mechanism. It was shown that inefficiency can arise due to both sellers withholding the good and selling to buyers of lower valuations despite the presence of higher valuation buyers. Moldovanu et al. (2008) studied a model of competing auctions where sellers decide on the amount of discrete supply of a homogeneous good with unit-demand buyers with privately known valuations. Specifically, they studied a model with two competing auctions where in the first stage both sellers simultaneously choose the number of items to sell, in the second stage buyers simultaneously choose in which auction to participate before they learn their individual valuations, and in the third stage, after they learn their individual valuations, buyers submit bids in their selected auctions. Moldovanu et al. (2008) provided conditions for the existence of a symmetric Bayes-Nash equilibrium and under some conditions characterized the equilibrium number of items sold by individual sellers. Azmat and Möller (2009) studied the question of what prize structure should contest owners use if the goal of each contest owner is to maximize the number of participants in his or her own contest. This was studied in a model with two identical players who incur linear production costs and where each contest allocates a prize purse by successive application of a Tullock contest success function with the value of the return to scale parameter common across different contests. It was shown that in the given model, contests will award multiple prizes if, and only if, the value of the return to scale parameter is sufficiently large, i.e., the sensitivity of a contest outcome is sufficiently sensitive to the invested efforts.

Another line of related work is that on competing auctions in the context of online services. Ellison et al. (2004) studied a model of competing auction sites with ex-ante identical unit-demand buyers with private valuations and sellers each with a single unit of a homogeneous good and a reservation value of zero. In the first stage, buyers and sellers simultaneously choose between two possible markets, buyers then learn their private values, and an auction is held at each market. A central question studied is that of the coexistence of different markets in equilibrium with motivating scenarios in the context of online services, e.g., the online auctions sites provided by eBay, Yahoo!, and Amazon, and in the context of the off-line world, e.g., Sotheby's and Christie's auction sites. Ellison and Fudenberg (2003) studied the same question of coexistence under more general assumptions. Peters and Severinov (2006) studied a game of simultaneous auctions as a model of eBay online auctions where each seller offers a homogeneous item by running a second-price auction with a reserve price set by each individual seller, and buyers are unit-demand with privately known valuations. The buyers are assumed to bid as often as they want across different auctions. In the first stage of the game, sellers simultaneously choose their reserve prices, then buyers arrive sequentially, and at each new buyer arrival the buyer submits one or more bids to any of the auctions; when a seller receives a bid he or she publishes the standing bid that corresponds to the second highest bid received by that time. After a buyer finishes submitting his or her bids, each buyer is given an opportunity to submit new bids or pass in the order of his or her entry into the market. Once each buyer in the market chooses to pass, a new buyer enters. After all buyers have entered the market, the bidding process continues by bidders updating their bids in the order of their original entry and this lasts until all buyers pass. Peters and Severinov (2006) provided an equilibrium characterization and established how sellers set their reserve prices in a large market. Anwar et al. (2006) provided the first empirical evidence in support of some of the hypotheses suggested by the theory of competing auctions using data from eBay online auctions. The empirical results indicated that a significant portion of bidders bid across competing auctions, that bidders tend to submit bids in auctions with the lowest standing bid, and that the winning bidders who cross-bid pay on average lower prizes than those who do not. Ashlagi et al. (2010) studied a system of two competing ad auctions focusing on the question of how advertisers would split their investments across different ad auction platforms. A similar model was studied by Ashlagi et al. (2011) under two different models, one with single-campaign advertisers and the other with multi-campaign advertisers who participate in both auctions. It was shown that in the first model there exists a unique symmetric equilibrium and that if the click-rates in the first auction are point-wise larger than those in the second auction, then the expected revenue in the first auction is larger than that in the second auction. This implication was shown to not necessarily hold in the second model.

The game with incomplete information that models a system of simultaneous standard all-pay contests as defined in Section 5.2.3 was proposed as a model of competition-based crowdsourcing services by DiPalantino and Vojnović (2009). A similar model was also studied by Bapna et al. (2010), and the special case of two simultaneous contests was studied by Amann and Qiao (2008). The analysis of the game with complete information that models a system of simultaneous standard all-pay contests as presented in Section 5.2 is new; it leverages the characterization of the expected payoffs in a mixed-strategy Nash equilibrium of the game that models the standard all-pay contest given in Chapter 2. Experimental evaluations of simultaneous contests in the context of crowdsourcing services were reported, e.g., by Yang et al. (2008), DiPalantino and Vojnović (2009), and Archak (2010). Specifically, Yang et al. (2008) and DiPalantino and Vojnović (2009) studied the popular crowdsourcing service Taskcn, and Archak (2010) and Lakhani et al. (2010) studied the competition-based software development platform TopCoder. These experimental evaluations found evidence suggesting strategic user behavior. In particular, Archak (2010) observed that coders use the registration phase of a contest as a mechanism to deter similarly skilled coders, which softens the competition by spreading the high-skilled coders across different contests.

The Colonel Blotto game was first introduced by Borel (1921). In this game, two colonels fight over a number of battlefields by simultaneously dividing their forces. A battlefield is won by the one with the most troops placed on it, and the winner of the game is the colonel who wins the most battlefields. The game was originally studied by Borel and Ville (1938) and subsequently by many authors, e.g., Tukey (1949), Gross and Wagner (1950), Blackett (1954, 1958), Bellman (1969), Shubik and Weber (1981), Roberson (2006), Hart (2008), Adamo and Matros (2009), Roberson and Kvasov (2012), Hortala-Vallve and Llorente-Saguer (2012), and Washburn (2013). The game was used as a model of two-party electoral competitions, e.g., Laslier (2002) and Laslier and Picard (2002), and as a model of system defense, e.g., by Shubik and Weber (1981). Borel and Ville (1938) provided a solution for the case of three battlefields with symmetric budgets and symmetric values of prizes, finding that at least two trivariate distributions constitute a mixed-strategy Nash equilibrium, one with the support on a disc and the other with the support on a hexagon inscribed in a simplex. Gross and Wagner (1950) provided a characterization of equilibrium for the following cases: (i) two battlefields with arbitrary budgets and values of prizes, (ii) three battlefields with symmetric budgets, and (iii) three or more battlefields with symmetric budgets and symmetric values of prizes. Roberson (2006) provided a full characterization for the case of three or more battlefields with arbitrary budgets and symmetric values of prizes. Concurrently and independently, Weinstein (2005) showed that an m-variate distribution that distributes its mass uniformly on a set of $m - 1$ line segments in the $(m - 1)$-simplex has all its univariate marginal distributions uniform on $[0, 2/m]$; see also Weinstein (2012). Theorem 5.22 and Theorem 5.23 are based on Roberson (2006).

A version of the game with discrete efforts was studied by Hart (2008). A game of simultaneous contests and two or more players with identical budgets as discussed in Section 5.3.2 was studied by Gradstein and Nitzan (1989); most of the results in that section are based on that work. A different version of the model where players incur linear production costs within a budget constraint was studied by Kvasov (2007). The analysis in Kvasov (2007) focused on the case of symmetric budgets that was later extended to asymmetric budgets by Roberson and Kvasov (2012). The Kolkata paise restaurant problem, posed in Exercise 5.14, is from Chakrabarti et al. (2009).

The game that models a system of simultaneous contests that allocate prizes according to proportional allocation and players with budget constraints as discussed in Section 5.4 was studied by, e.g., Feldman et al. (2005), Zhang (2005), and Pálvölgi et al. (2012). Sufficient conditions for the existence of a pure-strategy Nash equilibrium in Theorem 5.26 and the social efficiency bound in Theorem 5.32 are from Zhang (2005). Pálvölgi et al. (2012) considered the special case of linear utility functions; they established the existence of a pure-strategy Nash equilibrium under the assumption that the valuation parameters are strictly positive. The instance of the game that has multiple pure-strategy Nash equilibria with two players and two contests, shown in Section 5.4, was given in Feldman et al. (2005) and Zhang (2005), and a similar example was also presented in Pálvölgi et al. (2012).

The game of simultaneous contests that allocate prizes according to equal sharing mechanism of the type as defined in Section 5.5 and the example of online news posting competitions are from May et al. (2014).

CHAPTER 6

Utility Sharing and Welfare

In this chapter we consider systems that consist of individuals who generate some type of production outputs and are awarded shares of the resulting utility of production according to a *utility sharing mechanism*. Think of systems in which individuals make contributions to one or several projects that for each project amount to some value of *utility of production*. Contributors to each project are awarded according to a utility sharing mechanism that determines how the utility of production of each project is shared among those who contributed to it. Such systems arise in many real-life situations. For example, in the context of online services, users may contribute to activities such as online content creation or software development and may be awarded credits for their contributions in various kinds such as monetary payments, attention, and reputation. Another example is that of scientific collaborations where scientists work jointly on research projects and receive credits for the impact of their research results. In this case, the value of credit received may depend on some measure of the impact of the work on society and how much each individual contributed toward the success of the project. It is natural in such scenarios to consider strategic individuals who aim to selfishly maximize their individual payoffs, both in non-cooperative and cooperative strategic settings. A central question of interest here is that of the efficiency with respect to the social utility of production in environments where individual objectives are not necessarily aligned with the social objective. We are especially interested in evaluating the efficiency of utility sharing mechanisms that are simple and commonly deployed in practice; for example, sharing of the produced utility of production according to equal shares, sharing that is proportional to individual contributions, or sharing according to fixed shares depending on the ranks of individual contributions.

The class of contests considered in the present chapter differs from those in previous chapters in that prizes are shares of the utility of production, which is a function of effort investments, rather than shares of a fixed prize purse. Another important distinction is that in the present context we also consider collaborative environments where it is natural for players to form coalitions. This asks us to go beyond the solution concepts from non-cooperative game theory to consider those that account for strategic cooperation among players. Specifically, we shall consider the solution concept of a strong equilibrium, defined as a strategy vector under which no coalitional deviation exists that is beneficial for each member of the coalition. For most of our study, we shall consider the class of *local utility sharing mechanisms* that distribute the utility of production for each project to the contributors of the given project based solely on individual contributions to this project. For example, sharing equally among the contributors, proportionally to individual contributions, or assigning fixed shares in decreasing order of individual contributions to this project are instances of local utility sharing mechanisms. In the context of scientific collaborations, the author order that appears on a publication may signal information about shares of individual contributions. Here we find that different communities have adopted different norms. For example, alphabetical author order is a norm in mathematical sciences and theoretical computer science, while contribution order is a norm in computer systems. The class of local utility sharing mechanisms is more restrictive than those allowing for more general mappings of individual contributions to rewards.

Several factors may contribute to a loss of efficiency with respect to the social utility of production, and here we highlight four such factors: (i) the type of utility sharing mechanism, (ii) the type of utility of production functions, (iii) the type of production costs, and (iv) alternative options created by existence of several simultaneous projects. In general, for full efficiency the sharing of utility must depend on the players' outside options. The class of local utility sharing mechanisms that we consider do not account for players' outside options. The use of local utility sharing mechanisms may be a significant cause of inefficiency in cases where players split their efforts across a set of simultaneous projects. Simple local utility sharing mechanisms may reward players in some way that is related to their individual marginal contributions, but this may only be achieved approximately and may cause a loss of efficiency. We shall see that very different efficiency guarantees hold depending on whether individual contributions are substitutes or complements with respect to the utility of production. We shall also observe that the type of production costs has a significant effect on the social efficiency guarantees, e.g., whether individuals incur constant marginal costs of production or are endowed with effort budgets. The alternative options created by the existence of simultaneous projects across which an individual can split his or her effort investment may itself be a significant cause of inefficiency. Several examples in this chapter, in particular, will exploit this cause to exhibit instances of low efficiency.

6.1 Utility Maximization Games

A *utility maximization game* consists of a set of two or more players $N = \{1, 2, \ldots, n\}$. The strategy of player $i \in N$ is denoted by $\mathbf{b}_i$, assumed to take values in a set $\mathcal{B}_i$. The vector of strategies is denoted by $\mathbf{b} = (\mathbf{b}_i, \ i \in N)$, taking values in $\mathcal{B} = \mathcal{B}_1 \times \mathcal{B}_2 \times \cdots \times \mathcal{B}_n$. Given a utility function $u_i : \mathcal{B} \to \mathbf{R}_+$ and a production cost function $c_i : \mathcal{B}_i \to \mathbf{R}_+$, the payoff function is given by

$$s_i(\mathbf{b}) = u_i(\mathbf{b}) - c_i(\mathbf{b}_i), \quad \text{for } i \in N. \tag{6.1}$$

A *social utility function* $u : \mathcal{B} \to \mathbf{R}$ is given that quantifies the value of social utility for every given strategy vector. We refer to $\sum_{i \in N} u_i(\mathbf{b})$ as the *total utility of players*.

It is assumed that for every strategy vector, the social utility is at least as large as the total utility of players, i.e.,

$$u(\mathbf{b}) \geq \sum_{i \in N} u_i(\mathbf{b}), \quad \text{for all } \mathbf{b} \in \mathcal{B}. \tag{6.2}$$

A special case is the social utility function defined to be equal to the total utility of players. We shall consider specific assumptions for utility functions later in this chapter. For the production cost functions, we shall pay particular attention to the following two cases:

(i) *Hard effort constraints*: for every player $i \in N$, the production cost is zero in a compact set $\mathcal{B}_i$ and is infinite otherwise.

(ii) *Soft effort constraints*: the production cost of each player is a function of the total effort invested by this player.

A special case of hard effort constraints is that of *budget constraints* where each player $i \in N$ is endowed with a budget $c_i > 0$ and he or she incurs no production cost as long as his or her total effort investment is within his or her effort budget, and is infinite otherwise. A common special form of the soft effort constraints is that of linear production cost functions.

6.1.1 Simultaneous Projects

The game of *simultaneous projects* is a utility maximization game where players make strategic effort investments across a set of one or more projects $M = \{1, 2, \ldots, m\}$. Each project yields a utility according to a function of efforts invested in this project, $u_j : \mathcal{B} \to \mathbf{R}_+$, for $j \in M$. See Figure 6.1. The utility of investments into a project is shared among the players according to a utility sharing mechanism, which is specified for each $\mathbf{b} \in \mathcal{B}$ as follows:

$$x(\mathbf{b}) = \{x_{i,j}(\mathbf{b}), i \in N, j \in M\} \in \mathcal{X}$$

where

$$\mathcal{X} = \left\{ x \in [0, 1]^{n \times m} \mid \sum_{i \in N} x_{i,j} \leq 1, \quad \text{for all } j \in M \right\}.$$

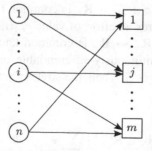

Figure 6.1. An example system of simultaneous projects: a circle represents a player, and a square represents a project. Each edge between a player and a project indicates an opportunity for effort investment.

We shall also use the function $u_{i,j}(\mathbf{b})$, which we define as the share of the utility of production of project j allocated to player i, i.e., $u_{i,j}(\mathbf{b}) = u_j(\mathbf{b})x_{i,j}(\mathbf{b})$, for $i \in N$, $j \in M$, and $\mathbf{b} \in \mathcal{B}$.

A utility sharing mechanism x is a *local utility sharing mechanism* if for every project $j \in M$, $x_{i,j}(\mathbf{b})$ depends only on the efforts invested into this project ($b_{i,j}$, $i \in N$).

Given a set of positive real numbers ($v_{i,j}$, $i \in N$, $j \in M$) where $v_{i,j}$ represents valuation of a unit utility share of project j by player i, the utility functions of players are defined by

$$u_i(\mathbf{b}) = \sum_{j \in M} v_{i,j} u_j(\mathbf{b}) x_{i,j}(\mathbf{b}), \quad \text{for } i \in N. \tag{6.3}$$

Special instances can be defined by imposing further restrictions on the values of the valuation parameters. We shall focus on the special case of binary valuations where each $v_{i,j}$ takes either value 0 or 1, exogenously specifying a subset of projects for each player from which he or she may receive a strictly positive share of utility. This allows us to model situations in which different projects require different skills and each player is skillful for some projects and not for the other, if any. The case of binary valuations can be completely defined by associating each player $i \in N$ with a subset of projects $M_i \subseteq M$ such that $j \in M_i$ if, and only if, $v_{i,j} = 1$, which we refer to as the set of *eligible projects*. For convenience, we shall also denote with N_j the set of *eligible players* for project j, where $i \in N_j$ if, and only if, $v_{i,j} = 1$.

For the case of binary valuations, note that the *total utility of projects* $u(\mathbf{b}) = \sum_{j \in M} u_j(\mathbf{b})$ satisfies condition (6.2). If each project transfers the entire utility of production to players, then the total utility of projects is equal to the total utility of players.

Game with Incomplete Information

In a game of simultaneous projects with incomplete information each player is assumed to be of a type that is private information and the vector of types is according to a prior distribution that is common knowledge. Specifically, we shall assume that the type t_i of player i takes values on a set of types $\mathcal{T}_i$. Given that the type of player i is t_i, the production output of this player is assumed to take values in a convex set $\mathcal{B}_i(t_i)$.

A special case of interest is that of players endowed with effort budgets, which are private information. Suppose that each player i of type t_i is endowed with an effort budget of value $c_i(t_i)$ where $c_i : \mathcal{T}_i \to \mathbf{R}_+$ is common knowledge. Suppose that each player $i \in N$ of type t_i requires an effort of value $e_{i,j}(t_i, b_{i,j})$ to produce an output of value $b_{i,j}$, where $e_{i,j} : \mathcal{T}_i \times \mathbf{R}_+ \to \mathbf{R}_+$ is common knowledge. Function $e_{i,j}(t, x)$ is assumed to be increasing, continuously differentiable, and a convex function in x such that $e_{i,j}(t, 0) = 0$ for every $t \in \mathcal{T}_i$. Then, the strategy set $\mathcal{B}_i(t_i)$ of player $i \in N$ can be represented as follows:

$$\mathcal{B}_i(t_i) = \left\{ \mathbf{b}_i \in \mathbf{R}_+^{|M_i|} \mid \sum_{j \in M_i} e_{i,j}(t_i, b_{i,j}) \le c_i(t_i) \right\}.$$

Since $e_{i,j}(t_i, e)$ is convex in e, the strategy set $\mathcal{B}_i(t_i)$ is convex.

6.1.2 Utility Functions

In this section we introduce some families of utility functions that are commonly studied in the literature. We shall consider a utility function $u : \mathbf{R}_+^n \to \mathbf{R}$, which represents how the production inputs by a set of n players into a project map onto the project utility value. For this reason, we sometimes refer to such a utility function as a *production function*. In the case of simultaneous projects, each project is associated with a production function that defines how the production inputs by the set of players who contribute to this project map onto the value of utility of this project.

A Catalog of Families of Utility Functions

A catalog of special families of utility functions is given as follows.

- **Total Contribution:** given an increasing function $f : \mathbf{R}_+ \to \mathbf{R}_+$,

$$u(\mathbf{b}) = f\left(\sum_{i \in N} b_i\right). \tag{6.4}$$

- **Sum of Individual Utilities:** given non-decreasing functions $f_i : \mathbf{R}_+ \to \mathbf{R}_+$, for $i \in N$,

$$u(\mathbf{b}) = \sum_{i \in N} f_i(b_i). \tag{6.5}$$

- **One Success Enough:** given increasing functions $f_i : \mathbf{R}_+ \to [0, 1]$ such that $f_i(0) = 0$, for $i \in N$,

$$u(\mathbf{b}) = 1 - \prod_{i \in N}(1 - f_i(b_i)). \tag{6.6}$$

- **Constant Elasticity of Substitution (CES):** given strictly positive real numbers c and $a_1, \ldots, a_n$, and $r \neq 0$,

$$u(\mathbf{b}) = c\left(\sum_{i=1}^{n} \left(\frac{b_i}{a_i}\right)^r\right)^{1/r}. \tag{6.7}$$

- **Cobb-Douglas:** given strictly positive real numbers c and $a_1, \ldots, a_n$,

$$u(\mathbf{b}) = c\prod_{i=1}^{n} b_i^{a_i}. \tag{6.8}$$

- **Leontief (or Weakest-Link):** given strictly positive real numbers c and $a_1, \ldots, a_n$,

$$u(\mathbf{b}) = c\min_{i \in N}\left\{\frac{b_i}{a_i}\right\}. \tag{6.9}$$

- **Best-Shot:** given strictly positive real numbers c and $a_1, \ldots, a_n$,

$$u(\mathbf{b}) = c\max_{i \in N}\left\{\frac{b_i}{a_i}\right\}. \tag{6.10}$$

The family of total contribution utility functions models situations where the utility of production of a project is a function of the total contribution invested in this project. A more general family is defined by $u(\mathbf{b}) = f(\sum_{i \in N} a_i b_i)$, for given positive real numbers $a_1, a_2, \ldots, a_n$. The best-shot family of functions models situations in which the utility of production corresponds to the best individual production input to the project. The CES family of utility functions can be seen as a relaxed version of the best-shot utility function because it converges to the the best-shot family of functions as the parameter r goes to infinity. The Cobb-Douglas family of functions is the limit of the CES family of functions as the parameter r goes to 0 and has *constant returns to scale* if $\sum_{i=1}^{n} a_i = 1$, *decreasing returns to scale* if $\sum_{i=1}^{n} a_i < 1$ and, *increasing returns to scale* if $\sum_{i=1}^{n} a_i > 1$. For the three cases, it respectively holds that $u(\lambda \mathbf{b}) = \lambda u(\mathbf{b})$, $u(\lambda \mathbf{b}) \leq \lambda u(\mathbf{b})$, and $u(\lambda \mathbf{b}) \geq \lambda u(\mathbf{b})$, for all $\lambda > 0$ and $\mathbf{b} \in \mathcal{B}$. The Leontief or the weakest-link family of functions models situations in which each contributor's production output is quintessential for the utility of production.

Substitutes, Complements, and Marginal Returns

We shall see that whether an equilibrium exists and, if it exists, how efficient it is depend strongly on the properties of project utility functions. In particular, it is important whether individual production inputs substitute or complement each other. The concept of *substitutes* formally corresponds to project utility functions that satisfy the *decreasing marginal returns* property. Conversely, the concept of *complements* formally corresponds to project utility functions that satisfy the *increasing marginal returns* property.

Definition 6.1. A function $f : \mathbf{R}^n \to \mathbf{R}$ is *submodular* on an Euclidean lattice, or we say it satisfies the *decreasing marginal returns* property, if for every two vectors $\mathbf{x}, \mathbf{y} \in \mathbf{R}^n$ such that $\mathbf{x} \leq \mathbf{y}$ holds coordinate-wise, we have

$$f(\mathbf{x} \vee \mathbf{z}) - f(\mathbf{x}) \geq f(\mathbf{y} \vee \mathbf{z}) - f(\mathbf{y}), \quad \text{for every } \mathbf{z} \in \mathbf{R}^n$$

where for two vectors $\mathbf{a}, \mathbf{b} \in \mathbf{R}^n$, $\mathbf{a} \vee \mathbf{b}$ denotes a vector with coordinates $\max\{a_i, b_i\}$ for $i = 1, 2, \ldots, n$.

If the reverse inequality holds, then f is *supermodular* on an Euclidean lattice, or we say it satisfies the *increasing marginal returns* property.

For example, the total contribution family of utility functions, defined in (6.4), satisfies the decreasing marginal returns property for every function f in (6.4) that is increasing and concave. Similarly, the utility function in (6.5) satisfies the decreasing marginal returns property if every function f_i in (6.5) is increasing and concave. The Leontief family of utility functions in (6.9) satisfies the increasing marginal returns property.

Elasticity and Substitution

An important property of utility of production functions is the *elasticity of production*, which is a standard concept used in economic theory.

Definition 6.2 (elasticity). Suppose $f : \mathbf{R}_+ \to \mathbf{R}_+$ is differentiable at $x \in \mathbf{R}_+$. The elasticity of f at x is defined by

$$e_f(x) = \left| \frac{f'(x)x}{f(x)} \right|.$$

We say that function f is of elasticity ξ, if $e_f(x) \leq \xi$, for all $x \in \mathbf{R}_+$.

For example, the power functions $f(x) = x^\alpha$, for $\alpha > 0$, are *iso-elastic*: $e_f(x) = \alpha$, for all $x \in \mathbf{R}_+$. For the family of functions $f(x) = 1 - e^{-\alpha x}$, for $\alpha > 0$, we have $e_f(x) = \alpha x/(e^{\alpha x} - 1)$, and hence, $\xi = 1$.

Another standard metric is the *elasticity of substitution* defined for a pair of production inputs.

Definition 6.3 (elasticity of substitution). Suppose $f : \mathbf{R}_+^n \to \mathbf{R}_+$ is differentiable at $\mathbf{x} \in \mathbf{R}_+^n$, where n is larger than or equal to two. Then, the elasticity of substitution for a pair $i \neq j$ at $\mathbf{x}$ is defined by

$$e_f^{i,j}(\mathbf{x}) = \frac{d \log \left(\frac{x_i}{x_j} \right)}{d \log \left(\frac{\frac{\partial}{\partial x_j} f(\mathbf{x})}{\frac{\partial}{\partial x_i} f(\mathbf{x})} \right)}.$$

In other words, the elasticity of substitution for a pair $i \neq j$ is defined as the ratio of the difference of the relative change of production inputs of i and j, and the difference of the relative change of the production output by the change of production inputs of i and j. For example, for the CES family of utility functions, we have $e_f^{i,j}(\mathbf{x}) = 1/(1 - r)$, for $r \neq 1$, for every $i \neq j$.

Another metric that captures the substitutability of production is the *degree of substitutability*, which naturally arises in the context of games that we study and is less standard.

Definition 6.4 (degree of substitutability). The degree of substitutability of a function $u : \mathcal{B} \to \mathbf{R}$ is defined as follows:

$$S_u = \sup_{\mathbf{b} \in \mathcal{B}} \frac{\sum_{i \in N} u(\mathbf{b}) - u(\mathbf{0}_i, \mathbf{b}_{-i})}{u(\mathbf{b})}.$$

Notice that $0 \leq S_u \leq n$ always holds. If the value of S_u is near to 0, then the function u is nearly constant. If u satisfies the decreasing marginal returns property, then $S_u \leq 1$. If $S_u = n$, then every player is quintessential for the utility of the project. It is left as Exercise 6.1 to the reader to show that the degree of substitutability for each of the families of utility functions in (6.4)-(6.10) is given as follows:

(i) Total contribution: $S_u \leq 1$, if f is a concave increasing function.
(ii) Sum of of individual utilities: $S_u \leq 1$, if each f_i satisfies the decreasing marginal returns property.
(iii) CES:

$$S_u = \begin{cases} n \left(1 - \left(1 - \frac{1}{r} \right)^{1/r} \right), & \text{if } 0 < r < 1 \\ 2, & \text{if } r \geq 1 \end{cases}.$$

(iv) Cobb-Douglas: $S_u = n$.
(v) Leontief: $S_u = n$.
(vi) Best shot: $S_u = 1$.

6.1.3 Utility Sharing Mechanisms

We present several well-known special forms of utility sharing mechanisms for a vector of efforts $\mathbf{b} \in \mathbf{R}_+^n$ such that $\sum_{i \in N} b_i > 0$, as follows:

- **Proportional to Marginal Contribution:**

$$x_i(\mathbf{b}) = \frac{u(\mathbf{b}) - u(0, \mathbf{b}_{-i})}{\sum_{l \in N}[u(\mathbf{b}) - u(0, \mathbf{b}_{-l})]}, \quad \text{for } i \in N. \tag{6.11}$$

- **Proportional Allocation:**

$$x_i(\mathbf{b}) = \frac{b_i}{\sum_{l \in N} b_l}, \quad \text{for } i \in N. \tag{6.12}$$

- **Equal-Share Allocation:**

$$x_i(\mathbf{b}) = \frac{1}{|N|}, \quad \text{for } i \in N. \tag{6.13}$$

- **Contribution Order:** Given fixed non-negative real numbers $a_1 \geq a_2 \geq \cdots \geq a_n \geq 0$ such that $\sum_{i \in N} a_i = 1$, players are ranked in decreasing order of marginal contributions and the t-th ranked player is assigned the share of a_t:

$$x_i(\mathbf{b}) = a_{\pi(i)}, \quad \text{for } i \in N, \tag{6.14}$$

where $\pi(i)$ is the rank of player i's production output.

- **Shapley-Shubik:** Let π be a permutation of the set of players $1, 2, \ldots, n$ and let Π be the set of all such permutations. Let $N_i(\pi)$ be the set of players who precede or are at the position of player i, i.e., $N_i(\pi) = \{j \in N \mid \pi(j) \leq \pi(i)\}$. The Shapley-Shubik allocation is defined by

$$x_i(\mathbf{b}) = \frac{1}{n!} \sum_{\pi \in \Pi}[u(\mathbf{b}_{N_i(\pi)}, \mathbf{0}_{N \setminus N_i(\pi)}) - u(\mathbf{0}_{N_i(\pi)}, \mathbf{b}_{N \setminus N_i(\pi)})], \quad \text{for } i \in N. \tag{6.15}$$

6.2 Examples of Efficient and Inefficient Production Systems

In this section we discuss four examples of production systems that illustrate how several factors contribute toward the social efficiency of the production; these factors include the form of the project utility functions, the form of production cost functions, the choice of the utility sharing mechanism, and the alternative options created by multiple projects in which a player may invest effort.

6.2.1 The Tragedy of the Commons

The well-known phenomenon of *the tragedy of the commons* refers to situations in which there is an inefficient use of congestive resources because of non-cooperative selfish behavior. The term was coined following the study by Hardin (1968), and the phenomenon was subsequently studied, for example, by Moulin and Watts (1996). The specific normal form game that we are going to consider is a special instance of a game of Cournot oligopoly that was studied as early as 1838 by Cournot and has been analyzed ever since in numerous studies. In the game of a Cournot oligopoly, players are producers of a good, strategies are the amounts of production, and the payoff for each producer is the revenue gained by selling the goods at a market price that is assumed to be a function of the total amount of goods produced by all producers. The example that we consider is a special instance of this game where the selling price is linearly decreasing in the total amount of production.

Consider a project with a utility function $u : \mathbf{R}^n_+ \to \mathbf{R}$ where the utility sharing is according to proportional allocation and the players are endowed with budgets of effort, so that the payoff functions of players are

$$s_i(\mathbf{b}) = u(\mathbf{b}) \frac{b_i}{\sum_{j \in N} b_j}, \quad \text{for } i \in N.$$

Assume that the project utility function is a concave function of the total effort of the following specific form: $u(\mathbf{b}) = (\sum_{j \in N} b_j)(1 - \sum_{j \in N} b_j)$. This is a utility function that has a diminishing rate of increase with the total effort investment up to a point, and then has a diminishing rate of decrease with the total effort investment. For this choice of the project utility function, the payoff functions of players can be written as

$$s_i(\mathbf{b}) = \left(1 - \sum_{j \in N} b_j\right) b_i, \quad \text{for } i \in N.$$

The social welfare function is defined to be the total payoff to players $s(\mathbf{b}) = (1 - \sum_{j \in N} b_j) \sum_{j \in N} b_j$. Obviously, the optimum social welfare is achieved for any vector of efforts $\mathbf{b}^*$ such that $\sum_{j \in N} b_j^* = 1/2$, which yields the optimum social welfare of value

$$\sum_{i \in N} s_i(\mathbf{b}^*) = \frac{1}{4}. \tag{6.16}$$

A vector of efforts $\mathbf{b}$ is a pure-strategy Nash equilibrium if no player can improve his or her payoff by unilaterally deviating from his or her effort investment:

$$\forall i \in N : b_i > 0 \text{ and } \frac{\partial}{\partial b_i} s_i(\mathbf{b}) = 0, \text{ or } b_i = 0 \text{ and } \frac{\partial}{\partial b_i} s_i(\mathbf{b}) \le 0. \tag{6.17}$$

Using this and the fact

$$\frac{\partial}{\partial b_i} s_i(\mathbf{b}) = 1 - \sum_{j \in N} b_j - b_i,$$

we have that there is a unique pure-strategy Nash equilibrium $\mathbf{b} = (1/(n+1), 1/(n+1), \ldots, 1/(n+1))$. The social welfare in the pure-strategy Nash equilibrium is equal to

$$\sum_{i \in N} s_i(\mathbf{b}) = \frac{n}{(n+1)^2}. \tag{6.18}$$

From (6.16) and (6.18), it follows that the social efficiency of the pure-strategy Nash equilibrium is $\Theta(1/n)$.

6.2.2 Social Inefficiency under a Monotone Utility of Production

The tragedy of the commons exhibits a socially inefficient production under a non-monotone project utility function. Can such an inefficiency occur for monotone project utility functions in total effort investment? The answer is affirmative: socially inefficient production can occur even if the project utility functions are monotone and with decreasing marginal returns due to production costs.

Consider a project with a utility function $u : \mathbf{R}_+^n \to \mathbf{R}_+$, the utility sharing mechanism according to proportional allocation, and players who incur unit marginal costs of production. The payoff functions of the players are given by

$$s_i(\mathbf{b}) = u(\mathbf{b}) \frac{b_i}{\sum_{j \in N} b_j} - b_i, \quad \text{for } i \in N.$$

Assume that the utility function is from the following specific family of monotone functions: $u(b) = b^\alpha$, for $\alpha > 0$. The payoff functions of players can be written as

$$s_i(\mathbf{b}) = \left(\left(\sum_{j \in N} b_j \right)^{\alpha-1} - 1 \right) b_i, \quad \text{for } i \in N. \tag{6.19}$$

The social welfare function is defined as the sum of payoffs of all players $s(\mathbf{b}) = (\sum_{j \in N} b_j)^\alpha - \sum_{j \in N} b_j$. If $\alpha < 1$, a socially optimum investment of efforts is any vector of efforts $\mathbf{b}^*$ such that $\sum_{j \in N} b_j^* = \alpha^{1/(1-\alpha)}$, which yields the optimum social welfare of value

$$\sum_{i \in N} s_i(\mathbf{b}^*) = \alpha^{\frac{\alpha}{1-\alpha}} (1 - \alpha). \tag{6.20}$$

Otherwise, if $\alpha = 1$, the optimum social welfare is zero and for $\alpha > 1$ it is infinite.

A vector of efforts $\mathbf{b}$ is a pure-strategy Nash equilibrium if, and only if, condition (6.17) holds true and the payoff for every player is non-negative. For the payoff functions (6.19), we have

$$\frac{\partial}{\partial b_i} s_i(\mathbf{b}) = R^{\alpha-1} \left(1 - (1 - \alpha) \frac{b_i}{R} \right) - 1$$

where $R = \sum_{j \in N} b_j$.

If $\alpha < 1$, in any pure-strategy Nash equilibrium, every player invests a strictly positive effort because any player who would invest a zero effort would have a beneficial unilateral deviation, and the efforts of any two players must be equal. It follows that $b_1 = b_2 = \cdots = b_n = R/n$, where

$$R = \left(1 - \frac{1-\alpha}{n} \right)^{\frac{1}{1-\alpha}}.$$

The social welfare in the pure-strategy Nash equilibrium satisfies

$$\sum_{i \in N} s_i(\mathbf{b}) = \frac{\left(1 - \frac{1-\alpha}{n} \right)^{\frac{1}{1-\alpha}}}{\frac{n}{1-\alpha} - 1} \sim \frac{1-\alpha}{n}, \quad \text{for large } n,$$

which combined with (6.20) shows that the social efficiency is $\Theta(1/n)$.

The case $\alpha = 1$ is degenerate as any investment of efforts is a pure-strategy equilibrium because for any strategy vector the payoff of every player is zero. The case $\alpha > 1$ is also degenerate because in this case there exists no pure-strategy Nash equilibrium.

If the players do not incur production costs as assumed herein but are endowed with effort budgets, then there is a unique pure-strategy Nash equilibrium, and in this equilibrium every player invests his or her entire effort budget. This coincides with the socially optimum investment of effort and thus has a full social efficiency. This demonstrates the importance of the form of production cost functions for the social efficiency of production.

6.2.3 Socially Efficient Production under Proportional Allocation

In this example we consider a system of production that consists of multiple projects. In this example we keep the same form of project utility functions and the same utility sharing mechanism as in the example in Section 6.2.2 but we replace the linear production costs with effort budgets of unit value. We shall see that such a production system is efficient in the sense that the social efficiency does not diminish to zero with the number of players. We shall use this particular example later in Section 6.2.4 to demonstrate the importance of the choice of the utility sharing mechanism.

Consider a system of two or more players, each endowed with a unit effort budget that can be split by each player between a private project available only to this player and a public project available to all players (see Figure 6.2). Assume that the utility function of each project is a function of the total effort invested in the project of the form $u(b) = b^\alpha$, for $0 < \alpha \le 1$. Assume that the utility sharing is according to proportional allocation. Let b_i denote the effort investment by player i to the public project. The payoff functions can be represented as follows:

$$s_i(\mathbf{b}) = \left(\sum_{j \in N} b_j\right)^{\alpha - 1} b_i + (1 - b_i)^\alpha, \quad \text{for } i \in N.$$

The social welfare function is defined to be the sum of payoffs of all players; hence, we have

$$s(\mathbf{b}) = \left(\sum_{j \in N} b_j\right)^\alpha + \sum_{j \in N}(1 - b_j)^\alpha.$$

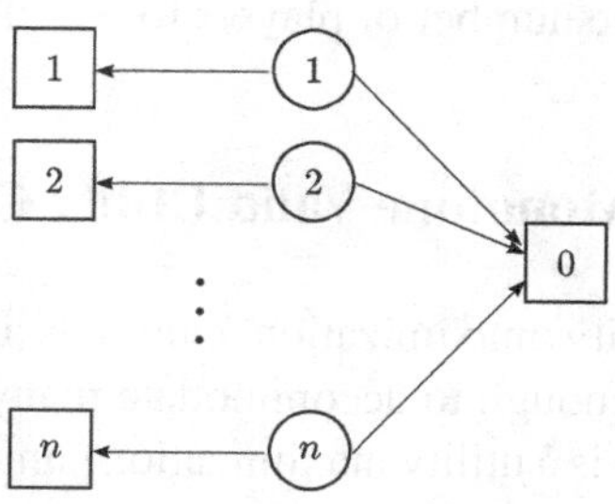

Figure 6.2. A system of n players (circles) and $n + 1$ projects (squares) such that each player is endowed with a unit budget of effort that he or she can split between a private project accessible only to this player and a public project accessible to all players.

There is a unique socially optimum investment of efforts $\mathbf{b}^*$ that is such that every player invests $1/(n+1)$ of his or her budget to the public project and the remaining part of the budget to his or her private project. Hence, $s(\mathbf{b}^*) \sim n$, for large n.

A vector of efforts $\mathbf{b}$ is a pure-strategy Nash equilibrium if, and only if, condition (6.17) holds true and the payoff for every player is non-negative. It is readily obtained that $\mathbf{b}$ is such that $b_1 = b_2 = \cdots = b_n$ and $R = \sum_{i \in N} b_i$ satisfies

$$R = \frac{\left(1 - \frac{1-\alpha}{n}\right)^{\frac{1}{1-\alpha}} n}{\alpha^{\frac{1}{1-\alpha}} n + \left(1 - \frac{1-\alpha}{n}\right)^{\frac{1}{1-\alpha}}} \sim \left(\frac{1}{\alpha}\right)^{\frac{1}{1-\alpha}}, \quad \text{for large } n.$$

Since $s(\mathbf{b}) = R^\alpha + n(1 - R/n)^\alpha$, it follows that $s(\mathbf{b}) \sim n$, for large n. This shows that full social efficiency holds asymptotically for large number of players n.

6.2.4 Socially Inefficient Production under Equal Sharing Allocation

The choice of a utility sharing mechanism is important. Full efficiency can be achieved in some instances if the utility sharing is according to proportional allocation, while it can be arbitrarily low under an equal sharing allocation.

Assume that the utility function of the public project is $u_0(b) = v_1 b$, and the utility function of each private project is $u_i(b) = v_2 b$, for $v_1, v_2 > 0$ such that $v_1/n < v_2 < v_1$. Assume that utility sharing is according to equal sharing allocation. The payoff functions of players are given by

$$s_i(\mathbf{b}) = \left(v_1 \sum_{j \in N} b_j\right) \frac{1}{n} + v_2(1 - b_i), \quad \text{for } i \in N.$$

The social welfare function is given by

$$s(\mathbf{b}) = (v_1 - v_2) \sum_{j \in N} b_j + v_2 n,$$

which is maximized by all players investing their entire effort to the public project, yielding the optimum social welfare of value $v_1 n$. In a pure-strategy Nash equilibrium, all players invest their entire effort budgets to private projects, which yields the social welfare of value $v_2 n$. Hence, the social efficiency of the pure-strategy Nash equilibrium is v_2/v_1, which can be made arbitrarily small by taking the value of marginal utility of the public project to be sufficiently large relative to the value of marginal utility of a private project and taking the number of players to be sufficiently large.

6.3 Monotone Valid Utility Games

An important class of utility maximization games is the class of *monotone valid utility games* that is broad enough to accommodate many interesting special cases. A monotone valid utility game is a utility maximization game that satisfies a *monotonicity* and a *marginal contribution condition*.

A utility maximization game is said to be *monotone* if for every strategy vector the social utility is at least as large as the social utility for the same strategy vector, but with an arbitrary player opted out from participation, i.e.,

$$u(\mathbf{b}) \geq u(\mathbf{0}_i, \mathbf{b}_{-i}), \quad \text{for all } \mathbf{b} \in \mathcal{B} \text{ and } i \in N. \tag{6.21}$$

A utility maximization game is *strongly monotone* if for every strategy vector, the utility for each player is at least as large as that when an arbitrary player opts out from participation, i.e., for every $i \in N$, $u_j(\mathbf{b}) \geq u_j(\mathbf{0}_i, \mathbf{b}_{-i})$, for all $\mathbf{b} \in \mathcal{B}$, and $j \in N$. Strong monotonicity implies monotonicity, but the converse is in general not true.

A utility maximization game satisfies the *marginal contribution condition* if for every strategy vector, the utility for each player is at least as large as the marginal contribution of this player to the utility, i.e., it holds that

$$u_i(\mathbf{b}) \geq u(\mathbf{b}) - u(\mathbf{0}_i, \mathbf{b}_{-i}), \quad \text{for all } \mathbf{b} \in \mathcal{B} \text{ and } i \in N. \tag{6.22}$$

A more general class of utility maximization games is defined by requiring the δ-approximate marginal contribution condition: there exists $\delta \geq 1$ such that every player is guaranteed to receive a utility in the amount of at least $1/\delta$ of his or her own marginal contribution, i.e. $u_i(\mathbf{b}) \geq (1/\delta)(u(\mathbf{b}) - u(\mathbf{0}_i, \mathbf{b}_{-i}))$, for all $\mathbf{b} \in \mathcal{B}$ and $i \in N$.

A utility maximization game is a *monotone valid utility game* if it is monotone and satisfies the marginal contribution condition. More generally, we say that a utility maximization game is a *δ-approximate monotone valid utility game* if it is monotone and satisfies the δ-approximate marginal contribution condition.

Observe that the concept of marginal contribution condition is related to the degree of substitutability of a utility function, which we introduced in Definition 6.4. If a utility maximization game satisfies the δ-approximate marginal condition, then the degree of substitutability satisfies $S_u \leq \delta$. For the utility sharing mechanism proportional to marginal contribution, we have $u_i(\mathbf{b}) \geq (1/S_u)(u(\mathbf{b}) - u(\mathbf{0}_i, \mathbf{b}_{-i}))$, for every player $i \in N$, meaning that the game satisfies the S_u-approximate marginal contribution condition.

6.3.1 Examples of Monotone Valid Utility Games

In this section, we provide several examples of monotone valid utility games that are defined by making certain assumptions about the utility sharing mechanism and the project utility functions. Specifically, we shall provide conditions under which a project utility function satisfies the marginal contribution condition or its relaxed version of the δ-approximate marginal contribution condition. If these conditions hold for every project of a simultaneous projects game, then the game is a monotone valid utility game. A recurrent assumption that we admit in all but one of the examples is as follows:

(A) Utility function u is a function of the total contribution that is increasing, concave, and such that $u(0) = 0$.

Marginal Contribution

Theorem 6.5. *Suppose that assumption (A) holds true. Then, the utility sharing mechanism proportional to marginal contribution (6.11) satisfies the marginal contribution condition.*

Proof. First, we note that

$$u\left(\sum_{j\in N}b_j\right) = \sum_{l=1}^{n}(u(b_1+\cdots+b_l)-u(b_1+\cdots+b_{l-1}))$$

$$\geq \sum_{l=1}^{n}\left(u\left(\sum_{j\in N}b_j\right) - u\left(\sum_{j\in N}b_j - b_l\right)\right) \qquad (6.23)$$

where the inequality is by the decreasing returns property. Combining this with (6.11), we obtain

$$u_i(\mathbf{b}) = u\left(\sum_{j\in N}b_j\right)x_i(\mathbf{b}) \geq u\left(\sum_{j\in N}b_j\right) - u\left(\sum_{j\in N}b_j - b_i\right).$$

$\square$

Proportional Allocation

Theorem 6.6. *Suppose that assumption (A) holds true. Then, the utility sharing mechanism according to proportional allocation (6.12) satisfies the marginal contribution condition.*

Proof. By assumption (A), it follows that

$$\frac{u(b)}{b} \geq \frac{u\left(\sum_{j\in N}b_j\right)}{\sum_{j\in N}b_j}, \qquad \text{whenever } 0 \leq b \leq \sum_{j\in N}b_j. \qquad (6.24)$$

The proof follows by

$$u_i(\mathbf{b}) = \frac{b_i}{\sum_{j\in N}b_j}u\left(\sum_{j\in N}b_j\right) \geq u\left(\sum_{j\in N}b_j\right) - u\left(\sum_{j\in N}b_j - b_i\right), \qquad \text{for all } i \in N,$$

where the equality is by the assumption that the utility sharing is according to proportional allocation, and the inequality is equivalent to the inequality in (6.24) for $b = \sum_{j\in N}b_j - b_i$. See Figure 6.3 for an illustration. $\square$

Winner-Take-All and One Success Enough

Theorem 6.7. *Suppose that the utility sharing mechanism is of the winner-take-all type with a uniform random tie break, which shares utility equally among successful contributors to the project, and the project utility function is of the one success enough form in (6.6). Then, the utility maximization game satisfies the marginal contribution condition.*

Proof. The allocation mechanism is such that players who succeed receive an equal share of the project utility where each player $i \in N$ succeeds independently and with

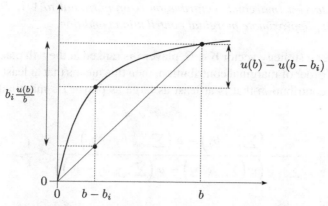

Figure 6.3. The marginal contribution condition holds for proportional allocation for any positive-valued, increasing, concave utility function.

probability $f_i(b_i)$. The utility function of player i is given by

$$u_i(\mathbf{b}) = f_i(b_i) \sum_{S \subseteq N \setminus \{i\}} \frac{1}{|S|+1} \prod_{l \in S} f_l(b_l) \prod_{l \in N \setminus \{i\} \setminus S} (1 - f_l(b_l)) \qquad (6.25)$$

where by definition $\prod_{l \in S} f_l(b_l) \equiv 1$, if $S = \emptyset$.

By the definition of the project utility function in (6.6),

$$u(\mathbf{b}) - u(\mathbf{0}_i, \mathbf{b}_{-i}) = \left(1 - \prod_{l \in N}(1 - f_l(b_l))\right) - \left(1 - \prod_{l \in N \setminus \{i\}}(1 - f_l(b_l))\right)$$

$$= f_i(b_i) \prod_{l \in N \setminus \{i\}} (1 - f_l(b_l)). \qquad (6.26)$$

Now, we note that

$$u_i(\mathbf{b}) = f_i(b_i) \sum_{S \subseteq N \setminus \{i\}: |S| > 0} \frac{1}{|S|+1} \prod_{l \in S} f_l(b_l) \prod_{l \in N \setminus \{i\} \setminus S} (1 - f_l(b_l))$$

$$+ f_i(b_i) \prod_{l \in N \setminus \{i\}} (1 - f_l(b_l))$$

$$\geq f_i(b_i) \prod_{l \in N \setminus \{i\}} (1 - f_l(b_l))$$

$$= u(\mathbf{b}) - u(\mathbf{0}_i, \mathbf{b}_{-i})$$

where the first equality is by (6.25) and the second equality is by (6.26).   □

Contribution Order Allocation

Theorem 6.8. *Suppose that assumption (A) holds true. Assume a utility sharing mechanism according to the rank-order allocation where the share allocated to the player* *with the t-th largest (marginal) contribution is proportional to* $1/t$. *Then, the game satisfies the* H_n-*approximate marginal contribution condition.*

Proof. If under a strategy vector $\mathbf{b} \in \mathcal{B}$, player i is ranked at the t-th place with respect to decreasing order of marginal contribution, then this means that at least t players have the marginal contribution that is at least as large as player i's marginal contribution. Hence,

$$\frac{u\left(\sum_{j\in N} b_j\right) - u\left(\sum_{j\in N} b_j - b_i\right)}{\sum_{l\in N}\left(u\left(\sum_{j\in N} b_j\right) - u\left(\sum_{j\in N} b_j - b_l\right)\right)} \leq \frac{1}{t}. \tag{6.27}$$

Now, note that

$$
\begin{aligned}
u_i(\mathbf{b}) &= \frac{1}{tH_{|N|}} u\left(\sum_{j\in N} b_j\right) \\
&\geq \frac{1}{H_{|N|}} \frac{u\left(\sum_{j\in N} b_j\right) - u\left(\sum_{j\in N} b_j - b_i\right)}{\sum_{l\in N}\left(u\left(\sum_{j\in N} b_j\right) - u\left(\sum_{j\in N} b_j - b_l\right)\right)} u\left(\sum_{j\in N} b_j\right) \\
&\geq \frac{1}{H_{|N|}}\left(u\left(\sum_{j\in N} b_j\right) - u\left(\sum_{j\in N} b_j - b_i\right)\right)
\end{aligned}
$$

where the first inequality is by (6.27) and the second inequality is by (6.23).   □

Some Non-Examples

Consider the class of utility functions such that $u(\mathbf{b}) = 0$, for every vector of efforts $\mathbf{b}$ such that $b_i = 0$ for some $i \in N$. For example, this class of utility functions accommodates the Cobb-Douglas and Leontief families of functions. For the given class of utility functions, the contribution of each player is essential for the utility of a project. The marginal contribution condition (6.22) corresponds to $u_i(\mathbf{b}) \geq u(\mathbf{b})$, for all $i \in N$. This clearly cannot hold under assumption (6.2) for any number of two or more players. Hence, the given class of utility functions cannot satisfy the marginal contribution condition.

6.3.2 Existence of a Pure-Strategy Nash Equilibrium

Corollary 6.9. *Consider an n-player utility maximization game such that* $u_i(\mathbf{b})$ *is a continuous function for* $\mathbf{b} \in \mathcal{B}$, *and concave in* b_i *for every given* $\mathbf{b}_{-i} \in \times_{j\neq i}\mathcal{B}_j$. *Suppose that the set* $\mathcal{B}_i$ *is convex and compact for every player* $i \in N$. *Then, there exists a pure-strategy Nash equilibrium.*

Proof. Under the given assumptions, the utility maximization game is a concave game and thus by Rosen's theorem (see Theorem 11.51 in Section 11.3.1) has a pure-strategy Nash equilibrium.   □

6.4 Social Efficiency and the Marginal Contribution Condition

Theorem 6.10. *Consider a utility maximization game that is monotone and satisfies the δ-approximate marginal contribution condition. If the utility function satisfies the decreasing marginal property, then in any pure-strategy Nash equilibrium, the social utility is at least $1/(\delta + 1)$ of the maximum social utility.*

Proof. Suppose that **b** is a pure-strategy Nash equilibrium and **b*** is a socially optimum strategy vector. The following relations hold true:

$$u(\mathbf{b}) \geq \sum_{i=1}^{n} u_i(\mathbf{b}) \tag{6.28}$$

$$\geq \sum_{i=1}^{n} u_i(b_i^*, \mathbf{b}_{-i}) \tag{6.29}$$

$$\geq \frac{1}{\delta} \sum_{i=1}^{n} u(b_i^*, \mathbf{b}_{-i}) - u(0, \mathbf{b}_{-i}) \tag{6.30}$$

$$\geq \frac{1}{\delta} \sum_{i=1}^{n} u((b_i^*, \mathbf{b}_{-i}) \vee (b_1^*, \ldots, b_{i-1}^*, b_i, \mathbf{0}))$$
$$- u((0, \mathbf{b}_{-i}) \vee (b_1^*, \ldots, b_{i-1}^*, b_i, \mathbf{0})) \tag{6.31}$$

$$= \frac{1}{\delta} \sum_{i=1}^{n} u(\mathbf{b} \vee (b_1^*, \ldots, b_i^*, \mathbf{0})) - u(\mathbf{b} \vee (b_1^*, \ldots, b_{i-1}^*, \mathbf{0})) \tag{6.32}$$

$$= \frac{1}{\delta}(u(\mathbf{b} \vee \mathbf{b}^*) - u(\mathbf{b})) \tag{6.33}$$

$$\geq \frac{1}{\delta}(u(\mathbf{b}^*) - u(\mathbf{b})) \tag{6.34}$$

where (6.28) is by condition (6.2) that the social utility function is at least as large as the total utility of players, (6.29) is by the assumption that **b** is a pure-strategy Nash equilibrium, (6.30) is by the assumption that the δ-approximate marginal condition holds, (6.31) is by the decreasing marginal returns condition, and (6.34) is by the assumption that the social utility function is an increasing function. Thus, $u(\mathbf{b}) \geq (1/(\delta + 1))u(\mathbf{b}^*)$, which proves the theorem. □

Corollary 6.11. *If the marginal contribution condition holds, then in any pure-strategy Nash equilibrium the social utility is at least $1/2$ of the maximum social utility.*

The Importance of the Monotonicity Condition In Section 1.3.5 we presented an example of a utility maximization game with one project whose utility function is non-monotonic, for which the social efficiency of pure-strategy Nash equilibrium diminishes to zero as the number of players grows large. This was an instance of the well-known phenomenon of *the tragedy of the commons* where the inefficiency arises due to over-utilization of resources because of non-cooperative strategic behavior of

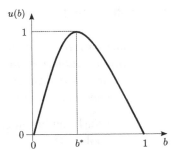

Figure 6.4. A non-monotone project utility function.

individual agents. We now show that the given observation holds for a broad class of non-monotonic utility functions.

Assume that the utility sharing is according to proportional allocation and players incur no production costs, so the payoff functions are given by

$$s_i(\mathbf{b}) = u\left(\sum_{j \in N} b_j\right) \frac{b_i}{\sum_{j \in N} b_j}, \quad \text{for } i \in N.$$

The utility function u is assumed to belong to a family of functions that satisfy the following conditions:

(i) Function u is concave and continuously differentiable.
(ii) There exists $b^* > 0$ such that u is increasing on $[0, b^*)$ and decreasing on (b^*, ∞).
(iii) $u(0) = 0$, $u(b^*) = 1$ and $u(1) = 0$.
(iv) $u'(1)$ is bounded.

Condition (iii) assumes specific values for the maximum value of the utility function and the value greater than zero at which the utility function assumes value zero. Note that these specific values are admitted merely for notational simplicity and one can allow for arbitrary strictly positive values. Figure 6.4 provides an illustration of the given family of utility functions.

Proposition 6.12. *Suppose that conditions (i)–(iv) hold. Then social welfare in the pure-strategy Nash equilibrium is $\Theta(1/n)$ of the maximum social welfare.*

Proof. Suppose that $\mathbf{b}$ is a pure-strategy Nash equilibrium. Then, $\partial s_i(\mathbf{b})/\partial b_i \leq 0$, for all $i \in N$, where equality holds whenever $b_i > 0$. By the symmetry of the game $b_1 = b_2 = \cdots = b_n = b/n$ where b is the unique strictly positive solution of the equation

$$\left(1 - \frac{1}{n}\right) u(b) + \frac{1}{n} u'(b)b = 0. \tag{6.35}$$

We show that $b^* < b < 1$. The lower bound $b^* < b$ holds because the left-hand side in equation (6.35) is strictly positive for every $b \in (0, b^*]$, it is equal to zero for $b = 0$, and $u(b)$ is increasing for $b \in [0, b^*)$ and $u(b^*) > 0$. The upper bound $b < 1$ holds because the left-hand side in (6.35) is negative for $b = 1$; hence, it must be $b < 1$.

By concavity of the function $u(x)$, we have

$$-u'(x)(1 - x) \leq u(x) \leq -u'(1)(1 - x), \quad \text{for every } x \in [b^*, 1]. \tag{6.36}$$

From (6.35) and the lower bound in (6.36) for $x = b$, it follows that $b \geq 1 - 1/n$. Since function $u(x)$ is decreasing for $x \in [1 - 1/n, b]$, we have

$$u(b) \leq u\left(1 - \frac{1}{n}\right). \tag{6.37}$$

It remains only to note that

$$\frac{u(b)}{u(b^*)} \leq u\left(1 - \frac{1}{n}\right) \leq \frac{-u'(1)}{n} = \Theta(1/n)$$

where the first inequality is by (6.37) and the assumption that $u(b^*) = 1$, and the second inequality is by the upper bound in (6.36). $\square$

The result in Theorem 6.10 can be established by using the framework of smooth games, which is presented in Appendix 11.3.2. This boils down to showing that every monotone valid utility game that satisfies the δ-approximate marginal contribution condition is $(1/\delta, 1/\delta)$-smooth. This implies that the social utility in any pure-strategy Nash equilibrium is at least $1/(\delta + 1)$ of the maximum social utility. In subsequent sections we shall extend the efficiency results to allow for games with coalitional deviations and with incomplete information where the type of each player is private information.

6.4.1 Strong Nash Equilibrium and Coalitional Smoothness

A bound on the social efficiency for monotone utility maximization games can also be established for strong Nash equilibria, a solution concept introduced in Definition 1.8. A strategy vector is a strong Nash equilibrium if there exists no deviation of a coalition of players such that every player in this coalition increases his or her payoff.

Theorem 6.13. *Consider a monotone utility maximization game that satisfies the δ-marginal contribution condition. Then, the social utility in every strong Nash equilibrium, whenever one exists, is at least $1/(\delta + 1)$ of the optimum social utility.*

Proof. Let π be a permutation specifying an arbitrary order of players, and let N_i^π be the subset of players at position larger than or equal to position i according to the order specified by the permutation π, i.e.

$$N_i^\pi = \{j \in N \mid \pi(j) \geq i\}.$$

Let **b** be a strong equilibrium strategy vector and **b*** be a utility-maximizing vector. Then, we have

$$u(\mathbf{b}) \geq \sum_{i \in N} u_i(\mathbf{b})$$

$$\geq \sum_{i=1}^{n} u_i(\mathbf{b}_{N_i^\pi}^*, \mathbf{b}_{-N_i^\pi})$$

$$\geq \frac{1}{\delta} \sum_{i=1}^{n} [u(\mathbf{b}_{N_i^\pi}^*, \mathbf{b}_{-N_i^\pi}) - u(0_{\pi^{-1}(i)}, \mathbf{b}_{N_{i+1}^\pi}^*, \mathbf{b}_{-N_i^\pi})]$$

$$\geq \frac{1}{\delta} \sum_{i=1}^{n} [u(\mathbf{b}^*_{N_i^\pi}, \mathbf{b}_{-N_i^\pi}) - u(\mathbf{b}_{\pi^{-1}(i)}, \mathbf{b}^*_{N_{i+1}^\pi}, \mathbf{b}_{-N_i^\pi})]$$

$$= \frac{1}{\delta} \sum_{i=1}^{n} [u(\mathbf{b}^*_{N_i^\pi}, \mathbf{b}_{-N_i^\pi}) - u(\mathbf{b}^*_{N_{i+1}^\pi}, \mathbf{b}_{-N_{i+1}^\pi})]$$

$$= \frac{1}{\delta} [u(\mathbf{b}^*) - u(\mathbf{b})]$$

where the first inequality is by condition (6.2) that the social utility function is at least as large as the total utility of players, the second inequality is by the assumption that vector $\mathbf{b}$ is a strong equilibrium, the third inequality is by the δ-approximate marginal contribution condition, the fourth inequality is by the monotonicity of the utility functions and the last equality is by a telescopic summation.

From the last sequence of relations, we have that $u(\mathbf{b}) \geq (1/(\delta + 1))u(\mathbf{b}^*)$. $\square$

Notice that the social efficiency bound for strong equilibria in Theorem 6.13 is exactly the same as that for the superset of pure-strategy Nash equilibria in Theorem 6.10. Note that the result in Theorem 6.13 does not require the utility functions to satisfy the decreasing marginal property, which is assumed in Theorem 6.10.

The result in Theorem 6.13 can be established using the framework of smooth games, in particular, the concept of coalitionally smooth games, defined in Section 11.3.3. A game is said to be (λ, μ)-coalitionally smooth if it has a strategy vector $\mathbf{a} \in \mathcal{B}$ such that for every $\mathbf{b} \in \mathcal{B}$ and a social-utility maximizing vector $\mathbf{b}^* \in \mathcal{B}$, the following condition holds for every permutation π of the players

$$\sum_{i=1}^{n} u_i(\mathbf{a}_{N_i^\pi}, \mathbf{b}_{-N_i^\pi}) \geq \lambda u(\mathbf{b}^*) - \mu u(\mathbf{b})$$

where recall N_i^π is the subset of players at position larger than or equal to position i according to the order specified by the permutation π. If a game is (λ, μ)-coalitionally smooth, then it guarantees social utility of value at least $\lambda/(\mu + 1)$ of the optimum value, in every strong equilibrium, which is shown in Section 11.3.3. The proof of Theorem 6.13 establishes that, under the given assumptions, the utility maximization game is a $(1/\delta, 1/\delta)$-coalitionally smooth game.

6.4.2 Game with Incomplete Information

In this section we consider utility maximization games with incomplete information using the concept of smooth games with incomplete information in Definition 11.80. A utility maximization game with incomplete information is said to be (λ, μ)-smooth with respect to a strategy $\beta : \mathcal{T} \to \mathcal{B}$, if for every pair of types $\mathbf{t}$ and $\mathbf{s} \in \mathcal{T}$ and every strategy vector $\mathbf{b}$ that is feasible under $\mathbf{s}$, it holds that

$$\sum_{i \in N} u_i(t_i, (\beta_i(t_i), \mathbf{b}_{-i})) \geq \lambda u(\mathbf{t}, \beta(\mathbf{t})) - \mu u(\mathbf{s}, \mathbf{b}).$$

If a game is (λ, μ)-smooth with respect to a strategy vector that for a given type of players maximizes a social utility function, then the expected value of the social utility function in every Bayes-Nash equilibrium of the game is at least $\lambda/(1+\mu)$ of the maximum expected social utility function, which is a result established in Theorem 11.81.

In the following theorem, we establish that if a utility maximization game with incomplete information satisfies the δ-approximate marginal contribution condition, then it is $(1/\delta, 1/\delta)$-smooth.

Theorem 6.14. *Suppose that a utility maximization game of simultaneous projects and local utility sharing mechanisms is such that the δ-approximate marginal contribution condition holds. Then, the game is $(1/\delta, 1/\delta)$-smooth.*

Proof. Let $\mathbf{t}$ and $\mathbf{s}$ be two vectors of types, let $\mathbf{b}^* \in \mathcal{B}(\mathbf{t})$ be a strategy vector that maximizes the social utility under the type vector $\mathbf{t}$, and let $\mathbf{b} \in \mathcal{B}(\mathbf{s})$ be an arbitrary strategy vector. We have

$$\sum_{i \in N} u_i(t_i, (b_i^*, \mathbf{b}_{-i})) = \sum_{i \in N} \sum_{j \in M_i} u_{i,j}(t_i, (b_{i,j}^*, \mathbf{b}_{N_j \setminus \{i\}})).$$

Since the δ-approximate marginal contribution condition is assumed to hold for every player and project, we have

$$u_{i,j}(t_i, (b_{i,j}^*, \mathbf{b}_{N_j \setminus \{-i\}})) \geq \frac{1}{\delta}(u_j(b_{i,j}^*, \mathbf{b}_{N_j \setminus \{i\}}) - u_j(0, \mathbf{b}_{N_j \setminus \{i\}})).$$

Combining the last two relations, we obtain

$$\sum_{i \in N} u_i(t_i, (b_i^*, \mathbf{b}_{-i})) \geq \frac{1}{\delta} \sum_{j \in M} \sum_{i \in N_j} (u_j(b_{i,j}^*, \mathbf{b}_{N_j \setminus \{i\}}) - u_j(0, \mathbf{b}_{N_j \setminus \{i\}})).$$

Now, by the same arguments as in the proof of Theorem 6.10, we have

$$\sum_{i \in N_j} (u_j(b_{i,j}^*, \mathbf{b}_{N_j \setminus \{i\}}) - u_j(0, \mathbf{b}_{N_j \setminus \{i\}})) \geq u_j(\mathbf{b}_{N_j}^*) - u_j(\mathbf{b}_{N_j}).$$

Hence,

$$u(\mathbf{t}, \mathbf{b}) = \sum_{i \in N} u_i(t_i, \mathbf{b}_i)$$

$$\geq \sum_{i \in N} u_i(t_i, (b_i^*, \mathbf{b}_{-i}))$$

$$\geq \frac{1}{\delta} \sum_{j \in M} u_j(\mathbf{b}_{N_j}^*) - \frac{1}{\delta} \sum_{j \in M} u_j(\mathbf{b}_{N_j})$$

$$= \frac{1}{\delta} \sum_{i \in N} u_i(t_i, \mathbf{b}^*) - \frac{1}{\delta} \sum_{i \in N} u_i(t_i, \mathbf{b})$$

$$= \frac{1}{\delta} u(\mathbf{t}, \mathbf{b}^*) - \frac{1}{\delta} u(\mathbf{t}, \mathbf{b}).$$

Thus, $u(\mathbf{t}, \mathbf{b}) \geq (1/(\delta + 1)) u(\mathbf{t}, \mathbf{b}^*)$. $\qquad\square$

The results of Theorem 6.14 and Theorem 11.81 imply the following corollary.

Corollary 6.15. *For any utility maximization game with incomplete information that consists of simultaneous projects and utility sharing mechanisms that satisfy the δ-marginal contribution condition, the expected social utility in every mixed-strategy Bayes-Nash equilibrium is at least $1/(\delta + 1)$ of the maximum expected social utility.*

The corollary implies that any such utility maximization game with incomplete information guarantees the social efficiency of value at least $1/2$ whenever it satisfies the marginal contribution condition.

Smooth Convex Production Cost Functions

Consider the case where the players incur production costs that are increasing and convex in their invested efforts. We consider the efficiency with respect to the social welfare function defined as the sum of the payoff functions of all the players. In the presence of production cost functions, the efficiency of an equilibrium can be arbitrarily low. We already encountered an example when this is so in Example 6.2.2. This example was for a single project game that satisfies the marginal contribution, the utility of production that satisfies the decreasing marginal returns property, and the players who incur linear production costs. We noted there that the social efficiency of pure-strategy Nash equilibrium of an n-player game can be as low as $O(1/n)$. In this section, we establish an interesting threshold property: if the production costs are strictly convex, the efficiency is lower bounded by a constant independent of the number of players. We shall establish this for the game with incomplete information. The results in this section allow for the prior distributions of the types to differ from one player to another.

The production costs of the players are assumed to be such that every player $i \in N$ incurs a production cost according to the given function $c_i : \mathcal{T}_i \times \mathbf{R}_+ \to \mathbf{R}_+$ that specifies the production cost for every given type t_i and the value of the total effort invested by this player:

$$e_i(t_i, \mathbf{b}_i) = \sum_{j \in M_i} e_{i,j}(t_i, b_{i,j}).$$

Here $b_{i,j}$ is the value of the production output of player i in project j, and $e_{i,j}(t_i, b_{i,j})$ is the amount of effort that player i needs to invest into project j to realize the production output of value $b_{i,j}$.

The payoff functions of the players are given by

$$s_i(t_i, \mathbf{b}) = \sum_{j \in M_i} u_{i,j}(\mathbf{b}_{N_j}) - c_i(t_i, e_i(t_i, \mathbf{b}_i)), \quad \text{for } i \in N.$$

We define the total utility and the total cost functions, respectively, as follows:

$$u(\mathbf{t}, \mathbf{b}) = \sum_{i \in N} \sum_{j \in M_i} u_{i,j}(\mathbf{b}_{N_j}) \text{ and } c(\mathbf{t}, \mathbf{b}) = \sum_{i \in N} c_i(t_i, e_i(t_i, \mathbf{b}_i)).$$

The social welfare function is defined as the sum of the payoff functions of the players and is given by

$$s(\mathbf{t}, \mathbf{b}) = u(\mathbf{t}, \mathbf{b}) - c(\mathbf{t}, \mathbf{b}).$$

The project utility functions are assumed to be monotonically increasing in each coordinate and to satisfy the decreasing marginal returns property in Definition 6.1. The production costs are assumed to obey the following assumptions. For every player $i \in N$ and type of this player $t_i \in \mathcal{T}_i$, $c_i(t_i, e_i)$ is assumed to be an increasing, continuously differentiable, convex function of elasticity at least of value $\mu + 1$, for parameter $\mu \geq 0$, in the effort investment e_i. The concept of elasticity of a function is introduced in Definition 6.2. This covers, as special cases, the linear production cost functions and the effort budget constraints as a limit of a sequence of convex production functions whose elasticity goes to infinity. For every player $i \in N$, type of this player $t_i \in \mathcal{T}_i$, and $j \in M_i$, $e_{i,j}(t_i, x)$ is assumed to be a strictly increasing, continuously differentiable, convex function in x, and such that $e_{i,j}(t_i, 0) = 0$.

We first present a lemma that is used shortly in the proof of Theorem 6.17. This lemma establishes a relation that holds for the expected social welfare and the expected utility in a Bayes-Nash equilibrium and the maximum expected social welfare, which may be of interest in its own right.

Lemma 6.16. *Suppose that the game is such that the project utility functions satisfy the decreasing marginal returns property and the marginal contribution condition holds. Then, in any Bayes-Nash equilibrium, the expected social welfare plus the expected total utility is at least the maximum expected social welfare, i.e.,*

$$\mathbf{E}[s(\mathbf{t}, \beta(\mathbf{t}))] + \mathbf{E}[u(\mathbf{t}, \beta(\mathbf{t}))] \geq \mathbf{E}[s(\mathbf{t}, \beta^*(\mathbf{t}))] \tag{6.38}$$

where $\beta(\mathbf{t})$ specifies Bayes-Nash equilibrium strategies and $\beta^*(\mathbf{t})$ specifies strategies that maximize the social welfare for every given type of players $\mathbf{t} \in \mathcal{T}$.

Proof. For every two vectors of types $\mathbf{t}, \mathbf{s} \in \mathcal{T}$ of players, we have:

$$\sum_{i \in N} s_i(t_i, (\beta_i^*(t_i), \beta_{-i}(\mathbf{s}))) = \sum_{i \in N} \sum_{j \in M_i} u_{i,j}(\beta_{i,j}^*(t_i), \beta_{N_j \setminus \{i\}}(\mathbf{s})) - \sum_{i \in N} c_i(t_i, e_i(t_i, \beta_i^*(t_i)))$$

$$\geq u(\mathbf{t}, \beta^*(\mathbf{t})) - u(\mathbf{s}, \beta(\mathbf{s})) - c(\mathbf{t}, \beta^*(\mathbf{t}))$$

$$= s(\mathbf{t}, \beta^*(\mathbf{t})) - u(\mathbf{s}, \beta(\mathbf{s}))$$

where the inequality follows by the assumption that the project utility functions satisfy the decreasing marginal returns property and the game satisfies the marginal contribution condition.

The assertion of the lemma follows by noting that for every player $i \in N$, we have

$$\mathbf{E}[s_i(t_i, (\beta_i^*(t_i), \beta_{-i}(\mathbf{s})))] = \mathbf{E}[s_i(t_i, (\beta_i^*(t_i), \beta_{-i}(\mathbf{t})))] \leq \mathbf{E}[s_i(t_i, (\beta_i(t_i), \beta_{-i}(\mathbf{t})))]$$

$$= \mathbf{E}[s_i(t_i, \beta(\mathbf{t}))]$$

where the first equality is by the fact that $\mathbf{t}$ and $\mathbf{s}$ are independent samples from the same product-form distribution and the second inequality is by the fact that $\beta(\mathbf{t})$ is a Bayes-Nash equilibrium. $\square$

The next theorem is the main result in this section, which establishes a lower bound on the efficiency of Bayes-Nash equilibrium for the case when the players incur production cost functions of the elasticity of value at least $\mu + 1$.

Theorem 6.17. *Under the prevailing assumptions on the project utility functions and the production cost functions, for every utility sharing mechanism such that the game* *satisfies the marginal contribution condition, the expected social welfare in any Bayes-Nash equilibrium is at least factor η of the maximum expected social welfare, where*

$$\eta = \frac{\mu}{2\mu + 1}.$$

Furthermore, the expected social utility is at least $\mu/(2(\mu + 1))$ of the expected utility produced in any outcome that maximizes the expected social welfare.

Proof. We claim that in any Bayes-Nash equilibrium $\beta(\mathbf{t}) = (\beta_{i,j}(t_i), \ i \in N, \ j \in M_i)$, the following inequality holds

$$\mathbf{E}[u(\mathbf{t}, \beta(\mathbf{t}))] \geq (1 + \mu)\mathbf{E}[c(\mathbf{t}, \beta(\mathbf{t}))], \tag{6.39}$$

which we establish at the end of the proof.

The first assertion of the theorem follows by

$$
\begin{aligned}
\mathbf{E}[s(\mathbf{t}, \beta^*(\mathbf{t}))] &\leq \mathbf{E}[s(\mathbf{t}, \beta(\mathbf{t}))] + \mathbf{E}[u(\mathbf{t}, \beta(\mathbf{t}))] \\
&= 2\mathbf{E}[s(\mathbf{t}, \beta(\mathbf{t}))] + \mathbf{E}[c(\mathbf{t}, \beta(\mathbf{t}))] \\
&\leq 2\mathbf{E}[s(\mathbf{t}, \beta(\mathbf{t}))] + \frac{1}{\mu}\mathbf{E}[s(\mathbf{t}, \beta(\mathbf{t}))] \\
&= \frac{2\mu + 1}{\mu}\mathbf{E}[s(\mathbf{t}, \beta(\mathbf{t}))]
\end{aligned}
$$

where the first inequality is by Lemma 6.16, the first equation is by the fact $\mathbf{E}[s(\mathbf{t}, \beta(\mathbf{t}))] = \mathbf{E}[u(\mathbf{t}, \beta(\mathbf{t}))] - \mathbf{E}[c(\mathbf{t}, \beta(\mathbf{t}))]$, and the second inequality is by the inequality (6.39).

The second assertion of the theorem follows by these relations:

$$
\begin{aligned}
2\mathbf{E}[u(\mathbf{t}, \beta(\mathbf{t}))] &\geq \mathbf{E}[u(\mathbf{t}, \beta(\mathbf{t}))] - \mathbf{E}[c(\mathbf{t}, \beta(\mathbf{t}))] \\
&\geq \mathbf{E}[u(\mathbf{t}, \beta(\mathbf{t}))] - \frac{1}{\mu + 1}\mathbf{E}[u(\mathbf{t}, \beta(\mathbf{t}))] \\
&= \frac{\mu}{\mu + 1}\mathbf{E}[u(\mathbf{t}, \beta(\mathbf{t}))]
\end{aligned}
$$

where the second inequality is by (6.39).

In the remainder of the proof, we establish claim (6.39). For every player $i \in N$, the expected payoff for this player conditional on his or her type and strategy is

$$
\begin{aligned}
&\mathbf{E}[s_i(t_i, (\mathbf{b}_i, \beta_{-i}(\mathbf{t}))) \mid t_i = t] \\
&= \sum_{j \in M_i} \mathbf{E}[u_{i,j}(b_{i,j}, \beta_{N_j \setminus \{i\}}(\mathbf{t})) \mid t_i = t] - c_i(t, e_i(t, \mathbf{b}_i)), \quad \text{for } t \in \mathcal{T}_i \text{ and } \mathbf{b}_i \in \mathbf{R}_+^m.
\end{aligned}
$$

For $\beta : \mathcal{T} \to \mathbf{R}^{n \times m}$ to be a Bayes-Nash equilibrium, the following condition must hold for $t = t_i, i \in N$ and $j \in M_i$:

$$\frac{\partial}{\partial b_{i,j}}\mathbf{E}[s_i(t_i, \beta(\mathbf{t})) \mid t_i = t] = 0,$$

which is equivalent to

$$\frac{\partial}{\partial e_i} c_i(t, e_i(t, \beta_i(t))) \frac{\partial}{\partial b_{i,j}} e_{i,j}(t, \beta_{i,j}(t)) = \frac{\partial}{\partial b_{i,j}} \mathbf{E}[u_{i,j}(\beta_{N_j}(\mathbf{t})) \mid t_i = t]. \quad (6.40)$$

Now,

$$(1 + \mu) c_i(t, e_i(t, \beta_i(t))) \leq e_i(t, \beta_i(t)) \frac{\partial}{\partial e_i} c_i(t, e_i(t, \beta_i(t)))$$

$$= \sum_{j \in M_i} e_{i,j}(t, \beta_{i,j}(t)) \frac{\partial}{\partial e_i} c_i(t, e_i(t, \beta_i(t)))$$

$$= \sum_{j \in M_i} \frac{e_{i,j}(t, \beta_{i,j}(t))}{\frac{\partial}{\partial b_{i,j}} e_{i,j}(t, \beta_{i,j}(t))} \frac{\partial}{\partial b_{i,j}} \mathbf{E}[u_{i,j}(\beta_{N_j}(\mathbf{t})) \mid t_i = t]$$

$$\leq \sum_{j \in M_i} \beta_{i,j}(t) \frac{\partial}{\partial b_{i,j}} \mathbf{E}[u_{i,j}(\beta_{N_j}(\mathbf{t})) \mid t_i = t]$$

$$\leq \sum_{j \in M_i} \mathbf{E}[u_{i,j}(\beta_{N_j}(\mathbf{t})) \mid t_i = t]$$

where the first inequality is by the fact that the elasticity of each production cost function is at least $1 + \mu$, the second equality is by the Bayes-Nash equilibrium condition (6.40), the second inequality is because $e_{i,j}(t_i, x)$ is convex, strictly increasing in x and $e_{i,j}(t_i, 0) = 0$, and the last inequality is by the fact that $u_{i,j}(\mathbf{b}_{N_j})$ is concave in $b_{i,j}$ and $u_{i,j}(\mathbf{b}_{N_j}) = 0$ whenever $b_{i,j} = 0$.   □

From the lower bound on the social efficiency in Theorem 6.17, we observe that for the case $\mu = 0$, which corresponds to linear production costs, the lower bound is equal to zero, which conforms to the observation that an equilibrium can be of arbitrarily low efficiency in this case. On the other hand, if the elasticity tends to infinity, which accommodates as a limit the case of effort budget constraints, then the limit lower bound on the efficiency is $1/2$, which conforms with the efficiency guarantee for the case of budget-limited players in Corollary 6.15 when the exact marginal contribution condition holds. Figure 6.5 shows a graph of the social efficiency lower bound in Theorem 6.17 versus the value of the parameter μ.

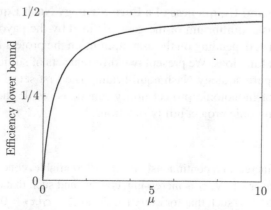

Figure 6.5. Social efficiency lower bound for production costs of elasticity at least $\mu + 1$.

6.5 Proportional Allocation

In this section we consider the utility sharing mechanism according to proportional allocation. For the case of a single project and suitable assumptions on the project utility function, the underlying game corresponds both to the well-known game of *Cournot oligopoly* and the game often referred to as a *surplus sharing game*. We shall provide different sets of conditions for the existence and uniqueness of a pure-strategy Nash equilibrium. We shall show that overdissipation of efforts occurs in a pure-strategy Nash equilibrium, a phenomenon sometimes referred to as the tragedy of the commons. We shall establish social efficiency bounds for the case of one or more simultaneous projects, each sharing the utility of production according to proportional allocation. We shall see how the properties of the project utility functions and the production cost functions affect efficiency in a pure-strategy Nash equilibrium.

6.5.1 Single Project

We consider a single project with utility function u of the total contribution under the utility sharing mechanism according to proportional allocation. The payoffs of players are given as follows:

$$s_i(\mathbf{b}) = u\left(\sum_{j \in N} b_j\right) \frac{b_i}{\sum_{j \in N} b_j} - c_i(b_i), \quad \text{for } i \in N. \tag{6.41}$$

Cournot Oligopoly and Surplus Sharing Games   The normal form game with payoff functions (6.41) is isomorphic to a classic model of a Cournot oligopoly. A Cournot oligopoly game consists of n producers of a good, where each producer $i \in N$ produces an amount of goods of b_i. The goods are sold in a market for the price per unit good of $\bar{u}(b)$, where $\bar{u} : \mathbf{R}_+ \to \mathbf{R}$, and $b = \sum_{i \in N} b_i$ denotes the total number of goods produced. In the parlance of economists, $\bar{u}$ is referred to as the *inverse demand function*. Each producer i incurs a production cost according to a production cost function $c_i : \mathbf{R}_+ \to \mathbf{R}_+$. The payoff of producer i is defined by $s_i(\mathbf{b}) = b_i \bar{u}(b) - c_i(b_i)$. Such defined payoff functions are of the same form as those of a utility maximization game with the project utility function $u(x) = \bar{u}(x)x$ and the payoff functions (6.41).

Existence and Uniqueness of a Pure-Strategy Nash Equilibrium

A pure-strategy Nash equilibrium of the game defined by the payoff functions (6.41) may or may not exist, depending on the assumptions on the project utility function and the production cost functions. We present two different sets of sufficient conditions for the existence of a pure-strategy Nash equilibrium. The first set of conditions accommodates a subset of monotonic project utility functions, while the second condition allows for non-monotonic project utility functions.

Sufficient Conditions I:

    (U) u is strictly increasing, continuously twice differentiable, concave, and $u(0) = 0$;

    (C) for every player $i \in N$, c_i is increasing, convex, and such that $c_i(0) = 0$;

    (S) there exists $b^* > 0$ such that for every $i \in N$, $u(x) - c_i(x) < 0$, for every $x > b^*$.

Theorem 6.18. *Under conditions (U), (C), and (S), there exists a pure-strategy Nash equilibrium. If, in addition, u is strictly concave, then there is a unique pure-strategy Nash equilibrium.*

Proof. We first establish the existence of a pure-strategy Nash equilibrium. This follows by showing that the game is a concave game, and thus by Rosen's Theorem 11.51, it has a pure-strategy Nash equilibrium. We need to show that (i) $s_i(\mathbf{b})$ is a continuous function, for every $i \in N$, (ii) $s_i(\mathbf{b})$ is concave in b_i, for every $i \in N$, and (iii) the set of strategy vectors is convex, closed, and bounded.

Condition (i) holds because by assumption u is differentiable and $u(0) = 0$, so the utility component $u(\sum_{j \in N} b_j)x_i(\mathbf{b})$ of every player i's payoff function is continuous at every point $\mathbf{b} \in \mathbf{R}_+^n$, and by assumption each production cost is convex; hence, it is continuous. Condition (ii) can be shown to hold as follows. Each payoff function is is equal to the utility component minus the production cost. Since the production cost is assumed to be a convex function, it suffices to show that the utility component $u(\sum_{j \in N} b_j)x_i(\mathbf{b})$ is a concave function in b_i, for every player $i \in N$. Note that for every $i \in N$,

$$\frac{\partial}{\partial b_i}\left(u\left(\sum_{j \in N} b_j\right)x_i(\mathbf{b})\right) = (1 - x_i(\mathbf{b}))f(\mathbf{b}) + x_i(\mathbf{b})g(\mathbf{b})$$

where

$$f(\mathbf{b}) = \frac{u\left(\sum_{j \in N} b_j\right)}{\sum_{j \in N} b_j} \text{ and } g(\mathbf{b}) = u'\left(\sum_{j \in N} b_j\right).$$

Now, note that

$$\frac{\partial^2}{\partial b_i^2}\left(u\left(\sum_{j \in N} b_j\right)x_i(\mathbf{b})\right)$$

$$= (g(\mathbf{b}) - f(\mathbf{b}))\frac{\partial}{\partial b_i}x_i(\mathbf{b}) + (1 - x_i(\mathbf{b}))\frac{\partial}{\partial b_i}f(\mathbf{b}) + x_i(\mathbf{b})\frac{\partial}{\partial b_i}g(\mathbf{b}) \leq 0$$

where the inequality holds because by the assumption that u is increasing, concave, and such that $u(0) = 0$, it follows that $f(\mathbf{b}) \geq g(\mathbf{b})$, and both $f(\mathbf{b})$ and $g(\mathbf{b})$ are decreasing in b_i, and by the definition of proportional allocation $x_i(\mathbf{b})$ is increasing in b_i.

Condition (iii) holds because every player is guaranteed a payoff of value zero by investing zero effort, so by assumption (S), we can define the set of strategy vectors to contain all vectors $\mathbf{b} \in \mathbf{R}_+^n$ such that $u(\sum_{j \in N} b_j) - c_i(\sum_{j \in N} b_j) \geq 0$, for every $i \in N$. This set is readily observed to be convex, closed, and bounded under the given assumptions on the utility function and the production cost functions.

We next show that under the additional assumption that the utility function is strictly concave, there is a unique pure-strategy Nash equilibrium. Suppose on the contrary that there exist two pure-strategy Nash equilibrium vectors $\bar{\mathbf{b}}$ and $\underline{\mathbf{b}}$ such that $\bar{b}_i \neq \underline{b}_i$, for some player $i \in N$. Without loss of generality, we assume that the players are enumerated such that the following relations hold, for some player $j \in N$,

$$\bar{b}_i \leq \underline{b}_i \quad \text{for } i \in \{1, 2, \ldots, j\} \tag{6.42}$$

$$\bar{b}_i > \underline{b}_i \quad \text{for } i \in \{j+1, j+2, \ldots, n\} \tag{6.43}$$

and

$$\sum_{i=1}^{n} \bar{b}_i \geq \sum_{i=1}^{n} \underline{b}_i. \tag{6.44}$$

We shall use the notation $\bar{u}(x) = u(x)/x$, $\bar{b} = \sum_{i \in N} \bar{b}_i$ and $\underline{b} = \sum_{i \in N} \underline{b}_i$. We next separately consider two different cases.

Case 1: $\bar{b} > \underline{b}$. Obviously, $1 \leq j < n$. We establish the following two properties:

$$\bar{u}(\bar{b})\bar{b}_i \leq \bar{u}(\underline{b})\underline{b}_i, \quad \text{for every } i \in \{1, 2, \ldots, j\} \tag{6.45}$$

and

$$\bar{u}(\bar{b})\bar{b}_i > \bar{u}(\underline{b})\underline{b}_i, \quad \text{for some } i \in \{j+1, j+2, \ldots, n\}. \tag{6.46}$$

The property (6.45) follows immediately from (6.42) and observing that $\bar{u}(\bar{b}) \leq \bar{u}(\underline{b})$ under the assumption $\bar{b} > \underline{b}$ because $\bar{u}(x)$ is decreasing in x under the assumption that the utility of production is an increasing, concave function such that $u(0) = 0$. The property (6.46) can be established by contradiction as follows. Suppose on the contrary that the given property does not hold. Then, we have that $\bar{u}(\bar{b})\bar{b}_i \leq \bar{u}(\underline{b})\underline{b}_i$, for every $i \in \{1, 2, \ldots, n\}$. Summing over $i \in N$, we obtain $u(\bar{b}) \leq u(\underline{b})$, which contradicts the assumptions that $\bar{b} > \underline{b}$ and u is a strictly increasing function.

Without loss of generality, we assume that the players are enumerated such that for some $j^* \in \{j, j+1, \ldots, n\}$, we have

$$\bar{u}(\bar{b})\bar{b}_i \leq \bar{u}(\underline{b})\underline{b}_i, \quad \text{for } j < j^* \text{ and } \bar{u}(\bar{b})\bar{b}_i > \bar{u}(\underline{b})\underline{b}_i \text{ otherwise.} \tag{6.47}$$

If a vector $\mathbf{b}$ is a pure-strategy Nash equilibrium, then $\partial s_i(\mathbf{b})/\partial b_i = 0$ and $b_i > 0$, or $\partial s_i(\mathbf{b})/\partial b_i \leq 0$ and $b_i = 0$. Note that

$$\frac{\partial}{\partial b_i} s_i(\mathbf{b}) = \left(1 - \frac{b_i}{b}\right) \bar{u}(b) + \frac{b_i}{b} u'(b) - c_i'(b_i)$$

where $b = \sum_{j \in N} b_j$.

Now, observe that for every player $i \in \{j^*, \ldots, n\}$, we have

$$\left(1 - \frac{\bar{b}_i}{\bar{b}}\right) \bar{u}(\bar{b}) + \frac{\bar{b}_i}{\bar{b}} u'(\bar{b}) = c_i'(\bar{b}_i) \geq c_i'(\underline{b}_i) \geq \left(1 - \frac{\underline{b}_i}{\underline{b}}\right) \bar{u}(\underline{b}) + \frac{\underline{b}_i}{\underline{b}} u'(\underline{b}) \tag{6.48}$$

where the first equality holds because $\bar{\mathbf{b}}$ is a pure-strategy Nash equilibrium and $\bar{b}_i > 0$, the first inequality is because $\bar{b}_i > \underline{b}_i$ and c_i is a convex function, and the last inequality is because $\underline{\mathbf{b}}$ is a pure-strategy Nash equilibrium.

Summing in (6.48) over $i \in \{j^*, \ldots, n\}$, we obtain

$$(1 - \lambda(\bar{\mathbf{b}}))\bar{u}(\bar{b}) + \lambda(\bar{\mathbf{b}})u'(\bar{b}) \geq (1 - \lambda(\underline{\mathbf{b}}))\bar{u}(\underline{b}) + \lambda(\underline{\mathbf{b}})u'(\underline{b}), \tag{6.49}$$

where $\lambda(\mathbf{b})$ is defined by

$$\lambda(\mathbf{b}) = \frac{\sum_{i=j^*}^{n} b_i}{(n - j^* + 1) \sum_{i=1}^{n} b_i}. \tag{6.50}$$

We note the following claim, which we establish shortly,

$$\lambda(\bar{\mathbf{b}}) \geq \lambda(\underline{\mathbf{b}}). \tag{6.51}$$

Combining (6.49), (6.51), and the facts $\bar{u}(\bar{b}) \geq u'(\bar{b})$ and $\bar{u}(\underline{b}) \geq u'(\underline{b})$ that hold under the assumptions on the utility function u, it follows that

$$(1 - \lambda(\bar{\mathbf{b}}))\bar{u}(\bar{b}) + \lambda(\bar{\mathbf{b}})u'(\bar{b}) \geq (1 - \lambda(\bar{\mathbf{b}}))\bar{u}(\underline{b}) + \lambda(\bar{\mathbf{b}})u'(\underline{b}).$$

This, however, is a contradiction to $\bar{u}(\bar{b}) < \bar{u}(\underline{b})$ and $u'(\bar{b}) < u'(\underline{b})$, which hold under the given assumptions on the utility function.

The claim in (6.50) is established as follows. If $j^* = 1$, then by the definition (6.50), the inequality in (6.51) trivially holds. Hence, we consider the case when $j^* > 1$. From (6.47), we have

$$\frac{\sum_{i=j^*}^{n} \underline{b}_i}{\sum_{i=j^*}^{n} \bar{b}_i} < \frac{\bar{u}(\bar{b})}{\bar{u}(\underline{b})} \leq \frac{\sum_{i=1}^{j^*-1} \underline{b}_i}{\sum_{i=1}^{j^*-1} \bar{b}_i}.$$

Hence, it follows that

$$\frac{\sum_{i=j^*}^{n} \bar{b}_i}{\bar{b}} > \frac{\sum_{i=j^*}^{n} \underline{b}_i}{\underline{b}}. \tag{6.52}$$

Combining with (6.50), we obtain that (6.51) holds.

Case 2: $\bar{b} = \underline{b}$. Obviously, $1 \leq j < n$ because the two vectors $\bar{\mathbf{b}}$ and $\underline{\mathbf{b}}$ would be equal otherwise. Since $\bar{u}(\bar{b}) = \bar{u}(\underline{b})$, from (6.42) and (6.43), we have $\bar{u}(\bar{b})\bar{b}_i \leq \bar{u}(\underline{b})\underline{b}_i$ if $i \leq j$ and $\bar{u}(\bar{b})\bar{b}_i > \bar{u}(\underline{b})\underline{b}_i$, otherwise. Hence, (6.49) and (6.52) must hold for $j^* = j + 1$. From (6.49), using the facts $u'(\bar{b}) = u'(\underline{b})$, $\bar{u}(\bar{b}) = \bar{u}(\underline{b})$, $\bar{u}(\bar{b}) \geq u'(\bar{b})$, and $\bar{u}(\underline{b}) \geq u'(\underline{b})$, it follows that $\lambda(\bar{\mathbf{b}}) \leq \lambda(\underline{\mathbf{b}})$. However, this contradicts $\lambda(\bar{\mathbf{b}}) > \lambda(\underline{\mathbf{b}})$, which follows from $1 < j^* \leq n$, (6.50), and (6.52). $\qquad\square$

Sufficient Conditions II:

(U1) $\bar{u}(x) = u(x)/x$ is continuous;

(U2) There exists a positive real number b^* such that $\bar{u}(x)$ is continuously twice differentiable and strictly decreasing for $x \in [0, b^*)$ and $\bar{u}(x) = 0$ for $x \geq b^*$;

(U3) For every $x \in [0, b^*)$, $[\bar{u}'(x)x]' \leq 0$;

(C') For every $i \in N$, c_i is increasing and lower-semi-continuous.

Note that unlike to the conditions in Theorem 6.18, the project utility function is allowed to be non monotonic and the production cost functions are not necessarily differentiable. Allowing for non monotonic project utility functions accommodates to model congestive resources. Condition (U2) and (U3) hold true for any project utility function $u(x) = \bar{u}(x)x$ such that $\bar{u}(x)$ is a decreasing, twice differentiable, concave function on $[0, b^*)$ and $\bar{u}(x) = 0$, for $x \geq b^*$, for some $b^* > 0$. See Figure 6.6 for an

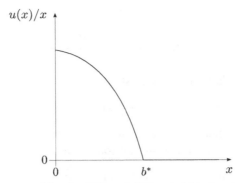

Figure 6.6. A sufficient condition for (U2) and (U3) to hold is that there exists $b^* > 0$ such that $u(x)/x$ is strictly decreasing, twice differentiable, and concave on $[0, b^*)$ and $u(x) = 0$ for $x \geq x^*$.

illustration. Under condition (U2), condition (U3) is equivalent to saying that for each player the marginal utility is non-increasing in the investment of any other player, i.e.

$$\frac{\partial^2}{\partial b_j \partial b_i} \left(\bar{u} \left(\sum_{l \in N} b_l \right) b_i \right) \leq 0, \quad \text{for all } i, j \in N \text{ such that } i \neq j.$$

This can be interpreted as a condition under which effort investments of players are substitutes. Conditions (U2) and (U3) can be interpreted in terms of the project utility function $u(x) = \bar{u}(x)x$ as follows. First part of condition (U2) means that $u(x) - u'(x)x > 0$, for $0 \leq x < b^*$. A sufficient condition is that u is strictly concave on $[0, b^*]$. Condition (U3) is equivalent to saying that $(u(x) - u'(x)x)/x$ is increasing, i.e. $u(x) - u'(x)x + u''(x)x^2 \leq 0$. Under conditions (U2) and (U3), the project utility function is necessarily strictly concave. Condition (C') imposes a weak assumption on the continuity of production cost functions: each production cost function c_i is assumed to be lower-semi-continuous, meaning that for every $x \geq 0$ and $\epsilon > 0$, there exists $\delta > 0$ such that $c_i(x) - c_i(y) < \epsilon$ for every y such that $|x - y| < \delta$. See Section 11.1.6 for a general discussion on semi-continuous correspondences. Notice that every non-decreasing left-continuous function is lower-semi-continuous. See Figure 6.7 for an illustration.

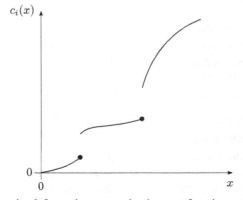

Figure 6.7. Any increasing left-continuous production cost function satisfies condition (C').

Theorem 6.19. *Under conditions (U1), (U2), (U3), and (C'), there exists a pure-strategy Nash equilibrium.*

Proof. The proof is based on a procedure for computing a point that satisfies a necessary and sufficient condition for a pure-strategy Nash equilibrium.

For every player $i \in N$, we denote with $\beta_i(b)$ the set of his or her best responses, given that the total effort of all other players is of value $b \in \mathbf{R}_+$. Note that for every $b \in [0, b^*)$, all the best responses are smaller than $b^* - b$. This is because every response larger than or equal to $b^* - b$ yields a zero utility, while investing any value x in $(0, b^* - b)$ yields a utility of value $\bar{u}(b + x)x > 0$ at a lower or equal production cost. For every player $i \in N$, given that the total effort of all other players is larger than or equal to b^*, his or her payoff is equal to $-c_i(b_i)$. Hence, any value $y \in \mathbf{R}_+$ such that $c_i(y) = \min\{c_i(x) \mid x \in \mathbf{R}_+\}$ is player i's best response; we assume that in this case, player i plays a unique response of value zero.

Formally, for every player $i \in N$, his or her best-response correspondence is defined by

$$\beta_i(b) = \begin{cases} \operatorname{argmax}\{\bar{u}(b + x)x - c_i(x) \mid x \in [0, b^*]\}, & \text{for } b \in [0, b^*) \\ \{0\}, & \text{for } b \geq b^*. \end{cases} \tag{6.53}$$

We denote with $\tilde{\beta}_i(b)$ the set of player i's best responses, given that the total effort of all players is equal to $b \in \mathbf{R}_+$, which is given by

$$\tilde{\beta}_i(b) = \{y \in \mathbf{R}_+ \mid y \in \beta_i(b - y)\}.$$

A vector $\mathbf{b} \in \mathbf{R}_+^n$ is a pure-strategy Nash equilibrium if, and only if,

$$b_i \in \tilde{\beta}_i\left(\sum_{j \in N} b_j\right) \text{ for all } i \in N. \tag{6.54}$$

We shall describe a procedure for finding a pure-strategy Nash equilibrium that computes a mapping $x \to \mathbf{b}(x)$ from $\mathbf{R}_+$ to $\mathbf{R}_+^n$ such that $b_i(x) \in \tilde{\beta}_i(x)$, for every $i \in N$, and finds a value $b \in \mathbf{R}_+$ such that $b = \sum_{i \in N} b_i(b)$. Hence, by (6.54), $\mathbf{b}(b)$ is a pure-strategy Nash equilibrium.

For every player $i \in N$, we also define the following two correspondences:

$$\beta_i^*(b) = [\min \beta_i(b), \max \beta_i(b)]$$

and

$$\tilde{\beta}_i^*(b) = \{y \in \mathbf{R}_+ \mid y \in \beta_i^*(b - y)\}.$$

We note some of the properties of the best-response correspondences. From (U2), (U3), and (6.53), it follows that for every player $i \in N$, β_i is a decreasing correspondence, i.e.,

$$\min \beta_i(b) \geq \max \beta_i(b'), \text{ if } 0 \leq b \leq b'.$$

Note that a downward jump in β_i corresponds to a 45-degree line jump for $\tilde{\beta}_i$, and that $\tilde{\beta}_i^*$ is identical to $\tilde{\beta}_i$ except for filling in any 45-degree line jump in $\tilde{\beta}_i$ with a straight

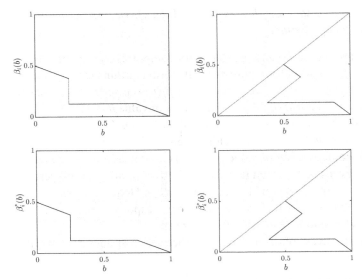

Figure 6.8. An example of best-response correspondences for a player i for the case of a project utility function $u(x) = x(1 - x)\mathbf{1}(x \in [0, 1])$ and production cost function $c_i(x) = (x/16)\mathbf{1}(x > 1/8)$.

line segment in the graph of $\tilde{\beta}_i$. Notice also that $\tilde{\beta}_i(b^*) = \tilde{\beta}_i^*(b^*) = \{0\}$. See Figure 6.8 for an example.

For every player $i \in N$, we denote with $(x_i(t), y_i(t))$, for $t \in [0, 1]$, the graph of the correspondence $\tilde{\beta}_i^*$. Note that

(i) $(x_i(0), y_i(0)) = (b^*, 0)$,
(ii) $y_i(t) \in \tilde{\beta}_i^*(x_i(t))$, for $t \in [0, 1]$,
(iii) $y_i(t)$ is increasing in t, and
(iv) $(x_i(1), y_i(1)) = (\max \beta_i(0), \max \beta_i(0))$.

Let T_i be the set of points (x_i, y_i) in the graph of $\tilde{\beta}_i^*$ at which the number of elements in $\tilde{\beta}_i$ decreases as x increases; for instance, in the example shown in Figure 6.8, there is one such point. Let $T = \cup_{i \in N} T_i$. Let X be the set that contains every value x such that $(x, y) \in T$ for some y. By convention, we define $X = \{x_1, x_2, \ldots, x_k\}$ such that $x_k < x_{k-1} < \cdots < x_1$, and also define $x_{k+1} = 0$ and $x_0 = b^*$.

We next describe a procedure that defines a mapping $x \to \mathbf{b}(x)$ starting from value $x = b^*$ and then for decreasing values of x until a point b is reached such that $\mathbf{b}(b)$ satisfies $b = \sum_{i \in N} \tilde{\beta}_i(b)$, which is a necessary and sufficient condition for a pure-strategy Nash equilibrium. This procedure terminates as soon as it finds an equilibrium, and is described as follows.

Initially, for $x = b^*$, we have that $\tilde{\beta}_i(b^*) = \{0\}$, and thus $b_i(b^*) = 0$, for every $i \in N$. Hence, $b^* - \sum_{i \in N} b_i(b^*) > 0$, which implies that $\mathbf{b}(b^*)$ is not an equilibrium. Suppose that the procedure was run for $x \in [x_{j-1}, b^*]$ and it was not terminated. We then describe the procedure for $x \in [x_j, x_{j-1})$. At $x = x_{j-1}$, we have $x_{j-1} - \sum_{i \in N} b_i(x_{j-1}) > 0$, because otherwise, the procedure would have already terminated. For $x \in (x_j, x_{j-1}]$, we define $\mathbf{b}(x)$ progressively for decreasing values of x starting from $x = x_{j-1}$ subject to the constraint that for every $i \in N$, $b_i(x) \in \tilde{\beta}_i(x)$ and that $b_i(x)$ is a continuous and

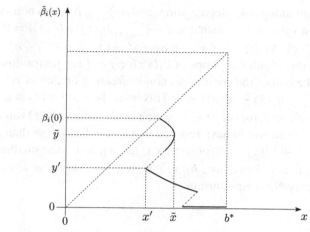

Figure 6.9. (x', y') is a point at which the process for constructing $b_i(x)$ cannot be continued.

decreasing function on $(x_j, x_{j-1}]$. If, for some $x \in (x_j, x_{j-1}]$, $x - \sum_{i \in N} b_i(x) = 0$, then $\mathbf{b}(x)$ is an equilibrium and the procedure terminates. Otherwise, the procedure is continued as follows. For $x = x_j$, we add discontinuities in $\mathbf{b}(x)$ as follows. For every player $i \in N$, let $a_i = \lim_{x \downarrow x_j} b_i(x)$. Let $I_j = \{i_1, i_2, \ldots, i_m\}$ denote the set of players that contains every player $i \in N$ such that $(x_j, y) \in T_i$ for some value y; by convention, we assume that $i_1 < i_2 < \cdots < i_m$. The elements of the vector $\mathbf{b}(x_j)$ are defined as follows. For every player $i \in N \setminus I_j$, we let $b_i(x_j) = a_i$. For other players, we do as follows. Let us define $A_0 = \emptyset$ and $A_l = \{i_1, i_2, \ldots, i_l\}$, for $l \in \{1, 2, \ldots, m\}$. We perform the following iterations for $l = 1, 2, \ldots, m$,

$$
b_{i_l}(x_j) = \max \left\{ y \mid y = a_{i_l} \text{ or both } (x_j, y) \in T_{i_l} \text{ and} \right.
$$

$$
\left. a_{i_l} \leq y \leq x_j - \sum_{i \in (N \setminus I_j) \cup A_{l-1}} b_j(x_j) - \sum_{i \in I_j \setminus A_l} a_j \right\}.
$$

If $x_j - \sum_{i \in (N \setminus I_j) \cup A_{l-1}} b_j(x_j) - \sum_{i \in I_j \setminus A_l} a_j = 0$, then $\mathbf{b}(x_j)$ is an equilibrium and the procedure terminates.

The procedure just described is run until an equilibrium is reached or a point x' is reached at which the procedure cannot be continued. The procedure cannot be continued at a point x', if for some player $i \in N$, $b_i(x)$ cannot be defined for $x < x'$ such that $b_i(x) \in \tilde{\beta}_i(x)$ and $b_i(x)$ is a continuous and decreasing function. Such a point can be reached only if some player $i \in N$ has a branch of the correspondence $\tilde{\beta}_i(x)$ that is increasing in x; see Figure 6.9 for an example. If a point x' is reached at which the procedure cannot be continued, the following steps are performed. Suppose that player $i \in N$ is a player for whom the process of decreasing x from value x' cannot be continued. For player i, we define a new response $b_i^*(x)$ for $x \geq x'$ that is continuous, non-decreasing, and such that $b_i^*(x) \in \tilde{\beta}_i^*(x)$. Notice that $x - (\sum_{j \neq i} b_j(x) + b_i^*(x))$ cannot change its sign along a 45-degree jump because it starts with a positive value,

$x - b_i^*(x)$ is constant along a 45-degree jump, and $-\sum_{j \neq i} b_j(x)$ is non-decreasing in x. Thus, the smallest value $x \geq x'$ such that $x - (\sum_{j \neq i} b_j(x) + b_i^*(x)) = 0$ must satisfy $b_i^*(x) \in \tilde{\beta}_i(x) \subseteq \tilde{\beta}_j^*(x)$. At the point x', we have $x' - (\sum_{j \neq i} b_j(x') + b_i^*(x')) > 0$. As x increases from value x', all the jumps of $b_j(x)$ for $j \neq i$ are jumps down and $b_i^*(x)$ is continuous. At the end of the continuous non-decreasing branch of $\tilde{\beta}_i^*$, say at point $\tilde{x}$, we have $\tilde{x} - (\sum_{j \neq i} b_j(\tilde{x}) + b_i^*(\tilde{x})) < 0$. This holds because $\tilde{\beta}_i(x)$ is decreasing on $[x', \tilde{x}]$ and $y' = \tilde{\beta}_i(x') < \tilde{y}$, for $(\tilde{x}, \tilde{y}) \in T_i$, which holds because $b_i(\tilde{x})$ was not assigned value $\tilde{y}$ because doing so would have resulted in a total effort larger than $\tilde{x}$. It follows that $x - (\sum_{j \neq i} b_j(x) + b_i^*(x)) = 0$ for some $x \in [x', \tilde{x}]$, and at the smallest such value x, $b_i(x) \in \tilde{\beta}_i(x) \subseteq \tilde{\beta}_i^*(x)$. Since also $b_j(x) \in \tilde{\beta}_j(x)$, for every $j \neq i$, it follows that $\mathbf{b}(x)$ is a pure-strategy Nash equilibrium.

$\square$

Over-Dissipation of the Total Effort

The tragedy of the commons occurs due to non-cooperative strategic behavior and is often associated with an excessive utilization of resources in comparison with a socially optimum utilization of resources. We are going to show that under a set of assumptions, which accommodates many cases of interest, the total effort in a pure-strategy Nash equilibrium outcome is larger than in a socially optimal outcome, and we demonstrate that this can be excessively large.

We shall use the concept of a left and a right derivative of a function, which for a function $f : \mathbf{R} \to \mathbf{R}$ at a point $x \in \mathbf{R}$, are respectively, denoted by $\partial_- f(x)$ and $\partial_+ f(x)$, and are defined as

$$\partial_- f(x) = \lim_{a \uparrow x} \frac{f(x) - f(a)}{x - a} \text{ and } \partial_+ f(x) = \lim_{a \downarrow x} \frac{f(a) - f(x)}{a - x}.$$

Specifically, we admit the following assumptions:

(i) The utility function u is non-negative, it has left and right derivatives, and is such that $\bar{u}(x) = u(x)/x$ is decreasing, and $\partial_+ u(0) > 0$.

(ii) For every player $i \in N$, his or her production cost function c_i is increasing, continuously differentiable, convex, and such that $c_i(0) = 0$.

(iii) $\bar{u}(\bar{b}) \leq \min_{i \in N} c_i'(0)$, for some $\bar{b} > 0$.

(iv) Function u is concave on any interval on which u is positive.

(v) $\bar{u}(0) > \min_{i \in N} c_i'(0)$.

For condition (i) observe that if the utility function u is continuously differentiable, then saying that $\bar{u}$ is decreasing is equivalent to saying that $u'(x)x \leq u(x)$, for every $x \geq 0$; in particular, this condition holds if the utility function is concave. Under conditions (i) and (ii), condition (iii) ensures the existence of a socially optimum solution $\mathbf{b}^*$ because it implies that $\mathbf{b}^* \in [0, \bar{b}]^n$. Condition (v) covers interesting cases because if this condition does not hold, then no player would have an incentive to invest a positive effort.

We define the social welfare function as the sum of the payoff functions of the players:

$$s(\mathbf{b}) = \bar{u}\left(\sum_{i=1}^n b_i\right) \sum_{i=1}^n b_i - \sum_{i=1}^n c_i(b_i), \text{ for } \mathbf{b} \in \mathbf{R}_+^n.$$

The following theorem establishes conditions for over-dissipation of the total effort in a pure-strategy Nash equilibrium.

Theorem 6.20. *Consider the game with the payoff functions (6.41) under the assumptions (i)-(v) on the utility of the production function and the production cost functions. For every pure-strategy Nash equilibrium vector of efforts* **b** *and every socially optimal vector of efforts* **b***, we have*

$$\sum_{i \in N} b_i > \sum_{i \in N} b_i^*$$

whenever $u(\sum_{i \in N} b_i) \neq u(\sum_{i \in N} a_i)$ *for every socially optimal vector of efforts* **a**.

Proof. Suppose that $\mathbf{b} \in \mathbf{R}_+^n$ is a pure-strategy Nash equilibrium vector of efforts and $\mathbf{b}^* \in \mathbf{R}_+^n$ is a socially optimal vector of efforts, and let us define $b = \sum_{i \in N} b_i$ and $b^* = \sum_{i \in N} b_i^*$. For vector **b**, for every $i \in N$, either of the following two conditions holds:

$$\bar{u}(b) + \partial_- \bar{u}(b) \cdot b_i \geq c_i'(b_i) \text{ and } b_i > 0, \tag{6.55}$$

$$\text{or, } \bar{u}(b) + \partial_+ \bar{u}(b) \cdot b_i \leq c_i'(b_i) \text{ and } b_i = 0. \tag{6.56}$$

On the other hand, for vector $\mathbf{b}^*$, for every $i \in N$, either of the following two conditions holds:

$$\bar{u}(b^*) + \partial_- \bar{u}(b^*) \cdot b^* \geq c_i'(b_i^*) \text{ and } b_i^* > 0, \tag{6.57}$$

$$\text{or, } \bar{u}(b^*) + \partial_+ \bar{u}(b^*) \cdot b^* \leq c_i'(b_i^*) \text{ and } b_i^* = 0. \tag{6.58}$$

We next establish several claims that are used to prove the theorem.

Claim 6.21. Under assumptions (i), (ii), and (v), $\sum_{i \in N} b_i > 0$.

Suppose on the contrary that $\mathbf{b} = (0, 0, \ldots, 0)$ is a pure-strategy Nash equilibrium. Then, under assumption (v), condition (6.56) cannot hold true, which contradicts the assumption that having all the players investing zero effort is a pure-strategy Nash equilibrium.

Claim 6.22. Under assumptions (i), (ii), and (v), $s(\mathbf{b}) \geq 0$.

We need to show that $s(\mathbf{b}) = \bar{u}(b)b - \sum_{i \in N} c_i(b_i) \geq 0$. This follows from the following relations:

$$\bar{u}(b)b = \sum_{i \in N} \bar{u}(b)b_i$$

$$\geq \sum_{i \in N} c_i'(b_i)b_i$$

$$\geq \sum_{i \in N} c_i(b_i)$$

where the first inequality follows from condition (6.55) and the second inequality follows by the assumption that for every player $i \in N$, c_i is an increasing, convex function such that $c_i(0) = 0$.

Claim 6.23. Under assumptions (i), (ii), and (v), $s(\mathbf{b}^*) > 0$.

This claim is established as follows. Let $k \in N$ be a player such that $c_k'(0) \leq c_i'(0)$, for every $i \in N$. By assumption (v), condition (6.55), and the continuity of functions $\bar{u}$ and c_i, for $i \in N$, there exists $\epsilon > 0$ such that $\bar{u}(\epsilon)\epsilon - c_k(\epsilon) > 0$. The proof of the claim follows by noting that

$$s(\mathbf{b}^*) \geq s(\epsilon e_k) = \bar{u}(\epsilon)\epsilon - c_k(\epsilon) > 0$$

where e_k is a n-dimensional vector with the k-th element equal to 1 and other elements equal to zero.

Claim 6.24. Under assumptions (i), (ii), and (v), $\bar{u}(b^*) > 0$.

The last claim is a straightforward implication of Claim 6.23.

Claim 6.25. $b_i < \sum_{j \in N} b_j$, for every $i \in N$.

This claim can be established by contradiction. Suppose that $\mathbf{b}$ is such that only one player invests a strictly positive effort. Then, the social optimality conditions coincide with those of the pure-strategy Nash equilibrium. In this case, $\mathbf{b}$ maximizes the social welfare, which is in contradiction to the assumption that $u(b) \neq u(b^*)$.

We now complete the proof of the theorem. In the case that $\mathbf{b}$ is such that $\bar{u}(b) = 0$, from Claim 6.24 and the assumption that $\bar{u}$ is decreasing, it follows that $b > b^*$, which establishes the statement of the theorem. In the remainder of the proof we consider the case when $\mathbf{b}$ is such that $\bar{u}(b) > 0$.

We establish that $b > b^*$. Suppose on the contrary that $b \leq b^*$. Since by assumption $u(b) \neq u(b^*)$, we have that $\bar{u}(b) \neq \bar{u}(b^*)$. Combining with the assumption that $\bar{u}$ is decreasing and the assumption $\bar{u}(b) > 0$, we have that $b < b^*$.

For every $i \in N$ such that $b_i^* > 0$, we have

$$c_i'(b_i^*) \leq \partial_- \bar{u}(b^*)b^* + \bar{u}(b^*) \leq \partial_+ \bar{u}(b)b + \bar{u}(b) \leq \partial_+ \bar{u}(b)b_i + \bar{u}(b) \quad (6.59)$$

where the first inequality follows from (6.57); the second inequality follows from $b < b^*$, $\bar{u}(b^*) < \bar{u}(b)$, and assumption (iv); and the last inequality follows from $\partial_+ \bar{u}(b) \leq 0$ and Claim 6.25. Note that all the equalities in (6.59) cannot hold simultaneously. If $\partial_+ \bar{u}(b) < 0$ then the last inequality in (6.59) is strict. On the other hand, if $\partial_+ \bar{u}(b) = 0$, then the second inequality in (6.59) is strict because $\bar{u}(b) > \bar{u}(\bar{b}^*)$ and $\partial_- \bar{u}(b) \leq 0$. Combining (6.59) with condition (6.55), we obtain

$$c_i'(b_i^*) < \partial_+ \bar{u}(b)b_i + \bar{u}(b) \leq c_i'(b_i).$$

Since by assumption (i), the production cost functions are convex, it follows that $b_i > b_i^*$ for every $i \in N$ such that $b_i^* > 0$, which implies a contradiction to the hypothesis that $b \leq b^*$. $\qquad \square$

The total effort in a pure-strategy Nash equilibrium can be arbitrarily larger than the total effort in a socially optimal outcome, which is shown by the following example.

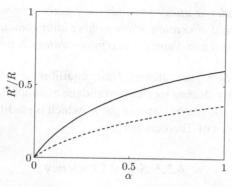

Figure 6.10. The ratio of the total effort in the socially optimal outcome and the total effort in the pure-strategy Nash equilibrium versus the parameter α for the game in Example 6.26. The solid line is for the case of two players, and the dashed line is for the limit of infinitely many players. The ratio can be arbitrarily small by taking the value of the parameter α small enough.

Example 6.26. Consider the example introduced in Section 6.2.2, which validates the assumptions of Theorem 6.20 for the specific choice of the project utility function $u(x) = x^\alpha$, for parameter $0 < \alpha < 1$, and production cost functions $c_i(b_i) = b_i$, for $i \in N$. In Section 6.2.2, we showed that the total efforts in a pure-strategy Nash equilibrium and a socially optimum outcome are given as follows:

$$R = \left(1 - \frac{1 - \alpha}{n}\right)^{\frac{1}{1-\alpha}} \text{ and } R^* = \alpha^{\frac{1}{1-\alpha}}.$$

It is readily observed that $R^* < R$, for every $\alpha \in (0, 1)$, which conforms with the statement of Theorem 6.20. The ratio of the total efforts, R^*/R, increases with α from value 0 for $\alpha = 0$ to value $\exp(-(1 - 1/n))$ for $\alpha = 1$. See Figure 6.10 for an illustration. In the limit as parameter α goes to zero, the socially optimal total effort goes to zero while that in the pure-strategy Nash equilibrium is at least a strictly positive constant. This shows that the total effort in a pure-strategy Nash equilibrium can be an arbitrarily larger factor of the total effort in a socially optimal outcome.

6.5.2 Arbitrary Number of Simultaneous Projects

In this section we consider the general case of one or more simultaneous projects where the utility sharing mechanism is according to proportional allocation and each project utility is a function of the total contribution invested in this project. The payoff functions are given as follows:

$$s_i(\mathbf{b}) = \sum_{j \in M_i} u_j \left(\sum_{l \in N_j} b_l\right) \frac{b_{i,j}}{\sum_{l \in N_j} b_{l,j}} - c_i \left(\sum_{l \in M_i} b_{i,l}\right), \text{ for } i \in N. \quad (6.60)$$

We provide sufficient conditions for existence of a pure-strategy Nash equilibrium in the following theorem.

Theorem 6.27. *Consider a utility maximization game where the utility sharing is according to proportional allocation where project utility functions u_j are increasing, concave, and $u_j(0) = 0$. Then, there exists a pure-strategy Nash equilibrium.*

Proof. The existence of a pure-strategy Nash equilibrium follows by showing that under the assumed utility sharing mechanism and the assumptions on the project utility functions the game is an n-player concave game, which is readily checked by the same arguments as in the proof of Theorem 6.18.   □

6.5.3 Social Efficiency

In this section we derive a bound on the worst-case social efficiency for a utility maximization game of simultaneous projects and then establish its tightness.

Theorem 6.28. *Suppose that each project utility function is an increasing concave function in the total effort invested in the project and is equal to zero in the case of no effort invested in the project. Then, the utility sharing defined by such project utility functions and the proportional sharing of utility satisfies the marginal contribution condition. Hence, in any pure-strategy Nash equilibrium, the social utility is at least $1/2$ of the maximum social utility.*

Proof. This is essentially a corollary of Theorem 6.6 and Corollary 6.11. Since each project allocates shares of utility according to proportional allocation with respect to the efforts invested in this project and the project utility function validates assumptions in Theorem 6.6, we have:

$$b_{i,j} \frac{u_j(b_{N_j})}{b_{N_j}} \geq u_j(b_{N_j}) - u_j(b_{N_j} - b_{i,j}), \quad \text{for all } i \in N \text{ and } j \in M_i$$

where by definition $b_{N_j} = \sum_{l \in N_j} b_{l,j}$. From this, it follows that

$$u_i(\mathbf{b}) = \sum_{j \in M} b_{i,j} \frac{u_j(b_{N_j})}{b_{N_j}} \geq \sum_{j \in M} u_j(b_{N_j}) - u_j(b_{N_j} - b_{i,j}) = u(\mathbf{b}) - u(\mathbf{0}_i, \mathbf{b}_{-i}).$$

The social utility function indeed validates $u(\mathbf{b}) \geq \sum_{i \in N} u_i(\mathbf{b})$ with equality, and it is monotone and with decreasing returns, since it is a sum of functions u_j that are monotone and concave.   □

The efficiency guarantee in Theorem 6.28 stands in sharp contrast to that of proportional allocation in the case of simultaneous projects where each project distributes a fixed value among participants in the project according to proportional allocation, which we studied in Section 5.4. There we found that the social utility in a pure-strategy Nash equilibrium can be arbitrarily small in comparison with the maximum social utility, while with increasing project value functions that validate the assumptions of Theorem 6.28, the social utility in any pure-strategy Nash equilibrium is guaranteed to be at least half of the maximum social utility.

Tight Example We construct an instance that achieves the worst-case social efficiency bound of $1/2$, hence showing the tightness of the result in Theorem 6.28. Consider a system with $n > 1$ players and n projects with proportional value sharing that is defined as follows. Each player is endowed with a budget of effort of value 1 that he or she can split in an arbitrary way over all projects. Project 1 is associated with the project utility function $u_1(x) = 1 - e^{-\alpha x}$ for $\alpha > 0$, and projects 2 through n are associated with identical project utility functions equal to $u_2(x) = q(1 - e^{-\beta x})$ for β and $q > 0$.

We shall identify a sufficient condition under which it is a pure-strategy Nash equilibrium for all players to invest their entire effort budgets in project 1. In this case the payoff for each player is $u_1(n)/n$. Consider a unilateral deviation by an arbitrary player $i \in N$ to an investment of efforts given by $\mathbf{b}_i = (b_{i,1}, b_{i,2}, \dots, b_{i,n}) \in \mathcal{B}_i$. We need to show that such a unilateral deviation cannot provide a larger payoff to player i, i.e.,

$$\frac{1}{n}u_1(n) \geq \frac{b_{i,1}}{n - 1 + b_{i,1}}u_1(n - 1 + b_{i,1}) + \sum_{j=2}^{n}u_2(b_{i,j}), \quad \text{for all } \mathbf{b}_i \in \mathcal{B}_i. \quad (6.61)$$

Suppose that player i invests a portion b of his or her budget to project 1 and the remaining portion of value $1 - b$ to other projects. Since the project utility function u_2 is concave, the payoff of player i is maximized by evenly distributing the portion of the effort budget $1 - b$ over projects 2 through n; hence, condition (6.61) is equivalent to

$$\frac{1}{n}u_1(n) \geq \frac{b}{n - 1 + b}u_1(n - 1 + b) + (n - 1)u_2\left(\frac{1 - b}{n - 1}\right), \quad \text{for all } 0 \leq b \leq 1.$$

Since the equality holds for $b = 1$, it is easy to observe that the inequality holds if, and only if, the derivative of the function defined by the right-hand side of the inequality is positive at $b = 1$.

From this, it follows that a necessary and sufficient condition for (6.61) to hold is

$$\frac{n - 1}{n^2} + \frac{1}{n}(\alpha - 1)e^{-\alpha n} \geq q\beta.$$

This condition means that for any given number of players n and the project utility functions of the admitted form, the product of $q\beta$ needs to be sufficiently small. Indeed, a sufficient condition is that $\alpha \geq 1$ and $(n - 1)/n^2 \geq q\beta$, and in the following we assume that these two conditions hold with equality in the last inequality. The social welfare in the pure-strategy Nash equilibrium is equal to $1 - e^{-\alpha n}$. The maximum social welfare is at least as large as that when each player invests his or her entire effort budget in one project and players make investments in different projects, in which case the social welfare is $1 - e^{-\alpha} + (n - 1)q(1 - e^{-\beta})$. Since $q\beta = (n - 1)/n^2$, the social efficiency is at most the following quantity:

$$\frac{1 - e^{-\alpha n}}{1 - e^{-\alpha} + \left(1 - \frac{1}{n}\right)^2 \frac{1 - e^{-\beta}}{\beta}}. \quad (6.62)$$

From this we observe that as n and α go to infinity, and β goes to zero, the upper bound on the social efficiency in (6.62) goes to $1/2$.

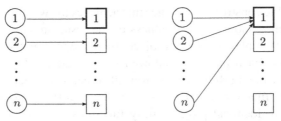

Figure 6.11. (Left) Socially optimal outcome, (right) a Nash equilibrium outcome.

See Figure 6.11 for an illustration. The intuition why in the pure-strategy Nash equilibrium all players invest their entire effort budgets in project 1 is because project 1 guarantees a marginal utility to each player that is at least as large as that in any alternative project. This yields a social welfare of 1 for large α. On the other hand, in the socially optimal outcome, project 1 yields a value of 1 while each other project adds a value of $1/n$, which in total yields an extra value of 1 compared with the pure-strategy Nash equilibrium outcome.

6.6 Contribution Order Allocation

We now consider utility sharing according to a contribution order allocation, which we defined in Section 6.1.3. In particular, we consider utility maximization games with incomplete information that consist of simultaneous projects that share utility according to a contribution order allocation. For the specific choice of a contribution order allocation that awards a share of the utility inversely proportional to the rank of the contribution, we have the following result.

Theorem 6.29. *Consider a utility sharing mechanism according to contribution order allocation where the share allocated to the player with the t-th largest (marginal) contribution is proportional to $1/t$, and each project utility is assumed to be an increasing, concave function of the total contribution. Then, the expected social utility in every Bayes-Nash equilibrium is at least $1/H_k$ of the maximum expected social utility, where H_k is the k-th harmonic number and k is the maximum number of players who can participate in a project.*

Proof. The statement of the theorem follows as a corollary of Theorem 6.8, from which it follows that under given assumptions the game satisfies the H_k-approximate marginal condition and the result in Corollary 6.15.   □

6.7 Equal-Share Allocation

In this section we focus on the equal-share allocation. We study the existence of equilibria and the efficiency under the equal-share utility sharing mechanism. We shall study the solution concept of setwise equilibrium, defined as follows.

A strategy vector $\mathbf{b}$ is a *setwise equilibrium* if for every project $j \in M$ and every non-empty subset of players $S \subseteq N_j$ we have that for every $\mathbf{b}'_S \in \times_{l \in S} \mathcal{B}_l$,

$$u_i(\mathbf{b}) \geq u_i((\mathbf{b}'_S, \mathbf{b}_{-S})) \text{ for some } i \in S.$$

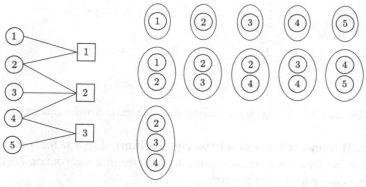

Figure 6.12. All admissible setwise coalitions for the given utility maximization game.

In other words, in a setwise equilibrium there exists no deviation by a coalition of players who all have at least one feasible project in common that is beneficial for every player in the coalition. A setwise equilibrium is resilient to unilateral deviations, so any setwise equilibrium is a pure-strategy Nash equilibrium, but the converse is in general not true. A setwise equilibrium is a weaker solution concept than a strong equilibrium. In a strong equilibrium, a strategy vector is required to be resilient to coalitional deviations for every non-empty subset of players. In a setwise equilibrium, the coalition sets are restricted to subsets of the players who can all participate in at least one common project. See Figure 6.12 for an illustration.

6.7.1 The Existence of Equilibria

We first consider the existence of a pure-strategy Nash equilibrium and then consider the existence of a setwise equilibrium.

Pure-Strategy Nash Equilibrium

Theorem 6.30. *Any utility maximization game of simultaneous projects that deploy equal-share utility sharing mechanism has a pure-strategy Nash equilibrium.*

Proof. The proof follows directly by the fact that the game is a potential game (see Appendix 11.3.2) with the potential function given by

$$\Phi(\mathbf{b}) = \sum_{j \in M} u_j(\mathbf{b}_{N_j}), \quad \text{for } \mathbf{b} \in \mathcal{B}.$$

□

Setwise Equilibrium

We first show a negative result that for the class of project utility functions of coordinate-wise increasing and convex functions, a setwise equilibrium is not guaranteed to exist. We then present a positive result showing that a narrower class of project utility functions that satisfy the additional condition of being equal to zero if the effort investment of at least one player from the set of players associated with this project is equal to zero, there exists a setwise equilibrium.

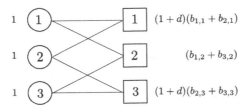

Figure 6.13. A utility maximization game that has no setwise equilibrium.

Theorem 6.31 (non-existence of setwise equilibrium). *Suppose that for every project $j \in M$, the utility function u_j is coordinate-wise increasing and convex. Then, a setwise equilibrium is not guaranteed to exist.*

Proof. The claim is established by showing non-existence of a setwise equilibrium for a simple instance shown in Figure 6.13. In this instance, there are three players each endowed with a unit budget and three projects. The feasible projects for the players are $M_1 = \{1, 2\}$ for player 1, $M_2 = \{1, 3\}$ for player 2, and $M_3 = \{2, 3\}$ for player 3. The project utility functions are linear functions of the total contributions given as follows:

$$u_1(\mathbf{b}) = (1 + d)(b_{1,1} + b_{2,1}), \; u_2(\mathbf{b}) = b_{1,2} + b_{3,2} \text{ and } u_3(\mathbf{b}) = (1 + d)(b_{2,3} + b_{3,3})$$

for a parameter $0 < d < 1$.

A setwise equilibrium must not have a beneficial unilateral deviation. For players 1 and 3 investing their entire effort budgets in projects 1 and 3, respectively, are dominant strategies. Therefore, any setwise equilibrium $\mathbf{b}$ must satisfy $(b_{1,1}, b_{1,2}) = (1, 0)$, $(b_{3,2}, b_{3,3}) = (0, 1)$, $0 \le b_{2,1} \le 1$, and $b_{2,1} + b_{2,3} = 1$. The payoff functions of players 1 and 3 are

$$s_1(\mathbf{b}) = (1 + d)(1 + b_{2,1}) \text{ and } s_3(\mathbf{b}) = (1 + d)(1 + b_{2,3}).$$

Any setwise equilibrium must not have a bilateral deviation by any pair of players that is beneficial to both players. However, this cannot be the case in the present example. Consider a strategy vector $\mathbf{b}'$ that results from $\mathbf{b}$ by a bilateral deviation of players 1 and 3 who invest their entire budgets to project 2. Having admitted such a deviation, the payoffs of players 1 and 3 are

$$s_1(\mathbf{b}') = 2 + (1 + d)b_{2,1} \text{ and } s_3(\mathbf{b}') = 2 + (1 + d)b_{2,3}.$$

From this, we observe that $s_1(\mathbf{b}') > s_1(\mathbf{b})$ and $s_3(\mathbf{b}') > s_3(\mathbf{b})$. Hence, the given bilateral deviation is beneficial to both player 1 and player 3, showing that $\mathbf{b}$ is not a setwise equilibrium. □

We next show that for a special class project utility functions, the equal-share utility sharing mechanism guarantees the existence of a setwise equilibrium.

Theorem 6.32 (sufficient conditions for existence of setwise equilibria). *Suppose that for every project $j \in M$, the utility function u_j is coordinate-wise increasing, and convex and such that $u_j(\mathbf{b}_{N_j}) = 0$ whenever $b_{i,j} = 0$ for some $i \in N_j$. Then there exists a setwise equilibrium.*

Proof. We define a strategy vector $\mathbf{b} \in \mathcal{B}$ by a procedure that we describe first, and then we show that $\mathbf{b}$ is a setwise equilibrium.

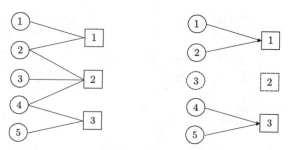

Figure 6.14. An example of a setwise equilibrium: budgets of players are $c_1 \geq c_2 \geq c_3 > c_4 \geq c_5 \geq 0$, and project utility functions are $u_j(\mathbf{b}_{N_j}) = \min_{i \in N_j} b_i$. The left figure shows all possible assignments of players to projects. In the right figure, solid and dashed circles, respectively, denote assigned and unassigned players, and solid and dashed squares, respectively, denote assigned and unassigned projects.

The procedure uses as input the information about the set of feasible projects and the budget of each player, namely M_i and c_i, for $i \in N$, and produces as output a strategy vector $\mathbf{b} \in \mathcal{B}$. The procedure is based on constructing an assignment of players to projects such that each player is assigned to at most one project, and each project is either assigned all the players from its feasible set of players or no players. This assignment is going to be maximal in the sense that each project that is not assigned players has at least one player from its feasible set of players already assigned to a different project. The strategy vector $\mathbf{b}$ is defined by letting each assigned player direct his or her entire budget to the project he or she is assigned to, and letting each unassigned player invest his or her effort budget in an arbitrary way across projects in the set of feasible projects to this player. The investments of the effort in the latter case do not affect any payoff of any player. This is because the assignment is maximal, so for each unassigned player, the set of feasible projects is such that every project in this set has at least one player in its feasible set of players already assigned to a different project. Hence, the utility of any such project is equal to zero.

Specifically, the assignment procedure is defined as follows. Let each project $j \in M$ be associated with value $v_j = u_j(\mathbf{c}_{N_j})$. This is exactly the utility of project j if all players in its feasible set N_j of players invest their entire budgets in project j. Initialize each project and each player to be in the state *unassigned*. Go through the projects in a decreasing order of values $u_j(\mathbf{c}_{N_j})$; for each project j inspected in this order, if none of the players from its feasible set N_j have already been assigned to it, (i) declare project j and all players in its feasible set N_j of players as *assigned*, and (ii) assign each player $i \in N_j$ to project j. The result of this procedure is an assignment of players that satisfies the aforementioned properties. See Figure 6.14 for an example.

We now show that any strategy vector $\mathbf{b}$ defined by this procedure is a setwise equilibrium. We need to show that for every project $l \in M$ the following condition holds: for every subset of players $S \subseteq N_l$, there exists no coalitional deviation that is beneficial for every player in this coalition. Let us first consider a unilateral deviation by a player $i \in N$. It suffices to consider only a player who is assigned to a project according to the assignment procedure, because otherwise, the payoff of the player is equal to zero no matter what deviation is deployed. Suppose that the player i is assigned to project j. The unilateral deviation consists of player i reallocating an amount of effort $x \in (0, c_i]$ from investing in project j to investing in some subset of projects

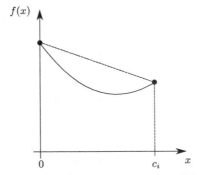

Figure 6.15. f convex and $f(0) \geq f(c_i) \Rightarrow f(x) \leq f(0)$, for every $x \in [0, c_i]$.

in $M_i \setminus \{j\}$. Since project utility functions are assumed to be coordinate-convex it is always a best response for player i to direct the entire amount of x to some project $j' \in M_i \setminus \{j\}$. Such a deviation is beneficial to player i only if

$$u_j(c_i - x, \mathbf{c}_{N_j \setminus \{i\}}) + u_{j'}(x, \mathbf{c}_{N_{j'} \setminus \{i\}}) > u_j(c_i, \mathbf{c}_{N_j \setminus \{i\}}) + u_{j'}(0, \mathbf{c}_{N_{j'} \setminus \{i\}}). \quad (6.63)$$

We note that

$$u_j(\mathbf{c}_{N_j}) \geq u_{j'}(\mathbf{c}_{N_{j'}}) \quad (6.64)$$

and

$$u_j(0, \mathbf{c}_{N_j \setminus \{i\}}) = u_{j'}(0, \mathbf{c}_{N_{j'} \setminus \{i\}}) = 0 \quad (6.65)$$

where (6.64) follows by the fact that project j' is unassigned by the given assignment procedure, and (6.65) follows by the assumption on the project utility functions.

Now, note that by the assumption that project utility functions are coordinate-wise convex, $f(x) := u_j(c_i - x, \mathbf{c}_{N_j \setminus \{i\}}) + u_{j'}(x, \mathbf{c}_{N_{j'} \setminus \{i\}})$ is a convex function on $[0, c_i]$. Function f is such that $f(0) = u_j(\mathbf{c}_{N_j})$ and $f(c_i) = u_{j'}(\mathbf{c}^{j'})$. Let $\lambda \in [0, 1]$ be such that $x = (1 - \lambda)c_i$. Note the following relations:

$$f(x) = f(\lambda \cdot 0 + (1 - \lambda)c_i)$$
$$\leq \lambda f(0) + (1 - \lambda)f(c_i)$$
$$\leq \max\{f(0), f(c_i)\}$$
$$= f(0)$$

where the first inequality is by the convexity of function f, the second inequality is obvious, and the last equality is by (6.64). See Figure 6.15. We have shown that $f(x) \leq f(0)$; that is,

$$u_j(c_i - x, \mathbf{c}_{N_j \setminus \{i\}}) + u_{j'}(x, \mathbf{c}_{N_j \setminus \{i\}}) \leq u_j(c_i, \mathbf{c}_{N_j \setminus \{i\}}) + u_{j'}(0, \mathbf{c}_{N_{j'} \setminus \{i\}}),$$

which contradicts equation (6.63), thus showing the non-existence of a beneficial unilateral deviation.

Showing that any setwise deviation cannot be beneficial for every player in the coalition follows by the following arguments. Consider an arbitrary non-empty set of players $S \subseteq N_l$, for some $l \in M$, that contains at least one player assigned to a project. Otherwise, if all players in S are unassigned, then each receives a zero payoff no matter how they distribute their efforts, so there exists no beneficial deviation. Let us consider a coalitional deviation by players in S such that each player $i \in S$ who is assigned to a project $j \in M_i$ reallocates an amount of effort $x_i \in (0, c_i]$ to other projects in his or her feasible set, namely $M_i \setminus \{j\}$. If player $i \in S$ is unassigned, then let x_i be equal to his or her effort budget c_i. In other words, we consider a coalitional deviation of players in S to $\mathbf{b}_S = (\mathbf{b}_i, i \in S)$ such that for each player $i \in S$ assigned to project $j \in M_i$, it holds that $\sum_{j' \in M_i \setminus \{j\}} b_{i,j'} = x_i$, and for each player $i \in S$ that is unassigned to a project, it holds that $\sum_{j' \in M_i} b_{i,j'} = c_i$.

Consider an arbitrary player $i \in S$ who is assigned to project $j \in M_i$. For the coalitional deviation $\mathbf{b}_S$ to be beneficial to player i, it must hold that

$$\sum_{k \in M_i \setminus \{j\}} u_k(\mathbf{b}_{S \cap N_k}, \mathbf{c}_{N_k \setminus S}) + u_j(c_i - x_i, \mathbf{c}_{N_j \setminus \{i\}}) > \sum_{k \in M_i \setminus \{j\}} u_k(0, \mathbf{c}_{N_k \setminus \{i\}}) + u_j(\mathbf{c}_{N_j}).$$

$$(6.66)$$

Since project utility functions are assumed to be coordinate-wise convex, for any coalitional deviation $\mathbf{b}_S$ the payoff of player i is at least as large by directing all his or her effort to one of the projects in $M_i \setminus \{j\}$. Let j' denote such a project. The payoff of player $i \in N$ can only increase by assuming that all players in $S \cap N_{j'}$ direct their entire effort budgets to project j'. Combining this with (6.66), observe that it must hold that

$$u_{j'}(x_i, \mathbf{c}_{N_k \setminus \{i\}}) + u_j(c_i - x_i, \mathbf{c}_{N_j \setminus \{i\}}) > u_{j'}(0, \mathbf{c}_{N_{j'} \setminus \{i\}}) + u_j(\mathbf{c}_{N_j}).$$

This is of the same form as (6.63). Since player i was assigned to project j and $j' \in M_i$, we have that project j' was unassigned, so, again, it must hold that $u_j(\mathbf{c}_{N_j}) \geq u_{j'}(\mathbf{c}_{N_{j'}})$. The proof is completed by using the same arguments as for the unilateral deviation. $\quad\square$

6.7.2 Social Efficiency

We first show that a pure-strategy Nash equilibrium can be arbitrarily inefficient and then establish a lower bound for the worst-case social efficiency in a setwise equilibrium.

Inefficiency of Pure-Strategy Nash Equilibrium

Social efficiency under utility sharing according to equal sharing can be arbitrarily low for simple special instances with natural choices for project utility functions. We have already encountered one such instance in Exercise 6.2.4 where each player has the option to either invest his or her budget in a private project or in a public project, and project utility functions were assumed to be linear functions of the total contribution. We now provide another example that shows that the worst-case social efficiency can be arbitrarily low.

Example 6.33. Consider an instance with three projects and four players as illustrated in Figure 6.16. The players are endowed with unit effort budgets. The projects available to them are $M_1 = \{1\}$ for player 1, $M_2 = \{1, 2\}$ for player 2, $M_3 = \{2, 3\}$ for player 3, and $M_4 = \{3\}$ for player 4. The project utility functions are given as $u_1(\mathbf{b}) = u(b_{1,1}, b_{2,1})$, $u_2(\mathbf{b}) = nu(b_{2,2}, b_{3,2})$, and $u_3(\mathbf{b}) = u(b_{3,3}, b_{4,3})$, where $n > 2$ is

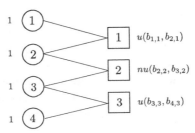

Figure 6.16. An instance of a utility maximization game with the worst-case social efficiency of $2/n$.

a parameter and $u(x, y)$ is any symmetric, coordinate-wise increasing, convex function such that $u(x, 0) = 0$. Special instances include (i) $u(x, y) = \min\{x, y\}$ and (ii) $u(x, y) = x^a y^b$, for $a, b \geq 1$.

The social utility is maximized by players 2 and 3 investing their entire effort budgets in project 2, which yields the maximum social utility of value $nu(1, 1)$. A pure-strategy Nash equilibrium occurs when players 1 and 2 invest their entire budgets in project 1 and players 3 and 4 invest their entire budgets in project 3, which yields the social utility of value $2u(1, 1)$. Therefore, social efficiency is at most $2/n$, which can be made arbitrarily small by taking a large enough value of parameter n.

The social inefficiency is caused by a lack of coordination that is intrinsic to non-cooperative strategic equilibria. If, instead, players 2 and 3 were to cooperate, a bilateral deviation from the given pure-strategy Nash equilibrium of players 2 and 3 to reallocate their entire effort budgets in project 2 would be beneficial to both players and, in the given example, would yield full social efficiency.

Efficiency of Setwise Equilibria

For the class of project utility functions that are coordinate-wise increasing, convex, and equal to zero if no effort is invested in the project, we shall show that an important factor that determines the worst-case social efficiency in a setwise equilibrium is the maximum number of players eligible to participate in a project.

Example 6.34. Consider a utility maximization game that consists of $k + 1$ projects, namely projects $0, 1, \ldots, k$, and k^2 players, namely players $1, 2, \ldots, k^2$. Each player is endowed with a unit budget of effort. Assume that players are partitioned into k equally-sized groups such that each player in the t-th group is eligible to participate in project t, and in each group the player with the smallest identifier can also participate in project 0. See Figure 6.17. Project 0 has a utility function equal to $(1 + \epsilon)$ times the minimum individual effort invested in this project, for parameter $\epsilon > 0$, and each project 1 through k has a utility function equal to the minimum individual effort invested in this project. Formally, this corresponds to the project utility function specified as follows:

$$u_0(\mathbf{b}_{N_0}) = (1 + \epsilon) \min\{b_{i,0} \mid i = 1, k + 1, 2k + 1, \ldots, (k - 1)k + 1\}$$

and

$$u_j(\mathbf{b}_{N_j}) = \min\{b_{i,j} \mid (k - 1)(j - 1) < i \leq kj\}, \quad \text{for } 1 \leq j \leq k.$$

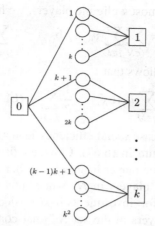

Figure 6.17. An instance of a utility maximization game with social utility in a setwise equilibrium equal to $(1 + \epsilon)/k$ of the optimum social utility.

A setwise equilibrium is for each player eligible to participate in project 0 to invest his or her entire effort budget in this project. This yields a social utility of value $1 + \epsilon$. The optimum social utility is achieved by letting each player invest his or her entire budget in projects other than project 0. This yields a social utility of value k. Thus, the social efficiency of setwise equilibrium, in the given example, is $(1 + \epsilon)/k$.

In the next theorem, we show a worst-case lower bound on the social efficiency of a setwise equilibrium for a class of project utility functions.

Theorem 6.35. *Consider a utility maximization game where each project utility function u_j is coordinate-wise increasing and convex, $u_j(\mathbf{0}_{N_j}) = 0$, and such that each project has at most $k \geq 1$ eligible players. Then, if a setwise equilibrium exists, the social utility in any setwise equilibrium is at least $1/k$ of the optimum social utility. Furthermore, this bound is tight.*

Proof. A strategy vector $\mathbf{b}$ is said to be extremal if it is such that every player invests his or her effort budget in exactly one project, i.e. for every player $i \in N$, $b_{i,j} \in \{0, c_i\}$ for every project $j \in M$ and $\sum_{l \in M} b_{i,l} = c_i$. The social utility function is defined as the sum of project utility functions, each of which is coordinate-wise increasing and convex. The optimization of the social utility function is over a convex separable set, which is such that the only constraint is that every player $i \in N$ splits his or her effort budget of value c_i in an arbitrary way over his or her set of feasible projects. Hence, it follows that there exists an optimal assignment of efforts that is extremal; if, in addition, each project utility function is coordinate-wise strictly convex, then any optimal assignment of efforts is extremal. Suppose that $\mathbf{b}^*$ is an extremal investment of efforts that is optimal with respect to the social utility. Suppose that $\mathbf{b}$ is an investment of efforts that is a setwise equilibrium.

We first claim the following inequality, which we will prove shortly,

$$\sum_{i \in N} s_i(\mathbf{b}) \geq \sum_{j \in M} u_j(\mathbf{b}^*_{N_j}). \tag{6.67}$$

Since each project has at most k eligible players, we have

$$\sum_{i \in N} s_i(\mathbf{b}) = \sum_{i \in N} \sum_{j \in M} v_{i,j} u_j(\mathbf{b}_{N_j}) \leq k \sum_{j \in M} u_j(\mathbf{b}_{N_j}). \tag{6.68}$$

From (6.67) and (6.68), it follows that

$$\sum_{j \in M} u_j(\mathbf{b}_{N_j}) \geq \frac{1}{k} \sum_{j \in M} u_j(\mathbf{b}_{N_j}^*)$$

which establishes the worst-case social efficiency lower bound of $1/k$.

We now establish the claim in (6.67). Consider first an arbitrary project $j \in M$ such that under $\mathbf{b}^*$ at least one player invests his or her entire effort budget in project j. Let N_j^+ be the subset of players in N_j who direct their entire effort budgets in project j according to the effort investments $\mathbf{b}^*$. Consider a coalitional deviation from the strategy vector $\mathbf{b}$ by players in the set N_j^+ that consists of every player $i \in N_j^+$ investing his or her entire effort budget to project j. Since $\mathbf{b}$ is assumed to be a setwise equilibrium, there must exist a player $i \in N_j^+$ such that

$$s_i(\mathbf{b}) \geq s_i(\mathbf{c}_{N_j^+}, \mathbf{b}_{-N_j^+}) \geq u_j(\mathbf{c}_{N_j^+}, \mathbf{b}_{-N_j^+}) \geq u_j(\mathbf{c}_{N_j^+}, \mathbf{0}_{-N_j^+}) = u_j(\mathbf{b}^*).$$

Let d_j denote one such player, and refer to this player as designated player for project j. Note that every player can be designated player for at most one project. Consider now a project $j \in M$ such that N_j^+ is empty. Then, it obviously holds that $s_i(\mathbf{b}) \geq u_j(\mathbf{b}_{N_j}^*) = 0$, for every player $i \in N_j$. It follows that

$$\sum_{i \in N} s_i(\mathbf{b}) \geq \sum_{i \in N} s_i(\mathbf{b}) \sum_{j \in M} \mathbf{1}(d_j = i)$$

$$\geq \sum_{i \in N} \sum_{j \in M} u_j(\mathbf{b}_{N_j}^*) \mathbf{1}(d_j = i)$$

$$= \sum_{j \in M} u_j(\mathbf{b}_{N_j}^*)$$

which establishes the claim asserted in (6.67).

The tightness claim follows by Example 6.34.

□

Summary

Utility Maximization Game A set of players $N = \{1, 2, \ldots, n\}$ with strategy vectors $\mathbf{b} = (b_1, b_2, \ldots, b_n)$ in the set of strategies $\mathcal{B} = \mathcal{B}_1 \times \mathcal{B}_2 \times \cdots \times \mathcal{B}_n$ and the payoff functions $u_i : \mathcal{B} \to \mathbf{R}$, for $i \in N$. A social utility function $u : \mathcal{B} \to \mathbf{R}$ is given such that $u(\mathbf{b}) \geq \sum_{i \in N} u_i(\mathbf{b})$, for every $\mathbf{b} \in \mathcal{B}$.

Simultaneous Projects A set of projects $M = \{1, 2, \ldots, m\}$ where each project is associated with a utility function of the effort investments in this project.

Local Utility Sharing Mechanisms Each project allocates shares of its utility of production to the contributors to this project, which are allowed to depend only on the production outputs directed to this project.

Monotone Game A utility maximization game is said to be *monotone* if for every investment of efforts, the social utility function is at least as large as when any given player opts out from participation.

Marginal Contribution Condition A utility maximization game is said to satisfy the *marginal contribution condition* if every player's utility is at least as large as his or her marginal contribution to the social utility. It is said to be an δ-approximate marginal contribution condition if every player's utility is at least factor $1/\delta$ of his or her marginal contribution to the social utility.

If project utility functions are such that production outputs of players are substitutes, then, utility sharing proportional to marginal contribution and proportional to the production output both satisfy the marginal contribution condition. If the utility sharing is inversely proportional to the rank of individual contributions, then the H_k-approximate marginal contribution condition holds, where k is the maximum number of participants in a project.

Efficiency Suppose that individual production outputs of players are substitutes. If the utility sharing mechanisms are such that the δ-approximate marginal contribution condition holds, the social utility in any pure-strategy Nash equilibrium is at least $1/(\delta + 1)$ of the optimum social utility.

The same guarantee holds for any strong Nash equilibrium, whenever one exists.

For the game with incomplete information where each player's production output is a type-specific concave increasing function of his or her effort, and the production cost is a function of the total effort invested by this player that has increasing returns and elasticity of value at least $1 + \mu$, in any Bayes-Nash equilibrium, the expected social utility is at least a factor $\mu/(2\mu + 1)$ of the optimum expected social utility.

If a project utility function is non-monotonic, the social utility in a pure-strategy Nash equilibrium can be $O(1/n)$ of the optimum social utility.

Proportional Allocation For project utility functions that are increasing, concave and are equal to zero for zero total effort investment, the game is a concave game and thus it has a pure-strategy Nash equilibrium. Under the same conditions, the game is a monotone valid utility game with utility functions that satisfy the decreasing returns property; thus, the social utility in any pure-strategy Nash equilibrium is at least $1/2$ of the optimum social utility. There exist examples for which the social efficiency can be arbitrarily close to $1/2$.

Equal-Share Allocation The game is a potential game with ordinal potential function $\Phi(\mathbf{b}) = \sum_{j \in M} u_j(\mathbf{b}_{N_j})$; hence, it has a pure-strategy Nash equilibrium. A setwise equilibrium is a strategy vector under which there exists no coalitional deviation of a subset of players who all participate in a common project that is beneficial to all members of the coalition. If project utility functions are coordinate-wise increasing and convex, then a setwise equilibrium is not guaranteed to exist. If, in addition, each project utility function is such that it is equal to zero whenever at least one participant invests no effort in this project, then there exists a setwise equilibrium. For project utility functions that are coordinate-wise increasing, convex, and have zero value for total effort investment of zero, the social efficiency of any setwise equilibrium is at least $1/k$, where k is the maximum number of participants in a project.

Exercises

6.1 **Degree of substitutability** Prove that the families of functions given in the catalog in Section 6.1.2 have the degree of substitutability as asserted therein.

6.2 **Degree of substitutability and skill types** Suppose a set of players $N = \{1, 2, \ldots, n\}$ and a set of skills $S = \{1, 2, \ldots, k\}$ are given such that each player possess one skill from S. Let N_s denote the subset of players of skill $s \in S$. Consider a utility of production function $u : \mathbf{R}_+^n \to \mathbf{R}$ that satisfies the decreasing marginal returns property skill-wise, meaning that for every skill $s \in S$, $u(\mathbf{b}_{N_s}, \mathbf{b}_{-N_s})$ satisfies the decreasing marginal returns property in $\mathbf{b}_{N_s}$ for every fixed $\mathbf{b}_{-N_s}$. Prove the following claims.

- The utility of production $u(\mathbf{b}) = \prod_{s \in S} u_s(\mathbf{b}_{N_s})$ satisfies the decreasing marginal returns property skill-wise, provided that each $u_s(\mathbf{b}_{N_s})$ satisfies the decreasing marginal returns property.
- Any utility of production function that satisfies the decreasing marginal property skill-wise has the degree of substitutability of value at most $|S|$.

6.3 **Degree of substitutability and marginal contribution** Suppose that utility sharing is proportional to marginal contribution and that the utility of production has the degree of substitutability of value δ. Prove that the δ-approximate marginal contribution condition holds.

6.4 **Worst-case social efficiency of local utility sharing mechanisms** Construct an instance of a utility maximization game to show that, without admitting any assumptions on the choice of the utility of production functions, there exists no local utility sharing mechanism that can guarantee a social utility of value larger than $1/k$ of the maximum social utility in a (strong) Nash equilibrium, where k is the maximum number of participants in a project.

6.5 **Efficiency and marginal contribution** Consider a utility maximization game that consists of simultaneous projects $M = \{1, 2, \ldots, m\}$, each with a utility of production function that satisfies the decreasing marginal returns property, and any local utility sharing mechanism that satisfies the δ-approximate marginal contribution condition. Suppose that the payoff functions of the players are given by

$$s_i(\mathbf{b}) = \sum_{j \in M} v_{i,j} u_j(\mathbf{b}_{N_j}) x_{i,j}(\mathbf{b}_{N_j}), \quad \text{for } i \in N$$

where $v_{i,j}$ are positive-valued valuation parameters such that there exist constants $0 < A \le B < \infty$ such that $v_{i,j} \in [A, B]$ whenever $v_{i,j} > 0$.

Prove that the social welfare, defined as the sum of the payoffs of players, in every pure-strategy Nash equilibrium is at least $(A/B)/(\delta + 1)$ of the optimal social welfare.

6.6 **El Farol bar problem** Consider a population of $n \geq 2$ people. Every Thursday night, each of these people wants to go to the El Farol bar. It is not fun to be in the bar if it is too crowded. If at most m people go to the bar, then they will have better time than if they stayed at home; otherwise, they will have a worse time. Specifically, assume that each individual i (whom we refer to as a player) receives a payoff of value $v_i \in (0, 1)$ if he or she decides to stay at home, a payoff of 1 if he or she decides to go to the bar and there are at most m people who came to the bar, and otherwise a payoff of value 0. Prove the following claims.

    (a) Every outcome in which an arbitrary subset of m players goes the bar and other players stay at home is a pure-strategy Nash equilibrium, and these are the only pure-strategy Nash equilibria. The social efficiency of every pure-strategy Nash equilibrium is at least

$$\max\left\{\frac{1}{2}, \frac{m}{n}\right\}$$

which can be achieved for some instances. For the special case $v_1 = v_2 = \cdots = v_n$, every pure-strategy Nash equilibrium has full social efficiency.

    (b) Suppose that $v_1 = v_2 = \cdots = v_n, 0 < m < n$, and that every player plays a mixed strategy. Then, there is a unique mixed-strategy Nash equilibrium, which is such that each given player goes to the bar with probability p and otherwise stays at home, where p is the unique solution to the equation

$$v_1 = \sum_{k=0}^{m-1} \binom{n-1}{k} p^k (1-p)^{n-1-k}.$$

The expected social welfare in the mixed-strategy Nash equilibrium can be an arbitrarily small fraction of the optimum social welfare.

    (c) Suppose that $v_1 = v_2 = \cdots = v_n$ and $0 < m < n$. Then the following properties hold in every Nash equilibrium. Either every player plays a pure strategy, or at least two players play a mixed strategy. In the latter case, at most $m - 1$ players play the pure strategy of going to the bar, and players who play mixed strategies play symmetric mixed strategies.

    (d) Suppose that the valuation parameters $v_1, v_2, \ldots, v_n$ are private information, independent and identically distributed according to a prior distribution F that has density on $[0, 1]$. A symmetric pure-strategy Bayes-Nash equilibrium is for every player $i \in N$ to go to the bar if $v_i < v^*$, and otherwise stay at home, where v^* is the unique solution to the equation

$$v^* = \sum_{k=0}^{m-1} \binom{n-1}{k} F(v^*)^k (1 - F(v^*))^{n-1-k}.$$

The expected social welfare in the symmetric pure-strategy Bayes-Nash equilibrium is

$$n\left(1 - \int_{v^*}^{1} F(x)dx\right).$$

On the other hand, the optimum expected social welfare is

$$\mathbf{E}[v_{(n,1)}] + \mathbf{E}[v_{(n,2)}] + \cdots + \mathbf{E}[v_{(n,n-m)}] + m.$$

6.7 **Cournot oligopoly** Consider an oligopoly system that consists of $n \geq 2$ producers of a good that is sold at a market price of value $\bar{u}(\sum_{i=1}^{n} b_i)$ per unit good given the amounts of

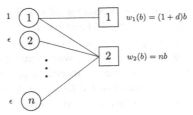

Figure 6.18. An example with a low and a high marginal value project.

production $\mathbf{b} = (b_1, b_2, \ldots, b_n)$. Suppose that $\bar{u}(x) = \max\{a - dx, 0\}$ for $a, d > 0$, and that each producer incurs a production cost of value c per unit good, where $c \in (0, a)$. Prove the following claims.

(a) There exists a unique pure-strategy Nash equilibrium $\mathbf{b} = (b_1, b_2, \ldots, b_n)$, which is given by

$$b_1 = b_2 = \cdots = b_n = \frac{a - c}{d} \frac{1}{n + 1}.$$

(b) The total payoff of players in the pure-strategy Nash equilibrium and the optimum total payoff of players are of respective values

$$\frac{(a - c)^2}{d} \frac{n}{(n + 1)^2} \quad \text{and} \quad \frac{(a - c)^2}{4d}.$$

Hence, the efficiency of the pure-strategy Nash equilibrium with respect to the total payoff is

$$\frac{4}{n}, \quad \text{for large } n.$$

(c) The utility of production in the pure-strategy Nash equilibrium and the optimum utility of production are of respective values

$$\frac{a - c}{d} \frac{a + cn}{(n + 1)^2} \quad \text{and} \quad \frac{a^2}{4d}.$$

Hence, the efficiency of the pure-strategy Nash equilibrium with respect to the utility of production is

$$\frac{c}{a}\left(1 - \frac{c}{a}\right)\frac{1}{n}, \quad \text{for large } n.$$

6.8 **Proportional allocation and linear utility of production** Consider the utility sharing game of two or more projects and players endowed with effort budgets in which all project utilities are linear functions in the total contribution. Prove that the utility of production in every pure-strategy Nash equilibrium is fully efficient.

6.9 **Equal-share allocation** Consider the utility maximization game with players endowed with effort budgets, utility sharing according to equal-share allocation, and utilities of production that are linear functions of the total contribution, as given in Figure 6.18. Identify conditions for the values of the parameters of the game under which the social efficiency of production in any pure-strategy Nash equilibrium is $O(1/n)$ of the optimum value.

6.10 **A paradox of power** Consider the game with a set $N = \{1, 2, \ldots, n\}$ of two more players endowed with effort budgets $c_1 \geq c_2 \geq \cdots \geq c_n > 0$. Suppose that the players can split their efforts between two types of activities: a production activity that results in a utility of production and a competition activity that determines the shares of the utility of production received by the players. Suppose that the utility of production is a function of the total effort invested in the production activity $u : \mathbf{R}_+ \to \mathbf{R}$ and that the shares of the utility of production are proportional to the efforts invested in the competition activity. Assume that $u(x)$ is an increasing, continuously differentiable function such that $u(0) = 0$ and that $u'(x)/u(x)$ is a decreasing function. Prove the following claims.

- There exists an instance of the game for which the following "strong paradox of power" holds: two players whose effort budgets have different values receive the same payoffs in a pure-strategy Nash equilibrium.
- There exists an instance of the game for which the following "weak paradox of power" holds: two players with the ratio $x > 1$ of their respective effort budgets receive respective payoffs whose ratio is smaller than x in a pure-strategy Nash equilibrium.
- A vector $\mathbf{b} = (b_1, b_2, \ldots, b_n)$ of efforts invested in the competition activity is a pure-strategy Nash equilibrium if the following conditions hold: b_1 is the largest positive value such that $b_1 \leq c_1$ and

$$\frac{u'\left(\sum_{i \in N}(c_i - b_1)^+\right)}{u\left(\sum_{i \in N}(c_i - b_1)^+\right)} b_1 \leq 1 - \frac{b_1}{\sum_{i \in N} c_i - \sum_{i \in N}(c_i - b_1)^+}$$

where $(x)^+ = \max\{x, 0\}$, and

$$b_i = \min\{b_1, c_i\}, \quad \text{for } i = 2, 3, \ldots, n.$$

6.8 Bibliographical Notes

Strategic games where the utility is shared among players according to a utility sharing mechanism have been studied in various contexts, including combinatorial auctions, e.g., Lehmann et al. (2001); market sharing games, e.g., Goemans et al. (2004); allocation of credit for scientific contributions, e.g., Kleinberg and Oren (2011); contribution games in social networks, e.g., Anshelevich and Hoefer (2012); and online collaboration services, e.g., Bachrach et al. (2013), Ghosh and Hummel (2012), and Ghosh and Kleinberg (2013). Some related studies are also found in the theory of contests where the reward of a contest is a function of invested efforts, e.g., Cohen et al. (2008). Utility sharing games studied in this chapter are closely related to the large body of literature on Cournot oligopolies, surplus sharing games, public goods, and congestion games, some of which we review later in this section. The issue of welfare efficiency has been one of the most central questions in economics, e.g., Pigou (1932), especially in systems where agents have alternative options, which creates externalities.

The concept of monotone valid utility games was originally introduced by Vetta (2002) for discrete strategy sets and submodular utility functions; this work established the bound on the price of anarchy of 2 for the class of monotone valid utility games with submodular utility functions. This framework was leveraged by several authors, e.g., Lehmann et al. (2001), Goemans et al. (2004), Kleinberg and Oren (2011), to derive the price of anarchy bounds for specific instances of monotone valid utility games. The framework of monotone valid utility games was extended to continuous strategies by Bachrach et al. (2013), who established the results relating the efficiency and the marginal contribution condition in Section 6.4 to the analysis of utility sharing according to proportional allocation in the case of one or more simultaneous projects in Section 6.5.2. The framework of smooth games and deriving the price of anarchy bounds using this framework was developed by Roughgarden (2009). In particular, it was shown therein that every monotone valid utility game is $(1, 1)$-smooth. The concept of universal smoothness was developed independently by Roughgarden (2012) and Syrgkanis (2012) for deriving the price of anarchy bounds for games with incomplete information. The efficiency bounds by using the universal smoothness in Section 6.4.2 are from Bachrach et al. (2013). The concept of coalitional smoothness was introduced by Bachrach et al. (2014) to derive bounds on the strong price of anarchy, along with other results such as identifying sufficient conditions for coalitional smoothness.

Specific families of utility of production functions have been studied in different contexts. The Cobb-Douglas utility of production function was introduced by Cobb and Douglas (1928) in the context of production in manufacturing to model the relationship between the inputs of capital and labor and the output volume of produced goods. Constant elasticity of substitution utility of production functions were introduced by Solow (1956) and later popularized by Arrow et al. (1961). An instance of this family of production functions was, for instance, studied by Hirshleifer (1991) in the context of competitive situations where players strategically split their effort budgets between productive and competitive activities. Exercise 6.10 is based on Hirshleifer (1991). In the context of public goods, Hirshleifer (1983) studied three different types of utility of production functions: the sum, minimum (weakest link), and maximum (best-shot) contribution. It was shown that under-provision of the public good tends to be considerately moderated under the weakest link function, and on the contrary, can be aggravated when the best-shot function is applicable. The minimum contribution utility of production function was studied in the context of *the minimum effort coordination games*, e.g., Huyck et al. (1990) and Anderson et al. (2001), and contribution games on graphs, e.g., Anshelevich and Hoefer (2012). Particular utility sharing mechanisms that are discussed in this chapter are from various sources: equal-share and proportional share allocation have been studied by many, e.g., see the references cited later for the work on surplus sharing and Cournot Oligopoly games; the marginal contribution allocation is motivated by the marginal contribution condition in the context of monotone valid utility games introduced by Vetta (2002); and the Shapley-Shubik allocation is from Shapley (1953) and Shubik (1962).

Proportional share allocation has been studied extensively in the context of surplus sharing games starting as early as in the work on oligopoly markets by Cournot (1897), which in our context corresponds to the case of a single project. The existence and uniqueness of a pure-strategy Nash equilibrium were studied by several authors under various assumptions, e.g., McManus (1962, 1964), Frank and Quandt (1963), Friedman (1977), Szidarovszky and Yakowitz (1977), Gabay and Moulin (1980), Murphy et al. (1982), Novshek (1984, 1985), Gaudet and Salant (1991), Watts (1996), Amir (1996), and Van Long and Soubeyran (2000). Debreu (1952) established the equilibrium's existence for a broader set of models. A textbook coverage of the topic includes Friedman (1983). McManus (1962, 1964) established the existence of a pure-strategy Nash equilibrium for the case of inverse demand functions that are decreasing, upper-semi-continuous, with bounded profit function, and symmetric production costs that are continuous increasing, and convex. Szidarovszky and Yakowitz (1977) established the existence of a pure-strategy Nash equilibrium for the case of inverse demand functions that are decreasing, twice continuously differentiable, and concave on the interval where they have a positive value, and for production costs that are increasing, twice continuously differentiable, and convex. The existence and uniqueness result in Theorem 6.18 is based on Watts (1996). Note that the conditions on the inverse demand function in Szidarovszky and Yakowitz (1977) imply those in Watts (1996). The necessary condition for existence in Theorem 6.19 is from Novshek (1985). The axiomatic approach for cost and surplus sharing games was studied by Friedman and Moulin (1999), Moulin (2002), and Friedman (2004). Social welfare losses under Cournot competition were studied by Corchón (2008) for aggregate welfare that includes the profits of firms and that of a representative consumer for particular families of inverse demand functions. Anderson and Renault (2003) quantified the efficiency loss in Cournot oligopoly models with concave demand functions. Amir (1996) showed that the log-concavity of inverse demand functions guarantees the existence of a Cournot equilibrium. The efficiency loss in Cournot games with convex demand functions was studied by Tsitsiklis and Xu (2012); they showed that for any production costs that are convex, increasing, continuously differentiable, and zero for zero investment, there exists a set of linear production cost functions under which the social efficiency is smaller. The price of anarchy in Cournot oligopolies was also studied by Guo and Yang (2005). Asymptotic efficiency for large markets was studied in Ushio (1985). Tsitsiklis and Xu (2013) derived lower bounds on the efficiency of Cournot games that are parametrized with some quantities of the inverse demand function at the equilibrium and a socially optimal outcome. Exercise 6.7 is about a model originally studied by Cournot (1897) and where the efficiency loss was characterized by Kluberg and Perakis (2012). Immorlica et al. (2010) studied the efficiency under coalitional deviations for the same model.

The term "the tragedy of the commons" was first introduced by Hardin (1968) to refer to situations where certain natural resources are the common property for a society of individuals and where the common property means that each individual has free access to the resources. The "tragedy" is the inefficiency resulting from the over-utilization of the resources when selfish individuals use more than their share of the resources. In particular, Moulin and Watts (1996) studied two versions of the tragedy of the commons: the *average return game* where each agent receives an output share proportional to his or her own contribution and the *average cost games* where each agent demands an amount of output and is charged proportionally to this demand. The El Farol bar problem, discussed in Exercise 6.6, was first formulated by Brian (1994). The over-dissipation of efforts in games where the produced value is shared according to proportional allocation was first established by Moulin and Watts (1996) in the context of average returns games. The over-dissipation of effort was also established by Chung (1996) for the special case of symmetric linear production cost functions and for the case of sharing according to a family of ratio-form contest success functions for a sufficiently large value of the return to scale parameter. More recently, the over-dissipation of effort was established for proportional allocation by Tsitsiklis and Xu (2013) as in Theorem 6.20 under the conditions stated therein.

The study of equal-share allocation in Section 6.7 is based primarily on the results in Anshelevich and Hoefer (2012) and Bachrach et al. (2013). Theorems 6.30, 6.31,

6.32, and 6.35 are from Anshelevich and Hoefer (2012). A related work is that on *network cost sharing* where the cost of each edge is shared equally among the flows that pass through the given edge. Anshelevich et al. (2004) showed that the price of stability for cost-sharing games is $H_n = \Theta(\log n)$ (the ratio of the smallest cost in a pure-strategy Nash equilibrium and the minimum cost), while Epstein et al. (2009) showed that H_n is the strong price of anarchy. Another related work is that on congestion games Rosenthal (1973), which many have studied focusing on the questions of the existence and uniqueness of equilibria, e.g., Bhaskar et al. (2009) and social efficiency, e.g., Cominetti et al. (2009).

The allocation of scientific credit and the division of cognitive labor have been studied across disciplines including psychology and computer science. The Matthew effect in science refers to a rich-get-richer phenomenon where, roughly speaking, two or more scientists independently or jointly make a scientific discovery and then the more famous of them receives a disproportionate share of the credit, even if their individual contributions were comparable; this was studied by Merton (1968, 1973). Kitcher (1990, 1993) studied some simple and insightful models to explain the division of cognitive labor. A model of simultaneous projects was more recently studied by Kleinberg and Oren (2011), where workers strategically invest indivisible unit efforts in a simultaneous moves fashion in one selected project, with project utility functions that satisfy the decreasing returns property and the sharing of a project utility according to equal-share allocation among successful workers in the given project. The game in Kleinberg and Oren (2011) was shown to be a monotone valid utility game that allows the derivation of social efficiency bounds, and the work focused on deriving non-local utility sharing mechanisms that achieve full social efficiency. The definition of the family of project utility functions in (6.6) is inspired by the studies in Kitcher (1990) and Kleinberg and Oren (2011).

Strategic games that involve production and utility sharing have also been studied extensively in the context of public goods, e.g., Ursprung (1990), Baik (1993), Gradstein (1993), and Riaz et al. (1995). Morgan (2000) studied lotteries as a fund-raising mechanism where a charity organization offers a fixed prize according to proportional allocation and the utility of each player is quasi-linear in the value of winning the prize and a convex increasing function of the surplus created by the charity organization. Bos (2011) studied the case of asymmetric valuations and a linear public good utility function. Courcoubetis and Weber (2006) studied the efficiency of public good provisioning with applications in the context of peer-to-peer file sharing and wireless local area networks. Public goods were also studied in networks including the seminal work by Bramoulle and Kranton (2007); and the effort games on graphs studied by Jackson and Wolinsky (1996), Bala and Goyal (2000), Goyal and Vega-Redondo (2005), Ballester et al. (2006), Galeotti et al. (2006), Corbo et al. (2007), Jackson (2008), Laoutaris et al. (2008), Galeotti and Goyal (2010), and Immorlica et al. (2012). These games share a great deal of similarity with those considered in this chapter. A notable distinction, though, is that in effort games on graphs an agent strategically makes an investment of effort in one activity that produces a good that is shared by neighbors of this agent and does not strategically split his or her effort across different activities. Another class of related games is that of the Nash bargaining problem (Nash 1950a), which in the basic two-player instance of the problem could be seen as a utility sharing game where the sharing is of a fixed value that is split between the two players through a negotiation. In the network version of the problem introduced by Kleinberg and Tardos (2008), a graph is given where each vertex corresponds to a player and each edge corresponds to a project. In the basic version of the problem, each player is assumed to choose at most one project, and the value of a project is realized only if both players at the end-vertices of the corresponding edge choose to participate in this project. The dynamics for the Nash bargaining on graphs was studied by Azar et al. (2009), Bateni et al. (2010), Draief and Vojnović (2010), Celis et al. (2010), and Kanoria et al. (2011). Hatfield and Duke Kominers (2011) studied the welfare properties in a game where agents engage in joint ventures via multilateral contracts.

In terms of experimental work, numerous studies have been conducted on the motives for contributions to online communities, including that of Wikipedia content creation, e.g., Forte and Bruckman (2005), Rashid et al. (2006), Adler et al. (2008), and Burke and Kraut (2008); contributions to open source software projects, e.g., Hars and Ou (2001), Hann et al. (2002), von Krogh et al. (2003), Ye and Kishida (2003), and Stiglitz (2006); rating of digital content, e.g., Chen et al. (2010); and online communities in general, e.g., Beenen et al. (2004), and Rashid et al. (2006). Specific case studies were conducted for Eclipse, Linux, SourgeForge, Gimp, and Perl, as well as the creation of some popular software applications, e.g., Freenet, by von Krogh et al. (2003). The questions that have been studied include the reasons for participation, the effects of governance structure, and the strategies to attract new contributors to the community. Several factors have been identified: the free software ideology, altruistism, and users' desire to satisfy their own needs, e.g., Stiglitz (2006); Hars and Ou (2001); career concerns; learning Ye and Kishida (2003); reputation and status within the community, affiliation and identity; reciprocation Stiglitz (2006); expected future returns and personal needs Hars and Ou (2001); and enjoyment and creativity Stiglitz (2006). The question of why a large number of talented developers voluntarily contribute to the creation, maintenance, and support of public goods was studied by economists, e.g., Lerner and Tirole (2002).

CHAPTER 7
Sequential Contests

In this chapter we consider contests among two or more players that proceed through multiple rounds and end either in a fixed number of rounds or as soon as a termination criteria is fulfilled; for example, as soon one of the players achieves a given point difference or the contest owner acquires a given quality of the production output. The players are awarded according to a prize allocation mechanism that is based on their effort investments. We shall consider prize allocation mechanisms that either award a prize at the end of the contest or some amount of that prize at the end of each round of the contest. We shall consider contests under different assumptions on the structure of the effort investments over rounds, including those in which each player invests effort in one round according to a given order of play or strategic decisions by the players, and contests in which each player can invest effort in each round having observed the efforts invested in earlier rounds. Sequential moves may either be imposed by the contest design, may endogenously arise as a strategic equilibrium, or may occur because players "psyche themselves up" in a contest. We shall consider such models of contests formulated as extensive form games and study the properties of subgame perfect Nash equilibria. These games differ with respect to the information available to the players about the abilities of other players; we shall consider both games with complete and incomplete information.

There are many contests in practice that are based on sequential effort investments. Traditional examples include R&D patent races in which individual firms compete in filing a larger number of patents than other firms, advertising campaigns in which firms try to maintain or increase their market shares at the expense of other firms through promotional competitions, political races in which candidates confront each other in a sequence of speeches, court trials in which it is customary for the plaintiff to present evidence prior to the defense lawyers and both sides make their final speeches in the same sequential order, and sport competitions such as team sports, gymnastic tournaments, and tennis matches. There are also numerous examples of sequential contests in the context of online services. For example, in online labor marketplaces and knowledge-sharing platforms, users submit solutions for tasks over a period of time until a deadline is reached or a given task is closed at the discretion of the task owner.

The solutions to tasks are made available for inspection to the public as soon as they are submitted, and individual solutions may build on those previously submitted. Another example of a sequential contest is that of scientific and technological challenges that are run until either a deadline or a given success criterion is reached and the intermediate success measures achieved by individual teams may be made available to the public through leaderboards and other means.

Most of the sequential contests, which in this chapter are formulated and studied as extensive form games, can be seen as natural extensions of normal form games in which players make simultaneous effort investments, as studied in preceding chapters. We shall show that there are instances of sequential games in which the equilibrium strategic behavior of players differs greatly from that in the corresponding games with simultaneous moves. On the one hand, there are instances of sequential contests that feature a discouragement effect in that lower ability players invest less effort than under simultaneous effort investments. On the other hand, there are instances of sequential contests that tend to elicit higher maximum individual effort and guarantee the same expected total effort as under simultaneous effort investments.

The remainder of this chapter is structured in five sections in which we study specific types of sequential contests as follows.

In Section 7.1, we consider a multi-round contest in which each player invests effort in one of the rounds according to the given order of play. We shall primarily consider the case of a two-player contest where one of the players undertakes the role of a leader and the other player undertakes the role of a follower with respect to the order of play: first, the leader invests effort, anticipating the response of the follower, and then the follower invests effort after having observed the effort investment of the leader. We shall separately consider two prize allocation mechanisms that are based on the realized individual effort investments. The first such mechanism awards the player who makes the largest effort investment with ties resolved in favor of the follower. The corresponding normal form game in this case is that of the standard all-pay contest that we studied in Chapter 2. The second prize allocation mechanism that we consider is that of smooth allocation of prizes according to a general-logit contest success function. The corresponding normal game in this case is studied in Chapter 4. For the prize allocation mechanism according to a general-logit contest success function, we shall also consider a two-round contest between two players such that both players make simultaneous effort investments in each round and the effort investments in the second round are made after the effort investments in the first round are revealed to both players. We shall see that under sequential moves the qualitative properties of equilibrium are, in general, different from those under simultaneous moves.

Section 7.2 studies the class of sequential contests known as *the war of attrition*. The war of attrition is a contest among two or more players that awards each player with at most one prize from a set of identical prizes. In this game, each player invests effort at a unit rate continuously in time until deciding to drop out from the competition, at which point all players remaining in the competition are informed that this player has dropped out. The game ends as soon as the number of players remaining in the competition becomes equal to the number of available prizes. In the case of a single prize and two players, the contest ends as soon as a player drops out from the competition. The production costs are such that each player incurs a unit marginal cost of production until dropping out from the competition or the end of the contest. In a contest that awards a single prize, both the prize allocation mechanism and production cost functions correspond to that of the standard all-pay contest, which is studied in Chapter 2. The game of the war of attrition between two players is akin to the standard second-price auction because the winner is a player who invests the largest effort and the production cost incurred by the winner is equal to the effort invested by the loser. A notable difference, however, is that the game of the war of attrition is of the all-pay type. The game of the war of attrition that awards one or more identical prizes in which valuation parameters are private information is closely related to the contest with a rank-order allocation of identical prizes where players make simultaneous effort investments and incur unit marginal costs of production, which we studied in Chapter 3.

Section 7.3 considers a multi-round contest between two players known as the *the tug of war*. In each round of the contest one of the players wins and the other loses. The winner of the contest is the player who first achieves a given number of wins more than the opponent. Specifically, in each round a player wins if in this round he or she invests larger effort than the opponent, with ties resolved uniformly at random, and players incur unit marginal costs of production. The game of the tug of war is a natural extension of the standard all-pay contest between a pair of players to multiple rounds. We shall see that, in general, the extension to multiple rounds favors the higher ability player. The expected total effort in a subgame perfect Nash equilibrium is less than or equal to that in the mixed-strategy Nash equilibrium of the standard all-pay contest.

In Section 7.4, we consider a multi-round contest among a set of players with each player endowed with a unit effort that he or she can invest in one of the rounds. The total effort investment up to a given round results in a utility of production to the contest owner. The contest ends as soon as the utility of production becomes larger than or equal to a threshold value that is private information to the contest owner or a given number of rounds is reached that is public information. The given contest termination rule is motivated by the fact that the contest owner may be impatient and thus would close the contest as soon as the utility of the total effort investment becomes larger than or equal to the threshold value. At the contest end time, a prize is awarded according to a prize allocation mechanism to a player who invested effort before the end of the contest. The given multi-round contest is motivated by applications in the context of user-generated content in online services, e.g., collaborative question-answering services such as Yahoo! Answers and StackOverflow. In such systems, individual submissions by users are made public as soon as they are submitted, and later submissions may be built on those previously submitted. An important factor that determines the chance of a submission being selected as the best submission is its order relative to other submissions. We consider the efficiency of prize allocation mechanisms with respect to the goal of incentivizing players to make early effort investments. The key is to understand how efficient are different prize allocation mechanisms under certain types of the utility of production: we shall consider individual contributions that are either substitutes or complements.

Finally, in Section 7.5, we consider a contest that awards a set of identical prizes in a given number of one or more rounds, with a given number of prizes being awarded in each round of the contest. In each round of the contest, players make simultaneous effort investments, and prizes are awarded to players who invest the largest efforts. In the contest, each player is awarded at most one prize, which is either imposed by the contest design or arises endogenously in the case of unit-demand players. In the case of unit-demand players, as soon as a player wins a prize in a round, he or she has no incentive to participate in any subsequent rounds. Such a sequential allocation of prizes is common in practice. For example, it is often used as a qualifying stage in a tournament. Such a qualifying stage consists of a given number of rounds, and in each such round a given number of players are selected to advance to the next stage of the tournament based on their relative individual performance in the given round. For example, such a qualifying stage is found in the design of the TopCoder Open Tournament whose structure is described in Section 1.1. We shall consider a formulation of an extensive form game with complete information where players have valuations of winning a prize whose values are common knowledge and are allowed to assume arbitrary but distinct values, and players incur unit marginal costs of production. The given extensive form game has a subgame perfect Nash equilibrium such that the subgame in each round corresponds to the normal form game that models a contest with rank-order allocation of identical prizes, which we studied in Section 3.2.3. We shall see that in a subgame perfect Nash equilibrium several quantities of interest, including the expected total effort and expected maximum individual effort, are within constant factors of those in the mixed-strategy Nash equilibrium of a single-round contest where all prizes are allocated based on simultaneous effort investments in one round.

7.1 Sequential Moves

In this section we consider a contest in which efforts are made sequentially, focusing on the case of a contest between two players. First, we shall consider the standard all-pay contest as introduced and studied in Chapter 2 but with sequential moves by players. Second, we shall consider a smooth allocation of prizes as introduced and studied in Chapter 4 but with sequential moves by players.

7.1.1 Standard All-Pay Contest

Two Players

Consider a contest between two players who invest efforts sequentially in two rounds. In the first round, one of the players takes a role of a leader and makes an effort investment whose value is revealed to the other player, and then, in the second round, this other player takes a role of a follower and makes his or her effort investment. The winner is the player who invests larger effort, with ties resolved in favor of the follower. The two players, player 1 and player 2, have positive valuations v_1 and v_2, respectively, of winning the contest and incur unit marginal costs of production. Without loss of generality, suppose that player 1 is the leader and player 2 is the follower. The payoff functions of the players are of the quasi-linear form:

$$s_i(b_1, b_2) = v_i x_i(b_1, b_2) - b_i, \quad \text{for } i \in \{1, 2\} \tag{7.1}$$

where

$$x_1(b_1, b_2) = \mathbf{1}(b_1 > b_2) \text{ and } x_2(b_1, b_2) = \mathbf{1}(b_1 \leq b_2).$$

The simultaneous-move version of the game corresponds to the normal form game that models the standard all-pay contest, studied in Chapter 2, which has the same payoff functions except for an unbiased resolution of ties that assigns the prize uniformly at random to one of the players. We shall observe that sequential moves can yield qualitatively much different equilibrium behavior than simultaneous moves.

The game with complete information Suppose that the valuation parameters are common knowledge. Consider first the case in which the valuation of the leader is larger than that of the follower. We show that $(b_1, b_2) = (v_2, 0)$ is a unique subgame perfect Nash equilibrium. In the subgame in which the follower makes his or her effort investment, having observed the effort investment b_1 of the leader, there are three possible cases: if $b_1 < v_2$, then matching the effort investment of the leader is a unique best response of the follower; if $b_1 > v_2$, then investing zero effort is a unique best response of the follower; and if $b_1 = v_2$, then the set of best responses of the follower consists of investing either 0 or v_2 which both yield him or her a zero payoff. Obviously, $(b_1, b_2) = (v_2, 0)$ is a subgame perfect Nash equilibrium, which is shown to be a unique subgame perfect Nash equilibrium as follows. Notice that any equilibrium strategy of the leader must be such that his or her effort investment is at least v_2. The effort investment of the leader must be equal to v_2 because for any larger value, the leader has a unilateral beneficial deviation to lower his or her effort to a value larger than or equal to v_2. The effort investment $(b_1, b_2) = (v_2, v_2)$ cannot be a subgame perfect Nash equilibrium because the leader has a unilateral beneficial deviation to increase his or her effort. Consider now the case in which the valuation of the leader is smaller than that of the follower. In this case, obviously, there is a unique subgame perfect Nash equilibrium $(b_1, b_2) = (0, 0)$ in which neither player invests a strictly positive effort. Finally, consider the case of players with equal valuations. In this case, there is a unique subgame perfect Nash equilibrium $(b_1, b_2) = (0, 0)$ in which neither player invests a strictly positive effort.

We now compare the sequential game outcome with that in the mixed-strategy Nash equilibrium of the corresponding game with complete information in which players make simultaneous effort investments, which we characterized in Theorem 2.3 in Chapter 2. Without loss of generality, assume that $v_1 \geq v_2$. In the mixed-strategy equilibrium, player 1 wins with a probability that is larger than or equal to the winning probability of player 2. The expected effort investments are $v_2/2$ and $v_2^2/(2v_1)$ by player 1 and player 2, respectively. Compare these effort investments with those of values v_2 and 0, in case player 1 is the leader and his or her valuation is larger than that of player 2, and those of zero values in case player 1 is the follower. See Figure 7.1 for an illustration. The comparison suggests that there are instances in which the sequential contest design is preferred over the simultaneous-move contest design with respect to both total effort and maximum individual effort. A natural question to ask is how the

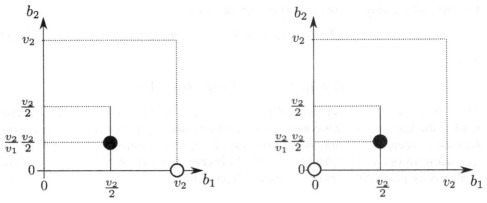

Figure 7.1. Subgame perfect Nash equilibrium points (white circles) and the expected points of mixed-strategy Nash equilibrium (black circles) for the standard all-pay contest between two players with valuations $v_1 \geq v_2 > 0$: (left) $v_1 > v_2$ with player 1 as the leader and player 2 as the follower, and (right) $v_1 > v_2$ with player 1 as the follower and player 2 as the leader, or $v_1 = v_2$ with any order of sequential play.

incomplete information about valuations affects the equilibrium outcome, which we study next.

The game with incomplete information Consider the game with incomplete information in which the valuation parameters are private information and are independent random variables with prior distributions F_1 and F_2 for players 1 and 2, respectively.

Theorem 7.1. *Assume that prior distributions F_1 and F_2 are strictly increasing and continuously differentiable on $[0, 1]$. If F_2 is strictly concave, then there is a subgame perfect Bayes-Nash equilibrium that is given as follows:*

$$\beta_1(v_1) = \begin{cases} 0, & \text{if } 0 \leq v_1 \leq \frac{1}{F_2'(0)} \\ F_2'^{-1}\left(\frac{1}{v_1}\right), & \text{if } \frac{1}{F_2'(0)} < v_1 \leq 1 \end{cases} \tag{7.2}$$

and

$$\beta_2(v_2, b_1) = \begin{cases} 0, & \text{if } 0 \leq v_2 \leq b_1 \\ b_1, & \text{if } b_1 < v_2 \leq 1. \end{cases} \tag{7.3}$$

If F_2 is convex, then $(0, 0)$ is the subgame perfect Bayes-Nash equilibrium.

Proof. We first consider the best response of the follower in the second round of the contest, and then that of the leader in the first round of the contest.

In the second round, having observed the effort investment of the leader, the payoff of the follower is given as follows:

$$s_2(v_2, \mathbf{b}) = v_2 \mathbf{1}(b_2 \geq b_1) - b_2.$$

Obviously, the best response for the follower is to invest b_1 if $b_1 < v_2$, and zero, otherwise.

In the first round of the contest, the leader anticipates the best response of the follower, and hence, the expected payoff of the leader is

$$\mathbf{E}[s_1(v_1, \mathbf{b}) \mid v_1, b_1] = v_1 \mathbf{Pr}[b_1 > b_2] - b_1$$
$$= v_1 \mathbf{Pr}[v_2 \leq b_1] - b_1$$
$$= v_1 F_2(b_1) - b_1.$$

Under the assumption that prior distribution F_2 is (strictly) concave, the expected payoff of player 1 is (strictly) concave in b_1 on $[0, 1]$. If $v_1 F_2'(0) - 1 \leq 0$, then the expected payoff of player 1 has maximum value at $b_1 = 0$. Otherwise, the expected payoff of player 1 has maximum value at a unique value b_1 in $(0, 1]$ such that $v_1 F_2'(b_1) - 1 = 0$.

On the other hand, under the assumption that prior distribution F_2 is convex, then $F_2(b) \leq b$ for all $0 \leq b \leq 1$; hence $v_1 F_2(b_1) - b_1 \leq (v_1 - 1)b_1 \leq 0$, where the inequality is strict whenever $v_1 < 1$ and $b_1 > 0$. It follows that the best response for player 1 is to invest zero effort, which is also followed by player 2 in the second round. $\quad\square$

A notable feature of the equilibrium is that there are instances in which the leader is pre-empted by the follower: the leader invests zero effort if his or her valuation is smaller than a threshold value that is fully determined by the prior distribution of the valuation of the follower. This is qualitatively much different from the behavior according to a Bayes-Nash equilibrium in the corresponding normal form game. If the prior distribution of the valuation of the follower is convex, then neither player invests strictly positive effort in equilibrium. In any case, the maximum individual effort is always invested by the leader, and this value of the effort investment is matched by the follower only if it is smaller than or equal to the follower's value of valuation.

We next consider two examples in which players have identical prior distributions of valuations to illustrate some of the properties of the subgame perfect Bayes-Nash equilibrium. We shall compare the subgame perfect Bayes-Nash equilibrium with the symmetric Bayes-Nash equilibrium in the corresponding normal form game with incomplete information. By Theorem 2.22 from Chapter 2, in the symmetric Bayes-Nash equilibrium, any given player with the valuation parameter of value v makes the effort investment of value

$$\beta(v) = \int_0^v x \, dF(x). \tag{7.4}$$

Example 7.2. Consider a family of distributions $F(v) = v^a$ for $v \in [0, 1]$, with parameter $0 < a \leq 1$. In the subgame perfect Bayes-Nash equilibrium, player 1 invests according to the strategy

$$\beta_1(v) = (av)^{\frac{1}{1-a}}$$

and player 2 invests $\beta_1(v_1)$ if $v_2 > \beta_1(v_1)$, and zero, otherwise. In the symmetric Bayes-Nash equilibrium both players invest according to the strategy

$$\beta(v) = \frac{a}{a+1} v^{a+1}.$$

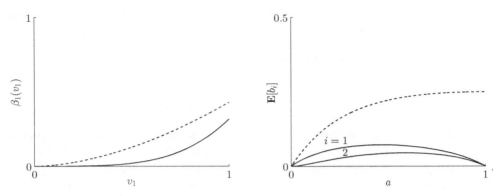

Figure 7.2. Subgame perfect Bayes-Nash equilibrium for the game in Example 7.2: (left) equilibrium strategy of player 1 for $a = 3/4$, and (right) the expected individual efforts versus a. The dashed lines show the quantities in the symmetric Bayes-Nash equilibrium.

Figure 7.2 shows graphs of $\beta_1(v)$ and $\beta(v)$ for particular values of parameter a, and the expected individual efforts in the two types of equilibria versus the value of parameter a.

Example 7.2 exhibits instances in which the effort investment of a player in the sequential game is less than or equal to the effort investment in the corresponding simultaneous-move game, conditional on the valuation of this player being fixed to a common value, i.e., $\beta_1(v) \leq \beta(v)$ for all $0 \leq v \leq 1$. This is a property that does not necessarily hold in general, which is demonstrated in the next example. Notice, however, that in Example 7.3, the expected individual effort of a player in the sequential game remains less than or equal to that in the game with simultaneous moves.

Example 7.3. Consider a family of distributions $F(v) = 1 - (1 - v)^a$ for $v \in [0, 1]$, with parameter $a \geq 1$. In the subgame perfect Bayes-Nash equilibrium, player 1 invests according to the strategy

$$\beta_1(v) = \begin{cases} 0, & \text{if } 0 \leq v \leq 1/a \\ 1 - \left(\frac{1}{av}\right)^{\frac{1}{a-1}}, & \text{if } 1/a < v \leq 1 \end{cases}$$

and player 2 invests $\beta_1(v_1)$ if $v_2 > \beta_1(v_1)$, and zero, otherwise. On the other hand, the symmetric Bayes-Nash equilibrium strategy is given by

$$\beta(v) = \frac{1}{a+1}(1 - (1 + av)(1 - v)^a).$$

In Figure 7.3, we observe that the equilibrium strategies $\beta_1(v)$ and $\beta(v)$ cross at an interior point and that the expected individual efforts in the sequential game are less than or equal to those in the game with simultaneous moves.

Comparison with simultaneous moves We next present three comparison results of the subgame perfect Bayes-Nash equilibrium in the sequential game and the symmetric Bayes-Nash equilibrium in the simultaneous-move game for the case of identical concave prior distributions.

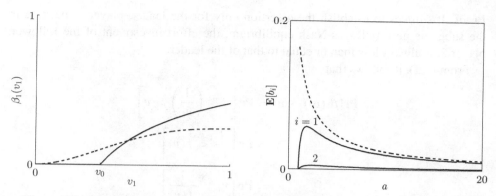

Figure 7.3. Subgame perfect Bayes-Nash equilibrium for the game in Example 7.3: (left) equilibrium strategy of player 1 for $a = 3$, and (right) the expected individual efforts versus a. The dashed lines show the quantities in the symmetric Bayes-Nash equilibrium.

Our first comparison is for the maximum possible effort investment in the sequential and simultaneous-move games.

Proposition 7.4. *A necessary and sufficient condition for $\beta_1(1) > \beta(1)$ to hold is*

$$\int_{v^*}^{1} (1 - F(v))\, dv > \int_{0}^{v^*} F(v)\, dv \tag{7.5}$$

where v^* is such that $f(v^*) = 1$.

The proof of this proposition is left to the reader as Exercise 7.2. A simple graphical interpretation of condition (7.5) is shown in Figure 7.4.

In the next proposition, we compare the sequential game and the simultaneous-move game with respect to expected individual efforts in equilibrium.

Proposition 7.5. *The expected individual effort of a player in the subgame perfect Bayes-Nash equilibrium of the sequential game is less than or equal to the expected individual effort of the player in the symmetric Bayes-Nash equilibrium of the simultaneous-move game.*

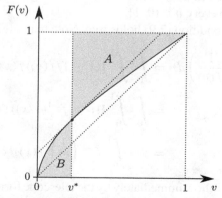

Figure 7.4. The maximum possible effort investment in the sequential game is larger than in the simultaneous-move game if, and only if, area A is larger than area B.

Proof. It suffices to establish the assertion only for the leader, player 1, because in the subgame perfect Bayes-Nash equilibrium, the effort investment of the follower, player 2, is always less than or equal to that of the leader.

From (7.2), it follows that

$$
\mathbf{Pr}[\beta_1(v_1) > v] = \mathbf{Pr}\left[f^{-1}\left(\frac{1}{v_1}\right) > v\right]
$$

$$
= \mathbf{Pr}\left[\frac{1}{v_1} < f(v)\right]
$$

$$
= \mathbf{Pr}\left[v_1 > \frac{1}{f(v)}\right]
$$

$$
= 1 - F\left(\frac{1}{f(v)}\right). \tag{7.6}
$$

Combining this with the telescope formula for the expected value, we have

$$
\mathbf{E}[\beta_1(v_1)] = 1 - \int_0^1 F\left(\frac{1}{f(v)}\right) dv. \tag{7.7}
$$

From (7.4) and some simple integral calculus, or directly as a special case of Corollary 2.57, we have

$$
\mathbf{E}[\beta(v_1)] = \frac{1}{2}\left(1 - \int_0^1 (2 - F(v))F(v)\,dv\right). \tag{7.8}
$$

From (7.7) and (7.8), the expected effort invested by the leader is smaller than or equal to the expected effort invested by a player in the simultaneous-move game if, and only if,

$$
\int_0^1 \left(F\left(\frac{1}{f(v)}\right) - F(v) + \frac{1}{2}F(v)^2 - \frac{1}{2}\right) dv \geq 0. \tag{7.9}
$$

The equality is achieved asymptotically by any sequence of distributions F^k that concentrates all the mass in an infinitesimally small neighborhood of value zero, i.e., $\lim_{k\to\infty} F^k(v) = 1$, for every $v \in (0, 1]$.

We next show that condition (7.9) holds true. Note that

$$
\int_0^1 F\left(\frac{1}{f(v)}\right) dv = \int_0^1 \int_0^1 \mathbf{1}(x \leq 1/f(v))f(x)\,dx\,dv
$$

$$
= \int_0^1 \int_0^1 \mathbf{1}(v \geq f^{-1}(1/x))f(x)\,dx\,dv
$$

$$
= 1 - \int_0^1 f^{-1}\left(\frac{1}{x}\right) f(x)\,dx.
$$

The next two identities follow immediately by the telescope formula for expected values and, in the last identity, by making use of the fact that $F^2(v)$ is the distribution of the maximum of two independent and identically distributed random variables according to distribution $F(v)$,

$$\int_0^1 F(v)\,dv = 1 - \int_0^1 xf(x)\,dx$$

$$\int_0^1 F^2(v)\,dv = 1 - \int_0^1 \int_0^1 \max\{x,y\}f(x)f(y)\,dx\,dy.$$

It follows that condition (7.9) can be written as

$$\int_0^1 \left(xf(x) - \frac{1}{2}\int_0^1 \max\{x,y\}f(x)f(y)\,dy - f^{-1}\left(\frac{1}{x}\right)f(x) \right) dx \geq 0.$$

The partial derivative of the left-hand side with respect to $f(v)$ is equal to

$$-\int_v^1 (1 - F(x))\,dx - f^{-1}\left(\frac{1}{v}\right) - \frac{1}{f'(v)}f\left(\frac{1}{f(v)}\right)$$

which vanishes to zero for f such that $F(x) = 1$ for $v \leq x \leq 1$. $\qquad\square$

Our third, and the last, comparison provides a necessary and sufficient condition for the effort investments to satisfy a stochastic order.

Proposition 7.6. *The effort investment of a player in the subgame perfect Bayes-Nash equilibrium of the sequential game is stochastically smaller than the effort investment of the player in the symmetric Bayes-Nash equilibrium of the simultaneous-move game if, and only if,*

$$\int_0^{1/f(v)} xf(x)\,dx \geq v \text{ for all } 0 \leq v < v^*$$

where v^* is the smallest x such that $f(x) = 1$.

Proof. The distribution of the effort investment by player 1 in the symmetric Bayes-Nash equilibrium is given as follows:

$$\mathbf{Pr}[\beta(v_1) \leq v] = F(\beta^{-1}(v)). \tag{7.10}$$

The random variable $\beta_1(v_1)$ is stochastically smaller than $\beta(v_1)$ if, and only if $\mathbf{Pr}[\beta_1(v_1) > v] \leq \mathbf{Pr}[\beta(v_1) > v]$ for all $0 \leq v \leq 1$. Using (7.6) and (7.10), this is equivalent to

$$F\left(\frac{1}{f(v)}\right) \geq F(\beta^{-1}(v)).$$

If $f(v) \leq 1$, then obviously the condition holds. Therefore, the necessary and sufficient condition is

$$\beta\left(\frac{1}{f(v)}\right) \geq v \text{ for all } v \in [0, 1] \text{ such that } f(v) > 1,$$

which in view of (7.4) is equivalent to the condition asserted in the proposition. $\qquad\square$

Arbitrary Number of Players

Consider a more general case of two or more players, $n \geq 2$, who sequentially submit efforts so that player 1 invests first, player 2 second, and so on until player n makes the last effort investment. The players have private valuations that are independent random variables with distribution functions $F_1, F_2, \ldots, F_n$ on $[0, 1]$. Suppose that each distribution function F_i is continuous, twice differentiable, and concave.

There exists a subgame perfect Bayes-Nash equilibrium that is characterized as follows. Let $G_i(x)$ be the probability of player i winning the contests if he or she exerts an effort of value x, given that none of the players in earlier rounds have invested more than x. It is readily observed that

$$
\begin{aligned}
G_{n-1}(x) &= F_n(x) \\
G_i(x) &= F_{i+1}\left(\frac{x}{G_{i+1}(x)}\right) G_{i+1}(x), \quad \text{for } 1 \leq i < n-1.
\end{aligned}
\tag{7.11}
$$

This admits an intuitive interpretation that goes as follows. If player $n - 1$ invests x and none of the players in earlier rounds invested more, then he or she wins if the valuation of player n is smaller than x, i.e., with probability $F_n(x)$. Consider now a player i such that $1 \leq i < n - 1$, given that he or she invests x, none of the players in earlier rounds invest more than x, and all players in subsequent rounds play according to the subgame perfect Bayes-Nash equilibrium strategies. Then, player i wins if two independent events happen: (i) the expected payoff of player $i + 1$ is negative, $v_{i+1} G_{i+1}(x) - x < 0$, which happens with probability $F_{i+1}(x / G_{i+1}(x))$, and (ii) the investment of x made up to this round eventually wins, which happens with probability $G_{i+1}(x)$.

Theorem 7.7. *There exists a subgame perfect Bayes-Nash equilibrium in which $G_i(x)$ is a continuous, twice differentiable, increasing, and concave function for all $1 \leq i < n$. The equilibrium strategies are given by*

$$
\beta_n(v_n, b_1, \ldots, b_{n-1}) = \begin{cases} 0, & \text{if } 0 \leq v_n < \bar{b}_{n-1} \\ \bar{b}_{n-1}, & \text{if } \bar{b}_{n-1} \leq v_n \leq 1 \end{cases}
\tag{7.12}
$$

$$
\beta_i(v_i, b_1, \ldots, b_{i-1}) = \begin{cases} 0, & \text{if } 0 \leq v_i < \underline{v}_i \\ \bar{b}_{i-1}, & \text{if } \underline{v}_i \leq v_i < \bar{v}_i, \quad \text{for } 1 < i < n \\ G_i'^{-1}\left(\frac{1}{v_i}\right), & \text{if } \bar{v}_i \leq v_i \leq 1 \end{cases}
\tag{7.13}
$$

$$
\beta_1(v_1) = \begin{cases} 0, & \text{if } 0 \leq v_1 < \underline{v}_1 \\ G_1'^{-1}\left(\frac{1}{v_1}\right), & \text{if } \underline{v}_1 \leq v_1 \leq 1 \end{cases}
\tag{7.14}
$$

where $\bar{b}_1 = 0$, $\underline{v}_1 = 1/G_1'(0)$, and

$$
\bar{b}_i = \max_{j \leq i} b_j, \underline{v}_i = \bar{b}_{i-1}/G_i(\bar{b}_{i-1}), \text{ and } \bar{v}_i = 1/G_i'(\bar{b}_{i-1}), \quad \text{for } 1 < i \leq n-1.
$$

The proof of this theorem can be established by backward induction and is left to the reader as Exercise 7.3, along with showing some of the following properties of the equilibrium. The expected maximum individual effort in the subgame perfect Bayes-Nash equilibrium is not necessarily monotonically increasing in the number of players. Adding a new player to the competition may increase or decrease the expected maximum individual effort depending on the order in which players make their effort investments and the distributions of the valuation parameters. If the new player is added to play first, then the expected maximum individual effort is guaranteed to be at least as large as before adding this player. On the other hand, there exist instances in which adding a player to play last can decrease the expected maximum individual effort. Intuitively, the latter case may occur when a high-ability player is added to play last, which discourages players from investing effort in earlier rounds.

7.1.2 Smooth Contest Success Functions

In this section we consider a two-player game with the payoff functions defined by (7.1) and the prize allocation according to a general logit contest success function:

$$x_i(b_1, b_2) = \begin{cases} \frac{f_i(b_i)}{f_1(b_1) + f_2(b_2)}, & \text{if } b_1 + b_2 > 0 \\ \frac{1}{2}, & \text{if } b_1 + b_2 = 0 \end{cases} \tag{7.15}$$

where $f_i : \mathbf{R}_+ \to \mathbf{R}_+$ is a strictly increasing, continuously twice-differentiable, and concave function such that $f_i(0) = 0$, for each player $i \in \{1, 2\}$. The version of this game that consists of a single round in which both players invest efforts simultaneously is an instance of the normal form game that we studied in Chapter 4; here, we refer to this game as the *normal form game*. In this section, we consider a sequential game that consists of two rounds such that each player makes an effort investment in exactly one of these two rounds according to a given order of play; we refer to this game as a *sequential play-once game*. We shall also consider a sequential game such that in each round both players simultaneously invest efforts, where the values of efforts invested in the first round are known to both players at the beginning of the second round; we refer to this game as a *sequential play-twice game*.

We denote with $\beta_i(b_j)$ the best response of a player i given that his or her opponent j plays strategy b_j, i.e.,

$$\beta_i(b_j) = \text{argmax}\{s_i(b_i, b_j) \mid b_i \in \mathbf{R}_+\}. \tag{7.16}$$

The normal form game has a unique pure-strategy Nash equilibrium (b_1^N, b_2^N), which follows from Theorem 4.4, and is a unique solution to

$$b_1^N = \beta_1(b_2^N) \text{ and } b_2^N = \beta_2(b_1^N). \tag{7.17}$$

Without loss of generality, we assume that the players are named such that in the pure-strategy Nash equilibrium of the normal form game, the winning probability of player 1 is larger than or equal to that of player 2, i.e., $f_1(b_1^N) \geq f_2(b_2^N)$. If the last inequality is strict, we say that the two players are *asymmetric*. Otherwise, if the equality holds, we say that the two players are *symmetric*. In the asymmetric case, we shall refer to player 1 as the *favorite* and to player 2 as the *underdog*.

We next present several lemmas that establish various properties of the payoff and best-response functions that are to be used in our subsequent analysis.

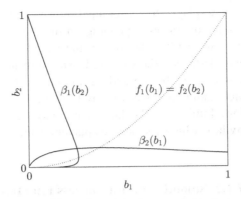

Figure 7.5. An illustration of the fact asserted in Lemma 7.9.

Lemma 7.8. *Suppose that f_1 and f_2 are strictly increasing, concave and such that $f_1(0) = 0$ and $f_2(0) = 0$. Then for every player i and his or her opponent j, $s_i(b_i, b_j)$ is concave in b_i, for every fixed value of $b_j \in \mathbf{R}_+$. Furthermore, this is strictly so if $b_j > 0$.*

Proof. Without loss of generality, consider the payoff function of player 1, and recall that it is defined as the difference of the utility function $v_1 x_1(b_1, b_2)$ and the production cost function b_1. The production cost is a linear function and thus concave. Since the sum of two concave functions is a concave function, it suffices to show that $x_1(b_1, b_2)$ is concave in b_1 for every given $b_2 \in \mathbf{R}_+$. Fix $f_2(b_2)$ to an arbitrary non-negative constant a. Note that $x_1(b_1, b_2) = f_1(b_1)/(f_1(b_1) + a)$ is a composition of two functions: function $h(x) = x/(x + a)$ and function $f_1(x)$. Since h is a non-decreasing function and f_1 is a strictly increasing and concave function, it follows that $x_1(b_1, b_2)$ is a concave function in b_1. If $a > 0$, function h is strictly increasing, and hence the composition of h and f_1 is a strictly concave function. Since f_2 is a strictly increasing function and $f_2(0) = 0$, we have that $a > 0$ if, and only if, $b_2 > 0$. $\qquad\square$

Lemma 7.9. *Suppose that f_1 and f_2 are strictly increasing, concave, and continuously differentiable functions. Then, the best-response functions β_1 and β_2 satisfy*

$$\beta_i'(b_j) \begin{cases} > 0 & \text{if } f_i(b_i) > f_j(b_j) \\ = 0 & \text{if } f_i(b_i) = f_j(b_j) \ , \\ < 0 & \text{if } f_i(b_i) < f_j(b_j) \end{cases} \quad \text{for } i, j \in \{1, 2\}, i \neq j.$$

See Figure 7.5 for an illustration.

Proof. Without loss of generality, consider the best-response function β_2 of player 2. By the definition of a best-response function, we have

$$\frac{\partial}{\partial b_2} s_2(b_1, \beta_2(b_1)) = v_2 \frac{\partial}{\partial b_2} x_2(b_1, \beta_2(b_1)) - 1 = 0.$$

Hence, we have

$$\frac{\partial}{\partial b_2} x_2(b_1, \beta_2(b_1)) = \frac{1}{v_2}.$$

By differentiating both sides in the last equation with respect to b_1, we obtain

$$\frac{d}{db_1}\frac{\partial}{\partial b_2}x_2(b_1, \beta_2(b_1)) = \frac{\partial^2}{\partial b_2^2}x_2(b_1, \beta_2(b_1))\beta_2'(b_1) + \frac{\partial^2}{\partial b_1 \partial b_2}x_2(b_1, \beta_2(b_1)) = 0.$$

$$(7.18)$$

Note that by Lemma 7.8, $\partial^2 x_2(b_1, \beta_2(b_1))/\partial b_2^2 \leq 0$ where the inequality is strict whenever $b_1 > 0$. Combining this with (7.18), we conclude that

$$\left(\frac{\partial^2}{\partial b_1 \partial b_2}x_2(b_1, \beta_2(b_1))\right)\beta_2'(b_1) \geq 0$$

where the inequality is strict whenever $b_1 > 0$. Hence, it follows that the sign of $\beta_2'(b_1)$ corresponds to that of $\partial^2 x_2(b_1, \beta_2(b_1))/(\partial b_1 \partial b_2)$. For a general-logit form contest success function, it is a routine calculus to establish that

$$\frac{\partial^2}{\partial b_1 \partial b_2}x_2(b_1, b_2) = \frac{f_1'(b_1)f_2'(b_2)(f_2(b_2) - f_1(b_1))}{(f_1(b_1) + f_2(b_2))^3}.$$

Since f_1 and f_2 are assumed to be strictly increasing functions, it follows that the sign of $\beta_2'(b_1)$ corresponds to the sign of $f_2(b_2) - f_1(b_1)$. $\square$

Lemma 7.10. *Suppose that f_1 and f_2 are strictly increasing and such that $f_1(0) = 0$ and $f_2(0) = 0$. Then, for every player i and his or her opponent j and every fixed value of $b_i \in \mathbf{R}_+$, the payoff function $s_i(b_i, b_j)$ is decreasing in b_j, and is strictly so if $b_i > 0$. Furthermore, if, in addition, f_1 and f_2 are continuously differentiable, then*

$$\frac{\partial}{\partial b_j}s_i(b_i, b_j) \leq 0$$

where the inequality is strict if $b_i > 0$.

Proof. Without loss of generality, consider the payoff function of player 1. If $b_1 = 0$, then the payoff for player 1 is equal to $v_1/2$ if $b_2 = 0$, and is equal to zero if $b_2 > 0$. Hence, it is a decreasing function in b_2. If $b_1 > 0$, then the payoff function $s_1(b_1, b_2) = v_1 f_1(b_1)/(f_1(b_1) + f_2(b_2)) - b_1$ is strictly decreasing in b_2, which readily follows because $f_1(b_1) > 0$ and $f_2(b_2)$ is strictly increasing in b_2. The last claim of the lemma follows trivially from $\partial s_1(b_1, b_2)/\partial b_2 = -v_1 f_1(b_1) f_2'(b_2)/(f_1(b_1) + f_2(b_2))^2$ and the assumptions imposed on functions f_1 and f_2. $\square$

Lemma 7.11. *Suppose that f_1 and f_2 are strictly increasing, concave, and continuously twice-differentiable functions such that $f_1(0) = 0$ and $f_2(0) = 0$. Then, for every player i and his or opponent j, the payoff function $s_i(b_i, \beta_j(b_i))$ is strictly concave in b_i.*

Proof. Without loss of generality, consider the payoff of player 1 conditional on that player 2 plays his or her best response to the effort investment by player 1. Since $s_1(b_1, b_2) = v_1(1 - x_2(b_1, b_2)) - b_1$, we have

$$\frac{\partial}{\partial b_2}s_1(b_1, b_2) = -v_1\frac{\partial}{\partial b_2}x_2(b_1, b_2).$$

By taking the derivative with respect to b_1 on both sides in the last equation, and using the identity in (7.18), it follows that

$$\frac{\partial^2}{\partial b_1 \partial b_2} s_1(b_1, b_2) + \frac{\partial^2}{\partial b_2^2} s_1(b_1, b_2) \frac{d}{db_1} b_2 = 0. \qquad (7.19)$$

The derivative of function $s_1(b_1, b_2)$ with respect to b_1 is equal to

$$\frac{d}{db_1} s_1(b_1, b_2) = \frac{\partial}{\partial b_1} s_1(b_1, b_2) + \frac{\partial}{\partial b_2} s_1(b_1, b_2) \frac{d}{db_1} b_2. \qquad (7.20)$$

Now, by taking the derivative with respect to b_1 in (7.20) and using the identity in (7.19), it follows that

$$\frac{d^2}{db_1^2} s_1(b_1, b_2) = \frac{\partial}{\partial b_1} \frac{d}{db_1} s_1(b_1, b_2).$$

From this equation, we observe that to establish the claim of the lemma, it suffices to show that $ds_1(b_1, b_2)/db_1$ is strictly decreasing in b_1, for every fixed value of b_2. We can do this as follows. From (7.19) and (7.20), it follows that

$$\frac{d}{db_1} s_1(b_1, b_2) = \frac{\partial}{\partial b_1} s_1(b_1, b_2) - \frac{\partial}{\partial b_2} s_1(b_1, b_2) \frac{\frac{\partial^2}{\partial b_1 \partial b_2} s_1(b_1, b_2)}{\frac{\partial^2}{\partial b_2^2} s_1(b_1, b_2)}.$$

Using this equation and some elementary calculus, we can obtain that

$$\frac{d}{db_1} s_1(b_1, b_2) = v_1 A(b_1) B(b_1, b_2) C(b_1, b_2) - 1 \qquad (7.21)$$

where

$$A(b_1) = f_1'(b_1),$$

$$B(b_1, b_2) = \frac{1}{f_1(b_1) + f_2(b_2)},$$

and

$$C(b_1, b_2) = \frac{f_2'(b_2)^2 - f_2''(b_2) f_2(b_2)}{2 f_2'(b_2)^2 - f_2''(b_2)(f_1(b_1) + f_2(b_2))}.$$

Under given assumptions on functions f_1 and f_2, it is readily observed that $A(b_1)$, $B(b_1, b_2)$, and $C(b_1, b_2)$ are all decreasing functions in b_1, and $B(b_1, b_2)$ is strictly so, for every fixed value of b_2. Hence, it follows that $ds_1(b_1, b_2)/db_1$ is strictly decreasing in b_1, for every fixed value of b_2.

$\square$

Sequential Play-Once Game

Consider the sequential play-once game in which player i is the leader and his or her opponent player j is the follower. Let b_i^L and b_j^F denote their respective effort investments. A vector of efforts (b_i^L, b_j^F) is a subgame perfect Nash equilibrium if the following two conditions hold true:

$$b_i^L = \arg\max\{s_i(b_i, \beta_j(b_i)) \mid b_i \in \mathbf{R}_+\} \text{ and } b_j^F = \beta_j(b_i^L). \qquad (7.22)$$

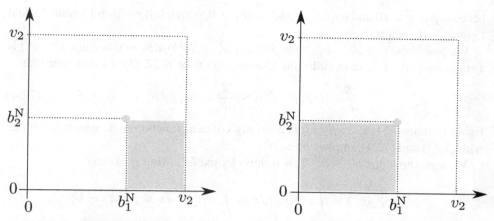

Figure 7.6. Sets of points containing the subgame perfect Nash equilibrium points: (left) the case of the favorite as the leader and (right) the case of the favorite as the follower.

The subgame perfect Nash equilibria of the sequential play-once game stand in the following relation with the pure-strategy Nash equilibrium of the normal form game.

Theorem 7.12. *Suppose that players are asymmetric. If player 1 is the leader then*

$$b_1^L > b_1^N \text{ and } b_2^F < b_2^N.$$

Otherwise, if player 1 is the follower, then

$$b_1^F < b_1^N \text{ and } b_2^L < b_2^N.$$

On the other hand, if the players are symmetric, then both subgame perfect Nash equilibria coincide with the pure-strategy Nash equilibrium.

Proof. We separately consider the cases of asymmetric and symmetric players.

Case 1: asymmetric players There are two different subgame perfect Nash equilibria depending on whether the favorite or the underdog player is the leader, which we separately consider as follows.

Case 1.1: the favorite is the leader We first show that

$$\frac{d}{db_1} s_1(b_1^N, \beta_2(b_1^N)) > 0. \tag{7.23}$$

This inequality follows by using the identity

$$\frac{d}{db_1} s_1(b_1^N, \beta_2(b_1^N)) = \frac{\partial}{\partial b_1} s_1(b_1^N, \beta_2(b_1^N)) + \frac{\partial}{\partial b_2} s_1(b_1^N, \beta_2(b_1^N)) \beta_2'(b_1^N)$$

and showing that the right-hand side of this equation is strictly positive by the following arguments. The first summation term in the right-hand side of the equation is equal to zero because (i) (b_1^N, b_2^N) is a pure-strategy Nash equilibrium and (ii) $b_1^N > 0$ that holds under the assumption that player 1 is the favorite, so $f_1(b_1^N) > f_2(b_2^N) \geq 0$. The second summation term in the right-hand side of the equation is strictly positive because $\beta_2'(b_1^N) < 0$ and $\partial s_1(b_1^N, \beta_2(b_1^N))/\partial b_2 < 0$, which follow from Lemma 7.9 and Lemma 7.10, respectively.

We now show that $b_1^L > b_1^N$. Note that $ds_1(b_1^L, \beta_2(b_1^L))/db_1 = 0$ because (b_1^L, b_2^F) is a subgame perfect Nash equilibrium. Combining this with (7.23), we conclude that

$$\frac{d}{db_1} s_1(b_1^N, \beta_2(b_1^N)) > \frac{d}{db_1} s_1(b_1^L, \beta_2(b_1^L)). \tag{7.24}$$

Using Lemma 7.11, $s_1(x, \beta_2(x))$ is a strictly concave function in x, which combined with (7.23) and (7.24), implies $b_1^L > b_1^N$.

We now show that $b_2^N > b_2^F$. This follows by the following relations:

$$b_2^N = \beta_2(b_1^N) = \int_0^{b_1^N} \beta_2'(x)\,dx > \int_0^{b_1^L} \beta_2'(x)\,dx = \beta_2(b_1^L) = b_2^F$$

where the first equation is by (7.17); the inequality is by the fact $b_1^N < b_1^L$ and Lemma 7.9, which implies $\beta_2'(b_1) < 0$, for $b_1 \geq b_1^N$; and finally, the last equation is by (7.22).

Case 1.2: the underdog is the leader The proof uses similar arguments as for the game in which the favorite is the leader, so we only outline the main steps. We first show that $b_2^N > b_2^L$. Note that

$$\frac{d}{db_2} s_2(\beta_1(b_2^N), b_2^N) = \frac{\partial}{\partial b_1} s_2(\beta_1(b_2^N), b_2^N)\beta_1'(b_2^N) + \frac{\partial}{\partial b_2} s_2(\beta_1(b_2^N), b_2^N)$$

$$\leq \frac{\partial}{\partial b_2} s_2(\beta_1(b_2^N), b_2^N)\beta_1'(b_2^N) + 0$$

$$< 0. \tag{7.25}$$

Since (b_1^F, b_2^L) is a subgame perfect Nash equilibrium, $ds_2(\beta_1(b_2^L), b_2^L)/db_2 = 0$, which combined with (7.25) and Lemma 7.11 implies $b_2^N > b_2^L$.

We next show that $b_1^N > b_1^F$. Note that by Lemma 7.9, we have $\beta_1'(b_2) > 0$, for $b_2 \geq b_2^N$. Hence,

$$b_1^N = \beta_1(b_2^N) > \beta_1(b_2^L) = b_1^F.$$

Case 2: symmetric players The pure-strategy Nash equilibrium (b_1^N, b_2^N) is such that $b_1^N = b_2^N$. Lemma 7.9 implies $\beta_1'(b_2^N) = \beta_2'(b_1^N) = 0$, which further implies

$$\frac{d}{db_1} s_1(b_1^N, \beta_2(b_1^N)) = \frac{d}{db_1} s_1(b_1^L, \beta_2(b_1^L)).$$

Combining with Lemma 7.11, we obtain $b_1^N = b_1^L$. A similar argument shows that $b_1^N = b_1^F$. $\qquad\square$

The comparison relations in Theorem 7.12 imply that in the equilibria of the sequential play-once game, the favorite invests more effort than in the equilibrium of the normal form game, if the favorite is the leader. On the other hand, the favorite invests less effort than in the normal form game if he or she is the follower. The effort invested by the underdog in the sequential play-once game is always smaller than in the normal form game, no matter whether he or she is the leader or the follower. The two contest designs can be ordered with respect to the maximum individual effort in the equilibria under consideration: the largest maximum individual effort is elicited in the sequential play-once game with the favorite being the leader, the second largest maximum individual effort is elicited in the normal form game, and finally, the smallest maximum individual effort is elicited in the sequential play-once game with the favorite being the follower.

Example 7.13 (proportional allocation). Consider a contest where the prize allocation is according to proportional allocation, which is a general-logit contest success function with $f_1(x) = f_2(x) = x$, for $x \in \mathbf{R}_+$. Assume that $v_1 \geq v_2 > 0$, so that player 1 is the favorite, and player 2 is the underdog. The subgame perfect Nash equilibria are specified as follows: if player 1 is the leader, then

$$(b_1^{\mathrm{L}}, b_2^{\mathrm{F}}) = \begin{cases} \left(\frac{v_1}{2} \frac{v_1}{2v_2}, \frac{v_1}{2} \left(1 - \frac{v_1}{2v_2} \right) \right), & \text{if } v_1 \leq 2v_2 \\ (v_2, 0), & \text{if } v_1 > 2v_2. \end{cases} \tag{7.26}$$

Otherwise, if player 1 is the follower, then

$$(b_1^{\mathrm{F}}, b_2^{\mathrm{L}}) = \left(\frac{v_2}{2} \frac{v_2}{2v_1}, \frac{v_2}{2} \left(1 - \frac{v_2}{2v_1} \right) \right). \tag{7.27}$$

We show that the asserted efforts are a subgame perfect Nash equilibrium only for the case when the favorite is the leader, as the other case follows along the same lines. Given that in the first round of the game, player 1 has made an effort investment of value b_1, in the second round of the game, player 2 plays his or her best response $\beta_2(b_1)$, which maximizes his or her payoff $s_2(b_1, b_2)$. This best response satisfies $\partial s_2(b_1, b_2)/\partial b_2 = 0$ and $b_2 > 0$, or $\partial s_2(b_1, b_2)/\partial b_2 \leq 0$ and $b_2 = 0$. Simple calculus yields that there is a unique best response that is given by

$$\beta_2(b_1) = \sqrt{b_1} \max \left\{ \sqrt{v_2} - \sqrt{b_1}, 0 \right\}.$$

In the first round of the game, player 1 anticipates the strategy that player 2 is going to play in the second round of the game, and chooses his or her effort b_1 that maximizes his or her payoff $s_1(b_1, \beta_2(b_1))$. Taking the derivative with respect to b_1, we obtain $(b_2 - b_1 d\beta_2(b_1)/db_1)v_1 = (b_1 + b_2)^2$, which after some calculus yields (7.26).

We compare the subgame perfect Nash equilibria of the sequential play-once game with the pure-strategy Nash equilibrium of the normal form game, which for a two-player contest is characterized in Theorem 4.9. Since proportional allocation validates the assumptions in Theorem 7.12, the equilibrium individual efforts in the sequential play-once game indeed satisfy the relations asserted therein. See Figure 7.7 for an illustration. The equilibrium total efforts in the sequential play-once game are given as follows:

$$R = \begin{cases} \min \left\{ \frac{v_1}{2v_2}, 1 \right\} v_2, & \text{if player 1 is the leader} \\ \frac{1}{2} v_2, & \text{if player 1 is the follower.} \end{cases}$$

Note that the total effort in equilibrium of the sequential play-once game with the favorite being the leader is at least as large as that in the normal form game. Specifically,

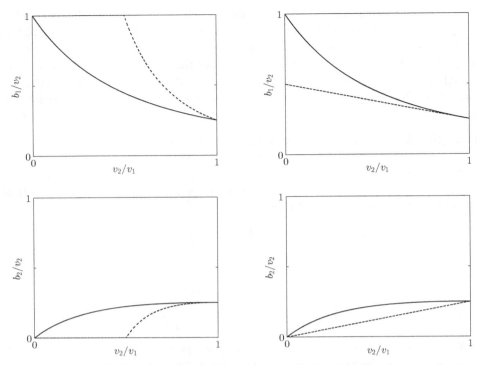

Figure 7.7. Equilibrium efforts in a two-player contest with the prize allocation according to proportional allocation for players with valuations $v_1 \geq v_2 > 0$: (left) the case of the favorite as the leader and (right) the case of the favorite as the follower. Solid lines show pure-strategy Nash equilibria and the dashed lines show subgame perfect Nash equilibria.

it achieves the second largest valuation v_2 whenever the ratio of the smaller valuation to the larger valuation v_2/v_1 is at most $1/2$, and it decreases to $v_2/2$ as the ratio v_2/v_1 increases from $1/2$ to 1. The total effort is at most a factor $3/2$ of that in the equilibrium of the normal form game, which is achieved for the case of valuation parameters such that $v_2/v_1 = 1/2$. On the other hand, in the case of the sequential play-once game with the favorite being the follower, the total effort in equilibrium is equal to $v_2/2$. Hence, it is at least half of that in the equilibrium of the normal form game.

Sequential Play-Twice Game

In this section we consider the sequential game that consists of two rounds where in each round both players simultaneously invest efforts. The amounts of efforts invested in the first round are assumed to be known by both players at the beginning of the second round. The prize is allocated at the end of the second round using the prize allocation mechanism in (7.15) based on the total effort investments made by the two players over the two rounds. We shall characterize the subgame perfect Nash equilibrium of this game.

Suppose that in the first round of the game, the effort investments are equal to $b_{1,1}$ and $b_{2,1}$ for player 1 and player 2, respectively. Then, in the second round of the game, their respective effort investments $b_{1,2}$ and $b_{2,2}$ must be such that for every player i and

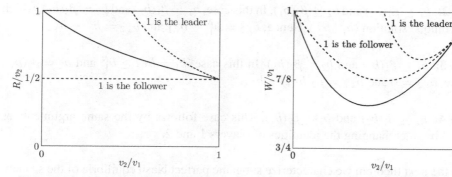

Figure 7.8. A two-player contest with prize allocation according to proportional allocation for players with valuations $v_1 \geq v_2 > 0$: (left) total effort, and (right) social efficiency. Solid lines are for the pure-strategy Nash equilibria and the dashed lines are for subgame perfect Nash equilibria.

his or her opponent j it holds that

$$s_i(b_{i,1} + b_{i,2}, b_{j,1} + b_{j,2}) \geq s_i(b_{i,1} + b'_{i,2}, b_{j,1} + b_{j,2}), \text{ for every } b'_{i,2} \geq 0.$$

This condition can be equivalently written as follows:

$$s_i(b_i, b_j) = \max\{s_i(b'_i, b_j) \mid b'_i \geq b_{i,1}\}.$$

Note that by Lemma 7.9, $s_i(b_i, b_j)$ is strictly concave in b_i, for every fixed value $b_j \in \mathbf{R}_+$. Observe also that $s_i(b_i, b_j)$ increases on $[0, \beta_i(b_j))$, achieves its maximum value at $\beta_i(b_j)$, and decreases on $(\beta_i(b_j), \infty)$. Hence, it follows that $s_i(b_i, b_j)$ achieves its maximum value on the interval $[b_{i,1}, \infty)$ at $\beta_i(b_j)$, if $b_{i,1} \leq \beta_i(b_j)$, and, otherwise, at $b_{i,1}$, if $b_{i,1} > \beta_i(b_j)$. In other words, for every player i and his or her opponent j, we have that

$$b_i = \max\{\beta_i(b_j), b_{i,1}\}. \tag{7.28}$$

Lemma 7.14. *The best responses of players in the subgame of the second round of the contest are given as follows, for every player i and his or her opponent j,*

$$\beta_{i,2}(b_{1,1}, b_{2,1}) = \begin{cases} 0, & \text{if } b_{i,1} \geq \beta_i(b_{j,1}) \text{ and } b_{j,1} \geq \beta_j(b_{i,1}) \\ b_i^N - b_{i,1}, & \text{if } b_{i,1} \leq b_i^N \text{ and } b_{j,1} \leq b_j^N \\ 0, & \text{if } b_{i,1} \geq b_i^N \text{ and } b_{j,1} \leq \beta_j(b_{i,1}) \\ \beta_i(b_{j,1}) - b_{i,1} & \text{if } b_{i,1} \leq \beta_i(b_{j,1}) \text{ and } b_{j,1} \geq b_j^N \end{cases} \tag{7.29}$$

or, in an equivalent, and more compact form,

$$\beta_{i,2}(b_{1,1}, b_{2,1}) = \max\left\{b_i^N - b_{i,1}, \beta_i(b_{j,1}) - b_{i,1}, 0\right\}.$$

Proof. The proof follows from the identity (7.28) by inspecting the following four possible cases:

Case 1: $b_1 \geq \beta_1(b_2)$ and $b_2 \geq \beta_2(b_1)$. In this case, $b_1 = b_{1,1}$ and $b_2 = b_{2,1}$. Hence, obviously, $b_{1,2} = b_{2,2} = 0$.

Case 2: $b_1 \leq \beta_1(b_2)$ and $b_2 \leq \beta_2(b_1)$. In this case, $b_1 = \beta_1(b_2)$ and $b_2 = \beta_2(b_1)$, which has a unique solution (b_1^N, b_2^N). Hence, $b_{1,2} = b_1^N - b_{1,1}$ and $b_{2,2} = b_2^N - b_{2,1}$.

Case 3: $b_1 \geq \beta_1(b_2)$ and $b_2 \leq \beta_2(b_1)$. In this case, $b_1 = b_{1,1} \geq b_1^N$ and $b_2 = \beta_2(b_1)$. Hence, $b_{1,2} = 0$ and $b_{2,2} = \beta_2(b_{1,1}) - b_{2,1}$.

Case 4: $b_1 \leq \beta_1(b_2)$ and $b_2 \geq \beta_2(b_1)$. This case follows by the same arguments as Case 3 by interchanging the identities of players 1 and 2. □

In the next theorem we characterize subgame perfect Nash equilibria of the sequential play-twice game.

Theorem 7.15. *Suppose that players are asymmetric; then (b_1, b_2) are the total effort investments by players in a subgame perfect Nash equilibrium if, and only if,*

$$b_1^N \leq b_1 \leq b_1^L \text{ and } b_2 = \beta_2(b_1). \tag{7.30}$$

On the other hand, if players are symmetric, then there is a unique subgame perfect Nash equilibrium that coincides with the pure-strategy Nash equilibrium.

Proof. The direct part of the statement is proven as follows. Suppose that (b_1, b_2) are total efforts in a subgame perfect Nash equilibrium. We first show that it must hold that $b_1 \geq \beta_1(b_2)$ and $b_2 = \beta_2(b_1)$, which is equivalent to that $b_1^N \leq b_1$ and $b_2 = \beta_2(b_1)$, via the following three claims.

Claim 1: $b_1 \geq \beta_1(b_2)$ and $b_2 \geq \beta_2(b_1)$. This follows directly from (7.28).

Claim 2: Either $b_1 = \beta_1(b_2)$ or $b_2 = \beta_2(b_1)$. Suppose on the contrary that $b_1 > \beta_1(b_2)$ and $b_2 > \beta_2(b_1)$. From (7.29), neither player invests a strictly positive effort in the second round. In the first round, using Lemma 7.8, $s_i(b_i, b_j)$ is concave in b_i and it achieves its maximum value at the point $\beta_i(b_j)$, for every player i and any given effort investment b_j of the opponent. It follows that both players have an incentive to unilaterally lower their efforts in the first round, which is a contradiction to the assumption that (b_1, b_2) are the total effort in a subgame perfect Nash equilibrium.

Claim 3: $b_1 \geq \beta_1(b_2)$ and $b_2 = \beta_2(b_1)$. Suppose on the contrary that $b_1 = \beta_1(b_2)$ and $b_2 > \beta_2(b_1)$. From (7.29), player 2 invests no effort in the second round. Suppose that player 2 lowers his or her effort in the first round by an infinitesimal amount. From (7.29), observe that there are two possibilities. (i) Player 1 responds to restore $b_1 = \beta_1(b_2)$. By Lemma 7.11, this will increase player 2's payoff because by lowering his or her effort, it is brought closer to the point b_2^F at which his or her payoff is the maximum. (ii) Player 1 may not be able to respond, in which case his or her effort remains unchanged. In this case, the deviation is beneficial to player 2 because of the facts in Lemma 7.8 and the deviation brings the effort investment closer to the point $\beta_2(b_1)$ at which his or her payoff is maximized for a fixed value of b_1.

We now show that $b_1 \leq b_1^L$. Suppose on the contrary that $b_1 > b_1^L$ and $b_2 = \beta_2(b_1)$. Then, it would be beneficial for player 1 to lower his or her effort by an infinitesimal amount, which is a contradiction.

The converse part of the statement of the theorem is established as follows. We first show that for every (b_1, b_2) satisfying condition (7.30), it holds that

$$b_2^F \leq b_2 \leq b_2^N. \tag{7.31}$$

The first inequality in (7.31) follows by

$$b_2 = \beta_2(b_1) = \beta_2(b_1^N) + \int_{b_1^N}^{b_1} \beta_2'(x)\,dx \leq \beta_2(b_1^N) = b_2^N$$

where we used (7.30) to note that $b_1^N \leq b_1$ and used Lemma 7.9 to note that $\beta_2'(x) \leq 0$, for every $x \geq b_1^N$. The second inequality in (7.31) follows similarly by

$$b_2 = \beta_2(b_1) = \beta_2(b_1^L) - \int_{b_1}^{b_1^L} \beta_2'(x)\,dx \geq \beta_2(b_1^L) = b_2^F.$$

Suppose that (b_1, b_2) satisfies condition (7.30). We next show that such a point corresponds to total efforts in a subgame perfect Nash equilibrium. Player 2 has no profitable deviation because by condition (7.30) it must hold that $b_2 = \beta_2(b_1)$, and playing $\beta_2(b_1)$ is the best response for player 2 for any effort investments by player 1 such that $b_{1,1} + b_{1,2} = b_1$. Player 1 has no profitable deviation either. Since by Lemma 7.9, $b_1 > \beta_1(b_2)$, player 1 has no incentive to change his or her investment in the subgame of round 2. If player 1 unilaterally deviates in round 1 to $b_{1,1}' < b_{1,1}$, then player 2 will increase his or her effort to b_2' such that $b_2' = \beta_2(b_{1,1}' + b_{1,2}) < b_2$. By Lemma 7.11, this will lower the payoff of player 1. If player 1 unilaterally deviates in round 1 to $b_{1,1}' > b_{1,1}$, then $b_2 > \beta_2(b_{1,1}' + b_{1,2})$, and player 2 will not respond in round 2. Player 1 will be worse off because of Lemma 7.8. $\square$

Theorem 7.15 tells us that, in general, the sequential play-twice game has a continuum of subgame perfect Nash equilibria. Any point on the graph of the underdog's best-response function between the pure-strategy Nash equilibrium point of the normal form game and the subgame perfect Nash equilibrium point of the sequential play-once contest with the favorite being the leader is a subgame perfect Nash equilibrium (see Figure 7.9 for an example). The effort investments made in individual rounds are fully determined by Lemma 7.14 and Theorem 7.15 and are as follows. Consider first the subgame perfect Nash equilibrium in which the total effort investment by the favorite, player 1, is larger than in the pure-strategy Nash equilibrium of the normal form game. In this case, player 1 makes no effort investment in the second round of the contest. The underdog, player 2, splits his or her effort between the two rounds in an arbitrary way such that it holds that $0 \leq b_{2,1} \leq \beta_2(b_1)$ and $b_{2,2} = \beta_2(b_1) - b_{2,1}$. Consider now the subgame perfect Nash equilibrium in which the total effort investment by player 1 is equal to that in the pure-strategy Nash equilibrium of the normal form game. In this case the total effort investments by players correspond to those in the pure-strategy Nash equilibrium of the normal form game and are split over the two rounds in an arbitrary way such that it holds that $0 \leq b_{i,1} \leq b_i^N$ and $b_{i,2} = b_i^N - b_{i,1}$ for player $i \in \{1, 2\}$.

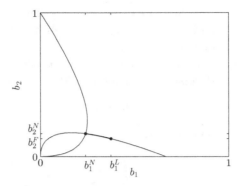

Figure 7.9. Subgame perfect Nash equilibria of a two-round contest are the points in the highlighted segment that lies on the graph of the underdog's best-response function.

In the next example we characterize the subgame perfect Nash equilibrium points of the sequential play-twice game where the prize is awarded according to proportional allocation. The subgame perfect Nash equilibrium points of the sequential play-once game with the prize allocation according to proportional allocation were characterized earlier in Example 7.13.

Example 7.16 (proportional allocation revisited). Under proportional allocation, the normal form game has a unique pure-strategy Nash equilibrium that is given in Theorem 4.9. The subgame perfect Nash equilibrium of the sequential play-once game with player 1 being the leader is given in (7.26). For the sequential play-twice game, by Theorem 7.15, the total efforts in a subgame perfect Nash equilibrium are any values b_1 and b_2 such that

$$v_2 \frac{1}{(1 + v_2/v_1)^2} \le b_1 \le v_2 \min \left\{ \frac{1}{4(v_2/v_1)^2}, 1 \right\} \tag{7.32}$$

and

$$b_2 = \sqrt{b_1} \max \left\{ \sqrt{v_2} - \sqrt{b_1}, 0 \right\}. \tag{7.33}$$

See Figure 7.9 for an illustration.

The total effort in the subgame perfect Nash equilibrium in which player 1 makes the total effort investment of value b_1 is given by

$$R(b_1) = \sqrt{v_2 b_1}.$$

The total effort in the subgame perfect Nash equilibrium is in between that in the pure-strategy Nash equilibrium of the normal form game and that in the subgame perfect Nash equilibrium of the sequential play-once game with the favorite being the leader. Any value of the total effort in between these two limit points is supported by a subgame perfect Nash equilibrium. The value of the total effort in the pure-strategy Nash equilibrium of the normal form game is the worst case for the total effort in a subgame perfect Nash equilibrium of the sequential play-twice game, and that in the subgame perfect Nash equilibrium of the sequential play-once game with the favorite being the leader is the best case.

Endogenous Selection of a Contest Design

Suppose that there is a preliminary round in which players choose a contest design according to which they are going to subsequently compete from among the following four choices: (i) a single-round contest with simultaneous effort investments, (ii) a sequential play-once game with the favorite being the leader, (iii) a sequential play-once game with the underdog being the leader, and (iv) a sequential play-twice game. In the next theorem, we identify which choices are a pure-strategy Nash equilibrium of the subgame in the preliminary round of the contest.

Theorem 7.17. *Suppose that in a preliminary round of a two-round contest players simultaneously choose whether or not to release the information about the values of their efforts in the first round of the contest. If players are asymmetric, then there is a unique pure-strategy Nash equilibrium, which is the one in which both the favorite and the underdog decide to release the information.*

On the other hand, if players are symmetric, then there are multiple pure-strategy Nash equilibria because of the fact that players are indifferent between releasing and not releasing the information, and in all these equilibria, the effort investments coincide with those in the pure-strategy Nash equilibrium of the normal form game.

Proof. We shall refer to the preliminary round of the contest as round 0. In round 0, each player selects one of the following two strategies: either 0 indicating not to reveal the information about his or her effort in round 1, or 1 otherwise. There are four cases to consider depending on the strategies $(b_{1,0}, b_{2,0})$ deployed by the players in round 0:

Case $(1, 1)$: both players decide to reveal the information. The subgame starting from round 1 of the contest corresponds to the sequential play-twice game whose subgame perfect Nash equilibria are specified in Theorem 7.15. The equilibrium payoffs conditional on playing $(1, 1)$ in round 0 of the extended game are as follows:

$$s_i(b_1, \beta_2(b_1)), \text{ for } b_1 \in [b_1^N, b_1^L], \text{ for } i \in \{1, 2\}. \tag{7.34}$$

Case $(0, 0)$: neither player decides to reveal the information. The subgame starting from round 1 coincides with the normal form game that has a unique pure-strategy Nash equilibrium (b_1^N, b_2^N). The equilibrium payoffs conditional on playing $(0, 0)$ in round 0 of the extended game are as follows:

$$s_i(b_1^N, b_2^N), \text{ for } i \in \{1, 2\}. \tag{7.35}$$

Case $(1, 0)$: the favorite chooses to reveal the information and the underdog decides not to reveal the information. In the subgame of the second round, the favorite plays according to the response function $b_1 = \max\{b_{1,1}, \beta_1(b_2)\}$, and the underdog plays according to $b_2 = \beta_2(b_1)$. The equilibrium outcome is for the favorite to direct all his or her effort to round 1, which results in the subgame perfect Nash equilibrium outcome of the sequential play-once game with the favorite being the leader. The equilibrium payoffs conditional on playing $(1, 0)$ in round 0 of the extended game are as follows:

$$s_i(b_1^L, b_2^F), \text{ for } i \in \{1, 2\}. \tag{7.36}$$

Case $(0, 1)$**:** the favorite chooses not to reveal the information and the underdog decides to reveal the information. In this case, we have $b_1 = \beta_1(b_2)$ and $b_2 = \max\{b_{2,1}, \beta_2(b_1)\}$. If $b_{2,1} \leq \beta_2(b_1)$, then $b_2 = \beta_2(b_1)$, and hence, the equilibrium outcome is (b_1^N, b_2^N). Otherwise, if $b_{2,1} > \beta_2(b_1)$, then player 2 directs all his or her effort to round 1. Player 2 has an incentive to decrease his or her effort, which would eventually reach the point (b_1^N, b_2^N). Any point in (b_1, b_2) such that $b_1 < b_1^N$ and $b_2 < b_2^N$ cannot be an equilibrium because at any such point it is beneficial for both players to unilaterally increase their efforts in round 2. Therefore, it follows that there is a unique subgame perfect Nash equilibrium that is (b_1^N, b_2^N). The equilibrium payoffs conditional on playing $(0, 1)$ in round 0 of the extended game are as follows:

$$s_i(b_1^N, b_2^N), \quad \text{for } i \in \{1, 2\}. \tag{7.37}$$

We next show that playing $(1, 1)$ in round 0 is a subgame perfect Nash equilibrium of the extended game. By Lemma 7.11, $s_1(b_1, \beta_2(b_1))$ is a strictly concave function in b_1; thus, it has a unique maximum value, which by definition is at the point b_1^L. From (7.34) to (7.37), it follows that playing 1 in round 0 is a (weakly) dominant strategy for the favorite.

Given that the favorite decided to play 1 in round 0, we show that a best response for the underdog is to play 1 as well. By (7.34) and (7.37), we need to show that

$$s_2(b_1, \beta_2(b_1)) \geq s_2(b_1^L, \beta_2(b_1^L)), \quad \text{for every } b_1^N \leq b_1 \leq b_1^L.$$

This is indeed true because $s_2(b_1, \beta_2(b_1)) \geq s_2(b_1, \beta_2(b_1^L))$ for every $b_1 \geq 0$, which obviously holds by the definition of the best-response function $\beta_2(b_1)$ in (7.16), and $s_2(b_1, \beta_2(b_1^L)) \geq s_2(b_1^L, \beta_2(b_1^L))$, for $b_1 \leq b_1^L$, which follows from Lemma 7.10. $\quad\square$

7.2 The War of Attrition

In the basic form of the game of *the war of attrition* there are two players who compete for a single prize. The players have positive valuations of the prize v_1 and v_2, for player 1 and player 2, respectively. The two players increase their effort investments continuously in time at a unit rate until one of the players drops out from the competition. The player who remained in the competition collects the prize. Both players incur a cost equal to the time elapsed from the beginning of the contest until the first time a player drops out from the competition. In other words, players incur unit marginal costs of production until the first time a player drops out from the competition. The payoff functions of the players are given by

$$s_i(b_1, b_2) = v_i x_i(b_1, b_2) - \min\{b_1, b_2\}, \quad \text{for } i = 1 \text{ and } 2 \tag{7.38}$$

where

$$x_1(b_1, b_2) = \mathbf{1}(b_1 > b_2) + \frac{1}{2}\mathbf{1}(b_1 = b_2) \text{ and } x_2(b_1, b_2) = 1 - x_1(b_1, b_2).$$

The payoff functions correspond to that of a standard auction in which a unit prize is allocated to the higher bidder and the payment is equal to the second highest bid. This standard auction is similar to the second-price auction with a notable difference being that it is of the all-pay type: unlike in the second-price auction, the payment is made by both players, not only by the winner.

We shall also consider a more general version of the game of the war of attrition that allows for $n \geq 2$ players and a set of $1 \leq m \leq n$ identical prizes. The players are assumed to have positive valuations for winning a prize with respective values $v_1, v_2, \ldots, v_n$ for players $1, 2, \ldots, n$. Each player is assumed to incur a unit marginal cost until dropping out from the competition and a marginal cost of value $0 \leq c \leq 1$ from the time this player drops out until the end of the contest. This definition of production costs accommodates both the special case in which each player incurs a zero marginal cost as soon as he or she drops out from the competition, and the case in which each player incurs a unit marginal cost until the end of the contest. The payoff functions can be written as follows:

$$s_i(\mathbf{b}) = v_i x_i(\mathbf{b}) - \left[(1-c)b_i + c \max_{j \in N} b_j \right], \quad \text{for } i \in N \qquad (7.39)$$

where $x_i(\mathbf{b})$ is the probability of player i winning a prize, conditional on the effort investments being $\mathbf{b} = (b_1, b_2, \ldots, b_n)$, under the allocation mechanism that awards prizes to m players who made the largest effort investments with uniform random tie breaks in the case of ties.

7.2.1 Game with Complete Information

In this section we consider the game with complete information where the valuation parameters are common knowledge. We shall see that in this case both a pure-strategy Nash equilibria and a mixed-strategy equilibria exist and, in general, are not unique.

Pure-Strategy Nash Equilibrium

For the game of the war of attrition there exists a continuum of pure-strategy Nash equilibria, which we demonstrate for the case of a contest between two players. Suppose first that one of the players values the prize more than the other player, and without loss of generality, assume that $v_1 > v_2 > 0$. From the definition of the payoff functions (7.38), observe that a pure-strategy Nash equilibrium is for player 1 to invest any amount of effort $b_1 \geq v_2$ and for player 2 to invest zero effort, $b_2 = 0$. All these pure-strategy Nash equilibria are payoff equivalent: the payoff for player 1 is equal to v_1 and for player 2 is equal to 0. For the case where the valuation parameters are identical, $v_1 = v_2 \equiv v$, there is also a continuum of pure-strategy Nash equilibria in which either player 1 invests any amount greater than or equal to v and player 2 invests a zero effort, or vice versa.

Mixed-Strategy Nash Equilibrium

For the game of the war of attrition there exists a continuum of mixed-strategy Nash equilibria as shown in the following theorem.

Theorem 7.18. *Suppose that the two players deploy mixed strategies according to a pair of distributions on* $\mathbf{R}_+$ *of the following form:*

$$B_1(x) = 1 - (1 - B_1(0))e^{-\frac{x}{v_2}} \text{ and } B_2(x) = 1 - (1 - B_2(0))e^{-\frac{x}{v_1}} \qquad (7.40)$$

where either $B_1(0) = 0$ *or* $B_2(0) = 0$. *Then, any such pair of mixed strategies is a mixed-strategy Nash equilibrium.*

Proof. Suppose that a pair of mixed strategies according to distributions B_1 and B_2 is a mixed-strategy Nash equilibrium. We show that neither B_1 nor B_2 has a positive atom at value $b > 0$. For the purpose of a contradiction, suppose that a player has a positive atom at $b > 0$, and without loss of generality, assume this is player 1. If $b_2 > b$, the payoff of player 1 is $-b$, and thus player 1 would benefit by investing less than b, which contradicts the assumption that he or she plays an equilibrium strategy.

Consider an arbitrary player $i \in \{1, 2\}$ and denote his or her opponent as $j \in \{1, 2\}$, $j \neq i$. Assume that player j deploys a mixed strategy according to a distribution B_j. The expected payoff of player i, conditional on the effort investment by this player, is given by

$$\mathbf{E}[s_i(b_1, b_2) \mid b_i = 0] = \frac{v_i}{2} B_j(0), \tag{7.41}$$

and for $x > 0$,

$$\mathbf{E}[s_i(b_1, b_2) \mid b_i = x] = v_i B_j(0) + \int_0^x (v_i - y)\, dB_j(y) + (-x)(1 - B_j(y)). \tag{7.42}$$

If a pair of distributions B_1 and B_2 constitutes a mixed-strategy Nash equilibrium, then player i is indifferent to playing any pure strategy in the support of distribution B_i, given that the opponent deploys a mixed strategy according to distribution B_j. Hence, for every x in the support of distribution B_i, it must hold that

$$\frac{\partial}{\partial b_i} \mathbf{E}[s_i(b_1, b_2) \mid b_i = x] = 0. \tag{7.43}$$

From (7.42), for $x > 0$,

$$\frac{\partial}{\partial b_i} \mathbf{E}[s_i(b_1, b_2) \mid b_i = x] = (v_i - x)\frac{d}{db} B_j(x) - (1 - B_j(x)) + x\frac{d}{dx} B_j(x).$$

Thus, (7.43) is equivalent to

$$v_i \frac{d}{dx} B_j(x) = 1 - B_j(x),$$

which is an ordinary differential equation with the solution given in (7.40).

We next show that it must be that either $B_1(0) = 0$ or $B_2(0) = 0$. Under the mixed strategies of the form in (7.40), we have that

$$\mathbf{E}[s_i(b_1, b_2) \mid b_i = 0] = \frac{v_i}{2} B_j(0),$$

and for $x > 0$,

$$\mathbf{E}[s_i(b_1, b_2) \mid b_i = x] = v_i B_j(0).$$

From this we observe that if both players invest zero efforts with a strictly positive probability, then for each player investing a strictly positive effort is preferred over investing a zero effort, so it must be that either $B_1(0) = 0$ or $B_2(0) = 0$. $\qquad\square$

The mixed-strategy equilibria in Theorem 7.18 are such that the mixed-strategy distribution of a player is parametrized only with the valuation parameter of the opponent.

In the mixed-strategy Nash equilibrium, the effort investment by a player is stochastically decreasing in the value of the valuation parameter of the opponent. The higher valuation player makes an effort investment that is stochastically smaller than that of the opponent. The individual effort investments made until a player concedes are a minimum of two independent random variables according to distributions B_1 and B_2. Hence,

$$\Pr[\min\{b_1, b_2\} \le x] = 1 - (1 - B_1(0))(1 - B_2(0))e^{-\left(\frac{1}{v_1} + \frac{1}{v_2}\right)x}.$$

The expected individual efforts made until a player concedes are equal to

$$\frac{1 - \max\{B_1(0), B_2(0)\}}{\frac{1}{v_1} + \frac{1}{v_2}}.$$

The winning probabilities are given by

$$\mathbf{E}[x_i(b_1, b_2)] = (1 - B_j(0))(1 - B_i(0))\frac{v_i}{v_1 + v_2} + B_j(0), \quad \text{for } i, j \in \{1, 2\}, j \ne i.$$

For the mixed-strategy Nash equilibrium in which neither player puts a mass at investing zero effort, the winning probabilities are proportional to the valuation parameters.

Symmetric valuations For players with symmetric valuations, say $v_1 = v_2 = v > 0$, there is a unique symmetric mixed-strategy Nash equilibrium in which neither player puts a mass at investing zero effort, where both players deploy mixed strategies according to the distribution

$$B(x) = 1 - e^{-\frac{x}{v}}.$$

The effort invested by each player until one of the players concedes is a minimum of two independent and identically distributed random variables according to exponential distribution with mean v; thus, it is a random variable with exponential distribution with mean $v/2$. It follows that the total effort investment until one of the players concedes is twice the value of an exponential random variable with mean $v/2$, and hence, the expected total effort is of value of v. In general, there is a continuum of asymmetric mixed-strategy Nash equilibria in which one of the players puts an atom at investing no effort.

7.2.2 Game with Incomplete Information

In this section we consider the game of the war of attrition with private valuations that are independent random variables according to prior distributions $F_1, F_2, \ldots, F_n$. We shall first consider the case of two players and one prize, and then a generalized version that allows for an arbitrary number of two or more players and any number of identical prizes.

Two Players

Consider the game of the war of attrition between two players with valuations according to prior distributions F_1 and F_2 that have strictly positive density functions f_1 and f_2, respectively, on the interval $[0, 1]$. Let $\beta_i(v_i)$ denote the strategy of player i conditional on his or her valuation being v_i.

The expected payoff for player i, conditional on his or her valuation being v_i and his or her effort investment being b_i, is given by

$$s(v_i, b_i) = \mathbf{E}[(v_i - \beta_j(v_j))\mathbf{1}(\beta_j(v_j) < b_i) \mid v_i] - b_i \mathbf{Pr}[\beta_j(v_j) \geq b_i] \quad (7.44)$$

where j denotes the identity of the opponent.

A pair of strategies (β_1, β_2) is a pure-strategy Bayes-Nash equilibrium if for every player $i \in \{1, 2\}$ and every value v_i in the support of the prior distribution F_i, we have

$$s(v_i, \beta_i(v_i)) \geq s(v_i, b_i), \quad \text{for every } b_i \in \mathbf{R}_+.$$

Lemma 7.19. *Every pure-strategy Bayes-Nash equilibrium (β_1, β_2) is such that β_1 and β_2 are strictly increasing and continuous functions.*

Proof. Showing that any equilibrium strategies are increasing functions can be done as follows. Suppose that (β_1, β_2) is a pure-strategy Bayes-Nash equilibrium. Without loss of generality, let us consider player 1. If player 1 has valuation v_1, then the strategy $b_1 = \beta_1(v_1)$ yields the expected payoff that is at least as large as under any other strategy $b_1' = \beta_1(v_1')$, i.e., $s(v_1, b_1) \geq s(v_1, b_1')$. Using (7.44), we have

$$\begin{aligned}
&v_1 \mathbf{Pr}[\beta_2(v_2) < b_1] - b_1 \mathbf{Pr}[\beta_2(v_2) \geq b_1] - \mathbf{E}[\beta_2(v_2)\mathbf{1}(\beta_2(v_2) < b_1)] \\
\geq\ &v_1 \mathbf{Pr}[\beta_2(v_2) < b_1'] - b_1' \mathbf{Pr}[\beta_2(v_2) \geq b_1'] - \mathbf{E}[\beta_2(v_2)\mathbf{1}(\beta_2(v_2) < b_1')].
\end{aligned} \quad (7.45)$$

If, on the other hand, player 1 has valuation v_1' then the strategy $b_1' = \beta_1(v_1')$ has the expected payoff that is at least as large as under the strategy $b_1 = \beta_1(v_1)$, i.e., $s(v_1', b_1') \geq s(v_1', b_1)$. Using (7.44), this can be written as

$$\begin{aligned}
&v_1' \mathbf{Pr}[\beta_2(v_2) < b_1'] - b_1' \mathbf{Pr}[\beta_2(v_2) \geq b_1'] - \mathbf{E}[\beta_2(v_2)\mathbf{1}(\beta_2(v_2) < b_1')] \\
\geq\ &v_1' \mathbf{Pr}[\beta_2(v_2) < b_1] - b_1 \mathbf{Pr}[\beta_2(v_2) \geq b_1] - \mathbf{E}[\beta_2(v_2)\mathbf{1}(\beta_2(v_2) < b_1)].
\end{aligned} \quad (7.46)$$

Summing up the left-hand sides and the right-hand sides in (7.45) and (7.46), we obtain

$$(v_1' - v_1)(\mathbf{Pr}[\beta_2(v_2) \geq b_1] - \mathbf{Pr}[\beta_2(v_2) \geq b_1']) \geq 0.$$

Hence, it follows that $v_1 \geq v_1'$ implies $b_1 \geq b_1'$, i.e., β_1 is an increasing function. Showing that any equilibrium strategies are strictly increasing can be done by contradiction. Suppose that the strategy of a player, say player 1, is not strictly increasing. Then, there would exist $b > 0$ such that $\mathbf{Pr}[\beta_1(v_1) = b] > 0$. In this case, player 2 would play just above value b. In turn, this implies that for any valuation v_1 of player 1 such that $\beta_1(v_1) = b$, it is better for player 1 to play slightly below b, which contradicts the assumption that β_1 is an equilibrium strategy.

The continuity of the equilibrium strategies can be established by contradiction as follows. Suppose that the strategy of a player, say player 1, is discontinuous. Then there must exist an interval $[a, b]$ such that $\mathbf{Pr}[\beta_1(v_1) \in [a, b]] = 0$ and $\beta_1(v_1^*) \in (a, b)$ for some value v_1^*. In this case, player 2 strictly prefers playing a to any value in (a, b) because his or her winning probability is unchanged and the expected cost is reduced. But then for player 1, dropping at or beyond value b is not optimal if his or her valuation is equal to v_1^*, which is a contradiction. $\qquad\square$

In the next theorem we provide a set of sufficient conditions for a pair of strategies to be a pure-strategy Bayes-Nash equilibrium.

Theorem 7.20. *Suppose that β_1 and β_2 satisfy*

$$\beta_1^{-1}(b)F_2'(\beta_2^{-1}(b))\frac{d}{db}\beta_2^{-1}(b) = 1 - F_2(\beta_2^{-1}(b)) \tag{7.47}$$

$$\beta_2^{-1}(b)F_1'(\beta_2^{-1}(b))\frac{d}{db}\beta_1^{-1}(b) = 1 - F_1(\beta_1^{-1}(b)) \tag{7.48}$$

and

$$\text{either } \beta_1^{-1}(0) = 0 \text{ or } \beta_2^{-1}(0) = 0. \tag{7.49}$$

Then, (β_1, β_2) is a pure-strategy Bayes-Nash equilibrium.

Proof. Since each strategy function β_i is strictly increasing and continuous, it has a well-defined inverse function β_i^{-1}. The expected payoff in (7.44), can be written as follows:

$$s(v_i, b_i) = \int_0^{b_i} (v_i - b_j)\,dF_j(\beta_j^{-1}(b_j)) - b_i(1 - F_j(\beta_j^{-1}(b_i))). \tag{7.50}$$

Since β_i is assumed to be a pure-strategy Bayes-Nash equilibrium, it must hold that

$$\frac{\partial}{\partial b_i}s(v_i, \beta_i(v_i)) = 0.$$

From (7.50), we have that

$$\frac{\partial}{\partial b_i}s(v_i, b_i) = v_i f_j(\beta_j^{-1}(b_i))\frac{d}{db_j}\beta_j^{-1}(b_i) - (1 - F_j(\beta_j^{-1}(b_i))),$$

which when set equal to zero, gives conditions (7.47) and (7.48).

It remains to show that (β_1, β_2) is such that either $\beta_1^{-1}(0) = 0$ or $\beta_2^{-1}(0) = 0$. For the purpose of a contradiction, suppose that on the contrary $\beta_1^{-1}(0) > 0$ and $\beta_2^{-1}(0) > 0$. Then, with a positive probability both players invest zero efforts or in other words immediately drop out. This, however, cannot be an equilibrium, because at the point where both players invest zero effort each player is better off by unilaterally increasing his or her effort. □

Symmetric prior distributions Consider the case of independent and identically distributed valuations according to a prior distribution F.

Corollary 7.21. *There exists a unique symmetric pure-strategy Nash equilibrium β that is given by*

$$\beta(v) = \int_0^v x\frac{dF(x)}{1 - F(x)}.$$

Proof. Under the assumption that the prior distributions are identical and equal to F and that the strategies are symmetric according to the function β, conditions (7.47) and (7.48) boil down to

$$\beta^{-1}(b)F'(\beta^{-1}(b))\frac{d}{db}\beta^{-1}(b) = 1 - F(\beta^{-1}(b)).$$

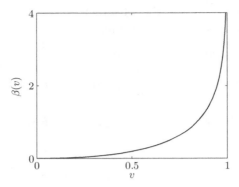

Figure 7.10. Equilibrium strategy in the game of the war of attrition for a uniform prior distribution.

Using the change of variables $b = \beta(v)$, it follows that

$$\frac{d}{dv}\beta(v) = v\frac{F'(v)}{1 - F(v)}.$$

By integrating, we obtain

$$\beta(v) = \beta(0) + \int_0^v x\frac{dF(x)}{1 - F(x)}$$

and by (7.49), we have that $\beta(0) = 0$.   □

Example 7.22 (uniform prior distribution). Suppose that the prior distribution is uniform on $[0, 1]$. Then, the symmetric Bayes-Nash equilibrium strategy is

$$\beta(v) = \log\left(\frac{1}{1 - v}\right) - v. \tag{7.51}$$

See Figure 7.10 for a graph of this function.

Since the prize allocation mechanism is such that a unit prize is allocated to the higher bidder, the game of the war of attrition is a standard auction, a concept introduced in Section 2.2.1. Under the prevailing assumptions, the valuations are independent and identically distributed, and the expected payment of a player with valuation zero is equal to zero; hence the revenue equivalence Theorem 2.20 applies. The revenue equivalence theorem says that standard auctions have equivalent expected payments. The all-pay auction is a standard auction and by Theorem 2.24 has the expected payment equal to the expected value of the second highest valuation. For the game of the war of attrition, the expected total effort R is equal to the expected payment, and hence

$$R = \mathbf{E}[v_{(2,2)}].$$

It is left as Exercise 7.11 for the reader to check that this holds true directly from the equilibrium strategies in Corollary 7.21. Since both players drop out from the competition at the same time it follows that individual efforts are equal. Hence, the expected values of individual efforts and the expected maximum individual effort are all equal to half of the expected value of the second highest valuation.

Continuum of asymmetric equilibrium strategies In Corollary 7.21 we characterized a symmetric pure-strategy Bayes-Nash equilibrium that is unique in the set of symmetric equilibria. In general, for the set of strategies that are allowed to be asymmetric, a pure-strategy Bayes-Nash equilibrium is not unique. In fact, there can exist a continuum of pure-strategy Bayes-Nash equilibria as shown by the following example.

Example 7.23 (uniform prior distribution). Assume that prior distributions are identical and are uniform distributions on the interval $[0, 1]$. From Theorem 7.20, it follows that there is a family of equilibrium strategies parametrized by a real-valued parameter θ such that (7.49) and the following condition hold:

$$\log\left(\frac{1 - \beta_1^{-1}(b)}{\beta_1^{-1}(b)}\right) = \log\left(\frac{1 - \beta_2^{-1}(b)}{\beta_2^{-1}(b)}\right) + \theta.$$

Equivalently, we can write

$$\beta_2^{-1}(b) = \frac{\beta_1^{-1}(b)}{(1 - e^{-\theta})\beta_1^{-1}(b) + e^{-\theta}}.$$

The symmetric equilibrium strategy corresponds to the value of the parameter $\theta = 0$, in which case $\beta_1 \equiv \beta_2 \equiv \beta$ with β specified in (7.51).

In general, a one-parameter family of equilibrium strategies can be characterized as follows. Let us define

$$H_i(x) = \int_x^1 \frac{F_i'(y)}{y(1 - F_i(y))} \, dy.$$

From (7.47) and (7.48), we have that $H_1'(\beta_1^{-1})d\beta_1^{-1} = H_2'(\beta_1^{-1})d\beta_2^{-1}$, which by integrating gives

$$H_1(\beta_1^{-1}) = H_2(\beta_2^{-1}) + \theta, \quad \text{for } \theta \in \mathbf{R}. \tag{7.52}$$

Equation (7.52) defines a one-parameter family of equilibrium strategies that we denote by $\beta_1(v, \theta)$ and $\beta_2(v, \theta)$. Since both H_1 and H_2 are strictly decreasing functions, we can write

$$\beta_2^{-1}(b, \theta) = H_2^{-1}(H_1(\beta_1^{-1}(b, \theta)) + \theta). \tag{7.53}$$

In the special case of uniform prior distributions, $(\beta_1^{-1}(b, \theta), \beta_2^{-1}(b, \theta))$ passes through $(0, 0)$, which means that for each player the probability of immediately dropping out from the competition is zero. By Theorem 7.20, either $\beta_1^{-1}(0, \theta) = 0$ or $\beta_2^{-1}(0, \theta) = 0$. Whether this holds for one or two players depends on the properties of the prior distributions and is characterized as follows. Let $\mathcal{F}$ be the class of distributions that contains all distributions that have strictly positive density functions on the interval $[0, 1]$, and let $\mathcal{F}_0$ be a subset of $\mathcal{F}$ that contains every distribution $F_i \in \mathcal{F}$ such that $\lim_{x \downarrow 0} H_i(x) = +\infty$.

Theorem 7.24. *For every pair of prior distributions F_1 and F_2 in $\mathcal{F}$ there is a one-parameter family of equilibrium strategies $(\beta_1^{-1}(b, \theta), \beta_2^{-1}(b, \theta))$ with the following properties:*

(i) *If $F_1 \in \mathcal{F}_0$ and $F_2 \in \mathcal{F}_0$, then $\beta_1^{-1}(0, \theta) = 0$ and $\beta_2^{-1}(0, \theta) = 0$ for all $\theta \in \mathbf{R}$.*

(ii) *If $F_1 \in \mathcal{F}_0$ and $F_2 \notin \mathcal{F}_0$, then $\beta_1^{-1}(0, \theta) > 0$ and $\beta_2^{-1}(0, \theta) = 0$ for all $\theta \in \mathbf{R}$.*

(iii) *If $F_1 \notin \mathcal{F}_0$ and $F_2 \notin \mathcal{F}_0$, then $\beta_1^{-1}(0, \theta) > 0$ and $\beta_2^{-1}(0, \theta) = 0$, or $\beta_1^{-1}(0, \theta) = 0$ and $\beta_2^{-1}(0, \theta) > 0$, for all $\theta \in \mathbf{R}$ except for $\theta = H_1(0) - H_2(0)$ such that $\beta_1^{-1}(0, \theta) = 0$ and $\beta_2^{-1}(0, \theta) = 0$.*

Proof. If $F_1 \in \mathcal{F}_0$ and $F_2 \in \mathcal{F}_0$, then $\lim_{v \downarrow 0} H_1(v) = +\infty$ and $\lim_{v \downarrow 0} H_2(v) = +\infty$. Hence, for every $\theta \in \mathbf{R}$, equation (7.53) is satisfied at $(\beta_1^{-1}(0, \theta), \beta_2^{-1}(0, \theta)) = (0, 0)$.

If $F_1 \in \mathcal{F}_0$ and $F_2 \notin \mathcal{F}_0$, then $\lim_{v \downarrow 0} H_1(v) = +\infty$ and $H_2(0)$ is finite. From (7.53), it follows that there exists no $\theta \in \mathbf{R}$ such that $\beta_1^{-1}(0, \theta) = 0$ and $\beta_2^{-1}(0, \theta) \geq 0$.

Finally, $F_1 \notin \mathcal{F}_0$ and $F_2 \notin \mathcal{F}_0$, then both $H_1(0)$ and $H_2(0)$ are finite. In this case by (7.52), $\beta_1^{-1}(0, \theta) > 0$ and $\beta_2^{-1}(0, \theta) = 0$ if $\theta < H_1(0) - H_2(0)$, $\beta_1^{-1}(0, \theta) = 0$ and $\beta_2^{-1}(0, \theta) = 0$ if $\theta = H_1(0) - H_2(0)$, and $\beta_1^{-1}(0, \theta) = 0$ and $\beta_2^{-1}(0, \theta) > 0$ if $\theta > H_1(0) - H_2(0)$. $\qquad\square$

For example, distribution $F(v) = 1 - (1 - v)^a$ for $v \in [0, 1]$, for parameter $a > 0$ is a member of the family of distributions $\mathcal{F}_0$, while distribution $F(v) = v^a$ for $v \in [0, 1]$, for parameter $a > 1$ is not a member of $\mathcal{F}_0$.

Arbitrary Number of Players and Identical Prizes

Consider the game of the war of attrition with $n \geq 2$ players and a given number of m prizes of identical values such that $1 \leq m < n$. The players have private valuation parameters according to a prior distribution such that their values are independent and identically distributed random variables with distribution F that has no atoms and has strictly positive density on the support $[0, 1]$. Each player incurs a unit marginal cost until either dropping out from the competition or the game ends and incurs a constant marginal cost of value $c \in [0, 1]$ from the time this player drops out from the competition until the end of the game. The payoff functions of the players are as given in (7.39).

We shall show that there exists a unique subgame perfect symmetric Bayes-Nash equilibrium, in which players drop out from the competition in increasing order of the values of their valuation parameters, so that the first player to drop out from the competition is the player with the lowest valuation, the second player to drop out from the competition is the player with the second lowest valuation, and so on. The game ends as soon as the number of players remaining in the competition is equal to the number of available prizes, with each such player being awarded a prize. See Figure 7.11 for an illustration.

Theorem 7.25. *There is a unique subgame perfect symmetric Bayes-Nash equilibrium for the game of the war of attrition, which is such that in each subgame with $j \in \{1, 2 \ldots, n - m\}$ players still to drop out from the competition, a player with valuation of value v who participates in this subgame waits for a duration*

$$\beta(v; j, \underline{v}_j) = c^{j-1} m \int_{\underline{v}_j}^{v} x \frac{dF(x)}{1 - F(x)}, \text{ for } v \in [\underline{v}_j, 1] \qquad (7.54)$$

where $\underline{v}_j$ is the largest valuation of a player who dropped out in an earlier subgame if any, and is otherwise equal to zero.

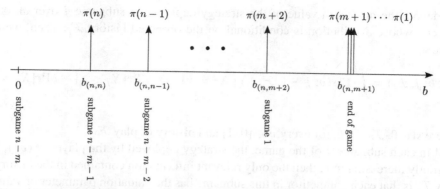

Figure 7.11. The dropouts of players in the game of the war of attrition is in increasing order of valuations in the subgame perfect symmetric Bayes-Nash equilibrium ($\pi(j)$ is the identity of the player with the j-th largest valuation).

Proof. The proof is organized in such a way so that we first introduce some notation, then present and prove several lemmas, and then finally prove the theorem.

We refer to a subgame in which there are j players who have yet to drop out from the competition as subgame j. The game starts with subgame $n - m$ and it ends at the end of subgame 1. For each subgame j, we denote with N_j the set of players who did not drop out in an earlier subgame, and refer to these players as *competing players* or *competitors* in this subgame. We denote with $\mathcal{F}_j$ the observed history of play by the players at the beginning of subgame j. We suppose that in each subgame, the competitors in this subgame play a common strategy, which for subgame j with history of play $\mathcal{F}_j$ is denoted as $\beta(v; j, \mathcal{F}_j)$ for a player who competes in this subgame and has a valuation parameter of value v.

At the end of each subgame j, each player observes the following new information about the valuation parameters of the players. Each player observes the value of the smallest time a player who competed in the given subgame decided to wait before dropping out. Hence, the new information available at the beginning of subgame $j - 1$ is that every player $i \in N_{j-1}$ has the valuation parameter of value v_i such that $\beta(v_i; j, \mathcal{F}_j) \geq \beta(\underline{v}_{j-1}; j, \mathcal{F}_j)$, where $\underline{v}_{j-1}$ is defined by $\beta(\underline{v}_{j-1}; j, \mathcal{F}_j) = \min_{l \in N_j} \beta(v_l; j, \mathcal{F}_j)$ for $j < n - m$, and $\underline{v}_{n-m} = 0$. The relevant history of play at the beginning of subgame j can be defined as $\mathcal{F}_j = \{\underline{v}_{n-m}, \underline{v}_{n-m-1}, \ldots, \underline{v}_j\}$. We refer to $\underline{v}_j$ as the *marginal valuation* in subgame j of the game. We denote with $s(v; j, \mathcal{F}_j)$ the expected continuation payoff for a player with the valuation parameter of value v from the beginning of subgame j until the end of the game. Similarly, we denote with $x(v; j, \mathcal{F}_j)$ the probability that a player who competes in subgame j with the valuation parameter of value v eventually wins a prize, and denote with $p(v; j, \mathcal{F}_j)$ his or her expected cost from the beginning of subgame j until the end of the game. Note that for every subgame j, history of play $\mathcal{F}_j$, and a valuation parameter of value v, we have

$$s(v; j, \mathcal{F}_j) = vx(v; j, \mathcal{F}_j) - p(v; j, \mathcal{F}_j). \tag{7.55}$$

For an arbitrary player with the valuation parameter of value v who competes in subgame j with history of play $\mathcal{F}_j$, we denote with $s(v, b; j, \mathcal{F}_j)$ the expected continuation payoff for this player conditional on that he or she plays strategy b in subgame j. Let

X_j denote the minimum value of the strategy deployed in subgame j over all other players, whose distribution is conditional on the observed history $\mathcal{F}_j$. Then, we can write

$$s(v, b; j, \mathcal{F}_j) = \int_0^b (\mathbf{E}[s(v; j-1, \mathcal{F}_{j-1}) \mid X_j = x] - x)\, d\mathbf{Pr}[X_j \le x] - b\mathbf{Pr}[X_j > b],$$
(7.56)

where $s(v; 0, \mathcal{F}_0) = v$, for every $v \in [0, 1]$ and history of play $\mathcal{F}_0$.

If in each subgame j of the game, the strategy deployed by the players $\beta(v; j, \mathcal{F}_j)$ is strictly increasing in v, then the only relevant information contained in the history of play $\mathcal{F}_j$ is that each competitor in this subgame has the valuation parameter of value at least $\underline{v}_j$. In this case, for each subgame j, we will denote the strategy deployed in this subgame with $\beta(v; j, \underline{v}_j)$. Similarly, we will replace $\mathcal{F}_j$ with $\underline{v}_j$ in the definitions of the expected cumulative payoffs, the probabilities of winning a prize, and the expected cumulative costs in subgame j.

We next present several lemmas that establish various properties of subgame perfect symmetric Bayes-Nash equilibria of the game, which are to be used at the end to complete the proof of the theorem.

Lemma 7.26. *For every subgame perfect symmetric Bayes-Nash equilibrium, for each subgame j and history of play $\mathcal{F}_j$, $\beta(v; j, \mathcal{F}_j)$ is strictly increasing in v.*

Furthermore, the probability that a player with the valuation parameter of value v who competes in subgame j eventually wins a prize is equal to the probability that his or her valuation is one of the m largest valuations among all competitors in this subgame conditional on that the valuation parameters of all competitors are of value at least $\underline{v}_j$, i.e.,

$$x(v; j, \underline{v}_j) = \sum_{i=j}^{m+j-1} \binom{m+j-1}{i} \left(\frac{F(v) - F(\underline{v}_j)}{1 - F(\underline{v}_j)} \right)^i \left(\frac{1 - F(v)}{1 - F(\underline{v}_j)} \right)^{m+j-1-i}.$$
(7.57)

Proof. We first establish that in every subgame perfect symmetric Bayes-Nash equilibrium, the expected continuation payoff $s(v; j, \mathcal{F}_j)$ is strictly increasing in v for every subgame j and history of play $\mathcal{F}_j$. This is shown by induction over the subgames of the game as follows. Base case: subgame $j = 1$. In this case the expected continuation payoff for each player who competes in this subgame is equal to the value of his or her valuation parameter, so the claim obviously holds. Induction step: suppose that the claim holds for subgame $j - 1$ for every history of play $\mathcal{F}_{j-1}$, and we then show that this implies that it holds for subgame j for every history of play $\mathcal{F}_j$. Suppose that v and $\tilde{v}$ are two values of valuations such that $v > \tilde{v}$ and $\beta(\tilde{v}; j, \mathcal{F}_j) > 0$. Since $\beta(\cdot; j, \mathcal{F}_j)$ is a symmetric Bayes-Nash equilibrium in subgame j with history of play $\mathcal{F}_j$, we have

$$s(v; j, \mathcal{F}_j) \ge s(v, \beta(\tilde{v}; j, \mathcal{F}_j); j, \mathcal{F}_j)$$

and

$$s(\tilde{v}; j, \mathcal{F}_j) = s(\tilde{v}, \beta(\tilde{v}; j, \mathcal{F}_j); j, \mathcal{F}_j).$$

Hence, combining with (7.56), we have that $s(v; j, \mathcal{F}_j) - s(\tilde{v}; j, \mathcal{F}_j) > 0$ is implied by

$$\int_0^{\beta(\tilde{v};j,\mathcal{F}_j)} \mathbf{E}[(s(v; j - 1, \mathcal{F}_{j-1}) - s(\tilde{v}; j - 1, \mathcal{F}_{j-1})) \mid X_j = x] \, d\mathbf{Pr}[X_j \leq x] > 0,$$

which holds by the induction hypothesis.

We now show that for every subgame j with history of play $\mathcal{F}_j$, $\beta(v; j, \mathcal{F}_j)$ is increasing in v. This is shown by induction over the subgames of the game. Base case: subgame $j = 1$. For every two values of valuations v and $\tilde{v}$, by the definition of a Bayes-Nash equilibrium, we have

$$s(v, \beta(v; 1, \mathcal{F}_1); 1, \mathcal{F}_1) \geq s(v, \beta(\tilde{v}; 1, \mathcal{F}_1); 1, \mathcal{F}_1)$$

and

$$s(\tilde{v}, \beta(\tilde{v}; 1, \mathcal{F}_1); 1, \mathcal{F}_1) \geq s(\tilde{v}, \beta(v; 1, \mathcal{F}_1); 1, \mathcal{F}_1).$$

By summing up the respective sides of the last two inequalities and using (7.56), it follows that

$$(v - \tilde{v}) \int_0^{\beta(v;1,\mathcal{F}_1)} d\mathbf{Pr}[X_1 \leq x] \geq (v - \tilde{v}) \int_0^{\beta(\tilde{v};1,\mathcal{F}_1)} d\mathbf{Pr}[X_1 \leq x].$$

Hence, if $v > \tilde{v}$, then $\beta(v; 1, \mathcal{F}_1) \geq \beta(\tilde{v}; 1, \mathcal{F}_1)$.

Induction step: suppose that for subgame $j - 1$ and every history of play $\mathcal{F}_{j-1}$, $\beta(v; j - 1, \mathcal{F}_{j-1})$ is increasing in v, and we then show that this implies that for subgame j and history of play $\mathcal{F}_j$, $\beta(v; j, \mathcal{F}_j)$ is increasing in v. By the same argument as in the base case, we can derive that

$$\int_0^{\beta(v;j,\mathcal{F}_j)} \mathbf{E}[(s(v; j - 1, \mathcal{F}_{j-1}) - s(\tilde{v}; j - 1, \mathcal{F}_{j-1})) \mid X_j = x] \, d\mathbf{Pr}[X_j \leq x]$$

$$\geq \int_0^{\beta(\tilde{v};j,\mathcal{F}_j)} \mathbf{E}[(s(v; j - 1, \mathcal{F}_{j-1}) - s(\tilde{v}; j - 1, \mathcal{F}_{j-1})) \mid X_j = x] \, d\mathbf{Pr}[X_j \leq x].$$

Since by the induction hypothesis the conditional expectation in the two integrands is strictly positive, it follows that if $v > \tilde{v}$, then $\beta(v; j, \mathcal{F}_j) \geq \beta(\tilde{v}; j, \mathcal{F}_j)$.

We now show that $\beta(v; j, \mathcal{F}_j)$ is strictly increasing in v for every subgame j and history of play $\mathcal{F}_j$. Suppose on the contrary that there exists a non-empty interval of valuations $[\underline{v}, \bar{v}]$ and a value $b > 0$ such that $\beta(v; j, \mathcal{F}_j) = b$, for $v \in [\underline{v}, \bar{v}]$. Then, all competing players in subgame j will decide to wait until b time units have elapsed since the beginning of this subgame with a strictly positive probability. However, then each such player will have a beneficial unilateral deviation to wait for a marginally larger value than b, which is a contradiction to that $\beta(\cdot; j, \mathcal{F}_j)$ is a symmetric Bayes-Nash equilibrium.

The second claim of the lemma is established as follows. Since in each subgame of the game, the symmetric Bayes-Nash equilibrium is strictly increasing, it follows that the marginal valuations are increasing over different subgames from the beginning until the end of the game. The players drop out in increasing order of their valuations until there are as many players as there are prizes, at which point the game ends. Hence, it follows that in every subgame of the game the equilibrium winning probabilities are as asserted in the lemma. $\qquad\square$

Lemma 7.27. *There is a unique symmetric Bayes-Nash equilibrium in subgame* 1 *of the game, which for every given value of marginal valuation* $\underline{v}_1$ *is given by*

$$\beta(v; 1, \underline{v}_1) = m \int_{\underline{v}_1}^{v} x \frac{dF(x)}{1 - F(x)}, \text{ for } v \in [\underline{v}_1, 1].$$

Proof. In subgame 1, there are $m + 1$ players who are in competition, and the game ends as soon as one of these players drops out from the competition. From (7.56), for every $v, v^* \in [\underline{v}_1, 1]$, we have

$$s(v, \beta(v^*; 1, \underline{v}_1); 1, \underline{v}_1) = \int_0^{\beta(v^*; 1, \underline{v}_1)} (v - \beta(x; 1, \underline{v}_1)) \, d\mathbf{Pr}[X_1 \leq x]$$
$$- \beta(v^*; 1, \underline{v}_1)\mathbf{Pr}[X_1 > \beta(v^*; 1, \underline{v}_1)].$$

For $\beta(\cdot; 1, \underline{v}_1)$ to be a symmetric Bayes-Nash equilibrium, it must hold that $\partial s(v, \beta(v^*; 1, \underline{v}_1); 1, \underline{v}_1)/\partial v^* = 0$, at $v = v^*$. By a straightforward calculus, we have

$$\frac{\partial}{\partial v^*} s(v, \beta(v^*; 1, \underline{v}_1); 1, \underline{v}_1) = v \frac{\partial \mathbf{Pr}[X_1 \leq \beta(v^*; 1, \underline{v}_1)]}{\partial v^*}$$
$$- \mathbf{Pr}[X_1 > \beta(v^*; 1, \underline{v}_1)] \frac{\partial}{\partial v^*} \beta(v^*; 1, \underline{v}_1).$$

Hence, we have

$$\frac{\partial}{\partial v^*} \beta(v^*; 1, \underline{v}_1) = v^* \frac{\partial \mathbf{Pr}[X_1 \leq \beta(v^*; 1, \underline{v}_1)]}{\partial v^*} \frac{1}{\mathbf{Pr}[X_1 > \beta(v^*; 1, \underline{v}_1)]}.$$

Combining with the fact

$$\mathbf{Pr}[X_1 > \beta(v^*; 1, \underline{v}_1)] = \left(\frac{1 - F(v^*)}{1 - F(\underline{v}_1)}\right)^m$$

we obtain that

$$\frac{\partial}{\partial v^*} \beta(v^*; 1, \underline{v}_1) = m v^* \frac{F'(v^*)}{1 - F(v^*)}$$

which by integrating corresponds to the expression asserted in the lemma. □

Lemma 7.28. *All subgame perfect symmetric Bayes-Nash equilibria are equivalent with respect to both the expected continuation payoffs and the expected continuation costs in each subgame of the game.*

Proof. The proof is by induction. Base case: subgame $j = 1$. For subgame 1, the claim follows by the uniqueness of the symmetric Bayes-Nash equilibrium in subgame 1, which is shown in Lemma 7.26. Induction step: suppose that the expected continuation payoffs are unique in subgame $j - 1$, and we then show that this implies that the expected continuation payoffs are unique in subgame j. Since in every Bayes-Nash equilibrium no player has a beneficial unilateral deviation, for every $v, v^* \in [\underline{v}_j, 1]$,

$$s(v^*; j, \underline{v}_j) \geq v^* x(v; j, \underline{v}_j) - p(v; j, \underline{v}_j),$$

which combined with (7.55) implies

$$s(v^*; j, \underline{v}_j) - s(v; j, \underline{v}_j) \geq (v^* - v)x(v; j, \underline{v}_j).$$

From this, it follows that

$$\frac{\partial}{\partial v}s(v;j,\underline{v}_j) = x(v;j,\underline{v}_j), \text{ for every } v \in [\underline{v}_j, 1].$$

By integrating, we obtain

$$s(v;j,\underline{v}_j) = s(\underline{v}_j;j,\underline{v}_j) + \int_{\underline{v}_j}^{v} x(y;j,\underline{v}_j)\,dy, \text{ for } v \in [\underline{v}_j, 1].$$

Combining with (7.55) and $s(\underline{v}_j;j,\underline{v}_j) = -p(\underline{v}_j;j,\underline{v}_j)$, we obtain

$$p(v;j,\underline{v}_j) = p(\underline{v}_j;j,\underline{v}_j) + \int_{\underline{v}_j}^{v} yx(y;j,\underline{v}_j)\,dy.$$

Note that by Lemma 7.26, in the right-hand side of the last equation, only the summation term $p(\underline{v}_j;j,\underline{v}_j)$ depends on the strategies deployed in subsequent subgames of the game. Since in subgame j a player of valuation $\underline{v}_j$ would instantly drop out, $p(\underline{v}_j;j,\underline{v}_j)$ is equal to the expected continuation cost in subgame $j-1$ for a player with valuation $\underline{v}_j$. Since by the induction hypothesis, the expected continuation payoffs and the expected continuation costs are unique in subgame $j-1$, it follows that so they are in subgame j of the game. $\qquad\square$

Lemma 7.29. *There is a unique subgame perfect symmetric Bayes-Nash equilibrium.*

Proof. The proof is by induction over the subgames of the game. Base case: subgame $j=1$. In subgame 1, by Lemma 7.26, there is a unique symmetric Bayes-Nash equilibrium. Induction step: suppose that there is a unique symmetric Bayes-Nash equilibrium in subgame $j-1$, and we then show that this implies a unique symmetric Bayes-Nash equilibrium in subgame j of the game.

We first show that every symmetric Bayes-Nash equilibrium strategy in subgame j of the game is continuous. Suppose on the contrary that there exists a finite interval in which every player drops out with zero probability. Then, a player who was due to drop out first after this interval would benefit from dropping out at the beginning of this interval. Since by the induction hypothesis, there is a unique equilibrium after the next dropout, its time cannot affect the subsequent development of the game. Hence, it follows that $\beta(\cdot;j,\underline{v}_j)$ is continuous and $\beta(\underline{v}_j;j,\underline{v}_j) = 0$.

We now show that there is a unique symmetric Bayes-Nash equilibrium strategy in subgame j of the game. Suppose on the contrary that in subgame j, there are two symmetric Bayes-Nash equilibrium strategies $\underline{\beta}$ and $\bar{\beta}$ and $0 \le \underline{v} < v^* \le 1$ such that $\underline{\beta}(v^*;j,\underline{v}) < \bar{\beta}(v^*;j,\underline{v})$. By the continuity of $\underline{\beta}$ and $\bar{\beta}$, it follows there exists $v \in [\underline{v}, v^*)$ such that

$$\underline{\beta}(v;j,\underline{v}) = \bar{\beta}(v;j,\underline{v})$$

and

$$\underline{\beta}(x;j,\underline{v}) < \bar{\beta}(x;j,\underline{v}), \text{ for every } x \in (v, v^*]. \tag{7.58}$$

Since $\underline{\beta}$ and $\bar{\beta}$ are symmetric Bayes-Nash equilibrium strategies, then, in particular, $\underline{\beta}(x;j,v)$ and $\bar{\beta}(x;j,v)$ are symmetric Bayes-Nash equilibrium strategies in subgame

j with the marginal valuation of value v. Note that

$$\underline{\beta}(v; j, \underline{v}) + \underline{\beta}(x; j, v) = \underline{\beta}(x; j, \underline{v})$$

and

$$\bar{\beta}(v; j, \underline{v}) + \bar{\beta}(x; j, v) = \bar{\beta}(x; j, \underline{v}).$$

Combining with (7.58), it follows that any player with valuation $x \in (\underline{v}, v^*]$ would have a smaller expected time until the next dropout of a player by using strategy $\underline{\beta}$ than by using strategy $\bar{\beta}$, and by the induction hypothesis, the same expected cumulative cost thereafter. This contradicts the equivalence of the expected cumulative payoffs of any subgame perfect symmetric Bayes-Nash equilibria shown in Lemma 7.28.   □

We now show that the strategies given by (7.54) specify a subgame perfect symmetric Bayes-Nash equilibrium. It suffices to consider an arbitrary subgame, say subgame j, and an arbitrary player, say of valuation v^*, and consider his or her unilateral deviations from the strategy given by (7.54) under the assumption that all other players play according to the strategy given by (7.54). There are two different deviations to consider depending on whether the given player decides to drop out from competition earlier or later than prescribed by the strategy given by (7.54).

Suppose first that the player drops out later than prescribed by (7.54). Then, note that this will not change his or her expected cost incurred while waiting for other players to drop out from the competition. This is because dropping out from the competition would reduce his or her cost per unit time by a factor c. However, by the definition of the strategy in (7.54), there would be one less player in the competition, which slows down the rate at which players drop out from the competition by factor c. The net effect is that the expected cost incurred by the player until the beginning of subgame 1 remains unchanged by the deviation. Now, if the player dropped out from the competition before subgame 1, then he or she will neither gained nor lost by the deviation. On the other hand, if the player is a competitor in subgame 1, then his or her valuation parameter is smaller than that of any other competitor in this subgame, which means that the player will incur a loss compared with making no deviation.

Suppose now that the player drops out earlier than prescribed by (7.54). Then, by the same argument as in the earlier case, this will not change his or her expected cost incurred until the beginning of subgame 1. In subgame 1 two events can happen. If v^* is smaller than the smallest valuation of a competitor in subgame 1, then the player's total payoff is not affected by the deviation. On the other hand, if v^* is larger than the smallest valuation of a competitor in subgame 1, then the player loses winning a prize by making the deviation.   □

For the special case $c = 0$, all players but the set of $m + 1$ players with the largest valuations immediately drop out from the competition and the contest ends as soon as one of the players from this set drops out from the competition. In the case $c = 0$ and a single prize, in the symmetric subgame perfect Bayes-Nash equilibrium, all players but the two with the largest valuations drop out immediately from the competition, and the contest ends as soon as one of these two players drops out.

In the remainder of this section we characterize some quantities of interest that hold in the subgame perfect symmetric Bayes-Nash equilibrium given in Theorem 7.25.

The individual effort investments are increasing in the valuation parameters of the players: they are increasing in the valuation of the players for the set of players with $n - m - 1$ smallest valuations and assume a common value for the set of players with $m + 1$ largest valuations. The ordered values of individual effort investments satisfy

$$b_{(n,n)} < b_{(n,n-1)} < \cdots < b_{(n,m+2)} < b_{(n,m+1)} = b_{(n,m)} = \cdots = b_{(n,1)}.$$

The individual effort investments are given by the following mapping of a vector of valuations onto a vector of individual effort investments:

$$b_{(n,i)} = \sum_{j=j^*(m,i)}^{n-m} \beta(v_{(n,m+j)}, v_{(n,m+j+1)}, j) \tag{7.59}$$

where $j^*(m, i) = \max\{i - m, 1\}$.

Corollary 7.30 (expected individual efforts). *The expected individual efforts in the subgame perfect symmetric Bayes-Nash equilibrium are given as follows:*

$$\mathbf{E}[b_{(n,i)}] = m \sum_{j=j^*(m,i)}^{n-m} \frac{c^{j-1}}{m+j} \mathbf{E}[v_{(n,m+j)}]. \tag{7.60}$$

Proof. The proof follows by taking the expectation in (7.59) and using the identity

$$\mathbf{E}[v_{(n,i)}] = i\mathbf{E}\left[\int_{v_{(n,i+1)}}^{v_{(n,i)}} x \frac{F'(x)}{1 - F(x)}\, dx\right], \quad \text{for } i \in \{1, 2, \ldots, n\}, \tag{7.61}$$

which follows by basic properties of the order statistics and is left to the reader as Exercise 7.20. □

For the special case $c = 0$, the $m + 1$ largest individual efforts assume a common value, which is a random variable with the expected value $m\mathbf{E}[v_{(n,m+1)}]/(m + 1)$, and all other individual efforts are equal to zero. For the case $c = 0$ and a single prize, only the two players with the largest valuations invest strictly positive efforts that are equal to the value of a random variable with the expected value $\mathbf{E}[v_{(n,2)}]/2$.

Corollary 7.31 (expected total effort). *The expected total effort in the subgame perfect symmetric Bayes-Nash equilibrium is given by*

$$R = m \sum_{j=1}^{n-m} c^{j-1} \mathbf{E}[v_{(n,m+j)}].$$

Proof. This follows by the identities

$$R = \sum_{j=1}^{n-m} (m + j)\mathbf{E}[\beta(v_{(n,m+j)}, v_{(n,m+j+1)}, j)] = m \sum_{j=1}^{n-m} c^{j-1} \mathbf{E}[v_{(n,m+j)}]$$

where the second equation follows by identity (7.61). □

For the special case $c = 0$,

$$R = m\mathbf{E}[v_{(n,m+1)}].$$

In the case of a single prize, the expected total effort is equal to the expected value of the second largest valuation $\mathbf{E}[v_{(n,2)}]$.

On the other hand, for the special case $c = 1$, we have

$$R = m \sum_{j=1}^{n-m} \mathbf{E}[v_{(n,m+j)}],$$

which shows that making all players pay a unit marginal cost until the contest ends can produce significantly larger expected total effort in comparison with the case in which players pay unit marginal costs only until either dropping out from the competition or the contest ends.

7.3 The Tug of War

The *tug of war* game refers to a contest between two players where a prize is awarded to the one who is first to achieve a given *winning margin* of $k \geq 1$ more wins than the opponent in a sequence of subgames played between the two players. In any given subgame, players make simultaneous effort investments, and the subgame is won by the player who invests a larger effort in this subgame, with resolution of ties according to a tie break rule. We shall study the game of tug of war as an extensive form game with quasi-linear payoff functions where players value the prize according to valuations $v_1 \geq v_2 > 0$, incur unit marginal costs of production, and in each subgame discount the expected payoff for participating in future subgames with a discount factor $0 < \delta \leq 1$. We shall study the subgame perfect Nash equilibrium of this game.

The extensive form game is specified more concretely as follows. The game proceeds through a sequence of subgames $t = 1, 2, \ldots$. The effort investments in each subgame t assume positive real values and are denoted by b_1^t and b_2^t for player 1 and player 2, respectively. We denote with X_t the difference between the number of subgames won by player 1 and player 2 in the first t subgames. We shall refer to X_t as the *point difference* in the first t subgames between the two players. Unless indicated otherwise, we assume that the initial point difference is equal to zero, i.e., $X_0 = 0$. In general, the initial point difference may assume an arbitrary value $-k \leq j \leq k$, which allows for giving a head start to one of the players. The game ends immediately after completion of subgame T, which by definition is the earliest subgame t such that either $X_t = -k$ or $X_t = k$. In the case $X_T = -k$, the winner of the contest is player 1, and otherwise, in the case $X_T = k$, the winner of the contest is player 2. Figure 7.12 provides an illustration. The payoff functions are given as follows:

$$s_1(\mathbf{b}) = \delta^T v_1 \mathbf{1}(X_T = -k) - \sum_{t=1}^{T} \delta^t b_1^t \text{ and } s_2(\mathbf{b}) = \delta^T v_2 \mathbf{1}(X_T = k) - \sum_{t=1}^{T} \delta^t b_2^t$$

where $\mathbf{b} = ((b_1^t, b_2^t), t = 1, 2, \ldots, T)$.

The extensive form game studied in this section accommodates as a special case the normal-form game of the standard all-pay contest between two players with complete information, which we studied in Chapter 2, for the value of the winning margin $k = 1$. In this special case, by Theorem 2.3, the game has a unique mixed-strategy Nash

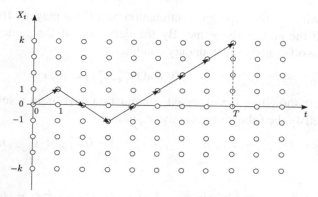

Figure 7.12. The tug of war: a sample realization of the point difference until the end of the game.

equilibrium that is fully characterized therein. In this section we study the subgame perfect Nash equilibrium of the game with the winning margin $k > 1$.

The extensive form game under consideration consists of a sequence of subgames $1, 2, \ldots, T$ in each of which players make strategic effort investments given a history of the effort investments in earlier subgames of the game. We consider the subgame perfect Nash equilibrium where in each subgame t of the game the only relevant part of the history is the point difference X_{t-1} just before this subgame. We shall refer to a subgame t such that $X_{t-1} = j$ as a *a subgame of type j*. For example, the outcome in Figure 7.12 consists of a sequence of eight subgames of respective subgame types

$$0, 1, 0, -1, 0, 1, 2, \text{ and } 3.$$

In each subgame of type j, the players make effort investments independently according to mixed strategies specified by distributions $B_{1,j}(x)$ and $B_{2,j}(x)$ for player 1 and player 2, respectively. We shall use the following definitions:

$$B_{i,j}(x-) = \lim_{\epsilon \downarrow 0} B_{i,j}(x - \epsilon) \text{ and } \Delta B_{i,j}(x) = B_{i,j}(x) - B_{i,j}(x-).$$

The ties of effort investments in a subgame of type j are resolved according to a tie break rule that selects one of the players to be the winner in the given subgame by sampling from the distribution $\mathbf{z}_j = (z_{1,j}, z_{2,j})$. The tie break rules are assumed to be unbiased so that $\mathbf{z}_j$ is a uniform distribution in all subgames of type j except in those in which one of the players has a strictly positive continuation valuation and the other player has a zero continuation valuation, in which case the winner in the subgame is the player with a strictly positive continuation valuation. For the given pair of mixed strategies and the given tie break rule, let $x_{i,j}$ denote the probability of player i winning in a subgame of type j.

In a subgame perfect Nash equilibrium, the sequence of subgame types $X_0, X_1, \ldots, X_{T-1}$ evolves according to a Markov chain with the state transition probabilities given by

$$X_t = \begin{cases} X_{t-1} - 1 & \text{with probability } x_{1,X_{t-1}} \mathbf{1}(X_{t-1} > -k) \\ X_{t-1} + 1 & \text{with probability } x_{2,X_{t-1}} \mathbf{1}(X_{t-1} < k) \end{cases}.$$

We denote with $s_{i,j}^*$ the expected continuation payoff for player i from a subgame of type j until the end of the game. By the definition of the game, the expected continuation payoffs satisfy the boundary conditions

$$(s_{1,-k}^*, s_{2,-k}^*) = (v_1, 0) \text{ and } (s_{1,k}^*, s_{2,k}^*) = (0, v_2). \qquad (7.62)$$

We shall next show that the expected continuation payoffs in a subgame of type $-k < j < k$ satisfy the following recursive equations:

$$s_{1,j}^* = \delta s_{1,j+1}^* + \delta \max\{(s_{1,j-1}^* + s_{2,j-1}^*) - (s_{1,j+1}^* + s_{2,j+1}^*), 0\} \qquad (7.63)$$

and

$$s_{2,j}^* = \delta s_{2,j-1}^* + \delta \max\{(s_{1,j+1}^* + s_{2,j+1}^*) - (s_{1,j-1}^* + s_{2,j-1}^*), 0\}. \qquad (7.64)$$

Without loss of generality, let us consider the expected continuation payoff of player 1 from a subgame of type $-k < j < k$. The expected continuation payoffs for player 2 follow by exactly the same arguments by swapping the identities of the two players. Let $b_{1,j}$ and $b_{2,j}$ denote the effort investments of player 1 and player 2 in a subgame of type j. There are three possible outcomes:

Outcome $b_{1,j} > b_{2,j}$: player 1 invests a larger effort than player 2. This event occurs with probability $B_{2,j}(b_{1,j}-)$ conditional on the effort investment of player 1 being of value $b_{1,j}$. The game switches from a subgame of subtype j to a subgame of type $j - 1$.

Outcome $b_{1,j} = b_{2,j}$: player 1 invests the same amount of effort as player 2. This event occurs with probability $\Delta B_{2,j}(b_{1,j})$ conditional on the effort investment of player 1 being of value $b_{1,j}$. The game switches from a subgame of type j to a subgame of type $j - 1$ with probability $z_{1,j}$ or to a subgame of type $j + 1$ with probability $z_{2,j}$.

Outcome $b_{1,j} < b_{2,j}$: player 1 invests a smaller effort than player 2. This event occurs with probability $1 - B_{2,j}(b_{1,j})$ conditional on the effort investment of player 1 being of value $b_{1,j}$. The game switches from a subgame of type j to a subgame of type $j + 1$.

In each of the three possible outcomes, player 1 incurs a production cost equal to the amount of his or her effort investment $b_{1,j}$. It follows that the expected continuation payoff $s_{1,j}(b_{1,j})$ for player 1 conditional on his or her effort investment being of value $b_{1,j}$ satisfies the following identity:

$$s_{1,j}(b_{1,j}) = \delta s_{1,j-1}^* B_{2,j}(b_{1,j}-) + (\delta s_{1,j-1}^* z_{1,j} + \delta s_{1,j+1}^*(1 - z_{1,j})) \Delta B_{2,j}(b_{1,j})$$
$$+ \delta s_{1,j+1}^*(1 - B_{2,j}(b_{1,j})) - b_{1,j}.$$

From this it follows that

$$s_{1,j}(b_{1,j}) = \delta s_{1,j+1}^* + v_{1,j} B_{2,j}(b_{1,j}-) + z_{1,j} v_{1,j} \Delta B_{2,j}(b_{1,j}) - b_{1,j} \qquad (7.65)$$

and

$$s_{2,j}(b_{2,j}) = \delta s_{2,j-1}^* + v_{2,j} B_{1,j}(b_{2,j}-) + (1 - z_{1,j}) v_{2,j} \Delta B_{1,j}(b_{2,j}) - b_{2,j} \qquad (7.66)$$

where, by definition,

$$v_{1,j} = \delta(s_{1,j-1}^* - s_{1,j+1}^*) \text{ and } v_{2,j} = \delta(s_{2,j+1}^* - s_{2,j-1}^*). \qquad (7.67)$$

From the form of the expected payoff functions in (7.65) and (7.66), it follows that each subgame of type j is strategically equivalent to the game that models the standard all-pay contest between two players with valuation parameters $v_{1,j}$ and $v_{2,j}$. By Theorem 2.3, the expected payoffs in the mixed-strategy Nash equilibrium of a subgame of type j are equal to $\max\{v_{1,j} - v_{2,j}, 0\}$ and $\max\{v_{2,j} - v_{1,j}, 0\}$ for player 1 and player 2, respectively. Using this fact in (7.65) and (7.66), it follows that the expected continuation payoffs in a subgame of type $-k < j < k$ satisfy the recursive equations (7.63) and (7.64).

7.3.1 Subgame Perfect Nash Equilibrium for $\delta = 1$

We separately consider the case of players with symmetric valuations and the case of players with asymmetric valuations.

Symmetric Valuations

Consider the case of players with symmetric valuations $v_1 = v_2 > 0$. It is readily observed that

$$(s_{1,j}^*, s_{2,j}^*) = \begin{cases} (v_1, 0), & \text{if } -k \le j < 0 \\ (0, 0), & \text{if } j = 0 \\ (0, v_1), & \text{if } 0 < j \le k \end{cases}$$

satisfies the boundary conditions (7.62) and equations (7.63) and (7.64).

Combining this with (7.67) we obtain a subgame perfect Nash equilibrium as summarized in Figure 7.13. The only non-trivial subgame is the first subgame between the two players, in which either player wins with equal probability because of the symmetry of valuations. In any subsequent subgame neither player invests a strictly positive effort, and eventually the winner of the game is the player who won in the first subgame of the game. It follows that the game of tug of war with symmetric valuations of value $v_1 > 0$ and any value of the winning margin $k > 1$ is equivalent to the standard all-pay contest between two players with symmetric valuations of value v_1 with respect to total individual efforts of players.

Asymmetric Valuations

Consider the case of players with asymmetric valuations $v_1 > v_2 > 0$. In this case, it is readily observed that

$$(s_{1,j}^*, s_{2,j}^*) = \begin{cases} (v_1, 0), & \text{if } -k \le j \le k - 2 \\ (v_1 - v_2, 0), & \text{if } j = k - 1 \\ (0, v_2), & \text{if } j = k \end{cases}$$

is a solution to the boundary conditions (7.62) and equations (7.63) and (7.64).

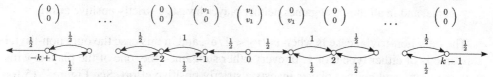

Figure 7.13. Subgame perfect Nash equilibrium of the game of tug of war with $\delta = 1$ and symmetric valuations. Each subgame type is represented by a circle with the corresponding valuations indicated near to the circle.

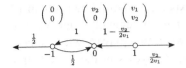

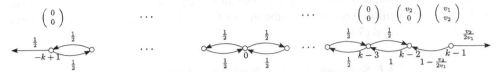

Figure 7.14. Subgame perfect Nash equilibrium of the game of tug of war with $\delta = 1$ and asymmetric valuations: (top) $k = 2$ and (bottom) $k > 2$. Each subgame type is represented by a circle with the corresponding valuations indicated near to the circle.

Combining this with (7.67) we obtain a subgame perfect Nash equilibrium as summarized in Figure 7.14. Starting from the initial point difference of zero, the subgame perfect Nash equilibrium is rather trivial: the player with the larger valuation, player 1, wins with certainty, and neither player invests a strictly positive effort in each subgame of the game. This stands in sharp contrast to the standard all-pay contest where in the mixed-strategy Nash equilibrium players invest strictly positive efforts with a positive probability and the winning probabilities of players are

$$(x_1, x_2) = \left(1 - \frac{v_2}{2v_1}, \frac{v_2}{2v_1}\right). \tag{7.68}$$

The effect of extending the game to a winning margin $k > 1$ is that the larger valuation player wins with certainty and neither player invests a strictly positive effort. We shall see in the next section that this is not preserved in the case where the expected continuation payoffs are discounted with a factor $0 < \delta < 1$, but it still holds that extending the game to a winning margin of $k > 1$ favors the larger valuation player.

7.3.2 Subgame Perfect Nash Equilibrium for $\delta < 1$

In this section we consider the game of tug of war with the discount factor $0 < \delta < 1$. We first provide a summary of the properties of the subgame perfect Nash equilibrium that we establish in this section.

We can distinguish two cases with respect to equilibrium strategies:

Case $v_1/v_2 < 1/\delta^2$: the game proceeds through a number of subgames until one of the players wins two more subgames than the other player.

Case $v_1/v_2 \geq 1/\delta^2$: player 1 wins in every subgame with certainty until winning the game, and in all these subgames neither player invests a strictly positive effort.

The only non-trivial case is when $v_1/v_2 < 1/\delta^2$, and in this case the only non-trivial subgame is of either type 0 or 1. In every other subgame type, one of the players wins with certainty, and neither player invests a strictly positive effort. See Figure 7.15 for an illustration.

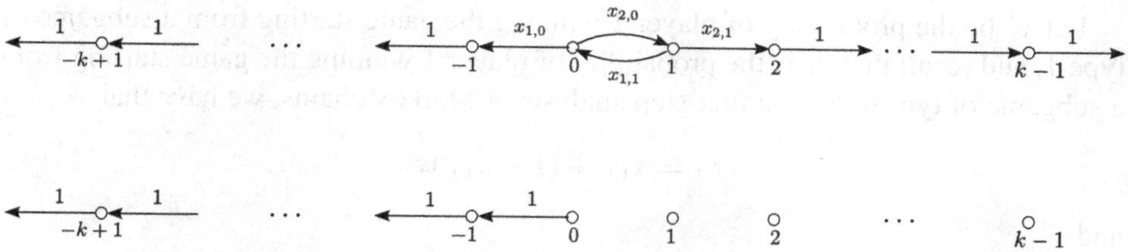

Figure 7.15. Subgame perfect Nash equilibrium for $\delta < 1$: (top) $v_1/v_2 < 1/\delta^2$ and (bottom) $v_1/v_2 \geq 1/\delta^2$.

In a subgame of type 0 the continuation valuations are

$$v_{1,0} = \delta^k v_1 \text{ and } v_{2,0} = \frac{\delta^k}{1 - \delta^2}(v_2 - \delta^2 v_1),\qquad(7.69)$$

and in a subgame of type 1 the continuation valuations are

$$v_{1,1} = \frac{\delta^{k+1}}{1-\delta^2}(v_1 - v_2) \text{ and } v_{2,1} = \delta^{k-1}v_2.\qquad(7.70)$$

The expected payoffs of players are

$$s_1^* = \begin{cases} \frac{\delta^k}{1-\delta^2}(v_1 - v_2), & \text{if } v_1/v_2 < 1/\delta^2 \\ \delta^k v_1, & \text{otherwise} \end{cases} \text{ and } s_2^* = 0.$$

For the case of the winning margin $k = 1$, the game corresponds to the game that models the standard all-pay contest between two players with valuation parameters $v_1 \geq v_2 > 0$. In this case, by Theorem 2.3, there is a unique mixed-strategy Nash equilibrium with the expected payoffs

$$s_1^* = v_1 - v_2 \text{ and } s_2^* = 0.$$

The winning probabilities of players (x_1, x_2) with the initial point difference of value zero are characterized as follows. If $v_1/v_2 \geq 1/\delta^2$ then obviously, $(x_1, x_2) = (1, 0)$ because player 1 wins in every subgame until winning the game. The case $v_1/v_2 < 1/\delta^2$ is more interesting and is characterized as follows. The only non-trivial subgames are of type 0, or 1. The game evolves starting from the first subgame of type 0, and it remains in a subgame of type 0 or 1 until hitting a subgame of type -1 or 2. In a subgame of type -1 player 1 is guaranteed to win in all subsequent subgames until winning the game, and in a subgame of type 2 player 2 is guaranteed to win in all subsequent subgames until winning the game. The probability of player 1 winning the game is thus equal to the probability of hitting a subgame of type -1 starting from a subgame of type 0.

By Theorem 2.3, the winning probabilities in a subgame of type 0 are

$$(x_{1,0}, x_{2,0}) = \left(1 - \frac{v_{2,0}}{2v_{1,0}}, \frac{v_{2,0}}{2v_{1,0}} \right)\qquad(7.71)$$

and in a subgame of type 1 are

$$(x_{1,1}, x_{2,1}) = \left(\frac{v_{1,1}}{2v_{2,1}}, 1 - \frac{v_{1,1}}{2v_{2,1}} \right).\qquad(7.72)$$

Let x_1^1 be the probability of player 1 winning the game starting from a subgame of type 1, and recall that x_1 is the probability of player 1 winning the game starting from a subgame of type 0. By the first-step analysis of Markov chains, we have that

$$x_1 = x_{1,0} + (1 - x_{1,0})x_1^1$$

and

$$x_1^1 = x_{1,1}x_1.$$

From the last two equations,

$$x_1 = \frac{x_{1,0}}{1 - (1 - x_{1,0})x_{1,1}}.$$

Combining with (7.71) and (7.72), it follows that the winning probabilities are given by

$$x_1 = \begin{cases} \dfrac{1 - \frac{1}{2(1-\delta^2)}\left(\frac{v_2}{v_1} - \delta^2\right)}{1 - \frac{1}{2(1-\delta^2)}\left(\frac{v_2}{v_1} - \delta^2\right)\frac{\delta^2}{2(1-\delta^2)}\left(\frac{v_1}{v_2} - 1\right)}, & \text{if } v_1/v_2 < 1/\delta^2 \\ 1, & \text{if } v_1/v_2 \geq 1/\delta^2 \end{cases}$$

and $x_2 = 1 - x_1$.

The winning probabilities are invariant to the value of the winning margin $k > 1$. The winning probability of player 1 increases in the value of the discount factor δ for $0 \leq \delta < \sqrt{v_2/v_1}$ and is equal to 1 for every $\sqrt{v_2/v_1} \leq \delta \leq 1$. In the limit of the discount factor going to zero, the winning probabilities correspond to those in the mixed-strategy Nash equilibrium in the standard all-pay contest in which case they are as given in (7.68); in the limit of the discount factor going to 1, the winning probabilities are $(x_1, x_2) = (1, 0)$. The winning probability of the larger valuation player, player 1, is larger than or equal to that in the standard all-play contest where the inequality is strict for any strictly positive value of the discount factor. The overall effect of extending the game to a winning margin $k > 1$ is making the higher valuation player more likely to win the game. In the case of the winning margin $k = 1$, the winning probability of the higher valuation player decreases linearly with the ratio of the lower to higher valuation. On the contrary, for any winning margin of value $k > 1$, the higher valuation player wins with certainty for any sufficiently large ratio of the higher to lower valuation. Otherwise, the winning probability of the higher valuation player decreases with the ratio of the lower to higher valuation. The threshold when this occurs is $v_2/v_1 = \delta^2$. See Figure 7.16 for an illustration.

A similar analysis can be carried out to characterize the expected total effort in a subgame perfect Nash equilibrium. Let r and q be the expected total efforts invested in a subgame of type 0 and 1, respectively. Let R and Q be the expected total efforts invested in the game started in a subgame of type 0 and type 1, respectively. Since a subgame of type 0 or 1 is strategically equivalent to a standard-all pay contest with valuations as specified by (7.69) and (7.70), respectively, it follows that the expected total efforts in each subgame of type 0 and 1 are given as

$$r = \frac{v_{2,0}}{2}\left(1 + \frac{v_{2,0}}{v_{1,0}}\right) \text{ and } q = \frac{v_{1,1}}{2}\left(1 + \frac{v_{1,1}}{v_{2,1}}\right). \tag{7.73}$$

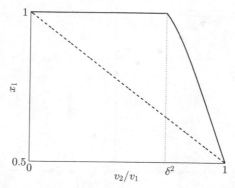

Figure 7.16. The winning probability of the higher valuation player: (dashed) winning margin $k = 1$ and (solid) winning margin $k > 1$.

Again, by the first-step analysis of Markov chains, we have

$$R = r + (1 - x_{1,0})Q \text{ and } Q = q + x_{1,1}R.$$

Hence, it follows that the expected total effort is equal to

$$R = \frac{r + (1 - x_{1,0})q}{1 - (1 - x_{1,0})x_{1,1}}. \tag{7.74}$$

In the case when $v_1/v_2 < 1/\delta^2$, it follows from (7.69)-(7.70), (7.71)-(7.72), (7.73), and (7.74) that the expected total effort depends on the winning margin k only through the factor δ^k and is proportional to this factor. Hence, the expected total effort decreases geometrically with the value of the winning margin k. Otherwise, in the case where $v_1/v_2 \geq 1/\delta^2$, the expected total effort is equal to zero because neither player invests a strictly positive effort in any subgame of the game.

Expected Continuation Payoffs in a Subgame Perfect Nash Equilibrium

In this section we first establish that the expected continuation payoffs in a subgame perfect Nash equilibrium are non-negative and increasing for a player the closer the point difference is for this player to win the game; we then provide an explicit characterization of the expected continuation payoffs in a subgame perfect Nash equilibrium.

Lemma 7.32 (non-negativity and monotonicity). *In a subgame perfect Nash equilibrium, the expected continuation payoffs are non-negative, and the following monotonicity properties hold in every subgame of type* $-k \leq j < k$,

(i) $s^*_{1,j} \geq s^*_{1,j+1}$ *with strict inequality if* $s^*_{1,j} > 0$, *and*
(ii) $s^*_{2,j} \leq s^*_{2,j+1}$ *with strict inequality if* $s^*_{2,j+1} > 0$.

Proof. In every subgame each player is guaranteed a non-negative continuation payoff by investing no effort in this and any subsequent subgame; thus, the expected continuation payoffs must be non-negative in any subgame perfect Nash equilibrium.

For the two monotonicity claims (i) and (ii), we establish only claim (i) because similar arguments apply for claim (ii). Consider the game starting from a subgame of type $j + 1$. There are two possible events from this subgame until the end of the game:

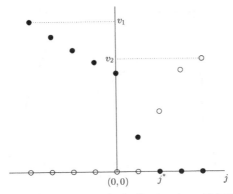

Figure 7.17. The equilibrium continuation payoffs $s^*_{1,j}$, denoted by black circles, and $s^*_{2,j}$, denoted by white circles. The tipping point j^* is in a subgame of type 2.

either a subgame of type j is reached in a finite number of subgames, or a subgame of type j is never reached. Conditional on the former event, we have $s^*_{1,j+1} \leq \delta s^*_{1,j}$ because before reaching a subgame of type j player 1 cannot gain a positive payoff and it takes at least one step to reach a subgame of type j. Conditional on the event that a subgame of type j is never reached, the expected continuation payoff of player 1 from a subgame of type $j + 1$ is non-positive; thus, obviously $s^*_{1,j+1} \leq \delta s^*_{1,j}$. It follows that in both cases $s^*_{1,j+1} \leq s^*_{1,j}$ where the inequality is strict whenever $s^*_{1,j} > 0$ because $\delta \in (0, 1)$.   □

From Lemma 7.32, there exists a *tipping point* $-k \leq j^* \leq k$ at which the expected payoffs of players cross over, i.e.,

$$s^*_{1,j} > s^*_{2,j} \quad \text{for} \ -k \leq j < j^* \text{ and } s^*_{1,j} \leq s^*_{2,j} \quad \text{for } j^* \leq j \leq k.$$

See Figure 7.17 for an illustration. An explicit characterization of the expected continuation payoffs in a subgame perfect Nash equilibrium can be established by finding a solution to the system of equations (7.63) and (7.64) with the boundary conditions (7.62) and is presented in the following lemma.

Lemma 7.33. *In any subgame perfect Nash equilibrium, the expected continuation payoffs are given as follows:*

(i) *If $v_1/v_2 > 1/\delta^{2(k-1)}$, then*

$$(s^*_{1,j}, s^*_{2,j}) = \begin{cases} \left(\delta^{k+j}v_1, 0\right), & \text{if} \ -k \leq j \leq k-2 \\ \left(\delta^{2k-1}v_1 - \delta v_2, 0\right), & \text{if } j = k-1 \\ (0, v_2), & \text{if } j = k. \end{cases}$$

(ii) *If $v_1/v_2 = 1/\delta^{2j^*}$, for an integer $-k + 1 < j^* < k$, then*

$$(s^*_{1,j}, s^*_{2,j}) = \begin{cases} \left(\delta^{k+j}v_1, 0\right), & \text{if} \ -k \leq j < j^* \\ (0, 0) & \text{if } j = j^* \\ \left(0, \delta^{k-j}v_2\right), & \text{if } j^* < j \leq k. \end{cases}$$

(iii) *If* $1/\delta^{2(j^*-1)} < v_1/v_2 < 1/\delta^{2j^*}$, *for an integer* $-k+1 < j^* < k$, *then*

$$(s_{1,j}^*, s_{2,j}^*) = \begin{cases} (\delta^{k+j}v_1, 0), & \text{if } -k \le j < j^* \\ \left(\frac{\delta^{k+j}}{1-\delta^2}v_1 - \frac{\delta^{k-j}}{1-\delta^2}v_2, 0\right), & \text{if } j = j^* - 1 \\ \left(0, \frac{\delta^{k-j}}{1-\delta^2}v_2 - \frac{\delta^{k+j}}{1-\delta^2}v_1\right), & \text{if } j = j^* \\ (0, \delta^{k-j}v_2), & \text{if } j^* < j \le k. \end{cases}$$

Proof. Case (i): in this case, there is a solution such that $v_{1,j} > v_{2,j}$ for $-k < j < k$. From equations (7.63) and (7.64) we have that for $-k < j < k$,

$$s_{1,j}^* = \delta s_{1,j-1}^* + \delta(s_{2,j-1}^* - s_{2,j+1}^*)$$

and

$$s_{2,j}^* = \delta s_{2,j-1}^*.$$

This is a system of linear equations with the solution such that $s_{2,j}^* = 0$ for $-k < j < k$, and $s_{1,j}^* = \delta s_{1,j-1}^*$ for $-k < j < k-1$ and $s_{1,k-1}^* = \delta s_{1,k-2}^* - \delta s_{2,k}^*$. The asserted expression in the lemma follows by combining with the boundary conditions $s_{1,-k}^* = v_1$ and $s_{2,k}^* = v_2$.

Case (ii): in this case, there is a solution such that $v_{1,j} > v_{2,j}$ for $-k \le j < j^*$, $v_{1,j^*} = v_{2,j^*}$, and $v_{1,j} \le v_{2,j}$ for $j^* < j \le k$, for some integer $-k < j^* < k$. The asserted expression in the lemma follows from (7.63) and (7.64) and the boundary conditions in (7.62).

Case (iii): in this case, there is a solution such that $v_{1,j} > v_{2,j}$ for $-k \le j \le j^*$, and $v_{1,j} < v_{2,j}$ for $j^* < j \le k$. The asserted expression in the lemma follows again from (7.63) and (7.64) and the boundary conditions in (7.62). □

From Lemma 7.33, the tipping point admits the following explicit characterization:

$$j^* = \min\left\{\left\lfloor \frac{1}{2}\log_{1/\delta}(v_1/v_2) \right\rfloor, k\right\}$$

where $\lfloor x \rfloor$ denotes the largest integer m such that $m \le x$. The tipping point is always a non-negative integer by the assumption that the valuation of player 1 is greater than or equal to the valuation of player 2, and is equal to zero in the case of symmetric valuations. The tipping point is increasing in the ratio of the higher to lower valuation and is equal to k for every sufficiently large ratio of the higher to lower valuation. In the first case in Lemma 7.33, the ratio of the higher to lower valuation is large enough for the tipping point to be of value k, while in the other two cases the tipping point is of value smaller than k.

Subgame Perfect Nash Equilibrium

In the following theorem we characterize a subgame perfect Nash equilibrium of the game of tug of war with the winning margin $k > 1$, the discount factor $0 < \delta < 1$, and the tie break rule that selects the winner uniformly at random, except in the case when one of the players has a strictly positive continuation valuation and the other player has a zero continuation valuation and so the former player is selected to be the winner in the given subgame.

Theorem 7.34. *The game of tug of war with the winning margin $k > 1$ and the discount factor $0 < \delta < 1$ has a subgame perfect Nash equilibrium with the outcome in each subgame of type $-k < j < k$ equivalent to that in the mixed-strategy Nash equilibrium of the game that models the standard all-pay contest with valuations $(v_{1,j}, v_{2,j})$ that are given as follows:*

(i) *If $v_1/v_2 > 1/\delta^{2(k-1)}$:*

$$
(v_{1,j}, v_{2,j}) = \begin{cases}
(v_1, 0), & \text{if } j = -k \\
\left((1-\delta)\delta^{k+j}v_1, 0\right), & \text{if } -k < j < k-2 \\
\left((1-\delta^2)\delta^{2(k-1)}v_1 + \delta^2 v_2, 0\right), & \text{if } j = k-2 \\
\left(\delta^{2k-1}v_1, \delta v_2\right), & \text{if } j = k-1 \\
(0, v_2), & \text{if } j = k.
\end{cases}
$$

(ii) *If $v_1/v_2 = 1/\delta^{2j^*}$:*

$$
(v_{1,j}, v_{2,j}) = \begin{cases}
(v_1, 0), & \text{if } j = -k \\
\left((1-\delta)\delta^{k+j}v_1, 0\right), & \text{if } -k < j < j^* - 1 \\
\left(\delta^{k+j^*-1}v_1, 0\right), & \text{if } j = j^* - 1 \\
\left(\delta^{k+j^*}v_1, \delta^{k-j^*}v_2\right), & \text{if } j = j^* \\
\left(0, \delta^{k-j^*-1}v_2\right), & \text{if } j = j^* + 1 \\
\left(0, (1-\delta)\delta^{k-j}v_2\right), & \text{if } j^* + 1 < j < k \\
(0, v_2), & \text{if } j = k.
\end{cases}
$$

(iii) *If $1/\delta^{2(j^*-1)} < v_1/v_2 < 1/\delta^{2j^*}$:*

$$
(v_{1,j}, v_{2,j}) = \begin{cases}
(v_1, 0), & \text{if } j = -k \\
\left((1-\delta^2)\delta^{k+j}v_1, 0\right), & \text{if } -k < j < j^* - 2 \\
\left(\frac{\delta^{k-j^*+2}}{1-\delta^2}v_2 - \delta^{k+j^*-2}\left(\frac{\delta^2}{1-\delta^2} - 1\right)v_1, 0\right), & \text{if } j = j^* - 2 \\
\left(\delta^{k+j^*-1}v_1, \frac{\delta^{k-j^*+1}}{1-\delta^2}v_2 - \frac{\delta^{k+j^*+1}}{1-\delta^2}v_1\right), & \text{if } j = j^* - 1 \\
\left(\frac{\delta^{k+j^*}}{1-\delta^2}v_1 - \frac{\delta^{k-j^*+2}}{1-\delta^2}v_2, \delta^{k-j^*}v_2\right), & \text{if } j = j^* \\
\left(0, \frac{\delta^{k+j^*+1}}{1-\delta^2}v_1 - \delta^{k-j^*+1}\left(\frac{1}{1-\delta^2} - \delta^2\right)v_2\right), & \text{if } j = j^* + 1 \\
\left(0, (1-\delta^2)\delta^{k-j}v_2\right), & \text{if } j^* + 1 < j < k \\
(0, v_2), & \text{if } j = k.
\end{cases}
$$

Proof. The proof of the first part of the theorem follows from the observation that each subgame of type j is strategically equivalent to the game that models the standard all-pay contest between two players with valuation parameters $v_{1,j}$ and $v_{2,j}$, and the assumption that the tie break rule is such that the player with a strictly positive valuation is favored in case one of the players has a zero valuation. The explicit characterization of valuations $(v_{1,j}, v_{2,j})$, for $-k \le j \le k$, follows by straightforward but tedious derivations using the boundary conditions in (7.62), relations in (7.67), and the characterization of the expected continuation payoffs in Lemma 7.33. $\qquad\square$

We discuss the equilibrium behavior of players for the initial point difference of value zero in the three cases identified in Theorem 7.34. In the first case the tipping point is at a subgame of type k; in this case player 1 wins every subgame against player 2 with certainty until winning the game and in all these subgames neither player invests a strictly positive effort. In the second case the tipping point is at a subgame of type $\log_{1/\delta}(v_1/v_2)/2$, and the game has the following two possible outcomes: if $v_1 > v_2$, the outcome is as in the first case with player 1 winning in every subgame until winning the game and neither player making a strictly positive effort investment, and otherwise, if $v_1 = v_2$, the competition in the first subgame is as in the mixed-strategy Nash equilibrium of the standard all-pay contest between two players with symmetric valuations of value $\delta^k v_1$, in which either player is equally likely to win and then wins in each subsequent subgame with certainty until winning the game and in all these subgames neither player invests a strictly positive effort. In the third case, there are two possible outcomes. If the tipping point is at a subgame of a type greater than 1, the outcome is as in the first case with player 1 winning in very subgame until the game ends and neither player invests a strictly positive effort. If the tipping point is either at a subgame of type 0 or 1, the players compete in subgames of type 0 or 1 until either reaching a subgame of type -1 from which point on player 1 wins in each subgame until winning the game and neither player invests a strictly positive effort, or reaching a subgame of type 2 from which point on player 2 wins in each subgame until winning the game and neither player invests a strictly positive effort.

7.4 Sequential Aggregation of Production

In this section we consider a contest among a set of players that runs through a sequence of rounds where each player strategically invests a unit effort in one of the rounds. In each round, the players who have not invested their efforts in an earlier round simultaneously decide whether or not to invest their efforts in the given round. The effort investments of the players accumulate and combine together to provide a utility of production to the contest owner. The contest ends as soon as the utility of production becomes larger than or equal to a threshold value that is private information to the contest owner. A prize is awarded to a set of players who invest their efforts before the end of the contest according to a prize allocation mechanism. The goal of the contest owner is to use a prize allocation mechanism that incentivizes players to make early effort investments; the assumption is that the contest owner may be impatient. The payoff of a player is assumed to be equal to the share of the prize that he or she is allocated.

We shall study the extensive form game that is defined as follows. The game consists of a set $N = \{1, 2, \ldots, n\}$ of two or more players and a sequence $1, 2, \ldots, m$ of one or more rounds. Each player is endowed with a unit budget of effort that he or she invests in one of the rounds. The effort investment of player i is given by a vector $\mathbf{b}_i = (b_{i,1}, b_{i,2}, \ldots, b_{i,m})$ that takes values in the set $\mathcal{B}_i = \{(y_1, y_2, \ldots, y_m) \in \{0,1\}^m \mid \sum_{t=1}^m y_t \leq 1\}$. For any given $\mathbf{b}_i = (b_{i,1}, b_{i,2}, \ldots, b_{i,m}) \in \mathcal{B}_i$, we have that $b_{i,t} = 1$ if player i invests his or her effort budget in round t, and $b_{i,t} = 0$, otherwise. Let N_t denote the set of players who invest their efforts in round t, i.e., $N_t = \{i \in N \mid b_{i,t} > 0\}$. Let b_t denote the total effort invested in rounds 1

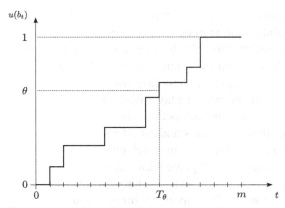

Figure 7.18. An illustration of the utility of aggregate production and the definition of a termination round.

through t, i.e., $b_t = \sum_{i \in N} \sum_{j \le t} b_{i,j}$. The utility of production to the contest owner is defined as follows: for every round $1 \le t \le m$ and effort investments $(b_{i,j}, i \in N, 1 \le j \le t)$, the utility of production to the contest owner is equal to $u(b_t)$ where $u : \{0, n\} \to [0, 1]$ is a given increasing function such that $u(0) = 0$ and $u(n) = 1$. The contest ends at the *termination round* $T_\theta(\mathbf{b})$ defined to be the earliest round in which the utility of production becomes larger than or equal to a threshold value $0 < \theta \le 1$:

$$T_\theta(\mathbf{b}) = \begin{cases} \min\{t \in \{1, 2, \ldots, m\} \mid u(b_t) \ge \theta\}, & \text{if } u(b_t) \ge \theta \text{ for some } 1 \le t \le m \\ +\infty, & \text{otherwise} \end{cases}$$

where $T_\theta(\mathbf{b}) = +\infty$ means that the prize is not allocated to the players. See Figure 7.18 for an illustration.

The value of the threshold θ is assumed to be private information to the contest owner. The players are assumed to have independent and identically distributed prior beliefs about the value of parameter θ according to prior distribution F, which is assumed to be a uniform distribution on $[0, 1]$. The distribution of the termination round is given as follows:

$$\Pr[T_\theta(\mathbf{b}) \le t] = \Pr[u(b_t) \ge \theta] = F(u(b_t)), \quad \text{for } 1 \le t \le m.$$

The prize allocation mechanism specifies the shares of the prize value that are allocated to the players. Without loss of generality, the prize is assumed to be of unit value. The shares of the prize value allocated to players correspond to the payoffs of the players. The payoff function of player i is given by $s_i : \mathcal{B}_i \times [0, 1] \to [0, 1]$ where $s_i(\mathbf{b}, \theta)$ denotes the payoff for player i given the effort investments being equal to $\mathbf{b}$ and the value of threshold being equal to θ. The payoff functions are such that $\sum_{i \in N} s_i(\mathbf{b}, \theta) \le 1$ for every $\mathbf{b} \in \times_{i \in N} \mathcal{B}_i$ and $\theta \in [0, 1]$. The expected payoffs functions are defined by taking the expected value with respect to the prior distribution of the threshold value,

$$s_i(\mathbf{b}) = \mathbf{E}[s_i(\mathbf{b}, \theta)], \quad \text{for } i \in N.$$

We present two examples of prize allocation mechanisms as follows:

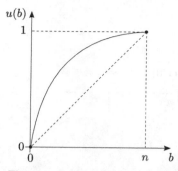 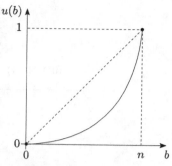

Figure 7.19. Two types of utility functions: (left) substitutes and (right) complements.

First to pass the post: This is a prize allocation mechanism that allocates the prize uniformly at random to one of the players who invests his or her effort in the termination round:

$$s_i(\mathbf{b}, \theta) = \frac{1}{|N_{T_\theta(\mathbf{b})}|} \mathbf{1}(i \in N_{T_\theta(\mathbf{b})}), \quad \text{for } i \in N.$$

Proportional to marginal contribution: This is a prize allocation mechanism that allocates the prize proportionally to the marginal contribution value:

$$s_i(\mathbf{b}, \theta) = \sum_{t=1}^{T_\theta(\mathbf{b})} \frac{1}{|N_t|} \frac{u(b_t) - u(b_{t-1})}{u(b_{T_\theta(\mathbf{b})})} \mathbf{1}(i \in N_t), \quad \text{for } i \in N.$$

We shall consider two types of utility functions. A utility function u is said to satisfy the condition of *substitutes* if

$$u(x + \delta) - u(x) > u(y + \delta) - u(y), \quad \text{for every } x < y \text{ and } \delta > 0.$$

A utility function is said to satisfy the condition of *complements* if

$$u(x + \delta) - u(x) < u(y + \delta) - u(y) \quad \text{for every } x < y \text{ and } \delta > 0.$$

An illustration is provided in Figure 7.19.

We shall consider a subgame perfect Nash equilibrium of the given game under specific prize allocation mechanisms. We refer to an equilibrium as a *pooling equilibrium* if there is a unique round in which all players direct their efforts.

7.4.1 Two Players

Consider the game with two players and two rounds; thus $n = 2$ and $m = 2$. There are four possible outcomes: either both players invest in the first round, player 1 invests in the first round and player 2 invests in the second round, player 1 invests in the second round and player 2 invests in the first round, or both players invest in the second round. We consider the class of prize allocation mechanisms that allocate equal shares to players if both invest in the same round, and award a share of $0 \le x \le 1$ to the player who invests in the first round if the two players invest in different rounds. The prize

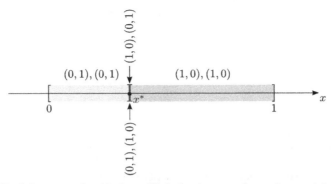

Figure 7.20. Subgame perfect Nash equilibria for the case of two players and two rounds.

allocation mechanisms first to pass the post and proportional to marginal contribution are accommodated as special cases for $x = 0$ and $x = u(1)$, respectively.

The expected payoffs are given as follows:

$$(s_1(\mathbf{b}_1, \mathbf{b}_2), s_2(\mathbf{b}_1, \mathbf{b}_2))$$

$$= \begin{cases} \left(\frac{1}{2}, \frac{1}{2}\right), & \text{if } (\mathbf{b}_1, \mathbf{b}_2) = ((1, 0), (1, 0)) \\ (u(1) + (1 - u(1))x, (1 - u(1))(1 - x)), & \text{if } (\mathbf{b}_1, \mathbf{b}_2) = ((1, 0), (0, 1)) \\ ((1 - u(1))(1 - x), u(1) + (1 - u(1))x), & \text{if } (\mathbf{b}_1, \mathbf{b}_2) = ((0, 1), (1, 0)) \\ \left(\frac{1}{2}, \frac{1}{2}\right), & \text{if } (\mathbf{b}_1, \mathbf{b}_2) = ((0, 1), (0, 1)) \end{cases}$$

There is a critical value of parameter x that determines the type of equilibrium outcomes, which is given by

$$x^* = 1 - \frac{1}{2(1 - u(1))}.$$

The outcome $((1, 0), (1, 0))$ is a unique subgame perfect Nash equilibrium if, and only if, $x > x^*$, each of the four possible outcomes is a subgame perfect Nash equilibrium if $x = x^*$, and the outcome $((0, 1), (0, 1))$ is a unique subgame perfect Nash equilibrium if, and only if, $x < x^*$. See Figure 7.20 for an illustration.

Notice that $u(1) > 1/2$ is equivalent to $x^* < 0$. If $u(1) > 1/2$ then there is a unique subgame perfect Nash equilibrium in which both players invest in the first round for every $0 \le x \le 1$. If $u(1) = 1/2$, then there are two different cases: if $0 < x \le 1$, then there is a unique subgame perfect Nash equilibrium in which both players invest in the first round of the game, and if $x = 0$, then any investment such that at least one player invests in the first round of the game is a subgame perfect Nash equilibrium.

First to Pass the Post
The prize allocation mechanism first to pass the post corresponds to the special case $x = 0$. There are three cases with respect to the existence of a subgame perfect Nash equilibrium:

$u(1) > 1/2$: in this case there is a unique subgame perfect Nash equilibrium in which both players invest in the first round.

$u(1) = 1/2$: in this case any possible outcome is a subgame perfect Nash equilibrium.

$u(1) < 1/2$: in this case there is a unique subgame perfect Nash equilibrium in which both players invest in the last round.

Proportional to Marginal Contribution

The prize allocation mechanism proportional to marginal contribution corresponds to the special case $x = u(1)$. There are three cases with respect to the existence of a subgame perfect Nash equilibrium:

$u(1) > 1 - 1/\sqrt{2}$: in this case there is a unique subgame perfect Nash equilibrium in which both players invest in the first round.

$u(1) = 1 - 1/\sqrt{2}$: in this case any possible outcome is a subgame perfect Nash equilibrium.

$u(1) < 1 - 1/\sqrt{2}$: in this case there is a unique subgame perfect Nash equilibrium in which both players invest in the last round.

Notice that the prize allocation mechanism that allocates proportionally to marginal contribution enlarges the set of utility functions for which the unique subgame perfect Nash equilibrium is for both players to invest in the first round. In this allocation mechanism case the set of utility functions includes all utility functions such that $u(1) > 1 - 1/\sqrt{2} \approx 0.29$. In contrast, in the allocation according to first pass the post, the set of utility functions includes all utility functions such that $u(1) > 0.5$.

In the next two sections we characterize the subgame perfect Nash equilibrium for particular prize allocation mechanisms. We identify conditions under which there exists a unique subgame perfect Nash equilibrium in which all players make their effort investments in the first round of the contest. The nature of the utility function – that is, whether the efforts represent substitutes or complements – will play a key role here.

7.4.2 First to Pass the Post

Theorem 7.35. *Suppose that the prize allocation mechanism is according to first to pass the post. If the utility function satisfies the substitutes condition, there is a unique subgame perfect Nash equilibrium in which all players make their investments in the first round. If the utility function satisfies the complements condition there is a unique subgame perfect Nash equilibrium in which all players make their investments in the last round.*

Proof. Consider first the case where the utility function satisfies the substitutes condition. Consider an arbitrary player $i \in N$ and an arbitrary strategy played by players $j \neq i$. Let δ_1 denote the number of the players other than player i who play in round 1. Under this strategy, the expected payoff for player i for playing in round 1 is

$$s_i = \frac{1}{\delta_1 + 1}\mathbf{Pr}[u(\delta_1 + 1) \geq \theta]. \tag{7.75}$$

Consider a unilateral deviation by player i to play in round $1 < t \leq m$. Let β denote the number of players who played before round t and let δ_t denote the number of players other than player i who play in round t. The expected payoff for player i is now

$$\tilde{s}_i = \frac{1}{\delta_t + 1} \mathbf{Pr}[u(\beta) < \theta \le u(\beta + \delta_t + 1)]. \tag{7.76}$$

We want to show that player i strictly prefers playing in round 1 than in round t, meaning that $s_i > \tilde{s}_i$. Since for each player the prior distribution of θ is uniform, from (7.75) and (7.76), we have that $s_i > \tilde{s}_i$ if, and only if,

$$\frac{u(\delta_1 + 1) - u(0)}{\delta_1 + 1} > \frac{u(\beta + \delta_t + 1) - u(\beta)}{\delta_t + 1}. \tag{7.77}$$

By the substitutes assumption, we have that

$$\frac{u(\delta_1 + 1) - u(0)}{\delta_1 + 1} = \frac{[u(\delta_1 + 1) - u(\delta_1)] + \cdots + [u(1) - u(0)]}{\delta_1 + 1} > u(\delta_1 + 1) - u(\delta_1)$$

and

$$\frac{u(\beta + \delta_t + 1) - u(\beta)}{\delta_t + 1} = \frac{[u(\beta + \delta_t + 1) - u(\beta + \delta_t)] + \cdots + [u(\beta + 1) - u(\beta)]}{\delta_t + 1}$$

$$< u(\beta + 1) - u(\beta).$$

Since $\delta_1 \le \beta$, by the substitutes assumption, it holds that $u(\beta + 1) - u(\beta) \le u(\delta_1 + 1) - u(\delta_1)$, and thus, (7.77) holds. This shows that it is the best response for player i to play in the first round, for any strategy of other players, and thus having all players playing in the first round is a unique subgame perfect Nash equilibrium.

Consider now the case where the utility function satisfies the complements condition. Consider a subgame in round $1 \le t < m$ given the history $\mathbf{b}_{t-1}$ and given that player i has not yet played. Assume that player i follows the strategy to play in the last round m. Let β be the number of players who play in rounds earlier than round t. Let δ_m denote the number of players other than player i who play in the last round. The expected payoff for player i is

$$s_i = \frac{1}{\delta_m + 1} \mathbf{Pr}[u(n - \delta_m - 1) < \theta \mid u(\beta) < \theta].$$

Consider now a deviation where player i plays in round t. Let δ_t denote the number of players other than player i who play in round t. The expected payoff for player i is then

$$\tilde{s}_i = \frac{1}{\delta_t + 1} \mathbf{Pr}[u(\beta) < \theta \le u(\beta + \delta_t + 1) \mid u(\beta) < \theta].$$

We show that because of the complements assumption, it holds that $s_i > \tilde{s}_i$, which is equivalent to

$$\frac{u(\beta + \delta_t + 1) - u(\beta)}{\delta_t + 1} < \frac{u(n) - u(n - \delta_m - 1)}{\delta_m + 1}. \tag{7.78}$$

By the complements assumption, we have that

$$\frac{u(\beta + \delta_t + 1) - u(\beta)}{\delta_t + 1} = \frac{[u(\beta + \delta_t + 1) - u(\beta + \delta_t)] + \cdots + [u(\beta + 1) - u(\beta)]}{\delta_t + 1}$$

$$< u(\beta + 1) - u(\beta)$$

and

$$\frac{u(n) - u(n - \delta_m - 1)}{\delta_m + 1} > u(n - \delta_m) - u(n - \delta_m - 1).$$

Since $\beta \leq n - \delta_m - 1$, it holds that $u(\beta + 1) - u(\beta) \leq u(n - \delta_m) - u(n - \delta_m - 1)$, and thus (7.78) holds.

We have thus shown that in each subgame, the strict best response for a player is to play in the last round, whatever the strategy of other players. Therefore, playing in the last round is a unique subgame perfect Nash equilibrium. □

Notice that Theorem 7.35 tells us that for utility functions that satisfy the substitutes condition, the simple prize allocation mechanism first to pass the post guarantees that all players investing in the first round is a unique subgame perfect Nash equilibrium. On the contrary, no such guarantee holds for utility functions that satisfy the complements conditions, and moreover, all players investing in the last round is a unique subgame perfect Nash equilibrium. One may wonder whether there exists a prize allocation mechanism that would guarantee the existence of a unique subgame perfect Nash equilibrium in which all players invest in the first round, for any utility function that satisfies the complements condition. We shall show this to be impossible for any utility function that satisfies a natural set of axioms.

7.4.3 Proportional to Marginal Contribution

We first establish sufficient conditions that ensure the non-existence of beneficial unilateral deviations to investing in an earlier and a later round from a strategy profile under which all players invest in the same round. This provides a sufficient condition for all players investing in the first round to be a subgame perfect Nash equilibrium, and a sufficient condition for all players investing in the last round to be a subgame perfect Nash equilibrium.

Lemma 7.36. *Given a utility function u and under a prize allocation mechanism proportional to marginal contribution and any strategy profile such that all players invest in the same round,*

(i) *If $u(1) \leq 1 - \sqrt{1 - 1/n}$, no player can profit by unilaterally deviating to investing in an earlier round.*

(ii) *If $u(n - 1) \geq 1 - 1/\sqrt{n}$, no player can profit by unilaterally deviating to investing in a later round.*

Proof. Consider first a strategy profile such that all players invest in round $1 < t \leq m$. Under such a strategy profile the expected payoff for each player is equal to $1/n$. Consider now a unilateral deviation of a player to investing in an earlier round. The expected payoff for this player after the deviation is equal to

$$\mathbf{Pr}[\theta \leq u(1)] + \mathbf{Pr}[\theta > u(1)]u(1) = u(1) + (1 - u(1))u(1).$$

This expected payoff is less than or equal to the expected payoff of the player before the deviation if, and only if, $u(1) \leq 1 - \sqrt{1 - 1/n}$.

Consider now a strategy profile such that all players invest in round $1 \leq t < m$. Under such a strategy profile the expected payoff for each player is equal to $1/n$. Consider a unilateral deviation of a player to investing in a later round. The expected payoff for this player after the deviation is equal to

$$\mathbf{Pr}[\theta > u(n-1)](1 - u(n-1)) = (1 - u(n-1))^2.$$

This expected payoff is less than or equal to the expected payoff of the player before the deviation if and only if $u(n-1) \geq 1 - 1/\sqrt{n}$.   □

We next show that the prize allocation mechanism proportional to marginal contribution guarantees that all players investing in the first round is a unique subgame perfect Nash equilibrium provided that the utility function satisfies the substitutes condition.

Theorem 7.37. *Suppose that the prize allocation mechanism is proportional to marginal contribution. If the utility function satisfies the substitutes condition there is a unique subgame perfect Nash equilibrium in which all players make their investments in the first round.*

Proof. We show first that it is a subgame perfect Nash equilibrium for all players to invest in the first round. Suppose that all players invest in the first round. By Lemma 7.36, if $u(n-1) \geq 1 - 1/\sqrt{n}$, no player can profit by unilaterally deviating to investing in a later round. Under the assumption that the utility function satisfies the substitutes condition we have that $u(n-1)/(n-1) \geq u(n)/n = 1/n$; hence

$$u(n-1) \geq 1 - \frac{1}{n}$$

which implies that $u(n-1) \geq 1 - 1/\sqrt{n}$.

We next show that all players investing in the first round is a unique subgame perfect Nash equilibrium, showing by contradiction that any other investment over rounds cannot be a subgame perfect Nash equilibrium.

Consider a strategy profile where all players invest in the same round other than the first round, say round $1 < t \leq m$, and assume that this is a subgame perfect Nash equilibrium. For this strategy profile the expected payoff of each player is equal to $1/n$. The expected payoff for a player who unilaterally deviates to investing in an earlier round is at least $u(1)$. Under the assumption that the utility function satisfies the substitutes condition we have that $u(1) > u(n)/n = 1/n$, which contradicts the assumption that all players investing in round t is a subgame perfect Nash equilibrium.

Consider now the remaining case where there are two different rounds such that in each of these two rounds at least one player makes an investment. Suppose that there are $i \geq 0$ players in the first round and $l > 0$ players in the last round with at least one player. The expected payoff of each player in the last round with at least one player making an effort investment is equal to

$$\mathbf{Pr}[\theta > u(n-l)]\frac{u(n) - u(n-l)}{l} = (1 - u(n-l))\frac{1 - u(n-l)}{l}.$$

Suppose that a player from the last round with at least one player making an investment in this round unilaterally deviates to investing in the first round. The expected payoff of such a player after the deviation is at least

$$\frac{u(i+1)}{i+1}.$$

Since the utility function satisfies the substitutes condition, we have

$$
\begin{aligned}
\frac{u(i+1)}{i+1} \\
= \frac{(u(i+1) - u(i)) + (u(i) - u(i-1)) + \cdots + (u(1) - u(0))}{i+1} \\
\geq \frac{(u(n) - u(n-1)) + (u(n-1) - u(n-2)) + \cdots + (u(n-l) - u(n-l-1))}{l} \\
= \frac{1 - u(n-l)}{l}
\end{aligned}
$$

it follows that $u(i+1)/(i+1) > (1 - u(n-l))^2/l$, which contradicts the assumption that the given strategy profile is a subgame perfect Nash equilibrium. $\qquad\square$

The prize allocation mechanism proportional to marginal contribution cannot in general guarantee that all players investing in the first round is a unique subgame perfect Nash equilibrium. A counterexample was shown for the case of two players and two rounds in Section 7.4.1 that is for any utility function such that $u(1) \leq 1 - 1/\sqrt{2}$. For specific instances of utility functions that satisfy the complements condition, the prize allocation mechanism proportional to marginal contribution can guarantee that all players investing in the first round is a unique subgame perfect Nash equilibrium. One instance of such a utility function is that with linear marginal values, which satisfies

$$u(1) - u(0) = c, \, u(2) - u(1) = 2c, \ldots, u(n) - u(n-1) = nc$$

where $c = 2/[(n+1)n]$. The claim that for the utility function with linear marginal values all players investing in the same round is a subgame perfect Nash equilibrium can be established by showing that the sufficient conditions in Lemma 7.36 are verified, which is left as Exercise 7.17.

7.4.4 Three Axioms

In this section we introduce a natural set of three axioms for the prize allocation mechanisms and show that there exists no prize allocation mechanism that satisfies all these three axioms and that has a unique subgame perfect Nash equilibrium in which all players make effort investments in the first round of the contest.

We shall use the concept of the α-marginal contribution, which is defined as follows: given a parameter $0 \leq \alpha \leq 1$, the α-marginal contribution to a utility function u at the value of total effort b is defined by

$$\partial^\alpha u(b) = \alpha(u(b) - u(b-1)) + (1 - \alpha)u(b).$$

Notice that for the extreme point $\alpha = 0$, the 0-marginal contribution corresponds to the total value contribution $u(b)$, and for the other extreme point $\alpha = 1$, the 1-marginal contribution corresponds to the marginal value contribution $u(b) - u(b - 1)$. For the intermediate points $0 < \alpha < 1$, the α-marginal contribution is a convex combination of the marginal and the total value contribution with the respective weights α and $1 - \alpha$.

For every given strategy profile $\mathbf{b}$, we define the α-marginal contribution of player i as follows:

$$\partial_i^\alpha u(\mathbf{b}) = \sum_{t=1}^{m} \partial^\alpha u(b_t)\mathbf{1}(b_{i,t} > 0).$$

We introduce the following three axioms:

Axiom 1: anonymity For every $1 \le t \le m$, $\theta \in [0, 1]$ and a permutation π of the elements $1, 2, \ldots, n$,

$$s_i(\mathbf{b}_{1,t}, \ldots, \mathbf{b}_{n,t}, \theta) = s_{\pi(i)}(\mathbf{b}_{\pi(1),t}, \ldots, \mathbf{b}_{\pi(n),t}, \theta), \quad \text{for } i \in N.$$

Axiom 2: time invariance For every integer $d > 0$ and $\theta \in [0, 1]$,

$$s_i\left(\sum_{j\in[t]} b_{1,j}, \ldots, \sum_{j\in[t]} b_{n,j}, \theta\right) = s_i\left(\sum_{j\in[t]+d} b_{1,j}, \ldots, \sum_{j\in[t]+d} b_{n,j}, \theta\right), \quad \text{for } i \in N.$$

Axiom 3: monotonicity For every utility function u there exists $\alpha \in [0, 1]$ such that for every $\mathbf{b} \in \times_{i\in N}\mathcal{B}_i$:

(i) For every pair of players $i, j \in N$ and every $\theta > \max\{u(b_t) \mid b_{i,t} > 0 \text{ or } b_{j,t} > 0\}$,

$$\partial_i^\alpha u(\mathbf{b}) \ge \partial_j^\alpha u(\mathbf{b}) \Rightarrow s_i(\mathbf{b}, \theta) \ge s_j(\mathbf{b}, \theta).$$

(ii) For every pair of players $i, j \in N$ such that $\partial_i^\alpha u(\mathbf{b}) - \partial_j^\alpha u(\mathbf{b}) \ge \partial_{i'}^\alpha u(\mathbf{b}) - \partial_{j'}^\alpha u(\mathbf{b})$ for every pair of players i' and j', there exists $\theta > \max\{u(b_t) \mid b_{i,t} > 0 \text{ or } b_{j,t} > 0\}$ such that

$$\partial_i^\alpha u(\mathbf{b}) > \partial_j^\alpha u(\mathbf{b}) \Rightarrow s_i(\mathbf{b}, \theta) > s_j(\mathbf{b}, \theta).$$

The given set of axioms accommodates two prize allocation mechanisms as asserted in the following theorem.

Theorem 7.38. *The prize allocation mechanisms first to pass the post and proportional to marginal contribution satisfy the axioms of anonymity, time invariance, and monotonicity.*

The proof of this theorem is left to the reader as Exercise 7.16.

Non-Existence

Theorem 7.39. *There exists no prize allocation mechanism that satisfies the three axioms of anonymity, time independence, and monotonicity and that has a unique subgame perfect Nash equilibrium in which all players play in the first round for every utility function.*

Proof. Suppose that there exists a prize allocation mechanism that satisfies each of the three axioms of anonymity, time independence, and monotonicity under which the game has a unique subgame perfect Nash equilibrium, where in this equilibrium all players make their effort investments in the first round. This implies that if all players invest in the first round, there is no profitable unilateral deviation to invest in a later round.

Consider a strategy vector $\mathbf{b}$ under which all players invest in a round t such that $1 < t \leq m$. By the axiom of anonymity, the expected payoffs of players are

$$\mathbf{E}[s_i(\mathbf{b}, \theta)] = \frac{1}{n}, \quad \text{for every } i \in N. \tag{7.79}$$

There cannot exist a profitable unilateral deviation to invest in a later round because under the time-independence axiom this would contradict the hypothesis that it is a subgame perfect Nash equilibrium for all players to invest in the first round of the game. Hence, it suffices to consider unilateral deviations to an earlier round. Suppose that the utility function satisfies the complements condition. Consider a strategy profile $\mathbf{b}'$ that results from $\mathbf{b}$ by player 1 unilaterally deviating to investing in a round t' such that $1 \leq t' < t$. By the complements assumption, we have that for every $\alpha \in [0, 1]$ and k such that $1 < k \leq n$,

$$u(1) - \alpha u(0) = u(1) < u(k) - u(k-1) \leq u(k) - \alpha u(k-1).$$

Hence, it follows that

$$\partial_1^\alpha u(\mathbf{b}') < \partial_i^\alpha u(\mathbf{b}'), \quad \text{for all } i \neq 1.$$

By the monotonicity axiom, we have that

$$s_1(\mathbf{b}', \theta) \leq s_i(\mathbf{b}', \theta), \quad \text{for all } i \neq 1, \text{ for some } \theta > u(n-1). \tag{7.80}$$

Let n be a player who invests in the latest round according to strategy profile $\mathbf{b}'$ in which a player makes an effort investment. By the complements assumption, the pair of players $(1, n)$ maximizes the difference $\partial_i^\alpha u(\mathbf{b}') - \partial_j^\alpha u(\mathbf{b}')$, over all $i, j \in N$ such that $i \neq j$. By the monotonicity axiom, we have that

$$s_1(\mathbf{b}', \theta) < s_n(\mathbf{b}', \theta), \quad \text{for some } \theta > u(n-1). \tag{7.81}$$

From (7.80) and (7.81), for every $i \in N$,

$$\mathbf{E}[s_1(\mathbf{b}', \theta)\mathbf{1}(\theta > u(n-1))] \leq \mathbf{E}[s_i(\mathbf{b}', \theta)\mathbf{1}(\theta > u(n-1))]$$

where the inequality is strict for $i = n$.

Since $\sum_{i \in N} \mathbf{E}[s_i(\mathbf{b}', \theta)\mathbf{1}(\theta > u(n-1))] \leq 1$, it follows that

$$\mathbf{E}[s_1(\mathbf{b}', \theta)\mathbf{1}(\theta > u(n-1))] < \frac{1}{n}.$$

The expected payoff of player 1 satisfies the following relations:

$$\mathbf{E}[s_1(\mathbf{b}', \theta)] = \mathbf{E}[s_1(\mathbf{b}', \theta)\mathbf{1}(\theta \leq u(n-1))] + \mathbf{E}[s_1(\mathbf{b}', \theta)\mathbf{1}(\theta > u(n-1))]$$

$$\leq \mathbf{Pr}[\theta \leq u(n-1)] + \mathbf{E}[s_1(\mathbf{b}', \theta)\mathbf{1}(\theta > u(n-1))]$$

$$= u(n-1) + \mathbf{E}[s_1(\mathbf{b}', \theta)\mathbf{1}(\theta > u(n-1))]. \tag{7.82}$$

In view of (7.79), the unilateral deviation by player 1 is non-profitable if $\mathbf{E}[s_1(\mathbf{b}', \theta)] < 1/n$, which by (7.82) is implied by the following conditions:

$$u(n-1) + \mathbf{E}[s_1(\mathbf{b}', \theta)\mathbf{1}(\theta > u(n-1))] < \frac{1}{n}. \qquad (7.83)$$

It follows that with any utility function u that satisfies the complements condition and condition (7.83), the strategy profile $\mathbf{b}$ under which all players invest in round t is a subgame perfect Nash equilibrium. Since we assumed $1 < t \leq m$, this contradicts the hypothesis that making all investments in the first round is a unique subgame perfect Nash equilibrium. $\qquad \square$

7.5 Sequential Allocation of Prizes

In this section we consider a model of a contest that awards a given number of identical prizes sequentially in one or more rounds. A given number of prizes is awarded in each round of the contest to players who invest the highest efforts in the given round by awarding each player at most one prize. Each player continues to compete in the round competitions until either winning a prize or the contest ends. This type of a multi-round contest is commonly used in practice. For example, it is often used as part of a larger tournament to determine a set of players to advance to the next round of the tournament where each "prize" corresponds to a place in the next round. The multi-round contest design considered in this section accommodates the one-round contest design where prizes are awarded in one single round as a special case, which under various assumptions we studied in earlier chapters of this book. Another special case of interest is that in which there are as many rounds as there are prizes, and thus prizes are awarded sequentially one after the other until all are allocated. Under additional assumptions to be made shortly, the game studied in this section can be seen as a generalization of the game with simultaneous investments of efforts and the rank-order allocation of multiple identical prizes that we studied in Section 3.2.3.

More formally, we consider an extensive form game with a set of two or more players $N = \{1, 2, \ldots, n\}$, a set of one or more prizes $M = \{1, 2, \ldots, m\}$, and the number of rounds k such that $1 \leq k < m$. The number of prizes awarded over different rounds is given by $m_1, m_2, \ldots, m_k$ where $m_j \geq 1$ for every round j, and $\sum_{j=1}^{k} m_j = m$. See Figure 7.21 for an illustration. Each player i has a valuation parameter of value v_i and incurs a unit marginal cost of production. The valuation parameters $v_1, v_2, \ldots, v_n$ are assumed to be of distinct values. A player is said to *participate* in a round if he or she has not won a prize in an earlier round. A player does not participate in a round if he or she has won a prize in an earlier round. This is either imposed by the

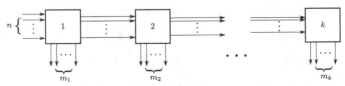

Figure 7.21. Sequential allocation of prizes in k rounds with m_j prizes awarded in round j.

contest rules or arises endogenously in the case of unit-demand players who have the same valuation for winning any subset of one or more prizes. We denote with N_j the set of players who participate in round j. All the players participate in the first round, and thus $N_1 = N$. The number of participants in the first round is equal to n and is equal to $n - (m_1 - m_2 - \cdots - m_{j-1})$ in round $1 < j \le k$. In each round, the participants in the given round simultaneously invest efforts. The effort investment by player i in round j is denoted by $b_{i,j}$, and the effort investments in round j are denoted by $\mathbf{b}^j = (b_{i,j}, i \in N)$. In each round the prize allocation is such that the prizes to be awarded in the given round are awarded to the set of players who invest the largest efforts. We denote with $x_{i,j}(\mathbf{b}^j)$ the probability of the event that player i wins a prize in round j, conditional on the effort investments in round j being $\mathbf{b}^j$. In each round, all individual effort investments that were made in earlier rounds are assumed to be public information. In each round, the expected payoff of a player to earn starting from the next round of the contest is discounted by a discount factor $0 < \delta \le 1$.

We shall characterize the subgame perfect Nash equilibrium of the given extensive form game where in each subgame players invest efforts according to mixed strategies. It is readily observed that the subgame of the last round of the contest corresponds to the game that models the standard all-pay contest with one or more identical prizes that we studied in Chapter 3, which has a unique mixed-strategy Nash equilibrium fully characterized in Theorem 3.44. It follows that the mixed-strategy Nash equilibrium in the subgame of the last round of the contest is such that the set of players who invest a strictly positive effort with a positive probability is the set of $m_k + 1$ players with the largest valuations among the participants in the last round of the game. The expected payoff of each such player i is equal to $v_i - v^k$ where v^k denotes the $(m_k + 1)$-st largest valuation among the participants in the last round of the contest. We next show that for each subgame of the game there is a correspondence to a game that models the standard all-pay contest with the rank-order allocation of one or more identical prizes. We denote with v^j the $(m_j + 1)$-st largest valuation among the participants in round j of the contest.

Lemma 7.40. *In the subgame perfect Nash equilibrium the subgame in each round j corresponds to a standard all-pay contest with the set N_j of players and m_j identical prizes, where each player $i \in N_j$ has a round-specific valuation:*

$$\phi_j(v_i) = \begin{cases} (1 - \delta)v_i + \delta \tilde{v}^j, & \text{if } 1 \le j < k \\ v_i, & \text{if } j = k \end{cases} \tag{7.84}$$

where

$$\tilde{v}^j = (1 - \delta) \sum_{l=j}^{k-2} \delta^{l-j} v^{l+1} + \delta^{k-1-j} v^k, \quad \text{for } 1 \le j < k. \tag{7.85}$$

Proof. The proof is by backward induction over the rounds of the game. Let $s(v_i, j)$ denote the expected payoff of a player with the valuation parameter of value v_i who participates in round j, which is earned from round j until the end of the game. We say that a player is active in a round if he or she invests a strictly positive effort in this round with a strictly positive probability.

Base case $j = k$: the subgame in the last round is a normal form game that models a standard all-pay contest among players in the set N_k where each player $i \in N_k$ has a valuation v_i of winning any one of the m_k prizes and incurs a unit marginal cost of production.

Induction step: suppose that the claim of the lemma holds for round $j + 1$ and we need to show that it holds for round j of the game, for $1 \leq j < k$. Consider an arbitrary round $1 \leq l < k$. For every player $i \in N_l$ and every point $a_{i,l}$ in the support of his or her mixed strategy in round l of the game, we have

$$s(v_i, l) = v_i \mathbf{E}[x_{i,l}(\mathbf{b}^l) \mid b_{i,l} = a_{i,l}] + \delta s(v_i, l + 1)(1 - \mathbf{E}[x_{i,l}(\mathbf{b}^l) \mid b_{i,l} = a_{i,l}]) - a_{i,l}$$

$$= [v_i - \delta s(v_i, l + 1)]\mathbf{E}[x_{i,l}(\mathbf{b}^l) \mid b_{i,l} = a_{i,l}] - a_{i,l} + \delta s(v_i, l + 1) \qquad (7.86)$$

$$= [v_i - \delta s(v_i, l + 1)] - [v^l - \delta s(v^l, l + 1)] + \delta s(v_i, l + 1) \qquad (7.87)$$

$$= v_i - v^l + \delta s(v^l, l + 1) \qquad (7.88)$$

where the equation in (7.87) holds because in every mixed-strategy Nash equilibrium, the expected payoff for a player conditional on the effort investment of this player being in the support of his or her mixed strategy is equal to the expected payoff of this player. By the form of the payoff functions in (7.86), these expected payoffs correspond to those in the game that models a standard-all pay contest with the rank-order allocation of m_l identical prizes of unit values, among players in the set of players N_l whose valuation parameters are given by

$$\phi_l(v_i) = v_i - \delta s(v_i, l + 1), \quad \text{for } i \in N_l. \qquad (7.89)$$

Combining with (7.84) for $l = j + 1$, we have

$$s(v_i, j + 2) = v_i - \tilde{v}^{j+1}. \qquad (7.90)$$

From (7.88), (7.90), and (7.85), we have

$$s(v_i, j + 1) = v_i - v^{j+1} + \delta s(v^{j+1}, j + 2)$$

$$= v_i - v^{j+1} + \delta[v^{j+1} - \tilde{v}^{j+1}]$$

$$= v_i - [(1 - \delta)v^{j+1} + \delta \tilde{v}^{j+1}]$$

$$= v_i - \tilde{v}^j.$$

Combining with (7.89), we obtain

$$\phi_j(v_i) = v_i - \delta s(v_i, j + 1) = v_i - \delta[v_i - \tilde{v}^j] = (1 - \delta)v_i + \delta \tilde{v}^j,$$

which completes the induction. $\qquad \square$

In the next corollary, we characterize the subgame perfect Nash equilibrium, which follows from Lemma 7.40 and Theorem 3.44.

Corollary 7.41. *There exists a unique subgame perfect Nash equilibrium for the game of sequential allocation of prizes that is characterized as follows:*

(i) *In each round j, the set of active players consists of $m_j + 1$ players with the largest valuations among players who have not won a prize in an earlier round.*

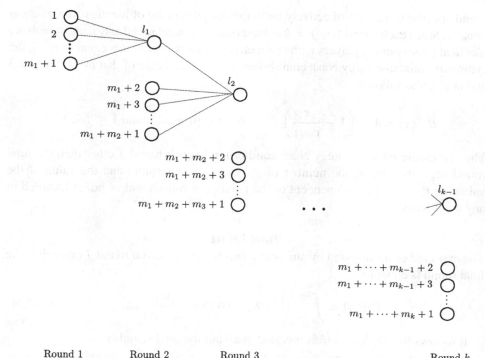

Round 1   Round 2   Round 3   Round k

Figure 7.22. Subgame perfect Nash equilibrium: in round 1 active participants are $m_1 + 1$ players with the largest valuation parameters, in each round $1 < j \le k$, the set of active participants consists of m_j players with largest valuation parameters who have not actively participated in an earlier round and loser from the previous round with his or her identity denoted by l_{j-1}.

(ii) *The loser in each round $1 \le j < k$ goes on to the next round to compete against m_{j+1} players with the largest valuations who have not actively participated in an earlier round.*

(iii) *In each subgame j there is a unique mixed-strategy Nash equilibrium, which is as in a standard all-pay contest with valuations $\phi_j(v_i)$, for $i \in N_j$.*

(iv) *The expected payoff for player i who actively participates in at least one round is $\delta^{j(i)-1}[(1 - \delta)(v_i - \tilde{v}^{j(i)}) + \delta(v_i - v^k)]$, where $j(i)$ denotes the first round in which player i actively participates and where $1 \le i \le m + 1$. (For each player $1 \le i \le m + 1$, $j(i) = l$, where l is a positive integer such that $m_1 + \cdots + m_{l-1} < i \le m_1 + \cdots + m_l$.)*

An illustration of the participation across different rounds of the contest in the subgame perfect Nash equilibrium is shown in Figure 7.22. In comparison with the single-round contest design, the total active participation of the players in the equilibrium of the sequential contest is $m + k$, while that in the single-round contest design is $m + 1$.

7.5.1 The Limit of No Discount

We consider the equilibrium in the limit as the discount factor δ goes to 1 from below. In this limit case, we observe from (7.84) and (7.85) that in each round $1 \le j < k$, the round-specific valuations of actively participating players are of identical values equal to v_{m+1}. Since each round $1 \leq j < k$ corresponds to a standard all-pay contest with m_j identical prizes among players with symmetric valuation parameters equal to v_{m+1}, the symmetric mixed-strategy Nash equilibrium is the special case of that in Section 3.2.3 and is given as follows:

$$B_{m_j}(x) = 1 - \left(1 - \frac{x}{v_{m+1}}\right)^{\frac{1}{m_j}}, \quad \text{for } x \in [0, v_{m+1}], \text{ and } 1 \leq j < k.$$

The symmetric mixed-strategy Nash equilibrium in each round j other than the final round depends only on the number of prizes m_j in this round and the value of the valuation v_{m+1}, and is independent of the number of rounds and of prizes awarded in any other round.

Total Effort

The expected effort invested by any active player i in any given round j other than the final round is equal to

$$\mathbf{E}[b_{i,j}] = \int_0^{v_{m+1}} (1 - B_{m_j}(b))db = \frac{m_j}{m_j + 1} v_{m+1}. \tag{7.91}$$

It follows that the total effort invested in all but the final round is

$$\mathbf{E}\left[\sum_{j=1}^{k-1}\sum_{i \in N_j} b_{i,j}\right] = \sum_{j=1}^{k-1}(m_j + 1) \cdot \frac{m_j}{m_j + 1} v_{m+1} = (m - m_k)v_{m+1}. \tag{7.92}$$

In the final round, there are $m_k + 1$ active players who consist of m_k players whose first active participation is in the final round and whose valuation parameters are the smallest among the players of $m + 1$ largest valuations, and one special player, say of identity X, who became an active participant in one of the earlier rounds 1 through $k - 1$ but lost in every round of his or her active participation. Note that this special player is one of the players 1 through $m_1 + \cdots + m_{k-1} + 1$. The expected total effort in the final round of the contest follows by the mixed-strategy Nash equilibrium characterization in Theorem 3.44 and taking the expectation with respect to the distribution of the identity of player X. Note that in each round $1 \leq j < k$, there are $m_j + 1$ actively participating players whose distributions of efforts are symmetric and all but one is awarded a prize; hence the probability that an actively participating player in round j loses and remains as an active player in the next round is $1/(m_j + 1)$. Therefore, we have that

$$\mathbf{Pr}[X = i] = \prod_{l=j(i)}^{k-1} \frac{1}{m_l + 1}, \quad \text{for } 1 \leq i \leq m_{k-1} + 1$$

where $j(i)$ is the first round in which player i is an active participant, i.e., $j(i) = t$, if $m_1 + \cdots + m_{t-1} + 1 < i \leq m_1 + \cdots + m_t + 1$.

Since in the final round there are m_k identical prizes and $m_k + 1$ active players with the smallest valuation parameter v_{m+1}, by Corollary 3.46, we have that the total expected effort in the final round is lower and upper bounded by $(m_k + 1 - H_{m_k+1})v_{m+1}$ and $m_k v_{m+1}$, respectively. Combining this with (7.92), we have that the expected total effort, R^M, in equilibrium over all rounds satisfies

$$(m + 1 - H_{m_k+1})v_{m+1} \leq R^M \leq mv_{m+1}. \tag{7.93}$$

Maximum Individual Effort

Using Corollary 3.49, the expected maximum individual effort, R_1^j, in round $1 \leq j \leq k$ satisfies

$$\left(1 - \frac{1}{m_j + 1}\right) v_{m+1} \leq R_1^j \leq v_{m+1}. \tag{7.94}$$

Since in the limit of no discount in all rounds but the final round the valuations of players are symmetric, we have that

$$R_1^j = \left(1 - \frac{1}{\binom{2m_j+1}{m_j}}\right) v_{m+1}, \quad \text{for } 1 \leq j < k$$

which is near to the maximum value v_{m+1} already for moderate values of the number of prizes awarded in a round.

For the expected maximum individual effort over all rounds, denoted as R_1^M, we have that

$$\left(1 - \frac{1}{k}\sum_{j=1}^{k}\frac{1}{m_j + 1}\right) v_{m+1} \leq R_1^M \leq v_{m+1} \tag{7.95}$$

where the lower bound follows by (7.94) and the fact that the maximum individual effort over all rounds is at least the mean of the maximum individual efforts invested in individual rounds.

Social Welfare

The expected social welfare in the subgame perfect Nash equilibrium is at least factor $1 - 1/(m_k + 1)$ of the maximum social welfare. Since each round awards at least one prize, it follows that the social efficiency is at least $1/2$. The asserted lower bound on the expected social welfare can be shown to hold as follows. From the characterization of the subgame perfect Nash equilibrium in Corollary 7.41, any efficiency loss occurs only if player $m + 1$, who participates in the last round and in none of the other rounds, wins a prize in the last round of the contest. Let x_i denote the probability that player i wins a prize in the subgame perfect Nash equilibrium of the game. Since there are $m_k + 1$ active participants in the last round of the contest and player $m + 1$ is the weakest among them, his or her winning probability is at most $1/(m_k + 1)$. Therefore, we have

$$\sum_{i=1}^{n} v_i x_i \geq \left(\sum_{i=1}^{m} v_i\right)(1 - x_{m+1}) \geq \left(\sum_{i=1}^{m} v_i\right)\left(1 - \frac{1}{m_k + 1}\right).$$

Comparison with a Single-Round Contest Design

We compare the multi-round contest design with the alternative contest design where players compete in one single round for a set of m identical prizes. The single-round contest design corresponds to the rank-order allocation of m identical prizes, which, in Chapter 2, we studied in the special case of one single prize and, in Section 3.2.3, we studied in the more general case of one or more identical prizes.

We observe that for both the multi-round contest and the single-round contest design, the expected total effort is approximately mv_{m+1}. More precisely, for the multi-round contest the expected total effort is within the bounds in (7.93), while the corresponding bounds for the expected total effort in the single-round contest are $(m + 1 - H_{m+1})mv_{m+1} \leq R^S \leq mv_{m+1}$. The lower bound for the multi-round contest is larger than the corresponding lower bound for the single-round contest design. For the special case of nearly identical valuations of players and an equal number of prizes across rounds, the efforts invested in the multi-round contest design correspond to $m + k$ samples from the distribution $B_{m/k}(x)$. On the other hand, the efforts in the single-round contest are m samples from the distribution $B_m(x)$. The expected total efforts are as follows:

$$\text{Multi-round contest:} \quad R^M = (m + k)\frac{m/k}{m/k + 1}v_{m+1} = mv_{m+1}$$

$$\text{Single-round contest:} \quad R^S = mv_{m+1}.$$

In this special case, the two contest designs are equivalent with respect to the expected total efforts. In fact, in the prevailing case of nearly identical valuations, the expected individual effort in each round is given by (7.91), and thus the expected total effort of value mv_{m+1} holds even more generally for an arbitrary distribution of the number of prizes across different rounds.

The expected maximum individual effort in both contest designs is near to the value v_{m+1}. The lower and upper bounds for the expected maximum individual effort in the multi-round contest (7.95) are exactly the lower and upper bounds for the single-round contest in Corollary 3.49 for the value of k equal to 1. For the special case of an equal number of prizes per round and nearly identical valuations, the expected maximum individual efforts in the two contest designs are given as follows:

$$\text{Multi-round contest:} \quad R_1^M = \left(1 - \frac{1}{\binom{m+m/k+k}{m/k}}\right)v_{m+1}$$

$$\text{Single-round contest:} \quad R_1^S = \left(1 - \frac{1}{\binom{2m+1}{m}}\right)v_{m+1}$$

where the latter is by Exercise 3.95 and the former is by similar arguments. From this we note that $R_1^M \leq R_1^S$ where the equality holds when $k = 1$, R_1^M is decreasing in k, and $R_1^M = (1 - 1/(2m + 1))v_{m+1}$ for $k = m$.

Summary

Sequential Moves

Standard all-pay contest A two-player contest with a prize allocation to the player who invests the largest effort with ties resolved in favor of the follower.

(i) The higher ability player preempts the lower ability player in a subgame perfect pure-strategy Nash equilibrium, meaning that the lower ability player invests an effort of value zero for any order of play.

(ii) For the game with incomplete information, the curvature of the prior distributions is an important factor that determines the qualitative properties of the subgame perfect Bayes-Nash equilibrium. For example, if the prior distribution of the follower is convex, then both players invest zero efforts.

Smooth allocation of prizes A two-player contest with a general-logit contest success function with production functions that are increasing, twice differentiable, concave, and zero at zero. Assume that player 1 is the favorite (more likely to win in the pure-strategy Nash equilibrium of the game with simultaneous moves), and player 2 is an underdog.

(i) For a pure-strategy Nash equilibrium (b_1^N, b_2^N), and two subgame perfect Nash equilibria (b_1^F, b_2^L) and (b_1^L, b_2^F):

$$b_1^F < b_1^N < b_1^L \text{ and } b_2^L < b_2^N, b_2^F < b_2^N.$$

(ii) For the two-round game such that in each round both players simultaneously make effort investments there is a continuum of subgame perfect Nash equilibria (b_1, b_2) specified as follows:

$$b_1^N \leq b_1 \leq b_1^N \text{ and } b_2 = \beta_2(b_1)$$

where $\beta_2(b_1)$ is the best response of player 2.

The War of Attrition

Two-player game: two players with valuations $v_1 \geq v_2 > 0$, each player incurs a unit marginal cost until deciding to drop out, and the winner is the player who drops out the last and earns the prize.

• There exists a continuum of pure-strategy Nash equilibria where the lower-valuation player drops out immediately, and the higher-valuation player invests any amount that is at least as large as the lower valuation.
• There exists a continuum of mixed-strategy Nash equilibria of the form $B_1(x) = 1 - (1 - B_1(0))e^{-\frac{x}{v_2}}$ and $B_2(x) = 1 - (1 - B_2(0))e^{-\frac{x}{v_1}}$ where at least one player places no atom at zero.

Game with incomplete information with n players and m identical prizes, where each player incurs a unit marginal cost until deciding to drop out, and a marginal cost in the amount of $0 \leq c \leq 1$ after dropping out until the end of the game.

- There exists a unique symmetric subgame perfect Bayes-Nash equilibrium.
- In the symmetric subgame perfect Bayes-Nash equilibrium, prizes are allocated to $m + 1$ players with the largest valuation parameters.
- The expected total effort:

$$R = m \sum_{j=m+1}^{n} c^{j-(m+1)} \mathbf{E}[v_{(n,j)}].$$

- The expected maximum individual effort:

$$R_1 = m \sum_{j=m+1}^{n} \frac{c^{j-(m+1)}}{j} \mathbf{E}[v_{(n,j)}].$$

- There exists a continuum of asymmetric subgame perfect Bayes-Nash equilibria.

The Tug of War A two-player contest between players with valuations $v_1 > v_2 > 0$ who incur linear production costs and the winner is whomever reaches first a point difference of value $k \geq 1$. Continuation values are discounted with a discount factor $\delta \in (0, 1]$.

There exists a subgame prefect mixed-strategy Nash equilibrium that admits an explicit characterization.

The expected payoffs for $k > 1$ and $\delta \in (0, 1)$:

$$s_1 = \begin{cases} \frac{\delta^k}{1-\delta^2}(v_1 - v_2), & \text{if } v_1/v_2 < 1/\delta^2 \\ \delta^k v_1, & \text{otherwise} \end{cases} \quad \text{and } s_2 = 0.$$

The winning probabilities are invariant to the value of the parameter k and player 1 preempts player 2 whenever $v_1/v_2 \geq 1/\delta^2$.

Sequential Aggregation of Production A prize is allocated according to a prize allocation mechanism in the earliest round in which a utility of production exceeds a threshold θ, which is private information to the contest owner with prior distribution F.

Examples of prize allocation mechanisms:

- First to Pass the Post: a unit prize is shared equally among players who invested in the first round in which the utility reached or exceeded the threshold value.
- Proportional to Marginal Contribution: same as First to Pass the Post but the prize is equal to the marginal contributed value in the first round in which the utility reached or exceeded the threshold value.

Substitutes: all the given prize allocation mechanisms have a unique subgame perfect Nash equilibrium and in this equilibrium all players make their contributions in the first round.

Complements: First to Pass the Post has a unique subgame perfect Nash equilibrium and in this equilibrium all players make their contributions in the last round.

Under axioms of anonymity, time invariance, and monotonicity, there exists no prize allocation mechanism that has a unique subgame perfect Nash equilibrium, in which all players make their contributions in the first round of the contest for every utility function.

Sequential Allocation of Prizes A k-round contest with n unit-demand players and $m < n$ identical prizes awarded in rounds 1 through k, where m_j prizes are awarded in round $1 \leq j \leq k$; the game is with complete information with valuation parameters $v_1 > v_2 > \cdots > v_n > 0$ and continuation values discounted with a factor $\delta \in (0, 1)$.

Subgame perfect Nash equilibrium: in each round the subgame is as in the standard all-pay contest among players who have not yet won a prize with valuations

$$\phi_j(v_i) = \delta \tilde{v}^j + (1 - \delta)v_i$$

where $\tilde{v}^j = (1 - \delta) \sum_{l=j}^{k-2} \delta^{l-j} v^{l+1} + \delta^{k-1-j} v^k$.

The limit of no discount:

The expected total effort: $(m + 1 - H_{m_k+1})v_{m+1} \leq R^M \leq m v_{m+1}$

The expected maximum individual effort:

$$\left(1 - \frac{1}{k} \sum_{j=1}^{k} \frac{1}{m_j + 1}\right) v_{m+1} \leq R_1^M \leq v_{m+1}.$$

Overall, the expected total effort and the expected maximum individual effort are near to those in the pure-strategy Nash equilibrium of the game that models a single-round contest.

The expected social welfare is at least $1 - 1/(m_k + 1)$ of the optimum social welfare.

Exercises

7.1   **Standard all-pay contest with sequential moves: two players** Consider the game that models a contest between two players who make sequential investments of effort as defined in Section 7.1.1, in the special case of independent and identically distributed valuation parameters with a prior distribution that has strictly positive density and is concave on $[0, 1]$. Prove that the following claims hold in the subgame perfect Nash equilibrium.

(a)   Conditional on the value of the valuation parameter, $v_1 = v$, player 1 is more likely to win than player 2 if, and only if,

$$v > \frac{1}{F'(F^{-1}(\frac{1}{2}))}.$$

(b)   The winning probability of player 1 is smaller than or equal to that of player 2.

7.2 **Maximum effort: sequential vs. simultaneous effort investments** Prove the claim in Proposition 7.4.

7.3 **Standard all-pay contest with sequential moves: two or more players** Consider the game that models the standard all-pay contest among two or more players who make sequential effort investments as defined in Section 7.1.1. Prove the following claims.

  (a) There exists a subgame perfect Bayes-Nash equilibrium as asserted in Theorem 7.7.
  (b) Adding a player to play first does not decrease the expected maximum individual effort.
  (c) There exists an instance in which adding a player to play last can decrease the expected maximum individual effort.

7.4 **Head starts** Consider the game that models a two-player contest with sequential effort investments as defined in Section 7.1.1, but assume that player 1 wins if $\theta b_1 > b_2$, and otherwise, player 2 wins, for value of parameter $\theta \geq 1$. Prove that the subgame perfect Bayes-Nash equilibrium is given as follows:

$$\beta_1(v_1) = \begin{cases} 0, & \text{if } 0 \leq v_1 \leq \frac{1}{\theta F_2'(0)} \\ \frac{1}{\theta} \min\left\{ F_2'^{-1}\left(\frac{1}{\theta v_1}\right), 1\right\}, & \text{if } \frac{1}{\theta F_2'(0)} < v_1 \leq 1 \end{cases}$$

and

$$\beta_2(v_1, v_2) = \begin{cases} 0, & \text{if } 0 \leq v_2 \leq \theta \beta_1(v_1) \\ \theta \beta_1(v_1), & \text{if } \theta \beta_1(v_1) < v_2 \leq 1 \end{cases}.$$

7.5 **Best responses under a difference-form contest success function** Consider the game between two players as defined in Section 7.1.2, but with a difference-form contest success function defining the winning probability of player 1 as

$$x_1(b_1, b_2) = H(f_1(b_1) - f_2(b_2))$$

where H is a distribution function on $\mathbf{R}$ that is continuously twice differentiable with an even density function, so that $H(-x) = 1 - H(x)$ for all $x \in \mathbf{R}$. Prove that the property of best-response functions asserted in Fact 7.9 holds.

7.6 **Sequential play-twice game: comparison with the single-round game** Consider the sequential play-twice game as defined in Section 7.1.2. Prove the following claims.

  (a) The total effort in the subgame perfect Nash equilibrium is strictly increasing in the effort investment b_1 of the favorite if, and only if,

  $$f_1(b_1)(f_1(b_1) + f_2(b_2))f_2''(b_2) < f_2'(b_2)((f_2(b_2) - f_1(b_1))f_1'(b_1) + 2f_1(b_1)f_2'(b_2))$$

  where $b_2 = \beta_2(b_1)$.
  (b) The total effort in any subgame perfect Nash equilibrium is larger than in the pure-strategy Nash equilibrium of the single-round game, if the following condition holds:

  $$f_1'(b_1) < 2f_2'(b_2) \text{ whenever } f_1(b_1) > f_2(b_2).$$

  (c) A sufficient condition for the last condition to hold is that the winning probabilities are according to an anonymous general-logit contest success function: $x_1(b_1, b_2) = f(b_1)/(f(b_1) + f(b_2))$, where f is an increasing, concave, continuously differentiable function such that $f(0) = 0$.

7.7 **Sequential moves and proportional allocation** Consider the game that models a contest among three players with unit-valued valuations and unit-valued marginal costs of production. The players invest their efforts sequentially with player 1 investing first, player 2 investing second, and player 3 investing last. A prize of unit value is allocated according to proportional allocation once all the effort investments are made.

(a) Show that there is a unique subgame perfect Nash equilibrium, given by

$$b_1 = (2a - 1)a^2, b_2 = 2(1 - a)a^2, b_3 = (1 - a)a^2$$

where

$$a = \frac{1}{2}\left(1 + \frac{1}{\sqrt{3}}\right).$$

(b) Compare the outcome in the subgame perfect Nash equilibrium with the outcome in the pure-strategy Nash equilibrium of the corresponding game with simultaneous moves.

7.8 **Single early mover and proportional allocation** Consider the game that models a contest among $n \geq 2$ players with unit-valued valuations and unit-valued marginal production costs, where a unit prize is allocated according to proportional allocation. Suppose that player 1 makes his or her effort investment first, whose value is revealed to all other players, who then simultaneously invest their efforts. Prove the following claims.

(a) There is a unique subgame perfect Nash equilibrium, which is given by

$$b_1 = \frac{1}{2}\left(1 - \frac{1}{2(n - 1)}\right) \text{ and } b_2 = \cdots = b_n = \frac{b_1}{n - 1}.$$

(b) The total effort in the subgame perfect Nash equilibrium corresponds to the total effort in the pure-strategy Nash equilibrium of the game in which all players make simultaneous effort investments but with $2(n - 1)$ players.

(c) The maximum individual effort in the subgame perfect Nash equilibrium is at least $1/4$, while in the pure-strategy Nash equilibrium of the game in which all players make simultaneous effort investments, it is smaller than $1/n$.

7.9 **King Solomon's dilemma**[1] Consider a contest between two players for an indivisible prize that is valued according to valuations v_1 and v_2 by player 1 and player 2, respectively. The valuations assume two distinct positive values that are common knowledge to both players and the contest owner, but which particular value is held by any specific player is known to the players and not to the contest owner. The payoff functions of the players are $s_1 = v_1 x_1 - p_1$ and $s_2 = v_2 x_2 - p_2$, where (x_1, x_2) determines the allocation of the prize such that $x_1 \in \{0, 1\}$ and $x_1 + x_2 = 1$, and (p_1, p_2) denotes payments. The goal is to design a mechanism under which it is a unique subgame perfect Nash equilibrium for the prize to be allocated to the player with the larger valuation and for neither player to make a payment. Prove that the following two-round mechanism is one such mechanism.

- Round 1: player 1 claims whether his or her valuation is higher. If player 1 claims that his or her valuation is higher, then the game proceeds to the second round. Otherwise, the prize is allocated to player 2, and neither player makes a payment.

---

[1] The King Solomon's dilemma refers to the following situation from the Old Testament, Kings A, Chapter 3: two mothers came to King Solomon with a baby they both claimed to be the baby's mother. King Solomon is faced with the problem of finding out which of the two women is the true mother of the baby.

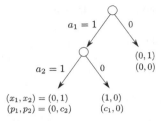

Figure 7.23. The extensive form game for the King Solomon's dilemma: in the first round player 1 claims whether his or her valuation is larger ($a_1 = 1$) or not ($a_1 = 0$); in the second round player 2 claims whether his or her valuation is larger ($a_2 = 1$) or not ($a_2 = 0$).

- Round 2: player 2 claims whether his or her valuation is higher. If player 2 claims that his or her valuation is higher, then he or she wins the item and makes a payment of value $\min\{v_1, v_2\} < c_2 < \max\{v_1, v_2\}$. Otherwise, the prize is allocated to player 1 who makes a payment of value $c_1 > 0$.

  See Figure 7.23 for a graphical representation of the given extensive form game.

7.10 King Solomon's dilemma and the standard all-pay contest Consider the King Solmon's problem in which there are two players with valuations v_1 and v_2 for player 1 and player 2, respectively, which can take arbitrary real values in a bounded interval, say in $[0, 1]$. Prove that for the following mechanism each subgame perfect Nash equilibrium is such that the prize is allocated to the player with a higher valuation if $v_1 \neq v_2$ or to either player if $v_1 = v_2$ and neither players incurs a payment.

- Round 1: player 2 announces a real number r in $[0, 1]$. If $r = 0$, then player 1 wins the prize and neither player incurs a payment. Otherwise, go to round 2.
- Round 2: player 1 claims whether his or her valuation is higher. If player 1 claims that his or her valuation is higher, then go to round 3. Otherwise, the prize is awarded to player 2, and neither player incurs a payment.
- Round 3: player 2 claims whether his or her valuation is higher. If player 2 claims that his or her valuation is higher, then both players compete in a standard all-pay contest with a sequential order of play such that player 1 is the leader and player 2 is the follower and both players incur a minimum cost of value r. Otherwise, if player 2 claims that his or her valuation is smaller, then player 1 wins the prize and neither player incurs a payment.

  See Figure 7.24 for an illustration.

7.11 The war of attrition Consider the two-player game of the war of attrition with incomplete information. Prove that the expected total effort in the symmetric pure-strategy Bayes-Nash equilibrium is equal to the expected value of the second highest valuation by using the characterization of the equilibrium given in Corollary 7.21.

7.12 The war of attrition with caps Consider a two-player game of the war of attrition with valuations $v_1 \geq v_2 > 0$ in which the strategy of each player is restricted to $[0, c]$, for $c > 0$. Prove that the points (b_1, b_2) asserted in what follows are pure-strategy Nash equilibrium points, and that these are the only pure-strategy Nash equilibrium points.

  (a) If $v_2 \leq c$, then (b_1, b_2) is such that either

$$b_1 = 0 \text{ and } b_2 \in [v_1, c]$$

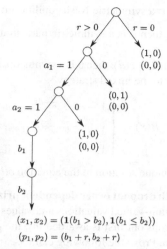

$$(x_1, x_2) = (\mathbf{1}(b_1 > b_2), \mathbf{1}(b_1 \le b_2))$$
$$(p_1, p_2) = (b_1 + r, b_2 + r)$$

Figure 7.24. The extensive form game for the King Solomon's dilemma: in the first round player 2 claims a positive real number r in $[0, 1]$, in the second round player 1 claims whether his or her valuation is larger ($a_1 = 1$) or not ($a_1 = 0$), in the third round player 2 claims whether his or her valuation is larger ($a_2 = 1$) or not ($a_2 = 0$), and in the fourth and the fifth rounds the players participate in a standard-all pay contest with a sequential order of play, with player 1 being the leader and player 2 being the follower in which both players incur a minimum cost of value r.

or

$$b_1 \in [v_2, c] \text{ and } b_2 = 0.$$

(b) If $c < v_2 < 2c$, then

- If $v_1 < 2c$, $(b_1, b_2) = (0, c)$ or $(c, 0)$
- If $v_1 = 2c$, $(b_1, b_2) = (c, 0)$.

(c) If $v_2 = 2c$, then

- If $v_1 = 2c$, $(b_1, b_2) = (0, c)$, or $(c, 0)$, or (c, c)
- If $v_1 > 2c$, $(b_1, b_2) = (0, c)$, or $(c, 0)$.

(d) If $v_2 > 2c$, then $(b_1, b_2) = (c, c)$.

7.13 A generalized war of attrition Consider a two-player game of the war of attrition with symmetric valuations of a prize whose value is equal to a function u of the first time until a player drops out from the competition, and assume that the production costs are according to a function c of the first time until a player drops out from the competition. Assume that the strategy set of each player is $[0, d]$, for some $d > 0$. Assume that function u is strictly positive and decreasing, and that function c is positive valued, increasing, continuously differentiable, bounded, and such that $c(0) = 0$. The payoff functions of the players are given as follows:

$$s_i(b_1, b_2) = u(\min\{b_1, b_2\})x_i(b_1, b_2) - c(\min\{b_1, b_2\}), \quad \text{for } i \in \{1, 2\}$$

where

$$x_1(b_1, b_2) = \mathbf{1}(b_1 > b_2) + \frac{1}{2}\mathbf{1}(b_1 = b_2) \text{ and } x_2(b_1, b_2) = 1 - x_1(b_1, b_2).$$

Prove that the following is a symmetric Nash equilibrium of the game.

(a) If $u(d)/2 > c(d)$, then it is a symmetric pure-strategy Nash equilibrium for both players to play d.

(b) Otherwise, if $u(d)/2 \leq c(d)$, then it is a symmetric mixed-strategy for both players to play according to the mixed strategy

$$
B(x) = \begin{cases} 1 - e^{-\int_0^x \frac{c'(y)}{u(y)} dy}, & \text{if } 0 \leq x \leq b^* \\ 1 - e^{-\int_0^{b^*} \frac{c'(y)}{u(y)} dy}, & \text{if } b^* < x < d \\ 1, & \text{if } x \geq d \end{cases}
$$

where b^* is the unique solution to the equation $c(b^*) = c(d) - u(d)/2$.

7.14 The war of attrition with dropout order dependent prizes Consider a n-player game of the war of attrition with unit-valued valuations and values of prizes $w_1 > w_2 > \cdots > w_n$ where the player who drops out first is awarded w_n, the player who drops out second is awarded w_{n-1}, and so on. Prove the following claims.

(a) There is a unique subgame perfect symmetric mixed-strategy Nash equilibrium where in each round with j players in the competition, each such player waits for an exponentially distributed time with mean

$$
\tau_j = (j-1)(w_{j-1} - w_j).
$$

(b) In each round with j players in the competition, the continuation value is w_j.

(c) The expected maximum individual effort is

$$
R_1 = \sum_{j=1}^{n-1} \frac{1}{j(j+1)} w_j - \left(1 - \frac{1}{n}\right) w_n.
$$

(d) The expected total effort is

$$
R = \sum_{j=1}^{n-1} (w_j - w_n).
$$

7.15 Pay-per-bid auctions (a.k.a. penny auctions or dollar auctions).[2] Consider the game of the pay-per-bid auction with $n \geq 2$ players that runs through one or more rounds $t = 1, 2, \ldots$ and is defined as follows. The auction is for a single item of value $v > 0$, which is assumed to be an integer. In each round, players simultaneously decide whether or not to place a bid in the given round. If at least one player places a bid in a round, then a candidate winner of the auction is selected uniformly at random from the set of players who placed a bid in this round. If none of the players placed a bid in a round, the auction ends and the winner is determined as follows: if the auction terminated in the first round then there is no winner, and otherwise, the winner is the candidate winner selected in the previous round. In the first round, all players are eligible to place a bid, and in each subsequent round, all players but the candidate winner selected in the previous round are eligible to place a bid. Thus, the number of players n_t who are eligible to bid in round t is equal to n in round $t = 1$ and is equal to $n - 1$, otherwise. In each round, the selected

---

[2] A pay-per-bid auction is a single-item auction in which each bidder incurs a fixed cost for placing a bid in addition to paying a final price for winning the item. A pay-per-bid auction is an *ascending price* auction if the final price is incremented for a fixed amount for each submitted bid and is a *fixed price* auction if the final price is an a priori fixed value. The auction ends as soon as no bidder places a bid within a time interval of fixed length since the last bid was placed by a bidder and the winner is the bidder who placed the last bid.

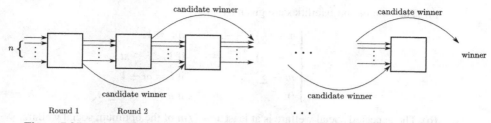

Figure 7.25. Structure of pay-per-bid auctions. At the end of each round the candidate winner is the player selected uniformly at random from the set of players who placed a bid in this round. The auction ends in the first round in which none of the players placed a bid, and in this round the winner of the auction is the candidate winner selected in the previous round if any. In each round all players are eligible to place a bid except for the current candidate winner.

candidate winner incurs a fixed cost of value c that is assumed to be an integer such that $0 \leq c < v$. The winner of the auction pays a final price for the item equal to the number of rounds in which at least one player placed a bid. See Figure 7.25 for an illustration of the structure of the pay-per-bid auction. Prove the following claims.

(a) A subgame perfect symmetric mixed-strategy Nash equilibrium is for each player eligible to bid in round t to place a bid in this round with probability a_t given by

$$a_t = \begin{cases} 1 - \left(\frac{c}{v-t+1}\right)^{\frac{1}{n_t}}, & \text{if } 1 \leq t \leq v - c \\ 0, & \text{if } t > v - c \end{cases}.$$

(b) The expected revenue to the auctioneer is equal to $v - c$.

7.16 Sequential aggregation of production Prove Theorem 7.38.

7.17 Sequential aggregation of production: allocation proportional to marginal contribution Show that for the case of a utility function with linear marginal values as considered in Section 7.4.3, all players investing in the same round is a subgame perfect Nash equilibrium.

7.18 Sequential allocation of prizes Consider a two-round contest with three players with valuations $v_1 > v_2 > v_3 > 0$ whose values are common knowledge. In each round, a unit prize is allocated to a player who invests the largest effort in the given round. In the first round, all three players participate. In the second round, only the two players who did not win in the first round participate. The players incur unit marginal costs of production. The payoffs are of quasi-linear form. Each player discounts any profit earned in the second round with a discount factor of value $\delta \in (0, 1)$.

(a) What is the probability that player 1 wins a prize in the subgame perfect Nash equilibrium?
(b) Is the probability that player 1 wins a prize monotonic in the discount factor, and if so how?
(c) What are the limit values of the probability that player 1 wins a prize as $\delta \downarrow 0$ and $\delta \uparrow 1$?

7.19 Sequential allocation of prizes Consider the sequential allocation of $m \geq 1$ identical prizes as defined in Section 7.5 such that one prize is awarded in each round of the contest among $n \geq 2$ players with valuation parameters $v_1 > v_2 > \cdots > v_n > 0$ for $1 \leq m < n$. Prove the following two claims.

(a) The winning probabilities are given by

$$
x_i = \begin{cases}
1 - \left(\frac{1}{2}\right)^m \frac{v_{m+1}}{v_1}, & \text{if } i = 1 \\
1 - \left(\frac{1}{2}\right)^{m+2-i} \frac{v_{m+1}}{v_i}, & \text{if } 1 < i \le m \\
m - \sum_{j=1}^{m} x_j, & \text{if } i = m + 1 \\
0, & \text{if } m + 1 < i \le n.
\end{cases}
$$

(b) The expected social welfare is at least $1 - 1/m$ of the optimum social welfare.

7.20 A mean value formula Prove that the identity asserted in Equation (7.61) holds.

7.6 Bibliographical Notes

An early study of a contest with precommitment in which one of the players is given the opportunity to make a strategic precommitment of effort was done by Dixit (1987). A central question here is whether such precommitments incentivize players to invest higher or lower efforts than in a single-round game with simultaneous moves. It was shown that for a symmetric two-player game there is no incentive for any strategic manipulation of the effort level. This is contrary to the case of asymmetric valuations where there exist prize allocation mechanisms such that the favorite player has an incentive to overcommit the effort and the opposite holds for the underdog player. This is presented more formally in Theorem 7.12, which is a result from Dixit (1987). The characterization of a subgame perfect Bayes-Nash equilibrium for the more general case that allows for an arbitrary number of players in Theorem 7.7 and the results left to the reader as Exercise 7.3 were established by Segev and Sela (2014). Further studies include that of Pérez-Castrillo and Verdier (1992) who studied the equilibrium behavior under sequential moves in contests with a ratio-form contest success function. Leininger (1993) studied equilibria in a sequential-move contest with proportional allocation. These papers endogenized the order of moves by extending the game with an initial announcement round in which players simultaneously decide according to which contest design to compete in subsequent rounds. Leininger (1993) showed that sequential equilibria arise endogenously as an equilibrium in contests where players choose the timing of moves. Fu (2006) considered the same problem, but under information asymmetry where the value of the prize is drawn from a commonly known prior distribution and then one of the players is informed about the prize value and the other player is not informed. Yildirim (2005) studied a two-round contest in which each player can make an effort investment in each round and a unit prize is allocated according to a general-logit contest success function of the total individual effort investments – Theorem 7.15 is from there. Yildirim (2005) showed that the precommitment by players to invest in each of the two rounds arises endogenously as a pure-strategy Nash equilibrium in the initial announcement round, which is presented in Theorem 7.17. The special case of proportional allocation was studied by Linster (1993) and Morgan (2003). Morgan and Vardy (2007) studied a model of sequential effort investments in which the follower incurs a fixed cost for observing the effort investment of the leader. Glazer and Hassin (2000) studied an n-player contest with symmetric valuations where a unit prize is allocated according to proportional allocation and where individual players sequentially invest efforts – they shown that early movers need not make larger payoffs than later movers and that the aggregate payoffs are lower than in the corresponding simultaneous-move game. Exercises 7.7 and 7.8 are from Glazer and Hassin (2000). Segev and Sela (2011) characterized the equilibrium for a sequential-move standard all-pay contest between two players with incomplete information, and studied how the equilibrium is affected by the use of head starts where the follower wins if his or her effort is larger than or equal to a fixed fraction of the leader's effort. This model is studied in Section 7.1.1. Exercise 7.4 is from Segev and Sela (2011). Favoritism and head starts in asymmetric contests were further studied in Kirkegaard (2012). A nice overview of various aspects of strategies in sequential contests is available in Konrad (2009). Sequential moves were also studied in the context of the Cournot oligopoly games, e.g., Saloner (1987), Pal (1991), Varian (1994), Romano and Yildirim (2005), and Aoyagi (2010), and the prizes that are functions of the invested efforts, e.g., Hoffmann and Rota-Graziosi (2012).

The game of the war of attrition was studied first as a model of animal conflict in the area of theoretical biology, e.g., Maynard Smith (1974), Bishop and Cannings (1978), Bishop et al. (1978), and Riley (1980), and later as a model in economic theory, e.g., Hendricks et al. (1988), Bulow and Klemperer (1997), and Gul and Lundholm (1995); private provisioning of public goods, e.g., Bliss and Nalebuff (1984); strikes, e.g., Kennan and Wilson (1989); firm exits from a declining industry, e.g., Ghemawat and Nalebuff (1985) and Fudenberg and Tirole (1986); and standard-setting games, e.g., Farrell and Simcoe (2012). The two-player game with symmetric valuations in Section 7.2.1 was perhaps first studied by Maynard Smith (1974). Haigh and Cannings (1989) studied equilibrium properties for different versions of the n-player games of the war of attrition. Exercise 7.14 is from Haigh and Cannings (1989). The equilibrium properties of the n-player game with incomplete information with symmetric prior distributions as presented in Section 7.2.2 are from Bulow and Klemperer (1997). Krishna and Morgan (1997) studied equilibrium properties for the game with incomplete information with affiliated types. The equilibrium properties under asymmetric prior distributions as in Section 7.2.2 are from Nalebuff and Riley (1985). Anderson et al. (1998) considered a two-player game of the war of attrition with a focus on the games where players choose strategies by sampling from a set of strategies according to a logit distribution function of payoffs of individual strategies. Exercise 7.12 is from Anderson et al. (1998). Konrad (2012) studied various designs of dynamic contests, including the game of tug of war, and argued that they cause a discouragement effect manifesting in the total effort falling considerably short of the prize at stake or leading to an intense competition in the early rounds and long periods of no competition. A nice chapter on the game of the war of attrition is available in Fudenberg and Tirole (1991). The related game of pay-per-bid auctions, also referred to as penny or dollar auctions, was studied in an early work by Shubik (1971) and more recently by, e.g., Augenblick (2011), Platt et al. (2013), and Byers et al. (2010). Exercise 7.15 covers a simple model with symmetric valuations and is from Augenblick (2011). Recent work has focused on trying to explain empirically observed large profit margins of pay-per-bid auctions by various factors, including risk aversion; risk loving, e.g., in Platt et al. (2013); and various information asymmetries such as asymmetry of beliefs about the number of opponents, e.g., Byers et al. (2010).

The game of tug of war was first introduced by Harris and Vickers (1987) as a model of patent races in R&D competitions. This model was subsequently studied by McAfee (2000), Konrad and Kovenock (2005), and Konrad and Kovenock (2009). Theorem 7.33 is from Konrad and Kovenock (2005). An alternative model that allows for draw outcomes in individual subgames was studied by McAfee (2000) and Agastya and McAfee (2006). Konrad and Kovenock (2009) studied a multi-round contest in which each round corresponds to a standard all-pay contest and, in addition to a player receiving a prize for winning the contest, each player is awarded for participating in individual rounds of the contest. Hörner (2004) studied a model of a dynamic competition between two players who engage in a sequence of competitions. In each competition each player either succeeds or fails, which happens independently and according to fixed probabilities that depend only on whether a player invested a high or a low effort and whether is ahead or behind with respect to the cumulative number of successes. The payoff for each player is a discounted sum of the payoffs earned in individual competitions, with the payoff in a competition being quasi-linear in the reward and the cost. Wolfgang and Chun-Lei (1994) studied a dynamic competition between two players in a game of alternating moves that proceeds through one or more rounds such that the first moving player plays in the odd-numbered rounds and the second moving player plays in the even-numbered rounds. For each player, the effort investments made in subsequent rounds are required to be an increasing sequence. The payoff of each player is defined to be as in a contest between two players with symmetric valuations where a unit prize is allocated based on individual efforts in the final round of the game according to a ratio-form allocation function and the players incur unit marginal costs of production. In each round of the game, all the effort investments made in previous rounds are assumed to be common knowledge. It was shown that higher total effort can be extracted than in the corresponding simultaneous-move contest. Konrad and Leininger (2007) studied equilibrium properties of an n-player game with complete information and symmetric valuations in which a unit prize is allocated based on individual efforts as in the standard all-pay contest and each player incurs production cost according to an increasing, twice continuously differentiable, and convex function. This is a two-round game where a fixed subset of players simultaneously invest efforts in the first round, and the remaining players simultaneously invest efforts in the second round of the game after having observing the effort investments in the first round.

The game of sequential aggregation of production was first formulated by Jain and Parkes (2008) and Jain et al. (2009) as a model to study how different prize allocation mechanisms provide incentives for early submissions in the context of online question-and-answer services. Most of the results in Section 7.4 are from Jain et al. (2009).

The game of sequential allocation of prizes with complete information as presented in Section 7.5 was studied by Clark and Riis (1998a). The bounds for the expected total effort and the expected maximum individual efforts are new. This specific contest design can be seen as to be in the spirit of sequential auctions that were studied in the economics literature following the works of Weber (1981) and Milgrom and Weber (1983), which analyzed the first-price and second-price sequential auctions with unit-demand bidders and private valuations. Other works assuming this model include Ashenfelter (1998), McAfee and Vincent (1993), and McAfee and Vincent (1997). A discussion of sequential moves in the context of a first-price auction is provided by Krishna (2002) and in the context of rent-seeking models is provided by Nitzan (1994). Recently, Leme et al. (2012) studied the social efficiency of sequential auctions, showing that for sequential first-price auctions with unit-demand bidders the price of anarchy is 2, which stands in contrast to the case of simultaneous first-price auctions where pure-strategy Nash equilibria are socially optimal; see Hassidim et al. (2011). McAfee and Vincent (1997) studied a sequential auction where a seller can post a reserve price and if the item fails to sell cannot commit to never attempt to resell the item. Revenue comparison results were obtained for the case of two optimal sequential auctions and one static auction in the limit when the time between the two auctions goes to zero and in the limit of asymptotically large number of bidders.

Sequential contests were used to study the implementation problem of allocating one or more prizes to players who value them the most, without payments made by the players in any equilibrium outcome. An early formulation of such a problem was posed as the King Solomon's dilemma by Glazer and Ma (1989), with the simplest version concerned with the case of one prize and two players. The problem formulations differ with respect to the information available to the players and the contest owner. The first formulation studied in Glazer and Ma (1989) was concerned with the case where all players know the values of two valuations and the only incomplete information is on the side of the contest owner, who knows the values of the valuations but does not know which player holds any specific value. For this problem formulation, a sequential contest was designed by Glazer and Ma (1989), described in Exercise 7.9, and shown to have the desired outcome as a unique subgame perfect Nash equilibrium. Glazer and Ma (1989) also studied the case with private valuations where each player knows whether his or her valuation is one of the largest, and an extension to two or more players. For this problem formulation, a sequential contest was proposed in Glazer and Ma (1989) that is based on using a standard all-pay contest with a minimum required effort that is selected by one of the players in the first round of the contest. This sequential contest is described in Exercise 7.10. The King Solomon's dilemma was subsequently studied by several authors. A simplification of the mechanism by Glazer and Ma (1989) was proposed by Moore (1992). Perry and Reny (1999) presented a mechanism that uses a second-price all-pay auction with a free winner-exit option. Olszewski (2003) presented a mechanism that uses a second-price auction with extra payments. Some more recent references are Bag and Sabourian (2005) and Qin and Yang (2009).

Other types of sequential contests were studied by various authors and under different assumptions. McAfee (1993) studied a system of players and contests that proceeds through multiple rounds: in each round players simultaneously decide in which contests to participate, at the end of a round players who lost in the given round strategically decide whether to continue competing in the next round, and the owners of the contests not selected by a player in this round strategically decide whether to make the contest available in the next round. Another example of a sequential contest is available in Fu and Lu (2010) who studied the effects of endogenous entry following the work of Fullerton and McAfee (1999). This was studied as a contest with two or more players with symmetric valuations where a prize is allocated according to an anonymous general-logit contest success function. Here the contest proceeds in three rounds: in the first round, the contest owner announces the rules and commits on the value of a prize purse and the value of an entry fee; in the second round, players sequentially decide whether to participate in the contest and at the time of this decision are informed about how many players have already decided to participate; and, finally, in the third round, players simultaneously invest efforts. It was found that the optimal contest design with respect to the total effort is such that two players actively participate. Clark and Nilssen (2013) studied a two-round contest between two players where a prize is awarded in each round according to proportional allocation, under the assumption that in the second round, the marginal cost of a player is a function of his or her effort investment in the first round. This assumption is motivated by scenarios in which players improve on their skills with experience.

CHAPTER 8

Tournaments

In this chapter we consider a competition among players organized as an *elimination tournament*, which is often referred to as a *knockout tournament*. An elimination tournament proceeds in one or more rounds. In each round, players who participate in the given round compete in contests of that round. In this chapter we focus on *single-elimination tournaments* where in each contest of a round, a single winner advances to the next round, and the winner of the tournament is the player who wins in all rounds. Prizes are awarded based on the number of successively passed rounds. A single-elimination tournament is defined by a tournament plan that specifies a schedule of matches and a seeding of players. Competitions organized as tournaments are commonplace not only in sports competitions but also in many other situations in life where the best player (or a set of best players) is selected by successive elimination.

A desired feature of a tournament competition is the efficiency with respect to the number of contests needed to determine a winner. For a tournament among $n = 2^r$ players that consists of two-player contests organized as a round-robin competition, where each player confronts each other player, the total number of the matches is

$$\binom{n}{2} = \frac{n(n-1)}{2}.$$

In contrast, the total number of matches in a single-elimination tournament is equal to

$$n - 1.$$

The number of matches is reduced from being quadratic in the number of players to being linear in the number of players. In practice, it is often infeasible to hold round-robin competitions because of the large number of matches that they require, and so one often deploys a more economical design in the form of an elimination tournament. However, this efficiency comes at the cost of increasing the chance of failing to identify the strongest player as the winner. The design of a tournament plan plays a critical role here by reducing the chance of early round upsets and ensuring some desired features such as *fairness* (the better the player the higher the chance of winning the tournament), *competitive balance* (a few one-sided matches), and *efficiency* (with respect to the number of contests).

We shall first consider properties of different seeding procedures for single-elimination tournaments that consist of matches between pairs of players. They will be studied under a probabilistic model where the outcomes of matches are assumed to be independent and according to fixed winning probabilities specific to each pair of players. From a strategic-behavior perspective, one may think of this as a setting in which the payoffs of players correspond to the value of winning the tournament, and the production costs are of no concern. The properties that we are going to study of various seeding procedures will formalize so far vaguely defined notions of the fairness and the competitive balance of a seeding procedure.

We shall also consider strategic behavior in tournaments with the payoffs of the players being quasi-linear in the value of rewards and production costs. This will be naturally studied using the concept of a subgame perfect Nash equilibria. There are several questions of interest in such strategic settings including the existence of an equilibrium and its properties, e.g., how the design of a tournament plan and allocation of prizes affect quantities of interest such as the total effort and the maximum individual effort, how they are affected by the form of the production costs, and how the informational assumptions about the abilities of the players affect equilibrium outcome.

8.1 Basic Concepts

A single-elimination tournament is a competition among a set of players divided into r successive rounds. Each round consists of one or more contests. In each contest of a round, one player wins and advances to the next round and other players lose and are eliminated from further competition. There is a single winner and this is the player who wins in each contest in which he or she participated.

Tournament Plan

A single-elimination tournament for a set of players $N = \{1, 2, \ldots, n\}$ is specified by a *tournament plan* (T, S) where T is a directed tree of depth r with a specified root node and n leaf nodes, and S is a seeding of players. Each leaf node of tree T represents a seeding position, and each internal node represents the winner of the subtournament defined by the subtree rooted at this internal node. A seeding S corresponds to a one-to-one mapping from the set of the leaf nodes of tree T to the set of players. We let $S(i)$ denote the player at the seeding position i. In particular, for two-player contests, a single-elimination tournament is specified by a tournament plan (T, S) where T is a *rooted binary tree*. See Figure 8.1 for an example. Each node of a *full binary tree* has either zero or two children, and a *complete binary tree* is generally defined as a full binary tree in which all the leaf nodes are at a depth of r or $r - 1$ for some positive integer r, and all the children on the last level occupy the left-most positions. A full binary tree is said to be *perfect* if all the leaf nodes are at the same depth. See Figure 8.2 for an illustration.

A single-elimination tournament (T, S) is said to be *balanced* if T is a regular tree, i.e., each contest consists of the same number of players, say m, and thus $n = m^r$.

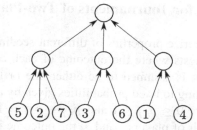

Figure 8.1. An instance of a tournament plan (T, S) where T is the given tree and S is the seeding specifying an assignment of players to the leaf nodes.

In the case of two-player contests, for a balanced single-elimination tournament plan (T, S), T is a perfect binary tree, i.e., each leaf node of this tree is at the same depth with respect to the root of the tree.

Prizes

The winner of a single-elimination tournament, which is the player who wins in all rounds of the tournament, is awarded a prize of value $w_r \geq 0$. Each player who wins in contests of round 1 through j and is eliminated in a contest in round $j + 1$ is awarded a prize of value $w_j \geq 0$, for $1 \leq j < r$. We assume that $w_r \geq w_{r-1} \geq \cdots \geq w_1 \geq w_0 = 0$. We may refer to w_r as the first prize, w_{r-1} as the second prize, and so on. Indeed, we can think of w_r as of the prize awarded to the winner of the tournament, w_{r-1} as the second prize awarded to the runner-up who participated and lost in the final round, w_{r-2} as the prize awarded to each player who participated and lost in the semifinal round, and so on and so forth. We define $\delta w_j = w_j - w_{j-1}$ to be the value of the prize awarded to a player for participating and winning in round j of the tournament.

Seeding Procedures

We distinguish static from dynamic seeding procedures. A static seeding procedure is defined by a tournament plan (T, S) that is determined and fixed prior to any matches. On the other hand, for the class of dynamic seeding procedures, the seeding of players in different rounds is allowed to change based on the observed outcomes of matches in previous rounds. A seeding can be either a deterministic or a randomized mapping from a prior information about the abilities of players to a seeding of players. Some standard seeding methods include random permutation seeding where the seeding is according to a random permutation, and standard seeding procedure where the seeding is according to a deterministic mapping that matches best players with worst players according to the prior information about the strengths of players.

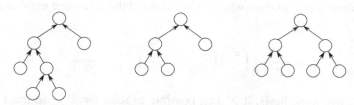

Figure 8.2. Binary trees: (left) full, (middle) complete, and (right) perfect.

8.2 Seedings for Tournaments of Two-Player Matches

In this section we characterize properties of different seeding procedures for tournaments of two-player contests where the outcome of each contest between a pair of players in the tournament is assumed to be either one or the other player winning independently and according to fixed probabilities given by a *matrix of winning probabilities* $\mathbf{P} = (p_{i,j})$, where $0 \leq p_{i,j} \leq 1$ and $p_{i,j} + p_{j,i} = 1$ for every $i, j \in N$. For each match between a pair of players i and j, the outcome is either player i winning and player j losing with probability $p_{i,j}$, or, otherwise, player i losing and player j winning with probability $p_{j,i}$. The diagonal elements $p_{i,i}$ can be defined arbitrarily, so without any loss of generality, we assume that the diagonal elements are equal to $1/2$. A player i is said to be *weakly stronger* than player j if $p_{i,j} \geq 1/2$, and is said to be *stronger* if $p_{i,j} > 1/2$. There are several special classes of the matrices of winning probabilities that are of particular interest, which we introduce in Section 8.2.3. We shall denote with $x_i((T, S), \mathbf{P})$ the probability of player i winning in a tournament with a tournament plan (T, S) and a matrix of winning probabilities $\mathbf{P}$. If the seeding S is chosen according to a randomized procedure, then we let $x_i(T, \mathbf{P}) = \mathbf{E}[x_i((T, S), \mathbf{P})]$ denote the winning probability for player i, ex-ante before the seeding of players is realized.

8.2.1 Number of Distinct Seedings for Two-Player Contests

The number of distinct seedings grows super-exponentially fast with the number of players n. More specifically, the number of distinct seedings for single-elimination balanced tournaments is specified as follows.

Theorem 8.1. *Suppose that the number of players is $n = 2^r$ for some integer $r \geq 1$. Then, the total number of distinct seedings is*

$$\frac{n!}{2^{n-1}}.$$

Proof. The proof is by induction. Let S_r be the set of all possible distinct seedings for $n = 2^r$ players. The claim of the theorem is

$$|S_r| = \frac{(2^r)!}{2^{2^r-1}}.$$

Base case: $r = 1$, trivially, $|S_1| = 1$. Induction step: assume that the claim holds for every $r' \in \{1, 2, \ldots, r - 1\}$, and we then show that the claim holds for $r' = r$. In the first round, there are 2^r players who can be paired in the following number of different ways:

$$\frac{1}{(2^{r-1})!}\binom{2^r}{2}\binom{2^r - 2}{2}\cdots\binom{2}{2} = \frac{2^r}{2^{2^r-1}}.$$

By the inductive hypothesis, it is then possible to seed the 2^{r-1} winners of the first round in $|S_{r-1}|$ different ways.

Table 8.1. Number of distinct seedings

n	$\frac{n!}{2^{n-1}}$
2	1
4	3
8	315
16	638, 512, 875
32	$1.2253 \; 10^{26}$
64	$1.37557 \; 10^{70}$

Therefore, the total number of distinct seedings for a balanced single-elimination tournament of r rounds is

$$|S_r| = |S_{r-1}| \left(\frac{2^r}{2^{2^{r-1}}} \right)$$

$$= \left(\frac{(2^{r-1})!}{2^{2^{r-1}-1}} \right) \left(\frac{2^r}{2^{2^{r-1}}} \right)$$

$$= \frac{(2^r)!}{2^{2^r-1}}. \qquad \square$$

The number of distinct seedings already assumes rather large values for some commonly observed numbers of competitors in single-elimination tournaments in practice. For example, for the common case of 16 competitors, the number of distinct seedings is larger than half a billion, and for the case of 32 competitors this number is as large as in the order of 10^{26}. See Table 8.1 for some numerical values.

8.2.2 Undesirable Properties of Random Permutation Seedings

Seeding procedure according to a uniform random permutation of players may be regarded as a fairest seeding of players. However, this seeding procedure is prone to early upsets because it may match a strong player against another strong player in an early round of the tournament, which may result in undesired effects such as the second best player having a small chance of reaching the final round of the tournament. Some properties of random permutation seeding procedures are characterized here assuming the existence of a ranking of players in decreasing strength, and noiseless comparisons where, in each match between a pair of players, the stronger player wins. The only element of randomness in such a model is due to random permutation seeding. In such a tournament, the strongest player wins with certainty. However, other players' probabilities of reaching a particular stage of the tournament are affected by the random permutation seeding procedure.

Second Best Player

An undesired property of a random permutation seeding procedure is that the second best player is eliminated before the final round with a probability of value nearly

Table 8.2. Probability of the event that the t-th strongest player reaches the round
with t players

t	2	4	8	16	$\cdots$	$+\infty$
$x_t(n, \log_2(n/t) + 1)$	0.5	0.422	0.393	0.380	$\cdots$	0.368
$(1 - 1/t)^{t-1}$	1/2	$(3/4)^4$	$(7/8)^7$	$(15/16)^{15}$	$\cdots$	$1/e$

1/2. More specifically, for any single-elimination tournament with $n = 2^r$ players
and random permutation seeding of players, the probability of the second best player
competing in the final round is equal to the probability of the event that the second best
player is not matched with the strongest player in an earlier round, which occurs with
probability

$$x_2(n, r) = \frac{n/2}{n - 1} = \frac{1}{2}\left(1 + \frac{1}{n-1}\right). \tag{8.1}$$

This is asymptotically equal to 1/2 as the number of players n grows large. For the
number of players equal to 4, 8, and 16, the second best player does not play in the
final with probability 1/3, 3/7, and 7/15, respectively.

t-th Best Player

The probability that the second best player reaches the final round of the tournament in
(8.1) can be generalized to the probability of the event that the t-th best player reaches
round j of the tournament as follows. In round j of the tournament, there are 2^{r-j+1}
competing players. The t-th strongest player reaches round j if, and only if, none of
the stronger players is assigned to a seeding position within a subtree originating at
the node in round $j - 1$ that contains player t. There are 2^{j-1} players in this subtree.
Therefore, the probability that none of the players stronger than the t-strongest player
fall in this subtree is equal to

$$x_t(n, j) = \frac{n - 2^{j-1}}{n - 1}\frac{n - 2^{j-1} - 1}{n - 2} \cdots \frac{n - 2^{j-1} - (t - 2)}{n - (t - 1)}$$

$$= \frac{(n - t)!(n - 2^{j-1})!}{(n - 1)!(n - 2^{j-1} - t + 1)!}.$$

In the case when the t-th strongest player is the weakest among 2^{r-j+1} players, that
is $t = 2^{r-j+1}$, we have $2^{j-1} = n/t$. If the t strongest players were to participate in
round j of the tournament, then the t-th player is the weakest among those players. In
this case, the probability of the t-th strongest player reaching round $j = \log_2(n/t) + 1$
is equal to

$$x_t(n, \log_2(n/t) + 1) = \frac{(n - t)!(n(1 - 1/t))!}{(n - 1)!(n(1 - 1/t) - t + 1)!}.$$

For fixed $t = 2^j$,

$$x_t(n, \log_2(n/t) + 1) \sim \left(1 - \frac{1}{t}\right)^{t-1}, \quad \text{for large } n.$$

In a tournament of many players, under random permutation seeding, the probability of the t-th strongest player reaching a round with t players is at most $1/2$, and it diminishes with t to value $1/e$ (see Table 8.1).

Top-t Best Players

Another metric of interest is the probability of the event that the top-t strongest players remain in the competition in the round of the tournament consisting of t players. It is easy to observe that the probability $p_n(t)$ of this event is equal to

$$p_n(t) = \frac{(n/t)}{n-1}\frac{(n/t)}{n-2}\cdots\frac{(n/t)}{n-t+1} = \frac{(n-t)!n^{t-1}}{(n-1)!}\frac{1}{t^{t-1}}.$$

For a fixed value of t,

$$p_n(t) \sim \frac{1}{t^{t-1}}, \quad \text{for large } n.$$

For example, for $t = 2, 4$, and 8, $p_n(t)$ is equal to $1/2$, $1/64$, and $1/(2, 097, 152)$, respectively. Hence, the event that the top t best players compete in the round of the tournament consisting of t players is highly unlikely even for small values of t.

8.2.3 Special Matrices of Winning Probabilities

We introduce three special classes of matrices of winning probabilities that satisfy the following properties: stochastic transitivity, strong stochastic transitivity, and the winning probabilities according to a generalized linear model. These properties are defined in the following and are shown to be in decreasing generality. These special classes of matrices of winning probabilities allow for a ranking of players in weakly decreasing strength that is used in the analysis of seeding procedures.

Definition 8.2. A matrix $\mathbf{P} = (p_{i,j})$ of winning probabilities is said to be *stochastically transitive* if for every triple i, k, and j such that $p_{i,k} \geq 1/2$ and $p_{k,j} \geq 1/2$, we have $p_{i,j} \geq 1/2$.

In other words, stochastic transitivity means that the following transitive relation holds: if for a pair of players i and j, player i is weakly stronger than some player k, and in turn player k is weakly stronger than player j, then player i is weakly stronger than player j. See Figure 8.3 for an illustration.

Stochastic transitivity implies the following property: for any stochastically transitive matrix of winning probabilities, there exists a ranking of players $(\sigma(1), \sigma(2), \ldots, \sigma(n))$, where $\sigma(i)$ denotes the rank of player i such that $\sigma(i) < \sigma(j)$ only if player i is weakly stronger than player $j \neq i$.

A stronger version of stochastic transitivity is defined by requiring that for every given player, the weaker the opponent is, the smaller the winning probability.

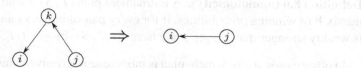

Figure 8.3. Transitivity.

Definition 8.3. A matrix $\mathbf{P}$ of winning probabilities is said to be *strongly stochastically transitive* if for every triple i, k and j, if $p_{i,k} \geq 1/2$ and $p_{k,j} \geq 1/2$, we have $p_{i,j} \geq p_{i,k}$ and $p_{i,j} \geq p_{k,j}$.

Another special class of matrices of winning probabilities is according to a generalized linear model, which is studied in some depth in Chapter 9.

Definition 8.4 (generalized linear models). Given is a parameter $\mathbf{v} = (v_1, v_2, \ldots, v_n) \in \mathbf{R}^n$ where v_i represents the strength of player i, and a distribution function $D : \mathbf{R} \to [0, 1]$ such that (i) $\lim_{x \to -\infty} D(x) = 0$, (ii) $\lim_{x \to \infty} D(x) = 1$, and (iii) $D(x) = 1 - D(-x)$, for every $x \in \mathbf{R}$. Then, $p_{i,j} = D(v_i - v_j)$ for all $i, j \in N$.

By Exercise 8.1, the three classes of matrices of winning probabilities introduced in this section satisfy the following relations:

$$\text{generalized linear model} \Rightarrow \text{strong stochastic transitivity}$$

$$\Rightarrow \text{stochastic transitivity} \qquad (8.2)$$

In other words, the set of stochastically transitive matrices is the most general. It contains the set of strongly stochastically transitive matrices, which in turn contains the set of matrices according to a generalized linear model.

8.2.4 Delayed Confrontation, Monotonicity, and Envy-Freeness

It is desired that a tournament plan is in some sense fair with respect to how the probabilities of winning the tournament or reaching a specific round of the tournament relate to the strengths of the players. For example, it may be desirable that a tournament plan maximizes the probability that the strongest player wins the tournament or that the two best players confront each other in the final round. At the same time, a good tournament plan may also need to assure an appreciable chance of winning for a weaker player in order to increase the interest of matches from the spectators' viewpoint. These vaguely defined goals are made more concrete by the concepts of delayed confrontation, monotonicity, and envy-freeness that we introduce as follows.

Definition 8.5 (delayed confrontation). A tournament plan (T, S) is said to satisfy the property of *delayed confrontation* if any two players from the top 2^q best players cannot be matched until the set of active players is reduced to 2^q or fewer players.

The delayed confrontation property is satisfied by a tournament plan according to a balanced single-elimination tournament with a standard seeding procedure, which is introduced in Section 8.2.5, and is not satisfied by a random permutation seeding procedure.

Definition 8.6 (monotonicity). A tournament plan (T, S) is said to be *monotone* for a matrix $\mathbf{P}$ of winning probabilities, if for every pair of players i and j such that player i is weakly stronger than player j, we have $x_i((T, S), \mathbf{P}) \geq x_j((T, S), \mathbf{P})$.

In other words, a tournament plan is monotone if any given player is at least as likely to win the tournament as any other player who is weaker or of the same strength. A monotone tournament plan may be considered fair in not discriminating against players so that no player has a larger chance of winning the tournament than a stronger player.

Definition 8.7 (envy-freeness). A tournament plan (T, S) is said to be *envy-free* if there exists no player who would prefer the seeding position of a weaker player, i.e., there exists no player i such that $x_i((T, S_{i,j}), \mathbf{P}) > x_i((T, S), \mathbf{P})$, for some weaker player $j \neq i$, where $S_{i,j}$ is the seeding of players derived from the seeding of players S by swapping the positions of players i and j.

8.2.5 Standard Seeding Procedure

The standard seeding procedure for a single-elimination tournament amounts to successively matching the strongest with the weakest unmatched player, and assigning the seeding positions such that in the absence of any upsets in the first round of the tournament, the seeding in the second round of the tournament corresponds to a standard seeding of players. More formally, the standard seeding procedure is defined recursively as follows. For $r = 1$, the standard seeding of the two players is $(1, 2)$. Suppose that for $n = 2^{r-1}$ players, the standard seeding of players is $(i_1, i_2, \ldots, i_{2^{r-1}})$. Then, the standard seeding for 2^r players is defined by $(i_1, n + 1 - i_1, i_2, n + 1 - i_2, \ldots, i_{2^{r-1}}, n + 1 - i_{2^{r-1}})$. See Figure 8.4 for standard seeding in a single-elimination tournament with two, four, and eight players.

Note that in a balanced single-elimination tournament, if in each match of a pair of players the stronger player wins, the standard seeding procedure guarantees that in every round j of the tournament, the competitors are the top 2^{r-j+1} strongest players.

Four Players

Consider the case of a single-elimination tournament with four players and a matrix $\mathbf{P}$ of winning probabilities. Denote the set of all possible seedings as $\mathcal{S} = \{S_1, S_2, S_3\}$ where $S_1 = (1, 4, 2, 3)$, $S_2 = (1, 3, 2, 4)$, and $S_3 = (1, 2, 3, 4)$. For brevity, let $x_i(S) \equiv x_i((T, S), \mathbf{P})$ denote the probability of player i winning the tournament under seeding $S \in \mathcal{S}$ and the matrix $\mathbf{P}$ of winning probabilities.

Theorem 8.8. *For every stochastically transitive matrix $\mathbf{P}$ of winning probabilities, the following properties hold.*

   (i) *Standard seeding S_1 maximizes $x_1(S)$ over $S \in \mathcal{S}$.*

   (ii) *The only monotone seeding is standard seeding, i.e., $x_1(S) \geq x_2(S) \geq x_3(S) \geq x_4(S)$, only if $S = S_1$.*

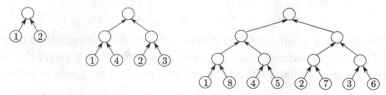

Figure 8.4. Standard seeding procedure for $n = 2, 4$, and 8.

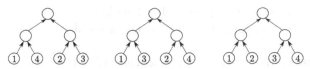

Figure 8.5. All possible seedings for a semifinal tournament.

(iii) *Standard seeding maximizes the probability that players 1 and 2 are the finalists if, and only if,*

$$p_{1,4}/p_{1,3} \geq p_{2,4}/p_{2,3},$$

otherwise, seeding S_2 maximizes this probability.

(iv) *For the scores defined by $v_i = \sum_{j \neq i} p_{i,j}$, $i \in N$, standard seeding maximizes the expected value for the winner given by $v_1 x_1(S) + v_2 x_2(S) + v_3 x_3(S) + v_4 x_4(S)$ over $S \in \mathcal{S}$.*

Proof of this theorem follows by simple arguments and is left as Exercise 8.2. The theorem tells us that for four-player single-elimination tournaments, the standard seeding procedure is the only static seeding procedure that is monotone. One may wonder whether the standard seeding procedure would remain monotone for the class of strongly stochastically transitive matrices of the winning probabilities, more generally, for tournaments with $n = 2^r$ for $r \geq 1$. One may ask whether this would be guaranteed by a static seeding procedure. We shall next see that the answer to this question is negative, with a counterexample for a tournament with just eight players.

Standard Seeding Procedure Can be Non-Monotone

The standard seeding procedure is not guaranteed to satisfy the monotonicity property as asserted in the following theorem.

Theorem 8.9. *For the standard seeding procedure in a balanced single-elimination tournament, there exists a strongly stochastically transitive matrix of the winning probabilities under which the seeding is non-monotone.*

Proof. The proof is by a counterexample. Let $\mathbf{P}_\alpha$ be a matrix of winning probabilities defined for parameter $\alpha \in (1/2, 1]$ as follows:

$$\mathbf{P}_\alpha = \begin{pmatrix} 1/2 & \alpha & \alpha & \alpha & \alpha & 1 & 1 & 1 \\ 1-\alpha & 1/2 & \alpha & \alpha & \alpha & 1 & 1 & 1 \\ 1-\alpha & 1-\alpha & 1/2 & \alpha & \alpha & \alpha & 1 & 1 \\ 1-\alpha & 1-\alpha & 1-\alpha & 1/2 & \alpha & \alpha & 1 & 1 \\ 1-\alpha & 1-\alpha & 1-\alpha & 1-\alpha & 1/2 & \alpha & 1 & 1 \\ 0 & 0 & 1-\alpha & 1-\alpha & 1-\alpha & 1/2 & 1 & 1 \\ 0 & 0 & 0 & 0 & 0 & 0 & 1/2 & 1 \\ 0 & 0 & 0 & 0 & 0 & 0 & 0 & 1/2 \end{pmatrix}. \quad (8.3)$$

Note that player 1 is stronger than player 2, player 2 is stronger than player 3, and so on, and player 7 is stronger than player 8; thus player 1 is stronger than any other player. The winning probabilities of player 1 and player 2 are given as follows

$$x_1((T, S), \mathbf{P}_\alpha) = \alpha^2 \text{ and } x_2((T, S), \mathbf{P}_\alpha) = 2\alpha(1-\alpha)(1-\alpha(1-\alpha)).$$

From this, observe that

$$\lim_{\alpha \downarrow \frac{1}{2}}(x_1((T, S), \mathbf{P}_\alpha), x_2((T, S), \mathbf{P}_\alpha)) = \left(\frac{1}{4}, \frac{3}{8}\right).$$

Thus, there exists $\alpha \geq 1/2$ such that $x_1((T, S), \mathbf{P}_\alpha) < x_2((T, S), \mathbf{P}_\alpha)$, which shows that for the given instance the standard seeding procedure S is not monotone.

The non-monotonicity arises because player 1 has a harder schedule than player 2: player 1 plays in the semi-final with either player 4 or 5 and in either case wins with probability α. On the other hand, player 2 plays in the semi-final with either player 3 or player 6, winning with probability α in the former case, and winning with certainty in the latter case. □

Static Seeding Procedures Cannot Guarantee Monotonicity

The existence of an instance for which a seeding procedure does not satisfy the monotonicity property can be established more generally for every static seeding procedure.

Theorem 8.10. *If there exists a seeding procedure for a balanced single-elimination tournament that guarantees monotonicity for every strongly stochastically transitive matrix of winning probabilities, then such a seeding procedure must be the standard seeding procedure.*

Proof. The proof is by induction on the tournament size $n = 2^r$.

Base case: $n = 2$. In this case, each of the two possible seedings is standard seeding, so the claim holds trivially.

Induction step: suppose that the claim holds for $n = m$, and we need to show that it holds for $n = 2m$. We assume the matrices of winning probabilities such that the set of players consists of a set of $2m - k$ top players and a set of k bottom players, for $1 \leq k \leq m$. The top players are ordered in decreasing order of their strenghts, so that player i is stronger than player j whenever $1 \leq i < j \leq 2m - k$. Specifically, we assume that $p_{i,j} = 1/2 + (2m - k - i + 1)\epsilon$ for $1 \leq i < j \leq 2m - k$ and parameter $0 \leq \epsilon < 1/(2m)$. We prove that the seeding must be such that in the first round of the tournament, each player i is matched with player $2m - i + 1$, for $1 \leq i \leq m$. This is shown by induction over $i = 1, 2, \ldots, m$.

Base case: $i = 1$. In this case, assume that the matrix of winning probabilities is such that there is one bottom player. We need to show that player 1 is matched with player $2m$. Notice that for the assumed matrix of winning probabilities, the players who advance to the second round of the tournament are from a set of top m players. Suppose that player 1 is matched with some player other than player $2m$; then player 1 wins the tournament with probability $1/(2m)$ for asymptotically small value of parameter ϵ. On the other hand, if player 1 is matched with player $2m$, then player 1 wins the tournament with probability at least $1/m$. Hence, it follows that player 1 must be matched with player $2m$. Induction step: assume that for $1 \leq j < m$, each player $i \in \{1, 2, \ldots, j\}$ is matched with player $2m - i + 1$. We need to show that player $j + 1$ is matched with player $2m - j$. Assume that the matrix of winning probabilities has $j + 1$ bottom players. By the induction hypothesis, each player $i \in \{1, 2, \ldots, j\}$ is matched to bottom player $2m - i + 1$. Thus, $2m - j$ is the only remaining unmatched bottom player. Notice that under the induction hypothesis, the players who advance to the second round of the tournament is a set of m top players. If player $j + 1$ is matched with a top player, then player $j + 1$ wins the tournament with probability $1/(2m)$ for asymptotically small value of parameter ϵ. On the other hand, if player $j + 1$ is matched with the bottom player $2m - j$, then player $j + 1$ wins the tournament with probability $1/m$ for asymptotically small value of parameter ϵ. This shows that player $j + 1$ must be matched with player $2m - j$. We have shown that each player $i \in \{1, 2, \ldots, m\}$ must be matched with player $2m - i + 1$. To complete the proof that the seeding of players must be according to the seeding procedure for a tournament of $2m$ players, we assume that the matrix of winning probabilities is such that there are m top players and m bottom players. In this case, each top player must be matched with a bottom player. The set of players who advance to the second round of the tournament is the set of top players. Since under the induction hypothesis, the seeding of players for a tournament of m players is according to the standard seeding procedure, this uniquely determines the seeding positions of the top m players in the first round of the tournament for $2m$ players, which conforms to that of the standard seeding procedure. $\square$

From Theorem 8.9 and Theorem 8.10, we have the following corollary.

Corollary 8.11. *For any static seeding of a balanced single-elimination tournament, there exists a strongly stochastically transitive matrix of winning probabilities under which the seeding is non-monotone.*

Static Seeding Procedures Cannot Guarantee Envy-Freeness
Theorem 8.12. *For every seeding S of a set of $n = 2^r$ players with $r \geq 3$ in a balanced single-elimination tournament, there exists a strongly stochastically transitive matrix of winning probabilities such that S is not envy-free.*

Proof. We establish the theorem by the following two observations. First, we shall show that for every seeding of a set of eight players in a balanced single-elimination tournament, there exists a strongly stochastically transitive matrix of the winning probabilities such that the seeding is not envy-free. This matrix of the winning probabilities will correspond to a set of players where there are six top players and two dummy players such that each dummy player loses against any top player with certainty. Second, we shall extend this case to $n = 2^r$ players, for any integer $r \geq 3$, by adding dummy players and then show that if a seeding is envy-free then it must correspond to a seeding in a balanced single-elimination tournament among eight players with the matrix of winning probabilities as in our original tournament with eight players.

For the tournament of $n = 8$ players, by extensive search, one can check that for the matrix winning probabilities (8.3) with $\alpha = 3/4$, there exists no seeding that is envy-free. We show this only for the case of the standard seeding $S = (1, 8, 4, 5, 2, 7, 3, 6)$; in this case, for the matrix of winning probabilities (8.3), player 1 envies player 2, for any $1/2 < \alpha < 1$. Indeed, under S, we observe that player 1 passes the first round with probability 1 while player 4 passes the first round with probability α and player 5 passes the first round with probability $1 - \alpha$. Since player 1 wins against either player 4 or player 5 with probability α, player 1 plays in the final with probability α. On the other hand, player 2 passes the first round with probability 1, player 3 with probability α, and player 6 with probability $1 - \alpha$. Since player 2 wins against player 3 with probability

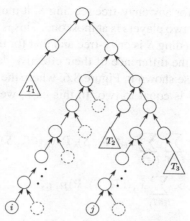

Figure 8.6. A balanced single-elimination tournament: players i and j are top players and in both T_2 and T_3 there is at least one top player; circles denote dummy players. The effective depth of player i is equal to 1 and that of player j is equal to 3.

α and against player 6 with probability 1, we have that player 2 plays in the final with probability $\alpha^2 + 1 - \alpha$ and player 3 with probability $\alpha(1 - \alpha)$. It follows that

$$x_1((T, S), \mathbf{P}_\alpha) = \alpha^2.$$

Next, we consider the seeding $S' = (2, 8, 4, 5, 1, 7, 3, 6)$, which is derived from S by swapping the positions of players 1 and 2. Simple calculations show that one of the finalists is player 2 with probability α, or player 4 with probability $\alpha(1 - \alpha)$, or player 5 with probability $(1 - \alpha)^2$, and the other finalist is player 1 with probability $\alpha^2 + 1 - \alpha$ or player 3 with probability $(1 - \alpha)\alpha$. It follows that

$$x_1((T, S'), \mathbf{P}_\alpha) = \alpha(1 - \alpha(1 - \alpha)).$$

Therefore, $x_1((T, S), \mathbf{P}_\alpha) < x_1((T, S'), \mathbf{P}_\alpha)$ which is equivalent to $(1 - \alpha)^2 > 0$. Since the parameter α is assumed to take values in $(0, 1/2]$, it follows that player 1 envies player 2 for any $1/2 < \alpha < 1$. The largest difference is achieved as α approaches $1/2$ from above and in this limit case,

$$(x_1((T, S), \mathbf{P}_\alpha), x_1((T, S'), \mathbf{P}_\alpha)) \rightarrow \left(\frac{1}{4}, \frac{3}{8}\right).$$

The underlying reason for the observed envy is a combination of the following two facts: (i) player 1 is a finalist with a larger probability under seeding S' than under seeding S, with probabilities $\alpha + (1 - \alpha)^2$ and α, respectively; and (ii) under either seeding, any possible opponent of player 1 in the final is a player against whom player 1 wins with the same probability of value α.

We now show how to generalize to the number of players $n = 2^r$, for any integer $r \geq 3$. Note that the set of players with the matrix of winning probabilities (8.3) is such that players 7 and 8 lose with certainty against any other player. Therefore, we can think of this set of players as consisting of six top players and two dummy players. We extend the matrix of winning probabilities to a set of 2^r players by adding dummy players. For a given seeding S, we shall say that a player is at effective depth d, if d is the smallest depth of the tree at which this player is matched with a non-dummy player.

A key observation is that for any envy-free seeding S, it must be that the difference of the effective depths of any two players is at most one. This is shown by contradiction as follows. Suppose that a seeding S is envy-free and that for this seeding there exist two players i and j such that the difference of their effective depths is larger than one. It suffices to consider the case shown in Figure 8.6, where the difference of the effective depths of players j and i is equal to two. In this case, we observe that the winning probability of player j is

$$x_j((T, S), \mathbf{P}) = \sum_{i_2 \in T_2} \sum_{i_3 \in T_3} x_{i_2}((T_2, S), \mathbf{P}) x_{i_3}((T_3, S), \mathbf{P}) p_{j,i_2} p_{j,i_3} p_{j,i}$$
$$\times \sum_{i_1 \in T_1} x_{i_1}((T_1, S), \mathbf{P}) p_{j,i_1}.$$

Now, let us consider a seeding S' that is derived from S by swapping the positions of player j and the dummy player that is matched in the first round with player i. This results in a situation as shown in Figure 8.7. For the seeding S', the winning probability of player j satisfies the following relations

$$x_j((T, S'), \mathbf{P}) = \sum_{i_2 \in T_2} \sum_{i_3 \in T_3} x_{i_2}((T_2, S), \mathbf{P}) x_{i_3}((T_3, S), \mathbf{P}) (p_{i_2,i_3} p_{j,i_2} + p_{i_3,i_2} p_{j,i_3}) p_{j,i}$$
$$\times \sum_{i_1 \in T_1} x_{i_1}((T_1, S), \mathbf{P}) p_{j,i_1}$$
$$\geq \sum_{i_2 \in T_2} \sum_{i_3 \in T_3} x_{i_2}((T_2, S), \mathbf{P}) x_{i_3}((T_3, S), \mathbf{P}) \min\{p_{j,i_2}, p_{j,i_3}\} p_{j,i}$$
$$\times \sum_{i_1 \in T_1} x_{i_1}((T_1, S), \mathbf{P}) p_{j,i_1}$$
$$> \sum_{i_2 \in T_2} \sum_{i_3 \in T_3} x_{i_2}((T_2, S), \mathbf{P}) x_{i_3}((T_3, S), \mathbf{P}) p_{j,i_2} p_{j,i_3} p_{j,i}$$
$$\times \sum_{i_1 \in T_1} x_{i_1}((T_1, S), \mathbf{P}) p_{j,i_1}$$
$$= x_j((T, S), \mathbf{P}).$$

Therefore, the difference of the effective depths of any two non-dummy players must be at most one. This implies that if a seeding S is envy-free, then it must be that it

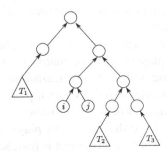

Figure 8.7. After a swap of player j and the player matched with player i in the first round.

corresponds to a seeding that is derived from a one-to-one mapping of the top six players to the leaves of a binary tree of depth three. □

8.2.6 Random Permutation Seeding Procedure

The winning probabilities for the random permutation seeding procedure are as follows:

$$x_i(T, \mathbf{P}) = \frac{1}{n!} \sum_{S \in \mathcal{S}} x_i((T, S), \mathbf{P})$$

We first establish a monotonicity property of the random seeding procedure for fixed seeding positions of a pair of players.

Theorem 8.13. *Suppose that* $\mathbf{P}$ *is strongly stochastically transitive and* T *is balanced. Then, for every pair of seeding positions* u *and* v *and* $i < j$, *we have*

$$\sum_{S \in \mathcal{S}:\, S(u)=i, S(v)=j} x_i((T, S), \mathbf{P}) \geq \sum_{S \in \mathcal{S}:\, S(u)=i, S(v)=j} x_j((T, S), \mathbf{P}).$$

As a corollary, we obtain the following monotonicity property.

Corollary 8.14. *Suppose that* $\mathbf{P}$ *is strongly stochastically transitive and* T *is balanced. Then, for every* $i < j$, *we have*

$$x_i(T, \mathbf{P}) \geq x_j(T, \mathbf{P})$$

Proof. We first establish two lemmas. The first lemma states an intuitive property and is presented without a proof. It states that if a player is replaced with a new player who in a pair comparison with each other player wins with a larger than or equal probability, then the winning probability of this new player is at least as large as that of the original player.

Lemma 8.15. *Let* $\mathbf{P}$ *be a strongly stochastically transitive matrix and let* $\mathbf{P}'$ *be identical to* $\mathbf{P}$ *except for replacing* $p_{i,k}$ *with* $p'_{i,k}$, *for fixed* i, *such that* $p'_{i,k} \geq p_{i,k}$ *for all* $k \neq i$. *Then,* $x_i((T, S), \mathbf{P}') \geq x_j((T, S), \mathbf{P}))$, *for every* T *and* S.

The second lemma establishes the monotonicity property for a pair of players who compete against each other in the first round of the tournament.

Lemma 8.16. *Given* T *and* S, *suppose that players* i *and* j *are assigned to two leaf nodes that are children of the same parent node; then* $i < j$ *implies* $x_i((T, S), \mathbf{P}) \geq x_j((T, S), \mathbf{P})$ *for every strongly stochastically transitive matrix* $\mathbf{P}$.

Proof. Let T' be the tournament tree obtained from T by removing the match between players i and j. Let S_{-i} be the seeding of players derived from S by removing player i and assigning player j to the parent node of the match (i, j) in the original tournament. Similarly, we define S_{-j}. Then, we have

$$x_i((T, S), \mathbf{P}) = p_{i,j} x_i((T', S_{-j}), \mathbf{P})$$

$$\geq p_{j,i} x_i((T', S_{-j}), \mathbf{P})$$

$$\geq p_{j,i} x_j((T', S_{-i}), \mathbf{P})$$

$$= x_j(T, S, \mathbf{P})$$

where the first inequality is by the assumption $i < j$ and the second inequality is by Lemma 8.15. □

We shall prove the theorem by induction on the number of players $n = 2^r$. Base case $r = 1$ holds trivially. Induction step: assume that the theorem holds for $n = 2^{r-1}$ and we need to show that it holds for $n = 2^r$. For each leaf node a of the tree T, denote with $p(a)$ the parent node of a, and denote with a' the other children node of $p(a)$. Suppose that players i and j are assigned to two leaf nodes u and v, respectively. If u and v are peer nodes, then the claim of the theorem holds by Lemma 8.16. Therefore, it suffices to consider the case where u and v are not peer nodes. For i' and j' such that $\{i', j'\} \cap \{i, j\} = \emptyset$, let us define

$$\mathcal{S}_{u,v,i',j'} = \{S \in \mathcal{S} \mid S(u) = i, S(v) = j, S(u') = i', S(v') = j'\}.$$

The inequality asserted in the theorem can be written as

$$\sum_{i'<j'} \sum_{S \in \mathcal{S}_{u,v,i',j'}} x_i((T, S), \mathbf{P}) + \sum_{S \in \mathcal{S}_{u,v,j',i'}} x_i((T, S), \mathbf{P})$$

$$\geq \sum_{i'<j'} \sum_{S \in \mathcal{S}_{u,v,i',j'}} x_j((T, S), \mathbf{P}) + \sum_{S \in \mathcal{S}_{u,v,j',i'}} x_j((T, S), \mathbf{P}).$$

Given i, j, i', j', let M denote the set of all possible matchings of all players except players i, j, i', j'. For $m \in M$, let $W(m)$ denote the set of all possible winners from the matches specified by m, and let $S(m)$ denote the set of all possible seedings of the leaf nodes of T by players in m such that (i) no player is assigned to the leaf nodes u and v, and (ii) every pair in m must be assigned to two nodes with the same parent node. Then, we have

$$\sum_{S \in \mathcal{S}_{u,v,i',j'}} x_i((T, S), \mathbf{P}) + \sum_{S \in \mathcal{S}_{u,v,j',i'}} x_i((T, S), \mathbf{P})$$

$$= \sum_{m \in M} \sum_{z \in W(m)} \mathbf{Pr}[z \mid m] \left(\sum_{S \in \mathcal{S}_{u,v,i',j'} \cap S(m)} x_i((T, S), \mathbf{P}) + \sum_{S \in \mathcal{S}_{u,v,j',i'} \cap S(m)} x_i((T, S), \mathbf{P}) \right)$$

$$= \sum_{m \in M} \sum_{z \in W(m)} \mathbf{Pr}[z \mid m] \left((p_{i,i'} p_{j,j'} + p_{i,j'} p_{j,i'}) \sum_{S' \in \mathcal{S}_{p(u),p(v)}} x_i((T', S'), \mathbf{P}) \right.$$

$$\left. + p_{i,i'} p_{j',j} \sum_{S' \in \mathcal{S}_{p(u),p(v)}} x_i((T', S'_{j',j}), \mathbf{P}) + p_{i,j'} p_{i',j} \sum_{S' \in \mathcal{S}_{p(u),p(v)}} x_i((T', S'_{i',j}), \mathbf{P}) \right)$$

where T' is the tournament tree for 2^{r-1} players obtained from T by removing the 2^r leaf nodes, and $S'_{a,j}$ is obtained from S' by swapping a and j.

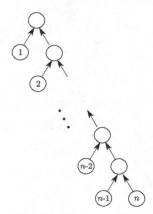

Figure 8.8. A ladder tournament plan.

Now, note the following three facts. First, by the induction hypothesis, we have

$$\sum_{S'\in\mathcal{S}} x_i((T', S'), \mathbf{P}) \geq \sum_{S'\in\mathcal{S}} x_j((T', S'), \mathbf{P}).$$

Second, by Lemma 8.15, we have

$$x_i((T', S'_{a,j}), \mathbf{P}) \geq x_j((T', S'_{a,i}), \mathbf{P}), \quad \text{for } a \in \{i, j\}.$$

Third, we have $p_{i,i'}p_{j',j} \geq p_{j,i'}p_{j',j}$ and $p_{i',j'}p_{i',j} \geq p_{j,j'}p_{i',i}$.
Therefore, it follows that

$$\sum_{S\in\mathcal{S}_{u,v,i',j'}} x_i((T, S), \mathbf{P}) + \sum_{S\in\mathcal{S}_{u,v,j',i'}} x_i((T, S), \mathbf{P})$$

$$\geq \sum_{S\in\mathcal{S}_{u,v,i',j'}} x_j((T, S), \mathbf{P}) + \sum_{S\in\mathcal{S}_{u,v,j',i'}} x_j((T, S), \mathbf{P}). \qquad \square$$

Non-Monotonicity for an Unbalanced Tournament Tree

For unbalanced tournament plans, there exist tournament plans that guarantee both monotonicity and envy-freeness for the class of strongly stochastically transitive matrices of winning probabilities. For example, one such tournament plan is a ladder tree, shown in Figure 8.8, where players are assigned seeding positions in decreasing order of their strength. One may be tempted to conjecture that random permutation seeding would guarantee monotonicity for any tournament tree, not only for balanced tournament trees. This, however, is not true, as shown in the following theorem.

Theorem 8.17. *There exist a strongly stochastically transitive matrix of winning probabilities and a tournament tree such that the random permutation seeding procedure is not ex-ante monotone.*

Proof. The proof follows by exhibiting an instance of a tournament tree and a strongly stochastically matrix of winning probabilities under which the random permutation seeding procedure is not ex-ante monotone. Suppose that the tournament tree is the unbalanced tournament tree given in Figure 8.9, which has 17 seeding positions.

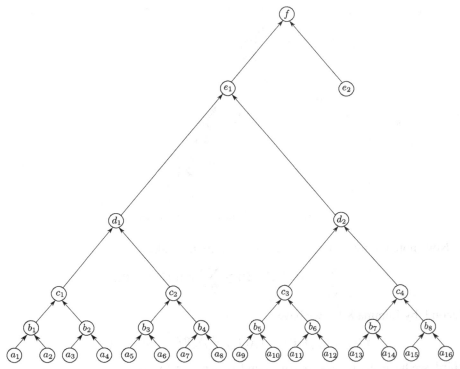

Figure 8.9. A counterexample used to establish non-monotonicity of the random permutation seeding procedure for a strongly stochastically transitive matrix of winning probabilities.

Suppose that the matrix of winning probabilities is for a set of 17 players such that there is a unique strongest player, 13 players of the second strongest strength, and 3 remaining players of the lowest and strictly decreasing strengths. Specifically, the winning probabilities for different types of players are given by

$$
\mathbf{P}_\epsilon = \begin{pmatrix}
1/2 & 3/5 & 1 & 1 & 1 \\
2/5 & 1/2 & 1 - 2\epsilon & 1 - \epsilon & 1 - \epsilon \\
0 & 2\epsilon & 1/2 & 1 - 2\epsilon & 1 - \epsilon \\
0 & \epsilon & 2\epsilon & 1/2 & 3/5 \\
0 & \epsilon & \epsilon & 2/5 & 1/2
\end{pmatrix}.
$$

We will show that under the random permutation seeding procedure, player 4 has a smaller probability of winning the tournament than player 5. Since player 4 is stronger than player 5, it follows that the random permutation seeding procedure is not ex-ante monotone.

For a node s of the tournament tree and a type t of a player, we denote with $\{s = t\}$ the event that a player of type t reaches position s in the tournament tree. In other words, the event $\{s = t\}$ holds if, and only if, a player of type t is assigned a seeding position in the subtree rooted at node s, and if he or she wins in all rounds before reaching the round of node s.

If a player of either type 4 or 5 is to win the tournament by starting from any seeding position other than e_2, this player must win at least four matches against a player whose type is either 1 or 2 or 3. The probability of this event is $O(\epsilon^4)$. Hence, the probability of winning the tournament for a player of type $t = 4$ or 5 satisfies

$$\mathbf{Pr}[f = t] = \frac{1}{17}\epsilon\,\mathbf{Pr}[e_1 = 2 \mid e_2 = t] + O(\epsilon^4).$$

Since under the given matrix of winning probabilities, the finalist at position e_1 is of either type 1 or 2 with probability 1, it follows that

$$\mathbf{Pr}[f = t] = \frac{1}{17}\epsilon\,(1 - \mathbf{Pr}[e_1 = 1 \mid e_2 = t]) + O(\epsilon^4).$$

From the last equation, we observe that to establish that $\mathbf{Pr}[f = 5] > \mathbf{Pr}[f = 4]$ it suffices to show that there exists a constant $c > 0$ such that

$$\mathbf{Pr}[e_1 = 1 \mid e_2 = 4] - \mathbf{Pr}[e_1 = 1 \mid e_2 = 5] \geq c\epsilon^2, \text{ for every small enough } \epsilon > 0.$$

$$(8.4)$$

In the remainder of the proof we establish that inequality (8.4) holds.

Since we will consider probabilities of events conditional on that the finalist at position e_2 is either of type 4 or 5, the player of type 1 is assigned to one of the seeding positions a_1 through a_{16} with probability 1. Since the subtree rooted at node e_1 is a perfect binary tree, without loss of generality, we can condition on the event that the player of type 1 is assigned to the seeding position a_1. For every given type τ of a player and an event A, we denote with $\mathbf{Pr}_\tau[A]$ the conditional probability of event A defined by

$$\mathbf{Pr}_\tau[A] = \mathbf{Pr}[A \mid e_2 = \tau, e_1 = 1].$$

Note that

$$\mathbf{Pr}[e_1 = 1 \mid e_2 = \tau] = \mathbf{Pr}_\tau[e_1 = 1], \text{ for } \tau \in \{4, 5\}.$$

By the definition of the tournament tree and the matrix of winning probabilities, it can be readily derived that for $\tau \in \{4, 5\}$, we have

$$\mathbf{Pr}_\tau[e_1 = 1] = \prod_{s=a_2,b_2,c_2,d_2} \left(1 - \frac{2}{5}\mathbf{Pr}_\tau[s = 2]\right)$$

where

$$\mathbf{Pr}_4[a_2 = 2] = \mathbf{Pr}_5[a_2 = 2],$$
$$\mathbf{Pr}_4[b_2 = 2] = \mathbf{Pr}_5[b_2 = 2],$$

and

$$\mathbf{Pr}_4[d_2 = 2] = \mathbf{Pr}_5[d_2 = 2] + O(\epsilon^3).$$

Therefore, it follows that

$$\mathbf{Pr}[e_1 = 1 \mid e_2 = 4] - \mathbf{Pr}[e_1 = 1 \mid e_2 = 5] = \kappa(\mathbf{Pr}_5[c_2 = 2] - \mathbf{Pr}_4[c_2 = 2]) + O(\epsilon^3)$$

$$(8.5)$$

where

$$\kappa = \frac{2}{5}\prod_{s=a_2,b_2}\left(1 - \frac{2}{5}\mathbf{Pr}_4[s = 2]\right).$$

Let us denote with $\alpha_\tau(\{a, b\}, \{c, d\})$ the probability of the event that the seeding of the players is such that for the leaf nodes of the subtree rooted at node c_2 of the tournament tree, one of the matches is between two players of types a and b, and the other match is between two players of type c and d, conditional on that $a_1 = 1$ and $e_2 = \tau$.

For $\tau, \tau' \in \{4, 5\}$ such that $\tau \neq \tau'$, we have

$$\mathbf{Pr}_\tau[c_2 = 2] = (p_{3,\tau'} p_{2,3} + p_{\tau',3} p_{2,\tau'})\alpha_\tau(\{2, 2\}, \{3, \tau'\})$$
$$+ (p_{2,\tau'} + p_{\tau',2} p_{2,\tau'})\alpha_\tau(\{2, 2\}, \{2, \tau'\})$$
$$+ (p_{2,3} + p_{3,2} p_{2,3})\alpha_\tau(\{2, 2\}, \{2, 3\})$$
$$+ (p_{2,3} p_{2,\tau'} + p_{2,3} p_{\tau',2} p_{2,\tau'} + p_{3,2} p_{2,\tau'} p_{2,3})\alpha_\tau(\{2, 3\}, \{2, \tau'\}).$$

Since by the definition of the matrix of winning probabilities, we have

$$p_{2,4} = p_{2,5}$$

and by the fact that the seeding is according to a random permutation, we have

$$\alpha_4(\{2, 2\}, \{3, 5\}) = \alpha_5(\{2, 2\}, \{3, 4\}),$$
$$\alpha_4(\{2, 2\}, \{2, 5\}) = \alpha_5(\{2, 2\}, \{2, 4\}),$$
$$\alpha_4(\{2, 3\}, \{2, 5\}) = \alpha_5(\{2, 3\}, \{2, 4\}),$$

it follows that

$$\mathbf{Pr}_5[c_2 = 2] - \mathbf{Pr}_4[c_2 = 2] = \alpha(p_{3,4} p_{2,3} + p_{4,3} p_{2,4} - p_{3,5} p_{2,3} - p_{5,3} p_{2,5}) = -\alpha\epsilon^2$$

where α is a strictly positive constant equal to $\alpha_4(\{2, 2\}, \{3, 4\})$.

Combining with (8.5), we have

$$\mathbf{Pr}[e_1 = 1 \mid e_2 = 4] - \mathbf{Pr}[e_1 = 1 \mid e_2 = 5] = -\kappa\alpha\epsilon^2 + O(\epsilon^3),$$

which establishes the inequality stated in (8.4). $\qquad\square$

8.2.7 Cohort Randomized Seeding Procedure

The cohort randomized seeding procedure is defined as follows. Suppose that $n = 2^r$ players are ordered in decreasing order of strength. The players are partitioned in cohorts such that players 1 and 2 are assigned to cohort 1, players 3 and 4 are assigned to cohort 2, and players are subsequently assigned to cohorts of doubling size as follows:

$$\underbrace{1, 2}_{1}, \underbrace{3, 4}_{2}, \underbrace{5, 6, 7, 8}_{3}, \underbrace{9, 10, 11, 12, 13, 14, 15, 16}_{4}, \ldots.$$

In other words, cohort 1 consists of players $N_1 = \{1, 2\}$, and cohort $1 < j \leq r$ consists of players $N_j = \{2^{j-1} + 1, \cdots, 2^j\}$. A seeding that satisfies the delayed-confrontation condition must be such that any two players in the same cohort j cannot be confronted in a match earlier than in round $r - j + 1$ of the tournament. A cohort randomized seeding procedure is defined recursively as follows. For a perfect binary tree of depth

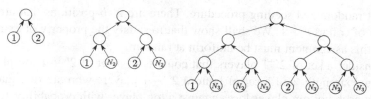

Figure 8.10. Cohort randomized seeding.

$k = 1$, the two players in cohort 1 are assigned arbitrarily to the two leaf nodes. For a perfect binary tree of depth $k = 2$, assign the two players from cohort 1 to the left children of the nodes to which these two players were assigned in the tree of depth 1, and assign players from cohort 2 uniformly at random to the two remaining leaf nodes. For the perfect binary tree of depth $k = 3$, similarly assign the players from cohort 1 and cohort 2 to the left children nodes of the nodes to which these players were assigned in the tree of depth 2, and assign players from cohort 3 uniformly at random to the remaining leaf nodes. Continuing this procedure to depth r defines a cohort randomized seeding for $n = 2^r$ players. See Figure 8.10 for an illustration.

An alternative way to define the cohort randomized seeding procedure for a set of $n = 2^r$ players is as follows: assign players according to the standard seeding procedure, and then randomly permute the assignment of players within each cohort 2 through r. For example, for the case of $n = 8$ players (shown in Figure 8.4), start with standard seeding $(1, 8, 4, 5, 2, 7, 3, 6)$; then (i) reassign players 3 and 4 to positions 3 and 7 according to a random permutation, and (ii) reassign players 5, 6, 7, and 8 to positions 2, 4, 6, and 8 according to a random permutation.

Theorem 8.18. *Consider a single-elimination tournament among $n = 2^r$ players for $r \geq 1$. A randomized seeding procedure satisfies the properties of delayed confrontation and ex-ante envy-freeness if, and only if, it is a cohort randomized seeding procedure.*

Proof. The proof is by induction. Base case $r = 2$. There are two possible tournament seedings $(1, 4, 2, 3)$ and $(1, 3, 2, 4)$. Let us assume that $(1, 4, 2, 3)$ is selected with probability p and $(1, 3, 2, 4)$ is selected with probability $1 - p$, for $0 \leq p \leq 1$. Suppose that players 1, 2, and 3 are of equal strength, and player 4 loses against any other player. Under $(1, 4, 2, 3)$, player 1 wins with probability $1/2$ while player 2 wins with probability $1/4$. Similarly, under $(1, 3, 2, 4)$, player 1 wins with probability $1/4$ while player 2 wins with probability $1/2$. It follows that $\mathbf{E}[x_1(T, S, \mathbf{P})] = 1/4 + p/4$ and $\mathbf{E}[x_2(T, S, \mathbf{P})] = 1/4 + (1 - p)/4$. Hence, if $p < 1/2$, then player 1 would prefer to swap with player 2, while for $p > 1/2$, player 2 would prefer to swap with player 1. Therefore, for the seeding to be ex-ante envy-free it must be $p = 1/2$.

Suppose that the statement of the theorem holds for $r \geq 1$; we then show that it holds for $r + 1$. In round $r + 1$ there are 2^{r+1} players, and the set of possible seedings that satisfy the delayed confrontations can be represented as

$$(a_1, b_1), (a_2, b_2), \ldots, (a_{2^{r-1}}, b_{2^{r-1}}), (a_{2^{r-1}+1}, b_{2^{r-1}+1}), \ldots, (a_{2^r}, b_{2^r}).$$

Here a-positions are assigned to players of cohorts 1 through r such that player 1 is assigned to position a_1, player 2 to position a_{2^r+1} and by our inductive hypothesis, the remaining a-positions are assigned to players of cohorts 2 through r according to the cohort randomized seeding procedure. There are 2^r b-positions that are assigned to players of cohort $r + 1$. We shall show that to satisfy the property of ex-ante envy-freeness, this assignment must be uniform at random.

We consider a set of 2^{r+1} players that consists of a set of $2^r + 1$ top players who are of equal strength, and a set of bottom $2^r - 1$ players who are of equal strength and where each bottom player loses against a top player with probability 1. Note that the set of top players consists of all players in cohorts 1 through r and one player of cohort $r + 1$, i.e., player $2^r + 1$. Let p_j denote the probability that player $2^r + 1$ is assigned to position b_j, for $j = 1, 2, \ldots, 2^r$. Denote with $\bar{x}_j$ the probability that the player assigned to position a_j wins the tournament. To win the tournament, a player in position a_j needs to win in r matches against equally strong players if his or her first match is a cohort $r + 1$ player other than player $2^r + 1$, and otherwise, he or she needs to win in $r + 1$ matches against equally strong players. Therefore,

$$\bar{x}_j = \frac{1}{2^r}(1 - p_j) + \frac{1}{2^{r+1}}p_j. \tag{8.6}$$

Since players 1 and 2 are assigned to positions a_1 and a_{2^r+1}, we have $\mathbf{E}[x_1(T, S, \mathbf{P})] = \bar{x}_1$ and $\mathbf{E}[x_2(T, S, \mathbf{P})] = \bar{x}_{2^r+1}$. For the seeding to be ex-ante envy-free, it must hold that $\mathbf{E}[x_1(T, S, \mathbf{P})] = \mathbf{E}[x_2(T, S, \mathbf{P})]$, i.e.,

$$p_1 = p_{2^r+1}. \tag{8.7}$$

Since players in cohorts 1 through r are of equal strength, $\mathbf{E}[x_i(S)] = \mathbf{E}[x_1(S)]$ for every $i \in N_2 \cup \cdots \cup N_r$. If the last condition does not hold, then player 1 would prefer the seeding of player i or vice versa. From the latter condition, (8.6) and (8.7), it follows that

$$\frac{1}{2^r} - \frac{1}{2^{r+1}}p_1 = \mathbf{E}[x_1(T, S, \mathbf{P})]$$

$$= \frac{1}{|N_2 \cup \cdots \cup N_r|}\sum_{i \in N_2 \cup \cdots \cup N_r} \mathbf{E}[x_i(T, S, \mathbf{P})]$$

$$= \frac{1}{2^r - 2}\sum_{j=2}^{2^r-1} \bar{x}_j$$

$$= \frac{1}{2^r} - \frac{1 - 2p_1}{2^{r+1}(2^r - 2)}$$

which is equivalent to $p_1 = 1/2^r$.

Finally, player 1 would not prefer a different a position than his or her own, i.e., $\bar{x}_1 \geq \bar{x}_j$, for every $j = 1, 2, \ldots, 2^r$. Combined with (8.6) and $p_1 = 1/2^r$, this means that $p_j \geq p_1$ for every $j = 1, 2, \ldots, 2^r$, which combined with $\sum_j p_j = 1$ means that $p_j = 1/2^r$ for every $j = 1, 2, \ldots, 2^r$. $\square$

Minimizing Favoritism

A randomized seeding procedure according to a probability distribution p over the set of all possible seedings S is said to *minimize favoritism* over all randomized seeding procedures according to probability distributions in a subset $\mathcal{P}$ if it minimizes the largest probability of winning by a player over $\mathcal{P}$, i.e.,

$$\max_{i \in N} \sum_{S \in \mathcal{S}} p(S) x_i((T, S), \mathbf{P}) \leq \max_{i \in N} \sum_{S \in \mathcal{S}} q(S) x_i((T, S), \mathbf{P}), \quad \text{for all } q \in \mathcal{P}.$$

A seeding is said to be *monotone with respect to seeding order* if the probability of winning by any higher seeded player is at least as large as the probability of winning by any lower seeded player.

This is a weaker version of monotonicity that allows for the probabilities of winning the tournament of two equally strong players to be different, but requires that the larger probability of winning is for the higher seeded player. If there is a strict order between the players, then the two versions of monotonicity are equivalent.

Theorem 8.19. *The cohort randomized seeding procedure is the only randomized seeding procedure that minimizes favoritism for all randomized seeding procedures that satisfy the conditions of delay confrontation and monotonicity with respect to seeding order.*

The proof of this theorem is left as Exercise 8.3. Under the condition of delayed confrontation, it is clear that the seeding must be such that cohorts of players are assigned to the leaves of the tournament tree as specified by the cohort randomized seeding procedure. The proof needs to establish that any other way to randomize within cohorts of players contradicts the conditions of minimizing favoritism and monotonicity with respect to the seeding order.

8.2.8 Dynamic Seeding Procedures

Consider a dynamic seeding procedure defined by seeding players in each round of a tournament according to the standard seeding procedure applied to the set of players participating in the given round with respect to their relative strengths. With a slight abuse of notation, let us define $x_i(N)$ to be the probability that player $i \in N$ wins the tournament under the dynamic seeding procedure.

Theorem 8.20. *The dynamic seeding procedure is monotone for every strongly stochastically transitive matrix of winning probabilities, i.e., if player i is weakly stronger than player j, then $x_i(N) \geq x_j(N)$.*

Proof. Suppose that the number of players is $n = 2^r$ for an integer $r \geq 1$. Let $x_i(N')$ be the probability that player i wins the tournament under the dynamic seeding procedure for the set of players $N' \subseteq N$. The following two lemmas can be shown to hold by induction on the number of rounds:

Lemma 8.21. *If player i is stronger than player j, then $x_i(N \setminus \{j\}) \geq x_j(N \setminus \{i\})$.*

and

Lemma 8.22. *If player i is stronger than player j, then $p_{k,j} x_k(N \setminus \{j\}) \geq p_{k,i} x_k(N \setminus \{i\})$, for any other player k.*

Let $\mathcal{T}$ be the set of all possible realizations in the elimination tournament under the dynamic seeding procedure, and let $\mathcal{T}_i$ denote the subset of realizations in $\mathcal{T}$ for which player i wins the tournament. Then, we have

$$x_i(N) = \sum_{t \in \mathcal{T}_i} \mathbf{Pr}[t].$$

Let o_i denote the first-round opponent of player i. Note that under the dynamic seeding procedure, player $o_i - 1$ is necessarily the first-round opponent of player $i + 1$. We distinguish two cases.

Case 1: $o_i = i + 1$. In the first round, player i is matched with player $i + 1$. Let j denote the winner of the match between players i and $i + 1$. Since the relative ranks in any future round remain the same regardless of whether player i or player $i + 1$ wins, there exists a one-to-one mapping between $\mathcal{T}_i$ and $\mathcal{T}_{i+1}$ such that if $t \in \mathcal{T}_i$ is mapped to $t' \in \mathcal{T}_{i+1}$, then t' can be obtained from t by replacing player i with player $i + 1$. Since $p_{i,k} \geq p_{i+1,k}$ for all k, it holds that $\mathbf{Pr}[t] \geq \mathbf{Pr}[t']$. Therefore,

$$x_i(N) = \sum_{t \in \mathcal{T}_i} \mathbf{Pr}[t] \geq \sum_{t' \in \mathcal{T}_{i+1}} \mathbf{Pr}[t'] = x_{i+1}(N).$$

Case 2: $o_i \neq i + 1$. We proceed by induction on the number of rounds r. Base case $r = 1$: the hypothesis trivially holds in this case. Induction step: assume that the hypothesis holds for $r \geq 1$ and consider now the case for the set of players N such that $|N| = 2^{r+1}$. Let N_2^* denote the subset of players who win in the first round excluding any matches involving either player i or player $i + 1$. Let $p(N') = \mathbf{Pr}[N_2^* = N']$. The following two identities hold:

$$x_i(N) = \sum_{N'} p(N')[p_{i,o_i} p_{i+1,o_i-1} x_i(N' \cup \{i\} \cup \{i + 1\})$$

$$+ p_{i,o_i} p_{o_i-1,i+1} x_i(N' \cup \{i\} \cup \{o_i - 1\})] \tag{8.8}$$

and

$$x_{i+1}(N) = \sum_{N'} p(N')[p_{i,o_i} p_{i+1,o_i-1} x_{i+1}(N' \cup \{i\} \cup \{i + 1\})$$

$$+ p_{o_i,i} p_{i+1,o_i-1} x_{i+1}(N' \cup \{o_i\} \cup \{i + 1\})]. \tag{8.9}$$

The proof follows by the following series of relations:

$$x_i(N) - x_{i+1}(N) \geq \sum_{N'} p(N')[p_{i,o_i} p_{o_i-1,i+1} x_i(N' \cup \{i\} \cup \{o_i - 1\})$$

$$- p_{o_i,i} p_{i+1,o_i-1} x_{i+1}(N' \cup \{o_i\} \cup \{i + 1\})]$$

$$\geq \sum_{N'} p(N')[p_{i,o_i} p_{o_i-1,i+1} x_{i+1}(N' \cup \{i + 1\} \cup \{o_i - 1\})$$

$$- p_{o_i,i} p_{i+1,o_i-1} x_{i+1}(N' \cup \{o_i\} \cup \{i + 1\})]$$

$$\geq \sum_{N'} p(N')[p_{i,o_i} p_{o_i-1,i+1} \frac{p_{i+1,o_i-1}}{p_{i+1,o_i}}$$

$$- p_{o_i,i} p_{i+1,o_i-1}] x_{i+1}(N' \cup \{o_i\} \cup \{i + 1\})]$$

$$\geq 0$$

where the first inequality follows by the induction hypothesis $x_i(N' \cup \{i\} \cup \{i + 1\}) \geq x_{i+1}(N' \cup \{i\} \cup \{i + 1\})$, the second inequality is by Lemma 8.21, the third inequality is by Lemma 8.22, and the last inequality is by the assumption that the matrix of winning probabilities is strongly stochastically transitive; hence $p_{i,o_i} \geq p_{i+1,o_i}$ and $p_{o_i-1,i+1} \geq p_{o_i,i}$.

8.3 Strategic Behavior and Production Costs

In this section we consider single-elimination tournaments where the probability that a player advances to the next round is determined endogenously as an equilibrium outcome of an underlying game that is defined in this section. In our analysis thus far a player would advance to the next round of the tournament if he or she won against the opponent in the given round, which was assumed to be with probability whose value is exogenously given. This accommodates cases in which players are endowed with some intrinsic abilities and their payoffs are equal to the value of the prize. In this section we consider strategic behavior in tournaments where the payoff of each player is quasi-linear in his or her expected valuation of winning the tournament and incurred production cost. In such a setting we shall consider a subgame perfect Nash equilibrium where in each round of the tournament the probability that a player wins in the given round is according to the subgame perfect Nash equilibrium. In each round of the tournament, the players who participate in the given round, simultaneously invest efforts aiming at selfishly maximizing their individual payoffs. The payoffs are assumed to be quasi-linear in the expected continuation value and the production cost incurred in the given round. In particular, we shall consider a single-elimination tournament where in each contest in a round of the tournament the player who invests the largest effort advances to the next round.

8.3.1 Four Players

Consider a balanced single-elimination tournament where the valuation parameters are common knowledge and players incur unit marginal costs of production. In each round of the tournament, the players who participate in the given round, make simultaneous effort investments. In a subgame perfect Nash equilibrium, each contest in a round is a standard all-pay contest. A complete characterization of the subgame perfect Nash equilibrium is rather involved for the general case of an arbitrary number of players. In this section, we therefore focus on the special case of a balanced single-elimination tournament with four players with valuations $v_1 \geq v_2 \geq v_3 \geq v_4 > 0$ and provide a complete characterization of the equilibrium in this case. In the subgame perfect Nash equilibrium, the equilibrium outcome in each contest of the tournament is as in a standard all-pay contest with valuations equal to the expected continuation payoffs conditional on advancing to the next round of the tournament. In the final round of the tournament, the expected payoff conditional on winning that round corresponds to the valuation of the prize, and the mixed-strategy equilibrium characterization is exactly as for the standard all-pay contest between two players in Theorem 2.3. The game considered in this section can be seen as an extension to studying equilibrium behavior in the semifinals of a balanced single-elimination tournament. There are three possible seedings of players as given in Figure 8.5, which we study separately in the following sections.

Throughout this section, we denote with $R(u, v)$ the expected total effort in the mixed-strategy Nash equilibrium of the normal form game that models the standard all-pay contest between two players with valuations $u \geq v > 0$. Recall that, by Theorem 2.3, we have

$$R(u, v) = \frac{v}{2}\left(1 + \frac{v}{u}\right). \tag{8.10}$$

Seeding: 1, 4, 2, 3

Theorem 8.23. *Consider a balanced single-elimination tournament among four players with the valuation parameters $v_1 \geq v_2 \geq v_3 \geq v_4 > 0$ under standard seeding $S = (1, 4, 2, 3)$. Then, in the subgame perfect mixed-strategy Nash equilibrium, we have the following properties.*

Case $v_1 > v_2$ or $v_2 > v_3$.

- *In the semifinal matches, player 1 wins with probability 1 and player 2 wins with probability $1/2$.*
- *Either players 1 and 2, or players 1 and 4 play in the final round.*
- *The winner of the tournament is player 1 with probability $1 - (v_2 + v_3)/(4v_1)$, player 2 with probability $v_2/(4v_1)$, or player 3 with probability $v_3/(4v_1)$.*
- *The expected payoff of player 1 is equal to $v_1 - (v_2 + v_3)/2$, and for all other players the expected payoffs are equal to zero.*
- *The expected total efforts in the semifinal matches are equal to zero.*
- *The expected total effort in the final match is $(R(v_1, v_2) + R(v_1, v_3))/2$.*

Case $v_1 = v_2 = v_3$.

- *In both semifinal matches, each player is equally likely to win.*
- *Any pair of players is equally likely to play in the final round.*
- *The winner of the tournament is player 1 with probability $1/4$, player 2 with probability $(3 - v_4/v_1)/8$, player 3 with probability $(3 - v_4/v_1)/8$, or player 4 with probability $v_4/(4v_1)$.*
- *The expected payoffs of the players are equal to zero.*
- *The expected total efforts in the semifinal matches are equal to zero.*
- *The expected total effort in the final match is $(R(v_1, v_1) + R(v_1, v_4))/2$.*

Proof. Assume that each participant in the semifinal round is awarded a prize of value $w > 0$ and the winner in the final is awarded a unit prize. We shall then consider the equilibrium in the limit as w goes to zero. This is needed to ensure that every player has a strictly positive continuation value in the semifinal round, and thus each contest in the tournament is a well-defined game with complete information that models the standard all-pay contest. Let $x_{i,j}(w)$ be the probability that player i wins in a semifinal match between players i and j. By Theorem 2.3, in the mixed-strategy Nash equilibrium of the game that models the standard all-pay contest between two players with valuation parameters $u \geq v > 0$, the expected payoffs of the two players are

$u - v$ and 0, respectively. It follows that the expected payoffs for players 1, 2, 3, and 4 conditional on winning in the semifinal matches are, respectively, given as follows:

$$\tilde{v}_1(w) = w + (v_1 - v_2)(1 - x_{3,2}(w)) + (v_1 - v_3)x_{3,2}(w)$$
$$\tilde{v}_2(w) = w + (v_2 - v_4)x_{4,1}(w)$$
$$\tilde{v}_3(w) = w + (v_3 - v_4)x_{4,1}(w)$$
$$\tilde{v}_4(w) = w. \tag{8.11}$$

Both semifinal matches correspond to standard all-pay contests: for the match between player 1 and 4 with respective valuation parameters $\tilde{v}_1(w)$ and $\tilde{v}_4(w)$, and for the match between players 2 and 3 with respective valuation parameters $\tilde{v}_2(w)$ and $\tilde{v}_3(w)$. By Theorem 2.3, the winning probabilities in the semifinal matches are given by $x_{4,1}(w) = \tilde{v}_4(w)/(2\tilde{v}_1(w))$ and $x_{3,2}(w) = \tilde{v}_3(w)/(2\tilde{v}_2(w))$. Combined with (8.11), we have

$$x_{4,1}(w) = \frac{1}{2} \frac{w}{w + (v_1 - v_2) + (v_2 - v_3)x_{3,2}(w)}$$
$$x_{3,2}(w) = \frac{1}{2} \frac{w + (v_3 - v_4)x_{4,1}(w)}{w + (v_2 - v_4)x_{4,1}(w)}.$$

For the case $v_1 = v_2 = v_3$, we have

$$x_{4,1}(w) = \frac{1}{2} \text{ and } x_{3,2}(w) = \frac{1}{2} \tag{8.12}$$

and otherwise, we have

$$\lim_{w \downarrow 0} x_{4,1}(w) = 0 \text{ and } \lim_{w \downarrow 0} x_{3,2}(w) = \frac{1}{2}. \tag{8.13}$$

By Theorem 2.3, the expected payoffs of players 1, 2, 3, and 4 are, respectively,

$$\tilde{v}_1(w) - \tilde{v}_4(w), \tilde{v}_2(w) - \tilde{v}_3(w), 0, \text{ and } 0,$$

which yield the expected payoffs asserted in the theorem in the limit as w goes to zero.

The probabilities of winning the tournament are derived as follows. We consider only the winning probability for player 1 because the same argument applies to the other players. Player 1 wins the tournament if he or she wins in the semifinal match against player 4 and he or she wins in the final match against either player 2 or 3. Therefore, we have

$$\mathbf{E}[x_1(\mathbf{b})] = (1 - x_{4,1}(w)) \left(\left(1 - \frac{v_2}{2v_1} \right) (1 - x_{3,2}(w)) + \left(1 - \frac{v_3}{2v_1} \right) x_{3,2}(w) \right)$$

where we used the expressions for the equilibrium winning probabilities in a match between player 1 and player 2, and in a match between player 1 and player 3, given by Theorem 2.3. By letting w go to zero, we obtain the winning probabilities asserted in the theorem.

The expected total effort invested in the semifinal match between player 1 and player 4 is equal to $R(\tilde{v}_1(w), \tilde{v}_4(w))$, and in the semifinal match between player 2 and player 3 it is equal to $R(\tilde{v}_2(w), \tilde{v}_3(w))$. Combined with (8.10) and (8.11), we obtain for the case $v_1 = v_2 = v_3$,

$$R(\tilde{v}_1(w), \tilde{v}_4(w)) = w$$

$$R(\tilde{v}_2(w), \tilde{v}_3(w)) = w + (v_1 - v_4)x_{4,1}(w),$$

and otherwise,

$$R(\tilde{v}_1(w), \tilde{v}_4(w)) = \frac{w}{2}\left(1 + \frac{w}{w + (v_1 - v_2) + (v_2 - v_3)x_{3,2}(w)}\right)$$

$$R(\tilde{v}_2(w), \tilde{v}_3(w)) = \frac{w + (v_3 - v_4)x_{4,1}(w)}{2}\left(1 + \frac{w + (v_3 - v_4)x_{4,1}(w)}{w + (v_2 - v_4)x_{4,1}(w)}\right).$$

Using the last expressions along with (8.12) and (8.13), we obtain the asserted limits for the expected total efforts in the semifinal matches.

The expected total effort in the final match follows from the observation that in the case $v_1 = v_2 = v_3$, any pair of players is equally likely to be the finalists, and otherwise, the final is equally likely between players 1 and 2, or between players 1 and 3. $\quad\square$

The expected payoff for the strongest player is equivalent to that in a standard all-pay contest in which the strongest player plays against a hypothetical player whose ability is equal to the mean ability of the second and the third strongest player. For the case when the valuation parameters are not all equal, this is because under the given seeding the equilibrium is such that the strongest player reaches the final with certainty and the winner of the semifinal match between the second and the third strongest player is equally likely to be either of these two players.

Seeding: 1, 3, 2, 4

Theorem 8.24. *Consider a balanced single-elimination tournament among four players with the valuation parameters $v_1 \geq v_2 \geq v_3 \geq v_4 > 0$ under seeding $S = (1, 3, 2, 4)$. Then, in the subgame perfect mixed-strategy Nash equilibrium, we have the following properties.*

Case $v_1 = v_2 > v_3 = v_4$ or $v_1 \geq v_2 > v_3 > v_4$.

- *In the semifinal matches, players 1 and 2 win with probability 1.*
- *Players 1 and 2 play in the final round.*
- *The winner of the tournament is either player 1 with probability $1 - v_2/(2v_1)$ or player 2 with probability $v_2/(2v_1)$.*
- *The expected payoff of player 1 is equal to $v_1 - v_2$ and for every other player is equal to zero.*
- *The expected total efforts in the semifinal matches are equal to zero.*
- *The expected total effort in the final match is $R(v_1, v_2)$.*

Case $v_1 = v_2 = v_3 = v_4$.

- *In both semifinal matches, each player is equally likely to win.*
- *Any two players are equally likely to play in the final round.*
- *The winner of the tournament is equally likely to be any of the players.*
- *The expected payoff of every player is equal to zero.*

- *The expected total efforts in the semifinal matches are equal to zero.*
- *The expected total effort in the final match is $R(v_1, v_1)$.*

Case $v_2 = v_3$ and either $v_1 > v_2$ or $v_3 > v_4$.

- *In the semifinal matches, player 1 wins against player 3 with probability*

$$x_{1,3} = 1 - \frac{1}{2}\frac{v_2 - v_4}{2v_1 - v_2 - v_4}$$

  and player 2 wins against player 4 with probability $1/2$.
- *The winner of the tournament is player 1 with probability $x_{1,3}(1 - (v_2 + v_4)/(4v_1))$, player 2 with probability $x_{1,3}v_2/(2v_1) + (1 - x_{1,3})(1 - v_3/(2v_2))$, player 3 with probability $(1 - x_{1,3})(1 - v_4/(2v_3) + v_3/(2v_2))/2$, or player 4 with probability $(1 - x_{1,3})v_4/(4v_3) + x_{1,3}v_4/(4v_1)$.*
- *The expected payoff of player 1 is equal to $v_1 - v_2$ and for every other player is equal to zero.*
- *The expected total efforts in the semifinal matches are equal to zero.*
- *The expected total effort in the final round is $(1 - x_{3,1})(R(v_1, v_2) + R(v_1, v_4))/2 + x_{3,1}(R(v_2, v_3) + R(v_3, v_4))/2$.*

Case $v_1 > v_2 > v_3 = v_4$.

- *In the semifinals matches, player 1 wins against player 3 with probability 1, and player 2 wins against player 4 with probability*

$$x_{2,4} = 1 - \left(\sqrt{\left(\frac{v_1 - v_2}{2(v_2 - v_3)}\right)^2 + \frac{v_1 - v_2}{2(v_2 - v_3)}} - \frac{v_1 - v_2}{2(v_2 - v_3)}\right).$$

- *The winner of the tournament is player 1 with probability $x_{2,4}(1 - v_2/(2v_1)) + (1 - x_{2,4})(1 - v_4/(2v_1))$, player 2 with probability $x_{2,4}v_2/(4v_1)$, player 3 with probability 0, or player 4 with probability $(1 - x_{2,4})v_4/(2v_1)$.*
- *The expected payoff of player 1 is equal to $v_1 - (v_2x_{2,4} + v_3(1 - x_{2,4}))$ and for every other player is equal to zero.*
- *The expected total efforts in the semifinal matches are zero.*
- *The expected total effort in the final round is $x_{2,4}R(v_1, v_2) + (1 - x_{2,4})R(v_1, v_4)$.*

Proof. The proof admits the same notation and follows the same main ideas as that of Theorem 8.23. Here we only derive the winning probabilities in the semifinal matches from which the rest follows easily.

The expected payoffs for players 1, 2, 3 and 4, conditional on winning in the semifinal round are, respectively, given as follows:

$$\begin{aligned}
\tilde{v}_1(w) &= w + (v_1 - v_2)(1 - x_{4,2}(w)) + (v_1 - v_4)x_{4,2}(w) \\
\tilde{v}_2(w) &= w + (v_2 - v_3)x_{3,1}(w) \\
\tilde{v}_3(w) &= w + (v_3 - v_4)x_{4,2}(w) \\
\tilde{v}_4(w) &= w.
\end{aligned} \tag{8.14}$$

By Theorem 2.3, the probabilities of advancing to the final round are given by $x_{4,2}(w) = \tilde{v}_4(w)/(2\tilde{v}_2(w))$ and $x_{3,1}(w) = \tilde{v}_3(w)(2\tilde{v}_1(w))$. Combined with (8.14), we have

$$x_{3,1}(w) = \frac{1}{2}\frac{w + (v_3 - v_4)x_{4,2}(w)}{w + (v_1 - v_2) + (v_2 - v_4)x_{4,2}(w)} \tag{8.15}$$

$$x_{4,2}(w) = \frac{1}{2}\frac{w}{w + (v_2 - v_3)x_{3,1}(w)}. \tag{8.16}$$

We separately consider five different cases.

Case 1: $v_1 = v_2 = v_3 = v_4$ In this case, we obviously have

$$x_{3,1}(w) = \frac{1}{2} \text{ and } x_{4,2}(w) = \frac{1}{2}.$$

Case 2: $v_2 = v_3$ and either $v_1 > v_2$ or $v_3 > v_4$ In this case, we have

$$\lim_{w\downarrow 0} x_{3,1}(w) = \frac{1}{2}\frac{v_2 - v_4}{2v_1 - v_2 - v_4} \text{ and } x_{4,2}(w) = \frac{1}{2}$$

which is readily observed from (8.15) and (8.16).

Case 3: $v_1 = v_2 > v_3 = v_4$ In this case, we have

$$\lim_{w\downarrow 0} x_{3,1}(w) = 0 \text{ and } \lim_{w\downarrow 0} x_{4,2}(w) = 0.$$

From (8.15) and (8.16) we have

$$x_{3,1}(w) = \frac{1}{2}\frac{w}{w + (v_2 - v_3)x_{4,2}(w)} \text{ and } x_{4,2}(w) = \frac{1}{2}\frac{w}{w + (v_2 - v_3)x_{3,1}(w)}.$$

From this, it follows that $x_{3,1}(w) = x_{4,2}(w)$, and

$$(v_2 - v_3)x_{3,1}(w)^2 + wx_{3,1}(w) - \frac{w}{2} = 0.$$

Hence,

$$x_{3,1}(w) = \frac{\sqrt{w^2 + 2(v_2 - v_3)w} - w}{2(v_2 - v_3)} = O(\sqrt{w}).$$

Case 4: $v_1 > v_2 > v_3 = v_4$ In this case, we have

$$\lim_{w\downarrow 0} x_{3,1}(w) = 0 \text{ and } \lim_{w\downarrow 0} x_{4,2}(w) = \sqrt{\left(\frac{v_1 - v_2}{2(v_2 - v_3)}\right)^2 + \frac{v_1 - v_2}{2(v_2 - v_3)}} - \frac{v_1 - v_2}{2(v_2 - v_3)}.$$

From (8.15) and (8.16) we have

$$x_{3,1}(w) = \frac{1}{2}\frac{w}{w + (v_1 - v_2) + (v_2 - v_3)x_{4,2}(w)} \text{ and}$$

$$x_{4,2}(w) = \frac{1}{2}\frac{w}{w + (v_2 - v_3)x_{3,1}(w)}.$$

From this, it follows that

$$(w + v_1 - v_2)x_{3,1}(w) = wx_{4,2}(w) \tag{8.17}$$

and

$$(v_2 - v_3)x_{3,1}(w)^2 + wx_{3,1}(w) - \frac{w^2}{2(w + v_1 - v_2)} = 0.$$

Hence,

$$x_{3,1}(w) = \frac{\sqrt{w^2 + 2(v_2 - v_3)\frac{w^2}{w + v_1 - v_2}} - w}{2(v_2 - v_3)} \sim \frac{\sqrt{1 + \frac{2(v_2 - v_3)}{v_1 - v_2}} - 1}{2(v_2 - v_3)}w, \quad \text{for small } w,$$

which combined with (8.17) gives

$$\lim_{w \downarrow 0} x_{4,2}(w) = \sqrt{\left(\frac{v_1 - v_2}{2(v_2 - v_3)}\right)^2 + \frac{v_1 - v_2}{2(v_2 - v_3)}} - \frac{v_1 - v_2}{2(v_2 - v_3)}.$$

Case 5: $v_1 \geq v_2 > v_3 > v_4$ In this case, we have

$$\lim_{w \downarrow 0} x_{3,1}(w) = 0 \text{ and } \lim_{w \downarrow 0} x_{4,2}(w) = 0.$$

From (8.15) and (8.16), it follows that

$$\frac{1}{2}\frac{x_{4,2}(w)(v_3 - v_4)}{w + v_1 - v_4} \leq x_{3,1}(w) \leq \frac{1}{2(v_2 - v_3)}\frac{w}{x_{4,2}(w)}.$$

Hence, $x_{4,2}(w) = O(\sqrt{w})$, and by (8.15), we have $x_{3,1}(w) = O(\sqrt{w})$. $\square$

Seeding: 1, 2, 3, 4

Theorem 8.25. *Consider a balanced single-elimination tournament among four players with the valuation parameters $v_1 \geq v_2 \geq v_3 \geq v_4 > 0$ under seeding $S = (1, 2, 3, 4)$. Then, in the subgame perfect mixed-strategy Nash equilibrium, we have the following properties.*

Case $v_1 > v_4$.

- *In the semifinal matches, player 1 wins with probability*

$$x_{1,2} = 1 - \frac{1}{2}\frac{2v_2 - v_3 - v_4}{2v_1 - v_3 - v_4}$$

  and player 3 wins with probability 1/2.
- *The winner of the tournament is either player 1 with probability $x_{1,2}(1 - (v_3 + v_4)/(4v_1))$, player 2 with probability $(1 - x_{1,2})(1 - (v_3 + v_4)/(4v_2))$, player 3 with probability $x_{1,2}v_3/(4v_1) + (1 - x_{1,2})v_3/(4v_2)$, or player 4 with probability $x_{1,2}v_4/(4v_1) + (1 - x_{1,2})v_4/(4v_2)$.*
- *The expected payoff of player 1 is equal to $v_1 - v_2$ and for every other player is equal to zero.*
- *The expected total effort in the semifinal match between player 1 and player 2 is $R(v_1 - (v_3 + v_4)/2, v_2 - (v_3 + v_4)/2)$ and is equal to zero in the other semifinal match.*
- *The expected total effort in the final match is $x_{1,2}(R(v_1, v_3) + R(v_1, v_4))/2 + (1 - x_{1,2})(R(v_2, v_3) + R(v_2, v_4))/2$.*

Case $v_1 = v_2 = v_3 = v_4$.

- *In both semifinal matches, each player is equally likely to win.*
- *Any two players are equally likely to play in the final round.*
- *The winner of the tournament is equally likely to be any of the players.*
- *The expected payoff of every player is equal to zero.*
- *The expected total efforts in the semifinal matches are equal to zero.*
- *The expected total effort in the final match is $R(v_1, v_1)$.*

Proof. Again, the proof admits the same notation and follows the same main ideas as that of Theorem 8.23. Here we only derive the winning probabilities in the semifinal matches from which the rest follows easily. The expected payoffs conditional on winning in the semifinal matches are

$$\tilde{v}_1(w) = w + (v_1 - v_4)(1 - x_{4,3}(w)) + (v_1 - v_3)x_{4,3}(w)$$
$$\tilde{v}_2(w) = w + (v_2 - v_4)x_{4,3}(w) + (v_2 - v_3)(1 - x_{4,3}(w))$$
$$\tilde{v}_3(w) = w \qquad\qquad\qquad\qquad\qquad\qquad\qquad\qquad\qquad (8.18)$$
$$\tilde{v}_4(w) = w.$$

By Theorem 2.3, the winning probabilities in the semifinal matches are given by $x_{2,1}(w) = \tilde{v}_2(w)/(2\tilde{v}_1(w))$ and $x_{4,3}(w) = \tilde{v}_4(w)/(2\tilde{v}_3(w))$. Hence, we have

$$x_{2,1}(w) = \frac{1}{2} \frac{w + (v_2 - v_3) + (v_3 - v_4)x_{4,3}(w)}{w + (v_1 - v_3) + (v_3 - v_4)x_{4,3}(w)} \qquad (8.19)$$

$$x_{4,3}(w) = \frac{1}{2}. \qquad (8.20)$$

Case $v_1 > v_4$ From (8.19) and (8.20), we have

$$\lim_{w \downarrow 0} x_{2,1}(w) = \frac{1}{2} \frac{2v_2 - v_3 - v_4}{2v_1 - v_3 - v_4}.$$

Case $v_1 = v_2 = v_3 = v_4$ In this case, we obviously have $x_{2,1}(w) = 1/2$. $\qquad\square$

Comparison of Different Seedings

We discuss how some of the equilibrium properties compare under different seedings of the players. This discussion is based on the characterization of the subgame perfect Nash equilibrium in Theorem 8.23, Theorem 8.24, and Theorem 8.25 for the seeding $(1, 4, 2, 3)$, $(1, 3, 2, 4)$, and $(1, 2, 3, 4)$, respectively.

Semifinal matches The winning probabilities for semifinal matches exhibit both extreme cases where the stronger player wins with certainty, and where the winner is equally likely to be either of the two players. Under the standard seeding of the players $(1, 4, 2, 3)$, we can distinguish two qualitative types of outcomes in the semifinal matches: in the first type, player 1 wins with certainty and either player 2 or player 3 wins equally likely, and in the second type of outcome, each player is equally likely to win. Under the seeding $(1, 3, 2, 4)$, players 1 and 2 win with certainty in the semifinal matches, for a broad set of values of the valuation parameters. In this case, the equilibrium essentially corresponds to that of a single all-pay contest between players 1 and

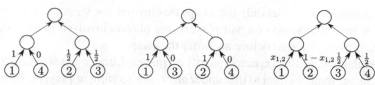

Figure 8.11. The equilibrium winning probabilities for semifinal matches: (left) under standard seeding of the players whenever $v_1 > v_2$ or $v_2 > v_3$, (middle) under the seeding of the players $(1, 3, 2, 4)$ whenever either $v_1 = v_2 > v_3 = v_4$ or $v_1 \geq v_2 > v_3 > v_4$, and (right) under the seeding of the players $(1, 2, 3, 4)$ whenever $v_1 > v_4$.

2. Under the seeding $(1, 2, 3, 4)$, none of the semifinal matches are such that one of the players wins with certainty, and it is always the case that in the match between player 3 and player 4 either is equally likely to win. See Figure 8.11 for a graphical illustration of equilibrium outcomes in semifinal matches.

The expected payoffs We first consider the monotonicity of different seedings with respect to the expected payoffs in a subgame perfect Nash equilibrium. Let s_i be the expected payoff of player i in a subgame perfect Nash equilibrium for a given seeding of players.

Corollary 8.26. *For each of the three seedings of players, $s_i \geq s_j$ whenever $v_i \geq v_j$. Moreover, the expected payoff for the strongest player under the standard seeding of players is larger than or equal to that under any other seeding of players.*

Proof. This corollary follows immediately from the characterization of the expected payoffs in Theorem 8.23, Theorem 8.24, and Theorem 8.25 under the seeding of players $(1, 4, 2, 3)$, $(1, 3, 2, 4)$, and $(1, 2, 3, 4)$, respectively. For every seeding of players S, for every player $i \neq 1$, the expected payoff is equal to zero, and that of player 1 is given as follows:

- If $S = (1, 4, 2, 3)$, then $s_1 = v_1 - (v_2 + v_3)/2$.
- If $S = (1, 3, 2, 4)$, then $s_1 = v_1 - v_2$ in all the cases except when $v_1 > v_2 > v_3 = v_4$, in which case $s_1 = v_1 - (v_2 x_{2,4} + v_3(1 - x_{2,4}))$ where $x_{2,4} \geq 1/2$.
- If $S = (1, 2, 3, 4)$, then $s_1 = v_1 - v_2$. $\qquad\square$

We next consider which of the three seedings satisfy the envy-freeness property with respect to the expected payoffs. Figure 8.12 indicates all possible swaps of the seeding positions of players that transform one seeding to another.

Corollary 8.27. *The standard seeding of players is the only seeding that can guarantee envy-freeness with respect to the expected payoffs.*

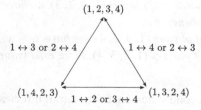

Figure 8.12. Switching between different seedings by swaps of the seeding positions.

Proof. It suffices to consider only the swaps that involve the strongest player, player 1, because for any other swap of a pair players, the players involved in the swap receive the expected payoff of zero before and after the swap.

By Corollary 8.26, the expected payoff of player 1 under the standard seeding of players is larger than or equal to that under any other seeding of players. Therefore, the standard seeding is envy-free with respect to the expected payoffs.

For either seeding $(1, 3, 2, 4)$ or $(1, 2, 3, 4)$ it is easy to observe that there exist valuation parameters such that a swap that results in the standard seeding is strictly beneficial to player 1. Suppose any valuation parameters such that $v_1 \geq v_2 > v_3 > v_4 > 0$. In this case, under either seeding $(1, 3, 2, 4)$ or $(1, 2, 3, 4)$, the expected payoff of player 1 is equal to $v_1 - v_2$. Swapping the positions of players 1 and 2 in the seeding $(1, 3, 2, 4)$ and swapping the positions of players 1 and 3 in the seeding $(1, 2, 3, 4)$ result in the standard seeding $(1, 4, 2, 3)$. Under the standard seeding, player 1 receives the expected payoff of value $v_1 - (v_2 + v_3)/2 > v_1 - v_2$. This shows that neither $(1, 3, 2, 4)$ nor $(1, 2, 3, 4)$ can guarantee the envy-freeness property for every valuation vector. $\square$

The tournament winning probabilities The probability that the strongest player wins under the standard seeding $(1, 4, 2, 3)$ is at least as large as under any other seeding of players. The probability that the strongest player wins under the seeding $(1, 3, 2, 4)$ is at least as large as under the seeding $(1, 2, 3, 4)$. The standard seeding is strictly superior with respect to maximizing the probability of the strongest player winning if, and only if, the strength of the third strongest player is strictly smaller than the strength of the second strongest player. The probability of the strongest player winning under the standard seeding $(1, 4, 2, 3)$ is decreasing in the strength of the third strongest player, and thus it has the largest value in the limit case as the strength of the third strongest player goes to zero. In this limit case, the probability of the strongest player winning under the standard seeding of players is larger than that under the seeding $(1, 3, 4, 2)$ for a factor that is decreasing in the ratio of the highest and the second highest valuation. From this it follows that the probability of the strongest player winning under the standard seeding $(1, 4, 2, 3)$ is at most factor $3/2$ of that under the seeding $(1, 3, 2, 4)$. This gain is realized in the limit case of the strongest and the second strongest player of nearly identical strengths and the third best player of nearly zero strength.

We now discuss the monotonicity properties of different seedings of players with respect to the probability of winning the tournament. We denote with x_i the probability that player i wins the tournament.

Corollary 8.28. *The following properties hold in the subgame perfect Nash equilibrium:*

- *Under the standard seeding of players $(1, 4, 2, 3)$, we have $x_i \geq x_j$ whenever $v_i \geq v_j$. Moreover, $x_i > x_j$ whenever $v_i > v_j$.*
- *Under the seeding of players $(1, 3, 2, 4)$, we have $x_i \geq x_j$ whenever $v_i \geq v_j$.*
- *Under the seeding of players $(1, 2, 3, 4)$, there exist valuation parameters such that $x_i < x_j$ and $v_i > v_j$.*

Proof. The first and the second statement follow straightforwardly from the equilibrium winning probabilities asserted in Theorem 8.23 and Theorem 8.24, respectively. For the seeding $(1, 3, 2, 4)$ we have $x_3 = x_4 = 0$, and thus it does not hold that $x_i > x_j$ whenever $v_i > v_j$.

The third statement, for the seeding $(1, 4, 2, 3)$, is established by showing that $x_2 < x_3$ for any valuation parameters $v_1 \geq v_2 \geq v_3 = v_4 > 0$ such that v_2/v_1 is sufficiently small and v_3/v_2 is sufficiently large. Fix the values of v_2 and v_3 and consider the limit of large v_1. From the characterization of the subgame perfect Nash equilibrium in Theorem 8.25, we obtain

$$1 - x_{1,2} \sim \frac{v_2}{2v_1} \left(1 - \frac{v_3}{v_2} \right), \quad \text{for large } v_1$$

and

$$x_2 \sim \frac{v_2}{2v_1} \left(1 - \frac{v_3}{v_2} \right) \left(1 - \frac{v_3}{2v_2} \right) \text{ and } x_3 \sim \frac{v_2}{2v_1} \left(3 - \frac{v_3}{v_2} \right) \frac{v_3}{4v_2}, \quad \text{for large } v_1.$$

For $x_2 < x_3$ to hold for sufficiently large v_1, it suffices that v_3/v_2 satisfies

$$\left(1 - \frac{v_3}{v_2} \right) \left(1 - \frac{v_3}{2v_2} \right) < \left(3 - \frac{v_3}{v_2} \right) \frac{v_3}{4v_2}$$

which is readily shown to be equivalent to $v_3/v_2 > (3 - \sqrt{9 - 16/3})/2 \approx 0.543$. $\quad\square$

We next consider the envy-freeness of different seedings with respect to the winning probabilities.

Corollary 8.29. *None of the three seedings can guarantee envy-freeness with respect to the probabilities of winning the tournament.*

Proof. We prove first that the seeding $(1, 3, 2, 4)$ is not guaranteed to be envy-free with respect to the probabilities of winning the tournament. Suppose that the valuation parameters are such that $v_1 > v_4 > 0$. By Theorem 8.24, under the seeding $(1, 3, 2, 4)$, player 3 has zero probability of winning the tournament. Swapping the seeding positions of player 3 and that of the weaker player 4 results in the standard seeding $(1, 4, 2, 3)$. By Theorem 8.23, under the standard seeding of players, player 3 wins the tournament with a strictly positive probability.

We next prove that the seeding $(1, 2, 3, 4)$ is also not guaranteed to be envy-free with respect to the probabilities of winning the tournament. Suppose that the valuation parameters are such that $v_2 > (v_3 + v_4)/2$. By Theorem 8.25, player 1 wins the tournament with probability $x_{1,2}(1 - (v_3 + v_4)/(4v_1)) < 1 - (v_3 + v_4)/(4v_1)$, where the inequality holds under the assumed condition. Swapping the seeding positions of player 1 and the weaker player 3 results in the standard seeding of players $(1, 4, 2, 3)$. By Theorem 8.23, under the standard seeding of players, player 1 wins with probability $1 - (v_3 + v_4)/(4v_1)$.

It remains only to prove that the standard seeding $(1, 4, 2, 3)$ is also not guaranteed to be envy-free with respect to the probabilities of winning the tournament. We show that there exist valuation parameters such that under the standard seeding of the players, player 2 can increase his or her winning probability by swapping his or her seeding position with player 4. Such a swap results in the seeding $(1, 2, 3, 4)$. By Theorem 8.23

and Theorem 8.25, we need to show that there exist valuation parameters such that

$$(1 - x_{1,2})\left(1 - \frac{v_3 + v_4}{4v_2}\right) > \frac{v_2}{4v_1}$$

where $x_{1,2} = (2v_2 - v_3 - v_4)/(2(2v_1 - v_3 - v_4))$. This is equivalent to the following condition:

$$\frac{1}{2}\frac{v_2 - a}{v_1 - a}\left(1 - \frac{a}{2v_2}\right) > \frac{v_2}{4v_1} \tag{8.21}$$

where $a = (v_3 + v_4)/2$. Notice that $0 < a \leq v_2$ and that the left-hand side of inequality (8.21) is decreasing in a. In the limit as a goes to 0, the left-hand side of inequality (8.21) is equal to $v_2/(2v_1)$, which is larger than the right-hand side of the inequality. Hence, it follows that the condition holds for every small enough a.   □

Total effort The expected total efforts in the semifinal matches are zero under all seedings of players, except for the semifinal match between players 1 and 2 under the seeding of players $(1, 2, 3, 4)$. In this special case, the expected total effort is as in the mixed-strategy Nash equilibrium of the game that models the standard all-pay contest between two players with valuations $v_1 - (v_3 + v_4)/2$ and $v_2 - (v_3 + v_4)/2$.

The expected total effort in the final match under the seeding $(1, 3, 2, 4)$ is at least as large as that under the seeding $(1, 4, 2, 3)$, which in turn is at least as large as that under the seeding $(1, 2, 3, 4)$.

8.3.2 Optimal Tournament Plan

In this section we consider the optimal design of a tournament plan with respect to the total effort in a subgame perfect Nash equilibrium. We consider a tournament that awards a single prize, which goes to the winner. The tournament plan is defined by a tree with $n = m^r$ leaf nodes, for some integers $m \geq 2$ and $r \geq 1$. Each contest of the tournament is among two or more players, and in each contest in each round of the tournament, a single player is selected to advance to the next round of the tournament. The winner in each contest is determined according to a contest success function of the effort investments made by the participants in that contest. Each player is assumed to have a unit valuation of the prize and a unit marginal cost of production.

Theorem 8.30. *Suppose that in each contest of the tournament there exists a symmetric pure-strategy Nash equilibrium and the total effort in this equilibrium is an increasing concave function of the number of players participating in the contest. Then, the total effort in the subgame perfect symmetric pure-strategy Nash equilibrium is largest when there is an equal number of players in different contests.*

Proof. We first show that in any given round of the tournament, it is optimal to evenly distribute the number of players over the contests in the given round. Consider an arbitrary round with m players and k contests. Suppose that players are assigned to different contests such that the number of players across different contests is given by $(n_1, n_2, \ldots, n_k)$. Note that $\sum_{i=1}^{k} n_i = m$. In the subgame perfect symmetric pure-strategy Nash equilibrium the total effort is equal to $v \sum_{i=1}^{k} R(n_i)$ where v is the payoff for continuing the competition in the next round conditional on winning in the current round, and $R(n_j)$ denotes the total effort in a contest among n_j players that offers a unit prize. Since R is assumed to be a concave function, the total effort is maximized for a balanced allocation of players to contests, i.e., for $n_1 = n_2 = \cdots = n_k$.

It remains to show that for a given number of rounds r and $n_1, n_2, \ldots, n_r$ denoting the number of players per contest in different rounds of the tournament, it is optimal to use the tournament design such that $n_1 = n_2 = \cdots = n_r$. The total effort invested by the players in the tournament in a subgame perfect pure-strategy Nash equilibrium can be characterized as follows. In the final round, the total effort is equal to $R(n_r)$. Since in equilibrium each finalist is equally likely to win the prize and each invests effort of value $R(n_r)/n_r$, each finalist has the expected payoff of value $(1 - R(n_r))/n_r$. In each contest of round $r - 1$, the total effort is $((1 - R(n_r))/n_r)R(n_{r-1})$, where the first factor accounts for the continuation value. Since there are n_r contests in round $r - 1$, the total effort in round $r - 1$ is equal to $(1 - R(n_r))R(n_{r-1})$. Continuing this argument to the first round of the tournament, the total effort in a subgame perfect pure-strategy Nash equilibrium is characterized as follows:

$$R(n_1, n_2, \ldots, n_r) = \sum_{j=1}^{r} R(n_j) \prod_{l=0}^{j-1} (1 - R(n_l)) \qquad (8.22)$$

where we define $n_0 = 0$, and note that $R(n_0) = 0$.

We shall show that

$$\frac{\partial}{\partial n_i} R(n_1, n_2, \ldots, n_r) = \frac{R'(n_i)}{1 - R(n_i)} \prod_{j=1}^{r} (1 - R(n_j)). \qquad (8.23)$$

Indeed, this follows by the following two facts. First, define

$$\varphi_i(x_1, x_2, \ldots, x_r) = \prod_{l=0}^{i} (1 - x_l) - \sum_{j=i+1}^{r} x_j \prod_{l=0}^{j-1} (1 - x_l),$$

and note that $\varphi_i(x_1, x_2, \ldots, x_r) = \varphi_{i+1}(x_1, x_2, \ldots, x_r)$, for $1 \leq i < r$. Hence $\varphi_i(x_1, x_2, \ldots, x_r) = \varphi_r(x_1, x_2, \ldots, x_r)$, for every $1 \leq i \leq r$, or equivalently,

$$\prod_{l=0}^{i} (1 - x_l) - \sum_{j=i+1}^{r} x_j \prod_{l=0}^{j-1} (1 - x_l) = \prod_{l=0}^{r} (1 - x_l), \quad 1 \leq i \leq r. \qquad (8.24)$$

Second, note that

$$\frac{\partial}{\partial n_i} R(n_1, n_2, \ldots, n_r) = R'(n_i) \prod_{l=0}^{i-1} (1 - R(n_l)) - R'(n_i) \sum_{j=i+1}^{r} R(n_j) \prod_{0 \leq l < j : l \neq i} (1 - R(n_l))$$

$$= \frac{R'(n_i)}{1 - R(n_i)} \left\{ \prod_{l=0}^{i} (1 - R(n_l)) - \sum_{j=i+1}^{r} R(n_j) \prod_{l=0}^{j-1} (1 - R(n_l)) \right\}$$

$$= \frac{R'(n_i)}{1 - R(n_i)} \prod_{l=0}^{r} (1 - R(n_l))$$

where the last equality is by (8.24).

Let L be the Lagrangian function defined, for $\lambda \geq 0$, as follows:

$$L(n_1, n_2, \ldots, n_r) = R(n_1, n_2, \ldots, n_r) - \lambda \left(\prod_{j=1}^{r} n_j - n \right).$$

Then, in view of (8.23), the first-order optimality condition

$$\frac{\partial}{\partial n_i} L(n_1, n_2, \ldots, n_r) = 0, \ i = 1, 2, \ldots, r$$

is equivalent to

$$\frac{n_i R'(n_i)}{1 - R(n_i)} \prod_{j=1}^{r} (1 - R(n_j)) = \lambda n, \ i = 1, 2, \ldots, r,$$

which necessitates that $n_1 = n_2 = \cdots = n_r$. □

Example 8.31. Consider the class of anonymous contest success functions of the general-logit form that we introduced in Chapter 4. For a contest among $m \geq 2$ players, given a positive-valued, increasing, and continuously differentiable function f, the winning probabilities are given by

$$x_i(\mathbf{b}) = \frac{f(b_i)}{\sum_{j=1}^{m} f(b_j)}, \quad \text{for } i = 1, 2, \ldots, m$$

whenever $\sum_{j=1}^{m} b_j > 0$, and $x_i(\mathbf{b}) = 1/m$, for $i = 1, 2, \ldots, m$, otherwise.

A necessary and sufficient condition for the existence of a pure-strategy Nash equilibrium is

$$\phi^{-1} \left(\frac{1}{m} \left(1 - \frac{1}{m} \right) \right) \leq \frac{1}{m}.$$

where $\phi(x) = f(x)/f'(x)$. If this condition holds true, the total effort in the pure-strategy Nash equilibrium is given by

$$R(m) = m\phi^{-1} \left(\left(1 - \frac{1}{m} \right) \frac{1}{m} \right)$$

Specifically, for the ratio-form contest success functions with the return to scale parameter $\alpha > 0$, we have $f(x) = x^\alpha$. In this case, a pure-strategy Nash equilibrium exists if, and only if, $\alpha \leq 1/(1 - 1/m)$, and in this case, the total effort is given by

$$R(m) = \alpha \left(1 - \frac{1}{m} \right).$$

An interesting question to ask is what is the optimal number of rounds of a balanced single-elimination tournament; the interested reader may check Exercise 8.4.

8.3.3 Optimal Prize Structure for Competitive Balance

In this section we consider what the optimal structure of prizes is for a single-elimination tournament with the objective of eliciting the same amount of effort in each contest of

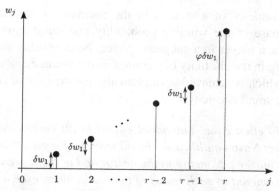

Figure 8.13. Optimal prize structure for a tournament among players of identical abilities that induces the same effort investment over different contests of the tournament in a subgame perfect Nash equilibrium.

the tournament. This is an objective of interest when attempting to maintain a competitive balance over different contests of a tournament. Specifically, we consider a single-elimination tournament with $r \geq 1$ rounds for a set of $n \geq 2$ players with valuation parameters denoted as $v_1, v_2, \ldots, v_n$, which are assumed to be common knowledge. Each contest of the tournament is assumed to be among $m \geq 2$ players; thus the number of players satisfies $n = m^r$. The players who participate in a round of the tournament make simultaneous effort investments in this round. In each contest, one player is selected as the winner and advances to the next round, which is assumed to be according to a smooth contest success function. Whenever a player i participates in a contest, he or she incurs a production cost according to a production cost function c, which is assumed to be increasing, continuously differentiable, and convex and such that $c(0) = 0$.

We shall establish what is the optimal structure of prizes for the case of players with symmetric valuation parameters in a subgame perfect Nash equilibrium. We shall show that the optimum prize structure is to award a common fraction of a prize purse to each player for advancing to the next round of the tournament, and to award an extra amount to the winner of the tournament. This means structuring the prizes as follows:

$$\delta w_r = \varphi \delta w_{r-1} \text{ and } \delta w_{r-1} = \cdots = \delta w_1 \tag{8.25}$$

for some value of parameter $\varphi \geq 1$. Note that a unit prize budget must be split according to (8.25) with

$$\delta w_1 = \frac{m-1}{n-1+(\varphi-1)(m-1)}.$$

The values of the prizes are thus

$$w_r = \delta w_1 \cdot (r + \varphi - 1) \text{ and } w_j = \delta w_1 \cdot j, \quad \text{for } 1 \leq j < r.$$

See Figure 8.13 for an illustration. For example, for a semifinals tournament, the prizes must be structured such that the values of the first place and the second place prize are in the ratio $(1 + \varphi) : 1$.

Specifically, the optimum value of parameter φ is

$$\varphi = \frac{1}{1 - \frac{1-\eta}{m}} \tag{8.26}$$

where η is the elasticity of a contest in the tournament, defined as the ratio of the marginal increase of the winning probability and the marginal increase of the production cost for a player in a subgame perfect Nash equilibrium. The factor φ in (8.26) is decreasing in the elasticity of a contest in the tournament, and this factor is at most of value 2, which is achieved asymptotically for the case of two-player contests for asymptotically small elasticity.

Theorem 8.32. *To elicit equal individual efforts in all contests of a tournament in the subgame perfect Nash equilibrium, the allocation of a prize budget must be of the following form: a player advancing to the next round of the tournament is awarded a common constant amount in each round of the tournament, except for the final round where an extra amount of prize is awarded to the winner of the tournament.*

Proof. We first introduce some notation. We denote by N_j the set of players participating in round j, and let $N_j(i)$ be the set of players in the contest of round j in which player i participates. Let $b_{i,j}$ be the effort invested by player i in a contest of round j. If player i is eliminated in an earlier round than round j, then let $b_{i,j} = 0$. Let $\mathbf{b}_{N_j}$ be the efforts invested by the players participating in round j of the tournament, i.e., $\mathbf{b}_{N_j} = (b_{i,j}, i \in N_j)$. Let $x_{i,j}(N_j(i), \mathbf{b}_{N_j})$ be the probability that player i wins in round j given that the set of players participating in this round is N_j and $i \in N_j$. Let $s_{i,j}(N_j, \mathbf{b}_{N_j})$ be the expected payoff for player i starting from round j of the tournament conditional on N_j being the set of players participating in round j and $i \in N_j$ and conditional on the values of efforts invested in round j.

The expected payoffs of the players satisfy a backward recursion. In the final round r of the tournament, the conditional expected payoffs satisfy

$$s_{i,r}(N_r, \mathbf{b}_{N_r}) = v_i w_r x_{i,r}(N_r(i), \mathbf{b}_{N_r})$$
$$+ v_i w_{r-1}(1 - x_{i,r}(N_r(i), \mathbf{b}_{N_r})) - c(b_{i,r}), \quad \text{for } i \in N_r.$$

For each round $1 \le j < r$, we have

$$s_{i,j}(N_j, \mathbf{b}_{N_j}) = v_i \mathbf{E}[s_{i,j+1}(N_{j+1}, \mathbf{b}_{N_{j+1}}) \mid i \in N_{j+1}] x_{i,j}(N_j(i), \mathbf{b}_{N_j})$$
$$+ v_i w_{j-1}(1 - x_{i,j}(N_j(i), \mathbf{b}_{N_j})) - c(b_{i,j})$$

where

$$\mathbf{E}[s_{i,j+1}(N_{j+1}, \mathbf{b}_{N_{j+1}}) \mid N_j, i \in N_{j+1}] = \sum_{N_{j+1}} p_i(N_{j+1} \mid N_j) s_{i,j+1}(N_{j+1}, \mathbf{b}_{N_{j+1}})$$

and $p_i(N_{j+1} \mid N_j)$ denotes the probability that the set of players who advance to round $j+1$ is N_{j+1} conditional on that the set of players who participate in round j is N_j and that player i is one of the players who advance to round $j+1$, i.e.,

$$p_i(N_{j+1} \mid N_j) = \prod_{l \in N_j \setminus \{i\}} x_{l,j}(N_j(l), \mathbf{b}_{N_j}).$$

A subgame perfect Nash equilibrium $\mathbf{b}^*$ is characterized as follows. Let

$$v_{i,j}(N_j) = v_i \mathbf{E}[s_{i,j+1}(N_{j+1}, \mathbf{b}^*_{N_{j+1}}) \mid N_j, i \in N_{j+1}] - v_i w_{j-1}.$$

The payoff functions in round j are given by

$$s_{i,j}(N_j, \mathbf{b}_{N_j}^*) = v_{i,j}(N_j)x_i(N_j(i), \mathbf{b}_{N_{j,i}}^*) - c(b_{i,j}^*) + w_{j-1}, \quad \text{for } i \in N_j.$$

A vector of efforts $\mathbf{b}^*$ is a subgame perfect Nash equilibrium, if for every $1 \le j \le r$, $i \in N_j$, and every feasible set N_j of the players in round j, we have

$$s_{i,j}(N_j, \mathbf{b}_{N_j}^*) \ge s_{i,j}(N_j, (b_{i,j}, \mathbf{b}_{N_j \setminus \{i\}}^*)), \quad \text{for every } b_{i,j} \ge 0.$$

Since the payoff functions are differentiable, we have

$$\frac{\partial}{\partial b_{i,j}} s_{i,j}(N_j, \mathbf{b}_{N_j}^*) = v_{i,j}(N_j)\frac{\partial}{\partial b_{i,j}}x_{i,j}(\mathbf{b}_{N_j(i),N_{j,i}}^*) - c'(b_{i,j}^*) = 0. \qquad (8.27)$$

By using the abbreviating notation

$$s_{i,j}(N_j) = s_{i,j}(N_j, \mathbf{b}_{N_j}^*), \quad x_i(N_j) = x_{i,j}(N_j(i), \mathbf{b}_{N_{j,i}}^*) \quad \text{and } c(N_j) = c(b_{i,j}^*),$$

we can write

$$s_{i,j}(N_j) = v_{i,j}(N_j)x_i(N_j) - c(N_j) + v_i w_{j-1}.$$

Let $\eta_i(N_j)$ be the *elasticity* defined by

$$\eta_i(N_j) = \frac{\dfrac{\frac{\partial}{\partial b_{i,j}}x_{i,j}(N_j(i), \mathbf{b}_{N_{j,i}}^*)}{x_{i,j}(N_j(i), \mathbf{b}_{N_j}^*)}}{\dfrac{c'(b_{i,j}^*)}{c(b_{i,j}^*)}}.$$

Condition (8.27) can be equivalently written as

$$v_{i,j}(N_j)x_i(N_j)\eta_i(N_j) = c(N_j), \quad \text{for } i \in N_j \text{ and } 1 \le j \le r.$$

The expected payoffs in a subgame perfect Nash equilibrium can be defined recursively as follows: $s_{i,r+1}(N_{r+1}) = w_r$, and

$$s_{i,j}(N_j) = \gamma_{i,j}(N_j)\mathbf{E}[s_{i,j+1}(N_{j+1}) \mid N_j] + (1 - \gamma_{i,j}(N_j))w_{j-1}, \; i \in N_j, \; 1 \le j \le r$$
$$(8.28)$$

where

$$\gamma_{i,j}(N_j) = (1 - \eta_i(N_j))x_i(N_j). \qquad (8.29)$$

Under the assumption that the valuation parameters have identical values, without loss of generality, assume that they are of unit value. In this case, we can write

$$s_{i,j}(N_j) \equiv s_j, \quad \mathbf{E}[s_{i,j+1} \mid N_i] \equiv s_{j+1}, \quad \text{and } \gamma_{i,j}(N_j) \equiv \gamma_j.$$

From (8.28), we obtain

$$s_{r+1} = w_r \qquad (8.30)$$

$$s_j = \gamma_j s_{j+1} + (1 - \gamma_j)w_{j-1}, \quad \text{for } 1 \le j \le r. \qquad (8.31)$$

Since the number of players in each contest is $m \geq 2$, $\gamma_j \equiv \gamma$ for $1 \leq j \leq r$. The effort investments by players in different contests of the tournament are equal if, and only if, the continuation values in different contests are equal, i.e., for some constant $c > 0$, $s_{j+1} - w_{j-1} = c$, for $1 \leq j \leq r$. From (8.30) and (8.31), we obtain

$$w_r - w_{r-1} = \frac{c}{\gamma} \quad \text{and} \quad w_j - w_{j-1} = (1-\gamma)\frac{c}{\gamma}, \quad \text{for } 1 \leq j \leq r.$$

From this, observe that (i) the prize for reaching and being eliminated in a round increases linearly with the number of rounds and (ii) the difference of the first and second prize is larger than the difference between any other two successive prizes. Since in each contest any of m contestants is equally likely to win, from (8.29), it follows that $1 - \gamma = 1 - 1/m + \eta/m$, which completes the proof. $\quad\square$

Example 8.33. Consider a balanced single-elimination tournament where contests are between pairs of players, players are of identical abilities, the winner in each contest is determined according to a ratio-form contest success function with the return to scale parameter $\alpha \in (0, 1]$, and each player incurs a unit marginal cost of production. In this case, in the subgame perfect Nash equilibrium, the elasticity is

$$\eta = \frac{\alpha}{2}$$

and

$$\varphi = \frac{4}{2+\alpha}.$$

In particular, in the case of proportional allocation, the prize awarded for winning in the final round of the tournament must be larger by the factor $4/3$ than the prize awarded for winning in any other round of the tournament.

8.3.4 Effort Budgets

In this section, we briefly consider a game with complete information for a single-elimination tournament with four players endowed with effort budgets. In particular, we shall show that it is optimal to award only the winner of the tournament when the objective is to maintain a competitive balance over different contests of the tournament.

Theorem 8.34. *Consider a two-round balanced single-elimination tournament with the values of the prizes $w_2 > w_1 \geq 0$ among four players with identical valuations where each player is endowed with a unit effort budget that can be arbitrarily split between the two rounds of the tournament. Suppose that in each match the winner is determined according to a general-logit contest success function with a production function f that is assumed to be increasing, continuously differentiable, concave, and such that $f(0) = 0$. Then, there exists a subgame perfect symmetric pure-strategy Nash equilibrium, and in this equilibrium, we have the following two properties:*

(i) *The effort invested in the first round is at least as large at that in the second round.*
(ii) *An equal individual effort is invested in each round of the tournament only if the prizes are of the winner-take-all form, i.e., $w_2 > w_1 = 0$.*

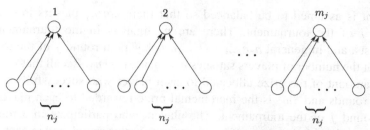

Figure 8.14. Round j of a tournament with $m_j = n_r n_{r-1} \cdots n_{j-1}$ contests each with n_j players.

Proof. We shall show that it is a subgame perfect symmetric pure-strategy Nash equilibrium for each participant in the first round to invest effort of value b, and for each participant in the second round to invest effort of value $1 - b$, where b is the solution to the equation

$$\frac{f'(b)}{f(b)}(w_2 + w_1) = \frac{f'(1-b)}{f(1-b)}(w_2 - w_1). \tag{8.32}$$

Consider a unilateral deviation of an arbitrary player in round 1 of the tournament, say player 1, to an alternative strategy of investing x in the first round and investing $1 - x$ in the second round. Then, the payoff of player 1 is

$$s_1(x, b) = (w_2 - w_1)\frac{f(x)}{f(x) + f(b)}\frac{f(1-x)}{f(1-x) + f(1-b)} + w_1\frac{f(x)}{f(x) + f(b)}.$$

It suffices to show that $s_1(x, b)$ is a concave function of x for any given $b \in [0, 1]$, which, along with the continuity of the payoff functions and convexity of the strategy sets, ensures the existence of a pure-strategy Nash equilibrium. Showing that $s_1(x, b)$ is a concave function in x is a routine exercise, and thus not performed here.

Note that

$$\frac{\partial}{\partial x}s_1(x, b) = \frac{f'(x)f(b)}{(f(x) + f(b))^2}\left((w_2 - w_1)\frac{f(1-x)}{f(1-x) + f(1-b)} + w_1\right)$$

$$- (w_2 - w_1)\frac{f(x)}{f(x) + f(b)}\frac{f'(1-x)f(1-b)}{(f(1-x) + f(1-b))^2}.$$

Condition (8.32) is equivalent to $\partial s_1(x, b)/\partial x = 0$, for $x = b$. Note that in (8.32), the left-hand side is decreasing in b and the right-hand side is increasing in b. The left-hand side is greater than or equal to the right-hand side in (8.32) for $b = 1/2$. Hence, it must be that $b \geq 1/2$.

It remains only to note that in view of (8.32), $b = 1/2$ can be an equilibrium only if $w_1 = 0$, i.e., the entire prize purse is allocated to the winner of the tournament. $\square$

8.3.5 Game with Incomplete Information

In this section we consider a single-elimination tournament among n players that consists of $r \geq 1$ rounds. The number of players per contest in each round of the tournament is assumed to be balanced so that there are n_j players in each contest in round j of the tournament. There are n_r finalists in the tournament, $n_r n_{r-1}$ semifinalists, and in general $n_r n_{r-1} \cdots n_{j-1} n_j$ players in round j of the tournament. Notice that the number of players satisfies $n = n_r n_{r-1} \cdots n_1$. Recall that w_j is defined to be the amount of the prize allocated to each player who successfully got through exactly j rounds and δw_j is the incremental prize rewarded to each player who got through round j of the tournament. The players who participate in a round of the tournament make simultaneous effort investments in this round, and in each contest of the round, the player who invests the largest effort is selected to advance to the next round of the tournament. In every round, a player who invests an effort in the amount b incurs a production cost of value $c(b)/v$ where $v > 0$ is the ability parameter of this player and c is a production cost function that is assumed to be increasing, continuously differentiable, and such that $c(0) = 0$. The ability parameters are assumed to be private information and are a sequence of independent and identically distributed random variables according to an atomless prior distribution F on the support $[0, 1]$.

We admit an important assumption of no revelation of the effort investments by a player to other players. The only information that is available to a player about the past contest outcomes of the tournament is who participated in any of the past contests and who won. Since we assume a prior distribution of the ability parameters under which they are independent and with identical distributions, the only relevant information about an opponent in a round j of the tournament is that the opponent won in past $j - 1$ rounds of the tournament. In a subgame perfect symmetric Bayes-Nash equilibrium, the winner in each contest of the tournament will be the player with the largest ability parameter. Hence, the prior distribution of the ability parameter of each participant in round j of the tournament corresponds to the distribution of the maximum ability of a player in a subtree rooted at a node at depth j of the tournament tree. Since in such a tree there are $n_{j-1} n_{j-2} \cdots n_1$ players, the prior distribution function of the ability parameter in round j of the tournament, denoted as F_j, is given by

$$F_j(v) = \begin{cases} F(v), & \text{for } j = 1 \\ F^{n_1 n_2 \cdots n_{j-1}}(v), & \text{for } 1 < j \leq r \end{cases}.$$

Characterization of Equilibrium

Theorem 8.35. *Consider a single-elimination tournament with $r \geq 1$ rounds among $n = n_r n_{r-1} \cdots n_1$ players such that in each round there are $m_j = n_r n_{r-1} \cdots n_{j+1}$ contests and each contest in this round consists of n_j players. Suppose that the ability parameters of the players are private information according to a sequence of independent and identically distributed random variables with an atomless distribution function F on the support $[0, 1]$, and that each player incurs a production cost according to a production cost function c in each contest in which this player participates.*

Then, there exists a subgame perfect symmetric Bayes-Nash equilibrium that is specified by

$$\beta_j(v) = c^{-1} \left(\sum_{l=j}^{r} \left(\int_0^v s_{j+1,l+1}(x) \, dF_j(x)^{n_j - 1} \right) \delta w_l \right), \quad \text{for } j \in \{1, 2, \ldots, r\}$$

$$(8.33)$$

where

$$s_{j,l}(v) = \int_0^v \frac{F_l(x)}{F_j(x)}\, dx. \tag{8.34}$$

The expected payoff $s_j(v)$ for a player with the ability parameter of value v for continuing to participate from round $j+1$ conditional on passing round j is given by

$$vs_j(v) = \sum_{l=j}^r s_{j,l+1}(v)\delta w_l, \quad \text{for } j \in \{1, 2, \ldots, r\}. \tag{8.35}$$

Proof. In the final round r, the subgame corresponds to a contest among n_r players for a prize of value δw_r with private valuations that are independent and identically distributed according to distribution function F_r. By the revenue equivalence theorem, Theorem 2.20, it follows that the symmetric Bayes-Nash equilibrium is given by

$$\beta_r(v) = c^{-1}\left(\delta w_r \int_0^v x\, dF_r(x)^{n_r-1}\right)$$

which corresponds to (8.33) for $j = r$.

Consider an arbitrary round $1 \le j < r$, and suppose that in each subsequent round players play according to the subgame perfect symmetric Bayes-Nash equilibrium strategies. Consider a unilateral deviation in round j by a player of ability v to a strategy according to ability parameter v'. The expected payoff for this player until the end of the game is given by

$$s(v, v') = [\delta w_j + s_{j+1}(v)]G_j(v') - \frac{1}{v}c(\beta_j(v'))$$

where $s_{j+1}(v)$ is the expected payoff for a player with valuation v conditional on this player participating in round $j+1$ and for brevity we define $G_j(v) = F_j(v)^{n_j-1}$, for $0 \le v \le 1$. Taking the partial derivative of the expected payoff with respect to v' and equating this to zero, we obtain

$$\frac{d}{dv'}c(\beta_j(v')) = v[\delta w_j + s_{j+1}(v)]G_j'(v').$$

For the equilibrium strategy, the last relation must hold for $v' = v$, and hence

$$\beta_j(v) = c^{-1}\left(\int_0^v [\delta w_j + s_{j+1}(x)]x\, dG_j(x)\right). \tag{8.36}$$

Combining (8.36) with the expected payoff of player of ability v in round j given by

$$s_j(v) = [\delta w_j + s_{j+1}(v)]G_j(v) - \frac{1}{v}c(\beta_j(v)),$$

we obtain

$$vs_j(v) = \int_0^v [\delta w_j(v-x) + vs_{j+1}(v) - xs_{j+1}(x)]\, dF_j(x)^{n_j-1}, \quad \text{for } j \in \{1, 2, \ldots, r\}.$$

Note that this is a linear recursion that, along with the boundary condition $s_{r+1}(v) = 0$ for $0 \le v \le 1$, has a unique solution given by (8.35). From (8.35) and (8.36), we obtain (8.33). $\square$

The characterization of the equilibrium in (8.33) and (8.34) admits an intuitive interpretation. $s_{j,l+1}(v)$ can be interpreted as the expected payoff per unit prize for a player to pass round l conditional on this player being of ability v and having passed round j. Note that $s_{j,l+1}(v)$ is defined as the integral of the probability of passing round l by a player of ability v conditional on this player passing round j. This event happens if all players under the subtree rooted at the node of round l are of ability less than v; there are $n_1 n_2 \cdots n_l$ such players. On the other hand, conditional on that a player of ability v has passed round j, his or her ability is the largest among the $n_1 n_2 \cdots n_{j-1}$ players under the subtree rooted at the node in round j that corresponds to the contest in which he or she participated. Hence, the given conditional probability of winning in round l corresponds to the probability of the event that in a sequence of $n_1 n_2 \cdots n_l - n_1 n_2 \cdots n_{j-1}$ independent samples from distribution F, all values are less than or equal to value v, which is equal to $F(v)^{n_1 n_2 \cdots n_l - n_1 n_2 \cdots n_{j-1}} = F_{l+1}(v)/F_j(v)$, as it appears in (8.34). The equilibrium effort functions in (8.33) are simply such that the production cost incurred in round j is equal to the expected payoff until the end of the game conditional on a player of ability v having passed round j.

Corollary 8.36. *For the winner-take-all prize allocation $w = \delta w_r > \delta w_{r-1} = \cdots = \delta w_1 = 0$, for $j \in \{1, 2, \ldots, r\}$, we have*

$$\beta_j(v) = c^{-1} \left(w \int_0^v F(x)^{n-n/m_j} (F(v)^{n/m_j - n/m_{j-1}} - F(x)^{n/m_j - n/m_{j-1}}) \, dx \right),$$

where $m_j = n_r n_{r-1} \cdots n_{j+1}$.

Total Effort

Corollary 8.37. *The expected total effort under unit marginal costs of production is given by*

$$R = \sum_{l=1}^r a_l \delta w_l$$

where

$$a_l = \sum_{j=1}^l m_{j-1} \int_0^1 s_{j+1,l+1}(x)(1 - F_j(x)) \, dF_j(x)^{n_j-1}, \quad \text{for } 1 \leq l \leq r.$$

Proof. The proof is as follows:

$$R = \sum_{j=1}^r n_r n_{r-1} \cdots n_j \int_0^1 \beta_j(v) \, dF_j(v)$$

$$= \sum_{j=1}^r n_r n_{r-1} \cdots n_j \int_0^1 \sum_{l=j}^r \left(\int_0^v s_{j+1,l+1}(x) \, dF_j(x)^{n_j-1} \right) \delta w_l \, dF_j(v)$$

$$= \sum_{l=1}^r a_l \delta w_l$$

where

$$a_l = \sum_{j=1}^{l} n_r n_{r-1} \cdots n_j \int_0^1 \left(\int_0^v s_{j+1,l+1}(x) \, dF_j(x)^{n_j-1} \right) dF_j(v)$$

$$= \sum_{j=1}^{l} n_r n_{r-1} \cdots n_j \int_0^1 s_{j+1,l+1}(x)(1 - F_j(x)) \, dF_j(x)^{n_j-1}.$$ $\square$

Corollary 8.38. *For the winner-take-all prize allocation* $w = \delta w_r > \delta w_{r-1} = \cdots = \delta w_1 = 0$, *and unit marginal costs of production, the expected total effort is given by*

$$R = w \sum_{j=1}^{r} \left[m_j \int_0^1 (F(x)^{n-n/m_j} - F(x)^n) \, dx - m_{j-1} \int_0^1 (F(x)^{n-n/m_{j-1}} - F(x)^n) \, dx \right].$$

$\square$

Maximum Individual Effort

Theorem 8.39. *Consider any single-elimination tournament among n players with independent and identically distributed valuations where the entire prize budget is allocated to the winner of the final round. Then, in the subgame perfect symmetric Bayes-Nash equilibrium, the expected maximum individual effort in the final round of the tournament is larger than that in a single standard all-pay contest among the same set of n players, whenever the number of players n is large enough.*

As a corollary, note that the expected maximum individual effort across all contests of the tournament in the subgame perfect symmetric Bayes-Nash equilibrium is larger than that in a single standard all-pay contest.

Proof. Since the subgame of the final round of the tournament corresponds to a standard all-pay contest among n_r players for a unit prize, by Corollary 2.27, in the symmetric Bayes-Nash equilibrium, the expected maximum individual effort in the final round satisfies

$$R_1(n, n_r) \le \frac{n_r}{2n_r - 1}.$$

We claim that for every $2 \le n_r \le n$, we have

$$R_1(n, n_r) \sim \frac{n_r}{2n_r - 1}, \quad \text{for large } n. \tag{8.37}$$

The standard all-pay contest is a special case of a tournament consisting of one round; hence by (8.37), $\lim_{n \to \infty} R_1(n, n) = 1/2$, which was already observed in Chapter 2. From this, and (8.37) we conclude that the expected maximum individual effort in the final round in a tournament with n players is larger than that in the single standard all-pay contest with the same set of n players, for every large enough number of players n.

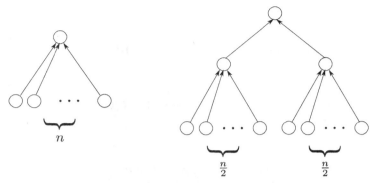

Figure 8.15. Two tournament plans: (left) a single-round tournament and (right) a two-round tournament with two finalists.

It remains to prove claim (8.37). Since the subgame in the final round of the tournament corresponds to a standard all-pay contest among n_r players with independent and identically distributed valuations according to distribution $F^{n_1 n_2 \cdots n_{r-1}}$, by Theorem 3.1, the equilibrium strategy is

$$\beta_r(v) = \int_0^v x \, dF(x)^{n - n/n_r}.$$

Using this, the expected maximum individual effort in the final round is given by

$$
\begin{aligned}
R_1(n, n_r) &= \int_0^1 \beta_r(v) \, dF(v)^n \\
&= \int_0^1 x(1 - F(x)^n) \, dF(x)^{n_1 \cdots n_{r-1}(n_r - 1)} \\
&= \int_0^1 x(1 - F(x)^n) \, dF(x)^{n - n/n_r} \\
&= \mathbf{E}[v_{(n - n/n_r, 1)}] - \frac{n_r - 1}{2n_r - 1} \mathbf{E}[v_{(2n - n/n_r, 1)}].
\end{aligned}
$$

Combining with the facts $\lim_{n \to \infty} \mathbf{E}[v_{(n - n/n_r, 1)}] = 1$ and $\lim_{n \to \infty} \mathbf{E}[v_{(2n - n/n_r, 1)}] = 1$, we obtain the asymptotic result in (8.37). □

By the asymptotic in (8.37), we have the following corollary.

Corollary 8.40 (optimality of two finalists). *In the limit of many players any balanced single-elimination tournament with two finalists is optimal with respect to the expected maximum individual effort in the final round of the tournament in a subgame perfect symmetric Bayes-Nash equilibrium. See Figure 8.15 for an illustration.*

The observed dominance of a single-elimination tournament contest design over a single standard all-pay contest design in the limit of many players is intuitive in view of the informational assumptions in the underlying games. For the standard all-pay contest, the game is with incomplete information where the valuations of players are independent and identically distributed according to the prior distribution F. In Chapter 2, we observed that in this case the expected maximum individual effort goes to a half of the maximum valuation as the number of players grows large. On the other hand, for a balanced single-elimination tournament, participants in the final round have private valuations that are independent and identically distributed according to a posterior distribution, which is conditional on the event that each finalist won in all previous rounds, and their valuations are the maximum valuation parameters among all players who competed for the given positions in the final round. There are in total $n_1 n_2 \ldots n_{r-1}$ such players, and thus the valuation parameters of the finalists are independent and identically distributed according to distribution $F^{n/n_r}(x)$. In the limit of many players, the valuation parameters are all identical and equal to 1, and the underlying game in the final round corresponds to a game with complete information. By Corollary 2.16, for every valuation vector, the expected maximum individual effort achieves the largest value in the mixed-strategy Nash equilibrium when only two players with the largest valuation parameters are active. From (2.47), in the case of n_r players with identical valuations of unit value, the expected maximum individual effort is equal to $n_r/(2n_r - 1)$. This is precisely the expected maximum individual effort obtained for the balanced single-elimination tournament with n_r finalists in the limit of many players. The largest expected maximum individual effort in the limit of many players is achieved for the case of two finalists, and in this case is equal to 2/3.

One may wonder whether, in fact, it may hold that $R_1(n, 2) \geq R_1(n, n)$ for every even number of players $n \geq 2$. This, however, is not true, which is shown as follows. By Exercise 8.5, we have

$$R_1(n, n_r) = (n - n/n_r) \int_0^1 F^{-1}(y) y^{n - n/n_r - 1}(1 - y^n)\, dy. \tag{8.38}$$

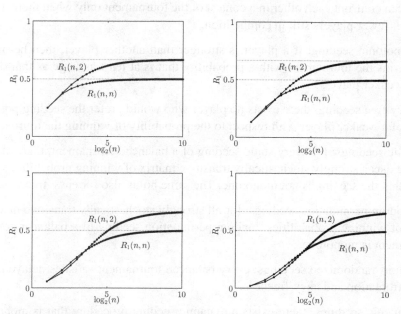

Figure 8.16. The expected maximum individual effort for Example 8.41 for the values of parameter $\alpha = 1$, 1/2, 1/4, and 1/8, from the upper-left corner clockwise.

Hence, we have

$$R_1(n, 2) - R_1(n, n) = \int_0^1 F^{-1}(y)\left(\frac{n}{2}y^{\frac{n}{2}-1} - (n-1)y^{n-2})(1-y^n)\right) dy. \quad (8.39)$$

The integrand is strictly positive on $[0, y^*)$, equal to zero at y^*, and strictly negative on $(y^*, 1]$ for some value $0 < y^* < 1$. Thus, for any fixed number of players n, there always exists a distribution F that has enough of mass on small values of valuations so that the integral in (8.39) is negative.

Example 8.41. Suppose $F(v) = v^\alpha$, for $v \in [0, 1]$, and parameter $\alpha > 0$. Then,

$$R_1(n, n_r) = \frac{\alpha(n - n/n_r)}{\alpha(n - n/n_r) + 1} - \frac{n_r - 1}{2n_r - 1}\frac{\alpha(2n - n/n_r)}{\alpha(2n - n/n_r) + 1}. \quad (8.40)$$

In this case, for every fixed number of players n, $R_1(n, 2) < R_1(n, n)$ for small enough α. See Figure 8.16 for numerical examples.

Summary

A tournament plan (T, S) for a set of players is defined by a tree T of directed edges to one single root and as many leaf nodes as the number of players, and seeding S that specifies an assignment of the players to the leaf nodes.

Seedings of tournaments of two-player contests

A tournament plan (T, S) for two-player contests is said to be balanced if T is a perfect binary tree.

Delayed confrontation: if two players belong to the top 2^q best players, then they can confront each other in a contest of the tournament only when there are 2^q or fewer players still in competition.

Monotonic seeding: if a player is stronger than another player, then he or she wins the tournament with a probability that is at least as large as that of the weaker player.

Envy-free seeding: there exists no player who would prefer the seeding position of a weaker player with respect to the probability of winning the tournament.

Static seedings: for every static seeding of a balanced tournament, there always exists a strongly stochastically transitive matrix of winning probabilities such that the seeding is not monotone. The same holds also for envy-freeness.

Random permutation seedings: for all strongly stochastically transitive matrices of winning probabilities, random permutation seeding of a balanced tournament is monotone.

Cohort randomized seedings: every balanced tournament satisfies delayed confrontation and envy-freeness.

Dynamic seedings: there exists a dynamic seeding procedure that is monotone for all strongly stochastically transitive winning probabilities.

Strategic behavior and production costs

For four-player tournaments with unit marginal cost of production:

 (i) The winning probability of the strongest player is maximized by the standard seeding procedure.

 (ii) The expected total effort in the final round is maximized by the seeding 1, 3, 2, 4.

 (iii) All seedings are monotonic with respect to the expected payoffs.

 (iv) Seedings 1, 4, 2, 3 and 1, 3, 2, 4 are ex-ante envy-free with respect to the expected payoffs while 1, 2, 3, 4 is not.

 (v) Seeding 1, 4, 2, 3 is monotone and envy-free with respect to winning probabilities.

For a single-elimination tournament among $n = m^r$ identical-ability players and a single prize awarded to the winner of the tournament, an optimal tournament plan is according to a regular tree with degree m and depth r with respect to the expected total effort in equilibrium.

For a balanced single-elimination tournament and identical-ability players, to guarantee competitive balance across all contests of the tournament, prizes must be structured such that they linearly increase with the number of successfully passed rounds and an extra prize is awarded to the winner of the tournament.

Effort budgets: competitive balance by the winner-take-all prize allocation.

Game with incomplete information: players with private valuations that are independent and identically distributed according to a distribution function F and unit marginal cost of production. Assume no revelation of the invested efforts in any of the rounds of the tournament.

 (i) The expected total effort in equilibrium is maximized by a one-round tournament (standard all-pay contest).

 (ii) The expected maximum individual effort is maximized by a tournament plan that consists of two finalists for sufficiently large number of players.

Exercises

8.1 Generalized linear model, strong stochastic transitivity, and stochastic transitivity
Prove that for every generalized linear model, the matrix of winning probabilities is strongly stochastically transitive and that every strongly stochastically transitive matrix of winning probabilities is stochastically transitive as asserted in (8.2).

8.2 Semi-finals tournament Prove the claims asserted in Theorem 8.8.

8.3 **Minimizing favoritism** Show that the cohort randomized seeding procedure minimizes the favoritism over all randomized seeding procedures that satisfy the conditions of delayed confrontation and monotonicity with respect to seeding order as asserted in Theorem 8.19.

8.4 **Optimal tournament plan** Consider a single-elimination tournament among $n = 2^k$ players, where k is a positive integer, under the assumption as in Section 8.3.2. Recall that $R(m)$ is the total effort in the pure-strategy Nash equilibrium of the game that models a contest among m players that awards a unit prize, assuming that a pure-strategy Nash equilibrium exists. Prove the following claims.

  (a) Consider balanced single-elimination tournaments with r rounds and such that each contest is among m players and $n = m^r$. Let $R_{r,m}$ be the total effort in the subgame perfect pure-strategy Nash equilibrium of the game, assuming that one exists. Then, we have

$$R_{r,m} = 1 - (1 - R(m))^r .$$

  (b) Suppose that the winner of each contest is determined according to the ratio-form contest success function with the return to scale parameter $0 < \alpha \le 1/(1 - 1/n)$. Then, the optimal number of rounds of a balanced tournament plan with respect to the total effort is as follows:

  • If $0 < \alpha < 1$, the optimal tournament plan is such that each contest is between a pair of players;
  • If $\alpha = 1$, then any number of rounds is optimal;
  • If $1 < \alpha \le 1/(1 - 1/n)$, then it is optimal that all players compete in a single contest.

8.5 **Maximum individual effort in the final round of a tournament** Prove that the expected maximum individual effort in the final round of a balanced single-elimination tournament, in the subgame perfect Bayes-Nash equilibrium, is as asserted in equation (8.38).

8.6 **Ladder tournament** Consider a single-elimination tournament among $n \ge 2$ players with $n - 1$ rounds, each consisting of a contest between a pair of players as depicted in Figure 8.8. There is a single prize of value $w > 0$, which is awarded to the winner of the tournament. In each contest of the tournament, the winner is determined according to a general-logit contest success function with a production function f that is increasing, continuously differentiable, and such that $f(0) = 0$. The players are assumed to have identical valuation parameters and incur unit marginal costs of production. Prove the following claims.

  (a) Suppose that f is such that $f'(x)x \le 2f(x)$ for $x \ge 0$. Then, there exists a unique subgame perfect pure-strategy Nash equilibrium, in which each player who participates in round j of the tournament makes an effort investment of value b_j given by

$$b_j = \begin{cases} \phi^{-1}(\frac{w}{4}), & \text{if } j = n - 1 \\ \phi^{-1}\left(\frac{1}{2}\phi(b_{j+1}) - \frac{1}{4}b_{j+1}\right), & \text{if } 1 \le j < n - 1 \end{cases}$$

  where $\phi(x) = f(x)/f'(x)$.

  (b) In particular, for the production function $f(x) = x^\alpha$, for $0 < \alpha \le 2$, there is a unique subgame perfect pure-strategy Nash equilibrium, in which each player in round j of the tournament makes an effort investment of value b_j given by

$$b_j = w\frac{\alpha}{4}\left(\frac{2-\alpha}{4}\right)^{n-1-j}, \quad \text{for } 1 \le j \le n-1,$$

and the total effort is equal to

$$R = w\frac{2\alpha}{2+\alpha}\left(1 - \left(\frac{2-\alpha}{4}\right)^{n-1}\right).$$

8.7 **Budgets of efforts and incomplete information** Consider a single-elimination tournament among four players where in the first round there are two matches between two players, and in the second round, there is a single match between two players who won in the first round. In each match between two players, the winner is the player who invests the larger effort, with a uniform random tie break. The winner of the tournament is awarded a prize of value w_2, the player who loses in the final round is awarded a prize of value w_1, and the two players who lose in the first round are awarded a prize of value w_0. The values of the prizes are assumed to satisfy $w_2 > w_1 \ge w_0 \ge 0$. The players are endowed with effort budgets whose values are private information and are assumed to be independent and according to an identical prior distribution F that has density function f. Prove the following claims.

(a) There exists a subgame perfect symmetric Bayes-Nash equilibrium $(\beta_1(x), \beta_2(x))$ that specifies the split of the effort budget by a player with effort budget of value x, which is specified by

$$\beta_1(x) = \frac{x}{3} + \frac{2}{3}\int_0^x \frac{\delta}{3F^2(y)+\delta}dy$$

and $\beta_2(x) = x - \beta_1(x)$, where $\delta = (w_1 - w_0)/(w_2 - w_1)$.

(b) For a tournament with a winner-take-all prize allocation, which awards the entire prize purse to the winner of the tournament, each player spends one third of his or her budget in the first round of the tournament, and the remaining two thirds of the budget in the second round of the tournament.

8.8 **Difference-form contest success function** Consider a single-elimination tournament among four players where in the first round there are two matches between two players, and in the second round, there is a single match between two players. In each match between two players, the winner is the player who exhibits the larger performance. The performance of a player in a round of the tournament is a sum of a costly effort and an independent random variable from a prior distribution F that has a even density function f. The winner of the tournament is awarded a prize of value w_2, and the player who loses in the final round is awarded a prize of value w_1. Suppose that $w_2 \ge w_1 \ge 0$ and that the total prize purse is of unit value, i.e., $w_2 + w_1 = 1$. By competing in a match, each player incurs a production cost of value equal to a function c of his or her effort investment in the given match, where c is an increasing, continuously differentiable, and strictly convex function and such that $c(0) = 0$.

(a) Suppose that the game is such that in each subgame, the payoff function of each player is concave in his or her own effort investment, for every given effort investment of the opponent. Show that there exists a subgame perfect symmetric pure-strategy Nash equilibrium, in which each player invests effort of value b_1 in the first round of the tournament, and each player playing in the second round of the tournament invests effort of value b_2, where b_1 and b_2 are unique solutions to

$$c'(b_2) = c_f(w_2 - w_1)$$

and

$$c'(b_1) = c_f\left(\frac{1}{2} - c(b_2)\right)$$

with c_f defined by

$$c_f = \int_{-\infty}^{\infty} f(x)^2\, dx.$$

(b) Exhibit an instance of the game for which it is optimal to award a runner-up prize of strictly positive value with respect to the expected total effort.

8.4 Bibliographical Notes

The study of how to design a tournament plan has a long and rich history. It dates back to as early as Dodgson (1883) in the context of lawn tennis tournaments. The design of tournament plans has attracted a lot of attention in the context of sports competitions, e.g., in the context of brackets used for NCAA basketball playoffs.

Seeding procedures for tournaments of two-player contests have been studied by several authors. The concepts of stochastically transitive, strongly stochastically transitive, and the generalized linear model of the matrices of winning probabilities were introduced by David (1963) to study properties of tournament plans. Chung and Hwang (1978) showed that, for a single-elimination tournament of two-player contests with outcomes according to the Bradley-Terry model, the stronger the player the larger his or her winning probability. Counterexamples were provided for cases when the matrix of winning probabilities is not of the Bradley-Terry type. The concept of a *monotone seeding* was introduced by Hwang (1982) who showed that the standard seeding procedure is not guaranteed to be monotone and that the dynamic seeding procedure in Section 8.2.8 ensures monotonicity. Theorem 8.20 is from Hwang (1982). Horen and Riezman (1985) studied how different seeding procedures compare with respect to different criteria, including the probability that the strongest player wins in single-elimination tournaments of four and eight players. Chung and Hwang (1978) conjectured that the random permutation seeding procedure is monotone for every stochastically transitive matrix of winning probabilities. The conjecture was disapproved for general tournament plans by Israel (1982) using the counterexample shown in the proof of Theorem 8.17. Chen and Hwang (1988) settled the conjecture for the case of balanced tournaments. Corollary 8.14 is from that work. Knuth (1987) contains some interesting results on the minimum number of comparisons for the k selection problem (identify the k-th strongest player) and some historical facts about the design of tournaments in sport competitions. Hwang et al. (1991) extended the result of Chung and Hwang (1978) to a broader class of generalized linear models that includes the Bradley-Terry model as a special case. Schwenk (2000) studied the general question of how to best seed a single-elimination tournament with respect to the criteria of delayed confrontation, monotonicity of seeding, and minimization of favoritism. He introduced the cohort randomized seeding procedure, studied in Section 8.2.7, and showed that this is the only randomized seeding procedure satisfying all three criteria. Theorem 8.2.7 is from therein. Using simulations, Appleton (1995) studied the effectiveness of various tournament designs with respect to maximizing the probability of the best player winning. Marchand (2002) also studied the winning probability of the best player winning for some specific matrices of winning probabilities under the standard seeding, random permutation seeding, and cohort randomized seeding procedures. Vu and Shoham (2011) studied the seeding procedures with respect to the criteria of monotonicity and envy-freeness. The Ph.D. thesis by Vu (2010) provides a good overview of known results on the design of elimination tournaments. Characterization of the number of distinct seedings for $n = 2^r$ players in Theorem 8.1 is a well-known result; e.g., Griffiths (2012) provides a proof for the more general case of tournaments for an arbitrary number of players $n \geq 2$, where some players receive byes.

A classic reference on the structure of prizes and incentives in elimination tournaments is Rosen (1986). In that work, it was shown that for a competitive balance to be maintained across all matches of a balanced single-elimination tournament in a subgame perfect pure-strategy Nash equilibrium, the prize purse must be allocated such that the prize allocated to a player is proportional to the number of successfully completed rounds by this player and an extra amount of prize is awarded to the winner of the tournament. This result is presented in Theorem 8.32. An important assumption under which this qualitative property holds is that players incur production costs according to a production cost function in different rounds of the tournament. Krishna and Morgan (1998) studied strategic behavior in two-round single-elimination tournaments with four identical players where performances of players consist of a sum of costly efforts and independently and identically distributed random variables from an atomless distribution. In that work it was shown that the winner-take-all prize allocation is not always optimal with respect to the expected total effort in equilibrium, i.e., there exist cases in which it is beneficial to allocate some portion of a prize purse to the runner-up prize. Exercise 8.8 is based on that work. Gradstein and Konrad (1999) studied how a tournament plan affects the total effort under assumptions that the prize allocation is of the winner-take-all type, the players have identical valuations, and the winner of each contest of the tournament is determined according to a ratio-form contest success function. It was shown that for any given number of rounds, the group sizes within each round should be equal across the competing groups and the optimal group size is the same across rounds. It was also shown that a single contest structure is optimal when the return to scale parameter α is greater than 1, any number of rounds is optimal when $\alpha = 1$, and the tournament design according to a perfect binary tree is optimal when α is smaller than 1. This is shown in Theorem 8.30. Fu and Lu (2012) studied elimination tournaments where in each contest a set of winners is determined by successive application of the ratio-form contest success function. It was found that, for identical players with unit marginal costs of production, multi-round tournaments elicit more of the total effort than a single-round contest whenever the contest success function is sufficiently imperfectly discriminating. It was also found that when the production functions are concave, the winner-take-all prize allocation is optimal with respect to the total effort and that increasing the number of rounds increases the total effort. This implies that for a set of n players, the total-effort maximizing design is a single-elimination tournament with $n - 1$ rounds with one contest held in each round between a pair of players. Moldovanu and Sela (2006) studied different contest architectures and how they compare with respect to the total effort and maximum individual effort in equilibrium in a game with incomplete information where the valuation parameters are private information and players incur production costs. For unit marginal costs of production, they found that (i) single contest design is optimal with respect to the total effort and (ii) a single-elimination tournament with two finalists is optimal with respect to the maximum individual effort provided that the number of players is sufficiently large. For strictly convex production costs, it may be beneficial to split the contestants among several subcontests. Theorem 8.39 is from Moldavan and Sela (2006). Groh et al. (2012) studied the subgame perfect mixed-strategy Nash equilibrium of the game with complete information that models single-elimination tournaments with four players focusing on three different criteria: the expected total effort, the probability that two strongest players play in the finals, and the probability of winning for the highest ability player. Most of the analysis in Section 8.3.1 is based on the results therein.

The study of strategic behavior in tournament contest structures with players endowed with effort budgets that are strategically split across different rounds of the tournament has been pursued by several authors. Matros (2004) studied a two-round single-elimination tournament with four players endowed with unit effort budgets. It was shown that for a class of contest success functions, there exists a subgame perfect pure-strategy Nash equilibrium as presented in Theorem 8.34. A game with incomplete information was also studied as given in Exercise 8.7. Harbaugh and Klumpp (2005) studied a two-round balanced single-elimination tournament among four players where players are endowed with unit effort budgets. The winner in a match is determined according to the weighted proportional allocation. A special case is studied of two types of players of high relative ability (favorites) and low relative ability (underdogs), and each semifinal match is between a favorite and an underdog player. It was shown that underdogs exert more effort in the semifinal round of the tournament while favorites save more effort for the final round.

The effects of information revelation in rounds of a tournament have also been studied by several authors. Matros and Lai (2006) considered two-round single-elimination tournaments where players' abilities are revealed before the competition in the final round. They found that the revelation always increases the first-round effort but decreases the final-round effort, and that the expected total effort in all contests of the tournament can increase for some instances and decrease for other instances with the revelation. Zhang and Wang (2009) studied how information revelation affects the existence and efficiency of equilibria in two-round elimination tournaments. Konrad and Kovenock (2010) studied several types of sequential games including a two-round elimination tournament in a game with incomplete information where there is an ex-ante uncertainty about abilities of the players. In particular, marginal costs of productions are assumed to be independent random variables that become common knowledge to players before they make their effort investments. Specifically, they considered a two-round tournament with three players where two players, say player 1 and player 2, meet in the semi-final round and the winner is confronted with the third player, player 3, in the final round. The marginal costs of productions of players 1 and 2 become common knowledge before the semi-final round, but the marginal cost of production of player 3 becomes common knowledge only at the beginning of the final round. The hypothesis of this work is that uncertainty about abilities of players may reduce the discouragement effect that may lower the effort in early stages for some players because of anticipated competition in later stages of the competition. Konrad (2012) discusses the discouragement effect in various types of games, including a game that models an elimination tournament.

Several studies of tournament plans have focused on various sports competitions. Annis and Wu (2006) compared various elimination tournament designs via simulations to examine potential playoff schemes for Division I-A football. Konig (2000) studied the competitive balance in the case study of Dutch soccer. Kaplan and Gartska (2001) considered the problem of estimating the number of correct predictions in single-elimination tournaments. Clarke et al. (2009) studied fairness, balance, and efficiency of the world professional snooker championship. Kendall et al. (2010) provides an annotated bibliography of the literature on sports scheduling.

A line of work on the analysis of tournament plans is focused on the manipulation of tournament plans, which is related to the general area of manipulations of voting systems in the context of social choice and sorting by pair comparisons. For example, manipulations were studied by Russell and Walsh (2009). Vu et al. (2009) considered computational complexity of a schedule control, i.e., designing a tournament plan that maximizes the winning probability of a given player. Altman et al. (2009) studied the choice rules that are monotonic (an alternative cannot get itself selected by losing in a pair comparison) and pairwise non-manipulable (a pair of alternatives cannot make one of them the winner by reversing the outcome of the match between them). Beygelzimer et al. (2009) studied error-correcting tournament plans. Altman and Kleinberg (2010) studied the problem of manipulation of randomized choice rules.

CHAPTER 9

Rating Systems

In this chapter we study fundamental principles that underlie the design of rating systems for rating of players' skills based on observed contest outcomes. Such rating systems have traditionally been used in the context of sports competitions. A canonical example is the rating of players' skills in the game of chess, but rating systems have also been used in other sports; for example, for rating individual players' strengths in the games of tennis and table tennis and for rating teams' strengths in the games of football, basketball, and baseball. The use of rating systems has also played an important role in the context of online services. For example, rating of coders' algorithmic and coding skills has been in use in popular competition-based crowdsourcing software-development platforms such as TopCoder. Another example is the rating of players' skills in popular online multi-player gaming platforms such as Xbox Live. The rating systems are used for various purposes such as determining which players or teams of players qualify to participate in a tournament, seeding of tournaments, and creation of leaderboards. The use of rating systems may stimulate competition among players and general interest in a contest. The use of rating systems for matchmaking that biases competitions to be among similarly skilled players may stimulate the participation and contribution of players and increase the interest of spectators. Rating systems can also be used for prediction of contest outcomes, which is of particular interest in the context of betting services. The ratings of players' skills can also be used as performance indicators for hiring and assigning work to skillful workers.

One of the main challenges for the design of a rating system is to accurately estimate players' skills based on sparse input data that contains information about contest outcomes. In many situations in practice, only a small portion of all distinct pairs of players face each other in a contest. In Figure 9.1, the input data sparsity is illustrated for the case of TopCoder competitions. Although the designs of some popular existing rating systems differ from each other in their details, we shall see that they all share a few fundamental design principles. A typical design assumes that the outcome of every given contest among a set of players is an independent sample from a distribution that is parametrized with a set of parameters that represent the skill of the players. The design aims to address the data sparsity problem by estimating

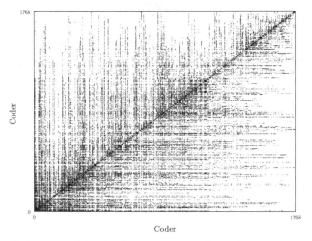

Figure 9.1. TopCoder co-participation in contests for software development tasks over a 10-year period from the end of 2003 until the beginning of 2013. The data consists of 1,768 coders and 3,018 tasks. The number of distinct pairs of coders who participated in at least one common contest is smaller than 2% of the total number of all possible pairs. The number of contests per coder has the mean value of 6.46, the median value of 2, the 90% quantile value of 17, and the maximum number as large as 264 contests. The number of coders per contest has the mean value of 3.79, the median value of 3, the 90% quantile value of 8, and the maximum number of 61 coders.

players' skills from given input data. An important aspect of the design is the choice of the method for statistical inference of unknown parameters; various statistical methods are in use, including those based on maximum likelihood estimation and approximate Bayesian inference. A common requirement is to design an online rating system, which updates the ratings of players or teams of players in an online fashion as soon as they have participated in a contest. Throughout this chapter, we shall refer to rating of *alternatives*, which allows for more generality, where an alternative may not only be a player or a team of players participating in contests but also some other kind of entity.

The remainder of this chapter is structured as follows. In Section 9.1 we introduce the basic concepts. Section 9.2 introduces some well known probabilistic models of contest outcomes. The relations between these models are discussed in Section 9.3. The statistical inference of the model parameters are discussed in Section 9.4 and Section 9.5, for maximum likelihood and Bayesian inference parameter estimation, respectively. Section 9.6 discusses the main elements of the design of some popular rating systems.

9.1 Basic Concepts

In this section we introduce some basic concepts in the context of rating systems. We first consider a simple problem of inferring the strengths of two alternatives. This will allow us to introduce the concept of a maximum likelihood estimation of unknown parameters and a Bayesian inference of latent variables. We then introduce the basic terminology and notation for the rating of two or more alternatives where the input is a sequence of observed rankings of pairs of alternatives, and we then cover the more general case where the input is a sequence of observed rankings of two or more alternatives.

9.1.1 Two Alternatives

Consider a universe of two alternatives, say named 1 and 2, who engage in a number of contests where in each contest one alternative wins and the other loses. Suppose that the outcomes of contests are according to a sequence $x_1, x_2, \ldots, x_m$ of independent and identically distributed Bernoulli random variables $\mathbf{Pr}[x_i = 1] = 1 - \mathbf{Pr}[x_i = 0] = p$, with unknown parameter $0 < p < 1$. Here $x_i = 1$ indicates that in contest i alternative 1 won, and $x_i = 0$ indicates that alternative 2 won. In the case of two alternatives, it is natural to interpret p as a parameter representing the skill of alternative 1 and $1 - p$ as a parameter representing the skill of alternative 2. The value of parameter p can be estimated by different methods given an observed sequence of contest outcomes. A natural prediction problem to consider is to estimate the probability of the event that alternative 1 wins in the $m + 1$-st contest given that alternative 1 won in w contests out of m past contests. In other words, we want to estimate the probability of the event $\{x_{m+1} = 1\}$ conditional on the observed event $\mathcal{F}_{m,w} = \{x_1 + x_2 + \cdots + x_m = w\}$, i.e.,

$$\mathbf{E}[x_{m+1} \mid \mathcal{F}_{m,w}].$$

There are two fundamentally different approaches for inference of the parameters of a probabilistic model: the standard frequentist approach using the concept of maximum likelihood estimation and a Bayesian approach using the framework of Bayesian inference, which for the simple problem considered in this section amounts to estimators of parameter p that are described as follows.

Maximum Likelihood

The standard frequentist approach is to use the maximum likelihood estimator of parameter p given the observation $\mathcal{F}_{m,w}$. Under the given probabilistic model of contest outcomes, the likelihood of observing $\mathcal{F}_{m,w}$ is equal to $L(p) = \binom{m}{w} p^w (1 - p)^{m-w}$. From this we observe the well-known fact that the maximum likelihood estimate of parameter p is

$$\hat{p} = \frac{w}{m}. \tag{9.1}$$

In other words, the maximum likelihood estimate of the probability that alternative 1 wins is equal to the observed fraction of wins by alternative 1 in past contests.

Bayesian Inference

The Bayesian approach is based on assuming that the unknown parameter is a latent random variable according to a prior distribution, and then the Bayesian inference amounts to computing its posterior distribution conditional on the observed data. For the simple probabilistic model considered in this section, the Bayesian approach suggests use of the following estimator:

$$\hat{p} = \frac{w+1}{m+2}.$$ (9.2)

The estimator in (9.2) can be derived as follows. Suppose that p is a latent random variable with a prior distribution F. Given the observation $\mathcal{F}_{m,w}$, the posterior distribution of p is obtained by Bayes' rule as follows:

$$\mathbf{Pr}[p \le x \mid \mathcal{F}_{m,w}] = \frac{\mathbf{Pr}[p \le x, \mathcal{F}_{m,w}]}{\mathbf{Pr}[\mathcal{F}_{m,w}]}$$

$$= \frac{\int_0^x \mathbf{Pr}[\mathcal{F}_{m,w} \mid p = y] \, dF(y)}{\mathbf{Pr}[\mathcal{F}_{m,w}]}$$

$$= \frac{\int_0^x y^w (1-y)^{m-w} dF(y)}{\int_0^1 y^w (1-y)^{m-w} dF(y)}.$$

Assume now that the prior distribution is a uniform distribution on $[0, 1]$. This is a non-informative prior that favors no particular value in the interval $[0, 1]$. For this choice of the prior distribution, it follows that

$$\mathbf{Pr}[p \le x \mid \mathcal{F}_{m,w}] = \binom{m}{w} \int_0^x y^w (1-y)^{m-w} dy.$$

In other words, the posterior distribution of the latent random variable p is a beta distribution with parameters $\alpha = w + 1$ and $\beta = m - w + 1$. Since the expected value of a random variable that has a beta distribution with parameters α and β is equal to $\alpha/(\alpha + \beta)$, the expected value of p with respect to the posterior distribution is as asserted in (9.2).

An appealing feature of the Bayesian estimator given by (9.2) is that it always holds that

$$0 < \hat{p} < 1.$$

The Bayesian estimator has a smoothening effect that avoids sticking to the boundary values 0 or 1 in case of an initial run of successive loses or wins by a alternative. The Bayesian estimate in (9.2) is always greater than or equal to the maximum likelihood estimate in (9.1). In the absence of any observations, its value is equal to $1/2$, and it converges to that of the maximum likelihood estimate in (9.1), asymptotically as the number of observations grows large. One may interpret the Bayesian estimator in (9.2) as a maximum likelihood estimate based on the observed data augmented with two hypothetical observations: one contest outcome in which alternative 1 won and another contest outcome in which alternative 2 won.

9.1.2 Pair Comparisons

A special case of interest in many sports competitions is that of two or more alternatives $N = \{1, 2, \ldots, n\}$, where contests are held between pairs of alternatives. The models of pair comparisons have also been studied more generally in statistics literature as a method for hypothesis testing by conducting relative comparisons between pairs of alternatives.

A standard assumption is that pair comparisons are independent random variables across different comparisons with binary outcomes, indicating which one of the two alternatives is ranked higher in a pair comparison. Under this assumption, a sufficient statistic for estimation of the model parameters is the count of the number of comparisons in which a given alternative is preferred over each other alternative, which we represent by the *number of wins matrix* denoted by

$$\mathbf{W} = (w_{i,j})$$

where $w_{i,j}$ is the number of pair comparisons in which alternative i is ranked higher than alternative j.

A special class of the number of wins matrices is that of *tournament matrices* where $\mathbf{W}$ is assumed to be such that $w_{i,j} \in \{0, 1\}$ and $w_{i,j} + w_{j,i} \leq 1$ for every $i, j \in N$. A tournament matrix $\mathbf{W}$ is said to be a *complete tournament matrix* if $w_{i,j} + w_{j,i} = 1$ for every $i, j \in N$. A tournament matrix can be equivalently defined by a *tournament graph* $G = (N, E)$ where $(j, i) \in E$ if, and only if, $w_{i,j} = 1$ for $i, j \in N$.

We also define the matrix of the number of pair comparisons $\mathbf{M} = (m_{i,j})$, where $m_{i,j}$ is the number of pair comparisons in which alternatives $\{i, j\}$ are compared. Notice that $\mathbf{M} = \mathbf{W} + \mathbf{W}^T$.

9.1.3 General Comparisons

Definition 9.1 (full ranking). A *full ranking* of a set of alternatives $N = \{1, 2, \ldots, n\}$ is defined by a one-to-one mapping $\rho : N \to N$, i.e., by a permutation of the alternatives. For every alternative $i \in N$, we refer to $\rho(i)$ as the *rank* of alternative i.

Every full ranking ρ of a set of alternatives N corresponds to a total ordering on the set of alternatives N defined by

$$\rho^{-1}(1) \succ \rho^{-1}(2) \succ \cdots \succ \rho^{-1}(n).$$

A ranking with ties is defined by using the concept of a partial ranking, which is a generalization of a full ranking and is defined as follows.

Definition 9.2 (partial ranking). A *partial ranking* of a set of alternatives $N = \{1, 2, \ldots, n\}$ is defined as a mapping $\rho : N \to M$ for a given *set of ranks M* associated with the usual total order.

For a partial ranking ρ on a set of alternatives N, alternative i is said to be ranked higher than j if, and only if, $\rho(i) < \rho(j)$, and i and j are said to be in a "tie" if, and only if, $\rho(i) = \rho(j)$. A full ranking is a partial ranking with no ties. A partial ranking corresponds to a weak ordering of alternatives.

A partial ranking can be defined by using the concept of a bucket ordering that is defined as follows.

Definition 9.3. A *bucket ordering* of a set of alternatives $N = \{1, 2, \ldots, n\}$ is a partition of alternatives in a collection of sets $N_1, N_2, \ldots, N_k$ for a given integer $k \geq 1$. A bucket ordering specified by $(N_1, N_2, \ldots, N_k)$ corresponds to a weak ordering on N defined by the following two conditions:

(i) $i \succ j$ if, and only if, $i \in N_a$ and $j \in N_b$ for $a, b \in \{1, 2, \ldots, k\}$ such that $a < b$.

(ii) $i \sim j$ if, and only if, $i, j \in N_a$ for some $a \in \{1, 2, \ldots, k\}$.

Notice that a bucket ordering specified by $(N_1, N_2, \ldots, N_k)$ is itself a partial ranking ρ with the set of ranks $M = \{1, 2, \ldots, k\}$ and

$$\rho(i) = a \quad \text{for } i \in N_a. \tag{9.3}$$

A bucket ordering defined by (9.3) is sometimes referred to as a *k-rating*.

Several standard partial rankings can be defined by using the concept of bucket ordering that we introduce as follows. Suppose that given is a bucket ordering specified by $(N_1, N_2, \ldots, N_k)$ of a set of alternatives $N = \{1, 2, \ldots, n\}$. We denote with $b(i)$ the identity of the set to which alternative i is assigned under the given bucket ordering, i.e., $b(i) = a$, for $a \in \{1, 2, \ldots, k\}$ such that $i \in N_a$. Then, we have the following definitions of standard partial rankings:

(i) *Standard competition ranking:*

$$\rho(i) = \sum_{a < b(i)} |N_a| + 1, \quad \text{for } i \in N.$$

For instance, if $1 \succ 2 \sim 3 \succ 4$, then $\rho = (1, 2, 2, 4)$.

(ii) *Modified competition ranking:*

$$\rho(i) = \sum_{a \leq b(i)} |N_a|, \quad \text{for } i \in N.$$

For instance, if $1 \succ 2 \sim 3 \succ 4$, then $\rho = (1, 3, 3, 4)$.

(iii) *Dense ranking:*

$$\rho(i) = \sum_{a \leq b(i)} \mathbf{1}(|N_a| > 0), \quad \text{for } i \in N.$$

For instance, if $1 \succ 2 \sim 3 \succ 4$, then $\rho = (1, 2, 2, 3)$.

(iv) *Fractional ranking:*

$$\rho(i) = \sum_{a < b(i)} |N_a| + \frac{1}{2}(|N_{b(i)}| + 1), \quad \text{for } i \in N.$$

For instance, if $1 \succ 2 \sim 3 \succ 4$, then $\rho = (1, 2.5, 2.5, 4)$.

The concept of a bucket ordering (or equivalently a k-rating) allows us to define some other well-known rankings. For example, the well-known five-star rating used for rating of movies is a 5-rating. A *top-k ranking* corresponds to a bucket ordering specified by a collection of sets $(N_1, N_2, \ldots, N_{k+1})$ such that $N_1, N_2, \ldots, N_k$ are singleton sets. A *top-k set* is a bucket ordering specified by a collection of sets (N_1, N_2) such that N_1 is of size at most k.

9.2 Probability Distributions over Rankings

In this section we overview some standard parametric distributions over a set of partial rankings. Some of these distributions have been used in the design of rating systems and in the general context of ranking of a set of alternatives. Given a set of alternatives $N = \{1, 2, \ldots, n\}$ and a set of parameters Θ_n, we consider a distribution F_θ with parameter $\theta \in \Theta_n$ on a set of partial rankings R_n. If the set of partial rankings R_n is a set of full rankings, then we may consider a distribution F_θ over the set of permutations S_n. A distribution F_θ over partial rankings may either be defined in an explicit closed form or by a sampling procedure over the set of partial rankings. The model considered in Section 9.2.1 is for a distribution over the set of partial rankings of two or more alternatives, those in Section 9.2.2 and Section 9.2.3 are for distributions over the set of top-1 rankings of two or more alternatives, and that in Section 9.2.4 is for distributions over the set of full rankings of pairs of alternatives.

9.2.1 Thurstone Models

In this section, we discuss a family of models that we refer to as *Thurstone models*, which are a generalization of the original model introduced by Thurstone (1927). The original Thurstone model is presented in this section, after we introduce some basic concepts that underlie the family of models that we refer to as Thurstone models.

A Thurstone model for full rankings specifies a distribution over the set S_n of full rankings of $n \geq 2$ alternatives by the following sampling procedure. Suppose a distribution F_θ on $\mathbf{R}^n$ is given for a parameter $\theta \in \Theta_n$. Then, a full ranking ρ over the set of alternatives is generated by sampling $\mathbf{b} = (b_1, b_2, \ldots, b_n)$ from F_θ and choosing ρ to be a full ranking of the alternatives such that

$$b_{\rho^{-1}(1)} \geq b_{\rho^{-1}(2)} \geq \cdots \geq b_{\rho^{-1}(n)}.$$

The distribution F_θ is commonly assumed to be such that a sample from F_θ corresponds to a unique full ranking of the alternatives. The random variables $b_1, b_2, \ldots, b_n$ are referred to as *discriminal processes* in the traditional contexts of statistics and choice theory and are referred to as *performances* in the context of modern rating systems. In this chapter, we shall use the latter terminology. The given sampling procedure corresponds to ordering the alternatives in decreasing order of their performances.

A Thurstone model can also be defined for rankings with ties. A common approach is to admit a parameter $\epsilon \geq 0$ and define relations between pairs of alternatives as follows: (i) $i \succ j$ if, and only if, $b_i - b_j > \epsilon$, (ii) $i \sim j$ if, and only if, $-\epsilon \leq b_i - b_j \leq \epsilon$, and (iii) $i \prec j$ if, and only if, $b_i - b_j < -\epsilon$. In particular, in a contest between a pair of alternatives, a draw outcome is declared whenever the absolute value of the difference of their performances is less than or equal to ϵ, and otherwise, the alternative with the higher performance is declared to be the winner and the other to be the loser. The case with no ties is a special case for the choice of the parameter value $\epsilon = 0$. See Figure 9.2 for an illustration.

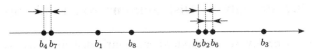

Figure 9.2. An example of a ranking with ties generated by a Thurstone model: $3 \succ 6 \sim 2 \sim$ $5 \succ 8 \succ 1 \succ 7 \sim 4$. The indicated lengths of intervals are those smaller than or equal to the given value of parameter ϵ.

The vector of performances $\mathbf{b} = (b_1, b_2, \ldots, b_n)$ can be decomposed into two components: a deterministic component that we refer to as the vector of the *strengths of the alternatives* $\mathbf{v} = (v_1, v_2, \ldots, v_n)$ and a random component that we refer to as the vector of *noise* $\varepsilon = (\varepsilon_1, \varepsilon_2, \ldots, \varepsilon_n)$ as follows:

$$\mathbf{b} = \mathbf{v} + \varepsilon. \tag{9.4}$$

The distribution of the vector of noise satisfies

$$\mathbf{Pr}[\varepsilon_1 \leq x_1, \varepsilon_2 \leq x_2, \ldots, \varepsilon_n \leq x_n] = F_\theta(\mathbf{v} + \mathbf{x}), \quad \text{for } \mathbf{x} = (x_1, x_2, \ldots, x_n) \in \mathbf{R}^n.$$

A special case of interest is a Thurstone model with independent noise $\varepsilon_1, \varepsilon_2, \ldots, \varepsilon_n$ with distributions $F_{\theta_1}, F_{\theta_2}, \ldots, F_{\theta_n}$. For this special case, for every pair of alternatives $i, j \in N$, we can define the function

$$p_{i,j}(x) = \int_\mathbf{R} F_{\theta_j}(x + y) \, dF_{\theta_i}(y), \quad \text{for } x \in \mathbf{R}, \tag{9.5}$$

which determines the probabilities of outcomes of pair comparisons

$$\mathbf{Pr}[i \succ j] = 1 - \mathbf{Pr}[j \succ i] = p_{i,j}(v_i - v_j), \quad \text{for every } i, j \in N, i \neq j. \tag{9.6}$$

An even more special case is a Thurstone model $\mathcal{T}_F$ with independent and identically distributed noise with a distribution function F from a parametric family of distributions. For a Thurstone model $\mathcal{T}_F$, for every pair of alternatives $i, j \in N$, we have

$$p_{i,j}(x) = D_F(x), \quad \text{for } x \in \mathbf{R} \tag{9.7}$$

where D_F is the *difference distribution* given by

$$D_F(x) = \int_\mathbf{R} F(x + y) \, dF(y), \quad \text{for } x \in \mathbf{R}. \tag{9.8}$$

The characterization of pair comparisons as given in (9.6) can be extended to the concept of the expected rank of an alternative according to a Thurstone model. Consider the standard competition ranking ρ generated by a Thurstone model that is defined by

$$\rho(i) = \sum_{j \in N} \mathbf{1}(b_i \geq b_j), \quad \text{for } i \in N.$$

For a Thurstone model with independent noise with distributions $F_{\theta_1}, F_{\theta_2}, \ldots, F_{\theta_n}$, taking the expected value, *the expected ranks of alternatives* admit the following explicit characterization:

$$\mathbf{E}[\rho(i)] = \sum_{j \in N \setminus \{i\}} p_{i,j}(v_i - v_j) + 1, \quad \text{for } i \in N. \tag{9.9}$$

Original Thurstone Model

The original Thurstone model was introduced by Thurstone (1927) for pair comparisons with the vector of performances of the form (9.4) where $\varepsilon = (\varepsilon_1, \varepsilon_2)$ is a bivariate Gaussian distribution with mean zero and covariance matrix Σ. The covariance matrix Σ can be represented in the following form:

$$\Sigma = \begin{pmatrix} \sigma_1^2 & \sigma_1 \sigma_2 r \\ \sigma_1 \sigma_2 r & \sigma_2^2 \end{pmatrix}$$

where σ_1^2 and σ_2^2 are variances of ε_1 and ε_2, respectively, and $r \in [-1, 1]$ is a correlation parameter.

The distribution of the performance differences $b_1 - b_2$ is a Gaussian random variable with mean $v_1 - v_2$ and variance $\sigma_i^2 + \sigma_j^2 - 2\sigma_i \sigma_j r$. It follows that the probability of the event that i is ranked higher than j is given by

$$p_{i,j} = \Phi\left(\frac{v_i - v_j}{\sqrt{\sigma_i^2 + \sigma_j^2 - 2\sigma_i \sigma_j r}} \right) \tag{9.10}$$

where Φ is the standard normal distribution.

In the original paper by Thurstone (1927), five types of comparative judgments are distinguished, which we describe as follows.

Type I This is the model of comparative judgment by a single observer whose judgments are independent random complete rankings of the two alternatives according to distribution (9.10).

Type II This is the model of comparative judgment by a panel of judges with each making a single judgment where individual judgments are independent random complete rankings of the two alternatives according to distribution (9.10).

Type III This is the model of comparative judgment according to distribution (9.10) with parameter $r = 0$. In other words, individual performances b_1 and b_2 are independent Gaussian random variables.

Type IV This is the model of comparative judgment in which the variances σ_1^2 and σ_2^2 are nearly identical, so that (9.10) is approximately $\Phi((v_i - v_j)/(\sqrt{2}(\sigma_i + \sigma_j)))$.

Type V This is the model of comparative judgment according to distribution (9.10) with $r = 0$ and $\sigma_i^2 = \sigma_j^2 = \sigma^2$. In other words, individual performances b_1 and b_2 are assumed to be independent Gaussian random variables with identical variances (see Figure 9.3).

The Thurstone Type V model is commonly assumed in the design of popular rating systems. Under the assumption of identical variances, which includes the Thurstone Type V model as a special case, the distribution in (9.10) boils down to the following

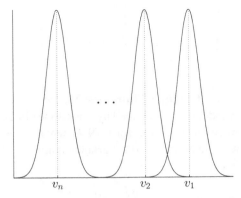

Figure 9.3. An illustration of a general Thurstone model with random independent performances with Gaussian distributions with identical variances.

form:

$$p_{i,j} = \Phi\left(\frac{v_i - v_j}{\sqrt{2}\beta}\right) \tag{9.11}$$

where by definition $\beta = \sigma\sqrt{1-r}$.

Bradley-Terry Model

The Bradley-Terry model was introduced as a probabilistic model of pair comparisons by Zermelo (1929) and was subsequently studied by Bradley and Terry (1952, 1954) and many others. For a given set of alternatives $N = \{1, 2, \ldots, n\}$, the model admits positive real-valued parameters $\theta_1, \theta_2, \ldots, \theta_n$ such that for every pair of alternatives $i, j \in N$, $i \neq j$, alternative i is ranked higher than alternative j with probability

$$p_{i,j} = \frac{\theta_i}{\theta_i + \theta_j} \tag{9.12}$$

and otherwise, alternative j is ranked higher than alternative i. This is naturally generalized to a model of choice of one alternative from a set of two or more alternatives as follows:

$$\mathbf{Pr}\left[\cap_{j \neq i}\{i \succ j\}\right] = \frac{\theta_i}{\sum_{j=1}^{n} \theta_j}, \quad \text{for } i \in N. \tag{9.13}$$

This model is a special case of Luce's choice model that we discuss in more detail in Section 9.2.2.

There are several Thurstone models that have the choice probability corresponding to that of the Bradley-Terry model. Such a Thurstone model is for the vector of performances $\mathbf{b} = (b_1, b_2, \ldots, b_n)$ defined such that $b_1, b_2, \ldots, b_n$ are independent random variables with the respective distributions $F_{\theta_1}, F_{\theta_2}, \ldots, F_{\theta_n}$, which are all according to one of the following three choices:

(i) Double-exponential (or Gumbel) distribution:

$$F_{\theta_i}(x) = e^{-\theta_i e^{-\alpha x}} \text{ for } x \in \mathbf{R}, \text{ and parameter } \alpha > 0.$$

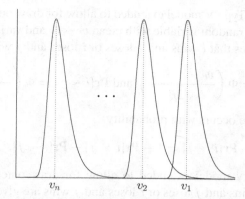

Figure 9.4. The general Thurstone model with independent random performances with double-exponential distributions.

(ii) Inverse-exponential distribution:

$$F_{\theta_i}(x) = e^{-\frac{\theta_i}{x^\alpha}} \text{ for } x \in \mathbf{R}_+, \text{ and parameter } \alpha > 0.$$

(iii) Exponential distribution:

$$F_{\theta_i}(x) = 1 - e^{-\theta_i x} \quad \text{for } x \in \mathbf{R}_+.$$

The Gumbel and inverse-exponential distributions have the choice probabilities as in (9.13) for any number of two or more alternatives, while the exponential distribution has the choice probabilities as in (9.13) for the case of pair comparisons. The reader may check this on his or her own or leverage the analysis in Section 4.2.2 to quickly become convinced of these facts.

The Bradley-Terry model is a *double-exponential Thurstone model* (see Figure 9.4), which can be observed as follows. Consider a Thurstone model with individual performances according to double-exponential distributions. Using the reparametrization $\theta_i = \exp(\alpha v_i)$ and the decomposition in (9.4), note that $b_i = v_i + \varepsilon_i$, where

$$\mathbf{Pr}[\varepsilon_i \leq x] = e^{-e^{-\alpha x}}, \quad \text{for } x \in \mathbf{R}. \tag{9.14}$$

Using this, the choice probabilities in (9.12) can be expressed as

$$p_{i,j} = \frac{1}{1 + e^{-\alpha(v_i - v_j)}}. \tag{9.15}$$

Thus, we observe that for pair comparisons, the Bradley-Terry model is quite similar to the Thurstone Type V model given in (9.11) except for replacing the Gaussian distribution with a logistic distribution.

Incidentally, the choice probabilities in equation (9.12) conform to the winning probabilities in the pure-strategy Nash equilibrium of the game that models a two-player contest with proportional allocation as given in Theorem 4.9.

Partial Rankings

In this section we show how the Thurstone Type V model and the Bradley-Terry model can be generalized to allow for draw outcomes in pair comparisons. We follow the Thurstone model for partial rankings as introduced at the beginning of Section 9.2.1.

For the Thurstone Type V model extended to allow for draw outcomes, we note that $b_i - b_j$ is a Gaussian random variable with mean $v_i - v_j$ and variance $2\beta^2$. Hence, the respective probabilities that i wins and j loses or i loses and j wins are given by

$$\mathbf{Pr}[i \succ j] = \Phi\left(\frac{v_i - v_j - \epsilon}{\sqrt{2}\beta}\right) \text{ and } \mathbf{Pr}[i \prec j] = \Phi\left(\frac{v_j - v_i - \epsilon}{\sqrt{2}\beta}\right) \quad (9.16)$$

and the draw outcome occurs with probability

$$\mathbf{Pr}[i \sim j] = 1 - \mathbf{Pr}[i \succ j] - \mathbf{Pr}[i \prec j]. \quad (9.17)$$

For the Bradley-Terry model extended to allow for draw outcomes, the respective probabilities that i wins and j loses or i loses and j wins are given by

$$\mathbf{Pr}[i \succ j] = \frac{\theta_i}{\theta_i + \theta\theta_j} \text{ and } \mathbf{Pr}[i \prec j] = \frac{\theta_j}{\theta\theta_i + \theta_j} \quad (9.18)$$

and the draw outcome occurs with probability

$$\mathbf{Pr}[i \sim j] = 1 - \mathbf{Pr}[i \succ j] - \mathbf{Pr}[i \prec j] = \frac{(\theta^2 - 1)\theta_i\theta_j}{(\theta_i + \theta\theta_j)(\theta\theta_i + \theta_j)} \quad (9.19)$$

where $\theta = e^\epsilon$. This can be shown by using the reparametrization $\theta_i = \exp(v_i)$ for $i \in N$ and assuming the double-exponential Thurstone model with $b_i = v_i + \varepsilon_i$ where ε_i is a random variable with the double-exponential distribution given in (9.14). It is an elementary calculus to show that the distribution of $\varepsilon_i - \varepsilon_j$ is logistic with parameter α, i.e.,

$$\mathbf{Pr}[\varepsilon_i - \varepsilon_j \leq x] = \frac{1}{1 + e^{-\alpha x}} \quad \text{for } x \in \mathbf{R}.$$

From this, we obtain

$$\mathbf{Pr}[i \succ j] = \mathbf{Pr}[b_i - b_j > \epsilon] = \frac{1}{1 + e^{-\alpha(v_i - v_j - \epsilon)}}$$

which by switching back to the initial parameters is equivalent to the expression in (9.14). The other probabilities of outcomes follow by similar arguments.

Home-Field Advantage

There are situations in which some of the alternatives may be in a more advantageous position than others because of some external factors. For example, in sports competitions a team playing on the home field may be in an advantageous position with respect to the away team. A way to account for the home-field advantage for the Bradley-Terry model is to amplify the skill of the home player by a factor $\theta \geq 1$. For pair comparison between alternatives i and j where alternative i has the home-field advantage, the extension of the Bradley-Terry model is given by

$$p_{i,j} = \frac{\theta\theta_i}{\theta\theta_i + \theta_j}.$$

A generalization of this model is a Thurstone model with parameter $\epsilon \geq 0$ such that $i \succ j$ if, and only if, $b_i - b_j \geq -\epsilon$ and otherwise $j \succ i$.

9.2.2 Luce's Choice Model

A model of choice over a set of alternatives is defined by an axiom for a system of win probabilities, which we introduce in this section.

Definition 9.4 (system of complete win probabilities). A *system of complete win probabilities* for a set of alternatives $N = \{1, 2, \ldots, n\}$ is defined by the set of probability distributions:

$$\mathcal{P}_{n,n} = \left\{ (p_S(i),\ i \in S) \in (0, 1)^{|S|} \ \Big| \ \sum_{i \in S} p_i(S) = 1, S \subseteq N, |S| \geq 2 \right\}$$

where we can intuitively interpret $p_S(i)$ as the probability of choosing alternative i from a subset of alternatives $S \subseteq N$.

A *system of pair comparisons* is defined as a more restrictive system of win probabilities that specifies only the winning probabilities for pairs of alternatives:

$$\mathcal{P}_{n,2} = \left\{ (p_{i,j}, p_{j,i}) \in (0, 1)^2 \ \big| \ p_{i,j} + p_{j,i} = 1, i, j \in N, i < j \right\}.$$

Definition 9.5 (Luce's Choice Axiom). A complete system of win probabilities is said to satisfy the Luce's Choice Axiom if, and only if, for every $i \in S$ and $S \subseteq N$,

$$p_S(i) = \frac{p_N(i)}{\sum_{j \in S} p_N(j)}.$$

Since $p_N(S) = \sum_{j \in S} p_N(j)$, note that the condition in Luce's Choice Axiom is equivalent to saying that for every $i \in S$ and $S \subseteq N$, $p_N(i) = p_S(i) p_N(S)$. This can be interpreted as requiring the probability of the event of selecting alternative i from the set N of all alternatives to be equal to the product of the probability of selecting first an arbitrary subset $S \subset N$ such that $i \in N$ and the probability of selecting alternative i from S.

The following theorem tells us that Luce's choice model is equivalent to a specific parametric family of distributions.

Theorem 9.6. *A system of complete win probabilities satisfies the Luce's Choice Axiom if, and only if, there exist positive real numbers* $\theta_1, \theta_2, \ldots, \theta_n$ *such that for every* $S \subseteq N$,

$$p_S(i) = \frac{\theta_i}{\sum_{j \in S} \theta_j}, \quad \text{for every } i \in S.$$

The scale of values $\theta_1, \theta_2, \ldots, \theta_n$ *is uniquely determined by the system* $\{p_S \mid S \subseteq N\}$ *up to multiplication by a constant.*

The part of the proof to establish that the asserted parametric distributions satisfy Luce's Choice Axiom follows straightforwardly. The converse follows by similar steps as those used to establish Theorem 4.2.

Plackett-Luce Model

The Plackett-Luce model is an extension of Luce's choice model from the choice of one alternative to a full ranking of alternatives. The model is defined by the probability distribution over the set of permutations given as follows:

$$\mathbf{Pr}[\rho^{-1}(1) \succ \rho^{-1}(2) \succ \cdots \succ \rho^{-1}(n)] = \prod_{i=1}^{n} \frac{\theta_{\rho^{-1}(i)}}{\theta_{\rho^{-1}(i)} + \theta_{\rho^{-1}(i+1)} + \cdots + \theta_{\rho^{-1}(n)}}, \text{ for } \rho \in S_n.$$

(9.20)

For the case of two alternatives, the model corresponds to Luce's choice model and the Bradley-Terry model.

Intuitively, the Plackett-Luce model can be interpreted as defining a distribution over the set of full rankings by a sampling procedure that samples alternatives without replacement proportional to their strength parameters, and defines the output full ranking ρ to be according to the order at which the alternatives are sampled.

9.2.3 Dawkins Choice Model

This model was introduced by Dawkins (1969) as a model of choice behavior for selecting one alternative from a given set of alternatives. Given a set of alternatives $N = \{1, 2, \ldots, n\}$, the model associates each alternative $i \in N$ with a threshold parameter $t_i \in \mathbf{R}$, where a smaller value of this threshold parameter indicates a larger preference for the corresponding alternative. Without loss of generality, assume that the alternatives are enumerated in increasing order of the values of their threshold parameters $t_1 \leq t_2 \leq \cdots \leq t_n$. The model postulates the existence of an "excitation" random variable T with a given distribution function $G(t) = \mathbf{Pr}[T \leq t]$, which is assumed to be strictly increasing for every $t \in \mathbf{R}$. An alternative is selected from the set of alternatives by using the following sampling procedure: first, sample T from distribution G until $t_1 \leq T$, and then sample an alternative uniformly at random from the set of alternatives $A(T) = \{i \in N \mid t_i \leq T\}$.

The Dawkins choice model can be equivalently defined by using the change of parameters $\theta_i = 1 - G(t_i)$, for $i \in N$. Under this change of parameters, we have $0 := \theta_{n+1} < \theta_n \leq \cdots \leq \theta_2 \leq \theta_1 < 1$. The model then corresponds to drawing a sample θ from a uniform distribution on $[0, 1]$ until $\theta \leq \theta_1$, and then sampling an alternative uniformly at random from the set of alternatives $A(\theta) = \{i \in N \mid \theta_i \geq \theta\}$. See Figure 9.5 for an illustration.

According to the Dawkins choice model, alternative $i \in N$ is preferred over other alternatives with probability

$$\mathbf{Pr}\left[\cap_{j \neq i}\{i \succ j\}\right] = \sum_{l=i}^{n} \frac{1}{l} \frac{\theta_l - \theta_{l+1}}{\theta_1}$$

$$= \frac{\theta_i}{i\theta_1} - \sum_{l=i+1}^{n} \frac{1}{(l-1)l} \frac{\theta_l}{\theta_1}.$$

(9.21)

$$0 \quad \theta_n \quad \cdots \quad \theta_{l+1} \quad | \quad \theta_l \quad \cdots \quad \theta_2 \quad \theta_1 \quad 1$$

$$\theta$$

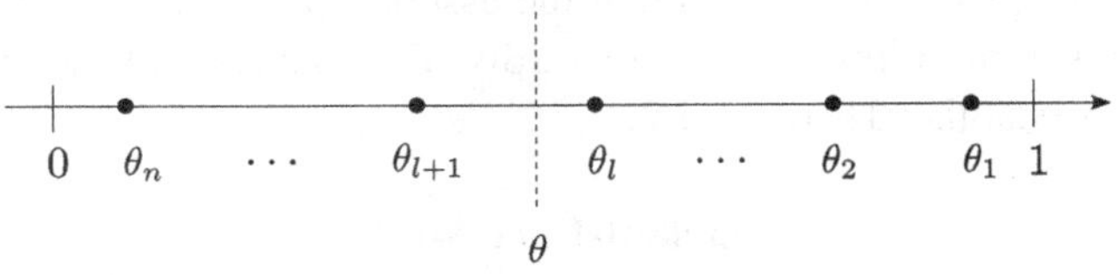

Figure 9.5. Dawkins choice model: for a given value of the threshold θ, an alternative is selected by sampling uniformly at random from the set of alternatives $A(\theta) = \{1, 2, \ldots, l\}$.

In particular, for comparison of a pair of alternatives 1 and 2 such that $0 \le \theta_2 \le \theta_1 \le 1$, the choice probabilities are given as follows:

$$p_{1,2} = 1 - \frac{1}{2}\frac{\theta_2}{\theta_1} \text{ and } p_{2,1} = \frac{1}{2}\frac{\theta_2}{\theta_1}. \tag{9.22}$$

Incidentally, the expressions in (9.22) conform to the winning probabilities in the mixed-strategy Nash equilibrium of the game that models the standard all-pay contest between two players with valuation parameters θ_1 and θ_2, as given in Theorem 2.3.

9.2.4 Generalized Linear Model

Given a strictly increasing function $D : \mathbf{R} \to [0, 1]$, which we call a *difference function*, a generalized linear model assumes that the probabilities of outcomes of pair comparisons satisfy

$$p_{i,j} = D(v_i - v_j) \tag{9.23}$$

where $\mathbf{v} = (v_1, v_2, \dots, v_n)$ is a vector of strength parameters. Most specific instances of difference functions considered in the context of generalized linear models are such that $D(-x) = 1 - D(x)$, for all $x \in \mathbf{R}$.

The class of general linear models accommodates several models of pair comparisons as special cases. Specifically, it is left as Exercise 9.7 to the reader to show that special cases include the Thurstone Type V model in (9.11), Bradley-Terry model in (9.12) and Dawkins choice model in (9.22). These models are accommodated by special forms of the difference functions, which are given in the following list of examples. Note that for the case of the Bradley-Terry and the Dawkins choice models, we use the change of parameters $\theta_i = \exp(v_i)$, for $i \in N$.

(i) *Gaussian*:

$$D(x) = \Phi\left(\frac{x}{\sqrt{2}\beta}\right), \quad \text{for } \beta > 0,$$

which accommodates the Thurstone Type V model in (9.11).

(ii) *Logistic*:

$$D(x) = \frac{1}{1 + e^{-x/s}}, \quad \text{for } s > 0,$$

which accommodates the Bradley-Terry model in (9.12) with $s = 1$.

(iii) *Laplace*:

$$D(x) = \begin{cases} \frac{1}{2}e^{x/s}, & \text{if } x < 0 \\ 1 - \frac{1}{2}e^{-x/s}, & \text{if } x \ge 0 \end{cases}, \quad \text{for } s > 0$$

which accommodates the Dawkins choice model in (9.22) with $s = 1$.

(iv) *Uniform*:

$$D(x) = \frac{1}{2} + sx, \quad \text{for } -1/(2s) \le x \le 1/(2s), \text{ and } s > 0. \tag{9.24}$$

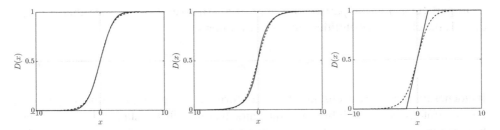

Figure 9.6. Function $D(x)$: (left) Gaussian, (middle) Laplace, (right) linear with a common value of variance and $2\beta^2 = 1$. The dashed line is the logistic function.

A numerical comparison of these specific difference functions is provided in Figure 9.6 for a fixed value of the variance.

Theorem 9.7. *For a generalized linear model $\mathcal{L}_D$ and any matrix of winning probabilities $\mathbf{P} = (p_{i,j})$ for two or more alternatives, there is a unique vector of strength parameters up to an arbitrary additive constant $c \in \mathbf{R}$, which is given by*

$$v_i = \frac{1}{n} \sum_{j \neq i} D^{-1}(p_{i,j}) + c, \quad for \ i \in N.$$

Proof. Since by (9.23), $v_i - v_j = D^{-1}(p_{i,j})$, the assertion follows by summing over $j \in N$. $\qquad \square$

For our catalog of examples, the vector of strengths are given as follows, up to an additive constant that is omitted. See also the graphical illustration in Figure 9.7.

(i) *Gaussian*:

$$v_i = \frac{\sqrt{2}\beta}{n} \sum_{j \neq i} \Phi^{-1}(p_{i,j}). \tag{9.25}$$

(ii) *Logistic*:

$$v_i = \frac{s}{n} \sum_{j \neq i} \log \left(\frac{p_{i,j}}{1 - p_{i,j}} \right). \tag{9.26}$$

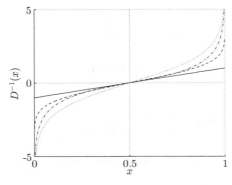

Figure 9.7. $D^{-1}(x)$ versus x for function $D(x)$ that is uniform (solid), Laplace (dashed-dotted), Gaussian (dashed), and logistic (dotted).

(iii) *Laplace*:

$$v_i = \frac{s}{n} \sum_{j \neq i} \log(2p_{i,j}) \mathbf{1}(p_{i,j} \leq 1/2) + \log\left(\frac{1}{2(1-p_{i,j})}\right) \mathbf{1}(p_{i,j} > 1/2). \qquad (9.27)$$

(iv) *Uniform*:

$$v_i = \frac{1}{2sn} \sum_{j \neq i} (2p_{i,j} - 1). \qquad (9.28)$$

In the case of the logistic model, the strength of an alternative corresponds to the sum of the log-odds ratios of this alternative winning against other alternatives. In the case of the uniform model, the strength of an alternative corresponds to the sum of the differences of the probability of winning and the probability of losing in matches with each other alternative.

Triples Function

For a generalized linear model $\mathcal{L}_D$, for every three alternatives $i, k, j \in N$, we have

$$p_{i,j} = t_D(p_{i,k}, p_{k,j})$$

where $t_D : (0, 1)^2 \to (0, 1)$ is the *triples function* defined by

$$t_D(x, y) = D(D^{-1}(x) + D^{-1}(y)).$$

Example 9.8. For Luce's choice model, for every three alternatives $i, k, j \in N$,

$$p_{i,j} = \frac{p_{i,k} p_{k,j}}{p_{i,k} p_{k,j} + (1 - p_{i,k})(1 - p_{k,j})}.$$

Example 9.9. For Dawkins choice model, for every three alternatives $i, k, j \in N$,

$$p_{i,j} = 1 - 2(1 - p_{i,k})(1 - p_{k,j}).$$

The triples function completely determines the set of winning probabilities that are admissible by a generalized linear model $\mathcal{L}_D$. This set consists of the winning probabilities for which $p_{1,2}, p_{2,3}, \ldots, p_{n-1,n}$ assume arbitrary values in $(0, 1)$, and all other winning probabilities are determined by the triples function as follows:

(i) $p_{1,3} = t_D(p_{1,2}, p_{2,3})$, $p_{1,4} = t_D(p_{1,3}, p_{3,4})$, $\ldots$, $p_{1,n} = t_D(p_{1,n-1}, p_{n-1,n})$.

(ii) $p_{i,j} = t_D(p_{i,1}, p_{1,j})$ for $1 < i < j \leq n$.

A Regression Model Formulation

A generalized linear model can be defined as a general statistical model as follows.

Definition 9.10. For every given vector of observations $\mathbf{y} = (y_1, y_2, \ldots, y_m) \in \mathbf{R}^m$, the generalized linear model is defined by the following three assumptions:

(i) $\mathbf{y}$ is a random variable with mean $\mu = \mathbf{E}[\mathbf{y}]$.

(ii) Given is a function $D : \mathbf{R} \to \mathbf{R}$ and a matrix $\mathbf{X} = (x_{t,i}) \in \mathbf{R}^{m \times n}$ such that

$$\mu_t = D\left(\sum_{i=1}^{n} x_{t,i} v_i\right), \quad \text{for } t = 1, 2, \ldots, m$$

where $\mathbf{v} = (v_1, v_2, \ldots, v_n) \in \mathbf{R}^n$ is a parameter of the model and the inverse of function D is referred as a *link function*.

(iii) Components of the vector $\mathbf{y}$ are independent random variables with distribution $f(y \mid \theta_t, \phi_t)$ for observation y_t from the exponential family of distributions, which is of the form

$$f(y \mid \theta, \phi) = \exp\left(\frac{y\theta - b(\theta)}{a(\phi)} + c(y \mid \phi)\right) \tag{9.29}$$

where θ and ϕ are parameters, and $a(\cdot)$, $b(\cdot)$, and $c(\cdot)$ are some specific functions.

If parameter ϕ is known, then this is the exponential family of distributions with canonical parameter θ. In the standard linear model, the link function is the identity function and each y_t is assumed to be according to a Gaussian random variable with mean μ_t and variance σ^2 so that we can write

$$\mathbf{y} = \mathbf{Xv} + \varepsilon$$

where ε is a Gaussian random vector with mean μ and covariance matrix $\sigma^2\mathbf{I}$.

The following two distributions are well-known distributions from the exponential family:

(i) **Gaussian distribution** Suppose y_t is a Gaussian random variable with mean μ and variance σ^2:

$$f(y \mid \theta, \phi) = \frac{1}{\sqrt{2\pi\sigma^2}}e^{-\frac{(y-\mu)^2}{2\sigma^2}} = \exp\left(\frac{y\mu - \mu^2/2}{\sigma^2} - \frac{y^2/\sigma^2 + \log(2\pi\sigma^2)}{2}\right).$$

In this case, we have

$$\theta = \mu, \ \phi = \sigma^2, \ a(\phi) = \phi, \ b(\theta) = \frac{\theta^2}{2}, \text{ and } c(y \mid \phi) = -\frac{y^2/\sigma^2 + \log(2\pi\sigma^2)}{2}.$$

(ii) **Binomial distribution** Suppose that ky_t is a binomial random variable with parameters k and p; then

$$f(y \mid \theta, \phi) = \binom{k}{ky}p^{ky}(1-p)^{k(1-y)}$$

$$= \exp\left(\frac{y\log\left(\frac{p}{1-p}\right) + \log(1-p)}{\frac{1}{k}} + \log\binom{k}{ky}\right).$$

In this case, we have

$$\theta = \log\left(\frac{p}{1-p}\right), \ \phi = \frac{1}{k}, \ a(\phi) = \phi, \ b(\theta) = \log\left(1 + e^\theta\right),$$

$$\text{and } c(y \mid \phi) = \log\binom{k}{ky}.$$

The generalized linearized model defined by Definition 9.10 specializes to a model of pair comparisons as follows. Each observation y_t is interpreted as the outcome of one or more comparisons for a pair of alternatives; hence, it is a binomial random variable up to a multiplicative factor. The identity of the pairs of comparisons being compared over different observations is encoded by matrix $\mathbf{X}$ such that if y_t is the outcome of comparison of alternative i and j, then $x_{t,i} = 1$ and $x_{t,j} = -1$, and $x_{t,k} = 0$, for $k \in N \setminus \{i, j\}$.

9.2.5 Distance Models

A distribution over full rankings with parameter $\theta = (\pi, \lambda)$, where π is a permutation in S_n and λ is a positive real number, is defined for a given distance function $d :$ $S_n \times S_n \rightarrow \mathbf{R}_+$ as follows:

$$f(\rho; \pi, \lambda) = \frac{1}{Z(\pi, \lambda)} e^{-\lambda d(\rho, \pi)}, \quad \text{for } \rho \in S_n \qquad (9.30)$$

where $Z(\pi, \lambda)$ is a normalization constant.

Two special well-known instances of the family of distributions (9.30) are

  (i) Mallows' ϕ model: the distance function is Kendall's τ distance.
 (ii) Mallow's θ model: the distance function is Spearman's footrule distance.

9.3 Relations between Different Models

In this section we establish some relations between different Thurstone models and discuss how they relate to the choice models of Luce and Dawkins that we introduced in the previous section. We first present some basic terminology and certain notions of equivalence between statistical models of rankings and then go on to discuss different relations.

A Thurstone model $\mathcal{T}_F$ is said to *admit the win probabilities* $p = \{(p_S(i), i \in S) \mid S \subseteq N\} \in \mathcal{P}_{n,n}$ if there exist strength parameters $v_1, v_2, \ldots, v_n$ such that

$$p_S(i) = \mathbf{Pr}[v_i + \varepsilon_i \geq v_j + \varepsilon_j \text{ for all } j \in S], \quad \text{for every } i \in S \subseteq N. \quad (9.31)$$

A Thurstone model $\mathcal{T}_F$ is said to *admit the system of complete win probabilities* $\mathcal{P}_{n,n}$ if equation (9.31) holds for every $p \in \mathcal{P}_{n,n}$.

Similarly, a Thurstone model $\mathcal{T}_F$ is said to *admit pair comparison probabilities* $p = \{(p_{i,j}, p_{j,i}), \mid i, j \in N, i < j\} \in \mathcal{P}_{n,2}$ if there exist strength parameters $v_1, v_2, \ldots, v_n$ such that

$$p_{i,j} = \mathbf{Pr}[v_i + \varepsilon_i > v_j + \varepsilon_j] = D_F(v_i - v_j). \qquad (9.32)$$

A Thurstone model $\mathcal{T}_F$ is said to *admit the system of pair comparison probabilities* $\mathcal{P}_{n,2}$ if equation (9.32) holds for every $p \in \mathcal{P}_{n,2}$.

Two Thurstone models $\mathcal{T}_F$ and $\mathcal{T}_G$ are said to be *equivalent for system* $\mathcal{P}_{n,n}$ if for every $p \in \mathcal{P}_{n,n}$ either both $\mathcal{T}_F$ and $\mathcal{T}_G$ admit the win probabilities p or neither $\mathcal{T}_F$ nor $\mathcal{T}_G$ admit the win probabilities p. The two Thurstone models, $\mathcal{T}_F$ and $\mathcal{T}_G$, are said to be *equivalent* if for every $n \geq 2$, they are equivalent for system $\mathcal{P}_{n,n}$.

Similarly, two Thurstone models $\mathcal{T}_F$ and $\mathcal{T}_G$ are said to be *equivalent for the system of pair comparisons* $\mathcal{P}_{n,2}$ if for every $p \in \mathcal{P}_{n,2}$ either, both $\mathcal{T}_F$ and $\mathcal{T}_G$ admit the win probabilities p, or neither $\mathcal{T}_F$ nor $\mathcal{T}_G$ admit the win probabilities p. The two Thurstone models, $\mathcal{T}_F$ and $\mathcal{T}_G$, are said to be *equivalent for pair comparisons* if for every $n \geq 2$, they are equivalent for system $\mathcal{P}_{n,2}$.

Two distributions F and G are said to be of the same *type* if there exist constants $a > 0$ and $b \in \mathbf{R}$ such that $F(x) = G(ax + b)$ for every $x \in \mathbf{R}$.

9.3.1 Conditions for Equivalence between Thurstone Models

There exist instances of different Thurstone models that have equivalent probabilities of ranking outcomes over a subset of alternatives. For example, in Section 9.2, we observed this to be the case for the probabilities of full rankings of pairs of alternatives according to the Bradley-Terry model. What is a necessary and sufficient condition for two Thurstone models to be equivalent with respect to pair comparisons or more generally for complete systems of win probabilities? This is the question studied in this section.

Equivalence of Thurstone Models for Pair Comparisons

A necessary and sufficient condition for two Thurstone models to be equivalent with respect to pair comparisons is given in the following theorem.

Theorem 9.11. *Two Thurstone models $\mathcal{T}_F$ and $\mathcal{T}_G$ are equivalent for pair comparisons if, and only if, their difference distributions satisfy*

$$D_F(x) = D_G(ax), \quad \text{for every } x \in \mathbf{R}$$

for some $a > 0$.

Proof. Since

$$p_{i,j} = \mathbf{Pr}[\varepsilon_j - \varepsilon_i \leq v_i - v_j] = D_F(v_i - v_j),$$

it follows that for any three pair comparison probabilities $p_{i,j}$, $p_{j,k}$, $p_{i,k}$ in a pair comparison system admitted by $\mathcal{T}_F$, we have

$$p_{i,j} = D_F(D_F^{-1}(p_{i,j}) + D_F^{-1}(p_{j,k})), \tag{9.33}$$

which is a triples function t_{D_F} (see Section 9.2.4).

The two models $\mathcal{T}_F$ and $\mathcal{T}_G$ are equivalent for pair comparisons if, and only if, they have the same triples functions, i.e.,

$$D_F(D_F^{-1}(p) + D_F^{-1}(q)) = D_G(D_G^{-1}(p) + D_G^{-1}(q)), \quad \text{for every } p, q \in (0, 1).$$

To solve this functional equation, let $x = D_F^{-1}(p)$ and $y = D_F^{-1}(q)$. Then,

$$D_G^{-1}(D_F(x + y)) = D_G^{-1}(D_F(x)) + D_G^{-1}(D_F(y)).$$

It follows that function $h(x) = D_G^{-1}(D_F(x))$ satisfies the Cauchy equation $h(x + y) = h(x) + h(y)$ for every $x, y \in \mathbf{R}$. Since h is continuous, by Theorem 11.16, the only solution is

$$D_G^{-1}(D_F(x)) = ax,$$

and thus, $D_F(x) = D_G(ax)$. Since $D_F(1) > 1/2$ because $D_F(0) = 1/2$ and D_F is strictly increasing by assumption, it follows that $a = D_G^{-1}(D_F(1)) > 0$. $\qquad\square$

The following corollary states two implications that we make use of later in this section.

Corollary 9.12. *If two Thurstone models $\mathcal{T}_F$ and $\mathcal{T}_G$ are equivalent for systems of win probabilities with three or more alternatives, then the following holds:*

(i) *They are equivalent for pair comparisons with any number of alternatives.*
(ii) *If $p \in \mathcal{P}_{n,n}$ is admitted by both models with the strength parameters $v_1, v_2, \ldots, v_n$ according to $\mathcal{T}_F$ and the strength parameters $u_1, u_2, \ldots, u_n$ according to $\mathcal{T}_G$ then*

$$u_i - u_j = a(v_i - v_j)$$

where a is a positive constant such that $D_F(x) = D_G(ax)$ for all $x \in \mathbf{R}$.

Proof. For the first item, note that equivalence for systems of three alternatives implies equivalence for pair comparisons for systems with three alternatives, which implies that the two models have the same triples functions. The proof of Theorem 9.11 implies pair comparison equivalence for any number of alternatives.

For the second item, note that pair comparison equivalence implies $D_F(x) = D_G(ax)$ for all $x \in \mathbf{R}$ for some $a > 0$. For $(p_{i,j}, p_{j,i})$, we have

$$p_{i,j} = D_F(v_i - v_j) = D_G(u_i - u_j).$$

It follows that

$$u_i - u_j = D_G^{-1}(p_{i,j}) = D_G^{-1}(D_F(v_i - v_j)) = a(v_i - v_j).$$

$\square$

Equivalence of Thurstone Models for Complete Comparisons

A necessary and sufficient condition for equivalence of two Thurstone models for systems of complete win probabilities is presented in the following theorem.

Theorem 9.13. *If two Thurstone models $\mathcal{T}_F$ and $\mathcal{T}_G$ are such that F and G are of the same type, then $\mathcal{T}_F$ is equivalent to $\mathcal{T}_G$. If $\mathcal{T}_F$ and $\mathcal{T}_G$ are equivalent for the complete win probabilities with three alternatives and the characteristic function of either F or G is never zero, then F and G are of the same type.*

For the proof of the converse implication asserted in the theorem, we need a lemma that we present first and then go on to prove the theorem. The lemma uses the concept of a characteristic function, which for a distribution function F is defined by

$$\psi_F(t) = \int_{\mathbf{R}} e^{itx} dF(x), \quad \text{for } t \in \mathbf{R}.$$

The real part and the imaginary parts of the characteristic function are given by

$$\text{Re}(\psi_F(t)) = \int_{\mathbf{R}} \cos(tx) \, dF(x) \text{ and } \text{Im}(\psi_F(t)) = \int_{\mathbf{R}} \sin(tx) \, dF(x),$$

where $\text{Re}(\psi_F(t))$ is an even function and $\text{Im}(\psi_F(t))$ is either an odd function and $\text{Im}(\psi_F(t)) \neq 0$ or $\text{Im}(\psi_F(t)) = 0$.

Lemma 9.14. *If two Thurstone models $\mathcal{T}_F$ and $\mathcal{T}_G$ are equivalent for $\mathcal{P}_{n,n}$ for every $n \geq 3$, the characteristic functions ψ_F and ψ_G of F and G, respectively, satisfy the equation*

$$\psi_G(t_1)\psi_G(t_2)\cdots\psi_G(t_{n-1})\psi_G\left(-\sum_{i=1}^{n-1} t_i\right)$$

$$= \psi_F(at_1)\psi_F(at_2)\cdots\psi_F(at_{n-1})\psi_F\left(-\sum_{i=1}^{n-1} at_i\right)$$

where a is a constant such that $D_F(x) = D_G(ax)$ for all $x \in \mathbf{R}$.

Proof. We prove the statement for the special case of three alternatives. The general case follows by the same arguments at the expense of some more cumbersome notation. Suppose that $\mathcal{T}_F$ and $\mathcal{T}_G$ are equivalent for complete win probabilities with three alternatives, and both admit an arbitrary $p \in \mathcal{P}_{3,3}$ with the strength parameters v_1, v_2, v_3 according to the model $\mathcal{T}_F$.

By Corollary 9.12, the strength parameters v_1', v_2', v_3' according to the model $\mathcal{T}_G$ satisfy

$$v_i' - v_j' = a(v_i - v_j),$$

where a is a positive constant such that $D_F(x) = D_G(ax)$ for all $x \in \mathbf{R}$.

Let $b_i = v_i + \varepsilon_i$, for $i = 1, 2, 3$, be the performances under the model $\mathcal{T}_F$ and $b_i' = v_i' + \varepsilon_i'$, for $i = 1, 2, 3$, be the performances under the model $\mathcal{T}_G$. Then,

$$p_{\{1,2,3\}}(1) = \mathbf{Pr}[\varepsilon_2 - \varepsilon_1 \leq v_1 - v_2, \varepsilon_3 - \varepsilon_1 \leq v_1 - v_3]$$

$$= \mathbf{Pr}[\varepsilon_2' - \varepsilon_1' \leq a(v_1 - v_2), \varepsilon_3' - \varepsilon_1' \leq a(v_1 - v_3)].$$

The last equation can be equivalently expressed as

$$J_F(x, y) = J_G(ax, ay), \quad \text{for } x, y \in \mathbf{R}$$

where

$$J_F(x, y) = \mathbf{Pr}[\varepsilon_2 - \varepsilon_1 \leq x, \varepsilon_3 - \varepsilon_1 \leq y] \text{ and } J_G(x, y),$$

$$= \mathbf{Pr}[\varepsilon_2' - \varepsilon_1' \leq x, \varepsilon_3' - \varepsilon_1' \leq y].$$

The proof follows by the following equations:

$$\psi_G(t_1)\psi_G(t_2)\psi_G(-(t_1 + t_2)) = \mathbf{E}[e^{it_1\varepsilon_2'}e^{it_1\varepsilon_3'}e^{-i(t_1+t_2)\varepsilon_1'}]$$

$$= \mathbf{E}[e^{i(t_1(\varepsilon_2'-\varepsilon_1')+t_2(\varepsilon_3'-\varepsilon_1'))}]$$

$$= \int_{\mathbf{R}}\int_{\mathbf{R}} e^{-i(t_1 x + t_2 y)}\, dJ_G(x, y)$$

$$= \int_{\mathbf{R}}\int_{\mathbf{R}} e^{-i(at_1 x' + at_2 y')}\, dJ_F(x', y')$$

$$= \mathbf{E}[e^{i(at_1(\varepsilon_2-\varepsilon_1)+at_2(\varepsilon_3-\varepsilon_1))}]$$

$$= \psi_F(t_1)\psi_F(at_2)\psi_F(-(at_1 + at_2)).$$

$\square$

Proof of Theorem 9.13. The first implication is easy to show as follows. Suppose that $\mathcal{T}_F$ admits the system of complete win probabilities $\mathcal{P}_{n,n}$ with the performances $b_i = v_i + \varepsilon_i$ for $i \in N$. Then,

$$
\begin{aligned}
p_S(i) &= \mathbf{Pr}[v_i + \varepsilon_i \geq v_j + \varepsilon_j, \text{ for all } j \in S] \\
&= \mathbf{Pr}[av_i + a\varepsilon_i + b \geq av_i + a\varepsilon_j + b, \text{ for all } j \in S] \\
&= \mathbf{Pr}[av_i + \tilde{\varepsilon}_i \geq av_j + \tilde{\varepsilon}_j, \text{ for all } j \in S]
\end{aligned}
$$

where

$$
\mathbf{Pr}[\tilde{\varepsilon}_i \leq x] = \mathbf{Pr}[a\varepsilon_i + b \leq x] = F\left(\frac{x-b}{a}\right) = G(x).
$$

Therefore, $\mathcal{P}_{n,n}$ is also admitted by Thurstone model $\mathcal{T}_G$ with the strength parameters $av_1, av_2, \ldots, av_n$.

The second implication can be shown as follows. Let $f(t)$ and $g(t)$ be the characteristic functions of F and G, respectively. By Lemma 9.14, for every $s, t \in \mathbf{R}$,

$$
g(s)g(t)g(-(s+t)) = f(as)f(at)f(-(as+at)). \tag{9.34}
$$

It suffices to show that it must hold that

$$
g(t) = e^{ict} f(at), \quad \text{for a constant } c \in \mathbf{R}. \tag{9.35}
$$

From (9.34) for $s = 0$, we have

$$
g(t)g(-t) = |g(t)|^2 = f(at)f(-at) = |f(at)|^2. \tag{9.36}
$$

If f satisfies $|f(t)|^2 > 0$ for all $t \in \mathbf{R}$, then so does g, and vice versa. Using the identity (9.36), we can rewrite (9.34) as

$$
\frac{g(s)}{f(as)} = \frac{g(t)}{f(at)} = \frac{g(s+t)}{f(as+at)}. \tag{9.37}
$$

Let

$$
h(x) = \frac{g(t)}{f(ax)}. \tag{9.38}
$$

Then, (9.34) corresponds to the following functional equation:

$$
h(s+t) = h(s)h(t). \tag{9.39}
$$

Using the notation $h(t) = h_1(t) + ih_2(t)$, we can write equation (9.39) as

$$
h_1(s)h_1(t) - h_2(s)h_2(t) = h_1(s+t) \tag{9.40}
$$

$$
h_1(s)h_2(t) + h_2(s)h_1(t) = h_2(s+t). \tag{9.41}
$$

From (9.38) and the fact that both f_1 and g_1 are even functions and each f_2 and g_2 is either an odd function or a constant equal to zero, it follows that h_1 is an even function and h_2 is either an odd function or a constant equal to zero. It follows that equation (9.40) is equivalent to the following well-known functional equation:

$$
h_1(s)h_1(t) + h_2(s)h_2(t) = h_1(t-s), \tag{9.42}
$$

which we discuss in more detail in Section 11.1.9. By Theorem 11.20, all the solutions to (9.42) such that h_1 is a continuous even function and h_2 is either a continuous odd function or a constant equal to zero are given by

$$h_1(t) = \cos(ct) \text{ and } h_2(t) = \sin(ct), \quad \text{for a constant } c \in \mathbf{R}. \tag{9.43}$$

By combining (9.38) and (9.43), we obtain equation (9.35) as claimed.   □

9.3.2 Relations between Thurstone and Luce's Models

We already observed that pair comparison probabilities according to Luce's choice model can be admitted by Thurstone models with distributions of the performances with distributions from different families of distributions. For example, the pair comparison probabilities according to the Bradley-Terry model are admitted by the Thurstone model $\mathcal{T}_F$ with F from the family of double-exponential distributions, as well by the Thurstone model $\mathcal{T}_G$ with G from the family of exponential distributions. This is because by Theorem 9.11, two Thurstone models are equivalent with respect to pair comparisons if, and only if, their difference distributions satisfy the condition asserted in the theorem, which may be satisfied by different families of distributions. On the other hand, two Thurstone models are equivalent with respect to the system of complete win probabilities if, and only if, they both belong to the double-exponential family of distributions as shown in the following theorem.

Theorem 9.15. *A Thurstone model $\mathcal{T}_F$ is equivalent to Luce's choice model for systems of complete win probabilities with three or more alternatives if, and only if, F is a double-exponential distribution, i.e.,*

$$F(x) = e^{-e^{-(ax+b)}} \text{ for } x \in \mathbf{R}, \text{ for some } a > 0 \text{ and } b \in \mathbf{R}.$$

Proof. For the direct part, suppose that a complete system $\{p_S \mid N\}$ is admitted by $\mathcal{T}_F$ for F a double-exponential distribution and the strength parameters $v_1, v_2, \ldots, v_n$. By Theorem 9.13, it suffices to consider only the particular case $a = 1$ and $b = 0$. Let $\theta_i = \exp(v_i)$ and $z_i = \exp(-\varepsilon_i)$; then z_i has the exponential distribution function. Then, we have for any $i \in S$ and $S \subseteq N$,

$$\begin{aligned} p_S(i) &= \mathbf{Pr}[v_i + \varepsilon_i \geq v_j + \varepsilon_j \text{ for all } j \in S] \\ &= \mathbf{Pr}[\theta_i/z_i \geq \theta_j/z_j \text{ for all } j \in S] \\ &= \mathbf{Pr}[z_i/\theta_i \leq z_j/\theta_j \text{ for all } j \in S] \\ &= \int_0^\infty \theta_i e^{-\theta_i z} \prod_{j \in S \setminus \{i\}} e^{-\theta_j z} \, dz \\ &= \frac{\theta_i}{\sum_{j \in S} \theta_j} \end{aligned}$$

which corresponds to Luce choice's model.

For the converse part, by Theorem 9.13, it suffices to show that for the double-exponential distribution with parameters $a = 1$ and $b = 0$, the characteristic function

$$\psi_F(t) = \Gamma(1 - it)$$

is such that $|\psi_F(t)| > 0$ for every $t \in \mathbf{R}$. This holds because

$$|\psi_F(t)|^2 = \Gamma(1 - it)\Gamma(1 + it) = \frac{it\pi}{\sin(it\pi)} = \frac{2\pi t}{e^{\pi t} - e^{-\pi t}}$$

which could be zero only at $t = 0$, but this is not true because $\psi_F(0) = 1$. □

9.3.3 Relations between Thurstone and Dawkins Models

The relation between a Thurstone model and a Dawkins choice model is such that there is a unique family of difference distributions for which there is equivalence between a Thurstone model and a Dawkins choice model for pair comparisons. On the other hand, no equivalence exists in the general case of systems of complete win probabilities with three alternatives.

Theorem 9.16. *A Thurstone model $\mathcal{T}_F$ is equivalent to Dawkins choice model for pair comparisons if, and only if, its difference distribution D_F is Laplace distribution*

$$D_F(x) = \begin{cases} \frac{1}{2}e^{ax}, & \text{if } x \le 0 \\ 1 - \frac{1}{2}e^{-ax}, & \text{if } x > 0 \end{cases} \tag{9.44}$$

for some constant $a > 0$.

Proof. It suffices to show that (9.44) implies the pair comparison probabilities of the Dawkins choice model:

$$p_{i,j} = 1 - 2p_{k,i}p_{j,k}$$

The uniqueness then follows by Theorem 9.11.

For any three alternatives i, k, j such that, without loss of generality, $p_{i,k}p_{k,j} \ge 1/2$, we have

$$p_{i,j} = D_F(v_i - v_k + v_k - v_j)$$

$$= 1 - \frac{1}{2}e^{-a(v_i - v_k)}e^{-(v_k - v_j)}$$

$$= 1 - 2\left(\frac{1}{2}e^{-a(v_i - v_k)}\right)\left(\frac{1}{2}e^{-a(v_k - v_j)}\right)$$

$$= 1 - 2p_{k,i}p_{j,k}.$$

□

For the complete system of win probabilities with three alternatives, the Dawkins choice model is not equivalent to any Thurstone model. To see this, suppose that alternative 1 is ranked higher than alternative 2, which is ranked higher than alternative 3. Therefore, for the threshold parameters of the Dawkins choice model, we have $\theta_1 > \theta_2 > \theta_3$ and for the strength parameters of Thurstone model, we have $v_1 > v_2 > v_3$.

For the Dawkins choice model, by (9.21) $p_{\{1,2,3\}}(3) = \theta_3/(3\theta_1)$ and $p_{\{1,3\}}(3) = \theta_3/(2\theta_1)$; hence,

$$p_{\{1,2,3\}}(3) = \frac{2}{3} p_{\{1,3\}}(3) \tag{9.45}$$

for every value $\theta_2 \in [\theta_3, \theta_1]$.

There exists no Thurstone model that would satisfy equation (9.45). Suppose that on the contrary there exists such a Thurstone model. Then,

$$p_{\{1,3\}}(3) = \mathbf{Pr}\,[v_3 + \varepsilon_3 \geq v_1 + \varepsilon_1] \tag{9.46}$$

and

$$p_{\{1,2,3\}}(3) = \mathbf{Pr}\,[v_3 + \varepsilon_3 \geq \max\{v_1 + \varepsilon_1, v_2 + \varepsilon_2\}]. \tag{9.47}$$

The right-hand side in equation (9.46) is independent of value v_2 and the right-hand side in equation (9.47) decreases in the value of the parameter v_2. This is in contradiction to equation (9.45).

9.4 Maximum Likelihood Estimation

In this section we consider maximum likelihood estimation (MLE) of parameters of a generalized linear model for pair comparisons. We shall establish necessary and sufficient conditions for the existence of a unique maximum likelihood estimate up to an additive constant. We shall also consider an iterative scheme for maximum likelihood estimation of parameters of the Bradley-Terry model and show that it converges to a maximum likelihood estimate from any initial value.

We consider a generalized linear model for pair comparisons specified by a difference function D and a vector of strength parameters $\mathbf{v} \in \mathbf{R}^n$. Given an observed matrix of wins $\mathbf{W} = (w_{i,j})$, the likelihood function is given by

$$L(\mathbf{v}) = \prod_{i,j \in N} \binom{m_{i,j}}{w_{i,j}} D(v_i - v_j)^{w_{i,j}} \tag{9.48}$$

where recall that $\mathbf{M} = (m_{i,j})$ is the matrix of the number of pair comparisons.

The log-likelihood function is equal to

$$\ell(\mathbf{v}) = \sum_{i,j \in N} w_{i,j} \log(D(v_i - v_j)) \tag{9.49}$$

up to an additive constant independent of parameter $\mathbf{v}$.

A vector of parameters $\mathbf{v} \in \mathbf{R}^n$ is a *maximum likelihood estimate* for the given generalized linear model if it maximizes the log-likelihood function (9.49).

For example, we may consider the log-likelihood function for the generalized linear model for pair comparisons with logistic difference function $D(x) = 1/(1 + \exp(-sx))$, for parameter $s > 0$. Using the change of parameters $\theta_i = \exp(sv_i)$, for

$i \in N$, we consider the log-likelihood function given by

$$\ell(\theta) = \sum_{i,j \in N} w_{i,j}[\log(\theta_i) - \log(\theta_i + \theta_j)]. \tag{9.50}$$

From the expression in (9.49), we observe that the log-likelihood function is *shift invariant*, meaning that for every vector of parameters $\mathbf{v} \in \mathbf{R}^n$, $\ell(\mathbf{v}) = \ell(\mathbf{v} + c)$ for all $c \in \mathbf{R}$. Hence, a maximum likelihood estimate may be unique only up to an additive constant. To show that the maximum likelihood estimate is unique up to an additive constant, without loss of generality, we fix the value of parameter v_1 to value 0 and consider the set of parameters $V = \{\mathbf{v} \in \mathbf{R}^n \mid v_1 = 0\}$.

9.4.1 Existence and Uniqueness

We first show that a necessary and sufficient condition for the log-likelihood function to be upper compact requires the matrix of wins to satisfy a certain property. We then show a necessary and sufficient condition for the log-likelihood function to be strictly concave, which requires the matrix of the number of pair comparisons and the difference function to satisfy certain properties. Given that the log-likelihood function is upper compact and strictly concave, there exists a unique maximum likelihood estimate of the vector of the strengths parameters up to an additive constant.

Upper Compactness of the Log-Likelihood Function

We first define the concepts of upper compactness of a function and irreducibility of a matrix.

Definition 9.17 (upper compact function). A function $f : \mathbf{R}^n \to \mathbf{R}$ is said to be *upper compact* if all its level sets are compact, i.e., for every $c \in \mathbf{R}$, the set $\mathcal{L}_c(f) = \{\mathbf{x} \in \mathbf{R}^n \mid f(\mathbf{x}) \geq c\}$ is compact. A set is compact if, and only if, it is *bounded* and *closed*.

The concept of an irreducible matrix is introduced in the following definition.

Definition 9.18 (irreducible non-negative matrix). Given a matrix $A \in \mathbf{R}_+^{n \times n}$, i and $j \in N = \{1, 2, \dots, n\}$ are said to *communicate* if there exists a sequence $i, i_1, i_2, \dots, i_{m-1}, j$ such that $a_{i,i_1} a_{i_1,i_2} \cdots a_{i_{m-1},j} > 0$. The matrix A is said to be *irreducible* if every i and $j \in N$ communicate.

Saying that a matrix A with non-negative elements is irreducible is equivalent to saying that for every possible partition of the set $N = \{1, 2, \dots, n\}$ into two non-empty sets S and $N \setminus S$, $a_{i,j} > 0$, for some $i \in S$ and $j \in N \setminus S$. For a matrix of wins $\mathbf{W}$, saying that the matrix is irreducible means that there exists no partition of alternatives into two non-empty sets such that none of the alternatives from either set won against every alternative from the other set.

Theorem 9.19. *The log-likelihood function given by (9.49) is upper compact if, and only if, the matrix of wins $\mathbf{W}$ is irreducible.*

Proof. We first show the direct part: if the log-likelihood function is upper compact, then the matrix of wins is irreducible. This is shown by contradiction by assuming that a matrix of wins is reducible and the log-likelihood function is upper compact. Since the matrix of wins is assumed to be reducible, there exists a partition of the set of alternatives into two non-empty sets S and $N \setminus S$ such that none of the alternatives in S ever won against any alternative in $N \setminus S$, i.e., $w_{i,j} = 0$, for all $i \in S$ and $j \in N \setminus S$. Under this assumption and (9.49), we have

$$\ell(\mathbf{v}) = \sum_{i,j \in S} w_{i,j} \log(D(v_i - v_j)) + \sum_{i,j \in N \setminus S} w_{i,j} \log(D(v_i - v_j))$$

$$+ \sum_{i \in N \setminus S, j \in S} w_{i,j} \log(D(v_i - v_j)). \tag{9.51}$$

Let $\mathbf{v} \in V$ and $c \in \mathbf{R}$ be such that $\mathbf{v} \in \mathcal{L}_c(\ell)$. Consider first the case when $1 \in S$. Define $\mathbf{v}^\delta \in V$ by $v_i^\delta = v_i$, for $i \in S$, and $v_i^\delta = v_i + \delta$, for $i \in N \setminus S$, and $\delta \geq 0$. From (9.51), note that $\ell(\mathbf{v}^\delta) \geq \ell(\mathbf{v})$ for every $\delta \geq 0$. Hence, $\mathbf{v}^\delta \in \mathcal{L}_c(\ell)$ for every $\delta \geq 0$. Combined with the fact that $\max_{i \in N} |v_i^\delta|$ can be made arbitrarily large by taking δ large enough, this shows that the set $\mathcal{L}_c(\ell)$ is unbounded, which is a contradiction to the assumption that ℓ is upper-compact. The same argument applies in the case when $1 \in N \setminus S$ by defining $\mathbf{v}^\delta \in V$ by $v_i^\delta = v_i - \delta$, for $i \in S$, and $v_i^\delta = v_i$, for $i \in N \setminus S$, for $\delta \geq 0$, and then again, it follows that the set $\mathcal{L}_c(\ell)$ is unbounded.

Conversely, we show that if the matrix of wins is irreducible, then the log-likelihood function is upper compact. This is shown by contradiction by assuming that the matrix of wins is irreducible and the log-likelihood function is not upper compact. Let $\mathbf{v} \in V$ and $c \in \mathbf{R}$ be such that $\mathbf{v} \in \mathcal{L}_c(\ell)$. Let $\mathbf{v}^1, \mathbf{v}^2, \ldots$ be a sequence in $\mathcal{L}_c(\ell)$ such that $\lim_{l \to \infty} v_i^l = -\infty$ and $\lim_{l \to \infty} v_j^l \in \mathbf{R}$, for some $i \neq j$. By the assumption that the matrix of wins is irreducible, there exits a path $i, i_1, \ldots, i_k, j$ such that $w_{i,i_1} w_{i_1,i_2} \cdots w_{i_k,j} > 0$. It follows that there exists a and b on this path such that $w_{a,b} > 0$, $\lim_{l \to \infty} v_a^l = -\infty$ and $\lim_{l \to \infty} v_b^l \in \mathbf{R}$. From (9.49), observe that

$$\ell(\mathbf{x}) \leq w_{a,b} \log(D(x_a - x_b)), \quad \text{for every } \mathbf{x} \in V.$$

From this, it follows that $\lim_{l \to \infty} \ell(\mathbf{v}^l) = -\infty$, which implies that the sequence $\mathbf{v}^1, \mathbf{v}^2, \ldots$ is not in $\mathcal{L}_c(\ell)$; thus there is a contradiction. $\qquad \square$

Example 9.20 (irreducible matrix of wins). Consider the generalized linear model for pair comparisons that correspond to the Bradley-Terry model and the matrix of wins:

$$\mathbf{W} = \begin{pmatrix} 0 & 1 & 2 \\ 1 & 0 & 2 \\ 1 & 2 & 0 \end{pmatrix}.$$

This matrix is clearly irreducible and thus the log-likelihood function is upper compact. Figure 9.8 illustrates this for a particular level set.

Example 9.21 (non-irreducible matrix of wins). Consider the generalized linear model for pair comparisons that correspond to the Bradley-Terry model and the

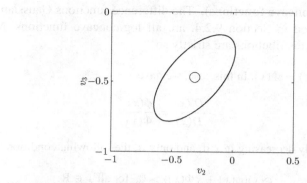

Figure 9.8. A compact level set of the log-likelihood function in Example 9.20.

matrix of wins:

$$\mathbf{W} = \begin{pmatrix} 0 & 1 & 2 \\ 1 & 0 & 2 \\ 0 & 0 & 0 \end{pmatrix}.$$

This matrix is clearly not irreducible and thus the log-likelihood function is not upper compact. Figure 9.9 illustrates this for a particular level set.

Strict Concavity of the Log-Likelihood Function

We identify a necessary and sufficient condition for the log-likelihood function to be strictly concave, which involves a requirement that the difference function is log-concave. The concepts of strictly concave and log-concave functions are defined in Section 11.1.5, which we quickly restate here.

A continuously differentiable function f is log-concave if, and only if, $\lambda(x) = f'(x)/f(x)$ is a decreasing function in x, and is *strictly* log-concave if $\lambda(x)$ is a strictly decreasing function in x. For a continuously differentiable distribution function F that satisfies $F(-x) + F(x) = 1$ for every $x \in \mathbf{R}$, saying that F is log-concave is equivalent to saying that F has an increasing hazard rate function, i.e., $h(x) = F'(x)/(1 - F(x))$ is an increasing function.

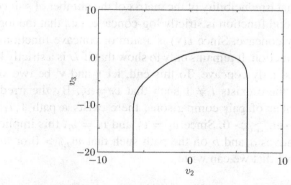

Figure 9.9. A non-compact level set of the log-likelihood function in Example 9.21.

Example 9.22 (log-concave functions). The difference functions Gaussian, logistic, and Laplace, discussed in Section 9.2.4, are all log-concave functions. Moreover, Gaussian and logistic distributions are strictly so.

(i) *Gaussian*: $D(x) = \Phi(x)$. In this case, we have

$$\frac{D'(x)}{D(x)} = \frac{\phi(x)}{\Phi(x)}$$

which is strictly decreasing in x if, and only if, the following condition holds:

$$\phi(x)(\phi(x) + x\Phi(x)) > 0, \text{ for all } x \in \mathbf{R}.$$

The last condition holds because $\phi(x) > 0$ and $\phi(x) + x\Phi(x) > 0$, where the latter inequality follows by noting that $\phi(x) + x\Phi(x)$ has derivative $\Phi(x) > 0$ and is equal to 0 asymptotically as x goes to $-\infty$.

(ii) *Logistic*: $D(x) = 1/(1 + e^{-x})$. In this case, we have

$$\frac{D'(x)}{D(x)} = \frac{1}{1 + e^x}$$

which is strictly decreasing in x.

(iii) *Laplace*: $D(x) = e^x/2$, for $x < 0$, and $D(x) = 1 - e^{-x}/2$, for $x \geq 0$. In this case, we have

$$\frac{D'(x)}{D(x)} = \begin{cases} 1, & \text{if } x < 0 \\ \frac{1}{2e^x - 1}, & \text{if } x \geq 0 \end{cases}$$

which is decreasing in x.

In the next theorem we establish a necessary and sufficient condition for the likelihood function to be strictly log-concave.

Theorem 9.23. *Suppose that the difference function D is strictly log-concave. Then, the log-likelihood function is strictly concave if, and only if, the matrix of the number of pair comparisons is irreducible.*

Proof. We first show that irreducibility of the matrix of the number of pair comparisons implies that the likelihood function is strictly log-concave, i.e., that the log-likelihood function $\ell(\mathbf{v})$ is strictly concave. Since $\ell(\mathbf{v})$ is a sum of concave functions, it follows that $\ell(\mathbf{v})$ is a concave function. It remains only to show that if D is a strictly log-concave function, then $\ell(\mathbf{v})$ is strictly concave. To this end, let $\mathbf{v}$ and $\mathbf{v}'$ be two vectors in V such that $\mathbf{v} \neq \mathbf{v}'$, i.e., there exists $i \neq 1$ such that $v_i \neq v_i'$. By the irreducibility of the matrix of the number of pair comparisons, there exists a path $1, i_1, \ldots, i_{k-1}, i$ such that $m_{1,i_1} m_{i_1,i_2} \cdots m_{i_{k-1},i} > 0$. Since $v_1 = v_1'$ and $v_i \neq v_i'$, this implies that there exists a pair of alternatives a and b on the path such that $w_{a,b} > 0$ or $w_{b,a} > 0$ and $v_a - v_b \neq v_a' - v_b'$. Note that we can write

$$\ell(\mathbf{v}) = \ell_{a,b}(\mathbf{v}) + \ell_{-(a,b)}(\mathbf{v})$$

where

$$\ell_{a,b}(\mathbf{v}) = w_{a,b} \log(D(v_a - v_b)) + w_{b,a} \log(D(v_b - v_a))$$

$$\ell_{-(a,b)}(\mathbf{v}) = \sum_{(i,j) \neq (a,b),(b,a)} w_{i,j} \log(D(v_i - v_j)).$$

From this note that $\ell_{a,b}$ is strictly concave, and $\ell_{-(a,b)}(\mathbf{v})$ is concave, which combined with the fact that $v_a - v_b \neq v_a' - v_b'$, implies that $\ell(\mathbf{v})$ is strictly concave.

Conversely, we show that strict log-concavity of the likelihood function implies irreducibility of the matrix of the number of pair comparisons. To contradict, suppose that the likelihood function is strictly log-concave and the matrix of the number of pair comparisons is reducible. Then, there exists a partition of the set of alternatives into two non-empty sets S and $N \setminus S$ such that $m_{i,j} = 0$, for every $i \in S$ and $j \in N \setminus S$,

$$\ell(\mathbf{v}) = \sum_{i \in S, j \in S} w_{i,j} \log(D(v_i - v_j)) + \sum_{i \in N \setminus S, j \in N \setminus S} w_{i,j} \log(D(v_i - v_j)), \quad \text{for } \mathbf{v} \in V.$$

$$(9.52)$$

Without loss of generality suppose that alternative 1 is an element of the set S. Let $\mathbf{v}$ be an arbitrary vector of strengths in V, and define vector $\mathbf{z} \in \mathbf{R}^n$ as follows: $z_i = 0$ for $i \in S$, and $z_i = c$ for $i \in N \setminus S$, for $c > 0$. Notice that $\mathbf{v} + \mathbf{z} \in V$. From (9.52), observe that

$$\ell(\mathbf{v}) = \ell(\mathbf{v} + \alpha \mathbf{z}) \text{ for all } 0 \leq \alpha \leq 1. \tag{9.53}$$

This contradicts the assumption that function ℓ is strictly concave. $\qquad\square$

The irreducibility of the matrix of the number of pair comparisons is equivalent to saying that for every partitioning of the set of alternatives into two non-empty sets, there exists a pair of alternatives in different such sets that competed against each other at least once. Since irreducibility of the matrix of wins $\mathbf{W}$ implies irreducibility of the matrix of the number of pair comparisons $\mathbf{M} = \mathbf{W} + \mathbf{W}^T$, the following corollary holds.

Corollary 9.24. *If the matrix of wins is irreducible and the difference function D is strictly log-concave, then the log-likelihood function is both upper compact and strictly concave.*

9.4.2 Necessary and Sufficient MLE Conditions

We identify a necessary and sufficient condition for a vector of parameters of a generalized linear model to be a maximum likelihood estimate in the following theorem.

Theorem 9.25. *Suppose that the difference function D is strictly log-concave and the matrix of wins is irreducible. Then, there exists a unique maximum likelihood estimate $\hat{\mathbf{v}}$ in $V = \{\mathbf{v} \in \mathbf{R}^n \mid v_1 = 0\}$, which is the solution of the following system of equations*

$$\sum_{j \in N} w_{i,j} \psi(\hat{v}_i - \hat{v}_j) = \sum_{j \in N} m_{i,j} \psi(\hat{v}_i - \hat{v}_j) D(\hat{v}_i - \hat{v}_j), \quad \text{for } i \in N$$

where

$$\psi(x) = \frac{D'(x)}{D(x)(1 - D(x))}, \quad for\ x \in \mathbf{R}.$$

Proof. From the expression of the log-likelihood function in (9.49), a sufficient condition is that D is log-concave. A necessary condition is that $\mathbf{v}$ is such that for the log-likelihood function given in (9.49), $\partial \ell(\mathbf{v})/\partial v_i = 0$ for all $i \in N$, which is equivalent to the condition asserted in the theorem. $\square$

For the particular case of a generalized linear model for pair comparisons that corresponds to the Bradley-Terry model, we have the following corollary.

Corollary 9.26 (logistic). *Consider the generalized linear model with $D(x) = 1/(1 + e^{-x})$ and $\psi(x) = 1$ for $x \in \mathbf{R}$. Then, the maximum likelihood estimate $\hat{\mathbf{v}} \in V$ is a unique solution of the following system of equations along with the condition $\hat{v}_1 = 0$:*

$$w_i = \sum_{j \in N} m_{i,j} \frac{e^{\hat{v}_i}}{e^{\hat{v}_i} + e^{\hat{v}_j}}, \quad for\ i \in N. \tag{9.54}$$

We observe that for the case of the Bradley-Terry model, a sufficient statistic for computing the maximum likelihood estimate of the model parameters is the number of wins for each alternative in comparisons with all other alternatives (assuming that the number of comparisons for each pair is a known parameter). In other words, for a given matrix of wins $\mathbf{W}$, a sufficient statistic for computing the maximum likelihood estimate of the model parameters are the row sums of the matrix of wins $\mathbf{W}$, i.e., $w_i = \sum_{j \in N} w_{i,j}$ for $i \in N$. From Corollary 9.26, we observe that for the Bradley-Terry model with parameters $\theta_1, \theta_2, \ldots, \theta_n$, the maximum likelihood estimate $\hat{\theta}_1, \hat{\theta}_2, \ldots, \hat{\theta}_n$ of the parameters is the unique solution (up to a multiplicative constant) of the system of equations:

$$w_i = \sum_{j \in N} m_{i,j} \frac{\hat{\theta}_i}{\hat{\theta}_i + \hat{\theta}_j} \quad for\ i \in N. \tag{9.55}$$

9.4.3 Iterative Method for the Bradley-Terry Model

In this section we consider an iterative method for computing a maximum likelihood estimate of the Bradley-Terry model parameters given as input a matrix of the number of wins. Specifically, we establish convergence of this iterative method to a maximum likelihood estimate from any initial value.

Since a maximum likelihood estimate of the Bradley-Terry model parameters is a fixed point of equation (9.55), it is natural to consider the following iterative method: given an arbitrary initial value $\hat{\theta}(0) \in \mathbf{R}_+^n$ such that $\sum_{i \in N} \hat{\theta}_i(0) > 0$, we recursively define, for $t = 0, 1, \ldots$,

$$\hat{\theta}_i(t + 1) = \frac{w_i}{\sum_{j \in N} \frac{m_{i,j}}{\hat{\theta}_i(t) + \hat{\theta}_j(t)}}, \quad for\ i \in N. \tag{9.56}$$

This is a gradient-ascend iterative scheme that we explain as follows. The gradient of the log-likelihood function has the components

$$\frac{\partial}{\partial \theta_i} \ell(\theta) = \frac{w_i}{\theta_i} - \sum_{j \in N} \frac{m_{i,j}}{\theta_i + \theta_j}, \quad \text{for } i \in N. \tag{9.57}$$

Using (9.57), the iterative scheme in (9.56) can be equivalently written as

$$\hat{\theta}_i(t+1) = \hat{\theta}_i(t) + \frac{\hat{\theta}_i(t)}{\sum_{j \in N} \frac{m_{i,j}}{\hat{\theta}_i(t) + \hat{\theta}_j(t)}} \frac{\partial}{\partial \theta_i} \ell(\hat{\theta}(t)) \quad \text{for } i \in N, \tag{9.58}$$

which is a gradient-ascend iterative scheme. Obviously, every point $\theta \in \mathbf{R}_+^n$ such that $\partial \ell(\theta)/\partial \theta_i = 0$ for every $i \in N$, i.e., θ is a maximum likelihood estimate, is a fixed point of the iterative system of equations (9.58). The following theorem establishes convergence to the maximum likelihood estimate from any initial point.

Theorem 9.27. *Suppose that the number of pair comparisons matrix is irreducible. Then, for any initial value $\hat{\theta}(0) \in \mathbf{R}_+^n$ such that $\sum_{i \in N} \hat{\theta}_i(0) > 0$, the sequence $\hat{\theta}(0), \hat{\theta}(1), \ldots$ defined by the iterative system of equations (9.56) converges to a unique limit point that corresponds to a unique maximum likelihood estimate (up to a multiplicative constant).*

Proof. The proof follows by showing that along any sequence generated by the iterative method (9.56), the value of the log-likelihood function is strictly increasing at any point that is not a fixed point of the system of equations (9.55) and it remains unchanged at any point that is a fixed point of the system of equations (9.55). This, along with the facts that the log-likelihood function is strictly concave and (9.55) is a necessary and sufficient condition for a point $\hat{\theta}$ to be a maximizer of the log-likelihood function, implies convergence to a unique limit point, which corresponds to the maximum likelihood estimate, for any initial point.

We need to show that for any initial point $\hat{\theta}(0) \in \mathbf{R}_+^n$, the sequence $\hat{\theta}(0), \hat{\theta}(1), \ldots$ defined by the iterative method (9.56) satisfies

$$\ell(\hat{\theta}(t+1)) - \ell(\hat{\theta}(t)) \geq 0, \quad \text{for every } t \geq 0 \tag{9.59}$$

where the equality holds only if $\hat{\theta}(t)$ is a fixed point of the system of equations (9.55).

Let us define the following family of functions:

$$\ell_{\mathbf{x}}(\theta) = \sum_{i,j \in N} w_{i,j} \left(\log(\theta_i) - \log(x_i + x_j) + 1 - \frac{\theta_i + \theta_j}{x_i + x_j} \right), \quad \text{for } \theta \in \mathbf{R}_+^n \tag{9.60}$$

where $\mathbf{x} = (x_1, x_2, \ldots, x_n)$ is a parameter with value in $\mathbf{R}_+^n$.

From (9.60), note that $\hat{\theta}(t+1)$ defined by the iterative method in (9.56) maximizes the value of function $\ell_{\hat{\theta}(t)}(\vartheta)$ over $\vartheta \in \mathbf{R}_+^n$. Hence, we have

$$\ell_{\hat{\theta}(t)}(\hat{\theta}(t+1)) \geq \ell_{\hat{\theta}(t)}(\hat{\theta}(t)),$$

which implies

$$\ell(\hat{\theta}(t+1)) \geq \ell(\hat{\theta}(t)).$$

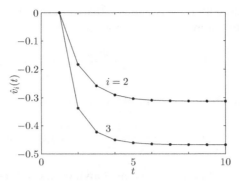

Figure 9.10. Convergence of the iterative method for computing the maximum likelihood estimate of the Bradley-Terry model parameters for the matrix of wins as in Example 9.20.

From the definition of the log-likelihood function in (9.50) and the fact that $\log(x) \leq x - 1$, for all $x \geq 0$, we have the following inequality:

$$\ell(\theta) \geq \ell_{\mathbf{x}}(\theta), \text{ for every } \theta \in \mathbf{R}_+^n \text{ and } \mathbf{x} \in \mathbf{R}_+^n \tag{9.61}$$

where the equality holds only if $\theta = \mathbf{x}$, in which case $\ell(\theta) = \ell_\theta(\theta)$. It follows that for every θ' and $\theta \in \mathbf{R}_+^n$ such that $\ell_\theta(\theta') \geq \ell_\theta(\theta)$, we have

$$\ell(\theta') \geq \ell_\theta(\theta') \geq \ell_\theta(\theta) = \ell(\theta),$$

which shows that $\ell_\theta(\theta') \geq \ell_\theta(\theta)$ implies $\ell(\theta') \geq \ell(\theta)$. $\qquad\qquad\square$

We illustrate the convergence of the iterative method (9.56) for a particular instance of the matrix of wins in the following example.

Example 9.28. Consider the generalized linear model for pair comparisons that corresponds to the Bradley-Terry model and the matrix of wins defined in Example 9.20. Since the given matrix of wins is irreducible and the underlying generalized linear model has the difference function D that is strictly log-concave, by Corollary 9.24, the log-likelihood function is strictly concave, and, hence, there is a unique maximum likelihood estimate of the vector of parameters $\mathbf{v}$ up to an additive constant.

We compute the maximum likelihood estimate of the vector of parameters $\mathbf{v}$ using the iterative method (9.56) as follows. First, we compute $\hat{\theta}(t) = (\hat{\theta}_1(t), \hat{\theta}_2(t), \hat{\theta}_3(t))$ for $t \geq 1$, using the iterative method (9.56), for a given initial point $(\hat{\theta}_1(0), \hat{\theta}_2(0), \hat{\theta}_3(0))$, which in this example we assume to be equal to $(1, 1, 1)$. Then, we use a change of parameters and normalization to obtain $(\hat{v}_1(t), \hat{v}_2(t), \hat{v}_3(t)) = (0, \log(\hat{\theta}_2(t)/\hat{\theta}_1(t)), \log(\hat{\theta}_3(t)/\hat{\theta}_1(t)))$, which is shown in Figure 9.10.

9.5 Bayesian Inference

In the framework of Bayesian inference, given a probabilistic model, a subset of the unknown parameters of the model are assumed to be random variables according to a prior distribution, and the inference is based on computing the posterior distribution of these random variables conditional on the observed data. Such variables can be either *observable*, meaning that their values can be observed from the given data, or *latent* (or hidden), meaning that their values cannot be directly observable from the given data. In the concrete context of ranking a set of alternatives, the observed data are a sequence of partial rankings over subsets of the alternatives. For example, each partial ranking may represent the outcome in a contest among the players who participated in it. We first discuss Bayesian inference for pair comparisons according to a generalized Thurstone model and then discuss how the framework applies to the more general setting of general comparisons.

Suppose that for a set of alternatives $N = \{1, 2, \ldots, n\}$, observations are given of full rankings $\mathbf{r} = (r_1, r_2, \ldots, r_m)$ of the respective pairs of alternatives $S = ((i_1, j_1), (i_2, j_2), \ldots, (i_m, j_m))$. Consider a generalized Thurstone model with the vector of strengths $\mathbf{v} = (v_1, v_2, \ldots, v_n)$ according to which a sequence of full rankings $R = (R_1, R_2, \ldots, R_m)$ of respective pairs of alternatives S is generated such that each full ranking R_t is in decreasing order of individual performances $b_{t,i_t} = v_{i_t} + \epsilon_{t,i_t}$ and $b_{t,j_t} = v_{j_t} + \epsilon_{t,j_t}$, where ϵ_{t,i_t} and ϵ_{t,j_t} are independent random variables from given parametric families of distributions. For concreteness, we consider Thurstone Type V model as an example, under which $\epsilon_{t,k}$ are normal random variables with mean zero and variance β^2.

The vector of strengths $\mathbf{v} = (v_1, v_2, \ldots, v_n)$ is assumed to be a latent variable with a prior density function $f_0(\mathbf{x}; \theta)$. In the design of rating systems it is common to assume a product-form prior density function $f_0(\mathbf{x}; \theta) = f_0(x_1; \theta_1) f_0(x_2; \theta_2) \cdots f_0(x_n; \theta_n)$, for $\theta = (\theta_1, \theta_2, \ldots, \theta_n)$. Specifically, it is common to assume that the prior distribution is such that individual strengths are independent Gaussian random variables with means and variances μ_i and σ_i^2 for $i \in N$.

The Bayesian inference of the strengths of alternatives is based on computing the univariate-marginal distributions of the posterior joint distribution of the strengths of alternatives conditional on the observed full rankings $\mathbf{r}$. This posterior joint distribution is given by Bayes's formula:

$$f(\mathbf{x} \mid R = \mathbf{r}) = \frac{\Pr[R = \mathbf{r} \mid \mathbf{v} = \mathbf{x}] f_0(\mathbf{x}; \theta)}{\Pr[R = \mathbf{r}]}. \tag{9.62}$$

In the last expression, the term $\Pr[R = \mathbf{r}]$ is just a normalizing constant of the joint posterior distribution. The term $\Pr[R = \mathbf{r} \mid \mathbf{v} = \mathbf{x}]$ is the likelihood of the observed set of full rankings $\mathbf{r}$ according to the given model conditional on the strengths of alternatives being $\mathbf{x} = (x_1, x_2, \ldots, x_n)$. Since the model assumes that full rankings between pairs of alternatives are independent conditional on the strengths of alternatives, we have

$$\Pr[R = \mathbf{r} \mid \mathbf{v} = \mathbf{x}] = \prod_{t=1}^{m} \Pr[R_t = r_t \mid v_{i_t} = x_{i_t}, v_{j_t} = x_{j_t}]. \tag{9.63}$$

where

$$\Pr[R_t = (1, 2) \mid v_{i_t} = x_{i_t}, v_{j_t} = x_{j_t}] = 1 - \Pr[R_t = (2, 1) \mid v_{i_t} = x_{i_t}, v_{j_t} = x_{j_t}]$$

$$= p_{i_t, j_t}(x_{i_t}, x_{j_t})$$

and

$$p_{i_t, j_t}(x_{i_t}, x_{j_t}) = \mathbf{Pr}[b_{t,i_t} > b_{t,j_t} \mid v_{i_t} = x_{i_t}, v_{j_t} = x_{j_t}]$$
$$= \mathbf{Pr}[x_{i_t} + \varepsilon_{t,i_t} > x_{j_t} + \varepsilon_{t,j_t} \mid v_{i_t} = x_{i_t}, v_{j_t} = x_{j_t}]$$
$$= \mathbf{Pr}[\varepsilon_{t,j_t} - \varepsilon_{t,i_t} < x_{i_t} - x_{j_t}].$$

In particular, for the Thurstone Type V model, $p_{i,j}(x, y) = \Phi((x - y)/(\sqrt{2}\beta))$. Notice that (9.63) can be equivalently written as

$$\mathbf{Pr}[R = \mathbf{r} \mid \mathbf{v} = \mathbf{x}] = \prod_{i<j} p_{i,j}(x_i, x_j)^{w_{i,j}(\mathbf{r})} (1 - p_{i,j}(x_i, x_j))^{m_{i,j}(\mathbf{r}) - w_{i,j}(\mathbf{r})}$$

where $w_{i,j}(\mathbf{r})$ is the number of full rankings in $\mathbf{r}$ for the pair of alternatives (i, j) such that $i \succ j$, and $m_{i,j}(\mathbf{r})$ is the number of full rankings in $\mathbf{r}$ for the pair of alternatives (i, j).

Example 9.29 (Gaussian product-form prior). Suppose that the observations of full rankings given by $\mathbf{r}$ are for a pair of alternatives, say alternative 1 and alternative 2, with the prior distribution of their strengths according to independent Gaussian random variables with means μ_1 and μ_2 and variances σ_1^2 and σ_2^2. For the Thurstone Type V model, the posterior joint density function of the strengths (v_1, v_2) is given by

$$f(x_1, x_2 \mid R = \mathbf{r}) \propto \Phi\left(\frac{x_1 - x_2}{\sqrt{2}\beta}\right)^{w_{1,2}(\mathbf{r})} \left(1 - \Phi\left(\frac{x_1 - x_2}{\sqrt{2}\beta}\right)\right)^{m_{1,2}(\mathbf{r}) - w_{1,2}(\mathbf{r})}$$
$$\times \phi\left(\frac{x_1 - \mu_1}{\sigma_1}\right) \phi\left(\frac{x_2 - \mu_2}{\sigma_2}\right).$$

We note two observations from the last example. First, the posterior joint distribution is not of a product form even though the prior distribution is of a product form. This implies that to compute a posterior univariate marginal distribution of the strength of an alternative, one needs to integrate the given posterior joint distribution over the values of the strengths of other alternatives. Second, the posterior joint density is not a Gaussian density even though the prior is a Gaussian density. This means that, in general, to represent the posterior distribution with a distribution from a specific family of distributions, one needs to use approximations.

9.5.1 Approximating the Posterior by a Gaussian Distribution

One way to approximate a distribution $p(x)$ by another distribution $q(x)$ from a given family of distributions Q is to choose a distribution q^* in Q that minimizes a given loss function $d(p, q)$, i.e., choose q^* such that $d(p, q^*) \le \min_{q \in Q} d(p, q)$. For example, one choice of a loss function is the Kullback-Leibler divergence defined by

$$D(p \parallel q) = \int_{-\infty}^{\infty} p(x) \log\left(\frac{p(x)}{q(x)}\right) dx.$$

The following theorem characterizes distributions that minimize the Kullback-Leibler divergence over the family of distributions Q that correspond to Gaussian distributions on $\mathbf{R}$.

Theorem 9.30 (matching moments). *Suppose that Q is the family of Gaussian distributions; then for every distribution $p(x)$, the Kullback-Leibler divergence is minimized by a Gaussian distribution $q^*(x)$ with the mean and the variance equal to the mean and the variance of the distribution $p(x)$, i.e.,*

$$\mu = \int_{-\infty}^{\infty} x p(x)\, dx \text{ and } \sigma^2 = \int_{-\infty}^{\infty} (x - \mu)^2 p(x)\, dx.$$

Proof. The family of Gaussian distributions Q contains the family of density functions $q(x) = \exp(-(x - \mu)^2/(2\sigma^2))/(\sqrt{2\pi}\sigma)$, for $-\infty < \mu < \infty$ and $\sigma \geq 0$. For $q \in Q$ with mean μ and variance σ^2, we have

$$D(p \parallel q) = \text{const} + \int_{-\infty}^{\infty} \left(\frac{(x - \mu)^2}{2\sigma^2} + \log(\sigma) \right) dx := d(\mu, \sigma).$$

From the first-order optimality conditions $\partial d(\mu, \sigma)/\partial \mu = 0$ and $\partial d(\mu, \sigma)/\partial \sigma = 0$, we obtain $\mu = \int_{-\infty}^{\infty} x p(x) dx$ and $\sigma^2 = \int_{-\infty}^{\infty} (x - \mu)^2 p(x) dx$, respectively. $\square$

Pair Comparisons with Win-or-Lose Outcomes

We consider approximation of the posterior univariate marginal distributions of strengths latent variables with Gaussian distributions for pair comparisons, which is optimal with respect to minimizing the Kullback-Leibler divergence over the family of Gaussian distributions. Consider a pair of alternatives (i, j) and suppose that a full ranking r is given for the given pair of alternatives. We admit the Thurstone Type V model according to which the two alternatives have respective strengths v_i and v_j and individual performances b_i and b_j according to two independent Gaussian random variables with respective means v_i and v_j and variances equal to β^2. The strengths of the alternatives are assumed to be latent variables with prior distribution according to which v_i and v_j are independent Gaussian random variables with respective means μ_i and μ_j and variances σ_i^2 and σ_j^2. The posterior joint distribution of the strengths is given in Example 9.29 where $m_{i,j}(r) = 1$ because the input is a single full ranking, and either $w_{i,j}(r) = 1$ if the given full ranking r is such that alternative i is ranked higher than j, and $w_{i,j}(r) = 0$, otherwise. The posterior univariate distributions of the strengths are not Gaussian so we approximate them with Gaussian distributions using the method of matching moments.

The posterior means and variances of the strengths of the alternatives are given as follows. Let $d_{i,j}$ be the ratio of the difference of the prior means of the strengths of alternatives i and j and the standard deviation of the difference of their performances, i.e., $d_{i,j} = (\mu_i - \mu_j)/\sigma_{i,j}$ where $\sigma_{i,j}^2 := \sigma_i^2 + \sigma_j^2 + 2\beta^2$. The posterior mean and variance of the strength of alternative i are given by the following mappings:

$$\mu_i \leftarrow \mu_i + \frac{\sigma_i^2}{\sigma_{i,j}} g(d_{i,j}, w_{i,j}) \tag{9.64}$$

$$\sigma_i^2 \leftarrow \sigma_i^2 \left(1 - \frac{\sigma_i^2}{\sigma_{i,j}^2} h(d_{i,j}, w_{i,j})\right) \tag{9.65}$$

where

$$g(d, w) = w\frac{\phi(d)}{\Phi(d)} - (1 - w)\frac{\phi(d)}{1 - \Phi(d)}$$

$$h(d, w) = w\frac{\phi(d)(\phi(d) + d\Phi(d))}{\Phi(d)^2} + (1 - w)\frac{\phi(d)(\phi(d) - d(1 - \Phi(d)))}{(1 - \Phi(d))^2}$$

and those for alternative j are given by analogous mappings obtained by swapping i and j in the last equations.

The expressions in (9.64) and (9.65) follow by computing the expected value and variance of the strength of an alternative conditional on the observed full ranking, which we explain as follows. Without loss of generality, assume that the input full ranking r is such that alternative i is ranked higher than alternative j, and consider the posterior expected value and variance of the strength of this alternative. According to the assumed model this corresponds to conditioning on the event $b_i - b_j > 0$. By Bayes's rule, the posterior expected value of the strength of alternative i is given by

$$\mathbf{E}[v_i \mid b_i - b_j > 0] = \frac{\mathbf{E}[v_i \mathbf{1}(b_i - b_j > 0)]}{\mathbf{Pr}[b_i - b_j > 0]}.$$

Under the assumed model, individual performances are random variables of the form $b_i = v_i + \varepsilon_i$ and $b_j = v_j + \varepsilon_j$ where $v_i, \epsilon_i, v_j,$ and ϵ_j are independent Gaussian random variables $v_i \sim f(\cdot; \mu_i, \sigma_i^2)$, $\varepsilon_i \sim f(\cdot; 0, \beta^2)$, $v_j \sim f(\cdot; \mu_j, \sigma_j^2)$, and $\varepsilon_j \sim f(\cdot; 0, \beta^2)$, respectively. We can write

$$\mathbf{E}[v_i \mathbf{1}(b_i - b_j > 0)] = \mathbf{E}[v_i \mathbf{1}(v_i - z > 0)]$$

where v_i and z are two independent Gaussian random variables $v_i \sim f(\cdot; \mu_i, \sigma_i^2)$ and $z \sim f(\cdot; \mu_j, \sigma_j^2 + 2\beta^2)$. By using the formula (11.52), we obtain

$$\mathbf{E}[v_i \mathbf{1}(b_i - b_j > 0)] = \mu_i + \frac{\sigma_i^2}{\sigma_{i,j}} \frac{\phi(d_{i,j})}{\Phi(d_{i,j})}.$$

This shows that the posterior expected value is according to the mapping (9.64) conditional on the observation that alternative i is ranked higher than alternative j. The other case follows by the same arguments. The posterior variance of the strength of an alternative follows by the same arguments and by making use of the formula (11.53).

We next discuss the updates of the mean and variance parameters given by (9.64) and (9.65) conditional on the observed full ranking of the two alternatives. Intuitively, the posterior mean strength is updated by incrementing the prior mean strength of the winner and decrementing the prior mean strength of the loser. The more unexpected the observed full ranking is with respect to the prior distribution, the higher the absolute value of the change. See the left graph in Figure 9.11. If, according to the prior distribution, an alternative is less likely to win, its posterior mean strength is incremented for a larger absolute amount in the event of winning; than it is decremented in the event of losing. Similarly, if according to the prior distribution, an alternative is more likely to win, then the update is for a larger absolute value in the event of this alternative losing. If an alternative wins against the other alternative, then the increment of its mean strength is for a larger value in the event of winning against a stronger alternative. Similarly, if an alternative loses, then the decrement of his or her mean strength is a larger value in the event of losing against a weaker alternative. The change of the mean strength is scaled with a factor that increases with the uncertainty about the strength of the alternative. The total mean strength does not necessarily remain constant. The difference between the sum of the posterior mean strength and the sum of the prior mean strengths is equal to $((\sigma_i^2 - \sigma_j^2)/\sigma_{i,j})h(d_{i,j}, w_{i,j})$, which may assume a positive or a negative value. The posterior variance of the strength of an alternative is always less than or equal to the prior variance. See the right graph in Figure 9.11. The variance parameter of the strength of an alternative is decremented for a larger amount when observing a more likely outcome according to the prior distribution.

Pair Comparisons with Win-Draw-Lose Outcomes

Consider a generalization of the model in the previous section that allows for draws in the observations. Given a parameter $\epsilon > 0$, this generalized model assumes that alternative i is ranked higher than alternative j if, and only if, $b_i - b_j > \epsilon$; alternative j is ranked higher than alternative i if, and only if, $b_i - b_j < -\epsilon$; and alternative i and alternative j draw if, and only if, $-\epsilon \le b_i - b_j \le \epsilon$. Assume that the observed partial ranking r is either $(1, 2)$, meaning that alternative i is ranked higher than alternative j; or $(2, 1)$, meaning that alternative j is ranked higher than alternative i; or $(1, 1)$ meaning that alternative i and alternative j are in a draw.

The posterior means and variances of the strengths of the alternatives are given as follows. Let $\mu_{i,j}$ denote the difference between the prior mean strengths $\mu_{i,j} = \mu_i - \mu_j$, and let $\sigma_{i,j}^2$ denote the variance of the difference of the performances $\sigma_{i,j}^2 = \sigma_i^2 + \sigma_j^2 + 2\beta^2$. The posterior mean and variance of the strength of alternative i are

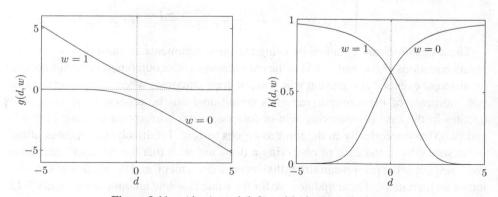

Figure 9.11. $g(d, w)$ vs. d (left) and $h(d, w)$ vs. d (right).

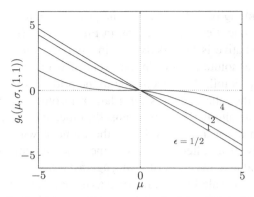

Figure 9.12. The update for the posterior mean strength of alternative i in the case of observing a draw with alternative j versus $\mu = \mu_i - \mu_j$ for the value of parameter $\sigma = 1$.

given by the following mappings:

$$\mu_i \leftarrow \mu_i + \frac{\sigma_i^2}{\sigma_{i,j}} g_\epsilon(\mu_{i,j}, \sigma_{i,j}, r)$$

and

$$\sigma_i^2 \leftarrow \sigma_i^2 \left(1 - \frac{\sigma_i^2}{\sigma_{i,j}^2} h_\epsilon(\mu_{i,j}, \sigma_{i,j}, r)\right)$$

with

$$g_\epsilon(\mu, \sigma, r) = \begin{cases} \frac{\phi\left(\frac{\mu-\epsilon}{\sigma}\right)}{\Phi\left(\frac{\mu-\epsilon}{\sigma}\right)}, & \text{if } r = (1,2) \\[2mm] -\frac{\phi\left(\frac{\mu+\epsilon}{\sigma}\right)}{1-\Phi\left(\frac{\mu+\epsilon}{\sigma}\right)}, & \text{if } r = (2,1) \\[2mm] \frac{\phi\left(\frac{\mu+\epsilon}{\sigma}\right)-\phi\left(\frac{\mu-\epsilon}{\sigma}\right)}{\Phi\left(\frac{\mu+\epsilon}{\sigma}\right)-\Phi\left(\frac{\mu-\epsilon}{\sigma}\right)}, & \text{if } r = (1,1) \end{cases}$$

and

$$h_\epsilon(\mu, \sigma, r) = \begin{cases} g_\epsilon(\mu, \sigma, r)\left(g_\epsilon(\mu, \sigma, r) + \frac{\mu-\epsilon}{\sigma}\right), & \text{if } r = (1,2) \\[2mm] g_\epsilon(\mu, \sigma, r)\left(g_\epsilon(\mu, \sigma, r) + \frac{\mu+\epsilon}{\sigma}\right), & \text{if } r = (2,1) \\[2mm] g_\epsilon(\mu, \sigma, r)^2 + \frac{\frac{\mu+\epsilon}{\sigma}\phi\left(\frac{\mu+\epsilon}{\sigma}\right)-\frac{\mu-\epsilon}{\sigma}\phi\left(\frac{\mu-\epsilon}{\sigma}\right)}{\Phi\left(\frac{\mu+\epsilon}{\sigma}\right)-\Phi\left(\frac{\mu-\epsilon}{\sigma}\right)}, & \text{if } r = (1,1). \end{cases}$$

These equations are obtained by using the same arguments as those that we used to obtain equations (9.64) and (9.65) in the case of win-or-lose outcomes, but conditioning on different events that represent win, loss, or draw outcomes when computing the first two moments of the strength variables conditional on the observed outcome. The updates in the case of observing win-or-lose outcomes correspond to those in (9.64) and (9.65) asymptotically in the limit as ϵ goes to zero. Intuitively, the updates of the mean strengths in the case of observing a draw are such that the stronger alternative (with respect to the prior mean strengths) incurs a decrement, and the weaker alternative incurs an increment. These updates are for the same absolute amounts. See Figure 9.12 for a graph.

9.5.2 Online Bayesian Inference

A Bayesian inference method is said to be online if it applies a Bayesian inference sequentially over successive rounds in which new input observations are made available. For the specific problem of inferring the strengths of alternatives, the online Bayesian inference method amounts to updating the posterior distributions of the strengths of the alternatives as soon as a new round of full or partial rankings is made available. In each round, the posterior distribution of the latent variables is computed by using, as the prior distribution, the posterior distribution computed in the previous round. The approximate Bayesian inference that is based on approximating a posterior distribution by a distribution from an assumed family of distributions is applied in the context of online Bayesian inference by successive application of such approximations. This is referred to as *assumed density filtering*. For example, to infer the strengths of alternatives by approximating their posterior distribution by a product-form Gaussian distribution, approximate online Bayesian inference amounts to computing a product-form Gaussian approximation of the underlying posterior distribution in each round and then using this approximation as the prior distribution in the subsequent round. For the special case of pair comparisons according to the Thurstone Type V model, this amounts to successively updating the mean and variance parameters along an input sequence of pair comparisons according to the iterative method specified by (9.64) and (9.65).

Example 9.31. Consider pair comparisons of three alternatives with the number of wins as given in Example 9.20 for specific sequence of pair comparisons as indicated in Figure 9.13. We assume Thurstone Type V model with the value of the parameter $\beta = 1/20$. The prior distribution is assumed to be such that the strengths of alternatives are independent and identically distributed according to a normal distribution with mean zero and variance $1/25$. The approximate posterior distributions of the strengths over different rounds are shown in Figure 9.13.

This example demonstrates how the univariate marginal distributions of the strengths latent variables concentrate around mean values as the number of observations increases. The example also demonstrates that, for an online Bayesian inference, the posterior distribution of latent variables depends on the order of input observations. Specifically, note that the first two comparisons are between alternatives 2 and 3 such that alternative 3 wins in the first round and alternative 2 wins in the second round. The approximate posterior distribution of the strengths in the second round is such that the mean strength of alternative 3 is larger than that of alternative 2. If the order of the first two pair comparisons is reversed, then the approximate posterior distribution in the second round will be such that the mean strength of alternative 2 is larger than that of alternative 3.

So far we have considered approximate Bayesian inference for the special case of pair comparisons. This special case allowed us to approximate posterior distribution with a product-form Gaussian distribution by using the method of matching moments and to determine the iterative method explicitly as given in (9.64) and (9.65). In general, other methods are needed. In the next section, we consider the concept of a factor

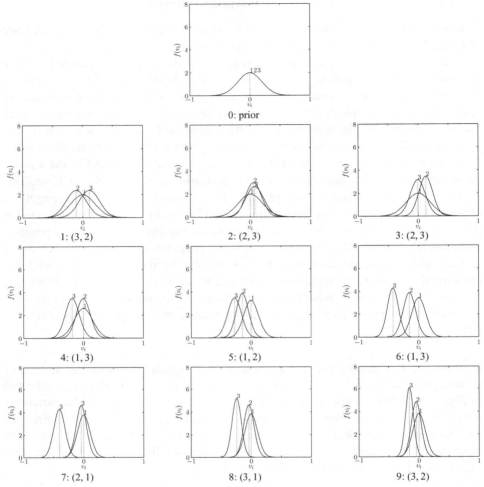

Figure 9.13. Online approximiate Bayesian inference: posterior distributions of skills for a given input sequence of full rankings (i_t, j_t) where i_t denotes the identity of the winner and j_t denotes the identity of the loser for the t-th input full ranking.

graph and an algorithm known as the sum-product algorithm for efficient computation of marginal distributions of a joint distribution.

9.5.3 Factor Graphs

A factor graph is a representation of a factorization of a function by a graph that is defined as follows. Suppose a function $g : \mathbf{R}^n \to \mathbf{R}$ is given that admits a factorization of the following form: given a set of indexes of variables $N = \{1, 2, \ldots, n\}$ and a set of indexes of factors $F = \{1, 2, \ldots, m\}$,

$$g(\mathbf{x}) = \prod_{f \in F} g_f(\mathbf{x}_{N(f)})$$

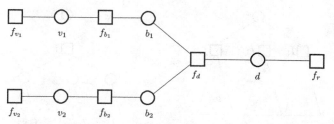

Figure 9.14. Factor graph for comparison of two alternatives.

where $g_f : \mathbf{R}^{|N(f)|} \to \mathbf{R}$ and $N(f) \subseteq N$ for $f \in F$, and we use the notation $\mathbf{x}_S = (x_i, i \in S)$ for $S \subseteq N$. A factor graph $G = (N, F, E)$ is defined as a bipartite graph that contains a variable vertex for each variable $i \in N$ and a factor vertex for each factor $f \in F$, and the set of edges E is defined to contain edges between variable vertex i and factor vertex f such that $i \in N(f)$. Such a graph representation contains full information about which variables affect each given factor. A convention is to graphically denote each variable vertex with a circle and to denote each factor vertex with a square.

Example 9.32 (two alternatives). Consider the posterior multivariate density function of the strength variables v_1 and v_2, performance variables b_1 and b_2, and performance difference $b_1 - b_2 = d$, with the prior distribution of the strengths being of product form such that $v_1 \sim f(\cdot; \mu_1, \sigma_1^2)$ and $v_2 \sim f(\cdot; \mu_2, \sigma_2^2)$. Suppose a full ranking is given such that alternative 1 is ranked higher than alternative 2. In this case, the posterior density function is

$$g(v_1, b_1, v_2, b_2, d) = \underbrace{f(v_1; \mu_1, \sigma_1^2)}_{f_{v_1}} \underbrace{f(b_1; v_1, \beta^2)}_{f_{b_1}} \underbrace{f(v_2; \mu_2, \sigma_2^2)}_{f_{v_2}} \underbrace{f(b_2; v_2, \beta^2)}_{f_{b_2}}$$

$$\underbrace{\mathbf{1}(b_1 - b_2 = d)}_{f_d} \underbrace{\mathbf{1}(d > 0)}_{f_r}$$

which contains five variables and six factors. See Figure 9.14 for a factor graph representation.

Sum-Product Algorithm

We describe a method for recursive computation of marginals of a joint distribution known as the sum-product algorithm. Suppose a probability density function $g : \mathbf{R}^n \to \mathbf{R}$ is given, and we want to compute the marginal probability density function

$$g(x_i) = \int_{\mathbf{x}_{N \setminus \{i\}}} g(\mathbf{x}) d\mathbf{x}. \tag{9.66}$$

We now show how to do this in an efficient way under the assumption that function g admits a factor graph representation by a tree. This is shown in the following two steps.

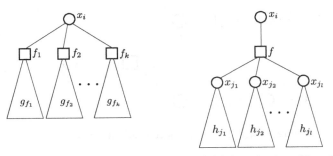

Figure 9.15. (Left) factorization of function g, (right) factorization of function g_f.

Step 1 Since the factor graph is a tree, there exists a factorization of function g of the following form:

$$g(x_i, \mathbf{x}_{N\setminus\{i\}}) = \prod_{f \in F(i)} g_f(x_i, \mathbf{x}_{N(f)\setminus\{i\}})$$

where each variable x_j, for $j \neq i$, appears in only one factor. To contradict, suppose that there exists $j \neq i$ such that variable x_j appears in two factors f and f'; then there exist two paths in the factor graph connecting factor vertices f and f', one through variable vertex i and the other through variable vertex j, which contradicts the assumption that the factor graph is a tree.

By the distributive law, we have

$$\int_{\mathbf{x}_{N\setminus\{i\}}} g(\mathbf{x})\, d\mathbf{x} = \int_{\mathbf{x}_{N\setminus\{i\}}} \prod_{f \in F(i)} g_f(x_i, \mathbf{x}_{N(f)\setminus\{i\}})\, d\mathbf{x}$$

$$= \prod_{f \in F(i)} \int_{\mathbf{x}_{N\setminus\{i\}}} g_f(x_i, \mathbf{x}_{N(f)\setminus\{i\}})\, d\mathbf{x}_{N(f)\setminus\{i\}}. \qquad (9.67)$$

We observe that the marginal function is a product of individual marginal functions as appears in (9.67).

Step 2 Each factor g_f can be further factorized in the following way:

$$g_f(x_i, \mathbf{x}_{N(f)\setminus\{i\}}) = h_f(\mathbf{x}) \prod_{j \in N(f)\setminus\{i\}} h_j(x_j, \mathbf{x}_{N(F(j)\setminus\{f\})})$$

where we refer to h_f as the kernel function. See Figure 9.15. The variable x_i appears only in the kernel function h_f, and each variable x_j appears at most twice, either in the kernel and in at most one of the factors $h_j(\cdot)$, $j \in N(f) \setminus \{i\}$. Again, by the distributive law, we have

$$\int_{\mathbf{x}_{N\setminus\{i\}}} g_f(x_i, \mathbf{x}_{N(f)\setminus\{i\}})\, d\mathbf{x} = \int_{\mathbf{x}_{N\setminus\{i\}}} h_f(\mathbf{x}) \prod_{j \in N(f)} h_j(x_j, \mathbf{x}_{N(F(j)\setminus\{f\})})\, d\mathbf{x}$$

$$= \int_{\mathbf{x}_{N\setminus\{i\}}} h_f(\mathbf{x}) \prod_{j \in N(f)} \int_{\mathbf{x}_{N(f)\setminus\{j\}}} h_j(x_j, \mathbf{x}_{N(F(j)\setminus\{f\})})\, d\mathbf{x}_{N(f)}.$$

$$(9.68)$$

We observe that the marginal function of g_f can be computed by multiplying the kernel function h_f by the marginal functions in (9.68) and then integrating over all the variables except variable x_i.

At the end of the second step, the factors $h_j(x_j, \mathbf{x}_{N(F(j)\setminus\{f\})})$ are of the same form as function g that we factorized in the first step. Thus, we can recursively apply the two steps further down the tree until the leaf vertices are reached. The marginal function g can be computed by applying the two steps in the reverse direction starting from the leaf vertices upward to the root of the tree.

The initialization of a leaf vertex is as follows. If a leaf vertex is a factor vertex f, then the function has the generic form $g_f(x_j)$ where j is the element of the singleton set $N(f)$, which means that the function sent by the leaf vertex f is the function $g_f(x_j)$ itself. If a leaf vertex is a variable vertex j connected to factor vertex f, which is an element of the singleton set $F(j)$, we have

$$g_f(x_i) = \int_{\mathbf{x}_{N\setminus\{i\}}} g_f(x_i, \mathbf{x}_{N(f)\setminus\{i\}})\, d\mathbf{x}.$$

For this to hold, from (9.68), we obtain that the message sent is equal to 1.

The sum-product algorithm is a message-passing method for the computation of marginal functions that we described earlier and is commonly represented as follows. Let $m_{x \to f}(x)$ denote the message passed from a variable vertex x to a factor vertex f, and let $m_{f \to x}(x)$ denote the message passed on from a factor vertex f to a variable vertex x. From our previous discussion, the initialization of messages is as follows: if a leaf vertex is a variable vertex x, then $m_{x \to f}(x) = 1$ for all factor vertices f with an edge to variable vertex x; otherwise, if a leaf vertex is a factor vertex f, then $m_{f \to x}(x) = h_f(x)$ for each factor vertex f with an edge to variable vertex x. From (9.67) and (9.68), the message updates are given as follows.

Sum-Product Algorithm:

$$m_{x_i \to f_k}(x_i) = \prod_{f_l \in F(i)\setminus\{f_k\}} m_{f_l \to x_i}(x_i) \tag{9.69}$$

$$m_{f_k \to x_i}(x_i) = \int_{\mathbf{x}_{-i}} h_{f_k}(\mathbf{x}) \prod_{j \in N(f_k)\setminus\{i\}} m_{x_j \to f_k}(x_j)\, d\mathbf{x}_{-i}. \tag{9.70}$$

The marginal function of variable x_i is given by

$$g(x_i) = \prod_{f \in F(i)} m_{f \to x_i}(x_i). \tag{9.71}$$

For every variable x_i and factor $f \in F(i)$, by (9.69) and (9.71), we have:

$$g(x_i) = m_{x_i \to f}(x_i) m_{f \to x_i}(x_i). \tag{9.72}$$

Example 9.33 (two alternatives revisited). Consider the two alternatives in Example 9.32 and how the sum-product algorithm is executed in this case. To compute the marginal density function of the strength variable v_1, we redraw the factor graph in

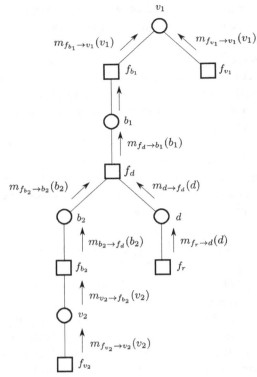

Figure 9.16. The messages of the sum-product algorithm used for computing the marginal distribution of variable v_1.

Figure 9.14 in an equivalent form given in Figure 9.16. The messages of the sum-product algorithm are defined as follows.

All the leaf vertices are factor vertices so the messages from these vertices are initialized as follows:

$$
\begin{aligned}
m_{f_{v_2} \to v_2}(v_2) &= f(v_2; \mu_2, \sigma_2^2) \\
m_{f_r \to d}(d) &= g_{f_r}(d) \\
m_{f_{v_1} \to v_1}(v_1) &= f(v_1; \mu_1, \sigma_1^2).
\end{aligned}
\tag{9.73}
$$

For the case of win-or-lose outcomes of pair comparisons, $g_{f_r}(d) = \mathbf{1}(d > 0)$ if alternative 1 wins, and $g_{f_r}(d) = \mathbf{1}(d < 0)$ otherwise.

The message-passing equations are given as follows:

$$
\begin{aligned}
m_{v_2 \to f_{b_2}}(v_2) &= m_{f_{v_2} \to v_2}(v_2) \\
m_{f_{b_2} \to b_2}(b_2) &= \int_{v_2} f(b_2; v_2, \beta^2) m_{v_2 \to f_{b_2}}(v_2)\, dv_2 \\
m_{b_2 \to f_d}(b_2) &= m_{f_{b_2} \to b_2}(b_2) \\
m_{d \to f_d}(d) &= m_{f_r \to d}(d) \\
m_{f_d \to b_1}(b_1) &= \int_d \int_{b_2} \mathbf{1}(b_1 - b_2 = d) m_{d \to f_d}(d) m_{b_2 \to f_d}(b_2)\, dd\, db_2 \\
m_{b_1 \to f_{v_1}}(b_1) &= m_{f_d \to b_1}(b_1)
\end{aligned}
\tag{9.74}
$$

An important observation is that all the messages from factor vertices f_{v_1} and f_{v_2} to factor vertex f_d correspond to Gaussian distributions; however, this is not the case for the messages from factor vertex f_d to variables vertices b_1 and b_2. The factor $g_{f_r}(d)$ makes the posterior distribution non-Gaussian.

9.5.4 Gaussian Density Filtering

Suppose that we want to approximate the posterior marginal distributions of the strength variables by Gaussian distributions. In Example 9.33, we observed that for the given model, the posterior marginal distribution of a strength variable is not Gaussian. If all factors were initialized to functions that are Gaussian distributions, then all the messages would correspond to univariate Gaussian densities, and the posterior marginal distributions of all variables would have been Gaussian. However, this is not true because of the factor that indicates the input ranking of the two alternatives. It is readily observed that the posterior marginal distribution of the performance difference of the two alternatives is a truncated Gaussian distribution. In this section, we describe an approximate message-passing method where the messages are approximated by Gaussian distributions. The key idea is to approximate the marginal distribution of the performance difference by a Gaussian distribution and, in particular, to choose a Gaussian distribution that minimizes the Kullback-Leibler divergence between the true posterior marginal distribution that corresponds to a truncated Gaussian distribution and a Gaussian distribution. By Theorem 9.30, we know that such an approximation corresponds to a Gaussian distribution that has the same mean and variance as the underlying true distribution.

For concreteness, we describe how this approximation is performed via message passing for the case in Example 9.33. The approximation consists of the following three steps:

(i) The messages are passed from the strength factor vertices and the input ranking factor vertex to the performance difference variable vertex according to the sum-product algorithm, as indicated in the left diagram in Figure 9.17.

(ii) The marginal distribution of the performance difference is approximated by a Gaussian distribution that minimizes the Kullback-Leibler divergence with the true marginal distribution of the performance difference.

(iii) The messages are passed from the performance difference variable vertex and the strength factor vertices to the strength variable vertices as indicated in the right diagram in Figure 9.17.

After the first step is completed, the marginal distribution of the performance difference is

$$g(d) = m_{d \to f_r}(d) m_{f_r \to d}(d) \tag{9.75}$$

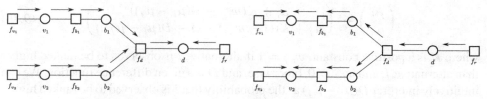

Figure 9.17. The schedule of messages for Gaussian density filtering.

where $m_{d \to f_r}(d) = f(d; \mu_1 - \mu_2, \sigma_1^2 + \sigma_2^2 + 2\beta^2)$ and $m_{f_r \to d}(d) = g_{f_r}(d)$. This is a truncated Gaussian density function, which in the second step is approximated by a Gaussian distribution $\hat{g}$ that minimizes the Kullback-Leibler divergence. This approximation is a Gaussian distribution with mean and variance given by (9.64) and (9.65). The approximation is implemented in the message-passing algorithm by replacing g in (9.75) with $\hat{g}$, and then computing message $\hat{m}_{f_r \to d}(d)$ such that

$$\hat{g}(d) = m_{d \to f_r}(d)\hat{m}_{f_r \to d}(d).$$

This defines the message $\hat{m}_{f_r \to d}(d)$ as the ratio of two Gaussian density functions, which itself is a Gaussian density function. In the third step, the sum-product algorithm is used on the original input but replaces the factor $g_r(d)$ with $\hat{m}_{f_r \to d}(d)$. With the given approximation, the message-passing algorithm follows the updates of the sum-product algorithm with all the messages from factor vertices initialized to Gaussian density functions, and all the messages corresponding to Gaussian density functions.

9.6 The Design Principles of Three Popular Rating Systems

In this section we discuss the main design principles of three popular rating systems. The first is the Elo rating system that was introduced by Arpad Elo and was first adopted by the United States Chess Federation (USCF) in 1960 and then by the World Chess Federation (FIDE) in 1970, and ever since has also been used for rating players or teams in other sport competitions. This rating system is defined for input full rankings of pairs of alternatives. The second rating system that we consider is TrueSkill that was developed for rating skills of players in the online multi-player gaming platform Xbox Live. This rating system generalizes the Elo rating system to allow for input to be partial rankings of two or more players and to allow competitions between teams of players. The third rating system is the one used for rating skills of coders in the competition-based software development platform, TopCoder. All these rating systems can be seen as particular instances of the generalized Thurstone model deploying different methods for the estimation of the model parameters.

9.6.1 Elo Rating System

The Elo rating system is an iterative method for estimating the strengths of alternatives assuming that observations are pair comparisons. The estimates of the strength parameters $\mu_1, \mu_2, \ldots, \mu_n$ are initialized to some specific values and then updated iteratively after each observed full ranking of a pair of alternatives (i, j) as follows:

$$\begin{pmatrix} \mu_i \\ \mu_j \end{pmatrix} \leftarrow \begin{pmatrix} \mu_i + K(w_{i,j} - D(\mu_i - \mu_j)) \\ \mu_j + K((1 - w_{i,j}) - (1 - D(\mu_i - \mu_j))) \end{pmatrix} \tag{9.76}$$

where K is a positive constant, $w_{i,j} = 1$ if alternative i is observed to be ranked higher than alternative j, and $w_{i,j} = 0$, otherwise, and D is a given difference function. We can intuitively interpret $D(\mu_i - \mu_j)$ as the probability that i is observed to be ranked higher than j, according to the assumed model, given that the strengths of the alternatives i and j are μ_i and μ_j, respectively.

The Elo rating system uses a particular inference method for estimating the unknown parameters of a generalized linear model that we introduced in Section 9.2.4 or of a generalized Thurstone model in view of our discussions in Section 9.2. This rating system provides point estimates of the strength parameters and no information about the uncertainty of these estimates. Specific instances of the Elo rating system may differ in the choice of the difference function D. For example, a Gaussian distribution has been used in the Elo rating system adopted by USCF. The same choice was made originally by FIDE, but was later changed to a logistic distribution.

The choice of the parameter K in the definition of the Elo rating system used to rate the strength of chess players has attracted a lot of debate. This parameter in some implementations may assume different values for different updates depending on various factors, such as the number of games in which a player has participated in the past and the type of the tournament in which the game takes place. The value of the K parameter is typically assumed to be decreasing in the number of games in which a player has participated in the past, with the underlying rationale of allowing for larger updates in an initial phase in which there is a greater uncertainty about the strength of the player.

The updates of the strength parameters are such that a larger change in the estimates of individual strength parameters occurs in the case of a more unlikely observation with respect to the estimates of the strengths prior to the observation. This means that if according to the estimates of the strengths prior to a contest between a pair of players, the weaker player is observed to win against a stronger player, then their strength parameters are changed by larger amounts. For the Elo rating system defined by the iterative equation (9.76), the sum of the values of the strength parameters remains unchanged because each update is such that the strength parameter of the winner and that of the loser are changed by the same amount.

9.6.2 TrueSkill

TrueSkill is a rating system designed for rating skills of players in a popular online multi-player gaming platform. Its design addresses several specific requirements that arise in online multi-player gaming, including the need to allow for contests among two or more players, for contests between teams of players, for draws in contest outcomes, and for computing point estimates of skills and uncertainty of these estimates. One of the primary purposes of a rating system in multi-player gaming scenarios is to enable the matchmaking of players of similar skills.

The TrueSkill rating system assumes a general Thurstone model with random independent performances according to Gaussian distributions. This rating system is based on using approximate online Bayesian inference that assumes a product-form Gaussian distribution as a prior distribution for the latent variables representing the skills of the players. The approximate online Bayesian inference is based on using the approximate message-passing inference discussed in Section 9.5.4 (see Figure 9.16). For the special case of contests between two players with win-draw-lose outcomes, the given approximate online Bayesian inference corresponds to the iterative method defined in Section 9.5.1.

The model accommodates contests between teams of players by assuming that the performance of a team is equal to the sum of individual performances of the team members. See Figure 9.18 for a graphical representation of this assumption.

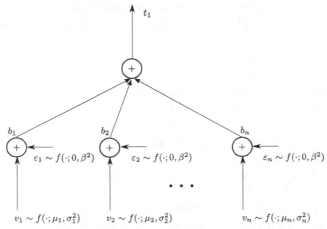

Figure 9.18. Team performance defined as the sum of individual performances of the team members.

9.6.3 TopCoder Rating System

TopCoder is a popular competition-based software development online platform that rates skills of coders based on observed performance in algorithm competitions, including so called single-round and marathon matches, and other competitions. The rating scores computed by this system are used to divide coders into two divisions: division 1 consisting of coders with a rating score larger than or equal to 1,200 and division 2 consisting of coders with a rating score smaller than 1,200. A histogram of the rating scores is shown in Figure 9.19. Competitions such as single-round matches are run separately and in parallel for coders in the two divisions. The rating scores are also used for determining which coders qualify to participate in specific tournaments, such as the annual TopCoder Open event that we discussed in Section 1.1.7. The rating scores are also used to create leaderboards. The rating score of a coder is prominently displayed in the user profile page where the user name appears in red for a rating score larger than or equal to 2,200, yellow for a score between 1,500 and 2,199, blue for a score of between 1,200 and 1,499, green for a score between 900 and 1,199, and gray color for a score between 0 and 899.

The TopCoder rating system maintains three variables for each coder: a rating score μ_i, volatility σ_i, and the number of times the coder was rated in the past t_i. The outcome of each contest is a ranking of coders in decreasing order of individual performances. The TopCoder rating system assumes that the outcome of a contest among coders in a set S is a full ranking $\rho : S \to \{1, 2, \ldots, |S|\}$ and that the expected rank of a coder is given by

$$\hat{\rho}(i) = \sum_{j \in S \setminus \{i\}} \Phi\left(\frac{\mu_j - \mu_i}{\sqrt{\sigma_i^2 + \sigma_j^2}}\right) + 1, \text{ for } i \in S. \tag{9.77}$$

These expected ranks correspond to those of a Thurstone model with independent individual performances where the performance of coder $i \in S$ is a Guassian random

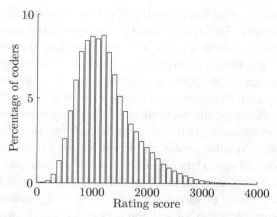

Figure 9.19. A histogram of TopCoder rating scores based on data collected in late 2012.

variable with mean μ_i and variance σ_i^2. This is readily observed from equation (9.9) with $p_{i,j}(x) = \Phi(x/\sqrt{\sigma_i^2 + \sigma_j^2})$.

The TopCoder rating system deploys an online inference of the model parameters described as follows. After each contest among coders in a set S, the following updates are applied for every $i \in S$:

$$\mu_i \leftarrow \mu_i + \Delta_i \tag{9.78}$$

$$\sigma_i^2 \leftarrow \sigma_i^2 + K(t_i)\left(\frac{1 - K(t_i)}{K(t_i)^2}\Delta_i^2 - \sigma_i^2\right) \tag{9.79}$$

$$t_i \leftarrow t_i + 1 \tag{9.80}$$

where

$$\Delta_i = K(t_i)G(\mu,\sigma)\left(\Phi^{-1}\left(\frac{1}{|S|}\left(\hat{\rho}(i) - \frac{1}{2}\right)\right) - \Phi^{-1}\left(\frac{1}{|S|}\left(\rho(i) - \frac{1}{2}\right)\right)\right) \tag{9.81}$$

$$K(t) = 0.18 + \frac{0.42}{t+1} \tag{9.82}$$

$$G(\mu,\sigma)^2 = \frac{1}{|S|}\sum_{j \in S}\sigma_j^2 + \frac{1}{|S|-1}\sum_{j \in S}(\mu_j - \bar{\mu})^2 \tag{9.83}$$

$$\bar{\mu} = \frac{1}{|S|}\sum_{j \in S}\mu_j. \tag{9.84}$$

The adjustment of the mean rating score in (9.78) can be interpreted as aiming at minimizing the prediction error for the ranks. The closer the coder is to the top or the bottom of the ranking according to the estimates prior to the contest, the more sensitive is the rating of this coder to his or her rank. There is an estimation bias favoring the coders at the top of the ranking to remain at the top of the ranking and favoring the coders at the bottom of the ranking to remain at the bottom of the ranking, which we shall elaborate on shortly. The parameter $K(t_i)$ affects the magnitude of the rating score change, which is decreasing in t_i from a positive constant to a smaller strictly positive constant. This is a standard parameter used in recursive estimation of parameters. The more contests a coder has participated in, the less his or her rating score will change. The parameter $G(\mu, \sigma)$, referred to as the *competition factor*, also controls the magnitude of the rating score change, and its definition is specific to the TopCoder rating system. This parameter increases the size of the change in relation to the following two elements: the uncertainty of the rating scores and the disparity of the ratings of coders according to the prior statistics. It increases the magnitude of the update when there is smaller confidence in the values of the rating scores and in the case of contests among coders of different skills according to the prior statistics. The update of the rating score variance as defined in (9.79) can be interpreted as a standard recursive estimate of variance based on observed prediction errors. Suppose that for the given input sequence of real numbers $x_t, x_2, \dots, x_t$, we have

$$\mu_t = \frac{1}{t} \sum_{s=1}^{t} x_s \text{ and } \sigma_t^2 = \frac{1}{t} \sum_{s=1}^{t} (x_s - \mu_t)^2. \tag{9.85}$$

Then, Exercise 9.15 shows that σ_t^2 obeys the following recursive equation:

$$\sigma_{t+1}^2 = t(\mu_{t+1} - \mu_t)^2 + \frac{t}{t+1} \sigma_t^2. \tag{9.86}$$

This recursive equation is of the same form as that in (9.79). It would have been exactly the same recursive equation if $K(t)$ was defined to be equal to $1/(t+1)$. Note that $K(t)$ as defined in (9.82) is a decreasing function, which is lower bounded by a strictly positive constant. This allows for the adaptation of the volatility parameter of coder i even for large values of t_i.

The TopCoder rating system underestimates the expected performance of higher ranked coders and overestimates the expected performance of lower ranked coders. As a result, it tends to favor higher ranked coders to remain higher ranked and the lower ranked coders to remain lower ranked. This bias is because of the non-linearity of the rating score update in (9.81), which we explain as follows. Suppose that the observed ranks are according to the underlying model, and consider a fixed point (μ, σ) of the iterative system given by (9.78)-(9.80), where for simplicity we assume that each coder participates in each contest. From equation (9.78), we obtain

$$\Phi^{-1}\left(\frac{1}{|N|} \sum_{j \in N} \Phi\left(\frac{\mu_j - \mu_i}{\sqrt{\sigma_i^2 + \sigma_j^2}} \right) \right) - \mathbf{E}\left[\Phi^{-1}\left(\frac{1}{|N|} \left(\rho(i) - \frac{1}{2} \right) \right) \mid \mu, \sigma \right] = 0.$$

From the last equation, we observe that the estimate of the rank is a biased estimate because of the non-linearity of function $\Phi^{-1}(x)$. Function $\Phi^{-1}(x)$ is strictly increasing in x and is concave on $[0, 1/2]$ and convex on $[1/2, 1]$. Hence, if the rank of a coder tends to take values in the top of the ranking, his or her expected rank would tend to be smaller or equal to his or her estimated rank. In other words, the rating system would bias toward predicting a lower placement for the coder, and thus favor the coder to realize a higher placement and further increase his or her rating score. The opposite bias holds for coders whose rank tend to be in the bottom half by predicting a higher placement and thus it favors the coder to remain in the bottom half. The existence of this bias is

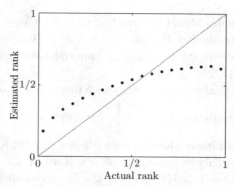

Figure 9.20. The observed rank versus expected rank normalized by the number of coders participating in the contest.

well supported by empirical observations shown in Figure 9.20 using historical rating scores of the coders.

Summary

Probabilistic Models of Rankings Given a set of two or more alternatives $N = \{1, 2, \ldots, n\}$, a ranking of alternatives is generated according to a probabilistic model.

(i) **Thurstone models** A full ranking of a subset of alternatives is generated to be in decreasing order of performance random variables, where the performance random variable of an alternative i is defined to be a sum of a deterministic strength parameter v_i and a noise random variable ε_i.

Classic Thurstone Model: noise random variables are independent, according to a Gaussian distribution with mean zero and variance β^2, i.e., with distribution $F(x) = \Phi(x/\beta)$, for $\beta > 0$.

Many probabilistic models of rankings correspond to a Thurstone model.

(ii) **Luce's Choice Model** Given positive-valued parameters $\theta_1, \theta_2, \ldots, \theta_n$, for every non-empty set $S \subseteq N$, alternative $i \in S$ is ranked higher than any other alternative in the set S with probability

$$\mathbf{Pr}[\cap_{j \in S \setminus \{i\}}\{i \succ j\}] = \frac{\theta_i}{\sum_{j \in S} \theta_j}, \quad \text{for } i \in S.$$

Bradley-Terry Model: for pair comparisons

$$\mathbf{Pr}[i \succ j] = \frac{\theta_i}{\theta_i + \theta_j}.$$

Plackett-Choice Model: for full rankings of two or more alternatives

$$\mathbf{Pr}[\rho^{-1}(1) \succ \rho^{-1}(2) \succ \cdots \succ \rho^{-1}(n)] = \prod_{i=1}^{n} \frac{\theta_{\rho^{-1}(i)}}{\theta_{\rho^{-1}(i)} + \cdots + \theta_{\rho^{-1}(n)}}.$$

where ρ is a one-to-one mapping from N to N, and $\rho(i)$ denotes the rank of alternative $i \in N$.

(iii) **Dawkins Choice Model** Suppose $0 < v_n \leq \cdots \leq v_2 \leq v_1 \leq 1$. Draw a uniform random number V until $v_{i+1} \leq V < v_i$, for some $1 \leq i \leq n$; then choose an alternative by sampling uniformly at random from the set of alternatives $\{1, 2, \ldots, i\}$.

For a pair of alternatives i and j such that $v_i \geq v_j$, we have

$$\mathbf{Pr}[i \succ j] = 1 - \frac{1}{2}\frac{v_j}{v_i} \text{ and } \mathbf{Pr}[i \prec j] = \frac{1}{2}\frac{v_j}{v_i}.$$

(iv) **Generalized Linear Models** Given is a function $D : \mathbf{R} \to [0, 1]$ satisfying (i) $D(x)$ is strictly increasing for all $x \in \mathbf{R}$, (ii) $\lim_{x \to -\infty} D(-x) = 0$, (iii) $\lim_{x \to \infty} D(x) = 1$, and (iv) $D(x) = 1 - D(-x)$ for all $x \in \mathbf{R}$. The probabilities of pair comparisons are according to the following model:

$$\mathbf{Pr}[i \succ j] = D(v_i - v_j).$$

Examples:
(a) *Classic Thurstone (Gaussian)*: $D(x) = \Phi(x/(\sqrt{2}\beta))$.
(b) *Logistic*: $D(x) = 1/(1 + e^{-x/s})$, $s > 0$.
(c) *Laplace*: $D(x) = e^{x/s}/2\mathbf{1}(x < 0) + (1 - e^{-x/s}/2)\mathbf{1}(x \geq 0)$, for $s > 0$.
Using a suitable change of variables, the logistic model corresponds to the Bradley-Terry model, and the Laplace model corresponds to the Dawkins choice model for pair comparisons.

Relations between Statistical Ranking Models

Systems of win probabilities: $\{p_S(i), i \in S, S \subseteq N, |S| \geq 2\}$. $p_S(i)$ is the probability of alternative i being selected from the subset of alternatives $S \subseteq N$.

Luce's Choice Axiom: $p_S(i) = \frac{p_N(i)}{\sum_{j \in S} p_N(j)}$, for $i \in S$, and $S \subseteq N$.

Luce's Choice Theorem: A system of win probabilities satisfies the choice axiom if and only if there exist real numbers $v_1, v_2, \ldots, v_n$ such that $p_S(i) = v_i / \sum_{j \in S} v_j$, for $i \in S$ and $S \subseteq N$.

A Thurstone model with distribution F is equivalent to the Luce's Choice Axiom if, and only if, F is a double-exponential distribution, i.e., $F(x) = \exp(-\exp(-(ax + b)))$, for $a > 0$ and $b \in \mathbf{R}$.

A Thurstone model is equivalent to Dawkins choice model for pair comparisons if, and only if, the distribution of the difference of two performance random variables is a Laplace distribution.

Maximum Likelihood Parameter Estimate for Pair Comparisons

The log-likelihood function: is given by

$$\ell(\mathbf{v}) = \sum_{i,j \in N} w_{i,j} \log(D(v_i - v_j)).$$

The log-likelihood function is

(i) Upper compact if, and only if, the matrix of wins $\mathbf{W} = (w_{i,j})$ is irreducible.

(ii) Strictly concave if D is strictly log-concave and the matrix of the number of pair comparisons $\mathbf{M} = \mathbf{W} + \mathbf{W}^T$ is irreducible.

If the log-likelihood function is upper compact and strictly concave, then there exists a unique maximum likelihood estimate of the strength parameters, up to an additive constant.

Iterative algorithm for the Bradley-Terry model:

$$\hat{\theta}_i(t+1) = \frac{\sum_{j \in N} w_{i,j}}{\sum_{j \in N} \frac{m_{i,j}}{\hat{\theta}_i(t) + \hat{\theta}_j(t)}}, \quad \text{for } i \in N.$$

Under the conditions for the existence and uniqueness, it is guaranteed to converge to the unique maximum likelihood estimate (up to a multiplicative constant).

Bayesian Inference

Bayesian inference principle: assume that some parameters of the model are random variables according to a prior distribution; then compute the posterior distribution of these random variables conditional on the observed set of rankings of the alternatives.

Common prior distribution: Gaussian.

Marginal distributions of a joint distribution can be efficiently computed using a factor graph representation and the sum-product message-passing algorithm.

A posterior distribution is not necessarily Gaussian. In practice, it is common to approximate a posterior distribution with a Gaussian distribution.

Popular Rating Systems

(i) Elo rating system

(ii) TrueSkill

(iii) TopCoder Rating System

All these rating systems are based on a Thurstone model of ranking outcomes. They differ in the type of rankings (e.g., pair comparison, multi-alternative comparisons, or team competitions) and in the details of the statistical estimation method for the parameters of the model.

Exercises

9.1 **Two players: who's better?** Consider a sequence of contests with win-or-lose outcomes between two players, which are independent and such that one of the players is better in the sense of having a larger winning probability $p > 1/2$ in each contest than the other player. Given $\delta \in (0, 1]$, show that a sufficient number of contests to correctly identify the better player based on observed outcomes of contests, with probability at least $1 - \delta$, is any m such that

$$m \geq \frac{\log_2(1/\delta)}{D(\frac{1}{2} \| p)}$$

where $D(\alpha\|\beta)$ is the Kullback-Liebler divergence between two Bernoulli distributions with parameters α and β.

9.2 **Multiple matches between two players** Consider a two-player game that proceeds through successive rounds, where in each round each player either succeeds or fails, which is assumed to occur independently with success probabilities p_1 and p_2 in $(0, 1)$, for players 1 and 2, respectively. The winner of the game is the player who first accumulates a larger number of successes than the other player.

(a) Show that the winning probabilities are

$$\mathbf{Pr}[1 \succ 2] = 1 - \mathbf{Pr}[1 \prec 2] = \frac{\frac{p_1}{1-p_1}}{\frac{p_1}{1-p_1} + \frac{p_2}{1-p_2}}.$$

(b) Consider a more general game in which the winner of the game is the player who first accumulates m more successes than the other player, for a given parameter $m \geq 1$. Show that the winning probabilities are given by

$$\mathbf{Pr}[1 \succ 2] = 1 - \mathbf{Pr}[1 \prec 2] = \frac{\left(\frac{p_1}{1-p_1}\right)^m}{\left(\frac{p_1}{1-p_1}\right)^m + \left(\frac{p_2}{1-p_2}\right)^m}.$$

Note that the winning probabilities of the given game correspond to those of a generalized linear model with logistic difference function $D(x) = 1/(1 + e^{-mx})$, with parameters $v_1 = \log(p_1/(1 - p_1))$ and $v_2 = \log(p_2/(1 - p_2))$, as well as to those of the Bradley-Terry model with parameters $\theta_1 = (p_1/(1 - p_1))^m$ and $\theta_2 = (p_2/(1 - p_2))^m$.

9.3 **Poisson performances** Suppose that two players score points according to independent Poisson processes with rates λ_1 and λ_2, respectively, and the winner is the player who is the first to accumulate a given number $r \geq 1$ of score points. Prove the following two claims.

(a) The winning probabilities are given by

$$\mathbf{Pr}[1 \succ 2] = 1 - \mathbf{Pr}[1 \prec 2] = \frac{\sum_{i=r}^{2r-1} \binom{2r-1}{i} \left(\frac{\lambda_1}{\lambda_2}\right)^i}{\left(\frac{\lambda_1}{\lambda_2} + 1\right)^{2r-1}}.$$

(b) The Bradley-Terry model is a special case for $r = 1$.

9.4 **Polya's urn process** Consider a sequence of matches between two players, say player 1 and player 2, with win-or-lose outcomes such that in each match a player wins with a probability proportional to his or her number of wins accumulated in previous matches. Suppose that the initial numbers of wins are θ_1 and θ_2 for player 1 and player 2, respectively, such that $\theta_1 + \theta_2 > 0$. Show that for every match $t \geq 1$, the winning probabilities are such that

$$\mathbf{Pr}[\text{player 1 wins in match } t] = \frac{\theta_1}{\theta_1 + \theta_2}.$$

9.5 **Poisson distribution and the probability of winning a game** Suppose that two players exhibit performances according to independent random variables such that the performance of player 1 is a Poisson random variable b_1 with mean v_1 and the performance of player 2 is a random variable b_2 with distribution on the set of positive integers. Prove the following two claims.

(a) The following identity holds:

$$\frac{\partial}{\partial v_1}\mathbf{Pr}[b_1 > b_2] = \mathbf{Pr}[b_1 = b_2]. \tag{9.87}$$

(b) If equation (9.87) is required to hold for a distribution of b_1 that has the mean of value v_1 and the distribution is differentiable in v_1, for every distribution of b_2 on the set of positive integers, then the distribution of b_1 must be Poisson with mean v_1.

9.6 **Brownian motion model of point score difference** Consider the point score difference in a two-player contest, say between player 1 and player 2, defined as the difference of the cumulative points scored by player 1 and player 2. The contest duration is for a fixed time, say of unit value, and the winner is the player who at the contest end time has accumulated a larger number of points. Suppose that the point score difference is according to a Brownian motion $X(t)$, $t \in [0, 1]$, with mean drift μ per unit time and variance σ^2 per unit time. Under the Brownian motion model, for every $0 \le s < t$, $X(s)$ and $X(t) - X(s)$ are independent random variables such that $X(s)$ is a Gaussian random variable with mean μs and variance $\sigma^2 s$, and $X(t) - X(s)$ is a Gaussian random variable with mean $\mu(t - s)$ and variance $\sigma^2(t - s)$. Prove the following claims.

(a) The winning probability of player 1, conditional on the point score difference being of value d at time t of the contest, denoted by $p(t, d)$, is given by

$$p(t, d) = \Phi\left(\frac{(1 - t)\mu + d}{\sqrt{(1 - t)\sigma^2}}\right).$$

(b) The winning probability of player 1, conditional on that he or she leads at time t of the contest, denoted by $p(t)$, is given by

$$p(t) = \frac{1}{\Phi\left(\frac{\mu}{\sigma}\sqrt{t}\right)} \int_0^\infty \Phi\left(\sqrt{\frac{t}{1 - t}}x + \frac{\mu}{\sigma}\sqrt{1 - t}\right) \phi\left(x - \frac{\mu}{\sigma}\sqrt{t}\right) dx.$$

In particular, for the case of two players of equal strengths, so that $\mu = 0$, we have

$$p(t) = \frac{1}{2} + \frac{1}{\pi}\tan^{-1}\left(\sqrt{\frac{t}{1 - t}}\right).$$

Specifically, conditional on player 1 leading at the half-time, he or she has the winning probability of 3/4.

9.7 **Special instances of the generalized linear model** Show that the Thurstone Type V model, Bradley-Terry model, and Dawkins choice model are all special instances of the generalized linear model, each with the difference function D as given in Section 9.2.4.

9.8 **Generalized linear model and stochastic transitivity** A matrix $\mathbf{P} = (p_{i,j})$ is said to be stochastically transitive if for every three elements i, k, j such that $p_{i,k} \ge 1/2$ and $p_{k,j} \ge 1/2$, it holds that $p_{i,j} \ge 1/2$. Prove that for every generalized linear model, the matrix of win probabilities is stochastically transitive.

9.9   **Ranking in decreasing order of the number of wins** Suppose that the number of wins matrix $W = (w_{i,j})$ is given for a set of alternatives $N = \{1, 2, \ldots, n\}$ with each distinct pair of alternatives having the same number of comparisons. Let us define $w_i = \sum_{j \in N} w_{i,j}$, for $i \in N$. Prove that for the Bradley-Terry model with parameters $\theta_1, \theta_2, \ldots, \theta_n$, the maximum likelihood estimates $\hat{\theta}_1, \hat{\theta}_2, \ldots, \hat{\theta}_n$ of the model parameters satisfy the following property: if $w_i > w_j$, then $\hat{\theta}_i > \hat{\theta}_j$.

9.10 **Pair comparisons with ties** Show that for the Thurstone Type V model and the double-exponential Thurstone model with ties, the probabilities of the outcomes are as given in Section 9.10.

9.11 **Linear regression estimation of the strength parameters** Suppose a matrix of empirical probabilities of wins $(\hat{p}_{i,j}, i, j \in N)$ is given such that $0 < \hat{p}_{i,j} < 1$ for every $i \neq j$. Show that the vectors of strengths as given in (9.25) through (9.28), with $p_{i,j}$ therein replaced with $\hat{p}_{i,j}$, minimize the mean square-error defined by

$$\mathrm{MSE}(\mathbf{v}) = \sum_{i \neq j} (D^{-1}(\hat{p}_{i,j}) - (v_i - v_j))^2.$$

9.12 **Elo rating: two players** Consider the updates of the rating scores in a series of contests between two players defined by the following system of ordinary differential equations:

$$\frac{d}{dt} v_1(t) = p_{1,2} - \hat{p}_{1,2}(v_1(t) - v_2(t)) \tag{9.88}$$

$$\frac{d}{dt} v_2(t) = (1 - p_{1,2}) - (1 - \hat{p}_{1,2}(v_1(t) - v_2(t))) \tag{9.89}$$

where $p_{1,2} \in (0, 1)$ is the winning probability of player 1 and $\hat{p}_{1,2}(x) = 1/(1 + e^{-x})$. Prove the following claims.

(a)   For $i, j \in \{1, 2\}$ such that $i \neq j$, we have

$$\lim_{t \to \infty} v_i(t) = \frac{v_i(0) + v_j(0)}{2} + \frac{1}{2} \log \left(\frac{p_{i,j}}{1 - p_{i,j}} \right).$$

(b)   The rate of convergence is characterized as follows:

$$v_1(t) - \lim_{s \to \infty} v_1(s) \sim e^{-p_{1,2}(1 - p_{1,2})t}, \quad \text{for large } t.$$

9.13 **Sum-product algorithm for pair comparisons** Show that the message-passing update equations in (9.73) and (9.74) indeed correspond to that of the sum-product algorithm for the given problem.

9.14 **The Bradley-Terry model parameter estimation** For a set $N = \{1, 2, \ldots, n\}$ of two or more alternatives, outcomes of pair comparisons are given with $\mathbf{W} = (w_{i,j})$ and $\mathbf{M} = (m_{i,j})$ denoting the matrix of wins and the matrix of the number of pair comparisons, respectively. Suppose that the input is generated according to the Bradley-Terry model with parameters $\theta = (\theta_1, \theta_2, \ldots, \theta_n)$. Let us define

$$\hat{p}_{i,j} = \begin{cases} \frac{w_{i,j}}{m_{i,j}}, & \text{if } m_{i,j} > 0 \\ 0, & \text{otherwise} \end{cases}, \quad \text{for } i, j \in N.$$

Suppose that $\hat{\theta} = (\hat{\theta}_1, \hat{\theta}_2, \ldots, \hat{\theta}_n)$ is a solution to the following system of linear equations:

$$\left(\sum_{j=1}^{n} \hat{p}_{j,i} \right) \hat{\theta}_i = \sum_{j=1}^{n} \hat{p}_{i,j} \hat{\theta}_j, \quad \text{for } i = 1, 2, \ldots, n.$$

Prove the following claims.

(a) Suppose that for each pair the number of observed pair comparisons tends to infinity; then $\hat{\theta} = \theta$ is a solution of the given system of linear equations.

(b) The vector $\hat{\theta}$ is an invariant measure of a Markov chain with the state space $\{1, 2, \ldots, n\}$ and the matrix $Q = (q_{i,j})$ of the transition probabilities given as follows:

$$q_{i,j} = \begin{cases} \frac{1}{d}\hat{p}_{j,i}, & \text{if } i \neq j \\ 1 - \frac{1}{d}\sum_{l \neq i} \hat{p}_{l,i}, & \text{if } i = j \end{cases}$$

where d is a real number such that $d \geq \max_{i \in N} \sum_{l \neq i} \hat{p}_{l,i}$.

9.15 Recursive estimation of variance Show that the variance σ_t^2 defined in (9.85) obeys the recursive form in (9.86).

9.7 Bibliographical Notes

The statistical estimation problem in Section 9.1.1 that we phrased as estimating the probability of a contest outcome between two players using a Bayesian formulation was considered already in the 18th century by Laplace; he treated the problem of estimating the probability of the event that sunrise would occur tomorrow, which is often referred as *Laplace's rule of succession*. Feller (1957) contains a discussion of this problem.

A model of a ranking of a set of alternatives induced from an order statistic was introduced by Thurstone (1927) and is often referred to as the Thurstone model or Thurstone-Mosteller model following the work by Mosteller (1951a). The original work in Thurstone (1927) assumed a multivariate Gaussian distribution, but Thurstone models often refer to more general models that derive a ranking from an order statistic. Daniels (1950) studied rankings induced from an order statistic of a sequence of independent random variables from distributions that belong to a family of distributions with location parameters. Yellott (1977) showed that such a model accommodates the Plackett-Luce model (Luce (1959)) if, and only if, the scores are distributed according to a double-exponential distribution. Henery (1983) and Stern (1990b) studied the same model of rankings for Gamma distributions. A more general class of these models was considered by Böckenholt (1993).

The model for pair comparisons where each alternative is associated with a strength parameter and in each comparison of a pair of alternatives one of the alternatives is preferred over the other with probability proportional to its strength parameter was perhaps first studied by Zermelo (1929). The model was subsequently studied by Bradley and Terry (1952, 1954), and following this work it is often referred to as the Bradley-Terry model. It is also sometimes referred to as the Bradley-Terry-Luce model, following the work on user choice models by Luce (1959) and as the multinomial logit model (McFadden (1973)). The iterative computation of the maximum likelihood estimate of the model parameters was studied by Zermelo (1929) and subsequently by several authors including Ford Jr. (1957) and Dykstra Jr. (1956, 1960). More recently, Hunter (2004) studied conditions for convergence of iterative algorithms for computing maximum likelihood parameter estimates for the Bradley-Terry model and its extensions and for other models such as the Plackett-Luce model. The proof of Theorem 9.27 is based on Hunter (2004). Comparison of the ranking orders according to the Bradley-Terry model and the number of wins in Exercise 9.9 are from Ford Jr. (1957). The least squares estimation of the model parameters was first proposed and studied by Mosteller (1951a,b,c). The concept of rankits was studied, by Bliss et al. (1956). Davidson and Solomon (1973) studied a Bayesian approach to the analysis of pair comparison experiments for multinomial and Bradley-Terry statistical models. Jech (1983) proposed a method that corresponds to the well-known Bradley-Terry model; a clarification of how this work stands in comparison with contemporaneous literature was provided by Stob (1984), which contains a nice account of historical developments. Diaconis (1988) showed that the logistic generalized linear model of pair comparisons holds for the Thurstone model with exponential distributions of performances. More recent work has focused on studying various aspects of the Bradley-Terry model and its extensions. Conner and Grant (2000) studied the existence of maximum likelihood estimates of the Bradley-Terry model parameters for a perturbed matrix of pair comparisons. Huang et al. (2006) studied a generalization of the Bradley-Terry model for contests between teams of individuals where the skill of a team is assumed to be the sum of skills of individual team members. Negahban et al. (2012) studied a parameter estimation method for the Bradley-Terry model that is considered in Exercise 9.14.

The linear model was perhaps first introduced by Noether (1960), and the term "generalized linear model" was perhaps first introduced by Nelder and Wedderburn (1972). McCullagh and Nelder (1989) provide an in-depth book treatment of this class of statistical models; the exposition in Section 9.2.4 is based on that work. McCullagh (1980) considered regression models for ordinal data and maximum likelihood estimation that subsume some of the models for random generation of permutations as special cases. Stern (1990b) provides a review of various models for random generation of permutations. Yellott (1977) and Latta (1979) considered the composition rules for the winning probabilities in pair comparisons under certain axioms. Cattelan (2012) provides an overview of extensions of the basic model of pair comparisons, in particular, allowing for dependent comparisons. Several authors argued that different models of pair comparisons lead to similar fits, e.g., Mosteller (1951a,b,c), Jackson and Fleckenstein (1957), Noether (1960), and Stern (1990a), and that the precise choice of the linear model does not matter much. For instance, Stern (1990a) studied a family of linear models based on a Gamma distribution that includes the Bradley-Terry and Thurstone-Mosteller models as special cases and found empirical evidence that, for the number of pair comparisons usually observed in practice, all linear pair comparison models appear to be equivalent for most practical purposes. Beasley (2006) discusses this particular issue as part of a more general exposition on some mathematical aspects of games. Several approaches have been studied to model draw outcomes. Glenn and David (1960) studied an extension of the Thurstone-Mosteller model to account for draw outcomes (used in TrueSkill), while Rao and Kupper (1967) and Davidson (1970) studied extensions to account for draw outcomes in the Bradley-Terry model.

Mallow's model was proposed by Mallows (1957). Plackett (1975) and Luce (1959) studied statistical models for multiple comparisons. Guiver and Snelson (2009) studied a message-passing algorithm for inferring parameters of a rating system based on the Plackett-Luce distribution.

There are several good references for the topic of factor graphs and the sum-product algorithm, which we discussed in Section 9.5.3; they include chapter 4 in MacKay (2003), chapter 8 in Bishop (2006), and chapter 2 in Richardson and Urbanke (2008). Kschischang et al. (2001) contains a nice survey of factor graphs and the sum-product algorithm. The sum-product algorithm was introduced by Pearl (1982). The Gaussian density filtering discussed in Section 9.5.4 is known as expectation propagation, which is due to Minka (2001).

The Elo rating system was developed by Arpad Elo and was first approved by the USCF in 1960 and then by FIDE in 1970 (World Chess Federation (2013)). Elo (1978) provided an overview of various aspects of this rating system as defined up to that time. The Elo rating system was also used for prediction of outcomes in various sports, such as football (Kirill 2013), and inspired the design of a number of rating systems that were developed later.

A large body of literature in statistics is devoted to studying various statistical models for predicting outcomes in sports competitions such as football, basketball, and tennis. Thompson (1975) considered a maximum likelihood ranking of players in two-player contests under a model that assumes that the winning probability of a higher ranked player in a contest with a lower ranked player is a function of the difference of the ranks of the two players. Specifically, a linear model and a non-linear model of quadratic form were considered. Stefani (1977) considered the rating of football teams as a linear regression problem. Stefani (1980) considered a modified model. Harville (1977) considered a linear model for the point spread in contests between pairs of teams and applied the model to rate high school and college football teams. In this model each team performance in a contest in assumed to consist of a sum of a parameter that represents the skill of the team and another parameter that accounts for the home-field advantage. A modified model was also considered with the limited use of point spreads. In this modified model the points earned are assumed to be linear in the point spread, but are capped beyond a given winning margin. A similar model was considered by Harville (1980) to predict outcomes in National Football League (NFL) games, with a notable difference in modeling the yearly variation of characteristic performance levels of individual teams by a first-order autoregressive process. The point spread is used in betting to reflect the perceived difference between two teams, e.g., team x may be a p-point favorite to defeat a team y. If team x wins by more than p points then those who bet on x win their bets. If x wins by less than p points or loses against y, then those who bet on x lose their bets. Finally, if x wins by exactly p points then no money is won or lost. The point spreads are typically set so that approximately the same amounts are bet on the favorite and the underdog to limit the risk for those who handle the bets. Stern (1991) considered the point spread as a predictor of the margin of victory in NFL games. The prediction error was shown to be well characterized by a normal distribution in data from several seasons in the 1980s. Stern (1994) studied a Brownian motion as a model of the progress of score difference in a two-player contest and provided goodness-of-fit results for data on professional basketball games.

Exercise 9.6 is from Stern (1994). Keller (1994) studied a model where the performance of a player is according to a Poisson distribution and established some characterization results. Exercise 9.5 is from Keller (1994). Keener (1993) considered how different methods for ranking teams of players depend in a fundamental way on the Perron-Frobenius theorem. Harville and Smith (1994) considered three linear models for the score difference that account for the home-court advantage. For the 1991–1992 college basketball season data reported in newspapers, the advantage of playing at home was estimated to be 4.68 ± 0.28 points relative to playing on a neutral court. Bassett (1997) considered the problem of rating teams based on minimizing the least absolute errors. Dixon and Coles (1997) developed a Poisson regression model that was fitted to English league and cup football data in the period 1992 to 1995. The model was shown to have positive returns when applied as a betting strategy. Mease (2003) proposed a penalized maximum likelihood approach that alleviates the issue of infinite likelihoods in the case of the existence of a player who won against any other player. The model was tested on college football team data. Reid (2003) considered a linear regression model in which each team is associated with two parameters, one to reflect the offense strength and the other the defense strength. The score of a team against an opponent is assumed to be the sum of an offense parameter of the team and a defense parameter of the opponent plus a random noise. The model parameters were estimated on college football scores data.

There are several books dedicated to statistical models for ranking data. David (1963) provides an excellent summary on pair comparisons. The book by Marden (1995) covers various types of statistical models for ranking data. McCullagh and Nelder (1989) provides an in-depth study of generalized linear models. The regression models for categorical data are covered by Tutz (2012) and Agresti (2013). In particular, the latter reference contains a discussion of a Bradley-Terry model that accounts for the home-field advantage. A survey of various ranking systems and their properties is available in Langville and Meyer (2012). Epstein (2013) provides an account on various aspects of gambling and statistics. The concepts from information theory and statistics such as the Kullback-Leibler divergence used in this chapter are standard; the interested reader may find more about these fundamental concepts in the book by Cover and Thomas (2006).

CHAPTER 10

Ranking Methods

In this chapter we consider the problem of ranking alternatives using as input a sequence of rankings of subsets of the alternatives. This problem arises in many situations including that of finding a global ranking of teams in a competition based on observed outcomes in contests involving subsets of teams, e.g., pairs of teams in many popular sports competitions. We may also think of rank aggregation where the goal is to find a consensus ranking for a set of input rankings from different sources, e.g., computing an aggregate ranking given as input a list of top-ranked search results by different search engines. The rank aggregation problem also accommodates the problem of identifying a ground-truth ranking based on noisy input judgments by a panel of experts. For example, such a problem arises in classification of objects that is now commonly performed by less-than-expert workers in paid-labor crowdsourcing online platforms.

We shall first consider the problem of rank aggregation where given a set of input rankings of a set of alternatives, the goal is to find an aggregate ranking of the alternatives that minimizes a given loss function. This optimization-based approach can be seen as finding a global ranking that minimizes the extent of disagreement with the input set of rankings. Specifically, we shall consider the problem of finding an aggregate ranking of alternatives that minimizes the sum of distances to individual input rankings of the alternatives. We shall see that some well-known distances are within a constant factor of each other, e.g., the well-known Kendall's τ and Spearman's Footrule distances. We shall consider the well-known Kemeny rank aggregation where the goal is to find an aggregate ranking of alternatives that minimizes the total number of disagreements of ranking of pairs of alternatives with respect to the input rankings of alternatives. This problem is known to be NP hard. We shall discuss some simple algorithms that guarantee a constant-factor approximation. We shall then consider the problem known as the minimum feedback arc set in tournaments, where the input is a tournament graph defined as a directed graph where there is exactly one directed edge between each pair of vertices, and the goal is to find a linear ordering of vertices that minimizes the number of backward edges. For example, a tournament graph may be defined as a majority tournament graph where the direction of an edge between a pair of alternatives indicates the majority winner between the two alternatives in a series of contests. A weighted tournament graph is a generalization that associates a weight to each ordered pair of alternatives; this weight, for example, may represent the number of times one of the alternatives won against the other alternative in a series of contests involving these two alternatives. We shall focus on the computational aspects and present some of the approximation algorithms known for this problem.

We shall then consider some well-known scoring methods for ranking a set of alternatives, which are based on assigning a score to each alternative and then ranking the alternatives in decreasing order of their scores. A popular scoring method, namely the point difference scoring method, defines the score for an alternative as the difference between the number of wins and the number of loses in comparisons with other alternatives. We shall show that the point difference scoring method is optimal with respect to minimizing a broad family of loss functions for pair comparisons according to a probabilistic model that satisfies certain assumptions.

Finally, we shall consider the problem of aggregation of judgments, a rank aggregation problem where the goal is to maximize the probability of identifying an underlying ground-truth ranking of alternatives based on noisy input judgments by a panel of experts. The problem can be formulated as a maximum a posteriori probability estimation of the ground-truth ranking. We shall show that for the special case of ranking two alternatives, the maximum a posteriori probability estimation is a weighted majority aggregation of judgments with a specific choice of the weights that represent the abilities of experts. We shall then consider the more general case of a collection of pairs of alternatives, where the goal is to minimize the total number of input judgments subject to guaranteeing a prescribed accuracy in identifying the ground-truth ranking for each pair of alternatives. A motivation for studying this problem is the classification of objects that is now commonly done using paid-labor crowdsourcing online platforms that recruit workers of varied expertise. In such settings, each judgment corresponds to a labeling instance that costs a fixed amount of money.

10.1 Basic Concepts

Suppose a set $N = \{1, 2, \ldots, n\}$ of alternatives is given. A full ranking of alternatives π is a one-to-one mapping $\pi : N \to N$, where $\pi(i)$ is the position of alternative i in the ordering of alternatives according to π. The set of full rankings of n alternatives is the set S_n of all permutations of n elements. By convention, an alternative i is said to be ranked higher than alternative j if $\pi(i) < \pi(j)$, i.e., a higher ranked alternative appears before a lower ranked alternative in the ordering of the alternatives according to π. The more general case of partial rankings allows for ties.

Let $d : S_n \times S_n \to \mathbf{R}$ be a given function that we refer to as a *distance function*. For two full rankings ρ and σ, $d(\rho, \sigma)$ quantifies the distance between the two full rankings ρ and σ.

10.1.1 A Catalog of Distances between Rankings

Some well-known distance functions for a pair of full rankings ρ and σ are given as follows:

(i) *Kendall's τ* distance function:

$$K(\rho, \sigma) = \sum_{i,j \in N: i < j} \mathbf{1}((\rho(i) - \rho(j))(\sigma(i) - \sigma(j)) < 0). \qquad (10.1)$$

This distance function corresponds to the number of pairwise disagreements in the two input full rankings of alternatives. It is equivalent to the minimum number of interchanges of adjacent pairs of the alternatives that is needed to transform the ordering of the alternatives according to ρ to the ordering of the alternatives according to σ. The maximum value of Kendall's τ distance function is $n(n-1)/2$, which is achieved when σ is the reverse of the full ranking ρ.

(ii) *Spearman's footrule* distance function:

$$F(\rho, \sigma) = \sum_{i \in N} |\rho(i) - \sigma(i)|. \qquad (10.2)$$

This distance function has the maximum value of $n^2/2$ when n is even and the maximum value of $(n^2 - 1)/2$ when n is odd, which are achieved when σ is the reverse of the full ranking ρ.

(iii) *Spearman's ρ* distance function:

$$d(\rho, \sigma) = \sum_{i \in N} (\rho(i) - \sigma(i))^2. \qquad (10.3)$$

(iv) A family of distance functions, for $0 < p < \infty$,

$$d(\rho, \sigma) = \sum_{i \in N} |\rho(i) - \sigma(i)|^p$$

which accommodates the Separman's footrule and Spearman's ρ distance as special cases for $p = 1$ and $p = 2$, respectively.

(v) *Cayley* distance function: defined as the number of interchanges of pairs of alternatives required to transform the input full ranking ρ to the input full ranking σ, allowing for interchanges of any pair of alternatives (not restricted to adjacent alternatives as in the definition of Kendall's τ distance function).

(vi) *Hamming's* distance function:

$$d(\rho, \sigma) = \sum_{i \in N} \mathbf{1}(\rho(i) \neq \sigma(i)). \qquad (10.4)$$

This distance function corresponds to the number of disagreeing ranks of the alternatives.

(N, d) is a metric space if the distance function d satisfies four conditions given in Definition 11.5, which include symmetry and triangle inequality. For Kendall's τ and Spearman's footrule distance functions, (N, d) is a metric space.

10.1.2 Diaconis-Graham Inequality

The definitions of the Kendall's τ and Spearman's footrule distance functions may appear to be quite different from each other. However, they are within a constant factor of each other for every pair of input full rankings as shown in the following theorem.

Theorem 10.1. *For every two full rankings σ and ρ of a set of alternatives N, we have*

$$K(\rho, \sigma) \le F(\rho, \sigma) \le 2K(\rho, \sigma). \tag{10.5}$$

Proof. We first prove the inequality $F(\rho, \sigma) \le 2K(\rho, \sigma)$. The proof is by induction on the value of the Kendall's τ distance. Base case: $K(\rho, \sigma) = 0$. Since both orderings are the same, we have $F(\rho, \sigma) = 0$, and the thus the hypothesis trivially holds. Induction step: suppose that the hypothesis holds for any two full rankings with the Kendall's τ distance of value $k - 1$ and we then show that this implies that it holds for any two full rankings with the Kendall's τ distance of value k. Let σ' be an ordering of the alternatives derived from σ by a swap of two alternatives, which reduces the Kendall's τ distance by 1. Then,

$$K(\rho, \sigma') = K(\rho, \sigma) - 1, K(\sigma, \sigma') = 1 \text{ and } F(\sigma, \sigma') = 2.$$

The proof follows by the following series of inequalities:

$$F(\rho, \sigma) \le F(\rho, \sigma') + F(\sigma, \sigma') \tag{10.6}$$

$$= F(\rho, \sigma') + 2K(\sigma, \sigma')$$

$$\le 2K(\rho, \sigma') + 2K(\sigma, \sigma') \tag{10.7}$$

$$= 2K(\rho, \sigma)$$

where (10.6) is by the triangle inequality applied to the distance function F, and (10.7) is by the induction hypothesis applied to ρ and σ' so it holds that $F(\rho, \sigma') \le 2K(\rho, \sigma')$.

We now prove the inequality $K(\rho, \sigma) \le F(\rho, \sigma)$. The proof is by induction on the value of the Spearman's footrule distance. Base case: $F(\rho, \sigma) = 0$. Since both orderings are the same, we have $K(\rho, \sigma) = 0$, and thus the hypothesis trivially holds. Induction step: suppose that the hypothesis holds for any two full rankings with the Spearman's footrule distance of value $k - 1$ and we then show that this implies that it holds for any two full rankings with the Spearman's footrule distance of value k. Without loss of generality, assume that ρ is the identity permutation, i.e., $\rho(1) = 1$, $\rho(2) = 2, \ldots, \rho(n) = n$. Then,

$$F(\rho, \sigma) = \sum_{i \in N} |\sigma(i) - i|.$$

Let i be the largest element in N such that $\sigma(i) \ne i$. Notice that by definition it must be $\sigma(i) < i$. Let j be the largest element in N such that $j \le \sigma(i) < \sigma(j)$. Such an element must exist because at positions $1, 2, \ldots, \sigma(i) - 1$ there can be at most $\sigma(i) - 1$ elements $1, 2, \ldots, \sigma(i)$. Notice that it must hold that $\sigma(j) \le i$ because otherwise we would have a contradiction to the definition of the element i. See Figure 10.1 for an illustration. Let σ' be the full ranking of alternatives obtained from σ by swapping

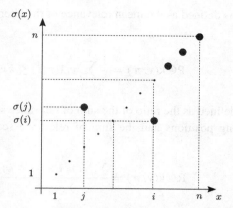

Figure 10.1. The definition of elements i and j for a full ranking σ.

the positions of alternatives i and j. For the full ranking σ', $\sigma'(i) \leq i$ and $\sigma'(j) \leq j$ because $j \leq \sigma(i)$ and $\sigma(j) \leq i$. The following identity holds:

$$F(\rho, \sigma) - F(\rho, \sigma') = |\sigma(i) - i| + |\sigma(j) - j| - (|\sigma(j) - i| + |\sigma(i) - j|)$$
$$= 2|\sigma(i) - \sigma(j)|. \tag{10.8}$$

The proof follows by the following series of relations:

$$F(\rho, \sigma) = 2|\sigma(i) - \sigma(j)| + F(\rho, \sigma') \tag{10.9}$$
$$\geq 2|\sigma(i) - \sigma(j)| + K(\rho, \sigma') \tag{10.10}$$
$$\geq K(\sigma, \sigma') + K(\rho, \sigma') \tag{10.11}$$
$$\geq K(\rho, \sigma) \tag{10.12}$$

where (10.9) is by the identity (10.8), (10.10) is by the induction hypothesis, (10.11) is by $K(\sigma, \sigma') \leq 2|\sigma(i) - \sigma(j)|$, and (10.12) is by the triangle inequality. $\square$

10.1.3 Standard Measures of Efficiency of a Ranking of Alternatives

Several definitions of efficiency of a full ranking of alternatives are used in the context of information retrieval systems, with respect to given positive-valued relevance scores $\mathbf{v} = (v_1, v_2, \ldots, v_n)$ of alternatives. For example, these relevance scores may be given as input by a set of experts, or they may be parameters of a probabilistic model of the full rankings of alternatives. The relevance scores may be binary, with value 1 indicating a relevant alternative, and value 0 indicating a non-relevant alternative. Typically, standard information retrieval measures of efficiency of a ranking of alternatives put a larger weight on the relevance of higher ranked alternatives. This is based on the intuition that in an information retrieval system, users tend to peruse the alternatives that appear high enough in the presented ranking of alternatives.

We introduce the following standard measures of efficiency of a full ranking of alternatives π that use as a parameter an integer $1 \leq k \leq n$.

(i) *Precision at k* is defined as the mean relevance of the alternatives at top k ranking positions:

$$P@k(\mathbf{v}, \pi) = \frac{1}{k} \sum_{i=1}^{n} v_i \mathbf{1}(\pi(i) \le k).$$

(ii) *Recall at k* is defined as the ratio of the sum of relevance scores of the alternatives at top k ranking positions and the sum of relevance scores over the set of all alternatives:

$$R@k(\mathbf{v}, \pi) = \frac{\sum_{i=1}^{n} v_i \mathbf{1}(\pi(i) \le k)}{\sum_{i=1}^{n} v_i}.$$

(iii) *F1 Measure at k* is a measure of efficiency of a ranking defined as a combination of precision and recall, specifically as the harmonic mean of precision and recall:

$$F1@k(\mathbf{v}, \pi) = \frac{2 \sum_{i=1}^{n} v_i \mathbf{1}(\pi(i) \le k)}{k + \sum_{i=1}^{n} v_i}.$$

(iv) *Average Precision* is defined as a weighted sum of precision at k with the weights proportional to the relevance scores of the alternatives:

$$AP(\mathbf{v}, \pi) = \frac{\sum_{j=1}^{n} v_j P@j(\mathbf{v}, \pi)}{\sum_{j=1}^{n} v_j}.$$

(v) *Reciprocal Rank at k* is defined for binary-valued relevance scores as the reciprocal rank of the highest ranked relevant alternative, if the rank of such an alternative is less than or equal to k, and otherwise, it is defined to be equal to zero:

$$RR@k(\mathbf{v}, \pi) = \frac{1}{r} \mathbf{1}(r \le k)$$

where $r = \min\{j \in N \mid v_{\pi^{-1}(j)} = 1 \text{ or } j = n\}$. Intuitively, we may think of this measure of efficiency of a full ranking of alternatives as reciprocal of the search cost for finding a relevant item by a user who inspects the top k ranked alternatives sequentially from the top to the bottom of the list.

(vi) *Normalized Discounted Cumulative Gain* The discounted cumulative gain at k is defined as

$$DCG@k(\mathbf{v}, \pi) = \sum_{i=1}^{n} \frac{2^{v_i} - 1}{\log(\pi(i) + 1)} \mathbf{1}(\pi(i) \le k).$$

The normalized discounted cumulative gain at k is defined as

$$NDCG@k(\mathbf{v}, \pi) = \frac{DCG@k(\mathbf{v}, \pi)}{DCG@k(\mathbf{v}, \pi_{\mathbf{v}})}$$

where $\pi_{\mathbf{v}}$ is a full ranking of alternatives in decreasing order of their relevance scores.

10.2 Rank Aggregation

We consider a specific formulation of a rank aggregation problem and the related optimization problem known as the minimum feedback arc set problem for tournaments.

10.2.1 Rank Aggregation Problem

The input to the problem is a sequence of one or more full rankings $\pi_1, \pi_2, \ldots, \pi_m$ that take values on the set of permutations S_n. Given a distance function $d : S_n \times S_n \to \mathbf{R}_+$, the *rank aggregation problem* is defined as follows: find a full ranking $\pi \in S_n$ that minimizes the loss function

$$L(\pi) = \sum_{i=1}^{m} d(\pi, \pi_i).$$

In particular, if d is the Kendall's τ distance function, then the rank aggregation problem is known as *the Kemeny rank aggregation*. The objective of the Kemeny rank aggregation problem is to find a full ranking of the alternatives that minimizes the total number of pairwise disagreements with the input sequence of full rankings of the alternatives.

Computational Complexity and Approximation Algorithms

The computational complexity of the Kemeny rank aggregation problem is asserted in the following theorem, which we state without a proof. The interested reader may find a brief review of the developments that led to this result in the bibliographical notes at the end of this chapter.

Theorem 10.2. *Finding a Kemeny optimal ranking is NP-hard.*

Although solving the Kemeny optimal rank aggregation is NP-hard, a constant-factor approximation in expectation is guaranteed by an algorithm as simple as returning as output one of the input rankings selected uniformly at random from the set of input full rankings.

Theorem 10.3. *The rank aggregation that outputs one of the input full rankings chosen uniformly at random from the set of input full rankings has the expected loss that is at most factor 2 of the optimum value of the loss function.*

Proof. Let π be a full ranking chosen uniformly at random from the set of input full rankings and let π^* be a full ranking that minimizes the Kemeny loss function. For the given sequence of input full rankings $\pi_1, \pi_2, \ldots, \pi_m$, let $w_{i,j}$ be the number of input full rankings for which alternative i is ranked higher than alternative j. The proof follows by the following series of relations:

$$\mathbf{E}[L(\pi)] = \mathbf{E}\left[\sum_{i,j \in N} w_{j,i}\mathbf{1}(\pi(i) < \pi(j))\right]$$

$$= 2\sum_{i<j} \frac{w_{j,i}w_{i,j}}{w_{i,j} + w_{j,i}} \tag{10.13}$$

$$\leq 2\sum_{i<j} \min\{w_{i,j}, w_{j,i}\}$$

$$\leq 2L(\pi^*) \tag{10.14}$$

where equation (10.13) holds because for any two distinct alternatives $i, j \in N$, the event $\{\pi(i) < \pi(j)\}$ occurs with probability proportional to the number of input rankings that rank alternative i higher than alternative j, i.e.,

$$\mathbf{Pr}[\pi(i) < \pi(j)] = 1 - \mathbf{Pr}[\pi(i) > \pi(j)] = \frac{w_{i,j}}{w_{i,j} + w_{j,i}}$$

and inequality (10.14) obviously holds because the Kemeny optimal ranking of alternatives must incur a cost of at least $\min\{w_{i,j}, w_{j,i}\}$ for every pair (i, j) of alternatives. $\qquad\qquad\square$

The factor 2 approximation in Theorem 10.3 is tight: for every given $\epsilon > 0$, there exists a sequence of input full rankings for which the algorithm has the loss function of value at least $2(1 - \epsilon)$ of the optimal value. This is shown by the following instance: let $\pi_1, \pi_2, \ldots, \pi_{n-1}$ be a sequence of input full rankings where π_i is the identity full ranking in S_n except for swapping the positions of alternatives i and $i + 1$, i.e.,

$$\pi_1 = (2, 1, 3, 4, 5 \ldots, n - 2, n - 1, n)$$
$$\pi_2 = (1, 3, 2, 4, 5, \ldots, n - 2, n - 1, n)$$
$$\vdots$$
$$\pi_{n-1} = (1, 2, 3, 4, 5, \ldots, n - 2, n, n - 1).$$

For this sequence of input full rankings, every input full ranking of alternatives has the Kemeny loss function of value $2(n - 2)$. On the other hand, the identity full ranking of the alternatives has the Kemeny loss function of value $n - 1$. Hence, it follows that taking any input full ranking as the output full ranking has the Kemeny loss function of value at least $2(1 - 1/(n - 1))$ of the optimum value of the Kemeny loss function.

10.2.2 Minimum Feedback Arc Set in Tournaments

The input for the minimum feedback arc set in tournaments problem is a tournament directed graph $G = (N, E)$ such that for every pair $i, j \in N$ either $(i, j) \in E$ or $(j, i) \in$

E, exclusively. We may intuitively interpret $(i, j) \in E$ as a binary relation that ranks alternative i higher than alternative j. The minimum feedback arc set problem is to find a full ranking π of alternatives that minimizes the number of pairs $(i, j) \in E$ such that $\pi(j) < \pi(i)$.

A generalization of the minimum feedback arc set in tournaments is the weighted minimum feedback arc set problem where the input is a matrix of positive real values $\mathbf{W} = (w_{i,j})$. In particular, w may intuitively interpret $w_{i,j}$ as the portion of observations in which alternative i is ranked higher than alternative j. The following two natural assumptions are sometimes imposed on the values of the elements of matrix $\mathbf{W}$:

(i) Probability constraints: $0 \le w_{i,j} \le 1$ and $w_{i,j} + w_{j,i} = 1$, for all $i, j \in N$.
(ii) Triangle inequality: $w_{i,j} \le w_{i,k} + w_{k,j}$, for all $i, j, k \in N$.

The *weighted minimum feedback arc set problem* is to find a full ranking π^* of alternatives that minimizes the loss function

$$L(\pi) = \sum_{i,j \in N} w_{j,i} \mathbf{1}(\pi(i) < \pi(j)) \tag{10.15}$$

over the full rankings $\pi \in S_n$.

Here the objective is to find a full ranking of alternatives that minimizes the total weight of the backward edges with respect to the order of alternatives according to the given full ranking of alternatives. The minimum feedback arc set problem for tournaments is a special case for the choice of the weights $w_{i,j} = 1$ if $(i, j) \in E$, and $w_{i,j} = 0$, otherwise. In this special case, the objective is to find a full ranking of alternatives that minimizes the number of backward edges with respect to the order of alternatives according to the given full ranking of alternatives.

The Kemeny rank aggregation problem is a special case of minimizing the weighted feedback-arc set in tournaments by defining $w_{i,j}$ as the portion of the input full rankings that rank alternative higher than alternative j, and observing that the objective function of the Kemeny rank aggregation problem corresponds to that in (10.15).

Probabilistic Justification of the Kemeny Rank Aggregation

The Kemeny rank aggregation is known to admit an interpretation as a maximum likelihood estimate of an underlying ground-truth full ranking of alternatives from noisy observations of pair comparisons according to the following probabilistic model. Given a ground-truth full ranking of alternatives π^*, pair comparisons are assumed to be independent according to the following distribution: for every comparison of a pair of alternatives, the observed order of the two alternatives is according to the ground-truth full ranking of alternatives π^* with probability $1/2 < p < 1$ and is in the reverse order, otherwise.

Let $\mathbf{W} = (w_{i,j})$ be the observed pair comparisons with $w_{i,j} = 1$ if alternative i is observed to be ranked higher than alternative j, and $w_{i,j} = 0$, otherwise. The likelihood of observing pair comparisons $\mathbf{W} = (w_{i,j})$ under the hypothesis that the ground-truth full ranking is π is given by

$$f(\pi) = \prod_{i,j \in N : \pi(i) < \pi(j)} p^{w_{i,j}}(1-p)^{w_{j,i}}$$

$$= (1-p)^{\sum_{i,j \in N} w_{j,i} \mathbf{1}(\pi(i) < \pi(j))} p^{\sum_{i,j \in N} w_{i,j} \mathbf{1}(\pi(i) < \pi(j))}$$

$$= p^{\sum_{i,j \in N} w_{i,j}} \cdot \left(\frac{1-p}{p} \right)^{\sum_{i,j \in N} w_{j,i} \mathbf{1}(\pi(i) < \pi(j))}.$$

Since by assumption $1/2 < p < 1$, we have $(1-p)/p \in (0, 1)$. Hence, maximizing the likelihood $f(\pi)$ is equivalent to minimizing $\sum_{i,j \in N} w_{j,i} \mathbf{1}(\pi(i) < \pi(j))$, which corresponds to the objective function of the weighted minimum feedback arc set problem given in equation (10.15).

QuickSort for Tournaments: A 3-Approximation

Consider an algorithm for tournaments that proceeds recursively by picking a pivot alternative and deriving a ranking by sorting the alternatives with respect to this pivot alternative: it puts all alternatives of higher rank than the pivot to the left and all alternatives of lower rank than the pivot to the right. See a formal definition in Algorithm 1.

QuickSort $(G = (N, E))$
if $N = \emptyset$ **then**
  return empty-list
end
Pick a random pivot $i \in N$;
$N_L \leftarrow \{j \in N : (j, i) \in E\}$;
$N_R \leftarrow \{j \in N : (i, j) \in E\}$;
return order QuickSort $(G(N_L))$, i, QuickSort $(G(N_R))$

Theorem 10.4. *QuickSort is a randomized algorithm for the minimum feedback arc set tournament problem with the expected cost of at most three times the optimal cost.*

Proof. Given as input a tournament graph $G = (N, E)$, let $\mathcal{T}$ be the set of directed triangles, and let T be the subset of $\mathcal{T}$ containing triangles whose all three vertices are part of the same recursive call and in this recursive call one of its vertices is selected to be the pivot. Let C_e be the cost incurred for edge $e \in E$ in the output of the algorithm: $C_e = 1$ if e is a backward edge and $C_e = 0$ otherwise. Note that the total cost of the algorithm amounts to a unit cost paid for each backward edge, and one backward edge is introduced by each directed triangle $t \in T$.

First, note that that the optimal value $L(\pi^*)$ is lower bounded by the solution of the following primal linear programming problem:

$$\text{minimize} \quad \sum_{e \in E} x_e$$

$$\text{subject to} \quad x_{e_1} + x_{e_2} + x_{e_3} \geq 1, \quad \text{for all } (e_1, e_2, e_3) \in \mathcal{T}$$

$$x_e \geq 0, \quad \text{for all } e \in E.$$

The optimum value of the primal problem is lower bounded by the optimum value of the dual linear programming problem that reads as follows:

$$\text{maximize} \quad \sum_{t \in \mathcal{T}} y_t$$

$$\text{subject to} \quad \sum_{t \in \mathcal{T}: e \in T} y_t \leq 1 \quad \text{for all } e \in E$$

$$y_t \geq 0, \quad \text{for all } t \in \mathcal{T}.$$

Therefore, we have

$$\sum_{t \in \mathcal{T}} y_t \leq L(\pi^*) \tag{10.16}$$

for every vector $\mathbf{y} = (y_t, t \in \mathcal{T})$ of non-negative real values such that $\sum_{t \in \mathcal{T}: e \in T} y_t \leq 1$ for all $e \in E$.

Second, note that $\mathbf{y} = (y_t, t \in \mathcal{T})$ with $y_t = \frac{1}{3}\mathbf{Pr}[t \in T]$ for $t \in \mathcal{T}$ is one such vector. Indeed,

$$\sum_{t \in \mathcal{T}: e \in t} \frac{1}{3}\mathbf{Pr}[t \in T] = \sum_{t \in \mathcal{T}: e \in t} \mathbf{Pr}[C_e = 1 \mid t \in T]\mathbf{Pr}[t \in T]$$

$$= \sum_{t \in \mathcal{T}: e \in t} \mathbf{Pr}[C_e = 1, t \in T]$$

$$= \mathbf{Pr}[C_e = 1]$$

$$\leq 1.$$

Third, and last, we have

$$\mathbf{E}[L(\pi)] = \mathbf{E}\left[\sum_{t \in \mathcal{T}} \mathbf{1}(t \in T)\right] \tag{10.17}$$

$$= \sum_{t \in \mathcal{T}} \mathbf{Pr}[t \in T]$$

$$= 3\sum_{t \in \mathcal{T}} \frac{1}{3}\mathbf{Pr}[t \in T]$$

$$\leq 3L(\pi^*) \tag{10.18}$$

where (10.17) is by the fact that there is a one-to-one mapping between the backward edges and the directed triangles in T, and the inequality (10.18) holds by (10.16) for the values $y_t = \frac{1}{3}\mathbf{Pr}[t \in T]$ for $t \in \mathcal{T}$. $\qquad\square$

Ordering in Decreasing Order of the Number of Wins:
A 5-Approximation

A common rank aggregation method deployed in various contests is to order the players in decreasing order of the number of wins, assuming that each player is confronted with each other player the same number of times. Given a weighted tournament matrix $\mathbf{W} = (w_{i,j})$ where each $w_{i,j}$ represents the portion of matches between players i and j that player i won, the ordering in decreasing number of wins corresponds to ranking of the players in decreasing order of the row-sums of matrix $\mathbf{W}$. How does this rank aggregation rule fare with respect to the objective of minimizing the feedback-arc-set problem? The following theorem provides an answer to this question.

Theorem 10.5. *Ranking in decreasing order of the number of wins yields a feedback-arc-set loss that is at most factor 5 of the optimal feedback-arc-set loss.*

Proof. Let $w(i) = \sum_{j \in N} w_{i,j}$ be the number of wins for alternative $i \in N$, and let ω be a permutation that orders the alternatives in decreasing order of the number of wins. Recall that L denotes the loss function for the weighted minimum feedback arc set problem defined in (10.15) and F denotes the Spearman footrule distance function defined in (10.2).

We claim that for every pair of permutations σ and ρ of the elements of the set N, we have the following three relations:

$$L(\sigma) \geq \frac{1}{2} F(n - \sigma, w) \tag{10.19}$$

$$F(n - \sigma, w) \geq F(n - \omega, w) \tag{10.20}$$

$$F(\sigma, \rho) \geq |L(\sigma) - L(\rho)|. \tag{10.21}$$

Using these claims, the proof follows from the following series of relations: let π be a permutation that minimizes the weighted feedback-arc-set loss function; then

$$4L(\pi) \geq \sum_{i \in N} |(n - \pi(i)) - w(i)| + |(n - \pi(i)) - w(i)|$$

$$\geq \sum_{i \in N} |(n - \pi(i)) - w(i)| + |(n - \omega(i)) - w(i)|$$

$$\geq \sum_{i \in N} |\pi(i) - \omega(i)|$$

$$\geq L(\omega) - L(\pi),$$

where the first inequality is by (10.19), the second inequality is by (10.20), the third inequality is by the triangle inequality, and finally, the fourth inequality is by (10.21) and the assumption that π minimizes the feedback-arc-set loss. We have shown that $L(\omega) \leq 5L(\pi)$.

It remains to establish claims (10.19), (10.20), and (10.21). First, we establish the inequality (10.19). For every permutation σ, the feedback-arc-set loss is equal to

$$L(\sigma) = \frac{1}{2} \sum_{i \in N} \sum_{j \in N} w_{i,j} \mathbf{1}(\sigma(i) > \sigma(j)) + w_{j,i} \mathbf{1}(\sigma(i) < \sigma(j)). \tag{10.22}$$

For every $i \in N$, we have the following relations:

$$\sum_{j \in N} w_{i,j} \mathbf{1}(\sigma(i) > \sigma(i)) + w_{j,i} \mathbf{1}(\sigma(i) < \sigma(j)) \tag{10.23}$$

$$= \sum_{j \in N} \mathbf{1}(\sigma(i) > \sigma(j)) + \sum_{j \in N} w_{j,i} - 2 \sum_{j \in N} w_{j,i} \mathbf{1}(\sigma(i) > \sigma(j)) \tag{10.24}$$

$$= (\sigma(i) - 1) + (n - 1 - w(i)) - 2 \sum_{j \in N} w_{j,i} \mathbf{1}(\sigma(i) > \sigma(j)) \tag{10.25}$$

$$= |(n - 1 - w_i) - (\sigma(i) - 1)|$$

$$+ 2 \left(\min\{n - 1 - w(i), \sigma(i) - 1\} - \sum_{j \in N} w_{j,i} \mathbf{1}(\sigma(i) > \sigma(j)) \right) \tag{10.26}$$

$$\geq |(n - 1 - w(i)) - (\sigma(i) - 1)| \tag{10.27}$$

$$= |n - \sigma(i) - w(i)| \tag{10.28}$$

where (10.24) follows by the fact $w_{i,j} + w_{j,i} = 1$ for every $i, j \in N$ such that $i \neq j$ and simple algebra; (10.26) follows by the elementary identity $x + y = |x - y| - 2\min\{x, y\}$ for every $x, y \in \mathbf{R}$, and (10.27) is because the term in brackets in (10.26) is non-negative. Summing the elements in (10.23) and (10.28) over $i \in N$ we obtain (10.19).

Second, the inequality in (10.20) holds because $\sum_{i \in N} |(n - \sigma(i)) - w(i)|$ is minimized by a permutation σ that orders the alternatives in decreasing order of the weights $w(1), w(2), \ldots, w(n)$, which by definition holds true for permutation ω.

Third, the inequality in (10.21) is shown as follows:

$$|L(\rho) - L(\sigma)|$$

$$= \left| \sum_{i,j \in N} w_{i,j} [\mathbf{1}(\sigma(j) < \sigma(i)) - \mathbf{1}(\rho(j) < \rho(i))] \right| \tag{10.29}$$

$$\leq \sum_{i,j \in N} w_{i,j} |\mathbf{1}(\sigma(j) < \sigma(i)) - \mathbf{1}(\rho(j) < \rho(i))| \tag{10.30}$$

$$= \sum_{i,j \in N} w_{i,j} |\mathbf{1}(\sigma(j) < \sigma(i), \rho(j) > \rho(i)) - \mathbf{1}(\sigma(j) > \sigma(i), \rho(j) < \rho(i))| \tag{10.31}$$

$$= \sum_{i,j \in N} w_{i,j} [\mathbf{1}(\sigma(j) < \sigma(i), \rho(j) > \rho(i)) + \mathbf{1}(\sigma(j) > \sigma(i), \rho(j) < \rho(i))] \tag{10.32}$$

$$= \sum_{i<j} \mathbf{1}(\sigma(j) < \sigma(i), \rho(j) > \rho(i)) + \mathbf{1}(\rho(j) < \rho(i), \sigma(j) > \sigma(i)) \tag{10.33}$$

$$= K(\sigma, \rho) \tag{10.34}$$

$$\leq F(\sigma, \rho) \tag{10.35}$$

where (10.29) follows by the definition of the feedback-arc-set loss in (10.22); the inequality in (10.30) is by the triangle inequality; the equality (10.34) is by the fact that

$w_{i,j} + w_{j,i} = 1$ for every $i, j \in N$ such that $i \neq j$; and finally, the inequality (10.35) is by the Diaconis-Graham inequality (10.5). This proves the relation in (10.21) and completes the proof of the theorem. □

10.3 Scoring-Based Ranking Methods

In this section, we present other scoring methods for ranking alternatives based on observed pair comparisons of the alternatives. The input is a set of two or more alternatives $N = \{1, 2, \ldots, n\}$, a matrix of wins $\mathbf{W} = (w_{i,j}) \subseteq \mathbf{R}_+^{n \times n}$, and a matrix of the number of pair comparisons $\mathbf{M} = (m_{i,j})$. We denote with $m_i = \sum_{j \in N} m_{i,j}$ the total number of observations in which alternative i is compared. A scoring method is defined by a mapping from the input matrix of wins and the matrix of the number of pair comparisons to a vector of scores. In the remainder of this section, we first introduce some well-known scoring methods and then discuss correspondences between some of these scoring methods and certain axioms.

10.3.1 A Catalog of Scoring Methods

In this section we introduce some well known scoring methods that are either in common use in practice or have been studied in literature.

Point Scores
The point scores are defined as the row-sums of the matrix of wins:

$$f_i = \sum_{j \in N} w_{i,j}, \text{ for } i \in N. \tag{10.36}$$

Intuitively, we may interpret the point score method as assigning each alternative a score that represents the cumulative number of points that this alternative gained in pair comparisons with other alternatives.

Point Difference Scores
The point difference scores are defined by

$$f_i = \sum_{j \in N} w_{i,j} - \sum_{j \in N} w_{j,i}, \text{ for } i \in N. \tag{10.37}$$

We may intuitively interpret the score assigned to an alternative as the difference between the total number of wins and the total number of loses in pair comparisons with other alternatives.

Accounting for Indirect Wins and Loses
Given a parameter $0 \leq \alpha < 1$, define

$$f_i = w_i - l_i, \text{ for } i \in N$$

where $\mathbf{w} = (w_1, w_2, \ldots, w_n)$ and $\mathbf{l} = (l_1, l_2, \ldots, l_n)$ are solutions of the following systems of linear equations:

$$w_i = \sum_{j \in N} w_{i,j} + \alpha \sum_{j \in N} w_{i,j} w_j, \text{ for } i \in N, \text{ and } l_i = \sum_{j \in N} w_{j,i} + \alpha \sum_{j \in N} w_{j,i} l_j, \text{ for } i \in N.$$

Fair Bets

The fair-bets scores are defined as a solution to the following systems of linear equations:

$$\left(\sum_{j \in N} w_{j,i} \right) f_i = \sum_{j \in N} w_{i,j} f_j, \text{ for } i \in N. \tag{10.38}$$

An example of a fair-bets scoring method is the estimator of the Bradley-Terry model parameters discussed in Exercise 9.14 where each element $w_{i,j}$ of the matrix of wins is defined as the fraction of matches won by alternative i in pair comparison with alternative j.

The fair-bets scoring method admits an intuitive interpretation as a fairness criterion in the context of betting systems. Suppose that in a betting system a bettor signs up for a contract on betting on alternative i such that he or she earns a profit of a value of f_j whenever alternative i wins against alternative j and otherwise incurs a loss of value f_i. Then, the fair-bets condition requires that each bettor has a zero expected profit.

Invariant Scores

The invariant scores are defined as a solution to the following system of linear equations:

$$\left(\sum_{l \in N} w_{l,j} \right) f_i = \sum_{j \in N} w_{i,j} f_j, \text{ for } i \in N. \tag{10.39}$$

For every irreducible matrix of wins $\mathbf{W}$ there exists a unique vector of invariant scores up to a multiplicative constant. This vector corresponds to the principal eigenvector of the stochastic matrix $\mathbf{P} = (p_{i,j})$ defined by

$$p_{i,j} = \frac{w_{j,i}}{\sum_{l \in N} w_{l,i}}, \text{ for } i, j \in N.$$

PageRank

The PageRank scoring method was originally introduced for ranking web documents using information about hypertext links connecting different documents. The PageRank scoring method is defined for an input matrix $\mathbf{W} = (w_{i,j})$ where $w_{i,j} = 1$ if document j has a link to document i and $w_{i,j} = 0$ otherwise, and a parameter $0 \le p \le 1$. The PageRank scores are defined as the solution to the following system of linear equations:

$$f_i = \sum_{j \in N} p_{j,i} f_j, \text{ for } i \in N$$

where

$$p_{i,j} = \begin{cases} (1-p)\frac{w_{j,i}}{\sum_{l \in N} w_{l,i}} + p\frac{1}{n}, & \text{if } \sum_{l \in N} w_{l,i} > 0 \\ p\frac{1}{n}, & \text{otherwise} \end{cases}.$$

The parameter p ensures that the transition matrix $\mathbf{P} = (p_{i,j})$ is irreducible by taking any value $0 < p \leq 1$, which implies the existence and uniqueness of the PageRank scores up to a multiplicative constant. We observe that for the special case $p = 0$, the PageRank scoring method is an invariant scores scoring method.

HITS

The original rating system HITS is defined for the matrix of wins $\mathbf{W} \in \{0, 1\}^{n \times n}$ that can be interpreted as the adjacency matrix of a directed graph with the alternatives in a one-to-one relationship with the vertices and $w_{i,j} = 1$ if, and only if, there is a directed edge from vertex i to vertex j. This rating system associates each alternative with two types of scores: an *authority score* and a *hub score*, respectively denoted by f_i and g_i, for alternative $i \in N$.

These scores are defined as the limit points of the following iterative system of equations: first, update

$$f_i \leftarrow \sum_{j \in N} w_{j,i} g_j, \text{ for } i \in N.$$

Then update

$$f_i \leftarrow \sum_{j \in N} w_{i,j} g_j, \text{ for } i \in N,$$

and then, normalize $\mathbf{f}$ and $\mathbf{g}$ such that $\sum_{i \in N} f_i^2 = 1$ and $\sum_{i \in N} g_i^2 = 1$.

Let $\lambda_1, \lambda_2, \ldots, \lambda_n$ be the eigenvalues of matrix $\mathbf{W}$ in decreasing order of absolute values. Under the assumption that $|\lambda_1| > |\lambda_2|$, the given iterative system of equations converges to a limit point $(\mathbf{f}, \mathbf{g})$, where $\mathbf{f}$ and $\mathbf{g}$ are the principal eigenvectors of matrices $\mathbf{WW}^T$ and $\mathbf{W}^T\mathbf{W}$, respectively. In other words, the authority and hub scores are defined as the solution to the following systems of linear equations:

$$f_i = \sum_{j \in N} \left(\sum_{k \in N} w_{i,k} w_{j,k} \right) f_j, \text{ for } i \in N$$

and

$$g_i = \sum_{j \in N} \left(\sum_{k \in N} w_{k,i} w_{k,j} \right) g_j, \text{ for } i \in N.$$

Callaghan, Mucha, and Porter's Scores

This scoring method was introduced by Callaghan et al. (2007) with the scores defined for a parameter $1/2 < p \leq 1$ as the solution to the following system of linear equations:

$$\left(\sum_{j \in N} p w_{j,i} + (1 - p) w_{i,j} \right) f_i = \sum_{j \in N} (p w_{i,j} + (1 - p) w_{j,i}) f_j, \text{ for } i \in N. \quad (10.40)$$

This is an instance of a fair-bets scoring method for the input matrix $\tilde{\mathbf{W}} = p\mathbf{W} + (1 - p)\mathbf{W}^T$. It is a fair-bets scoring method with respect to the matrix of wins in the special case for $p = 1$.

Accounting for the Difficulty of a Schedule

Many sport competitions are organized as tournaments in which each team plays in matches against some number of other teams according to a schedule. As a result some teams may face a more difficult schedule of matches than other teams. To account for the difficulty of the schedule, some of the existing scoring methods were defined as extensions of simple scoring methods, such as point score and point difference score. For example, several such scoring methods are used to rank U.S. college football teams, with the following three scoring methods being representative examples:

(i) *Masey's Scores*:

$$f_i = \frac{\sum_{j\in N} w_{i,j} - \sum_{j\in N} w_{j,i}}{m_i} + \sum_{j\in N} \frac{m_{i,j}}{m_i} f_j, \quad \text{for } i \in N. \tag{10.41}$$

(ii) *Maas's Scores*:

$$f_i = 2\frac{\sum_{j\in N} w_{i,l}}{m_i} - 1 + \sum_{j\in N} \frac{m_{i,j}}{m_i} f_j, \quad \text{for } i \in N. \tag{10.42}$$

(iii) *Colley's Scores*:

$$f_i = \frac{\sum_{j\in N} w_{i,j} - \sum_{j\in N} w_{j,i} + 2}{2(m_i + 2)} + \sum_{j\in N} \frac{m_{i,j}}{m_i + 2} f_j, \quad \text{for } i \in N \tag{10.43}$$

where $m_i = \sum_{j\in N} m_{i,j}$, for $i \in N$.

10.3.2 Axiomatic Characterizations

We consider axiomatic characterizations of some well-known scoring methods. The input is a set of two or more alternatives $N = \{1, 2, \ldots, n\}$ and a matrix of wins $\mathbf{W} = (w_{i,j}) \in \mathbf{R}_+^n$. A *scoring function* f is defined by assigning a non-negative score $f(i; S, \mathbf{W})$ to each alternative $i \in S$ for every non-empty subset of alternatives $S \subseteq N$. The scores are assumed to be normalized such that $\sum_{i\in S} f(i; S, \mathbf{W}) = 1$ for every $S \subseteq N$. We shall use the shortcut notation $f(i; \mathbf{W})$ in lieu of $f(i; N, \mathbf{W})$ for $i \in N$.

Point Scores

The point scores scoring function is given by

$$f(i; S, \mathbf{W}) = \sum_{j\in S} w_{i,j}, \quad \text{for } i \in S, \quad \text{and } S \subseteq N. \tag{10.44}$$

We introduce the following three axioms.

Anonymity A scoring function f is anonymous if for every pair of alternatives $i, j \in N$ and every permutation $\pi : N \to N$,

$$f(i; \mathbf{W}) \geq f(j; \mathbf{W}) \text{ if, and only if, } f(\pi(i); \mathbf{P}_\pi \mathbf{W}) \geq f(\pi(j); \mathbf{P}_\pi \mathbf{W})$$

where $\mathbf{P}_\pi = (p_{i,j})$ is a permutation matrix: $p_{i,j} = 1$ for $j = \pi(i)$ and $p_{i,j} = 0$, otherwise.

The axiom of anonymity merely ensures that the scoring function does not discriminate against alternatives based on their identities.

Strong monotonicity A scoring function f satisfies strong monotonicity if for every pair of alternatives $i, j \in N$ and every matrix $\mathbf{W} = (w_{i,k})$ such that $w_{i,k} = 0$ for some $k \in N \setminus \{i\}$, we have

$$f(i; \mathbf{W}) \geq f(j; \mathbf{W}) \text{ implies } f(i; \mathbf{W}') > f(j; \mathbf{W}')$$

where $\mathbf{W}' = (w'_{a,b})$ is defined by $w'_{a,b} = 1$ if $a = i$ and $b = k$, and $w'_{a,b} = w_{a,b}$, otherwise.

The axiom of strong monotonicity means that if for a given matrix of wins a scoring function gives a score to alternative i that is at least as large as that of another alternative j, then after adding one win to alternative i against some other alternative, the scoring function gives a larger score to alternative i than to alternative j.

Independence from other matches A scoring function f satisfies independence from other matches if for every two matrices of wins $\mathbf{W}$ and $\mathbf{W}'$ such that for a pair of alternatives $i, j \in N$, $w_{i,l} = w'_{i,l}$, for all $l \in N$ and $w_{j,l} = w'_{j,l}$, for all $l \in N$,

$$f(i; \mathbf{W}) \geq f(j; \mathbf{W}) \text{ if, and only if, } f(i; \mathbf{W}') \geq f(j; \mathbf{W}').$$

The axiom of independence from other matches ensures that the scoring function is such that the order of a pair of alternatives with respect to the scores assigned to these two alternatives is independent of the pair comparisons in which neither of the two alternatives participate.

Theorem 10.6. *A scoring function f satisfies the three axioms of anonymity, strong monotonicity, and independence from other matches, if, and only if, f is the point score scoring function.*

The proof of the direct part is obvious from the definition of the point score scoring function (10.44). The converse part is more involved and is not proved here.

Point Difference Scores

The point difference scores scoring function is given by

$$f(i; S, \mathbf{W}) = \sum_{j \in S} w_{i,j} - \sum_{j \in S} w_{j,i}, \quad \text{for } i \in S, \quad \text{and } S \subseteq N. \tag{10.45}$$

We shall present an axiomatization of the point difference scores using the previously introduced axioms of anonymity strong monotonicity, as well as the axiom of *independence of circuits*, which we introduce next. Before doing so, we need to define the concepts of circuits and admissible transformations of circuits. A circuit C_k of length k is an ordered collection of pairs of alternatives $((s_1, t_1), (s_2, t_2), \ldots, (s_k, t_k))$ such that $t_i = s_{i+1}$, for $i = 1, 2, \ldots, k - 1$, and $t_k = s_1$. A transformation on a circuit consists of adding a real value to each $w_{a,b}$ for (a, b) in C_k. Such a transformation is said to be *admissible* if after the transformation $w_{a,b} \in [0, 1]$ for every (a, b) in the circuit C_k.

Independence of circuits A scoring function f is *independent of circuits* if, and only if, for every two matrices of wins $\mathbf{W}$ and $\mathbf{W}'$ such that $\mathbf{W}'$ can be obtained from $\mathbf{W}$ through an admissible transformation on an elementary circuit of length two or three,

$$f(i; \mathbf{W}) \geq f(j; \mathbf{W}) \quad \text{if, and only if,} \quad f(i; \mathbf{W}') \geq f(j; \mathbf{W}'), \quad \text{for every } i, j \in N.$$

Theorem 10.7. *A scoring function f satisfies the three axioms of anonymity, strong monotonicity, and independence of circuits if, and only if, f is the point difference scoring function.*

The direct part of the proof is obvious using the definition of the point difference scores in (10.45). The proof of the converse part is more involved and is not given here.

Fair-Bets Scores

The fair-bets scoring function is defined as the solution to the system of linear equations (10.38). We shall use the following special types of matrix of wins. A matrix of wins $\mathbf{W}$ is said to be *balanced* if $\sum_{l \in N} w_{i,l} = \sum_{l \in N} w_{l,i}$ for all $i \in N$. If, in addition, $\sum_{l \in N} w_{i,l} = \sum_{l \in N} w_{j,l}$ for all $i, j \in N$, then $\mathbf{W}$ is said to be *regular*. In particular, a matrix of wins representing the number of win or lose outcomes in pair comparisons, is balanced if every alternative has a balanced number of wins and loses in pair comparisons with other alternatives. Such a matrix is regular if in addition every alternative has won (and lost) in the same number of pair comparisons.

Uniformity A scoring function f is *uniform* if for every regular matrix $\mathbf{W}$, $f(i; \mathbf{W}) = 1/n$ for all $i \in N$.

The axiom of uniformity requires that alternatives receive equal shares under the condition that each alternative has some common number of wins and loses in pair comparisons with other alternatives.

Strong uniformity A scoring function f is *strongly uniform* if for every balanced matrix $\mathbf{W}$, $f(i; \mathbf{W}) = 1/n$ for all $i \in N$.

The axiom of strong uniformity requires that alternatives receive equal shares under the weaker condition that each individual alternative has a balanced number of wins and loses in pair comparisons with other alternatives.

Neutrality A scoring function f is *neutral* if $f(i; \mathbf{W}) = 1/n$, for $i \in N$, implies $f(i; \mathbf{W} + \mathbf{A}) = 1/n$, for $i \in N$, for every symmetric matrix $\mathbf{A}$ with zero diagonal elements.

The axiom of neutrality means that if for a regular matrix of wins all alternatives are assigned the same score, then by extending the system with additional observations such that each alternative achieves the same number of wins and loses, the alternatives continue to be assigned equal scores.

Lemma 10.8. *A scoring function f is uniform and neutral if, and only if, it is strongly uniform.*

Inverse proportionality to losses A scoring function f is *inversely proportional to losses* if for every balanced matrix $\mathbf{W} = (\mathbf{w}_1, \mathbf{w}_2, \ldots, \mathbf{w}_n)$ such that $f(i; \mathbf{W}) = 1/n$, for $i \in N$, for every $\lambda_1, \lambda_2, \ldots, \lambda_n > 0$, we have

$$f(i; (\lambda_1 \mathbf{w}_1, \lambda_2 \mathbf{w}_2, \ldots, \lambda_n \mathbf{w}_n)) \propto \frac{1}{\lambda_i}, \quad \text{for } i \in N.$$

In other words, the axiom of inverse proportionality to loss holds for a scoring function f that for every balanced matrix of wins assigns equal scores to all alternatives, and if loss scores of each alternative i are multiplied by a strictly positive factor λ_i, the score value of this alternative is inversely proportional to the value of this factor.

Theorem 10.9. *A scoring function f satisfies the axioms of uniformity, neutrality, and inverse proportionality to losses, if, and only if, f is the fair-bets scoring function.*

An alternative axiomatization of the fair-bets scoring function is as follows.

Reciprocity A scoring function satisfies *reciprocity* if

$$f(i, \{i, j\}, \mathbf{W}) \propto w_{i,j} \quad \text{for all } \{i, j\} \subseteq N.$$

Consistency A scoring function f is *consistent* if for every matrix of wins $\mathbf{W}$ with three or more alternatives and $k \in N$, we have

$$f(i; N \setminus \{k\}, \mathbf{W}^k) \propto f(i; N, \mathbf{W}) \quad \text{for all } i \in N \setminus \{k\}$$

where $\mathbf{W}^k = (w_{i,j}^k, \ i, j \in N \setminus \{k\})$ and

$$w_{i,j}^k = \begin{cases} w_{i,j} + \frac{w_{i,k}}{\sum_{l \in N} w_{l,k}} w_{k,j}, & i \neq j \\ 0, & i = j \end{cases}.$$

Theorem 10.10. *A scoring function f satisfies the axioms of reciprocity and consistency, if, and only if, f is the fair-bets scoring function.*

Invariant Scores

The invariant scores scoring function is defined as the solution to the system of linear equations (10.39). We introduce the following two axioms.

Weak additivity A scoring function f is *weakly additive* if for every regular matrix $\mathbf{W}$ and every symmetric matrix $\mathbf{A}$ with main diagonal elements equal to zero, we have

$$f(i; \mathbf{W}) \propto \sum_{j \in N} w_{i,j} \text{ implies } f(i; \mathbf{W} + \mathbf{A}) \propto \sum_{j \in N} (w_{i,j} + a_{i,j}).$$

Invariance to scale of losses A scoring function f is *invariant to scale of losses* if for every matrix of wins $\mathbf{W} = (\mathbf{w}_1, \mathbf{w}_2, \ldots, \mathbf{w}_n)$ and $\lambda_i > 0$ for $i \in N$, we have

$$f(i; \mathbf{W}) = f(i; (\lambda_1 \mathbf{w}_1, \lambda_2 \mathbf{w}_2, \ldots, \lambda_n \mathbf{w}_n)), \quad \text{for all } i \in N.$$

Theorem 10.11. *A scoring function f satisfies the axioms of uniformity, weak additivity, and invariance to scale of losses, if, and only if, f is the invariant scores scoring function.*

10.3.3 Optimality of Point Difference Scores

In this section we consider the problem of ranking a set of alternatives where a matrix of scores that represent outcomes of pair comparisons is given as input. We shall show that ranking the alternatives using the point difference scores is optimal with respect to minimizing a broad class of loss functions under the assumption that outcomes of pair comparisons are independent and according to a specific family of distributions. We shall then show that for this to continue to hold, it is necessary that the pairwise scores have distributions from this specific family of distributions.

The input to the ranking problem is a set of alternatives $N = \{1, 2, \ldots, n\}$ and a matrix of real-valued *pairwise scores* $(d_{i,j}, i, j \in N)$, where we may intuitively interpret $d_{i,j}$ as the score attained by alternative i in pair comparisons with alternative j. The input pairwise scores are assumed to satisfy

$$d_{i,j} + d_{j,i} = 0, \quad \text{for every } i, j \in N, i \neq j. \tag{10.46}$$

This assumption accommodates many point rewarding schemes. For example, in a tournament in which every player plays against every other player exactly once and matches are with win or loss outcomes, we may assign $d_{i,j} = 1$ in case i wins against j, and $d_{i,j} = -1$, otherwise. For matches with win, draw, and loss outcomes, we may define $d_{i,j} = 0$ to represent the draw outcome. The pairwise scores of the given form also allow multiple matches between pairs of players as well as point rewarding schemes that assign real values depending on the observed performance of players, e.g., $d_{i,j} = b_i - b_j$ where b_i and b_j represent the performance of player i and player j, respectively.

The input pairwise scores $(d_{i,j}, i < j)$ are assumed to be a sequence of independent random variables with distribution functions

$$F_{i,j}(y; v_i, v_j) = \mathbf{Pr}[d_{i,j} \leq y \mid v_i, v_j]$$

where $\mathbf{v} = (v_1, v_2, \ldots, v_n)$ is a vector of parameters that represent individual strengths of the alternatives. The support of distribution $F_{i,j}$ is either $[-d, d]$ for a finite $d > 0$ or $(-\infty, \infty)$, or a symmetric discrete lattice $\{-m\Delta, \ldots, -\Delta, 0, \Delta, \ldots, m\Delta\}$ with $\Delta > 0$ and m either a positive integer or infinity. Note that the given assumptions on the pairwise scores accommodate pair comparisons according to a generalized linear model defined in Section 9.2.4.

We define a *true ranking* of alternatives to be a full ranking of the alternatives in decreasing order of the strength parameters. Given an input matrix of pairwise scores, the point difference scores of the alternatives are defined by

$$d_i = \sum_{j \in N} d_{i,j}, \quad \text{for } i \in N. \tag{10.47}$$

In the remainder of this section, we shall show that if the distributions of the input pairwise scores belong to the exponential family of distributions,

$$F_{i,j}(d) = c(v_i - v_j) \int_{-\infty}^{d} e^{(v_i - v_j)y} \mu(y) \, dy, \quad \text{for every } i, j \in N, i < j \quad (10.48)$$

where $\mu(\cdot)$ is a symmetric density function and $c(\cdot)$ is a normalizing constant; then the ranking of the alternatives in decreasing order of the point difference scores minimizes the expected loss for a broad class of loss functions that quantify the distance between every given ranking and a true ranking. Notice that for pairwise scores with distributions of the exponential form, the vector of point difference scores $\mathbf{d} = (d_1, d_2, \ldots, d_n)$ is a sufficient statistic for the distribution of the matrix of pairwise scores.

Moreover, we shall show that under certain regularity conditions, the distributions of the input pairwise scores must be of the exponential form for the ranking in decreasing order of point difference scores to be optimal.

A Catalog of Distributions from the Exponential Family

We demonstrate how some specific probabilistic models of outcomes of pair comparisons are accommodated by an input matrix of pairwise scores with distributions of pairwise scores from the exponential family of distributions given by (10.48). These probabilistic models of pair comparisons are discussed in Chapter 9. We consider the following four instances:

(i) *Bradley-Terry model*: given a set of of positive real valued parameters $\theta_1, \theta_2, \ldots, \theta_n$ that represent individual strengths of the alternatives, each comparison of a pair of alternatives (i, j) has a random independent outcome, either i being ranked higher than j or j being ranked higher than i, with probabilities $\theta_i/(\theta_i + \theta_j)$ and $\theta_j/(\theta_i + \theta_j)$, respectively. The former outcome is represented with the pairwise score $d_{i,j} = 1$, and the latter outcome is represented with the pairwise score $d_{i,j} = -1$. Using the change of parameters $v_l = \log(\theta_l)/2$ for $l \in N$, we have

$$\Pr[d_{i,j} = d \mid v_i, v_j] = \frac{e^{(v_i - v_j)d}}{e^{v_i - v_j} + e^{-(v_i - v_j)}}, \quad \text{for } d \in \{-1, 1\}, \quad (10.49)$$

which belongs to the exponential family of distributions.

(ii) *Bradley-Terry model with repetitions*: suppose that for each distinct pair of alternatives there are $m \geq 1$ independent outcomes of pair comparisons according to the Bradley-Terry model. Let $d_{i,j}$ be the difference between the number of wins and the number of loses for alternative i in pair comparisons with alternative j. Then, $d_{i,j}$ is a random variable with distribution

$$\Pr[d_{i,j} = d] = \binom{m}{\frac{m+d}{2}} \left(\frac{e^{v_i - v_j}}{e^{v_i - v_j} + e^{-(v_i - v_j)}} \right)^{\frac{m+d}{2}} \left(\frac{e^{-(v_i - v_j)}}{e^{v_i - v_j} + e^{-(v_i - v_j)}} \right)^{\frac{m-d}{2}}$$

$$= \frac{1}{(e^{v_i - v_j} + e^{-(v_i - v_j)})^{\frac{m}{2}}} e^{(v_i - v_j)d} \binom{m}{\frac{m+d}{2}}$$

for $d \in \{-m, -m+1, \ldots, -1, 0, 1, \ldots, m-1, m\}$. This, again, is a distribution that belongs to the exponential family of distributions.

(iii) *Thurstone model*: consider the Thurstone model with independent performances $b_1, b_2, \ldots, b_n$ where b_i is a Gaussian random variable with mean v_i and variance β^2. Let $d_{i,j} = b_i - b_j$. Then, the density function of $d_{i,j}$ is

$$e^{-\frac{(v_i-v_j)^2}{2(2\beta^2)}} \cdot e^{\frac{v_i-v_j}{2\beta^2}d} \cdot \frac{1}{\sqrt{2\pi}(\sqrt{2}\beta)} e^{-\frac{d^2}{2(2\beta^2)}} \quad \text{for } d \in \mathbf{R}$$

which belong to the exponential family.

(iv) *Correlated Gaussians*: consider the input pairwise scores $(d_{i,j}, i < j)$ that is a multivariate Gaussian random variable with the mean of $d_{i,j}$ equal to $v_i - v_j$ and the covariance matrix given by

$$\text{Var}[d_{i,j}] = \beta^2$$
$$\text{Cov}[d_{i,j}, d_{k,l}] = 0 \text{ if } i \neq j \neq k \neq l$$
$$\text{Cov}[d_{i,j}, d_{i,l}] = \delta \text{ for } j \neq l.$$

Then, the distribution of each $d_{i,j}$ is from the exponential family of distributions.

There are models of probabilistic outcomes of pair comparisons for which the distributions of pairwise scores $d_{i,j}$ are not members of the exponential family of distributions. Two such models are considered in Exercise 10.3.

Basic Definitions

Given a vector $\mathbf{x} \in \mathbf{R}^n$ and a permutation $\sigma \in S_n$, let $\mathbf{x}^\sigma = (x_1^\sigma, x_2^\sigma, \ldots, x_n^\sigma) \in \mathbf{R}^n$ be a vector defined by $x_i^\sigma = x_{\sigma(i)}$ for $i = 1, 2, \ldots, n$. A function $f : \mathbf{R}^{n \times k} \to \mathbf{R}$ is said to be *permutation invariant* if it satisfies

$$f(\mathbf{x}_1^\sigma, \mathbf{x}_2^\sigma, \ldots, \mathbf{x}_k^\sigma) = f(\mathbf{x}_1, \mathbf{x}_2, \ldots, \mathbf{x}_k), \text{ for every permutation } \sigma \in S_n.$$

A full ranking of alternatives is given by a vector $\mathbf{r}$ that corresponds to a permutation in S_n, with r_i being the rank of alternative $i \in N$.

Under the assumption that the sequence of pairwise scores $(d_{i,j}, i < j)$ is a sequence of independent random variables with distributions from the exponential family of distributions given by (10.48), the joint distribution of the pairwise scores $(d_{i,j}, i < j)$ satisfies

$$dF(\mathbf{y}) = c(\mathbf{v})e^{\sum_{i=1}^n v_i d_i} v(\mathbf{y})d\mathbf{y} \tag{10.50}$$

where $d_i = \sum_{i:i<j} y_{i,j} - \sum_{i:i>j} y_{j,i}$, $c(\mathbf{v}) = \prod_{i<j} c(v_i - v_j)$, and $v(\mathbf{y}) = \prod_{i<j} \mu(y_{i,j})$. Since $c(\mathbf{v})v(\mathbf{y})$ is a permutation-invariant function with respect to $(\mathbf{v}, \mathbf{y})$, it follows that $\mathbf{d}$ is a sufficient statistic for the joint distribution of the pairwise scores $(d_{i,j}, i < j)$.

A *loss function* is defined as a mapping $L : \mathbf{R}^n \times S_n \to \mathbf{R}_+$ where we intuitively interpret $L(\mathbf{v}, \mathbf{r})$ as the loss incurred by the ranking of alternatives $\mathbf{r}$ given that the true ranking is in decreasing order of the strength parameters $\mathbf{v}$.

Definition 10.12. A loss function $L : \mathbf{R}^n \times S_n \to \mathbf{R}_+$ is said to be *admissible* if it satisfies the following two conditions:

(i) *permutation invariance*: for every $\mathbf{v} \in \mathbf{R}^n$ and $\mathbf{r} \in S_n$, $L(\mathbf{v}, \mathbf{r}) = L(\mathbf{v}^\sigma, \sigma(\mathbf{r}))$, for every permutation $\sigma \in S_n$, and

(ii) *weak monotonicity*: for every $\mathbf{v} \in \mathbf{R}^n$ and $\mathbf{r} \in S_n$, if $v_i \geq v_j$ and $r_i < r_j$, then $L(\mathbf{v}, \mathbf{r}) \leq L(\mathbf{v}, \sigma(\mathbf{r}))$, for σ that is identity permutation except for transposing the positions of alternatives i and j. In other words, the loss function does not decrease if a full ranking of alternatives is made worse by transposing the positions of the two alternatives so that their resulting order is in discordance with their order in the true ranking.

The set of admissible loss functions is rather broad. For example, it accommodates Kendall's τ distance between a true ranking and a full ranking $\mathbf{r}$, which amounts to incurring a unit loss for every discordant ranking of a pair of alternatives with respect to the ranking in decreasing order of the strength parameters and the full ranking $\mathbf{r}$.

A *ranking method* is defined by a probability distribution $\varphi(\cdot \mid \mathbf{d})$ on the set of all possible full rankings S_n conditional on the value of the sufficient statistic $\mathbf{d}$. A ranking method φ is said to be permutation invariant if $\varphi(\mathbf{r} \mid \mathbf{d}) = \varphi(\sigma(\mathbf{r}) \mid \mathbf{d}^\sigma)$ for every permutation $\sigma \in S_n$. The *expected loss* of a ranking method φ is given by

$$\mathbf{E}_\varphi[L(\mathbf{v}, \mathbf{r})] = \int_{\mathbf{R}^n} L(\mathbf{v}, \mathbf{r}) \varphi(\mathbf{r} \mid \mathbf{d}) f(\mathbf{d} \mid \mathbf{v}) \, d\mathbf{d}. \tag{10.51}$$

Sufficiency of the Exponential Family of Distributions

We first establish a theorem that we use to show optimality of the ranking in decreasing order of the point difference scores with respect to minimizing the expected loss for every given admissible loss function and any given distributions of pairwise scores that are members of the exponential family of distributions.

Theorem 10.13. *Suppose that L is an admissible loss function and the joint distribution of the point difference scores $\mathbf{d}$ is of the following form*

$$f(\mathbf{d} \mid \mathbf{v}) = c(\mathbf{v}) a(\mathbf{v}, \mathbf{d}) p(\mathbf{d}) \tag{10.52}$$

where p is a permutation-invariant measure and a is a permutation-invariant measure that satisfies $a(\mathbf{v}, \mathbf{d}) \geq a(\sigma(\mathbf{v}), \mathbf{d})$, if $v_i \geq v_j$ and $d_i \geq d_j$, where σ corresponds to the identity permutation except for transposing the positions of i and j.

Then, the ranking in decreasing order of the point difference scores with random tie breaks minimizes the expected loss among all invariant ranking methods that depend on the pairwise scores $(d_{i,j}, i < j)$ only through the vector of the point difference scores $\mathbf{d}$.

Proof. Since the loss function is permutation invariant and we consider permutation-invariant ranking methods, the expected loss (10.53) is constant over permutations of $\mathbf{v}$, and thus we can write

$$\mathbf{E}_\varphi[L(\mathbf{v}, \mathbf{r})] = \frac{1}{n!} \sum_{\sigma \in S_n} \int_{\mathbf{R}^n} \sum_{\mathbf{r} \in S_n} L(\mathbf{v}^\sigma, \mathbf{r}) \varphi(\mathbf{r} \mid \mathbf{d}) f(\mathbf{d} \mid \mathbf{v}^\sigma) \, d\mathbf{d}.$$

This can be equivalently represented as follows:

$$\mathbf{E}_{\varphi}[L(\mathbf{v}, \mathbf{r})] = \int_{\mathbf{R}^n} \sum_{\mathbf{r} \in S_n} g(\mathbf{r} \mid \mathbf{d}) \varphi(\mathbf{r} \mid \mathbf{d}) p(\mathbf{d}) \, d\mathbf{d} \qquad (10.53)$$

where

$$g(\mathbf{r} \mid \mathbf{d}) = \frac{c(\mathbf{v})}{n!} \sum_{\sigma \in S_n} L(\mathbf{v}^\sigma, \mathbf{r}) a(\mathbf{v}^\sigma, \mathbf{d}).$$

Let $g^*(\mathbf{d}) = \min_{\mathbf{r} \in S_n} g(\mathbf{r} \mid \mathbf{d})$. Since the expected loss (10.53) is a linear function in $\varphi(\mathbf{r} \mid \mathbf{d})$, it follows that $\varphi(\mathbf{r} \mid \mathbf{d})$ minimizes the expected loss if, and only if, $\varphi(\mathbf{r} \mid \mathbf{d}) = 0$ whenever $g(\mathbf{r} \mid \mathbf{d}) > g^*(\mathbf{d})$. We now show that the minimum $g(\mathbf{r} \mid \mathbf{d}) = g^*(\mathbf{d})$ is reached if $\mathbf{r}$ corresponds to a full ranking in decreasing order of the point difference scores. Let ρ be the identity permutation except for a transposition of i and j. We claim that if $d_i \geq d_j$ and $r_i < r_j$, then $g(\mathbf{r} \mid \mathbf{d}) \leq g(\rho(\mathbf{r}) \mid \mathbf{d})$, which implies that the minimum is reached by ranking the alternatives in decreasing order of the point difference scores. The claim follows by the following arguments. First, note that

$$g(\mathbf{r} \mid \mathbf{d}) - g(\rho(\mathbf{r}) \mid \mathbf{d}) = \frac{c(\mathbf{v})}{n!} \sum_{\sigma \in S_n} a(\mathbf{v}^\sigma, \mathbf{d})[L(\mathbf{v}^\sigma, \mathbf{r}) - L(\mathbf{v}^\sigma, \rho(\mathbf{r}))]$$

$$= \frac{c(\mathbf{v})}{n!} \sum_{\sigma \in S_n} a((\mathbf{v}^\sigma)^\rho, \mathbf{d})[L((\mathbf{v}^\sigma)^\rho, \mathbf{r}) - L((\mathbf{v}^\sigma)^\rho, \rho(\mathbf{r}))]$$

$$= \frac{c(\mathbf{v})}{n!} \sum_{\sigma \in S_n} a((\mathbf{v}^\sigma)^\rho, \mathbf{d})[L(\mathbf{v}^\sigma, \rho(\mathbf{r})) - L(\mathbf{v}^\sigma, \mathbf{r})]$$

where the second equality is because of the sum over all permutations, and the third equality is by permutation invariance of the loss function L. Second, by taking the arithmetic mean of the first and the third equality in the last expression, we obtain

$$g(\mathbf{r} \mid \mathbf{d}) - g(\rho(\mathbf{r}) \mid \mathbf{d}) = \frac{c(\mathbf{v})}{2n!} \sum_{\sigma \in S_n} [a(\mathbf{v}^\sigma, \mathbf{d}) - a((\mathbf{v}^\sigma)^\rho, \mathbf{d})][L(\mathbf{v}^\sigma, \mathbf{r}) - L(\mathbf{v}^\sigma, \rho(\mathbf{r}))].$$

$$(10.54)$$

Third, and last, suppose that the ranking $\mathbf{r}$ is in decreasing order of the point difference scores, i.e., $r_i < r_j$ whenever $d_i > d_j$. Then, under the assumptions on functions L and a, we have

$$[a(\mathbf{v}^\sigma, \mathbf{d}) - a((\mathbf{v}^\sigma)^\rho, \mathbf{d})][L(\mathbf{v}^\sigma, \mathbf{r}) - L(\mathbf{v}^\sigma, \rho(\mathbf{r}))] \leq 0,$$

which combined with (10.54) implies $g(\mathbf{r} \mid \mathbf{d}) \leq g(\rho(\mathbf{r}) \mid \mathbf{d})$ for every permutation $\rho \in S_n$. This establishes the optimality of ranking in decreasing order of point difference scores. $\qquad \square$

The following result follows as a corollary of Theorem 10.13.

Corollary 10.14. *Suppose that L is an admissible loss function and pairwise scores $(d_{i,j},\ i < j)$ are independent random variables according to distributions from the exponential family of distributions. Then, every full ranking in decreasing order of* *the point difference scores minimizes the expected loss over all permutation-invariant ranking methods.*

Proof. We need to show that the assumptions of Theorem 10.13 hold. Under the assumption that pairwise scores $(d_{i,j}, i < j)$ are independent random variables with distributions from the exponential family (10.48), the joint distribution of the pairwise scores is given by (10.50), which is of the form (10.52) with

$$a(\mathbf{v}, \mathbf{d}) = e^{\sum_{i \in N} v_i d_i} \quad \text{and} \quad p(\mathbf{y}) = \prod_{i < j} \mu(y_{i,j}). \tag{10.55}$$

We next show that function a satisfies the two conditions imposed on function a in Theorem 10.13. Function a is clearly permutation invariant so the first assumption is satisfied. For the second assumption, we proceed as follows. Since σ is the identity permutation except for a transposition of i and j, we have

$$a(\mathbf{v}, \mathbf{d}) - a(\mathbf{v}^\sigma, \mathbf{d}) = e^{\sum_{l \in N} v_l d_l} - e^{\sum_{l \in N \setminus \{i,j\}} v_l d_l + v_i d_j + v_j d_i}$$

$$= e^{\sum_{l \in N \setminus \{i,j\}} v_l d_l} \left(e^{v_i d_i + v_j d_j} - e^{v_i d_j + v_j d_i} \right).$$

From this, we observe that $a(\mathbf{v}, \mathbf{d}) - a(\mathbf{v}^\sigma, \mathbf{d}) \geq 0$ if, and only if, $v_i d_i + v_j d_j \geq v_i d_j + v_j d_i$. The latter inequality holds because

$$(v_i d_i + v_j d_j) - (v_i d_j + v_j d_i) = (d_i - d_j)(v_i - v_j) \geq 0.$$

Finally, we need to show that $p(\mathbf{y})$ is permutation invariant, which in view of the second equation in (10.55) obviously holds. $\square$

Necessity of the Exponential Family of Distributions

We shall next establish that the point difference scores are a sufficient statistic for a permutation-invariant joint distribution of pairwise scores $(d_{i,j}, i < j)$ only if its univariate marginal distributions are from the exponential family (10.48). For the special case of pair comparisons with win or loss outcomes, this means that the point difference scores are a sufficient statistic for a permutation-invariant joint distribution of pairwise scores $(d_{i,j}, i < j)$, only if its univariate marginal distributions are as given in equation (10.49), i.e., they correspond to the Bradley-Terry model.

Theorem 10.15. *Suppose there are three or more alternatives and the pairwise scores $(d_{i,j}, i < j)$ are independent random variables with density functions $f_{i,j}$ that are assumed to be strictly positive and bounded on the support $(-a, a)$ for some $a > 0$. Let $f(\mathbf{y}) = \prod_{i<j} f_{i,j}(y_{i,j})$ be the joint density function of the pairwise scores $(d_{i,j}, i < j)$, and let $\mathcal{P}$ be the set of joint density functions generated from f by permutations of elements. Suppose that, $\mathbf{d} = (d_1, d_2, \ldots, d_n)$ is a sufficient statistic for the set of joint density functions $\mathcal{P}$, i.e.*

$$f(\mathbf{y}) = g(\mathbf{d})h(\mathbf{y}) \tag{10.56}$$

where h is a permutation-invariant function.

   Then, $f_{i,j}$ must satisfy

$$f_{i,j}(d) = c_{i,j} p(d) e^{(v_i - v_j)d} \tag{10.57}$$

where $c_{i,j}$ is the normalizing constant, v_i and v_j are some constants, and p is an even function.

Proof. Suppose that f is a joint density function of pairwise scores that satisfies (10.56). We need to show that its univariate marginal density functions satisfy (10.63). Let $\mathcal{D} = (-a, a)$ and $\mathcal{D}_u = (-a - u, a - u)$. We note the following basic fact:

$$f_{i,j}(d) = f_{j,i}(-d), \quad \text{for every } d \in \mathcal{D} \text{ and } i \neq j, \tag{10.58}$$

which follows by the assumption (10.46) on pairwise scores.

We define the following functions:

$$\varphi_{i,j}(d) = \sqrt{f_{i,j}(d) f_{j,i}(d)}, \quad \text{for } d \in \mathcal{D} \text{ and } i \neq j. \tag{10.59}$$

Each function $\varphi_{i,j}(d)$ satisfies the following properties:

$$\varphi_{i,j}(d) = \varphi_{j,i}(d), \quad \text{for } d \in \mathcal{D} \tag{10.60}$$

$$\varphi_{i,j}(d) = \varphi_{i,j}(-d), \quad \text{for } d \in \mathcal{D} \tag{10.61}$$

and

$$\varphi_{i,j}(d) = \varphi_{j,i}(-d), \quad \text{for } d \in \mathcal{D}. \tag{10.62}$$

The first property (10.60) obviously holds. The second and third properties, (10.61) and (10.62), follow by the fact (10.58).

The proof follows by the following three steps.

Step 1 We show that for every $i, j \in N$ and $d \in \mathcal{D}$,

$$f_{i,j}(d) = \varphi_{i,j}(d) e^{v_{i,j} d} \tag{10.63}$$

where $v_{i,j}$ is a real-valued constant.

Let k, l, m be a triplet of alternatives. Let $(d_{i,j}, i < j)$ and $(d'_{i,j}, i < j)$ be two vectors of pairwise scores such that $(d'_{i,j}, i < j)$ is identical to $(d_{i,j}, i < j)$, except for $d'_{k,l} = d_{k,l} + u$, $d'_{l,m} = d_{l,m} + u$, and $d'_{m,k} = d_{m,k} + u$. Notice that the two vectors of pairwise scores have equal values of point difference scores. For brevity, we use the following shortcut notation: $t = d_{k,l}$, $y = d_{l,m}$, and $z = d_{m,k}$. Since the two vectors of pairwise scores have equal point difference scores and the assumption that the joint distribution of pairwise scores is of the form (10.56), we have that for every $t, y, z \in \mathcal{D} \cap \mathcal{D}_u$,

$$\frac{f((d_{i,j}, i < j))}{f((d'_{i,j}, i < j))} = \frac{f_{k,l}(t + u) f_{l,m}(y + u) f_{m,k}(z + u)}{f_{k,l}(t) f_{l,m}(y) f_{m,k}(z)} = \frac{h((d_{i,j}, i < j))}{h((d'_{i,j}, i < j))}. \tag{10.64}$$

Since the right-hand side of the last equation in (10.64) is permutation invariant, we can divide both sides of the last equation in (10.64) by the same corresponding expressions but with alternatives k and l interchanged, which yields

$$\frac{f_{k,l}(t + u) f_{l,k}(t)}{f_{l,k}(t + u) f_{k,l}(t)} \frac{f_{l,m}(y + u) f_{k,m}(y)}{f_{k,m}(y + u) f_{l,m}(y)} \frac{f_{m,k}(z + u) f_{m,l}(z)}{f_{m,l}(z + u) f_{m,k}(z)} = 1. \tag{10.65}$$

The only term in equation (10.65) that is a function of t is the first fraction term. Hence, for some $\gamma_{k,l}(u)$, it holds that

$$\frac{f_{k,l}(t+u)f_{l,k}(t)}{f_{l,k}(t+u)f_{k,l}(t)} = \gamma_{k,l}(u), \quad \text{for } t \in \mathcal{D} \cap \mathcal{D}_u. \tag{10.66}$$

Now, in the last equation we replace u by v and t by $t+u$ to obtain

$$\frac{f_{k,l}(t+u+v)f_{l,k}(t+u)}{f_{l,k}(t+u+v)f_{k,l}(t+u)} = \gamma_{k,l}(v), \quad \text{for } t \in \mathcal{D} \cap \mathcal{D}_u \cap \mathcal{D}_{u+v}.$$

From the last two equations, we obtain

$$\gamma_{k,l}(u+v) = \gamma_{k,l}(u)\gamma_{k,l}(v), \tag{10.67}$$

which is valid for every u and v for which $\mathcal{D} \cap \mathcal{D}_u \cap \mathcal{D}_{u+v}$ has a strictly positive measure. Equation (10.67) is the Cauchy's exponential functional equation, as defined in Section 11.1.8, which has a solution $\gamma_{k,l}(x) = e^{2v_{k,l}x}$ for constant $v_{k,l} \in \mathbf{R}$. This is a unique solution under the assumption that the density functions $f_{i,j}$ are strictly positive and bounded on the support $(-a, a)$, which in view of (10.66) implies that $\gamma_{k,l}(x)$ is bounded on any finite interval. Combining with (10.66), if follows that

$$\frac{f_{k,l}(t)}{f_{l,k}(t)} = ce^{2v_{k,l}t} \tag{10.68}$$

where c is a constant $c > 0$. Without loss of generality, we assume that c is of unit value. From (10.59) and (10.68), it follows that

$$f_{k,l}(d) = \varphi_{k,l}(d)e^{v_{k,l}d}.$$

Step 2 We establish that $v_{i,j} = v_i - v_j$ for every $i \neq j$, for real-valued constants $v_1, v_2, \ldots, v_n$.

We first show that

$$v_{i,j} = -v_{j,i} \text{ for every } i \neq j. \tag{10.69}$$

From (10.63), we have

$$f_{i,j}(d) = \varphi_{i,j}(d)e^{v_{i,j}d}$$

and

$$f_{j,i}(-d) = \varphi_{j,i}(-d)e^{-v_{j,i}d} = \varphi_{i,j}(-d)e^{-v_{j,i}d} = \varphi_{i,j}(d)e^{-v_{i,j}d}$$

where in the last two equations we used properties (10.60) and (10.61). Since by (10.58), $f_{i,j}(d) = f_{j,i}(-d)$, it follows that $v_{i,j} = -v_{j,i}$.

We can rewrite (10.65) as follows:

$$e^{2(v_{k,l}+v_{l,m}+v_{m,k})u}A(y) = A(z) \tag{10.70}$$

where

$$A(x) = \frac{\varphi_{l,m}(x+u)\varphi_{k,m}(x)}{\varphi_{k,m}(x+u)\varphi_{l,m}(x)}. \tag{10.71}$$

We claim that all the factors in (10.70) are equal to 1. First, note that in (10.70) only factor $A(y)$ is a function of y. Thus, in view of (10.70), $A(y)$ itself is invariant to the value of y. Using this invariance and relations (10.62), we can write

$$A(y) = \frac{\varphi_{l,m}(y+u)\varphi_{k,m}(y)}{\varphi_{k,m}(y+u)\varphi_{l,m}(y)} = \frac{\varphi_{l,m}(-y)\varphi_{k,m}(-y-u)}{\varphi_{k,m}(-y)\varphi_{l,m}(-y-u)}$$

$$= \frac{\varphi_{m,l}(y)\varphi_{m,k}(y+u)}{\varphi_{m,k}(y)\varphi_{m,l}(y+u)} = \frac{1}{A(y)}.$$

Hence, $A(y) = 1$. By the same arguments, we have $A(z) = 1$. Hence, Equation (10.70) boils down to $e^{2(v_{k,l}+v_{l,m}+v_{m,k})u} = 1$, from which we conclude that

$$v_{k,l} + v_{l,m} + v_{m,k} = 0. \tag{10.72}$$

We can take an arbitrary alternative, say alternative l, and define $v_k = v_{k,l}$ for $k \neq l$ and $v_l = 0$. Using this in (10.72) along with the fact (10.69), we obtain $v_{m,k} = v_m - v_k$. Hence, we conclude that $v_{i,j} = v_i - v_j$, for $i, j \in N$.

Step 3 We show that $\varphi_{i,j}(d) = c_{i,j}h(d)$ for $i \neq j$ and $d \in \mathcal{D}$, where $c_{i,j}$ is a strictly positive constant and $h(d)$ is an even function.

From (10.71), note that $A(y) = 1$ is equivalent to

$$\frac{\varphi_{k,m}(y+u)}{\varphi_{k,m}(y)} = \frac{\varphi_{l,m}(y+u)}{\varphi_{l,m}(y)}.$$

From this equation, it follows that the left-hand side of the equation is invariant to the index (k, m). Hence, it must be that $\varphi_{k,m}(d) = c_{k,m}p(d)$ for some constant $c_{k,m} > 0$ and a positive-valued function $p(d)$. Since by (10.61), function $\varphi_{k,m}(d)$ is even, so is function $p(d)$. $\square$

10.4 Aggregation of Judgments

In this section we consider a rank aggregation problem where the input is a sequence of rankings of two or more alternatives, which are assumed to be independent noisy observations of a ground-truth ranking of the alternatives. The goal is to find a ranking that minimizes the expected value of a loss function, where this loss function quantifies the amount of loss incurred for each given pair of a ranking of the alternatives and the ground-truth ranking of the alternatives. Intuitively, we may think of this rank aggregation problem as that of the aggregation of judgments provided by a panel of experts. For example, individual judgments may be predictions of a final standing in a contest, or they may be relevance judgments for an object categorization task.

A general formulation of the rank aggregation problem considered in this section can be defined as follows. A set of alternatives $K = \{1, 2, \dots, k\}$ and a sequence $\mathbf{r} = (r_1, r_2, \dots, r_n)$ of input rankings of the alternatives are given, where each ranking r_i takes value in a set of rankings $\mathcal{R}_k$. For example, if the input rankings are full rankings, then $\mathcal{R}_k$ is the set of all distinct permutations of k alternatives. It is assumed that there exists a ground-truth ranking R^* of the alternatives that is a latent random variable with prior distribution p^0 on the set $\mathcal{R}_k$. The sequence of input rankings is

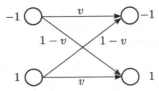

Figure 10.2. An input ranking of two alternatives is equal to the ground-truth ranking of the two alternatives with probability v, or is equal to the other ranking of the two alternatives with probability $1 - v$.

assumed to be a sequence of independent random variables $R = (R_1, R_2, \ldots, R_n)$ with given conditional probability distributions:

$$\mathbf{Pr}[R_i = r_i \mid R^* = r^*] = p_i(r^*, r_i), \quad \text{for } r^*, r_i \in \mathcal{R}_k, \ i = 1, 2, \ldots, n.$$

A *rank aggregation method* f is defined by a mapping $f : \mathcal{R}_k^n \to \mathcal{R}_k$, where $f(\mathbf{r})$ is the *aggregate ranking* of the alternatives given the sequence $\mathbf{r} = (r_1, r_2, \ldots, r_n)$ of input rankings of the alternatives. A *loss function* $L : \mathcal{R}_k \times \mathcal{R}_k \to \mathbf{R}_+$ is given that quantifies the amount of loss $L(f(\mathbf{r}), r^*)$ incurred by the rank aggregation method f for given input $\mathbf{r} = (r_1, r_2, \ldots, r_n)$ and given ground-truth ranking r^*. A particular choice of the loss function indicates whether the rank aggregation method fails to identify the ground-truth ranking of the alternatives, i.e.,

$$L(f(\mathbf{r}), r^*) = \mathbf{1}(f(\mathbf{r}) \neq r^*). \tag{10.73}$$

The rank aggregation problem is defined for a given set $\mathcal{F}$ of admissible rank aggregation methods as follows: find a rank aggregation method f in $\mathcal{F}$ that minimizes the expected value of the loss function over all rank aggregation methods in $\mathcal{F}$, i.e.,

$$\mathbf{E}[L(f(R), R^*)] \leq \mathbf{E}[L(g(R), R^*)], \text{ for every } g \in \mathcal{F}.$$

For the particular choice of the loss function in equation (10.73), the expected loss function is equal to the probability of error in identifying the ground-truth ranking of the alternatives, i.e.

$$\mathbf{E}[L(f(R), R^*)] = \mathbf{Pr}[f(R) \neq R^*].$$

We shall focus on the case of full rankings of a pair of alternatives in which the conditional probability distributions of the input rankings are given by

$$p_i(r^*, r_i) = v_i \mathbf{1}(r_i = r^*) + (1 - v_i)\mathbf{1}(r_i \neq r^*) \tag{10.74}$$

where $v_i \in [0, 1]$ for $i \in N$. We intuitively refer to v_i as the ability of expert i to identify the ground-truth ranking of the alternatives.

The problem of aggregation of judgments for a pair of alternatives is a binary hypothesis problem. For convenience of notation, we encode the full rankings $(1, 2)$ and $(2, 1)$ with hypotheses -1 and 1, respectively. We shall also redefine the notation slightly, so that $R = (R_1, R_2, \ldots, R_n)$ takes values in $\{-1, 1\}^n$, R^* takes values in $\{-1, 1\}$, and the rank aggregation method f is a mapping $f : \{-1, 1\}^n \to \{-1, 1\}$. We shall refer to $R = (R_1, R_2, \ldots, R_n)$ as input judgments and R^* as the ground-truth hypothesis. See Figure 10.2 for an illustration of a noisy input judgment.

10.4.1 Optimal Rank Aggregation

We consider the set of rank aggregation methods $\mathcal{F}$ that consists of all rank aggregation methods $f : \{-1, 1\}^n \to \{-1, 1\}$ that satisfy the following two conditions:

  (i) *full ranking*: $f(\mathbf{r}) \in \{-1, 1\}$ for every $\mathbf{r} \in \{-1, 1\}^n$, and
  (ii) *neutrality*: $f(-\mathbf{r}) = -f(\mathbf{r})$, for every $\mathbf{r} \in \{-1, 1\}^n$.

A rank aggregation in the set $\mathcal{F}$ is the *weighted majority rank aggregation method*, defined for given positive-valued weights $w_1, w_2, \ldots, w_n$ as

$$f(\mathbf{r}) = \begin{cases} \text{sign}\left(\sum_{i \in N} w_i r_i\right), & \text{if } \sum_{i \in N} w_i r_i \neq 0 \\ \tilde{r}, & \text{if } \sum_{i \in N} w_i r_i = 0 \end{cases}$$

where $\tilde{r}$ takes either value -1 or 1, arbitrarily. In other words, the weighted majority aggregate ranking is the full ranking that receives a larger total weight than the reverse full ranking, and in the case of a tie, it is one of the full rankings, arbitrarily. A special case of the weighted majority rank aggregation method is the *majority rank aggregation method* that has all the weights of equal value, which without loss of generality, are assumed to be of value 1. The class of weighted majority rank aggregation methods is special in that it contains a rank aggregation method that minimizes the expected loss function over the set of rank aggregation methods $\mathcal{F}$.

For an arbitrary rank aggregation method f, we have

$$\mathbf{Pr}[f(R) \neq R^*] = \sum_{\mathbf{r} \in \{-1,1\}^n} \sum_{r^* \in \{-1,1\}} \mathbf{1}(f(\mathbf{r}) \neq r^*) \ell(\mathbf{r}; r^*) p^0(r^*) \qquad (10.75)$$

where $\ell(\mathbf{r}; r^*)$ is the likelihood of observing the sequence of input judgments $\mathbf{r} = (r_1, r_2, \ldots, r_n)$ conditional on the ground-truth hypothesis being r^*:

$$\ell(\mathbf{r}; r^*) = \mathbf{Pr}[R = \mathbf{r} \mid R^* = r^*] = \prod_{i \in N: r_i = r^*} v_i \prod_{i \in N: r_i = -r^*} (1 - v_i). \qquad (10.76)$$

The likelihood function can be equivalently written as

$$\ell(\mathbf{r}; r^*) = \prod_{i \in N} v_i^{\frac{1 + r^* r_i}{2}} (1 - v_i)^{\frac{1 - r^* r_i}{2}}. \qquad (10.77)$$

The *weighted majority rank aggregation method with the log odds-ratio weights* is defined as the weighted majority rank aggregation with the weights

$$w_i = \log\left(\frac{v_i}{1 - v_i}\right), \quad i = 1, 2, \ldots, n.$$

From the expression of the likelihood function in (10.77) it is readily observed that the weighted majority rank aggregation method with the log odds-ratio weights is the maximum likelihood estimate of the ground-truth hypothesis. The weighted majority rank aggregation method with the log odds-ratio weights is also a maximum a posteriori probability estimate of the ground-truth hypothesis. A hypothesis r^* is a *maximum a posteriori probability estimate* of the ground-truth hypothesis for given input judgments $\mathbf{r} = (r_1, r_2, \ldots, r_n)$, if

$$\mathbf{Pr}[R^* = r^* \mid R = \mathbf{r}] \geq \mathbf{Pr}[R^* = -r^* \mid R = \mathbf{r}]. \qquad (10.78)$$

By Bayes's formula, the posterior distribution of the ground-truth hypothesis is given by

$$\Pr[R^* = r^* \mid R = \mathbf{r}] = \frac{\ell(\mathbf{r}; r^*) p^0(r^*)}{\ell(\mathbf{r}; r^*) p^0(r^*) + \ell(\mathbf{r}; -r^*) p^0(-r^*)}. \qquad (10.79)$$

Therefore, under a uniform prior distribution, condition (10.78) is equivalent to

$$\ell(\mathbf{r}; r^*) \geq \ell(\mathbf{r}; -r^*).$$

Using the expression for the likelihood function in (10.77), it follows that the last inequality is equivalent to saying

$$\left(\sum_{i \in N} \log\left(\frac{v_i}{1 - v_i} \right) r_i \right) r^* \geq 0,$$

which shows that the weighted majority rank aggregation with the log odds-ratio weights is a maximum a posteriori probability estimate of the ground-truth hypothesis.

The weighted majority rank aggregation with the log odds-ratio weights minimizes the probability of error in identifying the ground-truth hypothesis as shown by the following theorem.

Theorem 10.16. *Suppose that the prior distribution of the ground-truth hypothesis is uniform over the two hypotheses. Then, the optimal rank aggregation method within the set of rank aggregation methods $\mathcal{F}$ is the weighted majority rank aggregation method with the log odds-ratio weights.*

Proof. The expected loss in (10.75) is minimized by any rank aggregation method f such that $\ell(\mathbf{r}; r^*) < \ell(\mathbf{r}; -r^*)$ implies $f(\mathbf{r}) \neq r^*$, for every $\mathbf{r} \in \{-1, 1\}^n$ and $r^* \in \{-1, 1\}$. We need to show that this holds for f defined as the weighted majority rank aggregation method with the log odds-ratio weights. The proof follows by the following series of relations, which hold for every $\mathbf{r} \in \{-1, 1\}^n$ and $r^* \in \{-1, 1\}$:

$$\ell(\mathbf{r}; r^*) < \ell(\mathbf{r}; -r^*) \Leftrightarrow \prod_{i \in N: r_i = r^*} v_i \prod_{i \in N: r_i = -r^*} (1 - v_i) < \prod_{i \in N: r_i = -r^*} v_i \prod_{i \in N: r_i = r^*} (1 - v_i)$$

$$\Leftrightarrow \prod_{i \in N: r_i = r^*} \frac{v_i}{1 - v_i} < \prod_{i \in N: r_i = -r^*} \frac{v_i}{1 - v_i}$$

$$\Leftrightarrow \sum_{i \in N: r_i = r^*} \log\left(\frac{v_i}{1 - v_i} \right) (r^* r_i) < \sum_{i \in N: r_i = -r^*} \log\left(\frac{v_i}{1 - v_i} \right) (-r_0 r_i)$$

$$\Leftrightarrow \left(\sum_{i \in N} \log\left(\frac{v_i}{1 - v_i} \right) r_i \right) r^* < 0$$

$$\Leftrightarrow f(\mathbf{r}) r^* < 0$$

$$\Rightarrow f(\mathbf{r}) \neq r^*.$$

$\qquad\qquad\qquad\qquad\qquad\qquad\qquad\qquad\qquad\qquad\qquad\qquad\qquad\qquad\qquad\qquad\qquad\qquad\square$

The optimum probability of error has an upper bound as given in the following corollary.

Corollary 10.17. *Suppose that δ is the probability that the weighted majority rank aggregation method with the log odds-ratio weights results in a tie and in this case is equally likely to return either one of the two hypotheses. The optimal value of the expected loss is*

$$\min_{f \in \mathcal{F}} \mathbf{Pr}[f(R) \neq R^*] \leq \min \left\{ \frac{1}{2} \left[\delta + (1-\delta) 2^{-\sum_{i \in N} D(\frac{1}{2} \| v_i)} \right], \frac{1+\delta}{2} 2^{-\sum_{i \in N} D(\frac{1}{2} \| v_i)} \right\}$$

(10.80)

where $D(p \| q)$ is the Kullback-Leibler divergence between two Bernoulli distributions with parameters p and q.

Proof. We first show the upper bound in the first element of the minimum operator in (10.80). By the optimality of the weighted majority rank aggregation method with the log odds-ratio weights, denoted with f^*, we have

$$\min_{f \in \mathcal{F}} \mathbf{Pr}[f(R) \neq R^*] = \mathbf{Pr}[f^*(R) \neq R^*]$$

$$= \frac{1}{2} \mathbf{Pr}\left[f^*(R) = 0\right] + \mathbf{Pr}\left[f^*(R)R^* < 0\right]$$

$$= \frac{1}{2}\delta + \mathbf{Pr}\left[f^*(R)R^* < 0\right].$$

The first bound in the minimum operator in (10.80) follows by

$$\mathbf{Pr}\left[f^*(R)R^* < 0 \mid R^* = r^*\right] = \sum_{\mathbf{r} \in \{-1,1\}^n} \ell(\mathbf{r}; r^*) \mathbf{1}\left(f^*(\mathbf{r})r^* < 0\right)$$

$$= e^{-\frac{1}{2}\sum_{i \in N} \log\left(\frac{1}{v_i(1-v_i)}\right)} \sum_{\mathbf{r} \in \{-1,1\}^n : f^*(\mathbf{r})r^* < 0} e^{\frac{1}{2}\left(\sum_{i \in N} \log\left(\frac{v_i}{1-v_i}\right)r_i\right)r^*}$$

$$\leq e^{-\frac{1}{2}\sum_{i \in N} \log\left(\frac{1}{v_i(1-v_i)}\right)} \cdot \left|\{\mathbf{r} \in \{-1,1\}^n \mid f^*(\mathbf{r})r^* < 0\}\right|$$

$$= e^{-\frac{1}{2}\sum_{i \in N} \log\left(\frac{1}{v_i(1-v_i)}\right)} \cdot \frac{1}{2} 2^n (1-\delta)$$

$$= \frac{1}{2}(1-\delta) e^{-\frac{1}{2}\sum_{i \in N} \log\left(\frac{1}{4v_i(1-v_i)}\right)}$$

$$= \frac{1}{2}(1-\delta) 2^{-\sum_{i \in N} D(\frac{1}{2} \| v_i)}$$

where the second equality is by using (10.77), the first inequality is by the fact that each summation element is smaller than or equal to 1, and the third equality is by the fact that whenever $\mathbf{r}$ is such that the condition in the summation is true, then this condition is not true for $-\mathbf{r}$ and hence there can only be at most $2^n(1-\delta)/2$ elements in the given sum.

The second bound in the minimum operator in (10.80) follows by $\min_{f \in \mathcal{F}} \mathbf{Pr}[f(R) \neq R^*] \leq \mathbf{Pr}[(\sum_{i \in N} \log(\frac{v_i}{1-v_i})R_i)R^* \leq 0]$ and then using similar counting arguments as for the first bound. $\square$

The result in Corollary 10.80 tells us that in cases when there cannot be ties, the bound on the error probability of the optimum rank aggregation is $2^{-\sum_{i \in N} D(1/2 \| v_i)}/2$.

This is the case whenever there cannot exist a split of judgments so that the two hypotheses receive equal total weights. For example, in the case of experts of identical abilities, there cannot be a tie for any odd number of experts. In general, the second bound under the minimum operator is less than or equal to the first bound if, and only if, $\sum_{i \in N} D(1/2 \| v_i) \geq 1$, i.e., the discrimination of the two hypotheses by the panel of experts is large enough. In any case, the upper bound $2^{-\sum_{i \in N} D(1/2\|v_i)}$ holds for every value $\delta \in [0, 1]$, and this is exactly the bound that one would obtain by using a Chernoff's bound, which is left as Exercise 10.4 to the reader.

Arbitrary Prior Distribution

We consider a more general case that allows for arbitrary prior distribution of the ground-truth hypothesis. We shall establish optimality of the following weighted rank aggregation method, which we refer to as a *modified weighted majority rank aggregation with the log odds-ratio weights*:

$$f(\mathbf{r}) = \begin{cases} \text{sign}\left(\sum_{i \in N} w_i r_i + w_0 r_0\right), & \text{if } \sum_{i \in N} w_i r_i + w_0 r_0 \neq 0 \\ \tilde{r}, & \text{if } \sum_{i \in N} w_i r_i + w_0 r_0 = 0 \end{cases}$$

where

$$w_i = \log\left(\frac{v_i}{1 - v_i}\right), \text{ for } i = 0, 1, \ldots, n$$

and

$$r_0 = -\mathbf{1}(p^0(-1) \geq 1/2) + \mathbf{1}(p^0(1) > 1/2), \ v_0 = \max\{p^0(-1), p^0(1)\}$$

and $\tilde{r}$ takes either value -1 or value 1, arbitrarily. We may intuitively interpret this rank aggregation method as a weighted majority rank aggregation with the log odds-ratio weights with one extra expert who reports the more likely hypothesis according to the prior distribution, and whose weight is the log odds-ratio with respect to the ability parameter defined as the maximum probability of a hypothesis according to the prior distribution.

Theorem 10.18. *Suppose that the prior distribution of the ground-truth full ranking is given by p^0. Then, the optimal rank aggregation method within the set of rank aggregation methods $\mathcal{F}$ is the modified weighted majority rule with the log odds-ratio weights.*

Proof. From (10.75), we observe that any optimal rank aggregation method f is such that for every $\mathbf{r} \in \{-1, 1\}^n$ and $r^* \in \{-1, 1\}$,

$$\ell(\mathbf{r}; r^*)p^0(r^*) < \ell(\mathbf{r}; -r^*)p^0(-r^*) \text{ implies } f(\mathbf{r}) \neq r^*.$$

This implication holds for the modified weighted majority rank aggregation with the log odds-ratio weights following the same steps as in the proof of Theorem 10.16. □

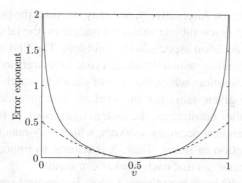

Figure 10.3. The optimal error exponent $D(1/2 \parallel v)$ (solid line), and the error exponent for the weighted majority rank aggregation with linear weights $(2v - 1)^2/2$ (dashed line).

10.4.2 Weighted Majority Rank Aggregation with Linear Weights

Consider the weighted majority rank aggregation method with the weights defined to be linear in the abilities of the experts: $w_i = 2v_i - 1$, for $i = 1, 2, \ldots, n$. This particular choice of weights has been studied in several instances in the literature.

Theorem 10.19. *Suppose that f is the weighted majority rank aggregation with weights $w_i = 2v_i - 1$, for $i = 1, 2, \ldots, n$. Then, the probability of error in identifying the ground-truth hypothesis satisfies*

$$\mathbf{Pr}[f(R) \neq R^*] \leq e^{-\frac{1}{2}\sum_{i \in N}(2v_i - 1)^2}.$$

The proof of this theorem is left as Exercise 10.4 to the interested reader. The error exponent with the linear weights is near to the optimal error exponent in Corollary 10.17 only when the ability parameters are near to the value of $1/2$ and becomes looser as the ability parameters are away from $1/2$. See Figure 10.3 for an illustration.

10.4.3 Budget Optimal Rank Aggregation

Insofar, we considered the aggregation of judgments for a single binary hypotheses. We shall now consider a more general case of a set of one or more binary hypotheses $M = \{1, 2, \ldots, m\}$, for $m \geq 1$. This case is of much interest in the context of online services; for example, in the context of labeling information items such as digital images or snippets of text where there are many items that require labeling and only a limited number of workers of varied expertise to perform the labeling tasks. In such settings, the expertise of the workers often varies across different workers, and thus, each item requires some number of repeated labeling inputs. Such labeling tasks are commonly performed by workers in paid-labor online crowdsourcing platforms, where the owner of a collection of items pays a fixed monetary price for each labeling instance. Thus, it is natural to consider the problem of minimizing the total number of labeling instances subject to a prescribed labeling accuracy. The accuracy could be defined in different ways. For example, one way is to require a bound on the probability of incorrect labeling for each item, and another way is to impose a bound on the portion of erroneously labeled items. Alternatively, one may consider the problem of maximizing a given measure of accuracy subject to a fixed budget on the labeling instances.

There are two key decision aspects in this problem. The first is the *task assignment*, which consists of deciding which labeling tasks to assign to which workers. The second is the *label estimation*, which consists of deciding which label to declare as the correct label for each given item once the workers have provided their judgments. In the absence of any other constraints, the task assignment will focus on assigning the labeling tasks to the highest accuracy workers, which may result in an overload when there is a large collection of items. Thus, it is natural to impose a constraint on the number of labeling instances that each worker can handle.

Assume that for each binary hypotheses j, there is a ground-truth hypothesis denoted with r_j^*. Let us define $x_{i,j} = 1$ if expert i is assigned to provide input judgment for binary hypothesis j, and $x_{i,j} = 0$, otherwise. If expert i is assigned to provide input judgment for binary hypothesis j, then let $r_{i,j}$ denote his or her input judgment. The input judgments are assumed to be independent over different binary hypotheses according to distributions,

$$\mathbf{Pr}[r_{i,j} = r_j^*] = 1 - \mathbf{Pr}[r_{i,j} \neq r_j^*] = v_{i,j}$$

where $v_{i,j} \in [0, 1]$ is the ability parameter of expert i for identifying the ground-truth hypothesis for binary hypothesis problem j. Assume that each expert can provide at most some positive integer number of input judgments, denoted with m_i for expert i.

We shall first consider a budget optimal rank aggregation for known ability parameters. This problem formulation is of interest in its own right and allows for the design of practical schemes in situations where the ability parameters are known up to a small margin of error.

Maximizing the Expected Number of Correctly Identified Hypotheses

Consider the problem of maximizing the expected number of correctly identified hypotheses subject to a budget constraint on the total number of judgments of value $b > 0$. Given an assignment of experts to binary hypothesis, by Theorem 10.16, it is optimal to use a weighted majority rank aggregation with the log odds-ratio weights for each binary hypothesis problem, using the input judgments provided for this binary hypothesis problem. Thus, using the bound on the error probability in Corollary 10.17, we can define the task assignment problem as the solution of the following integer programming problem:

$$
\begin{aligned}
\text{maximize} \quad & \sum_{j=1}^{m} \left(1 - \tfrac{1}{2} 2^{-\sum_{i=1}^{n} d_{i,j} x_{i,j}} \right) \\
\text{subject to} \quad & \sum_{j=1}^{m} x_{i,j} \leq m_i, \quad \text{for } 1 \leq i \leq n \\
& \sum_{i=1}^{n} \sum_{j=1}^{m} x_{i,j} \leq b \\
& x \in \{0, 1\}^{n \times m}
\end{aligned}
$$

where $d_{i,j}$ is the Kullback-Leibler divergence between two Bernoulli distributions with mean $1/2$ and $v_{i,j}$, respectively.

Guaranteed Accuracy for Each Binary Hypothesis

Consider now the problem of minimizing the total number of input judgments subject to that the probability of error for each binary hypothesis problem is at most ϵ, for given parameter $0 \le \epsilon < 1$. Define, for convenience, $c_\epsilon = \log_2(1/(2\epsilon))$. Under the given assumptions, the task assignment problem can be formulated as a linear integer programming problem with packing and covering constraints defined as follows:

$$
\begin{aligned}
\text{minimize} \quad & \sum_{i=1}^{n} \sum_{j=1}^{m} x_{i,j} \\
\text{subject to} \quad & \sum_{j=1}^{m} x_{i,j} \le m_i, \quad \text{for } 1 \le i \le n \\
& \sum_{i=1}^{n} d_{i,j} x_{i,j} \ge c_\epsilon, \quad \text{for } 1 \le j \le m \\
& x \in \{0, 1\}^{n \times m}
\end{aligned}
$$

where $d_{i,j} = D(\frac{1}{2} \| v_{i,j})$, for $i \in N$ and $j \in M$. This follows from the optimality of the weighted majority rank aggregation with the log odds-ratio weights shown in Theorem 10.16 and using the bound on the probability of error in Corollary 10.17. Notice that if, for some reason, one would prefer to use the weighted majority rank aggregation with the linear weights $2v_{i,j} - 1$, then using Theorem 10.19, the same formulation holds but with $d_{i,j}$ redefined to $(2v_{i,j} - 1)^2/2$ and $c_\epsilon = \log(1/(2\epsilon))$.

Bayesian Inference

Thus far, we considered the budget optimal rank aggregation problem under assumption that the ability parameters are known. This allowed us to formulate the problem as an integer programming optimization problem. In this section, we consider a Bayesian framework where the abilities of the experts are latent variables according to a prior distribution. A Bayesian estimation method is then considered that amounts to computing the maximum a posteriori hypothesis for each binary hypothesis problem, given a set of input judgments.

We focus on the special case in which the abilities of the experts can differ from one expert to another, but the ability of an expert assumes a common value for any input judgment task assigned to this expert. This means that if an expert $i \in N$ provides an input judgment for a binary hypothesis problem $j \in M$, his or her judgment is correct with probability v_i and is incorrect with probability $1 - v_i$, where $v_i \in [0, 1]$ is the ability latent variable. The prior distribution of the abilities is assumed to be of a product form with univariate marginal distributions $p_1^0, p_2^0, \ldots, p_n^0$. The input to the problem is a matrix $R = (r_{i,j}) \in \{-1, 0, 1\}^{n \times m}$, where for each binary hypothesis problem j, $r_{i,j} = -1$ if expert i reports -1, $r_{i,j} = 1$ if expert i reports 1, and $r_{i,j} = 0$ if expert i has not provided a judgment for binary hypothesis problem j. We denote with M_i the subset of binary hypotheses for which expert i provided a judgment, i.e., $M_i = \{j \in M \mid r_{i,j} \ne 0\}$. Similarly, we denote with N_j the set of experts who provided a judgment for binary hypotheses j, i.e., $N_j = \{i \in N \mid r_{i,j} \ne 0\}$.

The Bayesian estimation method considered in this section is based on a factor graph representation of the posterior joint distribution of the ground-truth hypotheses and the sum-product algorithm. The concept of a factor graph and the sum-product algorithm are defined in Section 9.5.3.

Factor graph The posterior joint distribution of the ground-truth hypotheses and the abilities of the experts follows by Bayes's rule and is given as follows:

$$p(\mathbf{r}^*, \mathbf{v}) \propto \prod_{i \in N} \prod_{j \in M_i} p(r_{i,j}; r_j^*, v_i) p_i^0(v_i) \tag{10.81}$$

where

$$p(r_{i,j}; r_j^*, v_i) = v_i \mathbf{1}(r_{i,j} = r_j^*) + (1 - v_i) \mathbf{1}(r_{i,j} \neq r_j^*).$$

If the prior distribution of the ability variables is discrete, the posterior joint distribution of the ground-truth hypotheses is obtained from (10.81) by summing over the values of the ability variables, so we have

$$p(\mathbf{r}^*) \propto \prod_{i \in N} h_i(\mathbf{r}_{M_i}^*) \tag{10.82}$$

where

$$h_i(\mathbf{r}_{M_i}^*) = \sum_{v_i} v_i^{\sum_{j \in M_i} \mathbf{1}(r_{i,j} = r_j^*)} (1 - v_i)^{\sum_{j \in M_i} \mathbf{1}(r_{i,j} \neq r_j^*)} p_i^0(v_i).$$

The same formulation holds if the prior distribution of an ability variable of an expert has a density, but with the summation in the last expression replaced with integration. Throughout this section, we use the notation for discrete prior distributions.

The univariate marginal distributions of the ground-truth hypotheses are given by

$$p_j(r_j^*) = \sum_{\mathbf{r}_{M \setminus \{j\}}^* \in \{-1,1\}^{m-1}} p(\mathbf{r}^*), \text{ for } r_j^* \in \{-1, 1\} \text{ and } j \in M.$$

The maximum a posteriori probability ground-truth hypotheses are

$$\hat{r}_j^* = \operatorname{argmax}\{p_j(x) \mid x \in \{-1, 1\}\}, \text{ for } j \in M.$$

The posterior joint distribution (10.82) admits a factor graph representation where each expert is represented with a factor vertex, and each latent variable r_j^* is represented with a variable vertex.

Example 10.20. Consider the matrix of input judgments:

$$R = \begin{pmatrix} -1 & 0 \\ 1 & 0 \\ -1 & 1 \\ 0 & 1 \\ 0 & -1 \end{pmatrix}.$$

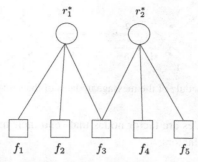

Figure 10.4. Factor graph for Example 10.20.

Then, the factor graph consists of five factor nodes and two variable nodes, and is of the structure given in Figure 10.4. The factors are given as follows:

$$h_1(r_1^*) = \sum_{v_1} v_1^{\mathbf{1}(r_1^*=-1)}(1-v_1)^{\mathbf{1}(r_1^*=1)} p_1^0(v_1)$$

$$h_2(r_1^*) = \sum_{v_2} v_2^{\mathbf{1}(r_1^*=-1)}(1-v_2)^{\mathbf{1}(r_1^*=1)} p_2^0(v_2)$$

$$h_3(r_1^*, r_2^*) = \sum_{v_3} v_3^{\mathbf{1}(r_1^*=-1)+\mathbf{1}(r_2^*=1)}(1-v_3)^{\mathbf{1}(r_1^*=1)+\mathbf{1}(r_2^*=-1)} p_3^0(v_3)$$

$$h_4(r_2^*) = \sum_{v_4} v_4^{\mathbf{1}(r_2^*=-1)}(1-v_4)^{\mathbf{1}(r_2^*=1)} p_4^0(v_4)$$

$$h_5(r_2^*) = \sum_{v_5} v_5^{\mathbf{1}(r_2^*=-1)}(1-v_5)^{\mathbf{1}(r_2^*=1)} p_5^0(v_5)$$

The sum-product algorithm The sum-product algorithm, defined in Section 9.5.3, for the posterior joint distribution in (10.82), corresponds to the following message updates for $i \in N$ and $j \in M_i$:

Sum-Product Algorithm:

$$m_{j\to i}(r_j^*) = \prod_{i'\in N_j\setminus\{i\}} m_{i'\to j}(r_j^*) \tag{10.83}$$

$$m_{i\to j}(r_j^*) = \sum_{\mathbf{r}_{M_i\setminus\{j\}}^*} h_i(\mathbf{r}_{M_i}^*) \prod_{j'\in M_i\setminus\{j\}} m_{j'\to i}(r_{j'}^*). \tag{10.84}$$

The marginal distributions of the ground-truth hypotheses are given by

$$p_j(x) = \prod_{i\in N_j} m_{i\to j}(x), \quad \text{for } x \in \{-1, 1\} \quad \text{and } j \in M. \tag{10.85}$$

Example 10.21. Revisit the factor graph in Example 10.20. The message updates of the sum-product algorithm are according to the schedule in Figure 10.5, and are specified as follows.

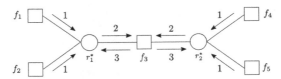

Figure 10.5. A schedule of the message updates of the sum-product algorithm.

Step 1 All the leaf nodes are factor nodes that send their messages initialized to their corresponding factors:

$$m_{f_1 \to r_1^*}(r_1^*) = h_1(r_1^*)$$

$$m_{f_2 \to r_1^*}(r_1^*) = h_2(r_1^*)$$

$$m_{f_3 \to r_2^*}(r_2^*) = h_3(r_2^*)$$

$$m_{f_4 \to r_2^*}(r_2^*) = h_4(r_2^*)$$

Step 2 The messages are from the two variable nodes computed according to (10.83) and using the messages received by the variable nodes in Step 1:

$$m_{r_1^* \to f_3}(r_1^*) = h_1(r_1^*)h_2(r_1^*)$$

$$m_{r_2^* \to f_3}(r_2^*) = h_4(r_2^*)h_5(r_2^*)$$

Step 3 The messages are from factor node f_3 computed according to (10.84) and using the messages received by node f_3 in Step 2:

$$m_{f_3 \to r_1^*}(r_1^*) = \sum_{r_2^* \in \{-1,1\}} h_3(r_1^*, r_2^*)h_4(r_2^*)h_5(r_2^*)$$

$$m_{f_3 \to r_2^*}(r_2^*) = \sum_{r_1^* \in \{-1,1\}} h_3(r_1^*, r_2^*)h_1(r_1^*)h_2(r_1^*)$$

The posterior marginal distributions of ground-truth hypotheses are given by (10.85), which for the computed values of the messages read as follows:

$$p_1(r_1^*) = h_1(r_1^*)h_2(r_1^*) \sum_{r_2^* \in \{-1,1\}} h_3(r_1^*, r_2^*)h_4(r_2^*)h_5(r_2^*)$$

and

$$p_2(r_2^*) = h_4(r_2^*)h_5(r_2^*) \sum_{r_1^* \in \{-1,1\}} h_3(r_1^*, r_2^*)h_1(r_1^*)h_2(r_1^*),$$

which are, indeed, the marginal distributions of the given joint distribution.

Alternative representation The sum-product algorithm given by (10.83) and (10.84) can be represented in an alternative form as follows. Let us define

$$a_i(x) = \sum_{v_i} v_i^x (1 - v_i)^{|M_i| - x} p_i^0(v_i), \quad \text{for } x = 0, 1, \ldots, |M_i| \qquad (10.86)$$

$$u_{j \to i}^{(t)} = \log \left(\frac{m_{j \to i}^{(t)}(+1)}{m_{j \to i}^{(t)}(-1)} \right) \tag{10.87}$$

and

$$w_{i \to j}^{(t)} = r_{i,j} \log \left(\frac{m_{i \to j}^{(t)}(+1)}{m_{i \to j}^{(t)}(-1)} \right). \tag{10.88}$$

The factorization of the posterior joint distribution of ground-truth hypotheses in (10.82) can be equivalently written as follows:

$$p(\mathbf{r}^*) \propto \prod_{i \in N} a_i \left(\sum_{j \in M_i} \mathbf{1}(r_{i,j} = r_j^*) \right).$$

The sum-product algorithm with message updates (10.83) and (10.84) can be expressed in the following form, which is left as Exercise 10.9 to the reader to show.

Sum-Product Algorithm (alternative formulation):

$$u_{j \to i}^{(t+1)} = \sum_{i' \in N \setminus \{i\}} r_{i',j} w_{i' \to j}^{(t)} \tag{10.89}$$

and

$$w_{i \to j}^{(t+1)} = \log \left(\frac{\sum_{k=0}^{|M_i|-1} a_i(k+1) f_{i,j,k}(u^{(t+1)})}{\sum_{k=0}^{|M_i|-1} a_i(k) f_{i,j,k}(u^{(t+1)})} \right) \tag{10.90}$$

where

$$f_{i,j,0}(u) = 1 \text{ and } f_{i,j,k}(u) = \sum_{M' \subseteq M_i \setminus \{j\}: |M'|=k} \exp \left(\sum_{j' \in M'} r_{i,j'} u_{j' \to i} \right),$$

$$\text{for } k = 1, 2, \dots, |M_i| - 1.$$

The maximum a posteriori probability ground-truth hypotheses are given by

$$r_j^{*(t+1)} = \text{sign} \left(\sum_{i \in N_j} w_{i \to j}^{(t)} r_{i,j} \right), \text{ for } j \in M. \tag{10.91}$$

Haldane prior distribution The message updates of the sum-product algorithm in (10.89) and (10.90), for the specific choice of the so-called Haldane prior distribution $p_i^0(0) = p_i^0(1) = 1/2$ for every $i \in N$, boils down to the following linear iterative system:

$$u_{j \to i}^{(t+1)} = \sum_{i' \in N \setminus \{i\}} r_{i',j} w_{i' \to j}^{(t)} \tag{10.92}$$

and

$$w_{i \to j}^{(t+1)} = \sum_{j' \in M \setminus \{j\}} r_{i,j'} u_{j' \to i}^{(t+1)} \tag{10.93}$$

which indeed follows from (10.89) and (10.90) and the fact that for the given choice of the prior distribution, it holds that

$$a_i(x) = \begin{cases} \frac{1}{2}, & \text{if } x = 0 \text{ or } x = |M_i| \\ 0, & \text{otherwise} \end{cases}.$$

The linear iterative system with a suitable initial value allows us to characterize the expected number of correctly identified ground-truth hypotheses for a given number of input judgments per binary hypotheses task. If the message updates are carried out according to (10.92) and (10.93) with the initialization according to the specification of the sum-product algorithm, then the posterior distribution of ground-truth hypotheses is such that $p(\mathbf{r}^*) = p(-\mathbf{r}^*)$. This is because the Haldane prior distribution is symmetric about $1/2$ (see Exercise 10.11). For instance, in Example 10.20, one would obtain that the posterior distribution is uniform over $(-1, 1)$ and $(1, -1)$. On the contrary, the simple majority aggregation of judgments would yield $(-1, 1)$ as the unique solution.

Density evolution equations Suppose that the assignment of the experts to the binary hypothesis tasks is according to a random bipartite graph with $\bar{n}$ experts assigned to each binary hypothesis task and $\bar{m}$ binary hypothesis task assigned to each expert. Notice that we have $\bar{n}m = \bar{m}n$. We define the following two parameters of the prior distribution:

$$\mu_1 = \mathbf{E}[2v_i - 1] \text{ and } \mu_2 = \mathbf{E}[(2v_i - 1)^2].$$

For brevity of notation, we also define the following parameter:

$$\delta = (\bar{n} - 1)(\bar{m} - 1)\mu_2^2.$$

This parameter will play a key role conditional on the event that the graph induced by the edges traversed by the execution of the iterative scheme for the first t iterations is a tree. It can be shown that, for fixed t, $\bar{n}$, and $\bar{m}$, this event occurs with probability $1 - O(1/m)$, which we don't prove here. Suppose that $w_{i \to j}^{(0)}$ are initialized to value 1. Let $w_{v,k}^{(t)}$ denote a random variable representing the message for a random edge (i, j) where i is a factor node and j is a variable node such that $v_i = v$. Similarly, let $u_k^{(t)}$ denote a random variable representing the message for a random edge (j, i).

The distributions of random variables $u_{j \to i}^{(t)}$ and $w_{i \to j}^{(t)}$ converge to the distributions of random variables $u^{(t)}$ and $w^{(t)}$, respectively, which are defined by the following density evolution equations:

$$u^{(t+1)} =_d \sum_{k=1}^{\bar{n}-1} a_{v_k, k} w_{v_k, k}^{(t)} \tag{10.94}$$

$$w_v^{(t+1)} =_d \sum_{k=1}^{\bar{m}-1} b_{v,k} u_k^{(t+1)} \tag{10.95}$$

where $=_d$ denotes equality in distribution. Here $a_{v_1, 1}, a_{v_2, 2}, \dots, a_{v_{\bar{n}-1}, \bar{n}-1}$ and $b_{v,1}, b_{v,2}, \dots, b_{v,\bar{m}-1}$ are independent random variables $a_{v_k, k}$ taking value 1 with probability v_k and value -1 with probability $1 - v_k$, and $b_{v,k}$ taking value 1 with probability v and value -1 with probability $1 - v$. The random variables $w_{v_1, 1}^{(t)}, w_{v_2, 2}^{(t)}, \dots, w_{v_{\bar{n}-1}, \bar{n}-1}^{(t)}$

are independent with the same distributions as $w_{v_1}^{(t)}, w_{v_2}^{(t)}, \ldots, w_{v_{\bar{n}-1}}^{(t)}$, respectively. Similarly, the random variables $u_1^{(t)}, u_2^{(t)}, \ldots, u_{\bar{m}-1}^{(t)}$ are independent with identical distributions corresponding to that of the random variable $u^{(t)}$. The random variables $a_{v_k,k}$ and $w_{v_k,k}^{(t)}$ are independent conditional on the value of random variable v_k. The random variables $b_{v,k}$ and $u_k^{(t)}$ are independent.

The distribution of random variable $r_j^{*(t)}$ in (10.91) corresponds to that of a random variable $r^{(t+1)}$ that satisfies the following distribution equality:

$$\hat{r}^{(t+1)} =_d \sum_{k=1}^{\bar{n}} a_{v_k,k} w_{v_k,k}^{(t)}. \tag{10.96}$$

Let us define

$$\mu(t) = \mathbf{E}[u^{(t)}] \text{ and } \sigma^2(t) = \text{Var}[u^{(t)}].$$

We claim that for $t = 1, 2, \ldots$, we have

$$\mu(t) = \mu(1)[(\bar{n} - 1)(\bar{m} - 1)\mu_2]^{t-1} \tag{10.97}$$

and

$$\sigma^2(t) = \begin{cases} \left(\sigma^2(1) + (1 - \mu_2)(1 + (\bar{m} - 1)\mu_2)\mu^2(1)(t-1)\right) \left(\frac{1}{\mu_2^2}\right)^{t-1}, & \text{if } \delta = 1 \\ \left(\sigma^2(1) + (1 - \mu_2)(1 + (\bar{m} - 1)\mu_2)\mu^2(1)\frac{1-\delta^{t-1}}{1-\delta}\right) \left(\frac{\delta}{\mu_2^2}\right)^{t-1}, & \text{if } \delta \neq 1 \end{cases} \tag{10.98}$$

where $\mu(1) = (\bar{n} - 1)\mu_1$ and $\sigma^2(1) = (\bar{n} - 1)(1 - \mu_1^2)$. A the end of this section, we briefly discuss how these expressions can be derived, and leave the details to the reader as Exercise 10.12.

From (10.94) and (10.96), we have

$$\mathbf{E}[\hat{r}^{(t+1)}] = \frac{\bar{n}}{\bar{n} - 1}\mu(t) \text{ and } \text{Var}[\hat{r}^{(t+1)}] = \frac{\bar{n}}{\bar{n} - 1}\sigma^2(t).$$

Combining this with the expressions in (10.97) and (10.98), we obtain that the coefficient of variation of random variable $\hat{r}^{(t+1)}$ satisfies

$$\frac{\sqrt{\text{Var}[\hat{r}^{(t+1)}]}}{\mathbf{E}[\hat{r}^{(t+1)}]} = \begin{cases} \Theta(1) & \text{if } \delta > 1 \\ \Theta(\sqrt{t}) & \text{if } \delta = 1 \\ e^{\Theta(t)} & \text{if } \delta < 1 \end{cases}.$$

This establishes the existence of a phase transition: if the following condition

$$(\bar{n} - 1)(\bar{m} - 1)\mu_2^2 > 1$$

holds true, then the coefficient of variation converges to a constant with the number of iterations. Otherwise, the coefficient of variation increases with the number of iterations. This implies that for the coefficient of variation to converge to a constant with the number of iterations, it is necessary that the total number of input judgments is at least $\sqrt{nm}/\mu_2$.

We conclude this section with a discussion on how to derive the expressions in (10.97) and (10.98). This follows from the density evolution equations (10.94) and

(10.95) by simple but tedious computations, whose main steps we describe as follows. Let us define

$$\mu_v(t) = \mathbf{E}[w_{v_k,k}^{(t)} \mid v_k = v] \text{ and } \sigma_v^2(t) = \text{Var}[w_{v_k,k}^{(t)} \mid v_k = v],$$

which are the mean and the variance, respectively, of random variable $w_{v_k,k}^{(t)}$ conditional on the value of v_k being equal to v.

Using the distribution equalities in (10.94) and (10.95) and the fact that the summation terms that appear in these two distribution equalities are independent, it is easy to observe that the following two recursive equations hold:

$$\mu(t) = (\bar{n} - 1)\mathbf{E}[(2v_i - 1)\mu_{v_i}(t - 1)] \tag{10.99}$$

and

$$\mu_v(t) = (\bar{m} - 1)(2v - 1)\mu(t). \tag{10.100}$$

An interesting side observation is that $\mu_v(t)$ is proportional to $2v - 1$. This means that we can interpret the given iterative method as that of a weighted majority aggregation of judgments defined by (10.96) with random weights whose expected values are linear in the ability of the experts.

Similarly, from the distribution equalities in (10.94) and (10.95), we obtain the following recursive equations for the variances:

$$\sigma^2(t + 1) = (\bar{n} - 1)(\mathbf{E}[\sigma_{v_i}^2(t) + \mu_{v_i}(t)^2] - \mathbf{E}[(2v_i - 1)\mu_{v_i}(t)]^2) \tag{10.101}$$

and

$$\sigma_v^2(t) = (\bar{m} - 1)(\sigma^2(t) + (1 - (2v - 1)^2)\mu(t)^2). \tag{10.102}$$

From (10.99) and (10.100), it immediately follows that

$$\mu(t + 1) = (\bar{n} - 1)(\bar{m} - 1)\mu_2\mu(t),$$

and, from (10.100)-(10.102), it follows that

$$\sigma^2(t + 1) = (\bar{n} - 1)(\bar{m} - 1)\sigma^2(t) + (\bar{n} - 1)(\bar{m} - 1)(1 - \mu_2)(1 + (\bar{m} - 1)\mu_2)\mu(t)^2.$$

The expressions in (10.97) and (10.98) follow from the last systems of recursive equations. The initial values $\mu(1)$ and $\sigma^2(1)$ follow, respectively, from (10.99) and (10.101) and $\mu_{v_i}(0) = 1$ and $\sigma_{v_i}(0) = 0$ with probability 1, by the assumption that the messages $w_{i \to j}^{(0)}$ are initialized to unit values.

Summary

Rank Aggregation Given an input sequence of rankings of n alternatives $\pi_1, \pi_2, \ldots, \pi_m$, find a ranking π that minimizes the function

$$L(\pi) = \sum_{i=1}^{m} d(\pi, \pi_i)$$

where $d : S_n \times S_n \to \mathbf{R}_+$ is a distance function.

Example distance functions:

(i) Spearman's footrule: $F(\sigma, \rho) = \sum_{i \in N} |\sigma(i) - \rho(i)|$

(ii) Kendall's τ: $K(\sigma, \rho) = \sum_{i,j \in N: i<j} \mathbf{1}((\sigma(i) - \sigma(j))(\rho(i) - \rho(j)) < 0)$

Diaconis-Graham inequality:

$$K(\sigma, \rho) \leq F(\sigma, \rho) \leq 2K(\sigma, \rho)$$

Kemeny rank aggregation: a rank aggregation with respect to Kendall's τ distances.

Computational complexity:

(i) Finding Kemeny optimal rank aggregation is NP-hard.

(ii) Taking as output an input ranking chosen uniformly at random from the set of input rankings is a 2-approximation for the Kemeny optimal rank aggregation.

Minimum Feedback Arc Set in Tournaments Given is a directed graph $G = (N, E)$ with a directed edge between every pair of vertices in one or the other direction, exclusively.

Minimum feedback arc set problem: find an ordering of vertices that minimizes the number of backward edges.

A weighted feedback arc set problem: given a matrix of non-negative values $\mathbf{W} = (w_{i,j})$, find an ordering π that minimizes

$$L(\pi) = \sum_{i,j} w_{j,i} \mathbf{1}(\pi(i) < \pi(j)).$$

Maximum likelihood estimation justification: given a tournament graph $G = (N, E)$ and parameter $1/2 < p < 1$, for each pair of vertices, the true ordering of the alternatives is observed with probability p, and the false ordering is observed otherwise. Let $\mathbf{W} = (w_{i,j})$ where $w_{i,j}$ is the number of times i was observed being ranked higher than j in pair comparisons of these two alternatives. The maximum likelihood ranking is a ranking π that minimizes $L(\pi)$.

Computation complexity:

(i) Minimum feedback arc set on tournaments is NP-hard.

(ii) QuickSort for tournaments with random pivot is a 3-approximation.

(iii) Ordering in decreasing order of the number of wins is a 5-approximation.

Rank aggregation in decreasing order of the number of wins: the number of wins per player is a sufficient statistic for minimizing the expected value of a loss function from a broad set of loss functions, if the distributions of pairwise scores are from the exponential family of distributions.

Aggregation of Judgments

Given a panel of n experts and two hypotheses each expert i reports r_i that is equal to the true hypothesis with probability v_i and is equal to the false hypothesis otherwise.

Optimal rank aggregation rule is the weighted majority rank aggregation with the log odds-ratio weights:

$$f(r_1, r_2, \ldots, r_n) = \text{sign}\left(\sum_{i=1}^{n} \log\left(\frac{v_i}{1 - v_i}\right) r_i\right).$$

The optimal value of the probability of error satisfies

$$\Pr[f(\mathbf{r}) \neq r_0] \leq 2^{-\sum_{i \in N} D(\frac{1}{2} \| v_i)}.$$

Given a panel of n experts and a collection of m binary hypotheses such that expert i reports the true hypothesis for the binary hypothesis j with probability $v_{i,j}$ and each expert is constrained to report at most m_i labels. Minimizing the number of labels subject to that each binary hypothesis is correctly identified with probability of at least $1 - \epsilon$ can be formulated as an integer programming problem.

Exercises

10.1   **Distances between full rankings** Prove the following claims about some well-known distances between full rankings.

(a) The maximum values of distances between two full rankings of $n \geq 2$ elements are given as follows:

distance	maximum value
Spearman's footrule	$n(n-1)$
Kendall's τ	$\frac{1}{2}n(n-1)$
Spearman's ρ	$\frac{1}{3}n(n-1)(2n-1)$
Hamming	n
Cayley	$n-1$

For the first three distances, the asserted maximum values are achieved for the identity full ranking and the reverse full ranking. For the last two distances, this is also so if n is even, and otherwise, the asserted maximum values are achieved for the identity full ranking and the full ranking that is equal to the reverse full ranking except for swapping the positions of elements $(n+1)/2$ and $(n+1)/2 + 1$.

(b) For every given full ranking ρ_n of $n \geq 2$ elements and a full ranking u_n chosen uniformly at random from the set of all possible full rankings of n elements, we

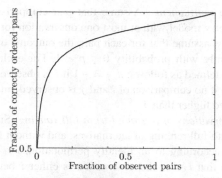

Figure 10.6. A lower bound on the fraction of correctly ordered pairs vs. the fraction of observed pairs using the ranking method based on the scores in Exercise 10.2 for a set of 100 players.

have

distance	$\mathbf{E}[d(\rho_n, u_n)]$	$\mathrm{Var}[d(\rho_n, u_n)]$
Spearman's footrule	$\frac{1}{3}(n^2 - 1)$	$\frac{1}{45}(n+1)(2n^2+7)$
Kendall's τ	$\frac{1}{4}n(n-1)$	$\frac{1}{72}n(n-1)(2n+5)$
Spearman's ρ	$\frac{1}{6}n(n^2-1)$	$\frac{1}{36}n^2(n^2-1)(n+1)$
Hamming	$n-1$	1
Cayley	$n - H_n$	$H_n - \sum_{i=1}^{n}\frac{1}{i^2}$

10.2 **Point difference scores** Consider a set $N = \{1, 2, \ldots, n\}$ of alternatives that obey a full ranking $\pi^*(1) < \pi^*(2) < \cdots < \pi^*(n)$. Let $w_{i,j} = \mathbf{1}(\pi^*(i) < \pi^*(j))$, for $i < j$. Suppose a set of noisy pair comparisons such that for given parameters $1/2 < p \le 1$ and $1 \le m \le n$, the outcome of comparison of a pair (i, j) is observed independently with probability m/n, and given that it is observed, the outcome $\hat{w}_{i,j}$ is equal to $w_{i,j}$ with probability p and is equal to $1 - w_{i,j}$, otherwise. Let $x_{i,j} = 1$, if the comparison of pair (i, j) is observed and $x_{i,j} = 0$, otherwise.

Consider the following rank aggregation rule: the output ranking π is defined to be a full ranking of the alternatives in decreasing order of the scores defined as follows:

$$s(i) = \frac{1}{2m}\sum_{j\ne i} x_{i,j}(2\hat{w}_{i,j} - 1), \text{ for } i = 1, 2, \ldots, n.$$

Show that for the given rank aggregation rule, there exists a constant $c > 0$ such that the expected Kendall's τ distance between π and π^* satisfies

$$\mathbf{E}[K(\pi, \pi^*)] \le \mathbf{E}\left[\sum_{i<j}\mathbf{1}(s(i) \ge s(j))\right] \le \frac{c}{(2p-1)\sqrt{m}}K_n$$

where $K_n = n(n-1)/4$ is the expected Kendall's τ distance between a full ranking sampled uniformly at random from the set of all permutations of n elements and the full ranking π^*. See Figure 10.6.

10.3 **Pairwise scores with distributions that are not of exponential form** Prove that for the following two models of pair comparisons, in general the distribution function of pairwise scores $d_{i,j}$ is not of the exponential form (10.48).

(a) *Incomplete tournaments*: Assume that pair comparisons are according to the Bradley-Terry model with at most one observation for each pair of alternatives. Specifically, assume that for each pair, the outcome of comparison is observed independently with probability $0 \le p < 1$. For each pair (i, j), the pairwise scores are defined as follows: $d_{i,j} = -1$ if i is observed to be ranked lower than j, $d_{i,j} = 0$ if no comparison of i and j is observed, and $d_{i,j} = 1$ if i is observed to be ranked higher than j.

(b) *Noisy observations of a ground-truth full ranking*: Suppose that there exists a ground-truth full ranking of alternatives, and without loss of generality, assume this to be according to an identity permutation. For each pair of alternatives (i, j) such that $i < j$, the observation is either i being ranked higher than j with probability p, or i being ranked lower than j with probability $1 - p$, for parameter $1/2 < p \le 1$.

10.4 **Aggregation of judgments** Prove the following two claims.

(a) For the weighted majority rank aggregation with the log odds-ratio weights as in Corollary 10.17, using Chernoff's bound, the error probability is smaller than or equal to

$$2^{-\sum_{i \in N} D(\frac{1}{2}\|v_i)}.$$

(b) The bound on the error probability asserted in Theorem 10.19 is obtained from a Hoeffding's inequality.

10.5 **Aggregation of judgments** Consider an aggregation of judgments provided by a panel of n experts. Suppose that the number of experts is odd and that the experts are of the same ability with parameter $0 \le v \le 1$. Show that the optimum rank aggregation results in a tie with probability equal to

$$\binom{n}{\frac{n}{2}} \frac{1}{2^n} e^{-n D(\frac{1}{2}\|v)} \sim \frac{\sqrt{2/\pi}}{\sqrt{n}} e^{-n D(\frac{1}{2}\|v)}, \text{ for large } n.$$

10.6 **Aggregation of judgments: a lower bound for the expected number of errors** Suppose there are a set of $m \ge 1$ binary hypothesis and a set of judges who can provide at most lm judgments in total, for a given integer $l \ge 1$. Each judgment for a given binary hypothesis is independent, equal to the ground-truth alternative with probability q, or equal to either of the two alternatives equally likely, with probability $1 - q$. Prove that for any aggregation rule, the expected fraction of incorrectly identified ground truths is at least

$$\frac{1}{2} e^{-2ql}, \text{ for every small enough } q > 0.$$

10.7 **Aggregation of judgments: a necessary number of judgments** Given a binary classification task, the task owner needs to hire a number of workers to provide judgments about which one of the two hypotheses is the true hypothesis. A large pool of workers is given such that each worker i in this pool provides an independent judgment that is correct with probability v_i and is incorrect otherwise. The abilities of the workers are according to the following prior distribution, which is known to the task owner,

$$\mathbf{Pr}\left[v_i = \frac{1+a}{2}\right] = 1 - \mathbf{Pr}\left[v_i = \frac{1}{2}\right] = \frac{q}{a^2}$$

where q and a are positive real-valued parameters such that $q \leq a^2 \leq 1$.

The task owner needs to decide how many workers to hire such that the probability of identifying the true hypothesis is at least $1 - \delta$, for given $\delta \in (0, 1]$. Once the task owner has decided how many workers to hire, the given number of workers is hired and the task owner is informed about the values of their ability parameters. Prove the following two claims.

(a) The prior distribution of the ability parameters is such that

$$\mathbf{E}\left[(2v_i - 1)^2\right] = q.$$

(b) The task owner must hire at least this many workers:

$$C_a \frac{\log(1/(2\delta))}{q}$$

where C_a is a constant that depends only on the parameter a.

This demonstrates the existence of an instance where it is necessary to acquire at least $\Omega(1/q)$ judgments.

10.8 **Maximum likelihood estimation of the best alternative** Suppose that there are $k \geq 2$ alternatives that obey a ground-truth full ranking, so that there is a single best alternative that in pair comparisons beats every other alternative. The goal is to estimate which one of the alternatives is the best alternative based on noisy pair comparisons by a set $N = \{1, 2, \ldots, n\}$ of experts. For each pair of alternatives, expert $i \in N$ provides an independent judgment, which is consistent with the ground-truth full ranking with probability v_i, and is otherwise inconsistent. Let $w_{i,a}$ be the number of pair comparisons for which expert i judged alternative a to be ranked higher than the other alternative. Prove that the maximum likelihood estimate of the best alternative is any alternative a^* that satisfies

$$\sum_{i \in N} \log\left(\frac{v_i}{1 - v_i}\right) w_{i,a^*} \geq \sum_{i \in N} \log\left(\frac{v_i}{1 - v_i}\right) w_{i,a}, \text{ for every } a \in \{1, 2, \ldots, k\}.$$

10.9 **Sum-product algorithm for the aggregation of judgments** Prove that the message-passing equations (10.89) and (10.90) follow from those in (10.83) and (10.84).

10.10 **Sum-product algorithm and the case of known abilities** Show that for a product-form prior distribution of the abilities of experts with univariate marginal distributions having all the mass on a value in $(0, 1)$, the weighted majority aggregation of judgments in (10.91) corresponds to the optimal weighted majority aggregation of judgments when the abilities of the experts are known as given in Theorem 10.16.

10.11 **The posterior distribution for symmetric prior distributions** In the problem of the aggregation of judgments, suppose that the prior distributions of the abilities are symmetric about $1/2$, i.e., $p_i^0(v_i) = p_i^0(1 - v_i)$, for every $v_i \in [0, 1]$ and $i \in N$. Prove that in this case the posterior joint distribution of the ground-truth hypotheses in Section 10.4.3 is symmetric, i.e., $p(\mathbf{r}^*) = p(-\mathbf{r}^*)$,

10.12 Sum-product algorithm: density evolution equations Derive the expressions for $\mu(t)$ and $\sigma^2(t)$ that are asserted in (10.97) and (10.98).

10.5 Bibliographical Notes

The study of distances between rankings of alternatives has a long history. Spearman's footrule distance was first proposed by Spearman (1904). Kendall's τ distance was introduced by Kendall and Smith (1939) and subsequently studied by Kendall (1955). The relations between the Spearman's footrule and Kemeny's τ distances in Theorem 10.1 are due to Diaconis and Graham (1977). Diaconis (1988) provides a good exposition of various properties of permutations. Fagin et al. (2003) and Fagin et al. (2006) developed a framework for the ranking of partial rankings (ranking with ties) based on different approaches. Kumar and Vassilvitskii (2010) studied generalized distances between rankings that allow for giving different weights to different positions, which is of interest in the context of information retrieval. The standard measures of efficiency of an information retrieval system were introduced by various authors, e.g., precision and recall by Cleverdon and Mills (1963), reciprocal rank by Voorhees and Harman (2005), and normalized cumulative discounted gain by Järvelin and Kekäläinen (2002). The effects of ties in a ranking on efficiency measures were first considered by Cooper (1968). McSherry and Najork (2008) adapted standard measures for partial rankings and provided closed-form expressions for the average measures computed over all possible permutations.

The Kemeny rank aggregation was introduced by Kemeny (1959) and subsequently studied by Kemeny and Snell (1972). This rank aggregation is sometimes also referred to as the Kemeny-Young rank aggregation following the line of work by Young (1986, 1988, 1995), and Young and Levenglick (1978), which provided an interpretation of this rank aggregation method as a maximum likelihood estimate under a probabilistic model for generating random permutations. Feigin and Cohen (1978) studied the rank aggregation problem assuming that each input ranking is generated independently from a distribution over permutations. Under condition that for fixed permutation π^*, every permutation π that has the same Kendall τ distance to π^* is equally probable, it was shown that there is a unique family of distributions that satisfies this condition, which is Mallow's distribution. More recently, Conitzer and Sandholm (2005) studied which common voting rules can be interpreted as maximum likelihood estimators under input rankings generated by adding noise to a fixed ranking. The NP-hardness of the Kemeny rank aggregation stated in Theorem 10.2 was established by Bartholdi et al. (1989), and this complexity result was further refined by Hemaspaandra et al. (2005). Dwork et al. (2001a) established that the problem is already NP-hard for an instance with four input rankings. Dwork et al. (2001a,b) showed that the rank aggregation with Spearman's footrule distance can be solved in polynomial time via a minimum cost matching. This combined with the Diaconis-Graham inequality yields a 2-approximation for Kemeny rank aggregation. Ailon et al. (2008) showed that taking the best of QuickSort and an input ranking is a $11/7$-approximation in expectation.

van Zuylen and Williamson (2009) showed a deterministic 8/5-approximation algorithm. Ailon (2007) introduced the rank aggregation problem of partial rankings, showed that the problem is NP-hard for top-m lists already for $m = 2$ and for p-ratings already for $p = 3$, and found 2- and 3/2-approximation algorithms. Schalekamp and van Zuylen (2009) provided a comparative analysis of different analytical and empirical methods and their combinations. Contizer (2006) studied a related but different problem of computing so-called Slater rank aggregation where the objective is to find a ranking of alternatives that minimizes the number of pairs of alternatives such that the ranking disagrees with the pairwise majority vote on these two alternatives. The study of rank aggregation using machine learning methods has also been pursued, e.g., Ailon and Mohri (2008), and Duchi et al. (2010).

The minimum feedback-arc-set problem in tournaments has been considered by several authors. It was shown to be NP-hard by Alon (2006). Ailon et al. (2008) established several approximation results for this problem including the 3-approximation for the unweighted version, and approximation ratios of 5, 2, and 2 for the weighted version under probability constraints, triangle inequality, and probability constraints and triangle inequality, respectively. van Zuylen et al. (2007) and van Zuylen and Williamson (2009) derived deterministic algorithms based on a derandomization of the pivot selection in the QuickSort algorithm introduced by Ailon et al. (2008), which guarantees an approximation ratio of 2 for the case of a weighted feedback arc set in tournaments that satisfies the triangle inequality and an approximation ratio of 3 for the case of a weighted minimum feedback arc set with the weights that satisfy the probability constraints. Coppersmith et al. (2006) showed that ordering in decreasing order of the number of wins guarantees a 5-approximation, which we studied in Section 10.2.2. This ordering is often attributed to Copeland (1951). Kenyon-Mathieu and Schudy (2007) established a polynomial time approximation scheme (PTAS) for the minimum feedback-arc-set problem in tournaments whose weighted generalization gives a PTAS for the Kemeny rank aggregation. Charon and Hudry (2010) is a nice and extensive survey on linear ordering problems. Newman and Vempala (2001) studied polyhedral relaxations for the linear ordering problem. Exercise 10.2 is based on the results in Wauthier et al. (2013). The optimality of ranking the alternatives in decreasing order of the point difference scores in decreasing order, as presented in Section 10.3.3, is from Buhlmann and Huber (1963) and Huber (1963). In Theorem 10.15, we admit more restrictive assumptions than those made in Huber (1963), which allow for point difference score distributions with support being a symmetric lattice.

A wide range of link-based ranking systems have been proposed by various authors. A link-based ranking system for publications was proposed by Pinski and Narin (1976). The PageRank rating system for web pages was introduced by Page et al. (1999) and Brin and Page (1998), and was subsequently studied by many including Langville and Meyer (2004, 2006). The HITS rating system was introduced by Kleinberg (1999). Link analysis was used to discover authorities and predict answer quality in question and answer communities by Jurczyk and Agichtein (2007), Shah and Pomerantz (2010), Tausczik and Pennebaker (2011), Paul et al. (2012), and Dror et al. (2011); for expertise matching for matching papers and reviewers in conference management systems by

Mimno and McCallum (2007); and for trust rating systems, e.g., EigenTrust, by Kamvar et al. (2003). Park and Newman (2005) proposed a rating system based on team scores defined by counting the number of direct and indirect wins and loses and tested it on a U.S. college football data. Callaghan et al. (2007) proposed a rating system where each player is assigned a score based on the stationary distribution of a random walk on a graph induced by the outcomes of pairwise contests. The online website maintained by Massey (2013) provides access to ratings of teams in various sports competitions including the National Football League, college football, the National Basketball Association, and the National Hockey League. Colley (2013) introduced a ranking method used for ranking of college football teams.

Several authors have studied axiomatic approaches for ranking systems. The ranking method based on point scores, which assigns a score to each player equal to the number of wins of this player, was first axiomatized for the score matrices that correspond to tournaments by Rubinstein (1980) and Henriet (1985); it was subsequently generalized to score matrices that correspond to arbitrary directed graphs by van den Brink and Gilles (2000, 2003). Theorem 10.6 is from van den Brink and Gilles (2003). Bouyssou (1992) provided an axiomatization of the Copeland scoring method. Saari and Merlin (1996) analyzed various properties of the Copeland scoring method. Theorem 10.7 is from Bouyssou (1992). Szymanski and Valletti (2005) and Slutzki and Volij (2006) provided an axiomatization of the fair-bets and invariant scoring methods proposed by Dawkins (1969) and Moon and Pullman (1970). An axiomatic approach was considered by Altman and Tennenholtz (2008). Andersen et al. (2008) studied an axiomatic approach for trust-based recommendation systems.

The problem of the aggregation of judgments was studied as early as by Dawid and Skene (1979) using the statistical inference method of expectation maximization. The optimality of weighted majority rank aggregation was first established by Nitzan and Paroush (1982), a result presented in Theorem 10.16. The error probability bound in Corollary 10.17 is new. Several papers addressed the optimality of common rank aggregation rules, including the expert rule (a weighted majority rule putting all the weight to the highest competence expert) and other weighted majority rules under partial information about the competencies of the experts, such as assuming that the competence weights are samples from a distribution, e.g., see Gradstein and Nitzan (1986), Sapir (1998), Berend and Sapir (2003), Berend et al. (2008), and the references therein. The weighted majority rule has also been considered in related but different contexts, such as in machine learning to make decisions based on inputs from a panel of experts, e.g., Littlestone and Warmuth (1994). The study of aggregation of judgments has recently been driven by application scenarios in the context of labeling of information items by less-than-expert workers in online crowdsourcing systems. Early work includes that by Sheng et al. (2008), Ipeirotis et al. (2010), and Donmez et al. (2009), with several subsequent studies in this direction, e.g. Raykar et al. (2009, 2010), Whitehill et al. (2009), Ertekin et al. (2011, 2012). Karger et al. (2014) introduced an approach based on a low-rank matrix approximation. The iterative message-passing method given by (10.89) and (10.90) in Section 10.4.3 was first proposed by Karger et al. (2011a). It was shown to be the sum-product algorithm for the Haldane prior distribution by Liu et al. (2012); the Haldane prior distribution is due to

Haldane (1932). A textbook account on the density evolution method applied in Section 10.4.3 is available in Richardson and Urbanke (2008). Ho and Vaughan (2012) formulated the online assignment of labeling tasks based on a linear integer programming problem that we discussed in Section 10.4.3 assuming a weighted majority rank aggregation with linear weights.

CHAPTER 11

Appendix

In the Appendix we define various mathematical concepts and state some of the theorems that are invoked at various places in the book. Most of the theorems are accompanied by proofs, with a few exceptions in which case we refer to the relevant literature.

Section 11.1 introduces the basic concepts of relations and orderings, sets, convex functions and optimization, the envelope theorem, some functional equations, and fixed-point theorems. The concept of a partial order is used in particular in Chapter 9 and Chapter 10. The convex optimization and the envelope theorem are used in Chapter 4. The Cauchy functional equations appear in the proofs of Theorem 4.2 and Theorem 10.15, and a functional equation related to trigonometric equations appears in the proof of Theorem 9.13. The fixed-point theorems are invoked in Section 11.3.

Section 11.2 covers some elements of probability and statistics including order statistics, distributions on a simplex, and Gaussian distributions. The order statistics are used throughout this book, but perhaps most prominently in Chapter 3. The distributions on a simplex are used in Chapter 5 to establish the existence of mixed-strategy Nash equilibria for the Colonel Blotto games. Some properties of Gaussian distributions are used in the context of approximate Bayesian inference for rating systems in Chapter 9.

In Section 11.3 we cover some special normal form games including concave, potential, and smooth games. The concept of a concave game that we discuss in Section 11.3.1 appears at several places in Chapter 4 and Chapter 6. In particular, we state and prove Rosen's theorem (Theorem 11.51) on the existence of a pure-strategy Nash equilibrium for concave games. The concept of a potential game, the existence of a pure-strategy Nash equilibrium for potential games, and conditions for a normal form game to be a potential game are discussed in Section 11.3.2. Some of these results are used in Chapter 5 to establish the existence of a pure-strategy Nash equilibrium of a normal form game that models a system of simultaneous contests, and in Chapter 6 for the utility sharing games with convex utility of production functions. The concept of a smooth game, different variants of smooth games, and the price of anarchy bounds that hold for smooth games are discussed in Section 11.3.3. This framework allows us to study the worst-case social efficiency for the class of smooth games for different equilibrium concepts. The concept of smooth games and the price of anarchy bounds are used in Chapter 6.

11.1 Real Analysis and Optimization

In this section we review some basic concepts of real analysis including relations and orderings, sets, topologies, metric spaces, convex sets and functions, correspondences, convex optimization, and some fixed-point theorems.

11.1.1 Relations and Orderings

Given a set X, a *relation* is a set R of ordered pairs $R \subseteq X \times X$. For every relation R, the inverse relation is defined by $R^{-1} = \{(y, x) \mid (x, y) \in R\}$. Given a relation R, one may write $x\,R\,y$, which is equivalent to $(x, y) \in R$. A relation R is said to be

(i) *reflexive* on X if, and only if, $x\,R\,x$ for all $x \in X$
(ii) *symmetric* if, and only if, $x\,R\,y$ and $y\,R\,x$ for all $x, y \in X$
(iii) *transitive* if, and only if, whenever $x\,R\,y$ and $y\,R\,z$ then $x\,R\,z$
(iv) *complete* if, and only if, for all $x, y \in X$, either $x\,R\,y$ or $y\,R\,x$.

A relation R on X is said to be an *equivalence relation* on X if, and only if, it is reflexive, symmetric, and transitive on X. An equivalence relation is denoted with equality $x = y$. A relation R is said to be *antisymmetric* if, and only if, whenever $x\,R\,y$ and $y\,R\,x$, then $x = y$.

Definition 11.1 (partial ordering). A *partial ordering* R on X is a relation R that is transitive and antisymmetric on X. For such a relation, the set (X, R) is called the a *partially ordered set*.

Definition 11.2 (weak ordering). A *weak ordering* R on X is a relation R that is transitive and complete on X. Then (X, R) is called a *weakly ordered set*.

Definition 11.3 (linear ordering or total ordering). A *linear ordering* (or *total ordering*) R on X is a relation R that is transitive, antisymmetric, and complete on X. Then (X, R) is called a *linearly ordered set* (or *totally ordered set*).

See Figure 11.1 for an illustration of the relationships between the three types of ordering. A partial ordering is called *strict* if $x\,R\,x$ does not hold for all $x \in X$. For any partial ordering R, we can define the relation $\preceq$ by $x \preceq y$ if, and only if, $x\,R\,y$ or $x = y$. Then $\preceq$ is a reflexive partial ordering. We can also define the relation $\prec$ by $x \prec y$ if, and only if, $x\,R\,y$ and not $x = y$. Then inequality is a strict partial ordering.

For every weak ordering R on X, we can define $x \preceq y$ if, and only if, $x\,R\,y$, $x \prec y$ if not $y\,R\,x$, and $x \sim y$ if, and only if, $x\,R\,y$ and $y\,R\,y$.

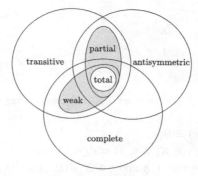

Figure 11.1. Orderings: partial, weak, and total.

11.1.2 Permutations

A *permutation* π of a set of elements $\{1, 2, \ldots, n\}$, for $n \geq 1$, is defined as a one-to-one function from the set $\{1, 2, \ldots, n\}$ to itself. Intuitively, for a given permutation π of a set $\{1, 2, \ldots, n\}$, we can interpret $\pi(i)$ as the position of element $i \in \{1, 2, \ldots, n\}$ according to the given permutation. The set of all permutations of n elements is denoted with S_n. The cardinality of this set is $n! := 1 \times 2 \cdots \times n$.

Given a permutation $\pi \in S_n$, the *inverse permutation* π^{-1} is defined as a one-to-one function from the set $\{1, 2, \ldots, n\}$ to itself such that $\pi^{-1}(\pi(i)) = i$ for every $i = 1, 2, \ldots, n$. Intuitively, $\pi^{-1}(i)$ is defined as the element in $\{1, 2, \ldots, n\}$ at position i according to permutation π.

11.1.3 Sets, Topologies, and Metric Spaces

Definition 11.4. Given a set X, a *topology* on X is a collection $\mathcal{T}$ of subsets of X such that

(i) $\emptyset \in \mathcal{T}$ and $X \in \mathcal{T}$
(ii) for every $U \in \mathcal{T}$ and $V \in \mathcal{T}$, we have $U \cap V \in \mathcal{T}$
(iii) for every $U \subset \mathcal{T}$, we have $\cup_{A \in U} A \in \mathcal{T}$.

For a given topology, the elements of X are called *points* and every $U \in \mathcal{T}$ is called an *open set*. For every given $U \in \mathcal{T}$, its complement $X \setminus U$ is called a *closed set*. A set $A \in \mathcal{T}$ is closed if for every sequence $x_1, x_2, \ldots, x_k$ such that $\lim_{k \to \infty} x_k = x$, if $x_1, x_2, \ldots, x_k \in A$ for every positive integer k, then $x \in A$.

For the set of real numbers $\mathbf{R}$ and the usual topology, an example of an open set is an open interval $(a, b) = \{x \in \mathbf{R} \mid a < x < b\}$. General open sets in $\mathbf{R}$ are unions of open intervals. An example of a closed set is the closed interval $[a, b] = \{x \in \mathbf{R} \mid a \leq x \leq b\}$. A set may be neither open nor closed, e.g., the half-open intervals $(a, b] = \{x \in \mathbf{R} \mid a < x \leq b\}$ or $[a, b) = \{x \in \mathbf{R} \mid a \leq x < b\}$.

Definition 11.5. Given a set X, a *pseudometric* for X is a function $d : X \times X \to \mathbf{R}_+$ such that

Figure 11.2. A convex set (left) and a non-convex set (right).

(i) for all $x \in X, d(x, x) = 0$
(ii) symmetry: for all $x, y \in X, d(x, y) = d(y, x)$, and
(iii) triangle inequality: for all x, y and $z \in X, d(x, z) \leq d(x, y) + d(y, z)$.
    If, also,
(iv) $d(x, y) = 0$ implies $x = y$, then d is called a *metric*.

(X, d) is called a (pseudo)*metric space*.

For every metric space (X, d) and $A \subset X$, the *diameter* of A is defined as diam$(A) =$ sup$\{d(x, y) \mid x \in A, y \in A\}$. The set A is said to be *bounded* if, and only if, it has a finite diameter. For example, in **R**, every interval $[a, b]$ such that $-\infty < a \leq b < \infty$ is bounded, and $[a, \infty)$ is unbounded for every $a \in \mathbf{R}$. For every metric space (X, d), a set $A \subseteq X$ is said to be *compact* if it is closed and bounded. For example, in **R**, for every positive integer k and $-\infty < a_1 < b_1 < \cdots < a_k < b_k < \infty$, $\cup_{i=1}^{k}[a_i, b_i]$ is a compact set.

A set $X \subseteq \mathbf{R}^n$ is said to be *convex* if for every two points $\mathbf{x}, \mathbf{y} \in X, \lambda\mathbf{x} + (1 - \lambda)\mathbf{y} \in X$, for every $0 \leq \lambda \leq 1$. In other words, a set $X \subseteq \mathbf{R}^n$ is said to be convex if for every two points in X, the line segment connecting the two points is contained in the set X (see Figure 11.2).

11.1.4 Continuous Functions

Consider a function $f : X \rightarrow \mathbf{R}$ on the domain X that is assumed to be a subset of a metric space.

Function f is said to be *continuous* at $x \in X$ if for every converging sequence $x_1, x_2, \ldots$ in X such that $\lim_{k \rightarrow \infty} x_i = x \in X$, $\lim_{k \rightarrow \infty} f(x_k) = f(x)$.

Under additional assumption that X is the set of real numbers, we define the concepts of a right-continuous and a left-continuous function as follows. A sequence $y_1, y_2, \ldots, y_k$ is said to converge to a point $x \in X$ from above if $y_i \in \{y \in X \mid y \geq x\}$ for every $i = 1, 2, \ldots, k$ and $\lim_{k \rightarrow \infty} y_i = x$. The last limit is denoted with $y \downarrow x$ and we use the notation

$$f(x+) = \lim_{y \downarrow x} f(y).$$

Function f is said to be *right-continuous* at point x, if $f(x+) = f(x)$.

Similarly, a sequence $y_1, y_2, \ldots, y_k$ is said to converge to a point $x \in X$ from below if $y_i \in \{y \in X \mid y \leq x\}$ for every $i = 1, 2, \ldots, k$ and $\lim_{k \rightarrow \infty} y_i = x$. The latter limit is denoted with $y \uparrow x$ and we use the notation

$$f(x-) = \lim_{y \uparrow x} f(y).$$

Function f is said to be *left-continuous* at point x, if $f(x-) = f(x)$.

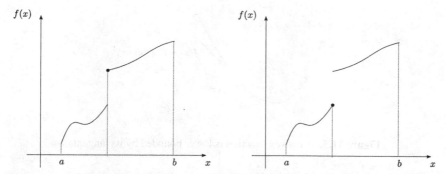

Figure 11.3. A right-continuous function on $[a, b]$ (left) and a left-continuous function on $[a, b]$ (right).

A graphical representation of a right-continuous and a left-continuous function is shown in Figure 11.3.

11.1.5 Convex Functions

Definition 11.6. A function $f : \mathbf{R}^n \to \mathbf{R}$ is *convex* on a set $D \subseteq \mathbf{R}^n$ if for every $\mathbf{x}, \mathbf{y} \in D$ we have

$$\lambda f(\mathbf{x}) + (1 - \lambda) f(\mathbf{y}) \geq f(\lambda \mathbf{x} + (1 - \lambda)\mathbf{y}), \quad \text{for all } 0 \leq \lambda \leq 1. \qquad (11.1)$$

The function f is *strictly convex* on a set $D \subseteq \mathbf{R}^n$ if for every $\mathbf{x}, \mathbf{y} \in D$ we have

$$\lambda f(\mathbf{x}) + (1 - \lambda) f(\mathbf{y}) > f(\lambda \mathbf{x} + (1 - \lambda)\mathbf{y}), \quad \text{for all } 0 < \lambda < 1. \qquad (11.2)$$

See a graphical illustration in Figure 11.4.

If function f is differentiable on a set $D \subseteq \mathbf{R}^n$, then saying that f is convex on the set D is equivalent to saying that for every $\mathbf{x}, \mathbf{y} \in D$,

$$f(\mathbf{y}) - f(\mathbf{x}) \geq (\mathbf{y} - \mathbf{x})^T \nabla f(\mathbf{x}). \qquad (11.3)$$

See Figure 11.5 for a graphical illustration. If f is convex on a set $D \subseteq \mathbf{R}^n$, then for every $\mathbf{x}, \mathbf{y} \in D$,

$$(\mathbf{y} - \mathbf{x})^T (\nabla f(\mathbf{y}) - \nabla f(\mathbf{x})) \geq 0. \qquad (11.4)$$

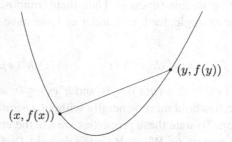

Figure 11.4. Every chord of a convex function lies at or above the function.

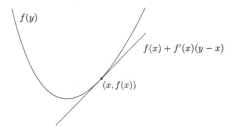

Figure 11.5. A convex function is lower bounded by its tangents.

Suppose that function f has the Hessian matrix defined as follows:

$$H(\mathbf{x}) = \left(\frac{\partial^2}{\partial x_i \partial x_j} f(\mathbf{x}), \; i, j = 1, 2, \ldots, n \right).$$

Then, function f is convex on a set $D \subseteq \mathbf{R}^n$ if, and only if, the matrix $H(\mathbf{x})$ is positive semi-definite for every $\mathbf{x} \in D$, i.e.,

$$\mathbf{y}^T H(\mathbf{x})\mathbf{y} \geq 0 \text{ for every } \mathbf{y} \in \mathbf{R}^n \text{ such that } \mathbf{y} \neq 0.$$

Definition 11.7. A function f is (strictly) concave on a set $D \in \mathbf{R}^n$ if $-f$ is (strictly) convex on the set D.

Operations that Preserve Convexity or Concavity

Sum Given two functions $g : \mathbf{R}^n \to \mathbf{R}$ and $h : \mathbf{R}^n \to \mathbf{R}$, we consider their *sum* $f(\mathbf{x}) = g(\mathbf{x}) + h(\mathbf{x})$ for $\mathbf{x} \in \mathbf{R}^n$.

If g and h are two convex (concave) functions on a set $D \subseteq \mathbf{R}^n$, then their sum f is a convex (concave) function on the set D. This property follows straightforwardly from the definition (11.1) of a convex (concave) function. It is also readily observed that if, in addition, either g or h is strictly convex (concave) on D (definition (11.2)), then $f(x) = g(x) + h(x)$ is strictly convex (concave).

Composition Given two functions $g : \mathbf{R}^k \to \mathbf{R}^n$ and $h : \mathbf{R}^n \to \mathbf{R}$, we consider the *composition* function $g \circ h : \mathbf{R}^n \to \mathbf{R}$ defined by $f(\mathbf{x}) = g(h(\mathbf{x}))$ for $\mathbf{x} \in \mathbf{R}^n$. The domain of f is $D(f) = \{\mathbf{x} \in D(h) \mid h(\mathbf{x}) \in D(g)\}$.

If g and h are convex (concave) functions, then under certain additional assumptions their composition is a convex (concave) function. Let us first consider the case where g is an increasing, concave, and continuously differentiable function and h is a concave and continuously twice differentiable function. Then their composition $f(\mathbf{x}) = g(h(\mathbf{x}))$ is a concave function. For example, for $k = 1$ and $n = 1$, we have $f'(x) = g'(h(x))h'(x)$, and

$$f''(x) = g''(h(x))h'(x)^2 + g'(h(x))h''(x).$$

Since $g''(h(x)) \leq 0$, $h'(x)^2 \geq 0$, $g'(h(x)) \geq 0$, and $h''(x) \leq 0$, we have $f''(x) \leq 0$.

These type of properties hold more generally without assuming that either g or h is a differentiable function. To state these properties we use the concept of the extended-value function, for a function $f : \mathbf{R}^n \to \mathbf{R}$ on the domain $D(f)$ denoted with f^* and defined by

$$f^*(\mathbf{x}) = \begin{cases} f(\mathbf{x}), & \text{if } \mathbf{x} \in D(f) \\ \Delta, & \text{otherwise} \end{cases}$$

where $\Delta = \infty$ if f is convex on $D(f)$ and $\Delta = -\infty$ if f is concave on $D(f)$. Requiring that, for a convex (concave) function f, the extended-value function f^* is increasing (decreasing) has the following implications. Consider the case $n = 1$. If f is convex, requiring that f^* is increasing implies that f is increasing on its domain and that its domain is $[a, \infty)$ or (a, ∞) for some $a \in \mathbf{R}$. Similarly, if f is concave, requiring that f^* is decreasing implies that f is decreasing on its domain and that its domain is $(-\infty, a]$ or $(-\infty, a)$ for some $a \in \mathbf{R}$.

The following properties hold for the composition $f = g \circ h$:

(i) If g is *concave*, g^* is increasing, and h is *concave*, then f is *concave*.
(ii) If g is *concave*, g^* is decreasing, and h is *convex*, then f is *concave*.
(iii) If g is *convex*, g^* is increasing, and h is *convex*, then f is *convex*.
(iv) If g is *convex*, g^* is decreasing, and h is *concave*, then f is *convex*.

We shall only show the first property because the other ones follow by the same arguments. Assume $\mathbf{x}, \mathbf{y} \in D(f)$ and $0 \leq \lambda \leq 1$. Since $\mathbf{x}, \mathbf{y} \in D(f)$, $\mathbf{x}, \mathbf{y} \in D(h)$ and $h(\mathbf{x}), h(\mathbf{y}) \in D(g)$. Since $D(h)$ is a convex set, we have $\lambda\mathbf{x} + (1 - \lambda)\mathbf{y} \in D(h)$.

By concavity of h, we have

$$h(\lambda\mathbf{x} + (1 - \lambda)\mathbf{y}) \geq \lambda h(\mathbf{x}) + (1 - \lambda)h(\mathbf{y}). \tag{11.5}$$

Since $h(\mathbf{x}), h(\mathbf{y}) \in D(g)$, we have $\lambda h(\mathbf{x}) + (1 - \lambda)h(\mathbf{y}) \in D(g)$. Given that g^* is increasing and the inequality (11.5), we have

$$g(h(\lambda\mathbf{x} + (1 - \lambda)\mathbf{y})) \geq g(\lambda h(\mathbf{x}) + (1 - \lambda)h(\mathbf{y})).$$

By concavity of g,

$$g(\lambda h(\mathbf{x}) + (1 - \lambda)h(\mathbf{y})) \geq \lambda g(h(\mathbf{x})) + (1 - \lambda)g(h(\mathbf{y})).$$

Hence, it follows that

$$g(h(\lambda\mathbf{x} + (1 - \lambda)\mathbf{y})) \geq \lambda g(h(\mathbf{x})) + (1 - \lambda)g(h(\mathbf{y})),$$

which establishes that $f(\mathbf{x}) = g(h(\mathbf{x}))$ is concave.

Quasiconvex Functions

Definition 11.8. A function $f : \mathbf{R}^n \to \mathbf{R}$ is *quasiconvex* if its domain and all its sublevel sets

$$S_\alpha = \{\mathbf{x} \in \text{ domain of } f \mid f(\mathbf{x}) \leq \alpha\}$$

for $\alpha \in \mathbf{R}$ are convex.

A function f is *quasiconcave* if $-f$ is quasiconvex, i.e., all its sublevel sets

$$S_\alpha = \{\mathbf{x} \in \text{ domain of } f \mid f(\mathbf{x}) \geq \alpha\}$$

for $\alpha \in \mathbf{R}$ are convex.

Any convex function f is quasiconvex, but the converse is not true. For example, consider the function $f : [0, 1] \rightarrow [0, 1]$ defined by

$$f(x) = \begin{cases} \frac{3}{2}x, & \text{if } x \in [0, 1/2] \\ \frac{1}{2}x + \frac{1}{2}, & \text{if } x \in [1/2, 1]. \end{cases}$$

This function is quasiconvex because all its sublevel sets are convex: $S_\alpha = [0, 2\alpha/3]$ for $\alpha \in [0, 1/2]$ and $S_\alpha = [0, 2\alpha - 1]$ for $\alpha \in [1/2, 1]$. However, this function f is not convex.

Log-Concave Functions

Definition 11.9. A function $f : \mathbf{R}^n \rightarrow \mathbf{R}$ is *logarithmically concave* or *log-concave* if $f(\mathbf{x}) > 0$ for all $\mathbf{x} \in D(f)$ and $\log f$ is concave. It is said to be *logarithmically convex* or *log-convex* if $\log f$ is convex.

An alternative equivalent definition is as follows: a function $f : \mathbf{R}^n \rightarrow \mathbf{R}$ with convex domain and $f(\mathbf{x}) > 0$ for every $\mathbf{x} \in D(f)$ is log-concave, if, and only if, for every $\mathbf{x}, \mathbf{y} \in D(f)$ and $0 \leq \lambda \leq 1$, we have

$$f(\lambda \mathbf{x} + (1 - \lambda)\mathbf{y}) \geq f(\mathbf{x})^\lambda f(\mathbf{y})^{1-\lambda}.$$

In particular, the value of a log-concave function at the arithmetic mean of two points is at least the geometric mean of the values at the two points.

11.1.6 Correspondences

Suppose X is a topological space. A correspondence $f : X \rightarrow \mathbf{R} \cup \{-\infty, +\infty\}$ is a mapping of each point $\mathbf{x} \in X$ to a set $f(\mathbf{x}) \subseteq X$.

Definition 11.10. A correspondence f is *upper semi-continuous* at a point $\mathbf{x} \in X$ if for every $\epsilon > 0$ there exists a neighborhood $N_\epsilon(\mathbf{x}) \subseteq X$ of point $\mathbf{x}$ such that $f(\mathbf{y}) \leq f(\mathbf{x}) + \epsilon$ for every $\mathbf{y} \in N_\epsilon(\mathbf{x})$. If X is a metric space, then this definition can be stated for the neighborhood set defined by $N_\epsilon(\mathbf{x}) = \{\mathbf{y} \in X : |\mathbf{x} - \mathbf{y}| \leq \delta\}$ for some $\delta > 0$. A function f is upper semi-continuous if it is upper semi-continuous at every point $\mathbf{x} \in X$.

A correspondence f is upper semi-continuous if, and only if, its level sets $\{\mathbf{x} \in X : f(\mathbf{x}) < \alpha\}$ are open sets for all $\alpha \in \mathbf{R}$. If a function f is right-continuous, then it is upper semi-continuous. The converse is in general not true: for example, the function in the left graph in Figure 11.3 remains upper semi-continuous by redefining the value of the function at point x to a larger value, but is then no longer right-continuous.

Definition 11.11. A correspondence f is *lower semi-continuous* at a point $\mathbf{x} \in X$ if for every $\epsilon > 0$ there exists a neighborhood $N_\epsilon(\mathbf{x}) \subseteq X$ of point $\mathbf{x}$ such that $f(\mathbf{y}) \geq f(\mathbf{x}) - \epsilon$ for every $\mathbf{y} \in N_\epsilon(\mathbf{x})$. If X is a metric space, then the latter definition can be stated for the neighborhood set defined by $N_\epsilon(\mathbf{x}) = \{\mathbf{y} \in X : |\mathbf{x} - \mathbf{y}| \leq \delta\}$ for some $\delta > 0$. A function f is lower semi-continuous if it is upper semi-continuous for all points $\mathbf{x} \in X$.

A correspondence f is lower semi-continuous if, and only if, its level set $\{\mathbf{x} \in X : f(\mathbf{x}) \leq \alpha\}$ is a closed set for all $\alpha \in \mathbf{R}$. If a function f is left-continuous, then it is lower semi-continuous. The converse is in general not true: for example, the function in the right graph in Figure 11.3 remains lower semi-continuous by redefining the value of the function at point x to a smaller value, but is then no longer left-continuous.

Definition 11.12. A correspondence f on $X \subseteq \mathbf{R}^n$ is *convex valued* if $f(\mathbf{x})$ is a convex set for all $\mathbf{x} \in X$.

11.1.7 Optimization

We consider the following optimization problem:

$$
\begin{aligned}
&\text{minimize } f(\mathbf{x}) \\
&\text{subject to } f_i(\mathbf{x}) \le 0, \ i = 1, 2, \ldots, k \\
&\qquad\qquad\; h_i(\mathbf{x}) = 0, \ i = 1, 2, \ldots, m
\end{aligned}
\tag{11.6}
$$

where $\mathbf{x} \in \mathbf{R}^n$ is the *optimization variable*, the function $f : \mathbf{R}^n \to \mathbf{R}$ is the *objective function*, the inequalities $f_i(\mathbf{x}) \le 0$ for $i = 1, 2, \ldots, k$ are the *inequality constraints* and $f_i : \mathbf{R}^n \to \mathbf{R}$ is the *inequality constraints function*, and $h_i(\mathbf{x}) = 0$ for $i = 1, 2, \ldots, m$ are the *equality constraints* and $h_i : \mathbf{R}^n \to \mathbf{R}$ is the *equality constraint function*.

The set of points D in $\mathbf{R}^n$ for which the objective and all constraints functions are defined is called the *domain* of the optimization problem (11.6). A point $\mathbf{x} \in D$ is *feasible* if it satisfies the constraints of the optimization problem (11.6). The problem (11.6) is said to be feasible if it has at least one feasible point, and otherwise it is said to be infeasible. The set of all feasible points of the optimization problem (11.6) is called the *feasible set* or the *constraint set*.

The *optimal value* f^* of the optimization problem (11.6) is given by

$$
f^* = \inf\{f(\mathbf{x}) \mid f_i(\mathbf{x}) \le 0, i = 1, 2, \ldots, k, h_i(\mathbf{x}) = 0, i = 1, 2, \ldots, m\}.
$$

A point $\mathbf{x}^*$ is an *optimal point* or a *solution* of the optimization problem (11.6) if $\mathbf{x}$ is a feasible point and $f(\mathbf{x}^*) = f^*$. A point $\mathbf{x}$ is said to be *locally optimal* if it is a feasible point and there exists $r > 0$ such that

$$
f(\mathbf{x}) = \inf\{f(\mathbf{y}) \mid f_i(\mathbf{y}) \le 0, i = 1, 2, \ldots, k,
$$

$$
h_i(\mathbf{y}) = 0, i = 1, 2, \ldots, m, \|\mathbf{y} - \mathbf{x}\|_2 \le r\}.
\tag{11.7}
$$

Convex Optimization

An optimization problem is said to be a *convex optimization problem* if it is of the form (11.6), functions $f, f_1, f_2, \ldots, f_k$ are convex functions, and functions $h_1, h_2, \ldots, h_m$ are affine functions, i.e., of the form $h_i(x) = \mathbf{a}_i^T \mathbf{x} - b_i$, for $i = 1, 2, \ldots, m$.

The feasible set of a convex optimization problem is a convex set, since it is an intersection of convex sets defined by the inequality and equality constraints.

The problem of maximizing a concave objective function f given by

$$
\begin{aligned}
&\text{maximize } f(\mathbf{x}) \\
&\text{subject to } f_i(\mathbf{x}) \le 0, \ i = 1, 2, \ldots, k \\
&\qquad\qquad\; \mathbf{a}_i^T \mathbf{x} = b_i, \ i = 1, 2, \ldots, m
\end{aligned}
\tag{11.8}
$$

is also referred to as a convex optimization problem.

Locally and globally optimal points Any locally optimal point of a convex optimization problem is globally optimal.

Suppose that $\mathbf{x}$ is a locally optimal point, i.e., there exists $r > 0$ such that (11.7) holds. Suppose that $\mathbf{x}$ is not globally optimal, i.e., there exists a feasible point $\mathbf{y}$ such that $f(\mathbf{y}) < f(\mathbf{x})$. It must be that $||\mathbf{y} - \mathbf{x}||_2 > r$ because otherwise $f(\mathbf{y}) \leq f(\mathbf{x})$. Consider $\mathbf{z}(\theta) = (1 - \theta)\mathbf{x} + \theta\mathbf{y}$ with $\theta = r/(2||\mathbf{y} - \mathbf{x}||_2)$. Observe that it holds that $||\mathbf{z}(\theta) - \mathbf{x}||_2 = r/2 < r$. By convexity of the feasible set, $\mathbf{z}(\theta)$ is a feasible point. By convexity of f we have

$$f(\mathbf{z}(\theta)) \leq (1 - \theta)f(\mathbf{x}) + \theta f(\mathbf{y}) < f(\mathbf{x}),$$

which contradicts (11.7). Hence, there exists no feasible point $\mathbf{y}$ such that $f(\mathbf{y}) < f(\mathbf{x})$, i.e., $\mathbf{x}$ is a globally optimal point.

An optimality condition for differentiable f Suppose that the objective function f in a convex optimization problem is differentiable so that

$$f(\mathbf{y}) \geq f(\mathbf{x}) + \nabla f(\mathbf{x})^T(\mathbf{y} - \mathbf{x}) \quad \text{for all } \mathbf{x}, \mathbf{y} \text{ in the domain of } f. \qquad (11.9)$$

Let $\mathcal{X}$ denote the feasible set of the optimization problem. Then, $\mathbf{x}$ is an optimal point if, and only if, $\mathbf{x} \in \mathcal{X}$ and

$$\nabla f(\mathbf{x})^T(\mathbf{y} - \mathbf{x}) \geq 0, \quad \text{for all } \mathbf{y} \in \mathcal{X}. \qquad (11.10)$$

This is shown as follows. Suppose that $\mathbf{x} \in \mathcal{X}$ and $\mathbf{x}$ satisfies (11.10). If $\mathbf{y} \in \mathcal{X}$ we have by (11.9) that $f(\mathbf{y}) \geq f(\mathbf{x})$. This shows that $\mathbf{x}$ is an optimal point.

Conversely, suppose that $\mathbf{x}$ is an optimal point and that the condition (11.9) does not hold, i.e., $\nabla f(\mathbf{x})^T(\mathbf{y} - \mathbf{x}) < 0$ for some $\mathbf{y} \in \mathcal{X}$. Consider $\mathbf{z}(\theta) = (1 - \theta)\mathbf{x} + \theta\mathbf{y}$ for a parameter $\theta \in [0, 1]$. Since the feasible set is convex, $\mathbf{z}(\theta)$ is a feasible point for every $\theta \in [0, 1]$. We now show that $f(\mathbf{z}(\theta)) < f(\mathbf{x})$ for small positive θ, which shows that $\mathbf{x}$ is not an optimal point. To show this, note that

$$\frac{d}{d\theta} f(\mathbf{z}(\theta))|_{\theta=0} = \nabla f(\mathbf{x})^T(\mathbf{y} - \mathbf{x}) < 0,$$

which implies $f(\mathbf{z}(\theta)) < f(\mathbf{x})$ for small positive θ.

Duality

Consider an optimization problem of the form (11.8). We define the *Lagrangian function* $L : \mathbf{R}^n \times \mathbf{R}^k \times \mathbf{R}^m \to \mathbf{R}$ associated with the problem (11.8) as

$$L(\mathbf{x}, \lambda, \nu) = f(\mathbf{x}) + \sum_{i=1}^{k} \lambda_i f_i(\mathbf{x}) + \sum_{i=1}^{m} \nu_i h_i(\mathbf{x})$$

with the domain $D \times \mathbf{R}^k \times \mathbf{R}^m$.

We refer to λ_i as the *Lagrange multiplier* associated with the constraint $f_i(\mathbf{x}) \leq 0$ and ν_i as the Lagrange multiplier associated with the constraint $h_i(\mathbf{x}) = 0$. The vectors $\lambda = (\lambda_1, \lambda_2, \dots, \lambda_k)$ and $\nu = (\nu_1, \nu_2, \dots, \nu_m)$ are called the *dual variables* or the *Lagrange multiplier vectors* associated with the problem (11.8).

We define the *Lagrange dual function* or the *dual function* $g : \mathbf{R}^k \times \mathbf{R}^m \to \mathbf{R}$ as the minimum value of the Lagrangian over $\mathbf{x}$ for a given $\lambda \in \mathbf{R}^k$ and $v \in \mathbf{R}^m$, i.e.,

$$g(\lambda, v) = \inf_{\mathbf{x} \in D} L(\mathbf{x}, \lambda, v).$$

Since the dual function is the point-wise infimum of a family of affine functions in λ and v it is a concave function, and this holds whether the optimization problem (11.8) is convex or not.

The dual function yields lower bounds on the optimal value f^* of the optimization problem (11.8), i.e., for any $\lambda \in \mathbf{R}^k_+$ and $v \in \mathbf{R}^m$,

$$g(\lambda, v) \le f^*.$$

To see this, suppose that $\mathbf{x}'$ is a feasible point for the optimization problem (11.8) and that $\lambda \in \mathbf{R}^k_+$. Then,

$$\sum_{i=1}^{k} \lambda_i f_i(\mathbf{x}) + \sum_{i=1}^{m} v_i h_i(\mathbf{x}) \le 0.$$

It follows that

$$L(\mathbf{x}', \lambda, v) = f(\mathbf{x}') + \sum_{i=1}^{k} \lambda_i f_i(\mathbf{x}) + \sum_{i=1}^{m} v_i h_i(\mathbf{x}) \le f(\mathbf{x}').$$

Hence,

$$g(\lambda, v) = \inf_{\mathbf{x} \in D} L(\mathbf{x}, \lambda, v) \le L(\mathbf{x}', \lambda, v) \le f(\mathbf{x}').$$

Since the last inequality holds for every feasible point $\mathbf{x}'$, it follows that $g(\lambda, v) \le f^*$.

The Lagrange dual problem The Lagrange dual problem associated with the (primal) optimization problem (11.8) is defined by

$$\begin{aligned} \text{maximize} \quad & g(\lambda, v) \\ \text{subject to} \quad & \lambda \in \mathbf{R}^k_+, v \in \mathbf{R}^m. \end{aligned} \tag{11.11}$$

We refer to (λ^*, v^*) as the *dual optimal* or the *optimal Lagrange multipliers* if they are optimal for the optimization problem (11.11).

The Lagrange dual problem (11.11) is a convex optimization problem since the objective is to maximize a concave objective function and the constraint set is a convex set. Note that this does not require the primal optimization problem be a convex optimization problem.

The optimal value of the Lagrange dual problem is the best lower bound on f^* that can be obtained from the Lagrange dual function.

If the optimum duality gap is zero, i.e., $f^* = g^*$, then we say that *strong duality* holds.

Sufficient conditions for the strong duality to hold are as follows:

(i) The primal optimization problem is a convex optimization problem, and
(ii) Slater's condition holds: there exists a feasible point $\mathbf{x}$ in the interior of the domain D such that $f_i(\mathbf{x}) < 0$ for some $i = 1, 2, \ldots, k$. Such a point is referred to as a *strictly feasible* point.

Optimality Conditions

Complementarity slackness Suppose that the strong duality holds. Let $\mathbf{x}^*$ be a primal optimal point and (λ^*, ν^*) be a dual optimal point. We have

$$
f(\mathbf{x}^*) = g(\lambda^*, \nu^*)
$$

$$
= \inf_{\mathbf{x} \in D} \left\{ f(\mathbf{x}) + \sum_{i=1}^{k} \lambda^* f_i(\mathbf{x}) + \sum_{i=1}^{m} \nu_i^* h_i(\mathbf{x}) \right\}
$$

$$
\leq f(\mathbf{x}^*) + \sum_{i=1}^{k} \lambda^* f_i(\mathbf{x}^*) + \sum_{i=1}^{m} \nu_i^* h_i(\mathbf{x}^*)
$$

$$
\leq f(\mathbf{x}^*).
$$

We conclude that the last two inequalities hold as equalities. Hence, $\mathbf{x}^*$ minimizes $L(\mathbf{x}, \lambda^*, \nu^*)$ over $\mathbf{x}$. We also observe that $\sum_{i=1}^{k} \lambda^* f_i(\mathbf{x}^*) = 0$. Since the Lagrange multipliers $\lambda_1^*, \lambda_2^*, \ldots, \lambda_k^*$ are non-negative, it follows that

$$
\lambda_i^* f_i(\mathbf{x}^*) = 0 \text{ for } i = 1, 2, \ldots, k.
$$

This is known as the *complementary slackness*, which holds for any primal optimal point $\mathbf{x}^*$ and any dual optimal point (λ^*, ν^*) whenever the strong duality holds. In other words, the complementary condition says that for any primal point $\mathbf{x}^*$ and any dual optimal point (λ^*, ν^*) either $\lambda_i^* = 0$ or $f_i(\mathbf{x}^*) = 0$ for all $i = 1, 2, \ldots, k$.

Karush-Kuhn-Tucker optimality conditions We assume that the functions f, $f_1, f_2, \ldots, f_k$ and $h_1, h_2, \ldots, h_m$ are differentiable. Let $\mathbf{x}^*$ be any primal optimal point and let (λ^*, ν^*) be any dual optimal point with the zero duality gap. Since $\mathbf{x}^*$ minimizes $L(\mathbf{x}, \lambda^*, \nu^*)$ over $\mathbf{x}$ it follows that it must hold that

$$
\nabla f(\mathbf{x}^*) + \sum_{i=1}^{k} \lambda_i^* \nabla f_i(\mathbf{x}^*) + \sum_{i=1}^{m} \nu_i^* \nabla h_i(\mathbf{x}^*) = 0.
$$

Thus, it follows that the following conditions, known as the Karush-Kuhn-Tucker (KKT) conditions, necessarily hold:

$$
f_i(\mathbf{x}^*) \leq 0, \quad \text{for } i = 1, 2, \ldots, k \tag{11.12}
$$

$$
h_i(\mathbf{x}^*) = 0, \quad \text{for } i = 1, 2, \ldots, m \tag{11.13}
$$

$$
\lambda_i^* \geq 0, \quad \text{for } i = 1, 2, \ldots, k \tag{11.14}
$$

$$
\lambda_i^* f_i(\mathbf{x}^*) = 0, \quad \text{for } i = 1, 2, \ldots, k \tag{11.15}
$$

$$
\nabla f(\mathbf{x}^*) + \sum_{i=1}^{k} \lambda_i^* \nabla f_i(\mathbf{x}^*) + \sum_{i=1}^{m} \nu_i^* \nabla h_i(\mathbf{x}^*) = 0. \tag{11.16}
$$

If the primal optimization problem is a convex optimization problem, the KKT conditions are also sufficient: for a convex optimization problem, any points $\mathbf{x}^*$, λ^*, and ν^* that satisfy the KKT conditions are primal and dual optimal with a zero duality gap. To see this, observe that (11.12) and (11.13) mean that $\mathbf{x}^*$ is primal feasible. Since by (11.14) the Lagrange multipliers $\lambda_1^*, \lambda_2^*, \ldots, \lambda_k^*$ are non-negative, the Lagrangian function $L(\mathbf{x}, \lambda^*, \nu^*)$ is convex in $\mathbf{x}$. The KKT conditions (11.16) mean that the gradient of the Lagrangian function is equal to zero at $\mathbf{x}^*$, so $\mathbf{x}^*$ minimizes $L(\mathbf{x}, \lambda^*, \nu^*)$. From this, we have

$$g(\lambda^*, \nu^*) = L(\mathbf{x}^*, \lambda^*, \nu^*)$$

$$= f(\mathbf{x}^*) + \sum_{i=1}^{k} \lambda_i^* f_i(\mathbf{x}^*) + \sum_{i=1}^{m} \nu_i^* h_i(\mathbf{x}^*)$$

$$= f(\mathbf{x}^*).$$

This shows that $\mathbf{x}^*$ and (λ^*, ν^*) have a zero duality gap and are thus primal and dual optimal.

If a convex optimization problem with differentiable objective and constraint functions satisfies Slater's condition, then the KKT conditions are necessary and sufficient for optimality. Slater's condition ensures that the optimum duality gap is zero.

The Envelope Theorem

Let $f : \mathbf{R}^n \times [0, 1] \to \mathbf{R}$ be a parametrized objective function for a parameter $t \in [0, 1]$. Let $\mathcal{X}$ be a feasible set of points, and let

$$V(t) = \max\{f(\mathbf{x}, t) \mid \mathbf{x} \in \mathcal{X}\}. \tag{11.17}$$

Let $x^* : [0, 1] \to \mathbf{R}^n$ be the correspondence: $x^*(t) = \{\mathbf{x} \in \mathcal{X} \mid f(\mathbf{x}, t) \geq V(t)\}$.

Theorem 11.13. *For every $t \in [0, 1]$ and $\mathbf{x} \in x^*(t)$, we have*

$$\frac{d}{dt} V(t) = \frac{\partial}{\partial t} f(\mathbf{x}, t).$$

Proof. We provide a proof that follows from a more general marginal value property that holds for linear programs. Observe that (11.17) can be written as

$$\begin{aligned} \text{minimize} \quad & y \\ \text{subject to} \quad & y \geq f(\mathbf{x}, t), \quad \text{for } \mathbf{x} \in \mathcal{X}. \end{aligned} \tag{11.18}$$

The dual linear program is

$$\begin{aligned} \text{maximize} \quad & \sum_{\mathbf{x} \in \mathcal{X}} f(\mathbf{x}, t)\lambda_\mathbf{x} \\ \text{subject to} \quad & \sum_{\mathbf{x} \in \mathcal{X}} \lambda_\mathbf{x} \leq 1 \\ & \lambda_\mathbf{x} \geq 0, \quad \text{for } \mathbf{x} \in \mathcal{X}. \end{aligned} \tag{11.19}$$

We also consider (11.18) with t replaced by $t + \epsilon$, with the corresponding dual problem given by

$$\begin{aligned} \text{maximize} \quad & \sum_{\mathbf{x} \in \mathcal{X}} f(\mathbf{x}, t + \epsilon)\lambda_\mathbf{x} \\ \text{subject to} \quad & \sum_{\mathbf{x} \in \mathcal{X}} \lambda_\mathbf{x} \leq 1 \\ & \lambda_\mathbf{x} \geq 0, \quad \text{for } \mathbf{x} \in \mathcal{X}. \end{aligned} \tag{11.20}$$

whose optimal value is $V(t + \epsilon)$. Note that λ such that $\lambda_\mathbf{x} = 1$ for some $\mathbf{x} \in x^*(t)$, and $\lambda_\mathbf{x} = 0$ otherwise, is an optimal point.

Let λ be an optimal point of the dual problem (11.19). Since λ is a feasible solution to the problem (11.20), we have

$$V(t + \epsilon) \leq \sum_{\mathbf{x} \in \mathcal{X}} f(\mathbf{x}, t + \epsilon)\lambda_{\mathbf{x}}^* = V(t) + \sum_{\mathbf{x} \in \mathcal{X}} (f(\mathbf{x}, t + \epsilon) - f(\mathbf{x}, t))\lambda_{\mathbf{x}}^*. \quad (11.21)$$

We now show that there exists $\epsilon_0 > 0$ such that in the last inequality, the equality holds for every $\epsilon \in [0, \epsilon_0]$. Let λ^* be the optimal solution of (11.20) that minimizes $\sum_{\mathbf{x} \in \mathcal{X}} [(f(\mathbf{x}, t + \epsilon) - f(\mathbf{x}, t))/\epsilon]\lambda_{\mathbf{x}}$, i.e.,

$$\begin{aligned}
\text{minimize} \quad & \sum_{\mathbf{x} \in \mathcal{X}} [(f(\mathbf{x}, t + \epsilon) - f(\mathbf{x}, t))/\epsilon]\lambda_{\mathbf{x}} \\
\text{subject to} \quad & \sum_{\mathbf{x} \in \mathcal{X}} f(\mathbf{x}, t)\lambda_{\mathbf{x}} = V(t) \\
& \sum_{\mathbf{x} \in \mathcal{X}} \lambda_{\mathbf{x}} \leq 1 \\
& \lambda_{\mathbf{x}} \geq 0, \quad \text{for } \mathbf{x} \in \mathcal{X}.
\end{aligned}$$

The dual optimization problem is

$$\begin{aligned}
\text{minimize} \quad & y + V(t)v \\
\text{subject to} \quad & y + vf(\mathbf{x}, t) \geq -[f(\mathbf{x}, t + \epsilon) - f(\mathbf{x}, t)]/\epsilon, \quad \text{for } \mathbf{x} \in \mathcal{X} \\
& y \geq 0 \\
& v \geq 0.
\end{aligned}$$

Let (y^*, v^*) be the optimal solution to this problem. By the duality, we have

$$y^* + V(t)v^* = \sum_{\mathbf{x} \in \mathcal{X}} [(f(\mathbf{x}, t + \epsilon) - f(\mathbf{x}, t))/\epsilon]\lambda_{\mathbf{x}}^*.$$

Let λ^0 be an optimal solution to (11.19). For $\epsilon \leq 1/v^*$, $\lambda = (1 - v^*\epsilon)\lambda^0 + \epsilon\lambda^*$, we have

$$\begin{aligned}
V(t + \epsilon) &\geq \sum_{\mathbf{x} \in \mathcal{X}} f(\mathbf{x}, t)\lambda_{\mathbf{x}} \\
&= (1 - v^*\epsilon) \sum_{\mathbf{x} \in \mathcal{X}} f(\mathbf{x}, t)\lambda_{\mathbf{x}}^0 + \epsilon \sum_{\mathbf{x} \in \mathcal{X}} f(\mathbf{x}, t)\lambda_{\mathbf{x}}^* \\
&= (1 - v^*\epsilon)V(t) + \epsilon \left(\sum_{\mathbf{x} \in \mathcal{X}} [(f(\mathbf{x}, t + \epsilon) - f(\mathbf{x}, t))/\epsilon]\lambda_{\mathbf{x}}^* - V(t)v^* \right) \\
&= V(t) + \sum_{\mathbf{x} \in \mathcal{X}} (f(\mathbf{x}, t + \epsilon) - f(\mathbf{x}, t))\lambda_{\mathbf{x}}^*. \quad (11.22)
\end{aligned}$$

From (11.21) and (11.22), we have

$$\begin{aligned}
\frac{d}{dt}V(t) &= \lim_{\epsilon \downarrow 0} \frac{V(t + \epsilon) - V(t)}{\epsilon} \\
&= \lim_{\epsilon \downarrow 0} \sum_{\mathbf{x} \in \mathcal{X}} \frac{f(\mathbf{x}, t + \epsilon) - f(\mathbf{x}, t)}{\epsilon}\lambda_{\mathbf{x}}^* \\
&= \lim_{\epsilon \downarrow 0} \frac{f(\mathbf{x}, t + \epsilon) - f(\mathbf{x}, t)}{\epsilon} \\
&= \frac{\partial}{\partial t}f(\mathbf{x}, t).
\end{aligned}$$

$\square$

11.1.8 Cauchy's Functional Equations

The following equations are known as Cauchy's equations:

$$a(x + y) = a(x) + a(y) \tag{11.23}$$

$$e(x + y) = e(x)e(y) \tag{11.24}$$

$$l(xy) = l(x) + l(y) \tag{11.25}$$

$$m(xy) = m(x)m(y) \tag{11.26}$$

They are referred to as Cauchy's *additive, exponential, logarithmic,* and *multiplicative* equation, respectively. Under suitable conditions, Cauchy's exponential, logarithmic, and multiplicative equations can be transformed to a Cauchy's additive equation.

It can be readily checked that $a(x) = cx$, for $x \in \mathbf{R}$, and a constant $c \in \mathbf{R}$ is a solution to equation (11.23). This, however, is not the only solution. In what follows we first provide sufficient conditions for uniqueness of the solution to the Cauchy's additive equation and then provide such conditions for other Cauchy's equations.

Cauchy's Additive Equation

Theorem 11.14. *If the functional equation (11.23) is supposed only for all x and y that are elements of the set of rational numbers* $\mathbf{Q}$*, then it has a unique solution given by*

$$a(x) = cx, \quad \text{for } x \in \mathbf{Q}, \text{ and a constant } c \in \mathbf{R}. \tag{11.27}$$

Proof. From (11.23), it follows that

$$a(x_1 + x_2 + \cdots + x_n) = a(x_1) + a(x_2) + \cdots + a(x_n).$$

In particular, if $x_1 = x_2 = \cdots = x_n = x$, then

$$a(nx) = na(x).$$

Using the last equation, and $x = (m/n)t$ for $m, n \in \mathbf{N}$ and $t \in \mathbf{Q}$, we have

$$na(x) = a(nx) = a(mt) = ma(t).$$

Hence,

$$ta(x) = xa(t).$$

By taking $t = 1$ and $a(1) = c$, we obtain $a(x) = cx$.

For $x = 0$, it immediately follows from (11.23) that $a(0) = 0$.

For negative x, by taking $y = -x$ in (11.23), we obtain

$$a(x) = a(0) - a(-x) = -a(-x) = cx$$

where the last equation is by the established result for positive rationals. $\qquad \square$

Theorem 11.15. *If the functional equation (11.23) is supposed for all real values x and y, then all solutions that are continuous at a point are given by*

$$a(x) = cx, \quad \text{for } x \in \mathbf{R} \text{ and a constant } c \in \mathbf{R}.$$

Proof. If function $a(x)$ is continuous at every $x \in \mathbf{R}$, then the claim is established for every given $x \in \mathbf{R}$ by taking a sequence of rational numbers that converges to x and then taking the limit along this sequence on both sides in equation (11.27).

If $a(x)$ is continuous for some $x_0 \in \mathbf{R}$, i.e., $\lim_{t \to x_0} a(t) = a(x_0)$, then, we have

$$\lim_{t \to x} a(t) = \lim_{t \to x_0} a(t + (x - x_0))$$

$$= \lim_{t \to x_0} (a(t) + a(x - x_0))$$

$$= a(x_0) + a(x - x_0)$$

$$= a(x)$$

where the second and the last equations hold by equation (11.23). □

The following theorem provides a set of equivalent conditions to the condition that a function is continuous at a point.

Theorem 11.16. *Suppose that $a : \mathbf{R} \to \mathbf{R}$ satisfies equation (11.23) with $c = a(1) > 0$. Then, the following conditions are equivalent:*

(i) *a is continuous at a point.*
(ii) *a is monotonically strictly increasing.*
(iii) *a is non-negative for non-negative x.*
(iv) *a is bounded from above on every finite interval.*
(v) *a is bounded from below on every finite interval.*
(vi) *a is bounded on every finite interval.*
(vii) *$a(x) = cx$.*

Proof. We prove the implications in the order that they are stated in the theorem and then prove that the last property implies the first one.

(i) $\Rightarrow$ (ii) Let $x > y$ and let r_n be a sequence of rationals such that $\lim_{n \to \infty} r_n = x - y$. Then, we have

$$0 = \lim_{n \to \infty} a(r_n + y - x + x_0) - a(x_0)$$

$$= \lim_{n \to \infty} (a(r_n) + a(y) - a(x))$$

$$= \lim_{n \to \infty} (cr_n + a(y) - a(x))$$

$$= c(x - y) + a(y) - a(x).$$

Hence, $a(x) - a(y) = c(x - y) > 0$, showing that a is montonically strictly increasing.

(ii) $\Rightarrow$ (iii) Suppose that $x \geq 0$. Then, by (ii) $a(x) \geq a(0) = 0$.

(iii) $\Rightarrow$ (iv) Suppose that $x \in [u, v]$ for an arbitrary finite interval $[u, v]$. By (iii) and (11.23), we have $a(x) \leq a(x) + a(v - x) = a(v)$ for every $x \in [u, v]$. This shows that $a(x)$ is bounded from above on $[u, v]$ with $a(v)$.

(iv) $\Rightarrow$ **(v)** Suppose that $x \in [u, v]$. By (11.23) and (iv), we have

$$a(x) = a(u) + a(u - x) = a(u) - a(x - u) \geq a(u) - a(v - u),$$

which shows that $a(x)$ is bounded from below on $[u, v]$ with $a(u) - a(v - u)$.

(v) $\Rightarrow$ **(vi)** Suppose that $x \in [u, v]$, for a finite interval $[u, v]$. Since by (v), a is bounded from below on $[u, v]$, it suffices to show that a is also bounded from above on $[0, v]$. This establishes the equivalence of (iv) and (v), and the conjuction of (iv) and (v) is equivalent to (vi). By (11.23), we have $a(x) = a(v) - a(v - x)$ for every $x \in [u, v]$. Since by (v), $a(v - x)$ is bounded from below on $[0, v - u]$, it follows that $a(x)$ is bounded from above on $[u, v]$.

(vi) $\Rightarrow$ **(vii)** Define $\phi(x) = a(x) - cx$. Notice that $\phi(x)$ satisfies equation (11.23), $\phi(r) = 0$ for every $r \in \mathbf{Q}$, and by (vi) ϕ is bounded on every finite interval $[u, v]$. Also, note that

$$\phi(x) = \phi(x + r), \quad \text{for } x \in \mathbf{R} \text{ and } r \in \mathbf{Q}. \tag{11.28}$$

Since for every real number x we can find a rational number r such that $x + r \in [u, v]$, we can conclude from (11.28) that ϕ is bounded on $\mathbf{R}$. We claim that $\phi(x) = 0$ for every $x \in \mathbf{R}$. If this does not hold, then there exists $x_0 \in \mathbf{R}$ such that $\phi(x_0) = \xi > 0$. Then, by (11.23), $\phi(nx_0) = n\xi$ holds for every integer n, so for an arbitrarily large value n, ϕ can take an arbitrarily large value, which is a contradiction to the assumption that ϕ is bounded.

(vii) $\Rightarrow$ **(i)** This implication obviously holds. □

Cauchy's Exponential Equation

Theorem 11.17. *If the functional equation (11.24) is supposed for all real values x and y, then all solutions that are continuous at a point are given by*

$$e(x) = e^{cx} \text{ for a constant } c \in \mathbf{R}, \text{ and } e(x) = 0.$$

If the functional equation (11.24) is supposed only for non-negative x and y, then for solutions that are continuous at a point, it has, in addition, the following solution:

$$e(x) = \begin{cases} 1, & \text{for } x = 0 \\ 0, & \text{for } x > 0. \end{cases}$$

Proof. We first prove that if $e(x)$ is a solution to equation (11.24) for $x \in \mathbf{R}$, then we have either $e(x) = 0$ for all $x \in \mathbf{R}$ or $e(x) > 0$ for all $x \in \mathbf{R}$. The same property holds also if (11.24) is supposed only for strictly positive x.

From (11.24), if $e(x_0) = 0$ for some $x_0 \in \mathbf{R}$, then for every $x \in \mathbf{R}$, we have

$$e(x) = e((x - x_0) + x_0) = e(x - x_0)e(x_0) = 0.$$

If equation (11.24) is supposed only for strictly positive x, then this shows that $e(x) = 0$ for $x \geq x_0$. To show that $e(x) = 0$ also for $x \in (0, x_0)$, we use a contradiction. Suppose that there exists $x \in (0, x_0)$ such that $e(x) \neq 0$. Then, we take n such that $nx \geq x_0$, and from (11.24) obtain the following contradiction:

$$0 = e(nx) = e(x_0)^n \neq 0.$$

On the other hand, by taking $x = y = t/2$ in (11.24), we obtain

$$f(t) = f(t/2)^2 > 0,$$

which shows that any non-trivial solution to (11.24) is positive everywhere. This justifies using the transformation $a(x) = \log(e(x))$, which yields a Cauchy's additive equation (11.23). By Theorem 11.15, there is a unique solution in this case given by $e(x) = e^{cx}$, for a constant $c \in \mathbf{R}$.

If equation (11.24) is supposed only for non-negative x and y, then we also have as a solution $e(0) = 1$ and $e(x) = 0$, for $x > 0$. $\qquad\square$

Cauchy's Logarithmic Equation

Theorem 11.18. *If the functional equation (11.25) is supposed only for all positive x and y, then all solutions that are continuous at a point are given by*

$$l(x) = c \log(x), \quad \text{for a constant } c \in \mathbf{R}.$$

If the functional equation (11.25) is supposed only for all real values such that $x \neq 0$ and $y \neq 0$, then all solutions that are continuous at a point are given by

$$l(x) = c \log(|x|), \quad \text{for a constant } c \in \mathbf{R}.$$

Proof. If equation (11.25) is supposed only for all positive x and y, then by using the transformation $a(x) = l(e^x)$, we obtain that a satisfies the Cauchy's additive equation (11.23), and the assertion follows from Theorem 11.15.

If function $l(x)$ satisfies equation (11.25) for $x = 0$, then we have

$$l(0) = l(x) + l(0),$$

which implies that there is only the constant solution $l(x) = 0$.

If we try to satisfy equation (11.25) for all real values x and y such that $x \neq 0$ and $y \neq 0$, then with $x = y = t$ and $x = y = -t$ we have $2l(t) = l(t^2) = 2l(-t)$, which yields the solution

$$l(x) = c \log(|x|), \quad \text{for } x \neq 0, \quad \text{for a constant } c \in \mathbf{R}.$$

$\qquad\square$

Cauchy's Multiplicative Equation

Theorem 11.19. *If the functional equation (11.26) is supposed only for all positive x and y, then all solutions that are continuous at a point are given by*

$$m(x) = x^c, \quad \text{for a constant } c \in \mathbf{R} \text{ and } m(x) = 0.$$

If the functional equation (11.26) is supposed for all real values x and y, then all solutions that are continuous at a point are given by

$$m(x) = \begin{cases} |x|^c, & \text{for } x \neq 0 \\ 0, & \text{for } x = 0 \end{cases}, m(x) = \begin{cases} -|x|^c, & \text{for } x \neq 0 \\ 0, & \text{for } x = 0 \end{cases}, \quad \text{for a constant } c \neq 0,$$

$$m(x) = 0, \ m(x) = 1, \ m(x) = \mathbf{1}(x \neq 0), \text{ and } m(x) = \mathbf{1}(x > 0) - \mathbf{1}(x < 0).$$

If the functional equation (11.26) is supposed only for all real values x and y such that $x \neq 0$ and $y \neq 0$, then all solutions that are continuous at a point are given by

$$m(x) = |x|^c, \ m(x) = \begin{cases} -|x|^c, & \text{for } x < 0 \\ |x|^c, & \text{for } x \geq 0 \end{cases}, \text{ and } m(x) = 0$$

for $x \neq 0$ and a constant $c \in \mathbf{R}$.

Proof. Suppose first that equation (11.26) is supposed only for positive x and y. In this case, using the transformation $e(x) = m(e^x)$, equation (11.26) can be transformed to equation (11.24), which we studied in Section 11.1.8. By Theorem 11.1.8, all solutions to (11.26) that are continuous at a point are given by

$$m(x) = x^c, \quad \text{for a constant } c \in \mathbf{R}, \text{ and } m(x) = 0.$$

Suppose now that equation (11.26) is supposed for all real values x and y. If function $m(x)$ satisfies equation (11.26) for $x = 0$, then we have

$$m(0) = m(x)m(0),$$

which implies that we have either $m(0) = 0$ or $m(x) = 1$ for all $x \in \mathbf{R}$.

If we try to satisfy (11.26) for all real x and y such that $x \neq 0$ and $y \neq 0$, then by taking $x = y = t$ and $x = y = -t$, we obtain $m(t)^2 = m(t^2) = m(-t)^2$, from which it follows that

$$m(-t) = m(t), \ m(-t) = -m(t), \ m(t) = t^c, \quad \text{for a constant } c \in \mathbf{R}, \text{ and } m(t) = 0. \tag{11.29}$$

This means that we have the following solutions for every $x \neq 0$:

$$m(x) = |x|^c, \ m(x) = \begin{cases} -|x|^c, & \text{for } x < 0 \\ |x|^c, & \text{for } x \geq 0 \end{cases}, \quad \text{for a constant } c \in \mathbf{R}, m(x) = 0. \tag{11.30}$$

The same expression is also valid if we try verify also for x and y such that $x = 0$ or $y = 0$, but with a constant $c > 0$.

Suppose now that equation (11.26) is supposed only for all real values x and y such that $x \neq 0$ and $y \neq 0$. In this case, solutions to (11.26) that are continuous at a point are given by (11.30). $\square$

11.1.9 Trigonometric Functions and Functional Equations

The trigonometric functions $f(x) = \cos(x)$ and $g(x) = \sin(x)$ satisfy these equations:

$$g(x)f(y) + f(x)g(y) = g(x + y) \tag{11.31}$$

$$f(x)f(y) - g(x)g(y) = f(x + y) \tag{11.32}$$

$$g(x)f(y) - f(x)g(y) = g(x - y) \tag{11.33}$$

$$f(x)f(y) + g(x)g(y) = f(x - y). \tag{11.34}$$

The last equation alone suffices to characterize the two trigonometric functions that none of the remaining equations are able to do.

Theorem 11.20. *The functional equation (11.34) has all continuous solutions given by*

$$f(x) = c \text{ and } g(x) = \pm\sqrt{c(1-c)}, \quad \text{for } c \in [0, 1]$$

and

$$f(x) = \cos(cx) \text{ and } g(x) = \sin(cx), \quad \text{for } c \in \mathbf{R}.$$

Proof. Suppose that $f(x) = c$, for a constant $c \in \mathbf{R}$. Then, equation (11.34) for $x = y$ gives $c^2 + g(x)^2 = c$, which has two solutions $g(x) = \sqrt{c(1-c)}$ and $g(x) = -\sqrt{c(1-c)}$, if $c \in [0, 1]$, and it has no solution otherwise.

Assume from now on that $f(x)$ is not a constant. If f and g are a solution to (11.34), then f is an even function and g is an odd function. To see that f is an even function, note that if in (11.34), we replace x with y and y with x, then the left-hand side of the equation remains unchanged. Hence, $f(x - y) = f(y - x)$, which shows that f is an even function. To see that g cannot be even, replace y with $-y$ in (11.34) to obtain $f(x + y) = f(x - y)$, which implies that f is a constant, which contradicts the assumption that it is not so. By replacing x with $-x$ and y with $-y$, we obtain

$$f(y - x) = f(-x)f(-y) + g(-x)g(-y).$$

Since f is even, we have

$$f(x - y) = f(x)f(y) + g(-x)g(-y).$$

Combining this with (11.34), we have

$$g(-x)g(-y) = g(x)g(y).$$

This implies $g(-x) = \pm g(x)$, which combined with the established fact that g is not even, implies that $g(x)$ is an odd function.

Since g is a continuous and odd function, we have $g(0) = 0$. Combining this with (11.34) for $y = 0$, we obtain $f(x) = f(x)f(0)$. Since $f(x)$ is a constant equal to zero, we have $f(0) = 1$. Equation (11.34) for $y = x$ yields

$$f(x)^2 + g(x)^2 = 1. \tag{11.35}$$

Therefore, we have

$$|f(x)| \leq 1. \tag{11.36}$$

By replacing y with $-y$ in (11.34), we obtain (11.32), which when added to (11.34), yields d'Alembert's equation:

$$f(x + y) + f(x - y) = 2f(x)f(y). \tag{11.37}$$

Theorem 11.21 (Aczél (1966)). *The functional equation (11.37) has all continuous solutions given by*

$$f(x) = 0, \ f(x) = \frac{1}{2}(e^{-cx} + e^{cx}), \ f(x) = \cos(cx)$$

for a constant $c \in \mathbf{R}$.

The solution $f(x) = (e^{-cx} + e^{cx})/2$ does not satisfy (11.36). Thus, the only non-constant solution to (11.37) is $f(x) = \cos(cx)$. Using (11.35), it follows that $g(x) = \sin(cx)$. $\qquad\qquad\qquad\qquad\qquad\qquad\qquad\qquad\qquad\qquad\qquad\qquad\qquad\square$

11.1.10 Fixed-Point Theorems

We make note of two fixed-point theorems. The first one is concerned with fixed points of continuous functions and is given as follows.

Theorem 11.22 (Brouwer's fixed-point theorem). *Let $X \subseteq \mathbf{R}^n$ be a convex, compact, and non-empty set. Then, every continuous function $f : X \to X$ has a point $\mathbf{x}^* \in X$ such that $\mathbf{x}^* = f(\mathbf{x}^*)$.*

The second fixed-point theorem is concerned with correspondences and reads as follows.

Theorem 11.23 (Kakutani's fixed-point theorem). *Let $X \in \mathbf{R}^n$ be a convex, compact, and non-empty set. Then, every correspondence f on X that is upper semi-continuous and convex valued, has a point $\mathbf{x}^* \in X$ such that $\mathbf{x}^* \in f(\mathbf{x}^*)$.*

We shall invoke the second theorem later in Section 11.3.1 to establish the existence of a pure-strategy Nash equilibrium for concave games.

11.2 Probability and Statistics

In this section we review the concepts of a distribution function and expected values, order statistics, distributions on a simplex with a specific form of a univariate marginal distribution, and some properties of Gaussian distributions.

11.2.1 Distribution Function and Expected Value

Let X be a random variable with *cumulative distribution function* $F(x) = \mathbf{Pr}[X \leq x]$ for $x \in \mathbf{R}$. Throughout this book, we often refer to $F(x)$ simply as a distribution function. The distribution function F satisfies the following properties:

 (i) $F : \mathbf{R} \to [0, 1]$.
 (ii) F is an increasing function.
 (iii) $\lim_{x \to \infty} F(x) = \mathbf{Pr}[X < \infty]$.
 (iv) $\lim_{x \to -\infty} F(x) = \mathbf{Pr}[X = -\infty]$.

A distribution function F is said to be *absolutely continuous* if there exists a function $f : \mathbf{R} \to \mathbf{R}_+$, called the *probability density function* of X, such that

$$F(x) = \int_{-\infty}^{x} f(y)\,dy \text{ for } x \in \mathbf{R}.$$

A distribution function F can be decomposed into a discontinuous component F_d and a continuous component F_c as follows. The discontinuity points of F are enumerable since the function is increasing and bounded. Let $x_1, x_2, \ldots, x_I$ denote the sequence of discontinuity points of F, where I is a strictly positive integer or infinity. Then, we can define

$$F_d(x) = \sum_{i=1}^{I} \mathbf{1}(x_i \le x)(F(x_i) - F(x_i-)) \text{ and } F_c(x) = F(x) - F_d(x), \quad \text{for } x \in \mathbf{R}$$

(11.38)

where by definition $F(x-) = \lim_{y \uparrow x} F(y)$. For every discontinuity point of F, x_i, we say that F has an *atom* (or a *mass*) at x_i.

Under the assumption that F_c is absolutely continuous, the *support set* of F is defined as

$$\text{supp}(F) = \{x \in \mathbf{R} \mid F_d(x) - F_d(x-) > 0 \text{ or } f_c(x) > 0\}.$$

We refer to $\underline{x} = \inf\{x \in \text{supp}(F)\}$ and $\bar{x} = \sup\{x \in \text{supp}(F)\}$ as the *lower end* and the *upper end of the support* of the distribution F, respectively.

Example 11.24. Consider the distribution function F defined in Figure 11.6. This distribution function can be decomposed in a discontinuous and a continuous component as follows:

$$F_d(x) = \begin{cases} 0, & \text{if } x < 0 \\ a, & \text{if } x \ge 0 \end{cases} \text{ and } F_c(x) = \begin{cases} 0, & \text{if } x < x^* \\ (1-a)\frac{x-x^*}{1-x^*}, & \text{if } x^* \le x < 1 \\ 1-a, & \text{if } x \ge 1 \end{cases}$$

The support set is $\text{supp}(F) = \{0\} \cup [x^*, 1]$ with the lower end of the support $\underline{x} = 0$ and the upper end of the support $\bar{x} = 1$.

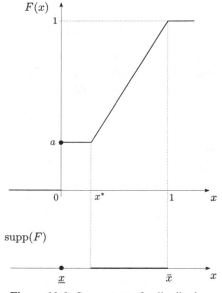

Figure 11.6. Support set of a distribution.

Given a function $g : \mathbf{R} \to \mathbf{R}$ and a random variable X with distribution function F, the expected value of g with respect to the distribution F is defined by

$$\mathbf{E}[g(X)] = \int_{\mathbf{R}} g(x) \, dF(x) \tag{11.39}$$

where the right-hand side in the equation is the Stieltjes-Lebesgue integral. For our purposes, we can admit the following identity:

$$\int_{\mathbf{R}} g(x) \, dF(x) = \sum_{i=1}^{I} g(x_i)(F(x_i) - F(x_i-)) + \int_X g(x) f_c(x) \, dx. \tag{11.40}$$

In particular, the mean of the random variable X is defined by (11.39) with $g(x) = x$, and the p-th moment by (11.39) with $g(x) = x^p$ for $p \in \mathbf{R}_+$.

Telescope Formula

Throughout the book, we use an alternative representation of the expected value of a non-negative random variable X that is known as the *telescope formula* and is given by

$$\mathbf{E}[X] = \int_0^\infty (1 - F(x)) \, dx.$$

This identity can be shown to hold as follows. First, we note that

$$\sum_{i=1}^{I} x_i(F(x_i) - F(x_i-)) = \sum_{i=1}^{I} x_i(F_d(x_i) - F_d(x_{i-1}))$$

$$= \sum_{i=1}^{I} (x_i - x_{i-1})(F_d(x_I) - F_d(x_{i-1})).$$

Second, by partial integration, we have for $a \geq 0$,

$$\int_0^a x f_c(x) \, dx = a F_c(a) - \int_0^a F_c(x) \, dx = \int_0^a (F_c(a) - F_c(x)) \, dx.$$

Taking the limit as a goes to infinity, we obtain

$$\int_0^\infty x f_c(x) \, dx = \int_0^\infty (F_c(+\infty) - F_c(x)) \, dx.$$

Now, from (11.40), we have

$$\int_0^\infty x \, dF(x) = \sum_{i=1}^{I} (x_i - x_{i-1})(F_d(x_I) - F_d(x_{i-1})) + \int_0^\infty (F_c(+\infty) - F_c(x)) \, dx$$

$$= \sum_{i=1}^{I} \int_{x_{i-1}}^{x_i} (F_d(x_I) - F_d(x_{i-1}) + F_c(+\infty) - F_c(x)) \, dx$$

$$+ \int_{x_I}^\infty (F_c(+\infty) - F_c(x)) \, dx$$

$$= \sum_{i=1}^{I} \int_{x_{i-1}}^{x_i} (1 - (F_d(x_{i-1}) + F_c(x)))\, dx + \int_{x_I}^{\infty} (1 - (F_d(x_I) + F_c(x)))\, dx$$

$$= \sum_{i=1}^{I} \int_{x_{i-1}}^{x_i} (1 - F(x))\, dx + \int_{x_I}^{\infty} (1 - F(x))\, dx$$

$$= \int_{0}^{\infty} (1 - F(x))\, dx$$

where we used the facts $F_d(x_{i-1}) + F_c(x) = F(x)$ for $x_{i-1} < x \le x_i$, for $i = 1, 2, \ldots, I$, and $F_d(x_I) + F_c(x) = F(x)$, for $x \ge x_I$.

Hazard Rate Function

Definition 11.25. Given an absolutely continuous distribution function F on the support X with density function f, the *hazard rate function* is defined as

$$h(x) = \frac{f(x)}{1 - F(x)}, \quad \text{for } x \in X.$$

The hazard rate function can be interpreted as the conditional density function of random variable $X \sim F$ conditional on the event $\{X > x\}$.

Stochastic Comparisons

Definition 11.26. For two random variables X and Y with respective cumulative distribution functions F and G, we say that X is *stochastically larger* than Y (or that F is stochastically larger than G), if $F(x) \le G(x)$ for every $x \in \mathbf{R}$. We say that X is *stochastically smaller* than Y (or that F is stochastically smaller than G), if $F(x) \ge G(x)$ for every $x \in \mathbf{R}$.

11.2.2 Order Statistics

Suppose $X_1, X_2, \ldots, X_n$ is a sequence of independent and identically distributed random variables with distribution function F that is absolutely continuous with the probability density function f. Let $X_{(n,1)} \ge X_{(n,2)} \ge \cdots \ge X_{(n,n)}$ be the rearrangement of the values $X_1, X_2, \ldots, X_n$ in decreasing order, which we refer to as *order statistics*. Let $F_{n,i}$ be the distribution function and $f_{n,i}$ be the density function of the random variable $X_{(n,i)}$, for $1 \le i \le n$.

Since $X_{(n,i)}$ is defined as the i-th largest value from n independent samples from the distribution function F that has density function f, its density function is given by

$$f_{n,i}(x) = \frac{n!}{(i-1)!(n-i)!} F(x)^{n-i}(1 - F(x))^{i-1} f(x), \quad \text{for } x \in \mathbf{R}. \tag{11.41}$$

From (11.41), we obtain the distribution function:

$$F_{n,i}(x) = n \int_{-\infty}^{x} \binom{n-1}{i-1} F(y)^{n-i}(1 - F(y))^{i-1} f(y)\, dy, \quad \text{for } x \in \mathbf{R}.$$

An alternative representation of the distribution $F_{n,i}$ is of the following form:

$$F_{n,i}(x) = \sum_{j=0}^{i-1} \binom{n}{j} F(x)^{n-j}(1 - F(x))^j, \quad \text{for } x \in \mathbf{R}. \tag{11.42}$$

This can be shown to hold as follows. Let $N_x(X_1, X_2, \ldots, X_n)$ denote the number of samples in $X_1, X_2, \ldots, X_n$ greater than $x \in \mathbf{R}$. Then, we can write

$$F_{n,i}(x) = \mathbf{Pr}[X_{(n,i)} \leq x]$$

$$= \mathbf{Pr}\left[\bigcup_{j \in \{0,1,\ldots,i-1\}} \{N_x(X_1, X_2, \ldots, X_n) = j\} \right]$$

$$= \sum_{j=0}^{i-1} \mathbf{Pr}\left[N_x(X_1, X_2, \ldots, X_n) = j\right]$$

$$= \sum_{j=0}^{i-1} \binom{n}{j} F(x)^{n-j}(1 - F(x))^j.$$

Moment Relations

Theorem 11.27. *For every $p \in \mathbf{R}_+$,*

$$i\mathbf{E}\left[X_{(n,i+1)}^p\right] + (n - i)\mathbf{E}\left[X_{(n,i)}^p\right] = n\mathbf{E}\left[X_{(n-1,i)}^p\right], \quad \text{for } 1 \leq i < n.$$

Proof. From (11.41), it follows that

$$\mathbf{E}\left[X_{(n,i)}^p\right] = \frac{n!}{(i-1)!(n-i)!} \int_0^1 F^{-1}(x)^p x^{x-i}(1 - x)^{i-1} dx, \quad \text{for } 1 \leq i \leq n.$$

For every $1 \leq i < n$, we can write

$$n\mathbf{E}\left[X_{(n-1,i)}^p\right] = \frac{n!}{(i-1)!(n-i-1)!} \int_0^1 F^{-1}(x)^p x^{n-i-1}(1 - x)^{i-1} dx$$

$$= \frac{n!}{(i-1)!(n-i-1)!} \int_0^1 F^{-1}(x)^p x^{n-i-1}(1 - x)^{i-1}[(1 - x) + x] dx$$

$$= \frac{n!}{(i-1)!(n-i-1)!} \left\{ \int_0^1 F^{-1}(x)^p x^{n-i}(1 - x)^i dx \right.$$

$$\left. + \int_0^1 F^{-1}(x)^p x^{n-i}(1 - x)^{i-1} dx \right\}$$

$$= i\mathbf{E}\left[X_{(n,i+1)}^p\right] + (n - i)\mathbf{E}\left[X_{(n,i)}^p\right]$$

which establishes the assertion of the theorem. $\qquad\square$

Asymptotic Order Statistics

Definition 11.28. A distribution function F that is either discrete or absolutely continuous is said to belong to the *domain of maximal attraction of a non-degenerate distribution function G* if there exist sequences a_n and $b_n > 0$ such that at every point x at which G is continuous, we have

$$\lim_{n \to \infty} F(a_n + b_n x)^n = G(x). \tag{11.43}$$

The domain of maximal attraction can be one of three possible types as given in the following theorem. The first type was first identified by Frechét (1927), and then a complete characterization was given by Fisher and Tippett (1928).

Theorem 11.29. *If a distribution function F belongs to the domain of maximal attraction of a non-degenerate distribution function G, then G is one of the following three types:*

(i) *Type 1 (Frechét): for $\theta < 0$,*

$$G_1(x;\theta) = \begin{cases} 0, & x \le 0 \\ e^{-x^\theta} & x > 0. \end{cases}$$

(ii) *Type 2 (Weibull): for $\theta > 0$,*

$$G_2(x;\theta) = \begin{cases} e^{-(-x)^\theta} & x \le 0 \\ 1 & x > 0. \end{cases}$$

(iii) *Type 3 (extreme value):*

$$G_3(x) = e^{-e^{-x}}, \quad -\infty < x < \infty.$$

The domains of maximal attractions are members of a single family of distributions of the following form:

$$G(x;\theta) = \exp\left(-\frac{1}{\left(1+\frac{x}{\theta}\right)^\theta}\right), \quad \text{for } 1 + \frac{x}{\theta} > 0 \text{ and } \theta \in \mathbf{R}.$$

A set of necessary and sufficient conditions for a distribution to be of a particular type was first found by Gnedenko (1943), and is covered in Galambos (1978).

Theorem 11.30 (necessary and sufficient conditions). *The following are necessary and sufficient conditions for a distribution function F to have the domain of maximal attraction of one of the three possible types.*

(i) *F is of type 1 if, and only if, $F^{-1}(1) = +\infty$ and there exists a constant $\theta < 0$ such that*

$$\lim_{t\to\infty} \frac{1 - F(tx)}{1 - F(t)} = x^\theta, \quad \text{for all } x > 0.$$

(ii) *F is of type 2 if, and only if, $F^{-1}(1)$ is finite and there exists a constant $\theta > 0$ such that*

$$\lim_{t\downarrow 0} \frac{1 - F(F^{-1}(1) - tx)}{1 - F(F^{-1}(1) - t)} = x^\theta, \quad \text{for all } x > 0.$$

(iii) *F is of type 3 if, and only if, $\mathbf{E}[X_i \mid X_i > c]$ is finite for some $c < F^{-1}(1)$ and*

$$\lim_{t\to F^{-1}(1)} \frac{1 - F(t + x\mathbf{E}[X_i - t \mid X_i > t])}{1 - F(t)} = e^{-x}, \quad \text{for all } -\infty < x < \infty.$$

For every distribution F that has the domain of maximal attraction of type 1, the upper limit of the support of F must be infinite. On the other hand, for every distribution F that has the domain of maximal attraction of type 2, the upper limit of the support of F is necessarily finite.

Sufficient conditions for a distribution to be of a particular type were established by von Mises (1936) and are given in the following theorem. A simple proof is available in Haan (1976).

Theorem 11.31 (von Mises's sufficient conditions). *Let F be an absolutely continuous distribution with the density function f, and let $h(x) = f(x)/(1 - F(x))$.*

(i) *F is of type 1 if*

$$\lim_{x \to \infty} x h(x) = -\theta, \quad \text{for large } x \text{ and some } \theta < 0.$$

(ii) *F is of type 2 if $F^{-1}(1) < \infty$ and*

$$\lim_{x \to F^{-1}(1)} (F^{-1}(1) - x) h(x) = 0, \quad \text{for some } \theta > 0.$$

(iii) *F is of type 3 if $h(x)$ is non-zero, differentiable for x close to $F^{-1}(1)$, and*

$$\lim_{x \to F^{-1}(1)} \frac{d}{dx} \left(\frac{1}{h(x)} \right) = 0.$$

One may also show that a distribution is of a particular type by direct derivation of the limit in (11.43) for a particular choice of the sequences a_n and b_n that appear therein. For such an approach, the following is a useful result.

Theorem 11.32. *The sequences a_n and b_n to establish the limit in (11.43) for a distribution can be chosen depending on the type of the distribution as follows:*

(i) *Type 1: $a_n = 0$ and $b_n = F^{-1}(1 - 1/n)$,*
(ii) *Type 2: $a_n = F^{-1}(1)$ and $b_n = F^{-1}(1) - F^{-1}(1 - 1/n)$,*
(iii) *Type 3: $a_n = F^{-1}(1 - 1/n)$ and $b_n = \mathbf{E}[X_i - a_n \mid X_i > a_n]$ or $b_n = F^{-1}(1 - 1/(ne)) - F^{-1}(1 - 1/n)$.*

We provide examples of specific distributions for each type of domain of maximal attraction in the following three examples.

Example 11.33 (Pareto distribution). Consider a Pareto distribution function $F(x) = 1 - x^\theta$ for $x \geq 1$ and $\theta < 0$. Since the hazard rate function is $h(x) = -\theta/x$, we have $xh(x) = -\theta$ for every $x \geq 1$, and hence, from Theorem 11.31 this distribution is of type 1 with parameter θ. One may also check this directly by taking $a_n = 0$ and $b_n = F^{-1}(1 - 1/n) = n^{-1/\theta}$ to obtain

$$F^n(a_n + b_n x) = \begin{cases} 0, & \text{if } x \leq n^{1/\theta} \\ \left(1 - \frac{x^\theta}{n}\right)^n, & \text{if } x > n^{1/\theta} \end{cases}$$

which has the limit of type 1 in Theorem 11.29 asymptotically as n grows large.

Example 11.34 (uniform distribution). Consider a uniform distribution function $F(x) = x$ for $x \in [0, 1]$. This is a type 2 distribution with parameter $\theta = 1$, which is easy to show in different ways as follows. The condition for a type 2 distribution in

Theorem 11.31 obviously holds because $F^{-1}(1) = 1$ and the hazard rate function is $h(x) = 1/(1 - x)$ for $0 \leq x < 1$. Alternatively, the condition in Theorem 11.30 for a type 2 distribution also obviously holds because

$$\frac{1 - F(F^{-1}(1) - tx)}{1 - F(F^{-1}(1) - t)} = \frac{1 - (1 - tx)}{1 - (1 - t)} = x, \quad \text{for } 0 \leq tx \leq 1 \text{ and } 0 \leq t \leq 1.$$

Yet another way is to take $a_n = f^{-1}(1) = 1$ and $b_n = F^{-1}(1) - F^{-1}(1 - 1/n) = 1/n$ to obtain

$$F^n(a_n + b_n x) = \begin{cases} \left(1 + \frac{x}{n}\right)^n, & x \leq 0 \\ 1, & x > 0 \end{cases}$$

which has the limit of type 2 in Theorem 11.29 for $\theta = 1$ asymptotically as n grows large.

Example 11.35 (logistic distribution). Consider a logistic distribution function $F(x) = 1/(1 + e^{-x})$ for $x \in \mathbf{R}$. This is a type 3 distribution that we show as follows. The hazard rate function of this distribution is equal to the distribution itself $h(x) = 1/(1 + e^{-x})$, which is non-zero and differentiable for every $x \in \mathbf{R}$. It follows that

$$\frac{d}{dx}\left(\frac{1}{h(x)}\right) = -e^{-x}$$

which converges to 0 asymptotically as x approaches $F^{-1}(1) = +\infty$. This completes showing that the condition for a type 3 distribution in Theorem 11.31 holds.

One may also take $a_n = F^{-1}(1 - 1/n) = \log(n - 1)$ and $b_n = F^{-1}(1 - 1/(ne)) - F^{-1}(1 - 1/n) = \log((ne - 1)/(n - 1))$ to obtain

$$F^n(a_n + b_n x) = 1/\left(1 + \frac{1}{n-1}\left(\frac{n-1}{ne-1}\right)^x\right)^n$$

which converges to the type 3 limit in Theorem 11.29 asymptotically as n grows large.

Asymptotic Joint Distribution of Extreme Order Statistics Suppose that F is absolutely continuous and that appropriate von Mises's sufficient conditions hold. Then, the density function of the n-variate random variable $((X_{(n,1)} - a_n)/b_n, \ldots, (X_{(n,i)} - a_n)/b_n)$ can be expressed as

$$F(a_n + b_n x_i)^{n-i} \prod_{j=1}^{i} (n - j + 1) b_n f(a_n + b_n x_j), \quad \text{for } x_1 > x_2 > \cdots > x_i.$$

In view of (11.43), it holds that

$$\lim_{n \to \infty} n b_n f(a_n + b_n x) = \frac{g(x)}{G(x)}.$$

Hence, it follows that the joint density function converges to

$$g_{(1,\ldots,i)}(x_1, \ldots, x_i) = G(x_i) \prod_{j=1}^{i} \frac{g(x_j)}{G(x_j)}, \quad \text{for } x_1 > x_2 > \cdots > x_i.$$

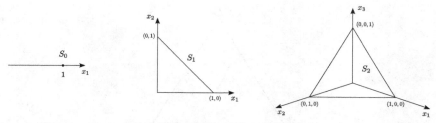

Figure 11.7. Simplexes S_0, S_1, and S_2.

11.2.3 Some Distributions on a Simplex

In this section we consider distributions on an $(m - 1)$-dimensional simplex that is defined by

$$S_m = \left\{ (x_1, x_2, \ldots, x_m) \in [0, 1]^m : \sum_{i=1}^m x_i = 1 \right\}$$

which have univariate marginal distributions of a specific form. See Figure 11.7 for a graphical representation of simplexes S_0, S_1, and S_2. These distributions are used to construct m-variate distributions with univariate marginal distributions that correspond to those of mixed-strategy Nash equilibira of the Colonel Blotto game, specified in Theorem 5.22. The existence of such distributions allows us to establish the existence of mixed-strategy Nash equilibria for these games.

Trivariate Hexa

We refer to a *trivariate hexa* as the distribution that has as support the hexagon inscribed in a 2-dimensional simplex and that is such that every point that lies on the boundary of the inscribed hexagon of a side length x has the density of value kx, where k is a normalizing constant equal to $k = 9\sqrt{3}/(2\sqrt{2})$. Figure 11.8 shows a graphical representation. The univariate marginal distributions of this distribution are uniform distributions on $[0, 2/3]$.

Trivariate Disc

We refer to *trivariate disc* as the distribution that has as support the disc inscribed in a 2-dimensional simplex of radius r and that is symmetric around the center point of the disc inscribed in the simplex, with each point in this disc at distance ρ from the center

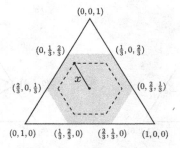

Figure 11.8. Trivariate hexa.

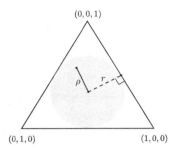

Figure 11.9. Trivariate disc.

of the disc having density of value

$$f(\rho) = \frac{1}{2\pi r} \frac{1}{\sqrt{r^2 - \rho^2}}, \quad \text{for } \rho \in [0, r]$$

where $r = 1/\sqrt{6}$. Figure 11.9 shows a graphical representation. The univariate marginal distributions of this distribution are uniform distributions on $[0, 2/3]$.

Multivariate with Uniform Marginals

Another distribution on a 2-dimensional simplex with uniform univariate distributions can be constructed as follows. Consider a distribution L_3 that splits a unit mass uniformly over a support that corresponds to the following two line segments:

$$\left[\left(0, \frac{1}{3}, \frac{2}{3}\right), \left(\frac{1}{3}, \frac{2}{3}, 0\right) \right] \text{ and } \left[\left(\frac{1}{3}, 0, \frac{2}{3}\right), \left(\frac{2}{3}, \frac{1}{3}, 0\right) \right].$$

Figure 11.10 (left) shows a graphical representation. This distribution has a univariate marginal distribution that is uniform on $[0, 2/3]$. A trivariate distribution $\bar{L}_3$ is defined by evenly splitting a unit mass over the support that consists of six line segments as depicted in Figure 11.10 (right). The univariate marginal distributions of this distributions are uniform distributions on $[0, 2/3]$.

This construction can be generalized to an m-variate distribution for an arbitrary positive integer m as follows. Let L_m be a distribution that uniformly distributes a unit

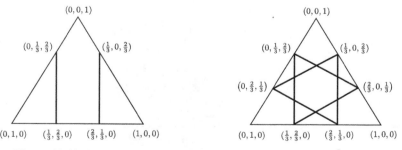

Figure 11.10. Supports of the 3-variate distributions L_3 (left) and $\bar{L}_3$ (right).

mass over the support that consists of the following $m - 1$ line segments:

$$\left[\tfrac{1}{c_m}(0, 1, \ldots, m - 2, m - 1), \quad \tfrac{1}{c_m}(1, 2, \ldots, m - 1, 0) \right]$$
$$\left[\tfrac{1}{c_m}(1, 2, \ldots, m - 2, 0, m - 1), \quad \tfrac{1}{c_m}(2, 3, \ldots, m - 1, 1, 0) \right]$$
$$\vdots$$
$$\left[\tfrac{1}{c_m}(m - 2, 0, 1, \ldots, m - 3, m - 1), \quad \tfrac{1}{c_m}(m - 1, 1, 2, \ldots, m - 2, 0) \right]$$

where $c_m = \binom{m}{2}$ is the normalizing constant. This distribution has a univariate marginal distribution that is a uniform distribution on $[0, 2/m]$.

Trivariate that has a Marginal with a Mass at Zero

Let T_θ^0 be a trivariate distribution with parameter $2/3 \le \theta \le 1$ that uniformly spreads a unit mass over a support that consists of the following three line segments:

$$[(\theta, 1 - \theta, 0), (1 - \theta, 0, \theta)] \text{ mass } \tfrac{1}{\theta} - 1$$
$$[(1 - \theta, \theta, 0), (0, 1 - \theta, \theta)] \text{ mass } \tfrac{1}{\theta} - 1$$
$$[(\theta, 1 - \theta, 0), (1 - \theta, \theta, 0)] \text{ mass } 3 - \tfrac{2}{\theta}$$

The support of this distribution is shown in Figure 11.11 (left). If $\theta = 2/3$, the whole mass is uniformly spread over the two line segments $[(2/3, 1/3, 0), (1/3, 0, 2/3)]$ and $[(1/3, 2/3, 0), (0, 1/3, 2/3)]$. If, on the other hand, $\theta = 1$, the whole mass is placed on the third line segment $[(1, 0, 0), (0, 1, 0)]$, and in this case the distribution is bivariate. The univariate marginal distributions are in general not identical: the univariate marginal distributions of x_1 and x_2 are identical and are uniform distributions on $[0, \theta]$, and the univariate marginal distribution of x_3 has an atom of mass $1 - 2(1 - \theta)/\theta$ at value zero and the remaining mass uniformly spread over $[0, \theta]$.

A distribution with identical univariate marginal distributions can be constructed as follows. Let $\bar{T}_\theta^0(x_1, x_2, x_3)$ be a trivariate distribution of a random variable that is defined as a random permutation of the values of a sample from the trivariate distribution $T_\theta^0(x_1, x_2, x_3)$. This distribution uniformly spreads mass over a collection of line segments shown in Figure 11.11 (right). The univariate marginal distributions of this distribution are identical and are such that they have an atom of mass $1 - 2/(3\theta)$

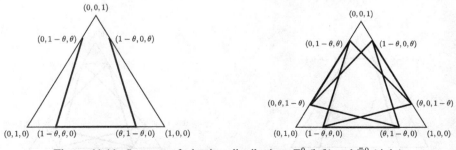

Figure 11.11. Supports of trivariate distributions T_θ^0 (left) and $\bar{T}_\theta^0$ (right).

at value zero and the remaining mass uniformly spread over $[0, \theta]$, i.e.,

$$\bar{T}_\theta^0(x) = \begin{cases} 0, & \text{if } x < \theta \\ 1 - \frac{2}{3\theta} + \frac{2}{3\theta}\frac{x}{\theta}, & \text{if } 0 \leq x < \theta \\ 1, & \text{if } x \geq \theta. \end{cases} \tag{11.44}$$

Trivariate that has a Marginal with a Mass at a Positive Value

Let T_θ^+ be a trivariate distribution with parameter $1/2 \leq \theta \leq 2/3$ that uniformly spreads a unit mass over a support that consists of the following three line segments:

$$[(\theta, 1 - \theta, 0), (1 - \theta, \theta, 0)] \text{ mass } 2 - \frac{1}{\theta}$$
$$[(1 - \theta, \theta, 0), (0, 1 - \theta, \theta)] \text{ mass } 2 - \frac{1}{\theta}$$
$$[(0, 1 - \theta, \theta), (1 - \theta, 0, \theta)] \text{ mass } \frac{2}{\theta} - 3$$

The support of this distribution is shown in Figure 11.12 (left). The univariate marginal distributions of x_1 and x_2, are uniform on $[0, \theta]$ and that of x_3 has an atom of mass $1 - 2(2 - 1/\theta)$ at value θ and the remaining mass uniform spread over $[0, \theta)$.

A distribution with identical univariate marginal distributions can be constructed as follows. Let $\bar{T}_\theta^+(x_1, x_2, x_3)$ be a trivariate distribution of a random variable that is defined as a random permutation of the values of a sample from the trivariate distribution $T_\theta^+(x_1, x_2, x_3)$. The support of this distribution is shown in Figure 11.12 (right). The univariate marginal distributions of distribution $\bar{T}_\theta^+$ are identical and are such that they have an atom of mass of $2/(3\theta) - 1$ on value θ and the remaining mass uniformly spread over $[0, \theta]$, i.e.,

$$\bar{T}_\theta^+(x) = \begin{cases} 0, & \text{if } x < 0 \\ 2\left(1 - \frac{1}{3\theta}\right)\frac{x}{\theta}, & \text{if } 0 \leq x < \theta \\ 1, & \text{if } x \geq \theta \end{cases} \tag{11.45}$$

Quadruple that has a Marginal with a Mass at Zero

Let Q_θ^0 be a quadruple distribution with parameter $1/2 \leq \theta \leq 2/3$ that spreads a unit mass uniformly over a support that consists of the following four line segments:

$$[(0, \theta, 1 - \theta, 0), (\theta, 1 - \theta, 0, 0)] \text{ mass } 2 - \frac{1}{\theta}$$
$$[(0, 1 - \theta, \theta, 0), (\theta, 0, 1 - \theta, 0)] \text{ mass } 2 - \frac{1}{\theta}$$
$$[(0, 0, 1 - \theta, \theta), (\theta, 1 - \theta, 0, 0)] \text{ mass } \frac{1}{\theta} - \frac{3}{2}$$
$$[(0, 1 - \theta, 0, \theta), (\theta, 0, 1 - \theta, 0)] \text{ mass } \frac{1}{\theta} - \frac{3}{2}$$

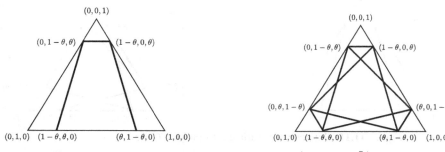

Figure 11.12. Supports of trivariate distributions T_θ^+ (left) and $\bar{T}_\theta^+$ (right).

The univariate marginal distributions of x_1, x_2, and x_3 are uniform on $[0, \theta]$, and the univariate marginal distribution of x_4 has an atom of mass $2(2 - 1/\theta)$ at value zero and the remaining mass uniformly spread over $[0, \theta)$. A distribution with identical univariate marginal distributions can be constructed as follows. Let $\bar{Q}_\theta^0$ be a quadruple distribution of a random variable defined as a random permutation of the values of a sample from the distribution Q_θ^0. The univariate marginal distributions of distribution Q_θ^0 are identical and are as follows:

$$\bar{Q}_\theta^0(x) = 1 - \frac{1}{2\theta} + \frac{1}{2\theta}\frac{x}{\theta}, \quad \text{for } x \in [0, \theta].$$

Quadruple that has a Marginal with a Mass at θ

Let Q_θ^+ be a quadruple distribution with parameter $2/5 \leq \theta \leq 1/2$ that spreads a unit mass uniformly over a support defined by the following four line segments:

$$[(0, \theta, 1 - 2\theta, \theta), (\theta, 1 - 2\theta, 0, \theta)] \text{ mass } \tfrac{1}{\theta} - 2$$
$$[(0, 1 - 2\theta, \theta, \theta), (\theta, 0, 1 - 2\theta, \theta)] \text{ mass } \tfrac{1}{\theta} - 2$$
$$[(0, \theta, 1 - 2\theta, \theta), (\theta, 1 - 2\theta, \theta, 0)] \text{ mass } \tfrac{5}{2} - \tfrac{1}{\theta}$$
$$[(0, 1 - 2\theta, \theta, \theta), (\theta, \theta, 1 - 2\theta, 0)] \text{ mass } \tfrac{5}{2} - \tfrac{1}{\theta}$$

The univariate marginal distributions of x_1, x_2, and x_3 are uniform on $[0, \theta]$, and the univariate marginal distribution of x_4 has an atom of mass $2(1/\theta - 2)$ at value θ and the remaining mass uniformly spread over $[0, \theta)$. A distribution with identical univariate marginal distributions can be constructed as follows. Let $\bar{Q}_\theta^+$ be the distribution of a random variable defined as a random permutation of the values of a sample from the distribution Q_θ^+. The univariate marginal distributions of distribution $\bar{Q}_\theta^+$ are identical and are as follows:

$$\bar{Q}_\theta^+(x) = \begin{cases} 0, & \text{if } x < \theta \\ \left(2 - \frac{1}{2\theta}\right)\frac{x}{\theta}, & \text{if } 0 \leq x < \theta \\ 1, & \text{if } x \geq \theta. \end{cases}$$

11.2.4 Gaussian Distribution

An n-variate Gaussian distribution is defined for a given mean vector $\mu \in \mathbf{R}^n$ and a positive-definite and symmetric *covariance matrix* $\Sigma \in \mathbf{R}^{n \times n}$ by the density function

$$f(\mathbf{x}; \mu, \Sigma) = \frac{1}{(2\pi)^{n/2}\sqrt{|\Sigma|}} \exp\left(-\frac{(\mathbf{x} - \mu)^T \Sigma^{-1}(\mathbf{x} - \mu)}{2}\right), \quad \text{for } \mathbf{x} \in \mathbf{R}^n, \quad (11.46)$$

where $|\Sigma|$ denotes the determinant of matrix Σ.

An alternative and equivalent definition is in terms of the *characteristic function* $\psi_\mathbf{X}(\mathbf{t}) = \mathbf{E}[e^{i\mathbf{t}^T\mathbf{X}}]$ for $\mathbf{t} \in \mathbf{R}^n$, which for a random vector according to a Gaussian distribution with mean vector μ and covariance matrix Σ has the following form

$$\psi_\mathbf{X}(\mathbf{t}) = \exp\left(i\mu^T\mathbf{t} - \frac{1}{2}\mathbf{t}^T\Sigma\mathbf{t}\right). \quad (11.47)$$

A special case is a univariate Gaussian distribution with mean μ and variance σ^2, often referred to as a *normal distribution*, which has the density of the form

$$f(x; \mu, \sigma^2) = \frac{1}{\sqrt{2\pi}\sigma} \exp\left(-\frac{(x-\mu)^2}{2\sigma^2}\right), \quad \text{for } x \in \mathbf{R}. \tag{11.48}$$

A normal distribution with mean zero and unit variance is referred to as *standard normal distribution*. We denote with $\Phi(x)$ the standard normal distribution and with $\phi(x)$ its density function.

In the remainder of this section, we present some facts about Gaussian distributions that are of interest in the context of approximate Bayesian inference.

The following fact can be established by showing that the characteristic function of random variable $\mathbf{y}$ corresponds to that of a Gaussian random variable with mean $\mathbf{A}\mu$ and covariance matrix $\mathbf{A}\Sigma\mathbf{A}^T$.

Fact 11.36 (linear transformation). Suppose that $\mathbf{x} \sim f(\cdot; \mu, \Sigma)$ and $\mathbf{y} = \mathbf{A}\mathbf{x} + \mathbf{b}$. Then,

$$\mathbf{y} \sim f\left(\mathbf{y}; \mathbf{A}\mu + \mathbf{b}, \mathbf{A}\Sigma\mathbf{A}^T\right).$$

The next fact follows by (11.48) and a straightforward calculus.

Fact 11.37 (product of two Gaussian densities). For every two Gaussian density functions with parameters (μ_1, σ_1^2) and (μ_2, σ_2^2), we have

$$f\left(x; \mu_1, \sigma_1^2\right) f\left(x; \mu_2, \sigma_2^2\right) = \kappa f(x; \mu, \sigma^2), \tag{11.49}$$

where $\kappa = f\left(\mu_1 - \mu_2; 0, \sigma_1^2 + \sigma_2^2\right)$, $\mu = (\mu_1\sigma_1^2 + \mu_2\sigma_2^2)/(\sigma_1^2 + \sigma_2^2)$, and $\sigma^2 = 1/(1/\sigma_1^2 + 1/\sigma_2^2)$.

The following fact derives from Fact 11.37 and a simple integration.

Fact 11.38. For every two Gaussian density functions with parameters (μ_1, σ_1^2) and (μ_2, σ_2^2), we have

$$\int_{\mathbf{R}} f(x; \mu_1, \sigma_1^2) f(x; \mu_2, \sigma_2^2) \, dx = f\left(\mu_1 - \mu_2; 0, \sigma_1^2 + \sigma_2^2\right) \tag{11.50}$$

and

$$\int_{\mathbf{R}} x f(x; \mu_1, \sigma_1^2) f(x; \mu_2, \sigma_2^2) \, dx = \frac{\frac{\mu_1}{\sigma_1^2} + \frac{\mu_2}{\sigma_2^2}}{\frac{1}{\sigma_1^2} + \frac{1}{\sigma_2^2}} f\left(\mu_1 - \mu_2; 0, \sigma_1^2 + \sigma_2^2\right). \tag{11.51}$$

The fact shown next is established in the rest of this section.

Fact 11.39. For two independent Gaussian random variables X_1 and X_2 with respective means μ_1 and μ_2 and variances σ_1^2 and σ_2^2, and $-\infty < a < b < \infty$, we have

$$E[X_1 \mid X_1 - X_2 \in (a, b)] = \mu_1 + \frac{\sigma_1^2}{\sqrt{\sigma_1^2 + \sigma_2^2}} g_{(a,b), \sqrt{\sigma_1^2 + \sigma_2^2}}(\mu_1 - \mu_2) \tag{11.52}$$

and

$$\text{Var}[X_1 \mid X_1 - X_2 \in (a, b)] = \sigma_1^2 \left(1 - \frac{\sigma_1^2}{\sigma_1^2 + \sigma_2^2} h_{(a,b), \sqrt{\sigma_1^2 + \sigma_2^2}}(\mu_1 - \mu_2) \right) \quad (11.53)$$

where

$$g_{(a,b),\sigma}(x) = \frac{\phi \left(\frac{x-a}{\sigma} \right) - \phi \left(\frac{x-b}{\sigma} \right)}{\Phi \left(\frac{x-a}{\sigma} \right) - \Phi \left(\frac{x-b}{\sigma} \right)}$$

$$h_{(a,b),\sigma}(x) = g_{(a,b),\sigma}(x)^2 + \frac{\frac{x-a}{\sigma} \phi \left(\frac{x-a}{\sigma} \right) - \frac{x-b}{\sigma} \phi \left(\frac{x-b}{\sigma} \right)}{\Phi \left(\frac{x-a}{\sigma} \right) - \Phi \left(\frac{x-b}{\sigma} \right)}.$$

We first show the identity in (11.52). By Bayes's formula, we have

$$\mathbf{E}[X_1 \mid X_1 - X_2 \in (a, b)] = \frac{\mathbf{E}[X_1 \mathbf{1}(X_1 - X_2 \in (a, b))]}{\text{Pr}[X_1 - X_2 \in (a, b)]}$$

$$= \mu_1 + \frac{\mathbf{E}[(X_1 - \mu_1)\mathbf{1}(X_1 - X_2 \in (a, b))]}{\text{Pr}[X_1 - X_2 \in (a, b)]}. \quad (11.54)$$

The difference $X_1 - X_2$ is a Gaussian random variable with mean $\mu := \mu_1 - \mu_2$ and variance $\sigma^2 := \sigma_1^2 + \sigma_2^2$. Hence, we have

$$\text{Pr}[X_1 - X_2 \in (a, b)] = \Phi \left(\frac{\mu - a}{\sigma} \right) - \Phi \left(\frac{\mu - b}{\sigma} \right). \quad (11.55)$$

Now, note that

$$\mathbf{E}[(X_1 - \mu_1)\mathbf{1}(X_1 - X_2 \in (a, b))]$$

$$= \sigma_1 \mathbf{E} \left[Y_1 \left(\Phi \left(\frac{\sigma_1 Y_1 + \mu - a}{\sigma_2} \right) - \Phi \left(\frac{\sigma_1 Y_1 + \mu - b}{\sigma_2} \right) \right) \right] \quad (11.56)$$

where Y_1 is a standard normal random variable. For $c, d \in \mathbf{R}$, we compute

$$\mathbf{E}[Y_1 \Phi(cY_1 + d)] = \int_{-\infty}^{\infty} \Phi(cy + d)y\phi(y)\, dy$$

$$= \int_{-\infty}^{\infty} \Phi(cy + d)(-\phi'(y))\, dy \quad (11.57)$$

$$= c \int_{-\infty}^{\infty} \phi(cy + d)\phi(y)\, dy \quad (11.58)$$

$$= \int_{-\infty}^{\infty} f(y; -d/c, 1/c^2) f(y; 0, 1)\, dy$$

$$= f(d/c; 0, 1/c^2 + 1) \quad (11.59)$$

$$= \frac{c}{\sqrt{c^2 + 1}} \phi \left(\frac{d}{\sqrt{c^2 + 1}} \right) \quad (11.60)$$

where (11.57) is by the fact $y\phi(y) = -\phi'(y)$ for all $y \in \mathbf{R}$, (11.58) is by partial integration, and (11.59) is by identity (11.50).

Using (11.60) in (11.56), we obtain

$$\mathbf{E}[(X_1 - \mu_1)\mathbf{1}(X_1 - X_2 \in (a, b))] = \frac{\sigma_1^2}{\sigma}\left(\phi\left(\frac{\mu - a}{\sigma}\right) - \phi\left(\frac{\mu - b}{\sigma}\right)\right). \quad (11.61)$$

The asserted identity in (11.52) follows from (11.63), (11.55), and (11.54).

We now show that identity (11.53) holds as well. Similarly, we use Bayes's formula to note that

$$\mathbf{E}[X_1^2 \mid X_1 - X_2 \in (a, b)] = \frac{\mathbf{E}[X_1^2 \mathbf{1}(X_1 - X_2 \in (a, b))]}{\mathbf{Pr}[X_1 - X_2 \in (a, b)]}$$

$$= \frac{\mathbf{E}[(X_1 - \mu_1)^2 \mathbf{1}(X_1 - X_2 \in (a, b))]}{\mathbf{Pr}[X_1 - X_2 \in (a, b)]}$$

$$+ 2\mu_1 \mathbf{E}[X_1 \mid X_1 - X_2 \in (a, b)] - \mu_1^2.$$

Since

$$\mathrm{Var}[X_1 \mid X_1 - X_2 \in (a, b)] = \mathbf{E}[X_1^2 \mid X_1 - X_2 \in (a, b)] - \mathbf{E}[X_1 \mid X_1 - X_2 \in (a, b)]^2$$

it follows that

$$\mathrm{Var}[X_1 \mid X_1 - X_2 \in (a, b)] = \frac{\mathbf{E}[(X_1 - \mu_1)^2 \mathbf{1}(X_1 - X_2 \in (a, b))]}{\mathbf{Pr}[X_1 - X_2 \in (a, b)]}$$

$$- (\mathbf{E}[X_1 \mid X_1 - X_2 \in (a, b)] - \mu_1)^2 \quad (11.62)$$

and

$$\mathbf{E}[(X_1 - \mu_1)^2 \mathbf{1}(X_1 - X_2 \in (a, b))]$$

$$= \sigma_1^2 \mathbf{E}\left[Y_1^2\left(\Phi\left(\frac{\sigma_1 Y_1 + \mu - a}{\sigma_2}\right) - \Phi\left(\frac{\sigma_1 Y_1 + \mu - b}{\sigma_2}\right)\right)\right] \quad (11.63)$$

where, again, Y_1 is a standard normal random variable. For $c, d \in \mathbf{R}$, we compute

$$\mathbf{E}[Y_1^2 \Phi(cY_1 + d)] = \int_{-\infty}^{\infty} y^2 \Phi(cy + d)\phi(y)\, dy$$

$$= \int_{-\infty}^{\infty} y \Phi(cy + d)(-\phi'(y))\, dy \quad (11.64)$$

$$= \int_{-\infty}^{\infty} \Phi(cy + d)\phi(y)\, dy + c\int_{-\infty}^{\infty} y\phi(cy + d)\phi(y)\, dy \quad (11.65)$$

$$= \mathbf{E}[\Phi(cY_1 + d)] + \int_{-\infty}^{\infty} yf(y; -d/c, 1/c^2)f(y; 0, 1)\, dy$$

$$= \mathbf{E}[\Phi(cY_1 + d)] - \frac{d}{c^2 + 1}f(-d/c; 0, 1/c^2 + 1) \quad (11.66)$$

$$= \mathbf{E}[\Phi(cY_1 + d)] - \frac{dc}{(c^2 + 1)^{3/2}}\phi\left(\frac{d}{\sqrt{c^2 + 1}}\right) \quad (11.67)$$

where equality (11.64) is by the fact $y\phi(y) = -\phi'(y)$ for all $y \in \mathbf{R}$, equality (11.65) follows by partial equation, and equality (11.66) follows by the identity (11.51).

Using (11.67) in (11.63), we obtain

$$\mathbf{E}[(X_1 - \mu_1)^2 \mathbf{1}(X_1 - X_2 \in (a, b))]$$

$$= \sigma_1^2 \mathbf{Pr}[X_1 - X_2 \in (a, b)] - \frac{\sigma_1^4}{\sigma^3} \left((\mu - a)\phi \left(\frac{\mu - a}{\sigma} \right) - (\mu - b)\phi \left(\frac{\mu - b}{\sigma} \right) \right).$$

Using the last equation and (11.55) in (11.63), we obtain the identity in (11.53).

11.2.5 Miscellaneous Inequalities

Theorem 11.40 (Jensen's inequality). *If f is a convex function on an interval $D(f)$ and X is a random variable with distribution concentrated on $D(f)$, then*

$$\mathbf{E}[f(X)] \geq f(\mathbf{E}[X]).$$

Proof. Let $(x_0, f(x_0))$ be a point on the graph of function f. Since f is convex on $D(f)$, there exists $a_{x_0} \in \mathbf{R}$ such that

$$f(x) \geq f(x_0) + a_{x_0}(x - x_0), \quad \text{for every } x \in D(f).$$

Choose $x_0 = \mathbf{E}[X]$, and then note that

$$\mathbf{E}[f(X)] \geq f(\mathbf{E}[X]) + a_{\mathbf{E}[X]}\mathbf{E}[(X - \mathbf{E}[X])] = f(\mathbf{E}[X]).$$

$\square$

Theorem 11.41 (Harris's inequality). *If X is a real-valued random variable and f and g are two increasing functions, we have*

$$\mathbf{E}[f(X)g(X)] \geq \mathbf{E}[f(X)]\mathbf{E}[g(X)].$$

Proof. Let Y be a random variable that is independent and that has the same distribution as random variable X. For every $x, y \in \mathbf{R}$, we have

$$(f(y) - f(x))(g(y) - g(x)) \geq 0.$$

Therefore, it follows that

$$\begin{aligned}
0 &\leq \mathbf{E}[(f(Y) - f(X))(g(Y) - g(X))] \\
&= \mathbf{E}[f(Y)g(Y)] - \mathbf{E}[f(X)g(Y)] - \mathbf{E}[f(Y)g(X)] + \mathbf{E}[f(X)g(X)] \\
&= \mathbf{E}[f(X)g(X)] - 2\mathbf{E}[f(X)]\mathbf{E}[g(X)] + \mathbf{E}[f(X)g(X)] \\
&= 2(\mathbf{E}[f(X)g(X)] - \mathbf{E}[f(X)]\mathbf{E}[g(X)]),
\end{aligned}$$

which establishes the asserted inequality.

$\square$

An immediate corollary of Theorem 11.41 is stated next.

Corollary 11.42. *If X is a real-valued random variable, f is an increasing function, and g is a decreasing function, then we have*

$$\mathbf{E}[f(X)g(X)] \leq \mathbf{E}[f(X)]\mathbf{E}[g(X)].$$

Theorem 11.43 (Markov's inequality). *If X is a non-negative random variable with a finite expected value, then*

$$\Pr[X > x] \leq \frac{\mathbf{E}[X]}{x}, \quad \text{for } x \geq 0.$$

Proof. The proof follows from the following sequence of relations:

$$\Pr[X > x] = \mathbf{E}[\mathbf{1}(X > x)] \leq \mathbf{E}\left[\frac{X}{x}\mathbf{1}(X > x)\right] \leq \mathbf{E}\left[\frac{X}{x}\right] = \frac{\mathbf{E}[X]}{x}.$$

$\square$

Theorem 11.44 (Chernoff's inequality). *If X is a random variable, then for every $\theta > 0$,*

$$\Pr[X > x] \leq e^{-\theta x}\mathbf{E}\left[e^{\theta X}\right], \quad \text{for } x \in \mathbf{R}.$$

Proof. By Markov's inequality in Theorem 11.43, for every $\theta > 0$, we have

$$\Pr[X > x] = \Pr\left[e^{\theta X} > e^{\theta x}\right] \leq \frac{\mathbf{E}\left[e^{\theta X}\right]}{e^{\theta x}} = e^{-\theta x}\mathbf{E}\left[e^{\theta X}\right], \quad \text{for } x \in \mathbf{R}.$$

$\square$

Theorem 11.45 (Hoeffding's inequality). *If $X_1, X_2, \ldots, X_n$ are independent real-valued random variables such that $\mathbf{E}[\sum_{i=1}^{n} X_i] = \mu n$ and $\Pr[a_i \leq X_i \leq b_i] = 1$ for $i = 1, 2, \ldots, n$, then for every $x > 0$,*

$$\Pr\left[\sum_{i=1}^{n} X_i - \mu n \geq xn\right] \leq e^{-2\frac{n^2 x^2}{\sum_{i=1}^{n}(b_i - a_i)^2}}.$$

Proof. We first state and prove the following lemma.

Lemma 11.46. *Suppose that X is a random variable such that $\Pr[a \leq X \leq b] = 1$ for $-\infty < a < b < \infty$. For every $\theta \in \mathbf{R}$, $\mathbf{E}[e^{\theta X}]$ is maximized by a distribution that puts a mass of weight $(b - \mathbf{E}[X])/(b - a)$ on a, and the remaining mass on b, and thus, it holds that*

$$\mathbf{E}[e^{\theta X}] \leq \frac{b - \mathbf{E}[X]}{b - a}e^{\theta a} + \frac{\mathbf{E}[X] - a}{b - a}e^{\theta b}, \quad \text{for } \theta \in \mathbf{R}.$$

Proof. For every given $\theta \in \mathbf{R}$, the function $f_\theta(x) = e^{\theta x}$ is convex. Hence, it is upper bounded on the interval $[a, b]$ by the chord connecting the points $(a, f_\theta(a))$ and $(b, f_\theta(b))$, i.e.,

$$e^{\theta x} \leq \frac{b - x}{b - a}e^{\theta a} + \frac{x - a}{b - a}e^{\theta b}, \quad \text{for } x \in [a, b].$$

It follows that

$$\mathbf{E}[e^{\theta X}] \leq \mathbf{E}\left[\frac{b - X}{b - a}e^{\theta a} + \frac{X - a}{b - a}e^{\theta b}\right] = \frac{b - \mathbf{E}[X]}{b - a}e^{\theta a} + \frac{\mathbf{E}[X] - a}{b - a}e^{\theta b}.$$

$\square$

Let $\mu_i = \mathbf{E}[X_i]$ for $i = 1, 2, \ldots, n$. By Chernoff's inequality in Theorem 11.44, the independence of the random variables $X_1, X_2, \ldots, X_n$, and Lemma 11.46, we have

$$\mathbf{Pr}\left[\sum_{i=1}^{n} X_i - \mu n \geq xn\right] \leq e^{-\theta xn}\mathbf{E}[e^{\theta \sum_{i=1}^{n}(X_i - \mu_i)}]$$

$$= e^{-\theta xn}\prod_{i=1}^{n}\mathbf{E}[e^{\theta(X_i - \mu_i)}]$$

$$= e^{-\theta xn}\prod_{i=1}^{n}\left(\frac{b_i - \mu_i}{b_i - a_i}e^{\theta a_i} + \frac{\mu_i - a_i}{b_i - a_i}e^{\theta b_i}\right)$$

$$= e^{-\theta xn}e^{\sum_{i=1}^{n} f_i(\theta_i)} \tag{11.68}$$

where

$$f_i(\theta_i) = -\theta_i p_i + \log\left(1 - p_i + p_i e^{\theta_i}\right), \theta_i = \theta(b_i - a_i), \text{ and } p_i = \frac{\mu_i - a_i}{b_i - a_i}.$$

Note that

$$f_i'(\theta_i) = -p_i + \frac{p_i}{p_i + (1 - p_i)e^{-\theta_i}}$$

and

$$f_i''(\theta_i) = \frac{p_i}{p_i + (1 - p_i)e^{-\theta_i}}\left(1 - \frac{p_i}{p_i + (1 - p_i)e^{-\theta_i}}\right).$$

We observe that $f_i''(\theta_i) \leq 1/4$. By a limited Taylor's series development, we have that

$$f_i(\theta_i) \leq f_i(0) + f_i'(0)\theta_i + \frac{1}{8}\theta_i^2 = \frac{1}{8}\theta_i^2 = \frac{1}{8}\theta^2(b_i - a_i)^2.$$

Combining this with (11.68), we have

$$\mathbf{Pr}\left[\sum_{i=1}^{n} X_i - \mu n \geq xn\right] \leq e^{-\theta xn + \frac{1}{8}\theta^2 \sum_{i=1}^{n}(b_i - a_i)^2}.$$

The right-hand side of the last inequality is minimum at value

$$\theta^* = \frac{4xn}{\sum_{i=1}^{n}(b_i - a_i)^2}$$

which yields the inequality asserted in the theorem. $\square$

Theorem 11.47 (Bennett's inequality). *Suppose that $X_1, X_2, \ldots, X_n$ is a sequence of independent real-valued random variables such that $\mathbf{E}[X_i] = 0$, $\mathbf{Pr}[X_i \leq b] = 1$ for $i = 1, 2, \ldots, n$, and $\sum_{i=1}^{n} \mathrm{Var}[X_i] = \sigma^2 n$. Then,*

$$\mathbf{Pr}\left[\sum_{i=1}^{n} X_i \geq xn\right] \leq e^{-n\frac{\sigma^2}{b^2}g\left(\frac{bx}{\sigma^2}\right)}, \quad \text{for every } x \geq 0$$

where $g(x) = (x + 1)\log(x + 1) - x$.

Proof. We first state and prove the following lemma.

Lemma 11.48. *Suppose that X is a random variable such that $\mathbf{E}[X] = 0$, $\mathbf{E}[X^2] = \sigma^2$, and $\mathbf{Pr}[X \le b] = 1$. Then, for every $\theta > 0$, $\mathbf{E}[e^{\theta X}]$ is maximized by a distribution that puts a mass of weight $b^2/(b^2 + \sigma^2)$ on $-\sigma^2/b$ and the remaining mass on b, and hence, we have that*

$$\mathbf{E}\left[e^{\theta X}\right] \le \frac{b^2}{b^2 + \sigma^2} e^{-\frac{\sigma^2}{b}\theta} + \frac{\sigma^2}{b^2 + \sigma^2} e^{b\theta}.$$

Proof. Fix an arbitrary $\theta > 0$. Let $f(x)$ be the unique parabola such that $h(x) = f(x) - e^{\theta x}$, for $x \in \mathbf{R}$, satisfies

$$h(b) = 0 \text{ and } h(-\sigma^2/b) = h'(-\sigma^2/b) = 0.$$

Then, we will establish that

$$e^{\theta x} \le f(x), \quad \text{for every } x \le b \tag{11.69}$$

where the equality holds for $x = -\sigma^2/b$ and $x = b$. From this it follows that

$$\mathbf{E}[e^{\theta X}] \le \mathbf{E}[f(X)]$$

where the equality is achieved by the distribution asserted in the lemma because it concentrates all its mass on $x \in \{-\sigma^2/b, b\}$, and for each such x, $e^{\theta x} = f(x)$.

We now establish the inequality in (11.69). Since $f''(x)$ is constant and $e^{\theta x}$ is strictly convex, it follows that there exists a unique value x_0 such that $h''(x_0) = 0$. Since $h(-\sigma^2/b) = 0$ and $h(b) = 0$, it must be that $h'(x_1) = 0$ for some $x_1 \in (-\sigma^2/b, b)$. Given that $h'(-\sigma^2/b) = 0$ and $h'(x_1) = 0$, it must be that $x_0 \in (-\sigma^2/b, x_1)$. Now, note that function h is convex on $(-\infty, x_0]$ becase for every $x \in (-\infty, x_0]$, $h''(x) = f''(x) - e^{\theta x} = h''(x) = f''(x_0) - e^{\theta x} \ge f''(x_0) - e^{\theta x_0} = h''(x_0) = 0$. Thus, function h achieves its minimum on the interval at the point $-\sigma^2/b$ and $h(-\sigma^2/b) = 0$. Function h is concave on $[x_0, \infty)$ because $h''(x) = f''(x) - e^{\theta x} = f''(x_0) - e^{\theta x} \le f''(x_0) - e^{\theta x_0} = h''(x_0) = 0$. Thus, function h achieves maximum value on $[x_0, \infty)$ at the point x_1. Since $h(b) = 0$, it follows that $h(x) \ge 0$ for every $x \le b$. $\square$

Let $\text{Var}[X_i] = \sigma_i^2$ for $i = 1, 2, \ldots, n$. We have the following relations:

$$\mathbf{Pr}\left[\sum_{i=1}^{n} X_i \ge xn\right] \le e^{-\theta xn} \prod_{i=1}^{n} \mathbf{E}\left[e^{\theta X_i}\right]$$

$$\le e^{-\theta xn} \prod_{i=1}^{n} \left(\frac{b^2}{b^2 + \sigma_i^2} e^{-\frac{\sigma_i^2}{b}\theta} + \frac{\sigma_i^2}{b^2 + \sigma_i^2} e^{b\theta}\right)$$

$$= e^{-\theta xn + \sum_{i=1}^{n} f(\sigma_i^2/b^2)} \tag{11.70}$$

where

$$f(x) = \log\left(\frac{1}{x+1} e^{-b\theta x} + \frac{x}{x+1} e^{b\theta}\right).$$

Function f is a concave function. Hence, by Jensen's inequality,

$$\frac{1}{n} \sum_{i=1}^{n} f(\sigma_i^2/b^2) \le f\left(\frac{1}{n} \sum_{i=1}^{n} \frac{\sigma_i^2}{b^2}\right) = f\left(\frac{\sigma^2}{b^2}\right) = \log\left(\frac{b^2}{b^2 + \sigma^2} e^{-\frac{\sigma^2}{b^2}\theta} + \frac{\sigma^2}{b^2 + \sigma^2} e^{b\theta}\right)$$

Combining this with (11.70), we obtain

$$\mathbf{Pr}\left[\sum_{i=1}^{n} X_i - \mu n \geq xn\right] \leq \left(\frac{b^2}{b^2+\sigma^2}e^{-\left(x+\frac{\sigma^2}{b}\right)\theta} + \frac{\sigma^2}{b^2+\sigma^2}e^{(b-x)\theta}\right)^n.$$

The right-hand side of the last inequality attains its minimum at

$$\theta^* = \frac{b}{b^2+\sigma^2}\log\left(\frac{1+\frac{xb}{\sigma^2}}{1-\frac{x}{b}}\right)$$

which yields the inequality asserted in the theorem. □

Theorem 11.49 (Bernstein's inequality). *Suppose that $X_1, X_2, \ldots, X_n$ is a sequence of independent real-valued random variables such that $\mathbf{E}[X_i] = 0$, $\mathbf{Pr}[-b \leq X_i \leq b] = 1$ for $i = 1, 2, \ldots, n$, and $\sum_{i=1}^{n} \text{Var}[X_i] = \sigma^2 n$. Then,*

$$\mathbf{Pr}\left[\sum_{i=1}^{n} X_i \geq xn\right] \leq e^{-n\frac{x^2}{2(\sigma^2+\frac{1}{3}bx)}}, \quad \text{for } 0 < x < b.$$

Proof. Note that

$$n\frac{x^2}{2\left(\sigma^2 + \frac{1}{3}bx\right)} = \frac{n\sigma^2}{b^2}\frac{\left(\frac{xb}{\sigma^2}\right)^2}{2\left(1 + \frac{1}{3}\frac{bx}{\sigma^2}\right)}.$$

Combining this with Theorem 11.47, the proof follows by the fact that

$$(x+1)\log(x+1) - x \geq \frac{x^2}{2\left(1+\frac{1}{3}x\right)}, \quad \text{for every } x \geq 0.$$

□

11.3 Some Special Types of Games

In this section we consider three special types of normal form games: concave, potential, and smooth games.

11.3.1 Concave Games

Definition 11.50 (concave game). A normal form game $G = (N, \{\mathcal{B}_i, i \in N\}, \{s_i, i \in N\})$ is a *concave game* if for every player $i \in N$,

    C1 The set of strategies $\mathcal{B}_i$ is a subset of Euclidean space $\mathbf{R}^{m_i}$ such that $\mathcal{B} = \times_{j \in N}\mathcal{B}_j$ is a convex and compact set.

    C2 The payoff function $s_i : \mathcal{B} \to \mathbf{R}$ is continuous and is concave in $\mathbf{b}_i$ for every $\mathbf{b}_{-i}$ such that $(\mathbf{b}_i, \mathbf{b}_{-i}) \in \mathcal{B}$.

According to Definition 1.3, a point $\mathbf{b} \in \mathcal{B}$ is a pure-strategy Nash equilibrium if, and only if,

$$s_i(\mathbf{b}) \geq s_i(\mathbf{b}_i', \mathbf{b}_{-i}), \quad \text{for all } \mathbf{b}_i' \in \mathcal{B}_i, \quad \text{for every } i \in N. \qquad (11.71)$$

The following theorem establishes the existence of a pure-strategy Nash equilibrium for concave games.

Theorem 11.51 (Rosen's theorem). *Every concave game has a pure-strategy Nash equilibrium.*

Proof. Let us define

$$s(\mathbf{b'}, \mathbf{b}) = \sum_{i=1}^{n} s_i(\mathbf{b'}_i, \mathbf{b}_{-i}), \quad \text{for } (\mathbf{b'}, \mathbf{b}) \in \mathcal{B} \times \mathcal{B}.$$

Consider the correspondence $f : \mathcal{B} \to \mathcal{B}$ defined as

$$f(\mathbf{x}) = \{\mathbf{x'} \in \mathcal{B} \mid s(\mathbf{x'}, \mathbf{x}) \geq s(\mathbf{y}, \mathbf{x}) \text{ for all } \mathbf{y} \in \mathcal{B}\}, \quad \text{for } \mathbf{x} \in \mathcal{B}.$$

By condition (C2), $s(\mathbf{x'}, \mathbf{x})$ is a continuous and concave function in $\mathbf{x'}$ for every fixed $\mathbf{x} \in \mathcal{B}$. Combined with condition (C1), it follows that f is an upper semi-continuous correspondence that maps every point of the convex, compact set $\mathcal{B}$ into a closed convex subset of $\mathcal{B}$. By the Kakutani fixed-point theorem, Theorem 11.23, there exists a point $\mathbf{b} \in \mathcal{B}$ such that $\mathbf{b} \in f(\mathbf{b})$, i.e., $\sum_{i=1}^{n} s_i(\mathbf{b}) \geq \sum_{i=1}^{n} s_i(\mathbf{b'}_i, \mathbf{b}_{-i})$ for every $\mathbf{b'} \in \mathcal{B}$. This implies the necessary and sufficient condition (11.71) for $\mathbf{b}$ to be a pure-strategy Nash equilibrium. $\square$

Socially Concave Games

Definition 11.52 (socially concave game). A normal form game $G = (N, \{\mathcal{B}_i, \ i \in N\}, \{s_i, \ i \in N\})$ is *socially concave* if it satisfies the following two conditions:

SC1 There exists $(\lambda_1, \lambda_2, \ldots, \lambda_n) \in \mathbf{R}_+^n$ such that $\sum_{i=1}^{n} \lambda_i = 1$ and $s(\mathbf{b}, \lambda) = \sum_{i=1}^{n} \lambda_i s_i(\mathbf{b})$ is a concave function in $\mathbf{b}$.
SC2 For every player $i \in N$ and $\mathbf{b}_i \in \mathcal{B}_i$, $s_i(\mathbf{b}_i, \mathbf{b}_{-i})$ is convex in $\mathbf{b}_{-i}$.

Corollary 11.53. *Every socially concave game with twice differentiable payoff functions is a concave game, and thus it has a pure-strategy Nash equilibrium.*

Proof. Condition (SC1) means that the Hessian matrix of function $s(\mathbf{b}, \lambda)$ with respect to $\mathbf{b}$ is negative semi-definite, i.e.,

$$\sum_{i \in N} \sum_{l_i=1}^{m_i} \sum_{j \in N} \sum_{l_j=1}^{m_j} x_{i,l_i} \left(\frac{\partial^2}{\partial b_{i,l_i} \partial b_{j,l_j}} s(\mathbf{b}, \lambda) \right) x_{j,l_j} \leq 0 \text{ for every } \mathbf{x} \neq 0.$$

It follows that for every player $i \in N$ and $(x_{i,k}, k = 1, 2, \ldots, m_i) \neq 0$,

$$\sum_{k=1}^{m_i} \sum_{l=1}^{m_i} x_{i,k} \frac{\partial^2}{\partial b_{i,k} \partial b_{i,l}} s(\mathbf{b}, \lambda) x_{i,l} \leq 0. \tag{11.72}$$

From condition (SC2), for every player $i \in N$ and $(x_{i,k}, k = 1, 2, \ldots, m_i) \neq 0$,

$$\sum_{k=1}^{m_i} \sum_{l=1}^{m_i} x_{i,k} \frac{\partial^2}{\partial b_{i,k} \partial b_{i,l}} \sum_{j \neq i} \lambda_j s_j(\mathbf{b}) x_{i,l} \geq 0. \tag{11.73}$$

From (11.72) and (11.73), it follows that

$$\sum_{k=1}^{m_i} \sum_{l=1}^{m_i} x_{i,k} \frac{\partial^2}{\partial b_{i,k} \partial b_{i,l}} s_i(\mathbf{b}) x_{i,l} \leq 0,$$

which shows that $s_i(\mathbf{b})$ is concave in $\mathbf{b}_i$. $\square$

Example 11.54 (generalized-logit contest success function). Consider a normal form game with the set of two or more players $N = \{1, 2, \ldots, n\}$ such that for $\epsilon > 0$, every player $i \in N$ has the strategy set $\mathcal{B}_i = [\epsilon, \infty)$ and the payoff function given by

$$s_i(\mathbf{b}) = v_i \frac{f_i(b_i)}{\sum_{j \in N} f_j(b_j)} - b_i$$

where $v_1 \geq v_2 \geq \cdots \geq v_n > 0$ and $f_i : \mathbf{R}_+ \to \mathbf{R}_+$ is an increasing, concave function such that $f_i(0) = 0$. This game is studied in Chapter 4. We can show that this game is socially concave as follows.

Condition (SC1) is shown to hold for $(\lambda_1, \lambda_2, \ldots, \lambda_n)$ such that $\lambda_i = (\sum_{j \in N} v_j)/v_i$, for $i \in N$:

$$s(\mathbf{b}, \lambda) = \sum_{i \in N} \lambda_i s_i(\mathbf{b})$$

$$= \sum_{i \in N} \frac{\sum_{j \in N} v_j}{v_i} \left(v_i \frac{f_i(b_i)}{\sum_{j \in N} f_j(b_j)} - b_i \right)$$

$$= \left(\sum_{j \in N} v_j \right) \left(1 - \sum_{i \in N} \frac{b_i}{v_i} \right)$$

which shows that $s(\mathbf{b}, \lambda)$ is a linear and hence a concave function in $\mathbf{b}$.

Condition (SC2) is shown to hold as follows. Fix an arbitrary player $i \in N$ and an arbitrary strategy $\mathbf{b}_i \in \mathcal{B}_i$. Saying that $s_i(\mathbf{b})$ is convex in $\mathbf{b}_{-i}$ is equivalent to saying that for every constant $c \geq 0$, $1/(c + \sum_{j \neq i} f_j(b_j))$ is convex in $\mathbf{b}_{-i}$. Function $x \to 1/(c + x)$ is decreasing and convex, and function $\sum_{j \neq i} f_j(b_j)$ is concave in $\mathbf{b}_{-i}$, from which it follows that $1/(c + \sum_{j \neq i} f_j(b_j))$ is convex in $\mathbf{b}_{-i}$.

Sufficient Conditions for Uniqueness

The conditions in Theorem 11.51 or those in Corollary 11.53 guarantee the existence of a pure-strategy Nash equilibrium, but do not imply uniqueness of a pure-strategy Nash equilibrium. In this section, we provide two sufficient conditions for uniqueness of a pure-strategy Nash equilibrium.

Diagonally Strictly Concave Games Assume that the set of strategies $\mathcal{B}$ is convex and defined as follows: given a collection of convex functions $h_j : \mathbf{R}^m \to \mathbf{R}$, for $j = 1, 2, \ldots, k$,

$$\mathcal{B} = \{\mathbf{x} \in \mathbf{R}^m \mid h_j(\mathbf{x}) \leq 0, \quad \text{for all } j = 1, 2, \ldots, k\}. \tag{11.74}$$

The KKT conditions in (11.12)-(11.16) for the optimization problem given by (11.71) with the set $\mathcal{B}$ given by (11.74) can be written as follows:

$$h_j(\mathbf{b}) \leq 0, \quad \text{for } j = 1, 2, \ldots, k \tag{11.75}$$

$$\sum_{j=1}^{k} \mu_{i,j} h_j(\mathbf{b}) = 0, \quad \text{for } i \in N \tag{11.76}$$

$$s_i(\mathbf{b}) \geq s_i(\mathbf{b}'_i, \mathbf{b}_{-i}) - \sum_{j=1}^{k} \mu_{i,j} h_j(\mathbf{b}'_i, \mathbf{b}_{-i}),$$

$$\text{for } i \in N \text{ for some } (\mu_{i,1}, \mu_{i,2}, \ldots, \mu_{i,k}) \in \mathbf{R}_+^k. \tag{11.77}$$

Since the payoff functions $s_1, s_2, \ldots, s_n$ are concave and differentiable and functions $h_1, h_2, \ldots, h_k$ are convex and differentiable, the condition in (11.77) is equivalent to

$$\nabla_i s_i(\mathbf{b}) - \sum_{j=1}^{k} \mu_{i,j} \nabla_i h_j(\mathbf{b}) = 0.$$

A weighted non-negative sum of the payoff functions is defined for every given $(\lambda_1, \lambda_2, \ldots, \lambda_n) \in \mathbf{R}_+^n$ as follows:

$$s(\mathbf{b}, \lambda) = \sum_{i=1}^{n} \lambda_i s_i(\mathbf{b}).$$

For every given $\lambda \in \mathbf{R}_+^n$, function $s(\mathbf{b}, \lambda)$ is said to be *diagonally strictly concave* in $\mathbf{b} \in \mathcal{B}$ if the following condition holds:

$$\sum_{i=1}^{n} \lambda_i (\mathbf{y}_i - \mathbf{x}_i)^T (\nabla_i s_i(\mathbf{y}) - \nabla_i s_i(\mathbf{x})) < 0, \quad \text{for every } \mathbf{x}, \mathbf{y} \in \mathcal{B}.$$

The following theorem identifies a set of sufficient conditions for the existence of a unique pure-strategy Nash equilibrium.

Theorem 11.55. *Suppose that an n-player concave game is such that $s(\mathbf{b}, \lambda)$ is diagonally strictly concave for some $\lambda \in \mathbf{R}_+^n$; then there exists a unique pure-strategy Nash equilibrium.*

Proof. A point $\mathbf{b}$ is a normalized pure-strategy Nash equilibrium if there exists $(\mu_1, \mu_2, \ldots, \mu_k) \in \mathbf{R}_+^k$ and $(\lambda_1, \lambda_2, \ldots, \lambda_n) \in \mathbf{R}_+^n$ such that conditions (11.75), (11.76), and (11.77) hold with $\mu_{i,j} = \mu_j/\lambda_j$, for all $j = 1, 2, \ldots, k$ and $i = 1, 2, \ldots, n$.

Claim 1: For every $\lambda \in \mathbf{R}_+^n$, there exists a normalized pure-strategy Nash equilibrium point. Let

$$s(\mathbf{y}, \mathbf{x}, \lambda) = \sum_{i=1}^{n} \lambda_i s_i(\mathbf{y}, \mathbf{x}_{-i}).$$

By the Kakutani's fixed-point theorem (Theorem 11.23), there exists $\mathbf{b} \in \mathcal{B}$ such that

$$s(\mathbf{b}, \mathbf{b}, \lambda) \geq s(\mathbf{b}', \mathbf{b}, \lambda), \quad \text{for all } \mathbf{b}' \in \mathcal{B}.$$

By the necessity of the KKT conditions, we have

$$h_j(\mathbf{b}) \leq 0 \text{ for all } j = 1, 2, \ldots, k \tag{11.78}$$

$$\sum_{j=1}^{k} \mu_j h_j(\mathbf{b}) = 0, \quad \text{for some } (\mu_1, \mu_2, \ldots, \mu_k) \in \mathbf{R}_+^k \tag{11.79}$$

$$\lambda_i \nabla_i s_i(\mathbf{b}) - \sum_{j=1}^{k} \mu_j \nabla_i h_j(\mathbf{b}) = 0, \quad \text{for all } i = 1, 2, \ldots, n. \tag{11.80}$$

The last three conditions correspond to conditions (11.77), (11.76), and (11.75) with $\mu_{i,j} = \mu_j/\lambda_i$, which are sufficient to ensure that $\mathbf{b}$ satisfies (11.71). Therefore, $\mathbf{b}$ is a normalized pure-strategy Nash equilibrium for a given vector λ.

Claim 2: Uniqueness. Assume that for some $\lambda \in \mathbf{R}_+^n$, there exist two normalized pure-strategy Nash equilibrium points $\mathbf{b}^1$ and $\mathbf{b}^2$. Then, we have for $l = 1$ and 2,

$$h_j(\mathbf{b}^l) \leq 0 \text{ for all } j = 1, 2, \ldots, k \tag{11.81}$$

$$\sum_{j=1}^{k} \mu_j^l h(\mathbf{b}^l) = 0 \tag{11.82}$$

$$\lambda_i \nabla_i s_i(\mathbf{b}^l) - \sum_{j=1}^{k} \mu_j^l \nabla_i h_j(\mathbf{b}^l) = 0, \quad \text{for all } i = 1, 2, \ldots, n. \tag{11.83}$$

Multiplying (11.83) by $(\mathbf{b}_i^2 - \mathbf{b}_i^1)^T$ for $l = 1$ and $(\mathbf{b}_i^1 - \mathbf{b}_i^2)^T$ for $l = 2$, we obtain

$$x + y = 0$$

where

$$x = \sum_{i=1}^{n} (\mathbf{b}^2 - \mathbf{b}^1)^T (\lambda_i \nabla_i s_i(\mathbf{b}^1) - \lambda_i \nabla_i s_i(\mathbf{b}^2))$$

and

$$y = \sum_{j=1}^{k} \sum_{i=1}^{n} \mu_j^1 (\mathbf{b}_i^2 - \mathbf{b}_i^1) \nabla_i h_j(\mathbf{b}^1) + \mu_j^2 (\mathbf{b}_i^1 - \mathbf{b}_i^2) \nabla_i h_j(\mathbf{b}^2)$$

$$\geq \sum_{j=1}^{k} \mu_j^1 (h_j(\mathbf{b}^2) - h_j(\mathbf{b}^1)) + \mu_j^2 (h(\mathbf{b}^1) - h(\mathbf{b}^2))$$

$$= \sum_{j=1}^{k} \mu_j^1 h_j(\mathbf{b}^2) + \mu_j^2 h_j(\mathbf{b}^1) \geq 0.$$

Since $s(\mathbf{b}, \lambda)$ is diagonally strictly concave, we have $x > 0$, which contradicts $x + y = 0$ and thus proves the theorem. $\qquad\square$

A Sufficient Condition for Diagonally Strict Concavity Let $J(\mathbf{b}, \lambda)$ be the Jacobian matrix of $g(\mathbf{b}, \lambda) = (\lambda_1 \nabla_1 s_1(\mathbf{b}), \ldots, \lambda_n \nabla_n s_n(\mathbf{b}))$ with respect to $\mathbf{b}$.

Corollary 11.56. *Suppose that for some $\lambda \in \mathbf{R}_+^n$, the symmetric matrix $J(\mathbf{b}, \lambda) + J^T(\mathbf{b}, \lambda)$ is negative definite for $\mathbf{b} \in \mathcal{B}$. Then, $s(\mathbf{b}, \lambda)$ is diagonally strictly concave for $\mathbf{b} \in \mathcal{B}$, and hence the n-player concave game has a unique pure-strategy Nash equilibrium.*

Proof. Let $\mathbf{b}^1$ and $\mathbf{b}^2$ be any two distinct points in $\mathcal{B}$, and let $\mathbf{b}(\theta) = (1 - \theta)\mathbf{b}^1 + \theta\mathbf{b}^2$ for $0 \le \theta \le 1$. Since $J(\mathbf{b}, \lambda)$ is the Jacobian matrix of $(\lambda_1 \nabla_1 s_1(\mathbf{b}), \ldots, \lambda_n \nabla_n s_n(\mathbf{b}))$ we have

$$\frac{d}{d\theta}g(\mathbf{b}(\theta), \lambda) = J(\mathbf{b}(\theta), \lambda)\frac{d\mathbf{b}(\theta)}{d\theta} = J(\mathbf{b}(\theta), \lambda)(\mathbf{b}^2 - \mathbf{b}^1).$$

Equivalently, we can write

$$g(\mathbf{b}^2, \lambda) - g(\mathbf{b}^1, \lambda) = \int_0^1 J(\mathbf{b}(\theta), \lambda)(\mathbf{b}^2 - \mathbf{b}^1)d\theta.$$

By multiplying both sides in the last equation by $(\mathbf{b}^1 - \mathbf{b}^2)^T$, we obtain

$$(\mathbf{b}^1 - \mathbf{b}^2)^T g(\mathbf{b}^2, \lambda) + (\mathbf{b}^2 - \mathbf{b}^1)^T g(\mathbf{b}^1, \lambda)$$

$$= -\int_0^1 (\mathbf{b}^2 - \mathbf{b}^1)^T J(\mathbf{b}(\theta), \lambda)(\mathbf{b}^2 - \mathbf{b}^1)d\theta$$

$$= -\frac{1}{2}\int_0^1 (\mathbf{b}^2 - \mathbf{b}^1)^T (J(\mathbf{b}(\theta), \lambda) + J(\mathbf{b}(\theta), \lambda)^T)(\mathbf{b}^2 - \mathbf{b}^1)d\theta$$

$$> 0,$$

which shows that $s(\mathbf{b}, \lambda)$ is diagonally strictly concave. $\qquad\square$

Another Set of Sufficient Conditions Based on Social Concavity A different set of sufficient conditions for the existence of a unique pure-strategy Nash equilibrium can be obtained for socially concave games as shown in the following corollary.

Corollary 11.57. *Assume that a normal form game is socially concave. If either in condition (SC1) $s(\mathbf{b}, \lambda)$ is strictly concave or in condition (SC2) $s_i(\mathbf{b})$ is strictly convex in $\mathbf{b}_{-i}$ for all $i \in N$, then $s(\mathbf{b}, \lambda)$ is diagonally strictly concave for $\mathbf{b} \in \mathcal{B}$ and thus the game has a unique pure-strategy Nash equilibrium.*

Proof. Assume that in (SC1) $s(\mathbf{b}, \lambda)$ is strictly concave. Then, for every $\mathbf{x}, \mathbf{y} \in \mathcal{B}$, we have

$$\sum_{i=1}^n \sum_{l=1}^{m_i}(y_{i,l} - x_{i,l})\frac{\partial}{\partial x_{i,l}}s(\mathbf{x}, \lambda) + (x_{i,l} - y_{i,l})\frac{\partial}{\partial y_{i,l}}s(\mathbf{y}, \lambda) > 0. \qquad (11.84)$$

Since $s(\mathbf{b}, \lambda) = \sum_{i=1}^{n} \lambda_i s_i(\mathbf{b})$ and by (SC2),

$$\sum_{i=1}^{n} \sum_{l=1}^{m_i} (y_{i,l} - x_{i,l}) \frac{\partial}{\partial x_{i,l}} \left(\sum_{j \neq i} \lambda_j s_j(\mathbf{x}) \right) + (x_{i,l} - y_{i,l}) \frac{\partial}{\partial y_{i,l}} \left(\sum_{j \neq i} \lambda_j s_j(\mathbf{y}) \right) \leq 0,$$

(11.85)

we have that

$$\sum_{i=1}^{n} \lambda_i \sum_{l=1}^{m_i} (y_{i,l} - x_{i,l}) \frac{\partial}{\partial x_{i,l}} s_i(\mathbf{x}) + (x_{i,l} - y_{i,l}) \frac{\partial}{\partial y_{i,l}} s_i(\mathbf{y}) > 0, \qquad (11.86)$$

which shows that $s(\mathbf{b}, \lambda)$ is diagonally strictly concave.

Assume now that (SC2) holds such that $s_i(\mathbf{b})$ is strictly convex in $\mathbf{b}_{-i}$ for all $i \in N$. Then, (11.85) holds with strict inequality. Since by (SC1), (11.84) holds with weak inequality, it follows that (11.86) must hold, and thus $s(\mathbf{b}, \lambda)$ is diagonally strictly concave. □

11.3.2 Potential Games

Consider a normal form game $G = (N, \{\mathcal{B}_i, \ i \in N\}, \{s_i, \ i \in N\})$. A function $\Phi : \mathcal{B} \to \mathbf{R}$ is an *ordinal potential function for* G if for every $i \in N$ and $\mathbf{b}_{-i} \in \mathcal{B}_{-i}$,

$$s_i(x, \mathbf{b}_{-i}) - s_i(y, \mathbf{b}_{-i}) > 0 \text{ if, and only if, } \Phi(x, \mathbf{b}_{-i}) - \Phi(y, \mathbf{b}_{-i}) > 0,$$

$$\text{for every } x, y \in \mathcal{B}_i.$$

Definition 11.58. A normal form game G is called an *ordinal potential game* if there exists an ordinal potential function for G.

Let $\mathbf{w} = (w_1, w_2, \ldots, w_n)$ be a vector of positive real numbers, which are referred to as weights. A function $\Phi : \mathcal{B} \to \mathbf{R}$ is a $\mathbf{w}$-*potential function for* G if for every $i \in N$ and for every $\mathbf{b}_{-i} \in \mathcal{B}_{-i}$,

$$s_i(x, \mathbf{b}_{-i}) - s_i(y, \mathbf{b}_{-i}) = w_i(\Phi(x, \mathbf{b}_{-i}) - \Phi(y, \mathbf{b}_{-i})), \quad \text{for every } x, y \in \mathcal{B}_i.$$

Definition 11.59. A normal form game G is called a $\mathbf{w}$-*potential game* if there exists a $\mathbf{w}$-potential function for G.

A function $\Phi : \mathcal{B} \to \mathbf{R}$ is an *exact potential function for* G if it is a $\mathbf{w}$-potential function for G with the values of the weights $w_i = 1$, for all $i \in N$.

Definition 11.60. A normal form game G is called an *exact potential game* (or simply, *potential game*) if it there exists an exact potential function for G.

The following theorem establishes the existence of a pure-strategy Nash equilibrium for every finite potential game.

Theorem 11.61. *Every finite potential game has at least one pure-strategy Nash equilibrium, which is a strategy vector that maximizes its potential function.*

Proof. Let Φ be a potential function of a normal form game G, and let $\mathbf{b}$ be a vector that maximizes Φ over the set $\mathcal{B}$. Consider a unilateral deviation of player $i \in N$

to a strategy $b_i' \in \mathcal{B}_i$. By assumption, $\Phi((b_i', \mathbf{b}_{-i})) \leq \Phi(\mathbf{b})$. Combining this with the definition of the potential function, we have

$$s_i(b_i', \mathbf{b}_{-i}) - s_i(\mathbf{b}) = \Phi(b_i', \mathbf{b}_{-i}) - \Phi(\mathbf{b}) \leq 0.$$

Hence, any unilateral deviation of a player cannot improve his or her payoff, showing that $\mathbf{b}$ is a pure-strategy Nash equilibrium. $\square$

Some normal form games are potential games, but it can be non-trivial to find a potential function for these games. For this reason, it is of interest to know equivalent conditions for a game to be a potential game that may be easier to verify. In the next subsection, we identify some of these conditions. The equivalent condition given later in Corollary 11.63 was used in the proof of Theorem 5.35 in Chapter 5.

Alternative Conditions for a Game to be a Potential Game

A *path* in $\mathcal{B}$ is a sequence of strategy vectors $\mathbf{p} = (\mathbf{b}^0, \mathbf{b}^1, \ldots)$ such that for every $t \geq 0$ there exists a unique player $i_t \in N$ such that $\mathbf{b}^{t+1} = (\mathbf{b}_{-i_t}^t, \mathbf{a})$ for some $\mathbf{a} \in \mathcal{B}_{i_t}$ such that $\mathbf{a} \neq \mathbf{b}_{i_t}^t$. $\mathbf{b}^0$ is called the *initial point* of $\mathbf{p}$, and if $\mathbf{p}$ is finite, the last element is called the *terminal point* of $\mathbf{p}$. $\mathbf{p}$ is an *improvement path* with respect to G if $s_{i_t}(\mathbf{b}^t) > s_{i_t}(\mathbf{b}^{t-1})$ for all $t > 0$. The finite path $\mathbf{p} = (\mathbf{b}^0, \mathbf{b}^1, \ldots, \mathbf{b}^T)$ is *closed* if $\mathbf{b}^0 = \mathbf{b}^T$. It is a *simple* closed path if, in addition, $\mathbf{b}^s \neq \mathbf{b}^t$ for all $0 \leq s < t < T$. The length of a simple closed path is defined to be the number of distinct points in it, i.e., the length of a simple closed path $\mathbf{p} = (\mathbf{b}^0, \mathbf{b}^1, \ldots, \mathbf{b}^T)$ is T.

For every finite path $\mathbf{p} = (\mathbf{b}^0, \mathbf{b}^1, \ldots, \mathbf{b}^T)$, we define

$$V(\mathbf{p}) = \sum_{t=0}^{T-1} [s_{i_t}(\mathbf{b}^{t+1}) - s_{i_t}(\mathbf{b}^t)]. \tag{11.87}$$

Theorem 11.62. *For a normal form game G, the following claims are equivalent:*

(i) *G is a potential game.*
(ii) *$V(\mathbf{p}) = 0$ for every finite closed path $\mathbf{p}$.*
(iii) *$V(\mathbf{p}) = 0$ for every finite simple closed path $\mathbf{p}$.*
(iv) *$V(\mathbf{p}) = 0$ for every finite simple closed path $\mathbf{p}$ of length four.*

Proof. Obviously, (ii) $\Rightarrow$ (iii) $\Rightarrow$ (iv). It is sufficient to prove that (i) $\Leftrightarrow$ (ii) and (iv) $\Rightarrow$ (ii) (see Figure 11.13).

Proof of Claim: (i) $\Rightarrow$ (ii). Suppose that Φ is a potential function of G. Let $\mathbf{p} = (\mathbf{b}^0, \mathbf{b}^1, \ldots, \mathbf{b}^T)$ be a closed path. By (11.87), we have

$$V(\mathbf{p}) = \sum_{t=0}^{T-1} [\Phi(\mathbf{b}^{t+1}) - \Phi(\mathbf{b}^t)] = \Phi(\mathbf{b}^T) - \Phi(\mathbf{b}^0) = 0.$$

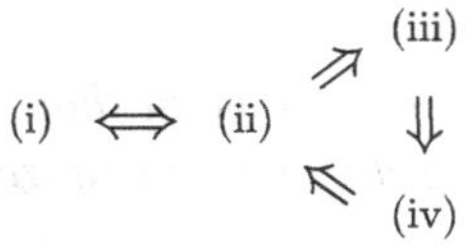

$$(i) \iff (ii) \quad \begin{array}{c} \nearrow (iii) \\ \Downarrow \\ \nwarrow (iv) \end{array}$$

Figure 11.13. A sufficient set of implications to establish the equivalence.

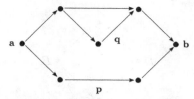

Figure 11.14. For every two paths **p** and **q** from **a** to **b**, $V(\mathbf{p}) = V(\mathbf{q})$.

Proof of Claim (ii) $\Rightarrow$ *(i).* Suppose that $V(\mathbf{p}) = 0$ for every finite closed path **p**. Fix $\mathbf{a} \in \mathcal{B}$. We show that for every two paths **p** and **q** that connect **a** to a point $\mathbf{b} \in \mathcal{B}$, $V(\mathbf{p}) = V(\mathbf{q})$. Let $\mathbf{p} = (\mathbf{a}, \mathbf{a}^1, \ldots, \mathbf{a}^T)$ and $\mathbf{q} = (\mathbf{a}, \mathbf{b}^1, \ldots, \mathbf{b}^S)$ such that $\mathbf{a}^T = \mathbf{b}^S = \mathbf{b}$. Let **r** be the closed path defined as

$$\mathbf{r} = (\mathbf{a}, \mathbf{a}^1, \ldots, \mathbf{a}^T, \mathbf{b}^{S-1}, \ldots, \mathbf{b}^1, \mathbf{a}).$$

Then, by our hypothesis, $V(\mathbf{r}) = 0$. Combining with (11.87), it follows that $V(\mathbf{p}) = V(\mathbf{q})$ (see Figure 11.14).

For every $\mathbf{b} \in \mathcal{B}$ choose a path $p(\mathbf{a}, \mathbf{b})$ that connects **a** and **b**, and let

$$\Phi(\mathbf{b}) = V(p(\mathbf{a}, \mathbf{b})).$$

We show that Φ is a potential function for G. We already proved that $\Phi(\mathbf{b}) = V(\mathbf{p})$ for every path **p** that connects **a** and **b**. Fix an arbitrary player $i \in N$, $\mathbf{b}_{-i} \in \mathcal{B}_{-i}$, and $\mathbf{x} \neq \mathbf{y} \in \mathcal{B}_i$. Let $\mathbf{p}_x = (\mathbf{a}, \mathbf{b}^1, \ldots, (\mathbf{x}, \mathbf{b}_{-i}))$ and $\mathbf{p}_y = (\mathbf{a}, \mathbf{b}^1, \ldots, (\mathbf{x}, \mathbf{b}_{-i}), (\mathbf{y}, \mathbf{b}_{-i}))$. Then, by (11.87), we have

$$\Phi(\mathbf{y}, \mathbf{b}_{-i}) - \Phi(\mathbf{x}, \mathbf{b}_{-i}) = V(\mathbf{p}_y) - V(\mathbf{p}_x) = s_i(\mathbf{y}, \mathbf{b}_{-i}) - s_i(\mathbf{x}, \mathbf{b}_{-i}).$$

Therefore, Φ is a potential function for G.

Proof of Claim (iv) $\Rightarrow$ *(ii).* Suppose that $V(\mathbf{p}) = 0$ for every simple closed path **p** of length four. Suppose that $V(\mathbf{p}) \neq 0$ for some closed path **p**. Such a path is of length T larger than or equal to five. Without loss of generality, assume that

$$V(\mathbf{q}) = 0 \text{ for every path } \mathbf{q} \text{ of length smaller than } T \qquad (11.88)$$

and that $i_0 = 1$. Since $i_0 = 1$ and $\mathbf{b}^0 = \mathbf{b}^T$, there exists $0 < t < T$ such that $i_t = 1$. If $t = 1$ or $t = T - 1$, then $V(\mathbf{q}) = V(\mathbf{p}) \neq 0$. Since the length of **q** is smaller than T this is in contradiction to (11.88). We now consider the case $1 < t < T - 1$. We show that there exists $\mathbf{z}^t \in \mathcal{B}$ such that the path $\mathbf{q} = (\mathbf{b}^0, \ldots, \mathbf{b}^{t-1}, \mathbf{z}^t, \mathbf{b}^{t+1}, \ldots, \mathbf{b}^T)$ satisfies

$$V(\mathbf{q}) = V(\mathbf{p}) \text{ and } j_{t-1} = 1 \qquad (11.89)$$

where j_{t-1} is the unique deviator at step $t - 1$ in the path **q**.

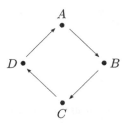

Figure 11.15. A closed path of length four.

Indeed, let $\mathbf{z}^t = (\mathbf{b}_{-1}^{t-1}, \mathbf{b}_1^{t+1})$ and then note that by the hypothesis that $V(\mathbf{r}) = 0$ for every closed path $\mathbf{r}$ of length four (see Figure 11.15), we have

$$V(\mathbf{p}) - V(\mathbf{q}) = V(\mathbf{b}^{t-1}, \mathbf{z}^t, \mathbf{b}^{t+1}) - V(\mathbf{b}^{t-1}, \mathbf{b}^t, \mathbf{b}^{t+1})$$

$$= [s_1(\mathbf{z}^t) - s_1(\mathbf{b}^{t-1})] + [s_{j_t}(\mathbf{b}^{t+1}) - s_{j_t}(\mathbf{z}^t)] - [s_{i_{t-1}}(\mathbf{b}^t) - s_{i_{t-1}}(\mathbf{b}^{t-1})]$$

$$- [s_1(\mathbf{b}^{t+1}) - s_1(\mathbf{b}^t)]$$

$$= - \{[s_{i_{t-1}}(\mathbf{b}^t) - s_{i_{t-1}}(\mathbf{b}^{t-1})] + [s_{i_t}(\mathbf{b}^{t+1}) - s_{i_t}(\mathbf{b}^t)] + [s_{j_t}(\mathbf{z}^t) - s_{j_t}(\mathbf{b}^{t+1})]$$

$$+ [s_1(\mathbf{b}^{t-1}) - s_1(\mathbf{z}^t)]\}$$

$$= -V(\mathbf{b}^{t-1}, \mathbf{b}^t, \mathbf{b}^{t+1}, \mathbf{z}^t, \mathbf{b}^{t-1}) = 0.$$

Continuing the same argument starting with path $\mathbf{q}$ we eventually obtain that there exists a path $\mathbf{r}$ of length T such that player 1 is the deviator at steps 0 and 1, which is in contradiction to hypothesis (11.88). $\qquad\square$

From Theorem 11.62, the following corollary is immediate.

Corollary 11.63. *A normal form game G is a potential game if, and only if, for every $i, k \in N$, $\mathbf{z} \in \mathcal{B}_{-\{i,k\}}$, $x_i, y_i \in \mathcal{B}_i$ and $x_k, y_k \in \mathcal{B}_k$,*

$$[s_i(B) - s_i(A)] + [s_k(C) - s_k(B)] + [s_i(D) - s_i(C)] + [s_k(A) - s_k(D)] = 0$$

$$(11.90)$$

where $A = (x_i, x_k, \mathbf{z})$, $B = (y_i, x_k, \mathbf{z})$, $C = (y_i, y_k, \mathbf{z})$, and $D = (x_i, y_k, \mathbf{z})$.

The Potential Games and the Price of Stability

The potential games allow us to use a potential function to derive bounds on the social efficiency as shown in the following theorem. This method for bounding the price of stability is known as the *potential function method*.

Theorem 11.64. *Suppose that a normal form game G has a potential function Φ such that for a given social utility function $u : \mathcal{B} \to \mathbf{R}$, there exist constants $\lambda, \mu > 0$ such that*

$$\lambda u(\mathbf{b}) \leq \Phi(\mathbf{b}) \leq \mu u(\mathbf{b}), \text{ for every } \mathbf{b} \in \mathcal{B}.$$

Then, the game G has a pure-strategy Nash equilibrium $\mathbf{b}$ such that for every utility-maximizing strategy vector $\mathbf{b}^*$, we have $u(\mathbf{b}) \geq (\lambda/\mu)u(\mathbf{b}^*)$.

Proof. Let $\mathbf{b} \in \mathcal{B}$ be a strategy vector that maximizes $\Phi(\mathbf{x})$ over $\mathbf{x} \in \mathcal{B}$, and let $\mathbf{b}^* \in \mathcal{B}$ be a strategy vector that maximizes $u(\mathbf{x})$ over $\mathbf{x} \in \mathcal{B}$. By Theorem 11.61, $\mathbf{b}$ is a pure-strategy Nash equilibrium for the game G. By the hypothesis of the theorem, we have

$$\Phi(\mathbf{b}) \leq \mu u(\mathbf{b}). \tag{11.91}$$

By the definition of the vector $\mathbf{b}$, we have $\Phi(\mathbf{b}^*) \leq \Phi(\mathbf{b})$, which combined with the hypothesis of the theorem implies

$$\lambda u(\mathbf{b}^*) \leq \Phi(\mathbf{b}). \tag{11.92}$$

From (11.91) and (11.92), it follows that $u(\mathbf{b}) \geq (\lambda/\mu)u(\mathbf{b}^*)$. $\qquad \square$

11.3.3 Smooth Games

In this section we introduce various definitions of smooth games and the efficiency properties that they imply for various types of a strategic equilibrium. The framework of smooth games provides a way for deriving worst-case bounds for the efficiency of strategic equilibria without requiring an explicit characterization of the underlying strategic equilibria. This framework also provides worst-case efficiency bounds for various notions of strategic equilibria, as we describe in this section. We first consider games with complete information and then games with incomplete information.

Games with Complete Information

We consider a normal form game $G = (N, \{\mathcal{B}_i, \ i \in N\}, \{s_i, \ i \in N\})$. A *welfare function* $s : \mathcal{B} \to \mathbf{R}$ is given that satisfies the following condition:

$$s(\mathbf{b}) \geq \sum_{i \in N} s_i(\mathbf{b}), \quad \text{for every } \mathbf{b} \in \mathcal{B}. \tag{11.93}$$

A strategy vector $\mathbf{b}^* \in \mathcal{B}$ is said to be *welfare optimal* if it maximizes the welfare function, i.e., $s(\mathbf{b}^*) \geq s(\mathbf{b})$, for every $\mathbf{b} \in \mathcal{B}$. The value $s(\mathbf{b}^*)$ for a welfare-optimal $\mathbf{b}^* \in \mathcal{B}$ is referred to as the optimal welfare.

Definition 11.65 (smooth game). A normal form game G is said to be (λ, μ)-*smooth* if it satisfies the following condition:

$$\sum_{i \in N} s_i(\mathbf{a}_i, \mathbf{b}_{-i}) \geq \lambda s(\mathbf{a}) - \mu s(\mathbf{b}), \quad \text{for every } \mathbf{a}, \mathbf{b} \in \mathcal{B}. \tag{11.94}$$

We shall next show that if a game G is (λ, μ)-smooth, then for every pure-strategy Nash equilibrium of G, the welfare is at least $\lambda/(\mu + 1)$ of the optimal welfare. Hence, it follows that in every pure-strategy Nash equilibrium of a normal form game G, the welfare is at least $\eta(G)$ of the optimal welfare where

$$\eta(G) = \max \left\{ \frac{\lambda}{\mu + 1} \,\middle|\, (\lambda, \mu) \in \mathbf{R}_+ \times \mathbf{R}_+ \text{ such that } G \text{ is } (\lambda, \mu)\text{-smooth} \right\}. \tag{11.95}$$

An important property of the worst-case efficiency bounds derived this way is that they are robust with respect to the choice of the solution concept. They hold for the solution concept of pure-strategy Nash equilibria, as well as for mixed-strategy Nash equilibria, correlated Nash equilibria, and coarse correlated Nash equilibria, which we demonstrate in the following four theorems.

Theorem 11.66 (pure-strategy Nash equilibria). *If a normal form game is (λ, μ)-smooth for $\lambda, \mu \geq 0$, then for every pure-strategy Nash equilibrium strategy vector $\mathbf{b}$ of this game and every welfare-optimal strategy vector $\mathbf{b}^*$, we have $s(\mathbf{b}) \geq (\lambda/(\mu + 1))s(\mathbf{b}^*)$.*

Proof. By the assumption on the welfare function in (11.93), the assumption that $\mathbf{b}$ is a pure-strategy Nash equilibrium, and the assumption that the game is (λ, μ)-smooth, we have

$$s(\mathbf{b}) \geq \sum_{i \in N} s_i(\mathbf{b}) \geq \sum_{i \in N} s_i(\mathbf{b}_i^*, \mathbf{b}_{-i}) \geq \lambda s(\mathbf{b}^*) - \mu s(\mathbf{b}),$$

which shows that $s(\mathbf{b}) \geq (\lambda/(\mu + 1))s(\mathbf{b}^*)$. $\qquad\square$

The efficiency lower bound also extends to the expected welfare in every mixed-strategy Nash equilibrium as shown in the following theorem.

Theorem 11.67 (mixed-strategy Nash equilibria). *If a normal form game is (λ, μ)-smooth for $\lambda, \mu \geq 0$, then for every mixed-strategy Nash equilibrium of this game and a welfare-optimal strategy vector $\mathbf{b}^*$, we have $\mathbf{E}[s(\mathbf{b})] \geq (\lambda/(\mu + 1))s(\mathbf{b}^*)$.*

Proof. By the definition of a mixed-strategy Nash equilibrium in Definition 1.4, in every mixed-strategy Nash equilibrium, the following condition holds for the expected payoff of every player $i \in N$,

$$\mathbf{E}[s_i(\mathbf{b})] \geq \mathbf{E}[s_i(\mathbf{b}) \mid \mathbf{b}_i = \mathbf{a}_i] = \mathbf{E}[s_i(\mathbf{a}_i, \mathbf{b}_{-i})], \quad \text{for every } \mathbf{a}_i \in \mathcal{B}_i \qquad (11.96)$$

where the last equality holds because in a mixed-strategy Nash equilibrium, the strategies of the players are independent. For every $\mathbf{a} \in \mathcal{B}$, we have

$$\mathbf{E}[s(\mathbf{b})] \geq \sum_{i \in N} \mathbf{E}[s_i(\mathbf{b})] \geq \mathbf{E}\left[\sum_{i \in N} s_i(\mathbf{a}_i, \mathbf{b}_{-i})\right] \geq \mathbf{E}[\lambda s(\mathbf{a}) - \mu s(\mathbf{b})]$$
$$= \lambda s(\mathbf{a}) - \mu \mathbf{E}[s(\mathbf{b})] \qquad (11.97)$$

where the first inequality is by assumption on the welfare function in (11.93), the second inequality is by (11.96), and the third inequality is by the assumption that the game is (λ, μ) smooth. Since $\mathbf{a}$ is an arbitrary strategy vector in $\mathcal{B}$, (11.97) holds in particular for a welfare-optimal strategy vector $\mathbf{b}^*$, which establishes the proof of the theorem. $\qquad\square$

The efficiency lower bound holds even more generally for the solution concept of a correlated Nash equilibrium defined in Definition 1.7 as shown in the following theorem.

Theorem 11.68 (correlated Nash equilibria). *If a normal form game G is (λ, μ)-smooth for $\lambda, \mu \geq 0$, then for every correlated Nash equilibrium and a welfare-optimal strategy vector $\mathbf{b}^*$, we have $\mathbf{E}[s(\mathbf{b})] \geq (\lambda/(\mu + 1))s(\mathbf{b}^*)$.*

Proof. Consider a correlated Nash equilibrium according to a distribution μ on $\mathcal{B}$. By the definition of a correlated Nash equilibrium in Definition 1.7, the expected payoff of every player $i \in N$ satisfies the following condition:

$$\mathbf{E}_{\mathbf{b}\sim\mu}[s_i(\mathbf{b})] \geq \mathbf{E}_{\mathbf{b}_{-i}\sim\mu_{-i}}[s_i(\mathbf{a}_i, \mathbf{b}_{-i})] = \mathbf{E}_{\mathbf{b}\sim\mu}[s_i(\mathbf{a}_i, \mathbf{b}_{-i})], \quad \text{for every } \mathbf{a}_i \in \mathcal{B}_i.$$

This shows that the inequality in (11.96) holds more generally for a correlated Nash equilibrium. The rest of the proof follows exactly the same steps as that of the proof of Theorem 11.67. $\qquad\square$

The lower bound on the efficiency extends even to the solution concept of a *coarse correlated equilibrium*, which is defined as a *no-regret sequence* of probability distributions $B^1, B^2, \ldots, B^T$ on the set $\mathcal{B}$ of strategies such that for every player $i \in N$ we have

$$\mathbf{E}\left[\sum_{t=1}^{T} s_i(\mathbf{b}^t)\right] \geq \mathbf{E}\left[\sum_{t=1}^{T} s_i(\mathbf{b}_i^*, \mathbf{b}_{-i}^t)\right] - o(T) \tag{11.98}$$

where $\mathbf{b}_i^*$ is the best fixed strategy in hindsight, i.e.,

$$\mathbf{E}\left[\sum_{t=1}^{T} s_i(\mathbf{b}_i^*, \mathbf{b}_{-i}^t)\right] \geq E\left[\sum_{t=1}^{T} s_i(\mathbf{a}_i, \mathbf{b}_{-i}^t)\right] \text{ for every } \mathbf{a}_i \in \mathcal{B}_i.$$

Theorem 11.69 (coarse correlated equilibrium). *If a normal form game G is (λ, μ)-smooth, then for every no-regret sequence of probability distributions $B^1, B^2, \ldots, B^T$ on the set of strategies $\mathcal{B}$ and every strategy vector $\mathbf{b}^* \in \mathcal{B}$, we have*

$$\frac{1}{T}\mathbf{E}\left[\sum_{t=1}^{T} s(\mathbf{b}^t)\right] \geq \left(\frac{\lambda}{\mu + 1} + o(1)\right)\mathbf{E}\left[s(\mathbf{b}^*)\right].$$

Proof. Let $B^1, B^2, \ldots, B^T$ be a no-regret sequence of probability distributions on the set of strategy vectors $\mathcal{B}$ and let $\mathbf{b}^* = (\mathbf{b}_1^*, \mathbf{b}_2^*, \ldots, \mathbf{b}_n^*)$ be a strategy vector such that for every player $i \in N$, $\mathbf{b}_i^*$ maximizes his or her cumulative payoff given that all the other players play according to the no-regret randomized strategies. Let $\epsilon_i(\mathbf{b}^t, \mathbf{b}_i^*) = s_i(\mathbf{b}_i^*, \mathbf{b}_{-i}^t) - s_i(\mathbf{b}^t)$ for $i \in N$.

Now, note that

$$s(\mathbf{b}^t) \geq \sum_{i\in N} s_i(\mathbf{b}^t)$$

$$= \sum_{i\in N} s_i(\mathbf{b}_i^*, \mathbf{b}_{-i}^t) - \sum_{i\in N} \epsilon_i(\mathbf{b}^t, \mathbf{b}_i^*)$$

$$\geq \lambda s(\mathbf{b}^*) - \mu s(\mathbf{b}^t) - \sum_{i\in N} \epsilon_i(\mathbf{b}^t, \mathbf{b}_i^*).$$

Hence, it follows that

$$\frac{1}{T}\mathbf{E}\left[\sum_{t=1}^{T} s(\mathbf{b}^t)\right] \geq \frac{\lambda}{\mu + 1}\mathbf{E}\left[s(\mathbf{b}^*)\right] - \frac{1}{\mu + 1}\sum_{i\in N}\mathbf{E}\left[\frac{1}{T}\sum_{t=1}^{T} \epsilon_i(\mathbf{b}^t, \mathbf{b}_i^*)\right].$$

The claim of the theorem follows because

$$\sum_{i \in N} \mathbf{E}\left[\frac{1}{T}\sum_{t=1}^{T}\epsilon_i(\mathbf{b}^t, \mathbf{b}_i^*)\right] = o(1).$$

$\square$

Example 11.70 (monotone valid utility games). We show that monotone valid utility games, introduced in Section 6.3, are $(1, 1)$-smooth. For every $\mathbf{a}, \mathbf{b} \in \mathcal{B}$, we have

$$\sum_{i=1}^{n} s_i(\mathbf{a}_i, \mathbf{b}_{-i}) \geq \sum_{i=1}^{n} s(\mathbf{a}_i, \mathbf{b}_{-i}) - s(\mathbf{0}, \mathbf{b}_{-i})$$

$$\geq \sum_{i=1}^{n} s((\mathbf{a}_i, \mathbf{b}_{-i}) \vee (\mathbf{a}_1, \ldots, \mathbf{a}_{i-1}, \mathbf{b}_i, \mathbf{0}))$$

$$- s((\mathbf{0}, \mathbf{b}_{-i}) \vee (\mathbf{a}_1, \ldots, \mathbf{a}_{i-1}, \mathbf{b}_i, \mathbf{0}))$$

$$= \sum_{i=1}^{n} s(\mathbf{b} \vee (\mathbf{a}_1, \ldots, \mathbf{a}_i, \mathbf{0})) - s(\mathbf{b} \vee (\mathbf{a}_1, \ldots, \mathbf{a}_{i-1}, \mathbf{0}))$$

$$= s(\mathbf{b} \vee \mathbf{a}) - s(\mathbf{b})$$

$$\geq s(\mathbf{a}) - s(\mathbf{b})$$

where the first inequality is by the marginal contribution condition, the second inequality is by the diminishing returns property, and the last inequality is by the monotonicity condition.

Locally Smooth Games A related concept of locally smooth games is introduced under the additional assumption that for every player $i \in N$, the set of strategies $\mathcal{B}_i$ is a convex subset of an Euclidean space and the payoff function s_i is continuously differentiable with bounded derivatives.

Definition 11.71 (locally smooth game). A normal form game G is *locally (λ, μ)-smooth with respect to a strategy vector* $\mathbf{a} \in \mathcal{B}$ if the following condition holds:

$$\sum_{i \in N}[s_i(\mathbf{b}) + \nabla_i s_i(\mathbf{b})^T(\mathbf{a}_i - \mathbf{b}_i)] \geq \lambda s(\mathbf{a}) - \mu s(\mathbf{b}), \quad \text{for every } \mathbf{b} \in \mathcal{B} \quad (11.99)$$

where $\nabla_i s_i(\mathbf{b})$ is the gradient of function $s_i(\mathbf{b})$ with respect to $\mathbf{b}_i$.

Locally smooth games imply a lower bound on the expected welfare for every correlated Nash equilibrium as stated in the following theorem. Since the set of mixed-strategy Nash equilibria is a subset of the set of correlated Nash equilibria, the same lower bound applies also to mixed-strategy Nash equilibria. Similarly, since the set of pure-strategy Nash equilibria is a subset of the set of mixed-strategy Nash equilibria, the same lower bound applies also to pure-strategy Nash equilibria.

Theorem 11.72. *If a normal form game is (λ, μ)-locally smooth with respect to a strategy vector* $\mathbf{a} \in \mathcal{B}$ *for* $\lambda, \mu \geq 0$, *then for every correlated equilibrium of this game* $\mathbf{E}[s(\mathbf{b})] \geq (\lambda/(\mu + 1))s(\mathbf{a})$.

Proof. We first prove that

$$\mathbf{E}[\nabla_i s_i(\mathbf{b})^T (\mathbf{a}_i - \mathbf{b}_i)] \le 0 \text{ for every } i \in N. \tag{11.100}$$

Suppose that on the contrary $\mathbf{E}[\nabla_i s_i(\mathbf{b})^T (\mathbf{a}_i - \mathbf{b}_i)] > 0$ for some player $i \in N$. Let $\mathbf{b}^\epsilon = ((1 - \epsilon)\mathbf{b}_i + \epsilon \mathbf{a}_i, \mathbf{b}_{-i})$ for $\epsilon \in [0, 1]$. Since the strategy sets are convex, $\mathbf{b}^\epsilon$ is in $\mathcal{B}$ for every $\epsilon \in [0, 1]$. Since $\mathbf{E}[(s_i(\mathbf{b}^\epsilon) - s_i(\mathbf{b}))/\epsilon]$ goes to $\mathbf{E}[\nabla_i s_i(\mathbf{b})^T (\mathbf{a}_i - \mathbf{b}_i)] > 0$ as $\epsilon \downarrow 0$, there exists $\epsilon > 0$ such that $\mathbf{E}[s_i(\mathbf{b}^\epsilon)] > \mathbf{E}[s_i(\mathbf{b})]$, which is a contradiction to the assumption that the distribution of $\mathbf{b}$ is a correlated Nash equilibrium.

The rest of the proof follows by this sequence of relations:

$$\begin{aligned}
\mathbf{E}[s(\mathbf{b})] &\ge \sum_{i \in N} \mathbf{E}\left[s_i(\mathbf{b}) + \nabla_i s_i(\mathbf{b})^T (\mathbf{a}_i - \mathbf{b}_i) \right] \\
&\ge \mathbf{E}[\lambda s(\mathbf{a}) - \mu s(\mathbf{b})] \\
&= \lambda s(\mathbf{a}) - \mu \mathbf{E}[s(\mathbf{b})]
\end{aligned}$$

where the first inequality is by the assumption on the welfare function in (11.93) and the fact (11.100) and the second inequality is by the assumption that the game is (λ, μ)-locally smooth with respect to the strategy vector $\mathbf{a}$. $\qquad \square$

There exist normal form games for which being a smooth game implies being a locally smooth game. For this class of games, one may obtain a tighter lower bound on the efficiency with respect to a given welfare function by optimizing over a larger set of parameters (λ, μ).

Theorem 11.73. *Suppose that a normal form game is such that for every player the strategy set is convex and the payoff function is continuously differentiable with bounded derivatives and is concave. Then, if the game is (λ, μ)-smooth, it is also (λ, μ)-locally smooth with respect to every strategy vector $\mathbf{a} \in \mathcal{B}$.*

Proof. Since for every player $i \in N$, the payoff function is assumed to be continuously differentiable and concave by (11.3), we have

$$s_i(\mathbf{a}_i, \mathbf{b}_{-i}) - s_i(\mathbf{b}) \le \nabla_i s_i(\mathbf{b})^T (\mathbf{a}_i - \mathbf{b}_i), \quad \text{for every } \mathbf{a}, \mathbf{b} \in \mathcal{B}.$$

Combining this with the assumption that the game is (λ, μ)-smooth, we obtain that for every $\mathbf{a}, \mathbf{b} \in \mathcal{B}$,

$$\sum_{i \in N} [s_i(\mathbf{b}) + \nabla_i s_i(\mathbf{b})^T (\mathbf{a}_i - \mathbf{b}_i)] \ge \sum_{i \in N} s_i(\mathbf{a}_i, \mathbf{b}_{-i}) \ge \lambda s(\mathbf{a}) - \mu s(\mathbf{b}),$$

which implies the game is (λ, μ)-locally smooth with respect to every strategy vector $\mathbf{a} \in \mathcal{B}$. $\qquad \square$

An Alternative Definition of Smooth Games An alternative notion of a smooth game can be defined for normal form games with payoff functions of quasi-linear form

$$s_i(\mathbf{b}) = u_i(\mathbf{b}) - c_i(\mathbf{b}), \quad \text{for } i \in N \tag{11.101}$$

where $u_i : \mathcal{B} \to \mathbf{R}_+$ is referred to as a utility function and $c_i : \mathcal{B} \to \mathbf{R}_+$ is referred to as a cost function. Let $u(\mathbf{b}) = \sum_{i \in N} u_i(\mathbf{b})$ be the total utility function, and let

$c(\mathbf{b}) = \sum_{i \in N} c_i(\mathbf{b})$ be the total cost function. Let $\mathbf{b}^*$ be a strategy vector that maximizes the total utility, i.e., $u(\mathbf{b}^*) \geq u(\mathbf{b})$, for all $\mathbf{b} \in \mathcal{B}$.

Definition 11.74 (smooth game with quasi-linear payoffs). A normal form game with quasi-linear payoff functions is (λ, μ)-*smooth with respect to quasi-linear payoffs* for $\lambda, \mu \geq 0$, if for every strategy vector $\mathbf{b} \in \mathcal{B}$, a utility-maximizing strategy vector $\mathbf{b}^*$, and every player $i \in N$ there exists a distribution A_i on the set $\mathcal{B}_i$ that is allowed to be parametrized with $\mathbf{b}_i$ and not with $\mathbf{b}_{-i}$ such that

$$\sum_{i \in N} \mathbf{E}_{\mathbf{a}_i \sim A_i}[s_i(\mathbf{a}_i, \mathbf{b}_{-i})] \geq \lambda u(\mathbf{b}^*) - \mu c(\mathbf{b}). \tag{11.102}$$

This definition of a smooth game provides the following lower bound on the efficiency with respect to the total utility.

Theorem 11.75 (correlated equilibrium). *If a normal form game is (λ, μ)-smooth with respect to quasi-linear payoffs and the strategy set of every player contains the strategy of no entry, then in every correlated Nash equilibrium and for every utility-optimal strategy $\mathbf{b}^*$, we have $\mathbf{E}[u(\mathbf{b})] \geq (\lambda/ \max\{\mu, 1\})u(\mathbf{b}^*)$.*

Proof. We first prove that

$$\sum_{i \in N} \mathbf{E}[s_i(\mathbf{b})] \geq \lambda u(\mathbf{b}^*) - \mu \mathbf{E}[c(\mathbf{b})]. \tag{11.103}$$

This follows from the following sequence of relations:

$$\sum_{i \in N} \mathbf{E}[s_i(\mathbf{b})] = \sum_{i \in N} \mathbf{E}[\mathbf{E}[s_i(\mathbf{b}) \mid \mathbf{b}_{-i}]]$$

$$\geq \sum_{i \in N} \mathbf{E}[\mathbf{E}_{\mathbf{a}_i \sim A_i}[s_i(\mathbf{a}_i, \mathbf{b}_{-i}) \mid \mathbf{b}_{-i}]]$$

$$= \mathbf{E}\left[\sum_{i \in N} \mathbf{E}_{\mathbf{a}_i \sim A_i}[s_i(\mathbf{a}_i, \mathbf{b}_{-i}) \mid \mathbf{b}_{-i}]\right]$$

$$\geq \mathbf{E}\left[\lambda u(\mathbf{b}^*) - \mu c(\mathbf{b})\right]$$

$$= \lambda u(\mathbf{b}^*) - \mu \mathbf{E}[c(\mathbf{b})]$$

where the first inequality is by the definition of the correlated equilibrium in Definition 1.7, the second inequality is by the assumption that the game is (λ, μ)-smooth with respect to quasi-linear payoffs, and all other relations hold by linearity of expectation.

From (11.103), we obtain

$$\mathbf{E}[u(\mathbf{b})] = \mathbf{E}\left[\sum_{i \in N} u_i(\mathbf{b})\right] = \sum_{i \in N} \mathbf{E}[s_i(\mathbf{b})] + \mathbf{E}[c(\mathbf{b})] \geq \lambda u(\mathbf{b}^*) + (1 - \mu)\mathbf{E}[c(\mathbf{b})].$$

$$\tag{11.104}$$

If $\mu \leq 1$, then from (1.7), we immediately have $\mathbf{E}[u(\mathbf{b})] \geq \lambda u(\mathbf{b}^*)$. Otherwise, if $\mu > 1$, then note that since every player is guaranteed a zero payoff by not participating, $\mathbf{E}[s(\mathbf{b})] = \mathbf{E}[u(\mathbf{b})] - \mathbf{E}[c(\mathbf{b})] \geq 0$, i.e. $\mathbf{E}[c(\mathbf{b})] \leq \mathbf{E}[u(\mathbf{b})]$. Combining this with

(11.104), we obtain

$$\mathbf{E}[u(\mathbf{b})] \geq \lambda u(\mathbf{b}^*) + (1 - \mu)\mathbf{E}[u(\mathbf{b})],$$

which is equivalent to $\mathbf{E}[u(\mathbf{b})] \geq (\lambda/\mu)u(\mathbf{b}^*)$. $\qquad\square$

We next present two examples showing that two games considered in this book, namely the game that models the standard all-pay contest in Chapter 2 and the game that models the contest with proportional allocation in Chapter 4, are smooth games.

Example 11.76 (standard all-pay contest). We show that the game that models the standard all-pay contest is $(1/2, 1)$-smooth with respect to quasi-linear payoffs. Hence, by Theorem 11.75, in every correlated equilibrium it has the expected total utility of at least $1/2$ of the optimal total utility. From the result in Theorem 2.19, we know that this lower bound is not tight for mixed-strategy Nash equilibria.

Recall that the game that models the standard all-pay contest consists of two or more players with valuation parameters $v_1 \geq v_2 \geq \cdots \geq v_n > 0$, and the payoff functions of the form $s_i(\mathbf{b}) = v_i x_i(\mathbf{b}) - b_i$ for $i \in N$. Hence, the payoff functions are of the quasi-linear form (11.101) with $u_i(\mathbf{b}) = v_i x_i(\mathbf{b})$ and $c_i(\mathbf{b}) = b_i$ for $i \in N$. The optimal total utility is achieved by assigning the entire prize to a player with the largest valuation, and, thus, it is of value v_1.

Consider unilateral deviations according to which a player with the largest valuation randomizes uniformly on $[0, v_1]$, say this is player 1, and all other players invest a zero effort with probability 1. Then, we have

$$\mathbf{E}[s_1(a_1, \mathbf{b}_{-1}) \mid \mathbf{b}] \geq v_1 \mathbf{Pr}[a_1 > \max_{i \neq 1} b_i \mid \mathbf{b}] - \mathbf{E}[a_1 \mid \mathbf{b}]$$

$$= v_1 \left(1 - \frac{\max_{i \neq 1} b_i}{v_1} \right) - \frac{v_1}{2}$$

$$\geq \frac{1}{2} v_1 - \sum_{i \in N} b_i$$

and

$$\mathbf{E}[s_i(a_i, \mathbf{b}_{-i}) \mid \mathbf{b}] = 0, \quad \text{for } i \neq 1.$$

Hence, it follows that

$$\sum_{i \in N} \mathbf{E}[s_i(a_i, \mathbf{b}_{-i}) \mid \mathbf{b}] \geq \frac{1}{2} v_1 - \sum_{i \in N} b_i,$$

which shows that the game is $(1/2, 1)$-smooth with respect to quasi-linear payoffs.

Example 11.77 (proportional allocation). We show that the game that models the contest with proportional allocation is $(1/2, 1)$-smooth with respect to quasi-linear payoffs. Hence, by Theorem 11.75, in every correlated equilibrium it has the expected total utility of value at least $1/2$ of the optimal total utility. From the result in Theorem 4.24, we know that this lower bound is not tight for pure-strategy Nash equilibria.

Recall that the game that models the contest with proportional allocation consists of two or more players with the payoff functions $s_i(\mathbf{b}) = u_i(b_i / \sum_{j \in N} b_j) - b_i$ if $b_i > 0$ and $s_i(\mathbf{b}) = u_i(0)$ if $b_i = 0$, where $u_i : \mathbf{R}_+ \to \mathbf{R}_+$ is a strictly increasing, concave function such that $u_i(0) = 0$ for every player $i \in N$. Note a slight abuse of notation in view of the definition of utility functions given earlier in this section. The optimal total utility is achieved by assigning the entire prize to a player with the largest valuation, and thus, it is of value v_1.

Suppose that $\mathbf{b}$ is a vector of efforts according to correlated equilibrium strategies. We use the shorthand notation $b_{-i} = \sum_{j \neq i} b_j$. We first show that for a unilateral deviation of player $i \in N$ to the strategy $a_i = \mu x \mathbf{E}[b_{-i}]$, for given $x \in [0, 1]$ and $\mu > 0$,

$$\mathbf{E}[s_i(a_i, \mathbf{b}_{-i})] \geq \frac{3\mu - 1}{4\mu} u_i(x) - \mu x \mathbf{E}[b_{-i}]. \tag{11.105}$$

Since

$$\mathbf{E}[s_i(a_i, \mathbf{b}_{-i})] = \mathbf{E}\left[u_i\left(\frac{a_i}{a_i + b_{-i}}\right)\right] - \mu x \mathbf{E}[b_{-i}],$$

it suffices to show that

$$\mathbf{E}\left[u_i\left(\frac{a_i}{a_i + b_{-i}}\right)\right] \geq \frac{3\mu - 1}{4\mu} u_i(x).$$

First, we note that

$$\mathbf{E}\left[u_i\left(\frac{a_i}{a_i + b_{-i}}\right)\right]$$

$$= \mathbf{E}\left[u_i\left(\frac{a_i}{a_i + b_{-i}}\right)\mathbf{1}\left(\frac{a_i}{a_i + b_{-i}} \geq x\right)\right] + \mathbf{E}\left[u_i\left(\frac{a_i}{a_i + b_{-i}}\right)\mathbf{1}\left(\frac{a_i}{a_i + b_{-i}} < x\right)\right]$$

$$\geq u_i(x)\left(1 - \mathbf{Pr}\left[\frac{a_i}{a_i + b_{-i}} < x\right]\right) + \mathbf{E}\left[u_i\left(\frac{a_i}{a_i + b_{-i}}\right)\mathbf{1}\left(\frac{a_i}{a_i + b_{-i}} < x\right)\right]$$

$$\geq u_i(x)\left(1 - \mathbf{Pr}\left[\frac{a_i}{a_i + b_{-i}} < x\right]\right) + \frac{u_i(x)}{x}\mathbf{E}\left[\frac{a_i}{a_i + b_{-i}}\mathbf{1}\left(\frac{a_i}{a_i + b_{-i}} < x\right)\right]$$

where the first inequality holds because u_i is an increasing function and the second inequality holds because u_i is a concave function.

Second, we have

$$\mathbf{E}\left[\frac{a_i}{a_i + b_{-i}}\mathbf{1}\left(\frac{a_i}{a_i + b_{-i}} < x\right)\right] \geq \frac{a_i}{a_i + \mathbf{E}\left[b_{-i} \mid \frac{a_i}{a_i+b_{-i}} < x\right]}\mathbf{Pr}\left[\frac{a_i}{a_i + b_{-i}} < x\right]$$

$$= \frac{a_i}{a_i \mathbf{Pr}\left[\frac{a_i}{a_i+b_{-i}} < x\right] + \mathbf{E}[b_{-i}]}\mathbf{Pr}\left[\frac{a_i}{a_i + b_{-i}} < x\right]^2$$

$$\geq x\frac{\mu}{\mu + 1}\mathbf{Pr}\left[\frac{a_i}{a_i + b_{-i}} < x\right]^2$$

where the first inequality is by Jensen's inequality because $x \to a_i/(a_i + x)$ is a convex function for every fixed $a_i > 0$ and the last inequality is obvious.

It follows that

$$\mathbf{E}\left[u_i\left(\frac{a_i}{a_i+b_{-i}}\right)\right] \geq u_i(x)\left(1 - \mathbf{Pr}\left[\frac{a_i}{a_i+b_{-i}} < x\right] + \frac{\mu}{\mu+1}\mathbf{Pr}\left[\frac{a_i}{a_i+b_{-i}} < x\right]^2\right)$$

$$\geq u_i(x)\frac{3\mu - 1}{4\mu}$$

where the last inequality follows by the fact $1 - z + (\mu/(\mu+1))z^2 \geq (3\mu - 1)/(4\mu)$ for all $z \in [0, 1]$. This completes the proof for the relation (11.105).

Suppose that $\mathbf{x}^* = (x_1^*, x_2^*, \ldots, x_n^*)$ is a socially optimum allocation and $\mu > 0$. Consider unilateral deviations of players such that player $i \in N$ unilaterally deviates to the strategy $a_i = \mu x_i^* \mathbf{E}[b_{-i}]$. By (11.105), we have

$$\sum_{i\in N} \mathbf{E}[s_i(a_i, \mathbf{b}_{-i})] \geq \frac{3\mu - 1}{4\mu} \sum_{i\in N} u_i(x_i^*) - \mu \sum_{i\in N} x_i^* \mathbf{E}[b_{-i}]$$

$$\geq \frac{3\mu - 1}{4\mu} \sum_{i\in N} u_i(x_i^*) - \mu\mathbf{E}\left[\sum_{i\in N} b_i\right]$$

which shows that the game is $((3\mu - 1)/(4\mu), \mu)$-smooth with respect to quasi-linear payoffs. By Theorem 11.75, the worst-case social efficiency for correlated equilibria is at least $\min\{\lambda/\max\{\mu, 1\} \mid \lambda = (3\mu - 1)/(4\mu), \mu > 0\} = 1/2$. See Figure 11.16 for a graph.

Coalitional Smoothness The concept of a smooth game can also be extended to imply lower bounds on the efficiency of strong equilibria, a solution concept that is defined in Definition 1.8. For a given set of players $N = \{1, 2, \ldots, n\}$ and a given permutation π of the elements of N, we define N_i^π to be the subset of players at position larger than or equal to i, i.e.,

$$N_i^\pi = \{j \in N \mid \pi(j) \geq i\}, \quad \text{for } i = 1, 2, \ldots, n.$$

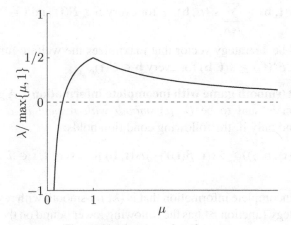

Figure 11.16. $\lambda/\max\{\mu, 1\}$ vs. μ.

Definition 11.78 (coalitionally smooth game). A normal form game is (λ, μ)-coalitionally smooth if there exists a strategy vector $\mathbf{a} \in \mathcal{B}$ such that for every strategy vector $\mathbf{b} \in \mathcal{B}$, a welfare-optimal strategy vector $\mathbf{b}^*$, and every permutation π of the players, the following condition holds:

$$\sum_{i=1}^{n} s_i(\mathbf{a}_{N_i^\pi}, \mathbf{b}_{-N_i^\pi}) \geq \lambda s(\mathbf{b}^*) - \mu s(\mathbf{b}).$$

Theorem 11.79. *If a game is (λ, μ)-coalitionally smooth for some $\lambda, \mu \geq 0$, then for every strong equilibrium $\mathbf{b} \in \mathcal{B}$ and every welfare-maximizing strategy vector $\mathbf{b}^*$, $s(\mathbf{b}) \geq (\lambda/(\mu + 1))s(\mathbf{b}^*)$.*

Proof. Consider a permutation of players π such that for every $i \in \{1, 2, \ldots, n\}$, the deviation of a coalition of players N_i^π from playing according to the strategy vector $\mathbf{b}$ to playing according to the strategy vector $(\mathbf{b}_{N_i^\pi}^*, \mathbf{b}_{-N_i^\pi})$ is blocked by player $\pi(i)$, i.e.,

$$s_{\pi(i)}(\mathbf{b}) \geq s_{\pi(i)}(\mathbf{b}_{N_i^\pi}^*, \mathbf{b}_{-N_i^\pi}).$$

Such a permutation always exists because of the assumption that the strategy vector $\mathbf{b}$ is a strong equilibrium.

Using this along with the assumption that the game is (λ, μ)-coalitionally smooth, we obtain

$$s(\mathbf{b}) \geq \sum_{i \in N} s_i(\mathbf{b}) \geq \sum_{i=1}^{n} s_i(\mathbf{b}_{N_i^\pi}^*, \mathbf{b}_{-N_i^\pi}) \geq \lambda s(\mathbf{b}^*) - \mu s(\mathbf{b}),$$

which implies $s(\mathbf{b}) \geq (\lambda/(\mu + 1))s(\mathbf{b}^*)$. $\qquad\square$

An example of a coalitionally smooth games is provided in Section 6.4.1.

Games with Incomplete Information

We consider a normal form game with incomplete information $G = (N, \{\mathcal{T}_i, \ i \in N\}, \{\mathcal{B}_i, \ i \in N\}, \{s_i, \ i \in N\})$ as introduced in Section 1.2.1. Given is a welfare function $s : \mathcal{T} \times \mathcal{B} \to \mathbf{R}$ that is assumed to satisfy

$$s(\mathbf{t}, \mathbf{b}) \geq \sum_{i \in N} s_i(t_i, \mathbf{b}), \quad \text{for every } \mathbf{b} \in \mathcal{B}(\mathbf{t}) \text{ and } \mathbf{t} \in \mathcal{T}. \tag{11.106}$$

Let $\beta^* : \mathcal{T} \to \mathcal{B}$ be a strategy vector that maximizes the welfare function; that is, for every $\mathbf{t} \in \mathcal{T}$, $s(\mathbf{t}, \beta^*(\mathbf{t})) \geq s(\mathbf{t}, \mathbf{b})$ for every $\mathbf{b} \in \mathcal{B}(\mathbf{t})$.

Definition 11.80 (smooth game with incomplete information). A game with incomplete information is said to be (λ, μ)-*smooth with respect to a strategy function* $\beta : \mathcal{T} \to \mathcal{B}$ if, and only if, the following condition holds:

$$\sum_{i \in N} s_i(t_i, (\beta_i(\mathbf{t}), \mathbf{b}_{-i})) \geq \lambda s(\mathbf{t}, \beta(\mathbf{t})) - \mu s(\hat{\mathbf{t}}, \mathbf{b}) \text{ for every } \mathbf{t}, \hat{\mathbf{t}} \in \mathcal{T} \text{ and } \mathbf{b} \in \mathcal{B}(\hat{\mathbf{t}}).$$

A game with incomplete information that is (λ, μ)-smooth with respect to a welfare-maximizing strategy function β^* has the following lower bound on the expected welfare in a Bayes-Nash equilibrium.

Theorem 11.81. *Suppose that a normal form game with incomplete information is* (λ, μ)*-smooth with respect to a strategy function* $\beta^* : \mathcal{T} \to \mathcal{B}$ *that maximizes the welfare function. Then, in every Bayes-Nash equilibrium the expected value of the welfare function is at least* $\lambda/(\mu + 1)$ *of the expected value of the welfare function under the strategy function* β^*.

Proof. For every given vector of types $\mathbf{t} \in \mathcal{T}$, let $B_1(\mathbf{b}_1; \mathbf{t}), B_2(\mathbf{b}_2; \mathbf{t}), \ldots, B_n(\mathbf{b}_n; \mathbf{t})$ be a mixed-strategy Bayes-Nash equilibrium strategies and let $B(\mathbf{b}; \mathbf{t}) = B_1(\mathbf{b}_1; \mathbf{t}) B_2(\mathbf{b}_2; \mathbf{t}) \cdots B_n(\mathbf{b}_n; \mathbf{t})$ for $\mathbf{b} = (\mathbf{b}_1, \mathbf{b}_2, \ldots, \mathbf{b}_n) \in \mathcal{B}(\mathbf{t})$. For every player $i \in N$, let $A_i(\cdot; t_i)$ be a mixed strategy defined by sampling the types of other players $\hat{\mathbf{t}}_i$ from the distribution μ_{-i} and then playing the strategy $\beta^*(t_i, \hat{\mathbf{t}}_i)$.

We have the following sequence of relations:

$$\mathbf{E}_{\mathbf{t} \sim \mu, \mathbf{b} \sim B(\cdot; \mathbf{t})}[s(\mathbf{t}, \mathbf{b})] \geq \mathbf{E}_{\mathbf{t} \sim \mu}\left[\mathbf{E}_{\mathbf{b} \sim B(\cdot; \mathbf{t})}\left[\sum_{i \in N} s_i(t_i, \mathbf{b})\right]\right] \qquad (11.107)$$

$$= \sum_{i \in N} \mathbf{E}_{\mathbf{t} \sim \mu, \mathbf{b} \sim B(\cdot; \mathbf{t})}[s_i(t_i, \mathbf{b})]$$

$$\geq \sum_{i \in N} \mathbf{E}_{\mathbf{t} \sim \mu, a_i \sim A_i(\cdot; t_i), \mathbf{b} \sim B(\cdot; \mathbf{t})}[s_i(t_i, (a_i, \mathbf{b}_{-i}))] \qquad (11.108)$$

$$= \sum_{i \in N} \mathbf{E}_{\mathbf{t} \sim \mu, \hat{\mathbf{t}}_i \sim \mu_{-i}, \mathbf{b} \sim B(\cdot; \mathbf{t})}[s_i(t_i, (\beta_i^*(t_i, \hat{\mathbf{t}}_i), \mathbf{b}_{-i}))]$$

$$= \sum_{i \in N} \mathbf{E}_{\mathbf{t} \sim \mu, \hat{\mathbf{t}} \sim \mu, \mathbf{b} \sim B(\cdot; \mathbf{t})}[s_i(t_i, (\beta_i^*(t_i, \hat{\mathbf{t}}_{-i}), \mathbf{b}_{-i}))]$$

$$= \sum_{i \in N} \mathbf{E}_{\mathbf{t} \sim \mu, \hat{\mathbf{t}} \sim \mu, \mathbf{b} \sim B(\cdot; \hat{\mathbf{t}})}[s_i(t_i, (\beta_i^*(t_i, \mathbf{t}_{-i}), \mathbf{b}_{-i}))] \qquad (11.109)$$

$$\geq \mathbf{E}_{\mathbf{t} \sim \mu, \hat{\mathbf{t}} \sim \mu, \mathbf{b} \sim B(\cdot; \hat{\mathbf{t}})}[\lambda s(\mathbf{t}, \beta^*(\mathbf{t})) - \mu s(\hat{\mathbf{t}}, \mathbf{b})]$$

$$= \lambda \mathbf{E}_{\mathbf{t} \sim \mu}[s(\mathbf{t}, \beta^*(\mathbf{t}))] - \mu \mathbf{E}_{\hat{\mathbf{t}} \sim \mu, \mathbf{b} \sim B(\cdot; \hat{\mathbf{t}})}[s(\hat{\mathbf{t}}, \mathbf{b})] \qquad (11.110)$$

where the inequality (11.107) follows from the assumption on the welfare function in (11.106), the inequality (11.108) is by the assumption that $B(\cdot; \mathbf{t})$ is a mixed-strategy Bayes-Nash equilibrium, (11.109) holds because $\mathbf{t}$ and $\hat{\mathbf{t}}$ are independent and identically distributed, and (11.110) is by the assumption that the game is (λ, μ)-smooth with respect to the strategy function β^*.

Therefore, it follows that

$$\frac{\mathbf{E}_{\mathbf{t} \sim \mu, \mathbf{b} \sim B(\cdot; \mathbf{t})}[s(\mathbf{t}, \mathbf{b})]}{\mathbf{E}_{\mathbf{t} \sim \mu}[s(\mathbf{t}, \beta^*(\mathbf{t}))]} \geq \frac{\lambda}{\mu + 1}$$

which establishes the claim of the theorem. $\qquad \square$

11.4 Bibliographical Notes

Comprehensive coverage of the topic of real analysis, some of which we reviewed in Section 11.1, is available in Dudley (2002). The topic of convex optimization is well covered in Boyd and Vandenberghe (2004), and an early reference by Rockafellar (1970). The proof of the envelope theorem (Theorem 11.13) is based on linear programming arguments from Vohra (2005). Some other versions of the envelope theorem, including a version with equality constraints, were established by Milgrom (1999) and Milgrom and Segal (2002). The topic of functional equations is covered in books by Aczél (1966) and Kannappan (2009). The results on the solutions of Cauchy's functional equations in Section 11.1.8 are standard. Theorem 11.16 is a partial version of Theorem 1.2 in Kannappan (2009), which contains equivalence claims for several other properties involving some concepts from measure theory. The discussion of the functional equations in Section 11.1.9 is based on Aczél (1966). The proofs of the fixed-point theorems asserted in Section 11.1.10 and other fixed-point theorems can be found, for example, in Border (1989), Vohra (2005), and Maschler et al. (2013).

There is an extensive literature on the topic of probability theory. A nice review of probability theory is available, for example, in Brémaud (2001). A comprehensive account on order statistics, which we discussed in Section 11.2.2, can be found in classic references such as Arnold et al. (2008). The distributions on a simplex with uniform univariate marginal distributions, discussed in Section 11.2.3, are from various references including Borel and Ville (1938), Weinstein (2005), and Roberson (2006). The inequalities in Section 11.2.5 are standard: Theorem 11.40 is by Jensen (1906); Theorem 11.41 is by Harris (1960); Theorem 11.44 is often attributed to Chernoff (1952) though it has roots in earlier work by Bernstein (1927); Theorem 11.45 is by Hoeffding (1963); Theorem 11.47 is by Bennett (1962), and Theorem 11.49 is by Bernstein (1927).

The class of concave games was introduced by Rosen (1986). The existence of a pure-strategy Nash equilibrium in Theorem 11.51 was established by Rosen (1986), along with the condition of diagonal strict concavity and showing that this condition ensures the uniqueness of a pure-strategy Nash equilibrium as presented in Theorem 11.55, and the sufficient condition in Corollary 11.56. The subclass of socially concave games was introduced, more recently, by Even-dar et al. (2009), along with the sufficient condition for uniqueness of a pure-strategy Nash equilibrium in Corollary 11.57. Example 11.54 is from Mirrokni et al. (2010). The first use of a potential function to establish the existence of a pure-strategy Nash equilibrium was done by Rosenthal (1973) who showed that every congestion game is a potential game. Monderer and Shapley (1996) provided further results and also covered other types of games. The exposition in Section 11.3.2 is based on Rosenthal (1973), with the only exception being the price of stability bounds in Theorem 11.64, which is a slight adaptation of a result in Nisan et al. (2007). The framework of smooth games as defined in Section 11.3.3 was first systematically formulated and studied by Roughgarden (2009). Theorems 11.66–11.69 showing the price of anarchy bounds derived using the smoothness framework were established by Roughgarden (2009). Cominetti et al. (2009) used the framework of locally smooth games to derive the price of anarchy bounds for splittable congestion games with a special case of local smoothness with $\lambda = 1$. The general concept of local smoothness was first introduced by Harks (2008) and was further developed by Roughgarden and Schoppmann (2011), who derived tight bounds on the price of anarchy for atomic splittable congestion games. The alternative framework of smooth games with quasi-linear payoffs and the price of an anarchy bound derived using this framework were established by Syrgkanis and Tardos (2013). The framework of coalitionally smooth games and the relation to the solution concept of strong Nash equilibria were introduced by Bachrach et al. (2014). The result in Theorem 11.79 also extends to correlated strong equilibria, as shown in Bachrach et al. (2014), which we did not cover in the Appendix. The worst-case efficiency bounds derived using the smoothness framework in Examples 11.70, 11.76, and 11.77 are from Roughgarden (2009), Syrgkanis and Tardos (2013), and Caragiannis and Voudouris (2014), respectively. The smoothness framework for games with incomplete information was developed independently by Roughgarden (2012) and Syrgkanis (2012). The composition theorems, identifying sufficient conditions under which a composition of smooth games remains a smooth game, e.g., a composition of simultaneous games or a composition of sequential games, were established in Syrgkanis and Tardos (2013) and are not covered in this chapter.

References

Aczél, J. 1966. *Lectures on Functional Equations and Their Applications*. New York: Academic Press.

Adamo, Tim, and Matros, Alexander. 2009. A Blotto game with incomplete information. *Economics Letters*, **105**(1), 100–102.

Adler, B. Thomas, de Alfaro, Luca, Pye, Ian, and Raman, Vishwanath. 2008. Measuring author contributions to the Wikipedia. Pages 1–15 of: *Proceedings of the 4th International Symposium on Wikis*. WikiSym '08. New York: ACM.

Agastya, Murali, and McAfee, R. Preston. 2006. *Continuing Wars of Attrition*. Working Papers.

Agresti, Alan. 2013. *Categorical Data Analysis*. 3 edn. New York: John Wiley & Sons.

Ailon, Nir. 2007. Aggregation of partial rankings, p-ratings and top-m lists. Pages 415–424 of: *Proceedings of the Eighteenth Annual ACM-SIAM Symposium on Discrete Algorithms*. SODA '07. Philadelphia: Society for Industrial and Applied Mathematics.

Ailon, Nir, and Mohri, Mehryar. 2008. An efficient reduction of ranking to classification. Pages 87–98 of: Servedio, Rocco A., and Zhang, Tong (eds), *COLT*. Lecture Notes in Computer Science. Madison, WI: Omnipress.

Ailon, Nir, Charikar, Moses, and Newman, Alantha. 2008. Aggregating inconsistent information: Ranking and clustering. *Journal of the ACM*, **55**(5), 23:1–23:27.

Albrecht, James, Gautier, Pieter, and Vroman, Susan. 2012. A note on Peters and Severinov: Competition among sellers who offer auctions instead of prices. *Journal of Economic Theory*, **147**(1), 389–392.

Allard, Richard J. 1988. Rent-seeking with non-identical players. *Public Choice*, **57**(1), 3–14.

Alon, Noga. 2006. Ranking tournaments. *SIAM Journal on Discrete Mathematics*, **20**(1), 137–142.

Altman, A., and Tennenholtz, M. 2008. Axiomatic foundations for ranking systems. *Journal of Artificial Intelligence Research*, **31**, 473–495.

Altman, Alon, and Kleinberg, Robert. 2010. Pages 686–690: *Proceedings of the 24th AAAI Conference on Artificial Intelligence*, Atlanta. Nonmanipulable randomized tournament selections. *Proceedings of the Twenty-Fourth AAAI Conference on Artificial Intelligence (AAAI-10)*.

Altman, Alon, Procaccia, Ariel D., and Tennenholtz, Moshe. 2009. Nonmanipulable selections from a tournament. Pages 27–32 of: *Proceedings of the 21st International Joint conference on Artifical Intelligence*. IJCAI'09. San Francisco: Morgan Kaufmann Publishers Inc.

Amann, E., and Leininger, W. 1996. Asymmetric all-pay auctions with incomplete information: The two-player case. *Games and Economic Behavior*, **14**(1), 1–18.

Amann, Erwin, and Qiao, Heng. 2008. *Parallel Contests*. TWI Research Paper Series 36. Thurgauer Wirtschaftsinstitut, Universitt Konstanz.

Amegashie, J. Atsu. 2006. A contest success function with a tractable noise parameter. *Public Choice*, **126**, 135–144.

Amir, Rabah. 1996. Cournot oligopoly and the theory of supermodular games. *Games and Economic Behavior*, **15**(2), 132–148.

Andelman, Nir, Feldman, Michal, and Mansour, Yishay. 2009. Strong price of anarchy. *Games and Economic Behavior*, **65**(2), 289–317.

Andersen, Reid, Borgs, Christian, Chayes, Jennifer, Feige, Uriel, Flaxman, Abraham, Kalai, Adam, Mirrokni, Vahab, and Tennenholtz, Moshe. 2008. Trust-based recommendation systems: An axiomatic approach. Pages 199–208 of: *Proceedings of the 17th International Conference on World Wide Web*. WWW '08. New York: ACM.

Anderson, Simon P., and Renault, Regis. 2003. Efficiency and surplus bounds in Cournot competition. *Journal of Economic Theory*, **113**(2), 253–264.

Anderson, Simon P., Goeree Jacob K., and Holt Charles A. 1998. The war of attrition with noisy players. Pages 15–29 of: *in Advances in Applied Microeconomics, Volume 7*. Bingley, UK: JAI Press.

Anderson, Simon P., Goeree, Jacob K., and Holt, Charles A. 2001. Minimum-effort coordination games: Stochastic potential and logit equilibrium. *Games and Economic Behavior*, **34**(2), 177–199.

Annis, David H., and Wu, Samuel S. 2006. A comparison of potential playoff systems for NCAA I-A football. *The American Statistician*, **60**, 151–157.

Anshelevich, E., Dasgupta, A., Kleinberg, J., Tardos, E., Wexler, T., and Roughgarden, T. 2004. The price of stability of network design with fair cost allocation. Pages 295–304 of: *Proceedings of the 45th Annual IEEE Symposium on Foundations of Computer Science*. FOCS'04.

Anshelevich, Elliot, and Hoefer, Martin. 2012. Contribution games in networks. *Algorithmica*, **63**(1–2), 51–90.

Anwar, Sajid, McMillan, Robert, and Zheng, Mingli. 2006. Bidding behavior in competing auctions: Evidence from eBay. *European Economic Review*, **50**(2), 307–322.

Aoyagi, M. 2010. Information feedback in a dynamic tournament. *Games and Economic Behavior*, **70**, 242–260.

Appelbaum, Elie, and Katz, Eliakim. 1986. Transfer seeking and avoidance: On the full social costs of rent seeking. *Public Choice*, **48**(2), 175–181.

Appleton, David R. 1995. May the best man win? *The Statistician*, **44**, 529–538.

Archak, Nikolay. 2010. Money, glory and cheap talk: analyzing strategic behavior of contestants in simultaneous crowdsourcing contests on TopCoder.com. Pages 21–30 of: *Proceedings of the 19th international conference on World wide web*. WWW '10. New York: ACM.

Archak, Nikolay, and Sundararajan, Arun. 2009. Optimal design of crowdsourcing contests. In: *Proc. of International Conference on Information Systems*.

Arnold, Barry C., Balakrishnan, N., and Nagaraja, H. N. 2008. *A First Course in Order Statistics*. SIAM Classics in Applied Mathematics.

Arrow, K. J., Chenery, H. B., Minhas, B. S., and Solow, R. M. 1961. Capital-labor substitution and economic efficiency. *Review of Economics and Statistics (The MIT Press)*, **43**(3), 225–250.

Arrow, Kenneth J. 1951. *Social Choice and Individual Values*. Yale University Press.

Ashenfelter, O. 1998. How auctions work for wine and art. *Journal of Economic Perspectives*, **3**(3), 23–36.

Ashlagi, Itai, Edelman, Benjamin, and Lee, Hoan Soo. 2010. *Competing Ad Auctions: Multi-Homing and Participation Costs*. Working Papers 10-055. Harward Business School.

Ashlagi, Itai, Monderer, Dov, and Tennenholtz, Moshe. 2011. Simultaneous ad auctions. *Mathematics of Operations Research*, **36**(1), 1–13.

Atlamaz, Murat, Berden, Caroline, Peters, Hans, and Vermeulen, Dries. 2011. Non-cooperative solutions for estate division problems. *Games and Economic Behavior*, **73**(1), 39–51.

Augenblick, Ned. 2011. *Consumer and Producer Behavior in the Market for Penny Auctions: A Theoretical and Empirical Analysis*. Working Papers.

Aumann, Robert J. 1974. Subjectivity and correlation in randomized strategies. *Journal of Mathematical Economics*, **1**(1), 67–96.

Auriol, Emmanuelle, and Renault, Regis. 2008. Status and incentives. *RAND Journal of Economics*, **39**(1), 305–326.

Azar, Yossi, Birnbaum, Benjamin, Celis, L. Elisa, Devanur, Nikhil R., and Peres, Yuval. 2009. Convergence of local dynamics to balanced outcomes in exchange networks. Pages 293–302 of: *Proceedings of the 2009 50th Annual IEEE Symposium on Foundations of Computer Science*. FOCS '09. Washington, DC: IEEE Computer Society.

Azmat, Ghazala, and Möller, Marc. 2009. Competition among contests. *RAND Journal of Economics*, **40**(4), 743–768.

Bachrach, Yoram, Syrgkanis, Vasilis, Tardos, Éva, and Vojnović, Milan. 2014. Strong price of anarchy, utility games and coalitional dynamics. Pages 218–230 of: *Proceedings of the 7th International Symposium on Algorithmic Game Theory*. SAGT 2014, Haifa, Israel.

Bachrach, Yoram, Syrgkanis, Vasilis, and Vojnović, Milan. 2013. Incentives and efficiency in uncertain collaborative environments. Pages 26–39 of: *Proceedings of the 9th Conference on Web and Internet Economics*. WINE 2013, Cambridge, MA.

Bag, Parimal Kanti, and Sabourian, Hamid. 2005. Distributing awards efficiently: More on King Solomon's problem. *Games and Economic Behavior*, **53**(1), 43–58.

Baik, Kyung Hwan. 1993. Effort levels in contests: The public-good prize case. *Economics Letters*, **41**(4), 363–367.

Baik, Kyung Hwan. 1994. Effort levels in contests with asymmetric players. *Southern Economic Journal*, **61**, 367–378.

Baik, Kyung Hwan. 1998. Difference-form contest success functions and effort levels in contests. *European Journal of Political Economy*, **14**(4), 685–701.

Baik, Kyung H., and Jason, F. 1992. Strategic behavior in contests: Comment. *The American Economic Review*, **82**(1), 359–362.

Bala, Venkatesh, and Goyal, Sanjeev. 2000. A noncooperative model of network formation. *Econometrica*, **68**(5), 1181–1229.

Ballester, Coralio, Calvó-Armengol, Antoni, and Zenou, Yves. 2006. Who's who in networks. Wanted: The key player. *Econometrica*, **74**(5), 1403–1417.

Bapna, Ravi, Dellarocas, Chrysanthos, and Rice, Sarah. 2010. Vertically differentiated simultaneous Vickrey auctions: Theory and experimental evidence. *Management Science*, **56**(7), 1074–1092.

Barclays Premier League. 2014. *The Official Website of the Barclays Premier League*. http://www.premierleague.com

Bartholdi, J., III, Tovey, C. A., and Trick, M. A. 1989. Voting schemes for which it can be difficult to tell who won the election. *Social Choice and Welfare*, **6**(2), 157–165.

Barut, Yasar, and Kovenock, Dan. 1998. The symmetric multiple prize all-pay auction with complete information. *European Journal of Political Economy*, **14**(4), 627–644.

Bassett, G. W. 1997. Robust sports ratings based on least absolute errors. *The American Statistician*, **51**(2), 99–105.

Bateni, MohammadHossein, Hajiaghayi, MohammadTaghi, Immorlica, Nicole, and Mahini, Hamid. 2010. The cooperative game theory foundations of network bargaining games. Pages 67–78 of: Proceedings of 37th International Colloquium on Automata, Languages and Programming, ICALP 2010, Bordeaux, France.

Baye, Michael R., Kovenock, Dan, and de Vries, Casper G. 1993. Rigging the lobbying process: An application of the all-pay auction. *American Economic Review*, **83**(1), 289–294.

Baye, Michael R., Kovenock, Dan, and de Vries, Casper G. 1994. The solution to the Tullock rent-seeking game when $R > 2$: Mixed-strategy equilibria and mean dissipation rates. *Public Choice*, **81**(3–4), 363–380.

Baye, Michael R., Kovenock, Dan, and de Vries, Casper G. 1996. The all-pay auction with complete information. *Economic Theory*, **8**(2), 291–305.

Baye, Michael R., Kovenock, Dan, and de Vries, Casper G. 1999. The incidence of overdissipation in rent-seeking contests. *Public Choice*, **99**(3/4), 439–454.

Beasley, John D. 2006. *The Mathematics of Games*. New York: Dover.

Beenen, Gerard, Ling, Kimberly, Wang, Xiaoqing, Chang, Klarissa, Frankowski, Dan, Resnick, Paul, and Kraut, Robert E. 2004. Using social psychology to motivate contributions to online communities. Pages 212–221 of: *Proceedings of the 2004 ACM Conference on Computer Supported Cooperative Work*. CSCW '04. New York: ACM.

Bellman, R. 1969. On Colonel Blotto and analogous games. *SIAM Review*, **11**(1), 66–68.

Bennett, George. 1962. Probability Inequalities for the Sum of Independent Random Variables. *Journal of the American Statistical Association*, **57**(297), pp. 33–45.

Berend, Daniel, Chernyavsky, Yuri, and Sapir, Luba. 2008. Ranking of Weighted Majority Rules. *Journal of Applied Probability*, **45**(4), 994–1006.

Berend, Daniel, and Sapir, Luba. 2003. Between the expert and majority rules. *Advances in Applied Probability*, **35**(4), 941–960.

Berry, Randall A., and Johari, Ramesh. 2013. Economic modeling in networking: A primer. *Foundations and Trends in Networking*, **6**(3), 165–286.

Bernstein, S. 1927. *Theory of Probability*. Moscow.

Bertoletti, Paolo. 2006 (Jan.). *On the reserve price in all-pay auctions with complete information and lobbying games*. MPRA Paper 1083. University Library of Munich, Germany.

Beygelzimer, Alina, Langford, John, and Ravikumar, Pradeep. 2009. Error-correcting tournaments. Pages 247–262 of: *Proceedings of the 20th International Conference on Algorithmic Learning Theory*. ALT'09. Berlin: Springer-Verlag.

Bhaskar, Umang, Fleischer, Lisa, Hoy, Darrell, and Huang, Chien-Chung. 2009. Equilibria of atomic flow games are not unique. Pages 748–757 of: *Proceedings of the Twentieth Annual ACM-SIAM Symposium on Discrete Algorithms*. SODA '09. Philadelphia: Society for Industrial and Applied Mathematics.

Bhattacharya, S., Goel, G., Gollapudi, S., and Munagala, K. 2010. Budget constrained auctions with heterogeneous items. Pages 379–388 of: *Proceedings of the 42nd ACM Symposium on Theory of Computing*, Cambridge, MA.

Bikhchandani, Sushil. 1999. Auctions of heterogeneous objects. *Games and Economic Behavior*, **26**(2), 193–220.

Bishop, Christopher M. 2006. *Pattern Recognition and Machine Learning*. New York: Springer.

Bishop, D. T., and Cannings, C. 1978. A generalized war of attrition. *Journal of Theoretical Biology*, **70**(1), 85–124.

Bishop, D. T., Cannings, C., and Smith, J. Maynard. 1978. The war of attrition with random rewards. *Journal of Theoretical Biology*, **74**(3), 377–388.

Blackett, D. W. 1954. Some Blotto games. *Naval Research Logistics Quarterly*, **1**(1), 55–60.

Blackett, D. W. 1958. Pure strategy solutions of Blotto games. *Naval Research Logistics Quarterly*, **5**(2), 107–109.

Bliss, C. I., Greenwood, Mary L., and White, Edna S. 1956. A rankit analysis of paired comparisons for measuring the effect of sprays on flavor. *Biometrics*, **12**(4), 381–403.

Bliss, Christopher, and Nalebuff, Barry. 1984. Dragon-slaying and ballroom dancing: The private supply of a public good. *Journal of Public Economics*, **25**(1–2), 1–12.

Böckenholt, Ulf. 1993. Applications of Thurstonian models to ranking data. *Probability Models and Statistical Analysis for Ranking Data*, Lecture Notes in Statistics Volume 80, 157–172.

Border, K. C. 1989. *Fixed Point Theorems with Applications to Economics and Game Theory*. Cambridge: Cambridge University Press.

Borel, E. 1921. La théorie du jeu et les équations inté grales á noyau symétrique. *Comptes Rendus de l'Académie des Sciences; English translation by L. Savage, The theory of play and integral equations with skew symmetric kernels, Econometrica 21 (1953), 97-100.*, **173**, 1304–1308.

Borel, E., and Ville, J. 1938. Application de la théorie des probabilitiés aux jeux de hasard. *Gauthier-Villars, Paris. Reprinted in E. Borel, A. Chéron, Théorie mathematique du bridge á la portée de tous, Editions Jacques Gabay, Paris, 1991*.

Bos, Olivier. 2011. How lotteries outperform auctions. *Economics Letters*, **110**(3), 262–264.

Bouyssou, Denis. 1992. Ranking methods based on valued preference relations: A characterization of the net flow method. *European Journal of Operational Research*, **60**(1), 61–67.

Boyd, Stephen, and Vandenberghe, Lieven. 2004. *Convex Optimization*. Cambridge: Cambridge University Press.

Bradley, Ralph Allan, and Terry, Milton E. 1952. Rank analysis of incomplete block designs: I. Method of paired comparisons. *Biometrika*, **39**(3/4), 324–345.

Bradley, Ralph Allan, and Terry, Milton E. 1954. Rank analysis of incomplete block designs: II. Additional tables for the method of paired comparisons. *Biometrika*, **41**(3/4), 502–537.

Bramoulle, Yann, and Kranton, Rachel. 2007. Public goods in networks. *Journal of Economic Theory*, **135**(1), 478–494.

Brémaud, Pierre. 2001. *Markov Chains: Gibbs Fields, Monte Carlo Simulation, and Queues (Text in Applied Mathematics)*. 2nd ed. New York: Springer.

Brian, W. 1994. Inductive reasoning and bounded rationality. *American Economic Review*, **84**(2), 406–411.

Brin, S., and Page, L. 1998. The anatomy of a large-scale hypertextual Web search engine. *Computer Networks and ISDN Systems*, **30**(1–7), 107–117.

Buhlmann, Hans, and Huber, Peter J. 1963. Pairwise comparison and ranking in tournaments. *Annals of Mathematical Statistics*, **34**(2), 501–510.

Bulow, Jeremy, and Klemperer, Paul. 1996. Auctions versus negotiations. *American Economic Review*, **86**(1), 180–94.

Bulow, Jeremy, and Klemperer, Paul. 1997. The generalized war of attrition. *American Economic Review*, **89**(1), 175–189.

Burke, Moira, and Kraut, Robert. 2008. Mopping up: Modeling Wikipedia promotion decisions. Pages 27–36 of: *Proceedings of the 2008 ACM Conference on Computer Supported Cooperative Work*. CSCW '08. New York: ACM.

Byers, John W., Mitzenmacher, Michael, and Zervas, Georgios. 2010. Information asymmetries in pay-per-bid auctions. Pages 1–12 of: *Proceedings of the 11th ACM Conference on Electronic Commerce*. EC '10. New York: ACM.

Callaghan, Thomas, Mucha, Peter J., and Porter, Mason A. 2007. Random Walker Ranking for NCAA Division I-A Football. *American Mathematical Monthly*, November.

Caragiannis, Ioannis, and Voudouris, Alexandros A. 2014. Welfare guarantees for proportional allocations. Pages 206–217 of: *Proceedings of the 7th International Symposium on Algorithmic Game Theory*. SAGT 2014.

Cattelan, Manuela. 2012. Models for paired comparison data: A review with emphasis on dependent data. *Statistical Science*, **27**(3), 412–433.

Celis, L. Elisa, Devanur, Nikhil R., and Peres, Yuval. 2010. Local dynamics in bargaining networks via random-turn games. Pages 133–144 of: Saberi, Amin (ed), *Internet and Network Economics*. Lecture Notes in Computer Science, vol. 6484. Springer: Berlin.

Chakrabarti, A. S., Chakrabarti, B. K., Chatterjee, A., and Mitra, M. 2009. The Kolkata Paise Restaurant problem and resource utilization. *Physica A Statistical Mechanics and its Applications*, **388**(June), 2420–2426.

Charon, Irne, and Hudry, Olivier. 2010. An updated survey on the linear ordering problem for weighted or unweighted tournaments. *Annals of Operations Research*, **175**(1), 107–158.

Chawla, Shuchi, and Hartline, Jason D. 2013. Auctions with unique equilibrium. Pages 181–196 of: *Proceedings of the 13th ACM Conference on Electronic Commerce*. EC '13, Philadelphia.

Chawla, Shuchi, Hartline, Jason D., and Sivan, Balasubramanian. 2012. Optimal crowdsourcing contests. Pages 856–868 of: Proceedings of the Twenty-Third Annual ACM-SIAM Symposium on Discrete Algorithms, SODA 2012, Kyoto, Japan.

Che, Yeon-Koo, and Gale, Ian L. 1998. Caps on political lobbying. *The American Economic Review*, **88**(3), 643–651.

Che, Yeon-Koo, and Gale, Ian. 2000. Difference-form contests and the robustness of all-pay auctions. *Games and Economic Behavior*, **30**(1), 22–43.

Chen, R., and Hwang, F. K. 1988. Stronger players win more balanced knockout tournaments. *Graphs and Combinatorics*, **4**(2), 95–99.

Chen, Yan, Harper, F. Maxwell, Konstan, Joseph, and Li, Sherry Xin. 2010. Social comparisons and contributions to online communities: A field experiment on MovieLens. *American Economic Review*, **100**(4), 1358–1398.

Chernoff, Herman. 1952. A Measure of Asymptotic Efficiency for Tests of a Hypothesis Based on the sum of Observations. *The Annals of Mathematical Statistics*, **23**(4), pp. 493–507.

Chung, F. R. K., and Hwang, F. K. 1978. Do stronger players win more knockout tournaments? *Journal of the American Statistical Association*, **73**(363), 593–596.

Chung, Tai-Yeong. 1996. Rent-seeking contest when the prize increases with aggregate efforts. *Public Choice*, **87**(1/2), 55–66.

Clark, Derek J., and Nilssen, Tore. 2013. Learning by doing in contests. *Public Choice*, **156**(1–2), 329–343.

Clark, Derek J, and Riis, Christian. 1998a. Competition over more than one prize. *American Economic Review*, **88**(1), 276–289.

Clark, Derek J., and Riis, Christian. 1998b. Contest Success Functions: An Extension. *Economic Theory*, **11**(1), 201–204.

Clark, Derek J., and Riis, Christian. 1998c. Influence and the discretionary allocation of several prizes. *European Journal of Political Economy*, **14**(4), 605–625.

Clarke, S. R., Norman, J. M., and Stride, C. B. 2009. Criteria for a tournament: The World Professional Snooker Championship. *Journal of the Operational Research Society*, **60**(Feb.), 1670–1673.

Cleverdon, C. W., and Mills, J. 1963. The testing of index language devices. *Aslib Proceedings*, **15**(4), 106–130.

Cobb, C. W., and Douglas, P. H. 1928. A theory of production. *American Economic Review*, **18**(1), 139–165.

Cohen, Chen, Kaplan, Todd R., and Sela, Aner. 2008. Optimal rewards in contests. *RAND Journal of Economics*, **39**(2), 434–451.

Colley, Wesley N. 2013 (November). *Colley Matrix*. http://colleyrankings.com.

Cominetti, Roberto, Correa, Jose R., and Stier-Moses, Nicolas E. 2009. The impact of oligopolistic competition in networks. *Operations Research*, **57**(6), 1421–1437.

Congleton, Roger D., Hillman, Arye L., and Konrad, Kai A. 2008a. *40 Years of Research on Rent Seeking 1: Theory of Rent Seeking*. New York: Springer.

Congleton, Roger D., Hillman, Arye L., and Konrad, Kai A. 2008b. *40 Years of Research on Rent Seeking 2: Applications: Rent Seeing in Practice*. New York: Springer.

Conner, Gregory R., and Grant, Christopher P. 2000. An extension of Zermelo's model for ranking by paired comparisons. *European Journal of Applied Mathematics*, **11**(December), 225–247.

Conitzer, Vincent, and Sandholm, Tuomas. 2005. Common voting rules as maximum likelihood estimators. Pages 145–152 of: *Proceedings of the 20th Conference on Uncertainty in Artifical Intelligence (UAI 2005)*, Edinburgh.

Contizer, Vincent. 2006. Computing Slater Rankings using similarities among candidates. In: *Proceedings of the American Association for Artifical Intelligence*. AAAI '06, Boston, MA.

Cooper, William S. 1968. Expected search length: A single measure of retrieval effectiveness based on the weak ordering action of retrieval systems. *American Documentation*, **19**(1), 30–41.

Copeland, A. 1951. *A 'reasonable' social welfare function*, Seminar on Applications of Mathematics to Social Sciences, University of Michigan, MI.

Coppersmith, Don, Fleischer, Lisa, and Rudra, Atri. 2006. Ordering by weighted number of wins gives a good ranking for weighted tournaments. Pages 776–782 of: *Proceedings of the Seventeenth Annual ACM-SIAM Symposium on Discrete Algorithm*. SODA '06. New York: ACM.

Corbo, Jacomo, Calvó-Armengol, Antoni, and Parkes, David C. 2007. The importance of network topology in local contribution games. Pages 388–395 of: Deng, Xiaotie, and Graham, FanChung (eds), *Internet and Network Economics*. Lecture Notes in Computer Science, vol. 4858. Springer: Berlin.

Corchón, Luis C. 2007. The theory of contests: A survey. *Review of Economic Design*, **11**(2), 69–100.

Corchón, Luis C. 2008. Welfare losses under Cournot competition. *International Journal of Industrial Organization*, **26**(5), 1120–1131.

Corchón, Luis, and Dahm, Matthias. 2010. Foundations for contest success functions. *Economic Theory*, **43**(1), 81–98.

Corcoran, William J., and Karels, Gordon V. 1985. Rent-seeking behavior in the long-run. *Public Choice*, **46**(3), 227–246.

Cornes, Richard, and Hartley, Roger. 2003. Risk aversion, heterogeneity and contests. *Public Choice*, **117**(1–2), 1–25.

Cornes, Richard, and Hartley, Roger. 2005. Asymmetric contests with general technologies. *Economic Theory*, **26**(4), 923–946.

Correa, José R., Schultz, Andreas S., and Stier-Moses, Nicolás E. 2013. The price of anarchy of the proportional allocation mechanism revisited. Pages 109–120 of: *Proceedings of the 9th International Conference on Web and Internet Economics, WINE 2013*. WINE '13, Cambridge, MA.

Courcoubetis, C., and Weber, R. 2006. Incentives for large peer-to-peer systems. *IEEE Journal on Selected Areas in Communications*, **24**(5), 1034–1050.

Cournot, A. A. 1838. *Recherches sur les principes mathematiques de la theorie des richesses [microform] / par Augustin Cournot*. Paris: L. Hachette.

Cournot, Augustin. 1897. *Researches into the Mathematical Principles of the Theory of Wealth*. London: MacMillan & Co., Ltd., translation of original book published in 1838.

Cover, Thomas M., and Thomas, Joy A. 2006. *Elements of Information Theory*. 2nd ed. New York: John Wiley & Sons.

Daniels, H. E. 1950. Rank correlation and population methods. *Journal of the Royal Statistical Society, Series B (Methodological)*, **12**(2), 171–191.

Dasgupta, A., and Nti, K. O. 1998. Designing an optimal contest. *European Journal of Political Economy*, **14**(4), 587–603.

Dasgupta, P. 1986. The theory of technological competition. In: J. E. Stiglitz and G. F. Mathewson (eds.) *New Developments in the Analysis of Market Structure*. Cambridge: MIT Press.

Dasgupta, P. S., and Heal, G. M. 1979. *Economic Theory and Exhaustible Resources*. Cambridge: Cambridge University Press.

Dasgupta, Partha, and Stiglitz, Joseph. 1980. Industrial structure and the nature of innovative activity. *Economic Journal*, **90**(358), 266–293.

David, H. A. 1963. *The Method of Paired Comparisons*. London: Charles Griffin & Company Limited.

Davidson, R. R. 1970. On extending the Bradley-Terry model to accommodate ties in paired comparison experiments. *Journal of the American Statistical Association*, **65**(329), 317–328.

Davidson, Roger R., and Solomon, Daniel L. 1973. A bayesian approach to paired comparison experimentation. *Biometrika*, **60**(3), 477–487.

Dawid, A. P., and Skene, A. M. 1979. Maximum likelihood estimation of observer error-rates using the EM algorithm. *Applied Statistics*, **28**(1), 20–28.

Dawkins, Richard. 1969. A threshold model of choice behaviour. *Animal Behaviour*, **17**(Part 1), 120–133.

Debreu, G. 1952. A social equilibrium existence theorem. *Proceedings of the National Academy of Sciences*, **38**(10), 886–893.

Dechenaux, Emmanuel, Kovenock, Dan, and Sheremeta, Roman. 2012. *A Survey of Experimental Research on Contests, All-Pay Auctions and Tournaments*. Working Papers 12-22. Chapman University, Economic Science Institute.

Diaconis, P. 1988. *Group Representation in Probability and Statistics*. IMS Lecture Series 11, Institute of Mathematical Statistics.

Diaconis, Persi, and Graham, R. L. 1977. Spearman's footrule as a measure of disarray. *Journal of the Royal Statistical Society. Series B (Methodological)*, **39**(2), 262–268.

DiPalantino, Dominic, and Vojnović, Milan. 2009. Crowdsourcing and all-pay auctions. Pages 119–128 of: *Proceedings of the 10th ACM Conference on Electronic Commerce*. EC'09. New York: ACM.

Dixit, Avinash. 1987. Strategic behavior in contests. *American Economic Review*, **77**(Dec.), 891–898.

Dixit, Avinash, and Nalebuff, Barry J. 2008. *The Art of Strategy*. New York: W. W. Norton & Co.

Dixon, Mark J., and Coles, Stuart G. 1997. Modelling association football scores and inefficiencies in the football betting market. *Journal of the Royal Statistical Society: Series C (Applied Statistics)*, **46**(2), 265–280.

Dodgson, Charles L. 1883. *Lawn Tennis Tournaments: The True Method of Assigning Prizes with a Proof of the Fallacy of the Present Method*. London: McMillan and Co.

Donmez, Pinar, Carbonell, Jaime G., and Schneider, Jeff. 2009. Efficiently learning the accuracy of labeling sources for selective sampling. Pages 259–268 of: *Proceedings of the 15th ACM SIGKDD International Conference on Knowledge Discovery and Data Mining*. KDD '09. New York: ACM.

Draief, M., and Vojnović, M. 2010. Bargaining dynamics in exchange networks. Pages 1303–1310 of: *the 48th Annual Allerton Conference on Communication, Control, and Computing (Allerton), 2010*. Allerton, IL.

Dror, Gideon, Koren, Yehuda, Maarek, Yoelle, and Szpektor, Idan. 2011. I want to answer, who has a question? Yahoo! answers recommender system. In: *Proceedings of the 17th ACM SIGKDD international conference on Knowledge discovery and data mining*, San Diego, CA, 1109–1117.

Duchi, John C., Mackey, Lester W., and Jordan, Michael I. 2010. On the consistency of ranking algorithms. Pages 227–234 of: *Proceedings of the 27th International Conference on Machine Learning Haifa*.

Dudley, R. M. 2002. *Real Analysis and Probability*. Cambridge: Cambridge University Press.

Dwork, Cynthia, Kumar, Ravi, Naor, Moni, and Sivakumar, D. 2001a. Rank aggregation methods for the Web. Pages 613–622 of: *Proceedings of the 10th International Conference on World Wide Web*. WWW '01. New York: ACM.

Dwork, Cynthia, Kumar, Ravi, Naor, Moni, and Sivakumar, D. 2001b. *Rank Aggregation Revisited*. Unpublished manuscript.

Dykstra Jr., Otto. 1956. A note on the rank analysis of incomplete block designs – applications beyond the scope of existing tables. *Biometrics*, **12**(3), 301–306.

Dykstra Jr., Otto. 1960. Rank analysis of incomplete block designs: A method of paired comparisons employing unequal repetitions on pairs. *Biometrics*, **16**(2), 176–188.

Ellingsen, Tore. 1991. Strategic buyers and the social cost of monopoly. *The American Economic Review*, **81**(3), 648–657.

Ellison, Glenn, and Fudenberg, Drew. 2003. Knife-edge or plateau: When do market models tip? *Quarterly Journal of Economics*, **118**(4), 1249–1278.

Ellison, Glenn, Fudenberg, Drew, and Möbius, Markus. 2004. Competing auctions. *Journal of the European Economic Association*, **2**(1), 30–66.

Elo, Arpad E. 1978. *The Rating of Chessplayers*. San Jose, CA: Ishi Press International.

Engelbrecht-Wiggans, R., and Weber, R. 1979. An example of a multiobject auction game. *Management Science*, **25**(12), 1272–1277.

English, James F. 2005. *The Economy of Prestige*. Cambridge, MA: Harvard University Press.

Epstein, A., Feldman, M., and Mansour, Y. 2009. Strong equilibrium in cost sharing connection games. *Games and Economic Behavior*, **67**(1), 51–68.

Epstein, Richard A. 2013. *The Theory of Gambling and Statistical Logic*. 2nd ed. New York: Academic Press.

Ertekin, Seyda, Hirsh, Haym, and Rudin, Cynthia. 2011. Approximating the wisdom of crowds. In: *Proceedings of the Second Workshop on Computational Social Science and the Wisdom of Crowds, Twenty-Fifth Annual Conference on Neural Information Processing Systems*. NIPS '11, Sierra Nevada, Spain.

Ertekin, Seyda, Hirsh, Haym, and Rudin, Cynthia. 2012. Learning to predict the wisdom of crowds. In: *Proceeding of Collective Intelligence*. CI '12, Cambridge, MA.

Even-dar, Eyal, Mansour, Yishay, and Nadav, Uri. 2009. On the convergence of regret minimization dynamics in concave games. Pages 523–532 of: *Proceedings of the 41st Annual ACM Symposium on Theory of Computing*. STOC '09, Bethesda, Maryland.

Fagin, Ronald, Kumar, Ravi, Mahdian, Mohammad, Sivakumar, D., and Vee, Erik. 2006. Comparing partial rankings. *SIAM Journal of Discrete Mathematics*, **20**(3), 628–648.

Fagin, Ronald, Kumar, Ravi, and Sivakumar, D. 2003. Comparing top k lists. Pages 28–36 of: *Proceedings of the Fourteenth Annual ACM-SIAM Symposium on Discrete Algorithms*. SODA '03. Philadelphia: Society for Industrial and Applied Mathematics.

Fang, H. 2002. Lottery versus all-pay auction models of lobbying. *Public Choice*, **112**(3–4), 351–371.

Farrell, Joseph, and Simcoe, Timothy. 2012. Choosing the rules for consensus standardization. *RAND Journal of Economics*, **43**(2), 235–252.

Feigin, P., and Cohen, A. 1978. On a model for concordance between judges. *Journal of the Royal Statistical Society*, **B**(40), 203–213.

Feldman, Michal, Fu, Hu, Gravin, Nick, and Lucier, Brendan. 2013. Simultaneous auctions are (almost) efficient. Pages 201–210 of: *Proceedings of the 45th Annual ACM Symposium on Theory of Computing*. STOC '13. New York: ACM.

Feldman, Michal, Lai, Kevin, and Zhang, Li. 2005. A price-anticipating resource allocation mechanism for distributed shared clusters. Pages 127–136 of: *Proceedings of the 6th ACM Conference on Electronic Commerce*, Vancouver, Canada.

Feller, William. 1957. *An Introduction to Probability Theory and Its Applications: Volume I*. 2nd ed. New York: John Wiley & Sons, Inc.

Fibich, Gadi, and Gavish, Nir. 2012. Asymmetric First-Price Auctions – A Dynamical-Systems Approach. *Mathematics Operation Research*, **37**(2), 219–243.

Finley, M. I., and Pleket, H. W. 2005. *The Olympic Games: The First Thousand Years*. New York: Dover Publications Inc.

Fisher, R. A., and Tippett, L. H. C. 1928. Limiting forms of the frequency distribution of the largest or smallest member of a sample. *Proceedings of the Cambridge Philosophical Society*, **24**, 180–190.

Ford Jr., L. R. 1957. Solution of a ranking problem from binary comparisons. *American Mathematical Monthly*, **64**(8), 28–33.

Forte, A., and Bruckman, A. 2005. Why do people write for Wikipedia? Pages 6–9 of: *Proceedings of the GROUP 05 Workshop - Sustaining Community: The Role and Design of Incentive Mechanisms in Online Systems*, Sanibel Island, FL.

Frank, C. R. Jr., and Quandt, R. E. 1963. On the existence of Cournot equilibrium. *International Economic Review*, **6**(1), 92–96.

Frank, Robert H. 1985. *Choosing the Right Pond: Human Behavior and the Quest for Status*. Oxford: Oxford University Press.

Frank, Robert H., and Cook, Philip J. 2010. *The Winner-Take-All-Society*. New York: Virgin Books.

Franke, Jr. Kanzow, Christian, Leininger, Wolfgang, and Schwartz, Alexandra. 2011. Effort maximization in asymmetric contest games with heterogeneous contestants. *Economic Theory*, **52**(2), 589–630.

Frechét, M. 1927. Su la loi de probabilitié de l'écart maximum. *Annals of the Society of Polonaise Mathematics*, **6**, 92–116.

Friedman, Eric J. 2004. Strong monotonicity in surplus sharing. *Economic Theory*, **23**(3), 643–658.

Friedman, Eric, and Moulin, Hervé. 1999. Three methods to share joint costs or surplus. *Journal of Economic Theory*, **87**(2), 275–312.

Friedman, James. 1977. *Oligopoly and the Theory of Games*. Amsterdam: North-Holland.

Friedman, James. 1983. *Oligopoly and Noncooperative Game Theory*. Cambridge: Cambridge University Press.

Fu, Qiang. 2006. Endogenous timing of contest with asymmetric information. *Public Choice*, **129**(1/2), 1–23.

Fu, Qiang, and Lu, Jingfeng. 2010. Contest design and optimal endogenous entry. *Economic Inquiry*, **48**(1), 80–88.

Fu, Qiang, and Lu, Jingfeng. 2012. The optimal multi-stage contest. *Economic Theory*, **51**(2), 351–382.

Fudenberg, Drew, and Tirole, Jean. 1986. A theory of exit in duopoly. *Econometrica*, **54**(4), 943–60.

Fudenberg, Drew, and Tirole, Jean. 1991. *Game Theory*. Cambridge, MA: MIT Press.

Fullerton, Richard L., and McAfee, R. Preston. 1999. Auctioning entry into tournaments. *Journal of Political Economy*, **107**(3), 573–605.

Gabay, D., and Moulin, H. 1980. On the uniqueness and stability of nash-equilibria in noncooperative games. In: *Applied Stochastic Control in Econometrics and Management Science (A. Bensoussan et al, Eds.)*. New York: North-Holland.

Galambos, J. 1978. *The Asymptotic Theory of Extreme Order Statistics*. New York: Wiley.

Gale, Ian, and Stegeman, Mark. 1994. *Exclusion in all-pay auctions*. Working Paper. Federal Reserve Bank of Cleveland.

Galeotti, Andrea, and Goyal, Sanjeev. 2010. The law of the few. *American Economic Review*, **100**(4), 1468–1492.

Galeotti, Andrea, Goyal, Sanjeev, and Kamphorst, Jurjen. 2006. Network formation with heterogeneous players. *Games and Economic Behavior*, **54**(2), 353–372.

Galton, Francis. 1902. The most suitable proportion between the value of first and second prizes. *Biometrika*, **1**(4), 385–399.

Garfinkel, Michelle R., and Skaperdas, Stergios. 2007. *Economics of Conflict: An Overview*. Handbook of Defense Economics, vol. 2. New York: Elsevier. Chap. 22, pages 649–709.

Gaudet, Gerard, and Salant, Stephen W. 1991. Uniqueness of Cournot equilibrium: New results from old methods. *Review of Economic Studies*, **58**(2), 399–404.

Gerchak, Yigal, and He, Qi-Ming. 2003. When will the range of prizes in tournaments increase in the noise or in the number of players? *International Game Theory Review*, **5**(2), 151–165.

Gerding, Enrico H., Dash, Rajdeep K., Byde, Andrew, and Jennings, Nicholas R. 2008. Optimal strategies for bidding agents participating in simultaneous Vickrey auctions with perfect substitutes. *Journal of Artificial Intelligence Research*, **32**(1), 939–982.

Ghemawat, Pankaj, and Nalebuff, Barry. 1985. Exit. *RAND Journal of Economics*, **16**(2), 184–194.

Ghodsi, Ali, Zaharia, Matei, Hindman, Benjamin, Konwinski, Andy, Shenker, Scott, and Stoica, Ion. 2011. Dominant resource fairness: Fair allocation of multiple resource types. Pages 24–24 of:

Proceedings of the 8th USENIX Conference on Networked Systems Design and Implementation. NSDI'11. Berkeley, CA: USENIX Association.

Ghosh, Arpita, and Hummel, Patrick. 2012. Implementing optimal outcomes in social computing: A game-theoretic approach. Pages 539–548 of: *Proceedings of the 21st International Conference on the World Wide Web.* WWW '12. New York: ACM.

Ghosh, Arpita, and Kleinberg, Jon. 2013. Incentivizing participation in online forums for education. Pages 525–542 of: *Proceedings of the Fourteenth ACM Conference on Electronic Commerce.* EC '13. New York: ACM.

Ghosh, Arpita, and McAfee, Preston. 2012. Crowdsourcing with endogenous entry. Pages 999–1008 of: *Proceedings of the 21st International Conference on the World Wide Web.* WWW '12. New York: ACM.

Glazer, Amihai, and Hassin, Refael. 1988. Optimal contests. *Economic Inquiry,* **26**(1), 133–143.

Glazer, Amihai, and Hassin, Rafael. 2000. Sequential rent seeking. *Public Choice,* **102**(3–4), 219–228.

Glazer, Jacob, and Ma, Ching-to Albert. 1989. Efficient allocation of a "prize": King Solomon's dilemma. *Games and Economic Behavior,* **1**(3), 222–233.

Glenn, W. A., and David, H. A. 1960. Ties in paired-comparison experiments using a modified Thurstone-Mosteller model. *Biometrics,* **16**(1), 86–109.

Gnedenko, B. 1943. Sur la distribution limite du terme maximum d'une serie aletoire. *Annals of Mathematics,* **44**, 423–453.

Goemans, Michel, Li, Li Erran, Mirrokni, Vahab S., and Thottan, Marina. 2004. Market sharing games applied to content distribution in ad-hoc networks. Pages 55–66 of: *Proceedings of the 5th ACM International Symposium on Mobile ad hoc Networking and Computing.* MobiHoc '04. New York: ACM.

Goyal, Sanjeev, and Vega-Redondo, Fernando. 2005. Network formation and social coordination. *Games and Economic Behavior,* **50**(2), 178–207.

Gradstein, Mark. 1993. Rent seeking and the provision of public goods. *Economic Journal,* **103**(420), 1236–1243.

Gradstein, Mark. 1995. Intensity of competition, entry and entry deterrence in rent seeking contests. *Economics and Politics,* **7**(1), 79–91.

Gradstein, Mark. 1998. Optimal contest design: Volume and timing of rent seeking in contests. *European Journal of Political Economy,* **14**(4), 575–585.

Gradstein, Mark, and Konrad, K. A. 1999. Orchestrating rent seeking contests. *Economic Journal,* **109**(458), 536–545.

Gradstein, Mark, and Nitzan, Shmuel. 1986. Performance evaluation of some special classes of weighted majority rules. *Mathematical Social Sciences,* **12**(1), 31–46.

Gradstein, Mark, and Nitzan, Shmuel. 1989. Advantageous multiple rent seeking. *Mathematical and Computer Modelling,* **12**(45), 511–518.

Griffiths, M. 2012. Knockout-tournament scenarios accounting for byes. *Mathematical Scientist,* **37**(1), 34–46.

Groh, Christian, Moldovanu, Benny, Sela, Aner, and Sunde, Uwe. 2012. Optimal seedings in elimination tournaments. *Economic Theory,* **49**(1), 59–80.

Gross, Oliver Alfred, and Wagner, R. A. 1950. A continuous Colonel Blotto game. *RAND Corporation,* **RM-408**.

Guiver, John, and Snelson, Edward. 2009. Bayesian inference for Plackett-Luce ranking models. Pages 377–384 of: *Proceedings of the 26th Annual International Conference on Machine Learning.* ICML '09. New York: ACM.

Gul, Faruk, and Lundholm, Russell. 1995. Endogenous timing and the clustering of agents' decisions. *Journal of Political Economy,* **103**(5), 1039–1066.

Guo, X., and Yang, H. 2005. The price of anarchy of Cournot oligopoly. Pages 246–257 of: *Workshop on Internet and Network Economics (WINE),* Hong Kong, China.

Haan, Laurens de. 1976. Sample extremes: An elementary introduction. *Statistica Neerlandica*, **30**(4), 161–172.

Haigh, John, and Cannings, Chris. 1989. The n-person war of attrition. *Acta Applicandae Mathematica*, **14**(1–2), 59–74.

Hajek, B., and Gopalakrishnan, G. 2002. *Do greedy autonomous systems make for a sensible Internet?* talk slides, Stochastic Networks Conference, Stanford University, http://www.ifp.illinois.edu/~hajek/Papers/stochnets02.pdf.

Haldane, J. B. S. 1932. A note on inverse probability. *Mathematical Proceedings of the Cambridge Philosophical Society*, **28**(1), 55–61.

Hann, Il-horn, Roberts, Jeff, and Slaughter, Ra. 2002. Why do developers contribute to open source projects? First evidence of economic incentives. In: *First Evidence of Economic Incentives, Proceedings of the 2nd Workshop on Open Source Software Engineering*, Orlando.

Harbaugh, Rick, and Klumpp, Tilman. 2005. Early round upsets and championship blowouts. *Economic Inquiry*, **43**(2), 316–329.

Hardin, Garrett. 1968. The tragedy of the commons. *Science*, **162**(3859), 1243–1248.

Hardy, G., Littlewood, J. E., and Pólya, G. 1952. *Inequalities*. 2nd ed. Cambridge: Cambridge University Press.

Harks, T. 2008. Stackelberg strategies and collusion in network games with splittable flow. Pages 133–146 of: *Proceedings of 6th International Workshop on Approximation and Online Algorithms*. WAOA '08, Karlsruhe, Germany.

Harris, T. E. 1960. A lower bound for the critical probability in a certain percolation process. *Mathematical Proceedings of the Cambridge Philosophical Society*, **56**(1), 13–20.

Harris, Christopher, and Vickers, John. 1987. Racing with uncertainty. *Review of Economic Studies*, **LIV**, 1–21.

Hars, A., and Ou, S. 2001. Working for free? motivations of participating in open source projects. Pages 7014– of: *Proceedings of the 34th Annual Hawaii International Conference on System Sciences (HICSS-34)-Volume 7 – Volume 7*. HICSS '01. Washington DC: IEEE Computer Society.

Harsanyi, John C. 1967. Games with incomplete information played by Bayesian players, III part I. The basic model. *Management Science*, **14**(3), 159–182.

Harsanyi, John C. 1968a. Games with incomplete information played by Bayesian players part II. Bayesian equilibrium points. *Management Science*, **14**(5), 320–334.

Harsanyi, John C. 1968b. Games with incomplete information played by Bayesian players, part III. The basic probability distribution of the game. *Management Science*, **14**(7), 486–502.

Harstad, Ronald M., Kagel, John H., and Levin, Dan. 1990. Equilibrium bid functions for auctions with an uncertain number of bidders. *Economics Letters*, **33**(1), 35–40.

Hart, Sergiu. 2008. Discrete Colonel Blotto and General Lotto games. *International Journal of Game Theory*, **36**(3), 441–460.

Hartline, Jason D. 2012. *Bayesian Mechanism Design*. Foundations and Trends® in Theoretical Computer Science, **8**(3), 143–263.

Harville, David A. 1977. The use of linear-model methodology to rate high school or college football teams. *Journal of the American Statistical Association*, **72**(358), 278–289.

Harville, David A. 1980. Predictions for national football league games via linear-model methodology. *Journal of the American Statistical Association*, **75**(371), 516–524.

Harville, David A., and Smith, Michael H. 1994. The home-court advantage: How large is it, and does it vary from team to team? *The American Statistician*, **48**(1), 22–28.

Hassidim, Avinatan, Kaplan, Haim, Mansour, Yishay, and Nisan, Noam. 2011. Non-price equilibria in markets of discrete goods. Pages 295–296 of: *Proceedings of the 12th ACM Conference on Electronic Commerce*. EC '11. New York: ACM.

Hatfield, John, and Duke Kominers, Scott. 2011. Multilateral matching. Pages 337–338 of: *Proceedings of the 12th ACM Conference on Electronic Commerce*. EC '11. New York: ACM.

Hemaspaandra, Edith, Spakowski, Holger, and Vogel, Jörg. 2005. The complexity of Kemeny elections. *Theoretical Computer Science*, **349**(3), 382–391.

Hendricks, Ken, Weiss, Andrew, and Wilson, Charles A. 1988. The war of attrition in continuous time with complete information. *International Economic Review*, **29**(4), 663–80.

Henery, Robert J. 1983. Permutation probabilities for Gamma random variables. *Journal of Applied Probability*, **20**, 822–834.

Henriet, D. 1985. The Copeland choice function: An axiomatic characterization. *Social Choice and Welfare*, **2**(1), 49–63.

Higgins, R., Shughart, W., and Tollison, R. D. 1885. Free entry and efficient rent seeking. *Public Choice*, **46**, 247–258.

Hillman, Arye L. 1988. *The Political Economy of Protectionism*. New York: Harwood.

Hillman, Arye L., and Katz, Eliakim. 1984. Risk-averse rent seekers and the social cost of monopoly power. *Economic Journal*, **94**(373), 104–110.

Hillman, Arye L., and Riley, John G. 1989. Politically contestable rents and transfers. *Economics and Politics*, **1**(1), 17–39.

Hillman, Arye L., and Samet, Dov. 1987. Dissipation of contestable rents by small number of contenders. *Public Choice*, **54**(1), 63–82.

Hirshleifer, Jack. 1983. From weakest-link to best-shot: The voluntary provision of public goods. *Public Choice*, **41**(3), 371–386.

Hirshleifer, Jack. 1989. Conflict and rent-seeking success functions: Ratio vs. difference models of relative success. *Public Choice*, **63**(2), 101–112.

Hirshleifer, Jack. 1991. The paradox of power. *Economics & Politics*, **3**(3), 177–200.

Hirshleifer, Jack, and Riley, John G. 1992. *The Analytics of Uncertainty and Information*. Cambridge: Cambridge University Press.

Ho, Chien-Ju, and Vaughan, Jennifer Wortman. 2012. Online task assignment in crowdsourcing markets. In: *Proceedings of the Twenty-Sixth AAAI Conference on Artifical Intelligence (AAAI 2012)*, Toronto, Canada.

Hoeffding, Wassily. 1963. Probability Inequalities for Sums of Bounded Random Variables. *Journal of the American Statistical Association*, **58**(301), pp. 13–30.

Hoffmann, Magnus, and Rota-Graziosi, Grégoire. 2012. Endogenous timing in general rent-seeking and conflict models. *Games and Economic Behavior*, **75**(1), 168–184.

Horen, Jeff, and Riezman, Raymond. 1985. Comparing draws for single elimination tournaments. *Operations Research*, **33**(2), 249–261.

Hörner, Johannes. 2004. A perpetual race to stay ahead. *Review of Economic Studies*, **71**(4), 1065–1088.

Hortala-Vallve, Rafael, and Llorente-Saguer, Aniol. 2012. Pure strategy Nash equilibria in non-zero sum colonel Blotto games. *International Journal of Game Theory*, **41**(2), 331–343.

Howe, Jeff. 2006a. *Crowdsourcing: A Definition*, http://crowdsourcing.typepad.com/cs/2006/06/crowdsourcing_a.html.

Howe, Jeff. 2006b. *Crowdsourcing: Why the Power of the Crowd Is Driving the Future of Business*. New York: Crown Business.

Huang, Tzu-Kuo, Weng, Ruby C., and Lin, Chih-Jen. 2006. Generalized Bradley-Terry models and multi-class probability estimates. *Journal of Machine Learning Research*, **7**(Jan), 85–115.

Huber, Peter J. 1963. Pairwise comparison and ranking: Optimum properties of the row sum procedure. *Annals of Mathematical Statistics*, **34**(2), 511–520.

Hunter, David R. 2004. MM algorithms for generalized Bradley-Terry models. *Annals of Statistics*, **32**(1), 384–406.

Huyck, John B. Van, Battalio, Raymond C., and Beil, Richard O. 1990. Tacit coordination games, strategic uncertainty, and coordination failure. *The American Economic Review*, **80**(1), 234–48.

Hwang, F. K. 1982. New concepts in seeding knockout tournaments. *American Mathematical Monthly*, **89**(April), 235–239.

Hwang, F. K., Zong-zhen, Lin, and Yao, Y. C. 1991. Knockout tournaments with diluted Bradley-Terry preference schemes. *Journal of Statistical Planning and Inference*, **28**(1), 99–106.

Immorlica, Nicole, Kranton, Rachel, and Stoddard, Gregory. 2012. Striving for social status. Page 672 of: *Proceedings of the 13th ACM Conference on Electronic Commerce*. EC '12. New York: ACM.

Immorlica, Nicole, Markakis, Evangelos, and Piliouras, Georgios. 2010. Coalition formation and price of anarchy in Cournot oligopolies. Pages 270–281 of: *Workshop on Internet and Network Economics (WINE)*, Stanford, CA.

Ipeirotis, Panagiotis G., Provost, Foster, and Wang, Jing. 2010. Quality management on Amazon Mechanical Turk. Pages 64–67 of: *Proceedings of the ACM SIGKDD Workshop on Human Computation*. HCOMP '10. New York: ACM.

Israel, R. 1982. Stronger players need not win more knockout tournaments. *Journal of the American Statistical Association*, **76**(376), 950–951.

Jackson, J. E., and Fleckenstein, M. 1957. An evaluation of some statistical techniques used in the analysis of paired comparisons. *Biometrics*, **13**(1), 51–64.

Jackson, Matthew O. 2008. *Social and Economic Networks*. Princeton, NJ: Princeton University Press.

Jackson, Matthew O., and Wolinsky, Asher. 1996. A strategic model of social and economic networks. *Journal of Economic Theory*, **71**(1), 44–74.

Jain, Shaili, Chen, Yiling, and Parkes, David C. 2009. Designing incentives for online question and answer forums. Pages 129–138 of: *Proceedings of the 10th ACM Conference on Electronic Commerce*. EC'09. New York: ACM.

Jain, Shaili, and Parkes, David C. 2008. A game-theoretic analysis of games with a purpose. Pages 342–350 of: *Proceedings of the 4th International Workshop on Internet and Network Economics*. WINE '08. Berlin: Springer-Verlag.

Järvelin, Kalervo, and Kekäläinen, Jaana. 2002. Cumulated gain-based evaluation of IR techniques. *ACM Transactions on Information Systems*, **20**(4), 422–446.

Jech, Thomas. 1983. The ranking of incomplete tournaments: A mathematician's guide to popular sports. *American Mathematical Monthly*, **90**(4), 246–264, 265–266.

Jensen, J. L. W. V. 1906. Sur les fonctions convexes et les inĝalités entre les valeurs moyennes. *Acta Mathematica*, **30**(1), 175–193.

Jia, Hao. 2008. A stochastic derivation of the ratio form of contest success functions. *Public Choice*, **135**(3), 125–130.

Joe-Wong, C., Sen, S., Lan, Tian, and Chiang, Mung. 2012 (March). Multi-resource allocation: Fairness-efficiency tradeoffs in a unifying framework. Pages 1206–1214 of: *Proceedings of IEEE Infocom 2012*.

Johari, Ramesh, and Tsitsiklis, John N. 2004. Efficiency loss in a network resource allocation game. *Mathematics of Operations Research*, **29**(3), 402–435.

Jurczyk, Pawel, and Agichtein, Eugene. 2007. Discovering authorities in question answer communities by using link analysis. Pages 212–22 of: *Proceedings of the Sixteenth ACM Conference on Information and Knowledge Management*. CIKM 2007, Lisbon.

Kamvar, S. D., Schlosser, M. T., and Garcia-Molina, H. 2003. The eigentrust algorithm for reputation management in P2P networks. Pages 640–651 of: *Proceedings of the 12th international conference on World Wide Web*, Budapest, Hungary.

Kannappan, Palaniappan. 2009. *Functional Equations and Inequalities with Applications*. Berlin: Springer.

Kanoria, Yashodhan, Bayati, Mohsen, Borgs, Christian, Chayes, Jennifer, and Montanari, Andrea. 2011. Fast convergence of natural bargaining dynamics in exchange networks. Pages 1518–1537 of: *Proceedings of the Twenty-Second Annual ACM-SIAM Symposium on Discrete Algorithms*. SODA '11. ACM-SIAM, San Francisco, CA.

Kaplan, Edward H., and Gartska, Stanley J. 2001. March madness and the office pool. *Management Science*, **47**(3), 369–382.

Karger, D. R., Sewoong, Oh, and Shah, D. 2011a. Budget-optimal crowdsourcing using low-rank matrix approximations. In: *49th Annual Allerton Conference on Communication, Control, and Computing (Allerton)*, Allerton, IL.

Karger, David R., Oh, Sewoong, and Shah, Devavrat. 2014. Budget-optimal task allocation for reliable crowdsourcing systems. *Operations Research*, **62**(1), 1–24.

Katz, Eliakim, Nitzan, Shmuel, and Rosenberg, Jacob. 1990. Rent-seeking for pure public goods. *Public Choice*, **65**(1), 49–60.

Keener, James P. 1993. The perron-frobenius theorem and the ranking of football teams. *SIAM Review*, **35**(1), 80–93.

Keller, Joseph B. 1994. A characterization of the Poisson distribution and the probability of winning a game. *American Statistician*, **48**(4), 294–298.

Kelly, Frank. 1997. Charging and rate control for elastic traffic. *European Transactions on Telecommunications*, **8**(1), 33–37.

Kelly, Frank, and Yudovina, Elena. 2014. *Stochastic Networks*. Cambridge: Cambridge University Press.

Kemeny, John. 1959. Mathematics without numbers. *Daedalus*, **88**(4), Quantity and Quality, 577–591.

Kemeny, John G., and Snell, J. Laurie. 1972. *Mathematical Models in the Social Sciences*. New York: Blaisdell, 1962. Reprinted by MIT Press, Cambridge, 1972.

Kendall, Graham, Knust, Sigrid, Ribeiro, Celso C., and Urrutia, Sebastián. 2010. Scheduling in sports: An annotated bibliography. *Computers & Operations Research*, **37**(1), 1–19.

Kendall, M. G. 1955. Further contributions to the theory of paired comparisons. *Biometrics*, **11**(1), 43–62.

Kendall, M. G., and Smith, B. Babington. 1940. On the method of paired comparions. *Biometrika*, **31**(3/4), 324–345.

Kennan, John, and Wilson, Robert. 1989. Strategic bargaining models and interpretation of strike data. *Journal of Applied Econometrics*, **4**(S1), 87–130.

Kenyon-Mathieu, Claire, and Schudy, Warren. 2007. How to rank with few errors. Pages 95–103 of: *Proceedings of the Thirty-Ninth Annual ACM Symposium on Theory of Computing*. STOC '07. New York: ACM.

Kirill. 2013 (October). *The World Football Elo Rating System*, http://www.eloratings.net.

Kirkegaard, René. 2012. Favoritism in asymmetric contests: Head starts and handicaps. *Games and Economic Behavior*, **76**(1), 226–248.

Kitcher, Philip. 1990. The division of cognitive labor. *Journal of Philosophy*, **87**(1), 5–22.

Kitcher, Philip. 1993. *The Advancement of Science*. Oxford: Oxford University Press.

Kleinberg, Jon. 1999. Authoritative sources in a hyperlinked environment. *Journal of the ACM*, **46**(5), 604–632.

Kleinberg, Jon, and Oren, Sigal. 2011. Mechanisms for (mis)allocating scientific credit. Pages 529–538 of: *Proceedings of the 43rd Annual ACM Symposium on Theory of Computing*. STOC '11. New York: ACM.

Kleinberg, Jon, and Tardos, Éva. 2008. Balanced outcomes in social exchange networks. Pages 295–304 of: *Proceedings of the 40th Annual ACM Symposium on Theory of Computing*. STOC '08. New York: ACM.

Klemperer, Paul. 1987. Markets with consumer switching costs. *Quarterly Journal of Economics*, **102**(2), 375–94.

Klemperer, Paul. 2004. *Auctions: Theory and Practice*. Princeton, NJ: Princeton University Press.

Kluberg, Jonathan, and Perakis, Georgia. 2012. Generalized quantity competition for multiple products and loss of efficiency. *Operations Research*, **60**(2), 335–350.

Knuth, D. E. 1987. A random knockout tournament: Problem 86-2. *SIAM Review*, **29** (March), 127–129.

Kolmar, Martin, and Wagener, Andreas. 2012. Contests and the private production of public goods. *Southern Economic Journal*, **79**(1), 161–179.

Konig, Ruud H. 2000. Competitive balance in Dutch soccer. *Journal of the Royal Statistical Society Series D*, **49**, 419–431.

Konrad, Kai, and Leininger, Wolfgang. 2007. The generalized Stackelberg equilibrium of the all-pay auction with complete information. *Review of Economic Design*, **11**(2), 165–174.

Konrad, Kai A. 2009. *Strategy and Dynamics in Contests*. Oxford: Oxford University Press.

Konrad, Kai A. 2012. Dynamic contests and the discouragement effect. *Revue d'économie politique*, **122**(2), 233–256.

Konrad, Kai A., and Kovenock, Dan. 2005. *Equilibrium and Efficiency in the Tug-of-War*. CESifo Working Paper Series 1564. CESifo Group Munich.

Konrad, Kai A., and Kovenock, Dan. 2009. Multi-battle contests. *Games and Economic Behavior*, **66**(1), 256–274.

Konrad, Kai A., and Kovenock, Dan. 2010. Contests with stochastic abilities. *Economic Inquiry*, **48**(1), 89–103.

Kooreman, Peter, and Schoonbeek, Lambert. 1997. The specification of the probability functions in Tullock's rent-seeking contest. *Economics Letters*, **56**(1), 59–61.

Koutsoupias, Elias, and Papadimitriou, Christos. 1999. Worst-case equilibria. Pages 404–413 of: *Proceedings of the 16th Annual Conference on Theoretical Aspects of Computer Science*. STACS'99. Berlin: Springer-Verlag.

Kreps, David M., and Wilson, Robert. 1982a. Reputation and imperfect information. *Journal of Economic Theory*, **27**(2), 253–279.

Kreps, David M., and Wilson, Robert. 1982b. Sequential equilibria. *Econometrica*, **50**(4), 863–894.

Krishna, Vijay. 2002. *Auction Theory*. New York: Academic Press.

Krishna, Vijay, and Morgan, John. 1997. An analysis of the war of attrition and the all-pay auction. *Journal of Economic Theory*, **72**(2), 343–362.

Krishna, V., and Morgan, J. 1998. The winner-take-all principle in small tournaments. *Advances in Applied Microeconomics*, **7**, 61–74.

Krishna, Vijay, and Rosenthal, Robert W. 1996. Simultaneous auctions with synergies. *Games and Economic Behavior*, **17**(1), 1–31.

Krueger, Anne O. 1974. The political economy of the rent-seeking society. *American Economic Review*, **64**(3), 291–303.

Kschischang, F. R., Frey, B. J., and Loeliger, H.-A. 2001. Factor graphs and the sum-product algorithm. *IEEE Transactions on Information Theory*, **47**(2), 498–519.

Kumar, Ravi, and Vassilvitskii, Sergei. 2010. Generalized distances between rankings. Pages 571–580 of: *Proceedings of the 19th International Conference on the World Wide Web*. WWW '10. New York: ACM.

Kvasov, Dmitriy. 2007. Contests with limited resources. *Journal of Economic Theory*, **136**(1), 738–748.

La, Richard J., and Anantharam, Venkant. 2002. Utility-based rate control in the Internet for elastic traffic. *IEEE/ACM Transactions on Networking*, **10**(2), 272–286.

Laffont, Jean-Jacques, and Martimort, David. 2001. *The Theory of Incentives: The Principal-Agent Model*. Princeton, NJ: Princeton University Press.

Laffont, Jean-Jacques, and Robert, Jacques. 1996. Optimal auction with financially constrained buyers. *Economics Letters*, **52**(2), 181–186.

Lakhani, Karim R., Garvin, David A., and Lonstein, Eric. 2010. TopCoder (A): Developing software through crowdsourcing. *Harvard Business School General Management Unit Case No. 610-032*.

Langville, Amy N., and Meyer, Carl D. 2004. Deeper inside PageRank. *Internet Mathematics*, **1**(3), 335–380.

Langville, Amy N., and Meyer, Carl D. 2006. *Google's PageRank and Beyond: The Science of Search Engine Rankings*. Princeton, NJ: Princeton University Press.

Langville, Amy N., and Meyer, Carl D. 2012. *Who's #1?: The Science of Rating and Ranking*. Princeton, NJ: Princeton University Press.

Laoutaris, Nikolaos, Poplawski, Laura J., Rajaraman, Rajmohan, Sundaram, Ravi, and Teng, Shang-Hua. 2008. Bounded budget connection (BBC) games or how to make friends and influence people, on a budget. Pages 165–174 of: *Proceedings of the Twenty-Seventh ACM Symposium on Principles of Distributed Computing*. PODC '08.

Laslier, J. F. 1997. *Tournament Solutions and Majority Voting*. Berlin: Springer.

Laslier, Jean-François. 2002. How two-party competition treats minorities. *Review of Economic Design*, **7**(3), 297–307.

Laslier, Jean-Francois, and Picard, Nathalie. 2002. Distributive politics and electoral competition. *Journal of Economic Theory*, **103**(1), 106–130.

Latta, R. B. 1979. Composition rules for probabilities from paired comparisons. *Annals of Statistics*, **7**(2), 349–371.

Law, Edith, and Ahn, Luis von. 2011. Human computation. *Synthesis Lectures on Artificial Intelligence and Machine Learning*, **5**(3), 1–121.

Lazear, Edward P., and Rosen, Sherwin. 1981. Rank-order tournaments as optimum labor contracts. *Journal of Political Economy*, **89**(5), 841–864.

Lee, Tom, and Wilde, Louis L. 1980. Market structure and innovation: A reformulation. *Quarterly Journal of Economics*, **94**(2), 429–436.

Lehmann, Benny, Lehmann, Daniel, and Nisan, Noam. 2001. Combinatorial auctions with decreasing marginal utilities. Pages 18–28 of: *Proceedings of the 3rd ACM Conference on Electronic Commerce*. EC '01. New York: ACM.

Leininger, Wolfgang. 1993. More efficient rent-seeking - A Münchhausen solution. *Public Choice*, **75**(1), 43–62.

Leme, Renato Paes, Syrgkanis, Vasilis, and Tardos, Éva. 2012. Sequential auctions and externalities. Pages 869–886 of: *Proceedings of the Twenty-Third Annual ACM-SIAM Symposium on Discrete Algorithms*. SODA '12. SIAM.

Lerner, Josh, and Tirole, Jean. 2002. Some simple economics of open source. *Journal of Industrial Economics*, **50**(2), 197–234.

Levin, Dan, and Ozdenoren, Emre. 2004. Auctions with uncertain numbers of bidders. *Journal of Economic Theory*, **118**(2), 229–251.

Levitt, Steven D. 1995. Optimal incentive schemes when only the agents' "Best" output matters to the principal. *RAND Journal of Economics*, **26**(4), 744–760.

Linster, Bruce G. 1993. Stackelberg rent-seeking. *Public Choice*, **77**(2), 307–321.

Littlestone, Nick, and Warmuth, Manfred K. 1994. The weighted majority algorithm. *Information and Computers*, **108**(2), 212–261.

Liu, Qiang, Peng, Jian, and Ihler, Alexander T. 2012. Variational inference for crowdsourcing. Pages 701–709 of: *Advances in Neural Information Processing Systems 25: 26th Annual Conference on Neural Information Processing Systems 2012*. Lake Tahoe, Nevada.

Long, Ngo Van, and Vousden, Neil. 1987. Risk-averse rent seeking with shared rents. *Economic Journal*, **97**(388), 971–985.

Loury, Glenn C. 1979. Market Structure and Innovation. *The Quarterly Journal of Economics*, **93**(3), 395–410.

Luce, R. Duncan. 1959. *Individual Choice Behavior: A Theoretical Analysis*. New York: John Wiley & Sons.

Münster, Johannes. 2006. Contests with an unknown number of contestants. *Public Choice*, **129**, 353–368.

MacKay, David J. C. 2003. *Information Theory, Inference, and Learning Algorithms*. Cambridge: Cambridge University Press.

Maheswaran, Rajiv T., and Basar, Tamer. 2003. Nash equilibrium and decentralized negotiation in auctioning divisible resources. *Group Decision and Negotiation*, **12**(5), 361–395.

Mallows, C. L. 1957. Non-null ranking models. *Biometrika*, **44**(1/2), 114–130.

Malueg, David A., and Yates, Andrew J. 2004. Rent seeking with private values. *Public Choice*, **119**(1/2).

Marchand, Éric. 2002. On the comparison between standard and random knockout tournaments. *The Statistician*, **51**, 169–178.

Marden, John I. 1995. *Analyzing and Modeling Rank Data*. Boca Raton, FL: Chapman and Hall.

Marshall, R. C., Meurer, M. J., , Richard, J.-F., and Stromquist, W. 1994. Numerical analysis of asymmetric first prize auctions. *Games and Economic Behavior*, **7**(2), 193–220.

Maschler, Michael, Solan, Eilon, and Zamir, Shmuel. 2013. *Game Theory*. Cambridge: Cambridge University Press.

Maskin, Eric, and Riley, John. 1984. Optimal auctions with risk averse buyers. *Econometrica*, **52**(6), 1473–1518.

Maskin, Eric, and Riley, John. 2003. Uniqueness of equilibrium in sealed high-bid auctions. *Games and Economic Behavior*, **45**(2), 395–409.

Massey. 2013 (November). *Massey Ratings*, http://masseyratings.com.

Matros, Alexander. 2004. Players with fixed resources in elimination tournaments. *Econometric Society 2004 North American Summer Meetings 295*. Econometric Society.

Matros, Alexander, and Lai, Ernest K. 2006 (Jan.). *Sequential Contests with Ability Revelation*. Working Papers 203. University of Pittsburgh, Department of Economics.

Matthews, Steven. 1987. Comparing auctions for risk averse buyers: A buyer's point of view. *Econometrica*, **55**(3), 633–646.

May, Avner, Chaintreau, Augustin, Korula, Nitish, and Lattanzi, Silvio. 2014. Filter & follow: How social media foster content curation. Pages 43–55 of: *Proceedings of the 2014 ACM SIGMETRICS International Conference on Measurement and Modeling Computer Systems*, Austin, TX.

Maynard Smith, J. 1974. The theory of games and the evolution of animal conflicts. *Journal of Theoretical Biology*, **47**(1), 209–221.

Maynard Smith, John. 1982. *Evolution and the Theory of Games*. Cambridge: Cambridge University Press.

McAdams, David. 2007. Uniqueness in symmetric first-price auctions with affiliation. *Journal of Economic Theory*, **136**(1), 144–166.

McAfee, R. Preston. 1993. Mechanism design by competing sellers. *Econometrica*, **61**(6), 1281–1312.

McAfee, Preston R. 2000. Continuing wars of attrition. *Available at SSRN: http://ssrn.com/ abstract=594607 or http://dx.doi.org/10.2139/ssrn.594607*.

McAfee, R. Preston, and McMillan, John. 1987. Auctions with a stochastic number of bidders. *Journal of Economic Theory*, **43**(1), 1–19.

McAfee, R. Preston, and Vincent, Daniel. 1993. The declining price anomaly. *Journal of Economic Theory*, **60**(1), 191–212.

McAfee, R. Preston, and Vincent, Daniel. 1997. Sequentially optimal auctions. *Games and Economic Behavior*, **18**, 246–276.

McCullagh, Peter. 1980. Regression models for ordinal data. *Journal of the Royal Statistical Society B*, **42**(2), 109–142.

McCullagh, P., and Nelder, J. A. 1989. *Generalized Linear Models*. 2nd ed. New York: Chapman & Hall.

McFadden, D. 1973. Conditional logit analysis of qualitative choice behavior. *Frontiers in Econometrics*, Academic Press: New York, 105–142.

McKinsey & Company. 2009. *And the winner is . . .* , http://mckinseyonsociety.com/downloads/reports/Social-Innovation/And_the_winner_is.pdf.

McManus, M. 1962. Numbers and size in Cournot oligopoly. *Bulletin of Economic Research*, **14**.

McManus, M. 1964. Equilibrium, numbers and size in Cournot oligopoly. *Bulletin of Economic Research*, **16**(2), 68–75.

McSherry, Frank, and Najork, Marc. 2008. Computing information retrieval performance measures efficiently in the presence of tied scores. Pages 414–421 of: Macdonald, Craig, Ounis, Iadh, Plachouras, Vassilis, Ruthven, Ian, and White, RyenW. (eds), *Advances in Information Retrieval*. Lecture Notes in Computer Science, vol. 4956. Berlin: Springer.

Mease, David. 2003. A penalized maximum likelihood approach for the ranking of college football teams independent of victory margins. *The American Statistician*, **57**(4), 241–248.

Merton, Robert K. 1968. The Matthew effect in science: The reward and communication systems of science are considered. *Science*, **159**(3810), 56–63.

Merton, Robert K. 1973. *The Sociology of Science: Theoretical and Empirical Investigations*. Chicago: University of Chicago Press.

Michaels, Robert. 1988. The design of rent-seeking competitions. *Public Choice*, **56**(1), 17–29.

Milgrom, Paul. 1999. *The Envelope Theorems*, Stanford: Stanford University Press.

Milgrom, Paul. 2004. *Putting Auction Theory to Work*. Cambridge: Cambridge University Press.

Milgrom, Paul, and Segal, Ilya. 2002. Envelope theorems for arbitrary choice sets. *Econometrics*, **70**(2), 583–601.

Milgrom, P., and Weber, R. 1983. *A theory of auctions and competitive bidding*. Tech. Rep. 5. Northwestern University.

Millner, Edward L., and Pratt, Michael D. 1991. Risk aversion and rent-seeking: An extension and some experimental evidence. *Public Choice*, **69**(1), 81–92.

Mimno, David, and McCallum, Andrew. 2007. Expertise modeling for matching papers with reviewers. In: *Proceedings of the 13th ACM SIGKDD International Conference on Knowledge Discovery and Data Mining*, KDD '07, New York, NY.

Minc, Henryk. 1988. *Nonnegative Matrices*. New York: John Wiley & Sons.

Minka, Thomas. 2001. Expectation propagation for approximate Bayesian inference. Pages 362–369 of: *Proceedings of the 17th Conference in Uncertainty in Artificial Intelligence*, Seattle, WA.

Mirrokni, Vahab S., Muthukrishnan, Muthu, and Nadav, Uri. 2010. Quasi-proportional mechanisms: Prior-free revenue maximization. In: *Proceedings of the 9th Latin American Theoretical Informatics Symposium*. LATIN'2010.

Mo, Jeonghoon, and Walrand, Jean. 2000. Fair end-to-end window-based congestion control. *IEEE Transactions on Networking*, **8**(5), 556–567.

Moldovanu, Benny, and Sela, Aner. 2001. The optimal allocation of prizes in contests. *American Economic Review*, **91**(3), 542–558.

Moldovanu, Benny, and Sela, Aner. 2006. Contest architecture. *Journal of Economic Theory*, **126**(1), 70–97.

Moldovanu, Benny, Sela, Aner, and Shi, Xianwen. 2007. Contests for status. *Journal of Political Economy*, **115**(2), 338–363.

Moldovanu, Benny, Sela, Aner, and Shi, Xianwen. 2008. Competing auctions with endogenous quantities. *Journal of Economic Theory*, **141**(1), 1–27.

Moldovanu, Benny, Sela, Aner, and Shi, Xianwen. 2012. Carrots and sticks: Prizes and punishments in contests. *Economic Inquiry*, **50**(2), 453–462.

Monderer, Dov, and Shapley, Lloyd S. 1996. Potential games. *Games and Economic Behavior*, **14**(1), 124–143.

Moon, J. W., and Pullman, N. J. 1970. On generalized tournament matrices. *SIAM Review*, **12**(3), 384–399.

Moore, J. 1992. Implementation in environments with complete information. Pages 182–282 of: Advances in Economic Theory: Sixth World Congress, Vol. 1, edited by Jean-Jacques Laffont. – Cambridge Collections Online © Cambridge University Press, 2006.

Morgan, John. 2000. Financing public goods by means of lotteries. *Review of Economic Studies*, **67**(4), 761–84.

Morgan, John. 2003. Sequential contests. *Public Choice*, **116**, 1–18.

Morgan, John, and Vardy, Felix. 2007. The value of commitment in contests and tournaments when observation is costly. *Games and Economic Behavior*, **60**(2), 326–338.

Mosteller, Frederick. 1951a. Remarks on the method of paired comparisons: I. The least squares solution assuming equal standard deviations and equal correlations. *Psychometrika*, **16**(1), 3–9.

Mosteller, Frederick. 1951b. Remarks on the method of paired comparisons: II. The efffect of an aberrant standard deviation when equal standard deivations and equal correlations are assumed. *Psychometrika*, **16**(2), 203–206.

Mosteller, Frederick. 1951c. Remarks on the method of paired comparisons: III. A test of significance for paired comparisons when equal standard deviations and equal correlations are assumed. *Psychometrika*, **16**(2), 207–218.

Moulin, Hervé. 1986. *Game Theory for the Social Sciences*. 2nd ed. New York: New York University Press.

Moulin, Hervé. 1988. *Axioms of Cooperative Decision Making*. Cambridge: Cambridge University Press.

Moulin, Hervé. 2002. Axiomatic cost and surplus sharing. Pages 289–357 of: Arrow, K. J., Sen, A. K., and Suzumura, K. (eds), *Handbook of Social Choice and Welfare*. New York: Elsevier.

Moulin, Hervé, and Watts, Alison. 1996. Two versions of the tragedy of the commons. *Review of Economic Design*, **2**(1), 399–421.

Muller, Wieland, and Schotter, Andrew. 2010. Workaholics and dropouts in organizations. *Journal of the European Economic Association*, **8**(4), 717–743.

Murphy, F., Sherali, H., and Soyster, A. 1982. A mathematical programming approach for determining oligopolistic market equilibrium. *Mathematical Programming*, **24**(1), 92–106.

Myerson, Roger B. 1981. Optimal auction design. *Mathematics of Operations Research*, **6**(1), 58–73.

Myerson, Roger B. 1991. *Game Theory: Analysis of Conflict*. Cambridge, MA: Harvard University Press.

Nalebuff, Barry, and Riley, John. 1985. Asymmetric equilibria in the war of attrition. *Journal of Theoretical Biology*, **113**(3), 571–527.

Nalebuff, Barry, and Stiglitz, J. 1983. Prizes and incentives: Towards a general theory of compensation and competition. *Bell Journal of Economics*, **14**(1), 21–43.

Nash, John. 1950a. The bargaining problem. *Econometrica*, **18**(2), 155–162.

Nash, John F. 1950b. Equilibrium points in n-person games. *Proceedings of the National Academy of Sciences*, **36**(1), 48–49.

Negahban, Sahand, Oh, Sewoong, and Shah, Devavrat. 2012. Iterative ranking from pair-wise comparisons. Pages 2483–2491 of: Bartlett, Peter L., Pereira, Fernando C. N., Burges, Christopher

J. C., Bottou, Lon, and Weinberger, Kilian Q. (eds), *Proceedings of the 26th Annual Conference on Neural Information Processing Systems 2012*, NIPS 2012, Lake Tahoe, Nevada.

Nelder, J. A., and Wedderburn, R. W. 1972. Generalized linear models. *Journal of the Royal Statistical Society, Series A*, **135**, Part 3, 370–384.

Newman, Alantha, and Vempala, Santosh. 2001. Fences are futile: On relaxations for the linear ordering problem. Pages 333–347 of: *Proceedings of the 8th International IPCO Conference on Integer Programming and Combinatorial Optimization*. London: Springer-Verlag.

Nguyen, Thành, and Tardos, Éva. 2007. Approximately maximizing efficiency and revenue in poly-hedral environments. Pages 11–19 of: *Proceedings of the 8th ACM Conference on Electronic Commerce*. EC '07. New York: ACM.

Nguyen, Thánh, and Vojnović, Milan. 2010a. *Prior-free Auctions without Reserve Prices*. Tech. rept. MSR-TR-2010-91. Microsoft Research.

Nguyen, Thánh, and Vojnović, Milan. 2010b. Weighted proportional allocation. *Proceedings of the 2011 ACM SIGMETRICS International Conference on Measurement and Modeling of Computer Systems*, San Jose, CA, **39**(1), 133–144.

Nguyen, Thánh, and Vojnović, Milan. 2011. Near Optimal Non-Truthful Auctions. *Microsoft Research Technical Report MSR-TR-2011-48*.

Nisan, Noam, and Ronen, Amir. 1999. Algorithmic mechanism design (extended abstract). Pages 129–140 of: *Proceedings of the Thirty-First Annual ACM Symposium on Theory of Computing*. STOC '99. New York: ACM.

Nisan, Noam, and Ronen, Amir. 2001. Algorithmic mechanism design. *Games and Economic Behavior*, **35**(1–2), 166–196.

Nisan, Noam, Rougharden, Tim, Tardos, Éva, and Vazirani, Vijay V. 2007. *Algorithmic Game Theory*. Cambridge: Cambridge University Press.

Nitzan, Shmuel. 1991a. Collective rent dissipation. *Economic Journal*, **101**(409), 1522–1534.

Nitzan, Shmuel. 1991b. Rent-seeking with non-identical sharing rules. *Public Choice*, **71**(1/2), 43–50.

Nitzan, Shmuel. 1994. Modelling rent-seeking contests. *European Journal of Political Economy*, **10**(1), 41–60.

Nitzan, Shmuel, and Paroush, Jacob. 1982. Optimal decision rules in uncertain dichotomous choice situations. *International Economic Review*, **23**(2), 289–297.

Noether, G. E. 1960. Remarks about a paired comparison model. *Psychometrika*, **25**(4), 357–367.

Novshek, William. 1984. Finding all n-firm Cournot equilibria. *International Economic Review*, **25**(1), 61–70.

Novshek, William. 1985. On the existence of Cournot equilibrium. *Review of Economic Studies*, **52**(1), 85–98.

Nti, Kofi O. 1999. Rent-seeking with asymmetric valuations. *Public Choice*, **98**(3–4), 415–430.

Nti, Kofi O. 2004. Maximum efforts in contests with asymmetric valuations. *European Journal of Political Economy*, **20**(4), 1059–1066.

O'Keeffe, Mary, Viscusi, W. Kip, and Zeckhauser, Richard J. 1984. Economic contests: Comparative reward schemes. *Journal of Labor Economics*, **2**(1), 27–56.

Olszewski, Wojciech. 2003. A simple and general solution to King Solomon's problem. *Games and Economic Behavior*, **42**(2), 315–318.

O'Neill, Barry. 1982. A problem of rights arbitration from the Talmud. *Mathematical Social Sciences*, **2**(4), 345–371.

Osborne, Martin J. 2003. *An Introduction to Game Theory*. New York: Oxford University Press.

Osborne, Martin J., and Rubinstein, Ariel. 1994. *A Course in Game Theory*. Cambridge, MA: MIT Press.

Pálvölgi, Dénes, Peters, Hans, and Vermeulen, Dries. 2012. A strategic approach to estate division problems with non-homogeneous preferences. *Games and Economic Behavior*, **85**, 135–152.

Page, Lawrence, Brin, Sergey, Motwani, Rajeev, and Winograd, Terry. 1999 (November). *The Page-Rank Citation Ranking: Bringing Order to the Web*. Technical Report 1999-66. Stanford InfoLab.

Pai, Mallesh M. 2009. *Competing Auctioneers*. Working Papers. Kellogg School of Management, Northwestern University.

Pal, D. 1991. Cournot duopoly with two production periods and cost differentials. *Journal of Economic Theory*, **55**(2), 441–448.

Papakonstantinou, Zinon. 2002. Prizes in early archaic Greek sport. *Nikephoros*, **15**, 51–67.

Park, Juyong, and Newman, M. E. J. 2005. A network-based ranking system for US college football. *Journal of Statistical Mechanics: Theory and Experiment*, **10**.

Parkes, David C., Procaccia, Ariel D., and Shah, Nisarg. 2012. Beyond dominant resource fairness: Extensions, limitations, and indivisibilities. Pages 808–825 of: *Proceedings of the 13th ACM Conference on Electronic Commerce*. EC '12. New York: ACM.

Parkes, David, and Seuken, Sven. 2016. *Economics and Computation: A Design Approach*. Cambridge: Cambridge University Press.

Paul, Chris, and Wilhite, Al. 1991. Rent-seeking, rent-defending, and rent dissipation. *Public Choice*, **71**(1/2), 61–70.

Paul, Sharoda A., Hong, Lichan, and Chi, Ed H. 2012. Who is authoritaive? Understanding reputation mechanisms in Quora. In: *Proc. of Collective Intelligence conference (CI)*.

Pearl, Judea. 1982. Reverend Bayes on inference engines: A distributed hierarchical approach. Pages 133–136 of: *Proceedings of the National Conference on Artificial Intelligence*. Pittsburgh, PA.

Pérez-Castrillo, J. David, and Verdier, Thierry. 1992. A general analysis of rent-seeking games. *Public Choice*, **73**(3), 335–350.

Perry, Motty, and Reny, Philip J. 1999. A general solution to King Solomon's dilemma. *Games and Economic Behavior*, **26**(2), 279–285.

Peters, Michael, and Severinov, Sergei. 1997. Competition among sellers who offer auctions instead of prizes. *Journal of Economic Theory*, **75**(1), 141–179.

Peters, Michael, and Severinov, Sergei. 2006. Internet auctions with many traders. *Journal of Economic Theory*, **130**(1), 220–245.

Pigou, Arthur C. 1932. *The Economics of Welfare*. London: MacMillan & Co.

Pinski, Gabriel, and Narin, Francis. 1976. Citation influence for journal aggregates of scientific publications: Theory, with application to the literature of physics. *Information Processing & Management*, **12**(5), 297–312.

Plackett, R. 1975. The analysis of permutations. *Applied Statistics*, **24**(2), 193–202.

Platt, Brennan C., Price, Joseph, and Tappen, Henry. 2013. The Role of Risk Preferences in Pay-to-Bid Auctions. *Management Science*, **59**(9), 2117–2134.

Posner, Richard A. 1975. The social costs of monopoly and regulation. *Journal of Political Economy*, **83**(4), 807–827.

Qin, Cheng-Zhong, and Yang, Chun-Lei. 2009. Make a guess: A robust mechanism for King Solomon's dilemma. *Economic Theory*, **39**(2), 259–268.

Rao, P. V., and Kupper, L. L. 1967. Ties in paired-comparison experiments: A generalization of the Bradley-Terry model. *Journal of the American Statistical Association*, **62**(317), 194–204.

Rashid, Al M., Ling, Kimberly, Tassone, Regina D., Resnick, Paul, Kraut, Robert, and Riedl, John. 2006. Motivating participation by displaying the value of contribution. Pages 955–958 of: *Proceedings of the SIGCHI Conference on Human Factors in Computing Systems*. CHI '06. New York: ACM.

Raykar, Vikas C., Yu, Shipeng, Zhao, Linda H., Jerebko, Anna, Florin, Charles, Valadez, Gerardo Hermosillo, Bogoni, Luca, and Moy, Linda. 2009. Supervised learning from multiple experts: Whom to trust when everyone lies a bit. Pages 889–896 of: *Proceedings of the 26th Annual International Conference on Machine Learning*. ICML '09.

Raykar, Vikas C., Yu, Shipeng, Zhao, Linda H., Valadez, Gerardo Hermosillo, Florin, Charles, Bogoni, Luca, and Moy, Linda. 2010. Learning from crowds. *Journal of Machine Learning Research*, **11**(Aug.), 1297–1322.

Reid, Michael B. 2003. *Least Squares Model for Predicting College Football Scores*. M.Phil. thesis, University of Utah.

Resnick, Paul, Kuwabara, Ko, Zeckhauser, Richard, and Friedman, Eric. 2000. Reputation systems. *Communications of the ACM*, **43**(1), 45–48.

Riaz, Khalid, Shogren, Jason F., and Johnson, Stanley R. 1995. A general model of rent seeking for public goods. *Public Choice*, **82**(3/4), 243–259.

Richardson, Tom, and Urbanke, Rudriger. 2008. *Modern Coding Theory*. Cambridge: Cambridge University Press.

Riley, J. G. 1980. Strong evolutionary equilibrium and the war of attrition. *Journal of Theoretical Biology*, **82**(3), 383–400.

Riley, John G. 1987. *An Introduction to the Theory of Contests*. Working Paper 469. UCLA Department of Economics.

Riley, John G., and Samuelson, William F. 1981. Optimal auctions. *American Economic Review*, **71**(3), 381–392.

Ritz, Robert A. 2008. Influencing rent-seeking contests. *Public Choice*, **135**(3–4), 291–300.

Roberson, Brian. 2006. The Colonel Blotto game. *Economic Theory*, **29**(1), 1–24.

Roberson, Brian, and Kvasov, Dmitriy. 2012. The non-constant-sum Colonel Blotto game. *Economic Theory*, **51**(2), 397–433.

Rockafellar, R. T. 1970. *Convex Analysis*. Princeton, NJ: Princeton University Press.

Romano, R., and Yildirim, H. 2005. On the endogeneity of Cournot-Nash and Stackelberg equilibria: Games of accumulation. *Journal of Economic Theory*, **120**(2), 73–107.

Rosen, J. B. 1965. Existence and uniqueness of equilibrium points for concave n-person games. *Econometrica: Journal of the Econometric Society*, **33**(3), 520–534.

Rosen, Sherwin. 1986. Prizes and incentives in elimination tournaments. *American Economic Review*, **76**(4), 701–715.

Rosenthal, Robert W. 1973. A class of games possessing pure-strategy Nash equilibria. *International Journal of Game Theory*, **2**(1), 65–67.

Rosenthal, Robert W., and Wang, Ruqu. 1996. Simultaneous auctions with synergies and common values. *Games and Economic Behavior*, **17**(1), 32–55.

Roughgarden, Tim. 2009. Intrinsic robustness of the price of anarchy. Pages 513–522 of: *Proceedings of the 41st Annual ACM Symposium on Theory of Computing*, Bethesda, MD.

Roughgarden, Tim. 2012. The price of anarchy in games of incomplete information. Pages 862–879 of: *Proceedings of the 13th ACM Conference on Electronic Commerce*. EC '12. New York: ACM.

Roughgarden, Tim, and Schoppmann, Florian. 2011. Local smoothness and the price of anarchy in atomic splittable congestion games. Pages 255–267 of: *Proceedings of the 22nd Annual ACM-SIAM Symposium on Discrete Algorithms*, San Francisco, CA.

Roughgarden, T., and Tardos, É. 2002. How bad is selfish routing? *Journal of the ACM*, **49**(2), 236–259.

Rowley, Charles, Tollison, Robert D., and Tullock, Gordon. 1988. *The Political Economy of Rent-Seeking*. New York: Springer.

Rubinstein, Ariel. 1980. Ranking the participants in a tournament. *SIAM Journal on Applied Mathematics*, **38**(1), 108–111.

Russell, Tyrel, and Walsh, Toby. 2009. Manipulating tournaments in cup and round robin competitions. Pages 26–37 of: Rossi, Francesca, and Tsoukias, Alexis (eds), *Algorithmic Decision Theory*. Lecture Notes in Computer Science, vol. 5783. Springer: Berlin.

Saari, Donald G., and Merlin, Vincent R. 1996. The Copeland method. *Economic Theory*, **8**(1), 51–76.

Saloner, G. 1987. Cournot duopoly with two production periods. *Journal of Economic Theory*, **42**(1), 183–187.

Sapir, Luba. 1998. The optimality of the expert and majority rules under exponentially distributed competence. *Theory and Decision*, **45**(1), 19–36.

Schalekamp, Frans, and van Zuylen, Anke. 2009. Rank aggregation: Together we're strong. In: *Workshop on Algorithm Engineering & Experiments*. ALENEX '09, New York, NY.

Schwenk, Allen J. 2000. What is the correct way to seed a knockout tournament? *American Mathematical Monthly*, **107**(February), 140–150.

Segev, Ella, and Sela, Aner. 2011. *Sequential All-Pay Auctions with Head Starts and Noisy Outputs*. Working Papers 1106. Ben-Gurion University of the Negev, Department of Economics.

Segev, Ella, and Sela, Aner. 2014. Multi-stage sequential all-pay auctions. *European Economic Review*, **70**(C), 371–382.

Shah, Chirag, and Pomerantz, Jefferey. 2010. Evaluating and predicting answer quality in community QA. In: *Proc. of SIGIR*.

Shapley, L. 1953. A value for n-person games. In: Kuhn, H., and Tucker, A. (eds.), *Contributions ot the Theory Of Games*. Princeton, NJ: Princeton University Press.

Sheng, Victor S., Provost, Foster, and Ipeirotis, Panagiotis G. 2008. Get another label? improving data quality and data mining using multiple, noisy labelers. Pages 614–622 of: *Proceedings of the 14th ACM SIGKDD International Conference On Knowledge Discovery and Data Mining*. KDD '08. New York: ACM.

Shubik, M. 1962. Incentives, decentralized control, the assignment of joint costs and internal pricing. *Management Science*, **8**(3), 325–343.

Shubik, Martin. 1971. The Dollar Auction game: A paradox in noncooperative behavior and escalation. *Journal of Conflict Resolution*, **15**(1), 109–111.

Shubik, Martin, and Weber, Robert James. 1981. Systems defense games: Colonel Blotto, command and control. *Naval Research Logistics Quarterly*, **28**(2), 281–287.

Singh, Nirvikar, and Wittman, Donald. 1988. Economic contests with incomplete information and optimal contest design. *Management Science*, **34**(4), 528–540.

Sisak, Dana. 2009. Multiple-prize contests – the optimal allocation of prizes. *Journal of Economic Surveys*, **23**(1), 82–114.

Skaperdas, Stergios. 1996. Contest success functions. *Economic Theory*, **7**(2), 283–290.

Slutzki, Giora, and Volij, Oscar. 2006. Scoring of web pages and tournaments axiomatizations. *Social Choice and Welfare*, **26**(1), 75–92.

Snyder, James M. 1989. Election goals and the allocation of campaign resources. *Econometrica*, **57**(3), 637–660.

Solow, R. M. 1956. A contribution to the theory of economic growth. *Quaterly Journal of Economics*, **70**(1), 65–94.

Spearman, C. 1904. The proof and measurement of association between two things. *American Journal of Psychology*, **15**, 72–101.

Stefani, R. T. 1977. Football and basketball predictions using least squares. *IEEE Transactions on Systems, Man and Cybernetics*, **7**(2), 117–121.

Stefani, R. T. 1980. Improved least squares football, basketball, and soccer predictions. *IEEE Transactions on Systems, Man and Cybernetics*, **10**(2), 116–123.

Stein, William E. 2002. Asymmetric rent-seeking with more than two contestants. *Public Choice*, **113**(3–4), 325–336.

Stern, Hal. 1990a. A continuum of paired comparison models. *Biometrika*, **27**(2), 265–273.

Stern, Hal. 1990b. Models for distributions on permutations. *Journal of the American Statistical Association*, **85**(410), 558–564.

Stern, Hal. 1991. On the probability of winning a football game. *The American Statistician*, **45**(3), 179–183.

Stern, Hal. 1994. A brownian motion model for the progress of sports scores. *Journal of the American Statistical Association*, **89**(427), 1128–1134.

Stiglitz, Joseph E. 2006. Give prizes not patents. *New Scientist*, September.

Stiglitz, Joseph E. 2008. Economic foundations of intellectual property rights. *Duke Law Journal*, **57**(6), 1693–1724.

Stob, Michael. 1984. A supplement to "A Mathematician's Guide to Popular Sports." *American Mathematical Monthly*, **91**(5), 277–282.

Stoica, I., Abdel-Wahab, H., Jeffay, K., Baruah, S. K., Gehrke, J. E., and Plaxton, C. G. 1996. A proportional share resource allocation algorithm for real-time, time-shared systems. Pages 288–299 of: *Proceedings of the 17th IEEE Real-Time Systems Symposium*. RTSS '96. Washington, DC: IEEE Computer Society.

Swaddling, Judith. 2011. *The Ancient Olympics*. 2nd ed. London: British Museum Press.

Syrgkanis, Vasilis. 2012. Bayesian games and the smoothness framework. *CoRR*, **abs/1203.5155**.

Syrgkanis, Vasilis, and Tardos, Eva. 2013. Composable and efficient mechanisms. Pages 211–220 of: *Proceedings of the 45th Annual ACM Symposium on Theory of Computing*. STOC '13. New York: ACM.

Szentes, Balázs. 2007. Two-object two-bidder simultaneous auctions. *International Game Theory Review*, **09**(3), 483–493.

Szentes, Balázs, and Rosenthal, Robert W. 2003a. Three-object two-bidder simultaneous auctions: Chopsticks and tetrahedra. *Games and Economic Behavior*, **44**(1), 114–133.

Szentes, Balazs, and Rosenthal, Robert W. 2003b. Beyond chopsticks: Symmetric equilibria in majority auction games. *Games and Economic Behavior*, **45**(2), 278–295.

Szidarovszky, Ferenc, and Okuguchi, Koji. 1997. On the existence and uniqueness of pure Nash equilibrium in rent-seeking games. *Games and Economic Behavior*, **18**(1), 135–140.

Szidarovszky, F., and Yakowitz, S. 1977. A new proof of the existence and uniqueness of the Cournot equilibrium. *International Economic Review*, **18**(3), 787–789.

Szymanski, Stefan. 2003. The economic design of sporting contests. *Journal of Economic Literature*, **XLI**, 1137–1187.

Szymanski, Stefan, and Valletti, Tommaso M. 2005. Incentive effects of second prizes. *European Journal of Political Economy*, **21**(2), 467–481.

Tausczik, Yla R., and Pennebaker, James W. 2011. Predicting the perceived quality of online mathematics contributions from users' reputations. Pages 1885–1888 of: *Proceedings of the International Conference on Human Factors in Computing Systems*, CHI 2011, Vancouver, BC, Canada.

Taylor, Alan D. 2005. *Social Choice and the Mathematics of Manipulation*. Cambridge: Cambridge University Press.

Thompson, Mark. 1975. On any given Sunday: Fair competitor orderings with maximum likelihood methods. *Journal of the American Statistical Association*, **70**(351), 536–541.

Thurstone, L. L. 1927. A law of comparative judgment. *Psychological Review*, **34**(2), 273–286.

Tirole, Jean. 1988. *The Theory of Industrial Organization*. Cambridge, MA: MIT Press.

Tsitsiklis, J. N., and Xu, Y. 2012. Efficiency loss in a Cournot oligopoly with convex market demand. Pages 63–76 of: Krishnamurthy, Vikram, Zhao, Qing, Huang, Minyi, and Wen, Yonggang (eds), *Game Theory for Networks*. Lecture Notes of the Institute for Computer Sciences, Social Informatics and Telecommunications Engineering, vol. 105. Springer Berlin Heidelberg.

Tsitsiklis, J. N., and Xu, Y. 2013. Profit loss in Cournot oligopolies. *Operations Research Letters*, **41**(4), 415–420.

Tukey, J. W. 1949. A problem of strategy. *Econometrica*, **17**, 73.

Tullock, Gordon. 1967. The Western costs of tariffs, monopolies, and theft. *Western Economic Journal*, **5**(3), 224–232.

Tullock, Gordon. 1975. On the efficient organization of trials. *Kyklos*, **28**(4), 745–762.

Tullock, Gordon. 1980. Efficient rent seeking. Pages 131–146 in Buchanan, J. M., Tollison, R. D., and Tullock, G. (eds.), *Toward a Theory of the Rent-Seeking Society*. Dallas: Texas A&M University Press.

Tutz, Gerhard. 2012. *Regression for Categorical Data*. Cambridge: Cambridge University Press.

Ursprung, Heinrich W. 1990. Public goods, rent dissipation, and candidate competition. *Economics & Politics*, **2**(2), 115–132.

Ushio, Yoshiaki. 1985. Approximate efficiency of Cournot equilibria in large markets. *Review of Economic Studies*, **52**(171), 547.

van den Brink, René, and Gilles, Robert P. 2000. Measuring domination in directed networks. *Social Networks*, **22**(2), 141–157.

van den Brink, René, and Gilles, Robert P. 2003. Ranking by outdegree for directed graphs. *Discrete Mathematics*, **271**(13), 261–270.

Van Long, Ngo, and Soubeyran, Antoine. 2000. Existence and uniqueness of Cournot equilibrium: A contraction mapping approach. *Economics Letters*, **67**(3), 345–348.

van Zuylen, Anke, Hegde, Rajneesh, Jain, Kamal, and Williamson, David P. 2007. Deterministic pivoting algorithms for constrained ranking and clustering problems. Pages 405–414 of: *Proceedings of the Eighteenth Annual ACM-SIAM Symposium on Discrete Algorithms*. SODA '07. Philadelphia: Society for Industrial and Applied Mathematics.

van Zuylen, Anke, and Williamson, David P. 2009. Deterministic pivoting algorithms for contrained ranking and clustering problems. *Mathematics of Operations Research*, **34**(3), 594–620.

Varian, Hal R. 1994. Sequential contributions to public goods. *Journal of Public Economics*, **53**(2), 165–186.

Vetta, Adrian. 2002. Nash equilibria in competitive societies, with applications to facility location, traffic routing and auctions. Page 416 of: *Proceedings of the 43rd Symposium on Foundations of Computer Science*. FOCS '02. Washington, DC: IEEE Computer Society.

Vickrey, William. 1961. Counterspeculation, auctions, and competitive sealed tenders. *Journal of Finance*, **16**(1), 8–37.

Vohra, Rakesh. 2005. *Advanced Mathematical Economics*. London: Routledge.

Vohra, Rakesh V. 2011. *Mechanism Design: A Linear Programming Approach*. Cambridge: Cambridge University Press.

von Krogh, Georg, Spaeth, Sebastian, and Lakhani, Karim R. 2003. Community, joining, and specialization in open source software innovation: A case study. *Research Policy*, **32**(7), 1217–1241.

von Mises, R. 1936. La distribution de la plus grande de *n* valeurs. *Review of the Mathematical Union Interbalcanique. Reproduced in Selected Papers of Richard von Mises, Am. Math. Soc. II (1964), 271–294*, **1**, 141–160.

von Neumann, J., and Morgenstern, O. 1944. *Theory of Games and Economic Behavior*. New York: John Wiley and Sons.

von Stackelberg, Heinrich. 1934. *Marktform und Gleichgewicht*. Berlin: Springer-Verlag.

Voorhees, E. M., and Harman, D. K. 2005. *TREC: Experiment and Evaluation in Information Retrieval*. Cambridge, MA: MIT Press.

Vu, Thuc, Altman, Alon, and Shoham, Yoav. 2009. On the complexity of schedule control problems for knockout tournaments. Pages 225–232 of: *Proceedings of the 8th International Conference on Autonomous Agents and Multiagent Systems (AAMAS)*.

Vu, Thuc D. 2010. *Knockout Tournament Design: A Computational Approach.* Ph.D. thesis, Stanford University.

Vu, Thuc, and Shoham, Yoav. 2011. Fair seeding in knockout tournaments. *ACM Transactions of Intelligent Systems Technology,* **3**(1), 9:1–9:17.

Washburn, Alan. 2013. OR Forum – Blotto politics. *Operations Research,* **61**(3), 532–543.

Wasser, Cédric. 2013. Incomplete information in rent-seeking contests. *Economic Theory,* **53**(1), 239–268.

Watts, Alison. 1996. On the uniqueness of equilibrium in cournot oligopoly and other games. *Games and Economic Behavior,* **13**(2), 269–285.

Wauthier, Fabian L., Jordan, Michael I., and Jojic, Nebojsa. 2013. Efficient ranking from pairwise comparisons. *International Conference on Machine Learning,* **28**(3). 109–117.

Weber, R. 1981. *Multiple-object auctions.* Discussion Paper 496. Kellogg Graduate School of Management, Northwestern University.

Weber, R. 1985. Auctions and competitive bidding. In Young, H. P. (ed.) *Fair Allocation. American Mathematical Society.* Providence, RI: American Mathematical Society.

Weinstein, Jonathan. 2005 (Jan.). *Two notes on the Blotto Game.* Tech. rept. Northwestern University (mimeo).

Weinstein, Jonathan. 2012. Two notes on the Blotto Game. *B. E. Journal of Theoretical Economics,* **12**(1), 1–11.

Whitehill, Jacob, Ruvolo, Paul, Wu, Tingfan, Bergsma, Jacob, and Movellan, Javier R. 2009. Whose vote should count more: Optimal integration of labels from labelers of unknown expertise. Pages 2035–2043 of: *Proceedings of 23rd Annual Conference on Neural Information Processing Systems, NIPS 2009,* Vancouver, BC, Canada.

Wolfgang, Leininger, and Chun-Lei, Yang. 1994. Dynamic rent-seeking games. *Games and Economic Behavior,* **7**(3), 406–427.

http://ratings.tide.com.

Wright, Brian Davern. 1983. The economics of invention incentives: Patents, prizes, and research contracts. *American Economic Review,* **73**(4), 691–707.

Yang, Jiang, Adamic, Lada A., and Ackerman, Mark S. 2008. Crowdsourcing and knowledge sharing: Strategic user behavior on Taskcn. Pages 246–255 of: *Proceedings of the 9th ACM Conference on Electronic Commerce.* EC '08. New York: ACM.

Ye, Yunwen, and Kishida, K. 2003. Toward an understanding of the motivation of open source software developers. Pages 419–429 of: *Proceedings of the 25th International Conference on Software Engineering, 2003.*

Yellott, John I. 1977. The relationship between Luce's choice axiom, Thurstone's theory of comparative judgement and the double exponential distribution. *Journal of Mathematical Psychology,* **15**(2), 109–144.

Yildirim, Huseyin. 2005. Contests with multiple rounds. *Games and Economic Behavior,* **51**(1), 213–227.

Young, H. P. 1986. Optimal ranking and choice from pairwise comparisons. In: Grofman, B., and Owen, G. (eds), *Information Pooling and Group Decision Making.* Binkley, UK: JAI Press.

Young, H. P. 1988. Condorcet's theory of voting. *American Political Science Review,* **82**(4), 1231–1244.

Young, H. P., and Levenglick, A. 1978. A consistent extension of Condorcet's election principle. *SIAM Journal of Applied Mathematics,* **35**(2), 285–300.

Young, Peyton. 1995. Optimal voting rules. *Journal of Economic Perspectives,* **9**(1), 51–64.

Zermelo, E. 1929. Die Berechnung der Turnier-Ergebnisse als ein Maximumproblem der Wahrscheinlichkeitsrechnung. *Mathematische Zeitschrift,* **29**, 436–460.

Zhang, Jun, and Wang, Ruqu. 2009. The Role of Information Revelation in Elimination Contests. *The Economic Journal*, **37**(3), 1–22.

Zhang, Li. 2005. The efficiency and fairness of a fixed budget resource allocation game. Pages 485–496 of: *Proceedings of the 32nd International Colloquium on Automata, Languages and Programming*, Lisbon, Portugal.

Index to Notations

Scalars and Vectors

- $\mathbf{R}$ is the set of real numbers, and $\mathbf{R}^n$ is the n-dimensional real Euclidean space
- $\mathbf{R}_+$ is the set of all positive numbers in $\mathbf{R}$, and $\mathbf{R}_+^n = \{\mathbf{x} \in \mathbf{R}^n \mid x_i \geq 0, \forall i = 1, 2, \ldots, n\}$
- $\mathbf{Z}$ is the set of integers, and $\mathbf{N} = \{x \in \mathbf{Z} \mid x \geq 0\}$
- Normal font letters $x, y, \ldots$ denote scalars
- Boldface letters $\mathbf{x}, \mathbf{y}, \ldots$ denote vectors in $\mathbf{R}^n$
- Boldface capital letters $\mathbf{A}, \mathbf{B}, \ldots$ denote matrices in $\mathbf{R}^{n \times m}$
- $\mathbf{x}^T$ denotes the transpose vector of vector $\mathbf{x}$
- $\mathbf{A}^T$ denotes the transpose matrix of matrix $\mathbf{A}$
- $\mathbf{x}_{-i}$ denotes vector $(x_1, x_2, \ldots, x_{i-1}, x_{i+1}, \ldots, x_n)$, given vector $\mathbf{x} = (x_1, x_2, \ldots, x_n)$
- Given two vectors $\mathbf{x}, \mathbf{y}$ of dimension n and a non-empty set $S \subseteq \{1, 2, \ldots, n\}$, $(\mathbf{x}_S, \mathbf{y}_{-S})$ is defined to be the vector with the i-th element equal to x_i if $i \in S$ and equal to y_i, otherwise

Functions and Real Analysis

- $f'(x)$ denotes the first derivative of function f that is differentiable at x

$$f'(x) = \frac{d}{dx} f(x)$$

- $\partial f(\mathbf{x})/\partial x_i$ denotes the partial derivative of function $f : \mathbf{R}^n \to \mathbf{R}$ with respect to variable x_i
- $f^{-1}(x)$ denotes the inverse function of function $f(x)$ whenever f is an invertible function, i.e.,

$$y = f(x) \Leftrightarrow f^{-1}(y) = x$$

Probability and Random Variables

- $\Pr[A]$ is the probability of event A
- $\Pr[A \mid B]$ is the probability of event A conditional on the occurrence of event B
- Random variables are denoted with the same style of notation as are scalar and vectors
- $\mathbf{x} \sim F$ means that random variable $\mathbf{x}$ has distribution F
- $E[\mathbf{x}]$ denotes the expected value of a random vector $\mathbf{x}$
- $E[f(\mathbf{x}, \mathbf{y}) \mid \mathbf{y}]$ means the expected value of $f(\mathbf{x}, \mathbf{y})$ conditional on the random variable $\mathbf{y}$ being equal to a particular value $\mathbf{y}$ (an abuse of notation for brevity)
- Given a sequence of values $x_1, x_2, \ldots, x_n$, the sequence $x_{(n,1)}, x_{(n,2)}, \ldots, x_{(n,n)}$ is defined to be values of $x_1, x_2, \ldots, x_n$ sorted in decreasing order
- Order statistics: given a sequence of independent and identically distributed random variables $x_1, x_2, \ldots, x_n$ according to distribution function F, $F_{(n,i)}$ and $f_{(n,i)}$ denote the distribution function and the density function of random variable $x_{(n,i)}$, respectively
- Gaussian multivariate random variable: given $\mu \in \mathbf{R}^n$ and $\Sigma \in \mathbf{R}^{n \times n}$, $f(\mathbf{x}; \mu, \Sigma)$ denotes the density of a multivariate Gaussian random variable with mean vector μ and covariance matrix Σ and is defined by

$$f(\mathbf{x}; \mu, \Sigma) = \frac{1}{(2\pi)^{n/2}|\Sigma|} \exp\left(-\frac{1}{2}(\mathbf{x} - \mu)^T \Sigma^{-1}(\mathbf{x} - \mu)\right)$$

  where $|\Sigma|$ is the determinant and Σ^{-1} is the inverse matrix of matrix Σ
- Standard normal random variable: $\Phi(x)$ denotes the cumulative distribution function, and $\phi(x)$ denotes the density funtion of a standard normal random variable $\phi(x) = f(x; 0, 1)$, i.e.,

$$\phi(x) = \frac{1}{\sqrt{2\pi}} \exp\left(-\frac{1}{2}x^2\right)$$

Common Functions and Sequences

- Indicator function: $\mathbf{1}(A) = 1$ if condition or event A is true; $\mathbf{1}(A) = 0$, otherwise
- Kullback-Leibler divergence between two distributions $p = (p_1, p_2, \ldots, p_n)$ and $q = (q_1, q_2, \ldots, q_n)$:

$$D(p \mid\mid q) = \sum_{i=1}^{n} p(i) \log\left(\frac{p(i)}{q(i)}\right)$$

- Kullback-Leibler divergence between two independent Bernoulli random variables with parameters $p, q \in [0, 1]$:

$$D(p \mid\mid q) = p \log\left(\frac{p}{q}\right) + (1 - p) \log\left(\frac{1 - p}{1 - q}\right)$$

- H_n denotes the n-th harmonic number: $H_n = \sum_{i=1}^{n} 1/i$

Order Notation

- $f(n) = O(g(n)) \Leftrightarrow \exists c > 0$ and $n_0 \in \mathbf{N}$ such that $f(n) \leq cg(n)$ for all $n \geq n_0$
- $f(n) = \Omega(n) \Leftrightarrow \exists c > 0$ and $n_0 \in \mathbf{N}$ such that $f(n) \geq cg(n)$ for all $n \geq n_0$
- $f(n) = \Theta(n) \Leftrightarrow f(n) = O(g(n))$ and $g(n) = O(f(n))$ hold true
- $f(n) = o(g(n)) \Leftrightarrow \lim_{n \to \infty} f(n)/g(n) = 1$
- $f(n) \sim g(n)$, for large $n \Leftrightarrow \lim_{n \to \infty} f(n)/g(n) = 1$

Index